ISBN 978-0-265-96191-9
PIBN 10916109

FB &c Ltd, Dalton House, 60 Windsor Avenue, London, SW19 2RR.
Company number 08720141. Registered in England and Wales.

For support please visit www.forgottenbooks.com

The Oldest English Texts.

EDITED

WITH INTRODUCTIONS AND A GLOSSARY

BY

HENRY SWEET, M.A.

LONDON:

PUBLISHED FOR THE EARLY ENGLISH TEXT SOCIETY,

BY N. TRÜBNER & CO., 57 & 59 LUDGATE HILL, E.C.

MDCCCLXXXV.

83

Oxford
PRINTED BY HORACE HART, PRINTER TO THE UNIVERSITY

PREFACE.

This collection is intended to include all the extant Old-English texts up to about 900 that are preserved in contemporary MSS., with the exception of the Chronicle and the works of Alfred. Most of the texts have been published before, but many of them, especially the glossaries, in a very inaccurate and defective form. All the texts here given have been corrected by the originals, except the runic ones.

I formed the plan of this undertaking many years ago, but it was not till 1878 that I was able to begin working at it continuously, for it was not till then that I had acquired palæographical knowledge enough to deal satisfactorily with the older texts, especially the charters. The printing of the texts lasted from May 1879 to January 1881. The labour of preparing the glossary, which would have been very severe in any case, was much increased by the time-wasting way in which, from a variety of unfortunate circumstances, I was obliged to carry it out. It was not till the beginning of 1884 that I was able to send it to press, and the printing took more than a year. So I was not able to begin working at the grammatical introduction till last spring.

Meanwhile, my interest in the work had been flagging more and more. When I first began it, I had some hopes of myself being able to found an independent school of English philology in this country. But as time went on it became too evident that the historical study of English was being rapidly annexed by the Germans, and that English editors would have to abandon all hopes of working up their materials themselves, and resign themselves to the more humble rôle of purveyors to the swarms of young program-mongers turned out every year by the German universities, so thoroughly trained in all the mechanical details of what may be called 'parasite philology' that no English dilettante can hope to compete with them—except by Germanizing himself and losing all his nationality. All this is of course inevitable—the result of our own neglect, and of the unhealthy over-production of the German universities—but it is not encouraging for those who, like myself, have had the mortification of seeing their favourite investigations forestalled one after another, while they are laboriously collecting their materials. But luckily the fields of linguistic science are wide, and there are regions as yet uninvaded by dissertations and programs, where I yet hope to do work that I need not be ashamed of. Indeed, my only regret now is that I did not abandon the historical study of English five years ago, so as to be able to devote myself entirely to the more important investigations which I have always carried on alongside of my Old English work. I am now resolved that I will take a rest from my long drudgery as soon as I have brought out the second edition of my *History of English Sounds.* I have therefore abandoned, for the present at least, my original intention of bringing out a grammar to accompany these texts. Meanwhile, some of the few original observations in which I have not been anticipated by the Germans will be found briefly abstracted in the Monthly Proceedings of the Philological Society; they will be given more at length in the *History of English Sounds.* The question of bringing out a supplementary volume of additional texts, notes, etc., will depend on external circumstances which I cannot undertake to predict.

The value of such a work as the present depends, of course, mainly on its accuracy. I am quite prepared to find many more errors in it than I should have expected; all I can say is, that I have put five times more labour into it than I ever anticipated, and am unable to give more. I may also remind my critics that I am not paid for my work, that I have no official position to make me responsible to any one, and that all my scientific work is a free gift to my countrymen—or rather to the Germans. Such errors and omissions as I have since discovered I have corrected and supplied at the end of this volume. The corrections to the Leiden Glossary are from Steinmeyer's text in the *Althochdeutsche Glossen*; this Glossary caused me especial difficulty because of my want of familiarity with the Continental hand.

The texts are printed exactly as in the MSS.; expanded contractions are denoted by italics, letters written above or below the line are enclosed in [ ], letters not in the MS. in ( ).

A great deal of what is said in the introductions to the texts must be considered as out of date, especially as regards the dialects: I now see that Cp, Lr, LP, Ps, and several of the shorter texts are Mercian.

It need scarcely be said that my knowledge of Low Latin has increased considerably since I first began to work at these texts, and that I am now able to explain several English words which I was not able to include in the Glossary.

The Glossary is exhaustive for all but those words in Ps which occur over and over again without variation, and some subordinate words, adverbs, prepositions, etc. Whenever the references are not exhaustive, an 'etc.' is added. The references to the proper names are intended to be exhaustive. All references were checked over again in my copy, so that I have considerable faith in their accuracy. Erroneous and anomalous forms are marked with †. The order I have adopted in the Glossary is one which I hope will facilitate its use in grammatical investigations, for which this work is mainly intended. The alphabetical index is of the roughest character, being intended merely to facilitate reference.

In conclusion I have to express my best thanks for the help I have had from many quarters. My obligations in connection with the Epinal Glossary I have already acknowledged in the preface to my edition of it. Especial thanks are further due to my friend Sievers for his very accurate transcript of the Erfurt Glossary (which he undertook quite spontaneously), and for his mediation in procuring the loan of the MS. itself; to the authorities of the Leiden library for their loan of the MSS. containing the Leiden Glossary and riddle; to M. Scheler for the loan of the Bede MS. in the Namur library; to Mr. Bradshaw, and to the Museum men, especially Messrs. Bond, Thompson, and Warner, for help and expressions of opinion on palæographical matters; to the well-known low Latinist, Mijnheer Hendrik Hessels, for the great trouble he has taken in testing the accuracy of my text of the oldest glossaries; and lastly to the Clarendon Press for the extraordinary accuracy with which the printing has been carried out.

HENRY SWEET.

LONDON, *January* 14, 1886.

CONTENTS.

OLDEST ENGLISH TEXTS.

OLDEST GLOSSARIES.

Description of MSS.

Epinal.

The Epinal MS. was first made known by Mone, and the English glosses in it were first published by him in his *Anzeiger für Kunde der Teutschen Vorzeit, hgg. von F. J. Mone* (VII jahrgang, I quartalheft, Karlsruhe, 1838), pp. 132–153. He states that he was first informed of the existence of the MS. by Professor Huguenin, of Metz. Mone's transcript had previously been sent by him to the Record Commission in London, who printed it in Appendix B to Mr. Cooper's Report, pp. 153–164—a collection of Old English texts (including the Andreas and Elene from the then lately discovered Vercelli MS.) which for some unknown reason was never published. Mone says that the text as given in this Report is accurate on the whole, but contains several errors, wherefore, and also on account of the rarity of the book in Germany, he has judged it advisable to reprint the Epinal glossary in his *Anzeiger*. Mone's second text repeats nearly all the errors and omissions of his first, as given in the Report, and is evidently a mere reprint of his original transcript without any re-collation of the MS.

The MS. (no. 17), which originally belonged to the monastery of Moyen-Moutier (Medianum Monasterium) near Senones, contains first the Sermones S. Augustini in a continental hand, and then at the end the glossary, written on fourteen folio leaves (28 pp.), with six columns in each page. The MS. is defective, the end of *v*, together with *y* and *z*, being wanting, but a comparison with the Erfurt MS. shows that this missing part probably contained only two English glosses. More serious is the loss of a sheet comprising part of *c* and the whole of *d* and *e*, by which we should have lost about 150 English glosses, had they not been preserved in the Erfurt MS. The tops of several of the later sheets have suffered somewhat from damp and wear, and the last page is very much worn. Mone has smeared these damaged places with some reagent which has almost blackened the vellum. He says: 'I must also remark that the last leaf of the MS. has suffered greatly from damp, the writing having disappeared here and there, and that I could not restore it even with a strong reagent.' Curiously enough, most of the glosses which Mone failed to read are now comparatively legible, and even on the last page there are few letters which I have not succeeded in making out with certainty.

The connection of the glossary with the text which precedes it is evidently purely external—due to the modern bookbinder. The handwriting shows the most archaic type of the Celtic-English writing—Hiberno-Saxon, as it is generally called, British, as I would call it—not in its purely uncial, nor yet in its most cursive form, but in one which is intermediate between the two, although occasionally breaking out into pure cursive, as is the case in most of the oldest MSS. Mone has incorrectly ascribed the cursively written words to a second hand. The character of the writing is shown in the photolithograph.

The scantiness of our materials, and the great diversity in the handwriting of documents which are certainly contemporary, must make us very cautious in assigning a date to any one of the oldest English MSS. on palæographical grounds alone. I intend to treat the subject fully in another place, and will therefore content myself for the present with stating my belief that the palæographical evidence *by itself*, as far as our present knowledge goes, points to a period not later than the beginning of the eighth century, and that the MS. may have been written any time between 600 and 700, in round numbers. As we shall see hereafter, the Corpus glossary shows a later recension of the same text as Epinal, containing a much larger number of words, which are also arranged in a more strictly alphabetical order. As Epinal and Corpus do not show any difference of dialect they were probably written in the same place. It is therefore highly improbable that any later scribe would copy the imperfect Epinal instead of the more complete and convenient Corpus text. The orthography of Corpus is more advanced and less clumsy than that of Epinal, substituting *þ* and *ð* for the ambiguous *d* and the digraph *th* of the latter, and introducing *w* for the cumbrous *uu* of Epinal. So also with the language, as shown by Corpus's disuse of *ae* in unaccented syllables, its levelling of inflectional *ae* and *i* under *e*, its development of fractures in such words as *heolstras* against the *helustras* of Epinal, and many other features. If, then, Corpus was written, as is, I believe, universally assumed, early in the eighth century, Epinal must have been written at least a generation earlier. The supposition of a later scribe having retained the older spelling and forms unchanged is untenable: if Epinal were a later copy of a much older glossary, we should expect either a mixture of older and later forms, or else a consistent modernization, as in Corpus, and there can be no doubt that the latter would have been the case: the language and spelling of Epinal are those of the period when it was written.

Erfurt.

This glossary was first published by Dr. Fr. Oehler in the *Neue Jahrbücher für Philologie* (Bd. xiii, pp. 256–297 and 325–387, 1847). His text gives the whole glossary, including those words which are glossed by Latin words only, although he himself states that he has omitted the commoner Latin words in Erf.^{2} and ^{3}. My text is based on a fresh copy of the English glosses made by Prof. E. Sievers, of Jena, which I afterwards carefully collated with the MS. itself.

The MS. is preserved in the Amplonian library at Erfurt (no. 42 fol.). It consists of 37 folio leaves with six columns on each page, and contains three alphabetical glossaries, the first of which is complete, while the second has lost a leaf, and the third extends only into *l*. The first glossary shows the same text as Epinal, whose gap it fills up. The first leaf of the MS. has suffered from exposure, and the lower margin of it, and, to a less extent, of the following leaves, has been considerably frayed and torn, additional portions having been torn and rubbed away since Oehler's time. The MS. is written in a continental hand, which the British

Museum men *I* showed it to ascribed to the end of the ninth century. The scribe was evidently unacquainted with English, as shown by his constant errors, and his nationality is unmistakeably betrayed by the intrusion of several Old High German words: 77 *alacris : blidi;* 104 *ablata : binoman;* 112 *adrogantissime : gelplih;* 397 *erugo : rost;* 512 *infandum : meinfol;* 730 *prætextatus : gigarauuit;* 926 *sella : satul.* The *uo* in *guoduueb* (441) is German, as also the *ph* in *lemphihalt* (589), and the pres. partic. *-enti* in 537, 575. In most cases a slight change of spelling has been enough to germanize the word, but in 112 the scribe has deliberately cut out the English word *uulanclicae* and substituted a pure German one. In 77 he has substituted *blidi* for the *snel* of Epinal and Corpus, and it is this substitution which makes me consider *blidi* to be a German gloss, although the word might otherwise be regarded as simply an archaic spelling of the English *blīðe.*

As regards the palæography of the MS. it may be noted that the *a* frequently has the *u*-like form, that *s* and *r* are formed rather alike, and that it is often almost impossible to distinguish between *m, ni* and *in.* In some places there seems to be another hand, larger and coarser, but without any apparent change of orthography.

In spite of the corruptness of the text, the language of the English glosses is evidently as old as in Epinal, and indeed, in some words, it is even more archaic, as in *brigdils* (127), *tuigin* (138). In fact, the very ignorance of the scribe has compelled him, as it were, to fossilize the archaisms of his original in a way which would have been impossible for a contemporary Englishman. It may be remarked that in the last two glossaries, where the English words are few and far between, the scribe has often indicated them by a waved line above them, or by adding *sax(onice).*

Corpus.

This precious glossary was first noticed by Wanley in his Catalogue (Hickes' Thesaurus, vol. ii. p. 115), who ascribes it to the eighth century: 'Cod. membr. vetustioribus litteris Saxonicis, seculo post Christum, ut videtur, octavo exaratus.' He also states that it formerly belonged to the monastery of St. Augustine at

Canterbury (quondam supellex Bibliothecæ Abbatiæ S. Augustini juxta muros Cantuariæ). It was first published by Mr. Thomas Wright in his Volume of Vocabularies (II, 96–124). Wright does not mention Wanley's account of the MS., but 'has no hesitation' in ascribing its writing to the eighth century. He remarks: 'Some one has written on the first leaf, in a hand perhaps of the thirteenth century, that it belonged to the church of Canterbury—*liber Sancti Augustini Cant.*—whence it no doubt came into the possession of Archbishop Parker. It is, therefore, not improbable that this vocabulary was originally compiled and written for the school of Canterbury.'

The MS., no. CXLIV (formerly S. 3), in the library of Corpus Christi College, Cambridge, has four columns on each page. It consists of two alphabetical glossaries, the former of which contains only a few English words. The handwriting is semi-uncial, occasionally running into cursive, not later than the first half of the eighth century. My text is based on repeated collation with the MS.

LEIDEN.

The Germanic portion of this glossary was first printed in Haupt's *Zeitschrift* (V, 194–198) by Bethmann, and was afterwards re-collated by E. Martin, who published his results in the same periodical (Neue folge II, 191–2). My own text is taken from the MS. itself. It is written in a scrubby, half-cursive, continental hand of the ninth century by a High German scribe, as shown by the glosses *sescuplum : dridehalpf* (28); *capitio : haubitloh* (48); *tenda : gez(e)lt* (63), and some others, together with the partic. pres. in *-enti* (14). The corruptions of the English words are of the same character as in Erfurt; the scribe excuses himself by the remark at the end, *sicut inveni scripsi, ne reputes scriptori.* The language is of the oldest type. The English words are often marked by a circumflex-like tick above them, or by the word *sax.*, as in Erf.

General Structure and Relations.

Before proceeding to discuss the general relations of the glossaries, it will be as well to enumerate the separate glossaries contained in the four MSS.—the Leiden, Epinal, Erfurt and Corpus. There are six of them :—

(1) Leiden (L.).
(2) Epinal-Erfurt (EE., Ep., Erf.[1]).
(3) Second Erfurt (Erf.[2]).
(4) Third Erfurt (Erf.[3]).
(5) First Corpus (C.[1]).
(6) Second Corpus (C.[2], C.).

It will be noted that for the sake of convenience I use C., without any exponent, to denote the (longer) second Corpus glossary, except when it is expressly contrasted with C.[1]. EE. is used to denote the text given by the agreement of Ep. and Erf.[1].

Alphabetical order.

All of these glossaries, except the first, are alphabetical. L. cannot, in fact, be strictly regarded as a single glossary, but rather as a collection of smaller glossaries, not yet digested into a single whole. The alphabetical order of the other glossaries is of two kinds. The first, and most primitive, is that of EE. and C.[1]. It consists in simply throwing the words together under their initial letter, without further alphabetical arrangement. Thus, the first four words in EE. show the following order of the first two letters: *am-*, *ax-*, *ar-*, *an-*. This we may call the *a-* order. The three other glossaries, E.[2], E.[3], and C.[2], follow a stricter, what may be called the *ab-* order, which throws together all words whose first two letters are the same, the third being disregarded. Thus, the first eight words in C.[2] show the following order of the first three letters: *abe-*, *abi-*, *abs-*, *abo-*, *abl-*, *abu-*, *abi-*, *abe-*. None of them has got so far as the strict *abc-* order of our modern dictionaries.

Method of compilation.

The way in which the alphabetical glossaries were compiled was evidently the following. The scribe had before him a glossary (or glossaries) of the L. type, which he wished, for convenience of reference, to throw into an alphabetical form. For this purpose he took as many sheets of parchment as there were letters of the alphabet, and marked them *a*, *b*, *c*, &c. in regular order. He then entered each gloss as it came under its initial letter, until the sheet for that letter was filled, when he took another, and so on, the result being a glossary of the EE. type. The *ab-* glossaries always presuppose one or more *a-* glossaries, which were recast on a plan similar to that on which the *a*- glossaries were constructed. The scribe took a number of sheets marked *a*, *b*, *c*, &c., and, beginning with *a*, he copied out all the words beginning with *ab*- in the order in which they came in his *a*-order glossary, and then proceeded to copy out those beginning with *ac*- in the same way, and so on.

Originally interlinear. The ultimate sources of a portion, at least, of these glossaries must be sought in interlinear and marginal glosses in Latin books. It is only on this supposition that we can explain the frequent appearance of nouns and adjectives in oblique cases, and different tenses &c. of verbs, such as *affectui vel dilectione*, *ære alieno*, *detractavit*, *promulgarunt*, *proterentem*, as also of groups of words, such as *ad expensas*, *ex phalange*, *pictus acu*, *tabida et putrefacta*, all entered under the first word. It is easy to trace some of these latter back to their literary sources, and, indeed, such a phrase as *verbere torto* at once betrays its Virgilian origin[1]. *Vi superum*, glossed *violentia deorum* in C., is also Virgilian. Equally familiar is the subject of a gloss in Erf.[2], which I give in full[2]:

Quousque tandem abutero Catellina patientia ? increpantium est principium libri Ciceronis, quod Catellina senator perditus civium sub consule Cicerone[3] male vivendo patientia ipsius Ciceronis male utebatur. Abutero, male uteris.

In the gloss *reciprocato : gistaebnendrae* (864)[4] we have a Latin masc. or neut. adjective glossed by an English fem. one, but in the same case (though it may also be genitive), showing that the Latin masc. or neut. substantive with which *reciprocato* agreed was glossed by an English feminine. Owing to defective word-division and the occasional necessary division at the end of a line in the prototype (whether a glossed book or an older glossary), it often happens that words are given in a truncated form. Thus under *c* we find *corax=nycticorax*, under *p* *petigo=impetigo*, all the MSS. agreeing. Conversely, unmeaning fragments of words are sometimes run on to English words, as in the gloss *axis : tumaex* (Erf. 13), where Ep. has simply *axis : aex*. The mysterious *scarpinat :*

1 This is pointed out by Wright in a note to C., but I learn from Prof. Skeat that he first reminded W. of the passage in Virgil.

2 After Oehler, the MS. itself being no longer accessible.

3 Cicepone *Oehler*.

4 References are to EE., unless otherwise implied or stated.

scripithaen occurs both in Ep. and Erf. (906), while C. has only *scripið*. A fruitful source of corruption is running two glosses into one, the subject of the second gloss being omitted, as in Erf. 608, where we have the mysterious gloss *lepus : hæra, quæ cum intro canit.* EE. 1089, 90 has the two glosses *verecundiæ concesserim : gilebdae* and *vadimonium : borg;* the scribe of C. copied the second of these under *va-*, and imagining the English word in the gloss above to be a continuation of *borg* written above the line, produced the unmeaning *vadimonium : borggilefde.* In some cases the separation of a compound gloss into its elements has led to a violation of the alphabetical order: EE. 729 has the gloss *percommoda matutinos : sua cendlic morgenlic,* which C. divides into *percommoda : sua cenlic* and *matutinos : morgenlic,* the latter thus coming under *p* instead of *m*. Similarly, we find under *m* in EE. (618) and C. *mendacio conposito : geregnodae,* and under *s* in C. (1329) *sempiterna moles : falthing,* the glosses applying only to the second words in both instances. Under *u* we find in Ep. (1084) *quinquefolium : hraefnaes fot,* the Latin word having probably been originally only an additional gloss to the preceding *viscus : mistil*, being afterwards itself glossed by *hraefnaes fot* and then written as an independent gloss.

Repetition of same gloss. A natural result of compiling glosses from various sources is that the same gloss is often repeated. The process of alphabetical arrangement—especially in the *ab-* order—tends, of course, to eliminate these repetitions, but it often happens that the same Latin word appears both in its correct and in some corrupted form, or, as is often the case, in two corrupted forms. Thus, we find (240, 1) first the correct *cornicula* and then **cornacula,* the former being omitted in C., although the two are glossed by different words in EE. So also **argillus* (3) and **argella* (48), in C. *argilla* and **argella, abilina* (15) and *avellanus* (50). C. has under *g gente,* under *c cente,* both=*ganta* and with the same gloss *wilde goos.* The alphabetical order shows that this last corruption, *cente* for *ganta,* must have existed in the non-alphabetical source of the gloss. So also all three (EE. and C.) agree in putting *arrius* (61) under *a,* while C. has also *farius* (842) under *f,* both words being glossed *fag,* and therefore probably corruptions of *varius.* In some cases corruptions common to EE. and C. actually do appear in the non-alphabetical L., such as *arpa* (40)=*harpe*, *berrus* (151)=*verres*, *netila* (675)=*nitela*. Often the same word appears in different cases in the different texts, especially in L. as opposed to the other three. Thus L. has *fibrarum* (27), *famfelucas* (171) against their *fibræ* (405) and C.'s *fibra* (870), and *famfaluca* (EE. 426, 447), and also *scropis* (150) (originally *scrobs*, *scrobis*) against *scrobibus* (948). Where the differences of case were sharply marked, as in these instances, the different cases of one and the same word were probably regarded as so many distinct glosses, and there was no attempt to reduce them to the common nominative, but rather to drop one of them. But where the difference was simply one of nom. and acc. in such endings as *-us*, *-um*, *-a*, *-am*, which were confounded very early in popular Latin, there may have been a tendency to substitute the nom. for the acc. in the process of compiling the glossaries, especially as in most cases this did not involve any alteration of the English gloss. At any rate, we find the following words which in L. are acc. but nom. in the others: *hederam* (44), *invisum* (104), *vitricum* (108), *decrepitam* (115), while the correct neuter *acrifolium* in L. (243) appears as a masc. nom. *acrifolus* in the others. The false masc. nom. *ruscus* (L. 127) is common to all of them. On the other hand, L. has *aquilius* (233) against *aquilium*, as also *auricula* (234) against *auriculum*, which may be due either to confusion in pronunciation or difference of source.

Repetitions of the same Latin word, but with a different English gloss, are very common, and are generally retained even in the latest digests, though sometimes two such glosses are rolled into one. Thus the two glosses *crabro : uaeps* (255) and *crabro : hirnitu* (275) of Erf. are united under the *crabro : waefs vel hurnitu* (603) of C. So also *fibula : sigil* (408) and *fibula : hringiae* (410) under *fibula : hringe, sigl* (C. 874).

Sources: literary.

We have already (p. 7) pointed out the literary sources of some of the glosses which consist of groups of words, and can therefore be easily identified. All doubt as to the literary and interlinear origin of the glosses in general is removed by a simple inspection of L., where each gloss is entered under the name of the book it was taken from. The scribe evidently had before him a library of Latin books containing a number of scattered interlinear glosses, some in Latin, some in English, which he copied out in parallel columns in the order of their occurrence. These non-alphabetical glossaries were probably at first intended only to serve the purpose of a running commentary and glossary to each text, and the plan of utilizing them for *general* reference was an afterthought. In order to give as much information as possible about the literary sources, I have in the text of L. preserved all the headings, even when there are no English glosses under them. It will be seen that most of the books are ecclesiastical: commentaries on various books of the Bible, lives of Saints (St. Martin), the works of the Fathers, and commentaries on them; also that most popular of Middle Age epitomes, the History of Orosius, and some purely profane writings. The heading *Incipit ex diversis libris* seems to point to an earlier collection of glosses out of different books, which was copied straight off.

Class-glossaries.

But it is evident that the glossaries were not compiled from literary sources alone; the purely colloquial half-Romance forms of many of the Latin words, such as *accearium* (steel), *morgit*=*mulget*, *roscinia*=*luscinia* (26), the number of technical words and names of animals and plants coming together in groups even in the alphabetical glossaries, cannot well have been taken out of ordinary books. In L. the latter class of words are thrown together under the headings *Verba de multis* and *Item alia*, and are evidently taken directly from class-glossaries, in which names of beasts, birds, fishes, minerals and other natural objects were collected in separate groups. Thus, 201–20 seem nearly all to be names of birds, the next three are names of fishes, then follow four names of animals, all of the same type. Again 238–41 give us four different swine-names, and further on we have a group of tree-names. 187–8 we find *argella, accearium* together, 196–8 three names of tools, and 144–5 *veru, cos*. This latter class of words is, however, rare and scattered. Evidences of other class-glossaries may be found in the juxtaposition of *simplex, bilex* and *triplex* (156–8), *aleo* (=*aleator*) and *alea* (140–1), *fidicen* and *fidis* (147–8), *striga* and *incuba* (228–9). But there are many scattered words which do not fall into any distinct class with the others. Further proof of these words being taken from class-glossaries is afforded by the fact of the great majority of them being in the nominative, while the literary words appear, as we have seen, as often, or oftener, in some oblique case.

There still remains the general question of the relations of the English to the Latin glosses, and the principles on which words were glossed generally. When we find a Latin word glossed by another Latin word, we may assume that the glosser had at least an elementary knowledge of the language, and, consequently, that he would generally gloss only the harder words, and would gloss these by commoner and simpler ones. On the other hand, when a Latin text is glossed by English words, there is at least a possibility of the glosser being almost completely ignorant of Latin. Such a glosser would be in the position of a schoolboy who scribbles *man*, *way*, over *ánthrōpos*, *hodós* in his Greek delectus in order to retain the newly learnt words in his memory. Hence it is that among the English literary glosses we find such everyday words glossed as *atqueve*, *pudor*, *petisse*, *trans*, and many others. But with technical words and names of natural objects the case is different. Here the English rendering was constantly employed to supplement and sum up the Latin definition. Thus L. 36 defines *perpendiculum* as *modica petra de plumbo, quam ligant in filo quando ædificant parietes*, and then adds the English equivalent *pundar*. Compare also *paliurus* (37) and *circino* (40). In all of these cases the later glossaries (EE. and C.) entirely omit the Latin definition, retaining only the English word. The same tendency to drop the Latin definition as soon as an English word has established itself may be observed in many other instances as well. Thus, *eumenides* are explained as *filiæ noctis* in L. 136, the English *hegitisse* being also added, while C. has simply *eumenides : haehtisse*. Sometimes, however, as in the case of *murica* (EE. 624), the Latin definition is retained in the later recensions as well. Even in comparing EE. with C., the tendency to drop superfluous words is very marked, as will be seen hereafter.

The English glosses.

In the case of names of animals, plants, &c., where accurate definition was difficult, if not impossible, there seems generally to be no trace of an intermediate Latin definition, and there can be little doubt that most of these words were taken from Latin-English class-glossaries, which may possibly have been compiled by the missionaries who first preached the gospel in Kent. Hence the marked preponderance of this class of words in the glossaries.

In many cases the English rendering was added in the alphabetical glosses themselves. Many of the purely Latin glosses in EE. appear in C. with an English word tacked on. Thus EE. has the gloss *apricitas : calor*, which is repeated in Erf.[2] (Oehl. 270. 297) in the corrupt form of *apricitas : color*. This last reappears in C. 188, the second word being deliberately glossed by the English 'hue'—*apricitas : color, hio.* Often also the same gloss appears twice, with and without an English rendering. An unmistakeable instance is C. 74, *adclinis : tohald, vel incumbens*, the original of which is seen in EE. *acclinis : resupinus vel incumbens.* In another place (96) EE. has *adclinis : tohald*, the Latin part of the gloss being entirely omitted. It is probable that the prototype of the English gloss both in EE. and C. had *adclinis : resupinus vel incumbens*, the English *tohald* being at first only a gloss on *resupinus*, and finally supplanting it. Even in comparing Ep. and Erf. we find the *colonus : gibuur* and *contribulus : meeg* (163, 4) of Ep. represented only by *colonus : vicinus* and *contribulus : consanguis* in Erf. These were no doubt the original glosses, the English words having at first been simply written above the second word in each. This is confirmed by C.'s reading of the second gloss—*contribulius : meig, vel sanguine*, the last two words being a corruption of *consanguis.* If the English rendering had been written after, instead of above, the Latin one, the order would have been the same as in *apricitas : color, hio.* The English word was written above simply because there was no room for it in the line, and when the whole gloss was copied out again in one line, the Latin word was omitted partly for the same reason.

We will now consider the structure and relation of the various texts more in detail.

Leiden. It is evident at the first glance that, although L. shows a more primitive text than EE. (and C.), the latter cannot have derived any portion of its literary glosses directly from L. Out of 145 glosses in L. which by their headings are referred to literary sources, only 49 appear in EE. and C., 20 out of these 49 being peculiar to C. (Note that C. contains nearly twice as many English glosses as EE.) Out of 40 literary headings in L. only 29 comprise English glosses, and 12 out of these 29 give only one English gloss. Of the remaining 17 there are 3 headings which consist entirely of glosses which do not appear in EE. and C.: *Item de ecclesiastica storia* (v), *De Ester* (xx), *Incipit in Esdra* (xxi). It will be noticed that the heading before v has out of 8 words only one that occurs also in EE. or C., and as this gloss appears again in another part of L., it is probable that the compiler of C. took it from the source there named (Eusebius); we may, therefore, conclude that there are 4 longer headings peculiar to L. There are, on the other hand, 6 headings at least half of whose glosses re-appear in EE. and C.: *In libro Isaie prophete* (xii), *In libro rotarum* (xxv), *Verborum interpretatio* (xxvii), *De Orosio* (xxxiii), *De dialogorum* (xxxvi), *Ex diversis libris* (xxxix). The rest of the 17 all have at least one gloss common also to EE. and C. Of the 12 headings comprising only a single gloss, 5 re-appear in EE. and C., 3 of these being peculiar to C. As it is impossible to determine with certainty the relations of some of the glosses, these statistics are not perfectly accurate, but they are quite enough so for our purposes. I have included *Incipit verborum interpretatio* among the literary sources, as it is probably the title of a book.

The repetition of the same glosses in EE. and C. may in some cases be fortuitous, but several of them are so marked in character that their appearance in L. and EE. is enough to prove that the two recensions must have drawn from common sources. Such a gloss is L. 78 *mauria, de auro facta in tonica: gespan*, where EE. has the slightly varied *murica: gespan, aureum in tunica.* So also the curious gloss C. 1660 *pronuba: heorðsuaepe* appears also in L. The truncated *petigo*, placed under *p* by EE. and C., is also in L.

In the class-glosses, *Verba de multis* (xliii), *Item lia* (xliv), *Item alia* (xlv) the connection between L. and the alphabetical glosses is much more intimate than in the literary glosses: out of over 100 glosses included under these three headings there are less than 20 which do not reappear in EE. and C., many of which either differ but slightly but others occurring in the latter, or else are of doubtful Englishness. The agreement of many of the most characteristic glosses shows that L. and the alphabetical glossaries not only drew from class-glossaries, but also from the same class-glossaries. Such glosses are *umbrellas: stalu to fuglum* (EE. 1067), *manticum: handful beouuaes* (645), *incuba: merae vel satyrus* (558).

It will be observed that of the words not peculiar to L. only 3 do not occur in EE., but in C., a much smaller proportion than in the case of the literary words.

Order in L. A sure and simple test of the affinity between L. and EE. is afforded by the gloss-order in both. If EE. were based on L. we should expect to find all the words beginning with the same letter which occur in both texts to come in the same order. The following are all the class-glosses beginning with *a* which occur both in L. and EE., arranged in the order in which they come in L., and with the number of their occurrences in EE. :—

EE.	7	6	15 (50)	47	48	49	4
L.	aleator	alea	abellana	alga	argella	accearium	andeda

39	40	41	43	44
auriculum : dros	arpa	acega	aquilius	auriculum : earuuigga

34	33	35	46
acrifolium	acerabulus	alnus	alneta.

It will be seen that in spite of discrepancies the general agreement is very remarkable. The transposition of two glosses in immediate succession (7,6 and 34,33) is natural, and frequent even in such closely allied texts as Ep. and Erf., as we shall see hereafter. Disregarding these variations, as also the isolated 4, we get three groups of glosses running on in regular order: 6–49, 39–44, 33–46. This cannot be chance, especially as the order of the words is often very arbitrary, and we cannot avoid the conclusion that both L. and EE. copied from the same class-glossary.

There are, on the other hand, a large number of plant-names, &c. in EE. which do not occur in L.

Groups of words in L. The relation of L. to the later glossaries in its treatment of those glosses which contain groups of words has already been touched upon (p. 11): it will be convenient to give the complete materia here. The words added or omitted are in italics, a † showing that the gloss appears in C. and not in EE.

A. Latin.

(1) *Omitted in the later glossaries.*

8 *antoni*, lacunar. 34 telum *orditus*. 35 viciam, *pisas agrestes*. †36 perpendiculum, *modica petra de plumbo, quam ligant in filo quando ædificant parietes*. 37 paliurus, *herba quæ crescit in tectis domorum, grossa folia habens*. 40 circino, *ferrum duplex, unde pictores faciunt circulos*. †136 eumenides, *filiæ noctis*. 221 tinct (=tinca): slii, *lupus brevis*. Also several whose identity is doubtful: 57 lagunculas, 79 lagonam, 82 prorigo, 93 callos, 154 cunæ.

(2) *Omitted in L.*

†10 ultro citro*que*. 159 *pedo*, paturum.

(3) *Retained.*

229 incuba: maerae vel satyrus (*om. in C.*).

(4) *Order changed.*

78 mauria, de auro facta in tonica: gespan—murica: gespan, aureum in tunica (*om. in C.*).

B. English.

(1) *Omitted in the later glossaries.*

34 telum *orditus: inuuerpan* uueb. †98 barathrum: *loh vel* da(e)l.

(2) *Omitted in L.*

?†13 callos: wearras *vel ill.* 216 picus: higre, *fina*.

Order changed.

114 exactio: monung gaebles—gaebles monung.

In one case L.'s gloss has been cut into two: L. 89 vexilla et labarum: segin, C. 2093 vexilla: seign, EE. 567 labarum: segn.

We may now sum up the relation between L. and EE. thus: L. and EE. took their literary glosses partly from the same books, all the class-glosses in L. and part of those in EE. being taken from the same glossary. The two glossers, in fact, evidently worked in the *General relation of L. to EE.*

same library or libraries, and, to a great extent, with the same books—in all probability, in the libraries of Canterbury.

Epinal-Erfurt.

EE. has been included above (p. 6) among the *a*- order glossaries, but this is only partly correct. If we go through the whole body of words given under any one letter in EE., we shall see that in the case of some of the letters it falls into two groups. The first, in which the great majority of the English glosses are contained, follows the *a*- order. Thus, in going through *a* we find considerable masses of English glosses interspersed with purely Latin ones, both often running on in uninterrupted succession through several numbers, and ending at *arcister : strelbora,* then a body of about 70 glosses, only two of which are English, and ending at *arx.* Then comes a group in regular *ab*- order, beginning with *aberuncat* and ending with *avena.* Although this second group is nearly as long as the first one down to *arcister,* it contains only three English glosses, which are lumped together nearly at the end, forming part of a small group in which the *ab*- order is completely ignored. This *ab*- group presupposes, of course, an earlier *a*- order alphabetical glossary. Not only do the same words appear in both groups, but also the same identical glosses. An unmistakeable instance is the gloss *acclinis,* already mentioned (p. 12). *Actionabatur : puplice vendebat* shows the same form of the verb as EE. 86 *actionabatur : scirde,* which can hardly be fortuitous. *Asotus : urbanus, luxurious* in the second group is clearly the same gloss as *asotus : luxuriosus* in the first. *Æstuaria : ubi duo maria conveniunt* and *altrinsecus : ex utraque parte,* both in the second group, may also be the same as EE. 107 and 51, and there are other instances. Both groups are, therefore, to some extent at least, independent recensions of glosses taken from the same books. The first group itself can be again subdivided, the first half consisting mainly of words taken from class-glossaries, and nearly always in the nominative, the second containing many verb-forms, oblique cases of adjectives and nouns, many of them abstract words. The *a*- group in EE. show occasional traces of the *ab*- order. 55–8 *albipedius, alvium, alviolum, alga* may be fortuitous, but in 186–214 there is an unmistakeable attempt to throw together all the words beginning with *con*-, although there is no separation of de- and *dis-* under *d*, or of the numerous *pers* and *pros* under *p*. There seems to be a tendency to throw the *ads* together (73–8, 95–102).

The connection between Ep. and Erf.[1] is so close that at first sight one might imagine Erf. to be a direct copy of Ep., although further examination shows that this is not the case. Epinal and Erfurt.

The following glosses of Ep. are omitted in Erf.: *cofinus* (222), *cariscus* (238), †*fitilium* (429), *favonius* (452), *hastilia* (489), *municeps* (620), *munifica* (621), †*millefolium* (639), *musiranus* (649), *maruca* (651), *majalis* (652), *maulistis* (654), *mastice* (655), *malva* (656), *marrubium* (657), *mulio* (658), *mango* (659), *matrix* (661), †*mergus* (662), †*occas* (713), †*occipitium* (720), *proscribit* (739), *patena : holopanne* (784), *perna* (804), †*pituita* (833), *sollicitat* (936), *viscus* (1083), *quinquefolium* (1084). Those marked with a † are wanting also in C. In Erf. the glosses *municeps* and *munifica* are rolled together into the single word *manificit* without any gloss, either English or Latin. The gloss *quinquefolium* is out of its alphabetical order in Ep., being originally simply a rendering of the preceding *viscus*. In some cases the gloss omitted in Erf. occurs over again in both Ep. and Erf. Thus *perna* reappears 774, and *patena* with a different rendering 786, as also *pituita* 775. The words *colonus* and *contribulus*, glossed by an English word in Ep., a Latin in Erf., have been noticed above (p. 12). In the case of (*h*)*alitus* (89) the space for the English word is left blank in Erf. It will be seen that half the omissions fall under *m*, where they mostly run on in uninterrupted succession. Omissions of Erf.

The following glosses which occur in Erf. are omitted in Ep. *genuinum* (487), †*occupavit : geonette* (717), *procuratio* (721), †*pedetemptim* (834), *sinapio : cressae* (922), those marked † being omitted in C. also. It will be observed that the gloss *occupavit* is repeated in both Ep. and Erf. with the only slightly different rendering *onettae* (712). Omissions of Ep.

In one case Erf. has a fuller gloss than Ep. 1050 via secta, *juvar* : iringaes uueg.

The order of the glosses sometimes differs in Ep. and Erf. The following gives the glosses in their Ep. order, the numbers above showing their place in Erf. Different order in Ep. and Erf.

31 57 56 163 (*end of* b)
11 amites. *56, 7 alvium, alviolum. 120 (*beginning of* b) buccula.
147 146 153 409 fraxinus
146, 7 ballena, broel. 161 bufo. 411 fenicia. *414–17 frixum,
fagus frixum ferinum 478 475 556
ferinum, fraxinus, fagus. 474 gracilis. 486 galmilla. 562 isca.
638[a] 637 636 638[b] 684
637, 8 myrtus, melarium. 641 mastigia. 646 mascus. 688 nodus.
742 741 766 765 827
*741, 2 per seudoterum, percitus. 765, 6 puncto, petigo. 828 palum-
1100 (*end of* u) 1088 1087
bes. 1057 vicatum. 1087, 8 vangas, virecta.

The * denotes agreement with C. in those cases in which its *ab*-order allows the original order to be seen. *It* will be observed that C. in every case supports the order of Ep. Also that Erf.'s transposition of 146, 7 separates *broel* from *broellarius*, which must originally have followed it, as in Ep. and C.

Epinal-Erfurt and Corpus.

The general relation of C. to EE. may be summed up by saying that C. is EE. arranged in *ab*- order, with as many more glosses from other sources. That C. was compiled directly from EE., as far as half of its matter is concerned, is proved beyond a doubt by its word-order. Thus, under *a*, we find the words beginning with *ab*- written out in the exact order of their occurrence in EE. The following are all the words beginning with *ab* in EE. in the order of their occurrence there: *abilina* (15), *abies* (37), *absinthium* (66), *abortus* (80), *ablata* (104). The first word in C. is *abelena*, and the others follow exactly in the same order as in EE. down to *ablata*. Then comes a fresh batch of words beginning with *ab*, none of which are in EE.—evidently taken from an *a*- order glossary of the same character as EE. It is, however, seldom that the order of the words of different sources is so regular. Thus, if we denote glosses occurring in EE. by *e*, and leave unmarked those occurring only in C., we find the following succession under *ac*-: 45*e*, 46, 47, 48, 49, 50, 51*e*, 52*e*, 53*e*, 54*e*, 55*e*, 56*e*, 57*e*, 58*e*, 59*e*, 60*e*, 61*e*, 62*e*, 63*e*, 64, 65, 66, 67. Here we have a long and unbroken series of *e*s in the middle, preceded and followed by smaller groups of *c*s, with an isolated *e* at the beginning. The order of *ad*- is much more regular, being broken only occasionally by isolated words: 68, 69*e*,

70*e*, 71, 72*e*, 73*e*, 74*e*, 75*e*, 76*e*, 77*e*, 78*e*, 79, 80*e*, 81, 82, 83, 84, 85*e*, 86, 87, 88, 89, 90, 91. The order of the short *ae-* is perfectly regular, with the exception of the first word: 92, 93*e*, 94*e*, 95*e*, 96*e*, 97, 98. *al-* is also almost perfectly regular, in spite of its length.

The explanation of these irregularities of order offers considerable difficulties. The supposition that the scribe deliberately copied out a few words first from one of the sources, then from another, afterwards returning to the first one, cannot be entertained. It is, however, possible that in copying, say words beginning with *ab* in EE., he may occasionally have missed a gloss, or even have skipped a whole column, which he would, on subsequent revision of the whole *ab-* group, discover and enter at the end of the *ab-* group. This may possibly be the explanation of the order of *am-*: 143*e*, 144, 145, 146, 147, 148, 149, 150*e*, 151, 152, 153, 154*e*, 155*e*, 156*e*. So also in *ar-*. Or the scribe may have entered the missed words at the top or foot of a column, between the lines—anywhere where he found room; indeed, no other course would be open to the revisor of a whole sheet or a whole letter. As we have seen, there are two cases in which the scribe of Erf., having missed a gloss in the middle of a letter, afterwards entered it at the end (*buccula* and *vicatum*).

The sources of the words peculiar to C. were, as already remarked, *a-* order (and *ab-*) glossaries like EE., one of which was almost certainly the original of Erf.[2], as shown by the history of the gloss *apricitas: calor* (p. 12). Here also there are distinct traces of class-glossaries. Thus out of seven words under *ab* four are names of winds: *ab euro, ad euronothum, ab affrico, a borea,* the connection of the second with the others being maintained only at the sacrifice of the strict alphabetical order, which would relegate it to *ad-*, as *a circio* and *a favonio* are regularly entered under *ac-* and *af-*.

C. omits the following Ep. glosses, those marked † being omitted in Erf. also, and those in brackets being parallel glosses, a † showing that the gloss occurs only in C.:—73 addicavit, 74 adstipulatus, 100 adempto: ginumni [102 adempta: binumni]; 176 celatum: utathrungaen [†424 cælatum: agraben, †451 celatum: abrectat], Omissions of C.

2—2

216 clunis, 234 cyathus: bolla [†627 cuppa: beodbolle], 240 cornicula: chyae [241 cornicula: crauuae], 296 cervical; 325 delibutus: gisalbot[1] [†676 delibutus: gesmirwid]; 400 flustra, 407 fax, 409 furca: uueargrod [†930 furcimen: waergrood], †429 fitilium, 443 feriatis: restaendum [†854 feriatus: gerested], 444 facundia; 480 genuino: gecyndilican [†961 genuino: tusc], 482 genas: hleor [†962 genas: heagaspen], 486 galmilla: limmolegn [477 galmum: molegn, C. 953 galmulum: molegnstycci, moling]; 505 ilium: neuunseada [†1041 ilia: midhridir]; 609 lacunar: hrof [597 lacunar: fiodae, †1180 lacunar: hebenhus]; †639 millefolium: gearuue [623 mirifillon: geruuae], †662 mergus: scalfr [647 mergulus: scalfr]; 674 nycticorax: naechthraebn [673 noctua: naechthraebn]; †713 occas.: fealga [†1427 occa: faelging], †719 occipitium: hnecca [715 occiput: hreacca]; 827 phitecus, †833 pituita: gillistrae [775 pituita: gibrec, †1575 petuita: sped]; 884 scrobibus: furhum [948 scrobibus: groepum], 904 scina: grima [902 scena: sceadu, †1818 scena: uuebung], 907 scalpellum: byris [883 scalpellum: bredisern, 891 scalprum: byris, thuearm, †1806 scalpellum: bor], 935 suffragium: mundbyrd [934 suffragator: mundbora], 953 scina, nitatio: grima [cp. 904 above], 981 scevus: sceolhegi [†1829 scevum: godureci]; 1044 tabida et putrefacta.

The following are wanting both in Ep. and C., occurring in Erf. only:

487 genuinum, intimum, dens: tusc [†961 genuino: tusc, naturale], 717 occupavit: geonette [712 occupavit: onettae], 834 pedetemptim.

The parallel glosses show that in many cases the omissions of C. are caused by the same Latin word reappearing with another, sometimes but slightly differing, rendering. The omissions were probably sometimes deliberate, sometimes the natural result of overlooking one of two similar glosses.

Groups of words in C. and EE.

The treatment of those glosses which contain groups of words offers many points of interest, words being added and omitted, and their order changed both in the Latin and English portions of the glosses. The following lists will give a general view, similar

[1] As this gloss is cut out in Ep., we do not know Ep.'s reading, and it is possible that *gisalbot* may be a German substitution for *gismirwid*.

changes being grouped together. The words omitted or added are in italics.

A. Latin.

(1) *omitted in C.*

103 arcessitus, *evocatus.* 177 cautere, *ferrum.* 370 e vestigio, *statim.* 379 (h)eptafyllon, *septemfolia.* 564 lepor, *subtilitas.* 568 lurcones, *avidi.* 571 lituus, *baculum augurale in prima parte curvum.* 581 lenta, *tarda.* 623 mirifillon, *millefolium.* 667 nausatio, *vomitus.* 685 nap(h)t(h)a, *genus fomenti.* 734 privigna, *filia sororis.* 765 puncto, *foramine, in quo pedes vinctorum tenentur in ligno cubitali, spatio interjecto.* 791 papula, *pustula.* 793 plantago, *septenerbia.* 835 petulans, *spurcus.* 878 rastros, *ligones.* 887 sarculum, *ferrum.* 967 stilium, *fusa.* 978 stilio, *vespertilio.* 981 *scevus,* strabus, *torbus.* 982 serum, *liquor casei.* 988 trutina, *statera.* 992 tropea, *signa.* 994 troc(h)leis, *modicis rotis.* 1001 tragelafus, *platocerus.* 1054 ventriculus, *stomachus avis.*

9 aulea: strel, *vel curtina ab aula.* 171 citropodes: crocha *super* IV *pedes.* 180 cercylus: aesc *vel navis.* 210 convenio: groetu *vel adjuro.* 277 culix: mycg *longas tibias habens.* 550 in mimo: in gliuuae, *quod tamen ad mimarios vel mimigraphos pertinet.* 558 incuba: merae *vel satyrus.* 624 murica: gespan, *aureum in tunica.* 874 rancor: throh *vel invidia vel odium.* 890 sentina: lectha, *ubi multæ aquæ colliguntur in unam*[1] *navem.* 894 scirpea: lebr, *de qua mat(t)a conficitur.* 998 tessera: tasol, *quadrangulum.* 1059 volvola: widuwindae, *herba similis hederæ, quæ vitibus et frugibus circumdari solet.*

9 aulea: strel, *vel curtina, ab aula.* 17 aneta, *a natando.* 391 esculus, *ab edendo.*

509 inlex: tyctaend, *ab inliciendo.* 620 municeps: burgleod, *a mu(ni)cipio.*

515 inritatus *in rixam.* 983 trux *palpitat.*

(2) *added in C.*

71 acris, *fortis.* 281 co(ho)rs, *numerus militum:* tuun. 288 crustallum *similis* haalstaan. 385 exta, *præcordia.* 406 fastidium

[1] om. in Ep.

[*odium*]. 441 fasces [*libri*]. 693 oppilavit, *clausit.* 772 praxinus (fr.), *viridus color.* 789 pittacium, *os peri.* 863 robor, *arbor.*

96 adclinis : tohald, *vel incumbens.* 101 adsæclum : pegn, *minister turpitudinis.* 181 chaos : duolma, *prima confusio omnium rerum.* 250 calt(h)a : reade clafre, *vel genus floris.* 966 salum : secg, *vel mare.* 1048 tipo : draca, *vel inflatio.*

(3) *omitted and added in C.*

172 calculus, ratio, sententia : tebelstan, vel lapillus EE.—calculus, ratio, sententia, numerus : teblstan C.

(4) *retained in both.*

26 achalantis, luscinia, roscinia. 329 deconfugione, statione. 376 echinus, piscis. 404 flavum, fulvum. 686 nanus, pumilio. 740 paludamentum, genus vestimenti bellici. 778 pedo, paturum (?). 837 perstromata, ornamenta. 1018 tuber, tumor. 1061 vulgo, passim.

608 lepus, leporis. 663 Mars, Martis. 664 mus, muris.

109 affectui : megsibbi, vel dilectione. 132 beta : berc, arbor dicitur. 164 contribulus : meeg, Ep.; contribulus : consanguis Erf.; contribulius : meig, vel sanguine C. 218 crepacula : claedur, tabula qua a segitibus territantur aves [1]. 453 fornix : boga super columnis. 501 inluvies secundarum : hama, in quo fit parvulus. 553 in æstivo cænaculo : yppae, ubi per æstatem frigus captant.

984 tonica polimita : hringfaag, a rotundidate circulorum.

529 in dies crudesceret : a fordh. 618 mendacio conposito : geregnodae. 727 pro captu : faengae. 984 tonica polimita : hringfaag [cp. C. †1612 polimita : hringfaag]. 1089 verecundiae concesserim : gilebdae.

(5) *order changed.*

42 ardea et dieperdulum : hragra—ardia : hragra, et dieperdulum. 367 exito : (endi)steb, vel perditio—exito [perditio] : endistaeb. 980 sortem, conditionem : uuyrd—sortem : wyrd, condicionem. 1092 vibrat, dirigat : borettit—vibrat : borettið, vel diregað.

[1] quae a segitibus territat C.

B. English.

(1) *omitted in C.*

5 arula: fyrpannae *vel herth.* 278 commentis: searuum *vel ordoncum.* 579 lenocinium: tychtin *vel scocha.* 583 lembum: listan *vel thres* [cp. C. †1228 limbus: thres, liste]. 673 noctua: naechthræbn, *alii dicunt nectigalae.* 928 strepitu: brectme *vel cliderme.* 997 testudo: bordhaca *vel sceldreda vel faerucæ.* 1042 termofilas: faestin *vel anstigan.*

962 stagnum: *staeg vel* meri. 1017 tilio: *lind vel* baest.

(2) *added in C.*

58 alga: scaldhyflas *vel sondhyllas.* 83 astu: facni *vel fraefeli.* 113 (h)auserunt: nomun, *hlodun.* 147 broel: edisc, *deortuun.* 238 cariscus: cuicbeam, *uuice.* 300 cladica: wefl *vel owef.* 324 dos: wituma *vel uuetma.* 332 delicatis et querulis: wrastum *end seobgendum.* 370 e vestigio: on lande[1], *on laste.* 402 fovet: feormat, *broedeth.* 446 fragor: suoeg, *cirm.* 711 obligamentum: lyb, *lybsn.* 789 pittacium, *os peri*: clut, *cleot.* 951 soccus: socc, *slebescoh.* 960 scirpea: eorisc, *leber.* 989 trulla: cruce, *turl, scofl.*

11 amites: *fugultreo vel* reftras. 256 cicadæ: *secggescere vel* haman. 286 cepa: *ynnilæc,* cipe. 360 emolumentum: [*lean,*] fultum. 372 expilatam: [*aþryid*], arytrid. 388 (h)elleborus: *þung,* woedeberge. 477 galmulum: *molegnstycci,* moling. 531 iners: *esuind,* asolcen. 656 malva: *hocc,* cottuc, gearwan leaf. 688 nodus: *wrasan,* ost. 706 obtenuit: *forcuom,* bigaet. 955 sponda: *benc,* selma. 1003 tridens: *auuel,* meottoc.

210 convenio: *ic* groetu.

461 cisil*stan.* 595 laquear: first*hrof.* 602 liciatorium: hebel*gerd.*

15 abelena: *hæsel*hnutu. 1056 urciolum: *wæter*cruce.

(3) *retained in both.*

(A star shows that *vel* is dropped in C.)

29 (h)arpago: auuel vel clauuo. *307 conpetum: tuun vel ðrop. 342 deferuntur: meldadun vel wrocgdun. *381 extale: snaedil

[1] [on lande] C.

vel thearm. *413 frugus: uncystig vel heamol. 419 fulix: ganot vel dopaenid. 430 falces: uudubil, sigdi, riftr. *473 glaucum: heuui vel grei. 544 index: taecnaendi, torctendi. 572 lacerna: haecilae vel lotha. *573 lumbare: gyrdils vel broec. 790 ptysones: berecorn berendae. *853 runcina: locaer vel sceaba. 862 rostrum: neb vel scipes celae. 873 rostris: foraeuuallum vel tindum. 891 scalprum: byris vel ut alii thuearm [ut alii *om. in C.*].

(4) *order changed.*

426 famfaluca: leasung vel faam—f.: [faam], leasung. 657 marrubium: hunae vel biouuyrt—m.: biowyrt vel hune. 808 picus: fina vel higrae—p.: higre, fina.

There are a few cases in which two glosses have been made into one, and the reverse. The former in

C. 603 crabro: waefs vel hurnitu=EE. 255 crabro: uuaeps, 275 crabro: hyrnitu. C. 874 fibula: hringe, sigl=EE. 408 fibula: sigil, 410 fibula: hringiae.

The latter in

EE. 554 jubar: leoma vel earendil=C. 1161 jubar: earendel, 1166 jubar: leoma. EE. 729 percommoda matutinos: sua cendlic morgenlic=C. 1534 percommoda: sua cenlic, 1535 matutinos: morgenlic [under *p*]. It will be observed that in two cases the order is reversed.

Corpus [1]. This glossary is of considerable length, but as it consists chiefly of Hebrew and other proper names whose meaning or etymology is explained in Latin, it contains but few English glosses. It follows a purely *a*- order, and is evidently entirely unconnected with C.[2] and EE., unless we compare its *scisca : eoforþrote* with the *scasa : eborþrote* of the latter (1816), appearing also in EE. In any case, it has no *special* connection with C.[2], except that of forming part of the same MS. and being written by the same hand. Its relations to the other texts are equally dubious. Its *vomer : scaer* reappears in Erf.[2] (1151) but under *b: bemer: scaer*, and its *tri(p)lex : ðrili* seems to be the same gloss as L.'s *triplex: drili* (158), although *trilex* may stand for *trilix.*

C.[1]'s *a*- order makes it probable that it was compiled from non-alphabetical sources, and that one of these was a class-glossary is shown by the appearance, within so small a compass, of three words relating to tides: *adsida, ledo, malina,* as also by the material meaning of most of the words, which are also nearly all in the nominative.

Although Erf.[2 3] contain many English glosses not in the others, they have evidently drawn partly from the same sources. For the repetition of EE.'s *calor : apricitas* in Erf.[2] see p. 12. Other glosses common to EE. and Erf.[2] are *omentum : mafa, pila : thothur* and several from class-glossaries. In Erf.[3] we find *aleator : tebleri* and *alea : tefil* reappearing both in EE. and in L., the order agreeing with the latter's against EE.'s, and *bucula : randbæg, humiliamanus* (pumilio, nanus): *duerh* reappearing with only slight discrepancies in EE. The gloss *baccula, vitula : cucælf* in Erf.[3] seems to be the original of C.'s *vitula : cucælf*, and there are several other class-glosses found in C. but not in EE., which reappear in Erf.[2 3]. *Lacerta* is an example in Erf.[2]. Erfurt.[2 3].

It is impossible to tell with certainty whether Erf.[2 3] formed part of the unmutilated Ep. MS., but their relation to C. makes it probable that they were included in the original MS. of EE.

Various Readings.

The vocabulary, general structure, and sources of the glossaries having been examined, there still remains the comparison of their divergent readings and the estimation of the value of the evidence of the different texts and MS. We must, of course, distinguish carefully between the text and the MS. which happens to represent it. The text EE. being preserved in two MSS., neither of which is a copy of the other, we are able by a comparison of these two MSS. to eliminate a large number of errors due merely to their scribes, and which did not exist in the prototype of both. For C. we have but one MS., and our only criterion of distinction between textual and scribal forms is the word-order, which admits, however, of only occasional application. But when we find *pilimita* entered under *po-*, we see that the error could not possibly have been made in the original text, and, at the same time, that the Corpus MS. is not the original one, but a copy. We will, therefore, begin with an examination of the obviously scribal errors of the MSS., which will, at the same time, make us acquainted with the idiosyncrasies of the scribes, and the value of their evidence.

Errors of Erfurt.

We will begin with Erf., which, being written by a foreign scribe, naturally contains the largest number of errors, especially in the English words, although it is evident that the British hand often puzzled him in the Latin as well.

The following are full—often exhaustive—examples of the errors of Erf., as far as they admit of classification, isolated errors being passed over, the English words following the Latin, from which they are separated by a stroke.

Addition. Much more in the English than the Latin. Consonants doubled, especially *s*: 41 *accega*, 242 *croccus*, 424 *fassianus*, 552 *invissus*—523 *unbrycci*, 1018 *assuollan*, 1036 *assuant*. Letter anticipated or repeated: 14 *ap(u)lustra*, 180 *cerci(c)lus*—581 *t(h)och*, 614 *t(h)oh*, 699 *bisiuui(si)di*, 728 *saeg(a)esetu*, 729 *morgen(d)lic* (from preceding *suacendlic*), 744 *faer(l)slaegmum*, 756 *s(c)ohtae*, 1020 *(h)ryhæ*, 1067 *f(l)uglum*, 1085 *f(l)ugles*. Addition of *n*: 207 *constipuisse(n)*, 578 *li(n)quentes*—69 *hindberge(n)*, 94 *ger(n)licae*, 245 *sci(n)ccing*, 490 *a(n)suand*. Addition of *c*: 585 *o(c)ter*, 1063 *toch(t)licae*. The former is probably due to the back curl of the *t* in the original. Addition of final vowel in English words: 66 *uermodae*, 193 *mondi*, 385 *becdermi*, 529 *a forthe*, 576 *etrinani*. Addition of *i*: 765 *uinctorium*, 794 *pastinacia*. Addition of *r*: 975 *sinfroniaca*, 983 *palpitrat*.

Omission. Double consonants: 31 *asses (s)corteas*, 145 *blat(t)is*—37 *sep(p)ae*, 93 *to nyt(t)um*, 586 *met(t)ocas*. Of repeated letters: 441 *fa(s)ces*—10 *frict(r)ung*, 41 *holt(h)ana*, 406 *cii(s)nis*. Endings: 461 *glare(a)*—84 *hrægl(i)*, 745 *caebis(ae)*. The unfamiliar thorn: 532 (þ)*ingungae*, 707 (þ)*a*. *h* before a consonant, probably from German analogies: 400 *(h)raen*, 537 *uuidir(h)linienti*.

Truncation: 582 *legu(la)*, 648 *mar(so)picus*, 1090 *vadi(monium)*—680 *unemo(tan)*, 762 *(si)funsterri*, 1050 *(ir)inges*. In some cases this may be the result of the omitted portions of the words having been written above the line in the prototype.

Transposition. 131 *badrigabo*, 923 *stronus* — 141 *art*, 225 *plaster*, 485 *frots*, 508 *hleodendri*, 559 *uuydublindæ*, 769 *spreui*, 798 *hrnigfaag*, 801 *ritf*, 824 *papoeg*.

Changes due to anticipation or repetition: 174 *cartalago*, 224 *cleatrum* (clathrum): *pearroc*, 678 *nugatitas*, 753 *pertinatiter*—177 *cautere, ferrum: fam* (ham), 541 *unasettæ* (-ddæ *from* 542 gisettan), 751 *scyccimelum* (st.), 885 *breitibannæ* (-pannæ).

Endings. *-æ* for *-e* in adverbs: 112 *adrogantissimæ*, 946 *strenuæ*. *-u* for *-i*: 56 *meelu*, 1075 *fletu*. *-is* for *-us*: 118 *affricis*, 796 *pictis*. *-us* for *-is*: 443 *feriatus*. Miscellaneous: 92 *aquila* (-æ), 923 *situlæ* (-a)—636 *apuldro* (-dr), 817 *buturfliogo* (-ae).

Special letters. *t* for *d*, &c.: 547 *intercapito*, 711 *oblicamentum*, 829 *palumpes*—528 *saltae*, 710 *hueolraat*, 1036 *assuant*, 1089 *gilepdae*. *d* for *t*, &c.: 172 *labillus*, 891 *scalbrum*—641 *suibæ*. These confusions may be partly due to German analogies. *ni*, *m*, &c., confused: 773 *panipinus* (pamp.)—714 *edischenim* (-henn), 744 *faerlslaegmum* (-inum), 769 *cinamelti* (un-), 777 uuorsin (uuorsm), 780 *triuumtri* (triuuintri). *m* for *n*: 65 *armiglossa*—493 *redgaesram*, 634 *lim*, 797 *fædum*, 837 *brum*, 852 *graemung* (nn). *n* for *m*: 78 *tilgendun*, 719 *naffa*. *n* for *r*: 5 *anula*, 910 *sandinas*—760 *buyrgenas*. *r* for *s*: 166 *cliborum*, 589 *lurdur*, 644 *murtacia*—643 *ruinsung*, 707 *girettan*, 770 *angreta*, 912 *ruga* (sugu). *s* for *r*: 103 *ascessitus*—619 *easbedlicust*. *r* for *p*: 861 *rodinare*. *s* for *p*: 32 *asueus* (ansueop), 131 *felduus* (-uuop). *f* for *p*: 33 *maefuldur*. *p* for *s*: 434 *ripendi*. *s* for *f*: 459 *hosr*, 807 *felusor*. *p* for *w*: 173 *pindil*. *p* for þ: 444 *puood*, 601 *popistil*. *a* for *u*: 153 *baculus*, 160 *babalis*—36 *falatreu*, 63 *gecaes sarae*, 732 *scoma*, 912 *ruga* (sugu). *u* for *a*: 88 *streumrad*, 162 *eust-*, 169 *-reud*. *a* for *cc*: 120 *bua*, 1008 *broa*. *oc* for *a*: 813 *floc* (=*flea*, the *e* being omitted). These mistakes are due to the *oc*-like shape of the *a*. *a* for *ae*: 474 *smal*, 742 *hrad*. German influence? *e* for *a*: 491 *habitavit*, 1023 *tebe* (tapete). Many other changes.

The errors of the other two MSS. being much fewer, we shall be able to enumerate them with greater fulness, beginning with Ep.

Errors of Epinal.

Addition. Letter anticipated or repeated: 960 *sc(r)irpea*—46 *al(t)erholt*, 124 *h(r)aebrebletae*, 207 *gesuidrad(r)ae*, 464 *quiquae*, 535 *anslegaen(g)rae*, 575 *woe(n)dendi*. Also in 89 *a(d)litus* (halitus), 417 *f(r)agus*, 1092 *vi(m)brat*, 913 *strig(i)a*—76 *gihiodum* (gieodun). Endings: 125 *stearn(o)*.

Omission: 26 *luscin(i)a*, 59 *ac(i)tula*, 819 *pal(i)urus*, 100 *ade(m)pto*, 102 *ade(m)pta*, 849 *qui(n)quenervia*, 220 *c(l)austella*—50 *(h)aesil*, 229 *g(e)leod*, 707 ð*(a)*, 773 *cro(u)s*, 999 *le(n)ctinadl*

1018 *(a)suul'en*, 1059 *wi(d)uwindae*. Two letters omitted: 561 *infri(gi)dat*, 729 *matu(ti)nos*—1051 *auund(en)re*. Endings: 558 *mera(e)*, 903 *cneorissa(e)*.

Transposition: 567 *seng*, 894 *lerb*, 579 *thyctin* (tychtin in prototype ?), 1063 *tholicae*.

Changes due to anticipation: 228 *gybyrdid*, 509 *tyctaend: anbinliciendi* (ab inliciendo).

Endings: 744 *profligatis* (-us), 839 *qualiis* (-lus), 67 *armos* (-us), 759 *provectæ* (-a), 830 *pastellas* (-us), 1051 *verbere torta* (-o).

Special changes. ni for *m*, &c.: 138 *tuum* (tuiin), 594 *multi* (milti). *m* for *n*: 635 *malagma*—76 *gihiodum*. *n* for *r*: 1034 *onsorg*. *r* for *n*: 15 *hrutu*, 437 *smitor*. *n* for *u*: 610 *men*.

Other changes: 62 *ascolonium* (asca.), 961 *sabulcus* (su.), 1069 *vitilago* (-igo), 567 *lobarum* (la.), 637 *martus* (my.)—421 *obtt* (obet), 553 *uppae* (y), 613 *cliþae* (f), 964 *teac* (g), 1038 *sclindinnae* (scild.), 1093 *unþyotgi* (-ctgi).

Errors of Corpus.

In C. it is impossible to distinguish between the errors of the latest scribe and those of his prototype, except in a few instances—marked with a star—where the word-order shows that they were introduced by the former, and only the more obviously clerical errors will therefore be given here.

Addition. 8 *ax(r)edones* (also † 258 *axredo*), 1020 *tapet(s)a*—39 *d(o)r(s)os*, 938 *f(r)aecni*, 983 *unhior(d)e*. Due to anticipation: 963 *sca(l)pula*.

Omission: *65 *a(r)naglosa*, 99 *agre(s)tis*, 101 *adsæc(u)lum*, *438 *f(r)ons*, 945 *ser(i)o*—454 *blaes(t)baelg*, 507 *(a)uundun*, 777 *uuor(s)m*, 915 *a(n)haebd*, 990 *georuuyrde(d)*. Two letters: 93 *ad (ex)pensas*. Ending: 623 *mirifillo(n)*—220 *clustorloc(ae)*.

Truncation: 837 *stefa(d brun)*.

Transposition: 529 *a forht*.

Changes due to anticipation or repetition: 12 *albulo* (-go), *309 *blohonicula* (bothon.), *798 *pilimita* (po.), 1092 *diregað* (-at, from borettið)—337 *handgand* (-ng).

Endings: 23 *aconito* (-a), 305 *corbus* (-is), 453 *fornis* (-ix), 641 *mastigium* (-ia), 652 *majales* (-is).

Special letters: 95 *adsensore* (ss), 110 *arbitus* (arcibus), 419 *funix* (l), 686 *nauus* (nanus), 969 *smus* (sinus), 758 *præfectæ* (prov.), 815 *præventus* (pro.), the last two being probably erroneous expansions of contractions—1 *laergae* (loe.), 4 *brandrod* (-rad), 479 *unaedilsa* (-ra), 535 *onligenre* (onslegenre), 625 *habae* (n.)

The following are errors common to Ep. and Erf., the correct form being in C. Errors of Epinal-Erfurt.

Omission: 26 *roscin(i)a*, 817 *papil(i)o*, 866 *rationat(i)o*, 87 *actuari(u)s*, 579 *lenoci(ni)um*—21 *dil(i)*, 196 *gegeruue(n)dnae*, 227 *mear(c)iseren*, 479 *(un)aedilra*, 831 *duergedost(l)ae*, 1046 *(h)ofr.*

Endings: 3 *argillus* (-a), 402 *fovit* (-et), 465 *genistæ* (-a), 610 *laris* (-us), 709 *omnimoda* (-o).

Special letters: 46 *almeta* (alneta), 226 *calear* (calcar), 497 *horodius* (her.), 565 *lagones* (lig.): *mettocas* (due to confusion with *lagoena: croog*, 584), 659 *margo* (mango), 883 *scalbellum* (scalpellum) [scabellum Erf.] — 123 *redisnae* (raedinne), 126 *handuyrp* (-uyrm), 840 *aehrian* (aegnan).

In comparing the more marked divergences of C. from EE., we cannot help noticing some cases of deliberate alteration in C., contrasting with the mechanical fidelity of the other two, whose divergence from their prototype is almost always unintentional—the result of mere scribal error or omission. The following are clear instances. EE. 540 has the correct *infractus: giuuaemmid*, where C., misled by the Latin *in-*, adds an *un-*, and writes *ungeuuemmid*, thus reversing the original meaning. EE. 750 has *permixtum: gemengidlice*, the *um-* standing, as in other instances, for the adverbial *-im*; C. takes it for an adjective termination, and cuts off the *e* of the English word, making it into the adjective *gemengetlic*. In EE. 781 *papiluus* (papyrus): *ilugsegg* the English word in its archaic spelling was not understood by the scribe of C., and he boldly substituted *wioluċscel* (whelkshell)! The change of *suadu* into *sceadu* in 972 *suesta: suina suadu* seems to be of the same kind. A gross error of C. is *wulfmod* for *colus: wullmod* 306 (*uuilmod*, preserved only in Erf.). Several doubtful cases, in which C. at first sight would seem to have the right reading, may also be explained as alterations. Thus Ep. 739 (om. in Erf.) has *proscribit: ferred*, where C. reads *proscripsit*. It is possible that *proscribit* may be an error for C.'s reading, but it is simpler to suppose that the former in the context it was taken from was a Alterations in Corpus.

historical present, altered to a preterite in C. In EE. 527 *industria: geornnissae* is evidently an ablative, but C. seems to have taken it for a nominative, and to have accordingly altered the English word to *geornis.* For the English adjective in EE. 933 *squalores: or-fiermae* C. has the literal substantive *orfeormnisse.* As EE.'s reading cannot have arisen from this by mere omission, it is possible that in the original context the Latin word was glossed either by the adjective alone or by the adjective with a subst., the latter being afterwards omitted. The change of the, as it stands, unintelligible Latin *in ebhatis* (854) into the English *in eobotum* of C. may also be a deliberate alteration. Note also the correction of the spellings of Latin words in 75 (number of C.) *atqueve,* 856 *foenus,* 857 *foederatus,* where the word-order demands *adqueve* (which is also Ep.'s reading), *fenus, federatus.*

Original errors of Corpus.

The following are errors of C., which probably existed already in the MS. from which it was copied.

164 *contribulius: meig vel sanguine.* E. has *contribulus: meeg.* Erf. substitutes *consanguis* for the English word, so that the original gloss was probably *contribulis: meeg vel consanguis.*

Endings: 336 *debita pensio: gedaebeni geabuli* (*gedebin gebil,* preserved only in Erf.). C. seems to have taken *pensio* for a dative or ablative. 622 *monarchia: anuualda* (anuuald). In 430, where EE. has *falcis* (= falx, falcis): *uudubil, sigdi, riftr,* C. makes the last into the plural *riftras,* leaving *siðe* in the sg. Perhaps he read *falcis* as *falces.* In 509 *inlex: tyctaend* C. has *tyctendi,* the substantival form without the *i* being probably the original. *tyhtin-gum* for the *tyctinnum* (513) of EE. is probably a mere error, due to some confusion with *-ung.*

Doubtful cases.

In the few remaining variations it is doubtful which text is right. For *saeppae* 37 C. has *etspe;* the original gloss was, perhaps, *abies: saeppae et espe. etspe* may, however, be a corruption of *saeppe.* For 1068 *eduualla* C. has *eduuelle,* which form appears again several times in C. (137, 908, &c.), and is, therefore, probably the correct one.

Special variations of Ep. and Erf.

We will now consider the special variations of Ep. and Erf., beginning with Ep.

Ep. right: 187 *conlatio* (conlato Erf. and C.), 411 *fenicia* (fin.), 733 *præpropera* (propropera C., propopera Erf.) = *præpropere.*

The remaining cases are doubtful: 6 *alea : teblae, tefil* Erf., *tebl* C.; the result of confusion between nom. and abl.; as an abl. might be changed into a nom., but not vice versa, Ep.'s reading is probably the original one. 829 *palumbes : cuscutan, cuscotae, -e* Erf., C. Here also the Latin ending is ambiguous, being both sg. and pl., and Ep.'s is probably the original reading.

In 206 *calentes : haetendae* Ep. seems to have changed the correct intransitive *hatende* of Erf. and C. into the trans. verb. In 1078 it has changed *smeruwyrt* into *speruwyrt*, both names of plants: in both cases the reading of Erf. and C. is probably the correct one.

In some few cases Erf. has the right reading of Latin words against Ep. and C.: 60 *accitulum* (*acitelum* Ep., C.; cp. 63 *accitulium* all), 188 *commeatus* (-os) pl., 232 *caractes* (caractis) = *cataractes*, 403 *fiscella* (-illa), 1016 *tabanus* (-unus), 1063 *viscide* (uscide). A few may be explained as corrections of the German scribe, but this will not apply to all of them.

The following divergences in the English words may be due to Erf.'s English original: 641 *suibæ* (suipan), 965 *bollae* (bolla), 1071 *vespa : uuaeps* (vespas: waeffsas), 676 *leccressae* (tuuncressa), 1059 *uuidubindae* (widuwindae). Also 108 *foetribarn* (fosturbarn)?

The close affinity of EE. and C. is attested by the numerous errors in the Latin words which run through all three MSS. There is, however, considerable difficulty in distinguishing scribal corruptions from Low Latin forms. The following lists do not, therefore, lay any claim to exhaustiveness. Those errors marked * reappear in L. also. Errors common to Erf.-Ep. and Corp. (and Leiden).

Endings: * 151 *berrus* (verres), 310 *cantarus* (cantharis), * 879 *ruscus* (-um); 186 *contemptum* (-im), 1023 *tabetum* (tapete); 17 *aneta* (anas), * *arpa* (harpe), 183 *camellea* (chamæleon), * 266 *cardella* (-uelis), 828 *progna* (procne), 733 *præpropera* (-e); 27 *asilo* (-us), * 293 *circinno* (-inus); 231 *capsis* (-a), 243 *culcites* (-as, -a?), 367 *exito* (-ium) perditio, 876 *rumex* (*-en*, from preceding *remex*).

Addition: 518 *in(t)ula*, * 1015 *tinc(t)i*, *tinct* L. (tinca); 952 *scienicis* (*scen-*, originally *scin-*, as in L., with *e* written above?).

Omission: 232 *ca(ta)ractes*, 233 *cer(v)us*, 244 *camis(i)a*, * 269 *cal(li)oma(r)c(h)us*, *calomachus* C., *calomaucus* L., 281 *co(ho)rs*, 303 *col(ch)icum*, 319 *dromidus* (-edarius), 714 *ortigome(t)ra*, 812 *peducla* (pediculus), 916 *sc(i)nifes*. Note, however, that 269–319 are not preserved in Ep.

Truncation: 285 *(nycti)corax*, * 766 *(im)petigo*.

Transposition: * 675 *netila* (nitela).

Special letters: 17 *aneta* (cp. 116 anate), 90 *œgit* (e), * 268 *cacomicanus* (-echanus), 666 *megale* (my.); * 43 *aquilium*, *-us* L. (aculeum), 182 *conquilium* (conchylium); 32 *atflarat* (ad.), 282 *cummi* (g), * 422 *ficetula* (d); 98 *adqueve* (Ep. and original of C.), 828 *progna* (procne), 1023 *tabetum* (tapete); 383 *epilenticus* (pt), 638 *melarium* (p), 697 *oridanum* (g., cp. 691 origanum), 61 *arrius* (*varius*, cp. C. 841 *farius*), * 649 *musiranus* (mus araneus).

The frequent *e* and *o* for *i* and *u* (*argella*, *cospis*, &c.) are no doubt anticipations of Romance forms. The use of *f* for *v* (*farius*, &c.) is common in British MSS., both Celtic and English. In *vicatum* the converse change has taken place.

Different words confounded: 361 *exaltavit* (exhalavit), 484 *gurgulio* (curculio). 235 *color : aac ; color=robur ?* but cp. C. 1651 *praxinus* (*fr.*), *viridus color : aesc.*

Relations of Leiden. The following forms, incorrect in EE. and C., are given correctly in L. (the numbers are L.'s): 35 *vicium* (-am), 243 *acrifolus* (-ium), 145 *cox* (cos), 167 *unibrellas* (umb.), 108 *vitricius* (-cum). In 40 *circino* the *n* is incorrectly doubled in EE. and C.

L. has, on the other hand, many errors of its own, which are corrected in the others: 34 *telam* (-um), 121 *elleus* (ebulum), 140 *aleo* (=*aleator*, from the following *alea ?*), 214 *perdulum* (diep.), 244 *acerafula* (-abulus), and many others.

The intimate relation between L. and C. is shown by the common omission in 107 *viti(li)ginem*. In three other divergences C. is right: 10 *ultro citro* (citroque C.), 110 *fledomum* (flebotoma), 124 *paranimphi* (-nymphus). These are all words which do not occur in EE. In 30 *flavescit, color olei : glitinot*, for which C. has *fl. : glitinat, albescit*, we probably have independent shortenings of a common fuller gloss.

L. and EE. agree partially in L. 248 *almenta*, EE. *almeta* for the correct *alneta* of C.

The innumerable scribal errors of L. in the English words are of the same character as those of Erf. A few examples must suffice: 104 *luad* (laað), 213 *scruc* (ii), 219 *umc* (uinc=finc), 76 *eburdnung* (-ðring), 169 *nordbaeg* (rond-), 55 *ymaeti* (sm.), 38 *uuitubil* (d), 77 *uuec* (g), the last two being probably germanisms. English errors in Leiden.

Summary.

All the glossaries are based on interlinear glosses, Latin and English, in Latin books, and on Latin-English class-glossaries, all at Canterbury, other English glosses being afterwards added in the process of copying and compilation.

Various independent glossaries were compiled from these sources, at first non-alphabetical. Two or more of them were afterwards fused together in various later digests, *a*- order being often made into *ab*- order.

L. is a German copy of an English non-alphabetical collection of literary and class glosses.

All the others are in the later alphabetical order, but are not based on L., though they all (except perhaps C.[1]) have drawn partly from the same sources.

Ep. and Erf.[1] are independent copies of probably the same MS. (EE.), the latter by a German scribe.

EE. itself was compiled partly from non-alphabetical glossaries, partly from *ab*- order ones, the former being thrown into *ab*-order, the two groups being kept apart under each letter.

C.[2] is a copy of a MS. which was compiled partly from the original of EE., partly from a group of other alphabetical literary and class glossaries, including the originals of Erf.[2] and probably of Erf.[3]. That C. was not compiled directly from EE. is proved by its often having the correct reading against both Ep. and Erf.[1]

Plan of Printing.

In printing the three closely-allied glossaries, Ep., Erf., and C., the most convenient arrangement appeared to be, to fuse Ep. and Erf. together, and to give C. on the opposite page. C. has twice as many words as EE., but as there is only one MS., it can be printed in double columns, and thus made to run tolerably even with the other text, which requires the whole breadth of the page. Reference from one MS. to the other is made perfectly easy by the numbers added to each gloss, those in C. referring also to L., which is also provided with an alphabetical index.

The reading of Erf. immediately follows that of Ep., being separated from it by a dash, both in the Latin and the English. When it has the same English reading as Ep., 'both' is added. Its reading of the Latin is the same as that of Ep., except when a variation is given. Thus in 17 the full reading of Erf. is *aneta : aenit a natando.* In order to save space unimportant variations are sometimes relegated to a note.

German words in Erf. and L. are in italics.

For the sake of convenience the ordinary spelling of the Latin words is given in parentheses, often only a single letter being added. Thus 166 *clibosum* (*v*) means that the word is written *clivosum* in our dictionaries. The spelling of the Latin is so far normalized that *j* and *v* are separated from *i* and *u*. Letters omitted are added in parentheses. Otherwise there is no alteration. The English words are left absolutely unaltered. Scribal errors and abnormal spellings are marked with a star both in the English and the Latin. Thus in 46 * *alterholt* the star refers the reader to Erf.'s reading, *alerholt*, as the correct one. This plan was suggested to me by that followed by Sievers in his edition of the Heliand. Those Latin words which require discussion will be treated of in another place, as also doubtful English words.

CORPUS[1].

Interpretatio nominum ebraicorum et grecorum.

Adsida : flood.
calvariae locus : cualmstou.
coliferte (*collibertus*) : geþofta.
clavis (*-us*) : helma.
5 *crepidinem* : neoþoúard [1].
doleus (*-ium*) : byden.
dasile : boor.
decurat : hornnaap.
ferula : hreod.
10 *fundus* : bodan.
foratorium : buiris.
gemellus : getuin.
gacila : snithstreo.
glebulum : hrider.
15 *jungula* : geocboga.
ledo : nepflod.
libitorium (*-atorium*) : saa.
lignarium : uuidubinde.
mantega : taeg.
20 *malina* : fylledflood.
mappa : cneoribt.
maculosus : specfaag.
ment(h)a : minte.
navum : gerinen.
25 *rastrum* : raece.
sicini (*siccine*) : ac ðus.
scisca : eoforþrote.
sublatorium (*suffl.*) : bloestbaelg.
tri(p)lex (or *trilix* ?) : ðrili.
30 *tantalus* : aelbitu.
va(e) : euwa.
vomer : scaer.

[1] *accent distinctly on the* u.

EPINAL-ERFURT.

[† Indicates words wanting in Corpus[2]. The numbers refer to C[2]; those in ( ) to repetitions in EE itself; those in [ ] to Leiden.]

Amites: loerge—loergae. 143[1].
axungia: rysil—risil. 256.
argillus[2] (*-a*): thohae—th[o]ę. 207.
andeda: brandrad—brondrad. 157.
5 *arula*—**anula*: fyrpannae *vel* herth—fyrponne *vel* h[erd]. 208.
alea: teblae—tefil. 110.
aleator[3]: teblere *both*. 111.
axedones[4]: lynisas[5]. 257.
a[*u*]*lea*[6] (*-aea*): strel *vel curtina, ab aula*[7]. 249.
10 (*h*)*ariolatus* (*-io*): *frictrung—frictung. 196.
amites: reftras *both*[8]. 150.
albugo: flio *both*. 112.
axis: aex—*tum*aex. 259.
aplustra (*-e* sg.)—**apulustra*: giroedro—geroedra. 178.
15 *abilina*: *hrutu—hnutu. 33.
al(*l*)*ium*: garlęc—garlec. 113.
aneta (*anas*): aenid, *a natando.*—aenit. 158.
armilausia: sercae *both*. 210.
alba spina: haeguthorn—hagudorn. 114.
20 *apiastrum*: biouuyrt—biuyrt (?). 181.
anet(*h*)*um*: dil *both*. 159.
aesculus[9]: boecae—boeccae. 93.
aconita[10]: thungas *both*. 45.
apio: merici[11]. 182.

[1] *first gloss in both apodixen:* fantasia. [2] i *indistinct in Ep., may be* e. [3] *all but the first* a *torn away in Erf.* [4] axedenes? *Ep.* [5] *whole gloss torn away in Erf.* [6] u *doubtful.* [7] *torn away in Erf., Oehler gives* A . . , . . baula. [8] *this gloss follows* areoli (30) *in Erf.* [9] a *torn off in Erf.* [10] *torn off in Erf.* [11] *Oehler gives* a . . . . meru; *nothing visible now in Erf.*

CORPUS 2.

Incipit glos(s)a secundum ordinem elimentorum alphabeti.

[† Indicates words wanting in Epinal-Erfurt. The numbers refer to Epinal-Erfurt; those in ( ) to repetitions of the gloss in C itself; those in [ ] to Leiden.]

Abelena: haeselhnutu. 15 (cp. 243).
abies: etspe (cp. Ep. 37).
35 *absinthium*: wermod. 66.
abortus: misbyrd. 80.
ablata: binumine. 104.
†*abunde*: *genycthlice.
†*abiget*: wereth.
40 †*ab euro*: eastansudan.
†*ad euronothum*: eastsuth.
†*abditis*: gehyddum.
†*ab affrico*: suðanwestan.
†*ab borea* (*a borea*): eastannorþan.
45 *aconito* (*-a*): þungas. 23.
†*acervus*: muha.
†*a circio*: norðanwestan.
†*actionari*(*i*)*s*: folcgeroebum.
†*acisculum*: piic.
50 †*acies, et ordo militum, et oculorum visus, et acumen ferri*: ecg *vel* scea[r]p*nis*.
a(*c*)*erabulus*: mapuldur. 33 [244].
achalantis, vel luscinia, vel roscinia: nehtęgale. 26 (cp. 1746).
acrifolus (*-ium*): holegn. 34 [243].
acega: holthona. 41 [209].
55 *accearium*: steli. 49 (1428) [188].
acitula: hromsa. 59.
acitelum: hromsan crop. 60.
accitulium: gęces sure. 63.
acinum (*-os*): hindberiae. 69.
60 *acris, fortis*[1], *vel*: from. 71.
actionabatur: scirde. 86.
actuarius: wraec. 87.
accetum(*i*): gefeotodne. 105.
†*acegia*: snite.
65 †*aceti cotilla* (*-ula*), *vas i.*: bolle.
†*acus*: netl *vel* gronuisc.
†*accidia, t*(*a*)*edium, vel anxietas i.*: sorg.
†*adsutae*: gesiuwide.
addictus: forscrifen. 52.
70 *adridente*: tyctende. 85.
†*aduncis*: gebegdum.
ad (*ex*)*pensas*[2]: tó nyttum. 93.
adsensore (*ss*): fultemendum. 95.
adclinis: tohald, *vel incumbens*. 96.
75 *atqueve*[3]: end suelce. 98 (238).
ademto: binumini[4]. 102.
adsaeclum[5] (*assecula*): þegn, *minister turpitudinis*. 101.

[1] fortio. [2] a *over* e. [3] *originally* adqueve, *as shown by alph. order.* [4] gebinumini. [5] u *er. after* c.

25 *alchior* : isęrn—isaern (?). 115.
achalantis vel luscinia[1] *vel roscina* : *nctigalae—nęctęgela[2]. 52.
asilo (*-us*) : briosa *both.* 225.
antiae : loccas *both.* 160.
(*h*)*arpago* : auuel *vel* clauuo *both.* 211.
30 *areoli* : sceabas—scebas. 197.
asses scorteas[3] : lidrinae trimsas—lidrinn : trynsas[4]. 226.
**atflarat—adflarat* : ansueop—*asueus[5]. 235.
acerabulus—**acterabulus* : mapuldur—*maefuldur. 51.
acrifolus (*-ium*) : holegn *both.* 53.
35 *alnus* : alaer—aler. 116.
alneum : fulae trea—*fala treu. 117.
abies : saeppae—*sępae. (cp. C. 34.)
ascella : ocusta *both.* 227.
auriculum—**ariculum* : dros *both.* 239.
40 *arpa* (*harpe*) : earngeat—*aerngeup. 212.
acega—**accega* : holthana—*holtana. 54.
ardea, et dieperdulum : hragra *both.* 198.
aquilium (*aculeus*) : anga *both.* 192.
auriculum : earuuigga—*aeruuica. 240.
45 *auriola* : stigu *both.* 242.
almeta (*aln.*) : *alterholt—alerholt. 119.
alga : uaar[6]—uar. 120.
argella (*-illa*) : laam—lam[7]. 199.
accearium : steeli—steli. 55.
50 *auellanus* : *aesil—haesl. 243.
altrinsecus : an ba halbae—on ba halbe. 121.
addictus : faerscribaen—faerscrifen. 69.
argutie—argutiae : thrauu—trafu. 200.
asfaltum (*ph*) : sp[a]ldr—spaldur. 228.
55 *allipedius* : huitfot *both.* 122.
alvium (*-eus*)—*albium* : meeli—*meelu[8]. 123, 250.
alviolum (*eo*)—*albiolum* : aldot *both.* 124.
**alga—alg*(*a*)*e* : scaldthyflas—scald[t]hyblas. 125.

[1] luscina *Ep.* [2] *open* a, *possibly* = u. [3] corteas *Erf.* [4] *vellum torn at* : . [5] *indistinct : Oehler reads* asuetis. [6] u *over* p. [7] l *over* sr. [8] *this gloss follows the next one in Erf.*

adgrediuntur : geeodun. 76.
†*adlido* : tonwinto.
80 *adnitentibus* : tilgendum. 78.
†*ad libidines* : wraene.
†*adtonitus* : hlysnende. (cp. 267.)
†*ad fasces* : to weorðmyndum.
†*adfligit* : gehuaeh.
85 *adrogantissime* : wlonclice. 112.
†*adplaudat* : on hlior rouuit.
*†*adcommodaturus* : uuoende.
†*adventio* : sarwo.
†*advocatus* : þingere. [113.]
90 †*adhibuit* : gelaðade *vel advocavit.*
†*adplicuit* : geþiudde.
†*aequatis* : efnum.
aesculus : boece. 22.
aegit (*egit*) : wraec. 90.
95 *aestuaria* : fleotas. 107.
aere alieno : geabuli. 115.
†*aegesta* : gors.
†*aequipensum* : ebnwege.
†*afiniculum* : [ellende], *a finibus procul.*
100 *afflarat* : ansuaep. (235).
†*a fafonio* (*v*) : suþanwestan.
affricus : westsuðwind. 118.
affectui : megsibbe, *vel dilectione.* 109.
agre(*s*)*tis* (*-es*) : wildę. 99.
105 †*agastrum* : aegmang (cp. 1435).
†*agitatio* : unstilnis.
†*agitat*(*a*)*e* : onettad.
†*agapem* : suoesendo.
†*agmen* : weorod.
110 *alea* : tebl. 6 [141].
aleator : teblere. 7 [140].
albulo (*-ugo*) : flio. 12.
al(*l*)*ium* : gaarleec. 16.
alba spina : hea[go]ðorn. 19.
115 *alcion* : isern. 25.
alnus : aler. 35 [246].
alneum : fulaetreo. 36.
†*alietum* (*haliaeetos*) : spaerhabuc.
alneta : alerholt. 46 [248].
120 *alga* : waar. 47 [175].
altrinsecus : on ba halfe. 51.
albipedius : huitfoot. 55.
aluuium (*alveum*) : meeli. 56 (250).
alviolum (*eo*) : aldaht. 57.
125 *alga*(*e*) : scaldhyflas *vel* sondhyllas. 58.
alternantium : staefnendra. 75.
alacris : snel. 77.
†*alacer* : swift.
alveus : streamraad. 88.
130 (*h*)*alitus* : aethm. 89.
alumnae : fostorbearn. 108.
†*alapiciosa* (*alopecia*) : calwa.
†*alvearia* : hyfi.
†*altilia* : foedils.
135 †*alcido* (*-edo*) : meau.
†*alcanus* : þoden.
†*alveum* : edúaelle.
†*alitudo* : fothur.
†*alligeo* (*-ego*) : recceo.
140 †*altor* : fostorfaeder.
†*allox* : tahae.
†*allauda* (*alauda*) : lauricae.
†*amites* : *la[e]rgae. 1.
†*amisionem* : forlor.
145 †*amentum*[1] : sceptog.

[1] ammentum.

actula—accitula: hramsa *both*. 56.
60 *acitelum—accitulum*: hramsa crop *both*[1]. 57.
arrius (*varius*): faag *both*. 201.
**ascolonium—ascalonium*: *hynnilaec—ynnilec. 229.
accitulium: geacaes surae—gecaes *sarae. 58.
ambila: laec *both*. 154.
65 *arniglosa—armiglossa* (*arnoglossa*): uuegbradae—uegbradae. 213.
absint(h)ium: uuermod—*uermodae. 35.
**armos—armus*: boog *both*. 215.
anguens: breer *both*. 161.
acinum (*-os*): hindberię—*hindbergen. 59.
70 *arbatae—arbate*: sibaed *both*. 216.
acris: fraam—from. 60.
**aucapatione—aucupatione*: setungae *both*. 244.
†*addicavit—*abdicavit*: bisceredae—bisceridae.
†*adstipulatus* (*-or*): fultemendi *both*.
75 *alternantium*: staefnęndra—staefnendra. 126.
adgrediuntur: *gihiodum—*gaeadun. 78.
alacris: snel—*blidi*. 127.
adnitentibus: tilgendum—tilgendun. 80.
anxius: soęr[g]ęndi—sorgendi. 169.
80 *abortus*: misbyrd *both*. 36.
ausus: gidyrstig—*gedurstip. 245.
appetitus: gitsung *both*. 184.
astu: fa[c]ni—facni. 230.
amiculo: hraecli—*hraegl. 155.
85 *adridente*: tyctendi *both*. 70.
*actionabatur—*accionabatur*: scirde *both*. 61.
actuaris (*-ius*): uuraec—uraec. 62.
alveus: streamrad—*streumrad. 129.
adlitus—(h)alitus: ethm[2]— . . .[3]. 130.
90 *aegit* (*egit*): uuraec—uraec. 94.
avehit: an uueg aferidae[4]—an uoeg *aueridae. 246.
*aquilae—*aquila*: segnas *both*. 194.
ad expensas: to nyttum—to *nytum. 72.

[1] o *written over first* a *of* hramsa *in Erf.* [2] dethm; *the* d *in a later hand.* [3] *left blank.* [4] f *over* u.

†*ambrones* : gredge.
†*ambages* : ymbsuaepe.
†*ambrosea* (-*ia*) : suoetnis.
†*amens* : emod.
150 *amites* : fugultreo *vel* reftras. 11.
†*amtes*: oemsetinne wiingeardes.
†*ambulas* : þiustra.
. †*amilarius* : mearh.
ambila : laec. 64.
155 *amiculo* : hregli. 84.
amentis : sceptloum. 106.
andeda : *bran[d]rod. 4 [192].
aneta (*anas*) : enid. 17.
anet(*h*)*um* : dili. 21.
160 *antiae* : loccas. 28.
anguens : breer. 68.
†*antefata* : forewyrde.
†*anastasis* : dilignissum.
†*antemn*(*a*)*e* : waede.
165 *antemna* : seglgerd. 111.
†*antedo* (*antidotum*) : wyrtdrenc.
†*ansatae* : aetgaere.
anten(*n*)*a* : boga.
anxius : sorgendi. 79.
170 *annua* : gerlice. 94.
anate (*anas*) : cladersticca. 116.
anser : goos. 117.
†*anus* : ald uuif.
†*anguil*(*l*)*a* : el.
175 †*anceps* : tuigendi.
†*antulus* : caecbora.
†*aporians*[1] : anscungendi.
aplustra (-*e* sg.) : geroeðro. 14.
†*aper* : eobor.
180 †*aporiamur* : biað þreade.
apiastrum : biowyrt. 20.
apio : merice. 24.
†*apo*(*s*)*tasia* : fraetgengian.
appetitus : gidsung. 82.
185 *apparitione* : getiunge. 97.
†*aparatu* : aexfaru.
†*applare* : eorscripel.
†*apricitas, color* : hio.
†*ap*(*p*)*aritio* : gethingio.
190 †*apparatum* : geþrec.
†*appotheca* (*apotheca*) : winfaet.
aquilium (*aculeus*) : onga. 43 [233].
†*aquemale* (*aquaemanalis*) : lebel.
aquilae : segnas. 92.
195 †(*h*)*armonia* : suinsung.
(*h*)*ariolatus* : frihtrung. 10.
areoli : sceabas. 30.
ardia (-*ea*) : hra[g]ra *et dieperdulum.* 42 [214].
argella (-*illa*) : laam. 48 [187].
200 *argutiae* : thrauuo. 53.
arrius (*varius*) : faag. 61.
†*arbutus* : aespe.
†*argutiae* : gleaunisse.
†*arx* : faestin.
205 †*archtoes* (*arctos*) : waegneþixl.
†*artura* : tot.
argilla : thoae. 3.
arula : fyrponne. 5.
†*artemon* : obersegl, *vel malus navis.*
210 *armilausia* : serce. 18.
(*h*)*arpago* : awel *vel* clauuo. 29.

[1] *second* a *over* e.

annua : gerlicae—*gernlicae. 170.
95 *adsessore*—**adsessores* : fultemendum *both.* 73.
adclinis[1] : tohald *both.* 74.
apparatione : gitiungi—*get[o]ing[2]. 185.
**adqueve*—*atqueve* : aend suilcae—end suilce. 75.
agrestes : uu[i]ldae—uuildae. 104.
100 †**adepto*—*ademto* : ginumni—:enumini[3].
adsaeculam (*assecula*)—**adsexulam* : thegn—degn. 77.
**adepta*—*ademta* : binumni *both.* 76.
arcessitus[4] *vel evocatus* : fetod—*fet[t]ad. 222.
ablata : binumini—*binoman.* 37.
105 *accetum* (*i*) : gefetodnae—*gefetatnae. 63.
amentis : sceptloum *both.* 156.
aestuaria : fleotas—fleutas. 95.
alumne—*alumnae* : fosturbearn—*foetribarn. 131.
affectui : megsibbi *vel dilectione* both. 103.
110 *arcibus* : faestinnum—fęstinnun. 223.
antempna—*antemna* : segilgaerd *both.* 165.
adrogantissime—**adrogantissimae* : uulanclicae—*gelplih.* 85.
(*h*)*auserunt* : naamun—*noumun. 247.
arcister : strelbora *both.* 224.
115 *aere alieno* : gaebuli *both.* 96.
anate (*-as*) : cladersticca—claderstecca[5]. 171.
anser : goos *both.* 172.
affricus—**affricis* : westsuþwind—uestsuduuind. 102.
atticus : dora *both.* 236.

120 *Buccula* : bucc—*bua[6]. 338.
balus : isęrnfetor—isaernfetor. 272.
bothonicula : stappa[7]—stoppa. 309.

[1] *last* i *over* a *in Erf.* [2] o *doubtful.* [3] *from Oehler; torn off now.* [4] ascessitus *Erf.* [5] d *from* t. [6] *in Erf. this gloss comes at the end of* b. [7] *first* a *altered; meant for* o (?).

arpa (*harpe*): earngeot. 40 [207].
anaglosa (*arnoglossa*): wegbrade. 65.
†*arpia*: ceber.
215 *armus*: boog. 67.
arbatae: sibaed. 70.
†*ars plumaria*: uuyndecreft.
†*archiatros*: healecas.
†*arvina*: risel.
220 †*ardebat*: scaan.
†*ar*(*r*)*ectas*: hlysnendi.
†*arcessitus*: feotod. 103.
arbitus (*arcibus*): faestinnum. 11
arcister: strelbora. 114.
225 *asilo* (-*us*): briosa. 27.
asses scorteas: liþrine trymsas. 31.
ascella: ocusta. 38.
asp(*h*)*altum*: spaldur. 54 [32].
ascalonium: ynnelaec. 62.
230 *astu*: facni *vel* fraefeli. 83.
†*ascop*(*er*)*a*: kylle.
†*aspera*: unsmoþi.
†*asapa*: earngeat.
†*astur*: haesualwe.
235 *atflarat* (*adfl.*): onsueop. 32 (100).
atticus: dora. 119.
†*attoniti*: hlysnende, afyrhte. (cp. 82.)
atqueve: *on suilce. (75)
auriculum: dorsos. 39 [200].
240 *auriculum*: earwicga. 44 [234].
†*avus*: aeldra faeder.
auriola: stigu. 45.
avellanus: hae[s]l. 50 (cp. 33) [161].
aucupatione: setunge. 72.
245 *ausus*: gedyrstig. 81.
avehit: on weg aferide. 91.
(*h*)*auserunt*: nomun, hlodun. 113.
†*avena*: atę.
aul(*a*)*ea*: stregl[1]. 9.
250 *a*(*l*)*v*(*e*)*um*: meli. (123).
†*auspicantur*: haelsadon.
†*auster*: suðuuind.
†*augur*: haelsere.
†(*h*)*ausurae*: brucende.
255 †*aurocalcum* (*orichalcum*): groeni [a]ar.
axungia: rysel. 2.
axredones (*axe.*): lynisas. 8.
†*axredo* (*axe.*): lynis.
axis: aex. 13.

260 *Bacidones*: raedinne. 123.
bagula: bridels. 127.
balsis: teter. 128.
ballista: staefliðre. 136.
basterna: beer. 137.
265 *bat*(*t*)*uitum*: gebeaten. 140.
baccinia: beger. 143.
ballena (*balaena*): horn. 146 (1522) [164].
†*barritus*: genung.
battat: geonath. 149 [194].
270 †*basterna*: scrid.

[1] g over a.

bacidones: redisnae—rędisnae. 260.
bicoca: *hraebrebletae—hebrebletae. 194.
125 *beacita—biacita*: *stearno—stęrn. 284.
briensis: *hand[u]yrp—*honduyrp. 320.
bagula[1]: bridils—brigdils[2]. 261.
basis—balsis: teter *both*. 262.
bobellum (*bovilla*): falaed *both*. 310.
130 *bratium*: malt *both*. 322.
*bradigabo—*badrigabo*: felduuop[3]—*felduus. 323.
beta (*betula*): berc, *arbor dicitur* both. 285.
bitumen: lim *both*. 295.
bulla: sigil *both*. 331.
135 *beneficium*: fremu *both*. 286.
ballista: staeblidrae—steblidrae. 263.
basterna: beer *both*. 264.
byssum: *tuum—tuigin. 343.
bitiligo (*v*): blec thrustfel *both*. 296.
140 *battuitum—*batuitum*: gibeataen—gebeatten. 265.
bile (*-is*): atr—*art. 297.
bubu (*-o*): uuf *both*. 334 (161).
bucina: begir *both*. 266.
blitum: clatae—clate. 306.
145 *blattis—*blatis*: bitulum *both*. 307.
ballena (*balaena*): hran—hron. 267.
broel: edisc *both*[4]. 324.
broelarius—broellearius: ediscueard[5]—ediscuard. 325.
batat—battat: ginath *both*[6]. 269.
150 *bruchus*: ce[f]r—cefr. 326.
berrus (*verres*): baar *both*. 287.
bruncus—brunchus (*broncus*): uurot—urot. 327.
*buculus—*baculus*: randbeag—rondbaeg. 335.
berruca (*v*): uue[a]rtae—uaertae. 288.
155 *byrseus—*byrreus*: lediruuyrcta—lediruyrhta. 344.
berna (*v*): higrae—higrę. 290.
bona: scaet *both*. 311.

[1] g *over* c *in Ep.* [2] g *from* s. [3] fe:l. [4] *comes before the preceding gloss in Erf.* [5] e:d. [6] *er. after* i *in Erf.*

†*balbus*: uulisp.
balus; isernfeotor. 121.
†*ba(c)chantes*: uuoedende.
†*barat(h)rum*: dael. [98].
275 †*basis*: syl.
†*ballationes*: cnop.
†*balbutus*: stomwlisp.
†*ban*: segn.
†*bapis* (*baptes*): treuteru.
280 †*baruina*: barriggae.
†*balneum*: stofa.
†*balatus*: bletid.
†*bariulus*: reagufinc.
beacita: stearn. 125.
285 *beta* (*betula*): berc, *arbor dicitur.* 132.
beneficium[1]: fre[o]mo. 135.
berrus (*verres*): baar. 151 [241].
berruca (*v*): ucarte. 154 [186].
†*bellicum*: slag.
290 *berna* (*v*): higrae. 156.
bena (*avena*): atę.
†*becta*: stęnt.
†*bettonica* (*betonica*): aturlaðe.
bicoca: haebreblete. 124.
295 *bitumen*: liim. 133.
bitiligo (*v*): blaec thrustfel. 139.
bile (*-is*): atr. 141.
†*bitulus* (*betula*): berc.
†*biothanatas*: seolfboran.
300 †*bitricius* (*vitricus*): steopfaeder.
†*birbicariolus* (*vervecariolus*): werna.
†*bitorius*: erdling.
†*bipertitum*: *herbid.
†*bilance*: tuiheolore.
305 †*bibulta*: billeru.
blitum: clate. 144.
blattis: bitulum. 145.
†*blessus* (*blaesus*): stom.
blohonicula[2] (*bothonicula*): stoppa. 122.
310 *bofellum* (*bovilla*): falud. 129.
bona: scaet. 157.
boreus (*-eas*): eastnorðwind. 162.
†*bobulcus* (*bu.*): hriðhiorde.
†*bovestra*: radre.
315 †*bacarius*[3] meresuin.
†*bofor*: lendislieg.
†*bombosa*: hlaegulendi.
†*botrum* (*botryo*): clystri.
†*bolides*: sundgerd in scipe *vel* metrap.
320 *briensis*: honduyrm. 126.
†*bra(c)hiale*: gyrdels.
bratium: malt. 130.
bradigabo: felduop. 131.
broel: edisc, deortuun. 147.
325 *broellarius*: ediscueard. 148.
bruchus: cefer. 150.
bruncus (*broncus*): wrot. 152.
bra(n)c(h)iae: cian. 158 [61].
†*brittia*: cressa.
330 †*braugina*: barice.
bulla: sigl. 134.

[1] aeneficium. [2] preceded by other *bo-* words. [3] *originally* bocarius, *as shown by alph. order.*

branc(h)iae—brancie : cian *both*. 328.
burrum : bruun—*bruum. 336.
160 *bubalis* (*-us*)—**babalis* : uusend—uesand. 337.
bufo (*bubo*)—*bubu* : uuf *both*[1]. (142.)
boreus (*-as*) : eastnorþwind—*eustnorduind. 212.

Colonus : gibuur—*vicinus*. 493.
contribulus (*-is*) : meeg—*consanguis*[2]. 495.
165 *calculus* : calc *both*. 345.
clibosum (*v*)—*cliborum* : clibecti *both*. 478.
colobium : ham—hom. 494.
caccabum : cetil *both*. 346.
coccum bis tinctum : uuilocre[a]d[3]—*u[u]slucreud. 496.
170 *cados* : ambras *both*. 347.
citropodes : crocha *super* IV *pedes*—*chroca. 461.
calculus, ratio vel sententia vel : tebelstan *vel lapillus*—*tebiltan *vel* **labillus*. 349.
cartellus : windil—*pindil. 348.
cartilaga (*-o*)—**cartalago* : naesgristlae *both*. 350.
175 *carbunculus* : spyrng[4]—spryng. 351.
†*celatum—caelatum* : utathru[n]gaen—utathrungen.
cautere (*-er*), *ferrum id est* : haam—*fam. 352.
cotizat : teblith *both*. 497.
convexum : hualb—*halb. 498.
180 *cercylus—cerciclus* (*cercurus*) : aesc *vel navis* both. 438.
chaos—**chos* : duolma—dualma. 457.
conquilium (*conchylium*) : uuilucscel—uuylucscel. 499.
camellea (*chamaeleon*) : uulfes camb *both*. 355.
canis lingua : ribbae *both*. 356.
185 *cicuta* : hymblicae—huymblicae. 462.
contemptum (*-im*) : heruuendlicae—haeruendlicae. 500.
conlatio—**conlato* : ambechtae *both*. 501.
**commeatos—commeatus* : sandae[5]—sondae. 502.

[1] *follows* brunchus (152) *in Erf.*
[2] *over er; g still visible.*
[3] read *from* raed.
[4] n *on er.*
[5] scandae; c *erased.*

†*bux*(*us*): box.
†*butio*: cyta.
bubo: uuf. 142.
335 *buculus*: rondbaeg. 153.
burrum: bruun. 159.
bubalis[1] (*-us*): weosend. 160.
buccula: buuc. 120.
†*bucitum* (*e*): seotu.
340 †*butio*: frysca.
†*bunia*: byden.
†*bubla*: flood.
byssum: tuin. 138.
byrseus: leðeruyrhta. 135 [190].

345 *Calculus*: calc. 165.
caccabum: cetil. 168.
cados: ambras. 170.
cartellus: windil. 173.
calculus, ratio, vel sententia, vel numerus vel: teblstan. 172.
350 *cartilago*: naesgristle. 174.
carbunculus: spryng. 175.
cautere (*-er*): aam. 177.
†*catapulta*: flaan.
†*cabillatio* (*v*): glio.
355 *camellea* (*chamaeleon*): wulfes camb. 183.
canes (*-is*) *lingua*: ribbe. 184.
calentes: hatende. 206.
caulem: steola. 215.
†*capulus*: helt.
360 *caumeuniae*: eordreste. 219.
calcar: spora. 226.
cauterium: merciseren. 227.
catasta[2]: geloed. 229.
†*capillatur* (*-io*): faexnis.
365 *capsis* (*-a*): cest. 231.
†*carcura* (*carceres*): craet.
caractis (*cataracta*): uuęterþruh. 232.
cariscus: cuicbeam, uuice. 238.
capitium: hood. 239.
370 *camis*(*i*)*a*: ha[a]m. 244.
carix (*-ex*): secg. 251 [151].
†*canalibus*: waeterðrum.
cappa: scicging. 245.
castanea: cistenbeam. 249.
375 *calt*(*h*)*a*: reade clafre *vel genus floris*. 250.
†*capistrum*: caebestr.
calcesta: huite clafre. 254.
†*cavanni*: ulae.
cancer: haebrn. 258.
380 *calciculium*: ieces surae. 263.
cardella (*-uelis*): þisteltuige. 266 [220].
cacomicanus (*kakomēkhanos*): lo[g]ðor. 268 [231].
calomachus (*calliomarchus*): haet. 269 [162].
cardu(*u*)*s*: þistel. 271.
385 *castorius*: beber. 272 [235].
†*caenum*: wase.
carectum: hreod. 290.
carpella: sadulboga. 283.
†*carina*: bythne.
390 *cant*(*h*)*i*: faelge. 292.
cassidele: pung. 297.
cappa: snod. 301.
carpasini: graesgroeni. 298.
calmetum: mer[s]c. 289.

[1] u *over the* a.

[2] *second* a *over* e.

contubernalis : gidopta[1]—*gidogta. 500.

190 *conjectura* : resung *both*. 501.

condidit : gisettae—gisette. 502.

convincens : obaer[s]taelendi—oberstęlendi. 503.

corben (*-is*) : mand—*mondi. 511.

convicta : obaerstaelid—oberstaelid. 515.

195 *concidit* : tislog—*gislog. 516.

conparantem : *gegeruuednae—*gegeruednae. 517.

censores : giroefan—geroefan. 439.

coaluissent : suornodun—*suarnadun. 518.

cuniculos : smigilas—smygilas. 608.

200 *concedam* : lytisna *both*. 519.

conjurati : gimodae—gimo[de]. 520.

contumax : anmod—onmod. 521.

confussione—*confusione* : gimaengiungiae—gem*en*giungae. 522.

concesserim : arectae[2] *both*. 523.

205 *conpar* : gihaeplice—gihaeplicae. 524.

calentes : haetendae—hattendae. 357.

constipuisse — **constipuissen* : *gesuidradrae[3] — *gisuderadae[4]. 525.

curiositas : feruuitgeornnis—feruitgernis 609.

clava : *stegn—stęng. 480.

210 *convenio* : groetu *vel adjuro*—*gloeto. 526.

contis : spreotum—spreutum. 527.

condiciones—*conditiones* : raedinnae—redinnae. 529.

crebrat—*crefrat* (*cribrat*) : siftit—siftid. 596.

consubrinus (*consobrinus*) : gesuirgion—gisuirgian. 530.

215 *caulem* : stela *both*. 358.

†*clunis* : lęndnum—*laendum.

coc(*h*)*leae* : lytlae sneglas *both*. 531.

crepacula : claedur, *id est tabula qua a segitibus territantur aves*—cledr. 599.

caum[*e*]*uniae*—*caumaeuniae* : eordrestae—eordraestae. 360.

[1] o *over* a. [2] e *erased after first* a *in Ep.* [3] *first* e *from* i. [4] *second* d *from t.*

395 †*caliga*: scoh.
carbo: gloed. 304.
carduelis: linetuige. 309.
cantarus (*cantharis*): wibil. 310.
†*caper*: heber.
400 †*callos*: weorras *vel* ill [13].
†*carula* (*garrula*): crauue.
cartilago: grun[d]sopa. 312.
†*capria* (*-ea*): raha.
†*cauda*: steort.
405 †*caldaria*: cetil.
†*cater*: suearth.
†*cartago* (*sartago*): braadponne.
†*caragios*[1] (*caragogos*): lyblaecan.
†*casla* (*casia*): heden.
410 †*canda*: boga.
†*campus*: brogdetende *vel* deppetende.
†*carbasus*: seglbosm.
†*cautionem*: gewrit.
†*capulum*: helt.
415 †*caumati*: suole.
†*caverniculis*: holum.
†*capistrinum*: geflit.
†*cassidis*: helmes.
†*casus*: fer.
420 †*casis*: ned.
†*casso* (*in cassum*): idle.
†*cassium* (*-is*): helm.
†*cardo*: heor.
†*caelatum*: agraben[2].
425 †*canthera* (*-arus*): trog.
†*callus*: waar.
†*calvarium*: caluuerclim.
†*cardiolus*: uudusnite.
†*callis*: paat.
430 †*capistro*: caefli.
†*calleo*: fraefeleo.
†*cauliculus*: steola.
†*carpebat*: sclat.
†*cavernas*[3]: holu.
435 *cartamo* (*cardamum*): lybcor[n]. 279 (459).
†*carc*(*h*)*esia*: bunan.
†*cessere*: *onwicum.
cercilus (*cercurus*): aesc. 180.
censores: geroefan. 197.
440 †*censeo*: doema.
†*cesuram*: gegandende.
celox: ceol. 230.
cer(*v*)*us*: elh. 233.
c(*a*)*erula*: heawi. 221.
445 *cerasius* (*-sus*): ciserbeam. 237.
cerefolium: cunelle. 246.
cĕfalus: heardhara. 270 [165].
c(*a*)*epa*: ynnilaec, cipe. 286.
†*c*(*a*)*ementum*: liim, *lapidum*.
450 †*cente* (*ganta*): wilde goos (*cp.* 963).
†*c*(*a*)*elatum*: abrectat.
†*cespites*: tyrb.
†*cessit*: gecode.
†*cereacus*: hornblauuere.
455 †*cernua*: hald.
†*cerefolium*: cerfelle.
chaus (*-os*): duolma, *prima confusio omnium rerum.* 181.
chaumos: suol. 274.
chartamo (*cardamum*): lybcorn (435).

[1] *o over* u. [2] *letter er. after second* a. [3] *second* a *over* u.

220 **caustella—clustella* : clustorlocae—clusterlocae. 481.
c(a)erula : haeuui—*haui. 444.
cofinus (*ph*) : mand. 532.
commentariensis[1] : giroefa—geroefa. 533.
*clat(h)rum—*cleatrum* : pearroc *both*. 486.
225 *cospis* (*u*) : palester—*plast*er*. 534.
calear (*calcar*) : spora *both*. 361.
cauterium : *mearisern—*merisaen. 362.
clabatum (*v*) : *gybyrdid—gebyrdid. 487.
catasta : gloed—geleod. 363.
230 *celox—*caelox* : ceol *both*. 442.
capsis (*-a*) : cest *both*. 365.
caractis—caractes (*cataractes*) : uua[e]terthruch—*uaeterthrouch. 367.
cer(v)us : elch *both*[2]. 443.
†*cyat(h)us—*cutus* : bolla—bollae.
235 *color* : aac *both*. 535.
corylus : haesil—haesl. 536.
cerasius[3]*—caerassius* (*cerasus*) : cisirbeam—cysirbeam. 445.
cariscus : cuicbeam. 368.
capitium : hood *both*. 369.
240 †*cornicula* : chyae—ciae.
cornacula[4] (*-icula*) : crauuae *both*. 537.
*crocus—*croccus* : gelu—gelo. 598.
culcites (*-ta*) : bedd *both*. 610.
camisa (*-ia*)*—camissa* : haam *both*[5]. 370.
245 *cappa* : scicing—*scinccing. 373.
cerefolium : cunillae *both*. 446.
corimbus (*y*) : leactrocas *both*. 540.
cicuta : uuodaeuistlae—*uuodeuuislae[6]. 463.
castania : *cistimbeam. 374.
250 *calt(h)a* : *rede clabre. 375.
carix (*-ex*) : *sech. 371.

[1] t *over* d *in Ep.* [2] c *over* e *in Erf.* [3] *might also be read* cerasrius. [4] a *over* i *in Ep.* [5] *second* a *in Ep. altered from* i (*probably first stroke of an* m). [6] *beginning of gap in Ep., this gloss being the last.*

460 †*chorus* (*caurus*): eostnorð-wind.
citropodes: chroa, croha. 171.
cicuta: hymlice. 185.
cicuta: wodewistle. 248.
cicad(*ae*): secggescere *vel* haman. 256.
465 *ciconia*: storc. 259 [206].
• *cicer*: bean. 284.
cisculus: heardheau. 262 [199].
cinoglosa (*cynoglossos*): ribbe. 280.
circinno (*circinus*): gabulrond. 293 [40].
470 *circius*: westnorðwind. 311.
†*cis*: biheonan.
†*cimiterium* (*coemeterium*), *pontiani*: licburg, *a nomine pon' pr' qui construxit.*
†*circinni*: windelocca[s].
†*circinatio*: oefsung.
475 †*cinnamomum*: [cymin], *resina.*
†*cicuanus* (*ciconia*): higrae.
†*citonium* (*cydonia*): goodaeppel.
clibosum (*v*): clibecti. 166.
†*clavia* (*-vus*): borda.
480 *clava*: steng. 209.
clustella: clustorloc. 220.
cladica: wefl *vel* owef. 300.
†*clinici*: faertyhted.
†*clavus caligaris* (*-ius*): scohnegl.
485 †*clas*(*s*)*is*: flota.
clatrum (*clathri*): pearuc. 224.
clabatum (*v*): gebyrded. 228.
†*clus*: teltreo.
†*clima*: half.
490 †*clavicularius*: caeghiorde.
†*commis*(*s*)*ura*: flycticlað.
†*conabulum* (*cunabula*): cilda trog [*cp.* 154].
colonus: gebuur. 163.
colobium: hom. 167.
495 *contribulius* (*-is*): meig, *vel sanguine.* 164.
coccum bis tinctum: wiolocread. 169.
cotizat: tebleth. 178.
convexu(*m*): hualf. 179.
conquilium (*conchylium*): wilocscel. 182.
500 *contemtum* (*-im*): *heuuendlice. 186.
conlato (*-io*): oembecht. 187.
commeatos (*-us*): sondę. 188.
contubernalis: geþofta. 189.
conjectura: resung. 190.
505 *condidit*: gesette[1]. 191.
convincens: oberstaelende. 192.
†*codices*: onheawas.
†*consutum*: gesiowed.
†*corimbos* (*y*): bergan.
510 †*commercium*: ceapstou, gestrion.
corben (*-is*): mand. 193.
†*conpactis*: gegaedradon.
corbus (*-is*): cauuel. 305.
†*consulo*: frigno.
515 *convicta*: oberstaeled. 194.
concidit: toslog. 195.
conparantem: gegaerwendne. 196.
coaluissent: suornadun. 198.

[1] *second e under the line.*

culmus: *uuryd. 612.
cucumis: popeg. 611.
calesta[1]: huitti clabre. 377.
c(r)abro: uaeps. 603.
cicad(a)e: haman. 464.
cu(r)culio: æmil. 613.
cancer: hafaern. 379.
ciconia: storc. 465.
cupa: bydin. 614.
colobostrum (*colostrum*): beost. 541.
ciscillus: heardheui. 467.
calciculium: *iaces *sura. 380.
cucuzata: laepaeuincæ. 619.
cuculus: gęc. 618.
cardella (*-uelis*): thistil. 381.
coc(h)leas: uuylocas. 542.
cacomicamus (*kakomēkhanos*): logdor. 382.
calomacus (*calliomarchus*): haeth. 383.
cefalus: heardhara. 447.
carduus: thistil. 384.
castorius: bebir. 385.
campos (*compos*): faegen. 543.
camos: suol. 458.
crabro: hirnitu. 603.
contentus: ginehord. 544.
culix (*-ex*): mi[c]hc, *longas tibias habens*. 617.
commentis: searuum *vel* ordoncum. 545.
cartamo (*cardamum*): lypbcorn. 435.
cynoglossa (*-os*): ribbae. 468.
co(ho)rs: tuun. 546.
cummi (*g*): teru. 616.
carpella: sadulbogo. 388.
cicer: bean. 466.
(*nycti*)*corax*: hraebn. 553.
caepa: cipae. 448.
culinia: *coacas. 620.
crustulla (*crustallum*): halstan. 604.

[1] o *over the* e.

concedam: lytesna. 200.
520 *conjurati*: gemode. 201.
contumax: anmood. 202.
confusione: gemengiunge. 203.
concesserim: arecte. 204.
conpar: gehaeplice. 205.
525 *constipuisse*: gesuedrade. 207.
convenio: ic groetu. 210.
contis: spreotum. 211.
†*contos*: speoru.
condicione: raedenne. 212.
530 *consobrinus*: gesuigran. 214.
coc(h)leae: lytle sneglas. 217.
coffinus (ph): mand. 222.
commentariensis: geroefa. 223.
cospis (u): palstr. 225 (622).
535 *color*: aac. 235.
corylus: haesl. 236.
cornacula (-icula): crauue. 241.
cornix: crawe. 308.
†*conglutinata*: gelimed.
540 *corimbos (y)*: leactrogas. 247.
colostrum: beost. 261 [178].
coc(h)leas: uuiolocas. 267.
conpos: faegen. 273.
contentus: geneorð. 276.
545 *commentis*: seorwum. 278.
co(ho)rs, numerus militum: tuun. 281.
†*confici*: gemęngan.
†*conpetentes portiunculas i.*: gelimplice daele.
†*conpagem*: gegederung.
550 †*coituras*: gegangendo.
†*commanipularius*: gescota, *vel conscius, socius, collega.*
†*consobrinus*: sueor.
(nycti)corax: hraefn. 285.
commis(s)ura: cimbing. 291.
555 *cox (cos)*: huet[e]stan. 294 [145].
coxa: thegh. 295.
conpetum: tuun, þrop. 307.
colicus (colchicum): eoburthrote. 303.
colus: *wulfmod. 306.
560 †*conc(h)is*: scellum.
†*conc(h)a*: mundleu.
†*coagolum (-ulum)*: ceselyb.
†*commolitio*: forgrindet.
†*concisium*: scelle.
565 †*confundit*: menget.
†*commentum*: aþoht.
†*conderetur*: gewarht.
†*conpedium*: gescroepnis.
†*coleandrum*: cellendre.
570 †*colomata (calliomarchus)*: haetcolae.
†*concha*: [beme].
†*convaluit*: geuaerpte.
†*consors*: orsorg.
†*comitavere*: to gelestunne.
575 †*conclamatus*, [*commotus*]: loma.
†*concessit*: geuuat[1].
†*commendabat*: trymide.
†*condebitores*: gescolan.
†*concussionibus*: raednisse.
580 †*confoti*: afoedde.
†*convenientes*: seruuende.
†*conlisio*: slaege.
†*coturno (-ix)*: *wodhae.
†*contio*: gemoot, *convocatio populi.*

[1] geuuatu.

cemetum : merisc. 394 (302).
290 *carectum* : hreod. 387.
commissuras : cimbing. 554.
cant(h)i : felge. 390.
circinno (*circinus*) : gabelrend. 469.
cox (*cos*) : huetistan. 555.
295 *coxa* : theoh. 556.
†*cervical* : *bol.
cassidele : pung. 391.
carpassini : gręsgro[e]ni. 393.
crus : scia. 602.
300 *caldica* : uuefl. 482.
cappa : snod. 392.
calmetum : *merix. 394 (289).
colicum (*colchicum*) : aebordrotae. 558.
carbo : gloed. 396.
305 *corvis* (*corbis*) : couel. 513.
colus : *uuilmod. 559.
conpetum : tuun *vel* ðrop. 557.
cornix : crauua. 538.
carduelis : *linaethuigae. 397.
310 *cantarus* (*cantharis*) : uuibil. 398.
circius : *uuestnorduuid. 470.
cartilago gg. : *grundsuopa. 402.

Dulcis sapa : *coerim. 709.
defructum (*defrutum*) : coerin. 628.
315 *dolatum* : gesnidan. 701.
dodrans : aegur. 702.
dumus : thyrnae. 710.
devotaturus : uuergendi. 632.
dromidus (-*edarius*) : afyrid *obbenda. 707.
320 *dromidarius* : se *oritmon. 708.
dalaturae (*dolatorium*) : *braedlaestu *aesc. 703.
decrepita : dobendi. 638.
desidebat : unsibbadae. 639.

585 †*costa*: rib.
†*contionatur*: maðalade, *declamat, judicat, contestatur.*
†*consobrinus, filius patruelis vel*: moderge.
†*confutat*: oberstaelid.
†*conpilat*: stilith.
590 †*cornu*: ceste.
†*con(n)ectit*: teldat.
†*concretum*: gerunnen.
†*conc(h)a*: musclan scel.
†*coccum*: wioloc.
595 †*cocilus*: ampre.
crebrat (cribrat): siftið. 213.
†*crebrum (cribrum)*: sibi.
crucus (crocus): gelo. 242.
crepacula: cleadur, *id est, tabula quae a segetibus territat*[1]. 218.
600 †*cratem*: flecta *vel* hyrþil.
†*crepido*: rimo.
crus: scia. 299.
crabro: waefs *vel* hurnitu. 255, 275.
crustula (-allum) similis: haalstaan. 288.
605 †*crama*: flete.
†*crates*: hegas.
†*cragacus*: styria.
cuniculos: smyglas. 199.
curiositas: feorwitgeornis. 208.
610 *culcites (-ta)*: bed. 243.
cucumis: popæg. 253.
culmus: wyrð. 252.
curculio: emil. 257.
cupa: byden. 260.
615 †*cuba (p)*: tunne.
cummi (g): teoru. 282.
culix (-ex): mygg. 277.
cuculus: gaec. 265.
cucuzata: lepeuuince. 264. [210].
620 *culinia*: cocas. 287.
†*cucuma*: fyrçruce.
cuspis: palstr (534).
†*cunae*: cildclaðas.
†*curtina*: wagryft.
625 †*culter*: saex.
†*cuneus*: waecg.
†*cuppa (ab) accipiendo i.*: beodbollę.

Defrutum: coerin. 314.
†*detulerat*: brohte.
630 †*delicatus*: wrast.
†*destituit*: obgibeht.
devotaturus: wergendi. 318.
†*desis (-es)*: suuęr.
†*desolutus*: onsaelid.
635 †*destituunt*: towuorpon.
†*destitutae*: toworpne.
†*decipula*: bisuicfalle.
decrepita: dobgendi. 322[115].
desidebat: unsibbade. 323.
640 †*defatiget*: suenceth.
delumentum: ðhuehl. 326.
deponile: wefta. 328.
deconfugione, statione: hyðae. 329.
deliberatio: ymbðriodung. 331.
645 *delicatis et querulis*: wrastum end seobgendum. 332.

[1] territant.

dos : uuituma. 704.
†*delibutus* : gisalbot. *cp.* 676.
delumentem (*-um*) : th[u]achl. 641.
ditor : gifyrdro. 678.
depoline : uueftan. 642.
deconfugione, statione : *hydde. 643.
disceptant : flitad[1]. 680.
deliberatio : *ymbdritung. 644.
delicatis et quaerulosis : urastum. 645.
disparuit : *ungiseem uard. 682.
defectura : aspringendi. 646.
decidens : geuuitendi. 647.
debita pensio : *gedębin gebil. 648.
deditio : hondgong. 649.
difficile : uernuislicæ. 686.
detractavit : forsoc. 650.
devia callis : horuaeg stiig. 651.
distabueret (*-unt*) : *asundum. 683.
deperuntur (*deferuntur*) : *meldadum *vel* *roactum. 652.
deshisciat (*dehiscit*) : tecinid. 653.
defecit : *tedridtid. 654.
detriturigine : agnidinne. 655.
digitalium musculorum[2] : fingirdo[c]cuna. 687.

[1] t *over* c. [2] munusculorum.

defectura: aspringendi. 334.
decidens: gewitendi. 335.
debita pensio: gedaebeni geabuli. 336.
deditio: *handgand. 337.
650 *detractavit*: forsooc. 339.
devia callus (*-is*): horweg stig. 340.
defferuntur (*deferuntur*): meldadun *vel* wroegdun. 342.
dehiscat (*-it*): tocinit. 343.
desicit: tetridit. 344.
655 *detriturigine*: agnidine. 345.
†*dentalia*: sules reost.
†*devinxit*: geband.
†*decerni*: scriben.
†*deglobere* (*u*) *i.*: flean.
660 †*defotabat* (*v*): forsuor.
†*depraehendo*: anfindo.
†*descivit*: wiðstylde, *pedem retraxit.*
†*defert*: wroegde.
†*delectum*: cyri, *vel electio.*
665 †*detestare* (*-i*): onseacan.
†*detrimentum*: wonung.
†*degeneraverat*: misthagch.
†*des*(*ed*)*isse*: tiorade.
†*degesto*: geraedit.
670 †*decreta*: geðoht.
†*devota*: cystig.
†*discidium*: [weggedal][1], *separatio.*
†*diem obiit*: asualt.
†*dictatorem*: aldur.
675 †*dilotis*: todaeldum.
†*delibutus*: gesmirwid *cp.* 325.
†*dilatio*: aelding.
ditor: gefyrðro. 327.
†*dispendium*: wom.
680 *disceptant*: flitat. 330.
†*dissimulat*: miðið.
disparuit: ungesene weã. 333.
distabuerunt: *asundun. 341.
†*discensor*: ungeðyre.
685 †*dilectum*: [meniu], *exercitum.*
difficile: wearnwislice. 338.
digitalium musculorum: fingr-[doccana]. 346.
†*disceptavero*: sciro.
†*dicam* (*-ax*): quedol.
690 †*dicas* (*-ax*): quedole.
†*difinis*: suiðe micel.
†*dispensatio*: scir.
†*dimis*(*s*)*is*: *asclaecadun.
†*dicimenta*: tacne.
695 †*dispectus*: fraecuð.
†*dignitosa*: meodomlice.
†*dis*(*s*)*olverat*: ascaeltte.
†*divinos*: uuitgan.
†*distitutum* (*dest.*): ofgefen.
700 †*distentus*: aðegen.
dolatum: gesniden. 315.
dodrans: egur. 316.
dolatura (*-orium*): braadlastęcus. 321.
dos: rwituma *vel* uuetma. 324.
705 †*domatis*: huses.
†*dolones*: hunsporan.
dromidus (*-edarius*): afyred olbenda. 319.
dromidarius: se eorodmon. 320.
dulcis sapa: caerin. 313.
710 *dumus*: þyrne. 317.

[1] below line; may belong to *difortium*: *repudium* below.

Echo : uuydumer. 715.
(*h*)*edera* : uuidouuindae. 717.
empticius : *ceapcnext. 742.
enunum (*aenulum*) : cetil. 749.
ebor (-*ur*) : elpendes ban. 712.
erimio : *hindbrere. 758.
expendisse : araebndae. 776.
egerere : *ascrefan. 730.
exundavit : uueol. 777.
eluderet : auęgdæ. 734.
exercitus (-*iis*) : bigongum. 779.
extorti : ath[r]aestae. 780.
exposito : geboronae. 781.
emolomentum (-*umentum*) : fulteam. 743.
exaltavit (*exhalavit*) : stanc. 782.
eviscerata : aeohed. 768.
(*a*)*egre* : erabedlicae. 729.
effossis : ach[l]ocadum. 721.
expendisse : throuadae. 783.
expedierant[1] : aręddun. 784.
exito (-*ium*) : *stęb *vel* perditio. 785.
exoleverunt[2] : *gesuedradum. 786.
ex falange (*ph*) : ob threatae. 787.
evertigo (*e vestigio*), *statim* : an landae. 769.
exauctoravit : giheldae. 788.
expilatam : aritrid. 789.
expeditio : *fertd[3]. 790.
elogio : geddi. 733.
egesta : ascrepaen. 731.
echinus, piscis : scel. 716.
extentera : anseot. 791.
emlemma (*emblema*) : fothr. 744.
(*h*)*eptafyllon*[4] (*ph*), VII*folia* : *gilodusr[t]. 753.
exagium : handmitta. 793.
extale (-*is*) : *snaedil *vel* thearm. 794.
emunctoria : *candelthuist. 745.

[1] expedier'. [2] exoleuer'. [3] r *dotted*. [4] eptasyllon.

†*Eatenus*: oð ðaet.
ebor (-*ur*): elpendbaan. 351.
†*ebredio*: hrisle.
ebulum: walhwyrt. 393 [121].
715 *echo*: wudumer. 347.
echinus, piscis vel: scel. 376.
(*h*)*edera*: uuduwinde. 348.
(*h*)*eder*(*a*): ifegn. 392 [44].
†(*a*)*edilitatem*: hámscire.
720 †*edissere* (*edixere*): asaecgan.
effos(*s*)*is*: ahlocadum. 364.
†*enebata* (*enervata*): asuond.
†*effetum*[1]: ontudri.
eftafolium (*heptaphyllon*): sinfulle (755).
725 *eftafylon* (*heptaphyllon*): gelodwyrt (753).
†*efficaciter*: fromlice.
†*efficax*: from.
†*effectum*: deid.
(*a*)*egre*: earfedlice. 363.
730 *egerere*: ascrepan. 354.
egesta: ascrepen. 375.
†(*a*)*egra*: slaece.
elogio: geddi. 374.
eluderet: auuægde. 356.
735 *electrum*: elotr. 386.
(*h*)*el*(*l*)*eborus*: þung, woedeberge. 388.
†*elogia*: laac.
†*elegans, loquax*: smicre.
†*eliminat*: aðytið.
740 †*elimat*: gesuirbet.
†*empta*: geboht.
empticius: ceapcneht. 349.
emolumentum: [lean], fultum. 360.
emblema: foth[r]. 378 [129].
745 *emunctoria*: candeltuist. 382.
†*emaones*: scinneras.
†*emenso*: oberfoerde.
†*enervat*: asuond.
enum (*aenulum*): cetil. 350.
750 †*enucleata*: geondsmead.
†*enixa*: beorende.
†*enixa est, genuit agnam i.*: ceolborlomb.
(*h*)*eptafyllon*[2]: gelodwyrt. 379 (725).
epilenticus (*epilepticus*): woda. 383.
755 *eptafolium* (*heptaphyllon*): sinfulle. 387 (724).
epimenia: nest. 389.
ependiten (*ependytes*): cóp. 390 (760).
erimio: hindberge. 352.
†*erenis* (*erinnys*): [haegtis], *furia*.
760 *erenditen* (*ependytes*): cop (757).
erpica: egðe. 395 [174].
erpicarius: egðere. 396.
(*a*)*erugo*: rust. 397.
†*errabiles*[3]: huerbende.
765 †*ericius*: iil.
(*a*)*esculus*: boece. 391.
†*essox* (*esox*): laex.
eviscerata: athed. 362.
e vestigio: [on lande], on laste. 370.
770 †*evidens*: seotol.
†*eurynis* (*erinnys*): walcyrge.
†*eumenides*: haehtisse [136].

[1] effetrum. [2] eptasyllon. [3] *second* e *over* i.

ephilenticus (*epilepticus*) : uuoda. 754.
excolat : siid. 800.
exta : bęcdermi. 801.
electirum (*electrum*) : elothr. 735.
eptafolium (*heptaphyllon*) : sinfullae. 755.
(*h*)*elleborus* : *poedibergæ. 736.
epimenia : nest. 756.
efetidem (*ependytes*) : cop. 757.
(*a*)*esculus, ab*[1] *edendo* : *beccae. 766.
(*h*)*edera* : ifeg. 718.
ebulum : uualhuyrt. 714.
exactio : gebles monung. 813.
erpica : egdae. 761.
erpicarius : egderi. 762.
(*a*)*erugo* : *rost*[2]. 763.

Facitiae (*facetiae*) : gliu *both.* 825.
fiber : bebr *both.* 867.
†*flustra, undae vel*—**frustra, unde vel* : hraen—*raen.
forfices : sceroro *both.* 898.
fovit (-*et*) : feormat—*caeormad[3]. 899.

[1] ob. [2] *End of gap in Ep.*; *begins again with the gloss* filoxsenia : philosophia. [3] d *from* t.

†*expeditus*: abundęn.
†*eximet*: alieset.
775 †*exegestus*: gebero.
expendisse: araef[n]de. 353.
exundavit: auueol. 355.
†*experimentum*: andwisnis.
exercitiis: bigangum. 357.
780 *ex*(*t*)*orti*: aðręsti. 358.
exposito: geborone. 359.
exaltavit (*exhalavit*): stonc. 361.
expe(*n*)*disset*: ðrowode. 365.
expedierant: araeddun. 366.
785 *exito* (*-ium*), [*perditio*]: endistaeb. 367.
exoleverunt: gesueðradun. 368.
ex phalange: [of ðreote], of foeðan. 369.
exauctoravit: geheende. 371.
expilatam: [aþryid], arytrid. 372 (817).
790 *expeditio*: faerd. 373.
exintera: ansceat. 377.
†*explodit*, *excludit*: atynið.
exagium: andmitta. 380.
extale (*-is*): snaedilþear*m*. 381 [101].
795 †*exilia*: gestin[c]cum.
†*expeditis*: gearụum.
†*exta*: iesen.

†*exenium* (*xenium*): laac.
†*exactor*: scultheta.
800 *excolat*: siid. 384.
exta, *praecordia*: baecþearm. 385.
†*examus*(*s*)*im*: [georn]ice], *absolute*, *certe*, *vel exquisite*.
†*exorbitans*: asuab.
†*exalaparetur*: suungen.
805 †*extipices* (*extispices*): haelsent.
†*expensa*: daeguuini.
†*ex*(*s*)*erta lingua*: naec[a]d tunge.
†*exces*(*s*)*us*: egylt.
†*exigebant*: araefndun.
810 †*expeditionibus*: ferdun.
†*examen*: sue[a]rm.
†*extorres*: wraeccan.
exactio: geabules monung. 394 [114].
†*excubias*: weardseld.
815 †*expendere*: to aseodenne.
†*exugia* (*axungia*): gescincio.
expilatam: arydid (789).
†*expresserunt*[1]: arehtun.
†*exerceri*: wesan draegtre.
820 †*exercitatae*: ðare getyhtan.
†*expeditio*: hergiung.
†*exactum*: baedde.
†*expeditus*: [snel], *velox*, *fortis*.

†*Favor*: herenis.
825 *facetia*(*e*)[2]: glio. 398.
†*falc*(*o*): walhhabuc.
fasces, [*libri*]: goduueb. 441.
fagus: boece. 417.

fastidium, [*odium*]: cymnis. 406.
830 *fasianus* (*ph*): worhona. 424.
†*fascias*: weðel.
famfaluca: [faam], leasung. 426 [*cp.* 171].

[1] exprae.

[2] e over i.

**fiscilla—fiscella* : taenil—tenil. 868.
flavum vel fulfum (*v*) : read—reod. 887
405 *fibrae* : librlaeppan *both.* 873.
fastidium : ciisnis—*ciinis. 829.
†*fax* : fæcilae—faecile.
fibula : sigil *both.* 874.
†*furca* : uue[a]rgrod—uaergrod.
410 *fibula* : hringiae—hringae. 874.
fenicia—finicia (*phoenicius*) : baeso—beoso[1]. 877.
flegmata (*ph*) : horh *both.* 888.
frugus : uncysti[g] *vel* heamol—uncystig *vel* *healful. 917.
frixum : afigaen—afigen. 918.
415 *ferinum* : hold *both.* 853.
**fraximus—fraxinus* : aesc—*aastc. 920.
**fragus—fagus* : boecae—boecce. 828.
*fusarius—*fagus* : uuananbeam—uuonanbeam. 935.
fulix : ganot *vel* dopaenid. *both*[2]. 936.
420 *filix* : fearn—*feran. 871.
fraga : *obtt—*obea. 919.
ficetula (*d*) : sugga—sucga. 878.
fringella[3] (*-illa*) : finc *both.* 921.
fasianus (*ph*)—**fassianus* : uuorhana—uuorhona. 830.
425 *furuncus* : mearth—meard. 937.
famfaluca : leasung *vel* faam—laesung *vel* faam. 832.
fungus : suamm—suamm. 938.
furfures : siuida *both.* 940.
†*fitilium* (*vitellus*) : aegergelu.
430 *falces—falcis* (*falx, falcis*) : uudubil, sigdi[4], riftr—uuidubil, sigdi, riftr. 834.
flabanus : suan *both.* 889.
flabum—flavum : gelu *both.* 890.
furvum : bruun *both.* 931.
fibrans (*v*) : risaendi—*ripendi. 879.
435 *fenus* : spearuua—spearua. 855.
foederatas : gitreeudae—getr[e]udæ. 900.

[1] *after* fibula : sigil (408) *in Erf.* [2] *The order of the last seven in Erf. is:* frugus, fraxinus, fagus : boecce, frixum, ferinum, fagus : uuonanbeam, fulix. [3] g *over* c *in Ep.* [4] si : g.

†*fasciarum*: suaeðila.
falcis: wudubil, siðe, riftras. 430.
835 *famfaluca*: wapul. 447.
falcastrum: wudubil. 449.
fa(v)onius: westsuðwind. 452.
†*fastinatio*[1] (*fascinatio*): malscrung.
†*falarica*: ætgęro[2].
840 †*falanx* (*ph*): foeða.
†*farius* (*v*): faag.
†*facessit*: sueðrað.
†*farsa*: acrummen.
†*favo* (*faba*): bean.
845 †*fasces*: cynedomas.
†*fastu*: uulencu.
†*fabrile*: smiðlice.
†*farelas* (*phalerae*): hryste.
†*falerata* (*ph*): gehyrsti.
850 †*feruginius* (*ferrugineus*): greig.
†*ferox*: roeðe.
†*ferculum*: disc.
ferinum: hold. 415.
†*feriatus*: gerested.
855 *fenus*: spe[a]rua. 435.
†*foenus*[3]: borg.
†*foederatus*[4]: getriowad.
†*faecce*: maere.
†*fespa* (*v*): waefs.
860 †*fefellit*: uuegið.
ferula: aescðrote. 450.
fellitat: suggit. 455.
†*fellus* (*felis*): catte.
†*f(o)enum*: graes.
865 †*ferrugine*: iserngrei.
†*ferruginem, obscuritatem ferri i.*: omei.
fiber: bebr. 399.
fiscilla (*-ella*): taenil. 403.
†*fida*: stearn.
870 †*fibra*: þearm [*cp.* 27].
filix: fea[r]n. 420.
†*fiscillus* (*-ella*): stictenel.
fibrae: librlaeppan. 405.
fibula: hringe, sigl. 408, 410.
875 †*fiscillis* (*-ellis*): sprinclum.
†*filum*: ðred.
finicia (*phoenicius*): beosu. 411.
ficetula (*ficedula*): sugga. 422 [218].
fibrans (*v*): risende. 434.
880 *finiculus* (*feniculum*): finulae. 451.
†*fiscalis, r(h)eda gebellicum*: wæ[g]nfearu.
†*fimum*: goor.
†*fictis*: facnum.
†*fistulis*: þeotum.
885 †*figite*: suiðigað.
†*filiaster*: steopsunu.
flavum, fulvum: read. 404.
flegmata (*ph*): horh. 412.
flabanus: suan. 431.
890 *flabum* (*v*): geolu. 432.
†*flagris*: suiopum.
flamma: blęd. 445.
floccus: loca. 448.
†*flavescit*: glitinat, *albescit* [30].
895 †*flagrans* (*fr.*): stincendi.

[1] *first* a *over* e. [2] ægtęro. [3] *originally* fenus, *as shown by alph. order.* [4] *originally* federatus, *as shown by alph. order.*

funestavere : *smitor—smiton. 941.
*frons—*fros* : hleor *both.* 923.
funestissima : tha deatlicostan—da deudlicustan. 942.
440 *framea* : aetgaeru—*aetgaru. 922.
*fasces—*faces* : goduuebb—guoduueb. 827.
fornicem : bogan *both*[1]. 901.
†*feriatis*[2], *quietis vel securis vel* : restaendum—restendum.
†*facundia, eloquentia vel* : þoot—*puoo[d].
445 *flamma* : blaeed—bled. 892.
fragor : suoeg *both.* 925.
*famfaluca—*fanfaluca* : uuapul *both.* 835.
floccus : loca *both.* 893.
falcastrum : uuidubil *both.* 836.
450 *ferula—*ferola* : aescthrotae—aescdrotae. 861.
finiculus (*feniculum*) : finugl *both.* 880.
fa(v)onius : uuestsuduuind. 837.
fornix[3] : boga *super columnis* both. 909.
follis : blestbaelg *both.* 910.
455 *fellitat* : suggit *both*[4]. 862.

Gurgulio : throtbolla—ðrotbolla. 1000.
gurgustium : cesol *both.* 1001.
gilvus : gelu *both.* 966.
*gibbus—*gypbus* : hofr—*hosr. 969.
460 *gipsus—gypsus* (*gypsum*) : sparaen—sparen. 968.
*glarea—*glare* : cisil—cisal. 975.

[1] *Erf.* bogant *with dot over* t. [2] feriatus *Erf.* [3] i *over* a *in Ep.* [4] t *from* d *in Erf.*

†*flebotoma* (*phlebotomus*): blod-saex. [110.]

†*fortuna*: wyrd.

forfices: scerero. 401.

fovet: feormat, broedeth. 402.

900 *foederatas*: getreuuade. 436.

fornicem: bogan. 442.

†*formido*: ano𝔡a.

†*forfex*: isernsceruru.

†*fors*: wyrd. [137.]

905 †*forceps*: tong.

†*fornacula*: cyline, heor𝔡e.

†*foras* (*-es*): bolcan.

†*fortex* (*v*): edwelle.

fornis (*-ix*): bogo, *super columnis*. 453.

910 *follis*: blaesbaelg. 454.

†*fornaculum* (*-la*): here. [126.]

†*formaticus*: cese, *a forma*.

†*fronulus*: linetuigle.

†*frat(r)uelis*: geaduling.

915 †*frat(r)uelis*: suhterga.

†*frat(r)uelis*: bro𝔡orsunu.

frugus: uncystig, heamul. 413.

frixum: afigaen. 414.

fraga: obet. 421.

920 *fraxinus*: aesc. 416.

fringella (*-illa*): finc. 423 [219].

framea: ætgaeru. 440.

f(r)ons: hleor. 438.

†*fretus*: bald.

925 *fragor*: suoeg, cirm. 446.

†*fraudulenter*: faecenlice.

†*frontuosus* (*frontosus*): bald.

†*frutina*: fultemend.

†*fuscinula*[1]: awel.

930 †*furcimen*: waergrood.

furbum (*v*): bruun. 433.

†*funalia*: *con*del.

†*fusum*: spinel.

†*fucus, faex*: taelg.

935 *fusarius*: wananbeam. 418.

funix (*fulix*): gonot *vel* dopp-aenid. 419.

furuncus: mear𝔡. 425 [*cp.* 224].

fungus: suom. 427.

†*funda*: li𝔡re.

940 *furfures*: sifi𝔡an. 428.

funestavere: smiton. 437.

funestissima: 𝔡a deadlicustan. 439.

†*funalia, cerei*: waexcondel.

†*ful(i)gine*: *sooth.

945 †*furia*: haehtis.

†*Gargarizet*: gagul suille.

†*garrit*: gionat.

†*gannatura*: gliu.

galla: g[all]uc. 466.

950 †*gar(r)ula*: cra[u]ue.

garbas: sceabas. 468.

galmaria: caluuer. 471.

galmulum (*galbanum*): mo-legnsty[cci], moling. 477.

†*galmilla*: liimcaluuer.

955 †*gabea* (*gavia*): me[a]u.

gabalacrum: calwer. 476.

†*gestus*: gebero.

†*generosus*: ae𝔡ile.

[1] *first* u *over* i.

glumula: scalu *both.* 976.
gladiolum: segg—secg. 977.
gramen: quiquae[1]—quicae. 989.
465 *genistae—geniste* (*-a*): broom *both.* 959.
galla: galluc *both*[2]. 949.
grassator: ferhergęnd—ferhergend. 990.
garbas: sceabas *both.* 951.
grallus (*graculus*): hrooc *both.* 991.
470 *glis*: eglae—egilae. 973.
galmaria: caluuaer—caluuer. 952.
glomer (*-us*): cleouuae—cleuuue. 979.
glaucum: hęuui *vel* grei—*hauui *vel* grei. 981.
gracilis: smael—*smal[3]. 992.
475 *glus*: frecnis *both.* 980.
*galbalacrum—*galmaria*: calu[u]aer—caluuer. 956.
galmum (*galbanum*): molegn—moleng. 953.
globus: leoma—leuma. 974.
gregariorum: *aedilra *both.* 993.
480 †*genuino*: gecyndilican[4] *both.*
gladiatores: caempan—cempan. 984.
†*genas—*genus*: hleor *both.*
gilvus: falu *both.* 970.
gurgulio (*curculio*): aemil *both.* 1003.
485 *gelum*: frost—*frots. 964.
†*galmilla* (*galbanum*): liimmolegn—limmolegn[5].
†——*genuinum, intimum vel dens*: tusc[6]. (*cp. C.* 961.)

**Hebitatus—hebetatus*: astyntid *both.* 1012.
hastilia telorum: scaeptloan. 1005.
490 *hebesceret*: asuand—*ansuand. 1013.
*hebitavit—*habitavit*: aslacudae *both.* 1014.
habitudines: geberu *both.* 1006.
hyadas (*-es*): raedgaesran—*redgaesram. 1035.
horno: thys geri *both.* 1028.
495 *hiulca*: cinaendi—cinendi. 1020.
hibiscum: biscopuuyrt *both.* 1021.

[1] *first* q *over* c. [2] c *from* s *in Erf.* [3] *after* galmum (477) *in Erf.*
[4] e *from* i *in Ep.* [5] *after* gracilis (474) *in Erf.* [6] *from* tunsc.

genista : brom. 465.
960 †*gente* (*ganta*) : wilde goos. (*cp.* 450.)
†*genuino* : tusc, *naturale.* (*cp. Erf.* 487.)
†*genas* : heagaspen.
†*gente* (*ganta*) : wilde goos. (*cp.* 450.)
gelum : forst. 485.
965 †*geumatrix* : geac.
gilvus : geolu. 458.
†*gillus* (*gilvus*) : grei.
gipsus (*gypsum*) : spaeren. 460.
gippus (*bb*) : hofr. 459.
970 *gilvus* : falu. 483.
†*gilbus* : gyrno.
†*gingria* : spon.
glis : egle. 470 [138].
globus : leoma. 478.
975 *glarea* : cisilstan. 461.
glumula : scala. 462.
gladiolum : saecg. 463.
†*glitilia* : clife.
glomer (*-us*) : *clouue. 472.
980 *glus* : frecnis. 475.
glaucum : heauui, grei. 473.

†*glandula* : cirnel.
†*glebo* : unwis.
gladiatores : cempan. 481.
985 †*gluten* : teoru.
†*gripem* (*gryps*) : gig.
†*grillus* (*y*) : hama.
†*gremen* (*gremium*) : faethm.
gramen : quice. 464.
990 *grassator* : forhergen[d]. 467.
grallus (*graculus*) : hrooc. 469 [201].
gracilis : smel. 474.
gregariorum : *unaeðilsa. 479.
†*gregatim* : wearnmelum.
995 †*grus, gruis* : cornoch.
†*gravis* (*grus*) : cornuc.
†*graffium* (*ph*) : gref.
†*grunnire* : grunnettan.
†*graticium* (*cr.*) : wagflecta.
1000 *gurgulio* : ðrotbolla. 456 [143].
gurgustium : ceosol. 457 [52].
†*gurgustione* : cetan.
gurgulio (*curculio*) : emil. 484.
†*gunna* : heden.

1005 *Hastilia telorum* : scaeptloan. 489.
habitudines : geberu. 492.
†*harundo* (*arundo*), *canna* : hreod.
†*haustum* : drync.
†*habenis* : gewaldleðrum.
1010 †*habile* : lioðuwac.
†*heus* : geheres thu.
hebitatus : astyntid. 488.
hebesceret : asuand. 490.

hebitabit (*-avit*) : asclacade. 491.
1015 †*heia* (*eja*) : welga.
herodius (*erōdiós*) : walchhabuc. 497 [50].
†*helleborus* : woidiberge.
†*herinis* (*erinnys*) : walcrigge.
†*hebetat* : styntid.
1020 *hiulca* : cinendi. 495.
hibiscum : biscopuuyrt. 496.
hirundo : sualuue. 498.

horodius (*erōdiōs*): uualh[h]ebuc—uualhhaebuc. 1016.
hirundo: sualuuae—sualuae[1]. 1022.

Indruticans: uura[e]stendi—*uraesgendi. 1045.
500 *inhians*: gredig *both.* 1046.
inluvies secundarum: hama, *in quo fit parvulus*[2] both. 1049.
inpetigo—**inpegit*: tetr[3]—*teg. 1047.
intestinum: thearm—thea[r]m. 1058.
interamen (*interaneum*): innifli—inifli. 1059.
505 †*ilium*: neuunseada—*naensida.
instites (*-as*): suedilas *both.* 1060.
intexunt: auundun *both.* 1062.
increpitans: hlaeodrindi—*hleodendri. 1065.
inlex: tyctaend, **anbinli*[*ciendi*]—tychtend, *ab inliciendo.* 1063.
510 *infestus*: flach *both.* 1066.
†**intercaeptum*—*interceptum*: araepsid—arepsit.
infandum: maanful—*meinfol.* 1069.
inlecebris: tyctin[n]um—tyctinnum. 1070.
ingratus: lath—laad. 1071.
515 *inritatus in rixam*: gigrę̄mid—gigremit. 1073.
incitamenta: tyctīnnae *both.* 1074.
jungetum (*juncetum*): riscthyfil—*rycthyfil. 1159.
intula (*inula*): uualhuuyrt—uua[l]huyrt. 1075.
inprobus: gimach—gemach. 1076.
520 *ingruerit*: anhriosith—onhrisit. 1077.
intractabilis: unlidouuac—*unliuduuac. 1079.
**incomodum*—*incommodum*: unbryci—*unbrycci. 1050.
interceptum est: r[a]ebsid uuaes—repsit uaes. 1084.

[1] *from* sualnuae. [2] *second* u *over* i *in Ep.* [3] e *partly written on er. after first* t.

†*histrix* (*hystrix*) : iil.
†*hinnitus* : hnaeggiung.
1025 †*hy*(*ae*)*na* : naectgenge.
†*holor* (*olor*) : suan.
†*hora* : sueg.
horno : þys gere. 494 (1030).
†*hoctatus* : gelaechtnad.
1030 †*horno* : þys gere. (1028.)
†*holido* (*olido*) : fule.
†*honeraria* (*oneraria*) : hlaestscip.
†*huscide* (*viscide*) : tolice.
†*humare*[1] : bimyldan.
1035 *hyadas* (*-es*) : raedgasram[2]. 493.
†*hymen*(*a*)*eos* : hęmedo.

Ibices : firgengaet. 560.
†*idoneus* : oxstaelde.
†*igni* (*-em*) *sacrum* : oman. [*cp.* 88.]
1040 *ign*(*i*)*arium* : aalgewerc. 556.
†*ilia* : midhridir, nioðanweard [hype].
†*illic* : þanan.
†*imbricibus* : þaectigilum.
†*inergumenos* (*energoúmenos*) : wodan.
1045 *indruticans* : wraestendi[3]. 499.
in(*h*)*ians* : gredig. 500.
inpetigo : teter. 502.
†*inextricabilis* : untosliten. [*cp.* 251.]
inluvies secundarum : hama, *in quo fit parvulus*. 501.
1050 *incommodum* : unbryce. 522.
†*inprovisu* : feringa.
†*infestatio* : unlioþuwacnis.
†*infula* : uueorðmynd.
†*inminente*(*m*) : aetweosendne.
1055 †*infestus* (*infectus*) : gemenged.
†*ingesta* : ondoen.
†*inola* (*-ula*) : eolene.
intestinum : þearm. 503.
interamen (*interaneum*) : innifli. 504.
1060 *instites* (*-as*) : sueðelas. 506 [*cp.* 72].
†*infima* : niol.
intexunt : wundun. 507.
inlex : tyctendi. 509.
†*interim* : þrage.
1065 *increpitans* : hleoþrendi. 508.
infestus : flach. 510.
†*interceptum* : arasad.
†*interceptio* : raepsung.
infandum : mánful. 512.
1070 *inlecebris* : tychtingum. 513.
ingratus : lað. 514.
†*incuda* (*incus*) : onfilti. [*cp.* 53.]
inritatus : gegremid. 515.
incitamenta : tyhtinne. 516.
1075 *intula* (*inula*) : uualhwyrt. 518.
inprobus : gemah. 519.
ingruerit : onhrioseð. 520.
†*inruens* : þerende.
intractabilis : unlioþuwac. 521.
1080 †*inmunes* (*immanes*) : orceas.
†*in procinctu* : in ðegnunge.
†*intercepit* : ręfsde.

[1] humase. [2] *first stroke of* m *added afterwards* (?). [3] i *over* e.

†*insimulatione*: uuroctae—uurochtae.

525 *inpendebatur*: gibaen uuaes—geben uaes. 1086.

interpellari: raefsed—refset. 1087.

industria: *geeornnissae[1]—*gyrnissæ. 1088.

inpendebat: saldae—*saltae. 1089.

in dies crudesceret: a fordh— a *forthe. 1090.

530 *in transmigratione—in transmigrationem*: in foernissae —in *fornissæ. 1091.

iners: asolcaen—asolcæn. 1092.

interventu: þingungae—*ingungae. 1093.

inlectus: gitychtid—getyctid. 1094.

interlitam[2]: bismiridae—bismirida. 1095.

535 *inpactae*: *a[n]slegaengrae—aslegenræ. 1096.

indigestae: unofaercumen[rae]—unofercum*en*ræ. 1097.

innitentes[3]: uuidirhliniendae—*uuidirlinienti. 1098.

insolesceret[4]: oberuuaenidae—oberuenedæ. 1099.

inpulsore: baedendrae—bedændræ. 1100.

540 *infractus*: giuuaemmid—geuemmid. 1101.

inopimum: unaseddae—*unasettæ. 1102.

inditas: þa gisettan[5]—ða gisettan. 1103.

infici: gimaengdae—gimengdæ. 1104.

index: taecnaendi, torcten[di]—taecnendi, torch[tendi]. 1105.

545 *inpostorem—*inposterem*: bisuicend—bisuiccend. 1106.

inter primores: *bitui[c]n aeldrum—bituichn ældrum. 1107.

intercapido (-*edo*)—**intercapito*: fristmearc—*fritmaerc. 1108.

insolens: feruuaenid—*feruendid. 1109.

incuria: inmaethlae—inmedlæ. 1110.

550 *in mimo*: in gliuuae, *quod tamen ad mimarios vel mimigraphos pertinet*—in *gluuiae. 1112.

jurisperiti: redboran *both*. 1160.

*invisus—*invissus*: laath—lath. 1113.

in aestivo caenaculo[6]: uppae, *ubi*[7] *per aestatem frigus captant*[8]—yppe. 1114.

[1] ge:or:n. [2] interlitan *Erf.* [3] innitent' *Erf.* [4] *last* e *over* i *in Ep.* [5] gise:t. [6] caenaculi *Ep.* [7] *om. in Erf.* [8] capiatur *Erf.*

†*intercepit*: fornoom.
interceptum est: raefsit waes. 523.
1085 †*insimulatione*: feringe.
inpendebatur: geben waes. 525.
interpellare (-*i*): raefsit. 526.
industria: geornis. 527.
inpendebat: salde. 528.
1090 *in dies crudesceret*: a *forht. 529.
in transmigrationem: in foernisse. 530.
iners: esuind, asolcen. 531.
interventu: þingunge. 532.
inlectus: getyhtid. 533.
1095 *interlitam*: bismiride. 534.
inpactae: *onligenre. 535.
indigestae: unobercumenre. 536.
innitentes: wiðerhlingende. 537.
insolesceret: oberuuenide. 538.
1100 *inpulsore*: baeden[d]re. 539.
infractus: ungeuuemmid. 540.
inopimum: unasaedde. 541.
inditas: ða gesettan. 542.
infici: gemengde. 543.
1105 *index*: tacnendi, torctendi. 544.
inposterem (*impostor*): bisuuicend. 545.
inter primores: *bitun aeldrum. 546.
intercapido (-*edo*): firstmaerc. 547.
insolens: foruuened. 548.
1110 *incuria*: iumaeðle. 549.
incuba: maere. 558 [229].
in mimo: in gliowe. 550.
invisus: lath. 552 [104].
in (*a*)*estivo coenaculo*[1]: yppe, *ubi per* (*a*)*estatem frigus captant.* 553.
1115 *involucus*: uulluc. 557 [172].
involuco: uudubinde. 559 [245].
†*inquilinis* (-*us*): genaeot.
†*indolis*: hyhtful *vel* ðiendi.
†*infri*(*gi*)*dat*: kaelið. 561.
1120 †*inruit*: raesde.
†*inpingit*: smat, gemaercode.
†*incentor*: tyhten[d].
†*incantata*: gegaelen.
†*incantatores*: galdriggan.
1125 †*infestationes*: tionan.
†*intercapidine* (-*edine*): ginnisse.
†*inundatio*: gyte.
†*incurrus* (*incursus*): ongong.
†*inbuit*: onreod.
1130 †*infastum*: sliden.
†*inruptio*: ongong.
†*innixus*: strimendi.
†*incanduit*: auucoll.
†*ineptus*: gemę[did].
1135 †*intrinicio* (*internecio*): forsliet.
†*in sirtim* (*y*): in sondgewearp.
†*innitor*: onhlingu[2].
†*inficio*: blondu.
†*infula*: uyrðo.
1140 †*inmoratur*: wunat.

[1] cenaculi.

[2] u *over* o.

juvar (b): leoma *vel* earendil—leoma *vel* oerendil. 1161, 1166.

555 *isic (issicius, esox)*: leax—lex. 1155.

ign(i)arium: algiuu[eo]rc—algiuerc. 1040.

involucus[1]—**invociucus*: uulluc *both.* 1115.

incuba: mera, *vel satyrus*—merae, *vel *saturnus.* 1111.

involuco — **involucu* : uuidubindlae — *uuydublindæ. 1116.

560 *ibices*: firgingaett *both.* 1037.

**infridat*—*infrigidat*: caelith—cælid. 1119.

isca: tyndirm—tyndrin[2]. 1156.

Lebes—**leves*: huuer *both.* 1197.

lepor, subtilitas vel: uuoþ—*vel pro*[3] uod. 1196.

565 *lagones*—*lagonas (ligones)*: mettocas *both.* 1211.

liburnices: gerec *both.* 1212.

**lobarum*—*labarum*: seng—segn. 1167.

lurcones, avidi vel: sigiras—*lurcones*: sigiras, *vel avidi.* 1241.

larbula (v): egisigrima *both*[4]. 1168.

570 *lunules (-as)*: menescillingas—meniscillingas. 1242.

lituus, baculum augurale in prima parte curvum[5], *id est*: crycc *both.* 1222.

lacerna: haecilae *vel* lotha[6]—hecile *vel* lotha. 1169.

lumbare: gyrdils *vel* broec—gyrdils, broec. 1244.

luculentum: torchtnis—torhtnis. 1243.

575 *lymphatico*: *uuoendendi—uuodenti. 1263.

livida toxica: tha uuannan aetrinan—tha uuannan *etrina[ni]. 1215.

ludi litterari(i)—*ludi *litterali*: staebplegan—*scæbplega. 1245.

[1] c *from* i. [2] *After* isic (555) *in Erf.* [3] p'. [4] *Erf. from* egisigrimma. [5] m *cut off by binder in Ep.* [6] th *from* d.

†*infectum* : geblonden.
†*indomitus* : wilde.
†*instincta* : onsuapen.
†*intransmeabili* : unoferfoere.
1145 †*inbellem* : orwige.
†*internicium* (*internecio*), *bellum dicitur quo nullus remanet* : utcualm.
†*inulus* (*vitulus*) : hindcaelf.
†*in catamo* : in bęce.
†*initiatum* : gestoepid.
1150 †*intimandum* : to cyðenne.
iota : sochtha.
†*jovem* : þuner.
†*irridabant* (*irritabant*) : tyhton.
†*irritum* : forhogd, *inanem*.
1155 *isic* (*esox*) : laex. 555.
isca : tyndrin. 562 [179].
†*istic* : uueðer.
†*istuc* : hider.
jungetum (*juncetum*) : riscðyfel. 517.
1160 *jurisperiti* : redboran. 551.
jubar : earendel. 554.
†*jugum* : cnol.
†*junctura* : foeging.
†*juventus* : midferh.
1165 †*juncus* : risc.
jubar : leoma. 554.

Lab(a)rum : segn. 567 [89].
larbula (*v*) : egisgrima. 569.
lacerna : haecile *vel* loða. 572.
1170 *lacessit* : gremið. 580.
laogoena (*lagena*) : crog. 584 [57].
†*latrina* : genge, groepe, *atque ductus cloacas*.
†(*a*)*laudae* : laurice.
lacessitus : gegremid. 593.
1175 *laexiva* (*lixivia*) : laeg. 591.
laquear : firsthrof. 595.
lanx : heolor. 607.
lacunar[1] : flode. 597 [8].
lactuca : þuðistel. 601.
1180 †*lacunar* : hebenhus.
lapatium (*lapathum*) : lelodrae. 606.
†*lacerta* : aðexe. [86].
larus : meau. 610.
lappa : clibe. 613.
1185 †*latex* : burne.
†*lacin*(*i*)*osum* : panhosum.
†*laena* : rift.
†*labat* : weagat.
†*lana* : uul.
1190 †*laquearia* : firste.
†*latratus* : baercae.
†*laudariulus* : frecmase.
†*ladascapiae, briensis i.* : hondwyrm.
†*lanterna* : lehtfaet.
1195 †*lacessere* : gremman.
lepor : wooð. 564.
lebes : huer. 563.
lenta : toh. 581.
lenocinium : tyhten. 579.
1200 †*legit, collegit* : lisit.
lembum (*limbus*): listan. 583.

[1] lauucar.

liquentes—**linquentes*: hlutrae *both.* 1216.
lenoc(in)ium—*lenotium*: *thyctin *vel* scocha—tyctin *vel* scocha. 1199.
580 *lacessit*: graemid—gremid. 1170.
lenta, tarda vel: toch—*thoch. 1198.
legula (i)—**legu*: gyrdislrhingae—gyrdilshringe. 1202.
lembum (limbus): listan *vel* thres—listan *vel* ðres. 1201.
lagoena (-ena): croog *both.* 1171.
585 *lutrus*[1] *(-a)*: otr—*octer. 1246.
ligones—**lagones*: mettocas—*metocas. 1211.
lucius: haecid *both.* 1247.
lucanica: maerh—mærh. 1249.
lurdus—**lurdur*: laempihalt—*lemphihalt. 1250.
590 *lendina*[2] *(lens)*: hnitu *both.* 1203.
lexiva (lixivia): leag—læg. 1175.
lupus: baers *both.* 1251.
lacessitus: gigraemid—gigremid. 1174.
lien: *multi—milti. 1217.
595 *laquear*: fierst—*firt. 1176.
ludari(u)s: steor *both.* 1252.
lacunar: flodae *both.* 1178.
levir: tacor *both.* 1204.
lolium: atae—atte. 1235.
600 *lodix*: lotha *both.* 1237.
lactuca: þuþistil—*popistil. 1179.
liciatorium—**licitorium*: hebild[3] *both.* 1219.
lihargum (lithargyrus): slęgu—slægu. 1230.
licidus—**lucidus*: huet—huaet. 1223.
605 *lectidiclatum*—*lectidicladum*: githuornae fleti—githuorne fleti. 1205.
lapatium (lapathum): lelodrae *both.* 1181.
lanx: helor *both.* 1177.
lepus, leporis[4]: hara—hæra[5]. 1206.

[1] *First* u *over* o *in Erf.* [2] *First* n *from* m *in Ep.* [3] *word er. before* hebild *in Ep.* [4] læporis *Erf.* [5] *Erf. adds* quae cum intro canit, *evidently taken from the gloss* liciter: qui cum lituo canit *in Ep.* (*four glosses on*), *but om. in Erf.*

legula (*lig.*) : gyrdilshringe. 582 (1226).
lendina (*lens*) : h[ni]tu [1]. 590 [232].
levir : tacur. 598.
1205 *lectidiclatum* : geþuorne flete. 605.
lepus, leporis : hara. 608.
lentum vimen : toh gęrd. 614.
†*lenticula* : piose.
†*lesta* : borda.
1210 †*lenirent* : afroebirdun.
ligones : meottucas. 565, 586.
liburnices : gerec. 566.
†*libor* (*v*) : uuam.
ligustrum : hunigsuge. 615.
1215 *livida toxica* : ðа wonnan aetrinan. 576.
liquentes : hlutre. 578.
lien : milte. 594 [146].
†*libertabus* : frioletan. [153].
liciatorium : hebelgerd. 602.
1220 *limax* : snegl. 611.
†*limphaticus* (*y*) : woed[endi] (*cp.* 1263).
lituus : cryc. 571.
licidus : huæt. 604.
†*libertus* : frioleta.
1225 †*linter* : baat.
lingula (=*ligula*) : gyrdilsbringe. (1202).
†*limus* : laam.
†*limbus* : ðres, liste.
†*liberalitas* : roopnis.
1230 *li*(*t*)*harg*(*yr*)*um* : slaegu. 603.
†*linea* : waebtaeg.
†*licium* : hebeld.
†*licia* : hebeldðred.
†*lima* : fiil.
1235 *lolium* : ate. 599.
†*lotium* : hlond.
lodix : loða. 600.
†*locusta* : lopust.
†*luscus* : anege.
1240 †*lucor* (*lurco*) : freceo.
lurcones : siras. 568.
lunulus (*-as*) : menescillingas. 570.
luculentum : torhtnis. 574.
lumbare : gyrdils, br[o]ec. 573.
1245 *ludi litterari*(*i*) : staefplagan. 577.
lutraos (*lutra*) : otr. 585.
lucius : haecid. 587.
†*lupatis* : bridelsum.
lucanica : mærh. 588.
1250 *lurdus* : lemphalt. 589 [195].
lupus : bre[r]s. 592.
ludarius : steor. 596.
lumbricus : regnwyrm. 612.
†*luteum* : crohha.
1255 †*lupercal* : haerg.
†*lumbus* : side.
†*luscinia* : naectegale.
†*luscinius* : for[s]c.
†*lupus* : wulf.
1260 †*lupa* : wylf.
†*lupinare* (*-anaria*) : uulfholu.
†*lumbulos* : lendebrede.
lymphatico : woedendi. 575 (*cp.* 1221).
†*lymbo* (*i*) : ðresi.

[1] i *over* u.

†*lacuna(r)*: hrof[1] *both.*

610 *laris (-us)*: *men—meu. 1183.

limax: snel—snegl. 1220.

lumbricus: regenuuyrm—regnuuyrm. 1253.

lappa: *cliþae—clifae. 1184.

lentum vimen: toch gerd—*thoh gerd. 1207.

615 *ligustrum*: hunaegsugae—hunegsugae. 1214.

Mordicos: bibitnae *both.* 1319.

manipulatim: threatmelum—*theatmelum. 1265.

mendacio conposito[2]: geregnodae[3]—*geradnodae. 1301.

molestissimum: earbetlicust—*easbedlicust. 1320.

620 *municeps*: burgleod, *a mu(ni)cipio.* 1334.

munifica: cistigian[4]. 1335.

monarchia: anuuald—anuald. 1321.

mirifillon (myriophyllon), millefolium: geruuae—geruę. 1315.

murica: gespan, *aureum in tunica*[5]—gespon. 1336.

625 *modioli*: nabae—nebæ. 1322.

mancus[6]: anhendi—anhaendi. 1266.

mafortae—maforte (Mafors): scybla[7] *both.* 1267.

morgit (mulgit): milciþ—milcid. 1323.

mossiclum—mossuclum: ragu *both.* 1324.

630 *mimoparo*: thebscib—thebscip. 1316.

manica: gloob—glob. 1268.

momentum: scytil *both.* 1325.

manile (manualis) lebil *both.* 1269.

*manitergium—*manutergium*: liin—*lim. 1270.

635 **malagna—malagma*: salb *both.* 1272.

malus: apuldur—*apuldro. 1273.

**martus—myrtus*: uuyr *both*[8]. 1356.

melarium (melapium): mi[l]scapuldr — *milcapuldr. 1302.

[1] *the* h *outside the line in Ep.* hroflititen *Erf. from* liciter *in Ep.* (*preceding note*). [2] conpsito *Erf.* [3] *from* gerenodae. [4] *For this and the foregoing Erf. has only* manificit. [5] tonica *Erf.* [6] mncus *Erf.* [7] y *over* i *and er. after* a *in Ep.* [8] *After* melarium *in Erf.*

1265 *Manipulatim*: þreatmelum. 617.
mancus: anhendi. 626.
maforte(*Mavors*): scyfla. 627.
manica: glof. 631.
manile . (*manualis*): lebil. 633.
1270 *manitergium*: lin. 634.
†*margo*: obr.
malagma: salf. 635.
malus: apuldur. 636.
†*mandras*: eouuistras.
1275 †*maceratus*: þreatende.
mastigium: suiopan. 641.
manubium: waelreaf. 642.
manticum: hondful beowes. 645 [184].
†*masca*: grima.
1280 *mascus*: grima. 646.
marsopicus: fina. 648 [217].
†*marsuppia* (*marsupium*): ceodas.
marruca: snegl. 651 [237].
majales (*-is*): bearug. 652 [238].
1285 *mango*: mengi[o]. 659.
maulistis: scyend. 654 [185].
mastice: huitcudu. 655.
malva: hocc, cottuc, *vel* gearwan leaf. 656.
mar(*r*)*ubium*: biowyrt *vel* hune. 657.
1290 *matrix*: quiða. 661.
†*massa*: clyne.
†*mapalia*: byre.
mars, martis: tiig. 663.
†*magalia*: byre. [155.]
1295 †*macilentus*: gefaested.
†*manere*: bidan.
†*madidum*: obðaenit.
†*madefacta*: geuueted.
†*machinamenta*: orðonc.
1300 †*mantega*: taeg.
mendacio conposito: geregna[de]. 618.
melarium (*melapium*): mircapuldur. 638.
melodium (*-ia*): suinsung. 643.
mergulus: scalfur. 647.
1305 †*mereo*: groeto.
merula: oslę. 665.
megale (*mugalê*): hearma. 666.
†*medulla*: merg.
†*mercurium*: Woden.
1310 †*mentagra*: bituihn.
†*merga* (*-us*): scraeb.
†*me*(*re*)*tricius*: mederwyrhta.
†*milvus*: glioda.

†*millefolium* : gearuuae.

640 *molibus* : ormetum *both.* 1326.

mastigia : suipan—*suibæ[1]. 1276.

manubium—*manuvium* : uuaelreab—uuelreab. 1277.

melodium (*-ia*) : suinsung—*ruinsung. 1303.

mustacia—**murtacia* : granae—granæ. 1343.

645 *manticum* : handful˙ *beouuas—handful beouaes. 1278.

mascus—**marcus* : grima *both*[2]. 1280.

mergulus : scalfr *both.* 1304.

marsopicus—**marpicus* : fina—*pina. 1281.

musiranus (*mus araneus*) : screuua. 1344.

650 *mustella* : uuesulae *both.* 1345.

maruca : snegl. 1283.

majalis : bearug. 1284.

mordacius : clofae—clofæ. 1327.

maulistis : scyhend. 1286.

655 *mastice* : huuitquidu. 1287.

malva : cotuc *vel* geormantlab. 1288.

marrubium[3] : hunae *vel* biouuyrt. 1289.

mulio : horsthegn. 1346.

margo (*mango*) : mengio. 1285.

660 *mugil* : haecid—hecid. 1342.

matrix : quiða. 1290.

†*mergus* : scalfr.

mars, martis : tiig *both.* 1293.

mus, muris : mus *both.* 1348.

665 *merula* : oslae *both.* 1306.

megale (*mugalê*) : hearma *both.* 1307.

Nausatio, vomitus[4] *vel* : uulatung—uulating. 1357.

(*g*)*naviter* : horsclicae—hor[s]clicae. 1358.

ninguit : *h*sniuuith—sniuidh. 1379.

670 *nomisma*—*nomysma* : mynit—munit. 1383.

nux : hnutbeam—hnutbeam. 1394.

nigra spina : slachthorn—slachdorn. 1380.

[1] *After* malagma (635) *in Erf.* [2] *After* myrtus (637) *in Erf.*
[3] a *over er.* u *in Ep.* [4] fomitus *Erf.*

†*milium* (*mille*) : miil.
1315 *mirifillo* (*myriophyllon*) : gearwe. 623.
mimopora : ðeofscip. 630.
†*minaci* : hlibendri.
†*mitra* : haet.
mordicos : bibitne. 616.
1320 *molestissimum* : earbetlicust. 619.
monarchia : anuualda. 622.
modioli : *habae. 625.
morgit (*mulgit*) : milcit. 628.
mosiclum : ragu. 629 (1332).
1325 *momentum* : scytel. 632.
molibus : ormetum. 640.
mordacius : clouae. 653 [173].
†*movebor* : styrið.
†*sempiterna moles* : falthing.
1330 †*molos(s)us* : roðhund.
†*morenula* : eil.
mosicum : ragu. (1324).
†*mora* : heorotberge.
municeps : burgliod. 620.
1335 *munifica* : cystigan. 621.
murica : gespon. 624 [78].
†*murenula* : bool.
†*muluctra* (*mulcra*) : ceoldre. [258].
†*munila* (*monile*) : baeg.
1340 †*muscipula* : muusfalle.
†*mucro* : mece.
mugil : haeced. 660.
mustacia : granae. 644 [182].
musiranus (*mus araneus*) : screauua. 649 [226].
1345 *mustela* : uueosule. 650.
mulio : horsðegn. 658.
†*mugil* : heardhara.
mus, muris : muus. 664.
†*multabitur* : uuitnath.
1350 †*murilium* : byrgen.
†*musca* (*masca*) : egesgrima.
†*musica* : myrgnis.
†*murice* : wurman.
†*musca* : flege.
1355 †*murus* (*morum*) : braer.
myrtus : uuir. 637.

Nausatio : uulatunc. 667.
(*g*)*naviter* : horsclice. 668.
nasturcium (*t*) : tuuncressa. 676.
1360 *nap(h)t(h)a* : blaecteoru. 677.
nap(h)t(h)a : tynder. 685.
nanus[1], *pumilio* : duerg. 686.
napis (*-us*) : naep. 687.
†*nazarei* : loccas.
1365 †*nabulum* (*naulum*) : ferescaet.
†*naviter* : suiðfromlice.
†*neptam* (*naphtham*) : tyndre.
†*nectar, mel, vinum* : *carere.
netila (*nitela*) : hearma. 675 [225].

[1] nauus.

noctua: naecht[h]raebn, **ali*[1] *dicunt* nectigalae—necthraebn, *nacthegelae. 1384.

†*nycticorax*—**nicticorax*[2]: naechthraebn—*nethhræbn.

675 *netila* (*nitela*): hearma *both.* 1369.

nasturcium (*nasturtium*): tuuncressa—leccressae. 1359.

nap(*h*)*t*(*h*)*a*: blaecteru *both.* 1360.

nugacitas—**nugatitas*: unnytnis *both.* 1395.

non subscivum[3]: unfaecni—unfecni. 1386.

680 *negotio*—*negotia*: unemotan—*unemo. 1371.

nebulonis[4]: sc[i]nlaecean—scinlecan. 1372.

nimbus: storm *both.* 1378.

**nequaquam*—*nequicquam*: holunga *both.* 1373.

nepa: habern—hafern. 1370.

685 *nap*(*h*)*t*(*h*)*a*, *genus fomenti, id est*: tyndir—*ryndir. 1361.

nanus vel pumilio[5]: duerg *both.* 1362.

napi (*-us*): naep—nep *nequam.* 1363.

nodus: ost *both*[6]. 1387.

Oscillae, oscille (*-a*): totridan *both.* 1466.

690 *oscitantes*: ganaendae—ganendæ. 1467.

origanum: uurmillae—uurmillæ. 1452.

osma: suicae *both.* 1468.

oppillavit: gigiscdae—gescdae. 1447.

obliquum: scytihalt—*sestihalth. 1403.

695 *obnixus*: strimaendi—strimendi. 1404.

obreptione: criopungae—cr[i]upungae. 1405.

oridanum (*origanum*): elonae *both.* 1453.

orcus—*orci* (*-a*): orc *both.* 1454.

opere plumario[7]: bisiuuidi uuerci—*bisiuuisidi uerci. 1450.

700 *olor*: suan *both.* 1436.

obuncans: genicldae—*gensccilde. 1408.

oligia: nettae—*nectae. 1437.

obestrum: beost—*beoth. 1406.

[1] alii *Erf.* [2] *the first* c *looks like an unfinished* x. [3] subciuum *Erf.* [4] u *over* o *in Ep.* [5] punilio *Erf.* [6] *After* nequicquam (683) *in Erf.* [7] plumari *Ep.*

1370 *nepa*: haebern. 684.
negotia: une[me]tta. 680.
nebulonis: scinlaecan. 681.
nequi(c)quam: holunga. 683.
†*netum*: gesiuwid.
1375 †*nervus*: sionu.
†*necabantur*: aqualdun.
†*nitorium*: spinil.
nymbus[1] (*i*): storm. 682.
ninguit: s[ni]uwið. 669.
1380 *nigra spina*: slaghðorn. 672.
†*nixu*: werðeode.
†*noctua, ulula*: ule.
nomisma: mynit. 670.
noctua: naehthraefn. 673 [204].
1385 †*navalia*: faelging.
non subscivum: unfaecni. 679.
nodus: wrasan, ost. 688.
†*notae*: speccan.
†*notatus*: oncunnen.
1390 †*noverca*: steopmoder.
†*noma*: nihtebr[ed].
†*numularius, nummorum prae-rogatur* (*-or*): miyniteri.
†*nurus*: snoro.
nux: hnutbeam. 671.
1395 *nugacitas*: unnytnis. 678.
†*nucl(e)i*: cir[n]las.
†*nullo negotio*: naenge earbeðe.
†*numquid*: ne huru is.

†*Obolitio*: eðung.
1400 †*obsides*: gislas.
†*obrizum* (*y*): smaete gold. [55].
†*obriguit*: gefreos.
obliquum: scytehald. 694.
obnixus: strimendi. 695.
1405 *obreptione*: cr[i]opunge. 696.
obestrum: beost. 703.
†*optimates*[2]: gesiðas.
obuncans: genyclede. 701.
obtenuit: forcuom, bigaet. 706.
1410 *obnixe*: geornlice. 708.
†*obunca*: crump.
†*obvix*: wiðerstal.
obligamentum: lyb, lybsn, 711.
†*obstruit*: fordytte.
1415 †*objecte*: ongen sette.
†*objectus*: uuitsetnis.
†*obruere*: oberu[u]recan.
†*obsedatus*: gislhada.
†*obturat*: *folclaemid.
1420 †*obtinuit*: ofercuom.
†*objectionibus*: gestalum.
†*obnoxius*: scyldig.
†*obex*: ogengel.
†*obicula*: geocstecca.
1425 *occupavit*: onette. 712.
†*ocreis*: baangeberg.
†*occa*: faelging.
†*occubuit*: gecrong.
occiput: hrecca. 715.
1430 †*occabat*: egide.
†*ocearium* (*a.*): staeli. (55).

[1] *originally* nimbus, *as shown by alph. order.*
[2] *originally* obtimates, *as shown by alph. order.*

ogastrum : aeggimang—aeggimong. 1435.

705 *oresta* : t[h]res—thres. 1455.

obtenuit : bigaet *both*. 1409.

ordinatissimam : *ð giset[t]an—*a *girettan. 1458.

obnixe—**obnixae* : geornlice—*geornlic*et*. 1410.

omnimoda (-*o*) : oeghuuelci ðinga[1]—oeghuelci *hadga[2]. 1442.

710 *orbita* : huueolrad—*hueolraat[2]. 1459.

obligamentum—**oblicamentum* : lybb—*libb[2]. 1413.

occupavit : onettae—*onete[2]. 1425.

†*occas* : fealga.

ortigomera (*ortygometra*) : edischaen — *edischenim[2]. 1460.

715 *occiput*—**occipud* : hreacca—hręca[2]. 1429.

ostriger : bru[u]nbesu—bruu*n*besu. 1469.

†——— *occupavit* : *geomette.

olor, cignus (*y*)—*olor gr*(*a*)*ece, latine cignus* : aelbitu—*ębitu. 1439.

omentum : maffa—*naffa. 1443.

720 †*occipitium* : *snecca.

——— *Procuratio* : *scur. 1625.

promulserit : lithircadae—lithircadæ. 1626.

profusis — **profussis* : genyctfullu*m* — genyctfullum. 1627.

promulgarunt : scribun *both*. 1628.

725 *provehit* : gifraemith—gifremit. 1629.

perfidia : treulesnis *both*[3]. 1533.

pro captu : faengae *both*. 1630.

promaritima : saegesetu—*saegaesętu. 1631.

percommoda matutinos[4] : sua cendlic morgen[lic]—sua cendlic *mor[gendlic]. 1534, 5.

[1] ði : nga. [2] *diff. hand.* [3] u *er. after sec.* u *in Ep.*
[4] matunos *Ep.*

†*offendit*: moette.
†*offirmans*: claemende.
†*officit*: werdit.
1435 *ogastrum*: aeggimong. 704 (1438, *cp.* 105).
olor: suon. 700.
oligia: nettae. 702.
olgastrum: aeggimong. (1435).
olor, cicnus (*y*): aelbitu. 718.
1440 †*olim*: singale.
†*olastrum*: staeb.
omnimodo: oeghwelce ðinga. 709.
omentum: maffa. 719.
†*omen*: hael.
1445 †*onocratallus* (*onocrotalus*): feolufer.
†*op*(*p*)*ilavit*: forclaemde.
oppilavit, clausit: gegiscte. 693 [177].
†*opinare* (-*i*): resigan.
†*op*(*p*)*ortunitatem*: gehydnis.
1450 *opere plumario*: bisiudi werci. 699.
†*oppilatae*: bisparrade.
origanum: wurmille. 691.
oridanum (*origanum*): eolone. 697.
orcus (-*a*): orc. 698.
1455 *oresta*: ðres. 705.
†(*h*)*or*(*r*)*ipilatio*: celiwearte.
†*orcus*: ðyrs, heldiobul.
ordinatissimam: þa gesettan. 707.
orbita: hueolrád. 710.
1460 *ortigomera* (*ortygometra*): edischen. 714.
†*oratores*: spelbodan.
†*ordinatus*: gehaeplice.
†*or*(*diens*): onginnendi.
†*orion*: eburðring. [76].
1465 †*orbitae*: last.
oscillae (-*a*): totridan. 689.
oscitantes: geongendi. 690.
osma: suice. 692.
ostriger: bruunbeosu. 716.

1470 †*Patrimonium*: gestrion.
partim: sume daeli. 731.
palpitans: brogdetende. 735.
particulatim: styccimelum. 751.
paludamentum, genus vestimenti bellici: haecile. 740.
1475 †*patrocinium*: mundbyrd.
†*paranimphus* (*y*): dryhtguma.
†*pal*(*a*)*estra*: plaega.
†*pastinare*: settan.
†*palatina*: raecedlic.
1480 *parcae*: wyrde. 764.
parcas: burgrune. 761.
†*palearibus*: deadraegelum.
†*palas*: scoble.
papilio: fiffalde. 768.
1485 *papula*: wearte. 771.
pampinus: crous. 773.
papilivus (*papyrus*): *wiolucscel. 781.
palingenesean (-*esis*): edscaeft. 783.
paneta (*patina*): holoponne. 784.

730 *praetextatus—pretextatus*: gigeruuid—*gigarauuit.* 1632.
partim: sume daeli—sumae dæli. 1471.
pudor: scamu—*scoma. 1679.
praepropera[1] (*-e*): fraehraedae *both.* 1633.
privigna, filia sororis, id est: nift *both.* 1634.
735 *palpitans*: brocda[e]ttendi—*brogdaethendi. 1472.
piraticum — piraticam: uuicingsceadan — uuicingsceadae. 1579.
percrebuit: mere uueard—mere uuard. 1536.
perduellium: þorgifect—*dorhgifecilae. 1537.
proscribit: ferred. 1635.
740 *paludamentum, genus vestimenti bellici, id est*: haecilae —hecæli. 1474.
per seudoterum—per seuduterum (*pseudothyrum*): þorh ludgaet—dorh ludgaet[2]. 1538.
percitus: hraed[3]—*hrad. 1539.
propensior[4]: tylg *both.* 1636.
**profligatus—profligatis*: forsleginum—*faerlslaegmum. 1637.
745 *pel(l)ices*: cebisae—*caebis. 1540.
phisillos (*physicus*): leceas *both.* 1578.
praerupta: staegilrae—stegelræ. 1638.
probus: ferth—fert. 1639.
proterunt[5]: treddun—*treodun. 1640.
750 *permixtum* (*-im*): gimengidlicę—gimaengidlicæ. 1542.
particulatim: styccimelum—*scyccimelum. 1473.
proterentem: naetendnae *both.* 1641.
pertinaciter[6]: anuuillicae *both.* 1543.
penduloso[7]: halði—*hahdi. 1541.
755 *pessu(lu)m*: spilth *both.* 1544.
petisse: sochtae—*scochtae. 1545.
per anticipationem: þorch obst—dorh obust. 1546.
provectae[8]: f[r]odrae—frodrae. 1642.
profetae — provecta (*perfecta*): gifraemid — gifremid. 1643.

[1] propopera *Erf., second* o *altered to* e. [2] *follows* percitus *in Erf.* [3] h *added out of line.* [4] or *from* us *in Erf.* [5] perterunt *Erf.* [6] pertinatiter *Erf.* [7] penduloro *Erf.* [8] u *over* f *in Ep.*

1490 *paneta* (*patina*): disc. 786.
†*paupilius* (*papyrus*): scaldhulas.
papula: spryng. 791.
†*pandis*: geapum.
†*patruus*: faedra.
1495 †*patruelis*: faedran sunu.
†*patruelis*: geaduling.
†*paxillum, palum*: naegl.
†*panpila*: wibl.
†*panuculum* (*panuncula*): uuefl.
1500 †*palagra*: ecilma.
†*pascsos*: geroscade.
pastinaca: walhmore. 794.
papirum (*y*): eorisc. 795.
pangebant: faedun. 797.
1505 *palla*: rift. 801.
par(*r*)*ula*: mase. 806 [202].
papilio: buterflege. 817.
paliurus: sinfulle. 819 [37].
pavo: pauua. 826.
1510 †*passus*: faeðm *vel* tuegen stridi.
palumbes: cuscote. 829.
pastellus (-*illus*): hunigaeppel. 830.
pansa: scaffo[o]t. 832.
†*paranymphus*: dryhtgum[a]. [124].
1515 †*parumper*: huonhlot*um*.
papaver: popei. (1621).
†*pariter*: gelice.
†*paruca*: hicae.
†*palpant*(*i*)*um*: olectendra.
1520 †*palmula*: steorroðor.
†*parricidio*: megcualm.
†*paciscitur*: geðingadon.
†*palagdrigus*: ecilmehti.
†*pantigatum* (*pantagathus*): uuduhona.
1525 †*palina* (*balaena*): hran. (267).
†*paleae*: aegnan.
†*pabulatores*: horshi[o]rdas.
†*passim*: styccimelum.
†*partica*: reodnaesc.
1530 †*perstrenue*: fromlice.
†*pedisequa*: ðignen.
†*perpessum est*: aðroten is.
perfidia: treuleasnis. 726.
percommoda: sua cenlic. 729.
1535 *matutinos*: morgenlic. 729.
percrebuit: mere wearð. 737.
perduellium: þorhgefeht. 738.
per seudoterum (*pseudothyrum*): ðorh ludgæt. 741.
percitus: hraed. 742.
1540 *pel*(*l*)*ices*: cebise. 745.
penduloso: haldi. 754.
permixtum: gemengetlic. 750.
pertinaciter: anuuillice. 753.
pessu(*lu*)*m*: spilth. 755.
1545 *petisse*: sohte. 756.
per anticipationem: ðorh obst. 757.
per vispell(*i*)*ones*: ðorh byrge[ras]. 760.
perpendiculum: colðred. 763.
†*per hironiam* (*ironiam*): ðorh hosp.
1550 (*im*)*petigo*: teter. 766 [91].
perna: flicci. 774 [166].
pedo, vel paturum: feotur. 778 [159].

760 *per vispell(i)ones*: þorch[1] by[r]geras—dorh *buyrgenas. 1547.

parcas: burgrunae—burgrunæ. 1481.

pliadas: sifunsterri—*funsterri. 1599.

perpendiculum: colþred—coldraed. 1548.

parcae—parce: uuyrdae *both.* 1480.

765 *puncto, foramine, in quo pedes vinctorum*[2] *tenentur*[3] *in ligno cubitali*[4], *spatio interjecto, id est*: cosp *both*[5]. 1680.

(im)petigo: tetr—te[t]r. 1550.

pulenta (*polenta*): briig *both.* 1681.

papilio—**papilici*: fifaldae—*uiualdra.* 1484.

pice, sevo(b): unamaelti sperþi—*cinamelti *spreui. 1581.

770 *pustula*: angseta[6]—*angreta. 1682.

papula: uueartae—uearte. 1485.

praxinus (*fraxinus*): aesc—esc. 1651.

pampinus—**panipinus*[7]: cros—crous. 1486.

perna: flicci *both.* (804) 1551.

775 *pituita*: gibrec—gibreec. 1580.

presetuas—praesetuas: byrgea *both.* 1652.

pus: uuorsm—*uuorsin. 1683.

pedo vel paturum: fetor *both.* 1552.

praetersorim—praetorsorum: paad *both.* 1654.

780 *prifeta*: thriuuuintri steo[r]—*triuumtri steur. 1655.

papiluus (*papyrus*): ilugsegg—*ilugseg. 1487.

pun(c)tus: brord—broord. 1685.

palingenesean — palingeneseon (*-esis*): edscaept *both.* 1488.

patena (*-ina*): holopannae. 1489.

785 *pingit*: faehit—*faethit. 1582.

patena (*-ina*): disc *both.* 1490.

pila: thothor—*thorr. 1584.

**prorigo—prurigo*: gycinis *both.* 1658.

pittacium: clut *both.* 1585.

790 *ptysones* (*ptisanas*): berecorn[8] berendae—berecorn berendæ. 1677.

[1] c *half* er. [2] uinctorium *Erf.* [3] tenetur *Erf.* [4] cubitalis *Erf.* [5] *follows* petigo *in Erf.* [6] an:g. [7] *second* i *from* a. [8] *second* e *over* i.

†*perpendiculum*: pundur. [36].
†*penuria*: weðl.
1555 †*percellitur*: bið slaegen.
†*pervicax*: ðro[e]htig.
†*pero* (-*a*): himming.
†*pessum*: clifhlep.
pessul(*um*): ha[e]ca. 803.
1560 *peducla* (*pediculus*): luus. 812.
petra[1] *focaria*: flint. 805.
pendulus: ridusende. 816.
pella: sadulfelge. 818.
pecten: camb. 825.
1565 †*percellitur*: slaegen.
†*pes*: fot.
†*perstant*: tioludun.
†*persolvio* (-*vo*): ic ðrouuio.
petulans: wraene. 835.
1570 *perpendit*: aehtað. 836.
perstromata, ornamenta: steba. 837.
pendulus: ohældi. 838.
†*pellis*: fel.
†*perpes*: hraed.
1575 †*petuita* (*pi.*): sped.
†*pectica*: slahae.
†*philosophus*: uðuuta.
phisillos (*physicus*): leceas. 746.
piraticam: wicincsceaðan. 736.
1580 *pituita*: gebrec. 775.
pice, saevo (*sebum*): unamaelte smeoruue. 769.
pingit: faehit. 785.
†*pistrimum* (-*num*): cofa.
pila: thothr. 787.
1585 *pittacium, os peri*: clut, cleot, 789.
†*pisum*: piosan.
†*pistrilla*: cofincel.
†*pillentes*: bere.
†*pirus*: pirge.
1590 †*pinus*: furhwudu.
pictus acu: mið nethle asiowid. 796.
picus: higre, fina. 808 [216].
pix, picis: pic. 820.
†*pilus*: her.
1595 †*piceca*: neb.
†*piscis*: fisc.
†*pistillus*: gnidil.
†*pluinas* (*prunus*): plumtreu.
pliadas: sibunsterri. 761.
1600 †*plumum* (*prunus*): plumae. (*cp.* 1664).
plantago: uuegbrade. 793.
platisa (-*essa*): flooc. 802 [163].
†*plectra*: auunden.
†*pla*(*n*)*taria*: setin.
1605 †*plus minus*: ymb ðæt.
†*polenta*: smeodoma.
†*postena*: boga.
†*portio*: hlyte.
populus: birce. 792.
1610 †*politis*: smoeðum.
†*portentum*: scin.
pilimita[2] (*po.*): hringfaag. 798.
porfyrio (*ph*): feolufer. 807.
porcopiscis: styrga. 809 [222].
1615 *porcaster*: foor. 810 [239].

[1] *e over* a.

[2] *originally* polimita, *as shown by alph. order.*

papula vel pustula: spryng *vel* tetr *both.* 1492.
populus: birciae *both.* 1609.
plantago vel septenerbia (*septemnerva*)—*plantaga, septinerbia*: uuaegbradae—uuegbradæ. 1601.
pastinaca—**pastinacia*: uualhmorae *both.* 1502.
795 *paperum*—*papirum* (*papyrus*): eorisc *both.* 1503.
pictus acu—**pictis acu*: mið naeðlae[1] [a]siuuid—mid nedlæ asiuuid. 1591.
pangebant: faedun—*fædum. 1504.
polimita: hringfaag—*hrnigfaag. 1612.
pronus: nihol *both.* 1659.
800 *prodimur*: birednae—biraednae. 1661.
palla: rift—*ritf. 1505.
platisa—*platissa* (*-essa*): flooc—floc. 1602.
pessul(*um*): haca *both.* 1559.
perna: *flicii. (774) 1551.
805 *petra focaria*: flint *both.* 1561.
parrula: masae *both.* 1506.
porfyrio (*ph*)—*porfirio*: felofor—*felusor. 1613.
picus: fina *vel* higrae *both.* 1592.
porcopiscis: styria *both.* 1614.
810 *porcaster*: foor—for. 1615.
porcellus: faerh *both.* 1616.
peducla (*pediculus*): luus *both.* 1560.
pulix[2] (*-ex*): fleah—*floc. 1683.
proflicta: forslaegen *both.* 1662.
815 *proventus*: spoed *both.* 1663.
pendulus: ridusaendi—ridusendi. 1562.
papilo (*-io*): buturfliogae—*buturfli[o]go. 1507.
pella: sadulfelgae *both.* 1563.
palurus—*palliurus* (*paliurus*): sinfullae—sinfullæ. 1509.
820 *pix, picis, id*: pic[3] *both.* 1593.
pollux (*-ex*): thuma—thumo. 1617.
prunus: plumae *both.* 1664.
pullis—*pollix* (*pollis* = *pollen*): g[r]ytt—gryt[4]. 1620.

[1] na *from* m. [2] i *over* u *in Ep.* [3] x *er. after* i *in Erf.* [4] *or* grytt (?).

porcellus: faerh. 811.
pollux (-*ex*) : ðuma. 821.
†*poleo* (-*io*): scaebe.
†*pollinis*: gruiit.
1620 *pollis*: grytt. 823. [*cp.* 149].
popaver (*pa.*) : popæg. 824 (1516).
†*posthumus*: unlab.
†*pons*: brycg.
†*procax*: huuæl.
1625 *procuratio*: sciir. 721.
promulserit: liðercade. 722.
profusis: genyhtfullum. 723.
promulgarunt: scribun. 724.
provehit: gefremið. 725.
1630 *pro captu* : fenge. 727.
promaritima: saegeseotu. 728.
praetextatus: gegeruuid. 730.
propropera (*praepropere*): fraehraeðe. 733.
privigna : nift. 733 [123].
1635 *proscripsit* : faerred. 739.
propensior : tylg. 743.
profligatis : forslaegenum. 744.
praerupta: staegilre. 747.
probus : ferht. 748.
1640 *proterunt*: tredun. 749.
proterentem: naetendne. 752.
praefectae (*provectae*) : frodre. 758.
profecta (*perfecta*): gefremid. 759.
†*praecipitat*: ascufið.
1645 †*praecipita*: afael.
†*praefaricator* (*v*) : reccileas.
†*praestantior*: fromra.
†*praesidium*: spoed.
†*praestante*: fremmendum.
1650 †*proteri*: brecan.
praxinus (*fr.*) *viridus color vel*: aesc. 772.
presetuas: byrga. 776.
†*pruina* : hrim.
pretersorim: paad. 779 (1676).
1655 *prifeta* : *ðriuuintra steor. 780.
†*provehit*: fremid.
†*prunas* : gloede.
prurigo: gycenis. 788 [*cp.* 82].
pronus: nihold. 799.
1660 †*pronuba*: heorðsuaepe. [73].
prodimur: birednae. 800.
proflicta: forslaegen. 814.
•*praeventus* (*pro.*): spoed. 815.
prunus: plumę. 821.
1665 *progna* (*procne*): su[u]aluue. 828.
†*praesorium*: pund.
†*prorostris*: haehsedlum.
†*praeceps*: trondendi.
†*procus*: brydguma.
1670 †*prodigus*: stryndere.
†*praesumptio*: forenyme.
†*propugnaculum*: briostbiorg.
†*proveho*: fyrðru.
†*proceres*: geroefan.
1675 †*propero* (-*e*): hraeðe.
praetersorium: paad. (1654).
ptysones (*ptisanas*): berecorn beorende. 790.
†*putamina*: hnyglan.
pudor: scomo. 732.

**popaver*—*papaver*: popaeg—*papoeg. 1621.

825 *pecten*: camb *both.* 1564.

pavo: pauua *both.* 1509.

†*phitecus* (*cercopithecus*): apa—*capa.

progna—*progina* (*procne*): suualuae—suualuuæ. 1665.

palumbes—**palumpes*: cuscutan—cuscotae[1]. 1511.

830 *pastellas*—*pastellus* (*pastillus*): hunaegaepl[2]—*cæneg-aepl. 1512.

pulium—*puleum* (*pulegium*): duuergaedostae—duer-gaedostae. 1686.

pansa: scabfoot—scaabfot. 1513.

†*pituita*: gillistrae.

†——— *pedetemptim, caute, quasi pede temptans*: [fot-melum][3].

835 *petulans vel spurcus*[4]: uuraeni—ureni. 1569.

perpendit: aecta[t]h—aechtath. 1570.

perstromata, ornamenta: stefad bru*n*—staefad *brum. 1571.

pendulus: ohaelðï—oheldi. 1572.

**Qualiis*—*qualus*: mand *both.* 1689.

840 *quisquiliae*: *aehrian—*ægrihan. 1696.

quadripertitum: cocunung *both.* 1690.

quocumquemodo[5]: gihuuelci[6] uuaega—gihuelci uuegi. 1700.

quacumque: suae suithae—suue suidae. 1691.

quantisper—**quantusper*: suae suithae—suue *sidae. 1692.

845 *quoquomodo* — **quoquemodo*: aengi þinga — ae[n]gi dinga. 1701.

quinetiam: aec þan—aec don. 1695.

quaternio—*quaterno*: quatern—quate*r*ni. 1693.

quinquefolium: hraebnęs foot—hræfnæs foot. 1697.

**quiquenervia*—*quinquenervia*: leciuuyrt—leciuyrt. 1698.

[1] *follows* pavo (825) *in Erf.* [2] g *over* er. [3] *Ep. has only the Latin:* pedetemtim caute quasi temtans pede. [4] purcus *Erf.*; *second* u *over* o. [5] *first* o *altered to* a *in Ep.* [6] gihuuuelci.

1680 *puncto* : cosp. 765.
pulenta (*polenta*) : briig. 767.
pustula : oncgseta. 770.
pus : *uuorm. 777.
pulix (-*ex*) : flęh. 813.
1685 *pun(c)tus* : *brond. 782.
pulleium (*pulegium*) : duergedostle. 831.
†*pullus* : brid.
†*pulla* : blaco.

Qualus : mand. 839.
1690 *quadripertitum* : cocunung. 841.
quacumque : suae suiðe. 843.
quantisper : suae suiðe. 844.
quaternio : quatern. 847.
†*quadrare* : geeblicadun.
1695 *quinetiam* : aec ðon. 846.
quisquiliae : aegnan. 840.
quinquefolium : hraefnes foot. 848.
quinquenervia : leciwyrt. 849.
†*quintus* : giululing.
1700 *quocumque modo* : gehwelci wega. 842.
quoquomodo : aenge þinga. 845.

850 *Renunculus*: lundlaga[1] *both.* 1712.
radium: hrisil—hrisl. 1704.
rictus: graennung[2]—*graemung. 1738.
runcina—**runtina*: locaer *vel* sceaba *both.* 1755.
rabulus (*-a*): flitere *in ebhatis both.* 1705.
855 *rema* (*rheuma*): stream *both.* 1714.
r(*h*)*euma*: gibrec—gebrec. 1717.
roscinia (*luscinia*): nectaegalae—*necegle. 1746.
resina: teru *both.* 1716.
respuplica (*respublica*): cynidom *both*[3].
860 *rien* (=*renes*): lęndino—lendino. 1740.
radinape—**rodinare*: lelothrae—lelothre. 1747.
rostrum: neb *vel* sci[p]es celae—neb *vel* scipes cæle. 1748.
robor (*-ur*): aac *both.* 1749.
reciprocato: gistaebnęndrae—*gistaebnen. 1721.
865 *reclines*: suae haldae—*suuaeldae[4]. 1722.
rationat(*i*)*o*: ambect—*ambaet. 1706.
recessus: helustras *both.* 1723.
rostratum: tindicti *both.* 1750.
relatu: spelli *both.* 1720.
870 *remota*: framadoenre—*framadoændrae. 1724.
rigore: heardnissae *both.* 1742.
reserat: andleac *both.* 1725.
rostris: foraeuuallum *vel* tindum—foreuuallum *vel* tindum. 1751.
rancor: throh, *vel invidia, vel odium*—throch. 1708.
875 *remex*: roedra *both.* 1726.
rumex (*-en*): edroc *both.* 1756.
ridimiculae—*ridimiculi* (*redimicula*): cyniuuithan *both.* 1743.
rastros, ligones, id: mettocas—*metticas. 1709.
ruscus (*-um*): cnioholaen—*cniolen. 1759.
880 *ramnus* (*rhamnos*): thebanthorn—*thebanthron. 1710.

[1] d *over* er. o *in Ep.*
[2] graen : n.
[3] i *from* o *in Erf.*
[4] *first* a *may be* o.

†*Raster* (*rastrum*): egiðe.
†*rancidis*: bitrum.
radius: hrisl. 851.
1705 *rabulus* (*-a*): flitere in eobotum. 854.
rationatio: ambaect. 866.
†*rabies*: geris.
rancor: troh. 874.
rastros: mettocas. 878.
1710 *ramnus* (*rhamnos*): ðeofeðorn[1]. 880.
†*radio*: gabulrond.
renunculus: lundlaga. 850.
†*retentare*: stouuigan.
rema (*rheuma*): stream. 855 [181].
1715 †*refugium*: geberg.
resina: teoru. 858.
r(*h*)*euma*: gebrec. 856.
†*reses*: slaec.
†*respuplica* (*b*): cynedoom. 859.
1720 *relatu*: spelli. 869.
reciprocato: gestaefnendre. 864.
reclines: suae halde. 865.
recessus: heolstras. 867.
remota: from adoenre. 870.
1725 *reserat*: onlaec. 872.
remex: roeðra. 875.
†*repagula*: sale.
†*reciprocis*: wrixlindum.
†*relatio*: eðcuide.
1730 †*retorto*: geðraune.
†*renis*: heðir.
†*rediva* (*reduvia*): aettaelg.
†*reverant*: spunnun.
†*respectus*: etsith.
1735 †*reponile*: gearnuuinde.
†*reciprocatu*: uurixlende.
†*retiunculas* (*ra.*): resunge.
rictus: grennung. 852.
†*rimosa*: cionecti.
1740 *rien* (= *renes*): laendino. 860.
†*rima* (*rythmus*): getael.
rigore: heardnisse. 871.
ridimiculae (*redimicula*): cynewiððan. 877.
†*rigentia*: forclingendu.
1745 †*ripariolus*: staeðsu[u]alwe.
roscinia (*luscinia*): naectegale. 857 [212]. (*cp.* 52).
rodinope: lelothrae. 861.
rostrum: neb *vel* scipes caeli. 862.
robor (*-ur*), *arbor*: aac. 863.
1750 *rostratum*: tindecte. 868.
rostris: foreuuallum *vel* tindum. 873.
†*roscido*: deawe.
†*rostri*: tindas.
†*rotnum*: nabogar.
1755 *runcina*: locer, sceaba. 853.
rumex (*-en*): edric. 876.
†*rubigo*: brondoom.
†*ruber*: read.
ruscus (*-um*): cnioholen. 879 [127].

[1] *letter er. after second* e.

Salebrae: thuerhfyri *both.* 1761.
sibba: sigil *both.* 1856.
scalbellum—*scabellum* (*scalpellum*): bredisern—bred isaern. 1793.
†*scrobibus*: furhum *both.*
885 *sartago*: bredipannae—*breitibannæ. 1762.
sarcinatum: gisiuuid—gesiuuid. 1763.
sarculum[1], *ferrum, id*: uueadhoc *both.* 1764.
sternutatio: fnora—*huora. 1909.
sarta tecta: gifoegnissae—*gefegnessi. 1765.
890 *sentina*: lectha, *ubi multae aquae colliguntur in navem*[2] *both.* 1833.
scalprum—**scalbrum*: byris, *vel ut* **ali* thuearm—byris, *vel ut alii* duæram. 1795.
salix: salch—salh. 1767.
sambucus: ellaen—ellae. 1775.
scirpea: *lerb, *de qua mat*(*t*)*a conficitur*—lebrae. 1804.
895 *serpillum* (*y*): bradae leac—brade lec. 1835.
stabula: seto *both.* 1903.
surum (*-a*): sparuua—sparua. 1944.
sagulum: loda *both.* 1779.
struere: stridae—streidæ. 1910.
900 *seditio*: unsibb—unsib. 1836.
secessum—*secessus*: helostr *both.* 1838.
scena: sceadu[3] *both.* 1801.
sanguinis: *cneorissa—cneorissae. 1780.
†*scina* (*scena*): grima *both.* (953).
905 *seta*: byrst *both.* 1837.
scarpinat: scripith *aen*—scripith *æn.* 1805.
†*scalpellum*: byris *both.* [198].
sturnus: staer—*sterm. 1911.
scorelus: emer *both.* 1810.
910 *sardinas*—**sandinas*: heringas *both.* 1781.
scira (*sciurus*): aqueorna—aquorna. 1811.
scrofa: sugu—*ruga. 1812.
**strigia*—*striga*: haegtis—hegtis. 1913.
sullus: otor—otr. 1945.

[1] surculum *Erf.* [2] unam navem *Erf.* [3] u *over* o *in Ep.*

1760 †*Sab(u)lo*: molde.
salebrae: þuerhfyri. 881.
sartago: brediponne. 885.
sarcinatum: gesiouuid. 886 (1774).
sarculum: uueodhoc. 887.
1765 *sarta tecta*: gefoegnisse. 889.
†*saevo* (*sebum*): unslit smeoro.
salix: salh. 892.
†*sagax*: gleu.
†*sarmentum*: spraec.
1770 †*salibaribus*: miðlum.
†*sarcofago* (*sarcophagus*): licbeorg.
†*sacellorum*: haerga.
†*sarcio*: siouu.
sarcinatum: gesiowid. (1763).
1775 *sambucus*: ellaern. 893.
†*sandalium*: scete, loða.
†*sambucus*: sueglhorn.
†*salum*: haeb.
sagulum: loða. 898.
1780 *sanguinis*: cniorisse. 903.
sardinas: heringas. 909 [223].
saginabant: maestun. 930.
sandix: uueard. 950.
sardas: smeltas. 949.
1785 †*saliunca*: sure.
salum: seeg *vel mare*. 966.
salsa: sure. 973.
†*sarabar(a)e*: braec[c]ę.
†*satiare*: asoedan.
1790 †*sacra, orgia*: edmelu.
†*scolonia* (*ascalonia*): cipe.
†*scabellum*: windfona.
scalpellum: bredisern. 883.
†*scopa(e)*: besma.
1795 *scalprum*: byrs *vel* þuarm. 891.
†*scamma*: feld.
†*saltuum*: feltha.
†*scylla*: eduuelle.
†*scansio*: scyrft.
1800 †*sceptra*: onwald.
scena: scadu. 902.
†*scotomaticus*: stae[r]blind.
†*scalpro*: bore. [*cp.* 259].
scirpea: lebr. 894.
1805 *scarpinat.*: scripið. 906 [189].
†*scalpellum*: bor.
†*scaturit*: criid.
†*scoria*: sinder.
†*scurra*: scond.
1810 *scorelus*: omer. 909 [208].
scirra (*sciurus*): aqueorna. 911 [236].
scrofa: sugu. 912 [240].
†*scara*: scaed.
sciniphes (*scinifes, ciniphes*): mygg. 916.
1815 *scilla*: glaedine. 920.
scasa: eborðrote. 927.
scindulis: scidum. 943.
†*scena*: uuebung.
scrobibus: groepum. 948. [*cp.* 150].
1820 †*scalmus*: thol.
sc(h)eda: taeg. 964.
scienices (*scenicus*): scinneras. 952 [118].
scirpea: eorisc, leber. 960.
scalpula (*scapulae*): sculdur. 963.
1825 †*scaphum* (-*a*): scip.

915 *suspensus*: anhaebd—anhæbd. 1947.
scnifes (*scinifes*, *ciniphes*): mygg—mycg. 1814.
sinapio (*sinapi*): cressae—cressa. (922) 1860.
sicalia—**sycalia*: rygi—*ryg. 1861.
simbulum—*symbulum* (*symbolum*): herebaecon—herebecon. 1873.
920 *scilla* (= *squilla*): gladinae—gledinae. 1815.
sequester: byrg[e]a—byrgea. 1840.
——— *sinapio*: cressae (917).
situla—**situlae*: ambaer—ember. 1859.
stornus—**stronus*: dropfaag—*drofaxg. 1914.
925 *sualdam* (*valvam*): durhere[1] *both*. 1948.
sella: sadol—*satul*. 1839.
scasa: eborthrotae *both*. 1816.
strepitu: brectme *vel* cliderme—*bretme *vel* clidrinnae. 1916.
stipatoribus: ymbhringendum—ymbdringendum. 1915.
930 *saginabant*: maestun—*mestum. 1782.
semigelato—**semigelatu*: ha[l]bclungni—halbclungni. 1844.
spatiaretur—**spatiareti*: suicudae-*both*. 1893.
squalores: orfiermae—orfermae. 1902.
suffragator[2]: mundbora *both*. 1949.
935 †*suffragium*—*subfragium*: mundbyrd *both*.
sollicitat: tyhtit[3]. 1883.
spiculis: flanum—flanum. 1894.
subscivum: faecni—fae[c]ni. 1950.
sinuosa—**sinuossa*: faetmaendi—faedmendi. 1862.
940 *successus*: spoed *both*. 1951.
sublustris—**sublustrus*: sciịr *both*. 1952.
sopitis[4]: ansuebidum—*ensuebitum. 1882.
scindulis: scidum—scidum. 1817.
sevo: smeruui *both*. 1846.
945 *serio*: eornęsti—eornesti. 1845.
strenue—**strenuae*: framlicae—fromlicae. 1917.
spina: bodęi *both*. 1891.

[1] *letter rubbed out after* u *in Ep.* [2] *second* a *from* o *in Erf.*
[3] h *over* c.; = tychtit (?). [4] p *from* b *in Erf.*

sciphus (*y*) : bolla. 965.
†*scintella* (*-illa*) : spærca.
†*scalpio* (*scalpo*) : scriopu.
†*sc*(*a*)*evum* : goduureci.
1830 †*scabro* : unsmoeði.
†*scenis* : scinnum.
†*semispatium* (*-spatha*) : þeohsaex.
sentina : lectha. 890.
†*sentes* : ðornas.
1835 *serpillum* (*y*): brade laec. 895.
seditio : unsib. 900.
seta : byrst. 905.
secessus : heolstr. 901.
sella : sadol. 926.
1840 *sequester* : byrga. 921.
†*sclabrum* : uuind.
†*scalpo* : clawe.
†*scuporum* : hliuða.
semigelato : halfclungni. 931.
1845 *ser*(*i*)*o* : eornisti. 945.
sevo : smeoru. 944.
serum : hwæg. 979.
†*sensim* : softe.
senon : cearricgge. 968.
1850 *senecen* (*senecio*) : gundesuilge. 976.
†*sepeliant* : onsuebbað.
†*sermo* : spręc.
†*sedulium* : rægu.
†*senex* : ald.
1855 †*senior* : aeldra.
sibba : sigl. 882.
†*singultat* : sicetit *vel* gesca slaet.
†*sicomoros* (*sycamorus*) : heopan.

[1] signaum.

situla : omber. 923.
1860 *sinapian* (*sinapi*) : cressa. 917.
sicalia : ryge. 918.
sinuosa : faeðmendi. 939.
†*simpla* : anfald.
†*sirina* (*siren*) : meremenin.
1865 *singultus* : gesca. 958.
†*sinnum* : cirm.
†*siliqua* : pisan hosa.
sisca : sniðstreo. 973.
sinfoniaca (*symphoniaca*) : belone. 975.
1870 †*signum*[1] : segn.
†*simultas* : unsib.
†*sinopede* : redestan.
simbulum (*symbolum*) : *herebenc. 918 (1971).
†*sinus* : byge.
1875 †*sinus* : faeðm.
smus (*sinus*) : wellyrgae. 969.
†*socrus* : sueger.
†*socer* : *sur.
soccus : socc, slebescoh. 951.
1880 †*solisequia* (*solsequium*) : sunfolgend.
†*sopio* : suebbo.
sopitis : onsuebdum. 942.
sollicitat : tyhteð. 936.
sorix (*-ex*) : mús. 977.
1885 *sortem* : wyrd, *condicionem*. 980.
†*sortilegos* : hlytan[2].
†*sollicito* : tyhto.
†*solvat* : *ondest.
†*sollicitare* : tyhtan.
1890 †*soricarius* : mushabuc.

[2] y *over* u.

scrobibus—**scropibus*: groepum *both.* 1819.
sardas: smeltas *both.* 1784.
950 *sandix*: uueard—uue[a]rd. 1783.
soccus: sooc *both.* 1879.
scienicis (*scenicus*): scinneras—*scineras. 1822.
†*scina* (*scena*) *nitatio vel*: grima *both.* (904).
stiria: gecilae—gecile. 1919.
955 *sponda*: selma *both.* 1895.
spina alba: haeguthorn—heguthorn. 1897.
spina nigra: slaghthorn—salachthorn. 1898.
singultus: iesca *both.* 1865.
stabulum: falaed *both.* 1920.
960 **scrirpea*—*scirpea*: eorisc *both.* 1823.
**sabulcus*—*subulcus*: suan—*suam. 1953.
stagnum: staeg *vel* meri *both.* 1921.
scapula (*-ae*): sculdur—*sculdra. 1824.
sc(*h*)*eda*: *teac—teag. 1821.
965 *scifus*—*sciffus* (*scyphus*): bolla—bollae. 1826.
salum: segg—seg. 1786.
stilium vel fusa: spinil *both.* 1922.
senon: cearruccae—cearricae. 1849.
sinus—*simus*: uuellyrgae *both.* 1876.
970 *slens*—*splenis* (*splen, splenis*): milti *both.* 1896.
spatula: bed *both.* 1899.
suesta—*sivesta*: suina suadu *both.* 1954.
sisca—*sista*: snidstreo—snidstreu. 1868.
salsa: surae *both.* 1787.
975 *sinfoniaca*[1] (*symphoniaca*): belonae *both.* 1869.
senecen (*-io*): gundaesuelgiae—gundaesuelgae. 1850.
sorix[2] (*-ex*), *id est*: mus *both.* 1884.
**stilio vel vespertilio*: hreathamus *both.* 1925.
seru(*m*): huaeg *both.* (982) 1847.
980 *sortem, condicionem*[3]: *uuyd—uyrd. 1885.
†*sc*(*a*)*evus, strabus, torbus* (*v*), *id est*: sceolhegi—sceolegi. 1939.
serum[4], *liquor casei, id*: huaeg—huuaeg. (979).

[1] sinfroniaca *Erf.* [2] sorid *Erf.* [3] conditionem *Erf.*
[4] *Only* um *visible in Ep.*

spina: bodeg. 947.
†*spicas*: ear.
spatiaretur: suicade. 932.
spiculis: flanum. 937.
1895 *sponda*: benc, selma. 955.
splenis: milte. 970.
spina alba: haeguðorn. 956.
spina nigra: slahðorn. 957.
spatula: bed. 971.
1900 †*spiramentum*: hol.
†*spiato*: matte. [81].
squalores: orfeormnisse. 933.
stabula: seto. 896.
†*stiba* (*v*): handle.
1905 †*stabulum*: stal.
†*strigillum* (*strigilis*): screope.
†*stragua* (*stragulum*): strel.
†*stuppa*: heordan.
sternutatio: fnora. 888 [60].
1910 *struerer*: streide. 899.
sturnus: staer. 908 [203].
†*strues*: heap.
striga: haegtis. 913 [228].
stornus: dropfaag. 924.
1915 *stipatoribus*: ymbhringendum. 929.
strepitu: braechtme. 928.
strenue: fromlice. 946.
†*strictis*: getogenum.
stiria: gecilae. 954.
1920 *stabulum*: falaed. 959.
stagnum: mere. 962.
stilium: spinel. 967.
†*stertens*: hrutende.
stilio (*vespertilio*): hraeðemu[u]s. 978.
1925 †*s*(*t*)*uppa*: ecambe.
†*st*(*r*)*angulat*: wyrgeð *vel* smorað.
†*stricta mac*(*ha*)*era*: getogone sueorde.
†*stamen*: wearp.
†*sternit*: gehnægith.
1930 †*strenas*: lybesne.
†*stellatus*: astaenid.
†*strut*(*h*)*io*: stryta.
†*stigmata*: picung.
†*stomachum*: maga.
1935 †*strigillus* (*-ilis*): aera, aeren scre[op].
†*stenax*: wurpul.
†*stiga*: gaad.
†*sturfus* (*sturnus*): fina.
strabus: scelege. 981.
1940 †*subplaudans*: gelpende.
†*suffundit*: ablendeð.
†*surculus*: tuig, ouuaestm.
†*susurio*: wrohtspitel.
surum (*-a*): spearua. 897.
1945 *sullus*: ottor. 914.
†*subarrata*: geuuetfaestae.
suspensus: ahaefd. 915.
sualdam (*valvam*): durhere. 925.
subfragator: mundbora. 934.
1950 *subscivum*: fraecni. 938.
successus: spoed. 940.
sublustris: scir. 941.
subulcus: suan[1]. 961.
suesta: suina sceadu. 972.
1955 †*surgit*: waexit.
†*sulforia* (*sulfur*): sue[f]l sueart.

[1] snan.

Trux palpitat[1], *vel* : hunhie[ri]—unhyri. 2040.
tonica polimita : hringfaag, *a rotunditate circulorum*—*hrinfag. 2029.
985 *torta* : auunden *both*. 2030.
tonsa : rothor—*rohr. 2031.
titio : brand—brond. 2018.
trutina vel statera : helor *both*. 2041.
trulla : crucae *both*. 2051.
990 *traductus* : georuuierdid *both*. 2042.
Tempe : scaedugeardas—sceadugeardas. 1998.
trop(a)ea, signa vel : sigbeacn—*beanc. 2043.
tortum : coecil *both*. 2032.
troc(h)leis, rotis modicis vel : stricilum *both*. 2044.
995 *triplia*[2] (*tripetia*) : lebil *both*. 2045.
tignarius **trigrarius* : hrofuuy[r]cta — *hrofhuyrihta. 2020.
testudo : *borohaca *vel* sceldreda *vel* faeru[cæ]—*brodthaca *vel* sceldhreða *vel* *fænucæ. 1999.
tessera : tasol, *quadrangulum*[3]—tasul. 2000.
tertiana : *lectinadl—lenctinadl. 2001.
1000 *tubo—tuba* (*-us*) : thruu[c]h—thruch. 2067.
tragelafus[4] *vel platocerus* (*platyceros*) : elch *both*. 2054.
torq(uet)[5]—**torquetur*[6] : uuraec *both*. 2033.
tridens : maettoc—mettoc. 2047.
tilia : lind *both*. 2019.
1005 *taxus* : iuu *both*. 1972.
tremulus : aespae—espę. 2048.

[1] palpitrat *Erf.* [2] p *from* b *in Erf.* [3] quadrungulum *Erf.*
[4] tragelafbus *Ep.* [5] *Rubbed out.* [6] torquet'.

†*suspenderat*: awenide.
†*sucini*: glaeres.
†*subigo*: wrotu.
1960 †*sub cono*: under haehnisse.
†*sudum*: lybt, *siccum*.
†*sutrinator*: scoere. [122].
†*subsannat*: hospetęt.
†*suffocacium*: cecil.
1965 †*subjugatis*: geðedum.
†*suis*: [suin].
†*suaeder*: butan toðum.
†*suellium*: suinin.
†*subtalaris*: steppescoh.
1970 †*sup(p)uratio*: gelostr.
symbulum (*symbolus*): herebæcun. (1873).

Taxus: iuu. 1005.
talpa: wond. 1014 [227].
taculus: brocc. 1008.
1975 *talpa*: wondeuueorpe. 1045.
tabunus (*tabanus*): briosa. 1016 [230].
tapetsa (*tapete*): rye. 1020.
tabetum (*tapete*): bred. 1023.
talumbus: gescadwyrt. 1032.
1980 *taxatione*: raedinne. 1035.
tabuisset: asuond. 1036.
tantisper: ðus suiðe. 1037.
taberna: winaern. 1040.
†*talaria*: feðrhoman.
1985 †*taurus*: fear.
†*taxaverat*: gierende.
†*talus*: oncleouue.
†*tabulata*: ðille.
†*tala*: webgerodes.
1990 †*tabulamen(tum)*: ðille.
†*taeni(i)s*: ðuaelum.
†*tegula*: tigule.
†*t(a)edis*: blesum.
†*teter*: duerc.
1995 †*territorium*: lond.
†*tentigo*: gesca.
†*tentorium*: geteld.
Tempe: sceadugeardas. 991.
testudo: bordðeaca. 997.
2000 *tessera*: tasul. 998. [*cp.* 84].
tertiana: *lenctinald. 999.
terebellus: nabogaar. 1010 [196].
tenticum: sprindel. 1025.
telum (-*a*): web. 1026 [34].
2005 *textrinum*: webb. 1030.
termofilas (*thermopylas*): fae[s]ten. 1042.
temonibus: þixlum. 1043.
teres: siunhuurful. 1047.
†*temperiem*: uueder.
2010 †*tehis*: tegum, fodrum.
†*teloniaris* (*telonarius*): uuicgeroebum.
thymus (-*um*): haet. 1007.
†*tholus*: hrof.
†*thadalus*: brooc.
2015 †*thessera*: beeme.
†*titica*: uuefl.
†*tisifone* (*ph*): uualcyrge.
titio: brond. 987.
tilia: lind. 1004 [247].
2020 *tignarius*: hrofuuyrhta. 996.
tincti (*tinca*): sli. 1015 [221].
tilio (-*a*): baest. 1017.
tignum: tin. 1024.
titulo: gata loc. 1028.

thymus (*-um*) : haeth—haedth. 2012.
toculus—*taculus* : brocc—*broa. 1974.
trifulus—*trufulus* : felospraeci—*felusp'ici. 2049.
1010 **terrebellus*—*terebellus* : nabfogar—*naboger[1]. 2002.
turdella : throstlae *both*. 2068.
tilaris—**itilaris* : lauuercae—lauuercæ. 2026.
turdus : scric—*screc. 2069.
talpa : wand—uuond. 1973.
1015 *tincti* (*tinca*) : sli *both*. 2021.
**tabu:us*—*tabanus* : briosa *both*. 1976.
tilio (*-a*) : lind *vel* baest—lind *vel* best. 2022.
tuber, tumor : suollaen—*assuollan. 2071.
**toreum*—*toreuma* : eduella—eduelli. 2034.
1020 *tapeta*[2] (*-e*) : ryae—*hryhae. 1977.
transtrum : ses *both*. 2050.
trulla : scofl—*scolf. 2051.
tabetum—*tebe* (*tapete*) : bred *both*. 1978.
tignum : tin *both*. 2023.
1025 *tenticum* : sprindil *both*. 2003.
telum (*-a*) : uueb *both*. 2004.
torax : felofearth—felufrech. 2035.
titule—*titulae* : gata loc—gatan loc. 2024.
tudicla—*tudica* (*tudicula*) : thuerae—thuere. 2072.
1030 *textrina* : uu[e]b—uueb. 2005.
tibialis : baanrift—baanryft. 2025.
talumbus : giscaduuyrt—*gescanuuyrt. 1979.
torrentibus : *streum—*streaumum. 2036.
tuta : *onsorg—orsorg. 2070.
1035 *taxatione* : raedinnae—redinnae. 1980.
tabuisset : asuand—*assuant. 1981.
tantisper : þus suiþae—dus suidae. 1982.
tutellam (*tutela*) : *sclindinnae[3]—scildinnae. 2073.
**triquarum*—*triquadrum* (*triquetrus*) : ðrifedor—*tri-foedur. 2052.
1040 *taberna* : uuinaern *both*. 1983.
trans : biginan—bigenan. 2053.

[1] b *from* o. [2] *First* a *from* e *in Erf.* [3] sclindi:n.

2025 *tibialis*: *baanrist. 1031.
tilares: lauricae. 1012 [211].
tipo (*typhon*): draca, *vel inflatio*. 1048.
†*tigillum*: first.
tonica polimita: hringfaag, *a rotund' circu'*. 984.
2030 *torta*: auunden. 985.
tonsa: roðr. 986.
torta: coecil. 993.
torquet: uuraec. 1002.
toreuma: eduuaelle. 1019.
2035 *torax*: feoluferð. 1027.
torrentibus: streamum. 1033.
†*torosa*: sionuualt.
†*toga*: goduuebbe.
†*torquent*: þrungun.
2040 *trux*: *unhiorde. 983.
trutina: heolor. 988.
traductus: georuuyrde. 990.
trop(*a*)*ea*: sigebecn. 992.
troc(*h*)*leis*: stricilum. 994.
2045 *triplia* (*tripctia*): lebl. 995.
†*trajectus*: ðorhbrogden.
tridens: auuel, meottoc. 1003.
tremulus: aespe. 1006.
trufulus: feluspreci. 1009 [170].
2050 *transtrum*: saes. 1021.
trulla: cruce, turl, scofl. 989, 1022.
triquadrum (*triquetrus*): ðrifeoðor. 1039.
trans: bigeonan. 1041.
tragelaphus: elch. 1001.
2055 †*trulla*: ponne.
†*transfert*: geuuendit.
†*tribuli*: braere.
†*tranant*: ðorhsuimmað.
†*tripes*: stool.
2060 †*tria*: huice.
†*tractibus*: naescum.
†*trita* (*turda*): ðrostle.
†*truitius*: ðraesce.
†*traigis*: higrae.
2065 †*tricent*(*ur*): ae[l]den.
†*tubera*: clate.
tubo (*-us*): ðruh. 1000.
turdella: ðrostle. 1011 [205].
turdus: scric. 1013 [213].
2070 *tuta*: orsorg. 1034.
tuber, tumor: asuollen. 1018.
tudic(*u*)*la*: thuaere. 1029.
tutellam (*tutela*): scildenue. 1038.
tuber: hofer. 1046.

termofilas—termopilas (*thermopylas*) : faestin *vel* anstigan—*festis *vel* anstiga. 2006.

temonibus : dislum—dixlum. 2007.

†*tabida et putrefacta* : afulodan, asuund[nan], aduinendanan—afulat ond asuunden.

1045 *talpa* : uuandaeuui[o]rpae—uuondæuuerpe. 1975.

tuber : ofr—o[f]r. 2074.

teres : sinuurbul[1]—*sinuulfur. 2008.

tipo (*typhon*) : *droco—draco. 2027.

Verruca : uueartae—uuertae. 2088.

1050 *via secta*[2] : iringaes uueg—*inges uueg. 2118.

verbere torto[3] : *auundre suipan—auundenre suipan. 2087.

venabula (*-um*) : eborspreot *both*. 2089.

valba[4] (*v*) : duerheri[5]—durheri. 2075.

ventriculus, stomachus avis vel : cesol *both*. 2090.

1055 *vescada*[6] : mundl : :—munleuu. 2091.

ur : : : *lum—urciolum* (*eo*) : : : : : ae—cruce. 2165.

vicat : *m—vicatum* (*ficatum*) : libr *both*[7]. 2119.

vestibulum : cebȩrtuun—*caebertuum. 2094.

volvola(*convolvulus*) : *wiuwindae, *herba similis hederae*[8], *quae vitibus et frugibus circumdari solet*—uuidubindae. 2158.

1060 *vit*(*t*)*as* : thuelan *both*. 2120.

vulgo, passim vel : oghuuaer—oeghuuer. 2173.

vitelli : suehoras—sueoras. 2121.

**uscidae—viscide* : *tholicae—*tochtlicae. 2170.

venetum : geolu—*geholu. 2095.

1065 *vatilla* (*batillum*) : gloedscofl *both*. 2076.

villis : uulohu*m*—uulohum. 2122.

unibrellas (*umb.*) : stalu to fuglu*m*[9]—stalu to *fluglum. 2153.

vertigo : edwalla—edualla. 2096.

**vitilago—vitiligo* : blectha *both*. 2123.

[1] b *over* f. [2] *Erf. adds* iuvar ; u *over the* a. [3] torta *Ep.*
[4] *Illeg. in Ep.* [5] *First* e *half erased* (?). [6] *Last* a *illeg. in Ep.*
[7] *Comes at the end of* u *in Erf.* [8] hedere *Erf.* [9] *First* u *from* l.

2075 *Valba* (*valva*) : durheri. 1053.
vatilla (*batillum*) : gloedscofl. 1065.
varix : ampre. 1073 [152].
varicat : stridit. 1086 [193].
vangas : spadan. 1087 [111].
2080 *vadimonium* : borg gilefde. 1089, 90.
†*vatilla* (*batillum*) : isernscobl.
†*vanus* : gemaeded.
†*vapore* : aethme.
†*vanna* (-*us*) : fon.
2085 †*vacca* : cuu.
†*vada brevia* : geuue[ada].
verbere torto : *awundere suiopan. 1051.
verruca : wearte. 1049.
venabula(-*um*) : eoborspreot. 1052.
2090 *ventriculus* : *ceonsol. 1054.
vescada : mundleu. 1055.
†*veror* : witro.
†*vexilla* : seign. [89].
vestibulum : caebrtuun. 1058.
2095 *venetum* : geolu. 1064.
vertigo : eduuelle. 1068 [168].
†*vectis* : *seng.
vespas : uuaefsas. 1071.
verberator(*i*)*um* : corthr. 1074.
2100 *verberatrum* : flete. 1075.
vesica : bledre. 1077.
veneria : smeoruwyrt. 1078.
vespertilio : hraeðemuus. 1098.
†*vernaculus* : frioleta.
2105 †*vecors* : gemaad.
†*vernacula* : menen.
vetellus : sueor. 1099.
†*vertil* : huerb.
†*vehiculum*[1] : wægn.
2110 †*vertiginem* : suinglunge.
†*vesper* : suansteorra.
†*veterno* : faecnum.
†*vermis* : eorðmata.
†*ve*(*r*)*miculus* : cornuurma.
2115 †*verbi gratia* : uuordes intinga.
†*violenter* : roeðelice.
†*viti*(*li*)*ginem* : bleci. [107].
via secta : iringes uueg. 1050 [77].
vicatum (*f*) : libr. 1057.

[1] veniculum.

1070 *vitricius* (*vitricus*) : steupfaedaer—*staupfotar. 2124.
vespas—vespa : waeffsas—uuaeps. 2098.
vorago : hool *both*. 2159.
varix : amprae—omprae. 2077.
verberatorium : cortr—cordr. 2099.
1075 *verberatrum* : fleti—*fletu. 2100.
urna : ambaer—*ombar. 2166.
vessica (*vesica*) : bledrae *both*. 2101.
veneria : *speruuuyrt—smeruuuyrt. 2102.
ulmus : elm *both*. 2149.
1080 *villosa* : ryhae *both*. 2126.
villa (*-us*) : linnin ryhae—linin ryhae. 2128.
viburna (*-um*) : uuiduuuindae—uuidubindae. 2129.
viscus : mistil. 2127.
quinquefolium : hraefnaes fot. (848).
1085 *vicium* (*vicia*) : fuglaes bean—*flugles bean. 2125.
varicat : stridit *both*. 2078.
vangas : spadan *both*[1]. 2079.
virecta : quicae[2]—*cuique. 2130.
verecundiae[3] *concesserim* : gilebdae—*gilepdae. 2080.
1090 *vadimonium—*vadi* : borg *both*. 2080.
vitiatum : auuaerdid[4]—auuerdid. 2131.
vibrat[5], *dirigat* (*-it*) : borẹt[t]it—boretit. 2147.
vitiato oculo : *unþyotgi egan—undyctgi ægan. 2133.
†*vesica* : blegnae—blegnæ.
1095 *undecunque—undecumque* : huuanan[6] huuoega—huuonan huuoega. 2155.
usurpavit : agnaettae—agnetæ. 2171.
uris : urum *both*. 2167.
vespertilio : hreadaemus—hreadamus[7]. 2103.
vetellus : sueor. 2107.

1100 *Yripeon* : haersearum. 2175.

[1] *After* virecta *in Erf.* [2] q *over* c. [3] vericundiae *Ep.*
[4] —di : d. [5] vimbrat *Ep.* [6] *Letter rubbed off after second* u.
[7] *Ep. ends with the gloss* veterator ; stroffosus, astutus.

2120 *vittas*: thuelan. 1060.
vitelli: sueoras. 1062.
villis: uuloum. 1066.
vitiligo: blectha. 1069.
vitricius (*vitricus*): steopfaeder. 1070 [108].
2125 *vicium* (*-ia*): fugles bean. 1085 [35].
villosa: rye. 1080.
viscus: mistel. 1083.
villa (*-us*): linin ryee. 1081.
viburna (*-um*): uuduuuinde. 1082.
2130 *virecta*: quicae. 1088.
vitiatum: awended. 1091.
†*vibrat*: brogde[t]teð.
vitiato oculo: unðyhtge egan. 1093.
†*virgultum*: gerd.
2135 †*viscera tosta*: gebreded flaesc.
†*vibice*: lelan.
†*vinco*: obersuiðo.
†*viresceret*: greouue.
†*viscellum*: broht.
2140 *viscera*: tharme, thumle.
†*vimen*: wearp.
†*villus*: u[u]loh.
†*virgo*: u[n]maelo.
†*vitulus*: caelf.
2145 †*vitula*: cucaelf.
†*vistula*: sugesweard.
vibrat: borettið *vel* diregað (*dirigit*). 1092.
†*ultroque citroque*: hider ond *hider. [10].
ulmus: elm. 1079.
2150 †*ulula*: ulae.
†*umbilicus*: nabula.
†(*h*)*umecta*: gibrec. [71].
unibrellas (*umb.*): stalu to fuglum. 1067 [167].
†*unguentum*: smeoru.
2155 *undecumque*: huonanhuegu. 1095.
†*unguana*: naegl[speru].
†*voti compos, voto ornatus i.*: fægen.
volvola (*convolvulus*): uuduuuinde. 1059.
vorago: hool. 1072.
2160 †*voragine*: suelgendi.
†*voluter, cupido votium*: oestful.
†*voluma*: gorst.
†*vordalium* (*sandalium*): laesti.
†*vox*: stebn.
2165 *urciolum* (*eo*): waetercruce. 1056.
urna: amber. 1076.
uris: urum. 1097.
†*verticeta*[1] (*urticeta*): netlan.
†*urguet*: threa[tade].
2170 *uscide* (*viscide*): tohlice. 1063.
usurpavit: agnette. 1096.
†*utensile*: geloma.
vulgo, passim: oeghuer. 1061.
†*uxorius*: ceorl.

2175 *Yryseon*: heresearum. 1100.
†(*h*)*ymnus*: loob.

[1] *Originally* urticeta, *as shown by alph. order.*

Erfurt[2].

Incipit[1] *conscriptio glos(s)arum in unam, quibus verba quoque vel nomina alia mixtim vel latina vel saxoniaè inseruntur.*

(14f) †*Acidus*: *acacsore.
(16b) †*avehit*: bernit.
(16c) *anser, auca*: gos.
(16d) †*anser silvatica*: gregos.
1105 (16f) †*argata*: ualtae.
(18d) *cancer*: *nefern.
†*ca[c]pinica*: hramsa.
(19a) †*cunabula*: cynna.
(19c) †*claucuIas*: uilucas.
1110 (20b) †*continuus*: ferstud.
(20c) †*conductium*: giindi.
(22d) †*epifates*: faerbenu.
(23d) †*fa(g)u(s), arbor*: boc.
†*fis(s)uras, scis(s)uras*: sloae *sax.*
1115 (23e) †*fidejus(sor)*: *brog *sax.*
(24c) †*gavia, avis qui dicitur*: stern *sax.*
(24d) †*genesco*: mušscel.
(26e) †*lapsanus (-a, -ium)*: coydic.
lacerta: adexe *sax.*
1120 (28b) †*muccus (mucus) sax.*: horch.
(28c) *nascurcium (nast.)*: cressa *sax.*
(29b) *omentum*: maffa.
(30a) †*patellas*: lempite *sax.*
(30e) *pila*: thothur.
1125 (31f) †*putrenum*: gandi.
(32c) †*ratis*: fliute *sax.*
†*racana*: huitil *sax.*

[1] incipitu.

(32e) *reniculus* (*-unculus*) : len libre da *sax.*
†ringitur : thrahit, *dic hoo more canum.*
1130 *†ricinus* : ticia *sax.*
(33a) *sambuca, lignum* : elle *sax.*
(33d) *†setes* (*-as*) : brysti *sax.*
(33e) *sinapiones* (*sinapi*) : cressa *sax. qui in aqua crescit.*
(33f) *†spalagius, musca venenosa est, aut*[1] *similis* fifeldae *sax.*[2]

Erfurt[3].

Nunc aliae XVI exiguae secuntur.

1135 (34f) *†Abusus* : foruerit.
(35a) *†adfectuosus, amabilis* : lebuendi *sax.*
(35b) *†aeditu(u)s templi vel (a)edis minister* : [rendegn].
†aequimanus : bylipti *sax.*
(35c) *alga marina* : uar.
1140 *†albeus* (*v*), *genus vasis* : trog.
aleator : tebleri *aleae.*
alia (*-ea*) : tefil.
†amisarius : stoeda *et homo* for[3].
†ampusatio, una lectio : fiit[4].
1145 (35e) *†aquiluus* (*aquilus*), *fulvus* : bruun locar.
†arca funeris, sarcofagum (*sacrophagus*) : [cest].
†arquamentum : dixl.
(35f) *†auctoracius i. g. monachus qui est ab exercitu electus* : [cempa].
axis : aex.
1150 (36a) *†battulus* : stam *sax.*
†biplex, duplex : tuili.
(36b) *†blat(t)a, pigmentum* : hauiblauum.
†blaciarius, primicularius : byrdistrae *sax.*

[1] aut*em.* [2] *After* 33 *a leaf is wanting.* [3] *Stroke over* r. [4] *Second* i *under line.*

†*bemer* (*vomer*) : scaer.
1155 *baccula* (*v*), *vitula* : cucaelf.
bucula, *umbo* : randbæg.
†*bustum*, *ustrina* : beel.
†*buris* : *scaes.
†*cata*, *bestiolae genus quod dicitur* : merth.
1160 †*casma* : caest.
(36c) †*capriolus* (*eo*) : raa.
†*calcatiosus* : spurul.
(36d) †*caper*, *porcus dimis*(*s*)*us* : baar.
calcar : sporonus spora.
1165 †*cervix*, *posteriora colli* : [hnecca].
†*cessius* (*caesius*), *glaucus* : ualde*n*negi.
†*censor*, *rimator*, *p'tiator* : ecƀtheri.
†*cista* : cest, *arcula*.
(36e) †*cella lignaria* : fin.
1170 *classis*, *navis* (*-es*) *collectae* : flota.
curnicula (*cornicula*), *genus avis* : crȩ.
†*colum* : lorg, couel.
(36f) †*colus* : lorg.
corbis : mond.
1175 †*colles* : bergas[1].
(37a) *humiliamanus* (*pumilio*, *nanus*) : duerh.
†*jaculum* : sciutil.
†*jactus* : bolt*io*.
†*sagitta* : sciutil.
1180 *ilium* : neisn' naensood.
(37d) †*inguen* : lesca hregresi.
†*juba*, *setes porci et leonis cabal*(*l*)*ique* : manu, brystæ.
(37e) †*lantantia* : beost.
†*lanna*, *angulus auris* : lappa.
1185 †*laxitas* : placūnis.
(37f) †*lignarium*, *ligneum* : fin.

[1] *Leaf cut out after* 36.

LEIDEN.

[† indicates words wanting in Corpus[2], to which also the numbers refer, a † before the number showing that the word does not occur in Ep.-Erf., and numbers in ( ) to repetitions in Leiden itself.]

(I)

Glos(s)ae verborum de canonibus.

(II)

Interpretatio sermonis de regulis.

(III)

Verba de sancti Martyni storia.

†*Anfibula* : oberlagu.
†*pro exercitu appuli* : huuitabar[1].
†*patescit* : briudid.
†*promontorium* : hog.
5 †*(h)abenis* : halsledir.
†*toracina* : haeslin.
†*murmur* : uastru[n]g.
antoni lacuna(r) : floda. 1178.
†*labefacare (-ere)* : agleddęgo.
10 *ultro citro* : hidir *an didir. †2148.
†*arguta* : ordancas.
†*exenia (xenia)* : madmas.

(IV)

Incipit in libris ecclesiasticae historiae.

Callas (-os) : uarras. †400 (93).
†*terebrantes* : borgenti.
15 †*per ipsima* : gaesuopę.
†*trogleis (trochleis)* : hlędrę.
†*latriuncula* : herst.
†*pusti* : brandas.
†*cautere* : tund[e]ri. (*cp.* 100).
20 †*ruder* : mixin.

(V)

Item de ecclesiastica storia.

†*Colomellas*[2] : lomum.
†*carbunculi* : poaas.
†*labrum, ambonem* : haet.
†*pruriginem* : bleci.
25 †*publite (poplite)* : hamme.
†*editiones* : thestisuir.
†*fibrarum* : darmana. (*cp.* C. †870).
†*sescuplum* : *dridehalpf.*

(VI)

Incipit brevis exsolutio de paralipomenon.

†*Lapides onichinos*[3] *(y)* : dunnę.

(VII)

De Salamone.

30 *Flavescit, color olei* : glitinot. †894.

[1] *The letters which follow in the MS. must be read as* r(h)eda : nomen vehiculi.
[2] e *from* o.
[3] *First* i *over some other letter.*

(VIII)

De ec(c)lesiasten.

(IX)

In cantico canticorum.

(X)

De Sapientia.

†*poderis, vestis sacerdotum a pedibus usque ad umbilicum pertingens, et ibi stringebatur cingulo, in cujus subteriore parte habebantur tintinnabula et mala punica in foribus visti*: *loth.

(XI)

De ecclesiastico.

asp(h)altum: spaldur. 228.

(XII)

In libro Isaie prophet(a)e.

†*Pilosi, incubi, monstri* (-*a*): *menae. (*cp.* 229.)

telam (-*um*) *orditus*: inuuerpan *uuep. 2004.

35 *viciam, pisas agrestes*: fugles beane. 2125 (183).

perpendiculum, modica petra de plumbo, qua(m) licant (*g*) *in filo quando* (*a*)*edificant parietes*: pundar. †1553.

paliurus, (*h*)*erba quae crescit in tectis domorum, grossa folia habens*: *fullae. 1508.

†*runtina* (*runcina*), *pidugio*: *uuitubil.

†*lima, qua limatur, ferri*: fiil.

40 *circino* (-*us*), *ferrum duplex, unde pictores faciunt circulos*: gabarind. 469.

†*delet*: hnabot.

(XIII)

Incipit in Hieremia.

(XIV)

Incipit in Danielem.

†*Cubitum*: elin.

(XV)

De Johel vel de prophetis minoribus.

†*ligones, ferrum fusorium*: tyrfahga.

hederam: ibaei. 718.

(XVI)

De Ose cynxronion (*synkhrônion*).

45 †*Lappa*: clate.

(XVII)

Incipit in Job.

Carectum: reod. 387.

†*oriona*: ebirdhring. (*cp.* 76).

†*capitio*: *haubitloh.*

†*hibicum* (*ibicum*): firgingata.

50 *herodion* (*erōdiós*): ualchefuc. 1016.

†*accipitres* (-*iter*): haefuc.

gurgustium: chelor. 1001.

†*incus*: osifelti. (*cp.* C. †1072).

†*armilla*: ermboeg.

55 *obrizum* (*y*): *ymaeti gold. †1401.

†*cartillago* (*cartilago*): uuldpaexhsue *vel* grost.

lagunculas vel lagina (*-ena*), *diminitivum*: croog. 1171 (79).
†*salices*: salhas.
†*ancillis, animalibus*: figl.
60 *sternutatio*: *nor. 1909.

(XVIII)

Incipit in Tobia.

brantie (*branchiae*): chyun. 328.

(XIX)

Incipit in Judith.

(XX)

De Ester.

†*Aeri*: haue.
†*tenda*: **gezlt.*
†*iacynt*(*h*)*ini*: *syitorheuuin.
65 †*lecti aurei*: berian beed.
†*purpuram*: uuylocbaso.
†*coccus*: uuyrmbaso.
†*rube*(*r*): uuretbaso.

(XXI)

Incipit in Esdra.

†*Lapide inpolito*: ungebatne stane, *non exciso.*
70 †*nemias, alio nomine*: atersatha.

(XXII)

Incipit in Matheum.

Umecta: *gebyraet. †2152.

(XXIII)

De Marco et Luco et Johanne.

†*Institis*: suithelon. (1060.)

(XXIV)

In libro officiorum.

Pronuba: herdusuepe. †1660.
†*simila*: smetuma.
75 †*mitras*: haetas.

(XXV)

In libro rotarum.

Orion: *eburdnung. †1464 (*cp.* 47).
via secta: iringes *uuec. 2118.

(XXVI)

In libro Antonii.

(XXVII)

Incipit verborum interpretatio.

Mauria de auro facta in tonica: gespan. 1336.
lagonam (*-enam*), *vas lapideum, ollo* (*-a*): crog. (57).

(XXVIII)

Decalogo Hieronimi in prologo.

(XXIX)

De ponderibus incipit.

80 †*Solidos tres*: trymisas *sax.*

(XXX)

De ponderibus secundum Eucherium.

(XXXI)

De Cassiano.

Spiathio: mattae. †1901.

(XXXII)

De Eusebio.

†*Prorigo* (*u*), *urigo cutis*: gyccae. (*cp.* C. 1658.)

†*tentigo, tenacitas ventris* : ebind.
†*tesseras* : tesulas. (*cp.* C. 2000.)
85 †*pedissequis* (*-us*); *conviator* : gegenta.
lacerta : adexa. †1182.
†*fornice* : scelb *vel* drep.
†*ignis* (*s*)*acer* : oma. (*cp.* C. †1039.)
vixilla (*vex.*) *et lab*(*a*)*rum* : segin. †2093. 1167.
90 †*codex* : stofun.
(*im*)*petigo* : tetr *afa.* 1550.
†*jugeres* : gycer.
callos, tensam cutem : uarras. (13.)
†*furtunam* (*fort.*), *fatum* : geuiif.
95 †*rogus* : beel *vel* aad.
†*fatum* : uyrd.
†*craticulis ferreis factis* : herst.
barat(*h*)*rum* : loh *vel* dal. †274.
†*laciniosa* : slitendę.
100 †*cautere, ferrum, melius* : tindre. (*cp.* 19.)
extale : snedildaerm. 794.
†*puplites* (*o*) : hommę.
†*lineolis* : dredum.
invisum : *luad. 1113.
105 †*ruderibus* : mixinnum.

(XXXIII)

De Orosio.

†*choncis* (*conchis*) : hebernum.
viti(*li*)*ginem* : bleci. †2117.
vitricum : *steuffeder. 2124.

(XXXIV)

De sancti *Augustini.*

†*Odonis vit*(*t*)*am* : mihes nostlum, *odon lineum est in pede.*

(XXXV)

De Clemente.

(XXXVI)

De dialogorum.

110 *Fledomum* (*phlebotomum*) : blodsaex. †896.
vangas : spaedum. 2079.
†*in mare Adriatico ab Adriano imperatore qui pensabat hoc mare cum catenis in profundum* rimis bord remum.
advocatus dicitur qui vocatur in adjutorium alicujus causa(*e*) *vel pro pecuniam* (*-ia*) : dingere. †89.
exactio : monung gaebles. 813.
115 *decrepitam* : dobend. 638.
†*arbor* : maest.
†*rimis* : cinum.
scinici (*scenici*) : *scinnenas. 1822.
†*histrionibus* : droccerum.

(XXXVII)

*Item incipi*unt *verba.*

(XXXVIII)

Item de nominibus diversis.

(XXXIX)

Incipit ex diversis libris.

120 †*Tapetibus* : rihum.

elleus (*ebulus*): ualuyrt. 714.
sutrinator: scoehere. †1962.
privigna: nift. 1634.
paranimphi (*paranymphus*): dryctguma. †1514.
125 †*seuit*: glimith.
fornaculum (*-la*): herth. †911.
ruscus (*-um*): cneholen. (250) 1759.
†*in pennias*: oberscoeiddo.

(XL)

Item de diversis nominibus.

(XLI)

iiii genera poetarum.

Emblema: fodor. 744.
130 †*cujatis*: huidirrynę.
†*nostratis*: hidirrinę.
†*quotus*: hu ald.
†*totus*: suæ ald.
†*perend*(*i*)*e*: ofer tua *nest.
135 †*animalus*: fifaldae.
eumenides, filiae noctis: hegitissę. †772.

(XLII)

Item alia de caelo.

(XLIII)

Verba de multis.

Fors: uyrd. †904.
glis: egle. 973.
†*damma* (*dama*): elha.
140 *aleo* (*aleator*): *teblheri. 111.
alea: tebl. 110.
†*histrio scurre* s lees.
gurgullio (*-ulio*): drohbolla. 1000.

(XLIV)

Item alia.

†*Veru*: snaas.
145 *cos*: *ueostun. 555.
lien: miltę. 1217.
†*fidicen*: harperi.
†*fidis*: sner.
†*pollis*: grot. (*cp.* C. 1620.)
150 †*scropis* (*scrobs, scrobis*): groop. (*cp.* C. 1819.)
carex: seic. 371.
varix: omprę. 2077.
libertabus: *friulactum. †1218.
†*cun*(*a*)*e*: *ciltrog, *unde cunabula.* (*cp.* C. †492.)
155 *magalia*: byrae. †1294.
†*simplex*: aenli.
†*bilex* (*-ix*): *tili.
†*triplex*: drili.
paturum: *fetor. 1552.
160 †*abctape*: tysse.

(XLV)

Item alia.

Abellana: *hel. 243.
calomaucus (*calliomarchus*): het. 383.
platissu (*-a*): *folc. 1602.
balera (*balaena*): hron. 267.
165 *caefalus*: haerdhera. 447.
perna: flicci. 1551.
umbrellas: stalo to *fuglam. 2153.
vertigo: eduallę. 2096.
buculus: *nordbaeg. 335.
170 *truffulus*: felospric. 2049.
†*famfelucas*: laesungac. (*cp.* C. 832.)

involucrus: uuluc. 1115.
mordatius (*-cius*): *clox. 1327.
erpica: *eg[i]ldae. 761.
175 *alga*: *uuac. 120.
†*pessul*: leer.
op(*p*)*ilavit*: *gigisdae. 1447.
colostrum: beust. 541.
isica: tyndri. 1156.
180 †*sicunia*: gibreci.
r(*h*)*euma*: streum. 1714.
mustacra (*-ia*): gronae: 1343.
vicias: *fuglues benae. (35.)
manticum: hondful baeues. 1278.
185 *maulistis*: scyhend. 1286.
berruca (*v*): uaert[a]ę. 288.
argella (*-illa*): la[a]m. 199.
accearium: stel. 55.
scarpmat (*-inat*): scribid.
190 *byrseus*: lediruyrcta. 344.
tubolo: fala.
andeda: *brondra. 157.
varicat: *stritęd. 2078.
battat: ginat. 269.
195 *lordus* (*u*): *lemphald. 1250.
terebellus: nębugaar. 2002.
dolabella: bradacus.
scalpellum: *biriis. (*Ep.* 907.)
ciscillus: haerdhaeu. 467.
200 *auriculum*: dros. 239.
garallus (*graculus*): hroc. 991.
par(*r*)*ula*: masae. 1506.
sturnus: stęr. 1911.
noctua: *necthtrefn. 1384.
205 *turdella*: drostlae. 2068.
ciconia: storhc. 465.
arpa (*harpe*): *arngeus. 212.
scorelus: emaer. 1810.
acega: holthona. 54.
210 *cucuzata*: *laepiumcę. 619.
tilaris: laurice. 2026.
ruscinia (*l*): nectigalae. 1746.
turdus: *scruc. 2069.
(*die*)*perdulum*: hragra. 198.
215 †*sticulus*: gaeuo.
picus: higrę. 1592.
marsopicus: *uinu. 1281.
ficetula (*-dula*): suca. 878.
fringella (*-illa*): *umc. 921.
220 *cardella* (*-uelis*): *distyltige. 381.
tinct (*tinca*): slii, *lupus brevis.* 2021.
porcopiscis: styra. 1614.
sardinus (*-as*): [h]eringas. 1781.
†*furunculas* (*-us*): maerth. (*cp.* C. 937.)
225 *netila* (*nitela*): herma. 1369.
musiranus (*mus araneus*): scraeua. 1344.
talpa: uoond. 1973.
striga: haegtis. 1913.
incuba: maerae *vel saturus.* (*cp.* 33) 1111.
230 *tabanus*: briusa[1]. 1976.
cacomicanus (*kakomēkhanos*): logdor. 382.
lendina (*lens*): hnitu. 1203.
aquilius (*aculeus*): onga. 192.
auricula: ęruigga. 240.
235 *castorius*: bebor. 385.

[1] mi *written over.*

scira (*sciurus*): acurna. 1811.
maruca: snægl. 1283.
majalis: bęrg. 1284.
porcastrum: foor. 1615.
240 *scrufa* (*o*): sugu. 1812.
berrus (*verres*): baar. 287.
†*philocain gr.*: scopon.
acrifolium: *holera. 53.
acerafula (-*abulus*): *mapaldurt. 51.
245 *involuco*: uudubindlae. 1116.
alnus: alaer. 116.
tilio (-*a*): lind. 2019.
almenta (*alnetum*): alerholt. 119.
†*putat*: snędit.
250 *ruscus*: *creholegn. (127.)

(XLVI)

Item de Cassiano.

†*Inextricabiles*: *anatreten. (*cp.* C. †1048.)
†*insolescit*: unstilli[t].
†*excellentiores*: gipparre.
†*sanguessuges* (*sanguisugae*): lecas.
255 †*citra*: bihina.
†*suricus*: brooc.
†*opere p'cium necessarium vel* neos.
multhra (*mulcra*): celdre. †1338.
†*scalpeum* (*scalprum*): boor[1]. (*cp.* C. †1803.)

[1] *The scribe adds* sicut inveni scripsi; ne reputes scriptori.

INDEX TO LATIN WORDS IN LEIDEN.

BLICKLING GLOSSES.

These glosses occur in the early eighth century psalter in the library at Blickling Hall, in Norfolk. They are apparently contemporary with the psalter itself, being written in the same red ink as that used for the rubrics. Their handwriting is of a very archaic, half-cursive type. Many of the glosses are much rubbed and worn away so as to be difficult to read. They were first published by Mr. E. Brock as an appendix to Dr. Morris's edition of the Blickling Homilies for the Early English Text Society (1874, 6). He has thrown them into alphabetical order, and printed them among the numerous later glosses in the MS. My own text is founded partly on his, partly on facsimiles made by me when the MS. passed through my hands. It will be seen that my readings occasionally differ from Brock's. For the sake of convenience I follow his order. On a leaf at the end of the book are written the names of several clerks of the city of Lincoln (Brock, p. 252). Brock does not tell us the age of the handwriting of this leaf, but it is, if I remember rightly, not earlier than the fourteenth century. We have no further clue to the origin of the MS., but there is every reason to believe it was written in Lincoln, and that the glosses here printed are in the East Mercian dialect of the first half of the eighth century, or possibly earlier.

inseparunt : þem ascadendu*m*.
inpulsus versatus sum : ascoben afeoll.
fecundae : berende.
plagae vestigia, cicatrices : dolgsuaþhe.
5 *cataracte* : forsceta.
in oportunitatibus : on geheplicnissum.
memoriale : gemyndelic.
novella olivarum : þa gingan eletri[o]w.
rugiebam : granode *vel* asten.
10 *promptuaria* : hordern.

ablactatus: from milcum adoen.
obdormiet: onhrernisse.
conplacebam: quemde.
in salsilaginem: on s.ltne mersc.
concidet: sliet.
torrens in austro: smoltregn[1].
australis: suþrador.
tetenderunt arcem: tinde bogan.
in auram: in wedr.
in salicibus: on *welgum.
incolatus meus: min wrecscype.

NORTHUMBRIAN BEDE-GLOSSES.

The glosses are written at the end of the Moore MS. of Bede's History in the Public Library at Cambridge, immediately after the fragment of Cædmon, and in the same hand of the first half of the eighth century. See notes on Cædmon.

Arula: hearth.
destina: feurstud.
jugulum: sticung.

[1] *Preceded by* toris (= torrens ?).

INSCRIPTIONS.

These inscribed texts, nearly all of which are in runes, most of them being also Northumbrian or Mercian, are all taken from Prof. G. Stephens' *Runic Monuments*, vol. i. To each inscription is added a reference to the page of Stephens' work, and the date assigned to it by him. In my transliteration, the rune *gifu* is represented by (g), *gár* by (*g*), *cén* by (c), the rune formed from it by repeating the side stroke on the other side by (k), and the still more complicated rune which is generally formed by inserting an upright stroke into the *gár*-rune by (*k*), the *ng*-rune by (q), the *ea*-rune by (*ea*).

I. BEWCASTLE COLUMN, Cumberland (398).

?670.

---

*G*essus *K*risttus.
Þis si*g*becn þun setton Hwætred,
Woþ*g*ar, Olwfwolþu aft Alcfriþu
ean *k*yniq eac Oswiuq.
*g*ebid heo sinna sowhula.

fruman *g*ear *k*ynin*g*es rices þaes[1]
Ec*g*friþu
lice

*K*ynnburu*g*
*K*yneswiþa
Myrcna *k*yn*g*
Wulfhere

*G*essus.

[1] ae *a bind-rune; might also be read* æe.

II. RUTHWELL CROSS, Dumfries (405).

? 680.

Letters inclosed in ( ) are given chiefly on the authority of the older editors, being now nearly gone.

Stephens bases his dating of the Cross mainly on his assumption of the poetry being Cædmon's, which he supports by translating lines 20–1, 'Cædmon made me.' He goes on to connect the mysterious word *fauœþo* with the verb *fēgan*, but if this were right, we should certainly find some such form as *fœgdœ*. The form *mœ* is equally anomalous; we should rather expect *mec* in a seventh century text. Even the name *Cædmon* is not quite certain, for Stephens reads *Cadmon*, which is an anomalous form. But assuming the name Cædmon, it can only be taken as that of the sculptor who devised the ornamentation and carved the cross. The ornamentation and the shape of the runes are, according to Stephens, different in some respects from those of the Bewcastle stone, whose date is not quite certain, although there is a general resemblance. All that the language teaches us is that the inscription cannot well be later than the middle of the eighth century. As regards the authorship of the poem, I hold fast to the opinion that it is a portion of the epilogue to the Elene, preserved entire in the Vercelli MS., and consequently is the work of Cynewulf. Also that the complete, original text of the Cross poem is that from which the Vercelli recension was copied. The sculptor or designer of the Ruthwell stone, having only a limited space at his command, selected from the poem such verses as he thought most appropriate, and engraved them wherever he had room for them.

(On)geredæ hinæ *G*od alme.tti*g*[1],
þa he walde on *g*al*g*u *g*isti*g*a

[1] *The fifth rune has the shape of the old* eu-*rune, which is impossible here, although Stephens reads* almeyottig; *we should expect* almecttig *or* almehttig, *and it is possible that the latter is the actual reading:* h *would easily become* eu *by the wearing away of some of its strokes.*

modi*g* fore . . .[1] men
(b)u*g*(a ic ni dars)te.
(ahof) ic riicnæ *k*yniqc,
he*a*funæs hlafard;
hælda ic (n)i darstæ.
bismæræedu uq*k*et men ba ætgad(r)e;
ic (wæs) miþ blodæ bistemi(d),
bi(*g*)ot(en) o(f) . . . .
Krist wæs on rodi.
hweþræ þer fusæ fe*a*rran kwomu
æþþilæ til anum: ic þæt al bi(he*a*)l(d).
s(are) ic wæs mi(þ) sor*g*u(m) *g*i(d)rœ(fe)d, h(n)a*g*(ic) . .
. . . miþ strelum *g*iwundad.
ale*g*dun hiæ hinæ limwœrignæ,
gistoddun him (æt) h(is l)icæs (h)*ea*f(du)m,
(bi)he*a*(l)du(n) hi(æ) þer h(*ea*fun) . . .

idægiscæf

*K*admon
mæfauœþo.

III. CASKET (470).

? 700–800.

The casket is made of whale-bone, the verses on it commemorating the capture of the whale. The two sentences refer to carvings of Romulus and Remus nursed by the wolf, and of the taking of Jerusalem by Titus. The two words which follow the latter are taken by Mr. Haig as the name of the artist, but Prof. Stephens supposes, with more probability, that they refer to the 'strong measures taken by Titus to ensure the obedience of the conquered city;' beneath them are representations of a tribunal, and of a person being led off to prison. The last word, *ægili*, stands over a carving of a man with a bow defending his house against his enemies, and is no doubt a proper name. The preceding line is all that remains of one side of the casket, so that the carving it probably refers to is lost.

[1] *Stephens reads* ale, *which he translates* 'all.'

Stephens identifies *fergenberig*, l. 5, with the present Ferry-hill in Durham, but it is possible that the word means simply 'mainland.' There are no distinctively Northumbrian forms.

Oþlæ unneg Romwalus and Reumwalus, twœgen gibroþæra,
fœddæ hiæ wylif in Romæcæstri.
Her fegtaþ Titus end Giuþeasu. dom. gisl.
Hronæs ban fiscflodu
ahof on fergenberig;
warþ gasric grorn,
þær he on greut giswom.
dr.g.þswi[1]. . . . . .
ægili.

IV. FALSTONE (biliteral), Northumberland (456).

? 700.

Roman.	*Runic.*
Eomaer the settae	Eomær þœ sœttœ
aeftaer Hroethberhtæ,	æftær Roetberhtæ[2],
becun aeftaer eomae.	be*k*un æftær eomæ.
gebidaed der saule.	*g*ebidæd der saule.

V. ALNMOUTH, Northumberland (461).

? 705.

Mixed uncials, minuscules and runes.

. . adulfes ð . .
. . . . . sav . .
myredah meh wo . .
. . vdwyg meh feg . .

[1] *The third and fifth letters resemble a sloping* s*-rune, like the* j *on the Charnay alphabet. Stephens, by confusing* j *with its modern English representation* y, *and the latter with the O. E. vowel* y, *gets the reading* drygyþ, *which he impossibly identifies with* dréogeð.

[2] *The* oe *in two letters.*

VI. MONK WEARMOUTH, Durham (477).

? 822.

Tidfirþ.

VII. LEAD RING, Coquet Island, Northumberland (480).

? 800–900.

þis is siuilfur(n ?)[1].

VIII. HARTLEPOOL, Durham (392, 6).

? 650–700.

Hildiþryþ
Hilddi[*g*]yþ.

IX. LANCASTER SLAB (375).

? 650–700.

Gibidæþ foræ Cynibalþ.
Cuþbœrec.

X. COLLINGHAM (Yorkshire) CROSS (390).

? 651.

Æftar Onswini cu.

[1] iu *doubtful: might also be read* e *as a single letter; or as an anticipation of the following* l.

XI. DEWSBURY, Yorkshire (464).

? 700.

Roman minuscules and uncials.

. . . .
. . . . . rhtae
becun aefter beornae
gibiddad der saule.

XII. THAMES KNIFE (361).

? 400–500.

B*ea*gnoþ[1].

XIII. SANDWICH, Kent (363).

? 428–597.

Assumed by Stephens to be heathen.

Ræhæbul.

XIV. DOVER, Kent (465).

? 700–800.

*G*islh*ea*rd.

XV. CHERTSEY DISH, Surrey (482).

? 800–900.

Mixed runes and decorated uncials.

Gætœh[2] uræcko.

[1] *If so old, the second rune must be read* eo. [2] œ *doubtful, may be* eu.

XVI. ÆTHRED'S RING (463).

? 700–800.

Mixed uncials and runes.

Æðred mec ah, Eanred mec agrof.

NAMES IN BEDE'S HISTORY.

The English person- and place-names occurring in Bede's Church History are here given from the following four MSS.

1. Moore (M.) in the Public Library at Cambridge, formerly at Ely. Written about 737. The forms of the English words are pure Northumbrian, and the fragment of Cædmon at the end of the MS. is in the same dialect.

2. Namur (N.) in the town-library of Namur in Belgium. The English names in this MS. were published by Mone in his *Quellen und Forschungen*, vol. i. The same MS. contains also Gregory of Tours. Mone says, 'the handwriting of both works belongs to the eighth century, but is of different nationality, for the Bede is written by an Anglo-Saxon, the Gregory by a Frank.' My attention was naturally attracted to the MS. by this statement, but when I inspected it myself, I found that it was written in a purely continental hand, without a trace of Old English influence. The errors of the scribe, of which I have given a few specimens, are alone enough to prove his not being an Englishman. But the MS. has an independent value, as being a copy of an English MS. of about the same age as M. It has a great gap in Book II.

3. Cotton Tiberius C II in the British Museum (I). MS. of the eighth century, the handwriting being less archaic than that of M. The orthography, with its *cht* and *ht* for *ct*, and *ð* for *th* and *d* is also later.

4. Cotton Tiberius A XIV (II). Of the first half of the ninth century. This MS. was badly burnt in the great fire, and much of it is lost and illegible. It is evidently a copy from a MS. of the same character as M., whose archaic spelling it repeats very faithfully.

As regards the relations of the MSS. it is certain that none of them are copied directly from any one of the others. It is self-evident that the oldest MS. M. cannot be a copy of any of the others, and that none of the others are copies of I, which has the least archaic forms of all. Again, the divergencies between M. and N. are such as would be impossible if N. were a direct copy of M. by an un-English scribe. In many cases all the three others agree against M., as in the form *Eduini* for M.'s *Aeduini*, *-gisl* for M.'s less archaic *-gils*. But N. has the latter form I, 15. In III, 21 and V, 24, where M. has the incorrect *Middilangli*, due to anticipation of the Latin *Angli*, they agree in giving the correct *Middilengli*. M.'s *Guruiorum* IV, 19, seems also to be an error for the usual *Gyruiorum*, which is the reading of the three others.

The omission of the same two names in II, 3, both in I and II shows that they must be copies of one MS. Unfortunately book II is wanting in N., or this passage would be decisive. In V, 19, N. and I both have *Cudbaldi* against M.'s *Cudualdi*, which Moberly has in his text. Here II leaves us in the lurch, and I have not investigated the relationship of the MSS. further, as not affecting the linguistic value of their various readings. The question can be definitely settled only by a detailed comparison of the Latin text, and this must be left to the next critical editor of Bede's History.

The various readings are separated by a stroke, and come in the following order, M., N., I, II, that of M. always coming first. When that of N. is not given, the reading that follows M.'s is marked I or II, as the case may be.

The names that come first in each book are taken from the elenchus or table of contents.

The numbers refer to the pages of Moberly's edition (Venerabilis Baedae Historia, Oxford 1869).

Names and readings which repeat the same forms without variation are not registered exhaustively. Celtic and other foreign names are given only when they throw light on Old English spellings.

Praefatio.

(1) *regi* ceoluulfo. baeda *famulus*—beda I. (2) cantuariorum (twice). nothelmum, -i, -us, -o. (3) nothelmo. nordanhymbrorum. ceddi *et* ceadda *g.* merciorum. *monasterii quod* læstinga eu *cognominatur*—*luestinga eu—lęstinga eu. *abbatis* esi. *in provincia* lindissi—*lindisi. (4) cynibercti *g.*—cynibericti[1]—

[1] u *over the* y.

cyniberhti. cudbercto—cudbericto[1]—cudberchto. *ecclesiae* lindisfarnensis.

Liber I.

ædilbercto—edilbericto—aeðilberchto. aedilfrid—aeðilfrid I.

1.

(6) *civitas quae dicitur rutubi portus, a gente anglorum* reptacęstir—reptacaester—reptacaestir. (7) brettonum—brittonum—•brettonum I, II. (8) brettones—brittones—brettones I, II.

7.

(21) *civitatem verolamium, quae nunc a gente anglorum* uerlamacæstir *sive* uaetlingacæstir *appellatur*—uerlamacaester, *uetlinguacáester—uerlamacaestir, uaetlingacęster.

12.

(28) *in loco qui sermone pictorum peanfahel, lingua autem anglorum* penneltun *appelatur*—pegneltuun—*peanuahel*, penneltuun. (29) *urbem* alcluith—alcluit I.

13.

(32) *cum* blaedla *et* attila—atila—bledla. blaedla *n.*—bledla I. attilae *g.*—a[t]tilę.

14.

(34) *rege* uurtigerno.

15.

(36) saxonibus, anglis, iutis. iutarum—iotarum. cantuari *et* uictuari *pl.*—contuari—cantuarii, uictuarii. iutarum *de illa patria quae* angulus *dicitur.* merci *pl.* nordanhymbrorum. humbri[2] *fluminis.* (37) hengist *et* horsa—haengist I. horsa. *filii* [u]uictgilsi, *cujus pater* uitta, *cujus pater* uecta, *cujus pater* uoden—uictgilsi, *uita—uictgisli—uictgisli, woðen[3].

25.

(52) aedilberct—ædilberich—aeðilbercht—aedilberct. (53) *fluvius* uuantsumu—uuantsamu I—u[u]antsumu[4]. aedilberctum—

[1] ic *underdotted.* [2] u *from* y *in N.* [3] uu *over the* w, *which is written on er.* [4] e *over the last* u *but one.*

aedilberictum—aeðilberchtum—aeðilberctum. *uxorem de gente francorum vocabulo* bercta—berchta I—bercta. *episcopo* liudhardo (Frankish name).

32.

(76) aedilbercto—aedibericto—aeðilberchto—aedilbercto. adilbercto (in a Latin letter)—aedilbericto—aeðilberhto—adiliberto.

33.

(79) aedilberct—aedilberict—aeðilbercht—aedilberct. *in sinu maris qui vocatur* amfleat.

34.

(80) aedilfrid—aedifrid—aeðilfrid—aedilfrid. *in loco qui dicitur* degsa stan, *id est*, degsa *lapis*—stán. (81) theodbald *frater* aedilfridi—*aedilbericti—aeðilfridi. aedilfrid—aeðilfrid—aedilfrid.

Liber II.

aedilbercto *et* sabercto *regibus*—sabericto—aeðilberhto *et* saberhto —aedilbercto *et* sabercto. aeodbaldum—*lauraldum—eadbaldum I, II. *regis* aeduini—*eduni—eduini I, II. aeduini *n.*—*ediuini—eduuine—eduini. *idem* aeduini—eduini—eduuine—eduini. *in provincia* lindissi—*lindisi—lindissi I, II. aeduini *g.*—eduini—eduuini—eduini. *occiso* aeduine—eduine—eduuine—eduine.

1.

(88) deiri *vocarentur iidem provinciales—so also* I, II. (89) *rex* aelli—aelle[1] I—aelle.

2.

(89) aedilbercti regis—aeðilberchti I—aedilbercti. augustinæs ac, *id est, robur augustini.*—agustinęs, agustini I—augustinaes, augustini. (90) huicciorum. (91) bancor[n]aburg—boncornaburg[2] I—bancornaburg. (92) aedilfrid—aeðilfrið I—aedilfrid. (93) *ad civitatem legionum, quae a gente anglorum* legacaestir, *a brettonibus autem rectius carlegion appellatur*—legacaester I, II. ædilfrid—aeðilfrið I—aedilfrid.

3.

(94) saberct, *nepos* aedilbercti, *ex sorore* ricula[3]—saberht, aeðilberchti I—saberct, aedilbercti. aedilbercti[3]. aedilberct—aeðil-

[1] a *er.* [2] a *over first* o. [3] *om. in* I, II.

berht I—aedilberct. (95) *in civitate dorubrevi, quam gens anglorum a primario quondam illius qui dicebatur* hrof hrofæscæstræ *cognominat*—hrofescaester I—hrofaescaestrae. aedilberct—aeðilberht I—aedilberct. berctualdi *g.*—berhtualdi I—berctualdi.

5.

(99) aelli *rex*—aelle I—aelli. caelin *rex occidentalium saxonum, qui lingua eorum* ceaulin *vocatur.* reduald—reduuald I—reduald. aeduini *rex*—eduuine I—eduine[1]. *nardahymbrorum — norðanhymbrorum I—nordanhymbrorum. (100) osuald—osuuald I—osuald. nordanhymbrorum—norðanhymbrorum I. osuiu—osuuiu I—osuiu. berctæ *regina n.*—berhtae I—berctae. aedilberct *filius* irminrici, *cujus pater* octa, *cujus pater* oeric, *cognomento* oisc, *a quo reges cantuariorum solent* oiscingas *cognominare*—aeðilbercht I. hengist *cum filio suo* oisc *invitatus a* uurtigerno *rege*—haengest I. eadbald. (101) sabercti *regis orientalium saxonum*—saeberhti I—sæbercti. *patri nostro* saba—sæba[2] II. (102) geuissorum.

6.

(104) *civitatem* hrofi.

7.

(105) aeodbaldo—eadbaldo I—eodbaldo.

8.

(107) adulualdi *regis* (in a Latin document)—aeðuluualdi[3] I.

9.

(108) *rege suo* aeduino—eduuine I—eduine. aedilbergae *filia* (nom.) aedilbercti *regis, quae alio nomine* tatae *vocabatur*—aeðilburgae[4], aeðilberchti, tatę I—aedilberge. (109) *fratre ejus* aeodbaldo — eadbaldo I — eodbaldo[5]. aeduino — eduuino I — eduino. (110) *sicarius vocabulo* eumer. cuichelmo—quichelmo I—cuichelmo. *amnem* deruuentionem—doruuentionem I—deruentionem. lilla *minister.* fordheri *n.*—forðheri I—fordheri. *filiam cui nomen* ęanfled—eanfled I, II.

10.

(112) ęduino. aeduino. audubaldi *regis* (in Latin document)—[e]adubaldi[6] I—audubaldi.

[1] *last* e *from* i. [2] æ *from* a (?). [3] i *over* c. [4] *last* e *er.*
[5] *first* o *altered to* a. [6] u *er.*

11.

(115) aedilbergam—aeðilburgam I—aedilbergam. ædibergæ *d.* —aeðilburgae I—aedilbergae. aedilbergæ—aeðilburgae I—aedilbergae. audubaldi (in Latin letter)—eadbaldi[1] I—audubaldi.

12.

(117) redualdum—rẹduualdum I—redualdum. (118) redualdum—reduualdum I—redualdum. (120) *amnis qui vocatur* idlæ—idlae I. rægenheri—raegnheri I, II.

13.

(121) *primus pontificum* coifi. (122) coifi. (123) *locus* godmunddingaham—godmundingaha*m*[2] I—godmundingaham.

14.

(124) osualdo—osualdo I, II. osfrid. eadfrid—eodfrid II. *regis* aeduini—eduine I—eduini. *de* quoenburga *filia* cearli *regis* merciorum. *de* aedilbergia *regina*—aeðilberga[3] I—aedilberga. (125) aedilhun—aeðilhun I—aedilhun. aedilthryd *filia*—aeðilðryð I—aedilthryd. *filius* uuscfrea—uúscfrea I—uuscfrea. yffi *filius* osfridi. *in villam regiam quae vocatur* ad gefrin—gebrin I—gefrin[4]. *in fluvio* gleni. *in loco qui vocatur* maelmin—mẹlmin[5] I—maelmin. berniciorum. deirorum. *in fluvio* sualua—sualwa I—sualua. *in regione quae vocatur* loidis. *abbatis* thryduulfi—thrythuulfi I, II. *in silva* elmete.

15.

(126) earpualdo *filio* redualdi—eorpuualdo, reduualdi I—earpualdo, redualdi. alduulf. *filius* tytili, *cujus pater fuit* uuffa, *a quo reges orientalium anglorum* uuffingas *appellant.* (127) eorpuald *all three.* ricbercto—ricberchto. eorpualdi—eorpuualdi I—eorpualdi. sigberct—sigbercht I—sigberct. *in civitate* domnoc—dommoc I, II.

16.

(128) lindocolinae *civitatis. praefectum, cui nomen erat* blaecca. *vir de monasterio* peartaneu[6] *vocabulo* deda. *in fluvio* treenta *all three. civitatem quae* tiouulfingacæstir *vocatur*—caestir I. (129)

[1] ea *over er.;* u *er. after first* d. [2] god *on er.* [3] u *over second* e. [4] vel b *written over.* [5] *accent over the* e. [6] u *made into* i *by er. in* II.

genus vexilli quod romani tufam, angli vero appellant thuuf—thuuf I—thuf.

20.

(136) caedualla *rex brettonum*—caeduualla I—caedualla. penda *viro de regio genere* merciorum. *in campo qui vocatur* haethfelth—haethfeld I—haethfelth. osfrid. eadfrid. (137) penda *regem.* osualdo—osuualdo I—osualdo. penda. caedualla—cęduualla. osualdus—osuualdus I—osuald. *regina* aedilberge *abl.*—aeðilburga I. eadbaldo. *duce* basso. *habens secum* eanfledam *filiam, et* uuscfrean *filium* æduini, *necnon et* yffi *filium* osfridi, *quos mater metu* eadbaldi *et* osualdi *misit in galliam rege* daegberecto—eanfledan, daegberhto I.

Liber III.

agilbercto (Frankish name)—aegilbericto—agilberhto. earconberct—erconberht I. *de filia ejus* ercongo[ta] *et propinqua* aedilbergæ. *regis* osuini—osuuini I. *ab* osuiu—*osino—osuio. *regis* sigbercti—sigberchti I. *rege* peada—peda. sigbercto—sigberchto I. *praedicante* ceddo. *idem* cedd—cedda I. oidilualdo—oedilualdo—oidiluualdo. *rege* penda. osuiu. tuda. ecgberct—egberc—ecgbercht. *defuncto* tuda. uilfrid. ceadda. *uighar—uighard—uuigheard.

1.

(139) *filius* aelfrici *vocabulo* osric. nordanhymbrorum—nordonhymbrorum I. eanfrid. (140) ceadualla—caeadualla—caeduualla. *in loco qui* denises burna, *id est rivus* denisi *vocatur*—denisaes brunna—dęnises burnna, dęnisi.

2.

(141) hefenfelth, *quod dici potest caelestis campus*—hefenfeld[1]—hefenfeld—hefenfelth. (142) hagustaldensis *ecclesiae. quidam de fratribus* hagustaldensis *ecclesiae nomine* bothelm.

4.

(147) ecgbercto—egbercto—ecgberchto.

6.

(151) regina *vocabulo* bebba. *ex sorore* acha.

[1] feld *from* fled.

7.

(151) *gens occidentalium saxonum qui antiquitus* geuissæ *vocabantur*—geuisse—geuisse. *regnante* cynigilso—cynigislo. *the other three.* (152) *civitatem quae vocatur* dorcic. haedde *episcopatum agente*—hędde I. coinualch—coinualach—coenualh. (153) pendan *regis. regem orientalium anglorum cui nomen erat* anna. coinualch—coinualach—coenualh. agilberctus *natione gallus*—agilberictus—agilberchtus. *episcopum vocabulo* uini—uuini I—uuine. *in civitate uenta, quae a gente saxonum* uintancæstir *appellatur*—uintancaestir—uintacaestir. agilberctus—egilberictus—agilberchtus. (154) uini—uini I—uine[1]. *regem merciorum vocabulo* uulfheri—uulfhere I.

8.

(155) earconbercto—earconbrecto—earconberhto. *filia* earcongotæ *n.*—earcongotę—eorcangotae[2]. saethryd *filia uxoris* annae *regis*—saethrith—saeðryth, annae[3]—saedryd, anna. *filia* aedilberg—edilberc—aeðilberg[4]. (156) sexburg, *uxor* earconbercti, *habuit filiam* earcongotam—sexburc—eorconberhti, eorcongotam—erconbercti. (157) aedilberg—aeðilberg I—aedilberg[5].

9.

(158) *in loco qui nuncupatur* maserfelth—maserfelth[6] I, II.

11.

(160) *reginae* osthrydae *g.*—ostrydę—osðryðę. osuiu. *monasterium* beardaneu[7]. aedilredo—aeðilredo I. (161) *abbatissa* aedilhild—aeðilhild I. *virorum* aediluini *et* alduini—aeðiluini, alduini I. *in monasterio quod vocatur* peartaneu—peartanea.

12.

(164) osuiu—osuuiu I.

13.

(164) *antistes* acca. uilbrordum. uilfrido.

[1] e *from* i. [2] *last* e *er.* [3] e *er.* [4] u *over second* e. [5] *second* e *dotted and* u *written over.* [6] th *over er. in* II. [7] ig *over* eu *in* II.

14.

(166) alchfrido—alhfrido I, II. oidilualdo—oedilualdo I. ithamar, *de gente* cantuariorum. osuini. osrici *g*. uilfarȩs dun, *id est mons* uilfari—uilfaraes duun—uilfares dún—uilfæraes dun. (167) tondheri—tondhere. hunualdi. ediluinum—aeðiluuinum I. *loco qui dicitur* in getlingum.

15.

(169) utta. regi osuio—osuuiu I. cynimund—cynemund I. (170) utta *presbytero*.

16.

(170) penda *duce*. bebbae *reginae g*. *in insula* farne.

18.

(173) *post* erpualdum, redualdi *successorem*, sigberct *frater ejus*. erpualdum, sigberch—eorpualdum, rȩdualdi, sigberht—erpualdum. (174) ecgrice *d*. sigberctum—sigberectum—sigberchtum. eni *g*.

19.

(174) sigberct—sigberech. (175) cnobheresburg, *id est urbs* cnobheri—c[o]nobheresburrug, c[o]nobhere—cnobheraesburg II. (179) ercunualdo—*hercun[u]aldo—ercunualdo I, II. ercunualdus—hercunualdus—erconualdus I, II.

20.

(179) *de provincia* gyruiorum. (180) berctgilsum—berechgislum—berchtgislum—berctgislum. ithamar *n*. ithamar *d*.

21.

(180) middilangli, *id est, mediterranei angli*—middilengli—middilȩngli—middilengli. *principe* peada—peoda[1] II. *filiam* alchfledam—alhfledam I. (181) *a filio regis* osuiu *nomine* alchfrido—alhfrido I. cyniburgam—cymburgam. *presbyteri* cedd *et* adda *et* betti—ced[2] I. uttan *g*. (182) *in regione quae vocatur* in feppingum. trumheri *viro*—triumhere. uulfheri *regis*—uulferi.

22.

(182) *rege* osuiu—osuuiu I. sigberct—sigberecth—sigberht. sigberctum—sigberectum—sigeberchtum. osuiu *regis*—osuiu I.

[1] *a over the* o. [2] *end of line.*

(183) *ecclesiam* lindisfaronensem—lindisfarnensem I—lindisfaronensem. ythancaestir — ythancaester I. tilaburg — tilaburug — tilaburg[1] — til[l]aburg. *in ripa* pentæ *amnis* — paentae — paente[2]. (184) *successit* sigbercto *in regnum* suidhelm, *filius* sexbaldi, *qui baptizatus est ab ipso* cedde *in vico regio qui dicitur* rendlæs ham, *id est, mansio* rendili—raendles, raendili I. (185) aediluald *frater* anna *regis*—ediluald—aeðiluald.

23.

(185) oidiluald—oediluald I. *in* derorum *partibus—so also Na.*, I. caelin. (186) cynibillum. laestinga eu—laestenga eu[3]. (187) ceadda *d.* cynibill—cynibil—cynibil. caelin *et* ceadda—cęlin I.

24.

(188) alc[h]frido. *reginam* cynuise—cynuisę. oidiluald—oidiluald I. aedilheri *frater* anna *regis*. (189) *prope flumen* uinuaed—uinued *the other three*. *filiam* aelffledam—aelbfledam—aelffledam—aelbfledam. heruteu, *id est, insula cervi*—heruteig[4] II. hild *abbattissa*. streanæs halch—streanes halh I—streonaes halch. (190) *mater* aeanfled—enflet—eanfled. trumheri[5]. *in monasterio quod dicitur* in getlingum. *rex* osuini. aeanfled—eanfled *the other three*. *dei famulo* trumherę—trumherę—trumherae—trumherę. (191) peada *filio regis* pendan—peadan, penda I—peoda[6]. *fluvio* treanta—treante. *idem* peada—peada II. *duces* immin *et* eafa *et* eadberct—eadbrect—eaba. uulfhere *filio ejusdem* pendan. *primum episcopum* trumheri, *secundum* iaruman, *tertium* ceaddan, *quartum* uynfridum.

25.

(193) *regina* eanfled. alchfridi. alchfrid. uilfridum. (194) *in loco qui dicitur* in hrypum. strenæs halc, *quod interpretatur sinus fari*—streanaes alch—strenes halch—streunaes halch. hild.

26.

(200) tuda. (201)eata *thrice*. osuiu *d.*—osuio *Na.*, I.

[1] ti[l]laburg; *later addition* (?). [2] *first* e *er*. [3] ig *over* eu *in* II. [4] *altered to* heortes ig *by a later hand*. [5] i *over* e *in* I. [6] a *over the* o; peoda *in margin*.

27.

(202) tuda. *in monasterio quod dicitur* pægnalaech—paegnalech—pęgnalech. (203) edilhun—aedelhun I. ediluini *g.*—aeðiluini I. ecgberct—egberct—ecbercht. (204) *o frater* ecgbercte!—egberct—ecberhte. edilhun—aeðilhun[1] I. ecgberect—ecgberct—ecberht.

28.

(205) agilberectum. *rex* osuio—osuiu—osuuiu. laestinga eu[2]. *presbyterum* eadhaedum—eadhedum—eadhaedum I, II. ecgfrido—ecfrido I. uini *n.*—uuini I. uine *d.*—uuine I.

29.

(206) ecgberct—ecgberict—ecberht. uighardum—*uigardum—uuigheardum. (207) uighard—uig[h]ar—uigheard. osuio[3] *d.*—osuiu I. osuio *d.*—osuiu *Na.*, I. (209) uighardo—uighardo I.

30.

(209) suidhelmum—*suidelmum—suithelmum. *reges* sigheri *et* sebbi—sighere I.` (210) *regi* uulfherę—uulfhere *Na.*, I. sigheri—sighere I. sebbi. uulfheri—uulfhere I. iaruman *episcopum*—iuruman I. trumheri *g.*

Liber IV.

uighard—uuigheard I. putta—put[t]a I. *ad locum* herutforda—heorutforda I. *deposito* uynfrido—*uinfrido—uynfrido. sæxuulf—saexuulf—saxulf—sexuulf. earconuald—erconuald I. *rex* sebbi. hæddi—heddi—haeddi. putta *d.*—*puta. cuichelm—quichelm I. gefmund—gebmund—gemmund—gebmund. *in campo* hæthfelda—haetfeldo I. edilthryd *regina*—aediltryd—aeðilðryt I. ecgfridum *et* aedilredum—ecfridum, aeðelredum I. hildae *g.*—hilde I. *de morte* ecgfridi *et* hlotheri—ecfridi, hlothere I. cudberct—cudbrect—cudbercht. heribercto—hereberchto.

1.

(211) erconberct—erconbercht I. osuio *d.*—osuiu *Nà.*, I. uighard—uigheard I. (213) raedfridum *all four*. *ad portum cui nomen est* quentauic (in France).

[1] i *altered to* e. [2] g *over* u *in* II. [3] *last* o *over* u.

2.

(215) aeddi. putta.

3.

(216) uulfheri—uulfheri I. iarumanno. *monasterio quod ęst in* læstingae—lestinga *he—laestinge. (217) *gentis* lindisfarorum. uulfheri—uulferi. *in loco qui dicitur* ad baruæ, *id est, ad nemus*—baruę—bearuae—baruae. *in loco qui vocatur* lyccidfelth—licidfelt liccidfeld—li[c]idfelth. ouini *twice*—ouuini I. (218) *cum regina* aedilthryde — aedyldrydę — aeðilðryda[1]. laestinga eu. (220) trumberct—trumbrect. (221) hygbald. ceadda—cedda. uynfridum—uymfridum. lindisfarorum.

5.

(224) herutford—*hęrutfrod—heorutford—herudford[2]. bisi. hrofescæstir—hrofaescaestir—hrofescaestir—hrofaescaest[e]r. uynfrid—uuinfrid. (225) *in loco qui appellatur* clofes ho[c]h—clofaes hooh—clofęs hooh—clofaes hooh. (226) hlothere *d.* bisi. (227) aecci *et* baduuini—baduini I.

6.

(227) sexuulfum—saexuulfum—saexulfum—sexuulfum. *monasterii quod dicitur* medeshamstedi, *in regione* gyruiorum—medeshamstede I. uynfrid—uymfrid. (228) *monasterium* ad baruæ—baruę I. sebbi *et* sigheri. earconualdum—eorcunualdum I. aedilburgæ[3] *d.* — aedilburge — aeðilburgae. *in regione* sudergeona — suðri[o]ena[4] I. cerotaes ei, *id est, ceroti insula*—ceortes ei I. *in loco qui nuncupatur* in berecingum—berecingun—bercingum—berecingum.

8.

(230) *puer* aesica. *eam alloquens,* eadgyd ! eadgyd ! eadgyd !—eadgyð *once* I.

9.

(231) *mater* aedilburga—aedilbur[u]g—aeðilburga. torctgyd—troctgyd — torchgyð. (232) torctgyd — *toragyd — to[r]chtgyð. (233) *matre* aedilburge—edilburge—aeðilburgę[5].

[1] i *altered to* e. [2] e *over the* u, *which is dotted.* [3] u *over* e. na *half* er. [5] a *over* ę.

10.

(233) aedilburgi *d.*—aeðilburgae I. hildilid—hildilit[1].

11.

(234) ualdheri—uualdhere I. erconualdo—ercunuualdo I. (235) sighardo—*so also* I. suefredo.

12.

(237) sexuulfum — saexuulfum — saexulfum. cuichelmum — c[u]uichelmum—quichelmum. gebmundum. ecgfridi—ęgfridi— ec[g]fridi. (238) bosa. eata. eadhaed—eadhaet I. eadgarum. cyniberctum. eadhaedum—eadhedum—ead[h]aedum. sexuulfum—sęxulfum I. (239) eadhaed, bosa, *et* eata—eadhed. tunberctum. *remanente* eata *et* trumuini. eadhaedum—eadhędum.

13.

(239) aedilualch—aedilualh I. meanuarorum *provinciam.* (240) *presbyteri* eappa, *et* padda, *et* burghelm, *et* oiddi. *regina* eabae *n.* eanfridi *g.* ænheri *g.*—aeanheri—eanheri—aenheri. bosanhamm—bo[o]sanhaam—bosanham I, II. (241) *aediluach—edilualch—aedilualh. selæseu, *quod dicitur latine insula vituli marini*—selaeseu—seleseu—selaesei.

14.

(242) acca. eappa. (243) eappan *a.*

15.

(244) caedualla—cædualla—ceadualla. (245) bercthuno *et* andhuno. caedualla *d.*—*sedualla—ceadualla. ini, *qui post* caeduallan *regnavit*—cęduallam *Na. C*[1].

16.

(246) caedualla—caeduualla I. bernuini. *presbyterum* hiddila. arualdi *regis.* (247) cyniberct—cyneberht I. hreutford, *id est, vadum harundinis*—hreudford—hreoutford—hreodford[2]. *pelago quod vocatur* soluente[3]. *fluminis* homelea—homelae[4] II.

17.

(248) *rege* hymbro■ensium — humbronensium. alduulfo *rege* estranglorum—eastranglorum I. (249) haethfelth—haethfeld I.

[1] t *over* o. [2] od *over* ut (u *dotted*). [3] u *dotted in* II. [4] vel a *written over.*

18.

(250) *abbate* biscopo. *fluminis* uiuri. ceolfrido.

19.

princeps guruiorum *vocabulo* tondberct—gyruiorum *the other three.* (253) aebbæ *abbatissae g.* *in regione quae vocatur* elge. (254) *soror* sexburg—saexburg I. earconberct—erconberht I. *regio* elge. grantacaestir—grantacęster I. cynifrid. (256) elge *regio a copia anguillarum nomen accepit.*

21.

(258) *juxta fluvium* treanta. aelfuini—aelbuini—aelfuine—aelbuini. osthryd—osthrid—osthryð. aedilred—ędilredh—aedilred.

22.

(259) imma *n.* tunna. tunnacaestir. (260) hlotheri *a.*

23.

(261) strenaes halc—streanaes halch—strenes halh. (262) hererici *g.*—heririci *Na. C*[1]. *soror* heresuid—heresuit I. alduulfi—aldulfi I. uiuri *fluminis.* heruteu—herutei II. (263) *civitatem calcariam, quae a gente anglorum* kælcacaestir *appellatur*—*faelcaestir—helcacęstir[1]. streaneshalch—streanaeshalch—streaneshalh—streanaeshalch. (264) bosa, aetla, oftfor. dorciccaestræ *g.*—dorcicæstrę—dorciccęstre. hildae *g.* *rex* osric. bosel. (265) boselum. tatfrid—tatfrið I. *mater* bregusuid—bregusuit I. hereric—heriric. *rege brettonum* cerdice. (266) *monasterio quod appellatur* hacanos. (267) frigyd—frigid—frigyð.

24.

(269) caedmon—cędmon, *Na.*, I.

25.

(273) *matri* aebbę. (275) aedgils.

26.

(275) bercto—berhto I. cudbercto—cudberchto I. (276) triumuini—trumuini—trumuini. (277) aelbfled—ęlffled I. *matre* eanflede—ęnflædæ. edric. uictred—uuichtred I.

[1] he *over er.*

27.

(278) *in insula quae appellatur* farne. tuidi *fluminis.* boisil—bosil I. (279) boisil—bosil I. eata.

28.

(281) *juxta fluvium* alne, *in loco qui dicitur* ad tuifyrdi, *quod significat ad duplicem vadum.* (282) trumuine *d.* boisil—boisel I.

29.

(283) hereberct. deruuentionis *fluvii*—doruuentionis I. (284) heriberct. cuthbercto. (285) *in insula* farne—farnę.

30.

(285) eadbercto. (286) *insulam* farne.

31.

(287) badudegn — badudeng — beaduðegn — baduðegn. cudbercti.

32.

(288) *amnem* dacore—dacor. suidberct—suitbercht I.. thruidred—*thryded—thrydred.

Liber V.

oidiluald—oið[il]uuald I. cudbercti—cuðberhti I. caedualla—*ceadulla I. ini. berctuald. uictberct—uictbercht I. uilbrord—uuilbrord—uilbrod. heuualdi *pl.* (two brothers). suidberct—suitbercht. uilbrord—uuilbrord—uilbrod. eollan *a.*—eallan—eollan. aldhelmum. coinred—coenred I. offa. acca. ceolfrid.

1.

(290) *oiduald—oidiluuald I. in hrypum—rypum II. gudfrid—gut[h]frid—gyðfrid. (291) aldfridi.

2.

(292) eata *episcopo.* bercthun. *monasterii quod vocatur* in derauuda, *id est, in silva* derorum—derauuda—derauudu—deirorum. tino *amne.*

(293) *dicito* gae, *id est, etiam*[1].

[1] gea *over er. in* I.

3.

(294) *in loco qui vocatur* uetadun. heriburg. quoenburg—quoinburg II.

4.

(295) *comitis qui vocabatur* puch.

5.

(296) addi—aeddi II.

7.

(300) caedualla—*ceadulla I—ceadualla. (301) caedual[1]—cædual—ceadual. caedual—cędual—ceadual. (This and the preceding quoted by Bede from C.'s epitaph.) (302) caedualla—ceadualla I. (303) berctuald. *fluminis* genladae. *monasterio quod* racuulfe *nominatur.* (304) ui[c]tredo *et* suæbhardo—uictredo, suębheardo I. goduine *d.*—goduino I. gebmundo.

9.

(306) boisili *g.*—boisili I. boisil—boisil I. *abbate* eata—æata. (307) uictberct—uictberht I. *regi* rathbedo (Frisian).

10.

(309) heuuald (4 times)—heuuald[2], heauald, heauuald, heuuald[3] I. (310) tilmon.

11.

(310) uilbrord—uilbrord I. (311) suidberctum—suidberchtum I. suidberct—suitberht I. bliththrydae *d.*—bliththryðe I. (312) uiltaburg, *id est, oppidum uiltorum.*

12.

(313) *in regione* nordanhymbrorum *quae vocatur* in cuneningum—cuniningum. (317) haemgils. (318) ediluald—aeðiluuald I. *frater* drycthelme!

13.

(321) pecthelmo—pehthelmo I.

18.

(328) osred. (329) haeddi. (330) fortheri—forðhere I. (331) selæseu. eolla.

[1] d *er. after* l. [2] *first* u *altered to* a. [3] *first* u *dotted, and* a *written over.*

19.

(332) *provincia quae vocatur* in undalum. (333) *adolescens* biscop. (334) baldhild *regina*—balthild—balthild[4]. (335) alchfridi. *in loco qui dicitur* stanford. (336) in læstinga æi—*luestingua—laestinga ei. aldgilso—aldgislo *Na.*, I. (337) uilbrord—uilbrod—uilbrord. (340) accan *a.* *juxta fluvium* nidd. *in provincia* undalum[1]. cudualdi *g.*—cudbaldi *Na.*, I.

21.

(343) *juxta amnem* tinam—tina *Na.*, I. *in loco qui vocatur* in gyruum.

22.

(356) coenred.

23.

(358) coenredo. alricum. (359) tatuini *n.* (360) ingualdo. alduino lyccitfeldensi — *licitfeldelsi — liccitfeldensi. alduulfo — aldulfo I. hrofensi—rofensi I. ingualdt. hadulac. fortheri—forthere I. ualchstod—uualstod I. hymbrę *fluminis*—hymbre—humbrę. ceoluulf—ceolulf.

24.

(363) *pugnatum ad* degsa stanæ—daegsa stanę I. saberctosaeberchto. middilangli—middilengli—middilaengli. (364) *ad* herutforda—herudforda *Na.*, I. eadhaeth—eadhaet I. ælfuini—aelfwine I. *in campo* hæthfeltha—haetfelda I. *in* streanæshalæ—streanaeshęlę—streaneshale. caeduald—cędualla—ceadualla. osthryd. berctred. (365) berctfrid. baeda—baeda—be:da. *ad* uiuraemuda—uiuraemuda—uuiuraemuda. (367) huaetbercti.

[1] t *over* er. [2] a *from* u *in*

NORTHUMBRIAN FRAGMENTS.

List of Kings.

From the Moore MS. of Bede's History, where it follows immediately after the fragment of Cædmon, in a hand which may well be the same as that of the History. These chronological notes must have been written either in 737 or else between 734 and 737—most probably in 737 (see preface to the Monumenta Historica Britannica, i. p. 73, and Zupitza, Ueber den Hymnus Cædmons, Zeitschrift für deutsches altertum, neue folge x), which is, of course, also the date of the Moore MS. of the History itself.

Anno DCLVII Ida *regnare coepit, a quo regalis* Nordanhymbrorum *prosapia originem tenet, et* XII *annos in regno permansit. Post hunc* Glappa I *annum,* Adda VIII, Aedilric IIII, Theodric VII, Friduuald VI, Hussa VII, Aedilfrid XXIIII, Aeduini XVII, Osuald VIIII, Osuiu XXVIII, Ecgfrid XV, Aldfrid XX, Osred XI, Coinred II, Osric XI, Ceoluulf VIII. *Baptizavit Paulinus ante annos* CXI. *Eclypsis ante annos* LXXIII. Penda *moritur ante annos* LXXIX. *Pugna* Ecgfridi *ante annos* LXIII ; Ælfuini *ante annos* VIII. *Monasterium* aet *U[i]uræmoda *ante annos* LXIIII. *Cometae visae ante annos* VIII ; *eodem anno pater* Ecgberct *transivit ad Xpm'. Angli in Brit' ante annos* CCXCII.

Cædmon's Hymn.

The hymn of Cædmon is written at the top of the page in a smaller hand than that of the List of Kings which follows it. It is not impossible that the hymn may have been written later than the List, to fill up the blank space. But the hand is evidently contemporary.

Nu scylun hergan[1] hefaenricaes uard,
metudæs maecti end his modgidanc,
uerc uuldurfadur; sue he uundra gihuaes,
eci Dryctin[2], or astelidæ.
He aerist scop aelda barnu*m*
heben til hrofe, haleg scepen.
Tha middungeard[3], moncynnæs uard,
eci Dryctin, æfter tiadæ
firum fold[u], frea allmectig.

Primo cantavit Caedmon *istud carmen.*

Bede's Death-song.

Preserved in the St. Gall MS. 254, of the ninth century, in the usual continental minuscule hand, evidently an accurate copy of an Old Northumbrian original. My text is from a photograph in the possession of Dr. J. A. H. Murray.

Fore the*re* neidfaerae naenig uuiurthit
thoncsnotturra than him thar[f] sie,
to ymbhycggannae, aer his hiniong[a]e,
huaet his gastae, godaes aeththa yflaes,
aefter deothdaege doemid uueorth[a]e.

Leiden Riddle.

The riddle is written at the end of the MS. Voss 106 in the University library of Leiden, immediately after the Latin riddles of Symposius and Aldhelm, in the same continental hand of the 9th century. The writing is much worn away, and has been made still more illegible by the use of reagents. It was first published by Bethmann in 1845 in the Zeitschrift für deutsches Alterthum, v. 199, together with the Leiden glosses, but very inaccurately, which is evidently partly due to his ignorance of the language. Then came Dietrich's critical text and facsimile in his University program *Commentatio de Kynewulfi poetae aetate*, Marburg, 1859–60. Dietrich's text was reprinted in Rieger's *Alt- und angelsächsis-*

[1] a *over dotted* e. [2] yc *from* in. [3] *first* d *from* n.

ches lesebuch (Giessen, 1861) with some critical amendments. Lastly, the Leiden librarian made a careful transcript of the riddle by the help of reagents in 1864, which he inserted at the end of the volume with the note 'Descripsi in Novemb. 1864. Medicinam adhibui Sulphuret. Ammonii. W. G. L.' This reading is of the highest value, giving many letters which in Dietrich's text are inserted only conjecturally—sometimes incorrectly. It is evidently entirely objective, giving nothing but the purely graphic evidence. Thus L. reads *membiað* for *menibiað*, *nuc* for *niic*, etc., where, indeed, it is hardly possible by mere inspection of the MS. to determine the true reading. In my own text I have, of course, carefully compared the results of my own study of the MS. with those of my predecessors, checking them by our knowledge of the language. The result has been to diminish the purely conjectural readings, and to introduce some corrections. The following are the readings which differ from those of Dietrich (D.'s following mine):

line 4. hygidoncum (minum)—bi hige minum.
7. hrutendum—hrutendi.

The first reading agrees with that of the Exeter text, the second differs. The reading of line 6 is still doubtful.

In my text the purely conjectural readings are enclosed in ( ). In the notes readings of L. in ( ) are those which he himself marks with a ?.

For the sake of comparison I add Thorpe's text of the Riddle from the Exeter Book, divergent readings being indicated by italics, and words omitted in Leiden enclosed in ( ).

Our text is evidently a direct copy of an original Old Northumbrian one.

A. Leiden Text.

Mec se ueta[1] uong, uundrum freorig,
ob his innaðae aerest[2] caend(æ).
Ni[3] uuat ic mec *biuorthæ uullan fliusum,

[1] *two letters er. after* a; *L. reads them as* n(e) *or* n(ae), *B. as* m.
[2] *so L.; may be* aerist (?).
[3] *only in D.'s facsimile; in his transliteration he has* m, *and omits the word in his critical text.*

herum ðerh hehcraeft bigido(n)cum[1] (minum).
Uundnae me ni bia𝔡 ueflæ, ni ic uarp hefæ,
ni ðerih ðrea(t)un[2] giðraec[3] ðret me hlimmith[4],
ne me hrutendum hrisil scelfaeð,
ni mec ou(ua)n(a)[3] aam sceal cnyssa.
Uyrmas mec ni auefun uyrdi craeftum,
ða ði gọelu godueb geatum fraetuath.
Uil mec hudrae suaeðeh uidæ ofaer eorðu
hatan mith hẹliðum hyhtlic giuæde[5].
Ni anoegun ic me aerigfaerae egsan brogum,
ðeh ði ni(man flanas frac)adlicae[6] ob cocrum.

B. Exeter Text.

Mec se wæta wong wundrum freorig
of his innaþe ærist cende.
Ne wat ic mec *beworhtne* wulle flysum,
hærum þurh heahcræft hygeþoncum *min.
Wundene me ne beoð wefle, ne ic wearp hafu,
ne þurh *þreata* geþræcu[7] þræd me (ne) hlimmeð,
ne (æt) me *hrutende* hrisil *scriþeð*,
ne mec ohwonan *sceal amas* cnyssan.
Wyrmas mec ne áwæfan *wyrda* cræftum,
þa þe geolo godwebb geatwum frætwað.
Wile mec (mon) hwæþre seþeah wide ofer eorþan
hatan *for* hæleþum hyhtlic gewæde.
(Saga soðcwidum, searoþoncum gleaw,
wordum wisfæst, hwæt þis *gewædu sy !)

Proverb.

From a letter by an anonymous monk to Boniface (Wynfrid) the Northumbrian missionary (Epistolae S. Bonifacii, ed. Würdtwein,

[1] *L. has* b(i) gido(cumt); *I read very doubtfully* . . gi(d.can.). *D. reads only* b. hi. *As* h *and* b *are rather like* (*L. reading* derb, *line* 4), *it is possible that the MS. really has* hygi-.
[2] *D. has* -an.
[3] *it is impossible to tell whether the last letter is followed by more letters or not.*
[4] -id *D.*, -(t)d *L.*
[5] giu(æ)de *L.*, giua *D.*
[6] *supplied partly by D., partly by Rieger.*
[7] *L.'s reading doubtful.*

n. 152[1]). Massmann in his *Abschwörungsformeln* gives a facsimile of the Vienna MS., from which my text is taken. The MS. is in the usual continental hand of the 9th century, to which is also due the *ga-* of *gahuem*. We should expect the dialect to be Northumbrian, but *daedlata* points clearly either to a West-Saxon original, or a West-Saxon scribe.

Memento Saxonicum verbum:
Oft daedlata domę foręldit,
sigisitha gahuem: suuyltit thi ana.

[1] I owe this reference to Rieger (Lesebuch, p. 129).

NINTH CENTURY.

Liber Vitae (Northumbrian).

The Cotton MS. Dom. A 7, the so-called Liber Vitae, first edited by J. Stevenson (with fewer and less gross errors than in his other editions, but with several omissions) for the Surtees Society under the title of *Liber Vitae ecclesiae Dunelmensis*, consists of a list of benefactors to the Durham church, the names being written alternately in gold and either silver or ordinary black ink, several names in succession being occasionally written in gold. The letters, especially the gold ones, are in many cases partly rubbed away, so as to be sometimes nearly or quite illegible. Letters given only on the authority of Stevenson are enclosed in ( ); the MS. may have been more legible in his time.

Besides the lists written in the first hand, other names have been added down to some centuries after the Conquest. I here give only those of the first hand, Celtic and other foreign names being in italics, in which I have been mainly guided by the opinion of Prof. Rhys. Naturalized Celtic names I have regarded as English.

The MS. is evidently of the beginning of the ninth century, or end of the preceding one; such, at least, is my impression, in which I was confirmed by the opinion of Messrs. Thompson and Warner, of the MS. department of the British Museum. A careful examination of the names would enable us to fix the date with certainty within a year or two. As this investigation will be shortly made by the Museum men, and as I am not competent to undertake it, I must reserve further details for the present.

It is worthy of note that the ð in this MS. has a very thin stroke, so that where the letters are partly worn away it is often impossible to distinguish between them. Wherever the stroke is invisible to my eyes, I have printed *d*.

Nomina regum vel ducum.

(12) Eduini. osuald. osuio. ecgfrith. alchfrith. aelfuini. anna. oslaf. eðilred. eðilberct. milred. beornhaeth. berctred. altfrith. alduini. eaduulf. coenred. osred. osric. beornred. tilfrith. berctred. eadberct. helmuald. coenred. cynimund. beornred. ecgberct. aeðilmod. ceolbald. casaer. friðubald. eanred. alchmund. aeðilbald. sigred. osuulf. suiðberct. eðilberct. eðilberct. eanbald. ricuulf. *unust.* aelfuald. cuthuulf. eadberct. pleguulf. eadred. sigsceat. aelfsig. uulfheard. uernfrith. hysca. cyniuulf. earduulf. alduulf. brorda. eadbald. uigfus. uulfhaeth. (12 *b*) helmbaed. helmgils. sigberct. cynibald. uulfheri. beornuini. helpric. helmuini. ceoluulf. sigberct. eanred. eðilred. osfrith. torctmund. aluuini. eðiluulf. mægenfrith. aelfuald. karlus. *custantin.* sigred. sigred. osberct. tonduini. alduulf. eadred. siguulf. sigred. sigred. alduulf. uada. heaðured. eanred. eadred. uulfred. ofa. aelfred. beorn. ecgbercht. uoenan. eanred.

Nomina reginarum et abbatissarum.

(13) Raegnmaeld. eanfled. iurminburg. aelfled. oeðilburg. cuthburg. nunnae. pendgith. inguburg. ualdgith. aluburg. badugyth. eaðryð. uincðryð. bilsuið. aestorhild. uilcumae. eðilgyth. osgyth. ricfolcyn. eðilhild. eangyth. eðilgyth. haðuburg. blaedsuith. eadgyð. cyniburg. osgyth. tatsuið. uerburg. osburg. hungyth. hrothuaru. cuoenburg. berchtae. aebbę. burgðryð. ðingu. heregyð. cyniðryth. uilcumae. burgðryð. uilðryth. ecgsuith. scirburg. uilsuith. cyniðryth. ceolðryth. eafu. uilgyth. redburg. redgyth. cuoenðryth. ricðryth. ythsuið. cyniburg. aldðryth. berctsuið. hildiðryth. berctgyth. (13 *b*) edgyth. uerngyth. tidburg. uilgyth. ecgburg. alchsuið. osburg. tatae. cyniðryð. huitae. uictgyth. hildiburg. uernðryth. ricðryth. aluburg. cuoendryth. cuoemlicu. aebbino. aluburg. beorngyth. hroeðburg. aluchburg. friðhild. eðilburg. bothild. heregyth. heaburg. eanburg. aldburg. uerburg. sigðryth. cyniburg. redburg. helmðryth. uernðryth. eðilðryth. altðryth. eðilðryth. uulfgyth. cuthburg. cuoenðryth. altsuith. aelfgyth. haðugyth. berctðryth. al[t]ðryth. eðilðryth. eadburg. burgsuith. altðryth. saegyth. tidburg. beorngyth. eardgyth. aldgyth. beorngyth. berctuaru. beorngyth. cyniðryth. aelfgyth. aelfled. saeðryth. eanðryth. (14) uulfhild. osðryth. uilðryth. uilsuið. eaðryth. tondburg.

eanðryth. aelfðryth. badugyth. siguaru. berctfled. eafu. ecguaru. *ostðryth. badu. eanburg. eatðryð. ecgsuið. eaðryð. uilgið. badusuið. cyniðryd. uilburg. hildigið. eadu. eardgyð. haðugið. edildryð. redburg. daegburg. uilburg. cynidryð. uynburg. hroeðgifu. aelfdryð. eatðryð. eandryð. hygðryð. eadburg. hygburg. berhtgið. eadburg. beorngið. osgið. hleoburg. hroeðgeofu. badusuið. saeðryð. osðryð. alburg. cynidryð. uichtburg. bettu. uulfhild. uildryð. alburg. eatcume. sigburg. seliburg. berhtðryð. eðilu. beonnu[1]. tidcume. (14 *b*) eðilsuið. eandryð. *eatdryd. hildidryð. osgid. eardgið. eandryð. ecgburg. tidhild. sigðryð. cynigyð. osgeofu.

Nomina anchoritarum.

(15 *a*) Oedilualdh *pr'*. uermund *pbr'*. baldhelm *pbr'*. feligeld *pbr'*. uichtbercht *pr'*. haemgils *pbr'*. eadualdh *pbr'*. herebercht *pr'*. boesel *pbr'*. herefrid *pbr'*. aethuini *pbr'*. eadhelm *pbr'*. balthere *pbr'*. tiluini *pbr'*. fronka *pbr'*. aldbercht *pr'*. echha *pbr'*. tilfrith *pbr'*. aldhaeth *pbr'*. *agustinus pbr'*. bilfrith *pbr'*. hadured *pbr'*. uilthegn *pbr'*. garuulf *pbr'*. cuthred *pbr'*. uulfsig *pr'*. hadumund *pr'*. uigbercht *pr'*.

*Nomina abbatum gradus *pbratus.*

(15 *b*) Ceolfrið *pbr'*. bacga *pbr'*. *elias pbr'*. haduberct *pr'*. aldhelm *pbr'*. eatfrith *pbr'*. herefrith *pbr'*[2]. garuald *pbr'*. tatbercht *pbr'*. thrythred *pbr'*. heardred *pbr'*. uichthaeth *pbr'*. cynibercht *pbr'*. eorpuini *pbr'*. huaetberct *pbr'*. uilbercht *pbr'*. ceolbercht *pbr'*. alchmund *pbr'*. aldred *pbr'*. frehelm *pbr'*. tatuini *pbr'*. uicbercht *pbr'*. hygbercht *pbr'*. cyniðegn *pbr'*. siguini *pbr'*. cyniuulf *pbr'*. uernbercht *pbr'*. eanuulf *pbr'*. balduini *pbr'*. uulfsig *pbr'*. cyniheard *pbr'*. hunsig *pbr'*. botuini *pbr'*. baldhere *pbr'*. albercht *pbr'*. botuulf *pbr'*. eaduald *pbr'*. uilfrith *pbr'*. torchtuini *pbr'*. uulfheard *pbr'*. uulfsig *pbr'*. uichtred *pbr'*. sigred *pbr'*. hunuini *pbr'*. *bressal pbr'*. beornfrið *pbr'*. headured *pbr'*. edilhech *pbr'*. frioduuini *pbr'*. berchtred *pbr'*. siguulf *pbr'*. cuthfrith *pbr'*. eanbercht *pbr'*. saeuald *pbr'*. tatuini *pbr'*. reduulf *pbr'*. uilferð *pbr'*. aelfuulf *pr'*. berchtuini *pr'*. ecgheard *pr'*. (16) saered *pr'*. ecgred *pr'*. eanuulf *pr'*. earduulf *pr'*. ecgred *pr'*. ecgheard *pr'*. eadmund *pr'*. eaduulf *pr'*.

[1] *written over remains of gold letters (the preceding and following names in gold).* [2] prb'.

Nomina abbatum gradus diaconatus.

(16 *b*) Beornuini *diac'*. berchthun *dia'*. cuthbercht *dia'*. cuthere *dia'*. sigbercht *dia'*. uulfheard *dia'*. alchuini *dia'*. eaduald *dia'*. ecguulf *diaco'*.

Nomina abbatum.

(17) Biscopus. cudda. oshere. aesturuini. siguini. billing. utta. bacga. forthuio. friodumund. hunuald. billing. ecguald. theodric. hiudu. inuald. cynibercht. maesuith. uilhelm. tilbercht. hygbald. buna. eanmund. hroðfrith. ethilbald. uigfrith. herebald. beadheard. aluuini. ricred. maeginuald. cuthuini. eadbercht. milred. osmund. altfrith. beornuini. redbald. eatfrith. eðilmund. berchtuini. cuthgar. heardred. eadbald. gefuini. uilbercht. pymma. beornfrith. hygbercht. eadberct *rex*. beorn. bada. eðilheard. suiðuulf. uulfhaeth. aelberct. alduini. bosa. helmuini. tilfrith. (17 *b*) cynigils. eðiluald *rex*. alchmund. leofuini. eanuulf. eanbercht. eaduulf. burghelm. berchtuulf. uilred. uernbercht. eatðegn. saebercht. osuulf. torchtmund. ofa. eduini. *eanulf. eðilbald. burghelm. alubercht. cynibald. ecga. eadbercht. beornheard. aelfsig. osbald. berchtred. tatuulf. heardberct. berchtuulf. reduulf. eanfrith. huaetred. uulfsig. beodufrith. osbercht. alduulf. huaetberht.

Nomina praesbyterorum.

(18 *b*) *Demma*. suiðbald. echha. hemma. scenuulf. ceolfrith. tathysi. dremka. ceolgar. alda. coenhere. tilisi. tidhere. maeðhelm. tulla. uulsig. tidhere. sigbald. brón. drycghelm. echha. frood. uiuti. uendilbercht. *faelfi*. tiduald. beadufrith. heaðuberct. daeghelm. cuthbercht. tella. coenhere. *aldceord. hygbald. beda. ceolbercht. aescuald. suiðmer. eanfrith. ini. eðilheard. hyni. hemma. tatberct. ceolhaeth. badumund. tella. hiuddi. *ultan*. londfrith. guthfrith. dycgfrith. cynimund. hygbald. hyssa. suitha. biscop. beoduca. tilthegn. uicfrith. (19) adding. plecgils. eaduald. ingild. uigbald. hiordi. aldhelm. inuald. tilisi. hildiberct. tiluini. bercht. ceolhere. londberct. pectuald. berctuald. dremca. beda. badumund. suiðgils. hysimonn. uilberct. helmuald. torchtmund. deduc. ðingfrith. londberct. tilberct. eaduald. cuthuulf. tiluini. bilhelm. daegfrið. betscop. helmuini. eatfrith. deneberct. liodberct. cynhelm. uitgils. frioðuuald. tilisi. cuðgar.

eðilberct. eðilberct. egilmund. cynimund. maethcor. streonberct. eðilberct. hroeðlac. aluberct. tatberct. tidbald. folcuini. hearduini. beoduuini. bothelm. berch[t]uald. penduulf. uilfrith. cuthfrið. liodberct. (19 *b*) cyniberct. alduulf. hildiberct. eanlac. friðuuini. eanberct. plegbrect. cuthgils. bercht. leofuini. bedhaeth. *tobeas*. tiluini. ualchstod. tilberct. cyniberct. dreamuulf. haðuulf. forthuald. hroðuald. eaduini. bynni. uigbald. tunna. uigbald. hyguini. eada. berchthelm. tungils. theodric. aluchsig. maegenric. tydi. uighaeð. helmuald. tiduini. eðilric. uerberct. hygbald. ealac. ceolmund. eaduini. saeuini. balðhelm. tiduulf. aldhaeth. piuda. geruald. burgfrið. cynifrið. hildiuald. garfrið. torchthelm. heaðuric. hygberct. burgfrið. uilberct. hunuulf. eanbercht. gyðhelm. ceoluulf. eðiluini. cyniðegn. (20) uilberct. forðhere. uernberct. tilfrið. alchmund. tilfrið. hyglac. uulfheard. uilðegn. uigberct. berctuini. titfrith. tathaed *lect'*. friðhelm. berctgils. hygberct. cynibald. alberct. berctuini. dycgfrith. sigberct. uulflaf. cynhelm. friouini. eadberct. huaetgils. alduulf. cyniuulf. lagudi *lect'*. uulfheard. eanfrith. *abniar lect'*. uulfsig. uilðegn. ecgmund. torctuulf. cynigils. eadberct. eanuini. eanuulf *lect'*. maegenuald. ecguulf. cyniberct. ceoluini. bedhelm. heardred. eanuulf. hygberct. eadbald. uulfheard *lect'*. hunberct. heaðured. eatdegn. cyna. uulfsig. ceolred. londfrið. osberct. uilðegn. berctred. ebbi. eðiluulf *lect'*. cuthberct. (20 *b*) eðilmund. cynheard. alduulf. tilberct. cuthbald. hroeðlac. eaduini. eatfrith. siguulf. alduulf. eanfrith. tatuini. r . . chchcriðe *l'*. hygberct. . . . . . heaðuuald. . . . dured. frioðuulf. beornred. hysiuulf. hygbald. cuðgar. eadberct. alduulf. guðmund. cynifrith. siguulf. eanred. eada. alduulf. tatuini. bercthun *lect'*. eadmer. baduulf. eanred. tidhaeth. ecgberct. cuthuulf. alberct. tidberct. eanuini. alduulf. eanbald *lect'*. haðuuini. hunfrith. uilgils. baduulf. beornred. beornuulf. uulfhaeth. heaðufrith. eaduulf. cyniuulf. cynibald. eadmer. alberct. aella. aluuini *lect'*. heaðuulf. cynigils. baduuald. tilberct. eanberct. (21) eaduulf. eaduini. haðuuini. eaduald. beornuini. earduulf. heaðuulf. berctmund. eaduald. eanred. berctuald. cyniuulf. uilmund. tiduini. beornuulf. ingeld. botuulf. hunbald. tiduini. beornuulf. ingild. botuulf. aldred. eadred. aelfuini. eadred. eaduulf. uchtred. saeuini. uulfheard. suiðred. hildigils. beornuulf. cuðred. uilðegn. aluðegn. headuulf. cynigils. uinibald. helpric.

eanbald. bercht. osbald. berhtuulf. torhtmund. uiluulf. uigbercht. eanred. aldred. alduini. uilðegn. berhtuulf. eaduulf. berhtuulf. eadred. eaduulf. berh[t]uulf. uigmund. beornuini. alduulf.

Nomina diaconorum.

(23) Haðuuald. daeghelm. daeghelm. daegmund. ecca. eanuini. eanmund. *iohannes.* tidberct. aeostoruini. eaduulf. torchtuini. eðiluini. eðilmund. uulfheard. ebbi. hunfrið. cuthberct. aelberct. bercthaeð. cuthred. bota. alchmund. sigsceat. tidbald. cynired. hygfrith. uulfsig. uilberct. cuthred. leofðegn. alduulf. eadred. cuthgar. alduulf. eadmaer. cuðhelm. *tonberct. eadmer. beornred.

Nomina clericorum.

(24) Eanuulf. tutta. byni. cunen. hadda. hiddi. cynifrith. huna. cyniberct. herefrith. cynifrith. tutta. uynhelm. kaenta. aldmon. tiduald. betti. hereberct. daeghelm. uach. cuddi. friðuald. berctfrith. aeðuini. bynni. utta. beorn. uach. heruuald. geruald. baldhelm. folcuald. forthhelm. cudda. egilmund. torcthelm. seuua. plegheri. eaduald. betti. taðhaeð. tiluuald[1]. helpric. pleoualch. aluych. eðilhech. snella. hroðuini. huaetgils. uilfrith. *finan.* aldheri. sigmund. coenualch. uont. hygberct. hleouald. hegaer. uychga[2]. beda. (24 *b*) hyglac. bofa. byda. uynna. friðuuald. berctfrith. heouald. aldhun. hereberct. sceutuald. hereric. bilhaeth. cuthelm. ecgbaeth. tilli. eadgar. friumon. torctsig. aetti. adda. ualch. eanberct. tilisi. torcthelm. riuualch. bercthelm. haeðberct. lutting. taetica. uigheard. eofa. haðuberct. tidhelm. baeglog. mucca. aluberct. uilgils. eadberct. liutfrith. hecci. uada. piichil. tatheri. alduini. eadhaeð. balduini. aluich. berctuulf. penduald. bacca. ecguald. tilbaeth. cynifrith. haleric. tathaeth. iubi. ecgi. hildigils. aethuini. alda. haðuberct. herefrith. cissa. (25) ingild. bercthelm. eanuulf. beornuini. cuthfrith. uiniberct. tatberct. uilmund. botuini. eada. abba. eadberct. backa. alberct. osuulf. eadberct. beonna. tidhelm. eðilberct. ecguini. eatfrith. hunsig. eanbald. hunberct. uidsith. atta. ceoluini. tatuini.

1 *dotted* u *after* i.

2 uydiga (?)

geruald. tatuini. beornuini. hungils. ecgberct. berctuini. haðured. eadberct. cuthgar. haðuulf. uulfheard. eanbald. ingild. hygberct. cuðuulf. beornfrith. beonna. haduulf. torctred. alchmund. tiluini. uigbald. haðumer. tilhaeth. aldheri. friðuberct. baduuini. uilberct. cynimund. beornuini. eadberct. eaduulf. dedhaeth. tathelm. liodberct. (25 *b*) tidhelm. eadbald. eatðegn. berctuini. eðilberct. berctmund. garberct. berctuini. cuthmund. blaedla. meguini. ceolfrith. suiðuulf. eatfrith. eanberct. hunberct. beornuini. •u(it)berct. friouini. ingild. badufrith. haðuulf. hygberct. eadgar. eatfrith. stiðuulf. uilgils. pleguini. hyguini. eanberct. uigberct. uiniberct. heremod. ceoluulf. badhelm. eanbald. uulfsig. eadberct. eosturuini. eada. uigbald. eaduini. beornfrith. pleguini. hygberct *lect'*. hyguini. daegbald. baduulf. cuthred. hearduini. badumund. uulfheard. cyniuulf. cyniðegn. eaduini. hyguini. beornuini. pecthelm. beornheard. earduulf. uulfsig. eatfrith. huaetred. (26) *adamnan. hogcin.* haðuberct. eaduald. ualchstod. alduini. brynca. bilgils. bosil. uurmeri. baduuald. haethi. berctgils. lefilla. uichtlac. cynhelm. hroeðlac. hildifrith. coenheri. uilfrith. eedric. ceolberct. berctuald. hleouald. hunberct. suiðhelm. plucca. dremca. tanduini. honoc. iuring. halegberct. eaduald. peuf. tidi. ona. tidhere. ecci. preed. beruulf. osmaer. betuald. lafa. uigheri. tiluuald. biluuald. caua. hysimon. homund. hecci. hleoberct. bilfrith. tiduini. imma. meguini. haemgils. uicfrith. herefrith. blaedla. beetfrith. cunen. hygberct. herebald. (26 *b*) cuga. ecgberct. eaduald. balðhere. sighaeth. badhelm. geruald. bilhaeth. uicfrith. bercthun. uictfrith. ceolberct. bacga. eota. haðberct. aldceorl. uigbald *pbr'*. eatfrith. uicthelm. tunfrith. suiðberct. tunna. lifna. guðhelm. heouald. tiuuald. boesil. ingild. bercthelm. suiðberct. baeglog. plegberct. daeguini. hynca. kentuald. snella. nytta. frioðuulf. eadberct. helmuald. tunuald. hyguini *pbr'*. eada *pbr'*. homund. hama. bercthelm *pbr'*. blaecmon. tungils *pbr'*. tilisi. haðuuald. ualdfrith. hyguald. riuuala. frioðugils. hroðfor. theodric *pbr'*. ceolberct. aluchsig *pbr'*. suiðgils. maegenric *pbr'*. suiðred. arduini. meiuald. (27) ael[f]uini. cynia. ualchstod. hereberct. una. ceoluald. esi. garmund. pecthelm. ycca. utta. aldmon. hildifrith. baduuini. bacca. alberct. bliðuald. tatfrith. beguini. arcanaen. beda. peufa. ecguio. tunfrith. ceolhelm. friðhelm. baduca. hunsig. offa. ingild.•brynca. ualchstod.

aluberct. uilberct. eanuini. inuald. eoforhuaet. hleouald. iidi. clyduini. eðiluini. utta. cut[h]berct. cyniberct. uitmęr. eedgils. cuda. frithhelm. torcthelm. eatferð. bacga. beornheard. eðilberct. domheri. tilfrith. uinilac. haðuuald. eadberct. ecgfrith. bryni. celin. garfrith. bralluc. (27 b) berctuini. huaetberct. pecthun. ceolheri. cynifrith. eonmund. tilberct. friðumund. haðuric. eðiluald. hearduini. hunuald. hygberct. cretta. tatuulf. hildigils. cuthuulf. suiðberct. alchmund. burra. hleouald. friðugeorn. suiðhelm. eonuald. hyguini. uicthaeth. preed. hygberct. bofa. berctuald. rimgils. bilaeth. folcheri. cynicin. hildiuald. leofrith. offa. tumma. hygberct. eoduald. cutheard. suiðualch. baduca. hyglac. lictuald. uiduc. helmuald. etla. sighard. hygberct. herebald. cyniðegn. uigfrith. tatuini. hilduini. hroeðuini. utta. berctfrith. friðumund. tatuualf. *adda*. *tuda*. eadberct. (28) cuthuulf. hereberct. cyniberct. berctmund. *dengus*. eanmund. eanmund. eatðegn. alduulf. cynimund. berctuini. suiðhelm. eaduulf. eadberct. uilmund. beornuini. sigfrith. cuthuulf. hygberct. hygfrith. uigberct. eðilberct. helmuini. berctfrith. daegberct. lefincg. badumund. haðuberct. eanfrith. coenberct. alduulf. uulfheard. eadberct. uilðegn. balduini. eadberct. helpric. eðiluulf. berctuini. eadbald. cuthuini. eanuini. sigberct. cynibald. cuthuulf. friðuulf. tiluini. hyssi. eda. tidberct. tunberct. alduulf. cyni. beonna. herebald. heaðfrith. beonna. tiduald. hyguald. beornuulf. leofuini *lect'*. eanuulf. cuthuulf. (28 b) hygbald. aldgils. eaduulf. redberct. huaetred. ecguulf. eaduini. cynimund. uilfrith. tatuini. eðilberct. helpuini. eanberct. beornuini. baldred. uigmund. ecguulf. tidbald. (coen)a. haðuulf. berctuulf. coenberct. helmgils. uulfheard. cyniðegn. betgils. cutberct. uilmund. eðiluini. berctred. eadberct. beornuulf. berctuini. uul[f]sig. berctred. eaduulf. beornuulf. eanuulf. berctgils. tidhaeth. eanred. uigberct. uulfheard. ecgred alric. earduulf. hunberct. uulfheard. cuthberct. uulfsig. uilberct. alberct. eanuini. alberct. cuthred. eadred. eatðegn. sigmund. beonna. ebbi. alberct. alberct. eanred. (29) alchuald. cyda. ofa. friðuric. uilfrith. trumuald. eadberct. bilfrith. infrith. eðilberct. uilberct. torchtfrith. arnan. baga. tidberct. eðiluini. eadgar. hiuddi. hildiberct. eaduald. tunberct. hygberct. tilfrith. nimstan. oshelm. cynifrith. beornfrith. aluchstan. cuthelm. londfrith. hygfrith. *aethan*. eadred. h[y]gberct. huaetmod.

adda. blaca. uicthaeth. domfrith. eata. eatfrith. uighaeth *pbr'*. dycguio. fexstan. berctuulf. berctuini. hildiberct. hygfrith. alda. eðiluini. hroeðuald. beornfrith. cynibald. cynifrith. hada. hygberct. edilberct. aldmon. berctuini. aluberct. badudegn. suiðgils. hel . r. . (29 *b*) heardred. helmuald. eanbald. cynhelm. eadgar. tondberct. uynfrith. eadhaeth. bilfrith. eadhaeth. aluchuald. pleguini. suiðgils. eðiluald. .... erct. eanuald *pbr'*. (aðilbald) eanfrith. ..... bercthelm. (cuthberct) berctuald. beeduini. eadberct. aldheri. friðuuald. cuthuulf. daegfrith. alberct. uilhaeth. alduini. cuthuald. balðheard. cuthuini. hyguald. siguald. sigred. ingild. tilberct. aldheri. tatberct. cuthric. eadberct. ceoluio. edilheri. betti. bilfrith. hygberct. heregeorn. hygberct. hyglac. burgfrith. cuthuulf. cada. eaduald. tiluuald. *cotten*. meifrith. alberct. alduini. eatfrith. bryni. berctheri. (30) forðheri. aluberct. hyguini. badufrith. cuthðegn. torctuini. beornuini. helmuini. uilmund. tilberct. uighelm. ceolberct. pectgils. betmon. cuthberct. leofuini. biluualch. egilmund *pr'*. uictfrith. baduini. eðiluini. haðuuini. haðuberct. cuðhelm. giuhaep. baduuini. cynifrith. beornuini. eada. herebald. alberct. eadberct. hidda. hygbald. berecht. uulfhard. beornhaeð. cueðilach. bilstan. berctuini. eadgar. cyniberct. pleouald. plecgils. pleguini. hygberct. uictbald. eanmund. tidberct. aldgils. guthmund. berctgils. uniberct. buna. alberct. alda. baduuini *pr'*. eadhun. osmund. eatfrith. adhysi. torctgils. eadbald. (30 *b*) beda. bilhaeth. berctred. eðiluini. milred. aeðuini. aðigils. eatðegn. eðilric. cynibald. friðumund. cuthric. uulfheri. tathelm. cuthuini. tatuini. eadhaeth. alchuald. b . oru . ini. heardred. berctuald. eadgar. sigheard. georored. tilmon. botuald. eaduald. pechtuald. berctuini. hroeðberct. eanuald. uitgils. eaduini. alberct. haðuberct. saeberct. uilhelm. berctuini. uynberct. eaduini. c(eo)luald. cynifrith. cuthuini. tunberct. aluca. bercthaeth. badheard. uernbald. aldheri. uicthelm. addul. frehelm. eaduald. baduuini. aldhun. eadbald. tatberct. alduulf. gut[h]berct. eðilric. berctfrith. eorupuald. tatberct. (31) cynifrith. eanuini. eðilmund. alduulf. tidberct. uilgils. sola. eðilmund. balðhun. helmuald. tatberct. eadberct. eatðegn. geonuald. beorn. badumund. baduuini. ceoluini. tilfrith. baeglug. siglac. eadberct. eðilberct. haðuberct. onboth. geruini. eanuini. utta. dene. sigberct. pechthelm. pleghelm. tiduini. haðuuini. suiðuald. helpric. haðuulf. badumund. hygberct. uergils. meguini. cuthuini.

berctuini. suiðhelm. eanfrith. badhelm. eanmund. cuthuald. eadberct. uerberct. eadberct. huaetberct. uynfrith. eadberct. coena. ceolberct. berctuald. suithuulf. eðilberct. hildiberct. beorn. eaduini. alduini. (31 *b*) hilduini. eadberct. eadgar. tili. bercht *ab'*. aldhun. eanberct. eanuulf. uilfrith. berchelm. beonna. aelfuald. haðuuald. uilfrith. eadgar. . . . . . eðilbald. . . l . . n. hygberct. . . . . . eanuini. eanuini. beguini. uigfrith. berctuini. ceoluini. eðilric. ingild. cuuen. streonuulf. ceoluini. tatuulf. uulfheard. aldhelm. guðhelm. geruald. haðuuini. hygbald. eatðegn. . . lfrith. bercht. (guð)uini. eanbald. eanuulf. huaetberct. uilberct. friðuuini. alduulf. cyniberct. uulfhaeth. tatmonn. hyguini. eðiluini. ualchard. ercinuald. cutberct. eanuulf. berct. uitta. uilðegn. seoluini. berctfrith. uulfsig. (32) tidberct. alduulf. eanred. cuthuulf. alduini. baduuini. cuthberct. *fergus*. eadberct. forðred. betuald. ecgberct. eðilberct. eaduini. eanbald. uilmund. earduulf. eaduulf. berctuulf. plegheard. earduulf. eadgar. forðred. eadred. haðuulf. balduini. uilmund. eanuulf. haðured. botuulf. plecga. alduulf. cuthðegn. earduulf. berctuulf. hunbald. bercthaeth. eanfrith. daegberct. altðegn. eaduald. hygferth. plegmund. cyniuulf. beaduðegn. uigbald. eadbald. herebald. alduulf. haðuberct. bercthaeð. aeðiluini. bercthaeð. cyniuulf. eanberct. ecgberct salrach. aldgils. h(ere)berct. eanberct. hygbald. eðiluulf. cuðmund. (32 *b*) cyniuulf. eanuulf. eaduulf. eadred. tilðegn. cuduulf. hearduulf. eanuulf. aldgils. hunberct. eanberct. eaduulf. hygbald. eadred. ediluulf. cuðmund. cuðuulf. cyniuulf. hearduulf. eanuulf. botuulf. uilric. saeberct. tilberct. aldhelm. uilðegn. hiordi. tilberct. fugul. tatuulf. tidberct. eadred. siguulf. cuðmund. cuðred. alberct. eanuulf. eðilberct. berctferð. tiluini. aldmund. cyniferð. berctuulf. badumund. siguulf. eadred. eðilmund. baduulf. eadred. haðuulf. eadgar. betuini. aldred. siguulf. beornuulf. berctuulf. eaduulf. hleofuini. eadgar. eoduulf. heaðured. ceolhere. berctferð. (33) eanbald. aldberct. hearduulf. berhtred. cuðred. hygred. tidhelm. eaduulf. eaduulf. eaduulf. berhtuulf. eðilbercht. osberht. eadbercht. alduulf. uada. haðuuini. eadred. beornred. eadbercht. eaduulf. helmuini. cyniuulf. hiodde. baðhun. berhtuulf. berhtuini. eanuulf. badigils. hygberht. eatðegn. uilmund. uulfhard. tilberht. eaduulf. eata. albercht. tidsig. uynbald. *ftadgus*. tidferð. cyniuulf. eadbercht. sigbald. haðumer.

Nomina monachorum.

(34) Herding. aligua. friubet. hiuddi. aldceorl. cuthelm. betuini. pecthaeth. uerenhaeth. tella. tiouald. hulan. bilhaeth. forthhelm. brynuald. pecthaeth. hemmi. cnobualch. hleouald. tilhaeth. uch[t]red. betti. m̃uul. cynifrith. tudda. uilfrith. cuðuald. torchtgils. efnuald. *coluduc.* inta. folcuini. alda. pega. berctuald. tu[u]nlic. baduuald. eðiluald. eadberct. haemgils. tatfrith. ylla. berctfrith. siguini. baca. bacga. eanuald. cuthric. leobhelm. suiðualch. ceoluulf. cynech. eðilberct. ceefi. cyni. paelli. offa. bryni. cuthuald. aldualch. (34 *b*) bercthelm. haeði. cuna. ingild. torcthelm. sigbald. bosa. friðugils. biu[u]ulf. *arthan.* eaduald. ingild. ceolfrith. berctgils. cyniðegn. baduuald. hleouald. friðuberct. torcthaeth. tunuald. eðiluini. suiðhelm. aldhelm. betuald. hunuald. bilhelm. uda. berctfrith. heregeorn. totta. eadberct. bilfrith. friðumund. cundigeorn. pleghelm. eatðegn. badufrith. snahard. tatfrith. helpuini. cuthelm. adda. laba. beornfrith. uilberct. gumuald. eadlac. cui[c]uald. uulfhaeth. cynhelm. uictfrith. siguini. eadgar. alberct. cynimund. cyniberct. eanuini. bercht. hama. hyguini. uilfrith. alduini. uynfrith. (35) cuthfrith. titfrith. eanberct. eodbald. haðuberct. pleguini. eaduald. aldceorl. hildiuald. heardred. aldmonn. helmuald. berctuini. eanberct. eaduini. friðubald. cynimund. baduca. hiuddi. burgfrith. geruald. bilhaeth. suiðberct. eodbald. theodric. eadgar. eaduald. uilberct. helpuini. deduini. berctfrith. hygberct. cyniberct. plecgils. hleoberct. friðuini. helpric. eata. haðuberct. alduulf. isernuulf. eata. pecthelm. cynimund. eðilric. uiniberct. *bercth. uynbald. berctuald. hygberct. liodberct. alduini. leofuini. badhelm. bercthun. lioda. ingild. tatuini. eanberct. haðuberct. pecthun. eanberct. *turpen.* (35 *b*) saeuini. tatberct. beornuini. uynberct. botuini. eaduald. eanuini. dycgberct. helmuini. siguulf. uinifrith. cuthuulf. berctsig. eata. diori. haðuuini. tilfrith. eadberct. berctuulf. daegberct. bercht. eadberct. helmuald. eanfrith. cuthfrith. bercthaeth. hygbald. *aberth.* berctgils. beduini. beornuini. berctgils. eadberct. uigberct. badhelm. eaduald. uynberct. uerenfrith. uigfrith. uulfgar. cuthelm. garuald. eanred. plegberct. badumund. eaduald. badumund. onna. hygberct. tidberct. cyniuulf. ecguini. eanuald. tilberct. eanberct. cyniberct. berctuini. uulfhaeth. eanuini. saeuini. daegberct. beornuini. hun-

frith. (36) beguini. uulfhaeth. diori. guða. eaduini. plegberct. earduulf. uermund. guðhelm. geruald. eaduini. uigfus. cuthbald. herebald. badhard. eadberct. tiduald. beonna. alberct. tidberct. uulfsig. cyniuulf. regnhaeg. bilhaeth. plegheard. eada. alcheri. alchuini. eadberct. cynibald. eaduulf. berctuini. eadberct. uilfrith. uulfsig. hygberct. haðuberct. cyniberct. cynimund. badumund. eaduulf. uilfrið. uulfheard. ingild. uilðegn. eaduini. hygberct. haðuferth. eatðegn. eanberct. badufrith. aluberct. badumund. cynifrith. beornuini. cuthgils. eanuulf. eanfrith. tiduini. helmuini. tathaeth. tiduini. tatmon. (36 *b*) suiðgils. eadbald. hearduini. altceorl. cuthðegn. eaduulf. tatuini. tidhelm. sigberct. titfrith. baduini. aelli. beorn. bercht. pectgils. eðiluini. cyniðegn. tiduini. *pobbidi.* cyniheard. alberct. uulfheard. cyniberct. tatuulf. alduulf. herebald. cyniuulf. cuthgar. daegberct. tidbercht. tiduulf. berct-uini. suiðberct. hildiberct. berctuulf. aldred. uulfheri. cuthuulf. haðuulf. tiduini. eanuini. beornuulf. berct. bercht. heardlac. hyg-berct. uiniberct. heardred. uulfsig. eanfrith. hysica. eadberct. aldmon. helmuald. ceolred. uilðegn. badumund. alric. beornuini. torctfrith. eðilhelm. aldulf. hygberct. (37) cyniberct. baduuini. siguini. hygbald. domuini. siguulf. tatuulf. haðuulf. cuthred. beornred. bercthun. koena. eadgar. hygbald. hygberct. eðiluini. tilfrith. heregils. tidberct. suiðuulf. tidberct. uigfrith. badhard. cyni-gils. eansig. eaduulf. eadbald. eanuulf. baduulf. eaduulf. ecguulf. alberct. botuulf. eada. bercthelm. cuthred. alduini. heaðured. earduulf. uulfsig. haduulf. cyniðegn. osuulf. alduulf. betuini. eaduulf. alduulf. uilmund. ceolred. bilðegn. uulfheard. eanbald. plegberct. berctfrith. uiglaf. cuðuulf. earduulf. alduulf. uighelm. eanbald. tidberct. haðuulf. h . . ðuulf. (37 *b*) hyguini. uulfsig. ceolred. alberct. eatðegn. hygmund. uigbald. herefrith. uulfsig. uigheard. eadbald. helmuald. eatfrith. eanred. cynimund. uulfsig. tidhelm. cyniuulf. osuulf. alduulf. eðilberct. alduulf. cyniuulf. cuthðegn. uicthelm. alberct. beornuulf. cyniheard. eadberct. cyniðegn. tid-helm. sigric. haðuulf. cuthgils. eðilfrith. eaduulf. eadbald. help-uini. berctuini. berctred. beornred. uigbald. seldred. alduulf. badufrith. eðiluulf. balduulf. eofuruulf. eanmund. baldred. tiduald. altceorl. berctuulf. ofa. uilðegn. berctuulf. beornred. baldhelm. badufrith. berctuini. cuðred. eaduald. gefuini. (38) eaduulf. ecguulf. eaduulf. aescuulf. alduulf. eanuulf. huaetberct. alduulf.

beornfrith. beornred. moll. sigred. berctuulf. eaduulf. eanuulf. eaduulf. diori. huaetred. eðiluulf. eanuulf. uigbald. bercht. eanuulf. seliberct. aldred. haðuberct. ecguulf. hleofrith. cuthred. cuðheard. alberct. hygberct. uulfheard. eanuulf. eanred. uchtred. eada. ingild. beornuini. earduulf. eaduulf. forðred. tidberct. earduulf. cuðuulf. siguulf. cuthgils. earduulf. eadred. ediluulf. rudda. eanuini. hunuulf. ecgred. ceolla. beornuulf. cyniuulf. uulfheard. herefrith. eadred. helpuini. cynifrith. tiluini. (38 b) liodfrith. eaduini. leofuini. tidberct. eanuini. cynhelm. hunberct. tatmonn. eada. eanuini. berctuulf. siguulf. eanuulf. alduulf. beornuulf. tatuulf. eaduulf. aelfsig. daeghelm. eanbald. aldred. eanuulf. hygberct. baduulf. cuðberct. eanred. aldhelm. haðuberct. uilbald. huita. cyniberct. beornuini. uilhaeth. eada. eadberct. cuthuulf. eanberct. eadhaeth. eadgar. baduuini. tatberct. liodfrith. aldgils. hygberct. alduulf. sigberct. uulfheard. haðuuini. cynigils. siguulf. eaduald. siguulf. meguulf. cuthmund. eadhaeth. eaduini. aelfsig. alduulf. baduulf. eada. cynimund. aescuulf. ecgberct (39) baldred. badufrith. cuthred. eaduulf. eadberct. eadberct. eaðugils. uilsig. torchtuulf. eðilbald. cuthuulf. eatfrith. beornuini. tiduulf. eðilbald. tondheri. eanberct. tilmonn. eaduulf. hygbald. berctuulf. suiðred. cynigar. eda. cyniuulf. eadbald. haðuulf. helmuini. alchsig. eðilheard. beornuulf. tiduulf. burghelm. eadberct. baduulf. eanfrith. baduuini. tiduini. berctred. cuðred. heaðured. uilhelm. eaduulf. berctred. eanred. eanlac. berctuini. alduulf. eanred. haðuberct. cuthlac. haðuulf. tidhelm. uulfheard. eanuulf. eaduulf. ecga. helmuini. cuthred. baede. uilberct. tatfrith. berctfrith. (39 b) eaduulf. tilfrith. huaetred. tidbald. beornred. beornuulf. hygfrith. eanred. alberct. ofa. cynimund. cuðheard. cuthðegn. eanferð. eanred. cyniferð. eanuulf. heaðuulf. berctuulf. aldred. eanuulf. eðilmund. aldred. cuðuulf. botfrith. heaðuberct. heaðuferth. hyguulf. liodbercht. hygberct. hygred. cuthðegn. aeðilmund. earduulf. hungils. haðubald. hereberct. eðilmund. siguulf. eaduulf *dux*. badured. eaduulf. baduulf. eaduulf. eadred. torchtred. eatferð. eaduulf. cyniuulf. herred. huita. eatðegn. tilferð. embe. heaðured. eanuulf. alduini. earduulf. uiniberct. haduuini. tilberct. alduulf. uilmund. (40) beornred. cuðuulf. hygferð. tilðegn. eaduulf. hleouini. tidhaeð. eduini. eaduulf. berctuulf. pechtuulf. hunberct. berchtuulf. tilberct. uulfheord. uulfheord. cyniðryð.

uilburg. hildigyð. eadu. eardgyð. ecgred. uilgils. osuulf. eaduulf. aldred. uigmund. beadugils. heardred. eadred. eonuulf. eanred. eadred. cuðuulf. herred. cyniferð. uulfred. cuðred. sigred. uilmund. eadhaeð. tatuulf. eardhelm. eðiluulf. berctred. eaduulf. reduulf. heaðuberct. eðiluini. eonuulf. uulfheard. eonuulf. beornhoð. tilberct. uilmund. uigmund. hygbald. eaduulf. eanred. heoðured. balduini. cynigils. tiduini. (40 *b*) albercht. berctmund. sigferð. sighelm. tiduulf. hleoberct. hyguini. alberct. eanberct. tatuulf. eanred. beornred. ebbe. uulfheard. berctuulf. tiduini. acuulf. alberct. eadberct. eanberct. berctred. siguulf. uulfhard. cyniuulf. hygberct. berctuulf. eadred. uilgils. haðuuini. eadred. haðuulf. cuðuini. hereferð. berctuulf. hroðuulf. uilhelm. bette. eaduulf. botuulf. pleghard. frioðuuini. tilne. aldred. hunberct. heardred. ingild. hunred. uulfhed. ofa. uilberct. berctferð. frioðuuini. uigferð. eanberct. eaduulf. hroðuulf. tidberct. torctuulf. alduulf. uuheard. uilmund. aldred. eanuini. eduini. (41) burgheard. reduulf. aelfsig. eadbald. eðiluulf. eanuulf. eaduulf. uini. reduulf. cuðuulf. eadbald. baduuini. eadred. huaetberct. badumund. tilðegn. tidbercht. eaduini. tidferd. cynibercht. eadred. eanred. ebbe. bearnhard. aldred. badumund. albercht. friuðuulf. friðubald. hygferð. ecgred. eaduulf. alduulf. hunbercht. uilferð. eadhelm. osbald. heardred. beornuulf. uulfred. beornuini. earnuulf. uigbeorn. uicga. torchtmund. berchtsig. eðiluulf. aldred. hunuald. berchtred. earduulf. tilbercht. botuulf. beonna. eadred. sigred. cuthelm. beornuini. uulfhard. hunferd. berchtuulf. headured. (41 *b*) eðilbercht. uigmund. uulfheard. hunred. eðilheard. eðiluulf. lioduini. aldred. tilred. brada. eanbercht. cuduulf. ecgred. berhtred. cuðuulf. bada. eanred. heardred. cyniuald. hygbald. aella. hygbercht. eanuulf. uilhaeð. cyniferð. saeuini. eanuulf. herred. uini. uillech. alduulf. tiduulf. tidbald. eðilberht. badumund. tatuulf. aluberct. siguulf. haðuulf. uulfhaeð. beornred. forðred. torchtmund. baldred. eanberht. uynbald. coenred. friouini. reduulf. tiduulf. aelfsig. hygberht. hungils. aldgils. berchtred. cyniferð. uulfsig. hroðuini. hygine. eda. eadred. uermund. gerferð. (42) berchtuald. eðiluini. eadgar. uichtbald. eanuulf. reduulf. tidberht. cuðgils. eadred. hyguulf. huita. kiona. cyniferð. siguulf. earduulf. eðilmund. eadred. hygine. berchtred. coenuulf. eðiluald. baldred. eadlac. eaduulf.

Genealogies (Northumbrian ?).

The following lists of bishops and genealogies of kings are taken from the Cotton MS. Vespasian B 6, fol. 108 foll. They are preceded by the Martyrologium poeticum of Bede, and miscellaneous notes, other works being bound up in the same volume. Plate 165 of the publications of the Palæographical Society (part 10, 1880) gives a facsimile of part of the MS. The letter-press gives the following information about the age of the MS. : 'Additions have been made to the lists in later times, but an examination of the portions due to the first hand proves that the MS. was written between the years 811 and 814. The last name in the list of popes, by the first hand, is that of Leo III, who died in 816; the last king is Coenuulf of Mercia, who died in 819; and among the latest of the bishops in the different dioceses are some who succeeded about the year 811, and others who died in 814. The fact that the latest recorded succession among the kings is one in the house of Mercia, points to that kingdom as the part of England, where the MS. was written. The character of the writing confirms this view, being of the same school as that of the Mercian charters of the same period.' The fact of the royal genealogies beginning with Northumbria is an equally strong argument in favour of the assumption of a Northumbrian scribe, which is further confirmed by their being preceded by a work of the Northumbrian Bede, and the want of Northumbrian charters makes the evidence of handwriting doubtful.

I have, of course, given only what is written by the first hand. In many places the original writing has been inked over again by a later hand. All these passages are here printed in italics.

Nomina arcepis(coporum) *dorober*(nensis) civ(itatis).

Augustinus. laurentius. mellitus. iustus. honorius. deusdedit. theodorus. berhtwaldus. tatuinus. noðhelmus. cuðberhtus. breguinus. iaenberhtus. aeðelheardus. uulfredus. *suiðredus. ceolnoðus.*

Nomina orientalium saxonum.

Mellitus. cedd. erconwald. . aldhere. incwald. ecguulf. sighaeh. eadberht. eadgar. coenwalh. eadbald. heaðoberht. osmund. aeðilnoð. *ceolberhtus.*

Nomina episcoporum hrofensis *ecclesiae.*

Paulinus. ithamar. putta. cuichelm. gebmund. tobias. alduulf. dunn. earduulf. diora. uærmund. beornmod.

Nomina episcoporum australium saxonum.

Eadberht. eolla. sicgga. aluberht. osa. gislhere. tota. uiohthun. aeðiluulf. *cyneredus.*

Nomina episcoporum occidentalium saxonum.

Primus occidentalium saxonum birinus fuit episcopus, qui cum consilio honorii papae venerat brittaniam. agilberht III. *uuine* IIII. leutherius. haedde. deinde in duas parochias divisus est, altera uuentanaecium ecclesiae, altera scirabur' ecclesiae.

In uenta' civitate.

Danihel. hunfrið. cynheard. aeðelheard. ecgbald. dudd. cyneberht. alchmund. wigðegn. *herefrið.*

In scira' ecclesia.

Aldhelm. forðhere. hereuuald. aeðelmod. denefrið. uuigberht. *alhstan.*

Nomina episcoporum orientalium anglorum.

Primus felix. thomas. * bertgils. bisi. postea in duas parrochias dividitur. beadwine. aecce. noðberht. aescuulf. heaðolac. eardred. aeðilferð. cuðuine. eanferð. aldberht. æðeluulf. ecglaf. heardred. alcheard. aelfhun. *uuermu*[*nd*]. tidferð. *uuilred. hunberht.*

Nomina episcoporum provinciarum merciorum.

Primus in provinciae merciorum et lindisfarorum ac mediteranerum anglorum episcopus diuma. cellah; ambo de scottia. trumhere de natione anglorum. gearomon. ceadda. wynfrið. saexwulf. postea vero in v parrochias dividitur. post sæxuulfum provinciae merciorum duos episcopos habuit headdan et wilfridum. postea uuilfridus ejectus. et headda praefatus regebat ambos parrochias. deinde alduine qui et uuor nominabatur. iterum divisa est in duas parrochias. totta. huita. eadberht. hemele. unuuona. cuðfrið. uuærenberht. berhthum. *rethhun.* hygberht. *aldred. ceolred.* alduulf. *hereuuine. oeðeluuald. hunberht.*

Nomina episcopo(rum) lind(is)farnorum post sæx[1].

Eadhaeð. aeðeluine. eadgar. cyneberht. alouuioh. alduulf. ceoluulf. eaduulf.

Nomina episcoporum huicciorum.

Bosel. oftfor. ecguuine. uuilfrið. milred. uęrmund. tilhere. heaðored. deneberht. *heaberht.*

Nomina episcoporum uest. r.

Putta. tyrhthel. torhthere. * walhston. cuðberht. podda. acca. • headda. aldberht. esne. ceolmund. utel. uulfheard. ....

(N)*om*(ina) ..... *genus nordanhymbrorum.*

Primus paulinus a justo archiepiscopo ordinatus. II aeðan. III fine. IIII colman. V tuda. postea in duas parrochias dividitur. cedda eboracensi ecclesiae ordinatum uilfrið hagstaldensiae ordina'. depositoque uilfrido a rege ecgfrido eota pro eo ordinatus epis' hag' pro ceddan bosa ebura ... defuncto eatan iohannis pro eo ordina' post longum vero exilium . ilfrið iterum in episcopatum hag' susceptus est et idem iohannis defunc' bosa eburaici substitutus est.

...... sis .....

Uilfrið. ecgberht. coen ... eanbald. eanbald. uulfwig.

Hag[u]staldensis ecclesiae.

I Acca. II frioðoberht. III alhmund. IIII tilberht. V aeðilberht. VI heardred. VII eanberht. tidferð[2].

Nomina episcoporum lindisfarorum.

Aeðan, fines. colman. eata. cudberht. eadberht. eatferð. oeðilwald. cynwulf. hygbald. ecgberht[2]. *eadmund.*

Nomina episcoporum ad candida casa.

I Pehthelm. II frioðowald. III pehtuine. IIII aeðilberht. V beaduulf. *heaðored.*

Haec genelogiae per partes brittaniae regum regnantium per diversa loca.

Nordanhymbra.

Eduine aelling. aelle yffing. yffi uuscfreaing. uuscfrea uilgilsing. uilgils . storualcning. uestorualcna soemling. soemel saefugling.

[1] *traces of letter over the* x; wulfum *added in later hand.* [2] *in smaller hand.*

saefugul saebalding. saebald siggeoting. siggeot suebdaeging. suebdaeg siggaring. siggar uegdaeging. uegdaeg uodning. uoden frealafing.

Item norðanhy(mb)r.

Ecgfrið osuing. Osuio eðilfriðing. eðilfrið eðilricing. eðilric iding. ida eopping. eoppa oesing. oesa eðilberhting. eðilberht angengeoting. angengeot alusing. alusa ingibranding. ingibrand wegbranding. wegbrand bernicing. beornic beldaeging. beldaeg wodning. uoden frealafing.

Item norðan'.

Ceoluulf cuðuining. cud . . . e liodwalding[1]. liod . ald ecgualding. ecguald edelming. edhelm ocgting. ocg iding. eadberht eating. eata li . dualding. lioduald ecgualding.

Item norðanhym'.

Albred eanuining. eanuine byrnhoming[2]. byrnhom bofing. bofa blaecmoning. blaecmon edricing. edric iding.

. . . .

Aeðilred *peding. penda pypbing. pypba crioding. crioda cynewalding. cynewald cnebbing. cnebba icling. . . il eamering. eamer angengeoting. . . g . . geot offing. off . . uærmunding. uermund uihtlaeging. uihtlaeg . að . . geoting. waðolgeot wodning. woden fr . . lafing.

(it)em mer . . .

Aeðelbald alwing. alwih eowing. eowa pybbing.

Item mercna.

Ecgfrið offing. offa ðincfri[ði]ing. ðincfrið eanuulfing. eanuulf osmoding. osmod eowing. eowa pybbing.

Item mercna.

Coenuulf cuðberhting. cuðberht bassing. bassa cynreowing. cynreou centwining. centwine cundwaling. cundwalh coenwaling. coenwalh pybbing.

lind . ar . a[3].

Aldfrið eatting. eatta eanferðing. eanferð biscoping. biscop beding. beda bubbing. bubba caedbaeding. caedbaed cuðdgilsing.

[1] w *doubtful.* [2] o *doubtful.* [3] l *and* n *doubtful.*

cueldgils cretting. cretta uinting. uinta wodning. uuoden frealafing. frealaf frioðulfing. frioðulf finning. finn goduulfing. godulf geoting.

Cantwar . .

Aeðelberht uihtreding. uihtred ecgberhting. ecgberht erconberhting. erconberht eadbalding. eadbald eðilberhting. eðilberht iurmenricing. iurmenric o . . . oese ocging. ocga hengesting. hengest uitting. uitta uihtgilsing. uihtgils uegdaeging. uegdaeg uodning. uoden frealafing.

Eostengla.

Aelfwald alduulfing. alduulf eðilricing. eðilric ening. eni tyttling. tyttla wuffing. wuffa wehing. wehha wilhelming. wilhelm hryping. hryp hroðmunding. hroðmund trygling. tryg.l t.ttwianing. tyt . . . . r . ing. care . . uodning. uoden frealafing.

Anno dominici incarnationis dcclvi aeðilbald rex occisus. eodem anno offa rex beornredum tyrannum bello superavit et regnum tenuit merciorum. anno ccc^{o}viii^{o} adventus anglorum in britanniam. adventus beati augustini c^{o}lx^{o} [1].

Lorica Glosses (Kentish).

These glosses to the Lorica of Gildas were first printed by Cockayne in his Leechdoms (I. LXVIII foll.) from MS. Bibl. Publ. Cantab. Ll. 1. 10, fol. 43. Cockayne says: 'The Latin text of the Cambridge MS. is of the eighth century; it was not intended to be glossed; the glosses were introduced afterwards in a small hand; the earlier ones marked with an asterisk belong to the end of the tenth century, the others to the eleventh.' He adds in a note: 'Mr. Bradshaw thinks the glosses contemporary.' I do not think the language of the earlier glosses can be earlier than the first half of the ninth century, although they are certainly older than the tenth. I learn from Mr. Bradshaw that he now considers the Latin text to be not older than the first half of the ninth century, so that we are in agreement. The dialect appears to be Kentish. The interpretations of some of the difficult words of the original are those given by C., with the help of Mr. Bradshaw.

[1] *note on fol.* 104 *in the same hand as the above lists.*

Mortalitas : wól.
lacerandum : to teorenne[1].
denso : ðicce[2].
ceteros agonithetas : cempan.
proretas : stioran.
anthletas (*ath.*) : cempan.
omne malum a me pereat : gewite.
pactum firmum feriat[3] : were trume fæstnie.
mei gibrae : mines lichoman.
pernas (=*artus*) : leower.
libera tuta (*tua*) *pelta* : gefria[4] ðine plægsceldæ.
librent : cueccen.
gygram (skull, top of forehead) : hnoll.
cephalem : heafudponnan.
iaris : loccum.
conas : egan.
patham : onwlite[5].
liganam : tungan.
sennas : toeð.
michinas : næsðyrel.
cladam : swiran[6].
crassum : breost.
madianum : sidan.
talias : lendana.
bathma : ðeeoh[7].
exugiam : midirnan.
binas idumas : twa honda.
fronti : h[n]eofulan.
rostro : nebbe.
labiae (-*o*) : weolure.
timpori (*te.*) : ðunnwengan[8].
mento : cinne.
supercili(*i*)*s* : oferbruum.
genis : heagospinnum.
buccis : smerum.

[1] *er., and* to slitenne *written over in the later hand.* [2] *altered to* þy ðiccan *by the later hand.* [3] i *on er.* [4] a *altered to* o. [5] *altered to* ondwlitan *later.* [6] *altered to* swioran *later.* [7] o *from* c (*later alteration*?). [8] e *altered to* o *later.*

internasso (*-aso*) : næsgristlan.
rotis : eghringum.
tautonibus (=*palpebrae*) : bruum[1].
ging(iv)is : toðreomum.
anile (*anhelae*) : oroðe.
uvae : hrectungan.
gurgilioni (*gurgu*) : ðrotbollan.
sublinguae : tungeðrum.
capitali : heafudponnan.
ceutro : swiran.
cartilagini : gristlan.
retrudas : ascufe.
cubitis : fæðmum.
pugnas : fyste.
spinam : hrycg.
renibus : lundleogum.
catacrinas : huppbaan.
nates : ersendu.
cambas : homme.
suras : speoruliran.
genuclis : : : : : : : banum[2].
talos : helan.
tibiis : sconcum.
calcibus : helum.
plantarum : illa.
jugulam : ðearmgewind.
reniculos : lundleogan.
fithrem : snedelðearm.
cum obligia (=*peritonaeum*) : nettan.
toleam (tonsil) : readan.
toracem : feoluferð.
fibras : smælðearmas.
bucliamine : heorthoman.
splenem : milte.
turtuosis (*to.*) : gebegdum.
intestinis : iscrnum.

[1] ofer *prefixed in the later hand.* [2] *the whole word er.; may be* hweorfbanum; *certainly not* speorbanum, *as suggested by Cockayne.*

pantes: alle[1].
lang(u)or: *ald.
vehor (*·ar*): ic sio wegen.

Lorica Prayer (Kentish).

The following form of prayer (of which the beginning is wanting) is written in a bold hand of the first half of the ninth century on fol. 2 *a* of the same MS. as the Lorica glosses. The dialect seems Kentish. The letters are much worn in many places, being sometimes quite illegible. Some I should not have read correctly at first sight without the help of Prof. Skeat and Mr. Bradshaw. My lines correspond to those of the MS.

7 ðe georne gebide gece 7 miltse fore alra his
haligra gewyrhtum 7 geeaṛningum 7 boenum b.
. . . . num, ða ðe *domino deo* gelicedon from fruman
middangeardes; ðonne gehereð he ðec ðorh hiora
ðingunge. do ðonne fiorðan siðe ðin hleor ðriga
to iorðan fore alle godes cirican, 7 sing ðas
fers: *domini est salus, salvum fac populum*
tuum, domine praetende misericordiam tuam.
sing ðonne *pater noster*. gebide ðonne fore
alle geleaffullę menn *in mundo*. ðonne bistu ðone
deg daelniomende ðorh dryhtnes gefe alra ðeara
goda ðe ænig monn for his noman gedoeð, 7 ðec alle
soðfestę fore ðingiað *in caelo et in terra, amen.*

Lorica Names.

The following names occur in the same MS.

(*fol.* 21) Aedelvald. (72) *ab* Alchfriðo[3]. (87 *b*) Oedelwald.

Codex Aureus Inscription (Kentish).

(About 870.)

From the facsimile in Westwood's Facsimiles of the Miniatures and Ornaments of Anglo-Saxon and Irish Manuscripts (London, 1868), from the MS. of the Gospels in the Royal Library at Stock-

[1] *second* e *er.*; e *prefixed by later hand.*

holm. The letters in ( ) have been cut away by the binder. Prof. Stephens was the first to identify this Aelfred with the Aelfred dux of the Charter given further on.

+ *Orate pro* Ceolheard *presbyteri*, Niclas 7 Ealhhun 7
Wulfhelm *aurifex*[1].

In nomine Domini nostri Ihesu Christi, ic Aelfred aldormon 7 Wérburg mín gefera begetan ðas béc æt haeðnu*m* herge mid uncre claene feo. ðæt ðonne wæs mid clæne golde. 7 ðæt wit ðeodan for Godes lufan 7 for uncre saule ðearf(e)[2], ond for ðon ðe wit *nolðan ðæt ðas halgan beoc lencg in ðære haeðenesse wunaden, 7 nu willað heo gesellan inn to Cristes circan Gode to lofe 7 to wuldre 7 to weorðunga, 7 his ðrowunga to ðoncunca, 7 ðæm godcundan geferscipe to brucen(ne)[2] ðe ín Cristes circan dæghwæmlice Godes lof rærað, to ðæm gerade ðæt heo mon árede eghwelce monaðe for Aelfred[2] 7 for Werburge 7 for Alhðryðe, heora saulum tó ecum lecedome, ða hwile ðe God gesegen haebbe ðæt fulwiht æt ðeosse stowe beon mote. Ec swelce ic Aelfred dux 7 Werburg biddað 7 halsiað ón Godes almaehtiges noman 7 on allra his haligra ðæt nænig mon seo to ðon gedyrstig ðætte ðas halgan beoc áselle oððe áðeode from Cristes circan ða hwile ðe fulwiht stondan mote

Aelfre(d). Werbur(g). Alhðryð *eorum* (*filia*).

Durham Admonition.

(Kentish.)

The Durham Ritual was first published by J. Stevenson for the Surtees Society (Rituale Ecclesiae Dunelmensis, 1840). This edition was collated with the MS. by Prof. Skeat, and the results are given in Appendix *II* to the Phil. Soc. Transs. for 1877–8–9. In spite of the Northumbrian interlinear gloss it contains, the main portion of the MS. was, as Prof. Skeat remarks, probably written in the South of England. He goes on to say: 'This is remarkably illustrated by the fact that a small portion of the *original* text is in Southern English. This passage, printed at p. 114, is in the large bold hand of the Latin text, and is entitled *halsuncge*, i.e.

[1] *this invocation is in a different hand from what follows.* [2] *end of line.*

a solemn charge addressed by the priest to the person or persons who were about to proceed to the ordeal. The words printed in square brackets are written above the line, being the alternative words of address, when only one person was to undergo the trial. The reader should also notice that the next nine rubrics are all in the same hand, and belong to the same period.' When *I* first saw the Admonition, *I* came to the conclusion that it was in the *Kentish* dialect of the ninth century, and Prof. Skeat agrees. But as to the date he says (probably after consulting with Mr. Bradshaw, whose help he acknowledges generally), that it 'cannot be placed earlier than the tenth century.' *I* have not access to the MS., and can only say that *I* do not see how the *language* of the present text can possibly be brought further down than the end of the ninth century: if a copy, it is of unparalleled accuracy.

I have omitted one of the rubrics, which is in Latin.

Halsuncge.

Ic eow [ðe] halsige on fæder naman, 7 on suna naman, ðaet is ure dryhten haelende Crist, 7 on ðaes halgan gastes, 7 for ðære cristnesse ðe ge [ðu] underfenge [underfengan], 7 for ða haligan ðrinesse, 7 fer ða IIII godspelleras, Matheus, 7 Marcus, 7 Lucas et Johannes, 7 fer ealle ða halgan reliquias ðe gind ealne middangeard sindon haligra martyra, 7 fer ealle ða halgan Godes ciricean * þ*æte* her on weorolde gehalgode sien, 7 fer naman ðaere halgan faemnan s*anct*a Marian þ*æt* ge tó þys[1] husle ne gangen ne to ðæm ordale, gif ge scyld on eow [ðe] witen, ðæs ðe eow [ðe] man tihð oððe on gewyrhtu*m* oððe on gewitnesse.

Gif men ferlice wyrde unsofte, oððe sprecan ne maege, halga him ðis wæter.

Wið egna sare sinc ðis.

Ðis mon sceall rede ofer drence *vel* ofer . . . . .[2]

. . . . . n scal reda ofer ða feta ðe ful infalleð.

To huntade 7 waeterhalguncge.

Salthalguncge to acrum *vel* to berenne *vel* in hvsvm.

Waeterhalgunc to ðon ilce.

Wið netena ungetionu 7 ðiofum.

1 y *over* u. 2 *illegible; Stevenson reads* smere (?).

Martyrology Fragment.

First published by Cockayne in his *Shrine*, p. 71 foll. from MS. Add. 23211 in the British Museum, consisting of two leaves, one containing the Martyrology fragment, the other having on one side the Genealogies which follow, on the other some astronomical notes in Latin. The MS. is evidently of the second half of the 9th century, which is confirmed by the West-Saxon genealogy not coming further down than Alfred. The genealogies being exclusively Saxon seems to point to that dialect, but both texts show several un-Saxon forms (*feringa, scealden; ceardicing, broðar*) alongside of specifically Saxon ones, such as *biscep, afierr, suæ;* perhaps the MS. is a copy of a West-Saxon original by a Kentish scribe.

The text of the Martyrology has been supplemented in italics from the later one given by Cockayne. Letters cut off on the margin are enclosed in ( ).

The cut off portions of the West-Saxon genealogy have been supplemented from that in the Parker Chronicle.

On ðone feowerteoðan dæg þæs monðes bið þara haligra gebroðra tid sancte Ualerianes 7 sancte Tiburties, ða Allmachius, Romeburge gerefa, nedde mid witum ðæt hi Criste wiðsocan. Ða hi þæt ne geþafodan, þa het he hi beheafdian. þa se man ðe þæt sceolde behealdan þæt hi man beheafdade, wepende 7 swergende he sæde þæt he gesawe heora sawla gongan ut of þæm lichoman fægre gefretwade, 7 þæt he gesawe Godes englas swa scinende swa sunne, 7 þa hi bæron to heofonum mid hiora fiðra flyhte; 7 se mon ða gele(fde) Gode, 7 he wæs *sungen on deað for Criste; 7 h(is) noma wæs Maximus.

On ðone eahtategðan dæg ðæs monðes (bið) ðæs halgan biscepes tid, *sancte* Eleutheri, (7 his) modor, ðære noma wæs *sancte* Anthiæ. He wæs (ðære) burge biscep ðe is nemned Mechania[1], in Ap(ulia) ðære mægðe, ah he geðrowade eft in Rom(e) martyrdóm for Criste. Adrianus se caser(e hine) ðreatade ðæt he Criste wiðsoce. Ða he ðæt (ne) walde, ða heht se casere gesponnan fiow(er) wildo hors to scride, 7 hine gebundenne in ð(æt scrid)

[1] ec *from* a.

*ásetton, ðæt ða wildan hors scealden iornan (on) hearde wegas in westenne, 7 him ða limo all (to)brecan. Ða cwom Godes engel of hiofonum, (7 ge)stillde ðæm horssum, 7 hio gelæddon ðæt scrid (on) hea dúne, ðær him cwom tó monigra cynn(a wil)deor, 7 wunedon mid hine, 7 ðonne he hóf (his) houd upp to hiofonum, ðonne hofon ða de(or he)ora fotas upp, 7 heredon god mid hine. Ð(a het) se casere his huntan hine ðær gefecca(n 7) hine mid sueorde ofslean. Ða cwóm stef(n of) hiofo[n]um, 7 cwæð: 'Cým, mín ðeow Eleuthe(rius), mine englas ðec lædað in ða hiofonlican (Hierusa)lem.' Ða feoll his modor ufan on his lic(homan), 7 cwæð: 'Mín sunu, gemyne ðu mec on ðære (ecean reste, 7) se casere hio heht gemartyria(n), 7 *God wuldriende heo ageaf hire gast.*

On ðone an 7 twentegðan dæg ðæs monðes bið þæs halgan anceran geleornes sancte Æþelwaldes. Se geset ancersetl on fearne ðæm ealonde ærest æfter Cuthbrihte ðæm halgan biscope, 7 æfter ðon ðe he tuelf gear ðær wunode ða eode he in ðone gefean ðære ecan eadinesse. Ðæs æðelwaldes wunder wæs ðæt he spræc to his liornæra sumum, 7 ða feringa oðsuigde he, suæ he hwæshwegu hercnade. Ða frægn se his ðegn hine[1] for hwon he suæ dede; ða cuæð he: 'Hú meahte ic bú somod ge in heofon geheran ge her spræcan?'

On ðone ðr[i]o 7 tuentegðan dæg ðæs monðes bið *sancte* Iorius tid, ðæs æðelan weres, ðone Datianus se casere seofon gear mid unasæcgendlicum[2] witum hine ðreade ðæt he Cris(te) wiðsóce, 7 he næfre hine ofersuiðan meahte; 7 ða æfter sefan[3] gearum heht he hine beheafdian. Ða he ða wæs læded to ðære beheafdunga, ða cuom fýr of heofonum, 7 forbęrnde ðone hæðnan casere, 7 alle ða ðe mid hine ær tintergedon ðone halgan wer. Ond he *sanctus* Georgius him to Dryhtne gebæd, 7 ðus cuæð: 'Hælende (C)rist, onfóh mi[n]um gaste! 7 ic ðec biddo ðæt suæ[4] (h)welc mon ðe mine gemynd on eorðan doe, ðonne afierr ðu from ðæs monnes húsum (æ)lce untrymnesse; ne him fiond sceððe, ne (h)ungor, ne monncwild; 7 gif monn minne (n)oman nemneð in ænigre frecennisse, oððe (o)n sǽ, oððe on siðfæte, ðonne gefylge se (ðin)*re mildheortnesse.*'

[1] e *er. after* i. [2] úná-; *accents in red ink.* [3] *space for one letter after* e. [4] e *nearly all cut off.*

Saxon Genealogies.

. . rice[1] 7 heold xxxvii wint, 7 vii monað; ond ða feng æ(ðelwulf) his sunu to, 7 heold xviiii healf gear; ond se æðe(lwulf) wæs ecgberhting, ecgberht ealhcmunding, ealh(mund) eabing, eaba eopping, eoppa ingilding, ingild co(enred)ing, coenred ceolwalding, ceolwald cuðuulfing, cuð(uulf) cuðwining, cuðwine *ceaulniing, ceaul[i]n cynnr(icing), cynnric crioding, criodo ceardicing; ond ða feng æðelbald his sunu to, 7 heold v gear; ða feng æðelbe(rht his) broðor to rice, 7 heold v gear; ða feng æðered his (broðor) to rice, 7 heold v gear, ða feng ælfred hira broðar (to rice), ond ða wæs agan his eldo xxiii wintra, ond ccc o(nd xcvi) wintra ðæs ðe his cynn ærest westseaxna bond o(n) walum geeodon.

de regibus orientalium seaxonum.

Offa sighering, sighere sigberhting, sigberht s(aweard)ing, saweard saberhting, saberht sledding, sle(dd) æscwining, æscwine offing, offa bedcing, bedca (sigefugling), sigefugl swæpping, swæppa antsecging, ants(ecg) gesecging, gesecg seaxneting.

item de regibus orientalium seaxonum.

Swiðred sigemunding, sigemund sigeharding, si(gehard) sebbing, sebbe seaxreding, seaxred sab(erhti)ng, saberht sledding.

item de regibus orientalium *seoxo(num).

Sigered sigericing, sigeric selereding, selered sigeberhting, sigeberht sigeb(aldi)ng, sigebald seleferðing, seleferð sigeferðing, sigeferð seaxing, seaxa sledding; ðonan forð . . .

Bede Glosses.

THE following glosses are written in the blank spaces at the end of each book in the MS. Cott. Tib. c. ii in a curiously twisted hand of the end of the ninth or beginning of the tenth century, apparently in the Kentish dialect, the last page in a rough cursive hand, quite different.

[1] *preceded by two lines of numbers.*

(fol. 3.) *Intemperans cupido* : mið ungemetlicre gitsunge.
exagitabat : styrede.
dementiam : ungemetnisse.
rethor : se [h]loðere[1].
serpere : snican.
liber edax sive utende · · ·.
farans (*pharus*) : bæcenfyr.
pontes : brycg.
stratae : st · · ·.
legatis : erendwrica.
adurit : bærnde.
obscuris cavernis : ðæm ðiostrum holum[2].
miserum anguiculum : ða earman nedran.
propulit : forðsceaf.
tollere : upahebban.
(*h*)*umo* : of foldan.
municeps : burgliod.
ex infima militiae : niðirlices compdomes.
(32 b.) *fertilitas* : wæstembiornis.
annonus : fodraðas.
cogunt : neddan.
funerum : hra.
jugulamur : we bioð stiocode.
invasisque : 7 gehergedum.
paupercula reliquia : ða earman lafe.
conroderet : gestread.
adficiens : dreccende.
ac famam : 7 ðone lisan.
investis (*f*) : ðæm reðum.
ac saltibus : 7 wudum.
retna aetis : nænig ældu.
adceleravit : geratade.
proprior : nior.
telaque : 7 strelas.
litigia : gecid.
uaemonibus : godwrecnissum.

[1] [hi]loðere?   [2] m *doubtful.*

diri sceleris : grimre synne.
contra inprobis : wið ðæm gemaum.
exitus : in siðas.
adjuncta : to geðioded.
defortii (*div.*) : towesnisse.
profusior : genihtsumra.
signius (*seg.*) : lætlicor.
superficiem : oferbliocan.
nonnulli : oft.
de miserandis reliquiis : of ðæm earmum lafum.
acerbatim : scearplice.
nunc : wilu*m*.
sane : cuðlice.
feda peste : fulre adle.
(58 b.) *ad succur*(*r*)*endum* : to gehelpenne.
caedebant : biotan.
nautarum : ðara nomementa.
et casu : 7 weas.
lassitudine : meðnisse.
pelagi : ðæs sæs.
baticinatio (*v*) : witedo[o]m.
per tribia (*v*) : ðorh wigas.
per rura : ðorh lond.
instar : onlicnis.
conflectum (*i*) : geflit.
conspicui : gesegenne.
tribunicae potestatis : alderdomes mȩhte.
ad(*ha*)*erentem* : æt cliðende.
capsulam : ceste.
evulsam : on[we]g alocene.
exultant : gefegan.
casualibus : ðæm fallendu*m*.
laquiis (*-eis*) : girenum.
palustria arundine : mið ðæm fenðacum.
tegebatur : wæs bewrigen.
slabris : windum.
(122 b.) *ma*(*c*)*hinam* : searwe.
repetitam : gesohte.

pernicitas : rædnis.
spolia : herereaf.
triumphant : sige fęston.
moliuntur : ðohton.
iter : siðfaet.
obtenueraδ (*t*) : ðynnade.
poplite : [h]omme.
adtrectat : grapade.
sucum : sea.
parumper : gewaer.
derutarum (*di-*) : gerorenra.
exterminia : ðara abreotnissa.
recente memoria : neowre gemynde.
calamitates : earfeðnisse.
et cladis : on waele.

VESPASIAN PSALTER.

THE Old English interlinear version of the Psalms contained in the Cottonian MS. Vespasian A. 1 is thus mentioned by Wanley in his Catalogue, p. 222: 'Psalterium D. Hieronymi Romanum elegantissime litteris capitalibus, in Anglia, annis abhinc circiter mille, ut videtur, scriptum et illuminatum, cui postea accedit interlineata versio Saxonica.

'Psalterio abscinduntur primus psalmus integer et pars secundi, nec non charta donationis Æthelbaldi R. Australium Saxonum, h. e. Merciorum, sive Suth-Anglorum (litteris capitalibus exarata) quae nunc habetur in prima pagina pretiosi libri collectionis cartarum qui inscribitur August. *II*.'

Of the portion of the MS. which precedes the psalter he says:

'Hucusque omnia scribuntur Latine litteris capitalibus tenuioribus, in *I*talia usitatis, a quibus ea quae in Anglia obtinebant paullum discrepant. Notandum quoque haec omnia ad amussim quadrare cum descriptione secundi psalterii quod ad Augustinum Cantuariensem transmisit Gregorius Magnus, uti supra videre licet pagg. 172 et 173.'

The reference is to his description of a MS. in the library of Trinity Hall, Cambridge:

'Cod. MS. in fol. grand. regnante Henrico V a monacho Abbatiae S. Augustini exaratus. In eo continetur historia fundationis et donationis monasterii S. Augustini, et ecclesiae Christi Cantuariae.

'Praeclarum hunc librum a me praedicandum censeo quod in eo describuntur codices quos S. Augustinus Episcopus Cant. ad se a Gregorio *I* Papa missos monasterio suo dedit, in quo, dum scriberetur hic codex, ut probabile est, extabant, et extitere deinceps usque ad tempus versi et direpti ejusdem monasterii, regnante Henrico Octavo.'

He then quotes the description of the books and enumeration of their contents given in the MS. It is quite clear that our MS. Vesp. A. 1 cannot be a copy of the Psalterium Augustini described in the Cambridge MS., for, although in both psalters the psalms are preceded by various miscellaneous matter, and followed by hymns, some of which are the same in both, there is in general a complete divergence.

Of the charter of Æthelbald, Wanley says in another place (p. 258):

'Haec carta litteris majusculis exaratur, et olim inserebatur in psalterio illo vetustissimo quod in hac bibliotheca inscribitur Vesp. A. 1, tandem autem, D. Rob. Cottono jubente, ex libro psalmorum exscindebatur, et hic una cum plurimis aliis affixa est.'

This charter (now marked Cott. Aug. *II*. 3) is an original one of 736, and bears every mark of a Mercian origin. Its handwriting, though uncial, is different from that of the Latin portion of the psalter, and is probably later.

The interlinear English gloss, extending also to the hymns at the end of the psalms, is mainly in a very fine hand, which cannot well be earlier or later than the first half of the ninth century, and this date is fully supported by the language, which shows a remarkably consistent type, uniformly but not excessively archaic. Some pages are glossed in a rougher but contemporary hand.

The dialect was, till quite lately, generally assumed to be Northumbrian, an opinion which will not bear the test of the most superficial comparison with the known Northumbrian texts. Dr. Murray in his 'Dialect of the Southern Counties of Scotland' was, *I* believe, the first to question it. In my 'Dialects of Old English' (Phil. Soc. Trans. 1875–6, p. 555), *I* claimed it to be Kentish, mainly on the ground of Wanley's assigning it to Canterbury, but also on account of the language. As we see, the external evidence points to Mercia, and if it could be proved that the charter was written on a blank page of the MS., and not merely bound up with it later, it would seem natural to assume at once that the later gloss is also Mercian. Yet there is no difficulty in supposing that the MS. may have been transferred to Canterbury any time between 736 and the beginning of the following century, and it will be safest to reserve the question of dialect till we come to the grammatical analysis of our texts.

The Latin text has been largely altered by erasures and otherwise, apparently in order to bring it more into conformity with the Vulgate readings and the conventional spellings.

In most cases the English gloss follows the original readings, which have, therefore, generally been restored as far as possible in my text. In those cases in which it agrees with the alterations, it is often doubtful whether the glosser may not have corrected the original reading himself by the context, as in 10. 5, *interrogant : frignað* with the *n* added later above the line: the original *interrogat*. is shown to be a plural by its subject *palpebrae*. The innumerable cases in which *-avit*=future has been altered to the regular *-abit* with the corresponding English gloss, as in *subsannabit : hyspeð* with the *b* on erasure, would seem at first sight to be cases of the glosser following the alteration, but as we sometimes find the unaltered *-avit* correctly glossed as a future (15. 9; 48. 16; 129. 5), it seems clear that he was accustomed to that spelling. The same *v* for *b* is frequent in *exacervaverunt*. In 90. 14 the future *speravit* has been wrongly glossed by the preterite *gehyhte*, the *v* having been afterwards erased and *b* substituted. Conversely, in 80. 17 the preterite was written with a *b*—*cibabit*, and consequently glossed with the English future *foedeð*, although the *b* has been erased and *v* substituted. These two cases are decisive. But 47. 8, where *conteres*, incorrectly made into *conterens* by the addition of *n*, is glossed *forðrę̄sten de*, seem equally decisive the other way. In 117. 35 the correct *prospera* has been made into *prosperare* by the addition of *re* in a cursive hand apparently the same as that of the gloss. Elsewhere the alterations are in the same uncial letters as the original, so that it is impossible to tell whether they are due to the glosser or not. The alterations are sometimes made by complete erasure and rewriting, sometimes only by partial alterations, the latter being apparently later than the former.

The innumerable alterations of the present endings *-is*, *-it(ur)* into the future *-es*, *-et(ur)* are evidently late, the *i* simply having three scratches added to it, so as to make it into a rough E. Examples are *loquitur* (2. 5), *perdis* (5. 7), *sedit* (9. 29), *abstrahit* (9. 30).

i for *e* is frequent in other unaccented syllables as well, as in *miserire* imper., *ori*, *nomini* abl., *cardinis* plur., *prodiat*, *periant*, *discendit*, *dilectatum*. In these cases the *i* has been altered to *e*, but in 10. 5 the sg. *sedis*, in 134. 10 the plural *fortis* have been kept unaltered. The converse *e* for *i* is also common, as in *perditiones* gen., *salutare*, *ore* abll., *oves* nom. sg., *sterelitatem*, *vendedisti*, especially in compound verbs, as in *intellege*, *intel-*

legere, dejeceret, sustenuit, eregens. ae for *e* occurs in *aequos, faciae* abl., in adverbs such as *vanae, supervacuae,* in *pretium,* and often in *conpraehendo.* A final *m* is often incorrectly added, as in *in magnificentiam* abl. (28. 4), *longitudinem* abl. (90. 16), *memoriam* nom. (108. 15). Among other spellings may be noted *bracchium* and *aput,* nearly always altered to *brachium* and *apud,* the omission of the *j* in *eicis, adiciat,* &c., the omission of the *s* in *exurgo* (*exsurgo* also occurring), *ammirabile, degluttivit.* Lastly, it may be noted that *os* very often has an acute accent, although there are none in the English gloss.

The English gloss contains many scribal errors, most of which, however, may be brought under a few definite groups, and are easily corrected.

The most remarkable peculiarity of the scribe is his tendency to omit not only single letters, but also syllables, and even groups of syllables. Thus we find *ðe(re), geh(yh)tað, forle(te)n, gefre(me)des, geswenced(nisse), soð(lice), Ef(rem),* some of which, especially the last but one, occur more than once. Among the omissions of single letters the most frequent is that of the *e* of *oe*: *socendra, socende, gemotes, toð,* the omission of the *o* being much less frequent: *gedrefde, sped.* Similar omissions occur in the other diphthongs: *ha(e)lu, gebra(e)dende, ma(e)hte; be(a)rn, sce(a)wað, de(a)ðes; ger(e)afien; h(e)ortum; we(o)rulde, cne(o)risse.* Doubled consonants are often simplified: *ic gebidu, eare, blisiað, from e, ic weoðu.* Final *m* is often omitted: *fro, ðeodu.* Final vowels are often dropped, even when they leave a single consonant behind: *streng(u), mong(e), ð(u), ð(a), n(e).* Initial letters are rarely dropped: *(n)oma, (u)sic.* The following are instances of the omission of one of two combined consonants: *(h)neapiu; ges(c)ild, s(c)eate; gereo(r)dnisse, gete(l)des; geli(m)plice, unbeore(n)dnesse, freo(n)d; cynin(g), mil(d)-heortnis; dus(t), gas(t)* (often); *rehtwi(s)nisse* (several times).

Some of these omissions may possibly correspond to the actual pronunciation, but it would evidently be hazardous to draw any positive inferences from the omissions of the MS., even when they occur more than once.

Additions of single letters are rare: *sa(l)wle, h(w)efie, sawul(f), onwend(e), syndri(n)g, of(f)ergeotul,* but there is a curious tendency to repeat monosyllables, such as *bið* (9. 24), *me, ðine.* In several cases (noticed in the text) what at first sight would be read *ie* appears to be only *e* with a tag before it.

Of substitutions, that of *d* for ð, as in *eordan, dreast, underdeodes, forweordað, det,* and (though less frequent) of ð for *d*, are so frequent that I have thought it unnecessary to star them. Of other errors the most important is a tendency to write *y* for *u*, as in *hyses, onscynedun,* the correct *u* having in some cases (67. 3; 77. 40) been written over the *y*. *u* for *y* in *forduttænde*. *s* for *f* in *ymbhwyrst, ester*. *e* for *o* in *ageten, recetunge* (=*roccetunge*). *c* for *t* in *gewicnade, gewicnendra*. There are also solitary instances of the interchange of *n* and *r*.

A frequent source of error is the repetition of part of the corresponding Latin word in the gloss, as in *montem* : *mont* (for *munt*), *conculcantes* : *fortreodendes* (for *-e*). Sometimes the whole of the Latin word is repeated, as in *nomen* : *nomen, meam* : *meam*. Often also the scribe has begun to write the Latin word and has then altered it into the English one. Thus we find *mare* : *sæ* with the *sæ* altered from an *m*, *tuae* : *ðine* with the ð altered from a *t*.

On the whole the gloss is accurate, such errors as *odorabunt* : *weorðiað* (113. 6), where *odorabunt* has been confused with *adorabunt*, being very rare. Sometimes, however, a case has been translated against the context, as in 105. 20, where the gen. sg. *vituli* has been glossed by the plural *calfur*.

Later glosses have occasionally been added in a hand apparently of the eleventh century. These I have put in the foot-notes.

The Vespasian Psalter was first published by the Surtees Society in 1843 (Anglo-Saxon and Early English Psalter), under the editorship of Mr. J. Stevenson. Mr. Stevenson's text abounds with such gross blunders, both in the English and Latin, as would lead an ordinary observer to suppose him to be entirely ignorant both of Old English and of Latin. He has also made many apparently deliberate alterations of the MS. text. Altogether his edition is a disgrace to English scholarship.

To save space, I have omitted the headings, which are never glossed. Stevenson follows the vulgate in counting them as the first verse of each psalm, and I have retained his numbering, to facilitate reference.

2.

1. *Quare fremuerunt gentes et populi meditati sunt inania*
2. *Astiterunt reges terrae et principes convenerunt in unum ad-*
versus Dominum et adversus Christum ejus 3. *Dirumpa-*
mus vincula eorum et projiciamus a nobis jugum ipsorum

se eardað in heofenum bismerað hie 7 dryhten hyspeð
4. *Qui habitat in caelis inridebit eos et Dominus subsannabit*

hie ðonne spriceð to him in eorre his 7 in hatheortnisse
eos 5. *Tunc loquitur ad eos in ira sua et in furore*

his ge-droefeð hie ic soðlice geseted ic eam cyning
suo conturbabit eos 6. *Ego autem constitutus sum rex*

from him ofer Sion *mont ðone halgan his bodiende
ab eo super Sion montem sanctum ejus praedicans

bibod dryhtnes dryhten cwæð to me sunu
praeceptum Domini 7. *Dominus dixit ad me Filius*

min ðu earð ic to dege ic cende ðec bide from me
meus es tu ego hodie genui te 8. *Postula a me*

7 ic sellu ðe ðeode erfeweardnisse ðine 7 onæhte ðine
et dabo tibi gentes hereditatem tuam et possessionem tuam

gemæru eorðan ðu reces hie in gerde *iserre 7 swe swe
terminos terrae 9. *Reges eos in virga ferrea et tamquam*

fęt lames ðu gebrices hie 7 nu cyningas ongeotað
vas figuli confringes eos 10. *Et nunc reges intellegite*

bi[o]ð gelærde alle ða ðe doemað eordan ðeowiað
erudimini omnes qui judicatis terram 11. *Servite*

dryhtne in ege 7 wynsumiað him mid cwaecunge[1]
Domino in timore et exultate ei cum tremore

gegripað ðylęs hwonne eorsie dryhten
12. *Adpraehendite disciplinam*[2] *ne quando irascatur Dominus*

7 ge forweorðen of wege ðonne beorneð in
et pereatis de via justa 13. *Cum exarserit in*

scortnisse eorre his eadge alle ða ðe getreowað in hine
brevi ira ejus beati omnes qui confidunt in eum

3.

dryhten hwet gemonigfaldade sindun ða ðe swencað mec
2. *Domine quid multiplicati sunt qui tribulant me*

[1] vel byfunge *added later.* [2] *glossed* styre, *later.*

monge arisað wið me monge cweoðað *salwle
multi insurgunt adversum me 3. *multi dicunt animae*

minre nis haelu[1] hire in *deo hire ðu soðlice
meae non est salus illi in Deo ejus 4. *Tu autem*

dryhten ondfenge min earð wuldur min ⁊ uphebbende heafud
Domine susceptor meus es gloria mea et exaltans caput

min mid[2] stefne minre to dryhtne ic cleopede ⁊
meum 5. *Voce mea ad Dominum clamavi et*

geherde mec of munte ðæm halgan his ic hneappade
exaudivit me de monte sancto suo 6. *Ego dormivi*

⁊ slepan ongon ⁊ ic eft aras forðon dryhten onfeng mec
et somnum coepi et resurrexi quoniam Dominus suscepit me

ne ondredu ic ðusend folces *ymsellendes me aris
7. *Non timebo milia populi circumdantis me exurge*

dryhten halne me doa god min forðon ðu sloge
Domine salvum me fac Deus meus 8. *Quoniam tu percussisti*

alle wiðerbrocan me butan intingan toeð synfulra
omnes adversantes mihi sine causa dentes peccatorum

ðu forðræstes dryhtnes is haelu ⁊ ofer folc ðin
conteruisti 9. *Domini est salus et super populum tuum*

bledsung ðin
benedictio tua

4.

midðy ic gecede ðe ðu geherdes me god rehtwisnisse minre
2. *Cum invocarem te exaudisti me Deus justitiae meae*

in [ge]swencednisse ðu gebręddes me mildsa me dryhten ⁊
in tribulatione dilatasti me Miserere mihi Domine et

geher gebed min bearn monnan hu longe *hwefie
exaudi orationem meam 3. *Filii hominum usque quo grave(s)*

on heortan to hwon lufiað ge idelnisse ⁊ soecað leasunge
corde ut quid diligitis vanitatem et queritis mendacium

weotað ðætte gemiclað dryhten ðone halgan his
4. *Scitote quoniam magnificavit Dominus sanctum suum*

dryhten gehereð me ðonne ic cleopiu to him eorsiað
Dominus exaudiet me dum clamavero ad eum 5. *Irascimini*

⁊ nyllað syngian ða ðe cweoðað in heortum eowrum
et nolite peccare qui dicitis in cordibus vestris

⁊ in bedcleofum eowrum bioð geinbryrde onsecgað
et in cubilibus vestris conpungimini 6. *Sacrificate*

[1] h *from* s.   [2] mid id.

onsegdnisse rehtwisnisse 7 gehyhtað in dryht*ne* monge
sacrificium justitiae et sperate in Domino Multi

cweoðað hwelc oteaweð us god getacnad is
dicunt Quis ostendit nobis bona 7. *Signatum est*

ofer us leht ondwlitan ðines dryht*en* ðu saldes blisse
super nos lumen vultus tui Domine Dedisti laetitiam

in heortan minre from tide hwętes wines 7 eles
in corde meo 8. *a tempore frumenti vini et olei*

his gemongfaldade[1] sindun in sibbe in ða ilcan
sui multiplicati sunt 9. *In pace in id ipsum*

ic*neapiu 7 gerestu forðon ðu dryht*en*
obdormiam et requiescam 10. *Quoniam tu Domine*

synderlice in hyhte gesettes me
singulariter in spe constituisti me

5.

word min mid earum onfoh dryht*en* onget cleopunge
2. *Verba mea auribus percipe Domine intellege clamorem*

mine behald . stefne gespreces mines *cynin min
meum 3. *intende voci orationis meae rex meus*

7 god min forðon to ðe ic *gebidu dryht*en*
et Deus meus 4. *Quoniam ad te orabo Domine*

on marne 7 ðu geheres stefne mine on marne ic ætstondu
mane et exaudies vocem mea(m)[2] 5. *Mane adstabo*

ðe 7 gesio forðon ne *wellende god unrehtwisnisse
tibi et videbo quoniam non volens Deus iniquitatem

ðu earð ne eardað neh ðe awerged ne
tu es 6. *Non habitabit juxta te malignus neque*

ðorhwuniað ða unręhtwisan biforan egum ðinum ðu fedest
permanebunt injusti ante oculos tuos 7. *Odisti*

dryht*en* alle ða ðe[3] wircað unrehtwisnisse ðu forspildes
Domine omnes qui operantur iniquitatem perdis

hie ða ða spreocað leasunge wer bloda 7 ðone fæcnan
eos qui loquuntur mendacium Virum sanguinum et dolosum

onscunað dryht*en* ic soðlice in mengu
abhominabitur Dominus 8. *Ego autem in multitudine*

mildheortnisse ðinre ic inga dryht*en* in hus ðin
misericordiae tuae introibo Domine in domum tuam

[1] e er *after second* g. [2] *cut off by binder.* [3] e *from some other letter.*

ic *gebidda to temple ðæm halgan ðinum in ege
adorabo ad templum sanctum tuum in timore

ðinum gelaed me dryht*en* in ðine rehtwisnisse fore
tuo 9. *Deduc me Domine in tua justitia propter*

feondum minum gerece in gesihðe ðinre weg minne
inimicos meos dirige in conspectu tuo viam meam

forðon nis in muðe heara soðfestnis heorte
10. *Quoniam non est in ore eorum veritas cor*

heara idel is byrgen open is hraece heara
eorum vanum est 11. *Sepulchrum patens est guttur eorum*

tungum heara *faccenlice dydun doem hie god gefallen
linguis suis dolose agebant judica illos Deus Decidant

from geðohtum heara efter mengu arleasnissa
a cogitationibus suis secundum multitudinem impietatum

heara onweg adrif hie forðon onscunedon ðe dryht*en*
eorum expelle eos quoniam exacervaverunt te Domine

7 blissien alle ða gehyhtað in ðe in ecnisse
12. *Et laetentur omnes qui sperant in te in aeternum*

gefioð 7 ðu ineardas in him 7 wuldriað in ðe
exultabunt et inhabitabis in eis et gloriabuntur in te

alle ða ðe lufiað noman ðinne forðon ðu dryht*en*
omnes qui diligunt nomen tuum 13. *Quoniam tu Domine*

ðu bledsas ðone rehtwisan dryht*en* swe swe mid scelde godes
benedices justum Domine ut scuto bonae

willan dines ðu gebegades usic
voluntatis tuae coronasti nos

6.

dryhten nales in eorre ðinum ðu dreast me ne in
2. *Domine ne in ira tua arguas me neque in*

hatheortnisse ðinre ðu ðreast[1] me mildsa me
furore tuo corripias me 3. *Miserire mihi*

dryht*en* forðon untrum ic eam hael me dryht*en* forðon
Domine quoniam infirmus sum sana me Domine quoniam

gedroefed sindun all ban min 7 sawl min
conturbata sunt omnia ossa mea 4. *et anima mea*

gedroefed is swiðe 7 ðu dryht*en* hu longe
turbata est valde Et tu Domine usque quo

[1] vel cid *added later*.

gecer 7 genere sawle mine halne me do
5. *convertere et eripe animam meam salvum me fac*

fore mildheortnisse ðine forðon nis in
propter misericordiam tuam 6. *Quoniam non est in*

ðeaðe se gemyndig sie ðin in helle soðlice hwelc
morte qui memor sit tui in inferno autem quis

ondetteð *ðæ ic won in geamrunge minre ic ðwea
confitebitur tibi 7. *Laboravi in gemitu meo lavabo*

ðorh syndrie nęht bed min mid tearum strene mine
per singulas noctes lectum meum lacrimis stratum meum

ic wetu gedroefed is fore eorre ege min
rigabo 8. *Turbatus est prae ira oculus meus*

ic aldade betwih alle feond mine gewitað
inveteravi inter omnes inimicos meos 9. *Discedite*

from me alle ða wircað unrehtwisnisse forðon
a me omnes qui operamini iniquitatem quoniam

geherde dryht*en* stefne wopes mines geherde
exaudivit Dominus vocem fletus mei 10. *Exaudivit*

dryht*en* boene mine dryht*en* gebed min
Dominus deprecationem meam Dominus orationem meam

genom scomien 7 sien gedroefde alle feond
adsumpsit 11. *Erubescant et conturbentur omnes inimici*

mine sien forcerred on bec 7 scomièn swiðe hreðlice
mei avertantur retrorsum et erubescant valde velociter

7.

dryht*en* god min in ðe ic gehyhte gefrea me from
2. *Domine Deus meus in te speravi libera me ab*

allu*m* oehtendu*m* me 7 genere me(c)[1] ðyles
omnibus persequentibus me et eripe m(e)[1] 3. *Ne*

æfre geslæcce[2] swe swe lea sawle mine ðonne nis
quando rapiat ut leo animam meam dum non est

se ðe alese ne se ðe hie hale gedoe dryht*en*
qui redimat neque qui salvum faciat 4. *Domine*

god min gif ic dyde ðis gif is unrehtwisnis in
Deus meus si feci istud si est iniquitas in

hondum minum gif ic agald ðaem geldendum me
manibus meis 5. *Si reddidi retribuentibus mihi*

[1] *cut off by binder.* [2] cce *in a diff. ink.*

yfel ic gefallu bi gewyrhtum from feondum minum
mala decidam merito ab inimicis meis

idelhende oehteð se feond sawle mine 7
inanis 6. *Persequatur inimicus animam meam et*

ge[g]ripeð hie 7 fortrideð in eorðan lif min 7
conpraehendat eam et conculcet in terra vitam meam et

wuldur min in dust gelaedeð aris dryhten
gloriam meam in pulverem deducat 7. *Exurge Domine*

in eorre ðinum 7 hefe up in endum feonda ðinra
in ira tua et exaltare in finibus inimicorum tuorum

aris dryhten god min in bebode ðæt ðu bibude
Exurge Domine Deus meus in praecepto quod mandasti

7 gesomnunge folca ymbseleð ðe 7 fore
8. *et synagoga populorum circumdabit te et propter*

ðissum in heanisse gaa eft dryhten doem folc
hanc in altum regredere 9. *Domine judica populos*

doem mec dryhten efter rehtwisnisse minre 7
judica me Domine Secundum justitiam meam et

efter unsceðfulnisse honda minra ofer me
secundum innocentiam manuum mearum super me

sie fornumen nið ðeara synfulra 7 gerece
10. *Consumetur nequitia peccatorum et dirige*

ðone rehtwisan smegende heortan et eðre god rehtwisne
justum scrutans corda et renes Deus Justum

fultum minne from dryhtne se hale gedoeð
11. *adjutorium meum a Domino qui salvos facit*

ða rehtan on heortan god doema rehtwis strong 7
rectos corde 12. *Deus judex justus fortis et*

longmod ah eorsað ðorh syndrie dægas
longanimis nunquid irascitur per singulos dies

nemne ge sien gecerde sweord his cweceð bogan
13. *nisi convertamini gladium suum vibrabit Arcum*

his ðeneð 7 gearwað ðone 7 in him gearwað
suum tetendit et paravit illum 14. *et in ipso paravit*

featu deaðes strelas his *beornedum[1] gefremede
vasa mortis sagittas suas ardentibus effecit

sehðe cenneð unrehtwisnisse ge:ecnað sar 7
15. *Ecce parturit injustitiam concepit dolorem et*

[1] u orer e.

cenneð unrehtwisnisse seað ontynde 7 dalf
peperit iniquitatem 16. *Lacum aperuit et effodit*

ðone ingefe[o]l in seað ðone ðe he dyde sie gecerred
eum incidit in foveam quam fecit 17. *Convertetur*

sar his in heafde his 7 in hnolle his unrehtwisnis
dolor ejus in capite ejus et in vertice ejus iniquitas

his astigeð ic ondettu dryhtne efter rehtwisnisse
ejus discendit 18. *Confitebor Domino secundum justitiam*

his 7 ic singu noman dryht*nes* ðæs hestan
ejus et psallam nomini Domini altissimi

8.

dryht*en* dryht*en* ur hu wundurlic is noma
2. *Domine Dominus noster quam ammirabile est nomen*

ðin in alre eorðan forðon upahefen is
tuum in universa terra Quoniam elevata est

micelnis ðin ofer heofenas of muðe cilda
magnificentia tua super caelos 3. *ex ore infantium*

7 milcdeondra ðu gefremedes lof fore feondum ðinum
et lactantium perfecisti laudem Propter inimicos tuos

ðæt ðu toweorpe feond 7 gescildend[1] forðon
ut destruas inimicum et defensorem 4. *Quoniam*

ic gesie heofenas werc fingra ðinra monan 7
videbo caelos opera digitorum tuorum lunam et

steorran ða ðu gesteaðulades hwet is mon ðæt
stellas quas tu fundasti 5. *Quid est homo quod*

gemyndig ðu sie his oððe sunu monnes forðon ðu neosas
memor es ejus aut filius hominis quoniam visitas

hine ðu gewonedes hine hwoene laessan from englum
eum 6. *Minuisti eum paulo minus ab angelis*

mid wuldre 7 mid are ðu gebegades hine 7
gloria et honore coronasti eum 7. *et*

gesettes hine ofer werc honda ðinra
constituisti eum super opera manuum tuarum

all ðu underdeodes under fotum his scep 7 oxan
8. *Omnia subjecisti sub pedibus ejus oves et boves*

all ec ðon 7 netenu feldes fuglas heofenes
universa insuper et pecora campi 9. *Volucres caeli*

[1] i *over dotted* e.

7 fiscas saes ða geondgað stige saes dryht*en*
et pisces maris qui perambulant semitas maris 10. *Domine*

dryht*en* ur hu wundurlic is noma ðin in
Dominus noster quam ammirabile est nomen tuum in

alre eorðan
universa terra

9.

ic ondetto ðe dryhten in alre heortan minre ic secgo
2. *Confitebor tibi Domine in toto corde meo narrabo*

all wundur ðin ic biom geblissad 7 ic gefie in
omnia mirabilia tua 3. *Laetabor et exultabo in*

ðe 7 singu noman ðinum ðu hehsta in
te et psallam nomini tuo altissime 4. *In*

forcerringe *fienda min on bec bioð geuntrumad 7
convertendo inimicum meum retrorsum infirmabuntur et

forweordað from onsiene ðinre forðon ðu dydest
perient a faciae tua 5. *Quoniam fecisti*

dom minne 7 intingan minne ðu sites ofer
judicium meum et causam meam sedis super

ðrymseld ðu doemes efennisse ðu ðreades ðeode
thronum qui judicas aequitatem 6. *Increpasti gentes*

7 forweorðed se arleasa noman heara ðu adilgades in
et periet impius nomen eorum delisti in

ecnisse in weoruld weorulde feond asprungun
aeternum et in saeculum saeculi 7. *Inimici defecerunt*

mid sweorde in ende 7 cestre heara ðu towurpe
framea in finem et civitates eorum destruxisti

forwearð gemynd heara mid swoege 7 dryht*en*
Peri(i)t memoria eorum cum sonitu 8. *et Dominus*

in ecnesse ðorhwunað gearwade in dome seld
in aeternum permanet Paravit in judicio sedem

his 7 he doemeð ymbhwyrft earðan in
suam 9. *et ipse judicabit orbem terrae in*

efennisse doemeð folc mid rehtwisnisse 7
aequitate Judicabit populos cum justitia 10. *et*

geworden is dryht*en* geberg ðearfena fultum in
factus est Domi[illegible]us refugium pauperum Adjutor in

gelimplicnissum in geswencednisse 7 *gehtað in ðe
oportunitatibus in tribulatione 11. *et sperent in te*

alle ðа cunnun noman ðinne forðon ðu ne forletes
omnes qui noverunt nomen tuum Quoniam non dereli(n)ques

ða soecendan ðe dryhten singað dryhtne se
quaerentes te Domine 12. *psallite Domino qui*

eardað in Sion secgað betwih ðeode wundur his
habitat in Sion Adnuntiate inter gentes mirabilia ejus

forðon soecende blod heara gemynd
13. *quoniam requirens sanguinem eorum memoratus*

is 7 nis ofergeotol gebed ðearfena
est et non est oblitus orationem pauperum

mildsa me dryhten 7 geseh eaðmodnisse mine
14. *Miserire mihi Domine et vide humilitatem meam*

of fiendum minum ðu uphest mec of geatum
de inimicis meis 15. *qui exaltas me de portis.*

deaðes ðæt ic secge all lofu ðin in geatum
mortis ut annuntiem omnes laudes tuas in portis.

doehter *Sine ic gefio in haelu ðinre gefestnade
filiae Sion 16. *Exultabo in salutari tuo infixae*

sindon ðeode in forwyrd ða dydun in *grin
sunt gentes in interitum quem fecerunt in laqueo

ðissum ða gedegladon gegripen is fot heara
isto quem occultaverunt conpraehensus est pes eorum

oncnaweð dryhten dryhtdomas donde in wercum
17. *Cognoscitur Dominus judicia faciens in operibus*

honda his bifongen bið se synfulla
manuum suarum conpraehensus est peccator

bioð gecerde ða synfullan in helle alle ðeode
18. *Convertantur peccatores in infernum omnes gentes*

ða ðe ofergeoteliað dryhten forðon nales in
quae obliviscuntur Dominum 19. *Quoniam non in*

ende ofergeotulnis bið ðearfena geðyld ðearfena ne
finem oblivio erit pauperum patientia pauperum non

forweorðeð in ende aris dryhten ne
peribit in finem 20. *Exurge Domine non*

meg mon sien doemed ðeode in gesihðe ðinre
praevaleat homo judicentur gentes in conspectu tuo

gesete dryhten aee ladtow ofer hie ðæt witen
21. *Constitue Domine legislatorem super eos ut sciant*

ðeode ðette men hie sindun tohwon dryhten
gentes quoniam homines sunt 22. *Ut quid Domine*

gewite ðu feor ðu forsist in gemalicnissum in geswen-
recessisti longe despicis in opportunitatibus in tribu-

cednisse ðonne oferhygdgað se arleasa bið inæled[1]
latione **23.** *Dum superbit impius incenditur*

ðearfa bioð bifongne in geðohtum heara ða
pauper conpraehenduntur in cogitationibus suis quas

hie ðencað forðon bið hered se synfulla in lustum
cogitant **24.** *Quoniam laudatur peccator in desideriis*

sawle his 7 se ða unrehtan doeð bið[2] bledsad
animae suae et qui iniqua gerit benedicitur

bismerað dryhten se synfulla efter mengu
25. *Irritavit Dominum peccator secundum multitudinem*

*eare his he ne soeceð nis god in gesihðe
irae suae non inquiret **26.** *Non est Deus in conspectu*

his bioð besmiten wegas his in alle tid bioð afirred
ejus polluuntur viae ejus in omni tempore Auferuntur

domas ðine from onsiene his allra fienda his
judicia tua a facie ejus omnium inimicorum suorum

waldeð cweð soðlice in heortan his ne biom
dominabitur **27.** *Dixit enim in corde suo Non*

ic onstyred of cneorisse in cneorisse butan yfle
movebor de generatione in generationem sine malo

ðes muð awergednisse 7 bitternisse ful is 7
28. *Cujus os maledictione et amaritudine plenum est et*

facne under tungan his gewin 7 sar siteð in
dolo Sub lingua ejus labor et dolor **29.** *sedit in*

searwum mid ðæm weoligum in degulnissum det he ofsle
insidiis cum divitibus in occultis ut interficiat

ðone unscyldgan egan his in ðearfan gelociað
innocentem **30.** *Oculi ejus in pauperem respiciunt*

setað in degulnisse swe swe lea in bedcleofan h[i]s
insidiatur in occulto sicut leo in cubili suo

setað þæt he geræafie ðearfan gereafian ðearfan ðonne
Insidiatur ut rapiat pauperem rapere pauperem dum

he atið hine in gerene his geeaðmodað hine onhęldeð
abstrahit eum **31.** *in laqueo suo humiliabit eum inclinabit*

hine 7 falleð ðonne he waldeð ðearfan cweð soðlice in
se et cadet dum dominabitur pauperi **32.** *Dixit enim in*

¹ inælled, *second* l *dotted*. ² bið *twice*.

his heortan ofergeotul is god forcerreð onsiene his ðæt
corde suo Oblitus est Deus avertit faciem suam ne

he ne gese oð ende aris dryhten god min 7
videat usque in finem 33. *Exurge Domine Deus meus et*

sie upahefen hond ðin ne ofergeotela ðu ðearfena in ende
exaltetur manus tua ne obliviscaris pauperum in finem

forðon bismirað se arleasa dryhten cwæð soðlice
34. *Propter quid irritavit impius Dominum dixit enim*

in heortan his ne soeceð god ðu gesist ðætte ðu
in corde suo Non requirit Deus 35. *Vides quoniam tu*

gewin 7 sar ðu sceawas ðæt ðu selle hie in honda ðine
laborem et dolorem consideras ut tradas eos in manus tuas

ðe soðlice *forlen is ðearfa feadurleasum ðu bist fultum
tibi enim derelictus est pauper pupillo tu eris adjutor

forðræst earm ðes synfullan 7 ðes awergdan bið soht
36. *Contere bracchium peccatoris et maligni requiretur*

scyld his ne bið gemoeted ricsað dryhten in
delictum ejus nec invenietur 37. *Regnabit Dominus in*

ecnisse 7 in weoruld weorulde forweorðað ðeode of
aeternum et in saeculum saeculi peribitis gentes de

eorðan his lust ðearfena geherde dryhten
terra ejus ·38· *Desiderium pauperum exaudivit Dominus*

lustas heortan heara geherde eare ðin doem
desideria cordis eorum exaudivit auris tua 39. *Judicare*

ðæm freondleasan 7 ðæm heanan ðætte no tosette. mae
pupillo et humili ut non adponat ultra

*gemicla hine mon ofer eorðan
magnificare se homo super terram

10.

in dryhtne ic getreowu hu cweaðað ge to minre sawle
2. *In Domino confido quomodo dicitis animae meae*

fer in *mont swe swe spearwa forðon sehde ða
Transmigra in montem sicut passer. 3. *Quoniam ecce pec-*

synfullan ðenedon bogan gearwadon strelas heara in cocere
catores tetenderunt arcum paraverunt sagittas suas in faretra

ðæt hie scoteden[1] in degelnisse ða rehtan on heortan forðon
ut sagittent in obscuro rectos corde 4. *Quoniam*

[1] d *from half-finished* n.

ða ðu *gefredes hie towurpun se rehtwisa soðlice hwęt dyde he
quae perfecisti destruxerunt justus autem quid fecit

dryht*en* in temple ðæm halgan his dryht*en* in heofene seld
5. *Dominus in templo sancto suo Dominus in caelo sedis*

his egan his in ðearfan gelociað bregas his frignað
ejus Oculi ejus in pauperem respiciunt palpebrae ejus interro-

bearn monna dryht*en* frigneð ðone rehtwisan 7
gant filios hominum 6. *Dominus interrogat justum et*

ðone arleasan se soðlice lufað unrehtwisnisse fiað sawle
impium qui autem diligit iniquitatem odit animam

his rineð ofer ða synfullan giren fyres 7 swefelrec 7
suam 7. *Pluet super peccatores laqueos ignis et sulphur et*

gast ysta dael calices heara forðon rehtwis
spiritus procellarum pars calicis eorum 8. *Quoniam justus*

dryht*en* 7 rehtwisnisse lufað rehtwisnesse gesið ondwleota his
Dominus et justitiam dilexit aequitatem vidit vultus ejus

11.

halne me doo dryht*en* forðon asprong se halga forðon
2. *Salvum me fac Domine quoniam defecit sanctus quoniam*

gewonade sind soðfestnisse from bearnum monna ða idlan
diminutae sunt veritates a filiis hominum 3. *Vana*

spreocende is anra gehwelc to ðæm nestan his welure faecne in
locutus est unusquisque ad proximum suum labia dolosa in

heortan 7 heortan spreocende sindun ða yflan tostrigdeð
corde et corde locuti sunt mala 4. *Disperdat*

dryhten alle weolure faecne 7 tungan yfel spreocende
Dominus universa labia dolosa et linguam maliloquam

ða cwedun tungan ure we micliað weolre ure
5. *Qui dixerunt Linguam nostram magnificabimus labia nostra*

from us sindun hwelc ur is dryht*en* , fore
a nobis sunt quis noster est Dominus 6. *Propter*

ermðe weðlena 7 geamrunge ðearfena nu ic arisu cwið
miseriam inopum et gemitum pauperum nunc exurgam dicit

dryht*en* ic setto ofer hęlu mine getrewlice ic dom in
Dominus Ponam super salutare meum fiducialiter agam in

hine gesprec dryhtnes gesprec clæne seolfur fyre
eo 7. *Eloquia Domini eloquia casta argentum igne*

amearad earðan geclasnad seofenfaldlice ðu dryhten
examinatum terrae purgatum septuplum 8. *Tu Domine*
*aldes usic 7 gehaldes usic from cneorisse ðisse in ecnisse
servabis nos et custodies nos a generatione hac in aeternum
in ymbhwyrfte ða arleasan gongað efter hehnisse
9. *In circuitu impii ambulant secundum altitudinem*
ðinre ðu gemonigfaldades bearn monna
tuam multiplicasti filios hominum

12.

hu longe dryhten ofergeotulas ðu mec in ende hu longe
Usque quo Domine oblivisceris me in finem quousque
acerres ðu onsiene ðine from me hu longe settu ic
avertis faciem tuam a me 2. *Quam diu ponam*
geðaeht in saule mine sar, in heortan minre ðorh deg
consilium in animam meam dolorem in corde meo per diem
hu longe bið upahefen se feond min ofer mec geloca
3. *Usque quo exaltabitur inimicus meus super me* 4. *respice*
7 geher me dryhten god min inliht egan min ne
et exaudi me Domine Deus meus Inlumina oculos meos ne
æfre ic aslepe in deaðe ne æfre cweðe feond
umquam obdormiam in mortem 5. *Ne quando dicat inimicus*
min ic strongade wið him ða swencað me gefiað
meus Praevalui adversus eum Qui tribulant me exultabunt
gif onstyred ic beam ic soðlice in ðinre *mildhertnisse
si motus fuero 6. *ego autem in tua misericordia*
ic gehyhtu gefið heorte min in haelu ðinre ic singu
sperabo Exultabit cor meum in salutari tuo cantabo
dryhtne se god selð me 7 ic singu noman ðinum
Domino qui bona tribuit mihi et psallam nomini tuo
ðu hehsta
Altissime

13.

cweð se unwisa in his heortan nis god gewemde sindun
Dixit insipiens in corde suo Non est Deus Corrupti sunt
7 onscuniendlice gewordne sind in lustum heara nis
et abominabiles facti sunt in voluntatibus suis Non est
se ðe doe god nis oð enne dryhten
qui faciat bonum non est usque ad unum 2. *Dominus*

of heofene forðlocað ofer bearn monna ðæt he gese hweðer
de caelo prospexit super filios hominum ut videat si

sie ongeotende oððe soecende god alle onhaeldon
est intelligens aut requirens Deum 3. *Omnes declinaverunt*

somud unnytte gewordne werun nis se ðe doe god
simul inutiles facti sunt non est qui faciat bonum

nis oð enne byrgen open is hraecae heara
non est usque ad unum Sepulchrum patens est guttur eorum

tungum heara faecenlice dydun atur nedrena under
linguis suis dolose agebant venenum aspidum sub

weolerum heara ðeara muð awergednisse 7 bitternisse
labiis eorum Quorum os maledictione et amaritudine

ful bið hreðe foet heara to ageotenne blod
plenum est veloces pedes eorum ad effundendum sanguinem

forðrę̨stednis 7 ungeselignis in wegum heara 7 weg sibbe ne
Contritio et infelicitas in viis eorum et viam pacis non

oncneowun nis ege godes biforan egum heara
cognoverunt Non est timor Dei ante occulos eorum 4.

ahne oncnawað alle ða ða wircað unrehtwisnisse ða
nonne cognoscent omnes qui operantur iniquitatem Qui

forswelgad folc min swe mete hlafes god ne
devorant plebem meam sicut escam panis 5. *Deum non*

gecedun der *forhtaðum mid ege ðer ne wes ege
invocaverunt illic trepidaverunt timore ubi non erat timor

forðon god in cneorisse ðere rehtan is geðaeht weðlan
6. *Quoniam Deus in generatione justa est consilium inopis*

ðu gescendes forðon god hyht his is hwelc seleð ofer
confudisti quia Deus spes ejus est 7. *Quis dabit ex*

Sion haelu Israel ðonne forcerreð dryhten heftned folces
Sion salutare Israhel dum avertit Dominus captivitatem plebis

his blissað 7 gefið
suae laetetur Jacob et exultet Israhel

14.

dry[h]ten hwelc eardað in selegescote ðinum oððe hwelc
Domine quis habitabit in tabernaculo tuo aut quis

gerested in munte ðæm halgan ð[i]num se ingę̨ð
requiescit in monte sancto tuo 2. *Qui ingreditur*

butan womme 7 wirceð rehtwisnisse se spriceð
sine macula et operatur justitiam 3. *Qui loquitur*
soðfestnisse in heortan his 7 nis facæn in tungan his
veritatem in corde suo et non egit dolum in lingua sua
ne he dyde ðæm nestan his yfel 7 edwit ne onfeng
Nec fecit proximo suo malum et opprobrium non accepit
wið ðæm nestan his to nowihte gelaeded bið in
adversus proximum suum 4. *Ad nihilum deductus est in*
gesihðe his se awergda ondredende soðlice *dryten gemiclað
conspectu ejus malignus timentes autem Dominum magnificat
se swereð ðæm nestan his 7 ne *bswac hine se feh
Qui jurat proximo suo et non decepit eum 5. *qui pecuniam*
his ne salde to westemscette 7 gefe ofer ðone unsceðfullan
suam non dedit ad usuram et munera super innocentem
ne onfeng se doeð ðas ne bið he onstyred in ecnisse
non accepit Qui facit haec non commovebitur in aeternum

15.

gehald me dryhten forðon in de ic gehyhte ic cweð
Conserva me Domine quoniam in te speravi 2. *dixi*
to dryhtne god min ðu earð forðon goda minra ðu ne
Domino Deus meus es tu quoniam bonorum meorum non
biðearft halge ða in eorðan sindun his gewundrade
indiges 3. *Sancti qui in terra sunt ejus mirificavit*
alle willan mine bitwih hie gemonigfaldade sindun
omnes voluntates meas inter illos 4. *Multiplicatae sunt*
soðlice medtrymnisse heara efter ðon hreaðedon ne
enim infirmitates eorum postea acceleraverunt Non
gesomniu ic gesomnunge heara of blodum ne gemyndig
congregabo conventicula eorum de sanguinibus nec memor
ic biom nomena heara ðorh weolure mine dryhten dael
ero nominum illorum per labia mea 5. *Dominus pars*
erfewordnisse minre 7 celces mines ðu earð ðu gesettes me
hereditatis meae et calicis mei tu es qui restituisti mihi
erfeweardnisse mine rapas gefeollun me in berhtnisse
hereditatem meam 6. *Funes ceciderunt mihi in praeclaris*
7 soðlice erfeweardnis min berht is me ic bledsiu
et enim hereditas mea praeclara est mihi 7. *Benedicam*

dryhten se me seleð ondget ec ðon · 7 oð
Dominum qui mihi tribuit intellectum insuper et usque ad

nẹht ðreadun me eðre mine ic foresaeh dryhten
noctem increpaverunt me renes mei 8. *Providebam Dominum*

in gesihðe minre aa forðon to ðere *swiðra is me ne
in conspectu meo semper quoniam a dextris est mihi ne

biom ic onstyred fore ðissum gelustfullad is heorte min
commovear 9. *Propter hoc dilectatum est cor meum*

7 gefilht tunge min ec ðon 7 flęsc min gereste𝑑 in
et exultavit lingua mea insuper et caro mea requiescit in

hyhte forðon ne *forletesde sawle mine in helle
spe 10. *Quoniam non derelinques animam meam in inferno*

ne ðu seles ðone halgan ðinne gesean gebrosnunge cuðe
nec dabis sanctum tuum videre corruptionem 11. *Notas*

me ðu dydest wegas lifes ðu gefylles me blisse mid
mihi fecisti vias vitae adimplebis me laetitia cum

ondwleotan ðinum gelustfullunge in ðere swiðran ðinre oð
vultu tuo delectationes in dextera tua usque

ende
in finem

16.

geher dryhten rehtwisnisse mine bihald boene
Exaudi Domine justitiam meam intende deprecationem

mine mid earum onfoh gebed min nales in weolerum
meam Auribus percipe orationem meam non in labiis

faecnum of ondwlitan ðinum dom minne forðyppeð
dolosis 2. *de vultu tuo judicium meum prodiat*

egan min gesiað efennisse ðu acunnadest heortan mine
oculi mei videant aequitatem 3. *Probasti cor meum*

7 neasades on næht mid fyre me amearedes 7 nis gemoeted
et visitasti nocte igne me examinasti et non est inventa

in me unrehtwisnis ðætte he ne sprece muð min *wirc
in me iniquitas 4. *Ut non loquatur os meum opera*

monna fore wordum weolura ðinra ic heold weagas
hominum propter verba labiorum tuorum ego custodivi vias

ða heardan gefreme gongas mine in stigum ðinum ðæt ne
duras 5. *Perfice gressos meos in semitis tuis ut non*

sien onwende sweðe mine ic cleapede forðon
moveantur vestigia mea 6. *Ego clamavi quoniam*

ðu geherdes me god onhæld eare ðin me 7 geher word
exaudisti me Deus inclina aurem tuam mihi et exaudi verba

min gewundra *mildheornisse ðine se hale gedoest
mea 7. *Mirifica misericordias tuas qui salvos facis*

ða gehyhtendan in ðec from ðæm wiðstondendum ðere swiðra[1]
sperantes in te 8. *a resistentibus dexterae*

ðinre gehald mec dryht*en* swe swe sean egan under scuan
tuae Custodi me Domine ut pupillam oculi sub umbra

fiðra ðinra *gesild me from onsiene arleasra ða me
alarum tuarum protege me 9. *a faciae impiorum qui me*

swencton fiond mine sawle mine ymbsaldun
adflixerunt Inimici mei animam meam circumdederunt

smeoru his bilucun muð heara spreocende wes in
10. *adipem suum concluserunt os eorum locutum est in*

oferhygde aweorpende me nu ymbsaldun me egan
superbia 11. *Projicientes me nunc circumdederunt me oculos*

heara gesetton onhældan in eorðan onfengun me
suos statuerunt declinare in terram 12. *Susceperunt me*

swe swe lea gearu to herehyðe 7 swe swe hwelp leon
sicut leo paratus ad praedam et sicut catulus leonis

eardiende in degulnissum aris dryht*en* forecym hie 7
habitans in abditis 13. *Exurge Domine praeveni eos et*

forcer hie genere sawle mine from ðæm arleasan sweorde
subverte eos eripe animam meam ab impio frameam

feonda of honda *ðinra dryht*en* from feam from eorðan
14. *inimicorum de manu tua Domine a paucis a terra*

todael hie 7 gescrenc hie in life heara of degelnissum
dispertire eos et supplanta eos in vita ipsorum De absconditis

ðinum gefylled is womb[1] heara gereorde sind ða swinnan 7
tuis adimpletus est venter eorum saturati sunt porcina et

forleortun ða to lafe werun lytlingum heara ic soðlice
reliquerunt quae superfuerunt parvulis suis 15. *Ego autem*

mid rehtwisnisse oteawu in gesihðe ðinre ic biom gereorded
cum justitia apparebo in conspectu tuo satiabor

ðonne bið gesweotulad wuldur ðin
dum manifestabitur gloria tua

[1] a *over dotted* e. [2] m *over* n.

17.

ic lufiu ðe dryhten megen min dryhten trymenis
2. *Dilegam te Domine virtus mea* 3. *Domine firmamentum*

min 7 geberg min 7 gefrigend min god min fultum
meum et refugium meum Et liberator meus Deus meus adjutor

min ic gebyhtu in hine gescildend min 7 horn haelu minre
meus sperabo in eum Protector meus et cornu salutis meae

fultum min hergende ic gecegu dryhten 7 from
adjutor meus 4. *laudans invocabo Dominum et ab*

feondum minum hal ic biom ymbsaldon me geamrunge
inimicis meis salvus ero 5. *Circumdederunt me gemitus*

deaðes 7 burnan unrehtwisnisse gedroefdon me sar
mortis et torrentes iniquitatis conturbaverunt me 6. *Dolores*

helle ymbsaldon me forecwomon me gerene deaðes 7
inferni circumdederunt me praevenerunt me laquei mortis et

in geswencednisse minre ic gecede dryhten 7 to gode
7. *in tribulatione mea invocavi Dominum et ad Deum*

minum ic cleopede 7 he geherde of temple ðæm hålgan his
meum clamavi Et exaudivit de templo sancto suo

stefne mine 7 cleopung min in gesihðe his ineode in
vocem meam et clamor meus in conspectu ejus introivit in

earan his 7 onstyred wes 7 cwęcede eorðe 7
aures ejus 8. *Et commota est et contremuit terra et*

steaðelas munta gedroefde sind 7 onstyrede sind forðon
fundamenta montium conturbata sunt et commota sunt quoniam

eorre[1] is him god astag rec in eorre his 7 fyr
iratus est eis Deus 9. *Ascendit fumus in ira ejus et ignis*

from onsiene his born colu onęlde sind from h[i]m
a faciae ejus exardescit Carbones succensi sunt ab eo

7 he onhaelde heofenas 7 ofdune astag 7 dimnis under
et 10. *inclinavit caelos et discendit et caligo sub*

fotum his 7 astag ofer cerubim 7 fleg
pedibus ejus 11. *Et ascendit super cherubin et volavit*

fleg ofer fiðru winda 7 sette ðeostru
volavit super pinnas ventorum 12. *Et posuit tenebras*

heolstur his in ymbhwyrfte his geteld his ðeostre
latibulum suum in circuitu ejus tabernaculum ejus tenebrosa

[1] *first* o *from* i.

weter in wolcnum lyfte fore sciman in gesihðe his
aqua in nubibus aeris **13.** *Prae fulgure in conspectu ejus*

wolcen leordon hegel 7 colu fyres 7 hleoðrað
nubes transierunt grando et carbones ignis **14.** *Et intonuit*

of heofene dryhten 7 se hehsta salde stefne his sende
de caelo Dominus et altissimus dedit vocem suam **15.** *Misit*

strele his 7 tostencte hie 7 legite gemonigfaldade 7
sagittas suas et dissipavit eos et fulgura multiplicavit et

gedroefde hie 7 oteawdon waellan wetra 7
conturbavit eos **16.** *Et apparuerunt fontes aquarum et*

onwrigen werun steaðelas ymbhwyrftes eorðan from ðreange
revelata sunt fundamenta orbis terrae Ab increpatione

ðinre dryhten from onoeðunge gastes earres ðines sende
tua Domine ab inspiratione spiritus irae tuae **17.** *Misit*

of heanisse 7 onfeng me 7 genom me of menge
de summo et accepit me et adsumpsit me de multitudine

wetra generede me of feondum minum ðæm stronges-
aquarum **18.** *Eripuit me de inimicis meis fortissimis*

tum 7 from ðissum ða fiodon me forðon gestrongade
et ab his qui oderunt me quoniam confortati

werun ofer me forecomun me in dege geswinces
sunt super me **19.** *Praevenerunt me in die adflictionis*

mines 7 geworden is dryhten gescildend min 7
meae et factus est Dominus protector meus **20.** *et*

utalaedde me in braedu halne me doo forðon walde
eduxit me in latitudinem salvum me fecit quoniam voluit

me 7 geedleanade me dryhten efter rehtwisnisse
me **21.** *Et retribuit mihi Dominus secundum justitiam*

mine 7 efter unsceðfulnisse honda minra geedleanad
meam et secundum innocentiam manuum mearum retribuit

me forðon ic heold weagas dryhtnes ne arleaslice
mihi **22.** *Quia custodivi vias Domini nec impie*

ic dyde from gode minum forðon alle domas his
gessi a Deo meo **23.** *Quoniam omnia judicia ejus*

in gesihðe minre sindun aa 7 rehtwisnisse his
in conspectu meo sunt semper et justitias ejus

ic onweg ne adraf from me 7 ic biom unwemme
non reppuli a me **24.** *Et ero inmaculatus*

*biom him 7 ic haldu me from unrehtwisnisse minre
coram eo et observabo me ab iniquitate mea

7 geedleanað me dryht*en* efter rehtwisnisse minre
25. *Et retribuit mihi Dominus secundum justitiam meam*

7 efter unsceðfulnisse honda minra in gesihðe
et secundum innocentiam manuum mearum in conspectu

egena his mid ðone halgan halig ðu *bis 7 mid
oculorum ejus 26. *Cum sancto sanctus eris et cum*

were unscedendu*m* unsceððende ðu bist 7 mid
viro innocente innocens eris (27.) *et cum*

ðy upahefenan upahefen ðu bist 7 mid ðy ðweoran ðu bist
electo electus eris et cum perverso subver-

forcerred forðon ðu folc eaðmod hal gedoest
teris 28. *Quoniam tu populum humilem salvum facies*

7 egan oferhygdigra ðu gehenes forðon ðu inlihtes
et oculos superborum humiliabis 29. *Quoniam tu inluminas*

lehtfet min dryht*en* god min inliht ðeostru min
lucernam meam Domine Deus meus inlumina tenebras meas

forðon from ðe ic biom genered from *ðe costunge 7
30. *Quoniam a te eripiar a temptatione et*

in gode minum ic ofergaa wall god min unbe-
in Deo meo transgrediar murum 31. *Deus meus inpol-*

smiten[1] weg his gespreocu dryht*nes* mid fyre amearad
luta via ejus eloquia Domini igne examinata

gescildend is alra gehyhtendra in hine forðon
protector est omnium sperantium in se 32. *Quoniam*

hwelc god butan dryht*ne* oððe hwelc god butan gode
quis Deus praeter Dominum aut quis Deus praeter Deum

urum god se bigyrde me mid megne 7 sette
nostrum 33. *Deus qui praecinxit me virtute et posuit*

unwemne weg minne se gefremede foet mine
inmaculatam viam meam 34. *Qui perfecit pedes meos*

swe swe heorutes 7 ofer ða hean gesette me se laered
tamquam cervi et super excelsa statuit me 35. *Qui docit*

honda mine to gefehte 7 sette swe swe bogan ærenne
manus meas ad proelium et posuit ut arcum aereum

earmas mine 7 ðu saldes me gescildnisse haelu
bracchia mea 36. *Et dedisti mihi protectionem salutis*

ðinre 7 sie swiðre ðin onfeng me 7 ðeodscipe ðin he me
tuae et dextera tua suscepit me et disciplina tua ipsa me

[1] e *er. after last* n.

lærde ðu gebraeddes gongas mine under me 7 ne sind
docuit 37. *Dilatasti gressos meos subtus me et non sunt*

geuntrumad sweðe mine ic oehtu feond mine 7
infirmata vestigia mea 38. *Persequar inimicos meos et*

gegripo hie 7 ic ne gecerru ær ðon hie aspringað
conpraehendam illos et non convertar donec deficiant

ic swencu *hio ne hie magun stondan fallað under
39. *adfligam illos nec potuerunt stare Cadent subtus*

foet mine 7 ðu bigyrdes me mid megne to gefehte
pedes meos 40. *et praecinxisti me virtute ad bellum*

7 gescrenctes alle arisende in me under me 7
Et supplantasti omnes insurgentes in me subtus me 41. *et*

feonda minra ðu saldes me bec et ða figendan me
inimicorum meorum dedisti mihi dorsum et odientes me

ðu tostenctes cleopedun ne wes se hale dyde
disperdidisti 42. *Clamaverunt nec erat qui salvos faceret*

to dryht*ne* ne he geherde hie 7 ic gebreocu hie
ad Dominum nec exaudivit eos 43. *Et comminuam illos*

swe swe dust biforan onsiene windes swe swe lam worðigna
ut pulverem ante faciem venti ut lutum platearum

ic adilgiu hie ðu *genes me of wiðcwedenisse folces
delebo eos 44. *Eripies me de contradictionibus populi*

ðu gesetes me in heafud ðieda folc ðæt
constitues me in caput gentium 45. *Populum quem*

ic ne oncnew ðeawde me from gehernisse earan hersumade
non cognovi servivit mihi obauditu auris obaudivit

me bearn fremðe ligende werun me bearn
mihi 46. *Filii alieni mentiti sunt mihi filii*

fremðe aldadon 7 haltadon from stigum heara
alieni inveteraverunt et claudicaverunt a semitis suis

leafað dryht*en* 7 gebledsad god min 7 sie up-
47. *Vivit Dominus et benedictus Deus meus et ex-*

pahefen god hęlu minre god ðu seles wrece
altetur Deus salutis meae 48. *Deus qui das vindictam*

me 7 underðeodes folc under me gefrigend min
mihi et subdidisti populos sub me Liberator meus

dryht*en* of ðeodum eorsendum 7 from ðæm arisendum
Dominus de gentibus iracundis 49. *et ab insurgentibus*

in me ðu upahefes me from were ðæm unrehtwisan
in me exaltabis me a viro iniquo

generes me fore ðon ic ondetto ðe in folcum
eripies me **50.** *Propter ea confitebor tibi in populis*

dryhten 7 noman ðinum salm ic cweoðu gemicliende
Domine et nomini tuo psalmum dicam **51.** *Magnificans*

haelu cyninges his 7 donde mildheortnisse criste his
salutare regis ipsius et faciens misericordiam Christo suo

7 sede his oð in weoruld
David et semini ejus usque in saeculum

18.

heofenas asecgað wuldur godes 7 werc honda his
2. *Caeli enarrant gloriam Dei et opera manuum ejus*

segeð trymenis deg dege roccetteð word 7
annuntiat firmamentum **3.** *Dies diei eructuat verbum et*

neht nehte getacnað wisdom ne sind gespreocu
nox nocti indicat scientiam **4.** *Non sunt loquellae*

ne word ðeara ne bioð geherde stefne heara in
neque sermones quorum non audientur voces eorum **5.** *In*

alle eorðan uteode swoeg heara 7 in endas ymbhwyrftes
omnem terram exivit sonus eorum et in fines orbis

eorðan word heara in sunnan he sette geteld his
terrae verba eorum **6.** *In sole posuit tabernaculum suum*

7 he swe swe brydguma forðgande of brydbure his
et ipse tamquam sponsus procedens de thalamo suo

gefaeh swe swe gigent to earnenne on weg from
Exultavit ut gigans ad currendam viam **7.** *a*

ðæm hean heofene utgong his 7 eftyrn his oð
summo caelo egressio ejus et occursus ejus usque ad

behnisse his ne is se ðe hine abyde from haeto his
summum ejus nec est qui se abscondat a calore ejus

ęew dryhtnes untelwirðe[1] gecerrende sawle cyðnis
8. *Lex Domini inrepraehensibilis convertens animas testimonium*

dryhtnes getreowu ···ro[2] gearwiende cilde rehtwis-
Domini fidele ···ientiam[2] praestans parvulis **9.** *Justi-*

nisse dryhtnes rehtlice blissiende heortan bibod dryhtnes
tiae Domini recte laetificantes corda praeceptum Domini

leht inlihtende egan ege dryhtnes halig
lucidum inluminans oculos **10.** *Timor Domini sanctus*

[1] i *altered to* y. [2] *cut away.*

ðorhwunað in weoruld weorulde domas godes soðe gereht-
permanet in saeculum saeculi judicia Dei vera. justifi-

wisade[1] in him seolfum wilsum ofer gold 7
cata in semet ipsa 11. *Desiderabilia super aurum et*

stan deorwyrðne swiðe 7 swoetran ofer hunig 7 biobread
lapidem praetiosum multum et dulciora super mel et favum.

weotudlice 7 ðeow ðin haldeð ða in gehælde ðere
12. *Nam et servus tuus custodiet ea in custodiendo illa*

edlean micel scylde hwelc ongeteð from degelnissum
retributio multa 13. *Delicta quis intellegit ab occultis*

minum geclasna me dryhten 7 from ðæm fremðum
meis munda me Domine 14. *et ab alienis*

*spreara ðiowe ðinum gif min ne bioð waldende ðonne
parce servo tuo Si mei non fuerint dominati tunc

unwemme ic biom 7 ic biom geclasnad from scylde[2]
inmaculatus ero et emundabor a delicto

ðere mæstan 7 bioð ðæt hie gelicien gespreocu mudes
maximo 15. *Et erunt ut conplaceant eloquia oris*

mines 7 smeang heortan minre in gesihðe ðinre aa
mei et meditatio cordis mei in conspectu tuo semper

dryhten fultum min 7 alesend min
Domine adjutor meus et redemptor meus

19.

gehere ðe dryhten in dege geswinces gescilde ðe
2. *Exaudiat te Dominus in die tribulationis protegat te*

noma godes Jacefes sende ðe fultum of halgum 7
nomen Dei Jacob 3. *Mittat tibi auxilium de sancto et*

of Sion gescilde ðe gemyndig sie dryhten alre onsegdnisse
de Sion tueatur te 4. *Memor sit Dominus omnis sacrificii*

ðinre 7 onsegdnisse ðine gefaettie selle ðe dryhten
tui et holocostum tuum pinguefiat 5. *Tribuat tibi Dominus*

efter heortan ðinre 7 all *gedaeh ðin getrymme
secundum cor tuum et omne consilium tuum confirmet

we bioð geblissade in haelu ðinre 7 in noman dryhtnes
6. *Laetabimur in salutari tuo et in nomine Domini*

godes ures we bioð gemiclade gefylleð dryhten alle
Dei nostri magnificabimur 7. *Impleat Dominus omnes*

[1] i *tagged: looks like* a. [2] s *from* h.

boene ðine nu ic oncneow ðætte halne doeð ðryhten
petitiones tuas nunc cognovi quoniam salvum faciet Dominus

Crist his 7 gehereð hine of heofene ðæm halgan his
Christum suum et exaudiet illum de caelo sancto suo

in maehtum haelu swiðran his ðas in creatum 7
in potentatibus salus dexterae ejus 8. *Hii in curribus et*

ðas in horsum we soðlice in noman dryhtnes godes ures
hii in equis nos autem in nomine Domini Dei nostri

we bioð gemiclade hie gebundne sindun 7 gefeollun we
magnificabimur 9. *Ipsi obligati sunt et ceciderunt nos*

soðlice *aresun 7 uparehte sindun . dryhten halne
vero resurreximus et erecti sumus 10. *Domine salvum*

do cyning 7 geher us in dege in ðæm we gecegað ðec
fac regem et exaudi nos in die qua invocaverimus te

20.

dryhten in megne ðinum bið geblissad cyning 7 ofer
2. *Domine in virtute tua laetabitur rex et super*

haelu ðine gefihð swiðlice lust sawle
salutare tuum exultabit vehementer 3. *Desiderium animae*

his ðu saldes him 7 willan weolera his ðu ne [bi]sceredes
ejus tribuisti ei et voluntate labiorum ejus non fraudasti

hine forðon ðu forecwome hine in bledsunge
eum 4. *Quoniam praevenisti eum in benedictione*

swetnisse ðu settes heafde his beg of stane deorwyrðem[1]
dulcidinis posuisti in capite ejus coronam de lapide praetioso

lif bed 7 ðu saldes him lengu dęga in weoruld
5. *Vitam petit et tribuisti ei longitudinem dierum in saecu-*

weorulde micel is wuldur his in haelu ðinre
lum saeculi 6. *Magna est gloria ejus in salutari tuo*

wuldur 7 micelne wlite ðu onsetes ofer hine forðon
gloriam et magnum decorem imponis super eum 7. *Quoniam*

ðu selest hine in bledsunge in weoruld weorulde
dabis eum in benedictionem in saeculum saeculi

ðu geblissas hine in gefian[2] mid ondwleotan ðinum for-
laetificabis eum in gaudio cum vultu tuo 8. *Quo-*

ðon cyning gehyhteð in dryhtne 7 in mildheortnisse
niam rex sperabit in Domino et in misericordia

[1] u *under the last* e. [2] g *on unerased* i.

ðes hestan ne bið onstyred sie *bið gimoeted hond
altissimi non commovebitur 9. *Inveniatur manus*

ðin allum feondum ðinum sie swiðre ðin gemoeteð alle
tua omnibus inimicis tuis dextera tua inveniit omnes

ða ðe ðe figað ðu setes hie swe swe ofen fyres in
qui te oderunt 10. *Pones eos ut clibanum ignis in*

tid ondwliotan ðines dryhten in eorre his gedroefeð
tempore vultus tui Dominus in ira sua conturbabit

hie 7 forswilgeð hie fyr westem heara of eorðan
eos et devorabit eos ignis 11. *Fructum eorum de terra*

ðu forspildes 7 sed heara from bearnum monna
perdis et semen eorum a filiis hominum

forðon hie onhaeldon in ðe yfel ðohtun geðaeht
12. *Quoniam declinaverunt in te mala cogitaverunt consilium*

ðæt hie ne maehtun gesteaðulfestian forðon ðu setes
quod non potuerunt stabilire 13. *Quoniam pones*

hie bec in lafum ðinum ðu gearwas ondwleotan heara
eos deorsum in reliquiis tuis praeparabis vultum illorum

hefe up dryhten in megne ðinum we singað 7
14. *Exaltare Domine in virtute tua cantabimus et*

singað megen ðin
psallimus virtutes tuas

21.

god god min geloca in me *forhon me forleorte ðu feor
2. *Deus Deus meus respice in me quare me dereliquisti longe*

from haelu minre word scylda minra god min
a salute mea Verba delictorum meorum 3. *Deus meus*

ic cleopiu ðorh deg ne ðu geheres 7 on naeht 7 nales to
clamabo per diem nec exaudies et nocte et non ad

unwisdome me ðu soðlice in halgum eardas lof
insipientiam mihi 4. *Tu autem in sancto habitas laus*

in ðe gehyhton fedras ure gehyhton 7
Israhel 5. *in te speraverunt patres nostri speraverunt et*

ðu gefreodes hie to ðe cleopedon 7 hale gewordne sind
liberasti eos 6. *Ad te clamaverunt et salvi facti sunt*

in ðe gehyhton 7 ne werun gescende ic soðlice eam
in te speraverunt et non sunt confusi 7. *Ego autem sum*

wyrm 7 nales mon edwit monna 7 aworpnes folces
vermis et non homo opprobrium hominum et abjectio plebis

alle ðа gesegun me herwdun me spreocende werun
8. *Omnes qui videbant me aspernabantur me locuti sunt*
mid weolerum 7 hrisedon heafud gehyhteð in dryht*ne*
labiis et moverunt caput 9. *Speravit in Domino*
genereð hine halne doe hine forðon he wile hine
eripiat eum salvum faciat eum quoniam vult eum
forðon ðu earð ðu atuge me of wombe hyht min
10. *Quoniam tu es qui abstraxisti me de ventre spes mea*
from breostum modur minre in ðe aworpen ic eam of innoðe
ab uberibus matris meae 11. *in te jactatus sum ex utero*
of wombe modur minre god min ðu earð ne gewit ðu
de ventre matris meae Deus meus es tu 12. *Ne discesseris*
from me forðon geswinc on neoweste is 7 nis se ðe
a me quoniam tribulatio proxima est et non est qui
gefultume ymbsaldon me calfur monig fearras faette
adjuvet 13. *Circumdederunt me vituli multi tauri pingues*
oferseton me ontyndon in me muð his swe swe leo
obsiderunt me 14. *Aperuerunt in me os suum sicut leo*
reafiende 7 grymetiende swe swe weter agotene sind 7
rapiens et rugiens 15. *sicut aqua effusa sunt et*
tostrogden sind all ban min geworden wes heorte min
dispersa sunt universa ossa mea Factum est cor meum
swe swe wæx gemaeltende in midle wombe minre adrugade
tamquam cera liquefiens in medio ventris mei 16. *Exaruit*
swe swe tigule megen min 7 tunge min ætfalh gomum
velut testa virtus mea et lingua mea adhesit faucibus
minum 7 in dust deaðes gelaeddon me forðon
meis et in pulverem mortis deduxerunt me 17. *Quoniam*
ymbsaldon me hundas monge geðaeht awergedra
circumdederunt me canes multi concilium malignantium
*oset mec dulfun honda mine 7 foet mine arimdon
obsedit me Foderunt manus meas et pedes meos 18. *dinumera-*
all ban min hie soðlice sceawedun 7
verunt omnia ossa mea Ipsi vero consideraverunt et
gelocadon me todaeldun him hregl min 7 ofer
conspexerunt me 19. *diviserunt sibi vestimenta mea et super*
hregl[1] min sendon *hlet ðu soðlice dryht*en* nales
vestem meam miserunt sortem 20. *Tu autem Domine ne-*

[1] r *from* l.

feor do ðu fultum ðinne from me to gescildnisse minre
longe facias auxilium tuum a me ad defensionem meam

geloca genere from sweorde sawle mine 7 of honda
aspice **21.** *Erue a framea animam meam et de manu*

hundes ða angan mine gefrea me of muðe leon 7 from
canis unicam meam **22.** *Libera me de ore leonis et a*

hornum anhyrnera eaðmodnisse mine ic secgu
cornibus unicornuorum humilitatem meam **23.** *Narrabo*

noman ðinne broðrum minum in midle cirican ic hergo ðe
nomen tuum fratribus meis in medio ecclesiae laudabo te

ða ðe ondreðað dryht*en* hergað hine all sed
24. *Qui timetis Dominum laudate eum universum semen*

Jacobes micliað hine ondrede hine all sed Israela
Jacob magnificate eum **25.** *Timeat eum omne semen Israhel*

forðon ne forhogde ne forsaeh boene ðearfena[1] ne
quoniam non sprevit neque dispexit precem pauperum neque

forcerreð onsiene his from me 7 midðy ic cleapade to him
avertit faciem suam a me et dum clamarem ad eum

geherde me mid ðe lof me in cirican micelre
exaudivit me **26.** *Aput te laus mihi in ecclesia magna*

gehat min dryht*ne* ic ageofu biforan ondredendum hine
vota mea Domino reddam coram timentibus eum

eatað ðearfan 7 bið gefylled 7 hergað dryht*en*
27. *Edent pauperes et saturabuntur et laudabunt Dominum*

ða soecað hine leofað heorte heara in weoruld weorulde
qui requirunt eum Vivit cor eorum in saeculum saeculi

gemynen 7 sien *gecered[2] to dryht*ne* alle
28. *reminiscentur et convertentur ad Dominum universi*

gemæru eorðan 7 gebiddað in gesihðe his alle oeðlas
fines terrae Et adorabunt in conspectu ejus omnes patriae

ðeoda forðon dryht*nes* is rice 7 he waldeð
gentium **29.** *quoniam Domini est regnum et ipse dominabitur*

ðeada eton 7 weorðadon alle weolie
gentium **30.** *Manducaverunt et adoraverunt omnes divites*

eorðan in gesihðe his forðgað alle ða astigað in
terrae in conspectu ejus procidunt universi qui discendunt in

eorðan 7 sawul min him leofað 7 sed min ðiowað
terram **31.** *Et anima mea ipsi vivit et semen meum serviet*

[1] *last* a *over dotted* e.

[2] g *on er.,* h *er. before it.*

him segeð dryht*ne* cneoris toword ⁊
illi **32.** *Adnuntiabitur Domino generatio ventura et*

secgað heofenes rehtwisnisse[1] his folce ðæt bið acenned
annuntiabunt caeli justitiam ejus populo qui nascitur

ðæt dyde dryht*en*
quem fecit Dominus

22.

dryht*en* receð me ⁊ nowiht me wonu bið in stowe
Dominus regit me et nihil mihi deerit **2.** *in loco*

leswe ðer mec gesteaðelade ofer weter *gereodnisse aledde
pascuae ibi me conlocavit Super aquam refectionis educavit

mec sawle mine gecerde gelaed[d]e me ofer stige
me **3.** *animam meam convertit Deduxit me super semitam*

rehtwisnisse fore noman his weotudlice ⁊ ðæhðe ic gonge
justitiae propter nomen suum **4.** *Nam etsi ambulem*

in midle scuan deaðes ne ondredu ic yfel forðon ðu mid me
in medio umbrae mortis non timebo mala quoniam tu mecum

erð gerd ðin ⁊ cryc ðin hie me froefrende werun
es Virga tua et baculus tuus ipsa me consolata sunt

ðu gearwades in gesihðe minre biod wið him ða
5. *Parasti in conspectu meo mensam adversus eos qui*

swencað mec ðu faettades in ele heafud min ⁊ drync
tribulant me Inpinguasti in oleo caput meum, et poculum

ðinne indrencende swide freaberht is ⁊ *milheortniss
tuum inebrians quam praeclarum est **6.** *Et misericordia*

ðin efterfylgeð mec allum degum lifes mines ðæt ic ineardie
tua subsequitur me omnibus diebus vitae meae Ut inhabitem

in huse dryht*nes* in lengu dęga
in domo Domini in longitudinem dierum

23.

dryht*nes* is earðe ⁊ fylnis his ymbhwyrft eorðena ⁊
Domini est terra et plenitudo ejus orbis terrarum et

alle ða eardiað in hire he ofer sęas gesteaðelade
universi qui habitant in ea **2.** *Ipse super maria fundavit*

hie ⁊ ofer flodas gearwað ða hwelc astigeð in
eam et super flumina praeparavit illam **3.** *Quis ascendit in*

[1] rehtwissnisse, *second* s *dotted.*

munt dryht*nes* oððe hwelc stondeð in stowe ðere halgan his
montem Domini aut quis stabit in loco sancto ejus

unsceððende on hondum 7 clænre heortan se ne onfeng in
4. *Innocens manibus et mundo corde qui non accipit in*

idelnisse sawle his ne he swor in facne ðæm nestan his
vano animam suam nec juravit in dolo proximo suó

ðes onfoeð bledsunge from dryht*ne* 7 mildheortnisse
5. *Hic accipiet benedictionem a Domino et misericordiam*

from gode ðæm halwendan his ðis is cneoris
a Deo salutari suo 6. *Haec est generatio*

soecendra dryht*en* *socendra onsiene godes Jacobes
quaerentium Dominum requirentium faciem Dei Jacob

onhebbað geatu aldres eowres 7 bioð upahefene geatu
7. *Tollite portas principes vestri*[1] *et elevamini portae*

ecelice 7 ingaeð cyning wuldres hwelc is ðes cyning
aeternales et introibit rex gloriae 8. *Quis est iste rex*

wuldres dryht*en* strong 7 maehtig dryht*en* maehtig in gefehte
gloriae Dominus fortis et potens Dominus potens in praelio

onhebbað geatu aldermen eoweres 7 bioð upahefene geatu
9. *Tollite portas principes vestri*[2] *et elevamini portae*

ecelice 7 ingaeð cyning wuldres hwet is ðes cyning
aeternales et introibit rex gloriae 10. *Quis es(t) iste rex*

wuld[ra]es dryht*en* megna he is cyning wuldres
gloriae Dominus virtutum ipse est rex gloriae

24.

to ðe dryht*en* ic upahof sawle minę god min in
Ad te Domine levavi animam meam 2. *Deus meus in*

ðe ic getreowu ne scomiu ic ne bismeriað mec feond
te confido non erubescam 3. *Neque inrideant me inimici*

mine 7 soðlice alle ða ðe bidað dryht*en* ne sien gescende
mei etenim universi qui te expectant Domine non confundentur

sien gescende ða unrehtwisan donde ða idlan wegas ðine
4. *Confundantur iniqui facientes vana vias tuas*

dryht*en* cuðe doo me 7 stige ðine lær me gerece
Domine notas fac mihi et semitas tuas edoce me 5. *Dirige*

[1] *altered to* vestras.

[2] as *over the* i.

me in soðfestnisse ðinre ⁊ lær me 'forðon ðu earð god
me in veritate tua et doce me quia tu es Deus.

haelend min ⁊ ðe ic arefnde alne deg gemyne
salvator meus et te sustinui tota die 6. *Reminiscere*

mildsa ðinra dryht*en* ⁊ mildheortnis ðin ða from
miserationum tuarum Domine et misericordia tua quae a

*werulde sind scyld *guiuðu ⁊ unondcyðignisse minre
saeculo sunt 7. *Delicta juventutis et ignorantiae meae*

ne ðu gemynes efter miclan mildheor[t]nisse ðinre
ne memineris secundum magnam misericordiam tuam

gemyndig bio ðu min god fore godnisse ðine dryht*en*
memor esto mei Deus Propter bonitatem tuam Domine

swoete ⁊ reht *dryt*en* fore ðissum aee gesette
8. *dulcis et rectus Dominus Propter hoc legem statuit*

gyltendum in wege gereceð ða mildan in dome lereð
delinquentibus in via 9. *dirigit mites in judicio docebit*

ða monðwęran wegas heara alle wegas dryht*nes*
mansuetos vias suas 10. *Universae viae Domini*

mildheortnis ⁊ soðfestnis soecendum cyðnisse his ⁊
misericordia et veritas requirentibus testamentum ejus et

cyðnisse his fore noman ðinum dryht*en* ðu gemildsas
testimonia ejus 11. *Propter nomen tuum Domine propitiaberis*

synne minre genyhtsum is soðlice hwelc is mon se ðe
peccato meo copiosum est enim 12. *Quis est homo qui*

ondrede dryht*en* ęe sette him in wege ðone geceas
timeat Dominum legem statuit ei in via quam elegit

sawul his in godum wunað ⁊ sed his erfeweardnisse
13. *Anima ejus in bonis demorabitur et semen ejus hereditate*

gesiteð eorðan trymenis is dryht*en* ondredendum
possidebit terram 14. *Firmamentum est Dominus timentibus*

hine ⁊ cyðnes[1] his ðæt sie *gesweocelad him egan
eum et testamentum ipsius ut manifestetur illis 15. *Oculi*

mine aa to dryht*ne* forðon he aluceð of girene foet
mei semper ad Dominum quoniam ipse evellit de laqueo pedes

mine geloca in mec ⁊ mildsa min forðon anga ⁊
meos 16. *Respice in me et miserire mei quoniam unicus et*

ðearfa ic eam geswencednisse heortan minre gebręd de
pauper sum ego 17. *Tribulationes cordis mei dilatatae*

[1] e *from* i (?).

sind of nedðearfnissum minum genere me geseh eað-
sunt de necessitatibus meis eripe me 18. *Vide humi-*

modnisse mine 7 gewin min 7 forlet alle synne mine
litatem meam et laborem meum et demitte omnia peccata mea

geloca feond mine forðon gemonigfaldade sind 7
19. *Respice inimicos meos quoniam multiplicati sunt et*

laeððu unrehtwisre fiedon mec hald sawle mine 7
odio iniquo oderunt me 20. *Custodi animam meam et*

genere mec ne biom ic gescended forðon ic gecede ðe
eripe me non confundar quoniam invocavi te

unsceððende 7 rehtwise ætfelun me forðon ic arefnde ðe
21. *Innocentes et recti adheserunt mihi quoniam sustenui te*

dryht*en* ales me god of allum nearenissum
Domine 22. *Redime me Deus Israhel ex omnibus angustiis*

minum
meis

25.

doem mec dryht*en* forðon ic in unsceðfulnisse minre in-
Judica me Domine quoniam ego in innocentia mea in-

gongende ic eam 7 in dryht*ne* gehyhtende ic ne biom geuntrumad
gressus sum et in Domino sperans non infirmabor

acunna me dryht*en* 7 costa me bern eðre mine 7 heortan
2. *Proba me Domine et tempta me ure renes meos et cor*

mine forðon mildheortnis ðin biforan egum minum is
meum 3. *Quoniam misericordia tua ante oculos meos est*

7 ic gelicade in soðfestnisse ðinre ic ne set in geðaehte
et conplacui in veritate tua 4. *Non sedi in concilio*

idelnisse 7 mid ða unrehtan ðondum ic in ne ga ic fiode
vanitatis et cum iniqua gerentibus non introibo 5. *Odivi*

gesomnunge awergedra 7 mid arleasum ic ne sitto
congregationem malignorum et cum impiis non sedebo

ic ðwea betwih alle unsceðende honda mine 7 ic ymbgaa
6. *Lavabo inter innocentes manus meas et circuibo*

wibed ðin dryht*en* ðæt ic geheru stefne lofes ðines 7
altare tuum Domine 7. *Ut audiam vocem laudis tuae et*

ic asecgu all wundur[1] ðin dryht*en* ic lufade wlite
enarrem universa mirabilia tua 8. *Domine dilexi decorem*

[1] *first* u *on* o.

huses ðines 7 stowe *getedes wuldres ðines ne
*domus tuae et locum *tabernaculis gloriae tuae* **9.** *Ne*

forspild ðu mid ðæm arleasum sawle mine 7 mid weorum
perdas cum impiis animam meam et cum viris

bloda lif min in ðeara hondum unrehtwisnisse
sanguinum vitam meam **10.** *in quorum manibus iniquitates*

sindun seo swiðre heara gefylled is geofum ic soðlice
sunt Dextera eorum repleta est muneribus **11.** *ego autem*

in unsceðfulnisse minre ingongende ic eam ales me 7 mildsa
in innocentia mea ingressus sum redime me et miserire

min fot soðlice min stod in wege ðæm rehtan in cirecum
mei **12.** *Pes enim meus stetit in via recta in ecclesiis*

ic bledsiu dryht*en*
benedicam Dominum

26.

dryht*en* inlihtnis mine 7 haelu min ðone ic ondredo
Dominus inluminatio mea et salus mea quem timebo

dryht*en* gescildend lifes mines from dæm ic forhtiu
Dominus defensor vitae meae a quo trepidabo

ðonne *toneolicað ofer me sceððende ðæt hie eten flæsc
2. *Dum adpropiant super me nocentes ut edant carnes*

min ða ðe me fiond mine hie geuntrumede sind 7
meas qui tribulant me inimici mei ipsi infirmati sunt et

gefeollun gif gestondað wið me ferdwic ne
caeciderunt **3.** *Si consistant adversum me castra non*

ondredeð heorte min gif ariseð in me gefeht in ðis
timebit cor meum si insurgat in me proelium in hoc

ic gehyhtu an ic bed from dryhtne ðas ic soecu ðæt
ego sperabo **4.** *Unam petii a Domino hanc requiram ut*

ic ineardie in huse dryht*nes* allum dægum lifes mines
inhabitem in domo Domini omnibus diebus vitae meae

ðæt ic gese willan dryht*nes* 7 ic siem gescilded from
ut videam voluntatem Domini et protegar a

*tempe ðæm halga(n)[1] forðon ahydeð me in
templo sancto ejus **5.** *Quoniam abscondit me in*

getelde his in dege ðæm[2] yfla gescilde me in degulnisse
tabernaculo suo in die malorum protexit me in abscondito

[1] *cut away.* [2] æm *altered from* æra (?)

geteldes his in stane upahof mec nu soðlice
tabernaculi sui 6. *in petra exaltavit me Nunc autem*

upahof heafud min ofer fiond mine ic ymbgaa 7
exaltavit caput meum super inimicos meos circuibo et

ageldu[1] in getelde[2] his onsegdnisse wynsumnisse[3] ic singu
immolabo in tabernaculo ejus hostiam jubilationis cantabo

7 salm ic cweoð(u)[4] geher dryht*en* stefne
et psalmum dicam Domino 7. *Exaudi Domine vocem*

mine mid ðere ic cleopede to de mildsa min 7 geher
meam qua clamavi ad te miserire mihi et exaudi

mec to ðe cweð heorte min ic sohte ondwleotan
me 8. *Tibi dixit cor meum Quisivi vultum*

ðin[n]e ondwleotan ðinne dryht*en* ic soecu ne acer ðu
tuum vultum tuum Domine requiram 9. *Ne avertas*

onsiene ðine from me 7 ne ahaeld ðu in eorre from ðiowe
faciem tuam a me et ne declines in ira a servo

ðinum fultum min ðu earð forlet ðu me ne forseh
tuo Adjutor meus es tu[5] *ne derelinquas me neque despicias*

me god se halwynda min forðon feder min 7
me Deus salutaris meus 10. *Quoniam pater meus et*

modur min forleorton mec dryht*en* soðlice genom mec
mater mea dereliquerunt me Dominus autem adsumpsit me

aee me gesete dryht*en* in wege ðinum 7 gerece
11. *Legem mihi constitue Domine in via tua et dirige*

mec in stige *ðe rehtan fore fiendum minum ne
me in semita recta propter inimicos meos 12. *Ne*

sele ðu mec in sawle oehtendra mec forðon
tradideris me in animas persequentium me quoniam

areosun in mec geweotan unrehte 7 legende wes
insurrexerunt in me testes iniqui et mentita est

unrehtwisnis him ic gelefu gesian god dryht*nes* in
iniquitas sibi 13. *Credo videre bona Domini in*

earðan lifgendra abid dryht*en* werlice doo 7
terra viventium 14. *exspecta Dominum viriliter age et*

sie gestrongad heorte ðin 7 abid dryht*en*
confortetur cor tuum et sustine Dominum

[1] vel offrige *added later.* [2] vel on eardungstowe *added later.* [3] vel lofes *added later.* [4] *cut away.* [5] esto, o *on er.*

27.

to ðe dryhten ic cleopiu god min ne swiga ðu from
1. *Ad te Domine clamabo Deus meus ne sileas a*

me 7 ic biom gelic[1] astigendum in seað geher
me et ero similis discendentibus in lacum 2. *Exaudi*

stefne boene minre ðonne ic gebiddu to ðe 7 ðonne
vocem deprecationis meae dum oro ad te et dum

ic uphebbu honda mine to temple halgum ðinum
extollo manus meas ad templum sanctum tuum

ne somud sele mec mid ðæm synfullum 7 mid wirc-
3. *Ne simul tradas me cum peccatoribus et cum ope-*

endum unrehtwisnisse ne forspild ðu me mid ðissum ða ðe
rantibus iniquitatem ne perdas me Cum his qui

spreocað sibbe mid ðone nestan his yfel soðlice sind in
loquuntur pacem cum proximo suo mala autem sunt in

*hortum heara sele him efter wercum heara 7
cordibus eorum 4. *Da illis secundum opera eorum et*

efter niðum teolunge heara geedleana him agef
secundum nequitias studiorum ipsorum retribue illis Redde

edlean heara him forðon hie ne ongetun
retributionem eorum ipsis 5. *quoniam non intellexerunt*

in werc dryhtnes 7 in werc honda his ne sceawiað
in opera Domini et in opera manuum ejus non considerant

toweorp hie ne ðu timbres hie gebledsad dryhten
Destrue illos nec aedificabis eos 6. *benedictus Dominus*

forðon geherde stefne boene minre dryhten
quoniam exaudivit vocem deprecationis meae 7. *Dominus*

fultum min 7 gescildend min 7 in hine gehyhteð heorte
adjutor meus et protector meus et in ipso speravit cor

min 7 gefultumad ic eam 7 bleow flęsc min 7 of
meum et adjutus sum Et refloruit caro mea et ex

willan minum ic ondetto him dryhten strengo folces
voluntate mea confitebor illi 8. *Dominus fortitudo plebis*

his 7 gescildend ðeara halwendra Cristes his is hal
suae et protector salutarium Christi sui est 9. *Salvum*

doo folc ðin dryhten 7 bledsa erfweardnisse ðine 7
fac populum tuum Domine et benedic hereditatem tuam et

rece hie 7 uphefe hie
rege eos et extolle illos usque in saeculum.

[1] *letter er. after* e.

28.

tobringað to dryhtne bearn godes tobringað to dryht*ne* bearn
Afferte Domino filii Dei afferte Domino filios

romma tobringað to dryht*ne* wuldur 7 are tobringað
arietum 2. *Afferte Domino gloriam et honorem afferte*

to dryht*ne* wuldur noman his wearðiað dryht*en* in halle
Domino gloriam nomini ejus Adorate Dominum in aula

ðere halgan his stefn dryht*nes* ofer weter god
sancta ejus 3. *vox Domini super aquas Deus*

megendrymmes hleoðrað dryht*en* ofer weter micel stefn
majestatis intonuit Dominus super aquas multas 4. *Vox*

dryht*nes* in megne stefn dryht*nes* in micelnisse stefn
*Domini in virtute vox Domini in *magnificentiam* 5. *Vox*

dryht*nes* gebreocendes cederbeamas 7 gebriceð dryht*en*
Domini confringentis cedros et confringit Dominus

cederbeamas ðes muntes 7 gescæneð hie swe swe
cedros Libani 6. *et comminuet eas tanquam*

caelf 7 se leofa swe swe sunu anhyrnra
vitulum Libani et dilectus sicut filius unicornuorum

stefn dryht*nes* betwihgongendes leg fyr stefn
7. *Vox Domini intercidentis flammam ignis* 8. *vox*

dryht*nes* *tosaecendes bihygdignisse 7 onstyreð dryht*en*
Domini concutientis solitudinem et commovebit Dominus

woesten stefn dryht*nes* gearwiendes heoretas 7
desertum Cades 9. *Vox Domini praeparantis cervos et*

biwrah ða ðiccan 7 in temple his alle cweoðað wuldur
revelavit condensa et in templo ejus omnes dicent gloriam

dryht*en* cwildeflod ineardað 7 siteð dryht*en* cyning in
10. *Dominus diluvium inhabitat et sedebit Dominus rex in*

ecnisse dryht*en* megen folce his seleð 7
aeternum 11. *Dominus virtutem populo suo dabit et*

bledsað folc his in sibbe
benedicit populum suum in pace

29.

ic uphebbu ðec dryht*en* forðon ðu onfenge me ne[1] ðu
2. *Exaltabo te Domine quoniam suscepisti me nec di-*

[1] d ne.

gelustfullades feond mine ofer mec dryhten god min
lectasti inimicos meos super me 3. *Domine Deus meus*

ic cleopade to ðe 7 ðu gehaeldes mec dryhten ðu atuge
clamavi ad te et sanasti me 4. *Domine abstraxisti*

from helwearum sawle mine ðu gehaeldes me from dune-
ab inferis animam meam salvasti me a discen-

stigendum in seað singað dryhtne halge his 7
dentibus in lacum 5. *Psallite Domino sancti ejus et*

ondettað *gemydde halignisse his forðon eorre in
confitemini memoriae sanctitatis ejus 6. *Quoniam ira in*

ebylgðu his 7 lif in willan his æt efenne
indignatione ejus et vita in voluntate ejus Ad vesperum

wunað wop 7 to margentide blis ic soðlice
demorabitur fletus et ad matutinum laetitia 7. *Ego autem*

ic *ceð in minre genyhtsumnisse ne biom onstyred in
dixi in mea abundantia Non movebor in

ecnisse dryhten in godum willan ðinum ðu gearwades
aeternum 8. *Domine in bona voluntate tua praestitisti*

wlite . minum megen ðu forcerdes onsiene ðine from me 7
decori meo virtutem avertisti faciem tuam a me et

geworden ic eam gedroefed to ðe dryhten ic cleopiu
factus sum conturbatus 9. *Ad te Domine clamabo*

7 to gode minum ic biddu hwelc nyttnis in
et ad Deum meum deprecabor 10. *quae utilitas in*

blode mine ðonne ic astigo in gebrosnunge ah
sanguine meo dum discendo in corruptionem Num quid

ondetteð ðe dust oððe seged soðfestuisse ðine
confitebitur tibi pulvis aut annuntiabit veritatem tuam

geherde dryhten 7 mildsiendie[1] is me dryhten geworden
11. *Audivit Dominus et misertus est mihi Dominus factus*

is fultum min ðu gecerdes wop minne in
est adjutor meus 12. *Convertisti planctum meum in*

gefean me ðu toslite sec minne 7 bigyrdes me
gaudium mihi conscidisti saccum meum et praecinxisti me

mid blisse ðæt singe ðe wuldur min 7 ic ne biom
laetitia 13. *ut cantet tibi gloria mea et non con-*

inbr(yrd)[2] dryhten god min in ecnisse ic ondettu ðe
pungar Domine Deus meus in aeternum confitebor tibi

[1] *last* i *doubtful, may be the beginning of an* e. [2] *cut off.*

30.

in ðe dryhten ic gehyhte ne biom ic gescended in ecnisse
2. *In te Domine speravi non confundar in aeternum*

in ðire rehtwisnisse gefrea me 7 genere me onhaeld to me
in tua justitia libera me et eripe me 3. *Inclina ad me*

eare ðin hreaða ðæt ðu generge mec bia ðu me in god
aurem tuam adcelera ut eripias me Esto mihi in Deum

gescildend 7 in stowe geberges ðæt halne mec ðu gedoe
protectorem et in locum refugii ut salvum me facias

forðon trymenis min 7 geberg min ðu earð
4. *Quoniam firmamentum meum et refugium meum es tu*

7 fore noman ðinum ladtow[1] me ðu bist 7 foedes
et propter nomen tuum dux mihi eris et enutries

me 7 utalędes mec of gerene ðisse ða gedegladon
me 5. *Et educis me de laqueo isto quem occultaverunt*

mec forðon ðu earð gescildend min dryht*en* in
mihi quoniam tu es protector meus Domine 6. *in*

honda ðine ic bibiodu gast minne ðu alesdes mec dryht*en*
manus tuas commendo spiritum meum Redimisti me Domine

god soðfestnisse · ðu fiodes haldende idelnisse idellice
Deus veritatis 7. *odisti observantes vanitatem supervacuae*

ic soðlice in dryht*ne* ic gehyhtu ic gefie 7 *blisie
Ego autem in Domino sperabo 8. *exultabo et laetabor*

in ðinre mildheortnisse forðon gelocades eaðmodnisse mine
in tua misericordia Quia respexisti humilitatem meam

hale ðu dydes of nedðearfnissum sawle mine ne
salvam fecisti de necessitatibus animam meam 9. *nec*

biluce me in honda feondes ðu gesettes in stowe
conclusisti me in manibus inimici Statuisti in loco

rumre foet mine mildsa me dryht*en* forðon
spacioso pedes meos 10. *miserire mihi Domine quoniam*

ic biom geswenced gedrefed is in eorre ege min sawul
tribulor Conturbatus est in ira oculus meus anima

min 7 womb min forðon asprong in sare lif min
mea et venter meus 11. *Quoniam defecit in dolore vita mea*

7 ger min in geamringum geuntrumad is in ðearfednisse
et anni mei in gemitibus Infirmata est in paupertate

[1] w *over* d.

megen min 7 ban min gedroefed sind ofer alle
virtus mea et ossa mea conturbata sunt 12. *Super omnes*

fiond mine geworden ic eam edwit nehgehusum minum
inimicos meos factus sum opprobrium vicinis meis

swiðe 7 ege cuðum. minum ða gesegun mec ute
nimium et timor · notis meis Qui videbant me foris

flugun from me ic gesnerc swe swe dead from
fugiebant a me 13. *excidi tamquam mortuus a*

heortan 7 geworden ic eam swe swe fet forloren[1] forðon
corde et factus sum sicut vas perditum 14. *Quoniam*

ic geherde telnisse monigra ymbeardiendra in
audivi vituperationem multorum circumhabitantium In

ðon ðonne bioð gesomnade alle somud wið me ðæt
eo dum congregarentur omnes simul · adversum me ut

hie onfoen sawle mine geðaehtende werun ic soðlice
acciperent animam meam consiliati sunt 15. *Ego vero*

in ðe gehyhte dryhten ic cweð ðu earð god min in
in te speravi Domine dixi. Tu es Deus meus 16. *in*

hondum ðinum tide mine gefrea me 7 genere me of
manibus tuis tempora mea Libera me et eripe me de

hondum feonda minra[2] 7 from oehtendum me
manibus inimicorum meorum et a persequentibus me

inliht onsiene ðine ofer ðiow ðinne 7 halne
17. *Inlumina faciem tuam super servum tuum et salvum*

mec doa ðinre mildheortnisse dryht*en* ne biom ic ge-
me fac in tua misericordia 18. *Domine non con-*

scended forðon ic gecede ðec scomien arleáse 7 sien gelęd‌de
fundar quoniam invocavi te Erubescant impii et deducantur

in helle dumbe sien gefremed ·weolere faecne ða
in infernum 19. *muta efficiantur labia dolosa quae*

spreocað wið ðæm rehtwisan unrehtwisnisse in oferhygde
loquuntur adversus justum iniquitatem in superbia

7 forhogadnisse swiðe micel mengu swoetnisse ðinre
et contemptu 20. *Quam magna multitudo dulcidinis tuae*

dryht*en* ða ðu ahydes ondredendum ðe 7 ðu gefremedes ða
Domine quam abscondisti timentibus te et perfecisti eam

gehyhtendum in ðec in gesihðe *bearn monna ðu
sperantibus in te in conspectu filiorum hominum 21. *Ab-*

[1] *second* o *from some other letter.* [2] i *over* c.

ahydes hie in degulnisse ondwleotan ðines from gedroefednisse
scondes eos in abdito vultus tui a conturbatione

monna gescildes hie in getelde ðinum from wiðcwedenisse
hominum Proteges eos in tabernaculo tuo a contradictione

geðieda gebledsad dryhten forðon gemiclade
linguarum **22.** *Benedictus Dominus quoniam mirificavit*

mildheortnisse his in cestre ymbstondnisse ic soðlice
misericordiam suam in civitate circumstantiae **23.** *Ego autem*

ic cweð in fyrhtu minre aworpen ic eam from[1] ondwleotan
dixi in pavore meo Projectus sum a vultu

egena ðinra forðon ðu geherdes stefne boene minre
oculorum tuorum Ideo exaudisti vocem depraecationis meae

mið ðy ic cleopiu to ðe lufiað dryhten alle
dum clamarem ad te **24.** *Diligite Dominum omnes*

halge his forðon soðfestnisse soeceð dryhten 7 geedleanað
sancti ejus quoniam veritatem requiret Dominus et retribuet.

*ðeossu ða[2] genyhtsumlice dooð oferhygd werlice
his qui abundanter faciunt superbiam **25.** *Viriliter*

doð 7 sie gestrongad heorte eower alle ða ðe gehyhtað
agite et confortetur cor vestrum omnes qui speratis

in dryhtne
in Domino

31.

eadge ðeara forletne sind unrehtwisnisse 7 ðeara biwrigen
1. *Beati quorum remissae sunt iniquitates et quorum tecta*

sind synne eadig wer ðæm ne geteleð dryhten
sunt peccata **2.** *Beatus vir cui non imputabit Dominus*

synne ne is in muðe his facen forðon ic swigade
peccatum nec est in ore ejus dolus **3.** *Quoniam tacui*

aldadon all ban min mid ðy ic cleapade alne deg
inveteraverunt omnia ossa mea dum clamarem tota die

forðon deges 7 naehtes gehefegad is ofer me hond ðin
4. *Quoniam die ac nocte gravata est super me manus tua*

gecerred ic eam in ermðu ðonne bið gebrocen ðorn scyld
conversus sum in erumna dum confringitur spina **5.** *Delic-*

min cuðe ðe ic dyde 7 unrehtwisnisse mine ic ne
tum meum cognitum tibi feci et injustitias meas non

oferwrah ic cweð ic forðsegcgo wið me unrehtwisnisse
operui Dixi Pronuntiabo adversum me injustitias

[1] ro *from other letters.* [2] þa; þ *on er.*

mine from dryht*ne* 7 ðu geedleanedes arleasnisse heortan
meas Domino et tu remisisti impietatem cordis

minre fore ðissum gebideð to ðe all halig in
mei 6. *Pro hac orabit ad te omnis sanctus in*

tid *geliplice hweðre[1] soðlice in cwildeflode wetra
tempore oportuno verum tamen in diluvio aquarum

micelra to him to ne geneolaecað ðu me earð
multarum ad eum non adproximabunt 7. *Tu mihi es*

geberg from ferðrycednisse[2] sie ymbseled salde me
refugium a pressura quae circumdedit me

wynsumnis min ales mec from ymbsellendum me
exultatio mea redime me a circumdantibus me

ondget ic sellu ðe 7 getimbru[3] ðe in wege
8. *Intellectum dabo tibi et instruam te in via*

ðissum ðæm ðu ingæst ic getrymmu ofer ðe[4] egan[5] min
hac qua ingredieris firmabo super te oculos meos

nyllað bion swe swe hors 7 mul in ðæm nis
9. *Nolite fieri sicut equus et mulus in quibus non est*

ondget in bridelse 7 haelftreo cecan heara geteh[6]
intellectus In freno et camo maxillas eorum constringe

ða to ne genehlaecað to ðe monge drea synfulra
qui non adproximant ad te 10. *Multa flagella peccatorum*

gehyhtende soðlice in dryhtne mildheortnis ymbseleð
sperantes autem in Domino misericordia circumdabit

*blisiað in dryhtne 7 gefiað rehtwise 7 wuldriað
11. *Laetamini in Domino et exultate justi et gloriamini*

alle rehte on heortan
omnes recti corde

32.

gefioð rehtwise in dryht*ne* rehtwise gedeofenað efen-
1. *Gaudete justi in Domino rectos decet conlau-*

herenis ondettað dryht*ne* in citra in hearpan
datio 2. *Confitemini Domino in cythara in psalterio*

ten strenga singað him singað him song neowne
decem cordarum psallite illi 3. *Cantate ei canticum novum*

[1] þeah *prefixed later.* [2] c *er. before* c. [3] vel lære *added later.*
[4] a *er. after* e. [5] a *over* e. [6] vel gewriþ *added later.*

wel singað in wynsumnisse forðon reht is word
bene psallite in jubilatione 4. *Quoniam rectus est sermo*

dryhtnes. 7 all werc his in geleafan lufað mild-
Domini et omnia opera ejus in fide 5. *Diligit mise-*

heortnisse 7 dom mildheortnisse dryhtnes ful is eorðe
ricordiam et judicium misericordia Domini plena est terra

worde dryhtnes heofenas getrymede sind 7 gaste
6. *verbo Domini caeli firmati sunt et spiritu*

muðes his all megen heara gesomnende swe swe in
oris ejus omnis virtus eorum 7. *Congregans sicut in*

cylle weter sæs settende in goldhordum neolnisse
utrem aquas maris ponens in thesauris abyssos

ondrede dryhten all eorðe from him soðlice bioð
8. *Timeat Dominum omnis terra ab ipso autem com-*

onstyred alle 7 alle ða eardiað *ymbhwyrst
moveantur universi et omnes qui habitant orbem

forðon he cweð 7 werun geworden[1] hie et 7
9. *Quoniam ipse dixit et facta sunt ipse mandavit et*

gecwicad werun dryhten tostenceð geðæht ðieda
creata sunt 10. *Dominus dissipat consilia gentium*

wiðceoseð soðlice geðohtas folca 7 wiðceoseð geðaeht
reprobat autem cogitationes populorum et reprobat consilia

aldermonna geðaeht soðli(ce)[2] dryhtnes wunað in
principum 11. *Consilium vero Domini manet in*

ecnisse geðohtas heortan his in weoruld weorulde
aeternum cogitationes cordis ejus in saeculum saeculi

eadigu ðiod ðere is dryhten god heara folc
12. *Beata gens cujus est Dominus Deus eorum populum*

ðæt geceas dryhten in erfeweardnisse him of *hiefene
quem elegit Dominus in hereditatem sibi 13. *De caelo*

gelocade dryhten 7 gesaeh alle bearn monna
prospexit Dominus et vidit omnes filios hominum

of ðæm gegearwedan eardunghuse his gelocað ofer alle
14. *de praeparato habitaculo suo respexit super omnes*

ða ðe eardiað ymbhwyrft se gehiewade[3] wrixendlice
qui habitant orbem 15. *Qui finxit singillatim*

heortan heara se ongiteð in all werc hiera
corda eorum qui intelligit in omnia opera eorum

[1] o *from* u. [2] *covered by a blot of ink.* [3] w *from some other letter.*

ne *bi gehęled cyning ðorh micel megen his ne
16. *Non salvabitur rex per multam virtutem suam nec*
gigent hal bið in mengu *streng his leas
gigans salvus erit in multitudine fortitudinis suae 17. *Falsus*
hors to haelu in genyhtsumnisse soðlice megnes his
equus ad salutem in abundantia autem virtutis suae
ne bið *halu sehðe egan dryhtnes ofer ða ondredendan
non erit salus 18. *Ecce oculi Domini super timentes*
hine gehyhtende soðlice in mildheortnisse his ðet
eum sperantes autem in misericordia ejus 19. *ut*
he ge:: from deaðe sawle heara 7 foedeð hie in hungre
eripiat a morte animas eorum et alat eos in fame
sawul soðlice ur abideð dryhten forðon fultum
20. *Anima autem nostra sustinet Dominum quoniam adjutor*
7 gescildend ur is 7 in him bið geblissad heorte
et protector noster es 21. *et in ipsa laetabitur cor*
ur 7 in noman ðæm halgan his we gehyhtað
nostrum et in nomine sancto ejus sperabimus
sie dryhten mildheortnis ðin ofer us swe swe we ge-
22. *Fiat Domine misericordia tua super nos sicut spera-*
hyhtað in ðe
bimus in te

33.

ic bledsiu dryhten in alle tid aa lof his in
2. *Benedicam Dominum in omni tempore semper laus ejus in*
muðe minum in dryhtne bið hered sawul min geheren
ori meo 3. *In Domino laudabitur anima mea audiant*
ða monðueran 7 blissien micliað dryhten mid me 7
mansueti et laetentur 4. *Magnificate Dominum mecum et*
uphebbað we noman his betwinum ic sohte dryhten
exaltemus nomen ejus in invicem 5. *Inquisivi Dominum*
7 he geherde me 7 of allum geswencednissum minum generede
et exaudivit me et ex omnibus tribulationibus meis eripuit
me togenehlaecað to him 7 bioð inlihte 7 ondwleotan
me 6. *Accedite ad eum et inluminamini et vultus*
eowre ne scomien ðes ðearfa cleopede 7 dryhten
vestri non erubescent 7. *Iste pauper clamavit et Dominus*
geherde hine 7 of allum geswencednissum his gefriode
exaudivit eum et ex omnibus tribulationibus ejus liberavit

hine insende engel dryht*en* in ymbhwyrfte ondredendra
eum 8. *Inmittit angelum Dominus in circuitu timentium*

hine 7 genereð hie bergað 7 gesiað ðætte wynsum is
eum et eripiet eos 9. *Gustate et videte quoniam suavis est*

dryht*en* eadig wer se gehyhteð in hine ondredað
Dominus beatus vir qui sperat in eum 10. *Timete*

dryht*en* alle halge his forðon nowiht wonu bið
Dominum omnes sancti ejus quoniam nihil deest

ðæm ondredendum hine weolie weðladon 7 hyn[g]radun
timentibus eum 11. *Divites eguerunt et esurierunt*

*socende soðlice dryht*en* ne aspringað ængum gode cumað
inquirentes autem Dominum non deficient omni bono 12. *Venite*

bearn geherað me ege dryht*nes* ic læru eow hwelc is
filii audite me timorem Domini docebo vos 13. *Quis est*

mon se wile lif 7 willað gesian dægas gode bewere
homo qui vult vitam et cupit videre dies bonos 14. *Cohibe*

tungan ðine from yfle 7 weolure ðylæs sprecen facen
linguam tuam a malo et labia tua ne loquantur dolum

acer from yfle 7 doa god soec sibbe 7 fyl[g] ða
15. *Diverte a malo et fac bonum inquire pacem et sequere eam*

egan dryht*nes* ofer rehtwise 7 earan his to boene heara
16. *Oculi Domini super justos et aures ejus ad preces eorum*

ondwleotan soðlice dryht*nes* ofer ða dondan yfel ðet
17. *Vultus autem Domini super facientes mala ut*

he forspilde of eorðan gemynd heara cleopedon
perdat de terra memoriam eorum 18. *Clamaverunt*

rehtwise 7 dryht*en* geherde hie 7 of allum geswencednissum
justi et Dominus exaudivit eos et ex omnibus tribulationibus

heara gefrede hie neh is dryht*en* ðissum ða
eorum liberavit eos 19. *Juxta est Dominus his qui*

geswencedre sind on heortan 7 eaðmode on gaste gehaeleð
tribulato sunt corde et humiles spiritu salvabit

*mong *geswenced rehtwisra 7 of ðissum allum gefreað
20. *Multae tribulationes justorum et de his omnibus liberabit*

hie dryht*en* dryht*en* haldeð all ban heara an
eos Dominus 21. *Dominus custodit omnia ossa eorum unum*

of ðæm ne bið fordręsted deað synfulra se wyrresta 7
ex eis non conteretur 22. *Mors peccatorum pessima et*

ða ða figað ðone rehtwisan agyltað aleseð dryht*en*
qui oderunt justum delinquent 23. *Redimet Dominus*

sawle ðiowa his 7 ne forleteð alle ða ðe gehyhtað
animas servorum suorum et non delinquit omnes qui sperant

in hine
in eum

34.

doem dryhten ða sceððendan me oferfeht ða onfehtendan mec
Judica Domine nocentes me expugna inpugnantes me

gegrip[1] wepen 7 sceld 7 aris in fultum me
2. *Adpraehende arma et scutum et exurge in adjutorium mihi*

ageot sweord 7 biluc wið him ða ðe me
3. *Effunde frameam et conclude adversus eos qui me per-*

oehtað cweð to sawle minre hælu ðin ic eam sien
sequuntur dic animae meae Salus tua ego sum 4. *Con-*

gescilde 7 onscunien feond mine ða soecað sawle mine
fundantur et revereantur inimici mei qui querunt animam meam

sien forcerred on bec 7 scomien ða ðencað me yfel
Avertantur retrorsum et erubescant qui cogitant mihi mala

sien swe swe *dus biforan onsiene windes 7 engel
5. *Fiant tamquam pulvis ante faciem venti et angelus*

dryhtnes swencende hie sien wegas heara ðeostre 7
Domini adfligens eos 6. *Fiant viae eorum tenebrae et*

*glidd 7 ængel dryhtnes oehtende hie forðon
lubricum et angelus Domini persequens eos 7. *Quoniam*

bi ungewyrhtum ahyddon me forwyrd girene heara idellice
gratis absconderunt mihi interitum laquei sui vanae

edwittun sawle mine cyme him giren ða
exprobraverunt animam meam 8. *Veniat illis laqueus quem*

hie neoton 7 geheftednis ða gedegladon gegripeð hie in
ignorant et captio quam occultaverunt adpraehendat eos in

girene ingefallen hie in ðæt ilce sawul soðlice min gefið
laqueo incidant in id ipso 9. *Anima autem mea exultabit*

in dryhtne 7 bið gelustfullað ofer haelu his all
in Domino et delectabitur super salutare ejus 10. *Omnia*

ban min cweodað dryhten hwelc gelic ðe genergende weðlan
ossa mea dicent Domine quis similis tibi eripiens inopem

of honda strongran[2] his weðlan 7 ðearfan from
de manu fortioris ejus egenum et pauperem a

[1] *second* g *over half-er. letter.* [2] ran *over dotted* es.

ðæm reafiendum hine arisende cyðeras unrehte ða
rapientibus eum 11. *Exsurgentes testes iniqui quae*

ic nysse frugnon mec 7 geedleanedun me yfel
ignorabam interrogabant me et 12. *retribuebant mihi mala*

fore godum 7 *unbeorednisse sawle minre ic soðlice
pro bonis et sterelitatem animae meae 13. *Ego autem*

ðonne me hefie werun ic gegerede mec mid heran 7
dum mihi molesti essent induebam me cilicio et

ic geeaðmodade in festenne sawle mine 7 gebed min in *seate
humiliabam in jejunio animam meam et oratio mea in sinu

minum sie forcerred swe ðone nestan swe broður urne
meo convertitur[1] 14. *Sicut proximum sicut fratrem nostrum*

swe ic gelicie swe swe hiofende 7 geunrotsad swe
ita conplacebam tamquam lugens et contristatus ita

ic wes geeaðmodad wið me geblissade werun 7
humiliabar 15. *Adversum me laetati sunt et*

tosomne bicwomun gesomnadon in mec ðrea 7 hie hit nyston
convenerunt congregaverunt in me flagella et ignoraverunt

tolesde sind ne geinbryrde sind costadon mec 7
16. *Dissoluti sunt nec conpuncti sunt temptaverunt me et*

bismeradon mid bismerunge grymetadon in mec mid toðum
diriserunt derisu striderunt in me dentibus

heara dryhten hwonne gelocas ðu gesete sawle mine
suis 17. *Domine quando respicies restitue animam meam*

from yfeldedum heara from þ leom ða angan mine
a malefactis eorum a leonibus unicam meam

ic ondetto ðe dryhten in cirican micelre in folce hefigum
18. *Confitebor tibi Domine in ecclesia magna in populo gravi*

ic hergu ðe ðæt ne bismerien in mec ða ðe wiðerbrociað
laudabo te 19. *Ut non insultent in me qui adversantur*

me unrehtlice ða ðe fiað me bi ungewyrhtum 7 becnadon mid
mihi inique qui oderunt me gratis et annuebant

egum forðon me efne sibsumlice spreocað 7
oculis 20. *Quoniam mihi quidem pacifice loquebantur et*

ofer eorre faecenlice ðohtun gebrę̨ddon in me muð
super iram dolose cogitabant 21. *Dilataverunt in me os*

his cwedon wel ðe wel ðe gesegan egan ur ðu gesege
suum dixerunt Euge euge viderunt oculi nostri 22. *vidisti*

[1] i *half-alt. to* e.

dryhten ne swiga ðu dryhten ne gewit*ð from me aris
Domine ne sileas Domine ne discedas a me 23. *Exsurge*

dryhten 7 bihald dom minne god min 7 dryhten min
Domine et intende judicium meum Deus meus et Dominus meus

in intingan minne doem me dryhten efter
in causam meam 24. *Judica me Domine secundum*

mildheortnisse ðinre dryhten god min þæt ne bismerien in
misericordiam tuam Domine Deus meus ut non insultent in

mec feond mine ne cweðen in heortum heara wel ðe
me inimici mei 25. *nec dicant in cordibus suis Euge*

wel ðe sawle ure ne cweðen we forswelgað hine
euge animae nostrae nec dicant Absorbuimus eum

scomien 7 onscunien somud ða blissiað yflum
26. *Erubescant et revereantur simul qui gratulantur malis*

minum sien gerede scome 7 awescnisse ða ða miclan spreocað
meis induantur pudore et reverentia qui magna loquuntur

wið me gefiað 7 blissiað ða willað *rehtwinisse
adversum me 27. *Exultent et laetentur qui volunt justitiam*

mine 7 cweoðað aa sie miclad dryhten ða willað
meam et dicant semper Magnificetur Dominus qui volunt

sibb ðeowes his ah 7 mid tungan min bið smegende
pacem servi ejus 28. *Sed et lingua mea meditabitur*

rehtwisnisse ðine alne deg lof ðin
justitiam tuam tota die laudem tuam

35.

cweð se unrehtwisa ðætte in him seolfum[1] nis
2. *Dixit injustus ut delinquat in semetipso non est*

ege godes biforan egum his forðon faccenlice dyde in
timor Dei ante oculos ejus 3. *Quoniam dolose egit in*

gesihðe his ðæt gemoette unrehtwisnisse his 7 laeðu
conspectu ejus ut inveniret iniquitatem suam et odium

word muðes his *unrehtwisse 7 facen nalde ongeotan ðæt
4. *Verba oris ejus iniquitas et dolus noluit intellegere ut*

wel dyde unrehtwisnisse smegende is in bedcleofan his
bene ageret 5. *iniquitatem meditatus est in cubili suo*

[1] l *over er.* f (?).

ætstod allum wege noht gode hete soðlice ne fiede
Adstitit omni viae non bonae malitiam autem non odivit

dryhten in heofene mildheortnis ðin 7 soðfestnis ðin oð
6. *Domine in caelo misericordia tua et veritas tua usque*

wolcen rehtwisnis ðin. swe swe muntas godes domas ðine
ad nubes 7. *Justitia tua sicut montes Dei judicia tua*

niolnis micelu men 7 neat hale ðu does dryhten
abyssus multa Homines et jumenta salvos facies Domine

to ðæm gemete gemonigfaldade mildheortnisse ðine god
8. *quemammodum multiplicasti misericordias tuas Deus*

bearn soðlice monna in gescildnisse fiðra ðinra ge-
Filii autem hominum in protectione alarum tuarum spe-

hyhtað bioð geindrencte from breostum huses ðines 7.
rabunt 9. *inebriabuntur ab ubertate domus tuae et*

burnan willan ðines drences hie forðon mid ðe
torrente voluntatis tuae potabis eos 10. *Quoniam aput te*

.is waelle lifes 7 in lehte ðinum we gesiað leht
est fons vitae et in lumini tuo videbimus lumen

ðene mildheortnisse ðine weotendum ðec 7 *rehwisnisse
11. *Praetende misericordiam tuam scientibus te et justitiam*

ðine ðissum ða rehte sind on heortan ne cyme me fot
tuam his qui recto sunt corde 12. *Non veniat mihi pes*

oferhygde 7 hond synfulra ne onwendeð mec ðer
superbiae et manus peccatorum non moveat me 13. *Ibi*

gefeollun alle ða ða wircað *unrehwisnisse onweg adrifene sind
ceciderunt omnes qui operantur iniquitatem expulsi sunt

ne hie maegon stondan
nec potuerunt stare

36.

nyl ðu elnian betwih awergde ne elnende ðu sie
Noli aemulari inter malignantes neque aemulatus fueris

donde unrehtwisnisse forðon swe swe heg hreðlice
facientes iniquitatem 2. *Quoniam tamquam faenum velociter*

adrugiað 7 swe swe leaf wyrta hreðe fallað gehyht in
arescent et sicut holera herbarum cito cadent 3. *Sperą in*

dryhtne 7 doa godnisse 7 inearda eorðan 7 ðu bist foeded
Domino et fac bonitatem et inhabita terram et pasceris

in weolum hire gelustfulla in dryht*ne* 7 seleð ðe
in divitiis ejus 4. *Delectare in Domino et dabit tibi*

boene heortan ðinre onwrih dryhtne *wig ðinne 7
petitiones cordis tui 5. *Revela Domino viam tuam et*

gehyht in hine 7 he doeð 7 utalędeð swe swe leht
spera in eum et ipse faciet 6. *Et educet tamquam lumen*

rehtwisnisse ðine 7 dom ðinne swe on midne deg
justitiam tuam et judicium tuum sicut meridie

underðioded bio ðu dryht*ne* 7 halsa hine ne elnende ðu sie
7. *Subditus esto Domino et obsecra eum ne aemulatus fueris*

hine se bið gesundfullad in wege his in men dondum
eum qui prosperatur in via sua in homine faciente

unrehtwisnisse blin[1] from eorre 7 forlet hatheortnisse ne
iniquitatem 8. *Desine ab ira et derelinque furorem ne*

elna ðu þætte nohtlice ðu doe forðon ða nohtlice
aemuleris ut nequiter facias 9. *Quoniam qui nequiter*

doð biað abreotte ða soðlice abidað dryht*en* he
agunt exterminabuntur qui vero expectant Dominum ipsi

erfewordnisse gesittað eorðan lytel nuget 7 ne
hereditate possidebunt terram 10. *Pusillum adhuc et non*

bið se synfulla 7 soeces stowe his ne ðu *gemotes
erit peccator et quaeris locum ejus nec invenies

ða monðuaeran soðlice gesittað eorðan 7 bioð gelustfullade
11. *Mansueti autem possidebunt terram et delectabuntur*

in menge sibbe haldeð se synfulla ðone rehtwisan 7
in multitudine pacis 12. *Observabit peccator justum et*

grymetad ofer hine mid toðum his dryht*en* soðlice
frement super eum dentibus suis 13. *Dominus autem*

bismerað hine forðon gelocað ðæt cymeð deg his
inridebit eum quoniam prospicit quod veniet dies ejus

sweord gebrugdun ða synfullan ðenedon bogan his
14. *Gladium evaginaverunt peccatores tetenderunt arcum suum*

ðæt hie awurpen weðlan 7 ðearfan ðæt hie cwaelmen ða reht-
ut dejiciant inopem et pauperem ut trucident rectos

heortan sweord heara ingaeð in heortan heara 7 boga
corde 15. *Gladius eorum intret in cor ipsorum et arcus*

heara bið forðrested bettre is lytel ðæm rehtwisan
eorum conteratur 16. *Melius est modicum justo*

[1] bl:in *rubbed; may have been* blinn, *as Stevenson reads.*

ofer weolan synfulra monge forðon earm
super divitias peccatorum multas 17. *Quoniam bracchia*

synfulra sien forðręsteð getrymeð soðlice ða rehtwisan dryht*en*
peccatorum conterentur confirmat autem justos Dominus

wat dryht*en* weagas unwemra 7 erfewordnis heara
18. *Novit Dominus vias inmaculatorum et hereditas eorum*

in ecnisse bið ne bioð gescende in tid yfle 7
in aeternum erit 19. *Non confundentur in tempore malo et*

in dægum hungres bioð gefylde forðon synfulle
in diebus famis saturabuntur 20. *quoniam peccatores*

forweorðað feond soðlice dryht*nes* sona gearade 7 upahefene
peribunt Inimici autem Domini mox honorati et exaltati

biað aspringende swe swe rec hie aspringað bið *onwende
fuerint deficientes ut fumus deficient 21. *Mutuatur*

se synfulla 7 ne onleseð se rehtwisa soðlice mildsað 7
peccator et non solvit justus autem miseretur et

geðwaerað forðon bledsiende hine gesittað eorðan
commodat 22. *Quoniam benedicentes eum possidebunt terram*

wercweoðende soðlice hine forweorðað from dryht*ne*
maledicentes autem illum disperient 23. *A Domino*

gong monnes bioð gereht 7 weg his gewillað swiðe
gressus hominis dirigentur et viam ejus cupiet nimis

ðonne gefalleð se rehtwisa ne bið *gedroefede forðon dryht*en*
24. *Cum ceciderit justus non conturbabitur quia Dominus*

trymeð hond his gungra ic wes 7 ic aldade 7 ic ne
*firmat *manuum ejus* 25. *Juvenior fui et senui et non*

gesaeh ðone rehtwisan forletenne ne sed his weðliende hlaf
vidi justum derelictum nec semen ejus egens panem

alne deg mildsað 7 geþwærað 7 sed his in bledsunge
26. *Tota die miseretur et commodat et semen ejus in benedictione*

bið onhaeld from yfle[1] 7 doo god 7 inearda in
erit 27. *Declina a malo et fac bonum et inhabita in*

weoruld weorulde forðon dryht*en* lufað dom 7
saeculum saeculi 28. *Quoniam Dominus amat judicium et*

ne forleteð halge his in ecnisse bioð gehaldne
non derelinquit sanctos suos in aeternum conservabuntur

ða unrehtwisan soðlice bioð wicnade 7 sed arleasra
Injusti autem punientur et semen impiorum

[1] l *from* n (?).

forweorðeð ða rehtwisan soðlice erfewordnisse gesittað
peribit 29. *Justi vero hereditate possidebunt*

eorðan 7 ineardiað in weoruld weorulde ofer hie
terram et inhabitabunt in saeculum saeculi super eam

muð ðes rehtwisan bið smead snyttru 7 tunge his
30. *Os justi meditabitur sapientiam et lingua ejus*

spriced dom ae godes his in heortan his 7 ne
loquitur judicium 31. *Lex Dei ejus in corde ipsius et non*

bioð gescrencte gongas his sceawað se synfulla
supplantabuntur gressus ejus 32. *Considerat . peccator*

ðone rehtwisan 7 soeceð forspildan hine dryhten soðlice
justum et querit perdere eum 33. *Dominus autem*

ne forleteð hine in hondum his ne geniderað[1] hine ðonne
non derelinquet eum in manibus ejus nec damnabit eum cum

bið *omed him abid dryhten 7 gehald wegas his
judicabitur illi 34. *Exspecta Dominum et custodi vias ejus*

7 hefeð up ðe þæt ðu ineardie eorðan ðonne forweorðað
et exaltabit te ut inhabites terram cum periant

ða synfullan ðu gesist ......[2] san upahefenne 7
peccatores videbis 35. *V . .*[2] *mpium superexaltatum et*

upahefenne ofer cederbeamas Libani 7 ic leorde 7 sehðe ne
elevatum super cedros 36. *Et transivi et ecce non*

wes 7 ic sohte hine 7 ne wes *gemoted stow his
erat et quaesivi eum et non est inventus locus ejus

hald soðfestnisse 7 geseh efennisse forðon sind
37. *Custodi veritatem et vide aequitatem quoniam sunt re-*

lafe męnn[3] ðæm sibsuman ða unrehtan soðlice forweorðað
liquiae homini pacifico 38. *Injusti autem disperient*

somud lafe arleasra forweorðað haelu soðlice
simul reliquiae impiorum peribunt 39. *Salus autem*

rehtwisra from dryhtne is 7 gescildend heara is on tid
justorum a Domino est et protector eorum est in tempore

geswinces 7 gefultumeð hie dryhten 7 gefreoð hie
tribulationis 40. *Et adjuvabit eos Dominus et liberabit eos*

7 genereð hie from synfullum 7 hale gedoeð hie forðon
et eripiet eos a peccatoribus et salvos faciet eos quoniam

gehyhton in hine
speraverunt in eum

[1] *last* e *on er.* [2] *rubbed away.* [3] ę *doubtful.*

37.

dryhten nales in eorre ðinum ðrea me *n in
2. *Domine ne in ira tua arguas me neque in*
hatheortnisse ðinre geðrea mec forðon strele ðine
furore tuo corripias me 3. *Quoniam sagittae tuae*
gefestnade sind me[1] 7 getrymedes ofer mec hond ðine
infixae sunt mihi et confirmasti super me manum tuam
ne is haelu in flesce minum *fro o[n]dwleatan eorres
4. *Nec est sanitas in carne mea a vultu irae*
ðines nis sib banum minum from onsiene synna minra
tuae non est pax ossibus meis a facie peccatorum meorum
forðon unrehtwisnisse mine ofergesetton heafud min
5. *Quoniam iniquitates meae superposuerunt caput meum*
swe swe byrðen hefig gehefegade sind ofer mec
sicut onus grave gravatae sunt super me
fuladun[2] 7 wyrsadon wundsweðe mine from onsiene
6. *Conputruerunt et deterioraverunt cicatrices meae a facie*
unwisdomes mines ermðum geswenced ic eam 7 gedroefed
insipientiae meae 7. *Miseriis afflictus sum et turbatus*
ic eam oð in ende alne deg geunrotsad ic ineode
sum usque in finem tota die contristatus ingrediebar
forðon sawul min gefylled is bismernissum 7 ne wes
8. *Quoniam anima mea conpleta est inlusionibus et non est*
haelu in flaesce minum gebeged ic eam 7 gehened[3]
sanitas in carne mea 9. *Incurbatus sum et humiliatus*
ic eam a hu lenge swiðu(r)[4] ic grymetede from geamrunge
sum usquequaque rugiebam a gemitu
heortan minre 7 biforan ðe is all lust[5] min 7
cordis mei 10. *et ante te est omne desiderium meum et*
gemrung min from ðe nis ahyded heorte min
gemitus meus a te non est absconditus 11. *Cor meum*
gedroefed is in me 7 forleort mec strengu min 7 leht
conturbatum est in me et deseruit me fortitudo mea et lumen
egena minra nis mid me *freod mine 7 ða nestan
oculorum meorum non est mecum 12. *Amici mei et proximi*

[1] *er. before* e. [2] vel rotedan *added later.* [3] vel geeadmet *added later.* [4] *rubbed out;* vel agehwær *added later.* [5] vel gewilnung *added later.*

mine wið me *tolehlaecað 7 stodon 7 ða nestan mine
mei adversum me adpropiaverunt et steterunt et proximi mei

feor stodon 7 ned dydun ða sohton sawle
a longe steterunt 13. *Et vim faciebant qui querebant animam*

mine 7 ða sohton yfel me spreocende werun idelnisse
meam et qui inquirebant mala mihi locuti sunt vanitatem

7 facen alne deg werun smegende ic soðlice swe swe
et dolos tota die meditabantur 14. *Ego autem velut*

deaf ic ne ge:::::[1] 7 swe swe dumb se ne ontyneð muð
surdus non audiebam et sicut mutus qui non aperiet os

•his 7 geworden ic eam swe swe mon no geherrende
suum 15. *Et factus sum ut homo non audiens*

7 nabbende in muðe his ðreange forðon in ðe
et non habens in ore suo increpationem 16. *Quoniam in te*

dryhten ic gehyhte ic cweð ðu geheres dryhten god min
Domine speravi dixi Tu exaudies Domine Deus meus

forðon ·ic cweð ne [a]h[w]onne bismerien in mec feond mine
17. *Quia dixi Ne quando insultent in me inimici mei*

7 mid ðy bioð onstyrede foet min in me ða miclan[2] spreocende
et dum commoverentur pedes mei in me magna locuti

sind forðon ic to ðream gearu ic eam 7 sar
sunt 18. *Quoniam ego ad flagella paratus sum et dolor*

min biforan me is aa forðon *unrehtwisniss mine
meus ante me est semper 19. *Quoniam iniquitatem meam*

ic forðsegcga 7 ðenco fore scylde minre feond
ego pronuntio et cogitabo pro peccato meo 20. *Inimici*

soðlice mine lifgað 7 gestrongade sind ofer me 7
autem mei vivent et confortati sunt super me et

gemonigfaldade sind ða ðe fiedon mec unrehtlice ða
multiplicati sunt qui oderunt me inique 21. *Qui*

geedleanedon[3] me yfel fore godum teldon[4] me forðon
retribuebant mihi mala pro bonis detrahebant mihi quoniam

*esterfylgende ic eam *rehtwinisse ne forlet ðu me
subsecutus sum justitiam 22. *Ne derelinquas me*

dryhten god min ne gewit ðu from me bihald in
Domine Deus meus ne discesseris a me 23. *intende in*

fultum minne dryhten god *halu minre
adjutorium meum Domine Deus salutis meae

[1] herde *on the er. in late hand.* [2] vel fela *added later.* [3] vel aguldon *added later* [4] hi *before* teldon *in later hand.*

38.

ic cweð ic haldu wegas mine ðet ic ne agylte in
2. *Dixi Custodiam vias meas ut non delinquam in*

tungan minre ic sette muðe minum gehaeld ðonne gestondeð
lingua mea Posui ori meo custodiam dum consistit

se synfulla wið me ic adumbade 7 geeaðmodad ic eam
peccator adversus me. 3. *Obmutui et humiliatus sum*

7 ic swigade from godum 7 sar min geedneowad is
et silui a bonis et dolor meus renovatus est

hatade heorte min binnan me 7 in smeange minre
4. *Concaluit cor meum intra me et in meditatione mea*

born fyr spreocende ic eam in tungan minre cuð me
exardescit ignis 5. *Locutus sum in lingua mea notum mihi*

doa dryht*en* ende minne 7 rim dæga minra hwelc is
fac Domine finem meum et numerum dierum meorum quis est

ðæt ic wite hwet wone sie me sehðe alde ðu settes dęgas.
ut sciam quid desit mihi 6. *Ecce veteres posuisti dies*

mine 7 spoede mine swe swe nowiht biforan ðe bið ah
meos et substantia mea tamquam nihil ante te est Verum

hweðre al idelnis ylc mon lifgende ðaehðe in
tamen universa vanitas omnis homo vivens 7. *quanquam in*

onlicnisse godes gonge mon hweðre idellice bið gedroefed
imagine Dei ambulet homo tamen vane conturbabitur

goldhordað[1] 7 nat hwæm gesomnað ða 7 nu hwet
Thesaurizat et ignorat cui congregat ea 8. *et nunc quae*

is bad min ahne dryht*en* 7 sie spoed min biforan ðe
est expectatio mea Nonne Dominus et substantia mea ante te

is from allum unrehtwisnissum minum genere mec
est 9. *Ab omnibus iniquitatibus meis eripe me*

edwit ðæm unwisan ðu[2] saldes mec ic adumbade 7
opprobrium insipienti dedisti me 10. *Obmutui et*

ne ontynde muð minne forðon ðu dydest awend from *e
non aperui os meum quoniam tu fecisti 11. *Amove a me*

witu ðin from strengu soðlice honda ðine ic asprong
plagas tuas 12. *a fortitudine enim manus tuae ego defeci*

in ðreangum[3] fore unrehtwisnisse ðu ðreades mon
in increpationibus Propter iniquitatem corripuisti hominem

[1] *second* d *from* ð. [2] u *from* a. [3] u *over* e.

7 aswindan ðu *des swe gongeweafran sawle his ah
et tabescere fecisti sicut aranea animam ejus Verum
hweðre all idelnis ylc mon *lifgen geher god
tamen universa vanitas omnis homo vivens 13. *Exaudi Deus*
gebed min 7 boene mine mid earum onfoh
orationem meam et deprecationem meam auribus percipe
tearas mine ne swiga ðu from me forðon londleod ic eam
lacrimas meas ne sileas a me Quoniam incola ego sum
mid ðe in eorðan 7 elðeoðig swe swe alle fedras mine
aput te in terra et peregrinus sicut omnes patres mei
• forletað me ðæt ic sie gecoeled ær ðon ic gewite 7
14. *Remitte mihi ut refrigerer priusquam abeam et*
męe ic ne biom
amplius non ero

39.

bidende ic abad dryht*en* 7 gelocade mec 7
2. *Expectans expectavi Dominum et respexit me* 3. *et*
gehcrde boene mine 7 ut alaedde mec of seaðe
exaudivit deprecationem meam et eduxit me de lacu
ermða 7 of lame derstan 7 sette ofer stan foet mine
miseriae et de luto fecis Et statuit super petram pedes meos
7 gerec : : : hte gongas mine 7 insende in muð minne
et direxit gressus meos 4. *et inmisit in os meum*
song niowne ymen gode urum gesioð monge 7
canticum novum hymnum Deo nostro Videbunt multi et
ondredað 7 gehyhtað in dryht*ne* eadig wer ðes is
timebunt et sperabunt in Domino 5. *Beatus vir cujus est*
noma dryht*nes* hyht his 7 ne gelocað in idelnisse 7 in
nomen Domini spes ejus et non respexit in vanitatem et in
*woedenheortnisse lease feolu ðu dydes ðu dryht*en* god
insanias falsas 6. *Multa fecisti tu Domine Deus*
min wundur ðin 7 geðohtum ðinum nis hwelc gelic
meus mirabilia tua et cogitationibus tuis non est quis similis
ðe ic segde 7 spreocende ic eam gemonigfaldade sind ofer
tibi Annuntiavi et locutus sum multiplicati sunt super
rim onsegdnisse 7 onsegdnisse naldes ðu lichoman
numerum 7. *sacrificium et oblationem noluisti corpus*
soðlice ðu gefremedes me onsegdnisse ec swelce fore scylde
autem perfecisti mihi Holocausta etiam pro delicto

ðu ne bede ða ic cweð sehðe ic cumu in heafde boec
non postulasti 8. *tunc dixi Ecce venio In capite libri*

awriten is bi me ðæt ic doe willan ðinne god
scriptum est de me 9. *ut faciam voluntatem tuam Deus*

min ic walde ⁊ ae ðine in midle heortan minre wel
meus volui et legem tuam in medio cordis mei 10. *Bene*

ic segde rehtwisnisse ðine in cirican micelre sehðe weolure
nuntiavi justitiam tuam in ecclesia magna ecce labia

mine[1] ic ne biwergu dryhten ðu oncneowe *rehtwinisse
mea non prohibebo Domine tu cognovisti 11. *justitiam*

ðine ic ne ahydde in heortan minre soðfestnisse ðine ⁊
tuam non abscondi in corde meo veritatem tuam et

haelu ðine ic segde ne hel ic mildheortnisse ðine ⁊
salutarem tuum dixi Non celavi misericordiam tuam et

soðfestnisse ðine from gesomnunge micelre ðu soðlice
veritatem tuam a synagoga multa 12. *Tu autem*

dryhten nales feor doa ðu mildheortnisse ðine from *e mildheortnis
Domine ne longe facias misericordias tuas a me misericordia

ðin ⁊ soðfestnis ðin aa onfengun me forðon
tua et veritas tua semper susciperunt me 13. *Quoniam*

ymbsaldon me yfel ðeara ne wes rim bi-
circumdederunt mȩ mala quorum non est numerus con-

fengon me unrehtwisnisse mine ⁊ ic ne maehte ðæt
praehenderunt me iniquitates meae et non potui ut

ic gesege gemonigfaldade sind ofer loccas *heasdes mines ⁊
viderem Multiplicati sunt super capillos capitis mei. et

heorte min forleort me gelicað ðe dryhten ðæt
cor meum dereliquit me 14. *Conplaceat tibi Domine ut*

ðu generge mec dryhten in fultum minne geloca
eripias me Domine in auxilium meum respice

sien gescende ⁊ onscunien somud ða ðe soecað sawle
15. *Confundantur et reveriantur simul qui quaerunt animam*

mine ðæt hie afirren hie sien forcerred on bec ⁊ s[c]omien
meam ut auferant eam Avertantur retrorsum et erubescant

ða ðencað me yfel forðberen sona scome
qui cogitant mihi mala 16. *Ferant confestim confusionem*

his ða cweoðað me wel ðæ[2] wel ðe gefen ⁊
suam qui dicunt mihi Euge euge 17. *Exultent et*

[1] minne; *first* n *dotted.*   [2] *altered from some other letter.*

blissien ðа soecað ðec dryhten 7 cweoðað aa sie gemiclad
laetentur qui quaerunt te Domine et dicant semper Magnificetur
dryhten ða lufiað haelu ðine ic soðlice weðla
Dominus qui diligunt salutare tuum **18.** *Ego vero egenus*
7 ðearfa ic eam dryhten gemnisse hafað min fultum min 7
et pauper sum Dominus curam habet mei adjutor meus et
gefrigend min wes *ðe dryhten ne leata ðu
liberator meus es tu Domine ne tardaveris

40.

eadig se ongiteð ofer weðlan 7 ðearfan in dege
2. *Beatus qui intellegit super egenum et pauperem in die*
yflum gefreað hine dryhten dryhten gehaldeð hine 7
mala liberabit eum Dominus 3. *Dominus conservet eum et*
*gelifesteð hine 7 eadigne gedoeð hine 7 geclasnað in eorðan
vivificet eum et beatum faciet eum et mundet in terra
sawle his 7 ne seleð hine in hond *feond his
animam ejus et non tradat eum in manus inimici ejus
dryhten weolan bireð him ofer bed sares his
4. *Dominus opem ferat illi super lectum doloris ejus uni-*
alle strene his ðu gecerdes in *untrynisse his ic
versum stratum ejus versasti in infirmitate ejus 5. *Ego*
ic cweð dryhten mildsa min hael sawle mine forðon
dixi Domine miserire mei sana animam meam quia
ic syngade ðe feond mine cwedon yfel me hwonne
peccavi tibi 6. *Inimici mei dixerunt mala mihi Quando*
swilteð 7 forweorðeð noma his 7 inneodan ðæt
morietur et periet nomen ejus 7. *Et ingrediebantur ut*
hie gesegen ða idlan spreocende wes heorte heara gesomnadon
viderent vana locutum est cor eorum congregaverunt
unreht him 7 uteodon ut 7 werun spreocende somud
iniquitatem sibi Et egrediebatur foras et loquebatur 8. *simul*
in *anisse hyspton alle feond mine wið me[1]
in unum susurrabunt Omnes inimici mei adversum me
ðohton yfel me word unreht onbudun wið
cogitabant mala mihi 9. *verbum iniquum mandaverunt adversum*
me ah se hneapað to ne geeceð þæt arise 7
me Num quid qui dormit non adiciet ut resurgat 10. *et*

[1] *repeated.*

soðlice mon sibbe minre in ðæm ic gehyhte se ðe et hlafas
enim homo pacis meae in quo sperabam qui edebat panes

mine gemonigfaldade wið me gescrencednisse ðu
meos ampliavit adversum me supplantationem **11.** *Tu*

soðlice dryhten mildsa min 7 awece me 7 ic geedleaniu him
autem Domine miserire mei et resuscita me et retribuam illis

in ðissum ic oncneow ðætte ðu waldes mec forðon ne
12. *In hoc cognovi quoniam voluisti me quia non*

gefið se feond min ofer me forðon unsceðfulnisse
gaudebit inimicus meus super me **13.** *Propter innocentiam*

soðlice[1] mine ðu onfenge mec 7 getrymedes mec in gesihðe
autem meam suscepisti me et confirmasti me in conspectu

ðinre in ecnisse gebledsad dryhten god from
tuo in aeternum **14.** *Benedictus Dominus Deus Israhel a*

weorulde 7 oð in weoruld sie sie
saeculo et usque in saeculum fiat fiat

41.

swe swe heorut gewillað to waellum wetra swę
2. *Sicut cervus desiderat ad fontes aquarum ita*

gewillað sawul min to ðe god ðyrsteð sawul min
desiderat anima mea ad te Deus **3.** *Sitivit anima mea*

to gode ðæm lifgendan hwonne ic cyme 7 oteawe biforan
ad Deum vivum quando veniam et parebo ante

*onsien godes werun me tearas mine hlafas
faciem Dei **4.** *Fuerunt mihi lacrimae meae panes*

deges 7 naehtes ðonne bið cweden to me deghwæmlice hwer
die ac nocte dum dicitur mihi cotidie Ubi

is god ðin ðas gemyndig ic eam 7 ageat in me
est Deus tuus **5.** *Haec recordatus sum et effudi in me*

sawle mine forðon ic inga in stowe geteldes
animam meam quoniam ingrediar in locum tabernaculi

wundurlic oð *godes hus godes in stefne wynsumnisse
ammirabilis usque ad domum Dei in voce exultationis

7 ondetnisse swoeg symbliendes forhwon unrot earðu
et confessionis sonus aepulantis **6.** *Quare tristis es*

sawul min 7 *forhon gedroefdes ðu me gehyht in
anima mea et quare conturbas me spera in

[1] i *over* e.

gode forðon ic ondetto him haelu ondwlitan *minis
Deum quoniam confitebor illi salutare vultus mei

7 god min from me seolfum sawul min gedroefed
7. *et Deus meus A me ipso anima mea turbata*

is forðon gemyndig ic biom ðin dryhten of eorðan
est propterea memor ero tui Domine de terra

7 from munte ðæm lytlan niolnis
Jordanis et Hermonis a monte modico 8. *Abyssus*

niolnisse geceð in stefne ðeotena[1] ðinra all
abyssum invocat in voce cataractarum tuarum omnia

ða hean ðin 7 yðe ðine ofer mec leordun in
excelsa tua et fluctus tui super me transierunt 9. *In*

dege onbead dryht*en* mildheortnisse his 7 on naeht
die mandavit Dominus misericordiam suam et nocte

gebirhte mid mec *gebe gode mines lifes ic cweoðu
declaravit Aput me oratio Deo vitae meae 10. *dicam*

gode ondfenga min ðu earð forhwon mec ofergeotul earð
Deo Susceptor meus es Quare me oblitus es

7 forhwon mec onweg adrife ðu 7 forhwon unrot ic ingaa
et quare me reppulisti et quare tristis incedo

ðonne swenceð mec fiond ðonne bioð gebrocen
dum affligit me inimicus 11. *Dum confringuntur*

all ban min edwiton mec ða swencað mec
omnia ossa mea exprobraverunt me qui tribulant me

ðonne bið cweden to me ðorh syndrie dægas hwer is
dum dicitur mihi per singulos dies Ubi est

god ðin forhwon unrot earðu sawul min 7
Deus tuus 12. *Quare tristis es anima mea et*

forhwon gedroefes ðu mec gehyht in god forðon ic on-
quare conturbas me spera in Deum quoniam confi-

detto him haelu ondwleotan mines 7 god min
tebor illi salutare vultus mei et Deus meus

42.

doem mec god 7 toscad intingan minne of ðeode
Judica me Deus et discerne causam meam de gente

noht haligre from men unrehtum 7 facnum genere me
non sancta ab homine iniquo et doloso cripe me

[1] a *over* e.

forðon ðu earð god min 7 strengu min forhwon
2. *Quia tu es Deus meus et fortitudo mea quare*

me onweg adrife ðu 7 forhwon unrot ic inga ðonne
me reppulisti et quare tristis incedo dum

swenceð mec se feond onsend leht ðin 7 soð-
adfligit me inimicus 3. *Emitte lucem tuam et veri-*

festnisse ðine hie mec *gelaedon 7 togelaeddon in
tatem tuam ipsa me deduxerunt et adduxerunt in

munte ðæm halgan ðinum 7 in getelde ðinum
monte sancto tuo et in tabernaculo tuo

ic ingaa to wibede godes to gode se geblissað
4. *Introibo ad altare Dei ad Deum qui laetificat*

iuguðe mine ic ondetto ðe in citran god god min
juventutem meam Confitebor tibi in cythara Deus Deus meus

forhwon unrot earðu sawul min 7 forhwon gedroefes[1]
5. *Quare tristis es anima mea et quare conturbas*

me gehyht in god forðon ic ondettu him haelu
me Spera in Deum quoniam confitebor illi salutare

ondwleotan mines 7 god min
vultus mei et Deus meus

43.

god mid earum urum we geherdun 7 fedras ure
2. *Deus auribus nostris audivimus et patres nostri*

segdun us werc ðæt wircende ðu earð in dægum
annuntiaverunt nobis Opus quod operatus es in diebus

heara 7 in dægum ðæm alldum honda ðine ðeode
eorum et in diebus antiquis 3. *Manus tuae*[2] *gentes*

tostenceð 7 ðu geplantades hie ðu *swenteṣ folc 7
disperdet et plantasti eos adflixisti populos et

onweg adrife hie nales soðlice in sweorde his
expulisti eos 4. *Nec enim in gladio suo*

gesittad eorðan 7 earm heara ne gehæleð hie
possidebunt terram et bracchium eorum non salvabit eos

ah sie swiðre ðin 7 earm ðin 7 inlihtnis
Sed dextera tua et bracchium tuum et inluminatio

o[n]dwleotan ðines forðon gelicade ðe in him ðu
vultus tui quoniam conplacuit tibi in illis 5. *Tu*

[1] d *on er.* [2] tua :.

earð se[1] ilca cyning min 7 god min ðu onbude
es ipse rex meus et Deus meus qui mandas

haelu in ðe fiond ure we windwiað
salutem Jacob 6. *In te inimicos nostros ventilavimus*

7 in noman ðinum we forhycgað arisende in us
et in nomini tuo spernimus insurgentes in nos

nales[2] soðlice[3] in bogan minum ic gehyhto 7 sweord
7. *Non enim in arcu meo sperabo et gladius*

min ne gehaeleð me ðu gefreades soðlice usic of
meus non salvabit me 8. *Liberasti enim nos ex*

ðæm swencendum usic 7 ða ða usic fiedon ðu gestea-
adfligentibus nos et eos qui nos oderunt confu-

ðelaðes in gode we bioð *here allne deg 7 in
disti 9. *In Deo laudabimur tota die et in*

noman ðinum we ondettað in weorulðe nu soðlice
nomini tuo confitebimur in saecula 10. *Nunc autem*

onweg adrife 7 ðu gescendes[4] usic 7 ne gæst god in
reppulisti et confudisti nos et non egredieris Deus in

megnum urum ðu forcerdes usic on bec fore
virtutibus nostris 11. *Avertisti nos retrorsum prae*

fiondum urum 7 ða ða usic fiedon gereafadon him
inimicis nostris et eos qui nos oderunt diripiebant sibi

ðu saldes′ usic swe swe scep metta 7 in *ðeodu
12. *Dedisti nos tamquam oves escarum et in gentibus*

ðu tostrugde usic ðu bibohtes[5] folc ðin butan
dispersisti nos 13. *Vendedisti populum tuum sine*

weorðe 7 ne wes mengo in onwendednissum heara
praetio et non fuit multitudo in commutationibus eorum

ðu settes usic in edwit nehgehusum urum mid
14. *Posuisti nos in opprobrium vicinis nostris de-*

bismerunge 7 forhogadnisse ðissum ða in *ymhwyrfte urum
risu et contemptu his qui in circuitu nostro

sin(d)[6] ðu settes usic in gelicnisse ðiodum on-
sunt 15. *Posuisti nos in similitudinem gentibus com-*

wendnisse heaf[d]es we gefyllað alne deg scomu
motionem capitis in plebibus 16. *Tota die verecundia*

min wið me is 7 gedroefednis ondwleotan mines oferwrah
mea contra me est et confusio vultus mei operuit

[1] *er. after* s. [2] l *on other letter.* [3] c *over dotted* s. [4] s (?) *er. before* g. [5] *first* b *from* h. [6] *cut off.*

mec from stefne *eðwetendes 7 *wiðspreocen from
me 17. *A voce exprobrantis et obloquentis a*

onsiene feondes 7 oehtendes ðas all cwomun
facie inimici et persequentis 18. *Haec omnia venerunt*

ofer usic 7 ofergeotele we ne sind ðec 7 unrehtlice
super nos et obliti non sumus te et inique

we ne doð in cyðnisse ðinre 7 ne gewat on bec
non egimus in testamento tuo 19. *et non recessit retro*

heorte ur 7 ðu onhældes stige ure from wege
cor nostrum Et declinasti semitas nostras a via

ðinum forðon ðu geeaðmodades usic in stowe
tua 20. *quoniam humiliasti nos in loco*

geswinces 7 oferwrah usic scua deaðes gif
afflictionis et operuit nos umbra mortis 21. *Si*

ofergeotulæ[1] we sind noma godes ures 7 gif we
obliti sumus nomen Dei nostri et si ex-

aðennað honda ure to gode ðæm fremðan ah ne
pandimus manus nostras ad deum alienum 22. *Nonne*

god soeceð ðas he soðlice wat ða deglan heortan
Deus requirit ista ipse enim novit occulta cordis

forðon fore ðe mid deaðe we biað geswencte alne deg
Quoniam propter te morte afficimur tota die

getalde we sind swe swe scep ofslegenisse aris
aestimati sumus ut oves occisionis 23. *Exurge*

forhwon *heppas[2] ðu dryhten aris ne forspild ðu usic oð
quare obdormis Domine exurge ne repellas nos usque

ende forhwon onsiene ðine ðu forcerrest ðu ofer-
in finem 24. *Quare faciem tuam avertis obli-*

geotelas wedelnisse ure 7 geswencednisse ure
visceris inopiam nostram et tribulationem nostram

forðon geeaðmodad is in dusðe sawul ur
25. *Quoniam humiliata est in pulvere anima nostra*

ætfalh in eorðan womb ur aris dryhten geful-
adhesit in terra venter noster 26. *Exurge Domine ad-*

tume us 7 gefrea us fore *nomen ðinum
juva nos et libera nos propter nomen tuum

[1] æ *from* u. [2] h *from some other letter.*

44.

roccetteð heorte min word god ic cweoðu ic werc
2. *Eructuavit cor meum verbum bonum dico ego opera*

min cyninge tunge min hreod *writ hreðlice writendes
mea regi Lingua mea calamus scribae velociter scribentis

wlitig on hiowe fore bearnum *mona[1] togoten is
3. *Speciosus forma prae filiis hominum diffusa est*

geofu in weolerum ðinum forðon bledsade ðe god
gratia in labiis tuis Propterea benedixit te Deus

in ecnisse begyrd sweord ðin *ym lendan
in aeternum 4. *accingere gladium tuum circa femur*

ða maehtgestan heow ðin 7 fegernisse ðine
potentissime 5. *Speciem tuam et pulchritudinem tuam*

beha[l]d gesundfullice forðgaa 7 ricsa fore soðfestnisse
intende prospere procede et regna Propter veritatem

7 monðwernisse 7 rechtwisnisse 7 gelaedeð ðec wundur-
et mansuetudinem et justitiam et deducet te mira-

lice sie swiðre ðin strele ðine scearpe ða
biliter dextera tua 6. *Sagittae tuae acutae poten-*

maehtgestan folc under ðe fallað in heortan fionda
tissime populi sub te cadent in corde inimicorum

cyninges seld ðin god in weoruld weorulde gerd
regis 7. *Sedis tua Deus in saeculum saeculi virga*

reht is *ger rices ðines ðu lufedes rehtwisnisse 7
recta est virga regni tui 8. *Dilexisti justitiam et*

feodes unrehtwisnisse forðon smirede ðec god god ðin
odisti iniquitatem propterea unxit te Deus Deus tuus

mid ele blisse fore gefoerraedennum ðinum myrre 7
oleo laetitiae prae consortibus tuis 9. *Mirra et*

dropa 7 smiring from hreglum ðinum from stepum
gutta et cassia a vestimentis tuis a gradibus

elpanbaennum of ðæm dec gelustfulladun dohtur
eburneis ex quibus te delectaverunt 10. *filiae*

cyninga in are ðinre ætstod cwoen to swiðran ðire
regum in honore tuo Adstitit regina a dextris tuis

in gegerelan bigyldum ymbswapen *misenlicnisse geher
in vestitu deaurato circumamicta varietate 11. *Audi*

[1] *from* mom.

dohtur 7 geseh 7 onhaeld eare ðin 7 forget
filia et vide et inclina aurem tuam et obliviscere.

folc ðin 7 gehusscipe feadur ðines forðon
populum tuum et domum patris tui **12.** *Quoniam*

gewillade cyning hiow *ðin forðon he is dryhten
concupivit rex speciem tuam quia ipse est Dominus

god ðin 7 weorðiað hine dohtur ðes londes in
Deus tuus et adorabunt eum **13.** *filiae Tyri in*

gefum ondwleotan ðinne biddað alle weolie
muneribus Vultum tuum deprecabuntur omnes divites

folces all wuldur his dohtur cyning from innan
plebis **14.** *omnis gloria ejus filiae regum ab intus*

in feasum gyldnum ymbswapen *misenlicnisse sien
In fimbriis aureis **15.** *circumamicta varietate Ad-*

togelaeded cyninge fęmnan efter ðon ða nestan his
ducentur regi virgines post eam proximae ejus

sien tobroht ðe in blisse 7 wynsumnisse sien
adferentur tibi **16.** *in laetitia et exultatione ad-*

togelaeded in tempel cyninges fore feodrum ðinum
ducentur in templum regis **17.** *Pro patribus tuis*

acende sind ðe bearn ðu gesetes hie aldermen ofer
nati sunt tibi filii constitues eos principes super

alle eorðan gemyndge bioð noman ðines in
omnem terram **18.** *Memores erunt nominis tui in*

ylcre cneorisse 7 cynne forðon folc ondet-
omni generatione et progeniae Propterea populi confite-

tað ðe in ecnisse 7 in weoruld weorulde
buntur tibi in aeternum et in saeculum saeculi

45.

god ur geberg 7 megen fultum in geswenced-
2. *Deus noster refugium et virtus adjutor in tribulation-*

nissum[1] ða *gemoetun usic swiðe forðon we ne ondredað
ibus quae invenerunt nos nimis **3.** *Propterea non timebimus*

ðonne bið *gedroed eorðe 7 bioð forcerred muntas in heortan
dum conturbabitur terra et transferentur montes in cor

sæs hleoðradan 7 gedroefde werun weter his gedroefde
maris **4.** *Sonaverunt et turbatae sunt aquae ejus conturbati*

[1] um *over* e.

werun muntas in fyrhtu his fiodes onraes geblissað
sunt montes in fortitudine ejus 5. *Fluminis impetus laetificat*

cestre godes gehalgað geteld his se hesta
civitatem Dei sanctificavit tabernaculum suum altissimus

god in midle his ne bið onstyred gefultumeð hie
6. *Deus in medio ejus non commovebitur Adjuvavit eam*

god mid ondwleatan his gedroefde *sin ðeade 7 onhaelde
Deus vultu suo 7. *conturbatae sunt gentes et inclinata*

sind rice salde stefne his se hesta 7 onstyred is eorðe
sunt regna dedit vocem suam Altissimus et mota est terra

dryhten megna mid us ondfenga ur god
8. *Dominus virtutum nobiscum susceptor noster Deus Jacob*

cumað 7 gesiað werc dryhtnes ða *sete tacen ofer
9. *Venite et videte opera Domini quae posuit prodigia super*

earðan afirrende gefeht oð oð endas eorðan bogan
terram 10. *Auferens bella usque ad fines terrae arcum*

forþreste[1] 7 gebriceð wepen 7 sceldas forberneð fyr(e)[2]
conteret et confringet arma et scuta conburet ign(i)[2]

aemetgiað 7 gesiað forðon ic eam dryhten
11. *Vacate et videte quoniam ego sum Dominus*

ic biom upahefen in ðiodum 7 ic biom upahefen in eorðan
exaltabor in gentibus et exaltabor in terra

dryhten megna mid us ondfenga ur
12. *Dominus virtutum nobiscum susceptor noster Deus Jacob*

46.

alle ðiode plagiað mid hondum wynsumiað gode in
2. *Omnes gentes plaudite manibus jubilate Deo in*

stefne wynsumnisse forðon god heh egesful
voce exultationis 3. *Quoniam Deus summus terribilis*

cyning micel ofer alle godas underðeodde folc
Rex magnus super omnes deos 4. *Subecit populos*

us 7 ðiode under fotum urum geceas usic in
nobis et gentes sub pedibus nostris 5. *Elegit nos in*

erfe him hiop ðæt he *luade astag
hereditatem sibi speciem Jacob quem dilexit 6. *Ascendit*

god in wynsumnisse 7 dryhten in stefne beman
Deus in jubilatione et Dominus in voce tubae

[1] þ *from* w.* [2] *cut off.*

singað gode urum singað singað cyninge urum
7. *Psallite Deo nostro psallite psallite regi nostro*

singað forðon cyning alre eorðan god singað
psallite 8. *Quoniam rex omni terrae Deus psallite*

snotterlice ricsað *dryh*en* ofer alle ðeode god
sapienter 9. *Regnabit Dominus super omnes gentes Deus*

siteð ofer seld halig his aldermen folces
sedet super sedem sanctam suam 10. *Principes populi*

gesomnadon mid[1] gode Abrahames forðon godas stronge
convenerunt cum Deo Abraham quoniam dii fortes

eordan swiðe upahefene werun
terrae nimium elevati sunt

47.

micel dryht*en* ⁊ *hergedlic swiðe in cestre godes
2. *Magnus Dominus et laudabilis nimis in civitate Dei*

ures in munte ðæm *hagan him *gebradende wyn-
nostri in monte sancto ejus 3. *Dilatans ex-*

sumnisse alre eorðan se munt Sion on sidan *noðdaeles
ultationis universae terrae mons Sion latera aquilonis

cestre cyninges ðes miclan god in grad*um* hire
civitas regis magni 4. *Deus in gradibus ejus*

bið oncnawen ðonne onfoeht hie forðon sehðe cyningas
dinoscitur dum suscipiet eam 5. *Quoniam ecce reges*

eorðan gesomnade sind ⁊ gesomnadun in annisse
terrae congregati sunt et convenerunt in unum

hie gesiende ða wundriende sindun gedroefde sindun
6. *Ipsi videntes tunc admirati sunt conturbati sunt*

⁊ onstyrede sind cwaecung bifeng hie ðer sar
et commoti sunt 7. *tremor adpraehendit eos Ibi dolores*

swe cennende in gaste strongum forðręstende sceopu
sicut parturientes 8. *in spiritu vehementi conterens*[2] *naves*

ðes londes swe we geherdun swe ⁊ gesegun in cestre
Tharsis 9. *Sicut audivimus ita et vidimus in civitate*

dryht*nes* megna in cestre godes ures god gesteaðelade
Domini virtutum in civitate Dei nostri Deus fundavit

ða in ecnisse we onfengun god mildheortnisse ðine
eam in aeternum 10. *Suscepimus Deus misericordiam tuam*

[1] *from* me. [2] *last* [n] *diff. hand.*

in midle temples ðines efter noman ðinum god
in medio templi tui 11. *Secundum nomen tuum Deus*

swe 7 lof ðin in endas eorðan rehtwisnisse ful is
ita et laus tua in fines terrae justitiae plena est

sie swiðre ðin blissie se munt Sion 7 gefen
dextera tua 12. *Laetetur mons Sion et exultent*

dohtur fore domas ðine *dryhen ymb-
filiae Judae propter judicia tua Domine 13. *Cir-*

sellað 7 clyppað hie secgað in torrum
cumdate Sion et conplectimini eam narrate in turribus

hire settað heortan eowre in megne his 7 to-
ejus 14. *ponite corda vestra in virtute ejus et distri-*

daelað stepas hire ðæt ge asecgen in cynne oðrum
buite gradus ejus ut enarretis in progeniae altera

forðon ðes is god ur in ecnisse 7
15. *Quoniam hic est Deus noster in aeternum et in*

*weorund weorulde 7 he receð usic in weorulde
saeculum saeculi et ipse reget nos in saecula

48.

geherað ðas alle ðeode mid earum onfoð ða ðe
2. *Audite haec omnes gentes auribus percipite qui habi-*

eardiað *ymbhwyrf gehwelce eorðcende 7 bearn monna
tatis orbem 3. *Quique terriginae et filii homi-*

somud in annesse weolig 7 ðearfa muð min
num simul in unum dives et pauper 4. *Os meum*

spriceð snytru 7 smea[n]g heortan minre gleawnisse
loquitur sapientiam et meditatio cordis mei prudentiam

ic onhaeldu to gelicnisse eare min ic ontynu in
5. *Inclinabo ad similitudinem aurem meam aperiam in*

hearpan foresetenisse mine to hwon ondredu ic in
psalterio propositionem meam 6. *Ut quid timebo in*

dege ðæm yflan unrehtwisnis helspuran minre ymbseleþ[1]
die mala iniquitas calcanei mei circumdedit

me ða ðe getreowað in megne heara 7 ða in
me 7. *Qui confidunt in virtute sua quique in*

genyhtsumnisse weolena heara bioð gewuldrade broður
abundantia divitiarum suarum gloriabuntur 8. *Frater*

[1] þ *from some other letter.*

ne aleseð aleseð mon ne seleð gode geðinge his
non redemit redemit homo non dabit Deo placationem suam

ne weorð alesnisse sawle his 7 won in
9. *nec praetium redemptionis animae suae et laboravit in*

ecnisse 7 leofað in ende forðon ne gesið
aeternum 10. *et vivit in finem* 11. *Quoniam non videbit*

forwyrd ðonne he gesið snotre sweltende somud se unwisa
interitum cum viderit sapientes morientes simul insipiens

7 se ðysga forweorðað 7 forletað fremðum weolan
et stultus peribunt Et relinquent alienis divitias

heara 7 byrgenne heara hus heara in ecnisse
suas 12. *et sepulchra eorum *domos eorum in aeternum*

geteld heara in c[n]eorisse 7 cynne gecegað
Tabernacula eorum in generatione et progeniae invocabunt

noman heara in eorðum heara 7 mon mid ðy
nomina eorum in terris ipsorum 13. *Et homo cum*

he on are wes ne onget he efenameten he is neatum ðæm
in honore esset non intellexit comparatus est jumentis insi-

unwisum 7 gelic geworden is him ðes weg heara
pientibus et similis factus est illis 14. *Haec via eorum*

eswic him 7 efter ðon in muþe[1] heara bledsiað
scandalum ipsis et postea in ore suo benedicent

swe swe scep in helle gesette sind 7 deað misfoedeð
15. *Sicut oves in inferno positae sunt et mors depascit*

hie 7 bigetað hie ða rehtwisan in margentid 7 fultum
eos Et obtinebunt eos justi in matutino et auxilium

heora aldað in helle 7 from wuldre his onweg
eorum veterascit in inferno et a gloria sua

adrifene sind hweðre sodlice god gefreað sawle
expulsi sunt 16. *Verum tamen Deus liberabit animam*

mine of honda helle ðonne onfoeð mec ne
meam de manu inferi dum acceperit me 17. *Ne*

ondred ðu ðonne weolig geworðen bið mon 7 ðonne
timueris cum dives factus fuerit homo et cum

gemonigfaldad bið wuldur huses his forðon nales
multiplicata fuerit gloria domus ejus 18. *Quoniam non*

ðonne he swilteð onfoð ðas all ne somud astigeð
cum morietur accipiet haec omnia neque simul descendit

[1] þ *on some other letter.*

mid hine wuldur huses his forðon sawul his
cum eo gloria domus ejus 19. *Quoniam anima ejus*

in life his bið gebledsad 7 we ondettað ðe ðonne ðu
in vita ipsius benedicitur et confitebitur tibi dum be-

bledsas him 7 ingaeð oð in cyn feddra
nefeceris ei 20. *Et introibit usque in progeniem patrum*

his 7 oð in ecnisse ne gesið leht 7
suorum et usque in aeternum non videbit lumen 21. *Et*

monn ða ðe he in are wes ne onget he efenmeten wes
homo cum in honore esset non intellexit comparatus est

neatum unwisum 7 gelic geworden is *his
jumentis insipientibus et similis factus est illis

49.

god goda dryhten spreocende wes 7 cede eorðan from
Deus deorum Dominus locutus est et vocavit terram A

sunnan upcyme oð setgong of Sione hiow
solis ortu usque ad occasum 2. *ex Sion species*

wlites his god sweotullice cymeð god ur 7 ne
decoris ejus 3. *Deus manifeste veniet Deus noster et non*

swigað fyr in gesihðe his beorneð 7 in ymbhwyrfte
silebit Ignis in conspectu ejus ardebit et in circuitu

his storm[1] strong togeceð heofen up 7 eorðan
ejus tempestas valida 4. *Advocavit caelum sursum et terram*

ðæt he toscade folc his gesomniað ðider halge
ut discerneret populum suum 5. *Congregate illic sanctos*

his ða geendebyrdun cyðnisse his ofer onsegdnisse
ejus qui ordinaverunt testamentum ejus super sacrificia

7 secgað heofenas rehtwisnisse his forðon god
6. *Et adnuntiabunt caeli justitiam ejus quoniam Deus*

doema is geher folc min 7 *sprecu to Israhela folce
judex est 7. *Audi populus meus et loquar Israhel*

7 ic cyðu ðe ðætte god god ðin ic eam nales
et testificabor tibi quoniam Deus Deus tuus ego sum 8. *Non*

ofer onsegdnisse ðine ic dregu ðe onsegdnisse *soð ðine
super sacrificia tua arguam te holocausta autem tua

in gesihðe minre sind aa ic ne onfoo of huse
in conspectu meo sunt semper. 9. *Non accipiam de domo*

[1] d storm.

ðinum calferu ne of eowdum ðinum buccan for-
tua vitulos neque de gregibus tuis hircos **10.** *Quo-*
ðon min sind all wildeor wuda neat in muntum
niam meae sunt omnes ferae silvarum jumenta in montibus
7 oexen ic oncneow all ða flegendan heofenes 7 hiow
et boves **11.** *Cognovi omnia volatilia caeli et species*
londes mid mec[1] is gif ic hyngriu ne cweoðu ic to ðe
agri mecum est **12.** *Si esuriero non dicam tibi*
min is soðlice ymbhwerft eorðan 7 fylnis his
meus est enim orbis terrae et plenitudo ejus
ah ic eotu flęsc ferra oððe blod
13. *Numquid manducabo carnes taurorum aut sanguinem*
buccena ic dri[n]co ageld gode onsegdnisse lofes 7
hircorum potabo **14.** *Immola Deo sacrificium laudis et*
geld ðæm hestan gehat ðin gece mec in dege ge-
redde Altissimo vota tua **15.** *Invoca me in die tri-*
swinces ðines ðæt ic generge ðec 7 ðu miclas mec
bulationis tuae ut eripiam te et magnificabis me
to ðæm synfullan soðlice cweð god forhwon ðu asagas
16. *Peccatori autem dixit Deus Quare tu enarras*
rehtwisnisse mine 7 genimes cyðnisse mine ðorh mud
justitias meas et adsumes testamentum meum per os
ðinne ðu soðlice ðu fiodes ðeodscipe 7 ðu awurpe
tuum **17.** *Tu vero odisti disciplinam et projecisti*
word min efter ðe gif ðu gesege ðeof somud
sermones meos post te **18.** *Si videbas furem simul*
ðu urne mid hine 7 mid unrehthæmderum ðæl ðinne
currebas cum eo et cum adulteris portionem tuam
ðu settes muð ðin genyhtsumað mid niðe 7 tunge
ponebas **19.** *Os tuum abundavit nequitia et lingua*
ðin hleoðrade facen sittende wið broeðer ðinum
tua concinnavit dolum **20.** *Sedens adversus fratrem tuum*
ðu teldes 7 wið suna moeder ðinre ðu settes eswic
detrahebas et adversus filium matris tuae ponebas scandalum
ðas ðu dydes 7 ic swigade ðu gewoendes on unrehtwis-
21. *Haec fecisti et tacui existimasti iniquitatem*
nisse ðæt ic were ðe gelic ic ðreu ðec 7 ic setto ða
quod ero tibi similis Arguam te et statuam illa

[1] e *from* id; *the* c *added later* (?).

ongegn onsiene ðinre ongeotað ðas alle ða ofer-
contra faciem tuam **22.** *intellegite haec omnes qui obli-*

geoteliað dryhten ne hwonne gereafie 7 ne sie se
viscimini Dominum ne quando rapiat et non sit qui

generge onsegdnis lofes gearað mec 7 ðer
eripiat **23.** *Sacrificium laudis honorificabit me et illic*

siðfet is ðider ic oteawu him haelu godes
iter est quo ostendam illi salutare Dei

50.

mildsa min god efter ðere miclan mildheortnisse
3. *Miserere mei Deus secundum magnam misericordiam*

ðinre 7 efter mengu mildsa ðinra adilga
tuam Et secundum multitudinem miserationum tuarum dele

unrehtwisnisse mine mae aðuaeh mec from un-
iniquitatem meam **4.** *Amplius lava me ab in-*

rehtwisnisse minre 7 from scylde minre geclasna mec
justitia mea et a delicto meo munda me

f[o]rðon unrehtwisnisse mine ic oncnawu 7 scyld
5. *Quoniam iniquitatem meam ego agnosco et delictum*

min biforan me is aa *ðc anum ic synngade
meum coram me est semper **6.** *Tibi soli peccavi*

7 yfel biforan ðe dyde[1] ðæt ðu sie gerehtwisad in
et malum coram te feci ut justificeris in

wordum ðinum 7 ðu wrices ðonne ðu ðoemes sehðe
sermonibus tuis et vincas dum judicaris **7.** *Ecce*

*soð in unrehtwisnissum geecnad ic eam 7 in scyldum
enim in iniquitatibus conceptus sum et in delictis

cende mec modur min sehðe *soð soðfestnisse
peperit me mater mea **8.** *Ecce enim veritatem*

ðu lufades ða uncuðan 7 ða deglan *syntru ðinre ðu ge-
dilexisti incerta et occulta sapientiae tuae mani-

sweo[tu]lades[2] me ðu onstrigdes mec mid ysopan 7
festasti mihi **9.** *Asperges me hysopo et*

ic biom geclasnad ðu ðwes mec 7 ofer snaw ic biom gehwitad
mundabor lavabis me et super nivem dealvabor

gehernisse minre ðu seles gefian 7 blisse 7
10. *Auditui meo dabis gaudium et laetitiam et*

[1] *Second* d *from* b. [2] *partly inked in by a later hand.*

gefiað ban ða *geeðmodedan acer onsiene ðine *fro
exultabunt ossa humiliata 11. *Averte faciem tuam a*

synnum minum 7 alle unrehtwisnisse mine adilga heortan
peccatis meis et omnes iniquitates meas dele 12. *Cor*

clæne gecwica in me god 7 gast rehtne geniowa
mundum crea in me Deus et spiritum rectum innova

innoðum minum ne aweorp ðu mec from onsiene
in visceribus meis 13. *Ne proicias me a facie*

ðin 7 gast haligne ðinne ne afir ðu from me
tua et spiritum sanctum tuum ne auferas a me

agef me blisse haelu ðinre 7 mid gaste alder-
14. *Redde mihi laetitiam salutaris tui et spiritu prin-*

lice getrime me ic lęru ða *urehtwisan wegas ðine
cipali confirma me 15. *Doceam iniquos vias tuas*

7 ða arleasan to ðe bioð gecerde gefrea mec of
et impii ad te convertentur 16. *Libera me de*

blodum god god hælu minre 7 gefið tunge
*sanguinibus Deus Deus salutis meae et *exultabit lingua*

min rehtwisnisse ðine dryhten weolere mine ontyn ðu
mea justitiam tuam 17. *Domine labia mea aperies*

7 muð min segeð lof ðin forðon
et os meum adnuntiabit laudem tuam 18. *Quoniam*

gif ðu walde onsegdnisse ic salde gewislice onsegdnisse
si voluisses sacrificium dedissem utique holocaustis

ðu ne gelustfullas onsegdnis gode *gas geswenced
non delectaberis 19. *Sacrificium Deo spiritus contribulatus*

heorte forðrested 7 geeaðmodad god ne forhogað
cor contritum et humiliatum Deus non spernit

freamsumlice doa dryhten in godum willan ðinum
20. *Benigne fac Domine in bona voluntate tua*

ðæt sien getimbred wallas ðonne
Sion ut aedificentur muri Hierusalem 21. *Tunc*

ðu onfoest onsegdnisse rehtwisnisse oflatan 7 onsegdnisse
acceptabis sacrificium justitiae oblationes et holocausta

ðonne onsettað ofer wibed ðin calfur
tunc inponent super altare tuum vitulos

51.

hwet wuldras ðu in hete . ðu maehtig erð[1] in
3. *Quid gloriaris in malitia qui potens es in*
unrehtwisnisse alne deg unrehtwisnisse ðohte tunge
iniquitatem 4. *Tota die injustitiam cogitavit lingua*
ðin swe swe scersaex scearp ðu dydes facen ðu lufedes
tua sic ut novacula acuta fecisti dolum 5. *Dilexisti*
hete ofer freamsumnisse unrehtwisnisse mae ðon
malitiam super benignitatem iniquitatem magis quam
spreocan rehtwisnisse ðu lufades all word fortru-
loqui aequitatem 6. *Dilexisti omnia verba praecipi-*
gadnisse in tungan faecenre forðon toweorpeð ðe god
tationis in lingua dolosa 7. *Propterea destruet te Deus*
in ende utaluceð ðe 7 utaleoreð ðe of getelde ðinum
in finem evellet te et emigrabit te de tabernaculo tuo
7 wyrtruman ðinne of eorðan lifgendra gesiað
et radicem tuam de terra viventium 8. *Videbunt*
rehtwise 7 ondredað 7 ofer hine hlæhað 7 cweoðað
justi et timebunt et super eum ridebunt et dicent
sehðe mon se ne sette god fultum him ah
9. *Ecce homo qui non posuit Deum adjutorem sibi sed*
*gehyte in mengu weolena heara 7 strongað
speravit in multitudine divitiarum suarum et praevaluit
in idelnisse his ic soðlice swe eletreow westembere
in vanitate sua 10. *Ego autem sicut oliva fructifera*
in huse dryht*nes* ic gehyhte in mildheortnisse godes mines
in domo Domini speravi in misericordia Dei mei
in ecnisse 7 in weoruld weorulde ic ondettu ðe
in aeternum et in saeculum saeculi 11. *Confitebor tibi*
dryht*en* in weoruld ðone ðu dydes 7 ic bidu noman
Domine in saeculum quem fecisti et expectabo nomen
ðinne forðon god is biforan gesihðe haligra ðinra
tuum quoniam bonum est ante conspectu sanctorum tuorum

52.

cweð se unwisa in heortan his nis god gewemde
Dixit insipiens in corde suo Non est Deus 2. *corrupti*

[1] a *over the* e.

sind 7 onscuniendlice gewordne sind in lustum hea(ra)[1]
sunt et abominabiles facti sunt in voluntatibus suis

nis se ðe doe god nis oð enne
Non est qui faciat bonum non est usque ad unum

dryhten of heofene forðlocade ofer bearn monna ðæt
3. *Dominus de caelo prospexit super filios hominum ut*

he gese hweðer sie ongeotende oððe soecende god
videat si est intellegens aut requirens Deum

alle onhaeldun somud *un gewordne werun nis
4. *Omnes declinaverunt simul inutiles facti sunt non est*

se doe god nis oð enne ah[2] ne on-
qui faciat bonum non est usque ad unum 5. *Nonne cogno-*

cnawað alle ða wircað unrehtwisnisse ða forswelgað
scent omnes qui operantur iniquitatem qui devorant

folc *meam swe swe mete[3] hlafes god ne ge-
plebem meam sicut escam panis 6. *Deum non invo-*

cedun ðer forhtadun ege ðer ne wes ege
caverunt illic trepidaverunt timore ubi non erat timor

forðon god tostenceð ban monna him liciendra
Quoniam Deus dissipat ossa hominum sibi placentium

gedroefde sind forðon god forhogde hie hwelc seleð
confusi sunt quia Deus sprevit eos 7. *Quis dabit*

of Sione haelu ðonne he forcerred dryhten
ex Sion salutare Israhel dum avertit Dominus

heftned folces his gefið iacob 7 bið geblissad
captivitatem plebis suae Exultabit Jacob et laetabitur

*is
Israel

53.

god in noman ðinum halne mec doa 7 in megne
3. *Deus in nomine tuo salvum me fac et in virtute*

ðinum gefrea mec god geher gebed min mid earum
tua libera me 4. *Deus exaudi orationem meam auribus*

onfoh word muðes mines forðon ða fremðan areosun
percipe verba oris mei 5. *Quoniam alieni insurrex-*

in mec 7 ða strongan sohtun sawle mine 7
erunt in me et fortes quesierunt animam meam et

[1] *cut off.* [2] h *from* n. [3] *second* e *from some other letter.*

no foresettun god biforan gesihðe heara sehðe
non proposuerunt Deum ante conspectum suum 6. *Ecce*

soðlice god gefultumeð me ⁊ dryh*ten* ondfenga is
enim Deus adjuvat me et Dominus susceptor est

sawle minre acer yfel feondum minum ⁊ in soð-
animae meae 7. *Averte mala inimicis meis et in veri-*

festnisse ðinre tostregd hie wilsumlice ic *onsecg ðe
tate tua disperde illos 8. *Voluntarie sacrificabo tibi*

⁊ ondetto noman ðinum dryht*en* forðon god he is
et confitebor nomini tuo Domine quoniam bonum est

forðon of alre geswencednisse ðu generedes mec ⁊
9. *Quoniam ex omni tribulatione eripuisti me et*

ofer feond mine gelocade ege ðin
super inimicos meos respexit oculus meus

54.

geher god gebed min ⁊ ne forseh ðu boene
2. *Exaudi Deus orationem meam et ne dispexeris depre-*

mine bihald in mec ⁊ geher mec geun-
cationem meam 3. *intende in me et exaudi me Con-*

rotsad ic eam in bigonge minum ⁊ gedroefed[1] ic eam
tristatus sum in exercitatione mea et conturbatus sum

from stefne feondes ⁊ from geswencednisse ðes synfvllan
4. *a voce inimici et a tribulatione peccatoris*

forðon onhældon in mec unrehtwisnisse ⁊ in eorre
Quoniam declinaverunt in me iniquitates et in ira

hefie werun me heorte min gedroefed is in me
molesti erant mihi 5. *Cor meum conturbatum est in me*

⁊ fyr[h]tu deaðes gefeol ofer mec ege ⁊ cwaecung
et formido mortis cecidit super me 6. *Timor et tremor*

cwomun ofer mec ⁊ biðehton mec ðeostro ⁊ cweð
venerunt super me et contexerunt me tenebrae 7. *Et dixi*

hwelc seleð me fiðru swe swe culfran ⁊ ic fligu ⁊
Quis dabit mihi pinnas sicut columbae et volabo et

gerestu sehðe ic afeorrade fleonde ⁊ ic wunade in
requiescam 8. *Ecce elongavi fugiens et mansi in*

woestenne ic bad hine se mec halne dyde
solitudine 9. *Expectabam eum qui me salvum faceret*

[1] *er. after first* e.

from lytelmodum 7 storme forbregd dryht*en* 7
a pusillanimo et tempestate **10.** *Praecipita Domine et*

todael tungan heara forðon ic gesæh unrehtwisnisse 7
divide linguas eorum quoniam vidi iniquitatem et

wiðcwedenisse in cestre deges 7 nęhtes ymb
contradictionem in civitate **11.** *die ac nocte Circum*

seleð hie ofer wallas his unrehtwisnis 7 gewin in
dabit eam super muros ejus iniquitas et labor in

midle his 7 unrehtwisnis 7 ne asprong of worðig-
medio ejus **12.** *et injustitia Et non defecit de plateis*

num his westemsceat 7 facen forðon gif feond
ejus usura et dolus **13.** *quoniam si inimicus*

min wergcweodelade me ic abere gewislice 7 gif ðes
meus maledixisset mihi supportassem utique Et si is

se ðe fiode mec ofer mec ða miclan spreocende were
qui oderat me super me magna locutus fuisset

ic ahydde mec gewislice fro*m* him ðu soðlice mon
absconderem me utique ab eo **14.** *Tu vero homo*

anmod ladtow min 7 cuða min ðu somud
unianimis dux meus et notus meus **15.** *qui simul*

mid mec swoet- nome mettas in huse dryht*nes* we
mecum dulces capiebas cibos in domo Domini ambu-

eodon mid geðeafunge cyme deað ofer hie 7
lavimus cum consensu **16.** *Veniat mors super illos et*

astigen hie in helle lifgende forðon nið in
descendant in infernum viventes Quoniam nequitia in

gesthusum heara in midle heara ic soðlice to
hospitiis eorum in medio ipsorum **17.** *Ego autem ad*

dryht*ne* cleopede 7 dryht*en* geherde mec on
Dominum clamavi et Dominus exaudivit me **18.** *Ves-*

efenne on marne 7 on midne deg[1] ic seggo 7 cyðu
pere mane et meridie narrabo et adnuntiabo

7 he gehereð stefne mine gefreað in sibbe sawle
et exaudiet vocem meam **19.** *Liberabit in pace animam*

mine from ðissum ða to ne geniolaecað me forðon bitwih
meam ab his qui adpropiant mihi quoniam inter

monge werun mid mec gehereð god 7 geeaðmodað
multos erant mecum **20.** *Exaudiet Deus et humiliabit*

[1] e *from* i (?).

hie se is ær weorulde 7 wunað in ecnisse nis
eos qui est ante saecula et manet in aeternum Non est

*soðl him onwendednis 7 hie ne ondreordun god
enim illis commutatio et non timuerunt Deum **21.** *ex-*

aðeneð hond his in geedleanunge him bismeotun
tendit manum suam in retribuendo illis contaminaverunt

cyðnisse his todaelde sind from eorre ondwleotan
testamentum ejus **22.** *divisi sunt ab ira vultus*

his 7 to nialaehte heorte his gehnistun word heara
ejus et adpropiavit cor ejus Mollierunt sermones suos

ofer ele 7 hie sind ða scotunge aweorp in god
super oleum et ipsi sunt jacula **23.** *Jacta in Deum*

gedoht ðinne 7 he ðe afoedeð ne seleð in ecnisse
cogitatum tuum et ipse te enutriet Non dabit in aeternum

yðgunge ðæm rehtwisan ðu soðlice god gelaedes
fluctuationem justo **24.** *tu vero Deus deduces*

hie in seað forwyrde weoras bloda 7 ða faecnan ne
eos in puteum interitus Viri sanguinum et dolosi non

gemidliað daegas heara ic soðlice in ðec gehyhto dryhten
dimidiabunt dies suos ego vero in te sperabo Domine

55.

mildsa me dryhten forðon fortred me mon
2. *Miserere mihi Domine quoniam conculcavit me homo*

alne deg fehtende swencton mec fortredon mec
tota die bellans tribulavit me **3.** *Conculcaverunt me*

feond mine alne dig from heanisse deges forðon
inimici mei tota die **4.** *ab altitudine diei Quoniam*

monge ða oferfehtað mec ondredað ic soð in ðec
multi qui debellant me timebunt ego vero in te

gehyhto dryhten in gode ic hergu word min alne
sperabo Domine **5.** *In Deo laudabo sermones meos tota*

dęg[1] in gode ic gehyhto ne ondredu ic hwet doe me
die in Deo sperabo non timebo quid faciat mihi

mon alne deg word min onscunedon wið
homo **6.** *Tota die verba mea execrabantur adversum*

me all geðaeht heara in yfel ineardiað
me omnia consilia eorum in malum **7.** *Inhabitabunt*

[1] d *from* t.

7 ahydað hie helspuran mine haldað swe
et abscondent ipsi calcaneum meum observabunt sicut

bad *sawulf min fore nowihte hale ðu gedoest
expectavit anima mea 8. *pro nihilo salvos facies*

hie in eorre folc ðu gebrices god lif min
eos in ira populos confringes Deus 9. *vitam meam*

ic segde ðe ic sette tearas mine in gesihðe ðinre swe
nuntiavi tibi posui lacrimas meas in conspectu tuo sicut

in gehate ðinum sien gecerde feond mine on bec
in promissione tua 10. *Convertantur inimici mei retrorsum*

on swe hwelcum dege ic geceigo ðec sehðe ic oncneow
in quacumque die invocavero te ecce agnovi

forðon god min ðu earð in gode ic hergu *wordum
quoniam Deus meus es tu 11. *In Deo laudabo verbum*

7. in dryhtne ic hergu word in gode ic gehyhtu ne
et in Domino laudabo sermonem in Deo sperabo non

ondredo ic hwet doe me monn in me sind god
timebo quid faciat mihi homo 12. *In me sunt Deus*

gehat ða ic ageofu herenisse ðe forðon ðu ge-
vota quae reddam laudationis tibi 13. *quoniam eri-*

neredes sawle mine of deaðe egan min from tearum
puisti animam meam de morte oculos meos a lacrimis

foet mine from slide ðæt ic licie biforan dryhtne in
pedes meos a labsu ut placeam coram Domino in

lehte lifgendra
lumine viventium

56.

mildsa min god mildsa min forðon in ðe getreoweð
2. *Miserere mei Deus miserere mei quoniam in te confidit*

sawul min 7 in scuan fiðra ðinra ic gehyhto oððet
anima mea et in umbra alarum tuarum sperabo donec

leoreð unrehtwisnis ic cleopiu to dryhtne ðæm hestan
transeat iniquitas 3. *Clamabo ad Dominum altissimum*

7 to dryhtne se wel dyde me sende of heofene
et ad Dominum qui benefecit me 4. *Misit de caelo*

7 gefreode mec salde in edwit *fortreodendes mec
et liberavit me dedit in opprobrium conculcantes me

sende god mildheortnisse his 7 soðfestnisse his
Misit Deus misericordiam suam et veritatem suam

generede sawle mine of midle hwelpa leona ic
5. *Eripuit animam meam de medio catulorum leonum dor-*

hneappade gedroefed bearn monna toðas heara wepen
mivi conturbatus Filii hominum dentes eorum arma

7 strelas 7 tunge heara mece scearp hefe up
et sagittae et lingua eorum machera acuta 6. *Exaltare*

ofer heofenas god 7 ofer alle eorðan wuldur ðin
super caelos Deus et super omnem terram gloria tua

girene gearwadon fotum minum 7 gebegdon sawle
7. *Laqueos paraverunt pedibus meis et incurvaverunt animam*

mine dulfun biforan onsiene minre seað 7 hie
meam Foderunt ante faciem meam foveam et ipsi

gefeollun in ðone gearu heorte min god gearu
inciderunt in eam 8. *Paratum cor meum Deus paratum*

heorte min ic singu 7 salm ic *weoðu dryh*tne*
cor meum cantabo et psalmum dicam Domino

aris wuldur min aris hearpe 7 citere ic
9. *Exurge gloria mea exurge psalterium et cythara ex-*

arisu on ærmargen ic ondetto ðe in folcum dryht*en*
urgam diluculo 10. *Confitebor tibi in populis Domine*

salm ic cweoðu ðe betwih ðeode forðon gemiclad
psalmum dicam tibi inter gentes 11. *Quoniam magni-*

is oð heofenas mildheortniss ðin 7 oð
ficata est usque ad caelos misericordia tua et usque

wolcenu soðfestnis ðin hefe up ofer heofenas
ad nubes veritas tua 12. *Exaltare super caelos*

god 7 ofer alle eorðan wuldur ðin
Deus et super omnem terram gloria tua

57.

gif soðlice gewislice rehtwisnisse spreocað ða rehtan
2. *Si vere utique justitiam loquimini justa*

doemað bearnum monna 7 soðlice in heortan
judicate filii hominum 3. *Et enim in corde*

unrehtwisnisse wircað in eorðan unrehtwisnisse honda
iniquitates operamini in terram iniquitatem manus

eowre hleoðriað afremðae sind ða synfullan from
vestrae concinnant 4. *Alienati sunt peccatores ab*

innoðe dwoledon from wombe spreocende sind ða leasan
utero erraverunt a ventre locuti sunt falsa

eorre him efter gelicnisse nedran swe nedran[1]
5. *Ira illis secundum similitudinem serpentis sicut aspides*

deafe 7 forduttænde earan hire sie ne gehered
surdae et obturantes aures suas 6. *quae non exaudient*

stefne galendra 7 galdurcreftas ða bioð agalene[2] from
vocem incantantium et venefici quae incantantur a

ðæm snottran god forþręsteð[3] *toð heara in mude
sapiente 7. *Deus conteret dentes eorum in ore*

heara wongtoeð leona gebriceð dryhten to
ipsorum molas leonum confringit Dominus 8. *Ad*

nowihte bicumad swe swe weter eornende bihaldeð bogan
nihilum devenient velut aqua decurrens intendet arcum

his oð ðet sien geuntrumad swe *sw wæx gemælted
suum donec infirmentur 9. *Sicut cera liquefacta*

bioð afirde ofer hie gefeol fyr 7 hie ne gesegun sunnan
auferentur super eos cecidit ignis et non viderunt solem

ær ðon forðgelaeden ðornas eowre twigu swe swe
10. *Priusquam producant spinae vestrae ramnos sicut*

lifgende swe in eorre forswilgeð hie bið geblissad
viventes sic in ira absorbet eos 11. *Laetabitur*

se rehtwisa ðonne he gesið wrece ðeara arleasra honda
justus cum viderit vindictam impiorum manus

his ðweð in blode synfulra 7 cweð mon
suas lavabit in sanguine peccatorum 12. *Et dicet homo*

hweðer gewislice is westem ðæm rehtwisan gewislice is god
si utique est fructus justo utique est Deus

*doende hie in eorðan
judicans eos in terra

58.

genere mec of feondum minum god min 7 from
2. *Eripe me de inimicis meis Deus meus et ab*

ðæm arisendum in mec gefrea mec genere of
insurgentibus in me libera me 3. *Eripe me de*

ðæm wircendum unrehtwisnisse 7 of weorum bloda
operantibus iniquitatem et de viris sanguinum

[1] nedram (?). [2] le *from* n. [3] þ *from* s.

hæl mec forðon sehðe ofersetun sawle mine
salva me 4. *Quia ecce occupaverunt animam meam*

onræsdun in mec stronge *nurehtwisnis min
inruerunt in me fortes 5. *neque iniquitas mea*

ne syn min ðryhten butan unrehtwisnisse ic orn
neque peccatum meum Domine Sine iniquitate cucurri

7 wes gereht aris ongegn yrn[1] me 7 geseh
et dirigebar 6. *exurge in occursum mihi et vide.*

7 ðu dryh*ten* god megna god israh*el* bihald to
et tu Domine Deus virtutum Deus Israhel Intende ad

niosenne alle deode ðu ne mildsas allum ða wircað
visitandas omnes gentes non miserearis omnibus qui operantur

unrehtwisnisse sien forcerrede to efenne 7 hungur
iniquitatem 7. *Convertentur ad vesperum et famem*

ðrowien swe swe hundas 7 ymbgad cestre sehðe
patientur ut canes et circuibunt civitatem 8. *Ecce.*

hie spreocað in muðe his 7 sweord is in weolerum
ipsi loquentur in ore suo et gladius est in labiis

heara forðon hwelc geherde 7 ðu dryhten bismeras
eorum Quoniam quis audivit 9. *et tu Domine deridebis*

hie fore nowiht ðu hafast alle ðeode strengo
eos pro nihilo habebis omnes gentes 10. *Fortitudinem*

mine to ðe ic halde forðon ðu god ondfenga min
meam ad te custodiam quia tu Deus susceptor meus

earð god min mildheortnis his forecymeð mec
es 11. *Deus meus misericordia ejus praeveniet me*

god min oteaw me god betwih mine fiond ne
12. *Deus meus ostende mihi bona inter inimicos meos ne*

slęh ðu hie ðy[2] læs hwonne ofergeotelien ęe ðinre to-
occideres eos ne quando obliviscantur legis tuae Dis-

stregd hie in megne ðinum 7 toweorp hie gescildend
perge illos in virtute tua et destrue eos protector

min dryht*en* scylde muðes heara word weolera
meus Domine 13. *Delicta oris eorum sermo labiorum*

heara 7 bioð bifongne in oferhygde heara 7 of
ipsorum et conpraehendantur in superbia sua et de

onscununge 7 leasunge sien nedde in eorre ge-
execratione et mendacio conpellantur 14. *in ira con-*

[1] :yrn. [2] y *from* u.

fyllnisse 7 hie ne bioð 7 weotun ðætte god
summationis et non erunt Et scient quia Deus domi-

waldeð iacobes 7 gemæra eorðan sien forcerred to
nabitur Jacob et finium terrae 15. *Convertentur ad*

efenne 7 hungur ðrowiað swe swe hundas 7 utan
vesperam et famem patientur ut canes et cir-

ymbgað cestre sehðe hie bioð tostrogdne to
cuibunt civitatem 16. *Ecce ipsi dispergentur ad*

eotenne gif soð ne bioð gefylde 7 gnorniað
manducandum si vero non fuerint saturati et murmurabunt

ic soðlice singu megen ðin 7 upphebbo on marne
17. *Ego autem cantabo virtutem tuam et exaltabo mane*

mildheortnisse ðine forðon geworden ðu earð ondfenga
misericordiam tuam Quia factus es susceptor

min 7 geberg min in dege geswinces mines
meus et refugium meum in die tribulationis meae

fultum min ðe ic singu forðon ðu god ondfenga
18. *adjutor meus tibi psallam Quia tu Deus susceptor*

min earð god min mildheortnis min
meus es Deus meus misericordia mea

59.

god ðu onweg adrife usic 7 towurpe usic eorre earð
3. *Deus reppulisti nos et destruxisti nos iratus es*

7 mildsende earð us ðu onstyredes eorðan 7 *ge-
et misertus es nobis 4. *Commovisti terram et con-*

drofdes hie gehael *forðrastnisse his forðon onstyred is
turbasti eam sana contritiones ejus quia mota est

ðu oteawdes folce ðinum *ðe heardan ðu *drentes usic
5. *Ostendisti populo tuo dura potasti nos*

mid wine onbryrdnisse ðu saldes ðæm [on]dredendum
vino conpunctionis 6. *Dedisti metuentibus*

ðec getacnunge ðæt hie flugen from onsiene bogan 7
te significationem ut fugiant a facie arcus et

sien gefriad ða gecorenan ðine halne mec doo
liberentur electi tui 7. *Salvum me fac*

mid ðinre dere swiðran 7 geher mec god spreocende
dextera tua et exaudi me 8. *Deus locutus*

is in ðæm halgan his ic biom geblissað 7 todęlu
est in sancto suo Laetabor et dividam

7 gemære getelda ic meotu min
Sicymam et convallem tabernaculorum metibor 9. *Meus*

is 7 min is[1] 7 strengu
est Galaad et meus est Manasses et Efrem fortitudo

heafdes mines cyning min hwer hyhtes
capitis mei Juda rex meus 10. *Moab olla spei*

mines ic aðennu gescoe min me
meae in Idumea extendam calciamentum meum mihi

sindun underðeoded hwelc gelaedeð mec in
allophili subditi sunt 11. *Quis deducet me in*

cestre getrymede oððe hwelc gelaeded mec oð in
civitatem munitam aut quis deducit me usque in

idumeam ah ne ðu god ðu onweg adrife usic 7
Idumeam 12. *Nonne tu Deus qui reppulisti nos et*

ðu ut ne gæst god in megnum urum sele us
non egredieris Deus in virtutibus nostris 13. *Da nobis*

fultum of geswencednisse 7 idel hælu monnes in
auxilium de tribulatione et vana salus hominis 14. *In*

gode don we megn 7 he to *niwihte gelaedeð
Deo faciemus virtutem et ipse ad nihilum deducet

*ð swencendan usic
tribulantes nos

60.

geher god boene mine bihald to gebede
2. *Exaudi Deus depraecationem meam intende orationi*

minum from gemærum eorðan to ðe ic cleopede ðonne
meae 3. *a finibus terrae ad te clamavi dum*

bið generwed heorte min in stane ðu uphofe mec ðu
anxiaretur cor meum in petra exaltasti me 4. *De-*

gelaedes mec forðon geworden ðu earð hyht min tor
duxisti me quia factus es spes mea turris

strengu from onsiene feondes ic ineardiu in getelde
fortitudinis a facie inimici 5. *Inhabitabo in taber-*

ðinum in weoruld ic *sion gescilded in wrigelse
naculo tuo in saecula protegar in velamento

[1] is *twice.*

fiðra ðinra forðon ðu god geherdes gebed
alarum tuarum 6. *Quoniam tu Deus exaudisti orationem*

min ðu saldes erfewordnisse ðæm ondredendum noman
meam dedisti hereditatem timentibus nomen

ðinne deg ofer dęgas cyninges ðu togeeces ger his
tuum 7. *Dies super dies regis adicies annos ejus*

oð in deg weorulde 7 weoruld ðorhwunað in
usque in diem saeculi et saecula 8. *permanebit in*

ecnisse in gesihðe godes mildheortnisse 7 soðfestnisse
aeternum in conspectu Dei Misericordiam et veritatem

hwelc soeceð heara swe ic singu noman ðinum god
quis requiret eorum 9. *sic psallam nomini tuo Deus*

in weoruld weorulde ðaet ic agefe gehat min of dege
in saeculum saeculi ut reddam vota mea de die

in deg
in diem

61.

ah ne gode underdeoded sawul min from him
2. *Nonne Deo subdita erit anima mea ab ipso*

soðlice haelu minre 7 soðlice he is god min 7
enim salutari meo 3. *Et enim ipse est Deus meus et*

se halwynda min fultum min ne biom ic onstyred mae
salutaris meus adjutor meus non movebor amplius

hu longe onraesað ge on men ofsleað alle
4. *Quo usque inruitis in homines interficitis universos*

swe swe walle onhaeldum 7 stanwalle oncnysede ah
tamquam parieti inclinato et macheriae inpulsae 5. *Ve-*

hweðre are mine ðohtun onweg adrifan ic orn
rumtamen honorem meum cogitaverunt repellere cucurri

in ðurst his mudes bledsadon 7 heortan heara werg-
in sitim ore suo benedicebant et corde suo male-

cweodon[1] ah hweðre gode underðioded bid sawul
dicebant 6. *Verumtamen Deo subdita erit anima*

min forðon from him is gedyld min 7 soðlice
mea quoniam ab ipso est patientia mea 7. *Et enim*

he is god min 7 se halwynda min fultum min
ipse est Deus meus et salutaris meus adjutor meus

[1] *second* o (a ?) *over* e.

ic ne leoru in gode ðæ*m* halwyndan minu*m* 7 wuldur
non emigrabo 8. *In Deo salutari meo et gloria*

min god fultumes mines hyht min in gode is
mea Deus auxilii mei et spes mea in Deo est

gehyhtað in hine all gemoeting folces ageotað biforan
9. *Sperate in eum omnis conventus plebis effundite coram*

him heortan eowre forðon god fultum ur is ah
illo corda vestra quia Deus adjutor noster est 10. *Ve-*

hweðre be[a]rn monna lease bearn monna
rum tamen vani filii hominum mendaces filii hominum

in wegum ðæt hie biswicen hie of idelnesse in ðæt ilce
in stateris . ut decipiant ipsi de vanitate in id ipsum

nyllað gehyhtan in unrehtwisnisse 7 in gestrodu nyllað
11. *Nolite sperare in iniquitate et in rapinis nolite*

gewillian weolan daehðe hie toflowen nyllað heortan
concupiscere Divitiae si affluant nolite cor

tosettan æne siða spreocende wes god tu ðas
adponere 12. *semel locutus est Deus duo haec*

ic geherde dette *maht godes is 7 ðe dryht*en*
audivi Quia potestas Dei est 13. *et tibi Domine*

mildheortnis forðon ðu agildes syndrigu*m* efter werce
misericordia quia tu reddes singulis secundum opera

heara
eorum

62.

god god min to ðe of lehte ic waecio ðyrsteð in
2. *Deus Deus meus ad te de luce vigilo Sitivit in*

ðe sawul min swiðe monigfaldlice 7 flęsc min in
te anima mea quam multipliciter et caro mea 3. *In*

woestenne 7 in ðæm ungefoernan 7 in wet[r]igre stowe swe
deserto et in invio et in inaquoso sic

in ðæm halgan ic oteawde ðe þæt ic gesege megen ðin
in sancto apparui tibi ut viderem virtutem tuam

7 wuldur ðin forðon betra is mildheortnis ðin
et gloriam tuam 4. *Quoniam melior est misericordia tua*

ofer lif weolere mine hergað ðec swe ic bledsie
super vitam labia mea laudabunt te 5. *Sic benedicam*

ðec in life minum 7 in noman ðinu*m* ic uphebbu honda
te in vita mea et in nomine tuo levabo manus

mine swe swe mid smeorwe ⁊ faetnisse sie gefylled
meas 6. *Sicut adipe et pinguidine repleatur*

sawul min ⁊ weolure wynsumnisse hergað noman ðinne
anima mea et labia exultationis laudabunt nomen tuum

gif gemyndig ic wes ðin ofer strene mine in margentid
7. *Si memor fui tui super stratum meum in matutinis*

ic smegu in ðe forðon geworden ðu earð fultum min
meditabor in te 8. *quia factus es adjutor meus*

⁊ in wrigelse fiðra ðinra ic gefie ætfalh sawul
Et in velamento alarum tuarum exultabo 9. *adhesit anima*

min efter ðe mec onfeng sie swiðre ðin hie soðlice
mea post te me suscepit dextera tua 10. *Ipsi vero*

in idelnisse sohtun sawle mine ingað in ða
in vanum quaesierunt animam meam introibunt in in-

nioðerran eorðan sien sald in hond sweordes daelas
feriora terrae 11. *tradentur in manus gladii partes*

foxa bioð cyning soðlice bið geblissad in dryhtne
vulpium erunt 12. *Rex vero laetabitur in Domino*

bioð hereð alle ða ðe swergað in hine forðon fortimbred
laudabuntur omnes qui jurant in eo quia obstructum

is muð spreocendra ða unrehtan
est os loquentium iniqua

63.

geher god gebed min ðonne geswenced from
2. *Exaudi Deus orationem meam cum tribulor a*

ege feondes genere sawle mine ðu gescildes mec
timore inimici eripe animam meam 3. *Protexisti me*

from gesomnunge awergedra from mengu wircendra
a conventu malignantium a multitudine operantium

unreht forðon ascerptun swe swe sweord tungan
iniquitatem 4. *Quia exacuerunt ut gladium linguas*

heara aðenedun bogan wisan bitre ðæt hie scoteden[1]
suas intenderunt arcum rem amaram 5. *ut sagittent*

in degelnisse ðone unwemman feringa scotedun hine
in occultis inmaculatum 6. *Subito sagittabunt eum*

⁊ ne ondreordun trymedun him word yfel fleotun
et non timebunt firmaverunt sibi verbum malum dispu-

[1] t *from* n.

ðæt hie ahydden girene cwedun hwelc gesiþ hie
taverunt ut absconderent laqueos dixerunt Quis videbit eos

smegende werun unrehtwisnisse asprungun smegende
7. *Scrutati sunt iniquitatem defecerunt scrutantes*

mid smeaunge togeneolaeced mon to heortan heran
scrutinio Accedit homo ad cor altum

7 bið upahefen god strelas cilda gewordne sind
8. *et exaltabitur Deus Sagittae parvulorum factae sunt*

witu heara 7 fore nowihte hefdun wið him tun-
plagae eorum 9. *et pro nihilo habuerunt contra eos lin-*

gan heara gedroefde sind alle ða ðe gesegun hie
guae ipsorum Conturbati sunt omnes qui videbant eos

7 ondreord *oghwelc mon 7 segdun werc godes
10. *et timuit omnis homo et adnuntiaverunt opera Dei*

7 dede his ongetun bið geblissad se rehtwisa in
et facta ejus intellexerunt 11. *Laetabitur justus in*

dryhtne 7 gehyhteð in hine 7 bioð herede alle ða reht-
Domino et sperabit in eo et laudabuntur omnes recti

wisan on heortan
corde

64.

ðe gedeafenað ymen god 7 ðe bið agefen
2. *Te decet hymnus Deus in Sion et tibi reddetur*

gehat geher gebed min to ðe
votum in Hierusalem 3. *Exaudi orationem meam ad te*

oeghwelc flæsc cymeð word unrehtwisra strongadun
omnis caro veniet 4. *Verba iniquorum praevaluerunt*

ofer us 7 arleasnissum urum ðu *gemilsas eadig
super nos et impietatibus nostris tu propitiaberis 5. *Beatus*

ðone ðu gecure 7 genome he ineardað in geteldum
quem elegisti et adsumpsisti inhabitabit in tabernaculis

*ðinnum we bioð gefylde in godum *hyses ðines halig is
tuis Replebimur in bonis domus tuae sanctum est

tempel din wundurlic in rehtwisnisse geher usic
templum tuum 6. *mirabile in aequitate Exaudi nos*

god se halwynda ur hyht alra gemæra eorðan 7 in
Deus salutaris noster spes omnium finium terrae et in

sae feor gearwiende muntas in mægne ðinum bi-
mari longe 7. *Praeparans montes in virtute tua ac-*

gyrded mid maehte ðu gedroefes grund sæs swo[e]g
cinctus potentia 8. *qui conturbas fundum maris sonum*

yða his hwelc arefneð bioð gedroefde ðiode ⁊
fluctuum ejus quis sustinebit Turbabuntur gentes 9. *et*

ondredað alle ða ðe eardiað endas eorðan from tacnum
timebunt omnes qui habitant fines terrae a signis

ðinum utgong margentide ⁊ on efenne ðu bist gelustfullad
tuis Exitus matutini et vespere delectaveris

ðu niosades eorðan ⁊ ðu indrenctes hie ðu gemonig-
10. *visitasti terram et inebriasti eam multiplicasti*

falddes geweolgian hie flod godes gefylled is mid wetre
locupletare eam Flumen Dei repletum est aqua

ðu gearwades mete heara forðon swe is gegearwung ðin
parasti cibum illorum quia ita est praeparatio tua

rinnellan his indrencende gemonigfalldende . cneorisse
11. *Rivos ejus inebrians multiplicans generationes*

his in dreapingum his bið geblissad ðonne he upcymeð
ejus in stillicidiis ejus laetabitur dum exorietur

bledsiende beg geres freamsumnisse ðinre ⁊ feldes
12. *Benedicens coronam anni benignitatis tuae et campi*

ðines bioð gefyld mid genyhtsumnisse faettiað endas
tui replebuntur ubertate 13. *Pinguiscent fines*

woestennes ⁊ wynsumnisse hyllas bioð bigyrde gegerede
deserti et exultatione colles accingentur 14. *Induti*

sind rommas scepa ⁊ gemæru ⁊ dene genyhtsumiað hwæte
sunt arietes ovium et convalles abundabunt frumento

⁊ soðlice cleopiað ⁊ ymen cweoðað
etenim clamabunt et hymnum dicent

65.

wynsumiað gode all eorðe salm cweoðað noman
Jubilate Deo omnis terra 2. *psalmum dicite nomini*

his sellað wuldur lofe his cweoðad gode hu
ejus date gloriam laudi ejus 3. *Dicite Deo Quam*

egesfulle sind werc ðin in mengu megnes ðines
terribilia sunt opera tua in multitudine virtutis tuae

legað ðe feond ðine all eorðe weorðað ðec
mentientur tibi inimici tui 4. *Omnis terra adoret te*

7 singeð ðe salm cwið noman ðinum ðu hesta
et psallat tibi psalmum dicat nomini tuo Altissime

cymað 7 gesiað werc dryht*nes* hu egesful in
5. *Venite et videte opera Domini quam terribilis in*

geðæhtum ofer bearn monna se gecerreð sae in
consiliis super filios hominum 6. *Qui convertit mare in*

dryge 7 flodas ðorhleoreð mid foet ðer we bioð geblissade
aridam et flumina pertransivit pede ibi laetabimur

in ðæt ilce se waldeð in megne his in ecnisse
in id ipso 7. *Qui dominatur in virtute sua in aeternum*

egan his ofer ðiode gelociað ða in eorre gegremedon
oculi ejus super gentes respiciunt qui in ira provocant

ne sien upahefen in him seolfum bledsiað ðiode god
non exaltentur in semetipsis 8. *Benedicite gentes Deum*

urne 7 hersumiað stefne lofes his se sette
nostrum et obaudite vocem laudis ejus 9. *Qui posuit*

sawle mine to life 7 ne salde onstyrgan foet mine
animam meam ad vitam et non dedit commoveri pedes meos

forðon ðu acunnades usic god mid fyre usic amearedes
10. *Quoniam probasti nos Deus igne nos examinasti*

swe mid fyre bið amearad seolfur ðu gelęddes usic in
sicut igne examinatur argentum 11. *Induxisti nos in*

gerene ðu settes geswencednisse in bece urum ðu
laqueum posuisti tribulationes in dorso nostro 12. *in-*

onsettes men ofer heafud ur we leordun ðorh fyr
posuisti homines super capita nostra Transivimus per ignem

7 weter 7 ðu ingelaeddes usic in coelnisse ic ingaa
et aquam et induxisti nos in refrigerium 13. *Introibo*

in hus ðin in onsegdnissum ic gelde ðe gehat min
in domum tuam in holocaustis reddam tibi vota mea

ða todęldun weolure mine ðas spreocende wes mud
14. *quae distinxerunt labia mea Haec locutum est os*

min in geswencednisse minre onsegdnisse merglice
meum in tribulatione mea 15. *holocausta medullata*

ic ofriu ðe mid inbernisse 7 rommum[1] ic ofriu ðe oxan
offeram tibi cum incensu et arietibus offeram tibi boves

mid buccum cumað 7 geherað mec 7 ic seg[c]o eow
cum hircis 16. *Venite et audite me et narrabo vobis*

[1] o *over* e.

alle ða ondredað dryhten hu feolu dyde sawle minre
omnes qui timetis Dominum quanta fecit animae meae

from him muðe minum ic cleopede 7 upahof under
17. *Ab ipso ore meo clamavi et exaltavi sub*

tungan minre unrehtwisnisse gif ic gelocade in heortan
lingua mea 18. *Iniquitatem si conspexi in corde*

minre ne gehereð god forðon geherde mec *go
meo non exaudiet Deus 19. *Propterea exaudivit me Deus*

7 bihaldeð stefne boene minre gebledsad dryhten
et intendit voci deprecationis meae 20. *Benedictus Dominus*

se onweg ne awende boene mine 7 mildheortnisse
qui non amovit deprecationem meam et misericordiam

his from me
suam a me

66.

god gemildsie us 7 bledsie usic inlihte ondwliotan
2. *Deus misereatur nobis et benedicat nos inluminet vultum*

his ofer usic 7 *gemilsie us ðæt we oncnawen in
suum super nos et misereatur nobis 3. *Ut cognoscamus in*

eorðan weg ðinne in allum ðiodum haelu ðin
terra viam tuam in omnibus gentibus salutare tuum

ondettigen ðe folc god ondettien ðe folc all
4. *Confiteantur tibi populi Deus confiteantur tibi populi omnes*

blissien 7 gefen ðiode forðon ðu doemest folc in
5. *Laetentur et exultent gentes quoniam judicas populos in*

rehtwisnisse 7 ðiode in eorðan ðu gereces *ondette[1]
aequitate et gentes in terra diriges 6. *Confiteantur*

ðe folc god ondettie ðe folc all eorðe
tibi populi Deus confiteantur tibi populi omnes 7. *Terra*

salde westem his bledsie usic god god ur 7
dedit fructum suum benedicat nos Deus Deus noster 8. *et*

bledsie usic god 7 ondreden hine alle endas eorðan
benedicat nos Deus et metuant eum omnes fines terrae

67.

arise god 7 sien tostrogdne feond his 7 flen from
2. *Exsurgat Deus et dissipentur inimici ejus et fugiant a*

[1] e *over* að.

onsiene his ðа fiodun hine swe asprong rec hie
facie ejus qui oderunt eum 3. *Sicut defecit fumus de-*

aspringen swe floweð wex from onsiene fyres swe
ficiant sicut fluit cera a facie ignis sic

forweorðen ða synfullan[1] from onsiene godes 7 ða reht-
pereant peccatores a facie Dei 4. *et justi*

wisan symbliað gefen in gesihðe godes sien gelustfullade
epulentur Exultent in conspectu Dei delectentur

in blisse singað gode salm cweodað noman his
in laetitia 5. *Cantate Deo psalmum dicite nomini ejus*

siðfet dood him se astag ofer setgong dryhten noma
iter facite ei qui ascendit super occasum Dominus nomen

is him gefiað in gesihðe his bioð gedroefde from onsiene
est ei Gaudete in conspectu ejus turbabuntur a facie

his fedras stepcilda 7 doeman widwena god in
ejus 6. *patres orfanorum et judices viduarum Deus in*

stowe ðere halgan his god se eardian doeð anmodde
loco sancto suo 7. *Deus qui inhabitare facit unanimes*

in huse se utalędeð gebundne in strengu gelice 7
in domo Qui educit vinctos in fortitudine similiter et

ða ða in eorre gegremmað ða eardiað in byrgennum
eos qui in ira provocant qui habitant in sepulcris

god mit te ðu utgæst biforan folce ðinum ðonne ðu
8. *Deus dum egredieris coram populo tuo dum trans-*

ofergæst ðorh woesten eorðe onstyred is 7 soðlice
gredieris per deserto 9. *terra mota est Etenim*

heofenas dreapedun from onsiene godes munt from
caeli distillaverunt a facie Dei mons Sina a

onsiene godes regn wilsumne toscadende
facie Dei Israhel 10. *Pluviam voluntariam segregans*

god erfewordnisse ðinre 7 soðlice geuntrumad is ðu soðlice
Deus hereditati tuae et enim infirmata est tu vero

*gefredes ða netenu ðin ineardiad in hire
perfecisti ea 11. *Animalia tua inhabitabunt in ea*

ðu gearwades in swoetnisse ðinre ðearfan god dryhten
parasti in dulcidine tua pauperi Deus 12. *Dominus*

seleð word godspelliendum megene micle cyning
dabit verbum evangelizantibus virtute multa 13. *rex*

[1] u *over* y.

megna ðes leofan 7 hiow huses todaelan herereaf
virtutum dilecti et species domus dividere spolia

gif ge slepað betwih midde ðreatas fiðru culfran
14. *Si dormiatis inter medios cleros pinnae columbae*

*besifrede 7 efterran beces his in hiowe goldes
deargentatae et posteriora dorsi ejus in specie auri

ðonne toscadeð des heofenlican cyninges ofer hie snawe
15. *Dum discernit caelestis regis super eam nive*

bioð gehwitte munt godes munt genyhtsum
dealvabuntur in Selmon 16. *Montem Dei montem uberem*

munt gerunnen munt fęt tohwon onfoð ge
mons coagulatus mons pinguis 17. *Ut quid suspicitis*[1]

muntas genyhtsume munt in ðæm wel gelicad is gode
montes uberes mons in quo bene placitum est Deo

eardian in him 7 soðlice dryhten eardað oð ende
habitare in eo et enim Dominus habitabit usque in finem

scrid godes ten ðusendum monigfald *ðused blis-
18. *Currus Dei *decim milium multiplex milia lae-*

siendra dryhten in him in ðæm halgan
tantium Dominus in illis in Sina in sancto 19. *as-*

stigende in heanisse gehefte laedde heftned salde gefe
cendens in altum captivam duxit captivitatem dedit dona

monnum 7 soðlice ða ne gelefað ineardian dryhten
hominibus Et enim qui non credunt inhabitare Dominus

god gebledsad gebledsad dryhten of dege in deg
Deus 20. *benedictus benedictus Dominus de die in diem*

gesundne siðfet doeð us god se *halwynde ur
Prosperum iter faciet nobis Deus salutaris noster

ur god hale to donne 7 dryhtnes utgong deaðes
21. *noster Deus salvos faciendi et Domini exitus mortis*

ah hweðre god· gescæneð heafudu feonda his
22. *Verumtamen Deus conquassavit capita inimicorum suorum*

cnol loccas geon[d]gongendra in scyldum his *cyð
verticem capilli perambulantium in delictis suis 23. *Dixit*

dryhten of Basan ic gecerru ic biom gecerred in *grud
Dominus Ex Basan convertam convertar in profundum

sæs oððæt sie bideped fot ðin in blode
maris 24. *donec intinguatur pes tuus in sanguine*

[1] *altered from* suscipitis (?).

tunge[1] hunda ðinra of feondum from him gesegene
Lingua canum tuorum ex inimicis ab ipso **25.** *visi*

sind gongas ðine god inngong godes mines cyninges se
sunt gressus tui Deus ingressus Dei mei regis qui

is in halgum his forecwomun aldermen tosomne
est in sancto ipsius **26.** *Praevenerunt principes con-*

*geðeode singendum in midle iungra[2] plægiendra timpanan
juncti psallentibus in medio juvenum tympanistriarum

in cirican bledsiað dryhten god of espryngum
27. *In ecclesiis benedicite Dominum Deum de fontibus*

ðer se gungesta in fyrhtu alder-
Israhel **28.** *Ibi Benjamin adulescentior in pavore prin-*

men heretogan heara aldermen 7 aldermen
cipes Juda duces eorum principes Zabulon et principes

onbiod god megen ðin getryme ðis
Neptalim **29.** *Manda Deus virtutem tuam confirma hoc*

god ðæt wircende ðu earð in us from temple
Deus quod operatus es in nobis **30.** *a templo*

ðinum ðæt is ðe ofredun cyningas gefe
tuo quod est in Hierusalem tibi offerent reges munera

ðu ðreades wuda gemot fearra betwih cye
31. *Increpa feras silvarum concilium taurorum inter vaccas*

folca dæt ne sien utatyned ðas ða gecunnade werun
populorum ut non excludantur hii qui probati sunt

seolfre tostenc ðiode ða gefeht willað cumað erend-
argento Dissipa gentes quae bella volunt **32.** *venient*

wrecan of Ægyptum sigelhearwan forcymeð hond his gode
legati ex Aegypto Aethiopia praeveniet manus ejus Deo

ricu eorðan singað gode singað dryhtne singað
33. *Regna terrae cantate Deo psallite Domino psallite*

gode se astag ofer heofenas heofena to eastdaele
Deo **34.** *qui ascendit super caelos caelorum ad orientem*

sehðe seleð stefne his stefne megnes his sellad
Ecce dabit vocem suam vocem virtutis suae **35.** *date*

are gode ofer Israel micelnis his 7 megen his
honorem Deo Super Israhel magnificentia ejus et virtus ejus

in wolcnum wundurlic god in halgum his god
in nubibus **36.** *Mirabilis Deus in sanctis suis Deus*

[1] u *over* o. [2] r *from some other letter.*

he seleð megen ⁊ strengu folces his ge-
*Israhel ipse dabit virtutem et fortitudinem *plebis suae bene-*

bledsad god
dictus Deus

68.

halne mec doa god forðon ineodun weter oð.
2. *Salvum me fac Deus quoniam introierunt aquae usque*

sawle mine gefestnad ic eam in lam grundes
ad animam meam 3. *infixus sum in limum profundi*

⁊ nis spoed cym in heanisse saes ⁊ storm
et non est substantia Veni in altitudinem maris et tempestas

bisencte mec ic won cleopiende hase gewordne werun
demersit me 4. *Laboravi clamans raucae factae sunt*

goman mine asprungun egan mine ðonne ic gehyhtu in
fauces meae defecerunt oculi mei dum spero in

god minne gemonigfaldade sindun ofer loccas heafdes
Deum meum 5. *Multiplicati sunt super capillos capitis*

mines ða fiodun mec bi ungewyrhtum gestrongade sind
mei qui oderunt me gratis Confortati sunt

ofer mec ða mec oehtað · feond mine unrehtwislice[1]
super me qui me persequuntur inimici mei injusti

ða ic ne reafade ða ic onlesde god ðu wast un-
qui non rapui tunc exsolvebam 6. *Deus tu scis in-*

wisdom minne ⁊ scylde mine from ðe ne sind
sipientiam meam et delicta mea a te non sunt

ahydde ne scomiað in mec ða ðe ðec bidað
abscondita 7. *Non erubescant in me qui te expectant*

dryhtne god megna ne onscunien ofer mec ða ðe
Domine Deus virtutum non revereantur super me qui

soecað ðec god forðon fore ðe ic
requirunt te Deus Israhel 8. *Quoniam propter te sup-*

aber edwit oferwrah mid scome onsiene mine
portavi improperium operuit reverentia faciem meam

fremðe geworden ic eam broðrum minum ⁊ cuma bearnum
9. *exter factus sum fratribus meis et hospis filiis*

moeder minre forðon hatheortnisse huses ðines
matris meae 10. *Quoniam zelus domus tuae*

[1] *dotted* e *after* s.

iteð mec 7 edwit edwitendra ðe gefeollun ofer
comedit me et opprobria exprobrantium tibi ceciderunt super

mec 7 oferwrah in festenne sawle mine 7 ge-
me 11. *Et operui in jejunio animam meam et fac-*

worden is me in edwit 7 ic sette hregl
tum est mihi in opprobrium 12. *Et posui vestimentum*

min heran 7 geworden ic eam him · in bispel
meum cilicium et factus sum illis in parabolam

wið mec bieodun ða ðe setun in gete 7 in
13. *Adversum me exercebantur qui sedebant in porta et in*

*mec sungun ða ðe druncun win ic soðlice *ge-
me psallebant qui bibebant vinum 14. *Ego vero ora-*

beded min to ðe dryht*en* tid welgelicade god in
tionem meam ad te Domine tempus beneplaciti Deus in

mengu mildheortnisse ðinre geher me in soðfestnisse
multitudine misericordiae tuae exaudi me in veritate

haelu ðinre *gere mec of lame ðæt ic in ne fele
salutis tuae 15. *Eripe me de luto ut non inhaeream*

gefrea mec of ðæm figendum mec 7 of grunde wetra
libera me ex odientibus me et de profundo aquarum

nales mec bisence storm wetres ne forswelge mec
16. *non me demergat tempestas aquae Neque absorbeat me*

grund ne ðrege ofer mec seað muð his ge-
profundum neque urgeat super me puteus os suum 17. *Ex-*

her mec dryht*en* forðon freamsum is mildheortnis ðin
audi me Domine quoniam benigna est misericordia tua

efter mengu mildsa ðinra geloca in mec
secundum multitudinem miserationum tuarum respice in me

ne acer ðu onsiene ðine from cnehte ðinum forðon
18. *Ne avertas faciem tuam a puero tuo quoniam*

ic bio geswenced hreðlice geher mec bihald to sawle
tribulor velociter exaudi · me 19. *Intende animae*

minre 7 gefrea hie fore fiondum minum genere mec
meae et libera eam propter inimicos meos eripe me

dryht*en* ðu soðlice wast edwit min gedroefnisse
Domine 20. *Tu enim scis improperium meum confusionem*

7 s[c]ome mine in gesihðe ðinre sind alle
et verecundiam meam 21. *in conspectu tuo sunt omnes*

geswencende mec edwit bad heorte min 7 ermðu
tribulantes me Improperium expectavit cor meum et mise-

⁊ ic arefnde ða somud mid mec were geunrotsad ⁊
riam et sustinui qui simul mecum contristaretur et

ne wes ⁊ froefrende mec ic sohte ⁊ ic ne gemoette
non fuit et consolantem me quisivi et non inveni

⁊ saldun in mete minne gallan ⁊ in ðurste minum
22. *Et dederunt in escam meam fel et in siti mea*

drynctun mec mid ecede sie biod heara biforan
potaverunt me aceto 23. *Fiat mensa eorum coram -*

him in girene ⁊ in edlean ⁊ in eswic
ipsis in laqueum et in retributionem et in scandalum

sien aðiostrade egan heara ðaet hie ne gesen ⁊ bec
24. *Obscurentur oculi eorum ne videant et dorsum*

heara aa gebeged ageot ofer hie eorre ðin
illorum semper incurva 25. *Effunde super eos iram tuam*

⁊ ebylgðu[1] eorres ðines ge[g]ripe hie sie
et indignatio irae tuae adpraehendat eos 26. *Fiat*

eardung heara woestu ⁊ in geteldum heara ne sie
habitatio eorum deserta et in tabernaculis eorum non sit

se ineardie forðon ðone ðu sloge hie oehtende
qui inhabitet 27. *Quoniam quem tu percussisti ipsi persecuti*

werun ⁊ ofer sar wunda minra otectun
sunt et super dolorem vulnerum meorum addiderunt

tosete unrehtwisnisse ofer unrehtwisnisse heara ⁊
28. *Adpone iniquitatem super iniquitatem ipsorum et*

in ne gað in ðinre rehtwisnisse sien hie adilgade of
non intrent in tua justitia 29. *Deleantur de*

boec lifgendra ⁊ mid ðæm rehtwisum ne bioð awriten
libro viventium et cum justis non scribantur

ðearfa ⁊ sargiende ic eam ⁊ haelu ondwlitan ðines
30. *Pauper et dolens ego sum et salus vultus tui*

god onfeng mec ic hergu noman godes mines mid
Deus suscepit me 31. *Laudabo nomen Dei mei cum*

songe ⁊ ic micliu hine in lofe licað gode ofer
cantico et magnificabo eum in laude 32. *Placebit Deo super*

caelf niowe hornas forðlędende ⁊ clea gesen
vitulum novellum cornua producentem et ungulas 33. *Videant*

ðearfan ⁊ blissien soecað dryhten ⁊ liofað sawul
pauperes et laetentur quaerite Dominum et vivet anima

[1] y *over* u.

eower forðon geherde ðearfan dryhten 7 ge-
vestra 34. *Quoniam exaudivit pauperes Dominus et*

bundne his ne forhogde hergað hine heofenas 7
vinctos suos non sprevit 35. *Laudent eum caeli et*

eorðe sae 7 all ða ðe in him sind forðon
terra mare et omnia quae in eis sunt 36. *Quoniam*

god halne *doð Sion 7 bioð timbrede cestre
Deus salvam faciet Sion et aedificabuntur civitates Judae

7 ineardiað ðer 7 erfeworðnisse bigeotað hie 7
et inhabitabunt ibi Et hereditate adquirunt eam 37. *et*

sed ðiowa his gesittað hie 7 ða ðe lufiað noman
semen servorum ejus possidebit eam et qui diligunt nomen

his ineardiad in hire
ejus inhabitabunt in ea

69.

god in *fultu minne bihald dryhten to gefultu-
2. *Deus in adjutorium meum intende Domine ad adju-*

miende me oefesta sien gescende 7 onscunien fiond
vandum me festina 3. *Confundantur et revereantur inimici*

mine ða ðe soecað sawle mine sien forcerde on bec
mei qui querunt animam meam 4. *Avertantur retrorsum*

7 scomien ða ðe me yfel sien forcerred sona
et erubescant qui cogitant mihi mala Avertantur statim

7 s[c]omiende ða ðe cweoðað me weolga weolga ge-
et erubescentes qui dicunt mihi Euge euge 5. *Ex-*

fen 7 blissien ða ðe soecað ðæc dryhten 7 cweðen
ultent et laetentur qui quaerunt te Domine et dicant

aa sie gemiclad dryhten ða ðe lufiað haelu ðine
semper Magnificetur Dominus qui diligunt salutare tuum

ic soðlice weðla 7 ðearfa ic eam god gefultume me
6. *Ego vero egenus et pauper sum Deus adjuva me*

fultum min 7 alesend min ðu earð dryhten ne leata
Adjutor meus et liberator meus es tu Domine ne retar-

ðu
daveris

70.

in ðe ic gehyhte dryhten ic ne sie ges[c]ended in ecnisse
In te speravi Domine ne confundar in aeternum

in ðinre rehtwisnisse gefrea mec 7 genere mec on-
2. *In tua justitia libera me et eripe me In-*

haeld to me eare ðin 7 gefrea mec bio ðu me
clina ad me aurem tuam et libera me 3. *esto mihi*

in god gescildend 7 in stowe getrymede ðætde[1] halne
in Deum protectorem et in locum munitum ut salvum

mec gedoe forðon trymenis min 7 geberg min
me facias Quoniam firmamentum meum et refugium meum

ðu earð god min genere mec of honda ðes synfullan
es tu 4. *Deus meus eripe me de manu peccatoris*

7 of honda wið ęe dondes 7 unrehtlice forðon
et de manu contra legem agentis et inique 5. *Quoniam*

ðu earð geðyld min dryhten hyht min from guguðe minre
tu es patientia mea Domine spes mea a juventute mea

in ðec getrymed ic eam of innoðe of wombe modur[2]
6. *In te confirmatus sum ex utero de ventre matris*

minre ðu earð min gescildend in ðec song min aa
meae tu es meus protector in te decantatio mea semper

swe swe forebecen geworden ic eam mongum 7 ðu
7. *Tamquam prodigium factus sum multis et tu*

fultum strong sie gefylled min muð lof ðin ðæt
adjutor fortis 8. *Repleatur os meum laudem tuam ut*

ic mege singan wuldur ðin alne deg micelnisse ðine
possim cantare gloriam tuam tota die magnificentiam tuam

ne aweorp ðu mec in tid aeldu ðonne aspringeð
9. *Ne proicias me in tempore senectutis dum defecerit*

megen min ne forlet ðu mec forðon cwedun feond
virtus mea ne derelinquas me 10. *Quia dixerunt inimici*

mine yfel me 7 ða ðe heoldun sawle mine geðęht
mei mala mihi et qui custodiebant animam meam consilium

dydun in annisse cweoðende god forleort hine
fecerunt in unum 11. *Dicentes Deus dereliquit eum*

oehtað 7 gegripað hine forðon nis se generge
persequimini et conpraehendite eum quia non est qui eripiat

[1] d *from* t. [2] o *from* u (?).

hine god ne afearra ðu from me god min in ful-
eum **12.** *Deus ne elongis a me Deus meus in auxi-*

tum minne geloca sien gescende ⁊ aspringen telende
lium meum respice **13.** *Confundantur et deficiant detrahentes*

sawle minre sien oferwrigen mid gedroefednisse ⁊ scome
animae meae operiantur confusione et pudore

ða ðe soecað yfel me ic soðlice aa in ðec
qui quaerunt mala mihi **14.** *Ego autem semper in te*

ic gehyhtu dryht*en* ⁊ geecu ofer all lof ðin
sperabo Domine et adiciam super omnem laudem tuam

muð min segeð rehtwisnisse ðine alne deg haelu
15. *Os meum pronuntiabit justitiam tuam tota die salutare*

ðine forðon ic ne oncneow scire ic inga in
tuum Quia non cognovi negotiationes **16.** *introibo in*

maehte dryhtnes dryht*en* ic biom gemyndgad rehtwisnisse
potentias Domini Domine memorabor justitiae

ðinre anes god ðu lærdes mec from guguðe minre
tuae solius **17.** *Deus docuisti me a juventute mea*

⁊ oð nu ic forðsecgu wundur ðin ⁊ oð in
et usque nunc pronuntiabo mirabilia tua **18.** *et usque in*

aeldu ⁊ aldra god ne forlet ðu ·mec ot ðet ic secge
senecta et senium Deus ne derelinquas me Donec adnuntiem

earm ðinne cneorisse alre ða toword is maehte
bracchium tuum generationi omni quae ventura est Potentiam

ðine ⁊ rehtwisnisse ðine god oð in heanisse
tuam **19.** *et justitiam tuam Deus usque in altissimis*

ða ðu[1] dydes micelnisse god hwelc gelic ðe hu monge
quae fecisti magnalia Deus quis similis tibi **20.** *Quantas*

ðu oteawdes me geswencednisse monge ⁊ yfle ⁊ gecerred
ostendisti mihi tribulationes multas et malas et conversus

ðu geliffestes mec ⁊ of neolnisse eorðan eft ðu alaedes
vivificasti me et de abysso terrae iterum reduxisti

mec ðu gemonigfaldades *rehwisnisse ðine ⁊ gecerred
me **21.** *Multiplicasti justitiam tuam et conversus*

trymmende earð mec ⁊ ic ondettu ðe in featum
exortatus es me* **22. *et ego confitebor tibi in vasis*

salma soðfestnisse ðine ic singu ðe in citran god
psalmorum veritatem tuam psallam tibi in cythara Deus

[1] ðu *twice.*

halig gefiað weolure mine ðonne ic singu
sanctus Israhel 23. *Gaudebunt labia mea dum cantavero*

ðe 7 sawul min ða ðu alesdes ah 7 tunge min
tibi et anima mea quam redemisti 24. *Sed et lingua mea*

bið smegende rehtwisnisse ðine ðonne gedroefde 7 onscuniende
meditabitur justitiam tuam dum confusi et reveriti

bioð ða ðe soecað yfel me
fuerint qui quaerunt mala mihi

71.

god dom ðinne cyninge sele 7 rehtwisnisse ðine
2. *Deus judicium tuum regi da et justitiam tuam*

suna cyninges doem folc ðin in ðinre rehtwisnisse
filio regis Judicare populum tuum in tua justitia

7 ðearfan ðine in dome onfoen muntas sibbe
et pauperes tuos in judicio 3. *Suscipiant montes pacem*

folce ðinum 7 hyllas rehtwisnisse in his rehtwisnis
populo tuo et colles justitiam 4. *In sua justitia*

doemeð ðearfan ðisses folces 7 hale gedoeð *bern ðear-
judicabit pauperes hujus populi et salvos faciet filios pau-

fena 7 geeaðmodað hearmcweoðendra 7 ðorhwunað
perum Et humiliabit calumniatorem 5. *et permanebit*

mid sunnan 7 ær monan in weoruld weorulde 7
cum sole et ante lunam in saeculum saeculi 6. *Et*

astag swe swe regn in fieos 7 swe swe dreapung
discendit sicut pluvia in vellus et sicut stillicidia

dropetende ofer eorðan upeorneð in dægum his
stillantia super terram 7. *Orietur in diebus ejus*

rehtwisnis 7 genyhtsumnis sibbe oð ðæt were upahefen mona
justitia et abundantia pacis donec extollatur luna

7 waldeð from sae oð sae 7 from flode
8. *Et dominabitur a mari usque ad mare et a flumine*

oð gemæru ymbhwyrftes eorðan biforan him forð-
usque ad terminos orbis terrae 9. *Coram illo proci-*

gað sigelhearwan 7 feond his eorðan *liciað cyningas
dent Aethiopes et inimici ejus terram lingent 10. *Reges*

7 ealondes gefe ofradun cyningas
Tharsis et insulae munera offerent reges Arabum et Saba

gefe togelaedað 7 weorðiað hine alle cyningas eorðan
dona adducent **11.** *Et adorabunt eum omnes reges terrae*

alle ðeoðe ðeowiað him forðon gefreode ðearfan
omnes gentes servient ei **12.** *Quia liberabit pauperem*

from ðæm maehtgan 7 weðlan ðæm ne wes fultum
a potente et inopem cui non erat adjutor

spearað dearfan 7 weðlan 7 sawle ðearfena hale
13. *Parcet pauperi et inopi et animas pauperum salvas*

gedoeð of westemsceattum 7 unrehtwisnisse gefreað
faciet **14.** *Ex usuris et iniquitate liberabit*

• sawle heara 7 berht noma heara biforan him 7
animas eorum et praeclarum nomen eorum coram ipso **15.** *Et*

leofað 7 bið sald him of golde 7 weorðiað of
vivet et dabitur ei de auro Arabiae et adorabunt de

him aa alne deg bledsiað hine 7 bið trymenis
ipso semper tota die benedicent eum **16.** *Et erit firmamentum*

in eorðan in heanissum munta ofer bið upahefen ofer
in terra in summis montium super extollitur super

Libanan munt westem his 7 blowað of cestre swe swe
Libanum fructus ejus et florebunt de civitate sicut

heg eorðan 7 sie *oma his gebledsad in
faenum terrae **17.** *Et sit nomen ejus benedictum in*

weorulde ær sunnan ðorhwunað noma his 7 ær monan
saecula ante solem permanebit nomen ejus et ante lunam

seld his 7 bioð gebledsade in him alle cyn eorðan
sedis ejus Et benedicentur in eo omnes tribus terrae

alle ðeode micliað hine gebledsad dryhten
omnes gentes magnificabunt eum **18.** *Benedictus Dominus*

god israela se doeð wundur micelu ana 7
Deus Israhel qui facit mirabilia magna solus **19.** *Et*

gebledsad noma megenðrymmes his in ecnisse 7 in weoruld
benedictum nomen majestatis ejus in aeternum et in sae-

weorulde 7 bið gefylled megendrymme his all eorðe
culum saeculi Et replebitur majestate ejus omnis terra

sie sie
Fiat Fiat

72.

swiðe god god israela ðissum ða ðe rehtre sind heortan
Quam bonus Deus Israhel his qui recto sunt corde

min soðlice fulneh onstyrede sind foet fulneh agotene
2. *Mei autem paene moti sunt pedes paene effusi*

sind gongas mine forðon ic elnade in ðæm synfullum
sunt gressus mei 3. *Quia zelavi in peccatoribus*

sibbe synfulra gesiende forðon nis onhęldednis deaðe
pacem peccatorum videns 4. *Quia non est declinatio morti*

heara ne trymenis in wite heara in gewinnun
eorum nec firmamentum in plaga eorum 5. *In laboribus*

monna ne sind 7 mid monnum ne *bið swungne
hominum non sunt et cum hominibus non flagellabuntur

forðon nom hie oferhygd heara oferwrigene sind mid un-
6. *Ideo tenuit eos superbia eorum operti sunt ini-*

rehtwisnisse 7 *arleas his forðyppeð swe swe of
quitate et impietate sua 7. *Prodiit quasi ex*

smeorwe unrehtwisnis heara leordun in geflite heortan
adipe iniquitas eorum transierant in disputatione cordis

ðohtun 7 spreocende werun niðas unrehtwisnisse in
8. *cogitaverunt et locuti sunt nequitias iniquitatem in*

heanisse spreocende werun settun in heofene mud
excelso locuti sunt 9. *Posuerunt in caelo os*

heara 7 tunge heara leorde ofer eorðan forðon
suum et lingua eorum transiit super terram 10. *Ideo*

cerreð hider folc min 7 dęgas fulle bioð gemoeted
revertetur huc populus meus et dies pleni invenientur

in him 7 cwedun hu wat god 7 gif is
in eis 11. *Et dixerunt Quomodo scivit Deus et si est*

wisdom in heanisse sehðe hie synfulle 7 genyht-
scientia in Excelso 12. *Ecce ipsi peccatores et abun-*

sumegende in weorulde bigetun weolan 7 ic cweð
dantes in saeculo optinuerunt divitias 13. *Et dixi*

soðlice butan intingan ic gerehtwisade heortan mine 7 ðwog
Ergo sine causa justificavi cor meum et lavi

betwih ða unsceððendan honda mine 7 ic wes geswungen
inter innocentes manus meas 14. *et fui flagellatus*

allne deg 7 gebecnend min in margentid gif ic cweð
tota die et index meus in matutino 15. *Si dicebam*

ic seggu swe sehðe cneoris bearna ðinra ðæm ic gestihtade
Narrabo sic ecce natio filiorum tuorum quibus disposui

ic gewoende ðæt ic oncneowe ðis gewin is biforan
16. *Existimabam ut cognoscerem hoc labor est ante*

me oððæt ic ingae in godes halig portic 7 ongete
me 17. *donec intrem in sanctuarium Dei et intellegam*

ða nestan heara ah hweðre fore facne ðu gestih-
novissima eorum 18. *Verumtamen propter dolos dispo-*

tades him yfel ðu awurpe hie ðonne werun upahefen
suisti eis mala dejecisti eos dum adlevarentur

hu gewordne werun in tolesnisse feringa asprungun
19. *Quomodo facti sunt in desolatione subito defecerunt*

forwurdun fore unrehtwisnisse heara swe swe from slepe
perierunt propter iniquitates suas 20. *velut a somno*

arisende dryhten in cestre ðinre onlicnesse heara to
exurgentes Domine in civitate tua imagines eorum ad

nowihte ðu gebeges forðon gelustfullad is heorte min
nihilum rediges 21. *Quia delectatum est cor meum*

7 eðre mine tolesde sind 7 ic to nowihte gebeged
et renes mei resoluti sunt 22. *et ego ad nihilum redactus*

eam 7 ic hit nyste swe swe neat geworden ic eam
sum et nescivi 23. *Ut jumentum factus sum*

mid dec 7 ic aa mid dec ðu nome hond ða
apud te et ego semper tecum 24. *Tenuisti manum dex-*

swiðran mine 7 in willan ðinum gelaedes mec 7 mid
teram meam et in voluntate tua deduxisti me et cum

wuldre genome mic hwet soðlice me to lafe *stodeð[1]
gloria adsumpsisti me 25. *Quid enim mihi restat*

in heofene 7 from ðe hwet walde ic ofer eorðan
in caelo et a te quid volui super terram 26. *De-*

asprong heorte min 7 flæsc min god heortan minre 7
fecit cor meum et caro mea Deus cordis mei et

dael min god min in weorulde forðon sehðe ða afirrað
pars mea Deus in saecula 27. *Quia ecce qui elongant*

hie from ðe forweorðað ðu forspildes alle ða dernliggað
se a te peribunt perdes omnes qui fornicantur

from ðe me soðlice ætfealan godc god is settan[2]
abs te 28. *Mihi autem adherere Deo bonum est ponere*

in dryhtne gode hyht minne ðæt ic secge all lofu
in Domino Deo spem meam Ut adnuntiem omnes laudes

ðin in geatum doehter
tuas in portis filiae Sion

[1] d *from* ð. [2] a *over* e.

73.

to hwon onweg adrife ðu us god in ende eorre is
Ut quid reppulisti nos Deus in finem iratus est

hatheortnis ðin ofer scep eowde ðinre gemyne ge-
furor tuus super oves gregis tui 2. *Memento con-*

somnunge ðinre ða ðu gescope from fruman ðu gefreades-
gregationis tuae quam creasti ab initio Liberasti

gerd erfes ðines munt sion in ðæm eardas in ðon
virgam hereditatis tuae mons Sion in quo habitas in id

ilcan ahefe hond ðine in oferhygde heara in ende
**ipso* 3. *Eleva manum tuam in superbia eorum in finem*

hu feolu wergende wes se feond in halgum ðinum 7
quanta malignatus est inimicus in sanctis tuis 4. *et*

gewuldrade sind ða ðe fiedon in midle ceafurtunes ðines
gloriati sunt qui te oderunt in medio atrio tuo

settun tacen heara tacen 7 ne oncneowun swe swe
Posuerunt signa sua signa 5. *et non cognoverunt sicut*

in wege ofer ða hean swe swe in wuda trea mid ęcesum
in via supra summum quasi in silva lignorum Securibus

curfun dura his in ðæt ilce twibille 7 eadesan
6. *exciderunt januas ejus in id ipsum bipinnae et ascia*

awurpun ða forberndun mid fyre halig portic ðin
dejecerunt eam 7. *Incenderunt igni sanctuarium tuum*

in eorðan bisme[o]ton[1] geteld noman ðines cwedun
in terra polluerunt tabernaculum nominis tui 8. *Dix-*

in heortan heara cneoris heara betwih hie cumað
erunt in corde suo cognatio eorum inter se Venite

forðryccen we alle daegas symbellice dryhtnes from earðan
conprimamus omnes dies festos Domini a terra

tacen ur we ne gesegun soðlice nis witga 7 usic
9. *Signa nostra non vidimus jam non est profeta et nos*

ne oncnaweð mę[2] hu longe god edwetede
non cognoscit amplius 10. *Usque quo Deus improperavit*

se feond bismerad *wiðerbrocað noman ðinne in ende
inimicus inritat adversarius nomen tuum in finem

to hwon *acers ðu onsiene ðine 7 ða swiðran ðine
11. *Ut quid avertis faciem tuam et dexteram tuam*

[1] *originally* bioð bismitene. [2] mę:.

of *midum[1] sceate ðinum in ende god soðlice cyning
de medio sinu tuo in finem 12. *Deus autem rex*

ur aer weorulde wircende is haelu in midle eorðan
noster ante saecula operatus est salutem in medio terrae

ðu getrymedes in megne ðinum sae ðu senctes
13. *Tu confirmasti in virtute tua mare tu contribulasti*

heafud dracena ofer weter ðu gebrece heafud
capita draconum super aquas 14. *Tu confregisti caput*

dracan micles 7 saldes hine in mete folce sigelhearwena
draconis magni et dedisti eum in escam populo Aethiopum

ðu toslite wællan 7 burnan ðu adrygdes flodas
15. *Tu disrupisti fontes et torrentes tu exsiccasti fluvios*

ðin is deg 7 ðin is naeht ðu dydes
Aetham 16. *Tuus est dies et tua est nox tu fecisti*

sunnan 7 monan ðu dydes all gemæru eorðan
solem et lunam 17. *tu fecisti omnes terminos terrae*

sumur 7 *lenten ðu dydes ða gemyndig bio ðu ðisse
aestatem et ver tu fecisti ea 18. *Memor esto hujus*

gescefte ðinre se feond edwitte dryhten 7 folc
creaturae tuae inimicus improperavit Domino et populus

unwis onscunade noman ðinne ne sele ðu wilde-
insipiens exacervavit nomen tuum 19. *Ne tradas bestiis*

orum sawle ondetende de sawle ðearfena ðinra ne
animam confitentem tibi animas pauperum tuorum ne

forget ðu in ende geloca in cyðnisse ðinre forðon
obliviscaris in finem 20. *Respice in testamento tuo quia*

gefylde sind ða aðeastrade sind eorðan husa unreht-
repleti sunt qui obscurati sunt terrae domorum iniqui-

wisnissa ne sie acerred eadmod geworden gedroefed
tatum 21. *Ne avertatur humilis factus confusus*

ðearfa 7 weðla hergað noman ðinne aris god
pauper et inops laudabunt nomen tuum 22. *Exurge Deus*

doem intingan ðinne gemyndig ðu earð edwita ðinra
judica causam tuam memor esto improperiorum tuorum

ðeara ða from ðæm unwisan sind alne deg ne
eorum qui ab insipiente sunt tota die 23. *Ne*

oferget ðu stefne soecendra ðec oferhygd[2] heara ða ðec
obliviscaris voces quaerentium te superbia eorum qui te

[1] midleum; le *erased.*

[2] oferferhygd, *the second* fer *dotted.*

fiodun astag aa to ðe
oderunt ascendat semper ad te

74.

we ondettað ðe god we ondettað ðe 7 gecegað
2. *Confitebimur tibi Deus confitebimur tibi et invocabimus*

noman ðinne ic secgo all wundur ðin ðonne ic onfo
nomen tuum Narrabo omnia mirabilia tua 3. *dum accepero*

tid ic rehtwisnisse ic doemu[1] gemaelted is eorðe
tempus ego justiciam judicabo 4. *Liquefacta est terra*

7 alle ineardiende in ðere ic getrymede syle his
et omnes inhabitantes in ea ego confirmavi columnas ejus

ic cweð to ðæm unrehtwisum nyllað unrehtlice don 7 ðæm
5. *Dixi iniquis Nolite inique agere et delin-*

agyltendum nyllað uphebban[2] horn
quentibus Nolite exaltare cornu 6. *Nolite extollere in*

7 nyllað spreocan wið gode un-
altum cornu vestrum et nolite loqui adversus Deum in-

rehtwisnisse forðon ne from eastdęle ne from westdæle
iquitatem 7. *Quia neque ab oriente neque ab occidente*

ne from woestum muntum forðon god doema is
neque à desertis montibus 8. *quoniam Deus judex est*

ðeosne geheneð 7 ðeosne uphefeð forðon calic in honda
Hunc humiliat et hunc exaltat 9. *quia calix in manu*

dryht*nes* scires wines ful is gemenged 7 onhaeldeð
*Domini vini meri plenus est *mixto Et inclinavit*

of ðissum in ðis ah hweðre drosne[3] his nis
ex hoc in hoc verumtamen fex ejus non est exi-

amællad drincað of ðæm alle synfulle eorðan ic
nanita Bibent ex eo omnes peccatores terrae 10. *ego*

soðlice in weorulde gefio singu gode Iacobes 7
autem in saecula gaudebo cantabo Deo Jacob 11. *Et*

alle hornas synfulra ic gebreocu 7 bioð upahefene hornas
omnia cornua peccatorum confringam et exaltabuntur cornua

ðæ[s] rehtwisan
justi

[1] *originally* doema. [2] *first* b *from* f. [3] *over* dearstan; *the scribe first wrote* der, *and then altered the* r *to* a.

75.

cuð in Iudea god in Israela folce micel noma his
2. *Notus in Judea Deus in Israhel magnum nomen ejus*

⁊ geworden is in sibbe stow his ⁊ eardung his
3. *Et factus est in pace locus ejus et habitatio ejus in*

ðer gebrec hornas bogan sceld sweord ⁊
Sion 4. *Ibi confregit cornua arcum scutum gladium et*

gefeht inlihtes ðu wundurlice from muntum ecum
bellum 5. *Inluminas tu mirabiliter a montibus aeternis*

*gedrefde sind alle unwise on heortan hneapedun[1]
6. *turbati sunt omnes insipientes corde dormierunt som-*

slep heara ⁊ nowiht gemoettun alle weoras weolena
num suum et nihil invenerunt omnes viri divitiarum

in hondum heara from dreange ðinre god Iacobes
in manibus suis 7. *Ab increpatione tua Deus Jacob*

hneapedon ða asteogun hors ðu egesful earð ⁊
dormitaverunt qui ascenderunt equos 8. *tu terribilis es et*

hwelc wiðstondeð ðe nu *seoðan from eorre ðinum of
quis resistit tibi extunc ab ira tua 9. *De*

heofene dom scotad is eorðe cwęcede ⁊ gestilde
caelo judicium jaculatum est terra tremuit et quievit

ða ðe aras in dome god ðætte hale gedyde alle
10. *dum exurgeret in judicio Deus ut salvos faceret omnes*

stille eorðan forðon geðoht monnes ondetteð ðe ⁊
quietos terrae 11. *Quia cogitatio hominis confitebitur tibi et*

lafe geþohta symbeldeg ðoð ðe gehatað ⁊
reliquiae cogitationum diem festum agent tibi 12. *Vovite et*

ageofað dryht*ne* gode eowrum alle ða ðe in ymbhwyrfte
reddite Domino Deo vestro omnes qui in circuitu

his sind ofriað gefe ðæm egesfullan ⁊ ðæm se afirreð
ejus sunt offertis munera Terribili 13. *et ei qui aufert*

gast aldermonna ðæm egesfullan mid cyningum eorðan
spiritum principum terribili apud reges terrae

76.

mid stefne minre to dryht*ne* ic cleopede stefn min to
2. *Voce mea ad Dominum clamavi vox mea ad*

[1] vel slypton *added in an almost contemp. hand.*

dryht*ne* 7 behaldeð me in dege geswencednisse minre
Deum et intendit mihi 3. *In die tribulationis meae*

god ic sohte hondum minum on naeht biforan him 7
Deum exquisivi manibus meis nocte coram eo et

ic neam biswicen ic wiðsoc *frofran sawle mine ge-
non sum deceptus Negavi consolari[1] *animam meam*

myndig ic wes godes 7 gelustfullad ic eam bigongen -
4. *memor fui Dei et delectatus sum Exercitatus*

ic eam 7 asprong hwon gast min forefengun
sum et defecit paulisper spiritus meus 5. *anticipaverunt*

waecene egan min gedroefed ic eam 7 ne a · · ·[2] ic ðohte
vigilias oculi mei turbatus sum et non · · ·[2] 6. *Cogitavi*

dęgas alde 7 ger ece in mode ic hefde 7 sme-
dies antiquos et annos aeternos in mente habui 7. *Et medi-*

gende ic eam on naeht mid heortan minre ic bieode 7
tatus sum nocte cum corde meo exercitabam et

windwade in me gast minne 7 ic cweð ah
ventilabam in me spiritum meum 8. *Et dixi Numquid*

in ecnisse aweorpeð god oððe no toseteð ðæt wel
in aeternum proiciet Deus aut non adponet ut bene

gelicad sie nuget oððe in ende mildheortnisse his
placitum sit adhuc 9. *aut in finem misericordiam suam*

acearf[3] from weorulde 7 cneorisse ah ofer-
abscidet a saeculo et generatione 10. *Numquid obli-*

geotelað mildsian god oððe bihafað in eorre mildheortnisse
viscetur misereri Deus aut continebit in ira misericordiam

his 7 ic cweð nu ic ongon ðeos onwendednis swiðran
suam 11. *Et dixi Nunc coepi haec inmutatio dexterae*

ðes hean gemyndig ic wes werca dryht*nes* forðon gemyndig
Excelsi 12. *memor fui operum Domini quia memor*

ic biom from fruman wundra ðinra 7 smegende
ero ab initio mirabilium tuorum 13. *Et meditatus*

ic eam in allum wercum ðinum 7 in gehaeldum ðinum
sum in omnibus operibus tuis et in observationibus tuis

mec ic bieode god in halgum weg ðin hwelc god
me exercebor 14. *Deus in sancto via tua quis Deus*

micel swe swe god ur ðu earð god ðu ðe doest
magnus sicut Deus noster 15. *tu es Deus qui facis*

[1] i *on er.* [2] *cut away.* [3] acceearf, *second* c *dotted.*

wundur ana cuðe ðu dydes in folcum megen ðin
mirabilia solus Notam fecisti in populis virtutem tuam

gefreodes in earme ðinum folc ðin bearn
16. *liberasti in bracchio tuo populum tuum filios Israhel et*

gesegun ðec weter god gesegun ðec weter
Joseph 17. *Viderunt te aquae Deus viderunt te aquae*

7 ondreordun gedroefde werun niolnisse mengu swoeges
et timuerunt turbati sunt abyssi 18. *multitudo sonitus*

wetra stefne saldun wolcen 7 soðlice strelas ðine
aquarum Vocem dederunt nubes et enim sagittae tuae

ðorhleordun stefn ðunurrade ðinre in hweole inlihton
pertransierunt 19. *vox tonitrui tui in rota Inluxerunt*

bliccetunge ðine eorðan ymbhwyrfte gesaeh 7 onstyred wes
coruscationes tuae orbi terrae vidit et commota est

eorðe in sae wegas ðine 7 stige ðine in wetrum
terra 20. *In mari viae tuae et semitae tuae in aquis*

miclum 7 sweðe ðine ne bioð oncnawen ðu gelaeddes
multis et vestigia tua non cognoscentur 21. *Deduxisti*

swe swe scep folc ðin in honda *Mosi 7 Aaron
sicut oves populum tuum in manu Moysi et Aaron

77.

bihaldað folc min ae mine onhaeldað eare eower
Adtendite populus meus legem meam inclinate aurem vestram

in word muðes mines ic ontynu in bispellum muð
in verba oris mei 2. *Aperiam in parabolis os*

minne ic spreocu foresetenisse from fruman weorulde
meum loquar propositiones ab initio saeculi

hu fiolu we geherdun 7 oncneowun ða 7 fedras ure
3. *Quanta audivimus, et cognovimus ea et patres nostri*

segdun us ne sind gedeglad from bearnum
narraverunt nobis 4. *Non sunt occultata a filiis*

in cneorisse oðerre secgende lofu dryhtnes 7
eorum in generatione altera Narrantes laudes Domini et

megen his 7 wundur his ða he dyde 7 awehte
virtutes ejus et mirabilia ejus quae fecit 5. *Et suscitavit*

cyðnisse in Iacob 7 ace sette ða
testimonium in Jacob et legem posuit in Israhel Quam

onbead fedrum urum ðætte cuðe dyde ða bearnum
mandavit patribus nostris ut notam faceret ea filiis

heara ðæt oncnawe cneoris oderu bearn ða bioð
suis 6. *ut cognoscat generatio altera Filii qui nas-*
acende 7 arisað 7 secgað ða bearnum heara ðæt
centur et exurgent et narrabunt ea filiis suis 7. *Ut*
hie setten in gode hyht his 7 no ofergeoteliað werca
ponant in Deo spem suam et non obliviscantur operum
godes his 7 bibodu his soecað ne sien swe swe
Dei sui et mandata ejus exquirant 8. *Ne fiant sicut*
fedras heara cyn ðuerh 7 bitur cyn ðæt ne
patres eorum genus pravum et peramarum genus quod non
gerehte heortan his 7 nis bifested mid gode *gas
direxit cor suum et non est creditus cum Deo spiritus
his bearn *Ef bihaldende bogan 7 sendende strelas
ejus 9. *Filii Efrem intendentes arcum et mittentes sagittas*
his gecerde in dege gefehtes ne heoldon
suas conversi sunt in die belli 10. *Non custodierunt*
cyðnisse godes his 7 in aee his naldun gongan
testamentum Dei sui et in lege ejus noluerunt ambulare
7 ofergeotule sind weldeda his 7 wundra his
11. *Et obliti sunt benefactorum ejus et mirabilium ejus*
ða he oteawde him biforan feadrum heara dyde[1]
quae ostendit eis 12. *coram patribus eorum Fecit*
wundur in eorðan Ægypta in felda toslat
mirabilia in terra Aegypti in campo Thaneos 13. *Inter-*
sae 7 gelaed[d]e hie 7 sette weter swe swe in
rupit mare et perduxit eos et statuit aquas quasi in
cylle 7 utalędde hie in wolcne deges 7 alle naeht
utrem 14. *Et eduxit eos in nube diei et tota nocte*
in inlihtnisse fyres toslat in *wostenne stan
in inluminatione ignis 15. *Interrupit in heremo petram*
7 gewetrade hie swe swe in niolnisse micelre 7
et adaquavit eos velut in abysso multa 16. *Et*
utaledde weter of stane 7 utalędde swe swe flodas
eduxit aquam de petra et eduxit tamquam flumina
weter 7 tosetton ðaget syngian him in eorre
aquas 17. *Et adposuerunt adhuc peccare ei in ira*
awehtun ðone hean in drugunge 7
concitaverunt Deum excelsum in siccitatem 18. *Et temp-*

[1] dydede.

costadon god in heortum heara ðæt hie beden mettas
taverunt Deum in cordibus suis ut peterent escas

sawlum heara 7 yfle spreocende sind bi gode 7
animabus suis 19. *et male locuti sunt de Deo et*

cwedun ah meg god gearwian biod in woestenne
dixerunt Numquid poterit Deus parare mensam in deserto

forðon slog stan 7 fleowun weter 7 burnan
20. *Quoniam percussit petram et fluxerunt aquae et torrentes*

yðgadun ah 7 hlaf meg sellan oððe gearwian
inundaverunt Numquid et panem poterit dare aut parare

• biod folce his forðon geherde dryhten 7 aelde
mensam populo suo 21. *Ideo audivit Dominus et distulit*

7 ofersette 7 fyr onaeled is in Iacob 7 eorre astag
et superposuit et ignis accensus est in Jacob et ira ascendit

forðon ne gelefdun in god heara ne
in Israhel 22. *Quia non crediderunt in Deum suum nec*

gehyhton in haelu his 7 onbead wolcnum
speraverunt in salutare ejus 23. *Et mandavit nubibus*

ufan 7 dura heofenes ontynde 7 rineð him
desuper et januas caeli aperuit 24. *et pluit illis*

heofenlic hlaf eotan hlaf heofenes salde him hlaf
manna manducare panem caeli dedit eis 25. *panem*

engla ętt mon hwętewestem sende him in
angelorum manducavit homo frumentationem misit eis in

genyhtsumnisse 7 awaehte suðanwind of hiofene 7
**abundantiam* 26. *Et excitavit austrum de caelo et*

ingelaedde in megne his westansuðanwind 7 rinde
induxit in virtute sua Africum 27. *Et pluit*

ofer hie swe swe dust flæsc 7 swe swe sond sæs
super eos sicut pulverem carnes et sicut harena maris

ða flegendan gefiðrede 7 gefeollun in midle ferdwica
volatilia pinnata 28. *Et ceciderunt in medio castrorum*

heara ymb ða geteld heara 7 eton 7
eorum circa tabernacula eorum 29. *Et manducaverunt et*

werun gefylde swiðe 7 lust heara brohte him
saturati sunt nimis et desiderium eorum obtulit eis

7 ne sind biscerede from luste his nuget mete
30. *et non sunt fraudati a desiderio suo Adhuc esca*

heara wes in muðe heara 7 eorre godes astag
eorum erat in ore ipsorum 31. *et ira Dei ascendit*

ofer hie 7 ofslog monge heara 7 gecorene Israela folces
super eos et occidit plurimos eorum et electos Israhel

amerde in allum ðissum syngadon ðaget 7 ne
impedivit **32.** *In omnibus his peccaverunt adhuc et non*

gelefdon in wundrum his 7 asprungun in idel-
crediderunt in mirabilibus ejus **33.** *Et defecerunt in vani-*

nisse daegas heara 7 ger heara mid oefestunge ðonne
tate dies eorum et anni eorum cum festinantia **34.** *Cum*

he sleð hie ðonne soecað hine 7 bioð gecerred ær
occiderit eos tunc inquirebant eum et convertebantur ante

lehte 7 cwomun to him 7 gemyndgade werun forðon
lucem et veniebant ad eum **35.** *Et memorati sunt quia*

god fultum heara is 7 god se hea alesend heara is
Deus adjutor eorum est et Deus excelsus liberator eorum est

7 lufedun hine in muðe his 7 in tungan heara
36. *Et dilexerunt eum in ore suo et in lingua sua*

legende werun him heorte soðlice heara ne wes
mentiti sunt ei **37.** *Cor autem eorum non erat*

reht mid hine ne geleafa hefd wes him in cyðnisse
rectum cum eo nec fides habita est illis in testamento

his he soðlice is mildheort 7 milde bið synnum
ejus **38.** *Ipse autem est misericors et propitius fit peccatis*

heara 7 ne *tostrigeded hie 7 gemonigfaldade ðæt he
eorum et non disperdet eos Et multiplicavit ut aver-

acerde eorre his from him 7 ne onælde all eorre his
teret iram suam ab eis et non accendet omnem iram suam

7 gemyndig is forðon flæsc hie sind *gas fearende
39. *Et memoratus est quia caro sunt spiritus vadens*

7 no eftcerrende swe oft swe onscunedun[1] hine in
et non rediens **40.** *Quotiens exacervaverunt eum in*

woestenne in eorre awehton hine in eorðan butan wetre
deserto in ira concitaverunt eum in terra sine aqua

7 gecerde sindun 7 costadun god 7 *ðon halgan
41. *Et conversi sunt et temptaverunt Deum et Sanctum*

Israel onscunedon ne sind gemyndge honda his
Israhel exacervaverunt **42.** *Non sunt recordati manus ejus*

hwelce dege gefreað hie of honda swencendes swe
qua die liberavit eos de manu tribulantis **43.** *Sicut*

[1] *first* u *over* y.

sette in *Ægypto tacen his 7 becen[1] his in ðæm felda
posuit in Aegypto signa sua et prodigia sua in campo

gecerde in blode flodas heara 7 ða
Taneos **44.** *Convertit in sanguine flumina eorum et plu-*

regnlican weter heara ðæt hie ne druncen insende in
viales aquas eorum ne biberent **45.** *Inmisit in*

him flegan hundlice 7 et hie 7 forsc 7 he abreotte
eis muscam caninam et comedit eos et ranam et exterminavit

hie 7 salde treowyrme westmas heara 7 gewin
eos **46.** *Et dedit erugini fructus eorum et labores*

heara gershoppan ofslog in hegle *wingeardes heara
eorum lucustae **47.** *Occidit in grandine vineas eorum*

7 *marbeamas heara in forste salde hegle net
et moros eorum in pruina **48.** *Tradidit grandini ju-*

heara 7 aehte heara fyre insende in him
menta eorum et possessiones eorum igni **49.** *Inmisit in eis*

eorre ebylgðe his ebylðu[2] 7 eorre 7 geswencednisse
iram indignationis suae indignationem et iram et tribulationem

onsonde ðorh englas yfle weg dyde styge eorres
immissiones per angelos malos **50.** *Viam fecit semitae irae*

his 7 *n spearede from deaðe sawlum heara 7 neat
suae et non pepercit a morte animabus eorum et jumenta

heara in deaðe belec 7 slog ylc frum-
eorum in morte conclusit **51.** *Et percussit omnem primo-*

bearn on eorðan fruman alles gewinnes heara
genitum in terra Aegypti primitias omnis laboris eorum

in geteldum 7 afirde swe swe scep folc
in tabernaculis Cham **52.** *Et abstulit sicut oves populum*

his 7 *gelaede hie swe swe eowde in woestenne 7
suum et perduxit eos tamquam gregem in deserto **53.** *Et*

utalaedde hie in hyhte 7 ne ondreordun 7 fiond heara
eduxit eos in spe et non timuerunt et inimicos eorum

oferwrah sae 7 ingelaedde hie in munt gehalgunge
operuit mare **54.** *Et induxit eos in montem sanctificationis*

his munt ðeosne ðone beget sie swiðre his 7 awearp
suae montem hunc quem adquisivit dextera ejus Et ejecit

from onsiene heara ðeode 7 hlete todaelde him eorðan
a facie eorum gentes et sorte divisit eis terram

[1] becen *er. before* becen. [2] ð *from* y.

in rape todales 7 eardade[1] in geteldum
in funiculo distributionis **55.** *Et habitavit in tabernaculis*

heara cyn 7 costadon 7 onscunedun
eorum tribus Israhel **56.** *et temptaverunt et exacervaverunt*

god ðone hean 7 cyðnisse his ne heoldun 7
Deum excelsum et testimonia ejus non custodierunt **57.** *Et*

onweg acerdon hie 7 ne heoldun to ðæm gemete fedras
averterunt se et non observaverunt quemadmodum patres

heara gecerde sind in bogan ðone ðweoran in eorre
eorum conversi sunt in arcum perversum **58.** *In ira*

awehton hine in hyllum his 7 in greftum his
concitaverunt eum in collibus suis et in sculptilibus suis

werun elniende hine geherde dryhten 7 forhogde 7
aemulati sunt eum **59.** *Audivit Dominus et sprevit et*

to nowihte gebegeð swiðe 7 onweg asceaf
ad nihilum redegit nimis Israhel **60.** *Et reppulit taber-*

geteld geteld his in ðæm eardade betwih
naculum Selom tabernaculum suum in quo habitavit inter

men salde in heftned megen heara 7
homines **61.** *Tradidit in captivitatem virtutes eorum et*

fegernisse heara in honda feondes 7 bilec in
pulchritudines eorum in manus inimici **62.** *Et conclusit in*

sweorde folc his 7 erfewordnisse his forhogde
gladio populum suum et haereditatem suum spraevit **63.** *Ju-*

gunge heara et fyr 7 faemnan heara ne sind
venes eorum comedit ignis et virgines eorum non sunt

cwiðde sacerdas heara in sweorde gefeollun 7
lamentatae **64.** *Sacerdotes eorum in gladio ceciderunt et*

widwan heara ne · weopun 7 awaeht is swe
viduae eorum non ploraverunt **65.** *Et excitatus est tam-*

swe slepende dryhten swe swe mæhtig geillerocad from
quam dormiens Dominus quasi potens crapulatus a

wine 7 slog feond his in ða efterran edwit
vino **66.** *Et percussit inimicos suos in posteriora oppro-*

ece salde him 7 onweg asceaf geteld
brium sempiternum dedit illis **67.** *Et reppulit taberna-*

7 cynn ne geceas ah geceas
culum Joseph et tribum Efrem non elegit **68.** *sed elegit*

[1] *first* d *from* ð.

cynn munt ðone lufude 7 timbrade
tribum Juda montem Sion quem dilexit 69. *Et aedificavit*

swe swe anhyrnra gehalgunge his in eorðan gestea-
sicut unicornuorum sanctificationem suam in terra fun-

ðelade hie in weorulde 7 geceas ðeow
davit eam in saecula 70. *Et elegit David servum*

his 7 ahof hine of eowdum scepa of ðæm siðborenum
suum et sustulit eum de gregibus ovium de postfaetantes[1]

onfeng hine foedan folc his 7 Israel
accepit eum 71. *Pascere Jacob populum suum et Israhel*

erfewordnisse his 7 foedde hie butan hete heortan
hereditatem suam 72. *Et pavit eos sine malitia cordis*

his 7 in ondgete honda his gelaedde hie
sui et in sensu manuum suarum deduxit eos

78.

god cwomun ðeode in erfewordnisse ðine bismeotun
Deus venerunt gentes in hereditatem tuam coinquinaverunt

tempel halig ðin settun swe swe eappultun
templum sanctum tuum Posuerunt Hierusalem velut pomorum

gehaeld settun ða deadlican ðiowa ðinra mettas
custodiam 2. *posuerunt mortalia servorum tuorum escas*

fuglum heofenes 7 flæsc haligra ðinra wildeorum eorðan
volatilibus caeli et carnes sanctorum tuorum bestiis terrae

aguton blod heara swe swe weter in ymbhwyrfte
3. *Effuderunt sanguinem eorum sicut aqua in circuitu*

7 ne wes se ðe bibyrgde gewordne we sind
Hierusalem et non erat qui sepeliret 4. *Facti sumus*

edwit nehgehusum urum on bismerunge 7 forhogdnisse
opprobrium vicinis nostris derisu et contemptu

ðissum ða in ymbhwyrfte urum sind hu longe
his qui in circuitu nostro su(nt)[2] 5. *Usque quo*

dryhten eorsas ðu in ende bið onaeled swe swe fyr
Domine irasceris in finem accenditur velut ignis

hatheortnis ðin ageot eorre ðin in ðeode ða ðec
zelus tuus 6. *Effunde iram tuam in gentes quae te*

[1] *last* e *on er.* [2] *cut off.*

ne oncneowun 7 in ricu ða ne gecedon noman
non noverunt et in regna quae non invocaverunt nomen

ðinne forðon etun 7 stowe his awoestun
tuum 7. *Quia comederunt Jacob et locum ejus desolaverunt*

ne gemyne ðu unrehtwisnisse ure ða aldan hreðe usic
8. *Ne memineris iniquitates nostras antiquas cito nos*

forefoe mildheortnis ðin forðon ðearfan gewordne we sind
anticipet misericordia tua quia pauperes facti sumus

swiðe gefultuma us god halwynde ur fore are
nimis 9. *Adjuva nos Deus salutaris noster propter honorem*

noman ðines dryht*en* gefrea usic 7 milde bio ðu synnum
nominis tui Domine libera nos et propitius esto peccatis

urum fore noman ðinum ne hwonne cweðen ðeode
nostris propter nomen tuum 10. *Ne quando dicant gentes*

hwer is god heara 7 cuðie in cneorissum biforan
Ubi est Deus eorum et innotescat in nationibus coram

egu*m* urum wrec blod ðiowa ðinra ðæt agoten
oculis nostris Vindica sanguinem servorum tuorum qui effusus

is ingæð in gesihðe ðine geamrung gecyspedra
est 11. *intret in conspectu tuo gemitus compeditorum*

efter micelnisse earmes ðines gesite bearn mid
Secundum magnitudinem bracchii tui posside filios morte

deaðe *gewicnedra agef nehgehusum uru*m* seofenfaldlice
punitorum. 12. *Redde vicinis nostris septuplum*

in sceat heara edwit heara ðæt edwitun
in sinus eorum inproperium ipsorum quod exprobraverunt

ðe we soðlice folc ðin 7 scep eowdes ðines
tibi 13. *Nos autem populus tuus et oves gregis tui*

we ondettað ðe in weorulde 7 in weoruld weorulde we
confitebimur tibi in saecula et in saeculum saeculi nar-

secgad lof ðin
rabimus laudem tuam

79.

ðu reces bihald ðu de gelaedes swe swe scep
2. *Qui regis Israhel intende qui deducis velut ovem*

ðu sites ofer Cerubin oteaw biforan Efrem 7
Joseph Qui sedis super Cherubin appare 3. *coram Efrem et*

Beniamen 7 Manasse awece maeht ðine 7 cym ðæt
Benjamin et Manasse Excita potentiam tuam et veni ut

hale ðu doe usic. dryhten god megna. gecer usic 7
salvos facias nos 4. *Domine Deus virtutum converte nos et*

oteaw onsiene ðine 7 hale we bioð dryhten god
ostende faciem tuam et salvi erimus 5. *Domine Deus*

megna hu longe eorsas ðu in gebed ðeowes dines
virtutum quousque irasceris in orationem servi tui

ðu foedes us hlafe teara 7 drync seles us in
6. *cibabis nos pane lacrimarum et potum dabis nobis in*

tearum in gemete ðu settes usic in wiðcwedenisse
lacrimis in mensura 7. *Posuisti nos in contradictionem*

nehgehusum urum 7 feond ure bismeredun *sic dryhten
vicinis nostris et inimici nostri deriserunt nos 8. *Domine*

god megna gecer usic 7 oteaw onsiene ðine 7 hale
Deus virtutum converte nos et ostende faciem tuam et salvi

we biað wingeard of *Agyptum ðu afirdes awurpe
erimus 9. *Vineam ex Aegypto transtulisti ejecisti*

ðeode 7 plantades hie weg ðu dydes in gesihde
gentes et plantasti eam 10. *Viam fecisti in conspectu*

his 7 plantedes wyrtwalan his 7 gefylled is eorðe
ejus et plantasti radices ejus et repleta est terra

oferwrah muntas scua his 7 trew his cederbeamas
11. *Operuit montes umbra ejus et arbusta ejus cedros*

godes ðu aðenedes twigu his oð sae 7
Dei 12. *Extendisti palmites ejus usque ad mare et*

oð flod setene his to hwon asetes ðu
usque ad flumen propagines ejus 13. *Utquid deposuisti*

stanwal his 7 winreopad ðæt alle ða leorad weg
maceriam ejus et vendemiant eam omnes qui transeunt viam

*abreoette hie eofur of wuda 7 *syndring wildeor
14. *Exterminavit eam aper de silva et singularis ferus*

ahiðende wes hie dryhten god megna gecer
depastus est eam 15. *Domine Deus virtutum convertere*

nu geloca of heofene 7 geseh 7 neosa wingeard ðeosne
nunc respice de caelo et vide et visita vineam istam

7 gerece ðone ðone plantade sie swiðre ðin 7 ofer
16. *et dirige eam quam plantavit dextera tua et super*

sunu monnes ðone ðu getrymedes ðe inaeled mid fyre
filium hominis quem confirmasti tibi 17. *Incensa igni*

7 agoten mid hond from dreange ondwliotan ðines for-
et effossa manu ab increpatione vultus tui peri-

weorðað sie hond ðin ofer wer ðere *swið ðinre
bunt 18. *Fiat manus tua super virum dexterae tuae*

7 ofer sunu monnes ðone ðu getrymedes ðe 7
et super filium hominis quem confirmasti tibi 19. *et*

we ne gewitað from ðe ðu geliffestes usic 7 *noma ðinne
non discedimus a te Vivificabis nos et nomen tuum

we gecegað dryhten god megna gecer usic 7 oteaw
invocabimus 20. *Domine Deus virtutum converte nos et ostende*

onsiene ðine 7 hale we bioð
faciem tuam et salvi erimus

80.

wynsumiað gode fultume urum wynsumiað gode Iacobes
2. *Exultate Deo adjutori nostro jubilate Deo Jacob*

niomað salm 7 sellað timpanan hearpan wynsume
3. *Sumite psalmum et date tympanum psalterium jucundum*

mid citran singað in fruman monðes horne in dege
cum cythara 4. *Canite in initio mensis tuba in die*

merum symbelnisse eowerre forðon bibod
insigni sollemnitatis vestrae 5. *Quia praeceptum in Israhel*

is 7 dom gode cyðnis
est et judicium Deo Jacob 6. *Testimonium in Joseph*

sette hine ðonne uteode of eorðan tungan
posuit eum dum exiret de terra Aegypti Linguam

ða ne wiste geherde acerde from byrðennum bec
quam non noverat audivit 7. *divertit ab oneribus dorsum*

his honda his in binne ðeowdun in geswince ðu
ejus manus ejus in cofino servierunt 8. *In tribulatione in-*

gecedes mec 7 ic gefreode ðec ic geherde dec in degelnisse
vocasti me et liberavi te exaudivi te in abscondito

stormes ic acunnade dec to wetre wiðcwedenisse
tempestatis probavi te ad aquas contradictionis

geher folc min 7 ic spreocu 7 cyðu ðe
9. *Audi populus meus et loquar Israhel et testificabor tibi*

gif mec ðu geheres ne bið in ðe god
Israhel si me audieris 10. *non erit in te deus*

niowe ne ðu weorðas god fremðne ic soðlice eam
recens neque adorabis deum alienum 11. *Ego enim sum*

dryhten god ðin se utaledde of eorðan abraed
Dominus Deus tuus qui eduxi te de terra Aegypti Dilata

muð ðinne 7 ic gefyllu ðone 7 ne geherde
os tuum et ego adimplebo illud 12. *et non audivit*

folc min stefne mine 7 ne bihaldeð me 7
populus meus vocem meam et Israhel non intendit mihi 13. *Et*

ne forleort hie efter lustum heortan heara 7 gað in
dimisi eos secundum desideria cordis eorum et ibunt in

lustum heara gif folc min geherde mec
voluntatibus suis 14. *Si plebs mea audisset me Israhel*

gif wegas mine eode to nowihte fiond heara
si vias meas ambulasset 15. *Ad nihilum inimicos eorum*

ic geeaðmodade 7 ofer ða swencendan hie ic sende hond
humiliassem et super tribulantes eos misissem manum

mine feond dryhtnes legende werun him 7 bið
meam 16. *Inimici Domini mentiti sunt ei et erit*

tid heara in ecnisse foedeð hie of smeorwe
tempus eorum in aeternum 17. *Cibabit eos ex adipe*

hwætes 7 of stane mid hunge gereordeð hie
frumenti et de petra melle satiavit eos

81.

god stod in gesomnunge goda in midle soðlice god
Deus stetit in synagoga deorum in medio autem Deus

toscadeð hu longe doemað ge unrehtwisnisse 7 onsiene
discernit 2. *Quousque judicatis iniquitatem et facies*

syngiendra geniomað doemað feadurleasne 7 weðlan
peccantium sumitis 3. *Judicate pupillum et egenum*

heanne 7 ðearfan gerehtwisiað genergað ðearfan 7
humilem et pauperem justificate 4. *Eripite pauperem et*

weðlan of honda synfulra gefrigað nystun ne
egenum de manu peccatorum liberate 5. *Nescierunt neque*

ongetun in *ðeostru gongað bioð onstyred alle stea-
intellexerunt in tenebris ambulant movebuntur omnia fun-

ðelas eorðan ic cweð godas ge earun 7 bearn ðes hean
damenta terrae 6. *Ego dixi Dii estis et filii Excelsi*

alle ge soðlice swe men sweltað 7 swe swe
omnes 7. *Vos autem sicut homines moriemini et sicut*

an of aldermonnum fallað aris god doem eorðan
unus de principibus cadetis 8. *Exurge Deus judica terram*
forðon ðu erfewordas in allum ðeodum
quoniam tu hereditabis in omnibus gentibus

82.

god hwelc gelic bið ðe ne swiga ðu ne biwere
2. *Deus quis similis erit tibi ne taceas neque conpescaris*
god forðon sehðe feond ðine hleoðradun 7 ða ðe
Deus 3. *Quoniam ecce inimici tui sonaverunt et qui*
ðec fiodun ahofun up heofud in folc ðin *gebreg-
te oderunt extulerunt caput 4. *In plebem tuam astute*
denlice ðohtun geþæht 7 ðohtun wið halgum
cogitaverunt consilium et cogitaverunt adversus sanctos
ðinum cwedon cumað tostrigden we hie of ðiode
tuos 5. *Dixerunt Venite disperdamus eos ex gente*
7 ne [bið] gemyndgað noma mae forðon
et non memorabitur nomen Israhel amplius 6. *Quoniam*
ðohtun geðeafunge in annesse wið ðe cyðnisse
cogitaverunt consensum in unum adversum te testamentum
gestihtadun geteld Idumea 7 Ismaela
disposuerunt 7. *Tabernacula Idumaeorum et Ismahelitum*
Moab 7 Aggareni Gebal 7 7 7 fremðes
Moab et Aggareni 8. *Gebal et Ammon et Amalech et alieni-*
cynnes mid ðæm eardiendum 7 soðlice somud
genae cum habitantibus Tyrum 9. *Et enim Assur simul*
cwom mid him gewordne sind in ondfengnisse bearnum
venit cum illis facti sunt in susceptione filiis Loth
doa him swe swe Madian 7 Sisarra swe swe Iabin in
10. *Fac illis sicut Madian et Sisarae sicut Jabin in*
burnan forwurdun gewordne werun
torrente Cison 11. *disperierunt in Endor facti sunt*
swe swe scearn eorðan sete aldermen heara swe
sicut stercus terrae 12. *Pone principes eorum sicut*
Oreb Zeb 7 Zebę 7 Salmana alle aldermen heora
Oreb Zeb et Zebeae et Salmana omnes principes eorum
ða cwedun on erfewordnisse gesitten we us halig
13. *qui dixerunt Hereditate possideamus nobis sanctu-*

portic godes god min sete hie swe swe hwiol 7
arium Dei 14. *Deus meus pone illos ut rotam et*

swe swe halm biforan onsiene windes 7 swe swe fyr
sicut stipulam ante faciem venti et 15. *sicut ignis*

ðæt forberneð wuda swe swe leg forberneð muntas
qui comburet silvas velut flamma incendat montes

swe ðu oehtes hie in storme ðinum 7 in eorre ðinum
16. *Ita persequeris eos in tempestate tua et in ira tua*

gedroefes hie gefyl onsiene heara mid orwyrðe 7
conturbabis eos 17. *Imple facies eorum ignominia et*

soecad noman ðinne dryht*en* sien gescende 7 ge-
quaerant nomen tuum Domine 18. *Confundantur et con-*

droefde in weoruld weorulde 7 onscunien 7 forweorðen
turbentur in saeculum saeculi et revereantur et pereant

7 oncnawen ðætte noma ðe dryhten ðu ana se hesta
19. *et cognoscant quia nomen tibi Dominus Tu solus altissi-*

ofer ˎ alle eorðan
mus super omnem terram

83.

swiðe lufiendlice sind geteld ðin *dryht megna
2. *Quam amabilia sunt tabernacula tua Domine virtutum*

gewillade 7 asprong sawul min in ceafurtune dryht*nes*
3. *Concupivit et defecit anima mea in atria Domini*

heorte min 7 fiesc min uphofun in god ðone lifgendan
Cor meum et caro mea exultaverunt in Deum vivum

7 soðlice speara gemoeted him hus 7 turtur nest
4. *Et enim passer invenit sibi domum et turtur nidum*

hwer gesetteð briddas his wibed ðin dryht*en* megna
ubi reponat pullos suos Altaria tua Domine virtutum

cyning min 7 god min eadge ða ðe eardiað in
rex meus et Deus meus 5. *Beati qui habitant in*

huse dinu*m* dryhten in weoruld weorulde hergad dec
domo tua Domine in saeculum saeculi laudabunt te

eadig wer ðes is fultum from ðe dryhten upstige
6. *Beatus vir cujus est auxilium abs te Domine ascensus*

in heortan his gestihtade in dene teara in stowe
in corde ejus disposuit 7. *in convalle lacrimarum in locum*

ða ðu gestihtades him 7 soðlice bledsunge seleð
quem disposuisti eis 8. *Et enim benedictionem dabit*

se ae salde gongað of megne in megen bið
qui legem dedit ambulabunt de virtute in virtutem vide-

gesegen god goda in Sion dryhten god megna
bitur Deus deorum in Sion 9. *Domine Deus virtutum*

geher boene mine mid earum onfoh god Iacobes ge-
exaudi precem meam auribus percipe Deus Jacob 10. *Pro-*

scildend ur geloca god 7 geloca in onsiene Cristes
tector noster aspice Deus et respice in faciem Christi

ðines forðon betre is deg an in *ceafultunum
tui 11. *Quia melior est dies una in *atris tuis*

ofer ðusend ic geceas aworpen bion in huse godes mae
super milia Elegi abjectus esse in domo Dei magis

*ðone eardian in geteldum synfulra forðon
quam habitare in tabernaculis peccatorum 12. *Quoniam*

mildheortnisse 7 soðfestnisse lufað dryhten gefe 7
misericordiam et veritatem diligit Dominus gratiam et

wuldur seleð god dryhten ne bis[c]ered godum
gloriam dabit Deus 13. *Dominus non privabit bonis*

gongende in unsceðfulnisse dryhten god megna eadig
ambulantes in innocentia Domine Deus virtutum beatus

mon se gehyhteð in ðec
homo qui sperat in te

84.

ðu bledsades dryhten eorðan ðine ðu acerdes heftned
2. *Benedixisti Domine terram tuam avertisti captivitatem*

Iacob ðu geedleanades unrehtwisnisse folces ðines[1] ofer-
Jacob 3. *Remisisti iniquitatem plebis tuae ope-*

wrige alle synne heara gestildes all eorre ðin
ruisti omnia peccata eorum 4. *Mitigasti omnem iram tuam*

acerdes from eorre ebylgðe ðinre gecer usic god
avertisti ab ira indignationis tuae 5. *Converte nos Deus*

halwynde ur 7 acer eorre ðin from us ðæt no
salutaris noster et averte iram tuam a nobis 6. *ut non*

in ecnisse eorsie us ne aðene ðu eorre ðin from
in aeternum irasceris nobis Neque extendas iram tuam a

[1] ð *from* t.

cynne in cynn god ðu forcerrende geliffestas usic
progenie in progeniem 7. *Deus tu convertens vivificabis nos*

⁊ folc ðin bið geblissad in ðec oteaw us dryhten
et plebs tua laetabitur in te 8. *Ostende nobis Domine*

mildheortnisse ðine ⁊ hælu ðine sele us ic gehere
misericordiam tuam et salutare tuum da nobis 9. *Audiam*

hwet sprece in me dryhten god forðon spriceð sibbe
quid loquatur in me Dominus Deus quoniam loquitur pacem

in folc . his ⁊ ofer halge his ⁊ in hie ða bioð
in plebem suam et super sanctos suos et in eos qui con-

gecerde to him ah hweðre neh *ondredendu
vertuntur ad ipsum 10. *Verumtamen prope timentibus*

hine haelu his ðæt ineardie wuldur in eorðan ure
eum salutare ipsius ut inhabitet gloria in terra nostra

mildheortnis ⁊ soðfestnis tosomne bicomun him rehtwisnis
11. *Misericordia et veritas obviaverunt sibi justitia*

⁊ sib clyppende werun hie soðfestnis of eorðan
et pax conplexae sunt se 12. *Veritas de terra*

upcumen wes ⁊ rehtwisnis of heofene forðlocade ⁊
orta est et justitia de caelo prospexit 13. *Et*

soðlice dryhten seleð freamsumnisse ⁊ eorðe ur seleð
enim Dominus dabit benignitatem et terra nostra dabit

westem his rehtwisnis biforan him gongeð ⁊
fructum suum 14. *Justitia ante eum ambulabit et*

seteð in wege gongas his
ponet in via gressus suos

85.

†·.onhaeld dryhten eare ðine to me ⁊ geher mec
1. *Inclina. Domine aurem tuam ad me et exaudi me*

forðon weðla ⁊ ðearfa ic eam hald sawle
quoniam egenus et pauper sum ego 2. *Custodi animam*

mine forðon halig ic eam halne doa ðiow ðinne god
meam quoniam sanctus sum salvum fac servum tuum Deus

min gehyhtendne in ðec mildsa me dryhten forðon
meus sperantem in te 3. *Miserere mihi Domine quoniam*

to ðe ic cleopade alne deg geblissa sawle ðeowes
ad te clamavi tota die 4. *laetifica• animam servi*

ðines forðon to ðe dryht*en* ic hof sawle mine
tui quia ad te Domine levavi animam meam

forðon ðu dryhten wynsum 7 milde earð 7 *geutsum
5. *Quoniam tu Domine suavis ac mitis es et copiosus*

in mildheortnisse allu*m* gecegendum ðec mid earum
in misericordia omnibus invocantibus te 6. *Auribus*

onfoh dryht*en* gebed min 7 behald stefne boene
percipe Domine orationem meam et intende voci deprecationis

minre in dege geswinces mines ic cleopede to ðe
meae 7. *In die tribulationis meae clamavi ad te*

forðon ðu geherdes me nis gelic ðe in godu*m*
quoniam exaudisti me 8. *Non est similis tibi in diis*

dryht*en* 7 nis efter werce ðinum alle ðeode
Domine et non est secundum opera tua 9. *Omnes gentes*

swe hwelce[1] ðu dydes cumað 7 weorðiað biforan ðe
quascumque fecisti venient et adorabunt coram te

dryht*en* 7 ariað noman ðinne forðon micel
Domine et honorificabunt nomen tuum 10. *Quoniam magnus*

ðu earð 7 donde wundur ðu earð god ana gelaed
es tu et faciens mirabilia tu es Deus solus 11. *Deduc*

mec dryht*en* in wege ðinu*m* 7 ic gongu in soðfestnisse
me Domine in via tua et ambulabo in veritate

ðinre blissie heorte min ðæt hie ondrede noman ðinne
tua Laetetur cor meum ut timeat nomen tuum

ic ondettu ðe dryht*en* god min in allre heortan
12. *confitebor tibi Domine Deus meus in toto corde*

minre 7 ariu noman ðinne in ecnisse forðon
meo et honorificabo nomen tuum in aeternum 13. *Quoniam*

mildheortnis ðin micelu is ofer mec 7 [ðu] generedes
misericordia tua magna est super me et eripuisti

sawle mine of helle ðere nioðerran god ða unreht-
animam meam ex inferno inferiori 14. *Deus injusti*

wisan areosun in mec 7 gesomnung mehtigra sohtun
insurrexerunt in me et synagoga potentium quaesi-

sawle mine 7 *non foresettun ðec biforan
erunt animam meam et non proposuerunt te ante

gesihðe his 7 ðu dryht*en* god min mildsend
conspectum suum 15. *Et tu Domine Deus meus miserator*

[1] ðu dydes (?) *er. after* hwelce.

7 mildheort geðyldig 7 swiðe mildheort 7 soðfest
et misericors patiens et multum misericors et verax

geloca in mec 7 mildsa min 7 sele maehte cnehte
16. *Respice in me et miserere mei et da potestatem puero*

ðinum 7 halne doa sunu menenes ðines doa mid
tuo et salvum fac filium ancillae tuae 17. *Fac me-*

mec dryhten tacen in gode ðæt hie gesen ða mec fiodun
cum Domine signum in bono ut videant qui me oderunt

7 sien gescended forðon ðu dryhten gefultumades mec 7
et confundantur Quoniam tu Domine adjuvasti me et

froefrende were mec
consolatus es me

86.

steaðelas his in muntum halgum lufað dryhten
Fundamenta ejus in montibus sanctis 2. *diligit Dominus*

geatu Sion ofer all geteld Iacobes wuldurfeste
portas Sion super omnia tabernacula Jacob 3. *Gloriosa*

cweden sind bi ðe cester godes gemyndig ic biom
dicta sunt de te civitas Dei 4. *Memor ero*

Rab 7 Babylon weotendum mec sehðe fremðes 7
Raab et Babylonis scientibus me Ecce alienigenae et

Tyrus 7 folc Sigelhearwena ðas werun in dere modur
Tyrus et populus Aethiopum hii fuerunt in ea 5. *Mater*

cwið mon 7 mon geworden wes in hire 7 he
Sion dicet Homo et homo factus est in ea et ipse

gesteaðelade hie se hesta dryhten segeð in gewreotum
fundavit eam Altissimus 6. *Dominus narravit in scripturis*

folca his 7 aldermonna heara ða werun in hire
populorum suorum et principum eorum qui fuerant in ea

swe blissiendra alra ur eardung is in ðe
7. *Sicut laetantium omnium nostrum habitatio est in te*

87.

*dryht god *halu minre in dege ic cleopede 7 on næht
2. *Domine Deus salutis meae in die clamavi et nocte*

biforan ðe ingeð gebed min in gesihðe ðinre onhęld
coram te 3. *Intret oratio mea in conspectu tuo inclina*

care ðin to boene minre dryht*en* forðon gefylled
aurem tuam ad precem meam Domine **4.** *Quia repleta*

is yflu*m* sawul min 7 lif min in helle toneolaeceð
est malis anima mea et vita mea in inferno adpropiabit

getald ic eam mid ðæm dunestigendum in seað ge-
5. *Aestimatus sum cum discendentibus in lacum*

worden ic eam swe swe mon butan fultume[1] betwih
factus sum sicut homo sine adjutorio **6.** *inter*

deade frea swe swe gewundade slepende aworpne in
mortuos liber Sicut vulnerati dormientes projecti in

byrgennum ðeara ðu ne gemundes mae 7 cuðlice hie
monumentis quorum non meministi amplius et quidem ipsi

of honda ðinre adrifene siud settun mec in seaðe
de manu tua expulsi sunt **7.** *Posuerunt me in lacu*

ðæm nioðerran in ðeostrum[2] 7 in scuan deaðes in
inferiori in tenebris et in umbra mortis **8.** *In*

mec getrymed is eorre ðin 7 alle upahefenisse ðine
me confirmata est ira tua et omnes elationes tuas

ofer mec ingelaeddes feor dydes cuðe mine fro*m*
super me induxisti **9.** *Longe fecisti notos meos a*

me settun mec in onscununge him sald eam 7
me posuerunt me in abominationem sibi traditus sum et

ut ne eode egan mine geuntrumade sind fore
non egrediebar **10.** *Oculi mei infirmati sunt prae*

weðelnisse ic cleopade to ðe dryhten[3] alne deg ic aðenede
inopia clamavi ad te Domine tota die expandi

honda mine to ðe ah deadum doest wundur
manus meas ad te **11.** *Numquid mortuis facies mirabilia*

oððe lecas *awecað 7 ondettað ðe ah
aut medici resuscitabunt et confitebuntur tibi **12.** *Num*

segeð ænig in byrgenne mildheortnisse ðine 7
quid narrabit aliquis in sepulchro misericordiam tuam et

soðfestnisse ðine in forlorenisse ah bioð oncnawne
veritatem tuam in perditione **13.** *Numquid cognoscentur*

in ðeostrum wundur ðin 7 rehtwisnis ðin in eorðan
in tenebris mirabilia tua et justitia tua in terra

ofergeotulnisse 7 ic to ðe dryht*en* ic cleopade 7
oblivionis **14.** *Et ego ad te Domine clamavi et*

[1] fultumie (?). [2] o *may be* a. [3] d *from* ð.

on marne gebed min forecymeð ðec to hwon dryhten
mane oratio mea praeveniet te 15. *Utquid Domine*

onweg adrifes ðu gebed min acerres ðu onsiene ðine from
repellis orationem meam avertis faciem tuam a

me weðla ic eam 7 in gewinnum from *guðe
me 16. *Egens sum ego et in laboribus a juventute*

minre upahefen soðlice geeaðmodad ic eam 7 gescended
mea exaltatus autem humiliatus sum et confusus

in mec ðorhleordun eorru ðin 7 brogan ðine ge-
17. *In me pertransierunt irae tuae et terrores tui con-*

droefdun mec ymbeodun mec swe swe weter alne
turbaverunt me 18. *Circuierunt me sicut aqua tota*

deg ymbsaldun mec somud ðu afeorrades from me
die circumdederunt me simul 19. *Elongasti a me*

freond 7 ðone nestan 7 cuðe mine from ermðe
amicum et proximum et notos meos a miseria

88.

mildheortnisse ðine *ðine in ecnisse ic singu in
2. *Misericordias tuas Domine in aeternum cantabo in*

*cnerisse 7 cynne ic forðsecgo soðfestnisse ðine in muðe
generatione et progenie pronuntiabo veritatem tuam in ore

minum forðon ðu cwede in ecnisse mildheortnis bið
meo 3. *Quoniam dixisti In aeternum misericordia ae-*

timbred in heofenum bið gearwad soðfes[t]nis ðin ic ge-
dificabitur in caelis praeparabitur veritas tua 4. *Dis-*

stihtade cyðnisse gecorenum minum ic swor Dauiðe ðeowe
posui testamentum electis meis juravi David servo

minum oð in ecnisse ic gearwigu[1] sed ðin 7
meo 5. *Usque in aeternum praeparabo semen tuum et*

ic timbriu in weoruld weorulde seld ðin ondettigað
aedificabo in saeculum saeculi sedem tuam 6. *Confite-*

heofenas wundur ðin dryhten 7 soðfestnisse ðine
buntur caeli mirabilia tua Domine et veritatem tuam

in cirican haligra forðon hwelc in wolcnum bið ge-
in ecclesia sanctorum 7. *Quoniam quis in nubibus aequa-*

[1] gearwi:gu.

efenlicad dryht*ne* oððe hwelc gelic bið gode betwih bearn
bitur Domino aut quis similis erit Deo inter filios

godes god se wuldrað in geðæhte haligra micel
Dei 8. *Deus qui glorificatur in consilio sanctorum magnus*

7 to ondredenne ofer alle ða in ymbhwyrfte his sind
et metuendus super omnes qui in circuitu ejus sunt

dryht*en* god megna hwelc gelic ðe[1] mæhtig earð
9. *Domine Deus virtutum quis similis tibi potens es*

dryht*en* 7 soðfestnis ðin in ymbhwyrfte ðinum ðu
Domine et veritas tua in circuitu tuo 10. *Tu*

waldes maehte sæs onstyrenisse soðlice yða his ðu
dominaris potestati maris motum autem fluctuum ejus tu

gemildgas ðu geeaðmodades swe swe ðone gewundedan
mitigas 11. *Tu humiliasti sicut vulneratum*

ðone oferhygdgan 7 in megne earmes ðines ðu tostenctes
superbum et in virtute bracchii tui dispersisti

fiond ðine ðine sind heofenas 7 ðin is eorðe
inimicos tuos 12. *Tui sunt caeli et tua est terra*

ymbhwyrft eorðena 7 fylnisse his ðu gesteaðelades
orbem terrarum et plenitudinem ejus tu fundasti

norðdæl 7 sæ ðu gescope 7 in
13. *Aquilonem et mare tu creasti Thabor et Hermon in*

noman ðinum gefeað ðinne earm mid maehte
nomine tuo exultabunt 14. *tuum bracchium cum potentia*

sie getrymed hond ðin 7 sie upahefen sie swiðre ðin
Firmetur manus tua et exaltetur dextera tua

rehtwisnis 7 dom gegearwung seldes ðines mild-
15. *justitia et judicium praeparatio sedis tuae Miseri-*

heortnis 7 soðfestnis foregað biforan onsiene ðinre eadig
cordia et veritas praeibunt ante faciem tuam 16. *beatus*

folc ðæt *wæt wynsumnisse dryht*en* in lehte ondwleotan
populus qui scit jubilationem Domine in lumine vultus

dines gongað 7 in noman ðinum gefiað alne
tui ambulabunt 17. *et in nomine tuo exultabunt tota*

deg 7 in ðinre rehtwisnisse bioð upahefen forðon
die et in tua justitia exaltabuntur 18. *Quoniam*

wuldur megnes heara ðu earð 7 in welgelicadum ðinum
gloria virtutis eorum tu es et in beneplacito tuo

[1] ð *from* t.

bið upahefen horn ur forðon dryht*nes* is ge-
exaltabitur cornu nostrum 19. *Quoniam Domini est ad-*

trugung 7 ðes halgan cyninges ures ða
sumptio et Sancti Israhel regis nostri 20. *Tunc*

spreocende ðu were in gesihde *bernu*m* ðinum 7 cwede
locutus es in aspectu filiis tuis et dixisti

ic sette fultum ofer ðone mæhtgan 7 upahof ðone ge-
Posui adjutorium super potentem et exaltavi electum

corenan of folce minum ic gemoette ðiow minne
de plebe mea 21. *Inveni David servum meum*

in ele halgu*m* minu*m* ic smirede hine hond[1] soðlice
in oleo sancto meo unxi eum 22. *Manus enim*

min fultumeð him 7 earm min gestrongað hine
mea auxiliabitur ei et bracchium meum confortabit eum

nowiht fromað se fiond in him 7 sunu unrehtwisnisse
23. *Nihil proficiet inimicus in eo et filius iniquitatis*

ne sceðeð him 7 ic forceorfu fiond his from onsiene
non nocebit ei 24. *Et concidam inimicos ejus a facie*

his 7 figende hine in fleam ic gecerru 7 soðfestnis
ipsius et odientes eum in fugam convertam 25. *Et veritas*

min 7 mildheortnis min mid[2] hine 7 in noman minum
mea et misericordia mea cum ipso et in nomine meo

bið upahefen horn his 7 ic settu in sae hond
exaltabitur cornu ejus 26. *Et ponam in mari manum*

his 7 in flodu*m* ða swiðran his he geceð
ejus et in fluminibus dexteram ejus 27. *Ipse invocabit*

mec feder min ðu earð god min 7 ondfenga hælu
me Pater meus es tu Deus meus et susceptor salutis

minre 7 ic frumcennedne settu hine heane fore
meae 28. *Et ego primogenitum ponam illum excelsum prae*

cyningu*m* eorðan in ecnisse ic haldu him mildheortnisse
regibus terrae 29. *In aeternum servabo illi misericordiam*

mine 7 cyðnisse mine getreowu*m* him 7 settu
meam et testamentum meum fideli ipsi 30. *Et ponam*

in weoruld weorulde seld his 7 ðrymseld his swe swe
in saeculum saeculi sedem ejus et thronum ejus sicut

dęgas heofenes gif hie forletað bearn his ae mine
dies caeli 31. *Si dereliquerint filii ejus legem meam*

[1] honda, a *er.* [2] mid:.

7 in domum minum ne gongað gif gerehtwisunge
et in judiciis meis non ambulaverint **32.** *Si justificationes*

mine besmitað 7 bibodu min ne haldað ic
meas profanaverint et mandata mea non custodierint **33.** *Visi-*

neosiu in gerde unrehtwisnisse heara 7 in swingum synne
tabo in virga iniquitates eorum et in verberibus peccata

heara mildheortnisse soðlice mine ic ne tostregdo
eorum **34.** *Misericordiam autem meam non dispergam*

from him ne ic sceððu in soðfestnisse minre ne
ab eo neque nocebo in veritate mea **35.** *neque*

ic besmitu cyðnisse mine 7 ða ðe forðgað of weolerum
profanabo testamentum meum et quae procedunt de labiis

minum ic ne do to bismere æne siða ic swor in halgum
meis non faciam irrita **36.** *Semel juravi in sancto*

minum gif ic Dauiðe legu sed his in ecnisse
meo si David mentiar **37.** *semen ejus in aeternum*

wunað 7 seld his swe swe sunne in gesihðe minre
manebit **38.** *et sedes ejus sicut sol in conspectu meo*

7 swe swe mona fulfremed in ecnisse 7 cyðere in heofene
et sicut luna perfecta in aeternum et testes in caelo

getreowe ðu soðlice onweg adrife 7 forhogdes 7
fidelis **39.** *Tu vero reppulisti et sprevisti et dis-*

aeldes Crist ðinne acerdes cyðnisse ðeowes ðines
tulisti Christum tuum **40.** *avertisti testamentum servi tui*

bismite in eorðan halignisse his towurpe alle
profanasti in terram sanctitatem ejus **41.** *Destruxisti omnes*

stanwallas his settes trymenisse his in fyrhtu ge-
macherias ejus posuisti munitiones ejus in formidine **42.** *Di-*

reafedon hine alle ða leorendan on weg geworden is in
ripuerunt eum omnes transeuntes viam factus est in

edwit nehgehusum his upahofe ða swiðran feonða
opprobrium vicinis suis **43.** *Exaltasti dexteram inimi-*

his geblissades alle fiond his acerdes
corum ejus laetificasti omnes inimicos ejus **44.** *Avertisti*

fultum sweordes his 7 ne ard[1] gefultemiende him in
adjutorium gladii ejus et non es auxiliatus ei in

gefehte tolesdes hine from geclasnunge 7 seld his
bello **45.** *Dissolvisti eum ab emundatione et sedem ejus*

[1] a *preceded by unfinished* a.

in eorðan gecnysedes gewonades daegas tida his
in terra conlisisti 46. *Minorasti dies temporum ejus*

ðorhgute hine gedroefednisse hu longe dryht*en*
perfudisti eum confusione 47. *Usque quo Domine*

eorsas ðu in ende beorneð swe swe fyr eorre ðin
irasceris in finem exardescit sicut ignis ira tua

gemyne dryht*en* hwet min spoed nales soðlice
48. *Memorare Domine quae mea substantia non enim*

idellice ðu gesettes bearn monna hwelc is mon se ðe
vane constituisti filios hominum 49. *Quis est homo qui*

lifge 7 ne gese deað oððe hwelc genereð sawle his
vivet et non videbit mortem aut quis eruet animam suam

of honda helle hwer sind mildheortnisse ðine ða
de manu inferi 50. *Ubi sunt misericordiae tuae anti-*

aldan dryht*en* swe ðu swore Dauide in soðfestnisse ðinre
quae Domine sicut jurasti David in veritate tua

gemyndig bio ðu edwita ðiowa ðinra ðæt ic ge-
51. *Memor esto opprobrium servorum tuorum quod con-*

singalade in sceate minum monigra ðioda ðæt
tinui in sinu meo multarum gentium 52. *Quod*

edwitun feond ðine dryht*en* ðæt edwiton on-
exprobraverunt inimici tui Domine quod exprobraverunt com-

wendednisse Cristes ðines gebledsad dryht*en* in
mutationem Christi tui 53. *Benedictus Dominus in*

ecnisse sie sie
aeternum Fiat fiat

89.

dryht*en* geberg geworden earð us from cneorisse 7
Domine refugium factus es nobis a generatione et

cynne ærðon weren muntas oððe were getrymed
progenie 2. *Priusquam fierint montes aut firmaretur*

ymbhwyrft eorðan from weorulde 7 oð in weoruld ðu
orbis terrae a saeculo et usque in saeculum tu

earð god ne acer ðu mon in eaðmodnisse 7 cwede
es Deus 3. *Ne avertas hominem in humilitatem et dixisti*

bioð gecerde bearn monna forðon ðusend gera bi-
Convertimini filii hominum 4. *Quoniam mille anni*

foran egum ðinum swe swe deg geostran se bileorde
ante oculos tuos sicut dies hesterna qui praeteriit

7 swe swe gehaeld in naeht ða fore nowihte
Et sicut custodia in nocte 5. *quae pro nihilo*

bioð hefd ger heara on marne swe swe wyrt leoreð
habentur anni eorum 6. *Mane sicut herba transeat*

on märne bloweð 7 ðorhleoreð on efenne gefalleð for-
mane floreat et pertranseat vespere decidat in-

heardað 7 adrugað forðon we asprungun in eorre ðinum
duret et arescat 7. *Quia . defecimus in ira tua*

7 in hatheortnisse ðinre *gedroefd we sind settes
et in furore tuo conturbati sumus 8. *Posuisti*

unrehtwisnisse ure in gesihðe ðinre weoruld ur
iniquitates nostras in conspectu tuo saeculum nostrum

in inlihtnisse ondwleotan ðines forðon alle degas
in inluminatione vultus tui 9. *Quoniam omnes dies*

ure asprungun 7 we in eorre ðinum asprungun ger
nostri defecerunt et nos in ira tua defecimus Anni

grytte[1]
ur swe swe gongeweafre werun smegende dægas
nostri sicut aranea meditabantur 10. *dies an-*

gera ura in him hundseofentigum gera gif soðlice
norum nostrorum in ipsis lxx annis Si autem

in maehtum hundaehtatiges gera 7 monigfald heara
in potentatibus lxxx anni et plurimum eorum

gewin 7 sar forðon ofercwom ofer usic monðuęrnis 7
labor et dolor Quoniam supervenit super nos mansuetudo et

we bioð gereafade hwelc wat maehte eorres ðines oððe
corripiemur 11. *Quis novit potestatem irae tuae aut*

fore ege eorre ðin ariman swiðre ðin
prae timore iram tuam 12. *dinumerare Dexteram tuam*

dryhten cuðe doa us 7 gelærde on heortan in snytru
Domine notam fac nobis et eruditos corde in sapientia

gecer dryhten sume hwile 7 bide ofer ðiowas
13. *Convertere Domine aliquantulum et deprecare super servos*

ðine gefylde we sind on marne mid mildheortnisse ðinre
tuos 14. *Repleti sumus mane misericordia tua*

7 we gefiað 7 geblissade sind in allum daegum urum
et exultavimus et delectati sumus in omnibus diebus nostris

gelustfullade we sind fore *dagum ðæm usic *geað-
15. *Delectati sumus pro diebus quibus nos humi-*

[1] *contemporary.*

modades ger in dæm· we gesegun yfel geloca in
liasti anni in quibus vidimus mala 16. *Respice in*

ðeowas ðine 7 in werc ðin dryhten 7 gerece beorn
servos tuos et in opera tua Domine et dirige filios

heara 7 sie birhtu dryhtnes godes ures ofer usic
eorum 17. *Et sit splendor Domini Dei nostri super nos*

7 werc honda ura gerece ofer usic
et opera manuum nostrarum dirige super nos

90.

se eardað[1] in fultume ðes hestan in gescildnisse godes
Qui habitat in adjutorio Altissimi in protectione Dei

heofenes wunað cwið to dryhtne ondfenga min
caeli commorabitur 2. *Dicet Domino Susceptor meus*

ðu earð 7 geberg min god min ic gehyhtu in hine
es et refugium meum Deus meus sperabo in eum

forðon he gefriað mec of girene huntiendra 7
3. *Quoniam ipse liberabit me de laqueo venantium et*

from worde mid gescyldrum[3] his ofersceadwad ðe
a verbo aspero[2] 4. *Scapulis suis obumbrabit tibi*

7 under fiðrum his gehyhtes mid scelde ymbseleð
et sub pinnis ejus sperabis 5. *Scuto circumdabit*

ðec soðfestnis his ne ondredes ðu ðe from ege naehtlicum
te veritas ejus non timebis a timore nocturno

from strele flegendum ðorh deg from sc[i]re geond-
6. *A sagitta volante per diem a negotio per-*

gongendum in ðeostrum from hryre 7 diofle middeglicum
ambulante in tenebris a ruina et daemonio meridiano

fallað from sidan ðire ðusend 7 ten ðusend to
7. *Cadent a latere tuo mille et decem milia a*

ðere swiðran ðinre ðe soðlice to ne geneolaeceð ah
dextris tuis tibi autem non adpropiabit 8. *Verum*

hweðre egum ðinum ðu sceawas 7 edlean synfulra
tamen oculis tuis considerabis et retributionem peccatorum

ðu gesist forðon ðu earð dryhten hyht min hest
videbis 9. *Quoniam tu es Domine spes mea Altis-*

[1] d *from* ð. [2] *glossed* grimmum *late.* [3] d *from* t.

settes geberg ðin to ne geniolaecað to ðe
simum posui refugium tuum **10.** *Non accedent ad te*
yfel 7 ðrea ne geneolaeceð getelde ðinum for-
mala et flagellum non adpropiabit tabernaculo tuo **11.** *Quo-*
ðon englum his onbead bi ðe ðæt hie hiolden ðec
niam angelis suis mandavit de te ut custodiant te
in allum wegum ðinum in hondum beorað ðec ne
in omnibus viis tuis **12.** *In manibus portabunt te ne*
æfre otspurne[1] to stane fot ðin ofer
umquam offendas ad lapidem pedem tuum **13.** *Super*
nedran 7 fagwyrm gonges 7 trides leon 7
aspidem et basiliscum ambulabis et conculcabis leonem et
dracan forðon in mec gehyhte 7 ic gefrigu hine
draconem **14.** *Quoniam in me speravit et liberabo eum*
gescildu hine forðon ic oncneow noman minne geceð
protegam eum quoniam cognovit nomen meum **15.** *Invo-*
me 7 ic geheru hine mid hine ic eam in ge-
cabit me et ego exaudiam eum cum ipso sum in tribu-
swince ic genergu hine 7 wuldriu hine lengu
latione Eripiam eum et glorificabo eum **16.** *longitudinem*
dæga gefyllu hine 7 oteowu him haelu mine
dierum adimplebo eum et ostendam illi salutare meum

91.

god is ondettan dryhtne 7 singan noman ðinum
2. *Bonum est confiteri Domino et psallere nomini tuo*
ðu hesta to seggenne on marne mildheortnisse ðine
Altissime **3.** *Ad adnuntiandam mane misericordiam tuam*
7 soðfestnisse ðine ðorh naeht in tenstrengre hearpan
et veritatem tuam per noctem **4.** *In decacordo psalterio*
mid songe 7 citran forðon ðu gelustfullades mec
cum cantico et cythara **5.** *quia delectasti me*
dryhten in gewerce ðinum 7 in wercum honda ðinra
*Domine in factura tua et in operibus *manum tuarum*
ic gefie hu micellice sind werc ðin dryhten
exultabo **6.** *Quam magnificata sunt opera tua Domine*

[1] t *over* f.

swiðe deope gewordne sind geðohtas ðine wer
nimis profundae factae sunt cogitationes tuae 7. *Vir*

unwis ne oncnaweð 7 dysig ne ongiteð ða mid ðy
insipiens non cognoscet et stultus non intelliget ea 8. *Cum*

upeornað ða synfullan swe swe heg 7 oteowdun alle
exorientur peccatores sicut faenum et apparuerunt omnes

ða ðe wircende werun unrehtwisnisse ðæt forweorðen in
qui operantur iniquitatem ut intereant in

weoruld weorulde ðu soðlice se hesta in ecnisse
•saeculum saeculi 9. *Tu autem altissimus in aeternum*

dryhten forðon · sehðe feond ðine dryhten forweorðað
Domine 10. *Quoniam ecce inimici tui Domine peribunt*

7 bioð *tostrodne alle ða ðe wircað unreht 7
et dispergentur omnes qui operantur iniquitatem 11. *Et*

bið upahefen swe swe anhornes horn min 7 aeldu min
exaltabitur sicut unicornis cornu meum et senectus mea

in mildheortnisse genyhtsumre 7 gelocade ege ðin
in misericordia uberi 12. *Et respexit oculus tuus*

fiond mine 7 arisende in mec wergende geherde eare
inimicos meos et insurgentes in me malignantes audivit auris

ðin se rehtwisa swe swe palma bloweð 7 swe swe
tua 13. *Justus ut palma florebit et sicut*

cederbeam noma bið gemonigfaldad geplantade in huse
cedrus Libani multiplicabitur 14. *Plantati in domo*

dryhtnes in ceafurtunum huses godes ures blowað nu
Domini in atriis domus Dei nostri florebunt 15. *Ad*

get bioð gemonigfaldade in aeldu genyhtsumre 7 wel ge-
huc multiplicabuntur in senecta uberi et bene pa-

ðyldge bioð ðæt hie secgen ðætte rehtwis dryhten
tientes erunt 16. *ut adnuntient Quoniam justus Dominus*

god ur 7 nis unrehtwisnis in him
Deus noster et non est iniquitas in eo

92.

dryhten ricsad wlite gegereð gegereð dryhten strengu
1. *Dominus regnabit decorem induit Induit Dominus forti-*

7 bigyrde hine mid megne 7 soðlice getrymeð
tudinem et praecinxit se virtutem Et •enim firmavit

ymbhwyrft eorðan ne bið onstyred gearu seld
orbem terrae qui non commovebitur 2. *Parata sedis*
ðin god nu hionan from weorulde ðu[1] earð uphofun
tua Deus ex tunc a saeculo tu es 3. *Elevaverunt*
flodas dryht*en* uphofun flodas stefne heara from
flumina Domine elevaverunt flumina voces suas 4. *a*
stefnum wetra micelra wundurlice upahefenisse *hæs
vocibus aquarum multarum Mirabiles elationes maris
wundurlic in heanisse dryht*en* cyðnisse ðine dryht*en*
mirabilis in excelsis Dominus 5. *Testimonia tua Domine*
*gelæfsume gewordne sind swiðe huse ðinum[2] gedeafineað
credibilia facta sunt nimis Domui tuae decent
ða halgan dryht*en* in lengu dęga
sancta Domine in longitudine dierum

93.

god wreca dryht*en* god wręca freolice dyde
1. *Deus ultionum Dominus Deus ultionum libere egit*
hefe up ðu doemes eordan ageld edlean oferhygdgum
2. *Exaltare qui judicas terram redde retributionem superbis*
hu longe synfulle dryht*en* hu longe synfulle bioð
3. *Usque quo peccatores Domine usque quo peccatores glo-*
gewuldrade secgað 7 spreocað unreht spre-
riabuntur 4. *Pronuntiabunt et loquentur iniquitatem lo-*
ocað alle ða wircað unrehtwisnisse folc ðin
quentur omnes qui operantur injustitiam 5. *Populum tuum*
dryht*en* geeaðmodedun 7 *erfwordnisse ðine *geswecton
Domine humiliaverunt et hereditatem tuam vexaverunt
widwan 7 *wrecan ofslogun 7 feadurlease ofslogun
6. *Viduam et advenam interfecerunt et pupillos occiderunt*
7 cwedun ne gesið dryht*en* ne ongiteð god Iacob
7. *Et dixerunt Non videbit Dominus nec intellegit Deus Jacob*
ongeotað nu ða ðe unwise earun in folce 7 dysge
8. *Intellegite nunc qui insipientes estis in populo et stulti*
hwilum hogiað se plantade eare ne gehered oððe
aliquando sapite 9. *Qui plantavit aurem non audiet aut*

[1] ð:u. [2] u *over* e.

se ðe hiowede ege ne *sceawað se ðreað ðeode
qui finxit oculum non considerat 10. *qui corripit gentes*

ne ðreað se læreð men wisdom dryhten wat
non arguet qui docet homines scientiam 11. *Dominus novit*

geðohtas monna[1] forðon idle sind eadig mon
cogitationes hominum quoniam vanae sunt 12. *Beatus homo*

ðone ðu gelæres dryhten 7 of ae ðinre læres hine
quem tu erudieris Domine et de lege tua docueris eum

ðæt ðu gemildgie hine from dęgum yflum oððet bið dolfen
13. *ut mitiges eum a diebus malis donec fodeatur*

ðæm synfullan seað forðon weg ne adrifeð dryhten
peccatori fovea 14. *Quia non repellit Dominus*

folc his 7 erfe his ne forleteð oð
plebem suam et hereditatem suam non derelinquit 15. *Quoad*

ðet rehtwisnis bið gecerred in dom 7 niomað hie
usque justitia convertatur in judicium. et qui tenent eam

alle ða rehtre sind heortan hwelc ariseð me
omnes qui recto sunt corde 16. *Quis exurget mihi*

wið wergendum oððe hwelc stondeð mid mec wið
adversus malignantes aut quis stabit mecum adversus

wircendum unreht nemne ðæt dryhten gefultumade
operantes iniquitatem 17. *Nisi quod Dominus adjuvasset*

mec hwoene læssan eardade in helle sawul min
me paulo minus habitaverat in inferno anima mea

gif ic cweð onstyred is fot min mildheortnis ðin
18. *Si dicebam Motus est pes meus misericordia tua*

dryhten gefultumað mec efter mengu sara
Domine adjuvabat me 19. *Secundum multitudinem dolorum*

minra in heortan minre frofre ðine dryhten *ge-
meorum in corde meo consolationes tuae Domine laetifi-

blisadon sawle mine ah ætfileð ðe seld
caverunt animam meam 20. *Numquid adheret tibi sedis*

*unrehtwisnise hiowas sar in bibode gehefta ð
iniquitatis qui fingis dolorem in praecepto 21. *captabunt*

in sawle ðes rehtwisan 7 blod *insceðende niðeriað
in animam justi et sanguinem innocentem condemnabunt

7 geworden is me dryhten in geberg 7 god min
22. *Et factus est mihi Dominus in refugium et Deus meus*

[1] a *over* e.

in fultum hyhtes mines 7 gildeð him dryhten
in auxilium spei meae **23.** *Et reddet illis Dominus*

unrehtwisnisse heara 7 in hetas heara tostrigdeð hie
iniquitates ipsorum et in malitias eorum disperdet illos

dryhten god ur
Dominus Deus noster

94.

cumað gefen we dryhtne wynsumie we gode ðæm hal-
1. *Venite exultemus Domino jubilemus Deo salutari*

wyndan urum abisgien we onsiene his in ondetnisse
nostro **2.** *Praeoccupemus faciem ejus in confessione*

7 in salmum wynsumie we him forðon god micel
et in psalmis jubilemus ei **3.** *Quoniam Deus magnus*

dryhten 7 cyning micel ofer alle godas forðon onweg
Dominus et Rex magnus super omnes deos Quoniam non

ne adrifeð dryhten folc his forðon in honda his
repellet Dominus plebem suam **4.** *quia in manu ejus*

sind alle endas eorðan 7 heanisse munta he gelocað
sunt omnes fines terrae et altitudines montium ipse conspicit

forðon his is sae 7 he dyde det 7 ða drygan
5. *Quoniam ipsius est mare et ipse fecit illud et arida*

honda his gesteaðeladun cumað weorðien we 7 forð-
manus ejus fundaverunt **6.** *Venite adoremus et pro-*

luten we biforan god woepen we biforan dryhtne se dyde
cidamus ante Deum ploremus coram Domino qui fecit

usic forðon he is dryhten god ur we soðlice
nos **7.** *Quia ipse est Dominus Deus noster nos autem*

folc his 7 scep leswe his to dege gif stefne his
populus ejus et oves pascuae ejus **8.** *Hodie si vocem ejus*

ge geherað nyllað aheardian heortan eowre swe in
audieritis nolite obdurare corda vestra **9.** *Sicut in*

onscununge[1] efter dege costunge in woestenne ðer
exacervatione secundum diem temptationis in deserto ubi

costadun mec fedras eowre cunnadun 7 gesegun werc
temptaverunt me patres vestri probaverunt et viderunt opera

min feowertigum gera on neoweste ic wes cneorisse
mea **10.** *Quadraginta annis proximus fui generationi*

[1] onscun:unge.

ðisse 7 cweð aa ðas dwoliað on heortan hie soðlice
huic et dixi Semper hii errant corde 11. *Ipsi vero*

ne oncnewun wegas mine ðæm ic swor in eorre minum
non cognoverunt vias meas quibus juravi in ira mea

gif ingað in reste mine
Si introibunt in requiem meam

95.

singað dryhtne song neowne singad dryhtne all eorðe
Cantate Domino canticum novum cantate Domino omnis terra

singað dryhtne 7 bledsiað noman his wel secgað of
2. *Cantate Domino et benedicite nomini ejus bene nuntiate de*

dege in deg haelu his secgað betwih ðeode
die in diem salutare ejus 3. *Adnuntiate inter gentes*

wuldur his in allum folcum wundur his forðon
gloriam ejus in omnibus populis mirabilia ejus 4. *Quoniam*

micel dryhten 7 *hergedlic swiðe egesful is ofer alle
magnus Dominus et laudabilis nimis terribilis est super omnes

godas forðon alle godas ðioda ðioful dryhten
deos 5. *Quoniam omnes dii gentium daemonia Dominus*

soðlice heofenas dyde ondetnis 7 fegernis in ge-
autem caelos fecit 6. *Confessio et pulchritudo in con-*

sihðe his halignis 7 micelnis in gehalgunge his
spectu ejus sanctitas et magnificentia in sanctificatione ejus

tobringað dryhtne oeðlas ðeoda tobringað dryhtne
7. *Adferte Domino patriae gentium adferte Domino*

wuldur 7 are tobringað dryhtne wuldur noman
gloriam et honorem 8. *adferte Domino gloriam nomini*

his uphebbað onsegdnisse 7 ingað in ceafurtunas his
ejus Tollite hostias et introite in atria ejus

weorðiað dryhten in halle ðere halgan his si[1] onstyred
9. *adorate Dominum in aula sancta ejus Commoveatur*

from onsiene his all eorðe cweoðað in *cneorisum
a facie ejus universa terra 10. *dicite in nationibus*

dryhten ricsað from treo 7 soðlice gereceð ymbhwyrft
Dominus regnabit a ligno et enim correxit orbem

[1] sic:, *the e er.*

eorðan se ne bið onstyred *domeð folc in rehtwisnisse
terrae qui non commovebitur Judicabit populos in aequitate

⁊ ðiode in eorre his blissien heofenas ⁊ gefee
et gentes in ira sua 11. *Laetentur caeli et exultet*

eorðe sie onstyred sae ⁊ fylnis hire gefiað
terra moveatur mare et plenitudo ejus 12. *Gaudebunt*

feldas ⁊ alle ða ðe in him sind ðonne gefiað all
campi et omnia quae in eis sunt tunc exultabunt omnia

trew wuda biforan onsiene dryht*nes* forðon cwom
ligna silvarum 13. *ante faciem Domini quoniam venit*

forðon cwom doeman eorðan doemeð ymbhwyrft eorðan
quoniam venit judicare terram Judicabit orbem terrae

in efennisse ⁊ folc in soðfestnisse his
in aequitate et populos in veritate sua

96.

dryht*en* ricsað[1] gefið eorðe blissien eolond micelu
Dominus regnabit exultet terra laetentur insulae multae

wolcen ⁊ dimnis in ymbhwyrfte hire rehtwisnis ⁊ dom
2. *Nubes et caligo in circuitu ejus justitia et judi-*

gerecenis seldes his fyr biforan him foregęð
cium correctio sedis ejus 3. *Ignis ante eum praeibit*

⁊ inaeleð in ymbhwyrfte fiond his inlihtun
et inflammabit in circuitu inimicos ejus 4. *Inluxerunt*

legite his ymbhwyrfte eorðan gesaeh ⁊ onstyred wes eorðe
fulgora ejus orbi terrae vidit et commota est terra

muntas swe swe wex tofleowun from onsiene dryht*nes* from
5. *Montes sicut cera fluxerunt a facie Domini a*

onsiene dryht*nes* cwaecade all eorðe segdon
facie Domini tremuit omnis terra 6. *Adnuntiaverunt*

heofenas rehtwisnisse his ⁊ *gesgun alle folc wuldur
caeli justitiam ejus et viderunt omnes populi gloriam

his sien gescende alle ða ðe weorðiað greftas ða
ejus 7. *Confundantur omnes qui adorant sculptilia qui*

wuldriað in hergu*m* heara weorðiað hine alle englas
gloriantur in simulacris suis Adorate eum omnes angeli

[1] i *over* e.

his geherde 7 geblissad is Sion 7 gefegun
ejus 8. *audivit et laetata est Sion et exultaverunt*

dohtur Iudan fore domum ðinum dryhten forðon ðu
filiae Judae propter judicia tua Domine 9. *Quoniam tu*

earð dryhten ðu hesta ofer alle eorðan swiðe upahefen
es Dominus altissimus super omnem terram nimis exaltatus

ðu earð ofer alle godas ða ðe lufiað dryhten fiað
es super omnes deos 10. *Qui diligitis Dominum odite*

yfel haldeð dryhten sawle ðeowa his of honda
malum custodit Dominus animas servorum suorum de manu

synfulra gefreað hie leht upcumen wes ðæm rehtan
peccatorum liberabit eos 11. *Lux orta est justo*

7 rehtheortum blis blissiað rehtwise in dryhtne 7
et rectis corde laetitia 12. *laetamini justi in Domino et*

ondettað gemynde halignisse his
confitemini memoriae sanctitatis ejus

97.

singað dryhtne song niowne forðon wundur dyde
Cantate Domino canticum novum quia mirabilia fecit

dryhten gehaelde hine mid ða swiðran his 7 earm
Dominus Salvavit eum dextera ejus et bracchium

haligne his cuðe dyde dryhten hælu his biforan
sanctum ejus 2. *Notum fecit Dominus salutare suum ante*

gesihðe ðioda onwrah rehtwisnisse his gemyndig
conspectu gentium revelavit justitiam suam 3. *Memor*

wes mildheortnisse his 7 soðfestnisse his gehuscipe
fuit misericordiae suae Jacob et veritatis suae domus

Israel gesegun alle endas eorðan haelu godes ures
Israhel Viderunt omnes fines terrae salutare Dei nostri

wynsumiað gode all eorðe singað 7 gefiað 7 singað
4. *jubilate Deo omnis terra cantate et exultate et psallite*

singað ´gode urum in citran in citran 7 stefne salmes
5. *Psallite Deo nostro in cithara in cithara et voce psalmi*

in hornum gelengdum 7 stefne hornes *hyrnes *wyn-
6. *in tubis ductilibus et voce tubae corneae jubi-*

sumiað in gesihðe cyninges dryhtnes sie astyred sȩ
late in conspectu regis Domini 7.• *Moveatur mare*

7 *fynis hire ymbhwyrft eorðena 7 alle[1] ða ðe eardiað
et plenitudo ejus orbis terrarum et universi qui habitant

in hire flodas plægiað mid hondum in þæt ilce muntas
in ea 8. *Flumina plaudent manibus in id ipsum montes*

gefegun biforan onsiene dryhtnes forðon cwom for-
exultaverunt 9. *ante faciem Domini quoniam venit quo-*

ðon cwom doeman eorðan doemæð *ymbhwyrf eorðan in
niam venit judicare terram Judicabit orbem terrae in

rehtwisnisse 7 folc in efennisse his
justitia et populos in aequitate sua

98.

dryhten ricsað eorsien folc ðu ðe sites ofer Cerubin
Dominus regnabit irascantur populi qui sedis super Cherubin

sie astyred eorðe dryhten in Sion micel 7 heh
moveatur terra 2. *Dominus in Sion magnus et excelsus*

ofer alle folc ondettað noman ðinum miclum
super omnes populos 3. *Confiteantur nomini tuo magno*

7 egesfullum forðon halig is 7 ar cyninges dom
et terribili quoniam sanctum est 4. *et honor regis judi-*

lufað ðu gearwades rehtwisnisse dom 7 rehtwisnisse
cium diligit Tu parasti aequitatem judicium et justitiam

in Iacob ðu dydest uphebbað dryhten god urne
in Jacob tu fecisti 5. *Exaltate Dominum Deum nostrum*

7 weorðiað scomul fota his forðon halig is
et adorate scabellum pedum ejus quoniam sanctum est

7 Aaron in biscopum his 7 Samuel betwih hie
6. *Moyses et Aaron in sacerdotibus ejus et Samuhel inter eos*

ða gecegað noman his gecedon dryhten 7 he geherde
qui invocant nomen ejus Invocabant Dominum et ipse exau-

hie in syle wolcnes sprec to him he-
diebat eos 7. *in columna nubis loquebatur ad eos Custo-*

oldun cyðnisse his 7 bibod his ða salde him
diebant testimonia ejus et praecepta ejus quae dederat illis

dryhten god ur ðu geherdes hie god ðu milde
8. *Domine Deus noster tu exaudiebas eos Deus tu propitius*

[1] ll *over some other letter.*

were him 7 wreocende in alle teolunge heara heb-
fuisti illis et vindicans in omnia studia eorum 9. *Ex-*
bað up dryhten god urne 7 weorðiað in munte
altate Dominum Deum nostrum et adorate in monte
halgum his forðon halig is dryhten god ur
sancto ejus quoniam sanctus est Dominus Deus noster

99.

wynsumiað gode all eorðe ðiowiað dryhtne in blisse
2. *Jubilate Deo omnis terra servite Domino in laetitia*
ingað in gesihðe his in wynsumnisse weotað ðæt
Intrate in conspectu ejus in exultatione 3. *scitote quod*
dryhten he is god he dyde usic 7 nales we usic we
Dominus ipse est Deus ipse fecit nos et non ipsi nos Nos
soðlice folc[1] his 7 scep leswe his ingað geatu
autem populus ejus et oves pascuae ejus 4. *intrate portas*
his in ondetnisse ceafurtunes his in ymenum ondetnissa
ejus in confessione atria ejus in hymnis confessionum
hergað noman his forðon wynsum is dryhten in
Laudate nomen ejus 5. *quoniam suavis est Dominus in*
ecnisse mildheortnis his 7 oð in weoruld weorulde
aeternum misericordia ejus et usque in saeculum saeculi
soðfestnis his
veritas ejus

100.

mildheortnisse 7 dom ic singu ðe dryhten ic singu
Misericordiam et judicium cantabo tibi Domine Psallam
7 ongeotu in wege ðæm unwemman ðonne ðu cymes to
2. *et intellegam in via inmaculata quando venies ad*
me ic geondgan[2] in unsceðfulnisse heortan minre in midle
me Perambulabam in innocentia cordis mei in medio
huses ðines ic no foresette biforan egum minum wisan
domus tuae 3. *Non proponebam ante oculos meos rem*
yfle donde oferleornisse ic fiode no ætfalh me
malam facientes praevaricationes odivi non adhesit mihi

[1] lc *from* n. [2] *last* n *may be* u (?).

heorte ðuerh onhaeldende *fro me awergde ic ne on-
4. *cor pravum Declinantes a me malignos non agnos-*
cneow telendne wið ðæm nestan his degullice
cebam 5. *detrahentem adversus proximum suum occulte*
ðeosne ic oehte oferhygdgum egan 7 ungereordedlicre heortan
hunc persequebar Superbo oculo et insatiabili corde
mitte ðis somud ic ne et egan min ofer ða ge-
cum hoc simul non edebam 6. *Oculi mei super fideles*
treowan eordan ðæt hie sitten ðas mid mec gongende in
terrae ut sedeant hii mecum ambulans in
wege ðæm unwemman ðes me ðegnade ne eardað
via inmaculata hic mihi ministrabat 7. *Non habi-*
in midle huses mines se doeð oferhygde se
tabit in medio domus meae qui facit superbiam qui
spriceð ða unrehtan ne gereceð in gesihðe egena
loquitur iniqua non direxit in conspectu oculorum
minra in margentid ic ofslog alle synfulle
meorum 8. *In matutinis interficiebam omnes peccatores*
eorðan ðæt ic tostregde of cestre dryhtnes alle ða
terrae ut disperdam de civitate Domini omnes qui
wircað unrehtwisnisse
operantur iniquitatem

101.

dryhten geher gebed min 7 cleopung min to ðe
2. *Domine exaudi orationem meam et clamor meus ad te*
becyme ne acer ðu onsiene ðine from me in swe
perveniat 3. *Ne avertas faciem tuam a me in qua-*
hwelcum dege geswenced onhaeld to me eare ðin in
cumque die tribulor inclina ad me aurem tuam in
swe hwelcum dege ic gecego ðec hr[e]ðlice geher mec
quacumque die invocavero te velociter exaudi me
forðon asprungun swe swe rec dægas mine 7 ban
4. *Quia defecerunt sicut fumus dies mei et ossa*
min swe in herstan herste sind slegen i■ eam
mea sicut in frixorium confrixa sunt 5. *Percussus sum*
swe swe heg 7 adrugað heorte min forðon *offergeotul
sicut faenum et aruit cor meum quia oblitus
ic eam eotan hlaf minne from stefne geamrunge
sum manducare panem meum 6. *a voce gemitus*

minre ætfelun[1] ban min flæsce minum gelic geworden
mei adheserunt ossa mea carni meae 7. *Similis factus*

ic eam stanegellan in woestenne geworden ic eam swe swe
sum pellicano in solitudine factus sum sic ut

næhthrefn in husincle ic waecade 7 geworden ic eam
nocticorax in domicilio 8. *Vigilavi et factus sum*

swe swe spearwa se anga in timbre alne deg ed-
sic ut passer unicus in aedificio 9. *Tota die ex-*

wittun[2] mec feond mine 7 ða ðe mec hergað wið
probrabant me inimici mei et qui me laudabant adver-

me sworun forðon escan swe swe hlaf
sum me jurabant 10. *Quia cinerem sic ut panem*

ic et 7 drync minne mid wope ic gemetgade from
manducabam et potum meum cum fletu temperabam 11. *A*

onsiene eorres 7 *ebylðu ðinre forðon uphebbende ðu ge-
facie irae et indignationis tuae quia elevans elisisti

cnysedes mec dægas mine swe swe scua onhaeldun
me 12. *Dies mei sic ut umbra declinaverunt*

7 ic swe swe heg adrugade ðu soðlice dryht*en* in
et ego sic ut faenum arui 13. *Tu autem Domine in*

ecnisse ðorhwunas 7 gemynd ðin in weoruld weorulde
aeternum permanes et memoriale tuum in saeculum saeculi

ðu arisende gemildsas *Sioene forðon cwom tid
14. *Tu exsurgens misereberis Sion quia venit tempus*

to mildsiende his forðon welgelicad hefdun ðeowas
miserendi ejus 15. *Quia beneplacitum habuerunt servi*

ðine stanas his 7 eorðan his mildsiað 7
tui lapides ejus et terrae ejus miserebuntur 16. *Et*

ondredað ðiode noman ðinne dryht*en* 7 alle cyningas
timebunt gentes nomen tuum Domine et omnes reges

eorðan wuldur ðin forðon timbreð dryht*en* Sion
terrae gloriam tuam 17. *Quoniam aedificabit Dominus Sion*

7 bið gesegen in megenðrymme his 7 gelocað in
et videbitur in majestate sua 18. *Et respexit in*

gebeodu ðearfena 7 ne forhogað *bene heara bioð
orationes pauperum et non sprevit preces eorum 19. *Scri-*

awriten ðas in cneorisse oðerre 7 folc ðæt bið gecwicad
bantur haec in generatione altera et populus qui creabitur

[1] vel ætclofodon *added later.* [2] vel hyspton *added later.*

hereð dryhten forðon gelocað of heanisse
laudabit Dominum **20.** *Quoniam prospexit de excelso*

ðæm halgan his dryhten of heofene on eorðan gelocade
sancto suo Dominus de caelo in terram prospexit

ðæt he geherde gemrunge gebundenra ⁊ onlese bearn
21. *Ut audiret gemitum vinculatorum et solvat filios*

ofslegenra ðæt sie segd in Sion noma dryhtnes
interemptorum **22.** *Ut adnuntietur in Sion nomen Domini*

⁊ lof his in Ierusalem in gemoetinge folc
et laus ejus in Hierusalem **23.** *In conveniendo populos*

in annesse[1] ⁊ ricu ðæt hie ðiowien dryhtne ondsweorede
in unum et regna ut serviant Domino **24.** *Respondit*

him in wege megnes his feanisse dega minra sege
ei in via virtutis suae paucitatem dierum meorum enuntia

me ⁊ ne gece ðu mec in midle dæga minra
mihi et **25.** *ne revoces me in dimidio dierum meorum*

in weoruld weorulde ger ðin in fruman eorðan ðu
in saeculum saeculi anni tui **26.** *Initio terram tu*

gesteaðelades dryhten ⁊ werc honda ðinra sind heofenas
fundasti Domine et opera manuum tuarum sunt caeli

hie forweorðað ðu soðlice ðorhwunas ⁊ alle swe swe
27. *Ipsi peribunt tu autem permanes et omnes sic ut*

hregl aldiað ⁊ swe swe wrigels onwendes hie ⁊
vestimentum veterescent et sic ut opertorium mutabis eos et

hie bioð onwende ðu soðlice se ilca[2] earð ⁊ ger ðin
mutabuntur **28.** *Tu autem idem ipse es et anni tui*

ne aspringað bearn ðiowa ðinra ineardiað ðer
non deficient **29.** *Filii servorum tuorum inhabitabunt ibi*

⁊ sed heara in weoruld[3] *werulde bið gereht
et semen eorum in saeculum saeculi dirigitur

102.

bledsa sawul min dryhten ⁊ all ða innerran *mi noman
Benedic anima mea Dominum et omnia interiora mea nomen

ðone halgan his bledsa sawul min dryhten ⁊ nyl
sanctum ejus **2.** *Benedic anima mea Dominum et noli*

ofergeotelian alle edlean his se milde bið
oblivisci omnes retributiones ejus **3.** *Qui propitius fit*

[1] a *from* u. [2] a *over dotted* e. [3] ld *from* n.

allum unrehtwisnissum dinum se haeleð alle aðle
omnibus iniquitatibus tuis qui sanat omnes languores

ðine se aleseð of forwyrde lif ðin se
tuos 4. *Qui redemit de interitu vitam tuam* 5. *qui*

gereordeð in godum lust ðinne se gebegað ðec in
satiat in bonis desiderium tuum qui coronat te in

mildse 7 mildheortnisse bið geedniowad swe swe earn
miseratione et misericordia renovabitur sic ut aquilae

*guðuð ðin donde mildheortnisse dryhten 7 dom
juventus tua 6. *Faciens misericordias Dominus et judicium*

allum tionan ðrowiendum cuðe dyde wegas his
omnibus injuriam patientibus 7. *Notas fecit vias suas*

Moysi bearnum willan his mildheort 7
Moysi filiis Israhel voluntates suas 8. *Misericors et*

mildsiend dryhten geðyldig 7 swiðe mildheort nales
miserator Dominus patiens et multum misericors 9. *Non*

in ende eorsað ne in ecnisse bið geebylged nales
in finem irascitur neque in aeternum indignabitur 10. *Non*

efter synne ure dyde us ne *efer unreht-
secundum peccata nostra fecit nobis neque secundum iniqui-

wisnisse urum geedleanað us forðon efter heanisse
tates nostras retribuit nobis 11. *Quia secundum altitu-*

heofenes from eorðan getrymede dryhten mildheortnisse
dinem caeli a terra confirmavit Dominus misericordiam

his ofer ondredende hine swe micel tostondeð eastdael
suam super timentes eum 12. *Quantum distat oriens*

from westdaele afeorrað from us unrehtwisnisse ure
ab occasu elongavit a nobis iniquitates nostras

swe mildsað feder bearnum swe mildsiende bið dryhten
13. *Sic ut miseretur pater filiis ita misertus est Dominus*

ondredendum hine forðon he wat geheowunge ure
timentibus se 14. *quia ipse sit figmentum nostrum*

gemyne dryhten ðæt dust we sind mon swe swe
Memento Domine quod pulvis sumus 15. *homo sic ut*

heg dægas his 7 swe swe blostme[1] londes swe bloweð
faenum dies ejus et sic ut flos agri ita floriet

forðon gast ðorhleoreð from him 7 ne bið 7 ne
16. *Quia spiritus pertransiit ab eo et non erit et non*

[1] lo *from* r.

oncnaweð mae stowe his mildheortnis soðlice
cognoscit amplius locum suum 17. *Misericordia autem*

dryht*nes* from weorulde is ⁊ oð in weoruld weorulde
Domini a saeculo est et usque in saeculum saeculi

ofer ondredende hine ⁊ rehtwisnis his ofer bearn
super timentes eum Et justitia ejus super filios

beorna haldendum[1] cyðnis his ⁊ gemynd
filiorum 18. *custodientibus testamentum ejus et memoria*

neomendum bibod his ðæt doen ða dryht*en* in
retinentibus mandata ejus ut faciant ea 19. *Dominus in*

heofene gearwade seld his ⁊ rice his alra waldeð
caelo paravit sedem suam et regnum ejus omnium domina-

bledsiað dryht*en* alle englas his maehtge
bitur 20. *Benedicite Dominum omnes angeli ejus potentes*

on megne ða ðe doð word his to geherenne stefne
virtute qui facitis verbum ejus ad audiendam vocem

worda his bledsiað dryht*en* alle megen his
sermonum ejus 21. *Benedicite Dominum omnes virtutes ejus*

ðegnas his ða doð willan his bledsiað
ministri ejus qui facitis voluntatem ejus 22. *Benedicite*

dryht*en* all werc his in ylcere stowe onwaldes his
Dominum omnia opera ejus in omni loco dominationis ejus

bledsa sawul min dryht*en*
benedic anima mea Dominum

103.

bledsa sawul min dryht*en* dryht*en* god min gemiclad
Benedic anima mea Dominum Domine Deus meus magni-

earð swiðlice ondetnisse ⁊ wlite ðu gegeredes
ficatus es vehementer Confessionem et decorem induisti

biswapen lehte swe swe mid hregle aðennende heofen
2. *amictus lumine sic ut vestimento Extendens caelum*

swe swe fel ðu biðeces in wetrum ða uferran his
sic ut pellem 3. *qui tegis in aquis superiora ejus*

se seteð wolcen upstige his se gongeð ofer fiðru
Qui ponit nubem ascensum suum qui ambulat super pinnas

winda se doeð englas his gastas ⁊ ðegnas
ventorum 4. *Qui facit angelos suos spiritus et ministros*

[1] *first* d *from* a (?).

his fyr bernende se steaðelade eorðan ofer steaðul-
suos ignem urentem 5. *Qui fundavit terram super stabili-*

festnisse his ne bið onhaelded in weoruld weorulde
tatem ejus non inclinabitur in saeculum saeculi

neolnis swe swe rift swæpels[1] his ofer muntas
6. *Abyssus sic ut pallium amictus ejus super montes*

stondað weter from ðreange ðinre fleoð from stefne
stabunt aquae 7. *Ab increpatione tua fugient a voce*

ðunurrade forhtiað astigað muntas 7 ofdune-
**tonitrui tui formidabunt* 8. *Ascendunt montes et dis-*

stigað feldas in stowe ða ðu gesteaðelades him
cendunt campi in locum quem fundasti eis 9. *Ter-*

gemære settes him ða hie ne[2] ofergongað ne
minum posuisti eis quem non transgredientur neque

bioð forcerde oferwrean eorðan se onsendeð waellan in
convertentur operire terram 10. *Qui emittet fontes in*

deanum betwih middel munta ðorhleorað weter
convallibus inter medium montium pertransibunt aquae

drencað ða alle wilddeor wuda bidað wilde assan
11. *Potabunt ea omnes bestiae silvarum expectabunt onagri*

in *ðurs heara ofer ða fuglas heofenes eardiað
in sitim suam 12. *super ea volucres caeli habitabunt*

of *mid stana sellað stefne heara leccende muntas
de medio petrarum dabunt voces suas 13. *Rigans montes*

of ðæm uferrum his of westme werca ðinra bið gereorded
de superioribus suis de fructu operum tuorum satiabitur

eorðe forð gelaedes heg neatum 7 wyrte ðeowdome
terra 14. *Produces faenum jumentis et herbam servituti*

monna ðæt he utalæde hlaf of eorðan 7 win ge-
hominum Ut educat panem de terra 15. *et vinum lae-*

blissað heortan monnes ðæt he gleadie onsiene in ele
tificet cor hominis Ut exhilaret faciem in oleo

7 hlafes heorte monnes getrymeð bioð gefylde all
et panis cor hominis confirmet 16. *Satiabuntur omnia*

trew wuda 7 cederbeamas ðes muntes ða ðu geplantades
ligna silvarum et cedros Libani quas plantasti

ðer spearwan *nistaðað heafuces hus ladtow is heora
17. *illic passeres nidificabunt Fulice domus dux est eorum*

[1] r (?) *er. after* e. [2] o (?) *er. before* n.

muntas heae heoretes stan geberg igles[1] dyde
18. *montes excelsi cervis petra refugium irinacis* 19. *Fecit*

monan in tid sunne oncneow setgong hire ðu
lunam in tempore sol cognovit occasum suum 20. *Po-*

settes ðeostru 7 geworden wes naeht in ðere ðorhleorað
suisti tenebras et facta est nox in ipsa pertransibunt

alle wilddeor wuda hwelpas leona grymetiende ðæt-
omnes bestiae silvarum 21. *Catuli leonum rugientes ut*

hie *gerafien 7 soecen from gode mete him upcumen
rapiant et quaerant a Deo escam sibi 22. *Ortus*

is sunne 7 gesomnade sind 7 in bedcleofum heara hie
est sol et congregati sunt et in cubilibus suis se

gesteaðeliað utgaeð mon to werce his 7 to gebede
conlocabunt 23. *Exiet homo ad opus suum et ad opera-*

his oð to efenne hu micellice
tionem suam usque ad vesperum 24. *Quam magnificata*

sind werc ðin dryht*en* all in snytru ðu dydes gefylled
sunt opera tua Domine omnia in sapientia fecisti repleta

is eorðe gescefte ðinre ðis sae micel 7 rum
est terra creatura tua 25. *Hoc mare magnum et spaciosum*

ðer snicende ðeara nis rim netenu lytelu 7
illic reptilia quorum non est numerus animalia pusilla et

micel ðer sceopu ðorhfearað draca ðes ðone
magna 26. *illic naves pertransibunt Draco iste quem*

ðu gehiowa[d]es to bismerenne him all from ðe
formasti ad inludendum ei 27. *omnia a te*

bidað dryht*en* ðæt ðu selle him mete in tid
expectant Domine ut des illis escam in tempore

sellendum ðe him gesomniað ontynendum ðe hond ðine
28. *Dante te illis colligent aperiente te manum tuam*

all bioð gefylde genyhtsumnisse forcerrendum soðlice ðe
omnia replebuntur ubertate 29. *Avertente autem te*

onsiene ðine bioð gedroefeð ðu afirres gast heara 7
faciem tuam turbabuntur auferes spiritum eorum et

aspringað 7 in dust heara eftcerrað onsend
deficient et in pulverem suum revertentur 30. *Emitte*

gast ðinne 7 bioð gecwicade 7 geedniowas onsiene eorðan
spiritum tuum et creabuntur et renovabis faciem terrae

[1] *from* iles.

sie wuldur dryhtnes in weoruld weoruldc bið geblissad
31. *Sit gloria Domini in saeculum saeculi laetabitur*

dryhten in wercum his se gelocað in eorðan 7
Dominus in operibus suis 32. *Qui respicit in terram et*

doeð hie cwaecian se gehrineð *untas 7 hie smicað
facit eam tremere qui tangit montes et fumigabunt

ic singu dryhtne in life minum ic singu gode minum
33. *Cantabo Domino in vita mea psallam Deo meo*

swe longe ic biom wynsum sie him- herenis min ic
quamdiu ero 34. *Suavis sit ei laudatio mea ego*

soðlice biom gelustfullad in dryhtne aspringen[1] syn-
vero delectabor in Domino 35. *Deficiant pecca-*

fulle from eorðan 7 unrehtwise swe ðæt [hie] ne sien
tores a terra et iniqui ita ut non sint

bledsa sawul min dryhten
benedic anima mea Dominum

104.

ondetað dryhtne 7 gecegað noman his secgað
1. *Confitemini Domino et invocate nomen ejus adnunciate*

betwih ðeode *wer his singað him 7 singað him
inter gentes opera ejus 2. *Cantate ei et psallite ei*

secgað all wundur his hergað in noman
narrate omnia mirabilia ejus 3. *Laudamini in nomine*

ðæm halgan his blissie heorte soecendra dryhten
sancto ejus laetetur cor quaerentium Dominum

soecað dryhten 7 bioð getrymede soecað onsiene his
4. *Quaerite Dominum et confirmamini quaerite faciem ejus*

aa gemunað wundra his ða he dyde becen
semper 5. *Mementote mirabilium ejus quae fecit prodigia*

7 domas muðes his sed ðeowes his bearn
et judicia oris ejus 6. *Semen Abraham servi ejus filii*

gecorenes his he dryhten god ur in alre
Jacob electi ejus 7. *Ipse Dominus Deus noster in uni-*

eordan domas his gemyndig wes in weoruld
versa terra judicia ejus 8. *Memor fuit in saeculum*

[1] að *over dotted* en.

cyðnisse his wordes ðæt onbead[1] in ðusend cneorrissa
testamenti sui verbi quod mandavit in mille generationes

ðæt gestihtade to Abraham 7 aðswyrde his to Isaace
9. *Quod disposuit ad Abraham et juramenti sui ad Isaac*

7 gesette ðæt in bebod 7 Israel in cyðnisse
10. *Et statuit illud Jacob in praeceptum et Israel in testa-*

ece cweoðende ðe ic selle[2] eorðan
mentum aeternum 11. *Dicens Tibi dabo terram Cha-*

rap erfes eowres mid[3] ðy hie werun
naan funiculum hereditatis vestrae 12. *Cum essent*

in rime scortum ða feastan 7 londleode in ðere 7
in numero brevi paucissimi et incolae in ea 13. *Et*

ðorhleordun of ðeode in ðeode 7 of rice to folce
pertransierunt de gente in gentem et de regno ad populum

oðrum ne forleort mon sceððan him 7 ðreade
alterum 14. *Non permisit hominem nocere eis et corripuit*

fore him cyningas nyllað gehrinan ða gehalgedan mine
pro eis reges 15. *Nolite tangere christos meos*

7 in witgum minum nyllað wergan 7 gecede hungur
et in profetis meis nolite malignari 16. *Et vocavit famem*

ofer eorðan 7 alle[4] trymenisse hlafes forðręste
super terram et omne firmamentum panis contrivit

sende biforan him wer in ðeow biboht wes Iosep
17. *Misit ante eos virum in servum venundatus est Joseph*

geeaðmodedun 7 gehendun in fotcospum foet his iren
18. *Humiliaverunt in conpedibus pedes ejus ferrum*

ðorhleorde sawle his oð ðet cwome word his
pertransivit animam ejus 19. *donec veniret verbum ejus*

gesprec dryht*nes* *inlegagede hine sende cyning 7
eloquium Domini inflammavit eum 20. *Misit rex et*

onlesde hine aldermon folca 7 forleort hine 7
solvit eum princeps populorum et dimisit eum 21. *Et*

gesette hine hlafard huses his 7 aldermon alre
constituit eum dominum domus suae et principem omnis

aehte his ðæt he gelærde aldermen his swe swe
possessionis suae 22. *Ut erudiret principes suos sic ut*

hine seolfne 7 uðwiotan his gleawnisse lærde 7
semet ipsum et seniores suos prudentiam doceret 23. *Et*

[1] g::::::: e *before* onbead. [2] ll *on er.* [3] d *from* ð. [4] *second* l *on er.*

bismarade Israel in Aegiptum 7 Iacob eardade in eorðan
intravit Israhel in Aegyptum et Jacob habitavit in terra

Chanaan 7 geecte folc his swiðe 7 getrymede
Chanaan **24.** *Et auxit populum suum nimis et confirmavit*

hit ofer feond his gecerreð heortan heara ðæt
eum super inimicos ejus **25.** *Convertit cor eorum ut*

hie fioden folc his 7 facen dyden in ðiowas his
odirent populum ejus et dolum facerent in servos ejus

sende Moysen ðiow his 7 Aaron ðone geceas hine
26. *Misit Moysen servum suum et Aaron quem elegit ipsum*

sette in him word tacna his 7 becna
27. *Posuit in eis verba signorum suorum et prodigiorum*

his in eorðan Chanaan sende ðeostru 7 aðeostrade
suorum in terra Chanaan **28.** *Misit tenebras et obscuravit*

hie forðon onscunedun word his gecerde
eos quia exacervaverunt sermones ejus **29.** *Convertit*

weter heara in blod 7 ofslog fiscas heara sende
aquas eorum in sanguinem et occidit pisces eorum **30.** *Misit*

in eorðan heara forscas 7 in bedcleofum cyninga heara
in terra eorum ranas et in cubilibus regum ipsorum

cweð 7 cwom hundes *pie 7 gneat in allum gemærum
31. *Dixit et venit cynomia et scinifes in omnibus finibus*

heara sette regnas heara in hegel fyr for-
eorum **32.** *Posuit pluvias eorum in grandinem ignem con-*

bernende in eordan heara 7 slog wingeardas
burentem in terra ipsorum **33.** *Et percussit vineas*

heara 7 fictrew heara 7 forðreste all trew gemæra
eorum et ficulneas eorum et contrivit omne lignum finium

heara cweð 7 cwom *gereshoppe 7 emel ðes ne
eorum **34.** *Dixit et venit lucusta et brucus cujus non*

wes rim 7 et all heg eorðan heara 7
erat numerus **35.** *et comedit omne faenum terrae eorum* **36.** *Et*

slog oelc frumbearn in eorðan Ægipta fruman
percussit omnem primogenitum in terra Aegypti primitias

ylces gewinnes heara 7 utalaedde hie in seolfre
omnis laboris eorum **37.** *Et eduxit eos in argento*

7 golde 7 ne wes in cyn heara untrum ge-
et auro et non erat in tribus eorum infirmus **38.** *Lae-*

blissad is in forðfromunge heara forðon gefeol
tata est Aegyptus in profectione eorum. quia cecidit

ege heara ofer hie aðeneð[1] wolcen in gescildnisse
timor eorum super eos **39.** *Expandit nubem in protectione*

heara ⁊ fyr ðæt hit lihte him ðorh næht bedun
eorum et ignem ut luceret eis per noctem **40.** *Petierunt*

flæsc ⁊ cwom him edeschen ⁊ hlafe heofenes gereorde
carnes et venit eis coturnix et pane caeli saturavit

hie toslat stan ⁊ fleowun weter ⁊ geweotun
eos **41.** *Disrupit petram et fluxerunt aquae et abierunt*

in drygum flodas forðon gemyndig wes wordes halges
in sicco flumina **42.** *Quia memor fuit verbi sancti*

his ðæt spreocende wes to his cnehte
sui quod locutus est ad Abraham puerum suum

⁊ utalędde folc his in wynsumnisse ⁊ ða gecorenan
43. *Et eduxit populum suum in exultatione et electos*

his in blisse ⁊ salde him lond dioda ⁊ gewin
suos in laetitia **44.** *Et dedit eis regiones gentium et labores*

folca gesetun ðæt hie halden rehtwisnisse his
populorum possederunt **45.** *Ut custodiant justificationes ejus*

⁊ aee his soecen
et legem ejus exquirant

105.

ondettað dryhtne forðon god forðon in weorulde
1. *Confitemini Domino quoniam bonus quoniam in saeculum*

mildheortnis his hwelc spriceð mæhte dryhtnes geherde
misericordia ejus **2.** *Quis loquitur potentias Domini auditas*

doeð all lofu his eadge ða haldað dom ⁊
faciet omnes laudes ejus **3.** *Beati qui custodiunt judicium et*

doð rehtwisnisse in alle tid gemyne ur
faciunt justitiam in omni tempore **4.** *Memento nostri*

dryhten in welgelicadum folces ðines niosa usic in
Domine in beneplacito populi tui visita nos in

haelu ðinrę to geseonne in godnisse gecorenra ðinra
salutari tuo **5.** *Ad videndum in bonitate electorum tuorum*

to blissiende in blisse ðeode ðinre ðæt ðu sie hered mid
ad laetandum in laetitia gentis tuae ut lauderis cum

erfe ðinum we syngadun mid fedrum urum un-
hereditate tua **6.** *Peccavimus cum patribus nostris in-*

[1] *last* ð *from* t.

rehtlice we dydun unrehtwisnisse we dydun fedras ure
juste egimus iniquitatem fecimus 7. *Patres nostri*

in *Ægypþum ne ongetun wuldur ðin 7 ne werun
in Aegypto non intellexerunt mirabilia tua et non fuerunt

gemyndge mengu mildheortnisse ðinre 7 bismeradun
memores multitudinis misericordiae tuae Et inritaverunt

hine astigende in dere readan sae 7 gefreode hie
eum ascendentes in Rubro Mare 8. *Et liberavit eos*

fore noman his ðæt cuðe dyde maeht his 7
propter nomen suum ut notam faceret potentiam suam 9. *Et*

ðreade sae *ðon readan 7 adrugad wes 7 utalaedde hie
increpavit Mare Rubrum et siccatum est et eduxit eos

in wetrum miclum swe in woestenne 7 gefreode hie
in aquis multis sicut in deserto 10. *Et liberavit eos*

of honda figendra 7 aleseð hie of honda feonda
de manu odientium et redemit eos de manu inimicorum

7 oferwrah mid wetre swencende hie an of him ne
11. *et operuit aqua tribulantes eos unus ex eis non*

awunede 7 gelefdun in wordum his 7 sungun
remansit 12. *Et crediderunt in verbis ejus et cantaverunt*

lofu his hreðe dydun 7 ofergeotule werun werca
laudes ejus 13. *cito fecerunt et obliti sunt operum*

his 7 ne arefndun geðeht his 7 gewilladun
ejus et non sustinuerunt consilium ejus 14. *Et concupierunt*

gewillunge in woestenne 7 costadon god in drugunge
concupiscentias in deserto et temptaverunt Deum in siccitate

7 salde him boene heara 7 sende gereordnisse in
15. *Et dedit eis petitiones eorum et misit saturitatem in*

sawle heara 7 bismeradun[1] in ferdwicum 7
animas eorum 16. *Et inritaverunt Moysen in castris et*

Aaron ðone halgan dryhtnes ontyned wes eorðe 7
Aaron sanctum Domini 17. *Aperta est terra et*

forswalg 7 oferwrah ofer gesomnunge Abirones
degluttivit Dathan et operuit super synagoga Abiron

born fyr in gesomnunge heara 7 leg forbernde
18. *Exarsit ignis in synagoga eorum et flamma conbusit*

ða synfullan 7 dydun cælf in Choreb 7 weorðadun
peccatores 19. *Et fecerunt vitulum in Choreb et adoraverunt*

[1] d *from some other letter.*

greftas 7 onwendun wuldur his in gelicnisse
sculptile **20.** *et mutaverunt gloriam suam in similitudinem*

calfur eotendes heg ofergeotule werun god se
vituli manducantis faenum **21.** *Obliti sunt Deum qui*

gefriode hie se dyde micelnisse in *Ægistum wundur
liberavit eos qui fecit magnalia in Aegypto **22.** *mirabilia*

in eorðan Chanaan ða egesfullan in ðæm readan sae 7
in terra Chanaan terribilia in Mari Rubro **23.** *Et*

cweð ðæt he tostrugde hie gif no Moyses se gecorena
dixit ut disperderet eos si non Moyses electus

his stode in gebroce in gesihðe his ðæt he forcerde
ejus stetisset in confractione in conspectu ejus ut averteret

eorre his 7 he ne tostrugde hie 7 fore nowiht
iram ejus et ne disperderet eos **24.** *Et pro nihilo*

hefdun eorðan wilsume 7 ne gelefdun in wordum
habuerunt terram desiderabilem et non crediderunt in verbis

his 7 gnornadun in geteldum heara ne hie
ejus **25.** *et murmuraverunt in tabernaculis suis nec ex-*

geherdun stefne dryht*nes* 7 upahof hond his
audierunt vocem Domini **26.** *Et elevavit manum suam*

ofer hie ðæt he gefælde hie in woestenne 7 ðæt
super eos ut prosterneret eos in deserto **27.** *et ut*

he awurpe sed heara in cneorissum[1] 7 tostrugde hie in
dejeceret semen eorum in nationibus et disperderet eos in

londum 7 gehalgade werun 7 eton
regionibus **28.** *Et consecrati sunt Belphegor et mandu-*

onsegdnisse deadra 7 bismeradun hine
caverunt sacrificia mortuorum **29.** *Et inritaverunt eum*

in teolungum his 7 gemonigfaldad is in him hryre
in studiis suis et multiplicata est in eis ruina

stod 7 gebed 7 blon sie styring 7
30. *Stetit Finees et exoravit et cessavit quassatio* **31.** *et*

getald wes hi*m* to rehtwisnisse in cneorisse 7 cne-
reputatum est illi ad justitiam in generatione et gene-

orisse oð in weoruld[2] in weoruld 7 bismeradu■ hine
ratione usque in saeculum **32.** *Et inritaverunt eum*

to wetre wiðcwedenisse 7 geswenced is *Moses fore
ad aquas contradictionis et vexatus est Moyses propter

[1] u *over* e. [2] ld *from* n.

him forðon onscunedon gast his 7 todaelde in
eos 33. *quia exacervaveruut spiritum ejus et distinxit in*

weolerum his ne todęldun ðeode ða cwaeð
labiis suis 34. *Non disperdiderunt gentes quas dixerat*

dryhten to him 7 gemengde werun betwih ðeode 7
Dominus illis 35. *et commixti sunt inter gentes et*

geleornadun werc heara 7 ðiowedun greftum
didicerunt opera eorum 36. *et servierunt sculptilibus*

heara 7 geworden is him in eswic 7 guldun
eorum et factum est illis in scandalum 37. *Et immo-*

bearn[1] his 7 bearn his deoflum 7 agu-
laverunt filios suos et filias suas daemoniis 38. *et effu-*

tun blod *insceððende blod bearna his 7
derunt sanguinem innocentem sanguinem filiorum suorum et

dohtra ða hie onsegdun greftum ofslegen wes
filiarum quos sacrificaverunt sculptilibus Chanaan Infecta est

eorðe in blodum 7 bismiten wes in wercum
terra in sanguinibus 39. *et contaminata est in operibus*

heara 7 dernlicgende werun in gehaeldum heara 7
eorum Et fornicati sunt in observationibus suis 40. *et*

eorre wes on mode *dominus in folc his 7 *onsuni-
iratus est animo Dominus in populum suum et abomi-

ende[2] wes erfewordnisse his 7 salde hie in
natus est hereditatem suam 41. *Et tradidit eos in*

hond ðeoda 7 waldende werun heora ða fiodun hie
manus gentium et dominati sunt eorum qui oderunt eos

7 swencton hie fiond heara 7 geeaðmodade werun
42. *Et tribulaverunt eos inimici eorum et humiliati sunt*

under hondum heara oft gefreode hie hie soðlice
sub manibus eorum 43. *sepe liberavit eos Ipsi autem*

onscunedun hine in geðaehte his 7 geeaðmodade werun
exacervaverunt eum in consilio suo et humiliati sunt

in heara unrehtwisnissum 7 gelocade hie mid ðy
in suis iniquitatibus 44. *Et respexit eos cum*

hie werun geswencte mit te he geherde gebeodu heara
tribularentur cum exaudiret orationes eorum

forðon gemyndig wes cyðnisse his 7 hreowsade hine
45. *Quia memor fuit testamenti sui et paenituit eum*

[1] bearn:, *um er.*

[2] u *from some other letter.*

efter mengu mildheortnisse his ⁊ salde hie
secundum multitudinem misericordiae suae 46. *Et dedit eos*

in mildheortnisse in gesihðe alra ða hie bifengun
in misericordias in conspectu omnium qui eos caeperant

hale usic doa dryht*en* god ur ⁊ gesomna usic
47. *Salvos nos fac Domine Deus noster et congrega nos*

of cneorissu*m* ðæt hie ondetten noman ðæm halgan ðinu*m*
de nationibus ut confiteamur nomini sancto tuo

⁊ wuldrien we in lofe ðinum gebledsad dryht*en*
et gloriemur in laude tua 48. *Benedictus Dominus*

god Israela from weorulde ⁊ oð in weoruld ⁊ cwið
Deus Israhel a saeculo et usque in saeculum et dicet

all folc sie sie
omnis populus Fiat fiat

106.

ondettað dryht*ne* dætte god ðætte in weoruld
1. *Confitemini Domino quoniam bonus quoniam in saeculum*

mildheortnis his cweðen nu ða alesde werun
misericordia ejus 2. *Dicant nunc qui redempti sunt*

f[r]om dryht*ne* ða aleseð of honda feondes ⁊ of
a Domino quos redemit de manu inimici et de re-

londum gesomnade hie from sunnan upcyme ⁊ setgonge
gionibus congregavit eos 3. *A solis ortu et occasu*

from norðdęle ⁊ sae dwoledun in woesten in
ab aquilone et mare 4. *erraverunt in solitudine in*

drugunge weg cestre eardunge ne gemoettun hyn-
siccitate viam civitatis habitationis non invenerunt 5. *Esu-*

grende ⁊ ðyrstende sawul heara in him asprong ⁊
rientes et sitientes anima eorum in ipsis defecit 6. *Et*

cleopedun to dryht*ne* ða ðe hie swenctun ⁊ of ned-
clamaverunt ad Dominum cum tribularentur et de ne-

ðearfnissum heara gefreade hie ⁊ utalaedde hie in
cessitatibus eorum liberavit eos 7. *Et eduxit eos in*

weg rehtne ðæt hie eoden in cestre eordunge on-
viam rectam ut irent in civitatem habitationis 8. *Con-*

dette dryht*ne* mildheortnis his ⁊ wundur his bearnu*m*
fiteantur Domino misericordia ejus et mirabilia ejus filiis

monna forðon gereorde sawle idle ⁊ sawle
hominum 9. *Quia satiavit animam inanem et animam*

hyngrende gereo[r]de mid godu*m* sittende in ðeostrum 7
esurientem satiavit bonis **10.** *Sedentes in tenebris et*

scuan deaðes 7 bendum gebundne in weðelnisse 7 irene
umbra mortis et vinculis ligatos in mendicitate et ferro

forðon *onscynedun gesprec dryht*nes* 7 geðæht ðes
11. *Quia exacervaverunt eloquium Domini et consilium Altis-*

*hesta bismeredun 7 geeaðmodad wes in gewinnu*m*
simi inritaverunt **12.** *Et humiliatum est in laboribus*

heortan heara geuntrumade sind ne wes se gefultumade
. *cor eorum infirmati sunt nec fuit qui adjuvaret*

7 cleopedun to dryht*ne* midðy hie werun geswencte 7
13. *Et clamaverunt ad Dominum cum tribularentur et*

of nedðearfnissu*m* heara gefreode hie 7 utalaedde
de necessitatibus eorum liberavit eos **14.** *Et eduxit*

hie of ðeostrum 7 of scuan deaðes 7 bende heara
eos de tenebris et umbra mortis et vincula eorum

toslat ondettað dryht*ne* mildheortnis his 7
disrupit **15.** *Confiteantur Domino misericordia ejus et*

wundur his bearnum monna forðon fordreste geatu
mirabilia ejus filiis hominum **16.** *Quia contrivit portas*

ða ęrnan 7 scyttels irenu gebrec onfeng hie of
aereas et vectes ferreos confregit **17.** *Suscepit eos de*

wege unrehtwisnisse heara fore unrehtwisnisse soðlice his
via iniquitatis eorum propter injustitias enim suas

geeaðmodade sind alne mete *onscuiende wes sawul
humiliati sunt **18.** *Omnem escam abominata est anima*

heara 7 to geniolaehtun geatu deaðes 7
eorum et adpropiaverunt usque ad portas mortis **19.** *Et*

cleopedun to dryht*ne* midðy hie werun geswencte 7 of
clamaverunt ad Dominum cum tribularentur et de

nedðearfnissu*m* heara gefreode hie sende word
necessitatibus eorum liberavit eos **20.** *Misit verbum*

his 7 gehaelde hie 7 generede hie of forwyrde heara
suum et sanavit eos et eripuit eos de interitu eorum

ondettað dryht*ne* mildheortnis his 7 wundur his
21. *Confiteantur Domino misericordia ejus et mirabilia ejus*

bearnu*m* monna ðæt hie onsecgen onsegdnisse lofes
filiis hominum **22.** *Ut sacrificent sacrificium laudis*

7 *segen werc his in wynsu*m*nisse ða astigað
et adnuntient opera ejus in exultatione **23.** *Qui discendunt*

sae in sceopum donde wircnisse in *wrum miclum
mare in navibus facientes operationes in aquis multis

hie gesegun werc dryhtnes 7 wundur his in
24. *Ipsi viderunt opera Domini et mirabilia ejus in pro-*

grunde cweð 7 stod gast ystes 7 upahefene werun
fundo 25. *Dixit et stetit spiritus procellae et exaltati sunt*

yðe his astigað ot heofenas 7 ofdune stigað-
fluctus ejus 26. *Ascendunt usque ad caelos et discendunt*

oð niolnisse sawul heara in yflum aswond
usque ad abyssos anima eorum in malis tabescebat

gedroefde werun 7 onstyrede werun swe swe druncen 7
27. *Turbati sunt et moti sunt sicut ebrius et*

all snyttru heara forswelgende wes 7 cleopedun
omnis sapientia eorum degluttita est 28. *Et · clamaverunt*

to dryhtne midðy hie werun geswencte 7 of nedðearfnissum
ad Dominum cum tribularentur et de necessitatibus

heara *gefre hie sette yst in weder 7
eorum liberavit eos 29. *Statuit procellam in auram et*

swigedon yðe his 7 blissende werun ðæt swigadon
siluerunt fluctus ejus 30. *et laetati sunt quod siluerunt*

7 utalędde hie in hyðe willan heara 7 of ned-
Et deduxit eos . in portum voluntatis eorum et de neces-

ðearfnissum heara gefreode hie onditien dryht*ne*
sitatibus eorum liberavit eos 31. *Confiteantur Domino*

*mildheortis his 7 wundur his bearnum monna 7
misericordia ejus et mirabilia ejus filiis hominum 32. *Et*

uphebben hine in cirican folces 7 in hehseotle aeldrena
exaltent eum in ecclesia plebis et in cathedra seniorum

hergen hine fordon sette flodas in woesten 7
laudent eum 33. *Quia posuit flumina in desertum et*

utgong wetra in ðurst eorðan westembere in salt-
exitus aquarum in sitim 34. *Terram fructiferam in salsi-*

nisse from hete ineardiendra in hire sette
laginem a malitia inhabitantium in ea 35. *Posuit*

woesten in mere wetres 7 eorðan butan wetre in utgong
desertum in stagnum aquae et terram sine aqua in exitus

wetra 7 gesteaðelade ðer hyngriende 7 gesetton
aquarum 36. *Et collocavit illic esurientes et constituerunt*

cestre eardunge 7 seowun lond 7 plantadon
civitatem habitationis 37. *Et seminaverunt agros et planta-*

wingeardas 7 dydun westem acennisse 7
verunt vineas et fecerunt fructum nativitatis 38. *Et*

bledsade hie 7 gemonigfaldade sind swiðe 7 neat
benedixit eos et multiplicati sunt nimis et jumenta

heara ne sind gewonad fea gewordne sindun 7
eorum non sunt minorata 39. *Pauci facti sunt et*

geswencte sind *fro geswencednisse yfla 7 sara
vexati sunt a tribulatione malorum et dolorum

*ageten is forhogadnis ofer aldermen heara 7 bi-
40. *Effusa est contemptio super principes eorum et sedux-*

sweocun hie in ungefoernum 7 nales in wege 7 gefultumade
erunt eos in invio et non in via 41. *Et adjuvavit*

ðeorfan of weðelnisse 7 sette swe swe scep *heoredas
pauperem de inopia et posuit sic ut oves familias

gesioð ða rehtan 7 blissiað 7 all unrehtwisnis
42. *Videbunt recti et laetabuntur et omnis iniquitas*

fordyt[t]ed muð his hwelc snottur 7 haldeð ðas
oppilavit os suum 43. *Quis sapiens et custodiet haec*

7 ðonne ongiteð mildheortnisse dryhtnes
et tunc intelligit misericordias Domini

107.

gearu heorte min god gearu heorte min ic singu
2. *Paratum cor meum Deus paratum cor meum cantabo*

7 salm ic cweoðu to dryhtne aris wuldur min aris
et psalmum dicam Domino 3. *Exurge gloria mea exurge*

hearpe 7 citre ic arisu on ærmargen ic ondettu ðe
psalterium et cythara exurgam diluculo 4. *Confitebor tibi*

on folcum dryhten salm ic cweoðu to ðe betwih ðeode
in populis Domine psalmum dicam tibi inter gentes

forðon gemiclad is oð heofenas mildheortnis ðin
5. *Quoniam magnificata est usque ad caelos misericordia tua*

7 oð wolcenu soðfestnis ðin hefe up ofer heofenas
et usque ad nubes veritas tua 6. *Exaltare super caelos*

god 7 ofer alle corðan mid wuldre ðine ðæt
Deus et super omnem terram gloria tua 7. *ut*

sien gefread ða gecorene ðine halne mec doa mid ða swiðran
liberentur electi tui Salvum me fac dextera

ðinre 7 geher mec god spreocende wes in halgum
tua et exaudi me 8. *Deus locutus est in sancto*

his ic biom geblissad 7 todaelu Sicimam 7 dene
suo laetabor et dividam Sicymam et convallem

getelda ic meotu min is Galaad 7 min is[1]
tabernaculorum metibor 9. *Meus est Galaad et meus est*

Manasses 7 Efrem strengu heafdes mines cyning min
Manasses et Efrem fortitudo capitis mei Juda rex meus

Moab hwer hyhtes mines in Idumeam ic aðennu
10. *Moab olla spei meae in Idumaea extendam calcia-*

gesc[o]e min me underðiodde sind hwelc
mentum meum mihi allophili subditi sunt 11. *Quis*

gelaedeð mec in cestre getrymede oððe hwelc gelaedeð
deducet me · in civitatem munitam aut quis deducet

mec oð in Idumeam ahne ðu god ðu ðe onweg
me usque in Idumaeam 12. *Nonne tu Deus qui reppul-*

adrife[2] usic 7 ut ne gęst god in megnum urum
isti nos et non egredieris Deus in virtutibus nostris

sele us fultum of geswencednisse 7 idelu hęlu monnes
13. *Da nobis auxilium de tribulatione et vana salus hominis*

in gode doen we megen 7 he to nowihte gelaedeð
14. *In Deo faciemus virtutem et ipse ad nihilum deducet*

swencende usic
tribulantes nos

108.

god lof min ne swiga ðu forðon muð ðes synfullan
2. *Deus laudem meam ne tacueris quia os peccatoris*

7 ðes *facnan ofer mec ontyned is spreocende sind
et dolosi super me apertum est 3. *Locuti sunt ad-*

wið me tungan faecenre 7 mid wordum læððu ymb-
versum me lingua dolosa et sermonibus odii circum-

saldun mec 7 oferfuhtun mec bi ungewyrhtum forðon
dederunt me et expugnaverunt me gratis 4. *Pro*

ðæt hie lufeden mec teldun me ic soðlice gebed
eo ut diligerent me detrahebant mihi ego autem orabam

settun wið me yfel fore godum 7 laeððu fore
5. *Posuerunt adversum me mala pro bonis et odium pro*

[1] *twice.* [2] i *over dotted* y.

lufan minre gesete ofer hine ðone synfullan 7
dilectione mea **6.** *Constitue super eum peccatorem et*

deoful stondeð to ðere swiðran his mit te bið doemed
diabolus stet a dextris ejus **7.** *Cum judicatur*

utgaeð geniðerad 7 gebed his sie in synne sie
exeat condemnatus et oratio ejus fiat in peccatum Fiat

eardung his *wostu 7 ne sie se eardie in ðere sien
habitatio ejus deserta et non sit qui habitet in ea **8.** *Fiant*

dægas his fea 7 biscophad his onfoeð oðer sien
dies ejus pauci et episcopatum ejus accipiat alter **9.** *Fiant*

bearn his asteapte 7 wif his widwe onstyrede sien on
filii ejus orfani et uxor ejus vidua **10.** *Commoti amo-*

weg awende bearn his 7 weðlien sien aworpne of
veantur filii ejus et mendicent ejiciantur de habita-

eardingum his smege borggelda alle *spode
tionibus suis **11.** *Scrutetur fenerator omnem substantiam*

his 7 reafien fremðe all gewin his ne sie him
ejus et diripiant alieni omnes labores ejus **12.** *Non sit illi*

fultum ne sie se mildsie feadurleasum his sien
adjutor nec sit qui misereatur pupillis ejus **13.** *Fiant*

bearn his in forwyrd in cneorisse anre sie adilgad
nati ejus in interitum in generatione una deleatur

noma his in gemynd *hwerfeð unrehtwisnis fedra
nomen ejus **14.** *In memoriam redeat iniquitas patrum*

his in gesihðe dryhtnes 7 syn modur his ne sie adilgad
ejus in conspectu Domini et peccatum matris ejus non deleatur

sie wið dryhtne aa 7 forweorðe of eorðan[1]
15. *Fiat contra Dominum semper et dispereat de terra*

gemynd heara forðon nis gemyndig
memoriam eorum* **16. *Pro eo quod non est recordatus*

don mildheortnisse 7 oehtende wes mon
facere misericordiam **17.** *et persecutus est hominem*

ðearfan 7 weðlan 7 inbryrdedne on heortan deaðe salde
pauperem et mendicum et conpunctum corde morti tradidit

7 lufade wergcweodulnisse 7 cymeð him 7 nalde
18. *Et dilexit maledictionem et veniet ei et noluit*

bledsunge 7 bið gelenged from him 7 gegereð hine
benedictionem et prolongabitur ab eo Et induit se

[1] e *er. before* a.

awergednisse swe swe hregle 7 ineode swe swe weter
maledictione sic ut vestimento et intravit sic ut aqua

in ða innerran his 7 swe swe ele in banum his
in interiora ejus et sic ut oleum in ossibus ejus

sie him swe swe hregl ðæt sie oferwrigen 7 swe
19. *Fiat ei sic ut vestimentum quod operietur et sic*

swe gyrdels mid ðy aa sie·bigyrded ðis werc heara
ut zona qua semper praecingitur 20. *Hoc opus eorum*

ða telað me mid dryht*ne* 7 ða ðe spreocað yfel·
qui detrahunt mihi apud Dominum et qui loquuntur mala

wið sawle minre 7 ðu dryht*en* dryht*en* doa
adversus animam meam 21. *Et tu Domine Domine fac*

mid mec mildheortnisse fore noman ðinum forðon wynsum
mecum misericordiam propter nomen tuum quia suavis

is mildheortnis ðin gefrea mec forðon weðla 7
est misericordia tua Libera me 22. *quoniam egenus et*

*ðearf ic eam 7 heorte min gedr[o]efed is in me
pauper ego sum et cor meum conturbatum est in me

swe scua ðonne *onhaeð *wiðlaedde eam 7 ascecen
23. *Sicut umbra cum declinat ablatus sum et excussus*

eam swe swe gershoppe cneow min geuntrumad sind
sum sic ut locusta 24. *Genua mea infirmata sunt*

fore festenne 7 flesc min inwended is fore ele
prae jejunio et caro mea inmutata est propter oleum

7 ic geworden eam edwit him. gesegun mec 7
25. *et ego factus sum opprobrium illis Viderunt me et*

hrisedon heafud heara gefultume mec dryht*en* god
moverunt capita sua 26. *adjuva me Domine Deus*

min halne ·mec doa fore mildheortnisse ðinre ðæt
meus salvum me fac propter misericordiam tuam 27. *Ut*

witen ðætte hond[1] ðin[2] ðeos is 7 ðu dryht*en* ðu dydest
sciant quia manus tua haec est et tu Domine fecisti

hie wergcweoðað him 7 ðu bledsas ða *ariað in
eam 28. *Maledicent illi et tu benedices qui insurgunt in*

mec sien gescende ðeo soðlice din bið geblissad sien
me confundantur servus autem tuus laetabitur 29. *In-*

gegerede ða telað me scome 7 sien oferwrigen swe
duantur qui detrahunt mihi reverentia et operiantur sic

[1] e *er. after* d. [2] e *er. after* n.

swe twitælgade gescendðe his ic ondettu dryhtne
ut deploide confusione sua 30. *Confitebor Domino*

swiðe in muðe minum 7 in midle monigra ic hergu
nimis in ore meo et in medio multorum laudabo

hine forðon ætstod to dere swiðran ðearfan þæt hale
eum 31. *Quia adstitit a dextris pauperis ut salvam*

dyde from oehtendum sawle mine
faceret a persequentibus animam meam

109.

cwið dryhten to dryhtne minum site to *ðe swiðran minre
Dixit Dominus Domino meo Sede a dextris meis

oð ðæt ic sette feond ðine scomul fota ðinra gerd
Donec ponam inimicos tuos scabellum pedum tuorum 2. *Vir-*

megnes ðines utsendeð dryhten of Sione 7 waldes
gam virtutis tuae emittet Dominus ex Sion et dominaveris

in midle feonda ðinra mid ðe fruma in dege
in medio inimicorum tuorum 3. *Tecum principium in die*

megnes ðines in birhtum haligra of innoðe ær
virtutis tuae in splendoribus sanctorum ex utero ante

margensteorran ic cende ðec swor dryhten 7 ne
luciferum genui te 4. *Juravit Dominus et non*

hreowsade hine ðu earð sacerd in ecnisse efter
paenitebit eum Tu es sacerdos in aeternum secundum

endebyrdnisse dryhten to ðere swiðran ðinre
ordinem Melchisedech 5. *Dominus a dextris tuis*

gebrec in dege eorres his cyningas doemeð in
confringit in die irae suae reges 6. *Judicabit in*

cneorissum gefylleð hryras gescænæð heafud monigu in
nationibus implebit ruinas conquassabit capita multa in

eorðan genyhtsumre of burnan in wege dronc fordon
terra copiosa 7. *De torrente in via bibet propterea*

up ahof heafud
exaltabit caput

110.

ic ondettu ðe dryhten in alre heortan minre in gedaehte
1. *Confitebor tibi Domine in toto corde meo in consilio*

rehtwisra 7 gesomnunge micelre werc dryht*nes*
justorum et congregatione 2. *magna opera Domini Ex-*

asoht in alle willan his ondetnis 7 micelnis
quisita in omnes voluntates ejus 3. *Confessio et magnificentia*

*wer his 7 rehtwisnis his wunað in weoruld weorulde
opus ejus et justitia ejus manet in saeculum saeculi

gemynd dyde wundra his mildheort 7 mildsend
4. *Memoriam fecit mirabilium suorum misericors et miserator*

dryht*en* mete salde ondredendu*m* hine gemyndig bið
Dominus 5. *escam dedit timentibus se Memor erit*

in weoruld cyðnisse his megen werca his
in saeculum testamenti sui 6. *virtutem operum suorum*

segeð folce his ðæt he selle him erfe
adnuntiabit populo suo 7. *ut det illis hereditatem*

ðioda *wer honda his soðfestnis 7 dom getreowe
gentium Opera manuum ejus veritas et judicium 8. *fidelia*

all bibodu his getrymed in weoruld weorulde geworden
omnia mandata ejus confirmata in saeculum saeculi facta

in soðfestnisse 7 rehtwisnisse alesnisse sende folce
in veritate et aequitate 9. *Redemptionem misit populo*

his onbead in ecnisse cyðnisse his halge 7
suo mandavit in aeternum testamentum suum sanctum et

egesful noma his fruma snyttru ege dryht*nes*
terribile nomen ejus 10. *Initium sapientiae timor Domini*

ondget god allu*m* dondum hie herenis his wunað[1]
intellectus bonus omnibus facientibus eam Laudatio ejus manet

in weoruld weorulde
in saeculum saeculi

111.

eadig wer se ðe ondredeð dryht*en* in bibodum his
1. *Beatus vir qui timet Dominum in mandatis ejus*

willað swiðe maehtig in eorðan bið sed his
cupiet nimis 2. *Potens in terra erit semen ejus*

cneorisse ðeara rehtra bið bledsad wuldur 7 weolan
generatio rectorum benedicetur 3. *Gloria et divitiae*

in huse his 7 rehtwisnis his wunað in weoruld weorulde
in domo ejus et justitia ejus manet in saeculum saeculi

[1] a *from* u.

upcumen wes in ðeostrum leht ðæm rehtheortum mild-
4. *Exortum est in tenebris lumen rectis corde mise-*

heort 7 mildsend 7 rehtwis dryht*en* wynsum mon
ricors et miserator et justus Dominus 5. *Jucundus homo*

se mildsað 7 geðwærað stihtað word his in dome
qui miseretur et commodat disponet sermones suos in judicio

forðon in ecnisse ne bið onstyred in gemynde
6. *quia in aeternum non commovebitur* 7. *In memoria*

æcre bið se rehtwisa from gehernisse yfelre ne ondredeð
aeterna erit justus ab auditu malo non timebit

gearu[1] is heorte his *gehtan in dryht*ne* getrymed
Paratum est cor ejus sperare in Domino 8. *Confirmatum*

is heorte his ne bið onstyred oð ðet gesieð fiond his
est cor ejus non commovebitur donec videat inimicos suos

tostregd[2] salde ðearfum rehtwisnis his wunað in
9. *Dispersit dedit pauperibus justitia ejus manet in*

weoruld weorulde horn his bið upahefen in wuldre
saeculum saeculi cornu ejus exaltabitur in gloria

se synfulla gesið 7 eorsað mid todu*m* his grymetað 7
10. *Peccator videbit et irascetur dentibus suis, fremet et*

aswindeð lust synfulra forweorðeð
tabescet desiderium peccatorum peribit

112.

hergað cnehtas dryht*en* hergað noman dryht*nes* sie
1. *Laudate pueri Dominum laudate nomen Domini* 2. *Sit*

noma dryht*nes* gebledsad of ðissum nu 7 oð in
nomen Domini benedictum ex hoc nunc et usque in

weoruld from sunnan upcyme oð setgong hergað
saeculum 3. *A solis ortu usque ad occasum laudate*

noman dryht*nes* heh ofer alle ðiode dryht*en* 7
nomen Domini 4. *Excelsus super omnes gentes Dominus et*

ofer heofenas wuldur his hwelc swe swe dryht*en*
super caelos gloria ejus 5. *Quis sicut Dominus*

god ur se in heanissum eardað 7 ða heanan ge-
*Deus noster qui in *altis habitat* 6. *et humilia re-*

[1] u *from* a. [2] e *from* i.

locað in heofene ⁊ in eordan aweccende from eorðan
spicit in caelo et in terra 7. *Suscitans a terra*

weðlan ⁊ of scearne araerende ðearfan ðæt he ge-
inopem et de stercore eregens pauperem 8. *Ut col-*

steaðelie hine mid aldermonnum mid aldermonnu*m* folces
locet eum cum principibus cum principibus populi

his se eardian doeð unbeorende in huse modur
sui 9. *Qui habitare facit sterilem in domo matrem*

bearna blissiende
filiorum laetantem

113.

in utgonge Israela of Ægyptu*m* hus of folce
1. *In exitu Israhel ex Aegypto domus Jacob de populo*

elreordum geworden wes *gehalgun his
barbaro 2. *Facta est Judaea sanctificatio ejus Israhel*

maeht his ricsað in hire sae gesaeh ⁊ fleh
potestas ejus Israhel regnavit in ea 3. *Mare vidit et fugit*

Iordan gecerred wes on bec muntas gefegun
Jordanis conversus est retrorsum 4. *Montes exultaverunt*

swe swe rommas ⁊ hyllas swe swe lombur scepa hwet
ut arietes et colles velut agni ovium 5. *Quid*

is ðe sae to hwon fluge ðu ⁊ ðu Iordan for hwon gecerred
est mare quod fugisti et tu Jordanis quare conversus

earðu on bec muntas for hwon uphofun ge swe swe
es retrorsum 6. *Montes quare exultastis ut*

rommas ⁊ hyllas swe swe lomberu scepa from onsiene
arietes et colles velut agni ovium 7. *A facie*

dryht*nes* onstyred is eorðe from onsiene godes
Domini commota est terra a facie Dei Jacob

se gecerreð steaðulfestne stan in mere wetres ⁊
8. *Qui convertit solidam petram in stagnum aquae et*

clif in wellan wetra nalas us dryht*en* nales us
rupem in fontes aquarum 1. *Non nobis Domine non nobis*

ah noman ðinu*m* sele wuldur *ofur mildheortnisse
sed nomini tuo da gloriam 2. *Super misericordiam*

ðine ⁊ soðfestnisse ðine ne hwonne cweðen ðiode hwer
tuam et veritatem tuam ne quando dicant gentes Ubi

is god heara god soðlice ur in heofene upp
est Deus eorum 3. *Deus autem noster in caelo sursum*

in heofene 7 in eorðan all swe hwet walde dyde
in caelo et in terra omnia quaecumque voluit fecit

hergas ðeoda seolfur 7 gold werc honda
4. *Simulacra gentium argentum et aurum opera manuum*

monna muð habbað 7 ne spreocað egan habbað
hominum 5. *Os habent et non loquentur oculos habent*

7 ne gesiað earan habbað 7 ne geherað nesðyrel
et non videbunt 6. *Aures habent et non audient nares*

habbað 7 ne weorðiað honda habbað 7 ne
habent et non odorabunt 7. *Manus habent et non*

grapiað fo[e]t habbað 7 ne gongað ne cleopiað
palpabunt pedes habent et non ambulabunt Non clamabunt

in hreacan his ne soðlice is gast in muðe heara
in gutture suo neque enim est spiritus in ore ipsorum

gelice him sien ða doð ða 7 alle ða getreowað
8. *Similes illis fiant qui faciunt ea et omnes qui confidunt*

in ðæm hus gehyhte in dryhtne fultum
in eis 9. *Domus Israhel speravit in Domino adjutor*

heara 7 gescildend[1] heara is hus gehyhte
eorum et protector eorum est 10. *Domus Aaron speravit*

in dryht*ne* fultum heara 7 gescildend[2] heara is ða
in Domino adjutor eorum et protector eorum est 11. *Qui*

ondredað dryht*en* gehyhtað in dryht*ne* fultum heara 7
timent Dominum sperent in Domino adjutor eorum et

gescildend heara is dryht*en* gemyndig wes ur 7
protector eorum est 12. *Dominus memor fuit nostri et*

bledsade usic bledsade hus bledsade hus
benedixit nobis benedixit domum Israhel benedixit domum

Aarones bledsade alle ondredende hine dryht*en* lytle
Aaron 13. *Benedixit omnes timentes se Dominum pusillos*

mid marum togeece *ryht*en* ofer eowic ofer eowic
cum majoribus 14. *Adiciat Dominus super vos super vos*

7 ofer bearn eowre gebledsade ge from dryht*ne* se
et super filios vestros 15. *Benedicti vos a Domino qui*

dyde heofen 7 eordan heofen heofenes dryht*ne* eorðan
fecit caelum et terram 16. *caelum caeli Domino terram*

soðlice salde bearnum monna nales deade hergað
autem dedit filiis hominum 17. *Non mortui laudabunt*

[1] gescilde : nd. [2] *first* d *from* b.

ðec dryhten ne alle ða astigað in helle ah
te Domine neque omnes qui discendunt in infernum 18. *Sed*

we ða ðe lifgað we bledsiað dryhten of ðissum nu ⁊
nos qui vivimus benedicimus Dominum ex hoc nunc et

oð in weoruld
usque in saeculum

114.

ic lufede forðon geherde dryhten stefne gebedes mines
1. *Dilexi quoniam exaudivit Dominus vocem orationis meae*

forðon onhaelde eare his me ⁊ in degum minum
2. *Quia inclinavit aurem suam mihi et in diebus meis*

ic gecegu hine ymbsaldun mec sar *deðes ⁊
invocabo eum 3. *Circumdederunt me dolores mortis et*

plihtas helle gemoettun mec geswencednisse ⁊ sar
pericula inferni invenerunt me Tribulationem et dolorem

ic gemoette ⁊ noman dryhtnes ic gecegu georstu dryhten
inveni 4. *et nomen Domini invocabo O Domine*

gefrea sawle mine mildheort dryhten ⁊ rehtwis ⁊
libera animam meam 5. *misericors Dominus et justus et*

god ur mildsað haldende cild dryhten
Deus noster miserebitur 6. *Custodiens parvulos Dominus*

geeaðmodad ic eam ⁊ gefreode mec gecer sawle
humiliatus sum et liberavit me 7. *Convertere anima*

mine in reste dine forðon dryhten wel dyde me
mea in requiem tuam quia Dominus benefecit mihi

forðon *genered sawle mine of deaðe egan min from
8. *Quia eripuit animam meam de morte oculos meos a*

tearum foet mine from slide ic liciu dryhtne in
lacrimis pedes meos a labsu 9. *Placebo Domino in*

londe lifgendra
regione vivorum

115.

ic gelefde forðon ðæt spreocende ic eam ic soðlice
10. *Credidi propter quod locutus sum ego autem*

geeaðmodad ic eam swiðe ic cweð in onweggewite
humiliatus sum nimis 11. *Ego dixi in excessu*

modes mines ylc mon leas hwet sellu ic
mentis meae omnis homo mendax 12. *Quid retribuam*

dryht*ne* fore allum ðа de he salde me calic
Domino pro omnibus quae retribuit mihi **13.** *Calicem*

haelu ic onfou 7 noman dryht*nes* ic gecegu deor-
salutaris accipiam et nomen Domini invocabo **15.** *Prae-*

wyrðe in gesihðe dryht*nes* deað haligra his georstu
tiosa in conspectu Domini mors sanctorum ejus **16.** *O*

dryht*en* ic ðiow ðin ic ðiow ðin 7 sunu menenes
Domine ego servus tuus ego servus tuus et filius ancillae

ðines ðu toslite bende mine ðe ic onsecgu *onsednisse
tuae Disrupisti vincula mea **17.** *tibi sacrificabo hostiam*

lofes gehat min dryht*ne* ic geldu in ceafur-
laudis **18.** *Vota mea Domino reddam* **19.** *in atriis*

tunum huses dryht*nes* in gesihðe alles folces his in
domus Domini in conspectu omnis populi ejus in

midle ðin
medio tui Hierusalem

116.

hergað dryht*en* alle ðiode 7 efenhergad hine alle
1. *Laudate Dominum omnes gentes et conlaudate eum omnes*

folc forðon getrymed is ofer usic mildheortnis his
populi **2.** *Quoniam confirmata est super nos misericordia ejus*

7 soðfestnis dryht*nes* wunað in ecnisse
et veritas Domini manet in aeternum

117.

ondettað dryht*ne* forðon god forðon in weoruld
1. *Confitemini Domino quoniam bonus quoniam in saeculum*

mildheortnis his cweðe nu ðætte god
misericordia ejus **2.** *Dicat nunc Israhel quoniam bonus*

forðon in weorulde mildheortnis his cweðe *ne
quoniam in saeculum misericordia ejus **3.** *Dicat nunc*

hus Arones forðon god forðon in weoruld mild-
domus Aaron quoniam bonus quoniam in saeculum mise-

heortnis his cweðen nu alle ða ðe ondredað dryht*en*
ricordia ejus **4.** *Dicant nunc omnes qui timent Dominum*

ðette god daette in weoruld mildheortnis his in
quoniam bonus quoniam in saeculum misericordia ejus **5.** *In*

geswi[n]cc *in gecede dryht*en* 7 he geherde mec in
tribulatione invocavi Dominum et exaudivit me in

braedu dryht*en* me fultum is ne ondredu ic hwet
latitudinem 6. *Dominus mihi adjutor est non timebo quid*

doe me mon dryht*en* me fultu*m* is 7 ic
faciat mihi homo 7. *Dominus mihi adjutor est et ego*

gesio fiond mine god is getreowan in dryht*ne*
videbo inimicos meos 8. *Bonum est confidere in Domino*

ðon getreowan in mon god is gehyhtan in
quam confidere in hominem 9. *Bonum est sperare in*

dryht*ne* ðon gehyhtan in aldermonnum alle ðeode
Domino quam sperare in principibus 10. *Omnes gentes*

ymbsaldon mec 7 in noman dryht*nes* wreocende ic eam
circumdederunt me et in nomine Domini ultus sum

hie ymbsellende ymbsaldon mec 7 in noman
eos 11. *Circumdantes circumdederunt me et in nomine*

dryht*nes* wreocende ic eam hie ymbsaldun mec swe
Domini ultus sum eos 12. *Circumdederunt me sic*

swe bian 7 burnun swe swe fyr in ðornu*m* 7 in noman
ut apes et exarserunt sic ut ignis in spinis et in nomine

dryht*nes* ic wreocu in him neded gehwerfed ic eam
Domini vindicabor in eis 13. *Inpulsus versatus sum*

ðæt ic feolle 7 dryht*en* onfeng mec strengu min
ut caderem et Dominus suscepit me 14. *Fortitudo mea*

7 herenis min dryht*en* 7 geworden is me in haelu
et laudatio mea Dominus et factus est mihi in salutem

*sefn blisse 7 haelu in geteldu*m* rehtwisra sie
15. *Vox laetitiae et salutis in tabernaculis justorum* 16. *Dex-*

swiðre dryht*nes* dyde megen sie swiðre dryht*nes* upahof
tera Domini fecit virtutem dextera Domini exaltavit

mec ne sweltu ic ah lifge 7 seggo werc dryht*nes*
me 17. *Non moriar sed vivam et narrabo opera Domini*

ðregende ðreade mec dryht*en* 7 deaðe ne salde
18. *Castigans castigavit me Dominus et morti non tradidit*

mec ontynað me geatu rehtwisnisse 7 ingong in ða
me 19. *Aperite mihi portas justitiae et ingressus in eas*

ic ondettu dryht*ne* ðis get dryht*nes* *rehtwisse ingað
confitebor Domino 20. *haec porta Domini justi intrabunt*

[1] ðæt ic ondettu ðe dryht*en* forðon ðu geherdes
per eam 21. *Confitebor tibi Domine quoniam exaudisti*

[1] *gloss illegible.*

mec 7 geworden earð me in haelu stan ðone
me et factus es mihi in salutem **22.** *Lapidem quem*

widcurun timbrende ðes geworden is in heafud hwommes
reprobaverunt aedificantes hic factus est caput anguli

from dryht*ne* geworden is[1] 7 is wundurlic in egu*m* uru*m*
23. *a Domino factus est et est mirabilis in oculis nostris*

ðes deg ðone dyde dryht*en* gefen we 7 blissien we
24. *Haec dies quam fecit Dominus exultemus et laetemur*

in ðæm[2] georstu dryht*en* halne mec doa eawla dryht*en*
in ea **25.** *O Domine salvum me fac O Domine*

wel gesundfulla gebledsad se ðe cwom in noman
bene prosperare[3] **26.** *benedictus qui venit in nomine*

dryht*nes* we bledsiað eowic of huse dryht*nes* god
Domini benediximus vos de domo Domini **27.** *Deus*

dryht*en* 7 inlihte us ic gese[t]te ðec deg symbel in
Dominus et inluxit nobis Constitui te diem sollemnem in

gelomlicnissu*m* oð horn wibedes god min
confrequentationibus usque ad cornua altaris **28.** *Deus meus*

ðu earð 7 ic ondetto ðe god min ðu earð 7 ic uphebbu ðe
es tu et confitebor tibi Deus meus es tu et exaltabo te

ic ondetto ðe dryht*en* fordon ðu geherdes mec 7 geworden
Confitebor tibi Domine quoniam exaudisti me et factus

ðu eard me in haelu ondettað dryht*ne* ðætte
es mihi in salutem **29.** *Confitemini Domino quoniam*

god ðætte in weoruld mildheortnis[4] his
bonus quoniam in saeculum misericordia ejus

118.

eadge unwęmme in wege ða de gongað in aee dryht*nes*
1. *Beati inmaculati in via qui ambulant in lege Domini*

eadge ða smegað cyðnisse his in alre heortan soecað
2. *Beati qui scrutantur testimonia ejus in toto corde exquirunt*

hine nales soðlice ða ðe wircað unrehtwisnisse in
eum **3.** *Non enim qui operantur iniquitatem in*

wegum his eodun ðu bibude bibodu ðin
viis ejus ambulaverunt **4.** *Tu mandasti mandata tua*

[1] wes (?) *er. before* is. [2] ð : : : æm, ere *er.* [3] *the* re *in cursive.* [4] mildheortnis : :.

haldan swiðe eala sien gereht weges mine to
custodiri nimis 5. *Utinam dirigantur viae. meae ad*

haldenne rehtwisnisse ðine ðonne ne biom ic ge-
custodiendas justificationes tuas 6. *Tunc non con-*

scended ðonne ic gelociu in alle bibodu ðin ic *ondett
fundar dum respicio in omnia mandata tua 7. *Confi-*

ðe dryhten in gerecenisse heortan in ðon ðet
tebor tibi Domine in directione cordis in eo quod

ic geleornade domas rehtwisnisse ðinre rehtwisnisse
didici judicia justitiae tuae 8. *Justificationes*

ðine ic haldu nales mec forlet a hu lenge swiður in
tuas custodiam non me derelinquas usquequaque 9. *In*

ðon gereceð *ging weg his in haldinge word ðin
quo corrigit juvenior viam suam in custodiendo sermones tuos

in alre heortan minre ic sohte ðec ne adrif ðu mec from
10. *In toto corde meo exquisivi te ne repellas me a*

bibodum ðinum in heortan minre ic ahyd[d]e gespreocu
mandatis tuis 11. *In corde meo abscondi eloquia*

ðin ðæt ic ne syngie ðe gebledsad earð dryhten
tua ut non peccem tibi 12. *Benedictus es Domine*

lær mec rehtwisnisse dine in weolerum minum
doce me justificationes tuas 13. *In labiis meis*

ic forðsegde alle domas muðes ðine in wege
pronuntiavi omnia judicia oris tui 14. *In via testi-*

cyðnissa ðinra gelusdfullad ic eam swe swe in allum
moniorum tuorum delectatus sum sicut in omnibus

weolum in bibodum ðinum mec ic beom[1] bigongen[2]
divitiis 15. *In mandatis tuis me exercebo*

7 sceawiu wegas ðine in ðinum rehtwisnissum
et considerabo vias tuas 16. *In tuis justificationibus*

ic smegu no ofergeoteliu word ðin sele ðiowe
meditabor non obliviscar sermones tuos 17. *Retribue servo*

ðinum ic lifgu 7 ic haldu word ðin onwrih
tuo vivam et custodiam sermones tuos 18. *Revela*

egan min 7 ic sceawiu wundur of ęe ðinre lond-
oculos meos et considerabo mirabilia de lege tua 19. *In-*

leod ic eam in eorðan ne ahyd ðu from me bibodu
cola ego sum in terra non abscondas a me mandata

[1] beom:::, g *first letter er.* [2] vel gerwige *added later.*

ðin gewillade sawul min gewillian rehtwisnisse ðine
tua **20.** *Concupivit anima mea desiderare justificationes tuas*

in alle tid ðu dreades ða *oferhygdan awergde ða
in omni tempore **21.** *Increpasti superbos maledicti qui*

onhaeldað from bibodum ðinum afir from me ędwit
declinant a mandatis tuis **22.** *Aufer a me oppro-*

⁊ forhogadnisse forðon cyðnisse ðine ic sohte
brium et contemptum quia testimonia tua exquisivi

⁊ soðlice setun aldermen ⁊ wið me sprecun
23. *Et enim sederunt principes et adversum me loquebantur*

ðiow soðlice ðin wes bigongen in ðinum rehtwisnissum
servus autem tuus exercebatur in tuis justificationibus

weotudlice ⁊ cyðnisse ðin[1] smeang min is ⁊ frofur
24. *Nam et testimonia tua meditatio mea est et conso-*

min rehtwisnisse ðine sind ætfalh *fyhtu
latio mea justificationes tuae sunt **25.** *Adhesit pavimento*

sawul min geliffeste mec efter *word dinum wegas
anima mea vivifica me secundum verbum tuum **26.** *Vias*

mine ic fordcyðde ⁊ ðu geherdes mec lær mec *rehtwis
meas enuntiavi et exaudisti me doce me justificationes

ðine weg rehtwisnissa ðinra getacna[2] me ⁊
tuas **27.** *Viam justificationum tuarum insinua mihi et*

ic biom bigongen in wundrum dinum hneapade sawul
exercebor in mirabilibus tuis **28.** *Dormitavit anima*

min fore longunge[3] getryme mec in wordum ðinum weg
mea prae tedio confirma me in verbis tuis **29.** *Viam*

unrehtwisnisse awend from me ⁊ of aee ðinre mildsa
iniquitatis amove a me et de lege tua miserere

min weg soðfestnisse ic geceas domas ðine neam ic
mei **30.** *Viam veritatis elegi judicia tua non sum*

ofergeotul ic ætfalh cyðnissum ðinum dryhten nyl mec
oblitus **31.** *Adhesi testimoniis tuis Domine noli me*

gescendan on weg biboda ðinra ic orn ða
confundere **32.** *Viam mandatorum tuorum cucurri cum*

ðu gebręddes heortan mine aee sete me dryhten
dilataris cor meum **33.** *Legem pone mihi Domine*

weg rehtwisnissa ðinra ⁊ ic soecu hie aa sele
viam justificationum tuarum et exquiram eam semper **34.** *Da*

[1] ðin:, e *er. added later.* [2] vel getæc *added later.* [3] vel for æþrote

me ondget 7 ic smegu aee ðine 7 haldu hie
mihi intellectum et scrutabor legem tuam et custodiam illam

in alre heortan minre gelaed mec in stige biboda
in toto corde meo **35.** *Deduc me in semita manda-*

ðinra forðon *ð ic walde onhæld heortan mine
torum tuorum quia ipsam volui **36.** *Inclina cor meum*

in cyðnisse ðine 7 nales in unrehte gitsunge acer
in testimonia tua et non in avaritiam **37.** *Averte*

egan min ðæt hie ne gesen idelnisse in wege ðinum gelif-
oculos meos ne videant vanitatem in via tua vivi-

festa mec gesete ðiowe ðinum gesprec ðin in ege
fica me **38.** *Statue servo tuo eloquium tuum in timore*

ðinum acerf edwit min ðæt resenðe ic eam
tuo **39.** *Amputa opprobrium meum quod suspicatus sum*

domas soðlice dine wynsume *sehð ic gewillade bi-
judicia enim tua jucunda **40.** *Ecce concupivi man-*

bodu ðin in rehtwisnisse ðinre geliffesta mec 7 cyme
data tua in aequitate tua vivifica me **41.** *Et veniat*

ofer mec mildheortnis ðin dryhten haelu ðine efter
super me misericordia tua Domine salutare tuum secundum

gesprece ðinum 7 ic ondsweoriu edwitendum me
eloquium tuum **42.** *Et respondebo exprobrantibus mihi*

word forðon ic gehyhte in wordum ðinum 7 ne
verbum quia speravi in sermonibus tuis **43.** *Et ne*

afir ðu of muðe minum word soðfestnisse a hu lenge swiður
auferas de ore meo verbum veritatis usquequaque

forðon in domum ðinum ic hyhte 7 haldu aee
quia in judiciis tuis speravi **44.** *Et custodiam legem*

ðine aee in aee 7 in weoruld weorulde 7
tuam semper in aeternum et in saeculum saeculi **45.** *Et*

gongu in bręde forðon bibodu ðin ic sohte 7
ambulabam in latitudine quia mandata tua exquisivi **46.** *Et*

sprec of cyðnissum ðinum in gesihðe cyninga 7 ne
loquebar de testimoniis tuis in conspectu regum et non

biom gescended 7 smegu in bibodum ðinum ða
confundebar **47.** *Et meditabor in mandatis tuis quae*

ic lufude swiðe 7 ahof honda mine to bibode
dilexi nimis **48.** *Et levavi manus meas ad mandata*

ðinum ða ic lufude swiðlice 7 biom bigongen in ðinum
tua quae dilexi vehementer et exercebor in tuis

rehtwisnissum gemyne wordes ðines ðiowe ðinum
justificationibus **49.** *Memento verbi tui servo tuo*

in ðon me hyht ðu saldes ðeos mec froefrende
in quo mihi spem dedisti **50.** *Haec me consolata*

wes in eaðmodnisse minre forðon gesprec ðin geliffesta
est in humilitate mea quia eloquium tuum vivificavit

mec ða oferhygdg[1] unrehtlice[2] dydun a hu lenge swiður
me **51.** *Superbi inique agebant usquequaque*

from ææ soðlice ðinre ic ne onhaelde gemyndig ic wes
• *a lege autem tua non declinavi* **52.** *Memor fui*

doma dinra from weorulde dryhten 7 *frofrende ic eam
judiciorum tuorum a saeculo Domine et consolatus sum

asprungnisse modes nom mec fore synfullum forle-
53. *Defectio animi tenuit me prae peccatoribus dere-*

tendum aee ðine singendlic me werun
linquentibus legem tuam **54.** *Cantabiles mihi erant*

rehtwisnisse ðine in stowe londbigonges mines gemyndig
justificationes tuae in loco incolatus mei **55.** *Memor*

ic wes in naeht noman ðines dryhten 7 heold aee
fui in nocte nominis tui Domine et custodivi legem

ðine ðeos me geworden wes forðon rehtwisnisse ðine
tuam **56.** *Haec mihi facta est quia justificationes tuas*

ic sohte dael min dryhten ic cweð haldan aee
exquisivi **57.** *Portio mea Domine dixi custodire legem*

ðine biddende ic eam onsiene ðine in alre heortan
tuam **58.** *Deprecatus sum faciem tuam in toto corde*

minre mildsa min efter gesprece ðinum forðon
meo miserere mei secundum eloquium tuum **59.** *Quia*

ic ðohte wegas ðine 7 bion gecerred foet mine in cyð-
cogitavi vias tuas et converti pedes meos in testi-

nisse ðine gearu[3] ic eam 7 neam gedroefed ðæt
monia tua **60.** *Paratus sum et non sum turbatus ut*

ic haldu bibodu ðin rapas synfulra ymbclyppende
custodiam mandata tua **61.** *Funes peccatorum circumplexi*

werun mec 7 aee ðine neam ic ofergeotul on midde
sunt me et legem tuam non sum oblitus **62.** *Media*

naeht ic aras to *ondetende ðe ofer domas rehtwisnisse
nocte surgebam ad confitendum tibi super judicia justitiae

[1] *last* g *on er.* [2] ða (?) *er. before* unr. [3] r *from unfinished* g (?).

ðinre daelniomend ic eam alra ondredendra ðec 7
tuae 63. *Particeps sum ego omnium timentium te et*

haldendra[1] bibodu ðin mildheortnisse ðinre dryht*en*
custodientium mandata tua 64. *Misericordia tua Domine*

ful is eorðe rehtwisnisse ðine lær mec godnisse
plena est terra justificationes tuas doce me 65. *Bonitatem*

ðu dydes mid ðeowe ðinu*m* dryht*en* eft*er* worde ðinum
fecisti cum servo tuo Domine secundum verbum tuum

godnisse 7 ðeodscipe 7 wisdom lær mec forðon in
66. *Bonitatem et disciplinam et scientiam doce me quia in*

bibodum ðinu*m* ic gelefde ær ðon geeaðmodad ic
mandatis tuis credidi 67. *Priusquam humiliarer ego*

agylte forðon gesprec ðin ic heold god ðu
deliqui propterea eloquium tuum custodivi 68. *Bonus es*

earð dryht*en* 7 in godnisse dinre lær mec rehtwisnisse ðine
tu Domine et in bonitate tua doce me justificationes tuas

gemonigfaldad is ofer mec unrehtwisnis oferhygdigra ic
69. *Multiplicata est super me iniquitas superborum ego*

soðlice in alre heortan minre ic smegu bibodu ðin
autem in toto corde meo scrutabor mandata tua

gerunnen is swe swe milc heorte heara ic soðlice
70. *Coagulatum est sicut lac cor eorum ego vero*

aee ðine smegende eam god me ðæt geeaðmo-
legem tuam meditatus sum 71. *Bonum mihi quod humi-*

dades mec ðæt ic leornade rehtwisnisse ðine god
liasti me ut discerem justificationes tuas 72. *Bonum*

me aee muðes ðines ofer ðusend goldes 7 seolfres
mihi lex oris tui super milia auri et argenti

honda dine dydun mec 7 gehiowadun mec sele me
73. *Manus tuae fecerunt me et plasmaverunt me da mihi*

ondget ðæt ic leornie bibodu ðin ða ðe ondredað
intellectum ut discam mandata tua 74. *Qui timent*

ðec gesiað mec 7 blissiað *forðo in worde ðinu*m*
te videbunt me et laetabuntur quia in verbo tuo

ic *gehte ic oncneow dryht*en* forðon rehtwisnis domas
speravi 75. *Cognovi Domine quia aequitas judicia*

dine 7 in soðfestnisse ðinre *geaðmodades mec sie
tua et in veritate tua humiliasti me 76. *Fiat*

[1] *last* d *from unfinished* n *or* r.

nu mildheortnis ðin ðæt he *frofrie mec efter ge-
nunc misericordia tua ut consoletur me secundum elo-

sprece ðinum ðiowe ðinum cymen me mildse
quium tuum servo tuo 77. *Veniant mihi miserationes*

ðine 7 ic lifge forðon aee ðin smeang min is
tuae et vivam quia lex tua meditatio mea est

sien *gesende ða *oferhydgan forðon unrehtlice unreht-
78. *Confundantur superbi quia injuste iniqui-*

wisnisse dydun in mec ic soðlice biom bigongen in
• *tatem fecerunt in me ego autem exercebor in*

bebodum ðinum sien gecerred to me ða ðe ondredað
mandatis tuis 79. *Convertantur ad me qui timent*

dec 7 ða ðe cunnun cyðnisse ðine sie heorte min
te et qui noverunt testimonia tua 80. *Fiat cor meum*

unwemme in ðinum rehtwisnissum ðæt ic ne sie gescended
inmaculatum in tuis justificationibus ut non confundar

asprong in haelu ðinre sawul min 7 in worde
81. *Defecit in salutare tuo anima mea et in verbo*

ðinum ic gehyhte asprungun egan min in gesprec
tuo speravi 82. *Defecerunt oculi mei in eloquium*

ðin cweoðende hwonne *frofres mec forðon ge-
tuum dicentes Quando consolaveris me 83. *Quia factus*

worden ic eam swe swe cylle in forste rehtwisnisse ðine
sum sic ut uter in pruina justificationes tuas

ne æam ic ofergeotul hu monge sind daegas ðiowes
non sum oblitus 84. *Quot sunt dies servi*

ðines ðonne ðu doest of oehtendum mec dom
tui quando facies de persequentibus me judicium 85. *Nar-*

segdun me ða unrehtan spellunge ah nales swe swe swe
raverunt mihi iniqui[1] *fabulationes sed non ita ut*

aee ðin dryhten all bibodu din soðfestnis ða
lex tua Domine 86. *Omnia mandata tua veritas ini-*

[un]rehtan oehtende werun mec gefultume mec *hwene
qui persecuti sunt me adjuva me 87. *Paulo*

lęssan fornomun mec in eorðan ic soðlice ne for-
minus consummaverunt me in terra ego vero non dere-

leort bibodu ðin efter mildheortnisse ðinre
liqui mandata tua 88. *Secundum misericordiam tuam*

[1] *last* i *on er.*

geliffesta mec ðæt ic halde cyðnisse muðes dines in
vivifica me ut custodiam testamenta oris tui **89.** *In*

ecnisse dryhten ðorhwunad[1] *wordum ðinum 7
aeternum Domine permanet verbum tuum in caelo **90.** *Et*

in weoruld weorulde soðfestnis ðin gesteadelades eorðan
in saeculum saeculi veritas tua Fundasti terram

7 ðorhwunað endebyrdnis ðin ðorhwuniað dægas
et permanet **91.** *ordinatione tua perseverant dies*

forðon al ðiowiað ðe nemne ðæt aee ðin
quoniam omnia serviunt tibi **92.** *Nisi quod lex tua*

smeang min is ðonne woeninga[2] ic forwurde in *eaðmod-
meditatio mea est tunc forsitan perissem in humili-

nise minre in ecnisse ic no ofergeoteliu rehtwisnisse
tate mea **93.** *In aeternum non obliviscar justificationes*

ðine forðon in him geliffestes mec ðin ic eam[3]
tuas quia in ipsis vivificasti me **94.** *Tuus sum*

halne mec doa forðon rehtwisnisse ðine ic sohte
ego salvum me fac quia justificationes tuas exquisivi

mec abiodun synfulle ðæt hie forspilden mec cyðnisse
95. *Me expectaverunt peccatores ut perderent me testimonia*

ðine ic onget alre gefylnisse ic gesaeh ende rum
tua intellexi **96.** *Omni consummatione vidi finem latum*

bibod ðin swiðe hu ic lufade aee ðine
mandatum tuum nimis **97.** *Quomodo dilexi legem tuam*

dryhten alne deg smeang min is ofer feond
Domine tota die meditatio mea est **98.** *Super inimicos*

mine gleawne mec dydes bibode ðinum forðon in ecnisse
meos prudentem me fecisti mandato tuo quia in aeternum

me is ofer alle lærende mec ic onget forðon
mihi est **99.** *Super omnes docentes me intellexi quia*

cyðnisse ðine smeang min is ofer uðweotan ic
testimonia tua meditatio mea est **100.** *Super seniores in-*

onget ðætte bibodu ðin ic sohte from allum wege
tellexi quia mandata tua exquisivi **101.** *Ab omni via*

yflum ic biwerede foet mine ðæt ic halde word ðin
mala prohibui pedes meos ut custodiam verba tua

from domum ðinum ic ne onhaelde forðon ðu ae
102. *A judiciis tuis non declinavi quia tu legem*

[1] wu *from* m. [2] en *from* m. [3] e *from* s.

settes me hu swoete gomum minum gespreocu
posuisti mihi 103. *Quam dulcia faucibus meis eloquia*

ðin ofer hunig 7 biabread muðe minum from bibodum
tua super mel et favum ore meo 104. *A mandatis*

ðinum ic onget forðon on fionge ic hefde alne weg un-
tuis intellexi propterea odio habui omnem viam ini-

rehtwisnisse forðon aee ðu settes me lehtfet[1]
quitatis quia tu legem posuisti mihi 105. *Lucerna*

fotum minum word ðin dryhten 7 leht stigum minum
pedibus meis verbum tuum Domine et lumen semitis meis

ic swor 7 sette haldan domas rehtwisnisse ðire
106. *Juravi et statui custodire judicia justitiae tuae*

geeaðmoddad eam a hu lenge swiður dryhten geliffesta
107. *Humiliatus sum usquequaque Domine vivifica*

mec efter worde ðinum wilsum mudes mines
me secundum verbum tuum 108. *Voluntaria oris mei*

welgelicade doa dryhten 7 domas ðine lær mec
beneplacita fac Domine et judicia tua doce me

sawul min in hondum ðinum aa 7 aee ðine
109. *Anima mea in manibus tuis semper et legem tuam*

ne eam ic ofergeotul setten synfulle gerene me
non sum oblitus 110. *Posuerunt peccatores laqueos mihi*

7 *bodum ðinum ic ne duolede erfewordnisse
et a mandatis tuis non erravi 111. *Hereditate*

ic biget cyðnisse ðine in ecnisse forðon gefea heortan
adquisivi testimonia tua in aeternum quia exultatio cordis

minre sind ic onhaelde heortan mine to donne
mei sunt 112. *Inclinavi cor meum ad faciendas*

rehtwisnisse ðine in ecnisse fore edleane ða
justificationes tuas in aeternum propter retributionem 113. *Ini-*

unrehtwisan on fienge ic hefde 7 aee ðine ic lufude
quos odio habui et legem tuam dilexi

fultum 7 ondfenga min ðu earð 7 in worde ðinum
114. *Adjutor et susceptor meus es tu et in verbo tuo*

ic *gehyte onhaeldað from me awergde 7 ic smegu
speravi 115. *Declinate a me maligni et scrutabor*

bibodu godes mines onfoh
mandata Dei mei 116. *Suscipe me secundum eloquium*

[1] *last* t *on er.*

tuum et vivam et ne confundas me ab expectatione mea
mec 7 hal ic biom 7 ic smegu in ðinum
117. *Adjuva me et salvus ero et meditabor in tuis*
rehtwisnissum aa ðu forhogdes alle stigende
justificationibus semper **118.** *Sprevisti omnes discendentes*[1]
from rehtwisnissum ðinum forðon unreht geðoht heara
a justificationibus tuis quia injusta cogitatio eorum
is oferliorende ic getalde alle synfulle eorðan forðon
est **119.** *Praevaricantes reputavi omnes peccatores terrae ideo*
ic lufude cyðnisse ðine gefestna mid ege ðinum flæsc
dilexi testimonia tua **120.** *Infige timore tuo carnes*
min from domum soðlice ðinum ic ondreord ic dyde
meas a judiciis enim tuis timui **121.** *Feci*
dom 7 rehtwisnisse ne sele mec oehtendum mec
judicium et justitiam ne tradas me persequentibus me
geceos ðeow ðinne in god ðæt ne hæarmcweodelien
122. *Elegi*[2] *servum tuum in bonum ut non calumnientur*
me oferhogan egan min asprungun in haelu ðinre
mihi superbi **123.** *Oculi mei defecerunt in salutari tuo*
7 in *gesp rehtwisnisse ðinre doa mid ðiowe
et in eloquium justitiae tuae **124.** *Fac cum servo*
ðinum efter mildheortnisse ðinre 7 rehtwisnisse ðine
tuo secundum misericordiam tuam et justificationes tuas
lær mec ðiow ðin ic eam sele me ondget
doce me **125.** *Servus tuus sum ego da mihi intellectum*
ðæt ic wite cyðnisse ðine tid to donne dryhten
ut sciam testimonia tua **126.** *Tempus faciendi Domine*
tostenctun unrehtlice aee ðine forðon ic lufade
dissipaverunt iniqui legem tuam **127.** *Ideo dilexi*
bibodu ðin ofer gold 7 gim *forðo to
mandata tua super aurum et topazion **128.** *Propterea ad*
allum bibodum ðinum ic gerehte *alme weg unrehtne
omnia mandata tua dirigebar omnem viam iniquam
on fionge ic hefde wundur cyðnis ðin dryhten
odio habui **129.** *Mirabilia testimonia tua Domine*
forðon scmegende wes ða sawul min birhtnis
ideo scrutata est ea anima mea **130.** *Declaratio*

[1] *first* n *er.* [2] *alt. to* elege.

worda ðinra inlihteð mec 7 ondget seleð cildum
sermonum tuorum inluminat me et intellectum dat parvulis

muð minne ic ontynde 7 togeteh gast forðon bibodu
131. *Os meum aperui et adtraxi spiritum quia mandata*

ðin ic gewillade geloca in mec 7 mildsa min
tua desiderabam **132.** *Aspice in me et miserere mei*

efter dome lufiendra noman ðinne gongas
secundum judicium diligentium nomen tuum **133.** *Gressus*

mine gerece efter gesprece ðinum 7 ne waldeð min
meos dirige secundum eloquium tuum et non dominetur mei

all unrehtwisniss ales mec from hearmum monna
omnis injustitia **134.** *Redime me a calumniis hominum*

ðæt ic halde bibodu ðin onsiene ðine inliht
ut custodiam mandata tua **135.** *Faciem tuam inlumina*

ofer ðiow ðinne 7 lær mec rehtwisnisse ðine ut-
super servum tuum et doce me justificationes tuas **136.** *Ex-*

gong wetra oferleordon egan min forðon ne heoldun
itus aquarum transierunt oculi mei quia non custodierunt

ę ðine rehtwis earð dryhten 7 reht dom
legem tuam **137.** *Justus es Domine et rectum judicium*

ðin ðu onbude rehtwisnisse cyðnisse ðine 7 soð-
tuum **138.** *Mandasti justitiam testimonia tua et veri-*

festnisse ðine swiðe aswindan mec dyde ellen
tatem tuam nimis **139.** *Tabescere me fecit zelus*

huses ðines forðon ofergeotule sind word ðin feond mine
domus tuae quia obliti sunt verba tua inimici mei

fyren gesprec ðin swiðlice 7 ðiow ðin lufade
140. *Ignitum eloquium tuum vehementer et servus tuus dilexit*

ðet iungra ic eam 7 forhogd rehtwisnisse
illud **141.** *Adolescentior ego sum et contemptus justificationes*

ðine ne eam ic ofergeotul rehtwisnis ðin rehtwisnis
tuas non sum oblitus **142.** *Justitia tua justitia*

in ecnisse 7 æe ðin soðfestnis geswencednis 7
in aeternum et lex tua veritas **143.** *Tribulatio et*

nearunis gemo[e]ttun mec bibod soðlice ðin smeang min
angustia invenerunt me mandata autem tua meditatio mea

is rehtwisnis cyðnis din in ecnisse ondget
est **144.** *Aequitas testimonia tua in aeternum intellectum*

sele me 7 ic lifgu ic cleopede in alre heortan
da mihi et vivam **145.** *Clamavi in toto corde*

minre geher mec dryht*en* rehtwisnisse ðine ic soecu
meo exaudi me Domine justificationes tuas requiram

ic cleopude to ðe halne mec doa ðæt ic halde
146. *Clamavi ad te salvum me fac ut custodiam*

bibodu ðin ic forecom[1] in ripunge 7 cleopede 7
mandata tua **147.** *Praeveni in maturitate et clamavi et*

in worde ðinum ic gehyhte forecomun egan min
in verbo tuo speravi **148.** *Praevenerunt oculi mei*

to ðe on ærmargen ðæt ic smege gesprecu ðin stefne
ad te diluculo ut meditarer eloquia tua **149.** *Vocem*

mine geher dryht*en* efter mildheortnisse ðinre 7
meam exaudi Domine secundum misericordiam tuam et

efter dome ðinum geliffesta mec toneolaehton
secundum judicium tuum vivifica me **150.** *Adpropiaverunt*

oehtende mec unrehtlice from ę ðe soðlice ðinre feor
persequentes me iniqui a lege autem tua longe

gewordne sind neh wes ðu dryhten 7 all
facti sunt **151.** *Prope es tu Domine et omnia*

bibodu ðin soðfestnis in fruman ic oncneow of cyð-
mandata tua veritas **152.** *Initio cognovi de testi-*

nissu*m* ðinu*m* forðon in ecnisse ðu gesteaðulades ða
moniis tuis quia in aeternum fundasti ea

geseh eaðmodnisse mine 7 genere mec forðon aee
153. *Vide humilitatem meam et eripe me quia legem*

ðine ne eam ic ofergeotul doem dom minne 7
tuam non sum oblitus **154.** *Judica judicium meum et*

ales mec fore gesprece ðinu*m* geliffesta mec feor
redime me propter eloquium tuum vivifica me **155.** *Longe*

is from ðæm synfullum haelu forðon rehtwisnisse ðine
est a peccatoribus salus quia justificationes tuas

ne sohtun mildse ðine micle swiðe
non exquisierunt **156.** *Miserationes tuae multae nimis*

dryht*en* efter dome ðinum geliffesta mec monge
Domine secundum judicium tuum vivifica me **157.** *Multi*

oehtende mec 7 swencende mec from 'cyðnissum ðinu*m*
persequentes me et tribulantes me a testimoniis tuis

ic ne onhaelde ic gesaeh no haldende were 7
non declinavi **158.** *Vidi non servantes pactum et*

[1] *last* o *from* u (?).

ic aswond forðon gesprec ðin ne heoldun geseh
tabescebam quia eloquia tua non custodierunt **159.** *Vide*

ðætte bibodu ðin ic lufude dryht*en* in ðinre mildheortnisse
quia mandata tua dilexi Domine in tua misericordia

geliffesta mec fruma worda ðinra soðfestnis
vivifica me **160.** *Principium verborum tuorum veritas*

in ecnisse alle domas rehtwisnisse ðinre aldermen
in aeternum omnia judicia justitiae tuae **161.** *Principes*

oehtende werun mec bi ungewyrhtu*m* 7 from wordum
persecuti sunt me gratis et a verbis

ðinu*m* forhtað heorte min ic biom geblissad ic ofer
tuis formidavit cor meum **162.** *Laetabor ego super*

gesprec ðin swe se gemoeteð herereaf micel un-
eloquia tua sicut qui invenit spolia multa **163.** *Ini-*

rehtwisnisse on fionge ic hefde 7 onscuniende ic eam aee
quitatem odio habui et abominatus sum legem

soðlice ðine ic lufade seofen siðum in dege lof
autem tuam dilexi **164.** *Septies in die laudem*

ic segde ðe ofer domas rehtwisnisse ðinre sib micelu
dixi tibi super judicia justitiae tuae **165.** *Pax multa*

lufiendu*m* noman ðinne 7 nis in hi*m* eswic
diligentibus nomen tuum et non est in illis scandalum

ic abad haelu ðine dryhten 7 bibodu ðin
166. *Expectabam salutare tuum Domine et mandata tua*

ic lufude heold sawul min cyðnisse ðine 7
dilexi **167.** *Custodivit anima mea testimonia tua et*

lufude ða swiðlice ic heold bibodu ðin 7 cyðnisse
dilexit ea vehementer **168.** *Servavi mandata tua et testi-*

ðine forðon alle wegas mine in gesihðe ðinre
monia tua quia omnes viae meae in conspectu tuo

*drhten toniolaeceð gebed min in gesihðe ðinre
Domine **169.** *Adpropiet*[1] *oratio mea in conspectu tuo*

dryht*en* efter gesprece ðinu*m* sele me ondget
Domine secundum eloquium tuum da mihi intellectum

ingaeð boen min in gesihðe ðinre dryht*en* efter
170. *Intret postulatio mea in conspectu tuo Domine secundum*

gesprece ðinu*m* genere mec roceteð weolre mine
eloquium tuum eripe me **171.** *Eructabunt labia mea*

[1] et *on er.*

ymen ðon[n]e ðu læres mec rehtwisnisse ðine forð-
hymnum cum docueris me justificationes tuas **172.** *Pro-*
segeð tunge min gespreocu ðin forðon all bibodu ðin
nuntiabit lingua mea eloquia tua quia omnia mandata tua
rehtwisnis sie hond ðin ðæt halne mec doe
aequitas **173.** *Fiat manus tua ut salvum me faciat*
forðon bibodu ðin ic geceas ic gewillade haelu ðine
quia mandata tua elegi **174.** *Concupivi salutare tuum*
dryht*en* 7 aee ðin smeang min is liofað sawul
Domine et lex tua meditatio mea est **175.** *Vivet anima*
min 7 hereð ðec 7 domas ðine gefultumað me
mea et laudabit te et judicia tua adjuvabunt me
ic duolude swe swe scep ðæt forwearð soec ðiow
176. *Erravi sic ut oves quae perierat require servum*
ðinne dryht*en* forðon bibodu ðin neam ic ofergeotul
tuum Domine quia mandata tua non sum oblitus

119.

to dryht*ne* mid ðy geswenced ic cleopude 7 geherde mec
Ad Dominum dum tribularer clamavi et exaudivit me
dryht*en* gefrea sawle mine from weoleru*m* unrehtwisu*m*
2. *Domine libera animam meam a labiis iniquis*
7 tungan faecenre hwet bið sald ðe oððe hwet
et a lingua dolosa **3.** *Quid detur tibi aut quid*
bið toseted ðe from tungan faecenre strelas maehtge
adponatur tibi a lingua dolosa **4.** *Sagittae potentes*
scearpe mid colu*m* tolesendes wæ me ðæt lond-
acutae cum carbonibus desolatoriis **5.** *Heu me quod inco-*
leod min afirred is ic eardade mid ðæm eardiendu*m*
latus meus prolongatus est habitavi cum habitantibus
swiðe londleod wes sawul min mid
Caedar **6.** *multum incola fuit anima mea* **7.** *Cum*
ðissum ða fiodun sibbe ic wes sibsu*m* ða ðe ic sprec
his qui oderunt pacem eram pacificus dum loquebar
to him oferfuhtun mec bi ungewyrhtu*m*
illis inpugnabant me gratis

120.

ic uphof egan min to muntum ðonan cymeð fultum
1. *Levavi oculos meos ad montes unde veniet auxilium*

me fultum min from dryhtne se dyde heofen
mihi 2. *Auxilium meum a Domino qui fecit caelum*

7 eorðan ne seleð in onstyrenisse fot ðinne ne
et terram 3. *Non det in commotione pedem tuum neque*

hneappað se ðe haldeð ðec sehðe ne hneapað ne ne
obdormiet qui custodit te 4. *Ecce non dormitabit neque*

slepeð se ðe haldeð Israela folc dryhten haldeð
obdormiet qui custodit Israhel 5. *Dominus custodit*

ðec ðryhten gescildnis ðin ofer hond ðere swiðran ðinre
te Dominus protectio tua super manum dexterae tuae

ðorh deg sunne ne berneð ðec ne mona ðorh naeht
6. *Per diem sol non uret te neque luna per noctem*

dryhten haldeð ðec from allum yfle gehaldeð sawle
7. *Dominus custodit te ab omni malo custodiat animam*

ðine dryhten dryhten haldeð ingong ðinne 7
tuam Dominus 8. *Dominus custodiat introitum tuum et*

utgong dinne of ðissum nu 7 oð in weoruld
exitum tuum ex hoc nunc et usque in saeculum

121.

geblissad ic eam in ðissum ða cweden sind me in huse
Laetatus sum in his quae dicta sunt mihi In domo

dryhtnes we gað stondende[1] werun foet ure in ceafur-
Domini ibimus 2. *Stantes erant pedes nostri in atriis*

tunum ðinum sie is timbred
tuis Hierusalem 3. *Hierusalem quae aedificatur*

swe swe cester ðere dælniomenis hire in det ilce ðider[2]
ut civitas cujus participatio ejus in id ipsum 4. *Illuc*

soðlice asteogun cyn cyn dryhtnes cyðnis in
enim ascenderunt tribus tribus Domini testimonium in

Israela folce to ondetenne noman ðinum forðon ðer
Israhel ad confitendum nomini tuo. 5. *Quia illic*

[1] on *on er*. [2] ði: yder.

setun seld in dome seld ofer hus Dauiðes
sederunt sedes in judicio sedes super domum David

biddað ða to sibbe sind 7 genyhtsumnis
6. *Rogate quae ad pacem sunt Hierusalem et abundantia*

lufiendum ðec sie sib in megne ðinum 7 genyht-
diligentibus te 7. *Fiat pax in virtute tua et abun-*

sumnis in torrum ðinum fore broðrum minum 7
dantia in turribus tuis 8. *Propter fratres meos et*

nestum minum ic sprec sibbe bi ðe fore huse
proximos meos loquebar pacem de te 9. *Propter domum*

dryhtnes godes mines ic sohte god ðe
Domini Dei mei quaesivi bona tibi

122.

to ðe ic uphof egan min ðu eardas in heofene
1. *Ad te levavi oculos meos qui habitas in caelo*

sehde swe swe egan ðiowa in hondum hlafarda
2. *Ecce sic ut oculi servorum in manibus dominorum*

heara 7 swe swe egan menenes hondum hlafdian
suorum Et sicut oculi ancillae in manibus dominae

hire swe egan ur to dryhtne gode urum oð ðet
suae ita oculi nostri ad Dominum Deum nostrum donec

mildsað us mildsa us dryhten mildsa us
misereatur nobis 3. *Miserere nobis Domine miserere nobis*

forðon swiðe gefylde we sind forhogadnis 7 swiðe
quia multum repleti sumus contemptione 4. *Et multum*

gefylled is sawul ur edwite genyhtsumum 7 for-
repleta est anima nostra opprobrium abundantibus et de-

segenis oferhogum
spectio superbis

123.

nymðe ðæt dryhten wes in us cweðe nu Israel
1. *Nisi quod Dominus erat in nobis dicat nunc Israhel*

nemne forðon dryhten wes in us ðonne arisað
2. *nisi quia Dominus erat in nobis Dum insurgerent*

men in usic woeninga cwice forswelgað usic
homines in nos 3. *forsitan vivos degluttissent nos*

ðonne ersade mod heara wið us woeninga
Dum irasceretur animus eorum adversus nos 4. *forsitan*

swe swe weter forswulgun usic burnan ðorhleorde
velut aqua absorbuissent nos 5. *Torrentem pertransivit*

sawul ur woeninga ðorhleorde sawul ur weter
anima nostra forsitan pertransisset anima nostra aquam

unarefnendlic gebledsad dryht*en* se ne salde usic in
intolerabilem 6. *Benedictus Dominus qui non dedit nos in*

heftned toðum heara sawul ur swe swe spearwa
captione dentibus eorum 7. *Anima nostra sic ut passer*

genered is of girene huntendra giren forðręsted is ⁊
erepta est de laqueo venantium Laqueus contritus est et

we gefreode sind fultum ur[1] in noman
nos liberati sumus 8. *adjutorium nostrum in nomine*

dryht*nes* se dyde heofen ⁊ eorðan
Domini qui fecit caelum et terram

124.

ða getreowað in dryht*ne* swe *se munt Sion ne
Qui confidunt in Domino sicut mons Sion non com-

bið onstyred in ecnisse se eardað in Ierusalem
movebitur in aeternum qui habitat 2. *in Hierusalem*

muntas in ymbhwyrfte his ⁊ dryht*en* in ymbhwyrfte
Montes in circuitu ejus et Dominus in circuitu

fol[c]es his of ðissu*m* nu ⁊ oð in weoruld fordon
populi sui ex hoc nunc et usque in saeculum 3. *Quia*

ne forleteð dryht*en* gerd synfulra ofer hlet
non derelinquit Dominus virgam peccatorum super sortem

rehtwisra ðæt ne aðennen rehtwise to unrehtwisnisse hond
justorum Ut non extendant justi ad iniquitatem manus

*hara wel doa dryht*en* godum ⁊ rehtu*m* on heortan
suas 4. *bene fac Domine bonis et rectis corde*

onhaeldende soðlice to ofergeotulnisse to gelaedeð dryht*en*
5. *Declinantes autem ad obligationem adducet Dominus*

mid ðæm wircendu*m* unrehtwisnisse sib ofer Israel
cum operantibus iniquitatem pax super Israhel

[1] urur.

125.

in forcerringe dryht*en* heftned Sione gewordne we sind
In convertendo Dominus captivitatem Sion facti sumus

swe swe *frofrende ðonne gefylled is mid gefian muð
sic ut consolati 2. *Tunc repletum est gaudio os*

ur 7 tunge ur wynsumnisse ðonne cweoðað betwih
nostrum et lingua nostra exultatione Tunc dicent inter

ðeode miclade dryht*en* don mid him miclade
gentes Magnificavit Dominus facere cum illis 3. *magnificavit*

dryht*en* don mid usic gewordne sind blissiende gecer
Dominus facere nobiscum facti sumus laetantes 4. *Con-*

dryht*en* heftned ure swe swe burnan in suððaele
verte Domine captivitatem nostram sic ut torrens in austro

ða sawað in tearu*m* in gefian hie reopað gongende
5. *Qui seminant in lacrimis in gaudio metent* 6. *euntes*

eodon 7 weopun sendende sed he(ara)[1] cumende soðlice
ibant et flebant mittentes semina sua Venientes autem

cumað in wynsu*m*nisse beorende reopan heara
venient in exultatione portantes manipulos suos

126.

nemðe dryht*en* timbrie hus in idelnisse winnað ða
Nisi Dominus aedificaverit domum in vanum laborant qui

timbriað ða nemðe dryht*en* halde cestre in idelnisse
aedificant eam Nisi Dominus custodierit civitatem in vanum

węciað ða haldað hie in idelnisse is eow ær
vigilant qui custodiunt eam 2. *In vanum est vobis ante*

lehte arisan arisað efter ðon gesittað ða ðe eotað
lucem surgere surgete postquam sederitis qui manducatis

hlaf sares ðonne seleð scyldum his slep sehðe
panem doloris Cum dederit dilictis suis somnum 3. *ecce*

erfewordnis dryht*nes* bearn meorde weste*m* wombe swe swe
hereditas Domini filii mercis fructus ventris 4. *Sicut*

strelas in honda maehtges swe 7 bearn witgena
sagittae in manu potentis ita et filii excussorum

[1] *cut off.*

eadig wer se gefylleð lust his of him ne
5. *Beatus vir qui implebit desiderium suum ex ipsis non*

bið gescended ðonne he spriceð to his feondu*m* in
confundetur dum loquetur inimicis suis in

ðæm gete
porta

127.

eadge alle ða ðe ondredað dryht*en* ða gongað in
Beati omnes qui timent Dominum qui ambulant in

weogu*m* his gewin westma ðinra ðu ites
viis ejus 2. *Labores *fructum tuorum manducabis*

eadig ðu earð 7 wel ðe bið wif ðin swe swe
beatus es et bene tibi erit 3. *Uxor tua sicut*

wintreow genyhtsumiende in sidum huses ðines bearn
vitis abundans in lateribus domus tuae Filii

din swe swe neowe plant eletrea in ymbhwyrfte beodes
tui sicut novella olivarum in circuitu mensae

ðines sehðe swe bið bledsad ylc mon se ondredeð
tuae 4. *Ecce sic benedicitur omnis homo qui timet*

dryht*en* bledsie ðec dryht*en* of Sione[1] 7 ðu gesee
Dominum 5. *Benedicat te Dominus ex Sion et videas*

ða god sind allum degum lifes ðines
quae bona sunt in Hierusalem omnibus diebus vitae tuae

7 gesee bearn bearna ðinra sib · ofer *I*srael
6. *Et videas filios filiorum tuorum pax super Israhel*

128.

oft oferfuhtun mec from guguðe minre cweðe nu
Saepe expugnaverunt me a juventute mea dicat nunc

Israela folc oft oferfuhtun mec from iuguðe minre
Israhel 2. *Saepe expugnaverunt me a juventute mea*

7 soðlice ne maehtun me ofer bec minne tim-
etenim non potuerunt mihi 3. *Super dorsum meum fabri-*

bradun synfulle afirdun unrehtwisnisse heara
caverunt peccatores prolongaverunt iniquitates suas

dryht*en* rehtwis ceorfeð swirban synfulra sien
4. *Dominus justus concidit cervices peccatorum* 5. *con-*

[1] o *made into* e (?).

gescended 7 onscunien alle ða fiodun Sion sien
fundantur et revertantur omnes qui oderunt Sion 6. *Fiant*
swe swe heg timbra ðæt ær ðon sie utaloceñ
sicut faenum aedificiorum quod priusquam evellatur
adrugiað of ðæm ne gefylleð hond his se ripeð
exaruit 7. *De quo non inplebit manum suam qui metit*
ne his sceat se ðe reopan *sonnað 7 ne cwedun
nec sinum suum qui manipulos colligit 8. *Et non dixerunt*
ða bileordun bledsung dryht*nes* ofer eowic we bledsiað
qui praeteribant Benedictio Domini super vos benediximus
eow in noman dryht*nes*
vobis in nomine Domini

129.

of grundum ic cleopude to ðe dryht*en* dryht*en* geher
De profundis clamavi ad te Domine 2. *Domine exaudi*
gebed min sien earan ðin bihaldende in gebed
orationem meam Fiant aures tuae intendentes in orationem
ðeowes ðines gif unrehtwisnisse haldes dryht*en* dryht*en*
servi tui 3. *Si iniquitates observaveris Domine Domine*
hwelc arefneð forðon mid ðec milds is 7 fore
quis sustinebit 4. *Quia apud te propitiatio est et propter*
aee ðinre ic arefnde ðec dryht*en* arefneð sawul min
legem tuam sustinui te Domine Sustenuit anima mea
in worde ðinum gehyhteð sawul min in dryht*ne*
in verbo tuo 5. *Speravit anima mea in Domino*
from gehaelde margentide oð naeht gehyhteð Israel
6. *A custodia matutina usque ad noctem speret Israhel*
in dryhtne forðon mid dryht*en* mildheortnis is 7
in Domino 7. *Quia apud Dominum misericordia est et*
genyhtsum mid hine alesnis 7 he aleseð Israel
copiosa apud eum redemptio 8. *Et ipse redimet Israhel*
of allu*m* unrehtwisnissum his
ex omnibus iniquitatibus ejus

130.

dryht*en* nis up ahefen heorte min ne up ahefen sind
Domine non est exaltatum cor meum neque elati sunt

egan min ne ic eode in miclum ne in wundurlicum
oculi mei Neque ambulavi in magnis neque in mirabilibus

ofer mec gif ne eaðmodlice ic hogade ah up ahof
super me **2.** *Si non humiliter sentiebam sed exaltavi*

sawle mine swe swe awened ofer modur his swe
animam meam Sicut ablactatus super matrem suam ita

geedleanas in sawle mine gehyhteð Israel in dryhtne
retribues in animam meam **3.** *Speret Israhel in Domino*

of ðissum nu 7 oð in weoruld
ex hoc nunc et usque in saeculum

131.

gemyne dryhten Dauides 7 alre monðuernisse
Memento Domine David et omnis mansuetudinis e(jus)[1]

swe swe swor dryhtne gehat geheht gode Iacobes
2. *Sicut juravit Domino votum vovit Deo Jacob*

gif ic inga in geteld huses mines gif ic astigu
3. *Si introiero in tabernaculum domus meae si ascendero*

in bed strene minre gif ic sellu slep egum minum
in lectum stratus mei **4.** *Si dedero somnum oculis meis*

oððe bregum minum hneappunge *oðð reste
aut palpebris meis dormitationem **5.** *aut requiem*

ðunwengum minum oððet ic gemoete stowe dryhtne
temporibus meis Donec inveniam locum Domino taber-

geteld gode Iacobes *seððe we geherdun ða
naculum Deo Jacob **6.** *Ecce audivimus ea in*

gemoettun ða in feldum wuda we ineodun
Eufrata invenimus ea in campis silvae **7.** *Introivimus*

in geteld his weorðadun in stowe ðer stodun foet
in tabernacula ejus adoravimus in loco ubi steterunt pedes

his aris dryhten in reste ðine ðu 7 erc
ejus **8.** *Exsurge Domine in requiem tuam tu et arca*

gehalgunge ðinre sacerdas ðine earun gegered reht-
sanctificationis tuae **9.** *Sacerdotes tui induantur jus-*

wisnisse 7 halge ðine blissiað fore Dauide ðieowe
titia et sancti t[illegible]i laetentur **10.** *Propter David servum*

ðinum ne acer ðu onsiene Cristes ðines swor
tuum non avertas faciem Christi tui **11.** *Juravit*

[1] *cut off.*

dryhten · soðfestnisse 7 ne biwaegde hine of westme
Dominus David veritatem et non frustrabitur eum De fructu

wombe ðinre ic settu ofer seld min gif haldað
ventris tui ponam super sedem meam **12.** *si custodi-*

bearn ðin cyðnisse mine 7 cyðnisse mine ðas
erint filii tui testamentum meum et testimonia mea haec

ða ic læru hie 7 bearn heara oð in weoruld sittað
quae docebo eos Et filii eorum usque in saeculum sedebunt

ofer seld min forðon geceas dryhten Sion ge-
super sedem meam **13.** *Quoniam elegit Dominus Sion pre-*

ceas hie in eardunge him ðeos rest min in
elegit eam in habitationem sibi **14.** *Haec requies mea in*

weoruld weorulde her eardung forðon ic geceas hie
saeculum saeculi hic habitabo quoniam preelegi eam

widwan his bledsiende ic bledsiu ðearfan his ic gereordu
15. *Viduam ejus benedicens benedicam pauperes ejus saturabo*

hlafum biscopas his ic gegerwu mid hælu 7 halge
panibus **16.** *Sacerdotes ejus induam salutare et sancti*

his wynsumnisse wynsumiað ðer ic forðgelaedu horn
ejus exultatione exultabunt **17.** *Illic producam cornu*

Dauides ic gearwade lehtfet Criste minum fiond
David paravi lucernam Christo meo **18.** *Inimicos*

his ic gegerwu scome ofer hine soðlice blóweð *ge-
ejus induam confusione super ipsum autem florebit sanc-

halgun min
tificatio mea

132.

sehðe swiðe god 7 swiðe wynsum eardian broður in
Ecce quam bonum et quam jucundum habitare fratres in

annisse swe swe smiring in heafde ðæt astag in
unum **2.** *Sicut unguentum in capite quod discendit in*

beard beard Aarones ðæt astag in leappan hregles
barbam barbam Aaron Quod discendit in ora vestimenti

his swe swe deaw se astigeð in munt
ejus **3.** *sicut ros Hermon quod discendit in montem*

forðon ðer bibead dryhten bledsunge 7 lif
Sion Quoniam illic mandavit Dominus benedictionem et vitam

oð in weor(uld)[1]
usque in sae(culum)[1]

[1] *cut off.*

133.

sehðe nu bledsiað dryhten alle ðiowas dryhtnes ða
Ecce nunc benedicite Dominum omnes servi Domini Qui

stondað in huse dryhtnes in ceafortunum huses godes
statis in domo Domini in atriis domus Dei

ures in naehtum uphebbað honda eowre in halgum
nostri 2. *In noctibus extollite manus vestras in sancta*

7 bledsiað dryhten bledsie ðec dryhten of Sione
et benedicite Dominum 3. *Benedicat te Dominus ex Sion*

se dyde heofen 7 eordan
qui fecit caelum et terram

134.

hergað noman dryhtnes hergað ðiowas dryhten ða ðe
Laudate nomen Domini laudate servi Dominum 2. *Qui*

stondad[1] in huse dryhtnes in ceafurtunum huses godes ures
statis in domo Domini in atriis domus Dei nostri

hergað dryhten forðon freamsum is dryhten singað
3. *Laudate Dominum quoniam benignus est Dominus psallite*

noman his forðon wynsum is forðon geceas
nomini ejus quoniam suavis est 4. *Quoniam Jacob elegit*

him dryhten in aeht him forðon ic on-
sibi Dominus Israhel in possessionem sibi 5. *Quia ego cog-*

cneow ðæt micel is dryhten 7 god ur fore allum
novi quod magnus est Dominus et Deus noster prae omnibus

godum all swe hwet walde dryhten dyde in
diis 6. *Omnia quaecunque voluit Dominus fecit in*

heofene 7 in eorðan in sae 7 in neolnissum 7
caelo et in terra in mare et in abyssis 7. *Et*

utlaedende wolcen from ðere ytmestan eordan legite in
educens nubes ab extremo terrae fulgura in

regn dyde se forðlaedeð[2] windas of goldhordum his
pluviam fecit Qui producit ventos de thesauris suis

se slog frumbearn Aegypta from men oð
8. *qui percussit primogenita Aegypti ab homine usque ad*

neat sende tacen 7 forebecen in midle ðinum
pecus 9. *Misit signa et prodigia in medio tui*

[1] o *over* a.

[2] d *from* ð.

egypti in Faraon 7 in alle ðiowas his se
Aegypti in Faraonem et in omnes servos ejus 10. *Qui*

slog ðiode monge 7 ofslog cyningas stronge Seon
percussit gentes multas et occidit reges fortis 11. *Seon*

cyning Amorrea 7 Og cyning Basan 7 all ricu
regem Amorreorum et Og regem Basan et omnia regna

Cananea ofslog 7 sal[d]e eorðan heara erfe
Chanaan occidit 12. *Et dedit *terra eorum hereditatem*

erfe Israel folce his dryhten noma ðin
hereditatem Israhel populo suo 13. *Domine nomen tuum*

in ecnisse dryhten gemynd ðin in weoruld weorulde
in aeternum Domine memoriale tuum in saeculum saeculi

forðon doemeð dryhten folc his 7 in ðiowum
14. *Quia judicabit Dominus populum suum et in servis*

his bið froefred hergas ðiada seolfur 7 gold
suis consolabitur 15. *Simulacra gentium argentum et aurum*

werc honda monna muð habbað 7 ne spreocað
opera manuum hominum 16. *Os habent et non loquentur*

egan habbað 7 ne gesieað earan habbað 7 ne
oculos habent et non videbunt 17. *Aures habent et non*

geherað nesðyrel habbað 7 ne stincad honda *habað
audient nares habent et non odorabunt Manus habent

7 ne grapiað foet habbað 7 ne gongað ne
et non palpabunt pedes habent et non ambulabunt Non

cleopiað in hracan heara ne soðlice is gast in mude
clamabunt in gutture suo neque enim est spiritus in ore

heara gelice him sien ða doð ða 7 alle
ipsorum 18. *Similes illis fiant qui faciunt ea et omnes*

ða ðe getreowað in him gehusscipe Israela folces bled-
qui confidunt in eis 19. *Domus Israhel bene-*

siað dryhten gehusscipe Aarones[2] bledsiað dryhten
dicite Dominum domus Aaron benedicite Dominum

gehusscipe Lefes bledsiað dryhten ða ondredað dryhten
20. *domus Levi benedicite Dominum Qui timetis Dominum*

bledsiað dryhten gebledsad dryhten of Sione se
benedicite Dominum 21. *benedictus Dominus ex Sion qui*

eardað in Hierusalem
habitat in Hierusalem

[1] o *from unfinished* a?

[2] *second* a *from* u.

135.

ondettað dryhtne ðet he is god dette in weorulde
Confitemini Domino quoniam bonus quoniam in saeculum

mildheortnis his ondettað gode goda dætte in
misericordia ejus 2. *Confitemini Deo deorum quoniam in*

weorulde mildheortnis his ondettað dryht*ne* hlafarda
saeculum misericordia ejus 3. *Confitemini Domino domi-*

dætte in weorulde mildheortnis his se dyde
norum quoniam in saeculum misericordia ejus 4. *Qui fecit*

wundur micelu ana forðon in weorulde[1] mildheortnis
mirabilia magna solus quoniam in saeculum misericordia

his se dyde heofen[2] in ondgete forðon in weorulde
ejus 5. *Qui fecit caelos in intellectu quoniam in saeculum*

mildheortnis his se steaðelade eorðan ofer weter
misericordia ejus 6. *Qui fundavit terram super aquas*

forðon in weorulde mildheortnis his se dyde
quoniam in saeculum misericordia ejus 7. *Qui fecit*

lehtfeatu micelu ana forðon in weoruld mildheortnis
luminaria magna solus quoniam in saeculum misericordia

his sunnan in *mahte deges forðon in weoruld
ejus 8. *Solem in potestatem diei quoniam in saeculum*

mildheortnis his monan 7 steorran in maehte
misericordia ejus 9. *Lunam et stellas in potestatem*

naehte forðon in weoruld mildheortnis his se
noctis quoniam in saeculum misericordia ejus 10. *Qui*

slog ęgipte mid frumbearnu*m* heara forðon in
percussit Aegyptum cum primitivis eorum quoniam in

weoruld mildheortnis his 7 utalædde of midle
saeculum misericordia ejus 11. *Et eduxit Israhel de medio*

his forðon in weoruld mildheortnisse his in honda
ejus quoniam in saeculum misericordia ejus 12. *In manu*

strongre 7 earme heam forðon in weorulde mildheortnis
forti et brachio excelso quoniam in saeculum misericordia

his se **todaelde** ðone readan sae in todælnisse
ejus 13. *Qui divisit Mare Rubrum in devisiones*

[1] ld *from* n. [2] o *from some other letter.*

forðon in weoruld mildheortnis his 7 utalaedde
quoniam in saeculum misericordia ejus **14.** *Et eduxit*

ðorh[1] middel his for*ðon* in weoruld mildheortnis
Israhel per medium ejus quoniam in saeculum misericordia

his 7 aswengde Pharaon 7 weorud his in ðæm
ejus **15.** *Et excussit Pharaonem et exercitum ejus in Mare*

readan sae forðon in weoruld mildheortnis his se
Rubro quoniam in saeculum misericordia ejus **16.** *Qui*

alaedde folc his ðorh *weosten forðon in weoruld
transduxit populum suum per desertum quoniam in saeculum

mildheortnis his se utalaedde weter of stane clifes
misericordia ejus **17.** *Qui eduxit aquam de petra rupis*

forðon in weorulde mild*heortnis* se slog cyningas
quoniam in saeculum Qui percussit reges

micle for*ðon* in weoruld[2] mil*dheortnis* 7 ofslog
magnos quoniam in saeculum **18.** *Et occidit*

cyningas wundurlice forðon in weoruld mildheo*rtnis*
reges mirabiles quoniam in saeculum

Seon cyning Amorrea forðon in weoruld mil*dheortnis*
19. *Seon regem Amorreorum quoniam in saeculum*

7 Og cyning Basan forðon in weoruld mildheortnis
20. *Et Og regem Basan quoniam in saeculum misericordia*

his 7 salde eorðan heara erfewordnisse forðon in
ejus **21.** *Et dedit terram eorum hereditatem quoniam in*

weoruld mildheortnis his erfe Israela ðiowe
saeculum misericordia ejus **22.** *Hereditatem Israhel servo*

his forðon in weorulde mildheortnis his forðon in
suo quoniam in saeculum misericordia ejus **23.** *Quia in*

eaðmodnisse ure gemyndig wes ur dryht*en* forðon in
humilitate nostra memor fuit nostri Dominus quoniam in

weorulde mildheortnis his 7 aleseð usic of honda
saeculum misericordia ejus **24.** *Et redimet nos de manu*

fionda ura forðon in weoruld mildheortnis his
inimicorum nostrorum quoniam in saeculum misericordia ejus

se seleð mete ylcum flęsce forðon in weorulde
25. *Qui dat escam omni carni quoniam in saeculum*

mildheortnis his ondettað gode heofenes forðon
misericordia ejus **26.** *Confitemini Deo caeli quoniam*

[1] h *from some other letter.*

[2] e *from* o.

in weorulde mildheortnis his ondettað dryht*ne* hlafarda
in saeculum misericordia ejus Confitemini Domino dominorum

ðætte in weorulde mildheortnis his
quoniam in saeculum misericordia ejus

136.

ofer flodas Babilones ðer we setun 7 weopun ða ðe
1. *Super flumina Babylonis illic sedimus et flevimus dum*

we werun gemyndge ðin Sion in salum in midle
recordaremur tui Sion 2. *In salicibus in medio*

hire we hengun organan ure forðon ðer frugnun
ejus suspendimus organa nostra 3. *Quia illic interro-*

usic ða gehefte laeddun usic word songa
gaverunt nos qui captivos duxerunt nos verba cantionum

7 ða ðe wiðlaeddun us *hymen singað us of songum
et qui abduxerunt nos Hymnum cantate nobis de canticis

Sione hu singað we song dryht*nes* in eorðan
Sion 4. *quomodo cantavimus canticum Domini, in terra*

fremðre gif ofergeotul ic biom ðin Hierusalem for-
aliena 5. *Si oblitus fuero tui Hierusalem obli-*

giteð mec sie swiðre min ætfileð tunge min gomum
viscatur me dextera mea 6. *Adhereat lingua mea faucibus*

minu*m* gif ic ne gemunu ðin gif ic no foresettu ðin
meis si non meminero tui Si non proposuero tui

*Hierusal in fruman blisse mine gemyne dryht*en*
Hierusalem in principio laetitiae meae 7. *Memento Domine*

bearna Edomes in dege ða cweoðað aidliað
filiorum Edom in die Hierusalem qui dicunt Exinanite

aidliað hu longe oð steadul in hire dohtur
exinanite quo usque ad fundamentum in ea 8. *Filia*

Babylones earm eadig se geedleanað ðe edlean
Babylonis misera beatus. qui retribuit tibi retributionem

ðæt ðu geedleanades us eadig se nimeð 7 gecnyseð
quam tu retribuisti nobis 9. *Beatus qui tenebit et adlidet*

ða lytlan his to stane
parvulos suos ad petram

137.

ic ondettu ðe dryht*en* in alre heortan minre forðon
Confitebor tibi Domine in toto corde meo quoniam

ðu geherdes all word muðes mines 7 in gesihðe
exaudisti omnia verba oris mei et in conspectu

engla ic singu ðe ic weorðiu [7] gebiddu to
angelorum psallam tibi 2. *Adorabo ad*

temple ðæm halgan ðinum 7 ondettu noman ðinu*m*
templum sanctum tuum et confitebor nomini tuo

ofer mildheortnisse ðine 7 soðfestnisse ðine forðon
Super misericordiam tuam et veritatem tuam quoniam

ðu gemiclades ofer usic noman haligne ðinne in
magnificasti super nos nomen sanctum tuum 3. *In*

swe hwelcum dege ic gecegu ðec geher mec ðu gemonig-
quacunque die invocavero te exaudi me multipli-

faldas in sawle minre megen ðin ondetten ðe
cabis in anima mea virtutem tuam 4. *Confiteantur tibi*

dryht*en* alle cyningas eorðan forðon hie geherdun all
Domine omnes reges terre quoniam audierunt omnia

word mudes ðines 7 singen in songum dryht*nes*
verba oris tui 5. *et cantent in canticis Domini*

forðon micel is wuldur dryht*nes* forðon heh
Quoniam magna est gloria Domini 6. *quoniam excelsus*

dryht*en* 7 *eaðmodan gelocað 7 ða hean feorran oncnaweð
Dominus et humilia respicit et alta a longe agnoscit

ðæh ðe ic gonge in midle geswinces ðu geliffestes me[1]
7. *Si ambulavero in medio tribulationis vivificabis me*

7 ofer eorre feonda minra ðu aðenedes hond ðine 7
et super iram inimicorum meorum extendisti manum tuam et

halne mec dyde swiðre ðin dryht*en* geedleanað
salvum me fecit dextera tua 8. **Domine retribuit*

fore me dryht*en* mildheortnis ðin in weoruld werc
pro me Domine misericordia tua in saeculum opera

honda dinra ne forseh du
manuum tuarum ne dispicias

[1] c *cut off* (?).

138.

dryhten gecunnades mec 7 oncnewe mec ðu oncneowe
Domine probasti me et cognovisti me 2. *tu cognovisti*

gesetenisse mine 7 ereste mine ðu ongete
sessionem meam et resurrectionem meam 3. *Intellexisti*

geðohtas mine feorran stige mine 7 gerecenisse
cogitationes meas a longe semitam meam et directionem

mine ðu aspyredes 7 alle wegas mine foresege
meam investigasti 4. *et omnes vias meas praevidisti*

forðon nis facen in tungan minre sehðe ðu dryhten
quia non est dolus in lingua mea 5. *Ecce tu Domine*

oncneowe all ða *nestan 7 ða aldan ðu gehiowades mec
cognovisti omnia novissima et antiqua tu formasti me

7 settes ofer mec hond ðine wundurlic geworden
et posuisti super me manum tuam 6. *Mirabilis facta*

is wisdom ðin[1] of me gestrongad is ne[2] ic meg to
est scientia tua ex me confortata est nec potero ad

him hwider gongu ic from gaste ðinum 7 from
eam 7. *Quo ibo a spiritu tuo et a*

onsiene ðinre hwider fleom ic gif ic astigu in heofen
facie tua quo fugiam 8. *Si ascendero in caelum*

ðu ðer earð gif ic dune stigu in helle ðu bist et gif
tu illic es si discendero in infernum ades 9. *Si*

ic niomu fiðru min ær lehte 7 eardiu in ðęm[3] ut-
sumpsero pinnas meas ante lucem et habitavero in postremo

mestan sæs 7 soðlice ðer hond ðin gelaeded mec
maris 10. *Etenim illuc manus tua deducet me*

7 nimeð mec *swið ðin 7 ic cweð woeninga
et tenebit me dextera tua 11. *Et dixi Forsitan*

on ðeostru bitreodað mec 7 naeht inlihtnis min in
tenebrae conculcabunt me et nox inluminatio mea in

wistum minum forðon ðeostru ne bioð aðeostrade
diliciis meis 12. *Quia tenebrae non obscurabuntur*

from ðe 7 nęht swe swe deg bið inlihted swe ðeostru
abs te et nox sic ut dies inluminabitur Sicut tenebrae

his swe 7 leht his forðon ðu dryhten gesete
ejus ita et lumen ejus 13. *quia tu Domine possedisti*

[1] ð:in. [2] ne:. *[3] *from* ðęre.

eðre mine onfenge mec of innoðe modur minre ic
renes meos suscepisti me de utero matris meae **14.** *Con-*
ondettu ðe dryhten forðon egesfullice *gewundra ðu earð
fitebor tibi Domine quoniam terribiliter magnificatus es
wundur werc ðin 7 sawul min wat swiðe nis
mira opera tua et anima mea novit nimis **15.** *Non est*
gedeglad muð min from ðe ðæt ðu dydes in degulnisse
occultatum os meum abs te quod fecisti in occulto
7 *sped min in ðæm[1] nioðerrum eordan unful-
et substantia mea in inferioribus terrae **16.** *Inper-*
fremednisse mine gesegun egan ðin 7 boec ðinre
fectum meum viderunt oculi tui et in libro tuo
alle earun awriten dægas bioð getrymed 7 nænig in him
omnes scribentur Dies firmabuntur et nemo in eis
me soðlice swiðe gearade sind freond ðine god
17. *Mihi autem nimis honorificati sunt amici tui Deus*
swiðe gestrongad is aldurdomes ḥear(a)[2] ic rimu
nimis confortatus est principatus eorum **18.** *Dinumerabo*
hie 7 ofer sond bioð gemonigfaldade ic aras 7 nu get
eos et super harenam multiplicabuntur resurrexi et adhuc
mid ðec ic eam hweðer· sles ðu god synfulle weoras
tecum sum **19.** *si occidas Deus peccatores Viri*
bloda onhaeldað from me forðon ge cweaðað in
sanguinum declinate a me **20.** *quia dicitis in*
geðohtum eowrum onfoen hie in idelnisse cestre his
cogitationibus vestris accipiant in vanitate civitates suas
ahne ða ðe ðec fiodun god ic fiode hie 7 ofer
21. *Nonne qui te oderunt Deus oderam illos et super*
fiond ðine ic aswond fulfremedre[3] fionge ic fiode hie
inimicos tuos tabescebam **22.** *Perfecto odio oderam illos*
fiond gewordne sind me gecunna mec god 7
inimici facti sunt mihi **23.** *Proba me Deus et*
wite ðu heortan mine frign mec 7 oncnaw stige mine
scito cor meum interroga me et cognosce semitas meas
7 geseh hweðer weg unrehtwisnisse in me is 7 gelaed
24. *Et vide si via iniquitatis in me est et deduc*
mec in wege ecum
me in via aeterna

[1] ðære (?) *er. before* ðæm. [2] *cut off.* [3] fulfre:medre.

139.

genere mec dryhten from men yflum from were un-
2. *Eripe me Domine ab homine malo a viro ini-*
rehtwisum gefria mec ða ðohtun heatas in heortan
quo libera me 3. *Qui cogitaverunt malitias in corde*
alne deg gesettun gefeht scerptun tungan heara
tota die constituebant proelia 4. *Acuerunt linguas suas*
swe swe nedran atur nedrena under weolerum heara
sic ut serpentes venenum aspidum sub labiis eorum
hald mec dryhten of honda synfulles from monnum
5. *Custodi me Domine de manu peccatoris ab hominibus*
unrehtwisum ales mec ða ðohtun gescrencan gongas
iniquis libera me Qui cogitaverunt subplantare gressus
mine ahyddun oferhogan girene me 7 rapas
meos 6. *absconderunt superbi laqueos mihi et funes*
aðenedon in girene fotum minum neh siðfete eswic
extenderunt in laqueo pedibus meis juxta iter scandalum
settun me ic cweð to dryhtne god min ðu earð
posuerunt mihi 7. *Dixi Domino Deus meus es tu*
geher dryhten stefne gebedes mines dryhten dryhten
exaudi Domine vocem orationis meae 8. *Domine Domine*
megen haelu minre ofersceadwa heafud min in dege
virtus salutis meae obumbra caput meum in die
gefehtes ne sele mec luste minum ðæm synfullan
belli 9. *Ne tradas me desiderio meo peccatori*
ðohtun wið me ne forlet ðu mec ne æfre
cogitaverunt adversum me ne derelinquas me ne umquam
sien upahefen heafud ymbhwyrftes heara gewin weolura
exaltentur 10. *Caput circuitus eorum labor labiorum*
heara oferwrið hie fallað ofer hie colu fyres
ipsorum operiet eos 11. *Cadent super eos carbones ignis*
in fyre ðu aweorpes hie in ermðum ne wiðstondað wer
in igne deicies eos in miseriis non subsistent 12. *Vir*
getynge ne bið gereht ofer eorðan wer ðone unrehtan
linguosus non dirigitur super terram virum injustum
yfel niomað in forwyrde ic oncneow forðon doeð
*mala capient in *interitum* 13. *Cognovi quoniam faciet*
dryhten dom weðlena 7 wrece ðearfena ah
Dominus judicium inopum et vindictam pauperum 14. *Verum*

hweðre rehtwise ondettað noman ðinum 7 eardiað
tamen justi confitebuntur nomini tuo et habitabunt
rehte mid ondwlitan ðinum
recti cum vultu tuo

140.

dryhten ic cleopude to de geher mec bihald stefne ge-
Domine clamavi ad te exaudi me intende voci ora-
bedes mines ðonne ic cleopiu to ðe sie geræht gebed
tionis meae dum clamavero ad te 2. *Dirigatur oratio*
min swe inbernisse in gesihde ð(inre)[1] uphefenis honda
mea sicut incensum in conspectu tu(o)[1] *Elevatio manuum*
minra onsegdnis efenlice sete dryhten gehaeld
mearum sacrificium vespertinum 3. *Pone Domine custodiam*
muðe minum 7 duru ymbstondnisse weo[le]rum minum
ori meo et ostium circumstantiae labiis meis
ðæt ðu ne onhaelde heortan mine in word yfel
4. *Ut non declines cor meum in verbum malum*
to acunnenne oncunnisse in synnum mid monnum
ad excusandas excusationes in peccatis Cum hominibus
wircendum unrehtwisnisse 7 ic ne genehlaecu mid gecorenum
operantibus iniquitatem et non conbinabor cum electis
heara ðreað mec rehtwis in mildheortnisse 7
eorum 5. *Corripiet me justus in misericordia et in-*
ðreað mec ele soðlice synfulles ne smireð heafud
crepabit me oleum autem peccatoris non inpinguet caput
min forðon nu get is gebed min in welgelicadum
meum Quoniam adhuc est oratio mea in beneplacitis
heara forswelgende werun gesingalede to stane doeman
eorum 6. *absorpti sunt continuati petrae judices*
heara geheren word min forðon maehtun swe swe
eorum audient verba mea quoniam potuerunt 7. *Sic ut*
faetnes eorðan wes tosliten ofer eorðan tostencte sind
crassitudo terrae erupta est super terram dissipata sunt
ban ur neh helle forðon to ðe dryhten dryhten
ossa nostra secus infernum 8. *Quia ad te Domine Domine*

[1] *cut off.*

egan min in dec ic gehyhte ne afir ðu sawle mine
oculi mei in te speravi non auferas animam meam

gehald mec from girene ða gesettun me 7 from
9. *Custodi me a laqueo quem statuerunt mihi et ab*

espicum wircendum unrehtwisnisse fallað in nette
scandalis operantibus iniquitatem 10. *Cadent in retiaculo*

his synfulle synderlice ic eam oððet ic *leareore
ejus peccatores singulariter sum ego donec transeam

141.

mid stefne minre to dryhtne ic cleopude mid stefne minre to
2. *Voce mea ad Dominum clamavi voce mea ad*

dryhtne biddende ic eam ic ageotu in gesihðe his
Dominum depraecatus sum 3. *Effundam in conspectu ejus*

gebed min geswencednisse mine biforan him ic forðsecgu
orationem meam tribulationem meam ante ipsum pronuntio

in aspringunge in me gast minne 7 ðu oncneowe
4. *In deficiendo in me spiritum meum et tu cognovisti*

stige mine in wege ðissum on ðæm ic ymbgongu
semitas meas In via hac qua ambulabam ab-

*ahydun girene me ic sceawade to ðere swiðran
sconderunt laqueos mihi 5. *considerabam ad dextris*

7 gesaeh 7 ne wes se oncneowe mec forwearð fleam
et videbam et non erat qui agnosceret me Periit fuga

from me 7 ne is se soece sawle mine ic
a me et non est qui requirat animam meam 6. *cla-*

cleopede to ðe dryhten cweð ðu earð hyht min dael
mavi ad te Domine dixi Tu es spes mea portio

min in eorðan lifgendra bihald in gebed min
mea in terra viventium 7. *Intende in orationem meam*

forðon geeaðmodad ic eam swiðe gefrea mec from ðæm
quia humiliatus sum nimis Libera me a per-

oehtendum mec forðon gestrongade sind ofer mec
sequentibus me quoniam confortati sunt super me

gelaed ut of carcerne sawle mine to ondetende noman
8. *Educ de carcere animam meam ad confitendum nomini*

ðinum mec bidað rehtwise oððet ðu geedleanie me
tuo Me expectant justi donec retribuas mihi

142.

dryhten geher gebed min mid earum onfoh halsunge
Domine exaudi orationem meam auribus percipe obsecra-
mine in soðfestnisse ðinre geher mec in ðinre
tionem meam in veritate tua exaudi me in tua
rehtwisnisse 7 ne ga ðu inn in dome mid ðiowe
justitia **2.** *Et non intres in judicio cum servo*
ðinum forðon ne bið[1] gerehtwisad in gesi[h]ðe ðinre
tuo quia non justificabitur in conspectu tuo
oeghwelc lifgende forðon *ohtende wes se feond sawle
omnis vivens **3.** *Quia persecutus est inimicus ani-*
mine *geaðmodade in eordan lif min gesteaðelade
mam meam humiliavit in terra vitam meam Collocavit
mec in degulnissum[2] swe swe deode weorulde 7
me in obscuris sicut mortuos saeculi **4.** *et*
generwed is in me[3] *gas min in me gedroefed is
ancxiatus est in me spiritus meus in me turbatum est
heorte min gemyndig ic wes dæga aldrá 7
cor meum **5.** *Memor fui dierum antiquorum et*
smegende ic eam in allum wercum ðinum 7 in dedum
meditatus sum in omnibus operibus tuis et in factis
honda ðinra ic smegu ic ðenede honda mine to
manuum tuarum meditabor **6.** *Expandi manus meas ad*
ðe sawul min swe swe eorðe butan wetre ðe hreðlice
te anima mea sicut terra sine aqua tibi **7.** *Velociter*
geher mec dryhten asprong gast min ne acer ðu
exaudi me Domine defecit spiritus meus non avertas
onsiene ðine from me 7 ic beom gelic astigendum in
faciem tuam a me et ero similis descendentibus in
seað geherde me doa on marne mildheortnisse ðine[4]
lacum **8.** *Auditam mihi fac mane misericordiam tuam*
forðon in ðec ic gehyhte dryhten cvðne[5] me doa weg
quia in te speravi Domine Notam mihi fac viam
in ðæm ic gonge forðon to ðe dryhten ic up ahof sawle
in qua ambulem quia ad te Domine levavi animam

[1] bið gebið. [2] vel þystrum *added later.* [3] m:me. [4] ð *from* t.
[5] v *from* y.

mine genere mec of feondum minum dryhten to ðe
meam 9. *Eripe me de inimicis meis Domine ad te*

ic gefleh lær mec doan willan ðinne forðon ðu
confugi 10. *doce me facere voluntatem tuam quia tu*

earð god min gast ðin god gelaedeð mec in wege
es Deus meus Spiritus tuus bonus deducet me in via

rehtum fore noman ðinum dryhten ðu geliffestes
recta 11. *propter nomen tuum Domine vivificabis*

mec in rehtwisnisse dinre 7 utalaedes of geswince sawle
me in aequitate tua Et educes de tribulatione animam

mine 7 in mildheortnisse ðinre tostences feond
meam 12. *et in misericordia tua disperdes inimicos*

mine 7 forspildes alle ða ðe swencað sawle mine forðon
meos et perdes omnes qui tribulant animam meam quoniam

ðiow ðin ic eam
servus tuus ego sum

143.

gebledsad dryhten god min se læreð honda mine to
Benedictus Dominus Deus meus qui docet manus meas ad

gefehte 7 fingras mine to gefehte mildheortnis min
proelium et digitos meos ad bellum 2. *Misericordia mea*

7 geberg min ondfenga min 7 *gefrigen min gescildend
et refugium meum susceptor meus et liberator meus Protector

min 7 in him ic gehyhte underðeodende folc under me
meus et in ipso speravi subiciens populos sub me

dryhten hwet is monn ðæt ðu cuðades him oððe sunu
3. *Domine quid est homo quid innotuisti ei aut filius*

monnes forðon getelest hine mon idelnisse gelic
hominis quoniam reputas eum 4. *Homo vanitati similis*

geworden is daegas his swe swe scua bileorað dryhten
factus est dies ejus sicut umbra praetereunt 5. *Domine*

*inhæld heofenas ðine 7 astig gehrin muntas 7 hie
inclina caelos tuos et discende tange montes et fumi-

smicað bliccette bliccetunge ðine 7 tostences hie
gabunt 6. *Corusca coruscationes tuas et dissipabis eos*

onsend strelas ðine 7 gedroefes hie onsend hond
emitte sagittas tuas et conturbabis eos 7. *Emitte manum*

ðine of heanisse genere mec 7 gefrea mec of wetrum
tuam de alto eripe me et libera me de aquis

miclum 7 of honda bearna fremðra ðeara muð
multis et de manu filiorum alienorum 8. *Quorum os*

spreocende is idelnisse 7 sie swiðre *hea swiðre un-
locutum est vanitatem et dextera eorum dextera ini-

rehtwisnisse god song niowne ic singu ðe in hearpan
quitatis 9. *Deus canticum novum cantabo tibi in psalterio*

ten strenga ic singu ðe ðu seles haelu cyningum
decem cordarum psallam tibi 10. *Qui das salutem regibus*

ðu gefreas ðiow ðinne of sweorde awergdum
qui liberas David servum tuum de gladio maligno

genere mec 7 gefrea mec of wetrum miclum of
11. *Eripe me et libera me de aquis multis et de*

honda bearna fremdra ðeara muð spreocende wes idel-
manu filiorum alienorum Quorum os locutum est vani-

nisse 7 swiðre heara swiðre unrehtwisnisse ðeara
tatem et dextera eorum dextera iniquitatis 12. *Quorum*

bearn swe swe niowe plant steaðelunge gesteaðulfestad from
filii sicut novella plantationis stabilita a

guguðe his ðohtur heara geglengde ymbgefretwade swe swe
juventute sua Filiae eorum compositae circumornatae ut

gelicnis temples hordern heara ful recetunge
similitudo templi 13. *Prumtuaria eorum plena eructuantia*

of ðissum in ðæt scep heara beorende genyhtsumiende in
ex hoc in illud Oves eorum fetosae abundantes in

siðfetum heara oxan heara faette nis hryre
itineribus suis 14. *boves eorum crassi Non est ruina*

stanwalles ne ferlet ne cleopung in *worðignum heara
macheriae neque transitus neque clamor in plateis eorum

eadig cwedun folc ðæm ðas *sin eadig folc
15. *Beatum dixerunt populum cui haec sunt beatus populus*

ðes is dryhten god heara
cujus est Dominus Deus eorum

144.

ic uphebbu ðec god cyning min 7 bledsiu noman ðinne
Exaltabo te Deus rex meus et benedicam nomen tuum

in ecnisse 7 in weoruld weorulde ðorh syndrie
in aeternum et in saeculum saeculi 2. *Per singulos*

daegas ic bledsiu ðec 7 hergu noman ðinne in ecnisse
dies benedicam te et laudabo nomen tuum in aeternum

7 in weoruld weorulde micel dryhten 7 hergendlic
et in saeculum saeculi **3.** *Magnus Dominus et laudabilis*

swiðe 7 micelnisse his nis ende cneoris 7
nimis et magnitudinis ejus non est finis **4.** *Generatio et*

cneoris hergað werc din 7 *maht ðine forðsecgað
generatio laudabunt opera tua et potentiam tuam pronuntiabunt

micelnisse megendrymmes ðines 7 halignisse ðine
5. *Magnificentiam majestatis tuae et sanctitatem tuam*

spreocað 7 wundur ðin secgað megen egesfulra
loquentur et mirabilia tua narrabunt **6.** *Virtutem terribili-*

ðinra cweoðað 7 micelnisse ðine secgað
orum tuorum dicent et magnitudinem tuam narrabunt

gemynd genyhtsumnisse wynsumnisse ðinre roccettað 7
7. *Memoriam abundantiae suavitatis tuae eructabunt et*

rehtwisnisse gefiað mildheort 7 mildsiend
justitiam tuam exultabunt **8.** *Misericors et miserator*

dryhten geðyldig 7 swiðe mildheort wynsum dryhten
Dominus patiens et multum misericors **9.** *Suavis Dominus*

allum 7 mildse his ofer all werc his
universis et miserationes ejus super omnia opera ejus

ondettað ðe dryhten all werc ðin 7 halge ðine
10. *Confiteantur tibi Domine omnia opera tua et sancti tui*

bledsiað ðec wuldur rices ðines cweoðað 7 maeht
benedicent te **11.** *Gloriam regni tui dicent et poten-*

ðine spreocað ðæt cuðe doen bearnum monna
tiam tuam loquentur **12.** *Ut notam faciant filiis hominum*

maehte ðine 7 wuldur micelnisse rices ðines rice
potentiam tuam et gloriam magnificentiae regni tui **13.** *Reg-*

ðin dryhten rice alra weorulda 7 waldnis
num tuum Domine regnum omnium saeculorum et dominatio

ðin in alre cneorisse 7 cynne getreowe dryhten in
tua in omni generatione et progenie Fidelis Dominus in

wordum his 7 halig in allum wercum his up-
verbis suis et sanctus in omnibus operibus suis **14.** *Ad-*

hefeð dryhten alle ða ðe hreosað 7 arceeð alle gecnysede
levat Dominus omnes qui ruunt et eregit omnes elisos

egan alra in ðec *gehyht[1] dryhten 7 ðu seles
15. *Oculi omnium in te sperant Domine et tu das*

mete him in tid gelimplice ðu ontynes hond
escam illis in tempore oportuno 16. *Aperis tu manum*

ðine 7 gefylles ylc neat bledsunge rehtwis
tuam et imples omne animal benedictione 17. *Justus*

dryhten in allum wegum his 7 halig in allum
Dominus in omnibus viis suis et sanctus in omnibus

wercum his neh is dryhten allum gecegendum
operibus suis 18. *Prope est Dominus omnibus invocantibus*

hine in soðfestnisse willan ondredendra hine doeð
eum in veritate 19. *voluntatem timentium se faciet*

7 gebeodu heara gehereð 7 hale gedoeð hie haldeð
et orationes eorum exaudiet et salvos faciet eos 20. *Custodit*

dryhten alle *lifiende hine 7 alle synfulle tostenceð
Dominus omnes diligentes se et omnes peccatores disperdit

lof dryhtnes spriceð muð min 7 bledsað ylc
21. *Laudem Domini loquitur os meum et benedicat omnis*

flesc noman haligne his in ecnisse 7 in weoruld
caro nomen sanctum ejus in aeternum et in saeculum

weorulde
saeculi

145.

here sawul min dryhten ic hergu dryhten in life
2. *Lauda anima mea Dominum laudabo Dominum in vita*

minum singu gode minum swe longe swe ic biom nyllað
mea psallam Deo meo quamdiu ero Nolite

getreowan in aldermonnum ne in bearnum monna
confidere in principibus 3. *neque in filiis hominum*

in ðæm ne wes haelu utgaeð gast his 7 eft-
in quibus non est salus 4. *Exiet spiritus ejus et rever-*

cerreð in eorðan his in ðæm dege forweorðað alle
tetur in terram suam in illa die peribunt omnes

geðohtas heara eadig ðes god fultum his
cogitationes eorum 5. *Beatus cujus Deus Jacob adjutor ejus*

hyht his in dryhtne gode his se dyde heofen 7
spes ejus in Domino Deo ipsius 6. *Qui fecit caelum et*

[1] gehyht::::::.

eorðan sae 7 all ða in ðæm sind se haldeð
terram mare et omnia quae in eis sunt 7. *Qui custodit*

soðfestnisse in weoruld doeð dom teonan geðyldgu*m*
veritatem in saeculum facit judicium injuriam patientibus

seleð mete hyngrendu*m* dryht*en* upreceð gecnysede dryht*en*
dat escam esurientibus Dominus eregit elisos Dominus

onleseð gecyspte dryht*en* inlihteð blinde dryht*en*
solvet conpeditos 8. *Dominus inluminat caecos Dominus*

gereceð rehtwise dryht*en* haldeð wręccan feadurleasne
diregit justos 9. *Dominus custodit advenam pupillum*

7 widwan onfoeð 7 weg synfulra abreoteð ricsað
et viduam suscipiet et viam peccatorum exterminabit 10. *Reg-*

dryht*en* in ecnisse god ðin Sion in weoruld
nabit Dominus in aeternum Deus tuus Sion in saeculum

weorulde
saeculi

146.

hergað dryht*en* forðon god is salm gode uru*m*
Laudate Dominum quoniam bonus est psalmus Deo nostro

wynsu*m* sie herenis timbriende dryht*en*
jucunda sit laudatio 2. *Aedificans Hierusalem Dominus*

7 tostencnisse[1] gesomniende se haeleð geðręste
et dispersiones Israhel congregans 3. *Qui sanat contritos*

on heortan 7 awriðeð forðręstnisse heara se rimeð
corde et alligat contritiones eorum 4. *Qui numerat*

mengu steorrena 7 allu*m* him noman ceð
multitudinem stellarum et omnibus eis nomina vocat

micel dryhten ur 7 micel megen his 7 snytre[2]
5. *Magnus Dominus noster et magna virtus ejus et sapientiae*

his nis rim onfonde monðwære dryht*en*
ejus non est numerus 6. *Suscipiens mansuetos Dominus*

geeaðmodað soðlice synfulle oð eorðan onginnað
humiliat autem peccatores usque ad terram 7. *Incipite*

dryht*ne* in ondetnisse singað gode uru*m* in citran
Domino in confessione psallite Deo nostro in cithara

se *oferw[i]rð heofen mid wolcnum 7 gearwað eorðan
8. *Qui operit caelum nubibus et parat terrae*

[1] to:st. [2] syn::: *er. before* snytre.

regn se forðlædeð in muntum heg 7 wyrte ðiow-
pluviam Qui producit in montibus faenum et herbam servi-

domes monna se seleð neatum mete heara 7
tuti hominum 9. *Qui dat jumentis escam ipsorum et*

briddum hrefna gecegendum hine nales in megnum
pullis corvorum invocantibus eum 10. *Non in viribus*

horses willan hafað ne in geteldum weres wel
equi voluntatem habebit neque in tabernaculis viri bene

gelicad is him welgelicad is dryhtne ofer on-
placitum est ei 11. *Beneplacitum est Domino super ti-*

dredende hine 7 in him ða gehyhtað in mildheortnisse
mentes eum et in eis qui sperant in misericordia

his
ejus

147.

here dryhten here god ðinne Sion
12. *Lauda Hierusalem Dominum lauda Deum tuum Sion*

forðon gestrongade scyttels geata ðinra bledsade
13. *Quoniam confortavit seras portarum tuarum benedixit*

bearn ðin in ðec se sette endas ðine sibbe 7
filios tuos in te 14. *Qui posuit fines tuos pacem et*

smeorwe hwætes gereordende ðec se utsendeð gesprec
adipe frumenti satians te 15. *Qui emittit eloquium*

his eorðan hreðlice eorneð word his se seleð
suum terrae velociter currit sermo ejus 16. *Qui dat*

snaw swe swe wulle geswerc swe swe eascan strigdeð
nivem sic ut lanam nebulam velut cinerem spargit

sendeð his swe swe stycce hlafes biforan
17. *Mittit christallum suum sic ut frusta panis ante*

onsiene celes his hwelc wiðstondeð sendeð word
faciem frigoris. ejus quis subsistit 18. *Mittit verbum*

his 7 gemaelteð ða bleow gast his 7 fleowun weter
suum et liquefaciet ea flavit spiritus ejus et fluent aquae

forðseggende word his rehtwisnisse 7 *doma
19. *Pronuntians verbum suum Jacob justitias et judicia*

his ne dyde swe ylcre cneorisse 7 domas
sua Israhel 20. *Non fecit taliter omni nationę et judicia*

his ne *gesweocoðade him
sua non manifestavit ęis

148.

hergað dryht*en* of heofenum hergad hine in heanissu*m*
Laudate Dominum de caelis laudate eum in excelsis

hergað hine alle englas his hergað hine alle
2. *Laudate eum omnes angeli ejus laudate eum omnes*

megen his hergað hine sunne ⁊ mona hergað hine
virtutes ejus 3. *Laudate eum sol et luna laudate eum*

alle steorran ⁊ leht hergað hine heofenas heofena
omnes stellae et lumen 4. *Laudate eum caeli caelorum*

⁊ weter ða ofer heofenas sind hergen noman dryht*nes*
et aquae quae super caelos sunt 5. *laudent nomen Domini*

forðon he cweð ⁊ geworden werun he onbead[1] ⁊ gescepen
Quia ipse dixit et facta sunt ipse mandavit et creata

werun gesette ða in ecnisse ⁊ in weoruld weorulde
sunt 6. *Statuit ea in aeternum et in saeculum saeculi*

bibod sette ⁊ no bileorde hergað dryht*en*
praeceptum posuit et non praeteribit 7. *Laudate Dominum*

of eorðan draecan ⁊ alle niolnisse fyr hegel snaw
de terra dracones et omnes abyssi 8. *Ignis grando nix*

is *gas ysta ða doð word his
glacies spiritus procellarum qui faciunt verbum ejus

muntas ⁊ alle hyllas treo westemberu ⁊ alle ceder-
9. *Montes et omnes colles ligna fructifera et omnes caedri*

beamas wilddeor ⁊ all netenu nedran ⁊ fuglas
10. *Bestiae et universa pecora serpentes et volucres*

gefiðrede cyningas eordan ⁊ alle folc aldermen ⁊
pennatae 11. *Reges terrae et omnes populi principes et*

alle doeman eordan gunge ⁊ *fęmman alde mid
omnes judices terrae 12. *Juvenes et virgines seniores cum*

gingru*m* hergen noman dryht*nes* forðon upahefen
junioribus laudent nomen Domini 13. *Quia exaltatum*

is noma his anes ondetnis his ofer heofen ⁊
est nomen ejus solius 14. *confessio ejus super caelum et*

eordan ⁊ uphefeð horn folces his ymen allu*m* halgu*m*
terram Et exaltabit cornu populi sui Hymnum omnibus sanctis

his bearnum Israel folce toneolaecendum him
ejus filiis Israhel populo adpropianti sibi

[1] be *on some other letters.*

149.

singað dryhtne song neowne herenis his in cirican
Cantate Domino canticum novum laudatio ejus in ecclesia

haligra *blisse Israel in hine se dyde hine
sanctorum 2. *Laetetur Israhel in eo qui fecit ipsum*

7 bearn Sione gefen ofer cyning heara hergen
et filii Sion exultent super regem suum 3. *Laudent*

noman his in ðreate in timpanan 7 hearpan singað
nomen ejus in choro in tympano et psalterio psallant

him forðon welgelicad is dryhtne in folce his
ei 4. *Quia beneplacitum est Domino in populo suo*

7 uphefeð monðuęre in haelu gefiað halge in
et exaltabit mansuetos in salutem 5. *Exultabunt sancti in*

wuldre blissiað in bedcleofum heara wynsumnisse
gloria laetabuntur in cubilibus suis 6. *Exultationes*

godes in gomum heara 7 sweord twiecge in hondum
Dei in faucibus eorum et gladii ancipites in manibus

heara to donne *wrec in cneorissum[1] ðreange
eorum 7. *Ad faciendam vindictam in nationibus increpa-*

in folce to gebindenne cyningas heara in
tiones in populis 8. *Ad alligandos reges eorum in*

fotcospum 7 eðele heara in bendum irnum ðæt
conpedibus et nobiles eorum in vinculis ferreis 9. *Ut*

doen in him dom awritenne wuldur ðis is allum
faciant in eis judicium conscriptum gloria haec est omnibus

halgum his
sanctis ejus

150.

hergað dryhten in halgum his hergað hine in try-
Laudate Dominum in sanctis ejus laudate eum in fir-

menisse megnes his hærgað hine in maehtum
mamento virtutis ejus 2. *Laudate eum in potentatibus*

his hergað hine efter mengu micelnisse his
ejus laudate eum secundum multitudinem magnitudinis ejus

hergað hine in *swoge hornes hergað hine in
3. *Laudate eum in sono tubae laudate eum in*

[1] u *over dotted* e.

hearpan 7 citran hergað hine in timpanan 7 ðreate
psalterio et cithara 4. *Laudate eum in tympano et choro*

hergað hine in strengum 7 organan hergað hine
laudate eum in chordis et organo 5. *Laudate eum*

in cymbalan *bel hleoðriendum hergað hine in cimbalan
in cymbalis bene sonantibus laudate eum in cymbalis

wynsumnisse ylc[1] gast hereð dryhten
jubilationis 6. *omnis spiritus laudet Dominum*

HYMNS.

1.

HIC PSALMUS PROPRIE SCRIBTUS DAVID EXTRA NUMERUM CUM PUGNAVIT CUM GOLIA.

lytel ic wes betwih broður[2] mine 7 *iugra in huse
Pusillus eram inter fratres meos et adolescentior in domo

feadur mines ic foedde scep feadur mines honda mine
patris mei pascebam oves patris mei manus meae

dydun organan fingras mine wyrctun hearpan 7 hwelc
fecerunt organum digiti mei aptaverunt psalterium et quis

segde dryhtne minum he dryhten he allra geherde
adnuntiavit Domino meo ipse Dominus ipse omnium exau-

mec he sende engel his 7 nom mec of scepum
divit me ipse misit angelum suum et tulit me de ovibus

feadur mines 7 smirede mec in mildheartnisse smirenisse
patris mei et unxit me in misericordia unctionis

his broður mine gode 7 micle 7 ne wes welgelicad
suae fratres mei boni et magni et non fuit beneplacitum

in him dryhtne ic uteode ongegn[3] fremðes cynnes men 7
in eis Domino exivi obviam alienigenae et

wergcweodelade mec in hergum he[a]ra ic soðlice ge-
maledixit me in simulacris suis ego autem eva-

brogdnum from him his agnum sweorde ic acearf heafud
ginato ab eo ipsius gladio amputavi caput

his 7 onweg afirde edwit of bearnum Israela
ejus et abstuli obprobrium de filiis Israhel

[1] l *from some other letter.* [2] b : : : : roður. [3] gn *from* m.

2.

CANTICUM ESAIAE PROPHETAE. II. FERIA.

ic ondettu ðe dryht*en* fordon eorre ðu earð me gecerred
Confitebor tibi Domine quoniam iratus es mihi conversus

is hatheortnis ðin 7 *frofrende earð mec sehðe god
est furor tuus et consolatus es mihi Ecce Deus

hęlend min getreowlice ic dom 7 ne ondredu forðon
salvator meus fiducialiter agam et non timebo Quia

strengu min 7 herenis min dryht*en* 7 geworden is
fortitudo mea et laudatio mea Dominus et factus est

me in haelu gehleadað weter in gefian of *wellu
*mihi in salutem *Aurietis aquas in gaudio de fontibus*

haelendes 7 cweoðað in ðæm dege ondettað dryht*ne* 7
salvatoris et dicitis in illa die confitemini Domino et

gecegað noman his *cyðe doð in folcu*m* gemoetinge
invocate nomen ejus Notas facite in populis adinventiones

his gemunað forðon heh is noma his singad
ejus mementote quoniam excelsum est nomen ejus Cantate

dryht*ne* forðon micellice dyde seggað ðis in alre
Domino quoniam magnifice fecit adnuntiate hoc in universa

eorðan gefeh 7 here eardung Sione forðon micel in
terra Exulta et lauda habitatio Sion quia magnus in

midu*m* ðin halig Israel
medio tui sanctus Israhel

3.

CANTICUM EZECHIAE. III. FERIA.

ic cweð in midu*m* daega minra ic fearu to gete
Ego dixi in medio dierum meorum vadam ad portas

helle ic sohte lafe gera minra ic cweð ic ne gesio
inferi Quaesivi residuum annorum meorum dixi non videbo

dryht*en* god in eorðan lifgendra ne gelociu ic mon
Dominum Deum in terra viventium Non aspiciam hominem

mae 7 eardiend gestilde cneoris min wiðlaeded is 7
ultra et habitatorem quievit generatio mea ablata est et

befalden is from me swe swe geteld heorda forcorfen
convoluta est a me quasi tabernaculum pastorum Praecisa

is swe swe fro*m* ðæm weofendan lif min mit te nuget
est velut a texente vita mea dum adhuc

gehefeldad acearf mec of marne oð efen geendas
ordirer · succidit me De mane usque ad vesperam finies

mec from efenne oð margen swe swe lea swe for-
me a vespere usque ad mane quasi leo sic con-

dręste all ban min of marne ot efen
trivit omnia ossa mea De mane usque ad vesperam

geendas mec swe swe brid swalwan swe ic cleopiu
finies me sicut pullus hirundinis sic clamabo

ic smegu swe swe culfre geðynnade sind egan min
meditabor ut columba Adtenuati sunt oculi mei

gelocende in heanis dryht*en* ned ic ðrowiu ondsweora fore
aspicientes in excelso Domine vim patior responde pro

me hwet ic cweðe oððe hwet ondsweorað me ðæt
me quid dicam aut quid respondebit mihi quod

ic *seofa doa ic ðencu all ger min in bitternisse
ipse fecerim Recogitabo omnes annos meos in amaritudine

sawle minre dryht*en* gif swe bið lifd oððe in weoleru*m*
animae meae Domine si sic vivitur aut · in talibus

lif gastes mines geðreas mec 7 geliffestes mec sehðe
vita spiritus mei corripies me et vivificabis me Ecce

in sibbe bitternis min sie bittreste ðu soðlice generedes
in pace amaritudo mea amarissima tu autem eruisti

sawle mine ðæt ic ne forwurde 7 awurpe on bec
animam meam ut non perirem Et projecisti post tergum

ðinne alle synne mine forðon nales hel ondetteð
tuum omnia peccata mea quia non infernus confitebitur

ðe ne deað hereð ðec ne bidað ða ofdune
tibi neque mors laudabit te Non expectabunt qui discen-

steogun in seað soðfestnisse ðine lifgende lifgende he
dunt in lacum veritatem tuam vivens vivens ipse

*onddetteð ðe swe 7 ic to dege feder bearnu*m* cuðe
confitebitur tibi sicut et ego hodie Pater filiis notam

*doð soðfestnisse ðine dryht*en* hale us doa 7 salmas
faciet veritatem tuam Domine salvos nos fac et psalmus

ure we singað allu*m* degum lifes ures in huse
nostros cantabimus cunctis diebus vitae nostrae in domo

dryht*nes*
Domini

4.

CANTICUM ANNAE VIDUAE. IV. FERIA.

gefaeh heorte min in dryht*ne* 7 upahefen is horn
Exultavit cor meum in Domino et exaltatum est cornu

min in gode mine[1] gebraeded is muð min ofer feond
meum in Deo meo Dilatatum est os meum super inimicos

mine forðon geblissad ic eam in haelu dinre nis
meos quia laetata sum in salutari tuo Non est

halig swe swe is dryht*en* ne soðlice is oðer butan
sanctus ut est Dominus neque enim est alius extra

ðe 7 nis strong swe swe god ur nyllað gemonigfaldian
te et non est fortis sicut Deus noster Nolite multiplicare

spreocan ða hean wuldrende gewiten ða aldan of muðe
loqui sublimia gloriantes recedant vetera de ore

eowrum forðon god wisdoma dryht*en* is 7 him earun
vestro Quia Deus scientiarum Dominus est et ipsi prae-

gegearwad geðohtas boga strongra oferswiðed is 7
parantur cogitationes Arcus fortium superatus est et

untrume bigyrde sind strengu gefylde ær fore hlafu*m*
infirmi accincti sunt robore Repleti prius pro panibus

*he bihyrdun 7 ðiowincelu werun gefylde o[ð] ðæt unbeo-
se locaverunt et familici saturati sunt Donec sterelis

rendu cende monge 7 sie monge hefde bearn ge-
peperit plurimos et quae multos habebat filios in-

untrumad wes dryht*en* cwælmeð geliffesteð gelaedeð to
firmata est Dominus mortificat et vivificat deducit ad

helwearum 7 eft alaedeð dryht*en* ðearfan doeð 7 ge-
inferos et reducit Dominus pauperem facit et ditat

weolegað geeaðmodað 7 geheð *awecende of duste
humiliat et sublimat Suscitans de pulvere

weðlan 7 of scearne upræren de ðearfan ðæt he sitte
egenum et de stercore eregens pauperem Ut sedeat

mid aldermonnu*m* 7 sundurseld wuldres nimeð dryht*en*
cum principibus et solium gloriae teneat Domini

soðlice sind heorras eorðan 7 sette ofer hie ymbhwyrft
enim sunt cardinis terrae et posuit super eos orbem

foet haligra his heold 7 arlease in ðeostru*m* ge-
Pedes sanctorum suorum servabit et impii in tenebris con-

[1] *letter cut off?*.

swigiað forðon nales in strengu his bið gestrongad wer
ticiscent Quia non in fortitudine sua roborabitur vir

dryhten forhtiað wiðerbrocan his 7 ofer him in
Dominum formidabunt adversarii ejus et super ipsis in

heofenum hleoðrað dryhten doemed endas eorðan 7 seleð
caelis tonabit Dominus judicabit fines terrae et dabit

cynedom cyninge his 7 geheð horn Cristes his
imperium regi suo et sublimabit cornu Christi sui

5.

CANTICUM EXODII. QUINTA FERIA.

singen we dryhtne wuldurlice soðlice gearad is hors
Cantemus Domino gloriose enim honorificatus est equum

7 onstigend awearp in sae fultum 7 gescildend geworden
et ascensorem projecit in mare adjutor et protector factus

is me in haelu ðes god min 7 ariu hine god
est mihi in salutem Hic Deus meus et honorabo eum Deus

feadur mines 7 ic *uphebu hine dryhten forðræstende
patris mei et exaltabo eum Dominus· conterens

gefeht dryhten noma is him scrid Pharaones 7 weoreda
bella Dominus nomen est ei Currus Pharaonis et exercitum

his awe[a]rp in sae gecorene upstigende ðreo foeðan
ejus projecit in mare Electos ascensores ternos statores

besencte in ðere readan sae widsae oferwrah hie bicwomun
demersit in Rubro Mare Pelago cooperuit eos devenerunt

in grund swe swe stan swiðre ðin dryhten gewuldrad
in profundum tamquam lapis Dextera tua Domine glorificata

is in megne sie swiðre honda· ðine dryhten gebrec feo[n]d
est in virtute dextera manus tua Domine confregit inimicos

7 ðorh mengu megenðrymmes ðines ðu fordręstes
Et per multitudinem majestatis tuae conteruisti ad-

wiðerbrocan ðu sendes eorre ðin 7 et hie swe swe
versarios Misisti iram tuam et comedit eos tamquam

halm 7 ðorh gast eorsunge ðinre todaeled is weter
*stipulam et per spiritum *iraecundiae tuae divisa est aqua*

heardadun swe swe wall weter heardadon yde in midre
Gelaverunt tamquam muros aquae gelaverunt fluctus in medio

sae cweð *feon oehtende ic befoo daellu herereaf
mare Dixit inimicus persequens conpraehendam partibo spolia*

gefyllu sawle mine ic ofslea sweorde minum waldeð
replebo animam meam interficiam gladio meo dominabitur

hond min ðu sendes gast ðinne 7 oferwrah hie sæ[1]
manus mea Misisti spiritum tuum et operuit eos mare

bisenctun swe swe lead in wetre ðæm strengestan hwelc
merserunt tamquam plumbum in aqua validissima Quis

gelic ðe in godum dryhten hwelc gelic ðe wuldurfest
similis tibi in diis Domine quis similis tibi gloriosus

in halgum wundurlic in megenðrymmum donde forebecen
in sanctis mirabilis in majestatibus faciens prodigia

ðu aðenedes ða swiðran ðine 7 forswalg hie eorðe
Extendisti dexteram tuam et devoravit eos terra

steordes mid *rehtwinisse dinre folc ðin ðis ðæt
gubernasti justitia tua populum tuum hunc quem

ðu gefreades ypped earð in *gre ðinum 7 in gereord-
liberasti Exortus es in virtute tua et in refec-

nisse ðere halgan ðinre geherdun ðiode 7 eorre werun
tione sancta tua Audierunt gentes et iratae sunt

sar befengun ineardiende Filisteos ða oefestun
dolores conpraehenderunt inhabitantes Philistim Tunc festina-

ladtowas Edomes 7 aldermen Moab gegrap
verunt duces Edom et principes Mohabitarum adprae-

hie cwaecung aswundun alle ineardiende
hendit eos tremor Tabuerunt omnes inhabitantes Chanaan

gefalle ofer hie ege 7 cwaecung micelnisse earmes ðines
decidat super eos timor et tremor magnitudinis brachii tui

sien swe swe stan oð ðæt leoreð folc ðin dryhten
Fiant tamquam . lapis donec transeat populus tuus Domine

oð ðæt ðonne geondfereð folc ðin ðis ðæt ðu bigete
usque dum pertranseat populus tuus hunc quem adquesisti

ingelaedes plantas hie in munt erfes . ðines
Induces plantas eos in montem hereditatis tuae in

gegearwadum eardunghuse ðinum ðæt gegearwades dryhten
praeparato habitaculo tuo quod praeparasti Domine

halignisse ðine dryhten ðæt gegearwadun honda ðine
Sanctimonium tuum Domine quod praeparaverunt manus tuae

dryhten ðu ricsas in ecnisse 7 in weoruld 7 nuget
Domine qui regnas in aeternum et in saeculum et adhuc

[1] sæ *from* m.

forðon ineode eorud · Faraones[1] mid feoðurtemum 7 up-
Quia introivit equitatus Farao cum quadrigis et as-

stigendum in sae 7 gelaedde ofer hie dryhten weter
censoribus in mare et induxit super eos Dominus aquas

sae bearn soðlice eodun ðorh dryge ðorh
maris Filii autem Israhel ambulaverunt per siccum per

midne[2] sę
medium mare

6.

CANTICUM ABACCU PROFETAE. SEXTA FERIA.

dryhten ic geherde gehernisse ðine 7 ondreord ic sceawade
Domine audivi auditum tuum et timui Consideravi

werc ðin 7 ic forhtade in midle twoega netna cuðas
opera tua et expavi In medio duorum animalium inno-

ðonne toniolaecað ger ðu oncnawes ðonne tocymeð
tesceris Dum adpropiaverint anni cognosceris Dum advenerit

tid odeawes in ðon ðonne gedroefed bið sawul min
tempu sostenderis in eo dum conturbata fuerit anima mea

in eorre mildheortnisse gemyndig[3] ðu bist god from Libano
in ira misericordiae memor eris Deus a Libano

cymeð 7 halig of munte scedehtum 7 ðiccum oferwrah
veniet et sanctus de monte umbroso et condenso Operuit

heofenas megenðrym his 7 lofe his ful is eorðe
caelos majestas ejus et laudi ejus plena est terra

birhtu his swe leht bið hornas sind in hondum
Splendor ejus sicut lumen erit cornua sunt in manibus

his ðer getrymed is megen wuldres his 7 sette
ejus ibi confirmata est virtus gloriae ejus et posuit

birhtu trume strengu his biforan onsiene his gæð
claritatem firmam fortitudini suae Ante faciem ejus ibit

word[4] 7 utgaeð in feldum foet his stodun 7 onstyred
verbum et exibit in campis pedes ejus steterunt et mota

wes eorðe gelocade 7 tofleowun ðeode tobrocene sind
est terra Aspexit et defluxerunt gentes confracti sunt

muntas swiðlice 7 tofleowun hyllas ecelice siðfetas
montes vehementer et defluxerunt colles aeternales itenera

ecnisse his fore gewinnum weres geteld Sigel-
aeternitatis ejus prae laboribus viri Tabernacula Aethi-

[1] *second* a *from* o. [2] ne *on* er. [3] d *from* t. [4] d *from* ð.

hearwena forhtiað geteld eorðan ah in
opum expavescent tabernacula terrae Madian Numquid in

flodum ðines earres dryhten oððe in flodum hatheortnis
fluminibus irae tuae Domine aut in fluminibus furor

ðin oððe in sae onræs ðin forðon astigende astiges
tuus aut in mare impetus tuus Quoniam ascendens ascendes

ofer hors ðin 7 eored ðin haelu ðennende ðu aðenes
super equos tuos et equitatus tuus sanitas Tendens extendes

bogan ðinne ofer cyneðrym cweð dryhten mid flodum
arcum tuum super sceptra dicit Dominus Fluminibus

bið tosliten eorðe geseað ðec 7 sargiað folc stregdende
scinditur terra videbunt te et dolebunt populi Aspargens

weter in siðfetum his salde niolnis stefne his from
aquas in itineribus suis dedit abyssus vocem suam ab

heanisse scinhiowes his upahefen is sunne 7 mona stod
altitudine fantasiae suae Elevatus est sol et luna stetit

in endebyrdnisse his in lehte scotunge ðine gað in
in ordine suo In lumine jacula tua ibunt in

birhtu legite wepna ðinra in neoweste ðinre
splendore fulgoris armorum tuorum In comminatione tua

gewonas eorðan 7 in *hatheortniss ðinre teles ðiode
minorabis terram et in furore tuo detrahes gentes

ðu gestode in haelu folces ðines ðæt hale gedoe cristas
Existi in salutem populi tui ut salvos facias christos

ðine sendes in heafudu unrehtra deað ðu awaehtes bende
tuos Misisti in capita iniquorum mortem excitasti vincula

oð swirban forcurfe in afremðunge heafud maehtigra
usque ad cervices Praecidisti in alienatione capita potentium

bið onstyred in ðon ðiode ontynað muðas heara swe
movebuntur in eâ gentes Adaperient ora sua sicut

ðearfa eotende in degulnisse sendes in sae hors ðin
pauper edens in occulto Misisti in mare aequos tuos

gedroefende weter micelu heold 7 forhtade womb min
turbantes aquas multas Custodivit et expavit venter meus

from stefne gebedes *beolera minra 7 ineode cwaecung
a voce orationis labiorum meorum et introivit tremor

in ban min 7 under me gedroefed is megen min
in ossa mea et subtus me turbata est virtus mea

gerestu in dege geswencednisse minre ðæt ic astige to
Requiescam in die tribulationis meae ut ascendam ad

folce leornisse minre forðon fictreo no tobringeð
populum transmigrationis (m)eae Quoniam ficus non adferet

westem 7 ne bið cneoris in wingeardum legað werc
fructum et non erit generatio in vineis Mentientur opus

eletres 7 feldas ne doð mettas asprungun from mete
olivae et campi non facient escas Defecerunt ab esca

scep 7 ne bioð in binne oexen[1] ic soðlice in dryhtne
oves et non erunt in praesepio boves Ego autem in Domino

wuldriu gefio in gode haelende minum dryhten god
gloriebor gaudebo in Deo Ihesu meo Domine Deus

megen min gesete foet mine in geendunge 7 ofer
virtus mea constitue pedes meos in consummatione et super

ða hean geseteð mec ðæt ic oferswiðe in birhtu his
excelsa statuit me ut vincam in claritate ipsius

7.

CANTICUM DE VIT.

bihald heofen 7 spreocu 7 gehere eorðe word of muðe
Adtende caelum et loquar et audiat terra verba ex ore

minum sie abiden swe *sw regn gesprec min 7 astigen
meo Exspectetur sicut pluvia eloquium meum et de-

swe swe deaw word min swe swe scur ofer
scendant sicut ros verba mea Sicut imber super

*gred 7 swe swe snaw ofer heg forðon noma dryhtnes
gramen et sicut nix super faenum quando nomen Domini

ic gecegu sellað[2] micelnisse gode urum god soðe werc
invocabo Date magnitudinem Deo nostro Deus vera opera

his 7 alle wegas his domas god getreowe 7 nis
ejus et omnes viae ejus judicia Deus fidelis et non est

unrehtwisnis in him rehtwis 7 halig dryhten syngadun
iniquitas in eo justus et sanctus Dominus Peccaverunt

nales him bearn unwemme cneoris ðweoru 7 forcerredu
non ei filii inmaculati natio prava et perversa

ðas dryhten geedleanades swe folc dysig 7 nales snottur
haec Domino retribuisti Sic plebs fatua et non sapiens

ahne ðes illce ðu *ear feder gesiteð ðec dyde ðec 7
nonne hic ipse tuus pater possedit te fecit te et

[1] *first* e *from unfinished* x. [2] s *from* f.

gescop ðec in mode habbað dægas weorulde ongeotað
creavit te In mente habete dies saeculi intellegite

ger cneorisse cneorissa frign feder ðinne 7 segeð
annos nationis nationum Interroga patrem tuum et adnun-

ðe ældran ðine 7 cweoðað ðe ðonne todaeleð
tiabit tibi seniores tuos et dicent tibi Cum dividerit

se hea ðiode to ðæm gemete tostrigdeð bearn Adames sette
excelsus gentes quemadmodum dispersit filios Adae Statuit

endas ðieda efter rime *enga godes 7
terminos gentium secundum numerum angelorum Dei Et

geworden wes dael dryhtnes folc his rap
facta est pars Domini populus ejus Jacob funiculum

erfewordnisse his genyhtsumiendne hine him dyde
hereditatis ejus Israhel Sufficientem eum sibi fecit

in woestenne in *ðurs haetu ðer ne wes weter ymb
in heremo in sitim caloris ubi non erat aqua Circum

laedde hine 7 gelærde hine 7 heold hine swe swe
duxit eum et erudivit eum et custodivit eum sicut

sian egan swe swe earn ðeceð nest his 7 ofer
pupillam oculi Sicut aquila tegit nidum suum et super

briddas his geset aðenede fiðru his 7 onfeng hie 7
pullos suos consedit Expandit alas suas et accepit eos et

onfeng hie ofer gescyldru his dryhten ana lærde hie
suscepit eos super scapulas suas Dominus solus docebat eos

7 ne wes mid him god fremðe togelaedde[1] hie in
et non erat cum eis deus alienus Adduxit eos in

strengu eordan fo[e]dde hie cennende londa[2] sucun
fortitudine terrae cibavit eos nascentias agrorum Suxerunt

hunig of stane 7 ele of trumum stane geclystre oxna
mel de petra et oleum de firma petra Botyrum boum

7 milc scepa mid smeorwe *lobra 7 romma bearna
et lac ovium cum adipe agnorum et arietum filiorum

fearra 7 buccena mid smeorwe eðra hwaetes 7
taurorum et hircorum cum adipe renium tritici et

blod winbergan drinceð win 7 et Iacob 7
sanguinem uvae Bibit vinum et manducavit Jacob et

gefylled wes 7 sporetteð se liofa faet geworden wes 7
satiatus est et recalcitravit dilectus Pinguis factus est et

[1] -d:de. [2] a *from* e.

faettade 7 *gebreded wes 7 forleort god se dyde
*incrassavit et dilatatus est et *dereliquid Deum qui fecit*

hine 7 gewat from gode ðæm halwyndan his onscunedun
eum et recessit a Deo salutari suo Exacerbaverunt

mec in fremðum in onscuningum heara awehtun
me in alienis in abhominationibus suis concitaverunt

mec onsegdun deoflum 7 nales gode godas ða hie
me Sacrificaverunt daemoniis et non Deo deos quos

ne cuðun niowinga cwomun to ðæm ða nystun feddras
non noverunt novi recentes venerunt quos nesciebant patres

heara god se ðec cende ðu forleorte 7 ofergeotul earð
eorum Deum qui te genuit dereliquisti et oblitus es

god foedendne ðec gesæh dryhten 7 wreocende wes 7
Deum alentem te Vidit Dominus et zelatus est et

onscunad wes fore eorre bearna his 7 dohtra 7
exacervatus est propter iram filiorum suorum et filiarum Et

cweð ic acerru onsiene mine from him 7 oteawu hwet
dixit avertam faciem meam ab eis et ostendam quid

bið him ot nestan forðon cneoris ðweoru 7 forcerredu
erit eis in novissimo Quia generatio prava et perversa

bearn in ðæm nis geleafa in him hie in hatheortnisse
filii in quibus non est fides in ipsis Ipsi in zelo

neddun mec 7 nales in gode in eorre awehtun
conpulerunt me et non in Deo in ira concitaverunt

mec in deofulgeldum hear(a)[1] 7 ic in hatheortnisse
me in idolis suis Et ego in zelo

onweg adrifu hie 7 nales in ðiode in ðiode unwise
expellam eos et non in gentem in gentem insipientem

bismeriu hie forþon fyr born from eorre minum 7
inritabo eos Quia ignis exarsit ab ira mea et

born oð helwearan ofdune et eorðe cennende
ardebit usque ad inferos deorsum Comedit terra nascentias

heara bernde steaðelas munta ic gesomniu in him
eorum concremavit fundamenta montium Congeram in ipsis

yfel 7 strelas mine gefyllu in him aswindende hungre
mala et sagittas meas consummabo in eis Tabescentes fame

7 mete werun fugla 7 aðenenes beces ungehaelendlic
et esca erunt avium et extensio dorsi insanibilis

[1] *cut off.*

toeð wildeora insendu in him mid hatheortnisse telendra
Dentes bestiarum inmittam in eis cum furore trahen-

ofer eorðan utan butan bearnum biscereð hie
tium super terram A foris sine filiis privavit eos

sweord 7 in *hondernum[1] ege gunge mid fæmnan
gladius et in prumptuariis timor Juvenes cum virgine

mid steaðulfestum aldum cweð ic tostregde hie biscergu
cum stabilito sene Dixit dispergam eos privabo

soðlice of monnum gemynd heara nybðe fore eorre
autem ex hominibus memoriam eorum Nisi propter iram

fionda ðy læs longe tid sien ofer eorðan ðæt hie
inimicorum ne longo tempore sint super terram Ne con-

ne gedeafien wiðerbrocum 7 cweðen honda ure hea
sentiant adversariis et dicant manus nostra excelsa

7 nales god dyde ðas all forðon ðiod forlorenum ge-
et non Deus fecit haec omnia Qui agens perdito con-

ðehte is 7 nis in him ðiodscipe ne hogedon
silio est et non est in eis disciplina Non sapuerunt

ongeatan ðas onfoð in towordre tide *h swe efter-
intellegere haec percipient in futuro tempore Quomodo perse-

fylgeð an ðusend 7 twegen onwendað ten ðusendu
quitur unus mille et duo transmovebunt dena milia

nemðe forðon dryhten underðiodde hie 7 god salde hie
Nisi quia Dominus subdidit eos et Deus tradidit illos

forðon nis god ur swe swe godas heara fiond soðlice
Quia non est Deus noster sicut dii illorum inimici autem

ure unondgetfulle of wingearde *soðl Sodomwearena wintreo
nostri insensati Ex vinea enim Sodomorum vitis

heara 7 owestem heara of Gomorra winbergan
eorum et propago eorum ex Gomorra Uva eorum

winbergan gallan hatheortnis draecena win
uva fellis amaritudinis ipsis Furor draconum vinum

heara 7 hatheortnis nedrena ungehaeledlic ahne ðas
eorum et furor aspidum insanabilis Nonne haec

gesomnade sind mid mec 7 getacnad in goldhordum
congregata sunt apud me et signata in thesauris

minum in dege wrece ic geldu him in tid on ða
meis In die ultionis reddam illis in tempore quo

[1] hondernum.

asliden bið fot heara forðon neh is deg forlorenisse
lapsus fuerit pes eorum Quia prope est dies perditiones

heara 7 ðas sind gearu eow forðon doemeð dryht*en*
eorum et haec sunt parata vobis Quia judicabit Dominus

folc his 7 in ðiowum his bið froefred gesaeh soðlice
populum suum et in servis suis consolabitur Vidit enim

hie geswencte 7 asprungne in wiðlaednisse 7 tolesde[1]
eos fatigatos et defectos in abductione et dissolutos

7 cweð hwer sind godas heara in ðæm ge getreowdun
• *Et dixit ubi sunt dii illorum in quibus confidebatis*

in him ðeara smeoru onsegdnissa ge eton[2] 7 druncun
in ipsis Quorum adipem sacrificiorum edebatis et bibebatis

win onsegdnisse heara arisen ne gefultumen eowic 7
vinum libationis eorum Exsurgant nunc adjuvent vos et

sien eow gescildend gesiað gesiað forðon ic eam god
fiant vobis protectores Videte videte quoniam ego sum Deus

7 nis oðer butan me ic ofslea 7 lifgan gedom
et non est alius praeter me Ego occidam et vivere faciam

slea 7 ic gehaelu 7 nis se ðe generge of hondum
*percutiam et ego sanabo et non est qui *eripiaat de manibus*

minu*m* forðon ic afirru in heofen hond mine 7 swergu
meis Quia tollam in caelum manum meam et jurabo

ðorh ða swiðran mine 7 cweoðu ic lifgu in ecnisse
per dexteram meam et dicam vivo ego in aeternum

forðon ic ascerpu swe swe legitu sweord min 7 doeð
Quia exacuam velut fulgur gladium meum et aget

dom hond min 7 geedleaniu dom feondu*m* 7
judicium manus mea Et retribuam judicium inimicis et

ðissu*m* ða fiodun mec ic *gildu indrencu strelas mine
his qui oderunt me reddam Inebriabo sagittas meas

in blode 7 sweord min iteð flęsc from blode
in sanguine et gladius meus manducabit carnes A sanguine

gewundedra 7 heftnede from heafde aldermonna feonda
*vulneratorum et captivitate a *capita principum inimi-*

blissiað heofenas somud mid hine 7 weorðien
corum Laetamini caeli simul cum eo et adorent

hine alle englas godes blissiað ðiode somud mid folce
eum omnes angeli Dei Laetamini gentes simul cum populo

[1] o *from beginning of some other letter.* •[2] t *made into* d.

his 7 getrymen hine all bearn godes forðon blod
ejus et confirment eum omnes filii Dei Quia sanguis
bearna his bið gescilded 7 he gescildeð 7 geedleanað dom
filiorum ejus defenditur et defendit et retribuit judi-
fiondum 7 ðissum ða fiodun hine gildeð 7
cium inimicis et his qui oderunt eum reddit et
geclasnað dryhten eorðan folces his
mundabit Dominus terram populi sui

8.

HYMNUM TRIUM PUERORUM.

bledsiað. all werc dryhtnes dryhten bledsiað heofenas
Benedicite omnia opera Domini Dominum Benedicite caeli
dryht*en* bledsiað englas dryhtnes dryhten bledsiað
Dominum benedicite angeli Domini Dominum Benedicite
weter ða ofer heofenas sind dryht*en* bledsiað all
aquae quae super caelos sunt Dominum benedicite omnes
megen dryhtnes dryhten bledsiað sunne 7 mona dryhten
virtutes Domini Dominum Benedicite sol et luna Dominum
bledsiað steorran heofenes dryht*en* bledsiað scur 7 deaw
benedicite stellae caeli Dominum Benedicite imber et ros
dryht*en* bledsiað alle gastas dryhten bledsiað fyr
Dominum benedicite omnes spiritus Dominum Benedicite ignis
7 sumur dryht*en* bledsiað naeht 7 deg dryht*en* bled-
et aestus Dominum benedicite noctes et dies Dominum bene-
siað deostru 7 leht dryhten bledsiað cele 7 haetu
dicite tenebrae et lumen Dominum benedicite frigus et caumas
dryht*en* bledsiað forstas 7 snaw dryht*en* bled*siað*
Dominum Benedicite pruina et nives Dominum benedicite
legite 7 wolcen dryht*en* bledsie[1] eorðe dryht*en* bled-
fulgora et nubes Dominum Benedicite terra Dominum bene-
siað muntas 7 hyllas dryht*en* bledsiað all acennende
dicite montes et colles Dominum Benedicite omnia nascentia
eorðan dryh*ten* bled*siað* sae 7 flodas dryht*en*
**terra Dominum Benedicite maria et flumina Dominum*
bledsiað wællan dryh*ten* bled*siað* hwalas 7 all ða
benedicite fontes Dominum Benedicite caeti et omnia quae

[1] *last* e *on er.*

bioð onstyred in wetrum · dryhten bledsiað fuglas heofenes
moventur in aquis Dominum benedicite volucres caeli

dryhten bledsiað wilddeor 7 all netenu dryhten
Dominum Benedicite bestiae et universa pecora Dominum

bledsiað bearn monna dryhten bledsie Israel dryhten
benedicite filii hominum Dominum Benedicat Israhel Dominum

bledsiað biscopas dryhtnes dryhten bledsiað ðiowas
Benedicite sacerdotes Domini Dominum benedicite servi

dryhtnes dryhten bledsiað gastas 7 *sawe rehtwisre
• Domini Dominum Benedicite spiritus et animae justorum

dryhten bledsiað halge 7 eaðmode on heortan dryhten
Dominum benedicite sancti et humiles corde Dominum

bledsiað 7 dryhten bledsien we
benedicite Ananias Azarias et Misahel Dominum Benedi-

feder 7 sunu 7 ðone halgan gast hergen we 7
camus Patrem et Filium et Sanctum Spiritum Laudaemus[1] *et*

up hebben we hi[n]e in weorulde gebledsad earð in
superexaltaemus[1] *eum in saecula Benedictus es in*

trymenisse heofenes 7 hergendlic 7 up ahefen in
firmamento caeli et laudabilis et superexaltatus in

weorulde
saecula

9.

CANTICUM ZACHARIAE SACERDOTIS.

gebledsad dryhten god Israel forðon neasede 7 dyde
Benedictus Dominus Deus Israhel quia visitavit et fecit

alesnisse folces his 7 arehte horn hælu us in huse
redemptionem plebis suae Et erexit cornu salutis nobis in domo

Dauiðes cnehtes his swe spreocende wes ðorh muð
David pueri sui Sicut locutus est per os sanc-

haligra his witgena ða from weorulde sind 7
torum suorum prophetarum qui a saeculo sunt Et

gefreade[2] usic from fiondum urum 7 of honda alra
liberavit nos ab inimicis nostris et de manu omnium

da usic fiodun to donne mildheortnisse mid fedrum
qui nos oderunt Ad faciendam misericordiam cum patribus

urum 7 gemunan cyðnisse his haligre ðone swergendan að
nostris et memorare testamenti sui sancti Jusjurandum

[1] ae *from* a. [2] d *from* ð.

ðone he swor to Abrahame feder urum sellende hine
quod juravit ad Abraham patrem nostrum daturum se

us ðet butan ege of hondum fionda ura
nobis Ut sine timore de manibus inimicorum nostrorum

gefreade we ðiwgen him in halignisse 7 rehtwisnisse biforan
liberati serviamus illi In sanctitate et justitia coram

him allum dægum urum 7 ðu cneht witga ðes hestan
ipso omnibus diebus nostris Et tu puer propheta Altissimi

ðu bist geced foregæst soðlice biforan onsiene dryhtnes
vocaveris preibis enim ante faciem Domini

gearwian wegas his to sellenne wisdom hælu folce his
parare vias ejus Ad dandam scientiam salutis plebi ejus

in forletnisse synna *minra ðorh innoðas mildheortnisse
in remissione peccatorum eorum Per viscera misericordiae

godes ures in ðæm neasade usic ufancumende of heanisse
Dei nostri in quibus visitavit nos oriens ex alto

inlihtan ðissum ða in ðeostrum 7 in *deaðes[1] deaðes
Inluminare his qui in tenebris et in umbra mortis

sittað to gereccenne foet ure in weg sibbe
sedent ad dirigendos pedes nostros in viam pacis

10.

CANTICUM SANCTAE MARIAE.

miclað sawul min dryhten 7 gefaeh gast min
Magnificat anima mea Dominum et exultavit spiritus meus

in gode halwyndum *minnum forðon gelocade eaðmodnisse
in Deo salutari meo Quia respexit humilitatem

menenes his sehðe soðlice of ðissum eadge mic cweoðað
ancillae suae ecce enim ex hoc beatam me dicent

alle cneorisse forðon dyde me ða miclan se maehtig
omnes generationes Quia fecit mihi magna qui potens

is 7 halig noma his 7 mildheortnis his from cynne
est et sanctum nomen ejus Et misericordia ejus a progenie

in cyn ondredendum hine dyde maehte in earme his
in progenie timentibus eum Fecit potentiam in bracchio suo

tostregd oferhogan on mode heortan his ofdune sette maehtge
dispersit superbos mente cordis sui Deposuit potentes

[1] d *from* ð.

of selde 7 upahof[1] eaðmode hyngrende gefylde godum
de sede et exaltavit humiles Esurientes implevit bonis

7 weolie[2] forleort idelhende onfoeð cneht his
et divites dimisit inanes Suscipit Israhel puerum suum

gemyndig mildheortnisse his swe spreocende wes to feadrum
recordatus misericordiae suae Sicut locutus est ad patres

urum Abram 7 sede his oð in weoruld
nostros Abraham et semini ejus usque in saeculum

11.

HYMNUM AD MATUTINOS.

birhtu federlices wuldres of lehte leht forðbringende
Splendor paternae gloriae De luce lucem praeferens

leht lehtes 7 waelle lehtes deg dæga inlihtende 7 soð
Lux lucis et fons luminis Dies dierum inluminans Verusque

sunne in wege scinende mid sciman ðrowian 7 lioma
sol in labere Micans nitore perpeti Jubarque

halges gastes ingeot urum gehygdum willum . cegen we ' to
Sancti Spiritus Infunde nostris sensibus Votis vocemus ad

feder feder eces wuldres feder męhtigre gefe
Patrem Patrem perennis gloriae Patrem . potentis gratiae

scyld gebegeð glidder gehiowað dede strece toð
Culpam redegit lubricam Informet actus strenuos Dentem

gebegeð efes(tigne)[3] fael gewynsumie roeðe selle to donne
retundat inv(idum) Casus secundet asperos Donet gerendi

gefe mod steoreð 7 receð clęne getreowum lichoman
gratiam Mentem gubernet et regat Castos fidele corpore

se rehta geleafa mid haetu walle facnes atur nyte 7 Crist
Fides calore ferveat Fraudis venena nesciat Christ-

us sie mete 7 drync ur sie geleafa bliðe
usque nobis sit cibus Potusque noster sit fides Laeti

drincen we geðungenlice *drincennisse gastes bliðe deg ðes
bibamus sobrie Ebrietatem spiritus Laetus dies hic

leore clęnnes sie ðæt on ærmargen se rehta geleafa swe swe
transeat Pudor sit ut deluculo Fides velut

midne deg degred . mod nyte degred ryne forðwegeð
meridies Crepusculum mens nesciat Aurora cursus provehit

[1] *preceded by* : : : : : : .   [2] *last* e *from* g.   [3] *cut off.*

degred all forðypeð in feder all sunu ⁊ all in worde
Aurora totus prodeat In Patre totus Filius Et totus in Verbo

feder wuldur ðe feder wuldur ðæm ancendan somud mid ðy
Pater Gloria tibi Pater Gloria Unigenito Una cum

halgan gaste in ðere ecan weorulde[1]
Sancto Spiritu In sempiterna saecula

12.

HYMNUM VESPERTINUM.

god sceppend alra ⁊ heofenes rec[c]ere gerwende deg mid
Deus creator omnium polique rector vestiens diem de-

wlitige lehte naeht slepes gefe liomu tolesde ðæt
coro lumine noctem soporis gratia Artus solutos ut

sie rest agefe gewinnes gewunan ⁊ mod woerigu gelihte
quies reddat labores usui mentesque fessas allevet

⁊ wopas onlese generwde ðoncas *gedoenu nu ða dege ⁊
luctusque solvat ancxios Gratis peracto jam die et

naehte upcyme boene gehatum scyldge ðæt ðu gefultume
noctis exortum praeces votis reos ut adjubes

*humen[2] singende we onlesað ðæc heortan ða niðerlican
hymnum canentes solvimus Te cordis ima

hleoðriað ðec stefn smoeðu hlydeð ðec lufað clęne
**concinat te vox canora concrepet te diligat castus*

lufe ðec mod weorðað geðungen ⁊ mit te grund
amor te mens adoret sobria Et cum profunda

biluceð deg dimnes naehta se rehta geleafa ðeostru nyte
clauserit diem caligo noctium fides tenebras nesciat

⁊ naeht getreowum lihteð slepan mod ne let ðu slepan
et nox fideli luceat Dormire mentem ne sinas dormire

scyld cunne clæne geleafa coelende slepes smec gemetgie
culpa noverit castus fides refrigerans somni vaporem temperet

ongered gehygde glidderre ðec heortan ða hean slepað ðylæs
Exuta sensu lubrico te cordis alta somnient nec

fiondes ðes efestgan[3] facne fyrhtu stille awecce Crist
hostis invidi dolo pavor quietos suscitet Christum

bidden we ⁊ feder Cristes ⁊ feadur gast an maehtig
rogemus et Patrem Christi Patrisque Spiritum unum potens

[1] *might be read* weoruldie. [2] u *on er.* [3] *second* e *from* s?

ðorh all hirt biddende ðrines wuldur ðe feder
per omnia fove precantes trinitas Gloria tibi Pater

13.

HYMNUM DIEBUS DOMINICIS.

cyning ece dryhten wisena sceppend alra ðu were ær
Rex aeterne Domine rerum creator omnium qui eras ante
weorulde aa mid feder sunu ðu middangeardes in fru-
saecula semper cum Patre Filius Qui mundi in pri-
man *gehiowadas mon ðæm ðinre onlicnisse
mordio Adam plasmasti hominem cui tuae imaginis
ondwliotan saldes gelicne ðone dioful biswac[1] fiond
vultum dedisti similem Quem diabolus deceperat hostis
mennesces cynnes ðes ðu hiow lichoman genioman
humani generis cujus tu formam corporis adsumere
*gemeode ðu were ðæt mon ðu alesdes ðone ær soðlice
dignatus es Ut hominem redemeris quem ante jam
gehiowades 7 usic to gode gegadrades *ðoh flæsces
plasmaveras Et nos Deo conjungeris per carnis con-
gemænnisse ðone acennedne of fæmnan forhtað ylc[2]
tubernium Quem editum ex virgine pavescit omnis
sawul ðorh ðone usic arisan holde mode we gelefað
anima per quem nos resurgere devota mente credimus
se us ðorh fulwiht forgefe forgefenisse we earun nu-
Qui nobis per baptismum donasti indulgentiam qui tene-
mene mid bendum gebundne mid ingehygde ðu
bamur vinculis ligati conscientia Qui crucem
fore men onfon gemeodemad were saldes ðin
propter hominem suscipere dignatus es Dedisti tuum
blod ure haelu weorð weotudlice[3] wagrift ðes
sanguinem Nostrae salutis praetium Nam velum templi
temples tosliten is 7 all eorðe cwaecade du monge
scissum est Et omnis terra tremuit Tu multos
slependra awehtes dryhten ðu fiondes ðes aldan
dormientium Resuscitasti Domine Tu hostis antiqui
megen ðorh rode deaðes fordrestende mid ðere usic ge-
vires Per crucem mortis conterens Qui nos sig-

[1] a *from* u. [2] *followed by* ::::. [3] t *from* d.

segnade onforanheafdum guðfonan *gelean we beorað ðu
nati frontibus Vexillum fidei ferimus Tu

hine from us aa onweg adrifan ðu were gemeodemad
illum a nobis Semper repellere dignaveris

ne æfre mege gedergan alesde mid ðine blode ðu
Ne umquam possit ledere Redemptos tuo sanguine Qui

fore us to helwearum[1] astigan gemeodemad ðu were
propter nos ad inferos Discendere dignatus es

ðæt deaðes borggeldu*m* lifes forgefe gefe ðe on margen
Ut mortis debitoribus Vitae donaris munera Tibi matutino

tid *hymen woepende we singað forgef[2] us dryht*en*
tempore Hymnum deflentes canimus Ignosce nobis Domine

forgef ondettendum forðon ðu geweota 7 doema earð[3]
Ignosce confitentibus Quia tu testis et judex es

ðone nænig meg biwægan ða deglan ingehygde ure
*Quem nemo potest fallere Secreta *conscientia *nostra*

gesionde sweðe ðu ura breosta ana aspyrgend
videns vestigia Tu nostrorum pectorum Solus investigator

earð ðu wunda lutiendra god ætstondes lece ðu earð
es Tu vulnerum latentium Bonus adsistis medicus Tu es

ðu on cuðe tid sellende ende weorulde ðu alra
qui certo tempore Daturus finem saeculi Tu cunctorum

geeorningum rehtwis geedleanend earð ðec soðlice ðu halga
meritis Justus remunerator es Te ergo sanctae

we halsiað ðæt ure haele wunde ðu earð mid feder
quaesumus Ut nostra cures vulnera Qui es cum Patre

sunu aa mid ðy halgan gaste wuldur ðe feder
Filius Semper cum Sancto Spiritu Gloria tibi Pater

wuldur ancendu*m*[4] somud mid halgu*m* gaste in ðere
Gloria Unigenito Una cum Sancto Spiritu In sempi-

ecan weorulde
terna saecula

[1] heol-, o *dotted out;* l *from some other letter.* [2] e *from* i. [3] e *from some other letter.* [4] *first* n *from other letter.*

CHARTERS.

THE first collective edition of the Old English charters and kindred documents was Kemble's *Codex Diplomaticus Aevi Saxonici* (1839–48), published by the Historical Society in six volumes. Thorpe afterwards (1865) published a collection, in one volume, under the title of *Diplomatarium Anglicum Aevi Saxonici*, consisting of those 'directly or indirectly bearing on our early history.'

Both of these collections were apparently intended mainly for historical and antiquarian purposes, and include Latin charters and those which are preserved only in later copies. Both editors employed other men to copy the charters for them, and did not attempt to deal with the palæographical evidence: the reader looks in vain for any statement of the date of the handwriting of the charters written on single sheets of vellum.

In my texts I give the English charters in full, and print only the English words and passages in the Latin ones, together with as much of the Latin context as is required to elucidate the English. I try to exclude all charters not preserved in contemporary MSS., as also later additions.

In eliminating the contemporary charters, the first step is to reject all documents preserved only in the monastic registers or *chartularies*, and to confine ourselves to those written on separate sheets. Of these, again, a large number are palpably later copies. When the copy is within half a century of its original, it becomes more difficult to detect its lateness. A contemporary copy, or one made within a few years, is, of course, as good as the original, as far as the language is concerned; as in the case of Ceolnoð (21, 2, 3), where we can trace the same scribes through two contemporary charters. The duplicates of Wihtred (5), Cuðred (34), and Wulfred[3] (58) are also apparently contemporary.

The main tests of age are the *handwriting*, and the *language* of the English portions. The age of a MS. written in or after the Alfred period in the South of England can generally be determined with ease by a mere inspection of the handwriting, which had then become tolerably uniform, MSS. being also common. But as we approach the seventh century, the number of varieties of handwriting increase, while the number of specimens decreases rapidly. Differences due to age are also liable to be crossed by those due to difference of place. In the later period, Northern MSS., such as the Durham gloss, are distinctly more archaic in character than contemporary Southern ones. How far this was the case earlier we have but little means of judging. It is quite possible, for instance, that the use of uncials may have lingered longer in some parts of the country than in others, but as there is an entire absence of Northumbrian charters and of uncially written West-Saxon ones (there being very few W. S. charters at all before 900), the total number of uncial charters being only *three*, all we can do is to state the fact that the latest uncial charter (no. 9) is dated 736, and that it is Mercian. The same uncertainty attends any general inferences drawn from the use of the other hands of the same period.

The evidence of the language is often clear and decisive. A copy of an earlier vernacular text generally shows a mixture of old and new: it never preserves the older forms throughout, and seldom modernizes consistently. If it does the latter, the discrepancy between date and language is at once apparent. The evidence of language being distinct from that of handwriting, the two naturally check one another: where they agree, a double probability is reached. Of course, where only a few English words are given, their evidence is often quite inadequate.

The next difficulty is to determine the *dialect* of a charter. Here we have to consider first the external evidence. In many this settles the question at once. When we have an original charter of a King of Kent, granting land in Kent to a Kentish retainer, we assume at once that the English words in it are in the Kentish dialect. Additional confirmation is often afforded by the place where the charter is kept, as when a Mercian charter can be traced to the archives of Worcester. In such a case as that of a Mercian or Saxon king granting land in Kent, doubt may arise. If the grant is to one of his own followers, it will naturally be in their own dialect; but if, say, a Mercian king grants land in Kent to a Kentish monastery, which party will draw up the deed? The antiquaries I have consulted agree in assuming that it was always written in the king's scriptorium. But, on the other hand, when, as in Ceolnoð (21, 2, 3), the monks bring a charter before several successive kings for confirmation, it seems natural to suppose that they would have a scribe of their own. Again, the boundaries would naturally be written, if possible, by a native of the district. There is, lastly, the possibility of the extant document being a duplicate written in the monastery itself. The last-mentioned charter well illustrates the complications that may thus arise, both by one part of a charter being written in a different dialect, and also by actual mixture. This mixture is generally graphic, as when a Mercian scribe copies Kentish boundaries, but may also be oral, as when he writes them down from the dictation of a man of Kent.

The internal evidence of handwriting and language is subject to the same doubts and difficulties in its bearings on dialect as on age. The uncertainty of the linguistic evidence is aggravated by the frequent possibility of a mixture of dialects, as already suggested. Handwritings are not easily mixed, and their evidence is very valuable when it enables us to distinguish groups of charters of the same place and period. Thus we have a tolerably well-defined group of 8th and early 9th century Mercian charters, written in a peculiar compromise between uncial and cursive, and a still more unmistakable group of Southern 9th century charters in a peculiar rough irregular hand. In the notes to each charter I often distinguish these hands as 'Mercian' and 'rough' respectively, and indicate briefly the character of the handwriting of many of the other charters as well. Most of the undescribed charters, especially those of the 9th century, are written in more or less regular pointed minuscules.

All my texts are taken either from the MSS. or from photographic reproductions. My main sources have been—

(1) The Facsimiles of Charters published by the Trustees of the British Museum (B. M.);

(2) Those published by the Palæographical Society (P. S.);

(3) The Facsimiles of A. S. MSS. photozincographed by Lieut. Gen. Cameron (Cam.).

Also some autotypes in periodicals. My texts of the Stowe

charters are from the MSS. themselves. Only a few of them were published by Kemble, and those only secondhand, from older printed texts. *I* have also revised the charters from photographs by the MSS. whenever it seemed advisable, especially the photozincographs of the Canterbury Charters (Cam.).

In excluding doubtful charters, *I* have been greatly helped by the investigations of Messrs. Bond and Thompson, as given in the B. M. series, which in most cases confirmed my own, begun several years before the publication of the B. M. series. *I* differ from them in maintaining the contemporariness of Wihtred (5) and of three charters written in the 'rough' hand: Æðelwulf[4] (20), Æðelwulf[1] (24), and Æðelberht[4] (29). *I* am, however, glad to learn from Mr. Thompson that he has since arrived independently at the same conclusion as *I* have about the contemporariness of the last three. All the others designated as late by Messrs. B. and T. *I* reject, and also (though more doubtfully) the following ones: 805. Æðelheard. Aug. ii. 55; 814. Coenwulf. Aug. ii. 77; 833. Ecgberht. Aug. ii. 102; 875. Eardwulf. Aug. ii. 89. The results are, of course, not free from uncertainty, but *I* have no doubt of the genuineness of the more important of the fifty-nine charters here given, especially the English ones.

I have classified the charters firstly by century, and secondly by dialect. Wherever the latter is not indicated unmistakably by the external evidence, I have put them into the special classes Saxon-Kentish and Mercian-Kentish. This *I* have done consistently even in those cases where the evidence of handwriting or language enables us to assign a charter with certainty to an unmixed dialect. In the dates *I* follow Kemble and my other predecessors; in assigning the original monastic archives *I* follow Messrs. Bond and Thompson. Where two dates are given, *I* go by the latest. Where useful, *I* have often added the modern equivalents (when identified) of the place-names, together with references to the volume, page, and number in Kemble's collection, and the page in Thorpe's, to the B. M. series, and to other sources, together with occasional notes on the handwriting and condition of the charter.

For convenience, I add a list of the charters, with their dates, titles, and MS. sources. Those marked * *I* do not find in Kemble, those marked † are printed by him only from later copies. Wherever the case of an English name is not noted, or to be inferred from the context, or is self-evident, it is the nominative.

Doubtful letters in the less legible charters, especially those which I give only on the authority of the B. M. (or other) transliterations, are in (   ).

VII–VIII. *Saxon.*

1. 692–3. Oeðelred. Aug. ii. 29.
*2. 693–731. Berhtwald. Aug. ii. 18.
3. 778. Cynewulf. Cott. Ch. viii. 4.

VII–VIII. *Kentish.*

4. 679. Hloðhere. Aug. ii. 2.
5. 700 or 715. Wihtred. Aug. ii. 88; Stowe.
6. 732. Æðelbert[1]. Aug. ii. 91.
7. 740. Æðelberht[2]. Aug. ii. 101.
*8. 770. Eardwulf. Stowe.

VIII. *Mercian.*

9. 736. Æðelbald[1]. Aug. ii. 3.
†10. 759. Eanberht. Add. Ch. 19,789.
11. 767. Offa[1]. Aug. ii. 26.
12. 799–802. Pilheard. Aug. ii. 27.
†13. 770. Uhtred. Worc. Arch.
14. 779. Offa[2]. Aug. ii. 4.
*15. 791–6. Offa[4]. Worc. Arch.
†16. 793–6. Offa[5]. Add. Ch. 19,790.

VIII. *Mercian-Kentish.*

*17. 742. Æðelbald[2]. Cant. Arch.
18. 788. Offa[3]. Cant. Arch.
19. 798. Coenwulf[1]. Aug. ii. 97.

IX. *Saxon.*

20. 847. Æðelwulf[4]. Cott. Ch. viii. 36.

IX. *Saxon-Kentish.*

21. 838. Ceolnoð[a]. Aug. ii. 21.
22. „ Ceolnoð[b]. Aug. ii. 20.
23. „ Ceolnoð[c]. Aug. ii. 37.
24. 839. Æðelwulf[1]. Aug. ii. 28.
*25. 843. Æðelwulf[2]. Stowe.
26. 845. Æðelwulf[3]. Aug. ii. 60.
27. 855. Æðelwulf[5]. Aug. ii. 71.
28. 858. Æðelberht[3]. Aug. ii. 66.
29. 862. Æðelberht[4]. Cott. Ch. viii. 32.
30. 863. Æðelberht[5]. Cant. Arch.
31. 867. Æðelred. Aug. ii. 95.
*32. 873. Ælfred[1]. Stowe.

IX. *Kentish.*

33. 803. Æðelheard[1]. Cant. Arch.
34. 805. Cuðred. Stowe; Aug. ii. 100.

35. 811. Wulfred[1]. Aug. ii. 47.

36. 824. Wulfred[2]. Aug. ii. 72.

37. 805–31. Oswulf. Aug. ii. 79.

38. 831. Eadwald. Aug. ii. 19.

39. 831. Ealhburg. Aug. ii. 52.

40. 832. Lufu. Aug. ii. 92.

41. 835. Abba. Aug. ii. 64.

42. 837. Badanoð. Aug. ii. 42.

43. 859. Plegred. Aug. ii. 16.

44. 888. Ceolwulf[3]. Aug. ii. 17.

IX. *Surrey.*

45. 871–89. Ælfred[2]. Stowe.

IX. *Mercian.*

46. 803. Æðelheard[2]. Aug. ii. 61.

47. 836. Wiglaf[2]. Aug. ii. 9.

48. 840. Berhtwulf. Cant. Arch.

IX. *Mercian-Kentish.*

*49. 805. Coenwulf[2]. Stowe.

50. 808. Coenwulf[3]. Aug. ii. 98.

51. 811. Coenwulf[4]. Aug. ii. 10.

52. 812. Coenwulf[5]. Cant. Arch.

53. 814. Coenwulf[6]. Aug. ii. 74.

*54. 815. Coenwulf[7]. Stowe.

55. 822. Ceolwulf[1]. Aug. ii. 93.

56. 823. Ceolwulf[2]. Aug. ii. 75.

*57. 824. Beornwulf. Stowe.

58. 825. Wulfred[3]. Aug. ii. 78; Stowe.

59. 831. Wiglaf[1]. Aug. ii. 94.

VII, VIII CENT. SAXON.

1.

Oeðelred. Cott. Aug. ii. 29.

692 or 693.

Uncial. Barking (Essex) archives. K. I. 39 (35). B. M. I. 2.

ego ho.ilredus *parens* sebbi *provincia* eastsexanorum. *tibi* hedilburge[1] *abbatissae. monasterii quae dicitur* beddanhaam. *terram quae appellatur* ricingahaam, budinhaam, dęccanhaam, angenlabeshaam. *in silva quae dicitur* uuidmundesfelt.—*termini sunt isti:* writolaburna, cęntinces triow *et* hanchemstede, *flumen tamisa* ..—sebbi *rex* eastsax'. oedelraedus. ercnuualdus. uuilfridus. *ego* haedde. guda. egcbaldus. hagona. hooc. sebbi *regis.* sigiheardi *regis.* suebredi *regis.*—odilredus[2].

[1] *only the upright stroke of the* b *visible.* [2] *later endorsement:* þis is seo boc to Bercingon.

2.

Berhtwald. Cott. Aug. ii. 18.

693–731.

Cursive. Brentford (Middlesex). Cant. arch. B. M. I. 5.

berctualdo. ualdharius. uestsęxanorum. *in loco qui dicitur* breguntford. coenredi *regis*. *de reconciliatione* (aelfdrydę)—*a* ualdh . .

3.

Cynewulf. Cott. Ch. viii. 4.

778.

Half-uncial, but distinct from Wihtred (5). Much worn. Bedwin (Wilts). Abingdon (Berks) archives. K. I. 161 (133). B. M. II. 3.

cynewulf *rex saxonum*. bican *comiti meo*. *in loco qui dicitur* bedewinde. . . erratuun. *vallem vocatam* cymenes denu. . . nes geat. *ad* peadan stigele. in filiðleage. *in quoddam vallu* in haran dene. *agellum qui dicitur* tatan edisc. in bedewindan. in horselget . . rames dene geate. to holhrygcgete. to (h)adfeldgeate. to baggan gete. to brad(an)leage. *illo septo* bradan leage. in standene. in puttan.ealh. to bulcan pytte. *in quoddam petrosum clivum et ex eo* baldwines healh *appellatur*. *austro* bulcan pyttes. *in illa antiqua monumenta in locum ubi a ruricolis dicitur* æt ðam holenstypbum, *sicque ad illos gabulos in longum* gemærweges to wadbeorge. *sicque* of wadb(eorge) *in illum fontem qui dicitur* forsca burna, *et ejus ex alveo intrat* bedewindan. in cymenes . . . — æðelmodus. egcbaldus. sc(illi)nges. (ham) . . æðelnoðes. ceolbrehtes. æðelmundes. . . (ser)des. fad(ol).

VII, VIII CENT. KENTISH.

4.

Hloðhere. Cott. Aug. ii. 2.

679.

Uncial. Cant. arch. 'Formerly inserted in the ancient Latin psalter of the Canterbury collection, now in the library of the University of Utrecht.' (Note added to the charter.) K. I. 20 (16). B. M. I. 1.

ego hlotharius rex cantuariorum. *terram in* tenid, *quae appellatur* uuestanae. *tibi* *bercuald. *cum meriscis, silvis. cum con-*

sensu theodori et ędrico, *filium fratris mei. in civitate* recuulf. *terram in* sturia——hlothari *regis.* gumbercti. gębredi. osfridi. irminredi. aedilmaeri. hagani. aeldredi. aldhodi. gudhardi. bernhardi. uelhisci.

5.

Wihtred. Cott. Aug. ii. 88 ; Stowe I.

700 or 715.

Both MSS. rounded half-uncial of an Irish type. Cott. from Cant. arch. K. I. 54 (47). B. M. I. 4.

ego uuihtredus[1] *rex* cantuariorum. *in loco qui dicitur* limingae. *terram quae dicitur* pleghelmes tun. *terminos, id est,* bereueg *et* meguuines paeð[2] *et* stretleg. *terrulae partem cujus vocabulum est* rumininngseta. *fluminis quae appellatur* liminaea——berhtuualdum[3]. berhtuualdus[4]. uuihtredi[5] *regis.* aethilburgae[6] *reginae.* enfridi (gen.) botta. frodi. adda. aedilfridi. bernhaerdi. aehcha. egisberhti[7]. hagana. theabul. aesica[8].

6.

Æðelberht[1]. Cott. Aug. ii. 91.

732.

Cant. arch. K. I. 92 (77). Th. 20. B. M. I. 6.

juxta liminaee. *ego* aethilberhtus *rex* cantuariorum. *antecessori tuo* (hymoran). *tu* dun. —— aethilberhtus. tatuuinus. aethilberhti *regis. rege* aethilberhto. balthhaeardi (gen.) bynnan. aeanberhti. aethiliaeardi[9].

7.

Æðelberht[2]. Cott. Aug. ii. 101.

740.

Fine, angular. Cant. arch. K. I. 103 (86). B. M. I. 8.

ego aethilberht *rex* cantuariorum. *fluminis cujus nomen* liminaea. *juxta marisco qui dicitur* biscopes uuic, *usque ad silbam*

[1] uihtredus *St.* [2] meguines paed *Stowe.* [3] berichtualdum *St.* [4] berichtualdus *St.* [5] uihtredi *St.* [6] aedilburgae *St.* [7] egisberichti. [8] aessica *St. Cott. indorsed in an old hand:* rumeningseta inn to limining-mynster. [9] *endorsed in an early hand:* Sandtunes boc.

qui apellatur ripp, *et ad terminos* suthsaxoniae. *in* liminiaeae. cuthberhto. *in loco qui dicitur* liminiaee——aethilberhtus. cuthberhtus. balthhardi (gen.) aeðelhuni. dunuualhi. duunuuallan. aldberhti. aethelnothi[1].

8.

Eardwulf. Stowe 3^{b}.

770.

Ego eardulfus *rex cantiae.* heaberhcto *abbate. in monasterio quod nominatur* ricuulfi. *in loco qui dicitur* perhamstede. *in regione* ęr[2] caestruuara, *ubi nominatur* heahhaam. *patre meo* *eadberhtuo—*episcopi* earduulfi. eardulfus. earduulfus. *signum manus* folcuuinis. byrnhames. *uuihtbrordis. uuealhhunes. aethelnothes.

VIII CENT. MERCIAN.

9.

Æðelbald[1]. Cott. Aug. ii. 3.

736.

Uncial. Worcester arch. Formerly inserted in the Vesp. Psalter (p. 184 above). K. I. 96 (80). B. M. I. 7.

Ego aethilbalt *rex marcersium et provinciarum quae* sutangli *dicuntur. comite meo* cyniberhtte. *in provincia cui nomen inditum est* husmerae, *juxta fluvium vocabulo* stur. *silvam quam nominant* cynibre, *aliam cui nomen est* moerheb — aetdilbalt. uuor. uuilfridus. aethilbaldo *rege.* aethilric. *principis* ęthilbal(di)[3] *ego* ibe. heardberht. ebbella. onoc. oba. sigibed. bercol. ealduuft. cusa. pede — *agrum in silva* moreb *cui vocabulum est* brochyl, *quem ego* edilbalt, *rex* suutanglorum, *comite meo* cyniberhttę *donavi*[4].

[1] *later endorsement:* Limenea boec. [2] *on er.* (?) [3] *cut off.*
[4] *later endorsement:* Norðstur.

10.

Eanberht. Add. Ch. 19,789.

759.

Half-uncial, Mercian hand. Rather worn. Worcester arch. K. I. 128 (105) from chartulary. B. M. II. 2.

regis offan *merciorum.* eanberht. uhctred. aldréd. *tibi* h(e)adda *abbati* æt onnan forda. uuisleag. rindburna. meosgelegeo. onnan duun — offa. eanberht. uhctred. aldred. milred. tilhere. cusa. (acan) (gen.) (dil)ran. bobban. bynnan. berhtuuald. tilberhti[1].

11.

Offa[1]. Cott. Aug. ii. 26.

767.

Free Mercian hand. Cant. arch. K. I. 142 (116). B. M. I. 9.

ego offa *rex mercior.* stidberhtae *venerabili viro terram* in middilsaexum bituih gumeninga hergae end liddinge *ab oriente torrentis* lidding *donabo.* stidberht. in ciltinne, *in loco ubi dicitur* wichama—offa. gengberht. eadberht. cuutfert.

12.

Pilheard's Endorsement. Aug. ii. 27.

799–802.

Mercian hand, more compact. Cant. arch. K. I. 142 (116). B. M. I. 9.

regum aethelbaldi *atque* offani. pilheardus **comis regis merciorum* coenuulfi. *locum qui dicitur* caelichyth — coenuulfus. æthelheardu[s]. unuuona. aldulf. utol. eadulf. deneberht. haðoberht. cyneberht. uuigberht. alhheard. tidferð. uuihthun. beonna. folðred. coenuulf. heaðoberht. æðelmund. esne. heardberht. ceolmund. wigga. cydda. cuðred. osulf. beornnoð. cyn[h]elm.

[1] *later endorsement:* Offa *rex.* to Onna forda.

13.

Uhtred. Worcester arch.

770.

Mercian hand. Autotype and transliteration by W. de G. Birch, in Transs. of Royal Soc. of Literature XI. pt. iii. New Series, (1878).

ego uhtredus *regulus* huicciorum *meo ministro* æðelmundo, *filio* ingeldi, *qui fuit dux et praefectus* æðelbaldi *regis merciorum cum licentia* offani *regis merciorum. juxta fluvium in orientale parte qui dicitur* salu(uerpe). æðelmundo.—eadbald. cyneðryð *regina.* ecgferð. ælfflæd *filia.*—*Hii sunt termini donationis istius* : saluuerpæ. cymedes halh. huitan stan. readan solo.

14.

Offa[2]. Cott. Aug. ii. 4.

779.

Mercian hand. Windrush (Glouc.), Widford (Glouc.), Turkdean (Glouc.). Evesham (Worc.) arch. K. I. 164 (137). B. M. I. 10.

offa *rex merciorum meo ministro* dud[d]onǫ. sulmonnes burg. *torrentis qui vocatur* theodningc. *fluvii qui nuncupatur* uuenrisc — uuithigford *usque* inwines burg. *vallis qui dicitur* turca denu. slohtran ford. *fluvius* uuęnrisc — *regis* offan. æt io[r]otlaforda — offa. eadber[h]tus. ceolulfus. tilherus. geberh(tu). aldberhtus. botuuine. brordan[1] (gen.) berhtuua[l]di. esne. eanberht. eadbaldi. esn(e). brordan. bynni. (eadbaldi)—godmundes leah[2].

15.

Offa[4]. Worcest. arch.

791–6.

Mercian hand. Westbury (Glouc.). Autotype in 'Journal of Archæological Association,' xxxii. (1876), p. 190.

ego offa *rex. in provincia* huuicciorum *ubi nominatur* uuestburg *prope flumen qui dicitur* aben aeðelmundo *meo ministro in loco qui nuncupatur* clobes hoas — offa *rex.* ecgferð *filius regis.* hygeberhti (gen.). æðelheardi. ceolulfi. haðoredi.

[1] broddan, *with* r *written over first* d. [2] *later endorsement:* Burhtunes boc.

unu[u]ona. cyneberhti. deneferði. ceolmundi. coenwalh *episcopi.* uuermundi. alhheardi. ælfhuni. uuiohtuni. alhmund *abbatis.* beonnan. uuigmundi. utel *abbatis* — brorda[1]. bynna. alhmund. esne. ædelmund. uuigberht. heardberht. uuynberht. ceolmund. ubba. lulling. eafing.

16.

Offa[5]. Add. Ch. 19,790.

(793–6).

Mercian hand, rather uncial. Westbury (Glouc.). Worcester arch. K. I. 203 (167) from a chartulary. B. M. II. 5.

offa *rex. terram in provincia* huuicciorum *ubi nominatur* uuestburg, *prope flumen qui dicitur* aben. aeðelmundo. *in loco qui nuncupatur* clobes hoas—offa. ecgferð. hygeberhti (gen.). æðelheardi. ceolulfi. haðoredi. unu[u]ona. cyneberhti. deneferði. ceolmundi. coenwalh. uuermundi. alhheardi. ælfhuni. uuiohtuni. alhmund. beonnan. uuigmundi. utel. brorda. bynna. alhmund. esne. æðelmund. uuigberht. heardberht. uuynberht. ceolmund. ubba. lulling. eafing[2].

VIII CENT. MERCIAN-KENTISH.

17.

Aeðelbald[3]. Cant. archives (Cam. i).

742.

æðelbaldi *regis merciorum. in loco ubi nominatur* clofes hos. æðelbaldus *rex.* cutberhtus. æðelberhti *regis cantiae.* wihtredi *regis.* æðelbald. æðelb[e]rhti *regis.* cutberhti *archiepiscopi* — æðelbald. cuðberhtus. uuita. torhthelm. willfredi. cuðberht. huetlac. eanfrið. ecglaf. aluuig. hunwald. daniel. aldwulf. æðelfrið. herewald. sigcga. redwulf. ofa. aldwulf. æðelmod. he[a]rdberht. eadbald. bercul. cyneberht. freoðorne. wermund. cuðred. buna[3].

[1] *from here to end not in facsimile.* [2] *later endorsement:* Westbyrig.
[3] *endorsed in a diff. (later?) hand:* eþelbaldi regis et cuþberti archiepiscopi.

18.

Offa[3]. Cant. Archives (Cam. ii).

788.

K. I. 184 (153).

offa *rex merciorum tibi* osberhto *ministro meo trado terram in provincia cantiae in regione* eastrgena *ubi nominatur* duningcland. *in loco ubi* (*nomin*)*atur* celchyð—offa. iaenberhtus. hygeberht. . . . . . lf. heardraed. aethilmod. cyneberht. unuuano. uuaer. hathor. ealgheard. ceolmund[1].

19.

Coenwulf[1]. Cott. Aug. ii. 97.

798.

Bobbing, Lyminge (Kent). Cant. arch. K. I. 211 (175). B. M. I. 12.

. . *merciorum.* oswulfo *duci. in loco qui vocatur* hrempingwíic *et alia nomine* hafingseota. *fluminis qui dicitur* liminea. *terrae qui dicitur* bobingseata—coenuulf. aeðelhard. hygeberht. haðored. unuuono. cyneberht. haðoberht. eaduulf. utel. alhhard. wiohthun. tidfrið. alhmund. beonna. uuigmund. forðred. brordan (gen.). heaberhti. esne. wigberhti. aeðelmundi. eadgari. uuicggan. ciolmundi. beornnoði. heardberhti. cyddan—osuulf. *conjugis* beornðryðe. *monasterio quod dicitur* aet liminge. æt limingge—hafingseotan boec.

IX CENT. SAXON.

20.

Æðelwulf[4]. Cott. Ch viii. 36.

847.

Ham (Wilts), Dorchester (Dorset). Cant. arch. K. II. 28 (260).
B. M. II. 30.

ætheluulf *occidentalium saxonum rex. territoria ista sunt cassatorum qui* ætheluulfe *regi* *om homme *senatores ejus concedissent*

[1] *later endorsement:* offa. .unninglaṅd.

in illo loco qui nuncupater dornuuaruna ceaster. ærest on merce cumb. ðonne on grenan pytt. ðonne on ðone torr æt mercecumbes æwielme. ðonne on denewaldes stan. ðonne on ðone díc, ðær esne ðone weg fordealf. ðonon ofdune on ðæs wælles heafod. ðonne ðær ofdune on broc oð tiddes ford. ðonne up on broc oð heottes dic to ðære fiodan. from ðære flodan ofdune ðær fyxan díc to broce gæð. 7 ðonne ofdune on broc oð sǽ. ðonne from ðyrelan stane up on broc oð smalan cumb. fram smalan cumbes heafde to græwanstane. ðonon wiðufan ðæs wælles heafod on odencolc. ðonon on ðone healdan weg wið huitan stanes. ðonon to ðæm beorge ðe mon hateð æt ðæm holne. ðonon an haran stan. ðonon on secgwælles heafod. ðonon an ða burg eastewearde. ðonon on ða lytlan burg westewearde. ðonon to stræte. ðonan benioðan wuda on geryhte ut on hreodpól. ðonne up on afene, oð ðæt ðe se alda suínhaga utscioteð to afene. ðonne be ðæm hagan on anne beorg. ðonne on sueordleage wælle. ðonon on wulfwælles heafod. ðonon on wealweg on ðone stan æt ðære flodan. from ðæm stane forð on ðone herepað on ðone díc. ðonon ofdune oð wealdenes ford. ðonon on ðone holan weg. ðonon ofdune on bróc on hunburge fleot 7 ðær to sǽ—ætheluulf. alhstan. æðelbaldi (gen.). osrici. osmundi. ecgheard. lulling. uulflafi. ecguulfi. lulluc. ceorli. uulfræd. alhstan. milræd.

IX CENT. SAXON-KENTISH.

21.

Ceolnoð[a]. Cott. Aug. ii. 21.

838.

Fine, regular. Kingston (Surrey), Malling (Kent). Cant. arch. (as also B and C). K. I. 318 (240). B. M. II. 26.

in illa famosa loco quae appellatur cyninges tún *in regione* suðregię. ceolnotho. *regibus* ecgberhto *et* aetheluulfo. ceolnotho. ecgberhto *et* aetheluulfo. *agrum* æt mallingum. *in dorovernia civitate.* baldredo *rege.* æt mallingum. ceolnotho. ecgberhtum. ecgberht *et* aetheluulf—ceolnoth. bægmund. uuerhard. brunhard. hysenoð. osmund. hunred. wigmund. beornnoð. heaberht. badonoð. wealhhere. ceolwulf. noðwulf. ceolwulf[1].

[1] *later endorsement:* Meallinga edgift.

22.

Ceolnoð b. Cott. Aug. ii. 20 (B. M. i. 17).

1. Same hand as A.

cyninges tún. suðregię. ceolnotho. ecgberhto *et* ætheluulfo. ceolnotho. ecgberhto *et* ætheluulfo. æt mallingum. baldredo. æt mallingum. ceolnotho. ecgberhtum. ecgberht *et* ætheluulf— *ceolnotht. bægmund. uuerhard. brunhard. hysenoth. hunred. wigmund. beornnoð. osmund. heaberht. badanoð. uuealhhere. noðwulf. ceolwulf.

2. Thicker, rougher. Wilton (Wilts.).

ætheluulfu*m* *regem*. úuiltún — æðeluulf. alhstan. eadhún. wulfhardi. æðeluulfi. eanwulfi. eadberhti. æðelheardi. ecgberhti. alhstani. osmundi. hudan. ósrici. ceolrædi. uulflafi.

3. Thinner, cursive.

eðeluulfi. *fluminis* humbrę. æt astran—ceolnoð. alhstani. helmstani. humberhti. cyrredi. cyneferði. ræðhuni. heaberhti. ceolberhti. beorhtredi. uuillredi. cuðuulfi.

23.

Ceolnoð c. Cott. Aug. ii. 37 (B. M. ii. 27).

1. Same hand as B 2.

kyninges tún. *regione* suðregiæ. ceolnoðo. ecgberhto, æðeluulfo. ceolnoðo. ecgberhto *et* æðeluulfo *agrum* et mallingu*m*. baldredo. et mallingu*m*. ceolnoðo. ecgberhtum. ecgberht *et* æðeluulf—ceolnoð. beagmund. uuærheard. brunheard. hysenoð. hunræd. uuigmund. beornoð. osmund. heaberht. badenoð. uualhhere. noðuulf. ceoluulf.

æðeluulfum. uuiltún—æðeluulf. alhstan. eadhun. uulfhardi. æðeluulfi. eanuulfi. eanuulfi. monnedi. æðelhelmi. eadberhti. æðelheardi. ecgberhti. alhstani. osmundi. hudan. osrici. ceolrædi. uulflafi.

2. Same hand as B 3.

æðeluulfi *regis*. *fluminis* humbre. æt astran—ceolnoð. alhstani. helmstani. humberhti. wigmundi. cyneferði. reðhuni. heaberhti. ceolberhti. beorhtredi. uuilredi. cuðulfi.

3. Different hand.

ðis sint ecgberhtes geðingeo 7 æðeluulfes uuið arcebiscep 7 uuið hiora leoda uuiotan . . eouuer gecor. gif eow h(ua) brocie for eouuere gecore, (ðonne) i(c) . . ge ðis geuurit[1].

24.

Æðelwulf[1]. Cott. Aug. ii. 28.

839.

Rough. Cant. arch. K. II. 1 (241). B. M. II. 28.

ego aeðeluulfus *rex occidentalium saxonum centuriorum. tibi* *iðdan. *civitate doroverniae. fluminae* st[u]ræ. *tibi* duddan. *in villa regia añ* uuiægenweoras. stur—aeðeu[u]lf. ceolnoð. aeðelstan. herebearht. aeðuulf. wulfred. alhhere. noðmund. uulfred. aeðelhard. noðuulf. ealhhun. oshere. modulf. boba. aeðered. uuina. aeðelm. duduc. uulflaf. aeðelric. huda. sigebearht. tucca. ceoluulf. tiruulf. dudda. uhtred—ælfred. æðered—lulla gebohte ðas boec 7 ðis lond æt æðewalde miþ ealra ðeassa *vel* portweorona gewitnisse—æðeluulfi *regis. ego* bægmund. wereard. osmund. abba. brunheard. hysenoð. hunred. uuigmund. lulling. heabearht. uueahhere. badenoð. noðuulf. ceoluulf. wer-bald. hwiting. freoðogeard. cichus.

25.

Æðelwulf[2]. Stowe 16.

843.

ego aetheluulf *rex occidentalium saxonum seu etiam* cantuuariorum *meo ministro* aethelmode *in regione cantiae que nominatur* on cert. on cert—hr..leag[2] [*in loca qui dicitur* noðfreðing] 7 suae cildebergas 7 tycan ora, ðonne mogan cumb. æt stenan steaple. þonne hearde méd. *silva quem nos* theodoice snad *nominamus. in loca qui vocatur* bean. gyldeburne. berhteningleag —*pastus porcorum qui in nostra saxonica lingua* denbera *vocantur:* aetingden. lidingden[3]. meredenn. uddanhom. cadacahrygc. heoratleag. hwitan[3] :::::. hildgaringdenn. tilgeseltha. hlifge-

[1] *later endorsement:* Meallingas. [2] *about* 14 *words erased after* hr . . leag. [3] *erased.*

sella—*actum in loco quae nominatur* meranworð—aetheluulf. aeðelstan *rex*. aeðeluulf. alahhere. freðoric. aeðelmod. di[o]ra. aeðelric. duduc. huda. eanuulf. lulluc. ceolnoð. uuaerheard. brunheard. hysenoð. hunred. wimund. beornferð. walahhere. noðwulf. wærbald.

26.

Æðelwulf[3]. Cott. Aug. ii. 60.

845.

Cant. arch. K. II. 26 (259). B. M. II. 29.

aeðeluulf *rex occidentalium saxonum necnon et* cantuariorum. badonoðe *apparitori meo. doroverniae civitatis.* et uuihtbaldes hlawe. uueowera get. *in confinio* deoringlondes. *fluminis qui dicitur* stúr. *prata,* aling med, longan med, *et jacit* be norðan hege. alchhere *ducis.* xv mancusas *auri. villa qui dicitur* on uueę—aeðeluulf. aeðelstan. tatnoð. alchhere. degberht. wynhere. aeðelmod. eadwulf. osberht. ęðelred. duduc. goda. wullaf. sig . . erht. ęðelric—badenoðingland.

27.

Æðelwulf[5]. Cott. Aug. ii. 71.

855.

Rough. Cant. arch. K. II. 48 (269). B. M. II. 31.

ego eðelwulf *rex occidentalium saxonum nec non et* cantuariorum. *meo ministro* ealdhere. *in provincia* cantuariorum, *ubi* ulaham *nominatur. terram et* ulaham. eðelwulf. *terra* ęt ulaham—hodo worða. winter bur[na]. *prata* to liminge. bromteag—eðelwulf. cialnoðus. eþelbearht. lullede. eðelmod. eadred. elfred. eðeric. duduc. cyneheard. wiohtgar. cialmund. milred. lulla. wullaf. eðelred—ðis sindan ðes landes bec et uluham, ealdheres landes.

28.

Æðelberht[3]. Cott. Aug. ii. 66.

858.

Rough. Mersham (Kent). Cant. arch. K. II. 64 (281). Th. 119. B. M. II. 33.

ego eðelbearht *rex dabo meo ministro* wullafe. *in illa loco ubi* *wasngwelle *nominatur. terrae* et mersa ham. *terram* et wassingwellan. eðelbearht. *terra* et mersaham. *quos* [h]ega *ante abuerat.* an wiwara wic. *subjecta* **erat* to wii ⁊ to leanaham ⁊ et febresham I sealtern ⁊ II wena gang mid cyninges wenum to blean ðem wiada ⁊ IIII oxnum gers mid cyninges oxnum an wiwarawic. *in alia* wiwarawic. xx lamba ⁊ xx fehta. *terra* et wassingwellan—cyninges folcland, *quod abet* wighelm ⁊ wulflaf. cuðrices dun. heregeðe land. wigh lmes land. biscepes land. to cert. an wassingwellan. an hwite celdan hec. *pascua porcorum quot nostra lingua* denbera *nominamus :* lamburnan den, orrices den. teligden. stanehtan denn, *et illa silva,* sandhyrst *nominatur quae pertinet* to wassingwellan. wullafe. et wassingwellan—*hec sunt prata* to wassingwellan : stocmed healf be norðan hegforde, be sture meda sue ðerto limpað—eðelbearht. eðelmod. eastmund. wullaf. eðered. sigenoð. beagmund. ese. dun. oslac. dudda. mucel. burgnoð. eðelweald. eadweald. lulla. acka. cynelaf. eðelhere. wighelm. noðmund. sigemund. hunfreð—ðis siondan ðes landes boec et wassingwellan ðet eðelbearht cyning wullafe sealde his ðegne wið oðrum sue miclum lande et mersaham. se cyning sealde ⁊ gebocade wullafe fif sulung landes et wassingwellan wið ðem fif sulungum et mersaham. ⁊ se cyning dyde ðet land et mersaham him to folclande, ða hie ðem landum iehwerfed hefdan butan ðem merscum ⁊ butan ðem sealtern et fefresham, ⁊ butan ðem wioda ðe to ðem sealtern limpð—ðis siondan ðes landes (boc et) wassingwellan.

29.

Æðelberht[4]. Cott. Ch. viii. 32.

862.

Rough. Bromley (Kent). Rochester arch. K. II. 72 (287). B. M. II. 36.

aeðælberht *rex occidentalium saxonum seu* cantu*ariorum.* dryhtwaldo *ministro meo.* bromleag—an norðan fram ceddan leage to langan leage bromleaginga mearc ⁊ liofs hema. ðanne fram langan leage to ðam wón stocce. ðanne fram ðam wón stocce be modinga hema mearce to cinta stiogole. ðanne fram cinta stiogole be modinga hema mearce to earnes beame. ðanne fram earnes beame cregsetna haga an easthalfe sced hit to liowsan dene. ðanne fram liowsan dene to swelgende. ðanne fram swelgende cregsetna haga to sioxslihtre. ðanne fram sioxslihtre to fearnbiorginga mearce.

fearnbiorginga mearc hit. sced to. cýstaninga[1] mearcę. cýstaninga[1] mearc hit sced suðan to weardsetle. ðanne fram weardsetle cýsstaninga[1] mearc to wichæma mearcę. ðanne sio westmearc be wichema mearcę ut to bipplestydæ. ðanne fram bipplestydę to acustydę to bioh[h]ahema mearcę. fram acustyde to ceddan leage—ðanne *belimpoð ðer to ðam londe fif denn an anutwalda. brocces ham ðes dennes nama. ðes oðres dennes nama sænget hryg. billan ora is ðes ðriddan nama. ðanne twa denn an gleppan felda—*in loco quae dicitur* willherestrio—aeðelberht. ciolnoð. aeðerred. aelfred. aeðælred. dryhtwald. heremod. alhhard. mucel. egcberht. eaduulf. æðæluulf. signoð. eanuulf. æsca. eastmund. orduulf. wiohtgar. æðelred. cynlaf. co(en)wald. cuðred. uulflaf. ælfhere.

30.

Æðelberht[5]. Cant. Archives (Cam. x).

863.

Rough. Mersham (Kent). K. II. 74 (288). Th. 121.

ego eðelbearht *rex occidentalium saxonum necnon et* cantuariorum *dabo meo ministro* eðelredo *aliquem partem terrae in illo loco ubi nominatur* mersaham. *cccctos* mancusas *auri. terram* et mersaham. eðelbearht—*ab occidente* stur *usque* blacan riðe. eadwealdes bocland to bradeburnan. *ab oriente* sture. *usque* garulfi *regis ministri* to mersaham 7 meda be eastan ee sue ðer mid riahte to ðem lande limpað *unamque salis coquinariam hoc est* I sealternsteall 7 ðer cota to *in illa loco ubi nominatur* herewic. *pascua porcorum, quae nostra lingua saxonica* denbera *nominamus: hoc est* husneah :::::: efreðingdenn herbedingenn pafingdenn :::::: widefingdenn bleccingdenn :::::: — *necnon xx statera casei* of mersce *ad* mersaham *reddatur — in illo loco que vocitatur* birenefeld — eðelbearht. eðered. eðered. dryhtweald. mucel. heahmund. heremod. garulf. eastmund. uulfred. wigstan. ecgferð. ealdred. sigenoð. elfstan. wighelm. wiahtred. ciolnoð. deimund. biarnulf. eðelweald. noðheard. osmund. iab. wighelm. tida. biarnheah. osulf. ealhstan. sigefreð. diarweald. sefreð. osmund. dudda. beagmund. osweald. lulla. oba. lulla. hunfreð. lulla. eadulf. osbearht. wealdhelm. ealdhere. diara. garulf. elric. dudda.

[1] *accent on* y *not certain.*

eðelwulf—ic eadwald sellò 7 forgeofu þis lond et wifeles *bergė agustines higum into hiora beode minre sawle to are 7 to *leedome; 7 iow fer godes lufe bidde þet ge hit minre sawle nyt gedeo, 7 me hit for gode leanie eow to elmessum, amen.

31.

Æðelred. Cott. Aug. ii. 95.

867.

St. Martin's, Canterbury. Cant. arch. K. II. 83 (294). B. M. II. 37.

ego eðelred *rex occidentalium saxonum* (*nec*)*non et* cantwariorum. *meo amico* wighelme. *in loco qui dicitur sancti martini ecclesia*—hina meteren. hina gemene weg—eðelred. *dorobernia*—eðelred. eastmund. ealhheard. heremod. mucel. beorhtnoð. forðred. eðelwulf. eðelred. acca. biarhtwulf. mannel. cialnoð. eðeredi *regis.* biarnhelm. noðheard. biarnfreð. osmund. wighelm. eðelweald. eardulf. biarnhelm. tidweald. beornred. sefreð. beornheah. sigefreð. sebearht. sigemund. torhthelm. herefreð. beornweald. wealdhere. elfstan. aldred. bearnulf. sigefred. bearnoð. herefreð. ealhheard. cialbearht. wealdhelm. tirweald —án setl æt *sancte* martine.

32.

Ælfred[1]. Stowe 18.

873.

Rough, irregular. Yalding, Bossingham (Kent).

ego elfred *rex, ego* eðered *archiepiscopus concedimus* liaban **fili* burgwines *agellam qoð nos nominamus* gilding. xx mancusa—crudes *silba. terra* *wer[f]eðes **monahis nostri. terra ad* bosingtune—*ego* æðelulf *rex occidentalium saxonum.* eanuulf. eðeluf. eðelbæld. uulfheard. æðelric. ceolmund. uuerenberht. lulling. uulffreð. eðeluf. eanulf. eðeluf. eðelbald. uulfeard. æðelric. ceolmund. *luling. ceolnoð. eðelstan. eðelulf. ealhhere. dryhtnoð. duduc. eðelmod. eðelric. eðelred. eðelhere. osmund. eðered. *gilsheard. eadberht. dudda. ealhhun. cyneberht.

IX. CENT. KENTISH.

33.

Æðelheard[1]. Cant. Arch. c. I.

803.

Pal. Soc. 23. K. v. 64 (1024). Th. 50.

ego aeðelheardus *dorobern[ens]is ecclesiae archiepiscopus*—aeðelheardus. aeþelheah. uulfheard. beornmod. feologeld. wernoð. uulfred. *aldulsus, liccedfeldensis *ecclesiae episcopus*. hygberht. monn. eadhere. lulla. wigferð. cuðberht. werenberht, legorensis *civitatis episcopus*. alhmund[1]. forðred. eadberht. eadred. eanred. beonna. uuigmund. berhthæð. æþelhæh. mon. eadwulf, syddensis *civitatis episcopus*. eadred. plegberht. hereberht. dæghelm. eaduulf. heaðored. deneberht, wegoranensis *civitatis episcopus*. hyseberht. pæga. coenferð. ðingcferð. freoðomund. selerẹd. wulfheard, herefordensis *ecclesiae episcopus*. cuðred. dycga. heaðobald. strygel. monn. wẹrferð. wigberht, scirabumensis *ecclesiae episcopus*. muca. berhtmund. eadberht. ealhmund, wintanæ *civitatis episcopus*. cuðberht. marcus. notheard. cufa. lulla. wigðegn. alhheard, elmhamis *ecclesiae episcopus*. folcberht. eadberht. hunfrið. freoðuberht. wulflaf. beornhelm. tidfrið, dammucae *civitatis episcopus*. uulfheard. ceolhelm. tilberht. lull. cynulf. eadberht. osmund, *lundonensis civitatis episcopus*. heahstan. tidhun. aeþelhelm. wighard. freoðored. wermund. lullingc. beagnoð. wigheard. tuda. heahberht. heared. uuihthun, selesegi *ecclesiae episcopus*. (c)eolmund[2]. eadberht. heahferð. dudd. beorcol. cynebald—*in loco qui vocatur* clofes hoas.

34.

Cuðred. Stowe 7, Cott. Aug. ii. 100.

805.

Æðelnoð's endorsement only in Stowe. K. I. 233 (191). B. M. II. 7 (Cott.).

ego cuðredus *rex* cantwariorum[3] *cum consensu* coenuulfi *regis* merciorum *dabo* æðelnoðo *praefecto meo in provincia cantiae terram in loco qui dicitur* æt heagyðe[4] ðorne—coenuulf. cuðred.

[1] *altered from* alumund. [2] c *cut off*. [3] cantuua. *C.* [4] hẹgyðe *C.*

uulfredus[1]. coenwald. osuulf. ealdberht. wealh. æðelieard[2]. berhtnoð. ceolnoð. wulfred. alduulf. uerenberht[3]. deneberht. tidferð. alhheard. eaduulf. wulfheard. beornmod. wigberht. alhmund. wiohthun. wigmund. beonna[4].

æðelnoð se *gerefa to éastorege 7 gænburg his wif aræddan hiora érfe beforan wulfre[de] arcebiscope 7 æðelhune his mæsseprioste 7 esne cyninges ðegne suæ hueðer hiora suæ leng lifes were foe[5] to londe 7 to alre æhte. gif hio bearn hæbbe, ðonne foe ðæt [ofer] hiora boega dagas to londe 7 to æhte. gif hio ðonne bearn næbbe, 7 wulfred archibiscop lifes sie, þonne foe he to ðæm londe, 7 hit forgelde 7 ðæt wiorð gedæle fore hiora gastas suæ ælmeslice 7 suæ rehtlice suæ he him seolfa on his wisdome geleornie, 7 ðas *prece nænig mon uferran dogor on nænge oðre halfe oncærrende sie nymne suæ þis gewrit hafað. wulfred. feologeld. æðelhun. cuðberht. æðelnoð. gænburg. esne.

þisses londes earan ðrie sulong æt hægyðe ðorne. 7 gif hiora oðrum oððe bæm suð fo[r]gelimpe, biscop ðæt lond gebycge suæ hie ðonne geweorðe.

35.

Wulfred[1]. Cott. Aug. ii. 47.

811.

Cant. arch. K. I. 238 (195). B. M. II. 11.

ego uulfred *christi ecclesiae antistes christi ecclesiae donabo terram in regione* easterege, *quae inibi ab incolis* folcuuininglond *vocatur. in regione* eosterege. *nostrae fraternitati* on byrg. ðæt folcwining lond on eosterge. *terrae* et liminum. coenuulf *rex.* on magonsetum æt geardcylle. *a* cyneðryðae *adquirere.* on liminu*m.* ðæt wynnhearding lond, 7 babbinglond, 7 an iocled on uppan *ufre. æt liminu*m*. on eosterge. on eostorege. *a* reacoluensae *ecclesiae.* dunwalinglond. æt burnan. aldhun. *domni* iaemberhti. ecgberht. aldhuno. offa. ecgberhto. aeðelheard. *rege* offa. aeðelheard. æt burnan. on easterege. æt burnan. on eostorege—uulfred. beornmodus. wernoð. beornwine. feologeld. aeðelhun. ceolstan. heamund. osuulf. heremod. tudda. deornoð. abba. guðmund. bada-

[1] wul. *C.* [2] *so also C.* [3] uue. *C.* [4] *later endorsement in C.* hegyðe ðorn. ðreo sulunga. [5] oe *on er.*

heard. cuðric. hunferð. uuilnoð. dryhtnoð. eangeard. aeðelheah. ealhun. deneberht. coenhere. tilred. billheard. dudd. goda. brunheard. uulfheard. osmund—coenuulfi *regis*. wulfredi. *in civitate dorovernia.*

36.

Wulfred[2]. Cott. Aug. ii. 72.

824?

Cant. arch. K. I. 290 (225). Th. 463. B. M. II. 17.

ego uulfred *arciepiscopus illa familia quae domino servitura est in dorouernia civitate aliquam partem meae terrae, hoc est iiii aratrorum, quod nominatur* æt sceldes forda—*terra quae pertinet ad* eastręge. osberhting lond. *terra quae pertinet ad* uuigincgga ham. sceldes ford. cynehard. ecgberhto *et* aeðeluulfo. dodda *monachus.* cynehardi *et* doddan—uulfred. ciolnoth. beagmund. uuerhard. aeðelhun. abba. hunred. osmund. wigmund. badanoð. heaberht. noðwulf. (b)runhard. (h)ysenoð. (daeg)mund. (biorn)-fer(ð). (eard)wulf. (oba). cichus. ealhheard. osmod. frioðogeard. (wi)ting. . . elered—sceldes fordæs boec 7 ðeara wica on byrg.

37.

Oswulf. Cott. Aug. ii. 79.

805–831.

Round, rather uncial. Cant. arch. K. I. 292 (226). Th. 459. B. M. I. 15.

ic osuulf aldormonn mid Godes gæfe ond beornðryð min gemecca sellað to cantuarabyrg to cristes cirican ðæt lond æt stanhamstede, xx swuluncga, gode allmehtgum 7 ðere halgon gesomnuncgæ fore hyhte 7 fore aedleane ðæs aecan 7 ðaes towardon lifes 7 fore uncerra saula hela 7 uncerra bearna. ond mid micelre eaðmodnisse biddað ðæt wit moten bion on ðem̄ gemanon ðe ðaer godes ðiowas siondan 7 ða menn *ða ðaer hlafordas wæron 7 ðara monna ðe hiora lond to ðaere cirican saldon. ond ðættæ mon unce tide ymb tuælf monað mon geuueorðiae on godcundum godum 7 æc on aelmessan suæ mon hiora doeð.

ic ðonne uulfred mid godes gaefe arc. epis. ðas forecuaedenan uuord fulliae, 7 bebeode ðæt mon ymb tuælf m̄onað hiora tid boega ðus geuueorðiae to anes daeges to osuulfes tide ge mid godcundum godum ge mid aelmessan ge aec mid higna suesendum. ðonne bebeode ic ðaet mon ðas ðing selle ymb tuælf monað of liminum, ðe ðis forecuaede[ne] lond to limpeð, of ðaem ilcan londe æt stanhamstede: cxx huaetenra hlafa ⁊ xxx clenra, ⁊ án hriðer dugunde ⁊ IIII scęp ⁊ tua flicca ⁊ v goes ⁊ x hennfuglas ⁊ x pund caeses, gif hit fuguldaeg sie. gif hit ðonne festendæg sie, selle mon uuęge cæsa ⁊ fisces ⁊ butran ⁊ aegera ðaet mon begeotan maege, ⁊ xxx ombra godes uuelesces aloð ð(et) limpeð to xv mittum, ⁊ mittan fulne huniges, oððа tuęgen uuines, suę hwaeder suae mon ðonne begeotan maege. ond of higna gemęnum godum ðaer aet ham mon geselle cxx gesufira hlafa to aelmessan for hiora saula suae mon aet hlaforda tidum doeð. ond ðas forecuędenan suęsenda all agefe mon ðęm reogolwarde, ⁊ he brytnię swæ higum maest red sie ⁊ ðaem sawlum soelest. aec mon ðaet weax ágæfe to *ciricican, ⁊ hiora sawlum nytt gedoe ðe hit man fore doeð. aec ic bebeode minum aefterfylgendum ðe ðaet lond hębben aet Burnan ðaet hiae simle ymb XII monað foran to ðære tide gegeorwien ten hund hlafa ⁊ swae feola sufla, ⁊ ðęt mon gedele to aelmessan aet ðere tide fore mine sawle ⁊ Osuulfes ⁊ beornðryðe [aet cristes cirican], ⁊ him se reogolweord on byrg gebeode foran to hwonne sio tid sie. aec ic bidde higon ðette hie ðas godcundan god gedon aet ðere tide fore hiora sawlum: ðaet ęghwilc messepriost gesinge fore osuulfes sawle twa messan, twa fore beornðryðe sawle; ⁊ aeghwilc diacon arede twa passione fore his sawle, twa fore hire; ond ęghwilc godes ðiow gesinge twa fiftig fore his sawle, twa fore hire, ðaette ge fore uueorolde sien geblitsade mid ðem weoroldcundum godum ⁊ hiora saula mid ðem godcundum godum. aec ic biddo higon ðaet ge me gemynen aet ðere tide mid suilce godcunde gode suilce iow cynlic ðynce, ic ðe ðas gesettnesse sette ge hueder ge for higna lufon ge ðeara saula ðe haer beforan hiora namon auuritene siondon. *valete in domino.*

þis is gesetnes (o)sulf(es ⁊) bearnðryðe.

38.

Eadwald. Cott. Aug. ii. 19.

831.

Roughish. Cant. arch. K. I. 295 (228). Th. 465. B. M. II. 19.

ðis is geðinge eadwaldes, osheringes, 7 cyneðryðe, eðelmodes lafe aldormonnes, ymbe ðet lond et cert ðe hire eðelmod hire hlabard salde. wes hit becueden *osbearte his broðar suna, gif he cyneðryðe oferlifde, 7 siððan *neniggra meihanda ma ðes cynnes, ac hia hit atuge yfter hira dege swe hit him boem rehtlicast 7 elmestlicast were.

ðonne hebfað eadwald 7 *cyne ðas wisan ðus fundene mid hira friandum. gib eadweald leng lifige ðonne cyneðryð, geselle et ðem londe et cert x ðusenda. gif he gewite er ðonne hia, his barna sue hwelc sue lifes sie agefe ðet feoh, ond[1] atee sue hit soelest sie for ða hit begetan. nis eðelmode enig meghond neor ðes cynnes ðanne eadwald, his modar, his broðar dohtar: mest cyn ðet he ðet lond hebbe 7 his beorn yfter him, 7 sue ateon sue him *nytlicas ðynce for ða ðe hit mid reohte begetan.

ego ceolnoð m.id godes gefe ercebiscop þis mid xps' rodetacne festnie 7 write. biarnhelm. eðelmund. osmund. biarnheah. sefreð. *ðelwald. *whelm. eðelwald. eardulf. biarnhelm. eadgar. elfstan. sigefreð. sigefreð. ealhstan. b(ia)rnnoð. cialbarht. wealdhelm. tirwald. oba. biarnhelm. sigemund. herefreð. wynhelm. wunbeald. wermund.

39.

Ealhburg. Cott. Aug. ii. 52.

About 831.

Rough, irregular. Cant. arch. K. I. 296 (229). Th. 468. B. M. II. 21.

ðis sindan geðinga ealhburge 7 eadwealdes et ðem lande et burnan hwet man elce gere ob ðem lande to cristes cirican ðem hiwum agiaban scel for ealhburge 7 for ealdred 7 fore eadweald 7 ealawynne: XL ambra mealtes, 7 XL 7 CC hlaba, I wege cesa,

[1] d *crowded in.*

I wege speces, I eald hriðer, IIII weðras, X goes, XX henfugla, IIII foðra weada. 7 ic ealhburg bebiade eadwealde minem mege an godes naman 7 an ealra his haligra ðet he ðis wel healde his dei 7 siððan forð bebeode his erbum to healdenne, ða[1] hwile ðe hit cristen se. 7 suelc mon se ðet lond hebbe eghwylce sunnandege X gesuflra hlafa to ðare[2] cirican for ealdredes saule 7 for ealhburge.

ðis is sia elmesse ðe ealhhere bebead ealawynne his doehter et ðenglesham, et III sulungum: elce gere C pen' to cristes cirican ðem higum. 7 suelc man se ðisses landes bruce, agebe ðis fiah an godes gewitnesse 7 an ealra his haligra, 7 suilc man sue hit awege ðonne se hit on his sawale nas on ðes ðe hit don het.

40.

Lufu. Cott. Aug. ii. 92.

832.

Rough. Cant. arch. K. I. 299 (231). Th. 474. B. M. II. 22.

ic lufa mid godes gefe *ancilla domini* wes soecende 7 smeagende ymb mine saulðearfe mid ceolnoðes ærcebiscopes geðeahte 7 ðara hiona et cristes cirican. willa ic gesellan of ðem ærfe ðe me god forgef 7 mine friond to gefultemedan ęlce gere LX ambra maltes 7 CL hlafa, L hwitehlafa, CXX *elmeshlafes, an hriðer, an suin, IIII weðras, II węga spices 7 ceses ðem higum to cristes *circcan for mine saule 7 minra frionda 7 mega ðe me to gode gefultemedan, 7 ðęt sie simle to adsumsio scæ[3] marie ymb XII monað. end sue eihwelc mon swe ðis lond hebbe minra ærbenumena ðis agefe 7 mittan fulne huniges, X goes, XX henfuglas.

ic ceolnoð mid godes gefe ercebisc*op* mid cristes rodetacne ðis festnie 7 write. beagmund pr' geðafie 7 mid write. beornfrið pr' geðafie 7 mid write. wealhhere. osmund. deimund. æðelwald. werbald. sifreð. swiðberht. beornheah. æðelmund. wighelm. lubo.

ic luba eaðmod godes ðiwen ðas forecwedenan god 7 ðas elmessan gesette 7 gefestnie ob minem erfelande et mundlingham ðem hiium to cristes cirican. 7 ic bidde 7 an godes libgendes naman bebiade

[1] the *a* blotted. [2] indistinct: may be *ðære*. [3] *no mark of contraction.*

ðæm men ðe ðis land ⁊ ðis erbe hebbe et mundlingham ðet he ðas god forðleste oð wiaralde ende. se man se ðis healdan wille ⁊ lestan ðet ic beboden hebbe an ðisem gewrite se him seald ⁊ gehealden sia hiabenlice b[l]edsung. se his ferwerne oððe hit agele se him seald ⁊ gehealden helle wite, bute he to fulre bote gecerran wille gode ⁊ mannum. *uene ualete.*

lufe þincggewrit.

41.

Abba. Cott. Aug. ii. 64.

835.

Cant. arch. K. I. 310 (235). Th. 469. B. M. II. 23.

ic abba geroefa cyðe ⁊ writan hate hu min willa ís þæt mon ymb min ærfe gedoe æfter minu*m* dæge.

ærest ymb min lond þe ic hæbbe, ⁊ me god lah, ⁊ ic æt minu*m* hlafordu*m* begæt, is min willa, gif me god bearnes unnan wille, ðæt hit foe to londe æfter me ⁊ his bruce mid minu*m* gemeccan, ⁊ sioððan swæ forð min cynn ða hwile þe god wille ðæt ðeara ænig sie þe londes weorðe sie ⁊ land gehaldan cunne. gif me ðonne gifeðe sie ðæt ic bearn begeotan ne męge, þonne is min willa þæt hit hæbbe min wiíf ða hwile ðe hia hit mid clennisse gehaldan wile, ⁊ min broðar alchhere hire fultume ⁊ þæt lond hire nytt gedoe. ⁊ him man sęlle an half swulung an ciollan dene to habbanne ⁊ to brucanne, wið ðan ðe he ðy geornliocar hire ðearfa bega ⁊ bewiotige. ⁊ mon selle him to ðem londe IIII oxan, ⁊ II cy, ⁊ L scępa, ⁊ æune horn. gif min wiíf ðonne hia nylle mid clennisse swæ gehaldan, ⁊ hire liofr[e] sie oðer hemed to niomanne, ðonne foen mine megas to ðem londe, ⁊ hire agefen hire agen. gif hire ðonne liofre sie.. . . nster to gánganne oððа suð to faranne[1], ðonne agefen hie twægen mine męgas, alchhere ⁊ aeðel . . . . hire twa ðusenda ⁊ fon him to ðem londe. ⁊ ágefe mon to liminge L eawa ⁊ V cy fore hie, ⁊ mon selle to folcanstane in mid minu*m* lice X oxan, ⁊ X cy, ⁊ C eawa, ⁊ C swina, ⁊ higum an sundran D pend' wið ðan ðe min wíif þær benuge innganges swæ mid

[1] first *a* from *o*: the scribe probably meant to write *foeranne*.

minu*m* lice swæ sioððan yferran dogre, swæ hwæder swæ hire liofre sie. gif higan ðonne oððe hlaford þæt nylle hire mynsterlifes geunnan, oððа hia siolf nylle, ⁊ hire oðer ðing liofre sie, þonne agefe mon ten hund pend' inn mid minu*m* lice me wið legerstowe ⁊ higum an sundran fif hund pend' fore mine sawle.

⁊ ic bidde ⁊ bebeode swælc monn se ðæt min lond hebbe ðæt he ælce gere agefe ðem higum æt folcanstane L ambra maltes, ⁊ VI ambra gruta, ⁊ III wega spices ⁊ ceses, ⁊ CCCC ħlafa, ⁊ an hriðr, ⁊ VI scep. ⁊ swælc monn se ðe to minum ærfe foe, ðonne gedele he ælcum messepreoste binnan cent mancus goldes, ⁊ ælcum godes ðiowe pend', ⁊ to *sancte* petre min wærgeld twa ðusenda. ⁊ freoðomund foe to minu*m* sweorde, ⁊ agefe ðer æt feower ðusenda; ⁊ him mon forgefe ðeran ðreotene hund pending[1]. ⁊ gif mine broðar ærfeweard gestrionen ðe londes weorðe sie, þonne ann ic ðem londes. gif hie ne gestrionen oððа him sylfu*m* ælles hwæt sęle, æfter hiora dege ann ic his freoðomunde, gif he ðonne lifes bið. gif him elles hwæt sæleð, ðonne ann ic his minra swæstar suna, swælcum se hit geðian wile ⁊ him gifeðe bið. ⁊ gif þæt gesele þæt min cynn to ðan clane gewite ðæt ðer ðeara nan ne sie ðe londes weorðe sie, þonne foe se hlaford to ⁊ ða higan æt kristes cirican, ⁊ hit minum gaste nytt gedoen. an ðas redenne ic hit ðider selle ðe se monn se ðe kristes cirican hlaford sie [se] min ⁊ minra erfewearda forespreoca ⁊ mundbora, ⁊ an his hlaforddome [we] bian moten.

ic ciolnoð mid godes gefe ærcebiscop ðis write ⁊ ðeafie, ⁊ mid cristes rodetacne hit festniæ. ic beagmund pr' ðis ðeafie ⁊ write. ic wærhard pr' ab' ðis ðeafie ⁊ write. ic abba geroefa ðis write ⁊ festnie mid kristes rodetacne. ic æðelhun pr' ðis ðeafie ⁊ write. ic abba pr' ðis þeafie ⁊ write. ic wigmund pr' ðis write ⁊ ðeafie. ic iof pr' ðis ðeafie ⁊ write.

ic osmund pr' ðis ðeafie ⁊ write. ic wealhhere diac' ðis write ⁊ ðeafie. ic badanoð diac' ðis write ⁊ ðeafie. ic heaberht diac' ðis write ⁊ þeafie. ic noðwulf subdiac' ðis write ⁊ ðeafie. ic wealhhere subdiac' ðis write ⁊ ðeafie. ic ciolwulf subdiac' ðis write ⁊ ðeafie.

heregyð hafað ðas wisan binemned ofer hire deg ⁊ ofer abban.

[1] *end of line;* pendinga (?).

ðæm higum et cristes cirican of ðæm londe et cealflocan: ðæt is ðonne ðritig ombra alað, ⁊ ðreo hund hlafa, ðeara bið fiftig hwitehlafa, an weg spices ⁊ ceses, an ald hriðr, feower weðras, an suin oððe sex weðras, sex gosfuglas, ten hennfuglas, ðritig teapera, gif hit wintres deg sie, sester fulne huniges, sester fulne butran, sester fulne saltes. ⁊ heregyð bibeadeð ðem mannu*m* ðe efter hire to londe foen on godes noman ðæt hie fulgere witen ðæt hie ðiss gelęsten ðe on ðissem gewrite binemned is ðęm higum to cristes cirican, [⁊ ðæt sie simle to higna blodlese ymb twelf monað agefen.] ⁊ se mann se to londe foe agefe hire erfehonda XIII pund pendinga; ⁊ hio forgifeð fiftene pund for ðy ðe mon ðas feorme ðy soėl gelæste.

(abban geroefan ærfegedal[1], his geðinga to kristes cirican.)

42.

Badanoð. Cott. Aug. ii. 42.

837.

Cant. arch. K. I. 316 (238). Th. 476. B. M. II. 25.

ic badanoð beotting cyðo ⁊ writan hato hu min willa is ðet min ærfelond fere ðe ic et aeðeluulfe cyninge begæt ⁊ gebohte mid fullum friodome on æce ærfe æfter minum dege ⁊ minra ærfewearda, ðet is, mines wifes ⁊ minra bearna. ic wille ærist me siolfne gode allmehtgum forgeofan to ðere stowe æt cristes cirican, ⁊ min bearn ðęr liffest gedoan, ⁊ wiib ⁊ cild ðæm hlaforde ⁊ higum ⁊ ðære stowe befestan ober minne dei to friðe ⁊ to mundbyrde ⁊ to hlaforddome on ðæm ðingum ðe him ðearf sie. ⁊ hie brucen londes hiora dei, ⁊ higon gefeormien to minre tide swæ hie soelest ðurhtion megen; ⁊ higon us mid heora godcundum godum swę gemynen swæ us arlic ⁊ him ælmeslic się.

⁊ ðonne ofer hiora dei, wifes ⁊ cilda, ic bebeode on godes noman ðæt mon agefe ðæt lond inn higum to heora beode him to brucanne on ece ærfe, swæ him liofast sie. ⁊ ic biddo higon for godes lufe ðæt se monn se higon londes unnen to brucanne ða ilcan wisan

[1] æ *doubtful; may be* a.

leste on swæsendum to minre tide, 7 ða godcundan lean minre saule mid gerece swę hit mine ærfenuman ær onstellen.

ðonne is min willa ðæt ðissa gewriota sien twa gelice: oðer habben higon mid boecum, oðer mine ærfeweardas heora dei.

ðonne is ðes londes ðe ic higum selle XVI gioc ærðelondes 7 medwe[1], all on æce ærfe to brucanne ge minne dei, ge æfter swæ to ationne swæ me mest red 7 liofast sie.

ceolnoð arc' episc' ðiss writo 7 festnię mid cristes rodetacne. alchhere dux ðiss writo 7 ðeafię. bægmund prb' ab' ðiss writo 7 ðeafię. hysenoð pr' ðiss writo 7 ðeafię. wigmund. badenoð. osmund. suiðberht. dyddel. cichus. sigemund. eðelwulf. tile. cyneberht. eðelred. badanoð.

43.

Plegred. Cott. Aug. ii. 16.

859.

Rough. Cant. arch. K. II. 66 (282). B. M. II. 34.

ego plegred *emi aliquam terre unculam* [et][2] eðelmode, *hoc est*, an healf tun *que ante pertinebat* to wilburgewellan, ðet land healf 7 healfne tun—cyniges hei weg. stret to scufelingforde. stur. cyninges land 7 halfne wer. *una prata* on burgwara medum suðeweardum, 7 an norðeweardum burgwara medum healfmed, 7 meahse log an cyninges strete—eðelmod. plegrede—eðelwulf. eanulf. eðelwulf. eðelmod. hunred. eðelbeald. eðeric. dudda. wimund. ceolmund. werenbearht. lulling. eadweald. wulfred. deimund. sebearht. diar. osulf. biarnhelm. hyse. duningcg. eð[el]noð.

44.

Ceolwulf[3]. Cott. Aug. ii. 17.

888 *or* 868.

Roughish. Cant. arch. K. II. 87 (296). B. M. II. 38.

cialulf. eanmunde *amico meo. in dorobernia—terminibus: in oriente* ęðelmund. deibearht. ciolulf. hemma—eanmunde—

[1] *space of about 16 letters erased here.*

[2] *written on margin.*

ęðered. ciolnoð. heahmund. ęðelwulf. dryhtweald. eastmund. garulf. ecgbearht. ecgferð. acca. wynsige. ęðered. dudda. lulla. ęðelweald. ęðelmund. eacca. ęðelweald. ęðelweald. osmund. ciolulf—ciolulf sealde eanmunde his mege ðisne tuun betwix eum wið cxx in *ęc ęrbe ęðeredes cyninges friols 7 his hand seten 7 sęlen.

IX CENT. SURREY.

45.

Ælfred[2]. Stowe 19.

871–889.

Horsley, Clapham, Chertsey, &c. (Surrey). K. II. 120 (317). Th. 480.

ic ęlfred *dux* hatu writan 7 cyðan an ðissum gewrite ęlfrede *regi* 7 allum his weotum 7 geweotan, 7 ec swylce minum megum 7 minum gefeorum, þa męn þe ic mines ęrfes 7 mines boclondes seolest onn, ðęt is þonne werburg min wif 7 uncer *ge*mene[1] b*earn*. *þæt* is þonne et ęrestan an sondenstede 7 on selesdune XXXII hida, 7 on westarham XX hida, 7 on cloppaham XXX hida, 7 on leangafelda VI hida, 7 on horsalęge X hida, 7 on netelam[styde] VI hida. ic ęlfred *dux* sello werburge 7 alhdryðe uncum *ge*menum bearne æfter minum dege þas lond mid cwice ęrfe 7 mid earðe 7 mid allum ðingum ðe to londum belimpað. 7 twa þusendu swina ic heom sello mid þem londum, gif hio hio gehaldeð mid þare clęnnisse þe uncer word*ge*cweodu seondan. 7 hio gebrenge ęt sancte petre min twa wergeld, gif ðet godes willa seo þet heo *þæt* fęreld age. ond ęfter werburge dęge seo alhðryðe þa lond unbefliten on sondemstyde 7 on selesdune 7 on leangafelda. ond gif heo bearn hębbe, feo ðęt bearn to ðęm londum ęfter hire ; gif heo bearn nębbe, feo ðonne an hire rehtfęderen sio neste hond to þem londe ond to ðem ęrfe, 7 swa hwylc minra fędrenmega swa ðęt sio *þæt* hine to ðan *ge*hagige *þæt* he þa oðoro lond begeotan męge 7 wille, þonne gebygcge he þa lond ęt hire mid halfe weorðe. ond swe hwylc mon swa ðęt sio þęt ðes londes bruce ofer minne dęg on cloppaham, þanne ge-

[1] *the ge is expressed here and below by a 7 with the direction of the upper stroke reversed.*

selle he cc peninga eghwylce gere to ceortesege for ęlfredes sawle to feormfultume[1]. ond ic sello ęðelwalde minum sunu III hida boclondes: II hida on huętedune, ...s hides an gatatune, 7 him sello þerto c swina; 7 gif se cyning him geunnan wille þęs folclondes to ðęm boclonde, þonne hębbe 7 bruce; gif hit þęt ne sio, þonne selle hio him swa hwaðer swa hio wille, swa ðęt lond an horsalege, swe ðęt an leangafelda. on[d] ic sello berhtsige minum mege án hide boclondes on lęncanfelda, 7 þerto c swina; 7 geselle hio c swina to cristes cirican for me 7 fer mine sawle, 7 c to ceortesege; 7 þone oferęcan mon gedęle gind mynsterhamas to godes ciricum in suþregum 7 in cęnt, þa hwile þe hio lestan willęn. ond ic sello sigewulfe minum mege ofer werburge dęg þęt lond an netelhæmstyde; ond sigulf geselle of ðem londe c pęninga to cristes cirican. ond eghwylc þara ęrfewearda þe ęfter him to ðęm londe foe, þonne ageofen hío þa ilcan elmessan to cristes cirican for ęlfredes sawle, þa hwile þe fulwiht sio, 7 hít man on ðęm londe begeotan męge. ond ic sello eadrede minum mege þet lond on fearnlege ęfter eðelredes dęge, gif he hit to him geearnian wile; 7 he geselle of ðem londe xxx .... cornes ęghwelce gere to hrofescestre; ond sio ðis lond *ge*writen 7 unbefliten ęfter eadredes dege in aelfredes rehtmeodrencynn ða hwile þe fulwihte[2] sio on angelcynnes ealonde. ðeos foresprec 7 þas gewriotu þe herbeufan awreotene stondað, ic ælfred willio 7 wille *þæt* hio sion soðfęstlice forðweard getrymed me 7 minum ęrfeweardum. gif ðęt ðonne god ællmęhtig *ge*teod habbe, ond me þęt on lęne gelið þęt me gesibbra ęrfeweard forðcymeð wepnedhades 7 acęnned weorðeð, ðanne ann ic ðęm ofer minne dęg alles mines ęrfes to brucenne swa him leofust sio. and swa hwylc mon swa ðas god 7 þas geofe 7 þas gewrioto 7 þas word mid rehte haldan wille ond *ge*lęstan, gehalde hine heofones cyning in þissum life ondwardum, 7 eac swa in þęm towardan life; ond swa hwylc mon swa hio wonie 7 breoce, gewonie him god almahtig his weorldare ond ea[c] swa his sawle are.

her sindon ðæra manna naman awritene ðe ðeosse wísan geweoton sindon. ic æðered ar' bisc' mid ðære halgan cristes rode tacne ðas word 7 ðas wisan fęstnie 7 write. ælfred *dux*. beorhtuulf *dux*. beornhelm ab'. earduulf ab'. wærburg. sigfreð pr. *beon-

[1] *accent on first* m. [2] *accent on the* w.

heah pr. beagstan pr'. wulfheah. æðelwulf pr'. earduulf pr'. beornoð diac'. wealdhelm diac'. wine sb' diac'. sæfreð. ceolmund m'. eadmund m'. eadwald m'. siguulf m'.

IX CENT. MERCIAN.

46.

Æðelheard[2]. Cott. Aug. ii. 61.

803.

Litchfield (Stafford.). Cant. arch. K. I. 224 (185). Th. 48. B. M. II. 6.

offa *rex* merciorum. iaenberhti. aeðelheardus. aeðelheardo. coenuulfus. aeðelheardus. clofes hoas. aeðelheardus. *in* liccidfeldensi *monasterio*. liccedfeldensi. æt clofes houm—aeðelheardus. alduulfus. uuerenberhtus. alcheardus. uuigberhtus. alhmundus. osmundus. eaduulfus. deneberhtus. uuihthunus. tidfriðus. uulfheardus. alhmundus. beonna. f[o]rðréd. uuigmundus.

47.

Wiglaf[2]. Cott. Aug. ii. 9.

836.

Hanbury (Worc.) arch. K. I. 314 (237). Th. 88. B. M. II. 24.

uuiglaf *rex merciorum. monasterium* in heanbyrg. in craeft. *liberabo a difficultate illa quam nos saxonice* faestingmenn *dicimus*—uuiglaf. cyneðryþ *regina*. ceolnoð. cyneferð. raeþhun. eaduulf. heaberht. eaduulf. alhstan. beormod. husa. cunda. ceolberht. cynred. eanmund. uueohtred. beornhelm. sigred. mucoel. tiduulf. aeþelhard. cyneberht. aeþeluulf. alhhelm. humberht. aelfstan. mucoel. wicga. aldred. aldberht. aelfred. hwithyse. werenberht. wulfred. wiglaf. eanuulf. alhmund. berhtuulf. ecghard—ðes friodom waes bigeten aet wiglafe cyninge mid ðaem tuentigum hida aet iddes hale end ðaes londes friodom aet haeccaham mid ðy ten hida londe aet felda bi weoduman. end mucele esninge ðaet ten hida lond aet Croglea—ðis is heanburge friodom, se waes bigeten mid ðy londe aet iddes hale, ⁊ aet heanbyrig ten hida ðaes londes, 7 aet felda ten hida on beansetum. 7 biscop gesalde sigrede aldormenn sex hund scillinga on golde, 7 mucele aldormenn ten hida lond æt croglea[1].

48.

Berhtwulf. Cant. Arch. c. 1280.

About 840.

Wootton (Glouces.). K. II. 5 (243). Pal. Soc. 24.

in nomine domini ego berchtwulf cyning sile forðrede minu*m* ðegne nigen higida lond in wudotune in ece erfe him to hiobbanne 7 to siollanne ðaem ðe hit wille mið eaðmodre hernisse him to geeornigan ofer his daeg cisseðebeorg feower treowe hyl, 7 eanburge mere, tihhan hyl, 7 utbigeht tu higida lond in erfe ece. 7 he salde to londceape xxx mancessan 7 nigen hund scill', wið ðaem londe hi*m* in ece erfe.

ic berhtwulf *rex* ðas mine gesaldnisse trymme 7 faestna in cristes rodetacne 7 in his ðaere haligran a 7 in his *wotona gewitnisse. aerist saeðryð *regina*, cyneferð *episcopus*, alchhun *episcopus*, berchtred *episcopus*, deorlaf *episcopus*, *ceored *episcopus*, *wichred *abbas*, aldred *abbas*, mucel *dux*, hunbercht *dux*, burgred *dux*, *aefstan, cyneberht *dux*, sigred *dux*, alberht *dux*, aldred *dux*, mucel *dux*, hunstan *dux*, eadwulf, beornoð, wulfred, mucel, aldred, wicga, eadgar, baldred, werenberht, eadred, aeðelwulf *presbyter*, heaberht *presbyter*, ecghun, ecgheard, beornhaeð, aldred.

7[2] we aec alle bibeodað ðe aet ðisse gewitnisse werun on cristes noman 7 on his ðaere haligra(n), gif aenig monn ðas ure gewitnisse incerre on owihte, ðaet he aebbe ðaes aelmaehtgan gode(s unhlis . .[3] 7) his ðaere haligran up in (heofnum) ðaes we him (ge)beod.n[4] maege.

[1] *later endorsm.* Wiglaf cinig.
[2] *this endorsm. is in places nearly illegible from wear; letters in ( ) are given on the authority of the Pal. Soc. transliteration.*
[3] unhlisse (?) *Pal.*
[4] gebeod in *Pal.*

IX CENT. MERCIAN-KENTISH.

49.

Coenwulf[2]. Stowe 10.

805.

Mercian hand.

ego coenuulfus *rex* merciorum *simul etiam et* cuðrędus *rex* cantuuariorum. uulfhardo *presbytero.* aeðelheardi *arhci' episc'. in cantia—ubi* sueordhlincas *vocitantur.* án sulung. *mediam partem unius mansiunculae, id est* an geocled. *ubi* *ecgheannglond *appellatur*—coenuulfus. *haec cartula scripta est in loco ubi nominatur* aclaeh, *atque eodem anno beatissimus* aeðilheardus *arh' epis' migrabat ad caelestia regna*—cuðredus. uulfredus. uuerenbe[o]rhti. alhmundi. tidfriði. osmundi. deneberhti. beornmodi. alduulfi. uigberhti. alh[e]ardi. eaduulfi. uuihthuni. uulfheardi. cynhelm. heaberht. tiduulf. ceoluuard. byrnuuald. beornnoð. heardberht. uuigga. uuigheard. feologeld. uuęrnoð. beorheard. haehferð. aeðilgeard. uihthere. wynbald. dudemon. ceolstan.

50.

Coenwulf[3]. Cott. Aug. ii. 98.

808.

Cooling (Kent), Tamworth (Staff.). Cant. arch. K. I. 237 (194). B. M II. 9.

coenuulf *rex* merciorum. *meo ministro* eaduulfo. *in loco quae appellatur* culingas. *haec sunt termina :* cyninges tuntih. genlad. biornheardes lond. ðorndun. *actum est in loco qui vocatur* tomeworðig—coenuulf. ęlfðryð *regina.* heaberht. beor[n]noð. ceolward. cynhelm. ecgferð. by[r]nwald. eadferð. heardberht. ceolberht. ðynne—culingaboc.

51.

Coenwulf[4]. Cott. Aug. ii. 10.

811.

Cant. arch. K. I. 242 (196). Th. 57. B. M. I. 14.

regis merciorum coenu[u]lfi. uulfredi (gen.). *in oppido regali lundaniae.* coen[u]ulf. uulfred. deneberht hu[u]icciorum *episcopus.* aeðeluulf *episcopus australium saxonum. regi* coenuulfo. uulfredi. *pro pecuniarum remuneratione, hoc est centum et viginti vi* mancosas. *cantiae* roeginga hám. appincglond. fefres hám. ðæt suiðhunincglond aet grafonàea. *duas possessiunculas et tertiam dimediam, id est in nostra loquella* ðridda half haga. sture *fluminis.* coenuulf. uulfredo. coenuulf.—coenuulf. aelfþryð *regina.* sigred. uulfred. deneberht. beornmod. aeðeluulf. heardberht. beornnoð. cynehelm. eadberht. ecguulf. eanberht. heahferð. cyneberht. coenwald. aeðelheah. cu[u]oenburg. seleburg. cuðred[1].

52.

Coenwulf[5]. Cant. Arch. c. 1278.

812.

Mercian hand. K. I. 249 (199). Pal. Soc. II.

merciorum *regis* coenuulfi. uulfredi *archiepiscopi.* coenuulfo. uulfredo. *in orientalis cantiae partibus.* uulfred. *aliquam terrae partiunculam, hoc est, duarum manentium in loco ubi* sueord hlincas *vocitantur, juxta distributionem suarum utique terrarum ritu cantiae* an sulung *dictum. mediam partem unius mansiunculae, id est,* an ioclet, *ab incolis ibi* ecgheanglond *appellatur.* uulfred. uulfhardo. aeðelheardi. uulfred. coenuulfo. fefresham. *terrae particula duarum manentium, id est,* an sulung, *ubi ab incolis* grafoneah *vocitatur, ab aquilone habens terminum* suuealuue *fluminis a plaga, oriente* suiðhuninglond, *a parte occidentali* ealh fleot, *ab austro* sigheardingmeduue ond eac suithhuninglond. *in regione* on liminum *et in loco ubi* kasingburnan *appellatur*

[1] *later endorsm.* Swiðhuningland, Grauanea; *in another hand* Grafenea.

demediam partem unius mansiunculae, id est, an ioclet. coenuulf. *has terrulas* æt grafonæa *atque iterum* æt casingburnan. aet sueordhlincum et ecgheanglond. uulfredo. uulfred. coenuulfo —coenuulf. uulfred. eaduulf. cuðredi. ploesa. cyneberhti. coenuualdi. aedelheah[1].

53.

Coenwulf[6]. Cott. Aug. ii. 74.

814.

Cant. arch. K. I. 253 (201). B. M. II. 13.

ego coenuulfus *rex merciorum* uulfredo *arciepiscopo dabo in provincia cantiae terram in regione quae dicitur* westanwidde *ubi nominatur* cynincges cua lond[2]—grafoneah, *et unum fretum qui nominatur nostra propria lingua* mearcfleot, 7 seleberhtincglond. *ad portum quae dicitur* cillincg. on grafon ęa. coenuulf. on blean. coenuulfi. æt bearwe—coenuulf. aelfþryþ *regina.* alduulf. heardberhti. ceoluulfi. uuighardi. reðhuni. torhthelmi. eaduulfi.

54.

Coenwulf[7]. Stowe 11.

815.

Wichbold (Worces.). Feversham (Kent).

coenuulf *rex merciorum meo archiepiscopo* uulfredo *in regione qui dicitur* febresham. seleberhtinglond—alhfleot. cyninges mersc. sualuę—*singulare praetium ad penam, id est* angylde. *ego* uulfred. coenuulfo. *viginti et tres* mancusas—*in vico regio qui dicitur* uuitbold — coenuulf. uulfred. deneberht. ceoluulf. mucel. uulfred.

[1] *later endorsm.* Grauanea. [2] *later endorsm.* be uuestanwuda cyncges culand.

55.

Ceolwulf[1]. Cott. Aug. ii. 93.

822.

Cant. arch. K. I. 272 (216). Th. 65. B.M. II. 15.

ego ceolwulf *rex merciorum vel etiam* contwariorum. uulfredo *arciepiscopo. in provincio cantiae ubi nominatur* mylentu[n] *hanc terram liberabo a refectione et habitu illorum qui dicuntur* fæstingmen. uulfredo—cymesinc. se *hole welle. *et occidente* diorente. scorham *silva. similiter qui dicitur* cert. greotan edesces lond. cymesinges cert. ondred. in ondrede. *iu hyrst. sc[i]ofingden. snadhyrst — LXXV mancusas. *in loco regale qui dicitur* bydictun—ceolwulf. wulfred. ęðelwald. reðhun. wulfheard. heaberht. sigered. eadberht. wulfred. muca. eatferð. bofa. piot. eadbald. cyneberht. wighelm. beadheard. tunred.

56.

Ceolwulf[2]. Cott. Aug. ii. 75.

823.

Cant. arch. K. I. 274 (217). B.M. II. 16.

ego ceolwulf *rex merciorum seu etiam* cantwariorum. *in provincia cantie.* wulfredo *arciepiscopo. urbis dorouerni.* coenwulf. ceolwulf — aldberhtingtun. stur — *actum est in villo regali qui dicitur* werburgingwic—wulfred. ceolwulf. æðelwald. beornmod. sigered. sigered. beornnoð. eadberht. alhheard. muca. elfwald. eatferð. mucel. bofa. beornwulf. eanmund. feologeld. biornhelm. piot. eadwulf. aldred. wighelm. cyneberht. eadbald. beadheard—londboc minra wica ⁊ ðritiges æcra be norðan byrg.

57.

Beornwulf. Stowe 12.

824.

Folkstone (Kent).

aet clofeshoum. beornuulfo *regi merciorum.* uulfredo. uulfredus. æt oesewalum[1]. aldberht. *ejus soror* seleðryð. seleðryð.

[1] *second* e *small* (*contemp. addition*).

aldberht. *monasterio quae nominatur* æt folcanstanę. aldberht. osuulf. æt oesewalum[1]. quoenðryðae (gen.). suðmynster. quoenðryðam. æt suðmynstre. aldberhto. uulfred. quoenðryðam. æt suðmynstre. quoenðryðe. wernoð. feologeld. aeðelhun — uulfred. beornuulf. aeðelwald. reðhun. heaberht. wigðegn. eadwulf. wermund. ciolberht. cynred. beonna. cuðulf. eanmund. eanmund. uuernoð. beornnoð. eadberht. eadwulf. aecgberht. sigered. cuðred. alchheard. mucael. ludęca. uhtred. eaduulf. bofa. aldred. bola.

58.

Wulfred[3]. Cott. Aug. ii. 78. Stowe 13.

825.

Reculver (Kent). Cott. from Cant. arch. K. I. 280 (220). Th. 73. B. M. II. 18.

de diversis saxoniae partibus congregatum est synodale concilium in loco quae nominatur aet[2] clofes houm, *praesidente huic concilio* uulfredo *arciepiscopo seu etiam* beornuulfo[3] *regi merciorum.* uulfredus. coenwulfi *regis. in monasteriis* aet[2] suðmynstre 7 æt ræculfo[4]. coenwulf. *terram* æt iognes homme. coenwulf. æt suðmynstre. beornwulfi *regis.* aet[2] clofes houm. uulfred. cwoenðryðam[5]. coenwulfi. coenwulf. beornwulfo. coenwulfi. æt hearge. herefreðing lond[6], 7 æt wemba lea, 7 æt geddincggum[7]. *abbatissa* cwoenðryð[8] *filia* coenwulfi. beornwulf. æt hearge. æt boclonde, 7 æt wemba lea, 7 æt herefreðinglonde. *in provincia* hwicciorum *in loco quae nominatur* oslafes hlau. æt hearge. *in provincia cantiae ubi dicitur* æt cumbe. coenwulfi. æt wincelcumbe. coenwulfi—cwoenðryð[9]. beornwulf. uulfredus. aeðelwald. reðhun. eadwulf. haeberht[10]. beornmod. beonna. wigðægn. alhstan. humberht. willred. ceolberht. cynred. cuðwulf. willferð. eanmund. eanmund. torhthelm. wiohtred. piott[11]. beornnoð. eadberht. eadwulf. ecgberht. alchhard[12]. cyneberht. sigered. mucel. cuðred. eadwulf. wulfred. bynna. aldred. wighelm. aldred. bola. alhstan. eadbald. feologeld. oswulf. hunferð.

[1] *second* e *small* (*contemp. addition*). [2] æt, *Stowe.* [3] -wulfo, *St.* [4] ręculfo, *St.* [5] -þryðam, *St.* [6] hęre-, *St.* [7] geddincgum, *St.* [8] coenþryð, *St.* [9] -þryð, *St.* [10] heaberht, *St.* [11] piot, *St.* [12] alhhard, *St.*

rocoena. osmund. tudda. brunhard. deornoð[1]. bægmund. hunred. cynehard. wigmund. dægmund. wihtred[2]. wærhard. eadwulf. duda. coenhard. alhhere. aelfgyð. beonne. aelfgyð. bægswið. aloburg. ęcgburg[3]—. is[4] earan cwænðryðe geðincgo 7 biscopes 7 þeara þegna on cantwarabyrg[5].

59.

Wiglaf[1]. Cott. Aug. ii. 94.

831.

Wichbold (Worces.). Cant. arch. K. I. 294 (227). B. M. II. 20.

ego uuiglaf *rex merciorum. in provincia* middelsaxanorum. *ab incolis nominatur* botewælle. uulfredo *arciepiscopo*—mercwælle. hygereðing tun 7 lullinges treo. colan homm. *terra pertinens* to hæse—uuiglaf. *actum est in regale villo quae nominatur* wicbold —uuiglaf. uulfred. cyneðryð *regina.* tidwulf. aeðelhard. eadwulf. sigered. aelfstan. wigmund. cyneberht. aelfred. headda. aldred. heahferð. aeðelhun. monna — botewællan boec.

[1] diornoð, *St.* [2] wiohtred, *St.* [3] æcgburg, *St.* [4] *this endorsm. not in Stowe.* *later endorsm. in Cott.* earg 7 wemban lea.

GLOSSARY.

AR—AL.

aron *vb* are. **VP** 81/6; 93/8 earun (estis). 131/9 §gegered (induantur); 138/16 §awriten (scribentur); **Hy** 4/7 §gegearwad (praeparantur). **Hy** 13/10 §numene (tenebamur). **Ct** 34/19; 58/23 earan.

hara *sm* hare. **Ep** 608 ~(lepus); **Cp** ~; **Ef** hæra.

Haran-dene Ct.

heard-hara *sm* a fish. **Ef** 270 ~(cefalus); **Cp** ~; **Ld** haerdhera. **Cp** 1347 ~(mugil).

sparian *wv* spare. **VP** 18/14 †spreara (parce!). 71/13 spearaδ. 77/50 §ede.

-waru

Berct-uaru *sf* **LV** 35.

Ecg-uaru *sf* **LV** 38.

Hrōth-uaru *sf* **LV** 23.

Sig-uaru *sf* **LV** 38.

-war- *spl.*

burg-war- *spl* citizens. **Ct** 43/4, 5 ~a medum.

caestr-uuar- *spl* citizens. **Ct** 8/3 *in regione* ꞡr ~a.

Cant-war- *spl* people of Kent. **BH** 1/1 cantuariorum. 21 cantuari —cont§—cantuarii. 162 cantuariorum. **Gn** 111 cantwar . . . *gpl.* **Ct** 4/1; 5/1; 6/1; 7/1 *etc* ~uariorum. 25/1 ~uuariorum. 31/1 ~wariorum. 34/1 ~wariorum (~uu§). 55/1 contwariorum. 56/1 cant§.

Cantwara-byrg Ct.

Dornuuarana-ceaster Ct.

hel-wearan *spl* hell-dwellers. **VP** 29/4; **Hy** 4/13; **Hy** 13/20 ~um (inferis, *etc*). **Hy** 7/45 oδ~.

Mēan-war- *spl* **BH** 275 ~uarorum *provinciam.*

Sodom-wear- *spl* people of Sodom. **VH** 7/62 ~ena (Sodomorum).

Wiht-war- *spl* **BH** 22 uictuari — uictuarii I.

faran *sv* go. **VP** 10/2 fer (transmigra!). 77/39 fearende (vadens). **Hy** 3/1 ic fearu (§am). **Ct** 41/18 to faranne. 42/2 fere *sbj.*

δorh-faran *sv* traverse. **VP** 103/26 ~fearaδ (pertransibunt).

faru *sf* course.

aex-faru *sf* axis-course. **Cp** 186 ~(aparatu).

earh-faru *sf* arrow-course. **Rd** 13 aerigfaerae *a.*

nēd-faru *sf* compulsory journey. **BDS** 1 there neidfaerae *d.*

wægn-faru *sf* chariot-journey. **Cp** 881 †gebellicum wæ[g]nfearu (fiscalis reda).

Lindis-far *spl* **BH** 241, 7 *gentis* ~orum. **Gn** 32, 64 §.

arn *prt* ran. **VP** 58/5; 61/5; 118/32 orn (cucurri).

barn *prt* burned. **VP** 17/9; 38/4; 105/18; **Hy** 7/44, 5 born (exardescit; §; exarsit; §; ardebit).

Marcus *sm* **Ct** 33/13 ~.

carcern *sm* prison. **VP** 141/8 ~e (carcere).

Martīn *sm* **Ct** 31/11 æt sce' ~e.

martyr *sm* martyr. **DA** 7 ~a.

martyrdōm *sm* martyrdom. **Mt** 14 ~dóm.

gemartyrian *wv* martyr. **Mt** 29 ~ia(n).

aler *s(m)* alder-tree. **Ep** 35 alaer (alnus); **Ld** §; **Ef**, **Cp** ~.

†alterholt **Ep**; aler§ **Ef**, **Cp**, **Ld**.

Aling-mēd Ct.

Alusa *sm* Gn 81 ~.

Alusing *sm* son of A. Gn 81 ~.

Aluca *sm* LV 285 ~.

Hale-rīc LV.

Sal-uuerpe Ct.

scalu scale, husk. Ep 462 ~(glumula); Ef ~; Cp ~a.

wyrt-wala *s*(*m*) root. VP 79/10 ~an(radices).

falod *s*(*m*) sheep-fold, cattle-pen. Ep 129 falaed (bobellum); Ef §; Cp falud. 959 falaed; Ef, Cp §.

gegalan *sv* sing, enchant. Cp 1123 gegaelen (incantata).

ā-galan *sv* enchant. VP 57/6 bioð agalene (incantantur).

galend *sm* enchanter. VP 57/6 ~ra (incantantium).

næhte-gale *sf* nightingale. Ep 26 †nctigalae (luscinia *etc*); Ef nęctęgela [*or* -gelu ?]; Cp nehtęgale. 673 nectigalae (noctua); Ef nacthegelae. 857 nectaegalae (roscinia); Ef necegle; Cp naectegale; Ld nectigalae. Cp 1257 naectegale (luscinia).

Aln *sf* river Alne. BH 318 *juxta fluvium* alne.

Aði-gils LV.

Hathor *sm* Ct 18/5 ~.

hraþe *av* quickly. Cp 1675 hraeðe (propero). VP 36/2; 78/8; 105/13 hreðe (cito).

hreaðian *wv* hasten. VP 15/4 ~edon (acceleraverunt). 30/3 ~a!

gelaðian *wv* summon, invite. Cp 90 ~ade (adhibuit vel advocavit).

swaþu *sf* track. Ep 972 suina suadu (suesta); Ef §; Cp §sceadu. VP 16/5; 17/37; Hy 13/25 sweðe (vestigia).

dolg-swaþu *sf* scar. Bl 4 ~suaþhe (plagae vestigia, cicatrices).

wund-swaþu *sf* scar. VP 37/6 ~sweðe (cicatrices).

scaþa *sm* thief.

wicing-scaþa *sm* pirate. Ep 736 uuicingsceadan (piraticum); Ef §ae (§am); Cp wicincsceaðan (§am).

staþol *sm* foundation. VP 17/8, 16; 81/5; 86/1; Hy 7/46 steaðelas (fundamenta). 136/7 oð steadul (§um).

staþol-fæst *aj* firm. VP 113/8 steaðulfestne (solidam). Hy 7/52 §um (stabilito).

staþolfæstnis *sf* firmness. VP 103/5 steaðulfestnisse (stabilitatem).

gestaþolfæstian *wv* make firm. VP 20/12 gesteaðulfestian (stabilire). 143/12 §ad (§ita).

staþolian *wv* establish. VP 103/5; 135/6 steaðelade (fundavit).

gestaþolian *wv* establish. VP 8/4; 118/152 gesteaðulades (fundasti). 22/2; 106/36; 142/3 §elade (collocavit). 23/2; 47/9; 77/69; 86/5 § (fundavit). 43/8 §elades (†confudisti). 88/12; 101/26; 103/8 § (fundasti). 118/90 gesteadelades (§). 94/5 gesteaðeladun (§averunt). 103/22 §iað (collocabunt). 112/8 §ie (§et).

staþelung *sf* founding, planting, VP 143/12 steaðelunge (plantationis).

eorþ-maþa *sm* earthworm. Cp 2113 eorðmata (vermis).

maþelian *wv* make a speech. Cp 586 maðalade (contionatur, declamat, judicat, contestatur).

Tað-haeth LV.

wase *sf* mud. Cp 386 ~(caenum).

Maser-feld BH.

Casing-burnan, kasing§ Ct.

tasol *sm* die. Ep 998 ~ (tessera, quadrangulum); Ef, Cp ~ul. Ld 84 tesulas (tesseras).

basu *aj* purple. Ep 411 baeso (fenicia); Ef beoso; Cp §u.

brūn-basu *aj* brownish purple. Ep 716 bru[u]nbesu (ostriger); Ef bruunbesu; Cp. §beosu.

weoloc-basu *aj* purple. Ld 66 uuylocbaso (purpuram).

wyrm-baso *aj* purple. Ld 67 uuyrmbaso (coccus).

assa *sm* donkey. VP 103/11 wilde ~an (onagri).

Wassing-welle Ct.

passio *sf* passion. Ct 37/37 twa passione.

Bassa *sm* BH 118 *duce* basso. Gn 103 ~.

Bassing *sm* son of Bassa. **Gn** 103 ~.

Astre *sf*? Ct 22/10; 23/11 æt ~an.

awel *s(m)* awl. **Ep** 29 auuel *vel* clauuo (arpago); Ef §; Cp ~. Cp 929 ~(fuscinula). 2047 auuel, meottoc (tridens).

Caua *sm* **LV** 201 ~.

cawel *s(m)* basket. **Ef** 305 couel (coruis); Cp cauuel. Ef 1172 lorg couel (colum).

clawu *sf* claw. **Ep** 29 auuel *vel* clauuo (arpago); Ef, Cp §. **VP** 68/32 clea (ungulas).

claw- **Cp** 1842 clawe (scalpo).

afen *sf* river. **Ct** 15/2; 16/2 *flumen qui dicitur* aben. 20/16, 7 up on ~e, to ~e.

haf- *vb* have. **Rd** 5 ic hefæ. **VP** 58/9 ~ast (habebis). 39/18; 146/10 ~að (§et; §ebit). **Ct** 34/17; 41/58 ~að. 38/7 ðonne hebfað eadwald ⁊ cyne(ðryð).

bi-hafað *vb* contains. **VP** 76/10 ~(continebit).

Hafing-seota Cp.

hafoc *sm* hawk. **Ld** 51 haefuc (accipitres). **VP** 103/17 heafuces (fulice).

mūs-hafoc *sm* mouse-hawk. **Cp** 1890 ~habuc (soricarius).

spær-hafoc *sm* sparrow-hawk. **Cp** 118 spaerhabuc (alietum).

wealh-hafoc *sm* **Ep** 497 uualh[h]ebuc (horodius); Ef uualhhaebuc; Cp walchhabuc. Ld 50 ualchefuc (herodion). Cp 826 walhhabuc (falc).

Lafa *sm* **LV** 200 ~. 347 laba.

þafian *wv* consent, agree. **Ct** 41/47 *etc* ic . . ðeafie. 51, 5 ic . . þeafie. 42/24, 5, 5 (ic) ðeafię.

geþafian *wv* consent. **VH** 7/55 gedeafien (consentiant). **Ct** 40/12, 3 (ic) geðafie.

geþafung *sf* consent. **VP** 54/15; 82/6 geðeafunge (consensu; §um).

scafan *sv* shave, scrape, polish. **Cp** 1618 scaebe (poleo).

scafa *sm* shaver, plane. **Ep** 853 sceaba (runcina); Ef, Cp §.

stafod *aj* (*ptc*) striped. **Ep** 837 stefad brun (perstromata, ornamenta); Ef staefad brun; Cp steba.

nafu *sf* nave (of wheel). **Ep** 625 nabae (modioli); Ef nebæ; Cp †habae.

nabfogaar Ep; naboger [a *from* e] Ef; naboga(a)r Cp; nębugaar Ld.

nafola *sm* navel. **Cp** 2151 nabula (umbilicus).

gafol *s(n)* tribute, tax. **Ep** 115 gaebuli (aere alieno); Ef §; Cp geabuli. **Ef** 394 gebles monung (exactio); Cp geabules§; Ld monung gaebles. Ef 336 gedębiu gebil (debita pensio); Cp gedaebeni geabuli.

gafollic *aj* fiscal. **Cp** 881 †gebellicum wægnfearu (fiscalis reda).

gafol *s(f)* fork.

†gafelrend Ef; gabulrond Cp; †gabarind Ld.

grafan *sv* dig.

āgrafan *sv* dig out. **Cp** 424 agra:ben (caelatum).

Grafon-sæa Ct.

gedafen *aj* (*ptc*) fitting, suitable. **Ef** 336 gedębin gebil (debita pensio); Cp gedaebeni geabuli.

gedafenian *wv* be fitting. **VP** 32/1 gedeofenað (decet). 64/2 gedeafenað. 92/5 gedeafineað (§ent).

Pafing-denn Ct.

maffa *sm* caul. **Ep** 719 ~(omentum); Cp ~; Ef †naffa. Ef 1122 ~(§).

anclēow *sf* ankle. **Cp** 1987 oncleouue (talus).

Hanchemstede Ct.

þanc *sm* (thought, pleasure) thanks. **VH** 12/4 ðoncas (gratis).

thoncsnotturra BDS.

hyge-þanc *sm* thought. **Rd** 4 hygido(n)cum (?).

or-þanc *sm* skill, cunning. **Ef** 278 ordoncum (commentis). Cp 1299 orðonc (machinamenta). Ld 11 ordancas (arguta).

mōd-geþanc *s(m)* thought. **CH** 2 modgidanc.

þancung *sf* thanking, thanks. **CA** 9 to ðoncunca.

scanca *sm* shank, leg. **Lr** 58 sconcum (tibiis).

stanc *prt* exhaled. **Ef** 782 ~(exaltavit); Cp stonc.

wlanclice *av* proudly. **Ep** 112 uulanclicae (adrogantissime); Cp wlonclice.

Franca *sm* **LV** 53 fronka.

mancus *sm* a coin. **Ct** 41/32 ~ *a.* 26/5; 30/3; 54/4; 55/7 ~as. 32/2 xx ~a. 51/5 mancosas. 48/6 xxx mancessan.

dranc *prt* drank. **VP** 109/7 dronc (bibet).

Bancorna-burg BH.

anga *sm* prick, goad. **Ep** 43 ~(aquilium); Ef ~; Cp onga; Ld § (§ius).

angseta Ep; ·§ Ef; oncg§ Cp.

Angel *s(f)* **BH** 23 *patria quae angulus dicitur.*

Angelcynnes Ct.

Angen-lābes-haam Ct. **Angengēot,** §ing Gn.

lang *aj* long. **VH** 7/54 longe tid (longo tempore). **Ct** 26/4 *prata* alingmed, longan med. 29/3, 3 to ~an leage. fram ~an leage.

Leangafeld Ct. **longmōd** VP.

lange *av* long. **VP** 4/3; 6/4; 12/1 *etc* hu longe (usque quo). 12/1; 61/4 *etc* hu § (quo usque). 12/2 hu § (quam diu). 103/33 swe § (§). 145/2 swe § swe (§). 37/9 a hu †lenge swiður (usque quaque).

langung *sf* longing. **VP** 118/28 fore longunge (taedio).

sang *sm* **VP** 70/6 song (decantatio). 32/3; 95/1 *etc* §neowne (canticum); 68/31; 91/4 §e (cantico). 136/3; 137/5 §um (§is). 136/3 §a (cantionum).

strang *aj* strong. **VP** 7/12; 23/8; 70/7; Hy 4/5 strong (fortis). 49/3 § (valida). 53/5 ða §an (fortes). 46/10; 58/4; 134/10 §e (§). 47/8 §um (vehementi). Hy 4/8 §ra (fortium). 135/12 §re (forti).

strangra *cp* **VP** 34/10 strongran (fortioris).

strangest *sp* **VP** 17/18 ðæm strongestum (fortissimis).

strangian *wv* prevail. **VP** 12/5 strongade (praevalui). 51/9 §að (§uit). 64/4 §adun (§uerunt).

gestrangian *wv* prevail. **VP** 88/22 gestrongað (confortabit). 26/14; 30/25 sie §ad (§etur). 138/6 §ad is (§ata est). 138/17 §ad is (§atus est). Hy 4/19 bið §ad (roborabitur). 17/18 §ade werun (confortati sunt). 37/20; 68/5; 141/7 §ade sind (§ati sunt).

āsprang *prt* failed. **VP** 38/12 asprong (defeci). 11/2; 30/11 *etc* § (§it).

wang *sm* plain. **Rd** 1 se ueta uong.

wong-toeð VP.

bi-fongen *ptc* seized. **VP** 9/17 ~bið (compraehensus est). 9/23; 58/13 bioð bifongne.

ǣg-mang *s* egg-mixture. **Cp** 105 aeg~(agastrum).

ǣg-gemang *s(n)* egg-mixture. **Ep** 704 aeggimang; Ef, Cp aeggimong (ogastrum). Cp 1438 § (olgastrum).

gecrang *prt* fell. Cp 1428 gecrong (occubuit).

gangan *sv* go. **VP** 85/11; 138/7 gongu(ambulabo; ibo). 118/45 § (ambulabam). 90/13 §es. 84/14; 103/3 §eð. 11/9; 83/8; 88/16, 31 §að *etc.* 22/4; 142/8; 137/7 §e (§em; §§; §avero). 38/7 §e (§et). 77/10 §an (§are). 83/13; 100/6; 125/6 §ende (§antes; §ans; euntes). **DA** 9 ~en *sbj pl.* **Ct** 41/17 to gánganne.

gongeweafre VP.

gegangan *sv* go, go together. **Cp** 441 †gegandende (cesuram). 550 gegangendo (coituras).

begangan *sv* practice, cultivate. **VP** 76/4 bigongen ic eam (exercitatus sum). 118/15, 27 ic beom§ (†§ebo, §ebor). 23 wes§. 48, 78 biom§.

betwīh-gangan *sv* go between. **VP** 28/7 ~gongendes (intercidentis).

geond-gangan *sv* go over, traverse. **VP** 67/22 ~gongendra (perambulantium). 90/6 §um.

in-gangan *sv* go in. **VP** 25/1, 11 ingongende eam (ingressus sum).

ofer-gangan *sv* go ovér. **VP** 103/9 ~gongað (transgredientur).

ymb-gangan *sv* go round. **VP** 141/4 ~gongu (ambulabam).

gang *sm* walking, step, course. **VP** 36/23 gong (gressus). 16/5;

17/37; 36/31 *etc* §as. Ct 28/5 11 wena ~.

begang *sm* practice, exercise. Ef 357 bigongum (exercitus); Cp bigangum (§iis).

land-begang *sm* land-culture, inhabiting. VP 118/54 londbigonges (incolatūs).

hand-gang *sm* surrender. Ef 337 hondgong (deditio); Cp †hand-gand.

• **hin-gang** *sm* departure. BDS 3 hiniong[a]e *d*.

inn-gang *sm* entrance. VP 67/25 inngong (ingressus). 117/19 ingong (§ *plur.*). 120/8 § ðinne (introitum). Ct 41/22 ~es.

on-gang *sm* assailing, incursion. Cp 1128, 31 ongong (†incurrus, inruptio).

set-gang *sm* setting (of sun). VP 49/1; 67/5; 103/19; 112/3 ~gong (occasum). 106/3 §e (§u).

ūt-gong *sm* going out. VP 18/7 ~(egressio). 64/9; 67/21 ~(exitus). 106/33, 5; 118/136 ~(§ūs *pl*). 120/8 ~ðinne. 113/1 ~e.

tang *s*(*f*) pincer, tong. Cp 905 tong (forceps).

Ona *sm* LV 200 ~.

anoða *sm* fear. Cp 902 ~(formido).

Onoc *sm* Ct 9/6.

Anut-walda Ct.

hana *sm* cock.

holt-hana *sm* woodcock. Ep 41 ~(acega); Ef †holtana; Cp ~hona; Ld §.

wōr-hana *sm* moorcock. Ep 424 uuor~(fasianus); Ef §hona; Cp worhona.

uudu-hona *sm* woodcock. Cp 1524 ~(pantigatum).

Honoc *sm* LV 199 ~.

hran *sm* whale. Ep 146 ~(ballena); Ef hron; Cp horn; Ld hron. Cp 1525 ~(palina). Rn 3/4 hronæs.

þanon *wv* thence, whence. Cp 1042 þanan (illic). VP 120/1 ðonan (unde). SG 23 ðonan. Ct 20/6, 11 *etc* ðonon. 15 ðonan.

swan *sm* swan. Ep 700 suan (olor); Ef §; Cp suon. Cp 1026 suan (holor).

ā-stan *prt* groaned. Bl 9 granode *vel* asten (rugiebam).

wana (*sbst*) *adj* wanting. VP 22/1; 33/10 nowiht wonu bið (deerit, deest). 38/5 hwet wone sie (desit).

wanian *wv* diminish, curtail. Ct 45/52 wonie *sbj*.

gewanian *wv* diminish, curtail. VP 8/6 gewonedes (minuisti). 11/2 §ade sind (diminutae). 88/46 §ades (minorasti). 106/38 sind §ad (§ata sunt). Hy 6/25 §as (§abis). Ct 45/52 §ie *sbj*.

wanung *sf* curtailment. Cp 666 wonung (detrimentum).

uuanan-bēam Ep; uuo§ Ef; uua§ Cp.

Un-wana *sm* Gn 39 unuuona. Ct 12/3; 15/5; 16/4 §. 19/4 unuuono. 18/4 unuuano.

hwanon *av* whence.

huuananhuuoega Ep; huuonan§ Ef; huonanhuegu Cp.

ā-hwanon *av* from anywhere. Rd 8 ou(ua)n(a).

gūð-fona *sm* (war)banner. VH 13/17 ~an (vexillum *a*).

wind-fona *sm* Cp 1792 ~(scabellum).

manung *sf* Ef 394 gebles monung (exactio); Cp geabules §; Ld §gaebles.

manig *aj* many. VP 21/13 monig (multi *pl*). 109/6 §u (§a *pl*). 30/14; 88/51; 108/30 §ra. 3/2, 3; 4/6 monge (multi) *etc*. 70/20 hu §(quantas). 118/84 hu § (quot). 77/31; Hy 4/11 §(plurimos). 33/20 †mong (multae). 70/7 §um (§is). Mt 21 monigra.

monigfald, §lice, gemonigfaldian, gemongfaldian VP.

manu *sf* mane. Ef 1182 ~(juba *etc*).

cranoc *s* crane. Cp 995 cornoch (grus, gruis). 996 cornuc (gravis).

ganot *sm* gannet. Ep 419 ~(fulix); Ef §; Cp. gonot.

granu *sf* moustache. Ep 644 ~ae (mustacia); Ef ~æ; Cp ~ae; Ld gronae.

gronuisc [*under* fisc] Cp.

self-bana *sm* suicide. **Cp** 299 †seolfboran (biothanatas).

ann *vb* grant. **Ct** 41/36, 8, 9; 45/47 ~ ic. 45/4 ic onn.

Anna *sm* **BH** 142 ~. 149 ~ae *regis* — § [e *er.*] I — anna. 192, 7 ~*regis.* **LV** 2 ~. 366 onna.

onnan-duun Ct. onnan-forda Ct.

gespannan *sv* buckle, harness. **Mt** 16 gesponnan.

gespan *s* buckle. **Ep** 1336 ~(murica, aureum in tunica); Ef, Cp gespon. Ld ~(mauria *etc*).

wann *prt* laboured. **VP** 6/7; 68/4 won (laboravi).

wann *aj* pale. **Ep** 576 tha uuannan (livida); Ef §; Cp wonnan.

fann *s* fan. **Cp** 2084 fon (vanna).

mann *sm* I man; II one. **Rn** 2/3, 8 men *pl.* **LP** 10 menn *pl* 12 monn. **CA** 16 mon. 11 § II. **DA** 10 man II. 15 mon II. 12 men *d.* **Mt** 8, 47 mon. 50 monn II. 48 monnes. **VP** 8/5; 9/20, 39 *etc* mon (homo). 38/12 § (§inem) *etc.* 48/21; 55/11; 143/3 monn (§o). 36/7; 42/1; 134/8; 139/2 men (§ine). Hy 1/8 fremðes cynnes men (alienigenae *d*). 36/37 męnn [ę *doubtful*] (homini). 8/5; 36/23 monnes. 9/21; 35/7; 61/4 *etc* men (§ines). 67/19 monnum. 10/5; 11/2, 9 §a *etc.* 4/3 †monnan (§inum). 44/3 †mona (§). **Ct** 20/13 mon II. 34/16 § I. 37/8, 9 *etc* § II. 28 man II. 39/2 man II 13, 14 § I. 9 mon. 40/9 §. 20 man. 41/11 § II. 1, 13, *etc* mon II. 28, 31, 44 monn. 68 mann. 42/13 mon II. 15 monn. 45/20, 49, 52 mon. 31 § II. 37 man II. 48/18 monn. 40/19 men *d.* 37/7 menn *pl.* 45/3 męn *pl.* 40/24; 41/64 ~um. 37/7 monna. 45/54 ~a.

monncwild Mt. moncynnæs CH. monðwǣre, §nis VP.

ealdor-mann *sm* chief. **CA** 3 aldormon. **VP** 104/20 aldermon (princeps) 21 § (§ipem). 23/9; 44/17; 46/10 *etc* §men (§ipes). 81/7; 112/8, 8 *etc* §monnum. 32/10; 75/13; 86/6 etc §monna. **Ct** 37/1 aldormonn. 38/2 §es. 47/15, 16 §menn *d.*

ēored-mann *sm* cavalry soldier. **Ef** 320 se oritmon; Cp se eorodmon (dromidarius).

fæsting-mann *sm* a kind of retainer. **Ct** 47/2 faestingmenn *pl.* 55/4 §men.

Mann *sm* **Ct** 33/4, 11 monn. 6 mon.

-man(n) *in pvoper names.*

Monn-ēd Ct.

Bet-mon *sm* **LV** 271 ~.

Blæc-mon *sm* **LV** 211 blæc ~. Gn 90 §.

Blæcmoning *sm* son of Blæcmon. Gn 90 blaec~.

Cæd-mon *sm* **Rn** 2/20 *kad*~. **BH** 311 caed~ — cęd~ — §. **CH** 10 caed~.

Dūde-mon *sm* **Ct** 49/12 ~.

Eald-mann *sm* **LV** 161; 215, 59; 386 aldmon. 352 §monn.

Freō-mon *sm* **LV** 169 friu~.

Gearo-mann *sm* **BH** 207 iaruman. 225 § — iur§ I. 240 iarumanno *d.* Gn 34 ~mon.

Hyse-mann *sm* **LV** 105 hysimonn. 201 §mon.

Sulmonnes-burg Ct.

Tāt-mann *sm* **LV** 304; 415 ~monn. 378 ~mon.

Til-mann *sm* **BH** 351 ~mon. **LV** 282 §. 426 ~monn.

Monna *sm* **Ct** 59/7 ~.

Mannel *sm* **Ct** 31/5.

on-gann *prt* began. **VP** 3/6; 76/11 ongon (coepi).

panne *sf* pan. **Cp** 2055 ponne (trulla).

brād-þanne *sf* frying-pan. **Cp** 407 braadponne (cartago).

brǣde-panne *sf* frying-pan. **Ep** 885 bredipannae (sartago); Ef †breitibannæ; Cp brediponne.

fȳr-panne *sf* fire-pan. **Ep** 5 ~pannae (arula); Ef, Cp ~ponne.

hēafod-panne *sf* scull. **Lr** 14, 44 ~udponnan (cephalem, capitali).

holo-panne *sf* pan. **Ep** 784 ~ae (patena); Cp ~ponne.

blann *prt* ceased. **VP** 105/30 blon (cessavit).

Want *sm* **LV** 166 uont.

Wantsumu *sf* a river. **BH** 28

fluvius uantsumu — uuantsamu 1 — u[u]antsemu [e *over* u].

Granta-caestir BH.

Cant-war- BH, Gn, Ct; cont§ BH, Ct. **cantwara-byrg** Ct.

plant *sn* plant. **VP** 127/3 neowe ~(novella *pl*). 143/12 niowe § (§).

plantian *wv* plant. **VH** 5/30 ~as (plantas). Ps 79/16; 93/9 ~ade (§avit). 79/9 ~ades (§asti). 106/37 ~adon (§averunt). 79/10 ~edes (§asti).

geplantian *wv* plant. **VP** 43/3; 103/16 ~ades (plantasti). 91/14 ~ade (§ati).

and *cj* and. **Ep** 98 aend suilcae (adqueve); Ef, Cp end. Cp 645 end (et). 2148 ond (que). Ef 1044 § (et). Cp 238 †on suilce (atqueve). Ld 10 bidir †an didir (ultro citro). **Rn** 3/1 ~. 3 end. **CH** 2 end. **BD**[2] 89 *on* (et). **CA** 6 ond. **Mt** 45 §. **SG** 1 *etc* §. **Ct** 37/1, 5, 8 *etc*; 38/10; 45/14, 5, 7; 52/11 §. 45/28 on[d]. 48 and. 11/2; 40/8; 47/10, 1 end.

and- ondsweorian [*under* a]. weard. ondwlita. mitta. ondget. ondfenga, §nis. wīsnis. unondcȳþignis.

And-hūn BH. **Ant-secg**, §ing SG.

andettan *wv* confess. **VP** 7/18; 29/13 ondettu (confitebor). 9/2; 17/50 *etc* §o. 118/7 ic ondett. 6/6; 29/10; 75/11 *etc* §eð. 29/5; 32/2; 43/9 *etc* §að. 105/47; 137/4 §en. 66/6; 106/8 §e [*last* e *over* að] (§eantur). 88/6 §igað. 66/4 §igen. 66/4 §ien. 66/6 §ie (§eantur). 91/2 §an (§eri). 121/4 to ondetenne (ad §endum). 118/62; 141/8 to ondetende (ad §endum). 73/19 ondetende (§entem). 104/1 ondetað. Hy 3/22 onddetteð. 106/31 onditien.

ondettend *sm* confessor. **VH** 13/23 ~um (confitentibus).

ondetnis *sf* confession. **VP** 95/6; 110/3; 148/14 ~(confessio). 41/5; 94/2; 99/4; 103/1; 146/7 ~se. 99/4 ~sa.

Andred *s* a forest. **Ct** 55/6/6 ondred, in §e.

hand *sf* hand. **Lr** 27 twa honda (binas idumas). **Mt** 22 hond *a*. **VP** 9/33; 20/9; 31/4 *etc* hond (manus) 40/3; 62/11; 105/41 in § (§ūs). 37/3; 73/3 §ðine (§um). 72/24 §ða swiðran *etc*. 16/14 of §a ðinra (§u). 21/21; 34/10 §a (§u). 135/12 in §a strongre *etc*. 9/35; 17/35; 21/17 *etc* §a (§ūs *pl*). 30/9 in §a (§ibus). 38/12 §a ðine (§ūs *g*). 7/4; 23/4 *etc* §um. 7/9; 8/7 *etc* §a (§uum). 79/17 mid hond (§u). 120/5 ofer § ðere swiðran (§um). **Ct** 45/17 sio neste hond.

handful Ep, Ef; hond- Cp, Ld. **hondgong** Ef; hand§ Cp. **handmitta** Ef; and§ Cp. **hondwyrm** Cp, Ef; hand§ Ep.

erfe-hand *sf* heir. **Ct** 41/68 ~onda *d*.

mǣg-hand *sf* relative. **Ct** 38/4 meihanda *gpl*, 11 meghond *n*.

handel *s* handle. **Cp** 1904 handle (stiba).

rand *sm*.

randbēag Ep, Ef; rond§ Ef, Cp; †nord§ Ld.

gafol-rand *sm* compasses. **Ef** 293 †gafelrend (circinno); Cp gabulrond; Ld †gabarind (circino, ferrum duplex, unde pictores faciunt circulos). Cp 1712 'gabulrond (radio).

land *sn* land. **Ef** 370 an ~ae; Cp on ~e (e vestigio, statim). Cp 1995 lond (territorium). **SG** 11 §. **Bd**[2] 59 ðorh § (per rura). **VP** 114/9 londe (regione). 44/13; 47/8 ðes §es (Tyri; Tharsis). 49/11; 102/15 §es (agri). 104/44; 106/37 lond (regiones; agros). 105/27; 106/2 §um (regionibus). Hy 7/24 §a (agrorum). **Ct** 24/8; 30/20; 37/16; 40/9; 45/41 þis lond. 34/20; 37/2, 29; 38/2, 13; 39/9; 41/10; 42/13; 45/27, 33, 8; 47/12 þæt §. 37/8; 41/3, 28; 47/16; 48/2, 5; 50/3; 53/3; 55/6 lond. 29/15; 34/11, 2, 4; 37/16; 38/9; 41/5, 13 *etc*; 45/17, 34 *etc*; 47/11, 3; 48/7 §e. 34/19; 41/7, 36, 7, 42; 42/9, 15, 20; 45/21; 47/10, 4 §es. 45/9, 14, 9, 20 lond *pl*. 45/10, 1, 6 §um. 28/9, 9, 9; 40/19; 41/7; 43/4 ~. 28/22; 43/2 ðet ~. 28/20; 30/7; 39/1, 2 ~e. 27/7, 7; 28/18, 21, 5; 39/13 ~es. 28/23 ~um.

Londberct LV. **londbōc** Ct. **londcēap** Ct. **Londfrith** LV. **londbigong** VP. **londlēod** VP.

Apping-land *sn* Ct 51/5 ~incg-lond.

Babbing-land *sn* Ct 35/6 ~ond.

Badenōðing-land *sn* Ct 26/8.

bōc-land *sn* book-land. Ct 30/5 ~. 45/26; 58/9 ~onde. 45/3, 24, 9 ~ondes.

Dēoring-land *sn* Ct 26/3 ~ondes.

Dūning-land *sn* Ct 18/3. duningc~.

Dūnwaling-land *sn* Ct 35/7 ~ond.

ēa-land *sn* island. VP 71/10 ~ondes (insulae). 96/1 eolond (§ *pl*). Ct 45/42 ~onde.

Ecghēang-land *sn* Ct 49/4 ~ngglond. 52/6, 15 ~ond.

erfe-land *sn* inherited land. Ct 40/17 ~e. 42/2 ærfelond.

erþ-land *sn* plough-land. Ct 42/20 ærðelondes.

folc-land *sn* public land. Ct 28/8, 23 ~, ~e. 45/25 ~ondes.

Folcwining-land *sn* Ct 35/2, 4 ~uuininglond, ~wininglond.

Herefreðing-land *sn* Ct 58/8, 10 ~ond (hę§), ~onde.

Seleberhting-land *sn* Ct 53/4 ~ncglond. 54/2 ~ond.

Swīþhūning-land *sn* Ct 51/6 suiðhunincglond. 52/10, 1 suiðhuninglond, suith§.

Wynnhearding-land *sn* Ct 35/6 ~ond.

hland *s*(*n*) urine. Cp 1236 hlond (lotium).

sand *sn* sand. VP 77/27 sond (harena). 138/18 § (§am).

sondhyllas Cp. **Sandhyrst** Ct. **Sondenstede** Ct. Sondemstyde Ct. sondgewearp Cp.

sand *sf* sending. **Ep** 188 ~ae (commeatos); Ef sondae; Cp sondę.

on-sand *sf* sending against. VP 77/49 onsonde (immissiones).

āswand *prt* diminished, became weak. **Ep** 490 asuand (hebesceret); Cp §; Ef ansuand. 1036 asuand (tabuisset); Ef †assuant; Cp. asuond. Cp 722 § (enebata). 748 § (enervat). VP 106/26 aswond (tabescebat). 118/158; 138/21 § (§ebam).

scand *sf* disgrace, ignominy. **Cp** 1809 scond (scurra).

standan *sv* stand. **VP** 23/3; 93/16; 108/6 stondeð (stabit; §; stet). 72/25 to lafe †stodeð (restat). 133/1 stondað. 134/2 stondad [o *ovĕr* a]. 17/39; 35/13 stondan. 121/2 §ende (stantes). **CA** 17 stondan. **Ct** 45/43 §að.

gestandan *sv* stand firm. **VP** 26/3 gestondað (consistant). 38/2 §eð.

æt-standan *sv* stand by. **VP** 5/5 ætstondu (adstabo). Hy 13/26 §es.

tō-standan *sv* stand apart. **VP** 102/12 tostondeð (distat).

wiþ-standan *sv* withstand. **VP** 75/8; 147/17 wiðstondeð (resistit; subsistit). 139/11 §að (§ent).

wiþstandend *sm* opponent. **VP** 16/8 ðæm wiðstondendum (resistentibus).

ymb-standnis *sf* standing round. **VP** 30/22; 140/3 ~stondnisse (circumstantiae).

wand *s* mole (animal). **Ep** 1014 ~(talpa); Ef uuond; Cp wond; Ld uoond.

uuandaeuuiorpae Ep; uuondæ§ Ef; wonde § Cp.

mand *sf* basket. **Ep** 193 ~(corben); Ef †mondi; Cp ~. 222 ~(cofinus); Cp ~. 839 ~; Ef, Cp ~(qualus). Ef 1174 mond (corbis).

candol *s*(*f*) candle. **Cp** 932 *con*del (funalia).

candeltuist Cp; candel§ Ef.

weax-candol *s*(*f*) wax-candle. **Cp** 943 waexcondel (funalia, cerei).

Tond-berct BH, LV; ton§ LV. Tondburg LV. Tondheri BH, LV. Tonduini, tand§ LV.

trand- *vb* be steep. **Cp** 1668 trondendi (praeceps).

geband *prt* bound. **Cp** 657 ~(devinxit).

brand *sm* brand, burning, sword. **Ep** 987 ~(titio); Ef, Cp brond. Ld 18 brondas (pusti).

brondoom Cp. **brandrād** Ep; brond§ Ep; brandrod Cp; brondra Ld.

Ingi-brand *sm* Gn 81 ~.

Ingibranding *sm* son of Ingibrand. Gn 81 ~.

Weg-brand *sm* Gn 82 ~.

Wegbranding *sm* son of Wegbrand. Gn 82 ~.

blandan *sv* Cp 1138 blondu (inficio). 1141 geblonden (infectum).

·omer *see* ęmer.

ham *s* shirt. Ep 167 ~(colobium); Ef, Cp hom. 244 haam (camisa); Ef §; Cp ha[a]m.

Byrn-ham *sm* Gn 89 ~hom. Ct 8/5 ~es.

Byrnhaming *sm* son of Byrnham. Gn 89 ~homing [o *doubtful*].

hama *sm* covering, coat, womb. Ep 501 ~(inluvies secundarum, *etc*); Ef, Cp §.

feðr-homa *sm* coat of feathers. Cp 1984 ~(talaria).

heort-homa *sm* heart-covering, pericardium. Lr 68 ~an (bucliamine).

līc-hama *sm* body. Lr 9 mines ~homan (mei gibrae). VP 39/7 § (corpus *a.*). Hy 11/8; 13/5 § (§ore; §oris).

Homel-ēa BH.

samod *av* together. VP 13/3; 27/3; 30/14 *etc* somud (simul). Hy 11/15; Hy 13/31 § mid (unā cum). Mt 37 somod.

tō-samne *av* together. VP 34/15 tosomne bicwomun (convenerunt). 67/26 §geðeode (conjuncti). 84/11 § bicomun (obviaverunt).

samnian *wv* collect, gather. VP 128/7 †sonnað (colligit).

gesamnian *wv* VP 15/4; Hy 7/46 gesomniu (congregabo; congeram). 38/7 §að (congregat). 49/5; 103/28 §iað (§ate; colligent). 106/2 §ade (congregavit) 34/15; 40/7 §adon (§averunt). 46[illegible]10 §adon (convenerunt). 47/5 §adun (convenerunt. 105/47 §a (congrega!). 32/7 §ende (§ans). 146/2 §iende (ans). 30/14 bioð ~ade. 47/5; 103/22 §ade sind. Hy 7/66 §ade sind.

gesamnung *sf* gathering. VP 85/14 gesomnung (synagoga). 7/8 §e (§ *n*). 39/11; 81/1; 105/17, 8 §e (§ā). 15/4 §e (conventicula *a*). 25/5 §e (congregationem). 73/2 §e ðinre (§ionis). 110/1 §e micelre (§ione). 63/3 §e (conventu). Ct 37/3 ðere halgon gesomnuncgæ *d.*

scamu *sf* shame. Ep 732 scamu; Ef scoma; Cp scomo (pudor). VP 43/16 scomu (verecundia). 68/20 s[c]ome (§iam). 34/26; 70/13 scome (pudore). 39/16; 131/18 §e (confusionem, §ione). 68/8; 108/29 §e (reverentiā).

scamian *wv* be ashamed. VP 24/2 scomiu (erubescam). 68/7 §iað (§ant). 6/11, 1; 30/18; 34/4, 26; 69/4 §ien (§ant). 33/6 §ien (§ent). 39/15 s[c]omien. 69/4 s[c]omiende.

scamol *s*(*m*) stool. VP 98/5; 109/1 scomul (scabellum *a*).

stam *aj* stammering. Cp 308 stom (blessus). Ef 1150 ~(battulus).

stomwlisp Cp.

fram *aj* vigorous. Ep 71 fraam; Ef, Cp from (acris). Cp 727 § (efficax). 1647 §ra (praestantior).

framlice *av* vigorously. Ep 946 ~ae; Ef fromlicae; Cp §e (strenue). Cp 726 § (efficaciter). 1530 § (perstrenue).

swīþ-framlice *av* very vigorously. Cp 1366 suiðfromlice (naviter).

framian *wv* prevail. VP 88/23 fromað (proficiet).

forðfromung *sf* prevailing. VP 104/38 ~e (profectione).

fram *av, prp* from. Ep 870 ~adoenre; Ef §; Cp from (remotu). Bl 11 from. LP 3 from. CA 17 §. Mt 48 §. VP 2/6 from him (ab). 2/8 §me. 4/8 §tide. 5/11 §geðohtum. 72/27 §ðe. 44/14 §innan (ab intus). 37/4; 50/11; 106/39 fro. 100/4 fro me. Ct 20/10 ~. 20/8, 9, 19 from. 29/2, 3, 4 *etc* ~.

nam *prt* took. VP 72/6; 118/53 nom (tenuit). Hy 1/5 § (tulit).

genam *prt* took. VP 6/10; 17/17; 26/10 genom (adsumpsit).

fornam *prt* destroyed. Cp 1083 ~oom (intercepit).

nama *sm* name. **LP** 12 for his noman. **CA** 15 § *d.* **DA** 2, 2 ~an *d.* 8 § *a.* **Mt** 9, 12 noma. 50 minne (n)oman. **VP** 8/2, 10; 40/6 noma (nomen). 43/21 § (§ *a.*). 91/13 § (Libani). 5/12; 9/11 *etc* §an ðinne. 79/19 noma ðinne. 7/18 §an (§ini). 9/3; 12/6 §an ðinum. 44/18 §an (§inis). 48/12 §an (§ina). 15/4 §ena. 43/26 †nomen ðinum (§en). 71/17 oma. **Ct** 29/16, 6, 7 ~. 39/7; 40/18 ~an *d.* 41/65; 42/12; 48/18 noman *d.* 37/43 ~on *pl.* 45/54 ~an §.

Tome-worðig Ct.

hamm *sf* ham. **Ld** 25 ~e (puplite). 102 homm̧e (puplites). **Bd**² 81 [h]omme (§e). **Lr** 54 homme (cambas).

Hamm *sf* Ham. **Ct** 20/2 †om homme.

Bōsan-hamm *sf* **BH** 277 ~ - bo[o]sanhaam - ~ ham - §.

Colan-homm *sf* **Ct** 59/3 ~.

Iognes-homm *sf* **Ct** 58/5 æt ~e.

Uddan-hom *sf* **Ct** 25/8 ~.

ramm *sm* ram. **VP** 64/14; 113/4, 6 rommas (arietes). 28/1; **Hy** 7/26 §a. 65/15 §um [o *over* e].

geswamm *prt* swam. **Rn** 3/7 giswom.

swamm *sm* mushroom. **Ep** 427 suamm (fungus); **Ef** §; **Cp** suom.

wamm *sm* stain, defect. **Cp** 679 wom (dispendium). 1213 uuam (libor) **VP** 14/2 womme (maculā).

hwamm *sm* corner. **VP** 117/22 hwommes (anguli).

Dammoc *s* Dunwich. **BH** 106 *in civitate* domnoc — dommoc 1 — §. **Ct** 33/16 dammucae *civitatis.*

hramsa *sm* ramsons, wild garlic. **Ep** 59 ~; **Ef** ~; **Cp** hromsa (acitula). 60 † ~ crop (acitelum); **Ef** †hromsa §; **Cp** hromsan §. **Ef** 1107 ~ (ca[c]pinica).

campdōm *sm* warfare. **Bd**² 18 compdomes (militiae).

ampre *sf* dock. **Ep** 1073 amprae (varix); **Ef** omprae; **Cp** ~; **Ld** ompŗe. **Cp** 595 ~ (cocilus).

amber *sm* pail; II a measure. **Ep** 170 ambras (cados); **Ef**, **Cp** §. 923 ambaer (situla); **Ef** ember; **Cp** omber. 1076 ambaer (urna); **Ef** ombar; **Cp** omber. **Ct** 39/4; 40/4; 41/29, 30 ambra *gpl* II. 37/21; 41/60 ombra § II.

ambiht *sn* office. **Ep** 187 ambechtae (conlatio); **Ef** §; **Cp** oembecht. 866 ambect; **Ef** ambaet; **Cp** ambaect (rationatio).

lamb *sn* lamb. **Cp** 752 lomb (agnam). **VP** 113/4, 6 lombur, lomberu (agni *pl*). **Hy** 7/26 †lobra (§orum). **Ct** 28/7 XX ~a.

wamb *sf* stomach, womb. **VP** 16/14; 30/10; 43/25; **Hy** 6/31 womb (venter). 21/10, 1; 57/4; 70/6 §e (§re). 126/3 §e (§ris). 21/15 §minre (§). 131/11 §ðinre (§).

camb *sm* comb. **Ep** 183 uulfes~ (camellea); **Ef** §; **Cp.** wulfes §. 825 ~(pecten); **Ef**, **Cp** §.

ǣ-cambe *sf* oakum. **Cp** 1925 ecambe (stuppa).

ac *av* but. **Cp** 26 ~ðus (sicini). **Mt** 14 ah. **VP** 34/28; 43/4; 51/9 *etc* ah (sed). 38/6, 12 *etc* §hweðre (veruntamen). **Ct** 38/4 ~.

ah *interr.* **VP.** 7/12; 29/10; 40/9 *etc* ~(numquid). 13/4; 38/8; 43/22 *etc* ~ne (nonne).

Aca *sm* **Ct** 10/4 (acan) *g.*

haca *sm* hook. **Ep** 803 ~(pessul); **Ef** §; **Cp** ha[e]ca.

Hacanōs BH.

hrace *sf* throat. **VP** 5/11 hraece (guttur). 13/3 §ae (§). 113/7 hreacan (§e). 134/17 hracan (§e).

hŗectungan Lr.

bord-þaca *sm* shield-covering, testudo. **Ep** 997 †borohaca *etc* (testudo); **Ef** brodthaca; **Cp** bordðeaca.

on-sacan *sv* deny. **Cp** 665 onseacan (detestare).

sacerd *sm* priest. **VP** 77/64; 131/9 ~as (sacerdotes). 109/4 ~ (~os).

ā-slacian *wv* become slack. **Ep** 491 aslacudae (hebitavit); **Ef** §; **Cp** asclacade. **Cp** 693 asclaecadun (dimisis).

ā-scacan *sv* shake off. **VP** 108/23 ascecen (excussus).

tō-scacan *sv* shake asunder. **VP** 28/8 †tosaecendes (concutientis).

wacian *wv* watch. **VP** 62/2 waecio (vigilo). 101/8 waecade (§avi). 126/1 węciað (§ant).

wracu *sf* revenge, punishment. **VP** 17/48; 57/11; 139/13 wrece (vindictam). 149/7 †wrec (§). **Hy** 7/67 §e (ultionis). 93/1, 1 §a, wręca (§onum).

fracodlice *av* basely, wickedly. **Rd** 14 (frac)adlicae.

nacod *aj* naked. **Cp** 807 naec[a]d tunge (exerta).

cwacian *wv* quake. **VP** 17/8; 75/9 cwęcede (contremuit; tremuit). 96/5; **Hy** 13/14 cwaecade (tremuit). 103/32 §ian (§ere).

cwacung *sf* trembling. **VP** 2/11 cwaecunge (tremore). 47/7; 54/6; **Hy** 5/26, 7; 6/32 cwaecung (tremor).

Dacor *sf* river Dacre. **BH** 325 *amnem* ~e — ~.

draca *sm* dragon. **Ep** 1048 droco (tipo); Ef draco; Cp ~ (§, vel inflatio). **VP** 73/13 ~ena (draconum). 14 ~an micles (§onis), 90/13 § (§onem). 103/26 ~a (§o). 148/7 draecan (§ones). **Hy** 7/64 §ena.

Baca *sm* **LV** 339 ~.

Blaca *sm* **LV** 256 ~.

Acca *sm* **BH** 160, 281, 331 ~. 365 ~an *a*. **Gn** 49, 62 ~. **Ct** 28/17 acka. 31/5; 44/4 ~. 5 eacca.

Bacca *sm* **LV** 174; 215 ~. 177 backa.

Agustin *sm* **BH** 47 augustinæs ac, *id est, robur augustini*—agustinęs, *agustini* 1—augustinaes, *augustini*. **Ct** 30/21 ~es higum.

haga *sm* enclosure, measure of land. **Ct** 20/17 ðæm ~an. 29/7, 8 cregsetna~. 51/7 *duas possessiunculas et tertiam dimediam, id est in nostra loquella* ðridda half ~.

swīn-haga *sm* enclosure for swine. **Ct** 20/17 se alda suín~.

hagu-

Hagustaldensis BH; hag[u]§, hagstaldensiae, hag' Gn. **haeguthorn** Ep; hagu-, hegu- Ef.; haegu-, hea[go]- Cp.

gehagian *wv* suit. **Ct** 45/19 ~ige *sbj*.

Hagona *sm* **Ct** 1/7 ~. 4/5 ~ani *g*. 5/7 ~ana.

ragu *s* lichen. **Ep** 629 ~(mossiclum); Ef, Cp §. **Cp** 1332 ~(mosicum). 1853 rægu (sedulium).

reagufinc Cp.

hlagolian *wv* sound. **Cp** 317 hlaegulendi (bombosa).

lund-laga *sm* kidney. **Ep** 850 ~(renunculus); Ef, Cp §. **Lr** 51, 62 ~leogum, ~leogan (renibus, reniculos).

ofer-lagu *sf* cloak. **Ld** 1 ober~ (anfibula).

ā-sagas *prs* sayest. **VP** 49/16 ~(enarras).

slagu *sf* slag. **Ep** 603 slęgu (lihargum); Ef slægu; Cp slaegu.

wagian *wv* wag. **Cp** 1188 weagat (labat).

maga *sm* stomach. **Cp** 1934 ~(stomachum).

gagul-swillan Cp.

Baga *sm* **LV** 252 ~.

Bacga *sm* **LV** 58, 79; 205, 20; 339 ~. **Ct** 3/6 baggan gete.

hratian *wv* rush, hasten. **Bd**[2] 32 geratade (adceleravit).

latian *wv* delay. **VP** 39/18; 69/6 ne leata ðu (tardaveris; re§).

cwatern *s* number four (quatre) on dice. **Ep** 847 quatern (quaternio); Ef quaterni; Cp quatern.

Atta *sm* **LV** 179 ~.

catte *sf* cat. **Cp** 863 ~(fellus).

adese *sf* adze. **VP** 73/6 eadesan (ascia).

sūþ-rador *sm* south sky. **Bl** 17 ~(australis).

gehladan *sv* draw water. **VH** 2/5 gehleadað weter (aurietis).

sadol *sm* saddle. **Ep** 926 ~(sella); Ef †satul; Cp ~.

sadulbogo Ef; Cp §a. **sadulfelgae** Ep; § Ef, Cp.

spade *sf* spade. **Ep** 1087 ~an (vangas); Ef, Cp §. **Ld** 111 spaedum (§).

Wada *sm* **LV** 14; 173; 326 uada.

Fadol *sm* **Ct** 3/14 fad(ol).

Cadaca-hrygc Ct.

clador *s* rattle. **Ep** 218 claedur (crepacula *etc*); Ef cledr; Cp cleadur.

cladersticca Ep, Ef; § Cp.

gladian *wv* gladden. **VP** 103/15 gleadie (exhilaret).

Badu *sf* **LV** 39 ~.

Baduca *sm* **LV** 217, 28; 353 ~.

Adda *sm* **BH** 181 ~. **LK** 3 ~. **LV** 170; 347 ~. **Ct** 5/6 ~.

Adding *sm* **LV** 102 ~.

Addul *sm* **LV** 286 ~.

Padda *sm* **BH** 276 ~.

apa *sm* ape. **Ep** 827 ~(phitecus); Cp~; Ef †capa.

apuldor *s(f)* appletree. **Ep** 636 ~ur (malus); Cp §; Ef apuldro.

milsc-apuldor *s(f)* sweet-apple-tree. **Ep** 638 §apuldr (melarium); Ef milcapuldr; Cp mircapuldur.

wapul *s* bubble. **Ep** 447 uuapul (famfaluca); Ef §; Cp ~.

mapuldor *sm* maple. **Ep** 33 ~ur (acerabulus); Ef †maefuldur; Cp mapuldur; Ld †mapaldurt.

tapor *sm* taper. **Ct** 41/62 ðritig teapera.

Appincg-lond Ct.

Glappa *sm* **LK** 3 ~.

Abba *sm* **LV** 177 ~. **Ct** 24/10; 35/12; 36/7; 41/1, 49, 51 ~. 58, 71 ~an *g*.

habban *wv* have. **VP** 113(2)/5, 5, 6, 6, 7, 7 etc ~að (habent). **Hy** 7/11 § (§ete). 134/17 †habað (§ent). **Ct** 41/12 to ~anne. 48/2 to hiobbanne.

nabban *wv* not to have. **VP** 37/15 ~ende (non habens).

Babbing-lond Ct.

hæring *sm* herring. **Ep** 910 heringas (sardinas); Ef, Cp, Ld §.

scær *s(n)* plough-share. **Cp** 32 scaer (vomer). **Ef** 1154 § (bemer). 1158 †scaes (buris).

scersaex VP.

stær *s(m)* starling. **Ep** 908 stær (sturnus); Ef †sterm; Cp staer; Ld stęr.

staer-blind Cp.

spaer-habuc Cp.

spæren *s* spar. **Ep** 460 sparaen (gipsus); Ef sparen; Cp spaeren.

Wær *sm* **Ct** 18/5 uuaer.

geond-færeþ *vb* traverses. **VH** 5/29 ~fereð (pertranseat).

færeld *sn* journey. **Ct** 45/13 þæt fęreld.

Wil-fær *sm* **BH** 162 uilfaręs dun, *id est, mons* uilfari.

Uilfaręs-dūn — uilfaraes§ — uilfares§ — uilfæraes§ BH.

ā-bær *prt* endured. **VP** 68/8 aber (supportavi).

gærs *sn* grass. **Cp** 864 graes (fenum). **Ct** 28/6 gers.

gręsgroeni Ef; graes§ Cp. **geres-hoppe**, gers§ VP.

bærs *s* bass (a fish). **Ep** 592 baers (lupus); Ef §; Cp †bre[r]s.

ærn *sn* house.

rendegn Ef.

bere-ærn *sn* barn. **DA** 18 to berenne.

hord-ærn *sn* storehouse. **Bl** 10 ~ern (promptuaria). **VP** 143/13 § (prumptuaria). **Hy** 7/57 †hondernum (§iis).

mete-ærn *sn* refectory. **Ct** 31/3 hina ~ren.

sealt-ærn *sn* saltern. **Ct** 28/5 ~ern. 24, 5 ðem §.

sealternsteall Ct.

win-ærn *sn* tavern. **Ep** 1040 uuinaern (taberna); Ef §; Cp ~aern.

hærn *s* wave. **Ep** 400 hraen (flustra, undae); Ef †raen.

bærnan *wv* burn. **VP** 25/2 bern (ure). 103/4 §ende (§entem). 120/6 §eð. **Hy** 7/46 §de (concremavit). **Bd**[2] 11 ~de (adurit).

for-bærnan *wv* burn up *trans.* **VP** 45/10; 82/15, 5 ~berneð (comburet; §, incendat). 105/18 §de (combusit). 73/7 §dun (incenderunt). 104/32 §ende (comburentem). **Mt** 44 ~bęrnde.

in-bærnes *sf* burning. **VP** 65/15; 140/2 inbernisse (incensu; §um).

ærce-biscop, erce§, arce§, archi§ Ct.

æl- all.

Aelberct, al§ LV. **alme'ttig** Rn; allmectig CH; almaehtig CA; all§, æll§, al§, ael§ Ct. **Alrīc** BH, LV; el§ Ct. [Alwīch *under* ealu.]

hæl *prt* concealed. **VP** 39/11 hel (celavi).

hæle *sm* man. **Rd** 12 hęliðum.

smæl *aj* narrow, slender. **Ep** 474 smael (gracilis); Ef smal; Cp smęl. **Ct** 20/10, o oð smalan cumb, smalan cumbes.

smælðearmas Lr.

scæl *vb* shall. **Rd** 8 sceal. **DA** 15 sceall. 16 scal. **Ct** 39/3 sçel.

stæl *sn* place. **Ep** 1067 stalu to fuglum; Ef, Cp §; Ld stalo (umbrellas).

wæl *sn* slaughter. **Bd**² 89 *on* waele (et cladis).

walcyrge, walcrigge, uualcyrge Cp. uuaelreab Ep; uuel§ Ef; waelreaf Cp.

hwæl *sm* whale. **VH** 8/13 hwalas (caeti).

hwæl *aj* noisy. **Cp** 1624 huuæl (procax).

getæl *sn* number. **Cp** 1741 getael (rinia).

dæl *sn* valley. **Cp** 274 dael (baratrum); Ld dal.

æelf-

Aelfflēd, aelb§ BH; aelfled LV; ælffled Ct. **Aelfgȳth** LV; §gyð Ct. **Ælfhere** Ct. **Aelfhūn** LV; ælf§ Ct. **Aelfrēd** LV, CA, Ct; ælf§ SG, Ct. **Aelfrīc** BH. **Aelfsig** LV. **Aelfstān**, æ§, e§, †aefstan Ct. **Olwfwolþu** Rn; aelfuald LV; aelfwald Gn; elf§ Ct. **Aelfðrȳth** LV; aelfþryð, ęlf§ Ct. **Aelfuini**, aelb§ BH; ælf§ LK; aelfuini LV. **Aelfuulf** LV.

ælmesse *sf* alms. **Ct** 37/9 on aelmessan. 14 mid§. 37/24, 31 to §. 30/23 elmessum. 39/11 sia §e. 40/16 ðas §an *a.* 45/36 ða §an *a.*

elmeshlāf Ct.

ælmeslic *aj* charitable. **Ct** 42/11 swæ him ~sie. 38/5 elmestlicast.

ælmeslice *av* charitably. **Ct** 34/15 ~.

æþele *aj* noble. **Cp** 958 aeðile (generosus). **Rn** 2/13 æþþilæ *pl.* **Mt** 40 ðæs æðelan weres. **VP** 149/8 eðele (nobiles).

Aeðilbald, ethil§, eðil§ (aðil§), LV; æðel§, aeðil§ Gn; æðel§ SG; aethilbalt, aetdil§, edil§, ęthilbald, aethel§, æðel§, eðel§ Ct. **Aedilberg**, ædil§, aeðil§, edil§ BH [*under* eo]. **Aedilberct**, ædil§, aeðil§, edil§, adil§ [*in Lat. doc.*], adiliberto, aedibericto BH; eðilberct, edil§ LV; aeðilberht, eðil§, aeðel§ Gn; æðel§ SG; aethilberht, aeðæl§, aeðel§, æðel§, eþel§, eðel§ Ct; eðilberhting Gn. **Aedilburg**, aeðil§, edil§ BH; eðil§ LV; hedil§, aethil§ Ct. **Aedilfrid**, ædil§, aeðil§ BH; aedil§ LK; eðilfrith LV; aeðilferð, eðilfrið, §ing Gn; aedilfrid, æðelfrið Ct. **Aeðilgeard**, æðelieard (§), aethil§ Ct. **Aðigils** LV. **Eðilgȳth** LV. **Edilhēch**, eðil§ LV; aeþelheah, aeðel§, aedel§ Ct. **Eðilheard** LV; aeðel§ Gn; aeðil§, aeðel§, aeþel§, æthel§, æðel§ Ct. **Eðilhelm** LV; æþel§, æðel§, aeðelm Ct. **Aedilheri**, edil§ BH; eðelhere Ct. **Aedilhild**, aeðil§ BH; eðil§ LV. **Aedilhūn**, aeðil§, edil§, aedel§ BH; aeðel§, æðel§ Ct. **Aedilmāeri** Ct. **Aeðilmōd** LV; aeðel§ Gn; aethil§, aethel§, æðel§, eðel§ Ct. **Aeðilmund**, eðil§ LV; æðel§, aeðel§, ęðel§, eðel§, ædel§ Ct. **Aeðilnōð** Gn; æðel§, aethel§, eð[el]§ Ct. **Aedilrēd**, aeðil§, ędil§, aeðel§ BH; aeðil§, eðil§ LV; aeðil§ Gn; æðered SG; aeðæl§, æðel§, ęðel§, eðel§, aeðerred, æðered, ęðered, eðered Ct. **Aedilrīc**, LK; eðil§ LV; §§ Gn; aethil§, aeðel§, æðel§, ęðel§, eðel§, eðeric Ct; eðilricing Gn. **Aeðelstān**, eðel§ Ct. **Eðilsuīð** LV. **Aedilthrȳd**, aeðilðryð, edilthryd, aedyldrydę BH. **Aediluald**, aeðil§, edil§, adul§, aeðul§ [*these two in Lat. doc.*] BH; eðil§ LV; aedel§ LN; æðelwaldes Mt; æðelwald, aeðel§, ęðel§, æðe§, †ðel§ Ct. **Aedilualch**, edil§ BH. **Aediluini**, aeðil§ BH; §§, eðil§, aethuini, aeð§ LV; aeðeluine Gn. **Eðiluulf**, edil§ LV; aeðil§, æðil§ Gn; æ(ðelwulf), æðe(l§) SG; aetheluulf, æthel§, aeþel§, aeðel§, æðel§, ęðel§, eðel§, æðælwulf, eðeluf, aeðeu[u]lf, aeðuulf Ct.

un-æþele *aj* not noble, plebeian. **Cp** 993 †unaeðilsa (gregariorum); †aedilra Ep, Ef.

Æþelu *sf* **LV** 46 eðilu.

Reth-hūn Gn; raeþ§, ræð§, reð§ Ct.

staeð-suualwe Cp.

hwæþer *prn* whether. **Ct** 34/10

suæ hueðer suæ. 37/22 suę huaeder suae. 41/23 swæ hwæder swæ. 45/27 swa hwaðer swa.

hwæþer *cj* whether. **VP** 13/2; 52/3; 57/12; 138/19, 24 hweðer (si).

gehwæþer *av* both. **Ct** 37/42 gehueder ge .. ge.

hwæþre *av* however. **Rn** 2/12 hweþræ. **Rd** 11 hudrae. **VP** 38/7 *etc* hweðre (tamen); 6, 12 *etc* ah § (veruntamen); 31/6 *etc* §soðlice (§).

fæðm *s(m)* embrace, lap, fathom. **Cp** 988 faethm (gremen). 1510 faeðm *vel* tuegen stridi (passus). 1875 faeðm (sinus). **Lr** 48 ~um (cubitis).

fæþman *wv* embrace, encompass. **Ep** 939 faetmaendi (sinuosa); Ef faedmendi; Cp faeð§.

cwæþ *prt* said. **Mt** 25, 7 cwæð. 37, 46 cuæð. **VP** 2/7; 9/34 cwæð (dixit). 105/34 cwaeð (dixerat). 9/27, 32; 15/2; 72/15 *etc* cweð (dixit, §; §i; dicebam). 29/7 †ceð (dixi). 67/23 cyð (§it).

pæþ *sm* path. **Cp** 429 paat (callis). **Ct** 5/3 paeð (paed).

here-pæþ *sm* army-path. **Ct** 20/20 ðone ~pað.

hæsel *s(m)* hazel. **Ep** 50 †aesil (avellanus); Ef, Cp haesl; Ld †hel. 236 haesil; Ef, Cp haesl.

haeselhnutu Cp.

þæs *g* of the. **Rn** 1/6 þaes. **DA** 3 ðaes. 10 ðæs. **Mt** 11, 34 *etc* §. **Bd**²56 §. **VP** 9/36, 6 *etc* ðes. 9/28; 39/5 § (cujus) *etc*. 67/15 des. 7/18; 74/11 ðæs. **Ct** 20/6, 11; 37/4 ðæs. 37/4; 47/10, 4; 48/19 ðaes. 45/25 þęs. 27/7; 28/18, 25; 29/16, 6, 7; 38/4, 12; 39/15; 42/20; 45/21 ðes.

þæs *av* **SG** 10 ðæs ðe 'since.' **Ct** 48/20 ðaes.

wæs *prt* was. **Ep** 523, 5 uuaes; Ef uaes; Cp waes. **Rn** 2/9 (wæs). 11, 4 ~. **CA** 5 ~. **Mt** 9, 10 *etc* ~. **SG** 2, 10 ~. **Bd**² 71 ~. **VP** 13/5; 16/10; 17/8 *etc* wes. 36/36; 37/8; 78/3 *etc* ne§. **Ct** 38/3; 40/1 wes. 47/9, 13 waes.

næs *av* not. **Ct** 39/15 nas.

hwæs *gen* whose.

hwæshwegu Mt.

gehwæs *g* of each. **CH** 3 gihuaes.

fæs *sn* fringe. **VP** 44/14 feasum (fimbriis).

naes-gristlae Ep; Ef, Cp §; næsgristlan Lr. næsðyrel Lr; nes§ VP.

mæsse *sf* mass. **Ct** 37/36 twa messan.

mæssepriost, messe§ Ct.

æsc *sm* ash, war-ship. **Ep** 180 aesc (cercylus vel navis); Ef, Cp §. 416 aesc; Cp § (fraxinus); Ef †aastc. 772 aesc (praxinus); Cp §; Ef esc.

aescthrotae Ep, Ef, Cp. **Aescuald** LV. **Æscwine**, §ing SG. **Aescuulf** LV, Gn.

Æsca *sm* Ct 29/20 ~.

æsce *sf* ashes. **VP** 101/10 escan (cinerem). 147/16 eascan (§).

naesc *s* **Cp** 2061 ~um (tractibus).

rēod-naesc *s* **Cp** 1529 ~(partica).

Læsting *s* Lastingham. **BH** 241 *monasterio in* ~ae — lestinga he — laestinge.

Læstinga-ēu, laestinga§, laestenga§, luestinga§, luestingua§, lęstinga§, lestinga§ BH.

hlaest-scip Cp.

wæstm *sm* growth, fruit. **VP** 20/11; 57/12; 66/7 *etc* westem (fructum; §us; §um). 103/13; 131/11 westme (§u). 77/46 §as (§ūs). 127/2 §a (§um = uum).

westemsceat VP.

hwǣte-wæstm *sm* crop of wheat. **VP** 77/25 hwętewestem (frumentationem).

ō-wæstm *sm* shoot, twig. **Cp** 1942 ouuaestm (surculus). **VH** 7/63 owestem (propago).

wæstmbǣre *aj* fertile. **VP** 51/10; 106/34 westembere (fructifera; §am). 148/9 §beru (§a *fem.*)

wæstmbǣrnis *sf* fertility. **Bd**² 19 wæstembiornis (fertilitas).

fæst *aj* firm.

staþolfest, §nis, §ian. **wuldurfest**. **sōþfest**, §nis; soþfęstlice.

liffæst *aj* settled. Ct 42/6 liffest.

be-fæstan *wv* make firm, commit, entrust. VP 77/8 bifested (creditus). Ct 42/7 befestan.

geliffestan *wv* VP 84/7 ~as (vivificabis). 118/107, 49, 54, 6, 9 ~a (§a!). 137/7; 142/11; Hy 3/16 ~es (§abis). Hy 4/12 ~eð (§at). 118/93 ~es (§asti). 118/25 ~e (§a!).

sige-fæstan *wv* triumph. Bd² 77 ~fęston (triumphant).

geuuetfaestan *wv* betroth. Cp 1946 ~ae (subarrata).

faestingmenn, fæsting§ Ct.

fæsten *sn* fastness, fort. Ep 110 faestinnum (arcibus); Cp §; Ef fęstinnun. 1042 faestin (termofilas); Ef †festis; Cp faesten. Cp 204 faestin (arx).

fæstenian *wv* confirm. Lr 8 were fæstnie (pactum feriat). Ct 38/16; 40/12; 41/50 (ic) festnie. 41/48 ic festniæ. 42/23 ic festnię. 45/56 ic fęstnie. 48/8 ic faestna.

gefæstnian *wv* fasten, fix, confirm. VP 9/16; 37/3 gefestnade (infixae). 68/3 §ad (§us). 118/120 §a (infige!). Ct 40/17 ic gefestnie.

fæstan *wv* fast. Cp 1295 gefaested (macilentus).

fæsten *sn* fast. VP 34/13; 68/11; 108/24 festenne (jejunio).

festendæg Ct.

mæst *sm* mast (of ship). Ld 116 maest (arbor).

mæstan *wv* feed, pasture. Ep 930 maestun (saginabant); Cp §; Ef mestum.

cæster *sf* city. VP 86/2; 121/3 cester (civitas). 45/5 cestre (§atem); 59/11 §getrymede (§atem) *etc.* 30/22 § (§ate); 72/20 §ðinre (§ate) *etc.* 106/4 § (§atis). 9/7; 68/36; 138/20 § (§ates).

Caestruuara Ct.

Celca-cæster *sf* BH 304 *civitatem calcariam quae a gente Anglorum* kælca caestir *appellatur* — faelcaestir — helcacęstir (he *on er*).

Dorcic-cæster *sf* Dorchester. BH 306 ~caestræ *g* — dorcicæstrę — ~cęstre.

Dornwarena-cæster *sf* Dorchester. Ct 20/3 ~uuarana ceaster.

Granta-cæster *sf* Granchester. BH 295 ~caestir — ~cęster I.

Hrōfes-cæster *sf* Rochester. BH 57 ~æscæstræ *a.* — ~escaester I — ~aescaestrae. 249 ~cæstir — hrofaescaestir — ~caestir — hrofaescaest[e]r. 372 hrofensi — rofensi I. Gn 9 hrofensis. Ct 45/40 to ~cestre.

Lega-cæster *sf* Chester. BH 51 *civitatem Legionum, quae a gente Anglorum* ~caestir *appellatur* — §er I, II. Ct 33/4 legorensis *civitatis.*

Repta-cæster *sf* Richborough. BH 10 ~cęstir — ~caester — ~caestir.

Rōme-cæster *sf* Rome. Rn 3/2 in romæcæstri.

Tēowulfinga-cæster *sf* BH 110 tiouulfinga cæstir — §caestir I.

Tunna-cæster *sf* BH 300 ~caestir.

Wætlinga-cæster *sf* Verolamium. BH 13 uaetlinga cæstir — uetlingua cáester — uaetlinga cęster.

Werlama-cæster *sf* Verolamium. BH 12 uerlama cæstir — §caester — §caestir.

Wintan-cæster *sf* Winchester. BH 145 *civitate venta, quae a gente saxonum* uintan cæstir *appellatur* — §caestir — uinta caestir. Ct 33/13 wintanæ *civitatis.*

Yþan-cæster *sf* BH 187 ythan caestir — §er I.

bæst *s* bast. Ep 1017 lind *vel* baest (tilio); Cp §; Ef best.

æspe *sf* aspen, white poplar. Ep 1006 aespae (tremulus); Ef espę; Cp aespe. Cp 34 †etspe (abies). 202 aespe (arbutus).

ūpā-hæfen *ptc* raised. VP 8/2; 9/33 *etc* ~hefen is, sie§ (elevata est; exaltetur). 71/7 were§ (extollatur). Hy 8/23 § (superexaltatus). 130/1 §sind (elati sunt). 72/18 werun§ (adlevarentur). 36/20 §e biað (exaltati fuerint) *etc.* 23/7, 9 bioð §e (elevamini). 46/10 §e werun (elevati sunt). 17/27, 7 mid ðy §an upahefen ðu bist (cum electo §us eris). 36/35, 5 §ne (superexaltatum, elevatum).

ūpāhefenis *sf* elevation. **VP** 87/8; 92/4 ~isse (elationes).

ūp-hefenis *sf* elevation. **VP** 140/2 ~(elevatio).

hæf *sn* sea. **Cp** 1778 haeb (salum).

hæfer *sm* goat. **Cp** 399 heber (caper).

†**hraebrebletae** Ep; hebre§ Ef; haebre§ Cp.

hæfern *s* crab. **Ef** 258 hafaern (cancer); Cp haebrn. Ep 684 habern (nepa); Ef hafern; Cp haebern. Ef 1106 †nefern (cancer). Ld 106 hebernum (choncis).

ā-ræfnan *wv* endure. **Ef** 353 araebndae (expendisse); Cp araef[n]de. Cp 809 araefndun (exigebant). **VP** 24/5, 21; 68/21; 129/4 arefnde (sustinui). 105/13 §dun (§uerunt). 64/8; 129/3, 4 §eð (§ebit; §§; §uit).

unāræfnendlic *aj* intolerable. **VP** 123/5 ~refnendlic (intolerabilem).

hræfn *sm* raven. **Ef** 285 hraebn (corax); Cp hraefn. Ep 848 hraebnęs foot (quinquefolium); Ef hræfnæs§; Cp hraefnes§. 1084 hraefnaes fot (§). **VP** 146/9 hrefna (corvorum).

næht-hræfn *sm* night-raven. **Ep** 673 naecht[h]raebn (noctua); Ef necthraebn; Cp naehthraefn; Ld †nechtrefn. 674 naechthraebn (nycticorax); Ef nethhræbn. **VP** 101/7 næhthrefn (nocticorax).

læfer *s* rush. **Ep** 894 †lerb (scirpea *etc*); Ef lebrae; Cp lebr. Cp 1823 leber (§).

læfel *sm* basin. **Ep** 633 lebil (manile); Ef, Cp §. 995 § (triplia); Ef §; Cp lebl. Cp 193 lebel (aquemale).

scræf *s* cormorant. **Cp** 1311 scraeb (mergus).

stæf *sm* staff. **Cp** 1441 staeb (olastrum).

staeblidrae Ep; steb§ Ef.; staefliðre Cp. **staebplegan** Ep; scæb- Ef; staefplagan Cp.

ende-stæf *sm* end. **Ef** 367 †stęb (exito, perditio); Cp endistaeb.

fræfel *s* cunning. **Cp** 230 facni *vel* fraefeli (astu).

fræfelian *wv* be cunning. **Cp** 431 fraefeleo (calleo).

cæfer *sm* cockchafer. **Ep** 150 cefr (bruchus); Ef §; Cp cefer. Cp 214 ceber (arpia).

ceber-tuun Ep; caeber§ Ef; caebr§ Cp; ceafurtun, ceafor§, ceaful§ VP.

cæfel *s* halter. **Cp** 430 caefli (capistro).

cæfester *s* halter. **Cp** 376 caebestr (capistrum).

for-gæf *prt* granted. **Ct** 40/4 ~gef.

græf *s* writing-style. **Cp** 997 gręf (graffium).

tæfl *sf* die. **Ep** 6 teblae (alea); **Ef** tefil; Cp, Ld tebl. Ef 1142 tefil (alia).

tebelstān Ep; tebil§ Ef; tebl§ Cp.

tæflan *wv* gamble. **Ep** 178 teblith (cotizat); Ef §; Cp tebleth.

tæflere *sm* gambler. **Ep** 7 teblere (aleator); Ef, Cp §; Ld †teblheri. Ef 1141 tebleri (§).

wæfs *sm* wasp. **Ef** 255 uaeps; Cp waefs (crabro). Ep 1071 waeffsas (vespas); Ef uuaeps; Cp uuaefsas. Cp 859 waefs (fespa).

æfter *prp, av* after. **Rn** 1/3 aft. 4/2, 3 æftær (aeftaer). 11/2 aefter. 10/1 æftar. **CH** 8 ~*av*. **BDS** 5 aefter. **Mt** 42 ~. **VP** 5/11; 7/9, 9 efter (secundum) *etc*. 15/4 §ðon (postea). 102/10 †efer. **Ct** 41/2, 5, 38; 42/3; 45/9 ~. 42/21 ~*av*. 45/14, 6, 35, 8, 41 ęfter. 41/64 efter. 38/5, 13 yfter.

efterfylgan, §end; †esterfylgan.

æfterra *aj compar* behind. **VP** 67/14 efterran (posteriora). 77/66 ða § (§).

hæft

heftnēd VP.

gehæftan *wv* capture. **VP** 93/21 geheftað (captabunt).

gehæftednis *sf* captivity. **VP** 34/8 geheftednis (captio).

gehæft *aj* captive. **VP** 67/19; 136/3 gehefte (captivam; §os).

ræfter *sm* rafter, beam. **Ep** 11 reftras (amites); Ef, Cp §.

ed-scæft *s(f)* regeneration. **Ep** 783 edscaept (palinginesean); Ef §; Cp edscaeft.

gescæft *sf* creation, creature. **VP** 73/18 ðisse gescefte (creaturae *g*). 103/24 ðinre§ (§ā).

scæft *s*(*m*) shaft.

scaeptlōan Ep, Cp; sceptloum Ep, Ef, Cp; sceptog Cp.

cræft *sm* skill.

gealdor-cræft *sm* magic skill. **VP** 57/6 galdurcreftas (vocem venefici).

hēah-cræft *sm* high skill. **Rd** 4 • ðerh hehcraeft.

wynde-cræft *sm* art of embroidery. **Cp** 217 uuyndecreft (ars plumaria). **Rd** 9 † uyrdicraeftum.

Cræft *s* **Ct** 47/1 in craeft.

græft *sm* carving. **VP** 77/58; 105/36, 8 greftum (sculptilibus). 96/7; 105/19 §as (§ia; §e).

hæfde *prt* had. **VP** 76/6; 118/104, 13, 28, 63 hefde (habui). **Hy** 4/11 § (habebat). 63/9; 101/15; 105/24 §un (habuerunt). 77/37 hefd (habita). 89/5 bioð§ (§entur). **Ct** 28/23 hefdan.

on-hæfd *ptc* **Ep** 915 anhaebd (suspensus); Ef anhæfd; Cp ahaefd.

æcer *sm* I field. II acre. **DA** 18 acrum. **Ct** 56/8 ðritiges æcra II.

hæcele *sf* cloak. **Ep** 740 haecilae (paludamentum); **Ef** hecæli; **Cp** haecile. 572 haecilae (lacerna); **Ef** hecile; Cp haecile.

ræce *sf* rake. **Cp** 25 raece (rastrum).

Ræculf *s*. Reculver. **BH** 346 *monasterio quod* racuulfe *nominatur*. **Ct** 4/3 *in civitate* recuulf. 8/2 *monasterio quod nominatur* ricuulfi. 35/7 *a* reacoluensae *ecclesiae*. 58/4 æt ræculfo (ręculfo).

þæc *s*(*n*) thatch, covering.

þaectigilum Cp.

fenn-þæc *s*(*n*) fen-covering. **Bd**[2] 70 fenðacum (palustria arundine).

geþræc *sn* tumult. **Cp** 190 geþrec (apparatum). **Rd** 6 giðraec *a*.

slæc *aj* slack, languid. **Cp** 732 slaece (egra). 1718 slaec (reses).

slæcnes *sf* slackness. **Ef** 1185 †placūnis (laxitas).

spræc *s* twig, shoot. **Cp** 1769 spraec (sarmentum).

spræc *prt* spoke. **Mt** 34 ~. **VP** 98/7; 118/46; 119/7; 121/8 sprec (loquebatur *etc*).

wæcen *sf* watch. **VP** 76/5 waecene (vigilias).

wræc *prt* drove, persecuted. **Ep** 90 uuraec (aegit); **Ef** uraec; **Cp** wraec. 1002 uuraec (torquet); **Ef**, Cp §.

wraec *s* **Ep** 87 uuraec; **Ef** uraec; Cp wraec (actuarius).

wrecscype *sm* exile. **Bl** 21 ~(incolatus).

fæcele *sf* torch. **Ep** 407 fæcilae (fax); Ef faecile.

bæc *sn* back. Cp 1148 in bęce (in catamo). **VP** 17/41; 68/24; 80/7 bec (dorsum). 128/3 § minne (§). 13/20 § (deorsum). 6/11; 9/3 *etc* on § (retrorsum). 43/19 on § (retro). **Hy** 3/18 on § (post tergum). 65/11 §e (dorso). 67/14; **Hy** 7/48 §es (§i).

baecþearm **Cp**; bęcdermi Ef.

gebræc *prt* broke. **VP** 75/4; 106/16; 109/5; **Hy** 5/9 (confregit *etc*).

blæc *aj* black. **Ep** 139 blec thrustfel (bitiligo); Ef blec; Cp blaec. 677 blaec teru (napta); Ef, Cp §. Cp 1688 blaco (pulla). **Ct** 30/4 blacan riðe.

Blaecmon LV, Gn; §ing Gn.

Æcce *sm* **BH** 252 aecci. **Gn** 28 aecce.

sæcc *sm* sack. **VP** 29/12 sec minne (saccum).

Blæcca *sm* **BH** 108 blaecca.

æx *s*(*f*) axe. **VP** 73/5 ęcesum (securibus).

Acustyde Ct.

brād-æx *s*(*f*) broad axe. **Ld** 197 bradacus (dolabella).

blādlāst-æx *sf* broad axe. **Ef** 321 braedlaestuaesc; Cp braadlastęcus (dolatura).

næht *sf* night. **Ld** 134 ofer tua †nest (perendie). **VP** 73/16; 103/20; 138/11; **Hy** 12/10 naeht (nox). **Hy** 12/2 § (noctem). 77/14 alle § (§e). 91/3; 120/6 ðorh § (§em). 129/6 oð § (§em). 21/3; 41/9; 76/3, 7 on § (§e). 118/62 on midde § (media §e). 89/4; 118/55 in § (in §e). 16/3; 87/2 on næht (§e). 104/39 ðorh § (§em). 138/12 nęht (nox). 15/7 oð § (noctem). 18/3 neht (nox). 18/3 §e (nocti). 135/9; Hy 12/5 naehte (§is). 31/4; 41/4 deges ⁊ §es (§e). 54/11 deges ⁊ nęhtes (§e). 6/7 nęht (§es). Hy 8/7 naeht (§es). 133/2 naehtum. Hy 12/9 §a (§ium).

†noctigalae, necti§, nectae§ Ep; nęctę§, nacthe§, necegle Ef; nehtęgale, naecte§ Cp; nectigalae Ld. **naectgenge** Cp. **naechthraebn** Ep; nect§, neth§ Ef; naeht§ Cp; necthtrefn Ld; næhthrefn VP.

næhtlic *aj* nocturnal. **VP** 90/5 naehtlicum (nocturno).

mæhte *prt* could. **Mt** 37, 42 meahte. **VP** 39/13 maehte (potui). 20/12; 128/2; 140/6 §un (§uerunt).

mæht *sf* power. **CH** 2 maecti *pl.* **BD**[2] 63 męhte (potestatis). **VP** 113/2 maeht (potestas). 105/8 § (potentiam). 144/11 § ðine (§). 85/16; 89/11 §e (potestatem). Hy 10/6 §e (potentiam). 70/18; 79/3; 144/12 §e ðine (§am). 135/9 in §e (potestatem). 64/7; 88/14 mid §e (potentiā). 88/10 waldes §e (dominaris potestati). 70/16 §e (potentias). 105/2 mæhte (§as). 19/7; 89/10; 150/2 maehtum (potentatibus). 61/12; 144/4 maht. 135/8 §e.

mæhtig *aj* powerful. **VP** 23/8, 8; 51/3; 111/2; Hy 10/4; Hy 12/14 maehtig (potens). 77/65; 88/9 mæhtig. 102/20; 119/4; Hy 10/7 maehtge. 71/12 ðæm §an. 88/20 ðone mæhtgan. 126/4 mæhtges. 44/4, 6 ða §estan. Hy 6/28 maehtigra. 85/14 mehtigra. Hy 11/5 męhtigre.

æl-mæhtig *aj* almighty. **Rn** 2/1 alme·ttig. **CH** 9 allmectig. **CA** 15 almaehtiges. **Ct** 37/3; 42/5 allmehtgum. 45/45 ællmęhtig, 52 almahtig. 48/19 aelmaehtgan.

bræhtm *s* noise. **Ep** 928 brectme *vel* cliderme (strepitu); Ef bretme; Cp braechtme.

ægnan *spl* chaff. **Ep** 840 †aehrian (quisquiliae); Ef †ægrihan; Cp aegnan. Cp 1526 § (paleae).

hægl *sm* hail. **VP** 17/13; 148/8 hegel (grando). 104/32 § (§inem). 77/47, 8 hegle.

hrægl *sn* dress. **Ep** 84 hraecli (amiculo); Ef hraegl; Cp hręgli. **VP** 21/19; 68/12; 101/27; 108/19 hregl (vestem; (vestimentum; §; §) 103/2; 108/18 §e. 132/2 §es (§i). 21/19 hregl (§a). 44/9 §um.

dēad-raegel *sn* grave clothes. **Cp** 1482 ~um (palearibus).

Uiht-laeg *sm.* **Gn** 95 ~.

Uihtlaeging *sm* son of W. **Gn** 95 ~.

slægen *ptc* struck. **Cp** 1555 bið slaegen (percellitur). 1565 slaegen (§). **VP** 101/5 slegen (percussus).

for-slægen *ptc* beaten. **Ep** 744 forsleginum; Ef †faerlslaegmum (profligatis); Cp forslaegenum. 814 forslaegęn (proflicta); Ef §; Cp forslaegen.

of-slægen *ptc* killed. **VP** 101/21 ofslegenra (interemptorum). 105/38 ofslegen wes (†infecta est).

on-slægen *ptc* beaten on. **Ep** 535 †a[n]slegaengrae (inpactae); Ef †aslegenræ; Cp †onligenre.

ofslægennis *sf* slaughter. **VP** 43/22 ofslegenisse (occisionis).

stæg *s* pond, pool. **Ep** 962 staeg *vel* meri (stagnum); Ef §.

wægn *sm* carriage, chariot, cart. **Cp** 2109 wægn (veniculum). **Ct** 28/5, 5 11 wena gang mid cyninges wenum.

wægnfearu Cp. **waegneþixl** Cp.

fægernes *sf* beauty. **VP** 95/6 fegernis (pulchritudo). 44/5; 77/61 §nisse (§inem; §ines).

fægen *aj* glad. **Ef** 273 faegen; Cp §(conpos). Cp 2157 ~ (voti compos, voto ornatus).

frægn *prt* asked. **Mt** 36 ~.

nægl *sm* nail. **Cp** 1497 naegl (paxillum, palum).

naeglsperu Cp.

scōh-nægl *sm* shoe-nail. **Cp** 484 ~negl (clavus caligaris).

mæg *vb* can. **DA** 12 maege. **VP** 9/20 meg (praevaleat); 77/19, 20 § (poterit); 138/6 § (§ero); Hy 13/24 § (§est). 70/8 §e (possim); Hy 13/19 §e (§it). 17/39 magun (potuerunt). 35/13 maegon (§). **Ct** 37/20, 3 maege. 41/8; 45/19, 37 męge. 42/10 megen. 48/21 we maege.

mægen *sn* power. **VP** 17/2; 21/16 megen (virtus); 32/16 micel § (§utem); 58/17 § ðin (§utem) *etc.* 59/14 megn. 17/33, 40; 20/2 *etc* megne. 67/12 megene. 32/17; 65/3; 67/34 *etc* megnes. 20/14 megen ðin (§utes); 102/21 alle § (§utes); 77/4 § (§utes) *etc.* Hy 13/16§ (vires). 43/10; 59/12 megnum. 23/10; 45/8, 12 *etc* §a. 64/7 mægne.

Mægenfrith LV. **Mægenric** LV. **megenðrym** VP. **Mægenuald**, mægin§ LV.

on-gægn *prp w. dat.* towards, against. **VP** 49/21; Hy 1/8 ongegn (contra; obviam). 58/6 § yrn (in occursum).

ongensettan.

dæg *sm* day **LP** 11 ðone deg. **Mt** 11, 39 ðone ~. **VP** 18/3; 36/13 *etc* deg (dies). 12/2 *etc* § (§em). 24/5; 31/3 *etc* alne § (tota §e). 36/6 on midne § (meridie). Hy 11/13 swe swe midne § (§es). 2/7; 94/8; Hy 3/22 to §e (hodie). 17/19 §e (die). 18/3 §e (§ei) *etc.* 31/4; 54/11 §es ⁊ naehtes (§e ac nocte). 55/4; 77/14; 135/8 §es (§ei). 89/9 §as (§es). 22/6; 114/2; 127/5; Hy 3/24 §um. 101/24 §a. 55/5 dęg. 54/24; 73/8; 77/33 *etc* daegas. 89/14 §um. Hy 3/1 §a. 7/12; 33/13; 41/11 *etc* dægas. 26/4; 36/19; 43/2, 2 *etc* §um. 38/5; 90/16; 101/25 §a. 38/6; 60/7; 72/10 *etc* dęgas. 93/13 §um. 20/5; 22/6; 92/5 §a. 89/15 dagum. 55/3 dig. 54/18 deg *from* dig (?). **Ct** 39/7; 42/7, 9, 12, 9, 21 dei. 41/58, 63 deg. 45/21, 33, 48 dęg. 48/4 daeg. 38/5; 41/38; 42/3; 45/9, 41 dege. 45/14, 39 dęge. 41/2 dæge. 37/13 daeges. 34/12 dagas.

Daegbald LV. **Daegberct** BH, LV; degberht, deibearht Ct. **Daegburg** LV. **Daegfrið** LV. **Daeghelm** LV; dæg§ Ct. **Daegmund** LV, Ct; dæg§ Ct; dei§ Ct. degred VP. **daeguuini** Cp. **Daeguini** LV.

Bel-daeg *sm* **Gn** 82 ~.

Beldaeging *sm* son of Beldæg **Gn** 82 ~.

dēaþ-dæg *sm* day of death **BDS** 5 deothdaege *d.*

fæsten-dæg *sm* fast-day **Ct** 37/19 festen~.

fugol-dæg *sm* fowl-day. **Ct** 37/19 fuguldaeg.

sunnan-dæg *sm* Sunday **Ct** 39/9 ~dege *d.*

Swǣf-dæg *sm* **Gn** 76 suebdaeg.

Swǣf-dæging *sm* son of S. **Gn** 75 suebdaeging.

symbel-dæg *sm* feast-day. **VP** 75/11 ~deg (diem festum).

Weg-dæg *sm* **Gn** 76, 115 uegdaeg.

Wegdæging *sm* son of Wegdæg **Gn** 76, 115 uegdaeging.

dæg-hwǣm-lice *av* daily. **CA** 10 ~. **VP** 41/4 deg~ (cotidie).

mid-dæg-lic *aj* midday. **VP** 90/6 middeglicum (meridiano).

hægtis *sf* witch, hag. **Ep** 913 haegtis; Cp, Ld § (striga); Ef hegtis. Cp 759 haegtis (erenis, furia). 772 haehtisse (eumenides); Ld 136 hegitissę. 945 haehtis (furia).

sægde *prt* said. **VP** 39/6; Hy 1/4 segde (adnuntiavi; §avit). 39/10; 55/9 § (nuntiavi). 39/11; 118/164 § (dixi). 43/2; 63/10 §un. 77/3; 118/85 §un (narraverunt). 96/6 §on. 101/22 sie segd.

forð-segde *prt* proclaimed. **VP** 118/13 ~(pronuntiavi).

on-segde *prt* sacrificed. **VH** 7/33 ~un (sacrificaverunt).

onsegdnis *sf* sacrifice. **VP** 4/6; 49/23; 50/19 *etc* ~(sacrificium). 19/4 ~se ðine (holocostum *a.*). 26/6 § (hostiam) *etc.* 39/7, 7 § ⁊ § (sacrificium et oblationem). 50/18 § (†holocaustis). 19/4 § ðinre (sacrificii). Hy 7/74 § (libationis). 39/7; 95/8 § (holocausta; hostias) *etc.* 65/13 §sum (holocaustis). Hy 7/73 §sa (sacrificiorum). 115/17 onsednisse (hostiam).

to-strægd *prt* scattered. **VH** 10/7 tostregd (dispersit). Ps 111/9 § [e *from* i].

æt *prp av* at. **Rn** 2/17 (æt). **BH** 242, 55 ad baruæ, *id est, ad nemus.* 318 ad tuifyrdi, *quod significat ad duplicem vadum.* **LK** 9 aet. **CA** 4, 13 ~. **VP** 29/6 ~ (ad). 138/8 ðu bist et (ades). Hy 7/39 ot nestan (in novissimo). Ct 3/9; 10/2; 14/4; 19/9; 20/4, 13, 9; 21/3, 4; 22/2, 2, 10; 23/11; 24/8; 25/4; 31/11; 34/3, 19; 35/5, 6, 8 *etc*; 36/3; 37/2. 16; 41, 3, 29, 42; 42/5; 46/3; 47/16; 52/14, 4; 53/6; 57/2, 3, 4 *etc*; 58/4, 5, 5 *etc* æt. 41/34 ðer-æt. 19/8; 37/23, 5, 9 *etc*; 48/17; 51/6; 52/14; 57/1 aet. 58/2, 4, 6 § (æt). 27/3; 45/12, 20 ęt. 23/2, 3; 26/2; 27/3, 7; 28/2, 2, 3 *etc*; 30/3, 20; 35/4; 38/2, 8, 9; 39/1, 1, 11, 2; 40/3, 17, 9; 41/59; 42/2; 43/1; 45/5 et.

ætstandan, ætgædre, ætwesan, ætfeolhan, aettaelg, otspurne, æt-gāeru otēcan, **ætfēlun, otēowan, ætclīþan, ætstōd.**

æt *prt* ate. **VP** 32/9; 40/10; 77/45; 101/10 *etc* et (†mandavit; edebat; comedit; manducabam). 77/25 ętt (manducavit).

Ætla *sm* **BH** 18 attila *dat.*—atila. 19 attilae *gen.*—at[t]ilę. 306 ætla. **LV** 229 etla.

læt *aj* slow.

dǣd-læt *aj* slow of deeds. **Pv** 1 daedlata *nom.*

lætlice *av* slowly, slothfully. **Bd²** 43 ~or (signius).

þæt *prn aj* that, the. **Cp** 1605 ymb ðæt (plus minus). **Rn** 2/13 ~. **CA** 5, 5 ðæt. **DA** 2 ðaet. **Mt** 16, 20 ðæt. **VP** 7/7; 17/45; 21/31, 2 ðæt (quod; quem; qui, §) *etc.* 79/13; 104/10 § (eam; illud) *etc.* 34/8 *etc* ðæt ilce (id ipsum). 97/8 þæt. 118/140 ðet. 9/29; 94/5; 121/3 det. **Ct** 34/12, 4, 20; 35/3, 5; 37/2; 41/59, 67; 42/13; 51/6 ðæt. 41/10, 24, 40 þæt. 37/15, 20, 7, 9; 47/12 ðaet. 40/8; 45/4, 16, 8 *etc* ðęt. 45/26, 33, 46 þęt. 28/19, 22; 38/2, 10, 3; 39/9; 40/21; 42/4; 43/2; 45/13 ðet. 37/21 ð(et). 45/38 þet. 45/5 þ'.

þæt *cj* that. **CA** 7, 11, 3, 6, ðæt. **DA** 9 þ'. **Mt** 15, 8, 34 *etc* ðæt. **VP** 8/3, 5 *etc* ðæt (ut, quod). 9/32 *etc* § he ne gese (ne videat). 67/31 dæt (ut). 60/9; 68/24 ðaet (ut; ne). 67/31 dæt (ut). 9/30; 34/24; 36/34 *etc* þæt (ut). 32/19; 33/17; 38/2 *etc* ðet (ut). 135/1 § (quoniam). 9/29 det (ut). **Ct** 37/6, 12; 41/5, 6, 8 *etc*; 42/13, 5, 8 ðæt. 40/9; 41/1, 9, 41 þæt. 37/29, 35, 41; 48/19 ðaet. 37/31 ðęt. 45/21, 46 þęt. 38/13; 39/7; 40/19; 42/1 ðet. 30/22; 45/13 þet. 45/18, 9, 44 þ'.

oþ-þæt *cj* until. **Cp** 711 oð ðaet (eatenus). **VP** 67/24; 71/7; 72/17; 109/1; Hy 5/28 oð ðæt (donec). Hy 5/29 § (usque). Hy 4/10 o[ð]ðæt. 56/2; 57/8; 93/13; 104/19; 111/8; 122/2; 131/5; 140/10; 141/8 oð ðet. 93/15 § (quoadusque). 70/18 otðet (donec).

oþ-þæt-þe *cj* until. **Ct** 20/16 oð ðæt ðe.

þætte *cj* that. **CA** 16 ðætte. **DA** 8 þe'. **VP** 4/4; 9/35, 9; 58/14 *etc* ðætte (quoniam; §, ut; quia). 36/8 þætte (ut). 106/1; 135/2, 3 dætte (quoniam). 117/4 daette (quoniam). 9/21; 117/4 ðette (§). 61/12; 135/1 dette (quia; quoniam). 70/3 ðætde [d *from* t] (ut). **Ct** 37/8 ðættæ. 34 ðette. 39 ðaette.

sæt *prt* sat. **VP** 25/4 set (sedi).

gesæt *prt* sat down. **VH** 7/21 geset (consedit).

on-sæt *prt* assailed, besieged. **VP** 21/17 oset (obsedit).

wæter *sn* water. **DA** 13 ðis ~. **VP** 17/12; 22/2; 57/8 *etc* weter (aqua; §am; §a). 64/10; 77/40 wetre. 80/8; 105/32 to § (ad §as). 68/16; 113/8 wetres. 28/3, 3; 45/4 *etc* (§as *etc*). 76/20 wetrum. 106/23 †wrum. 17/16, 7; 31/6 *etc* wetra.

waetercrūce Cp. **waeterhālgung** DA. **uua[e]terthrūch** Ep; **uaeter§** Ef; uuęter§ Cp; waeterðrum Cp.

gewæterian *wv* water. **VP** 77/15 gewetrade (adaquavit).

wæterig *aj* watery. **VP** 62/3 in wet[r]igre stowe (in inaquoso).

Uaetlinga-cæstir, uetlingua§ **BH.**

hwæt *prn* what. **BDS** 4 huaet. **VP** 3/2; 8/5; 38/5 *etc* hwet (quid). 23/10; 38/8; 88/48 § (quis *etc*). 113(2)/3; 134/6 swe § (quaecumque *pl*). 10/4 hwęt (quid). **Ct** 39/2 hwet.

elles-hwæt *prn* anything else. **Ct** 41/37, 9 ælles~, elles~.

hwæt *aj* brisk, bold. Ep 604 huet (licidus); Cp huæt (§); Ef huaet (lucidus).

Huaetberct BH, LV. Huaetgils LV. Huetlāc Ct. Hwætrēd Rn; huæt§ LV. Huaetmōd LV.

Eofor-hwæt *sm* LV 218 ~huaet.

fæt *sn* vessel. DA 16 feta *pl.* VP 2/9 fęt (vas). 30/13 fet (§). 7/14 featu (vasa). 70/22 §um (§is).

leoht-fæt *sn* lantern. Cp 1194 lehtfaet (lanterna). VP 17/29; 131/17 lehtfet (lucernam). 118/105 § (§a). 135/7 §featu (luminaria).

wīn-fæt *sn* wine-vessel. Cp 191 ~faet (appotheca).

sīþ-fæt *sm* journey. Mt 51 on siðfæte. Bd² 79 siðfaet (iter). VP 49/23; 67/5, 20 siðfet (iter). 139/6 §e. Hy 6/13 §as. 143/13; Hy 6/21 §um.

fraet-gengian Cp.

cræt *sn* carriage, chariot. Cp 366 craet (carcura). VP 19/8 creatum (curribus).

be-gæt *prt* obtained. Ep 706 bigaet (obtenuit); Ef, Cp §. VP 77/54; 118/111 beget, biget (adquisivit; §i). Ct 41/4; 42/2 begæt.

on-gæt *prt.* understood. VP 48/13, 21; 118/95, 9, 100, 4 onget (intellexi *etc*).

gæt *sn* gate. VP 117/20 ðis get (porta). 68/13; 126/5; Hy 3/1 ~e (portā; §; †§as). 23/7, 7, 9, 9; 86/2; 99/4; 106/16, 8; 117/19 geatu. 9/15, 5; 72/28 §um. 147/13 §a. Ct 3/3 ..nes geat. 5 ..rames dene §e.

Baggan-gæt *sn* Ct 3/6 to ~gete.

Hādfeld-gæt *sn* Ct 3/5 to (h)adfeldgeate.

Holhrycg-gæt *sn* Ct 3/5 to holhrygcgete.

Horsel-gæt *sn* Ct 3/5 ~get.

lud-gæt *sn* side-gate. Ep 741 þorh ~gaet (seudoterum); Ef §; Cp ~.

Uuēowera-get *sn* Ct 26/3 ~.

hætt *sm* hat. Cp 1318 haet (mitra). Ld 75 haetas (§as). Ld 23 haet (labrum, ambonem).

scætt *sm* payment, tribute. Ep 157 scaet (bona); Ef, Cp §.

fere-scætt *sm* passage-money, fare. Cp 1365 ~scaet (nabulum).

wæstm-scætt *sm* usury. VP 14/5 to westemscette (usuram). 54/12 §sceat (§a). 71/14 §sceattum.

gnætt *s(m)* gnat. VP 104/31 gneat (scnifes).

frætwian *wv* adorn. Rd 10 fraetuath *pl.*

ymbe-gefrætwian *wv* adorn around. VP 143/12 ymbgefretwade (circumornatae).

hræd *aj* quick. Ep 742 [h]raed (percitus); Ef hrad; Cp hraed. Cp 1574 hraed (perpes). VP 13/3 hreðe (veloces).

frǣ-hræd *aj* very quick. Ep 733 fraehraedae (propropera); Ef §; Cp fraehraeðe.

hrædlice *av* quickly. VP 6/11; 36/2; 68/18 *etc* hreðlice (velociter).

hrædnes *sf* quickness. Cp 579 raednisse (concussionibus). Bd² 75 rædnis (pernicitas).

gewæd *sn* ford, shallow. Cp 2086 geuueada (vada brevia).

Uin-uaed *s* BH 197 *prope fluvium* ~ — uinued *other three.*

fæder *sm* father. Cp 241 aeldra faeder (avus). DA 2 ~*g.* VP 26/10; 88/27; 102/13; Hy 3/22; 7/10; 11/15, 5; 12/15; 13/30 feder (pater). Hy 8/21; 11/5, 5; 12/14 § (patrem). Hy 7/12 §ðinne (§). Hy 11/14; 13/2, 29 § (patre). Hy 9/8; 11/5. to §. 44/11; Hy 1/2, 2, 6; 5/4; 12/14 feadur (patris). 21/5; 38/13; 43/2; 67/6; 77/3; 77/8, 57; 94/9; 105/7 fedras. Hy 7/34 feddras. 77/12; Hy 10/10 feadrum. 44/17 feodrum. 77/5; 105/6; Hy 9/6 fedrum. 48/20 feddra. 108/14 fedra.

fōstor-faeder *sm* foster-father. Cp 140 ~(altor).

stēop-fæder *sm* stepfather. Ep 1070 steupfaedaer (vitricius); Ef †staupfotar; Cp steopfaeder; Ld †steuffeder. Cp 300 ~faeder (bitricius).

wuldor-fæder *sm* glorious father. CH 3 uuldurfadur *gen.*

fæderlēas *aj* fatherless. VP 9/35; 108/12 feadurleasum (pupillo,

§is). 81/3; 145/9 §ne (§um) 93/6 §e (§os).

fæderlic *aj* paternal. **VH** 11/1 federlices (paternae).

fædera *sm* paternal uncle. **Cp** 1494 faedra (patruus). 1495 faedran sunu (patruelis).

fędren-mēga Ct.

reht-fæderen *sn* direct paternal line. **Ct** 45/17 an hire rehtfęderen.

Caed-baed, §ing Gn. **Kadmon** Rn; Caedmon BH, CH; cęd§ BH. **Caed-ualla**, cæd§, cęd§, cead§, cæad§, caead§, †sed§ BH.

gædeling *sm* companion, relative. **Cp** 914 geaduling (fratuelis). 1496 § (patruelis).

æt-gædre *av* together. **Rn** 2/8 ætgad(r)e.

gegædrian *wv* gather. **Cp** 512 gegaedradon (conpactis). **VH** 13/7 gegadrades (conjungeris).

gegæderung *sf* gathering. **Cp** 549 gegederung (conpagem).

glædene *sf* gladden, iris. **Ep** 920 gladinae (scilla); Ef gledinae; Cp glaedine.

for-træd *prt* trod down. **VP** 55/2 ~tred (conculcavit).

bæd *prt* prayed, asked. **VP** 20/5; 26/4 bed (petit; §ii).

gebæd *prt* prayed. **Mt** 46 ~. **VP** 105/30; 108/4 gebed (exoravit; orabam).

Blædla *sm* **BH** 18 blaedla *d* — bledla I. 18 blaedla — bledla. **LV** 186; 203 blaedla.

Gīu-haep *sm* **LV** 273 ~.

læpe-wince Ep; laepae§ Ef; lepe§ Cp; laepi§ Ld.

gescæpen *ptc* created. **VP** 148/5 gescepen werun (creata sunt).

æppel *s(m)* apple.

eappultūn VP.

codd-æppel *s(m)* quince. **Cp** 477 †goodaeppel (citonium).

hunig-æppel *s(m)* honey apple. **Ep** 830 hunaegaepl; Ef †cænegaepl (pastellus); Cp hunigaeppel.

gehæpplic *aj* convenient. **Ep** 205 gihaeplice (conpar); Ef §ae; Cp gehaeplice. Cp 1462 § (ordinatus).

gehæpplicnes *sf* convenience. **Bl** 6 geheplicnissum (oportunitatibus).

læppa *sm* lap, end. **Ef** 1184 lappa (lanna, angulus auris). **VP** 132/2 in leappan hregles (in ora vestimenti).

lifer-læppa *sm* fibre. **Ep** 405 librlaeppan (fibrae); Ef, Cp §.

sæppe *sf* white poplar. **Ep** 37 saeppae (abies); Ef sępae.

Swæppa *sm* **SG** 15 ~.

Swæpping *sm* son of S. **SG** 15 ~.

hnæppian *wv* doze. **VP** 3/6; 56/5 hneappade (dormivi). 120/3 §að (obdormiet). 43/23 †heppas [h *from some other letter*] (obdormis). 4/9 †neapiu (§iam). 40/9 hneapað (dormit). 120/4 § (dormitabit). 75/6 hneapedun (dormierunt). 7 §on (dormitaverunt). 118/28 hneapade (§avit).

hnæppung *sf* dozing. **VP** 131/4 hneappunge (dormitationem).

Æbbe *sf* **BH** 293 ~æ *g*. 312 *matri vocabulo* aebbę. **LV** 23 aebbę.

Aebbino *sf* **LV** 29 ~.

hæbbe *prs* have. I) *indic.* **Ct** 40/21 ic hebbe. 41/3 ic ~. II) *subj.* **CA** 13 haebbe. **Ct** 34/11; 41/9 ~. 45/16, 26 hębbe. 37/29 §en. 38/13; 39/9; 40/9, 19; 41/28 hebbe. 45/46 habbe. 42/19 §en. 48/19 aebbe.

næbbe *prs sbj* Ct 34/13 ~. 45/16 nębbe.

be-spearrian *wv* bar. **Cp** 1451 bisparrade (oppilatae).

wearr *sm* callosity, corn. **Cp** 400 weorras *vel* ill (callos); Ld uarras. Ld 93 § (callos, tensam cutem). Cp 426 waar (callus).

cearricge *sf* **Ep** 968 cearruccae (senon); Ef ~ae; Cp cearricgge.

fearr *sm* bull. **Cp** 1985 fear (taurus). **VP** 21/13 fearras (§i). 49/13 ferra (§orum). 67/31; Hy 7/27 fearra (§§).

pearroc *sm* enclosure. '24 ~(clatrum); Ef §; Cp pearuc.

bearrige *sf* Cp 282 barrigae (baruina) 330 barice (braugina).

Cearl *sm* **LV** 13 karlus.

earð *s(f)* plough-land, crop. **Ct** 45/9 mid ~e.

wearþ *prt* became. **Ep** 737 mere uueard (percrebuit); Ef uuard; Cp wearð. Ef 333 †ungiseem uard (disparuit); Cp wea'. **Rn** 3/6 warþ.

for-wearð *prt* perished. **VP** 9/7; 118/176; 141/5 ~(periit *etc*).

felo-fearth *s* fieldfare (a bird). **Ep** 1027 ~(torax); Ef felufrech; Cp feoluferð. **Lr** 66 § (toracem).

mearþ *s* marten. **Ep** 425 mearth (furuncus); Ef meard; Cp mearð. Ef 1159 merth (cata, bestiolae genus). Ld 224 maerth (furunculas).

Sigel-hearwan *pl* Ethiopians. **VP** 67/32; 71/9 ~(aethiopia; aethiopes). 73/14; 86/4; Hy 6/15 §ena (§um).

searu *sn* artifice, stratagem. **Ef** 278 searuum *vel* ordoncum (commentis); Cp seorwum. Cp 88 sarwo (adventio). **Bd**[2] 73 searwe (mahinam). **VP** 9/29 searwum (insidiis).

here-searu *sn* war-stratagem. **Ef** 1100 haersearum (yripeon); Cp heresearum.

spearwa *sm* sparrow. **Ep** 435 spearuua (fenus); Ef spearua; Cp spe[a]rua. **VP** 10/2; 101/8; 123/7 ~(passer). 83/4 †speara (§). 103/17 ~an (§es).

spaerhabuc Cp.

spearwa *sm* calf of leg. **Ep** 897 sparuua (surum); Ef sparua; Cp spearua.

nearunis *sf* narrowness. **VP** 24/22 nearenissum (angustiis). 118/143 ~(§ia).

gearu *aj* ready. **Cp** 796 gearuum (expeditis). **VP** 16/12; 37/18; 56/8, 8; 92/2; 107/2, 2; 118/60 ~(parat-). Hy 7/69 ðas sind ~(§a). 111/7 ~[u *from* a] (§um).

Iaruman, iuru§ **BH**; gearomon Gn. **Geororéd** LV.

ful-geare *av* fully. **Ct** 41/65 ~gere.

gearwian *wv* prepare. **VP** 88/5 ~ (praeparabo). 20/13 ~as (§abis). 7/13, 4; 23/2; 146/8 ~að (paravit, §; prae§; parat). 9/8; 102/19; 131/17 ~ade (paravit; §; §avi). 22/5; 29/8; 64/10; 67/11; 98/4 ~ades (§asti; praestitisti; parasti; §; §). 10/3; 56/7 ~adon (§averunt). 77/19, 20; Hy 9/13 ~(§are). 18/8; 64/7 ~iende (praestans; praeparans). 28/9 ~iendes (§antis). 88/3 bið ~ad (§abitur).

gegearwian *wv* **VH** 5/31, 2 ~ades, ~adun (praeparasti, §averunt). Hy 4/8 earun ~ad (§antur). Hy 5/31 ~adum (§ato). 32/14 ðæm ~edan (§§). **Ct** 37/30 gegeorwien *sbj pl.*

gegearwung *sf* preparation. **VP** 64/10; 88/15 ~(praeparatio).

gearwe *sf* yarrow. **Ep** 623 geruuae (mirifillon, millefolium); Ef gerue; Cp ~. 639 gearuuae (millefolium). Cp 1288 ~an leaf *etc* (malva).

bearu *s(m)* grove. **BH** 242 ad baruæ, *id est, ad nemus* — barue — bearuae — baruae. 255 ad baruæ—barue 1. **Ct** 53/6 æt Bearwe.

earfoþ *s(n)* hardship, trouble. **Cp** 1397 naenge earbeðe (nullo negotio).

earfoþlic *aj* troublesome. **Ep** 619 earbetlicust (molestissimum); Ef †easbedlicust; Cp earbetlicust.

earfoþlice *av* with difficulty. **Ef** 363 erabedlicae (egre); Cp earfedlice.

earfeðniss *sf* trouble. **Bd**[2] 88 ~e (calamitates).

be-þearf *vb* need. **VP** 15/2 biðearft (indiges).

þearf *sf* need. **BDS** 2 tharf. **CA** 6 for ðearf(e). **Ct** 41/12 ðearfa *pl.* 42/8 ðearf.

sāwol-þearf *sf* soul-need. **Ct** 40/2 ymb mine saulðearfe.

ðearfa *sm* poor man, pauper. **VP** 9/23, 35 *etc* ~(pauper). 33/7 ðes ~ (§). 9/30, 0, 0 *etc* ðearfan (§em). 9/31 *etc* § (§i). 108/31 § (§is). 21/27 *etc* § (§es). 111/9 §um (§eribus). 9/10, 3 *etc* §ena (§um). 71/13 dearfan (§i). 106/41 ðeorfan (§em). 108/22 †ðearf (pauper).

ðearfednis *sf* poverty. **VP** 30/1 ~nisse (paupertate).

nēd-þearfnis *sf* need. **VP** 24/17; 30/8; 106/6, 13, 9, 28, 30 ~nissum (necessitatibus).

ā-cearf *prt* cut off. **VP** 76/9; Hy 1/10; 3/7 ~(abscidet; amputavi; succidit).

earn *sm* eagle. **VP** 102/5; Hy 7/20 ~(†aquilae; §a). Ct 29/6, 6 ~es beame.

earngēat Ep; §, §geot Cp; aerngeup Ef; arngeus Ld. **Earnuulf** LV.

ge-earnian *wv* earn, deserve. **Cp** 45/39 ~. 48/4 geeornigan.

geearnung *sf* merit. **LP** 2 ~ingum. **VH** 13/28 geeorningum (meritis).

scearn *s* dung. **VP** 82/11 ~(stercus). 112/7; Hy 4/15 ~e (§ore).

stearn *s* stern (bird). **Ep** 125 ~o (beacita); Ef stęrn; Cp ~. Ef 1116 stern (gavia, avis). Cp 869 ~(fida).

wearn-wīslice Cp; uernuislicæ Ef.

wearn-mēlum Cp.

fearn *s*(*n*) fern. **Ep** 420 ~(filix); Ef †feran; Cp ~.

Fearnbeorginga Ct. **Fearnlēge** Ct.

Farn *s* Farne. **BH** 168 *in insula* farne. 316 ~e *nom.* 321 *insulā* ~e — ~ę. 322 *insulam* ~e.

Lindis-farn *s* Lindisfarne. BH 7 ~ensis. 186 ~faronensem — ~farnensem 1 — ~faronensem.

gearn-uuinde Cp; †giindi Ef.

bearn *sn* child. **CH** 5 barnum. **VP** (*only in pl*) 4/3; 10/5; 11/9 *etc* ~(filii *etc*). 105/37 ~ ⁊ ~(§ios et §ias). 108/13 ~(nati). 11/2 *etc* ~um. 105/38 ~a ⁊ dohtra (filiorum et filiarum). 61/10 be[a]rn. 71/4 bern. 88/20 §um. 89/16 beorn. 102/17 §a. **Ct** 34/11, 3; 41/8; 45/15, 6, 6 ~. 42/6 ~ *pl.* 45/8 ~e. 41/4 ~es. 37/5; 42/4 ~a. 38/10 barna. 13 beorn. 45/4 b'.

fōstor-bearn *sn* foster-child. **Ep** 108 fostur~(alumne); Ef †foetribarn; Cp ~.

frum-bearn *sn* first child. **VP** 77/51; 104/35; 134/8 ~(primogenitum; §; §a). 135/10 ~um (primitivis).

earm *sm* arm. **VP** 9/36; 88/22 *etc* ~(bracchium). 70/18; 88/14 ~ðinne. 36/17 ~(§ia). 76/16 ~e ðinum *etc.* 78/11 *etc* ~es. 17/35 ~as.

ermboeg [*under* ēa] Ld.

earm *aj* wretched, poor. **Bd**[2] 13 ~an (miserum). 25 § (paupercula *pl*). 46 ~um (miserandis). **VP** 136/8 ~(misera).

hearm *sm* harm. **VP** 118/134 ~um (calumniis).

hearmcweoðendra VP; hæarmcweodelien VP.

hearma *sm* ermine. **Ep** 666 ~(megale); Ef, Cp §. 675 ~(netila); Ef, Cp §; Ld herma.

þearm *sm* gut. **Ep** 503 thearm (intestinum); Ef §; Cp ~. Cp 870 ~(fibra). 2140 tharme (viscera). Ld 27 darmana (fibrarum).

ðearmgewind Lr.

bæc-þearm *sm* entrails. **Ef** 385 bęcdermi (exta); Cp baec ~(§, praecordia).

smæl-þearm *sm* small entrails. **Lr** 67 ~ðearmas (fibras).

snǣdel-þearm *sm* entrails. **Ef** 381 snaedil *vel* thearm (extale); Cp snaedil~; Ld snedildaerm. **Lr** 63 snędelðearm (fithrem).

þwearm *s* borer. **Ep** 891 byris, thuearm (scalprum); Ef duæram; Cp þuarm.

swearm *sm* swarm. **Cp** 811 sue[a]rm (examen).

earc *sf* ark. **VP** 131/8 erc (arca).

gesnearc *prt* dwindled. **VP** 30/13 gesnerc (excidi tamquam mortuus).

spearca *sm* spark. **Cp** 1827 spærca (scintella).

mearc *sf* mark, boundary. **Ct** 29/3, 10, 1, 2 ~. 5, 6, 9 ~e *d.* 10, 3, 4 ~ę *d.*

Mearcflēot Ct. †**mearīsern** Ep; Ef †merisaen; Cp merciseren.

frist-mearc *sf* respite, interval. **Ep** 547 ~(intercapido); Ef †fritmaerc; Cp first§.

west-mearc *sf* west boundary. **Ct** 29/12 sio ~.

gemearcian *wv* mark. **Cp** 1121 smat, gemaercode (inpingit).

bearce *sf* barking. **Cp** 1191 baercae (latratus).

earh *s* arrow.

aerigfaerae Rd.

fearh *sm* hog. **Ep** 811 faerh (porcellus); Ef, Cp §.

mearh *sm* horse. **Cp** 153 ~(amilarius).

hearg *sm* temple, altar, idol. **Cp** 1255 haerg (lupercal). 1772 §a (sacellorum). **VP** 96/7; Hy 1/9 hergum (simulacris). 113/4 (2) §as (§a). **Ct** 11/2 gumeninga hergae *dat.* 58/7, 9, 11 æt Hearge.

uue[a]rgrōd Ep; uaerg§ Ef; waerg§ Cp.

mearg *s*(*n*) marrow. **Ep** 588 maerh (lucanica); Ef, Cp mærh. Cp 1308 merg (medulla).

mearglic *aj* marrowy. **VP** 65/15 merglice (medullata).

bearg *sm* hog. **Ep** 652 bearug (majalis); Cp §; Ld bęrg.

eart *vb* art. **VP** 2/7; 3/4 *etc* earð (es). 117/28 eard. 22/4 erð. 51/3 e[a]rð. 88/44 ne ard [a *preceded by unfinished* a]. 41/6, 12; 42/5 *etc* earðu. Hy 7/10 ðu ear (†tuus).

sweart *aj* black. **Cp** 1956 suefl sueart (sulforia).

wearte *sf* wart. **Ep** 154 uue[a]rtae (berruca); Ef uaertae; Cp uearte; Ld uaert[a]ę. 771 uueartae (papula); Ef uearte; Cp wearte. 1049 uueartae (verruca); Ef uuertae; Cp ~.

celi-wearte *sf* (chill-wart) gooseskin. **Cp** 1456 ~(horripilatio).

eard *s*(*m*) native-land.

Eardgȳð LV. **Eardhelm** LV. **Eardrēd** Gn. **Arduini** LV. **Earduulf** LV, Gn, Ct.

eardian *wv* dwell. **VP** 138/9 ~iu (habitavero). 21/4; 73/2 *etc* ~as. 2/4; 5/6 *etc* ~að. 23/1; 48/2 ~iað *etc.* 108/7 ~ie. 77/55, 60; 93/17 *etc* ~ade. 67/7, 17 ~ian (inhabitare, habitare) *etc.* 16/12 ~iende (§ans). 82/8; 119/5 ~iendum.

in-eardian *wv* inhabit, dwell. **VP** 60/5 ~iu (habitabo). 5/12 ~as (inhabitabis). 28/10 *etc* ~að (§at). 36/29 ~iað *etc.* 67/11 *etc* ~iad. 22/6; 36/34 *etc* ~ie. 36/3, 27 ~a! 67/19 ~ian. 74/4; Hy 5/24, 6 ~iende (§antes). 106/34 ~iendra.

ymb-eardian *wv* dwell around. **VP** 30/14 ~iendra (circumhabitantium).

eardiend *sm* dweller. **VH** 3/4 ~(habitatorem).

eardung *sf* dwelling. **VP** 68/26; 75/3 *etc* ~(habitatio). 131/14 ~(†habitabo). 131/13 in ~unge (habitationem). 106/4, 36 ~unge (§ionis). 108/10 ~ingum. 106/7 eordunge (§ionis).

eardunghūse VP.

heard *aj* hard. **Mt** 18 ~e *pl.* **VP** 16/4 ða ~an (duras). 59/5 ðe [= ða] ~an (~a *pl*). **Ct** 25/5 ~e méd.

Heardberht LV, Ct. **heardhara** Ef, Cp; haerdhera Ld. **heardhēau** Cp; Ef §; Ld haerd§. **Heardlāc** LV. **Heardrēd** LV, Gn, Ct. **Hearduini** LV. **Hearduulf** LV.

Æþel-heard *sm* **LV** 85, 99; 428, 70 eðil~. **Gn** 4 aeðel ~us. 21 aeðel~. **Ct** 12/3 æthelheardu[s]. 15/4; 16/4; 22/8; 23/9 æðel~i. 35/9, 9 aeðel~. 33/1, 2; 46/1, 2, 2, 3 aeðel~us. 46/1 §o. 49/2; 52/7 §i. 49/6 aeðil ~us. 19/3; 59/5 aeðelhard. 24/5 aeðel§. 47/6 aeþel§.

Beadu-heard *sm* **LV** 82 beadheard. 285 bad§. 371, 90 badhard. **Ct** 35/13 bada~. 55/10; 56/8 bead~.

Beald-heard *sm* **LV** 265 balð~. **Ct** 6/3 balthhaeardi. 7/5 balthhardi.

Beorn-heard *sm* **LV** 90; 194; 220 ~. 464 bearnhard. **Ct** 4/6 bernhardi. 5/6 §haerdi. 49/11 †beorheard. 50/3 biorn ~es.

Bill-heard *sm* **Ct** 35/14~.

Brūn-heard *sm* **Ct** 23/4; 24/10; 25/13; 35/15 ~. 21/5; 22/4; 36/8; 58/20 ~hard.

Burg-heard *sm* **LV** 460~.

Cēol-heard *sm* **CA** 1~.

Cœ̄n-heard *sm* **Ct** 58/22 coenhard.

Cūþ-heard *sm* **LV** 228 cutheard. 410, 34 cuð~.

Cyne-heard *sm* **LV** 65; 381; 400 cyni~. 131 cynheard. **Gn** 21 cynheard. **Ct** 27/6 ~. 36/5; 58/21 ~hard. 36/6 §i.

Ealg-heard *sm* **Ct** 18/5 ~.

Ealh-heard *sm* **Gn** 30 alc~. **Ct** 15/6; 16/5 alhheardi. 12/4;

33/14; 34/6; 56/5 alh~. 46/4 alcheardus. 57/10 alch~. 31/4, 10; 36/9 ~. 19/4; 29/19 alhhard. 58/17 alchhard (alhhard). 49/9 alh[e]ardi.

Ecg-heard *sm* **LV** 71, 2 ~. **Ct** 20/23; 48/16 ~. 47/9 ~hard.

Gīsl-heard *sm* **Rn** 14 *gislheard*. **Ct** 32/9 gils~.

Gūþ-heard *sm* **Ct** 4/5 gudhardi.

Lēod-heard *sm* **BH** 30 liudhardo [*Frankish name*].

Nōþ-heard *sm* **Ct** 30/16; 31/6 noð~. 33/14 not~.

Pīl-heard *sm* **Ct** 12/1 ~us.

Pleg-heard *sm* **LV** 309, 72 ~. 457 ~hard.

Sige-heard *sm* **BH** 268 sighardo — § 1. **LV** 229 sighard. 282 sigheard. **SG** 18 si(gehard). **Ct** 1/8 sigi~i.

Sige-hearding *sm* son of Sigeheard. **SG** 18 ~harding.

Sigheardingmēduue Ct.

Snā-hard *sm* **LV** 346 ~.

Swǣf-heard *sm* **BH** 346 suæbhardo — suębheardo 1.

Uu-heard [=uīg§?] *sm* **LV** 460 ~.

Wǣr-heard *sm* **Ct** 21/5; 22/4; 36/7 uuerhard. 41/49; 58/21 ~hard. 23/4 uuær~. 25/12 uuaer~. 24/9 wereard.

Wealh-heard *sm* **LV** 304 ualchard.

Wīg-heard *sm* **BH** 127 uighar — uighard — uuig~. 220 uighardum — uigardum — uuigheardum. 221 uighard — uig[h]ar — §heard. 222 uighardo — § 1. 227 uighard — uuigheard 1. 237 uighard — uigheard 1. **LV** 171; 397 uig~. **Ct** 33/18, 9 ~hard, ~. 49/11 uuig~. 53/7 §i.

Wulf-heard *sm* **LV** 9; 66, 75; 122, 6, 9, 45, 54, 81, 93; 236, 45, 8, 8; 301, 75, 81, 94; 410, 3, 21, 31, 49, 53, 70 uulf~. 274; 329; 454, 69 uulfhard. 444, 4 uulfheord. **Gn** 50 uulf~. **Ct** 22/8 ~hardi. 23/7 uulfhardi. 49/2; 52/7 §o. 32/5; 33/2, 16; 35/15 uulf~. 46/6 §us 49/9 §i. 33/10; 34/6; 55/9 ~. 32/6 uulfeard.

Wynn-heardinglond Ct.

heardnis *sf* hardness. **Ep** 871 heardnissae (rigore); **Ef** §; **Cp** heardnisse.

heardian *wv* harden. **VH** 5/13, 3 ~adun, ~adon (gelaverunt).

ā-heardian *wv* harden. **VP** 94/8 ~ (obdurare).

for-heardian *wv* harden. **VP** 89/6 ~að (induret).

sweard *s* skin. **Cp** 406 swearth (cater). 2146 suge ~(vistula).

weard *sm* guardian. **Ep** 950 uúeard (sandix); **Ef** uue[a]rd; **Cp** uueard. **CH** 1, 7 uard.

weardseld Cp. **weardsetle** Ct.

Cēol-weard *sm* **Ct** 49/10 ~uuard; 50/5 ~ward.

edisc-weard *sm* gardener. **Ep** 148 ~ueard (broelarius); **Cp** §; **Ef** ~uard.

erfe-weard *sm* heir. **Ct** 41/36 ærfe~. 42/4, 19 ærfewearda, §as. 45/46 ęrfe~. 35, 45 §a, §um. 41/45 erfewearda.

regol-weard *sm* regulator. **Ct** 37/26 reogolwarde. 33 §weord.

Sǣ-weard *sm* **SG** 14 sa ~.

Sǣ-wearding *sm* son of Sæweard. **SG** 13 s(aweard)ing.

erfe-weardian *wv* inherit. **VP** 81/8 ~wordas (hereditabis).

erfe-weardnis *sf* heritage. **VP** 15/6 ~(hereditas). 2/8; 15/5; 24/13; 32/12 ~nisse. 27/9 erfweardnisse. 36/18; 126/3 ~wordnis. 15/5; 36/9, 29; 60/6 *etc* §nisse. 67/10 §§ ðinre. 93/5 erfwordnisse. 68/36 erfeworðnisse.

and-weard *aj* present. **Ct** 45/51 ondwardum.

ēaste-weard *aj* east. **Ct** 20/14 ~e.

forð-weard *aj* future. **Ct** 45/44 ~.

neoþo-weard *aj* lower. **Cp** 5 neoþoúard (crepidinem).

neoþan-weard *aj* lower. **Cp** 1041 nioðan~ hype (ilia).

norðe-weard *aj* north. **Ct** 43/5 ~um.

sūðe-weard *aj* south. Ct 43/5 ~um.

tō-weard *aj* future. VP 21/32; 70/18 toword (ventura). Hy 7/58 §re (futuro). Ct 37/4 towardon. 45/51 §an.

weste-weard *aj* west. Ct 20/15 ~e.

geard *sm* court, enclosure, dwelling.

Geardcylle Ct.

Æþel-geard *sm* Ct 6/4 aethil-iaerdi *g.* 34/4 æðelieard (§). 49/12 aeðil~.

Ēan-geard *sm* Ct 35/13.

Friþu-geard *sm* Ct 24/12 freo-ðo~. 36/9 frioðo~.

middan-geard *sm* world. CH 7 middun~. . LP 4 ~es. DA 7 ealne ~. VH 13/2 ~es (mundi).

sceadu-geard *sm* shade-dwelling. Ep 991 scaedugeardas (Tempe); Ef, Cp sceadu§.

wīn-geard *sm* vineyard. Cp 151 oemsetinne wiingeardes (amtes). VP 79/15 ~ ðeosne (vineam). Hy 7/62 ~e. 77/47 ~es (†vineas). 104/33; 106/37 ~as (§). Hy 6/36 ~um (§eis).

beard *sm* beard. VP 132/2, 2 ~(barbam).

Beardan-ēu BH.

hearpe *sf* harp. VP 56/9; 107/3 ~(psalterium). 80/3; Hy 1/3 ~an (§ *a*). 32/2; 48/5; 143/9; 149/3 § (§io). 91/4 tenstrengre § (§io).

hearpere *sm* harper. Ld 147 harperi (fidicen).

scearp *aj* sharp. VP 51/4; 56/5 ~(acuta). 44/6; 119/4 ~e (§ae *pl*).

scearplice *av* sharply. Bd² 47 ~(acerbatim).

scearpnis *sf* sharpness. Cp 50 scearpn' (acies, acumen ferri *etc*).

ā-wearp threw out. VH 5/2 ~(projecit). 6 awe[a]rp.

wearp *s* warp. Cp 1928 ~(stamen). 2141 ~(vimen). Rd 5 uarp.

sand-gewearp *s* sand-bank. Cp 1136 in sond~ (in sirtim).

eall *aj* all. Rn 2/13 al. Lr 72 alle (pantes). LP 6, 10, 2 §. 1, 11 alra. CA 15 allra. DA 6, 7 ~e. 6 ealne. Mt 19 all. 44 §e. VP 19/5 all (omne). 31/6 § (§is). 21/24 § (universum). 6/3 § (omnia). 8/8, 8 § (§, universa *pl*) *etc.* 38/6 al (§*sg*). 118/91 § (omnia). 18/5; 44/17 alle (§em). 2/10, 3 §e (§es). 25/6 §e unsceðende (innocentes). 9/18 §e ðeode *etc.* 35/5 §um (§i). 7/2 §um (§ibus) *etc.* 8/2, 10 alre (universā). 9/1 § (toto). 19/4 § (omnis). 47/3 § (universae *g*) *etc.* 17/31; 86/7 alra. Hy 13/27 § (cunctorum) *etc.* 24/5; 31/3; 34/28 *etc* alne. 85/12 allre. 9/26; Hy 1/4 allra. 43/9; 72/14 allne. 118/128 †alme (omnem). Ct 37/26; 42/21 all. 45/2, 10 §um. 48 §es. 48/17 §e. 34/11 alre. 24/8; 39/7, 14 ealra.

heall *sf* hall. VP 28/2; 95/9 halle ðere halgan (aulā).

steall *sm* stall. Cp 1905 stal (stabulum).

sealtern-steall *sm* saltern. Ct 30/8 *unamque salis coquinariam, hoc est* I ~.

wiðer-stal *sm* opposition. Cp 1412 ~(obvix).

weall *sm* wall. VP 17/30 wall (murum). 50/20; 54/11 §as (§i; §os). 61/4 §e onhaeldum (parieti). Hy 5/13 wall (muros = §us). Ct 20/6, 11 wælles. 18 on sueordleage §e.

wealweg Ct.

fore-weall *sm* rampart. Ep 873 foraeuuallum (rostris); Ef, Cp foreuuallum.

Secg-weall *sm* Ct 20/14 ~wælles.

stān-weall *sm* stone wall. VP 61/4 ~walle (macheriae). 79/13 ~wal (§am). 88/41 ~wallas (§as). 143/14 §es (§ae).

Wulf-weall *sm.* Ct 20/18 ~wælles.

weallan *sv* boil. VH 11/9 walle (ferveat).

Cæd-wealla *sm* BH 113 caedualla *rex brettonum* — §uualla I — §ualla. 116 § — cęduualla. 130 ceadualla — caeadualla — caeduualla. 282 caedualla — cæd§ — cead§. 283 caedualla *d* — †sedualla — cead§. 283 *post* caeduallan — cęduallam — §. 285 caedualla — §uualla I. 327 §ualla — †ceadulla I. 342 caedualla

— ceadulla I. 342 caedual [*fr.* *epitaph*] — cæd§ — cead§. 343 caedual [*fr. ep.*] — cęd§ — cead§. 344 caedualla — cead§ I. 379 caeduald — cęd̄ualla — cead§.

Dūn-wealla *sm* **Ct** 7/5 duunuuallan *g*

feallan *sv* fall. **Bd**[2] 68 fallendum (casualibus). **VP** 9/31 falleð (cadet). 17/39; 36/2; 81/7 *etc* §að.

in-feallan *sv* fall in. **DA** 16 in falleð.

gefeallan *sv* fall. **VP** 7/5 gefallu (decidam). 36/24; 89/6 §eð (ceciderit; decidat). **Hy** 5/27 §e. 5/11 §en.

in-gefeallan *sv* fall in. **VP** 34/8 ingefallen (incidant).

muus-falle *sf* mousetrap. **Cp** 1340 ~(muscipula).

bisuic-falle *sf* trap. **Cp** 637 ~(decipula).

Meallingas *spl.* **Ct** 21/3, 4 *agrum* æt mallingum. 22/2, 3; 23/2, 3 §.

gealla *sm* gall. **VP** 68/22 gallan (fel *a*). **Hy** 7/64 § (fellis).

gealluc *sm* comfrey. **Ep** 466 galluc (galla); Ef, Cp §.

Bralluc *sm* **LV** 222 ~.

hals-ledir Ld.

healsian *wv* conjure, entreat. **CA** 15 halsiað. **DA** 2 ic §ige. **VP** 36/7 halsa (obsecra!). **Hy** 13/29 §iað (quaesumus).

halsung *sf* conjuring. **DA** 1 halsuncge. **VP** 142/1 halsunge (obsecrationem).

malscrung *sf* charm. **Cp** 838 ~(fascinatio).

palster *s* spike. **Ep** 225 palester (cospis); Ef plaster; Cp palstr. **Cp** 622 § (cuspis).

ealu *s*(*n*) ale.

Aluberclt LV; ealuberht Gn. **Aluburg,** al§ LV; alo§ Ct. **Aluðegn** LV. **Aluych,** aluīch LV; alouuioh, alwih, alwing Gn. **Aluuini** LV. **Ealawynne** Ct.

ealoþ *s*(*n*) ale. **Ct** 37/21 aloð *g*. 41/60 alað *g*.

swealwe *sf* swallow. **Ep** 498 sualuuae (hirundo); Ef sualuae; Cp sualuue. 828 suualuae (progna); Ef suualuuæ; Cp su[u]aluue. **VH** 3/10 swalwan (hirundinis).

sǣ-swealwe *sf* sea-swallow. **Cp** 234 †haesualwe (astur).

stæþ-swealwe *sf* bank-swallow. **Cp** 1745 staeðsu[u]alwe (ripariolus).

Swealwe *sf* the river Swale. **BH** 99 *in fluvio* sualua — sualwa I — sualua. **Ct** 52/9 suuealuue *fluminis.* 54/3 sualuę.

fealu *aj* fallow. **Ep** 483 falu (gilvus); Ef, Cp §.

cealwa *sm* baldness. **Cp** 132 calwa (alapiciosa); **Ep** 116 b calua (alapiosa).

calwer *s* **Ep** 471 caluuaer (galmaria); Ef, Cp caluuer. 476 calu[u]aer (galbalacrum); Ef caluuer (galmaria); Cp calwer (gabalacrum).

caluuerclīm Cp.

liim-caluuer *s* **Cp** 954 ~(galmilla).

healf *aj* half. **SG** 2 ~. **Ct** 28/14; 43/2, 3, 6 ~. 43/3 ~ne. 41/11; 51/7 half. 43/4 §ne. 45/20 §e.

halbclungni Ep; Ef §; Cp half§.

healf *sf* side, quarter. **Ep** 51 an ba halbae (altrinsecus); Ef halbe; Cp halfe. **Cp** 489 half (clima). **Ct** 34/16 on oðre halfe.

east-healf *sf* east side. **Ct** 29/7 an ~halfe.

sealf *sf* salve. **Ep** 635 salb (malagma); Ef §; Cp salf.

gesealfian *wv* **Ef** 325 gisalbot (delibutus).

scealfor *s* diver (bird). **Ep** 647 scalfr (mergulus); Ef §; Cp scalfur. 662 scalfr (§).

hwealf *aj* convex. **Ep** 179 hualb (convexum); Ef †halb; Cp hualf.

cealf *sn* calf. **Cp** 2144 caelf (vitulus). **VP** 28/6; 68/32 § (§um). 105/19 cælf (§). 21/13 calfur monig (§i). 50/21; 105/20 § (§os; §i †*g*). 49/9 calferu (§os).

Cealflōcan Ct.

cū-cealf *sn* cow-calf. **Ef** 1155 cucaelf (vitula). **Cp** 2145 ~ (§).

hind-cealf *sn* fawn. **Cp** 1147 ~caelf (inulus).

dealf *prt* dug. **VP** 7/16 dalf (fodit).

for-dealf *prt* dug up (read). Ct 20/6 ~.

healm *s* halm, straw. VP 82/14; Hy 5/12 halm (stipulam).

sealm *sm* psalm. VP 17/50; 26/6 *etc* salm (psalmum). 97/5 §es. Hy 3/23 §as. 94/2 §um. 70/22 §a.

cwealm *s*(*m*) death, destruction.

cualmstōu Cp.

ūt-cwealm *s*(*m*) utter destruction. Cp 1146 utcualm (internicium bellum *etc*).

mǣg-cwealm *s*(*m*) murder of a relation. Cp 1521 megcualm (parricidio).

palm *s*(*m*) palm. VP 91/13 ~a (palma).

Westor-wealcna *sm* Gn 74 uestorualcna.

Westorwalcning *sm* son of W. Gn 74 ·storualcning.

cealc *sm* lime. Ep 165 calc (calculus); Ef, Cp §.

ealh *s*(*m*) temple.

Aluchburg LV; ealh§ Ct. **Alchflēd**, alh§ BH. **Ealhflēot**, alh§ Ct. **Alcfriþu** Rn; alchfrid, alc[h]§, alch§, alh§ BH; alchfrith LV; alchfriðo LN. **Alcheard** Gn, Ct; alchheard, alhheard, alheardi Ct. **Alhhelm** Ct. **Alhhere**, alchhere, alahhere, ealhhere Ct. **Ealhhūn**, ealhun, alchhun Ct. **Alchmund** LV, Gn; alh§ Gn, Ct; ealh§ SG, Ct; ealhcmunding SG. **Aluchsig**, alch§ LV. **Aluchstān** LV; alh§ Gn, Ct; ealh§ Ct. **Alchsuið** LV. **Alhðrȳð** CA, Ct. **Alchuald**, aluch§ LV. **Alchuini** LV.

Baldwines-healh *s*(*m*) Ct 3/8 *in quoddam petrosum clivum, et ex eo ~ appellatur.*

Cymedes-halh *s*(*m*) Ct 13/6 ~ *a*.

Iddes-healh *s*(*m*) Ct 47/10, 3 aet ~hale.

Puttan-healh *s*(*m*) Ct 3/7 *in* puttan·ealh.

Strēones-healh *s*(*m*) Whitby. BH 200 streanæs halch—§es halh 1—streonaes halch. 210 strenæs halc, *quod interpretatur sinus fari*—streanaes †alch—strenes halch—streunaes halch. 301 strenaes halc—streanaes halch—strenes halh. 305 streanes halch—streanaes §—§es halh—§aes halch. 378 *in* streanæs halæ—§aes hęlę—§es hale.

sealh *sm* willow. Ep 892 salch (salix); Ef, Cp salh. Ld 58 salhas (salices). VP 136/2 salum (§).

wealh *sm* foreigner, Briton. SG 11 Walum.

uualhhebuc Ep; §haebuc Ef; walchhabuc, walh§ Cp; ualchefuc Ld. **Ualchard** LV. **Wealhhere**, uu§, †uueah§, uualh§, walah§ Ct. **Uuealhhūnes** Ct. **uualhmorae** Ep; § Ef; walh§ Cp. **Ualchstod**, uualstod BH. **uualhuuyrt** Ep; Ef, Cp §; walhwyrt Cp; ualuyrt Lp.

Wealh *sm* LV 170 ualch. Ct 34/4 ~.

Æþel-wealh *sm* BH 275 aedilualch — §ualh 1. 278 †§uach—edilualch—aedilualh.

Bil-uualch *sm* LV 271 ~.

Cnof-wealh *sm* LV 335 cnobualch.

Cœ̄n-wealh *sm* BH 141/2 coinualch—§ualach—coenualh. LV 166 coenualch. Gn 7, 105 §walh. Ct 15/5; 16/5 §§.

Cœ̄n-wealing *sm* son of C. Gn 104 coenwaling.

Cund-walh *sm* Gn 104 ~.

Cund-waling *sm* son of C. Gn 104 ~.

Dūn-wealh *sm* Ct 7/5 dunualhi *g*.

Dūnwaling-lond Ct.

Eald-wealh *sm* LV 341 aldualch.

Œ̄se-wealas *pl* Ct 57/2, 4 oes[e]walum.

Plēo-ualch *sm* LV 165 ~.

Rīu-ualch *sm* LV 170 ~.

Suið-ualch *sm* LV 228; 340 ~.

æt-fealh *prt* adhered. VP 21/16; 43/25; 62/9; 100/3; 118/25, 31 ~falh (adhaesit *etc*).

Ealg-heard Ct.

for-swealg *prt* swallowed up. VP 105/17 ~swalg (deglutivit). Hy 5/20 § (devoravit).

fealg *sf* felloe (of wheel). Ep 713

~a(occas). Ef 292 felge (canti); Cp faelge.

gealga *sm* gallows. **Rn** 2/2 *galgu a.*

healt *aj* lame.

lemp-healt *aj* lame, limping. **Ep** 589 laempihalt (lurdus); Ef †lemphi§; Cp lemp§; Ld †lemphald.

healtian *wv* limp. **VP** 17/46 haltadon (claudicaverunt).

sealt *sn* salt. **Ct** 41/64 saltes.

sealtern Ct. **salthalguncge** DA. sealternsteall Ct.

sealt *aj* salt. **Bl** 14 s·ltne mersc (salsilaginem).

sealtnis *sf* saltness. **VP** 106/34 saltnisse (salsilaginem).

ā-sualt *prt* died. **Cp** 673 ~(diem obiit).

sinu-wealt *aj* round. **Cp** 2037 sionuualt (torosa).

mealt *s* malt. **Ep** 130 malt (bratium); Ef, Cp §. **Ct** 39/4 ~es. 40/4; 41/29 maltes.

eald *aj* old. **Cp** 173 ald·uuif (anus). 1854 § (senex). Ld 132 hu § (quotus). 133 suæ § (totus). **VP** 38/6; 76/6; 148/12 §e (veteres; antiquos; seniores). 78/8; 88/50; 138/5; Hy 4/6 ða §an (antiquas; §ae; §a *pl*; vetera). Hy 13/15 ðes §an (antiqui *g*). 43/2 alldum (§is). Hy 7/52 aldum (sene). 142/5 §ra (antiquorum). **Ct** 20/17 alda. 39/5 eald. 41/61 ald.

Aldbercht LV; §berht Gn; §berht, ealdberht, aldberhting-tūn Ct. **Aldburg** LV. **Aldceorl**, alt§ LV. **Aldfrid** BH, LK; altfrith LV; aldfrið Gn. **Aldgīsl** BH, LV. **Aldgȳth** LV. **Aldhāeth** LV. **Aldhelm** BH, LV, Gn. **Aldheri** LV; §here Gn; ealdhere Ct. **Aldhōdi** Ct. **Aldhūn** LV, Ct. **Aldmonn** LV. **Aldmund** LV. **Aldrēd** LV, Gn, Ct; aeld§, eald§ Ct. **Altsuīð** LV. **Altðegn** LV. **Aldðrȳth**, alt § LV. **Aldualch** LV. **Alduini** BH, LV; §uine Gn. **Ealduuft** Ct. **Alduulf** BH, LV, Gn, Ct; alduulfing Gn.

Ealda *sm* LV 95; 175; 257, 77; 337 alda.

ealdian *wv* grow old. **VP** 48/15 aldað (veterascit). 101/27 §iað (veterescent). 6/8 §ade (inveteravi). 36/25 §ade (senui). 17/46; 31/3 §adon (inveteraverunt).

ealdor *sm* prince. **Cp** 674 aldur (dictatorem). **VP** 23/7 aldres (principis). 70/18 aldra (senium).

aldormon CA; aldermon VP; aldormonn Ct.

ealdordōm *sm* authority. **Bd**[2] 63 alderdomes męhte (tribuniciae potestatis). **VP** 138/17 aldurdomes (principatus *n*).

ealdorlic *aj* princely. **VP** 50/14 alderlice (principali).

aldot *s* vessel. **Ep** 57 ~(alviolum); Ef §; Cp aldaht.

healdan *sv* hold. **VP** 17/24; 38/2; 88/29 *etc* haldu (observabo; custodiam; servabo). 129/3 §es (observaveris). 18/12; 33/21 *etc* §eð (custodiet; §it). 55/7; 88/32 *etc* §að (observabunt; custodierint). 58/10; 118/88 *etc* §e (§iam). 126/1 §e (§ierit). 104/45 §en (§iant). 24/20; 36/37 *etc* hald (§i!). 30/7; 114/6; 118/158 §ende (observantes; custodiens; servantes). 102/18 §endum (custodientibus). 118/63 §endra (§ientium). 118/4, 57, 106 §an (§iri, §ire, §ire). 118/5 to §enne (ad §iendas). 11/8 aldes (servabis). **Ct** 39/7, 8 ~e; to ~enne. 40/20 ~. 45/50 haldan.

gehealdan *sv* **VP** 11/8 gehaldes (custodies). 40/3; 120/7 §eð (conservet; custodiat). 15/1; 16/8; 36/34; 140/9 gehald (conserva!; custodi!); §; §). 36/28 bioð gehaldne (conservabuntur). **Ct** 40/22, 3 se ~en. 41/7, 10, 5 gehaldan. 45/11 §eð. 50 §e *sbj*.

behealdan *sv* behold; attend to. **VP** 57/8; 65/19; 80/12 bihaldeð (intendet *etc*). 16/1; 34/23 *etc* bihald (intende!). Hy 7/1 § (ad§!). 77/1 §að (§§ite!). 77/9; 129/2 §ende (intendentes). 5/3; 44/5 behald (§e!). 76/2 §eð (§it).

healdung *sf* keeping. **VP** 118/9 in haldinge (in custodiendo).

heald *aj* sloping. **Ep** 754 halði (penduloso); Ef †hahdi; Cp haldi. 865 suae haldae; Ef suuaeldae; Cp suae halde (reclines). Cp 455 hald (cernua). **Ct** 20/12 ðone ~an weg.

ni-hold *aj* sloping. **Ep** 799 nihol (pronus); Ef §; Cp ~. Cp 1061 niol (infima).

scyte-heald *aj* oblique. **Ep** 694 scytihalt; Ef sestihalth; Cp scytehald (obliquum).

tō-heald *aj* inclined. **Ep** 96 tohald (adclinis); Ef, Cp §.

sealde *prt* gave. **Ep** 528 saldae (inpendebat); Ef †saltae; Cp salde. **VP** 14/5; 77/48; 115/12 *etc* salde (dedit; tradidit; retribuit). 4/7; 20/3, 5 *etc* §es (dedisti; tribuisti, §). 68/22; 76/18 §un (dederunt). 62/11; 71/15 *etc* sien sald; bið § (tradentur; dabitur). **Ct** 38/3; 48/6 salde. 28/19, 21; 44/6 ~. 37/8 saldon. 40/21, 3 seald *ptc.*

gesalde *prt* gave. **Ct** 47/15 ~.

ymb-salde *prt* surrounded. **VP** 16/9, 11 *etc* ~un (circumdederunt). 17/5, 6; 21/13, 7 *etc* ~on.

gesaldnis *sf* grant. **Ct** 48/8 ðas ~se.

scald-thȳflas Ep; Ef scald[t]hyblas; Cp scaldhyflas. scaldhulas Cp.

Hagu-steald(es hām) *sm* Hexham **BH** 134/5 ~staldensis. **Gn** 54 hagstaldensiae. 55, 7 hag'. 61 *hag[u]-staldensis.*

spaldr *s* asphalt. **Ep** 54 ~(asfaltum); Ef, Cp, Ld spaldur.

weald *sm* forest.

Anut-weald *sm* **Ct** 29/15 an ~walda.

wealdan *sv* wield, rule. **VP** 88/10; 109/2 waldes (dominaris; §averis). 9/26, 31 *etc* §eð. 18/14 bioð §ende. 105/41 §ende werun.

wealdnis *sf* rule. **VP** 144/13 waldnis (dominatio).

gewald-leðrum Cp.

-weald

Ualdfrith LV. **Ualdgith** [*under* ȳ] LV. **Wealdhelm** Ct. **Ualdheri** BH, Ct; wealdhere Ct; †wealdenesford.

Ælf-weald *sm* **Rn** 1/3 olwfwolþu. **LV** 8, 13; 298 aelfuald. **Gn** 118 aelfwald. **Ct** 56/5 elfwald.

Æsc-weald *sm* **LV** 99 aescuald.

Æþel-weald *sm* **BH** 73 aduluualdi *g* [*in Latin document*]—aeðuluualdi I. 191 aediluald — ed§ — aeð§. 356 ediluald — aeðiluuald I. **LV** 87; 224, 62; 338; 481 eðiluald. **LN** aedeluald. **Mt** 34 aeðelwaldes. **Ct** 38/17 eðelwald. 40/14; 56/4 æðel§. 57/7; 58/13 aeðel§. 55/8 ęðel§. 45/23 ęðel§e. 24/8 æðewalde. 38/17 †ðelwald. 28/17; 30/16; 31/7 eðel~. 44/5, 5 ęðel ~.

ān-weald *s(n)* single rule, monarchy. **Ep** 622 anuuald; Ef anuald; Cp anuualda (monarchia).

Ar-weald *sm* **BH** 286 ~ualdi *g*.

Beadu-weald *sm* **LV** 140, 96; 338, 43 baduuald.

Beorht-weald *sm* **BH** 59 berctualdi *g* — berht§ I. 328, 45 berctuald. **LV** 111 berch[t]uald. 478 bercht§. 104, 42, 98; 227, 63, 81, 96; 337, 57 berct§. **Gn** 2 berhtwaldus. **Ct** 2/1 berctualdo *d*. 4/2 bercuald. 5/5, 5 berhtuualdum (berichtualdum), berhtuualdus (berichtualdus). 10/4 §uuald. 14/6 § uua[l]di.

Beorn-weald *sm* **Ct** 31/9 ~.

Bet-weald *sm* **LV** 200; 307, 44 ~uald.

Bil-weald *sm* **LV** 201 ~uald.

Bliš-weald *sm* **LV** 215 ~uald.

Bōt-weald *sm* **LV** 282 ~uald.

Byrn-weald *sm* **LV** 335 bryn uald. **Ct** 49/10 ~uuald. 50/5 by[r]nwald.

Cent-weald *sm* **LV** 209 kentuald.

Cēol-weald *sm* **LV** 214 ~uald. 284 c(eo)luald. **SG** 5 ~wald

Cēol-wealding *sm* son of Cēolweald. **SG** 4 ~walding.

Cœ̄n-weald *sm* **Ct** 29/21 co(en)-wald. 34/4; 51/11 coen§. 52/17 §uualdi *g*.

Cūþ-weald *sm* **BH** 366 cudualdi — §baldi—§baldi. **LV** 264, 94; 341 cuthuald. 336 cuðuald.

Cwic-weald *sm* **LV** 348 cui[c]-uald.

Cyne-weald *sm* **LV** 472 cyniuald. **Gn** 93 ~wald.

Cyne-wealding *sm* son of Cyneweald. **Gn** 93 ~walding.

Dene-weald *sm* Ct 20/5 ~waldes stan.

Dēor-weald *sm* Ct 30/17 diar~.

Dryht-weald *sm* Ct 29/19 ~wald. 2 ~waldo. 30/13; 44/3 ~.

Ēad-weald *sm* LV 51, 66, 75; 103, 6, 41, 2, 64, 95, 9; 204, 53, 68, 82, 6; 312, 42, 51, 4, 60, 4, 6; 405, 22 ~uald. 228 eod§. Ct 28/17; 38/8; 39/3; 43/8 ~. 30/4; 39/1 ~es. 39/6 ~e. 30/20; 38/7, 12; 45/60 ~wald. 38/1 §es.

Ealh-weald *sm* LV 251, 81 alchuald. 261 aluchuald.

Ēan-weald *sm* LV 226 eonuald 262, 83; 339, 67 ean§.

Ecg-weald *sm* LV 79; 174 ~uald. Gn 86 §.

Ecg-wealding *sm* son of Ecgweald. Gn 85, 7 ~ualding.

Efen-weald *sm* LV 337 efnuald.

Eorcen-weald *sm* BH 174 ercunualdo *d*—hercun[u]aldo—ercunualdo—§. 174 §us—hercunualdus—erconualdus—§. 229 earconuald—er§ I. 256 earconualdum—eorcun§ I. 267 erconualdo *d*—ercunuualdo I. LV 305 ercinuald. Gn 6 erconwald. Ct 1/6 ercnuualdus.

Eorp-weald *sm* BH 102 earpualdo — eorpuualdo I — earpualdo. 105 ~uald—§I—§II. 105 ~ualdi—~uualdi. 169 erpualdum—§—eo§—erp§. LV 287 eorupuald.

Folc-weald *sm* LV 163 ~uald.

Forþ-weald *sm* LV 115 forthuald.

Friþu-weald *sm* LK 4 friduuald. LV 162, 68; 264 friðuuald. 108 frioðuuald. Gn 68 frioðowald.

Gār-weald *sm* LV 59; 365 ~uald.

Gēr-weald *sm* LV 119, 63, 80; 204; 302, 53, 70 ~uald.

Geon-weald *sm* LV 289 ~uald.

Gum-weald *sm* LV 347 ~uald.

Heaþo-weald *sm* LV 134 heaðuuald. 152; 211, 21, 99 haðuuald.

Helm-weald *sm* LV 5; 105, 17; 209, 29, 60, 89; 352, 62, 86, 98 ~uald.

Hēo-weald *sm* BH 329 heuualdi *pl.* 350 heuuald *four times*—heauald [*first* a *from* u], heauald, heauuald, heauuald [*first* a *over dotted* u]. LV 168; 207 heouald.

Heoru-weald *sm* LV 162 heruuald.

Here-weald *sm* Gn 24 ~uuald Ct 17/6 ~wald.

Hilde-weald *sm* LV 119; 227; 351 ~iuald.

Hlēo-weald *sm* LV 166, 98; 218, 25; 335, 43 ~uald.

Hrœþ-weald *sm* LV 258 hroeðuald.

Hrōþ-weald *sm* LV 115 hroðuald.

Hūn-weald *sm* BH 164 ~ualdi *g.* LV 79; 224; 344; 467 ~uald. Ct 17/5 ~wald.

Hyge-weald *sm* LV 211, 40, 65 hyguald.

In-weald *sm* LV 80; 103; 218 ~uald.

Ing-weald *sm* BH 372 ~uald. 370 §o. Gn 6 incwald.

Lēod-weald *sm* Gn 85 liod·ald. 87 §uald.

Lēod-wealding *sm* son of Lēodweald. Gn 85 liodwalding. 87 li·dualding.

Liht-weald *sm* LV 229 lictuald.

Mǣg-weald *sm* LV 213 meiuald.

Mægen-weald *sm* LV 82 maeginuald. 128 maegen§.

Œþel-weald *sm* BH 125 oidilualdo *d*—oe§—oidiluualdo. 161 oidilualdo—oe§ I. 193 oidiluald—oe§ I. 196 oidiluald—§ I. 327 oidiluald—oið[il]uuald I. 332 oiduald—oidiluuald I. LV 50 oediluald. Gn 41 *oeðeluuald.* 66 oeðilwald. LN oedelwald.

onwald *sn* authority. Cp 1800 ~(sceptra). VP 102/22 ~es (dominationis).

Ōs-weald *sm* BH 63 osuald—osuuald I—osuald. 92 osualdo *d*—I, II §. 115 §—osuualdo I—osualdo II *etc.* LK 4 osuald. LV 2 osuald. Ct 30/18 ~.

Pend-weald *sm* LV 174 ~uald.

Peoht-weald *sm* LV 104 pectuald. 282 pecht§.

Plēo-weald *sm* LV 275 ~uald.

Rǣd-weald *sm* BH 61 reduald —reduuald I—reduald. 87 redualdum — rędualdum I — redualdum. 87 §—reduualdum—redualdum. 102 §i *g*—§uualdi I. 103 redualdi. 169 §i *g*—rędualdi I.

Sǣ-weald *sm* LV 69 saeuald.

Scēot-weald *sm* LV 168 sceutuald.

Sige-weald *sm* LV 265 siguald.

Swīþ-weald *sm* LV 292 suiðuald.

Tēo-weald *sm* LV 207 tiuuald. 334 tiouald.

Tīd-weald *sm* LV 97; 161; 240; 371; 403 ~uald. Ct 31/7 ~.

Til-weald *sm* LV 164 [u *dotted out after* i]; 201, 68 ~uuald.

Tīr-weald *sm* Ct 31/10; 38/19 ~wald.

Trum-weald *sm* LV 251 ~uald.

Tūn-weald *sm* LV 209; 344 ~uald.

†**Waldenes-ford** Ct.

be-fealdan *sv* fold. **VH** 3/5 befalden (convoluta).

ān-fald *aj* simple. Cp 1863 ~(simpla).

monig-fald *aj* manifold. VP 67/18; 89/10 ~ (multiplex; plurimum).

monigfaldlice *av* manifoldly. VP 62/2 ~(multipliciter).

seofen-faldlice *av* sevenfold. VP 11/7; 78/12 ~(septuplum).

gemonig-faldian *wv* multiply. VP 137/3 ~as (multiplicabis). 17/15 ~ade (§avit) *etc.* 11/9 ~ades (§asti) *etc.* Hy 4/5 ~ian (§are). 48/17; 91/13 *etc* ~ad bið. 3/2; 15/4 *etc* ~ade sindun. 4/8 gemongfaldade [e *er after sec.* g]. 64/10, I gemonigfalldes, §ende.

fīfalde [*under* ī].

ā-cwealdon *prt* killed. Cp 1376 aqualdun (necebantur).

ā-gald *prt* repaid. VP 7/5 ~(reddidi).

gealdor *sn* incantation, magic.

galdurcreftas VP.

galdrigge *sf* [*or* §a *sm*?] enchantress. Cp 1124 ~an (incantatores).

getealde *prt* counted, accounted. VP 43/22 getalde sind (aestimati sumus). 87/5 eam getald (§atus sum). 105/31 § wes (§atum est). 118/119 §e (reputavi).

beald *aj* bold. Cp 924, 7 bald (fretus, frontuosus).

Balðheard LV; balthhaeardi, §hardi Ct. **Baldhelm**, balð§ LV. **Baldhere**, balð§, balt§ LV. **Baldhild**, balt§ BH. **Balðhūn** LV. **Baldrēd** LV, Ct. **Balduini** LV; §wines Ct. **Balduulf** LV.

Æþel-beald *sm* LV 6 aeðilbald. 81 ethil§. 89; 299; 425, 6 eðil§. 262 (aðilbald). Gn 98 aeðel§. 122 aeðil§. SG 7 æðel§. Ct 9/5 aethil§o. 9/6 ęthilbal(di). 12/1 aethelbaldi. 13/2 æðelbaldi. 17/1 §i. 2 §us. 3, 4 æðelbald. 20/22 §i. 32/6 eðelbald. 9/1 aethilbalt. 4 aetdil§. 8 edil§. 32/5 eðelbæld. 43/7 eðelbeald.

Cēol-beald *sm* LV 6 ~bald.

Cūþ-beald *sm* BH 366 cudualdi — §baldi — §. LV 132; 370 cuthbald.

Cyne-beald *sm* Rn 9 cynibalþ. LV 11; 90; 124, 39; 238; 58, 80; 373 cynibald. Ct 33/21 ~bald.

Dæg-beald *sm* LV 192 daegbald.

Ēad-beald *sm* BH 40 aeodbaldum — ead§ I — ead§. 69 eadbald. 72 aeodbaldo — ead§ I — eod§. 77 aeodbaldo — ead§ — ead§ [a *from* o]. 82 audubaldi [*in Latin document*] — eadbaldi [*from* adubaldi] I — audubaldi. 86 § — eadbaldi [ea *on er.*; u *er. after first* d] I — audubaldi. 69 eadbald. 117 §o. 119 §i. LV 10, 84; 129, 85; 238, 78, 86; 313, 78, 91, 8; 401, 27, 61, 2 ~bald. 351, 4 eodbald. Gn 7, 113 ~bald. Ct 13/4; 17/7; 55/10; 56/7; 58/19 ~bald. 14/7, 7 §i.

Ēad-bealding *sm* son of Eadbeald. Gn 113 ~balding.

Ēan-beald *sm* LV 7; 137, 47, 79, 81, 90; 260; 303, 8, 24, 94, 5; 417. Gn 60, 0 ~bald.

Ecg-beald *sm* Gn 21 ~bald. Ct 1/7; 3/13 egcbaldus.

Friþu-beald *sm* LV 6; 352; 464 friðubald.

Heaþu-beald *sm* **LV** 438 haðubald. **Ct** 33/11 heaðo§.

Here-beald *sm* **LV** 81; 203, 30, 40, 73; 313, 71, 82 ~bald.

Hūn-beald *sm* **LV** 143; 311 ~bald.

Hyge-beald *sm* **BH** 246 hygbald. **LV** 80, 98; 101, 18, 34; 241, 74; 302, 15, 7, 63, 88, 9; 426, 50, 72 hygbald. **Gn** 66 §.

Ōs-beald *sm* **LV** 91; 147; 465 osbald.

Rǣd-beald, *sm* **LV** 83 redbald.

Sǣ-beald *sm* **Gn** 75 saebald.

Sǣ-bealding *sm*. son of Sǣbeald. **Gn** 75 saebalding.

Seax-beald *sm* **BH** 189 sexbaldi.

Sige-beald *sm* **LV** 96; 331; 42 sigbald. **SG** 22 ~bald.

Sige-bealding *sm*. son of Sigebeald. **SG** 22 ~b(aldi)ng.

Swīþ-beald *sm* **LV** 94 suiðbald.

Tīd-beald *sm* **LV** 110, 55; 244; 433, 74 ~bald.

þēod-beald *sm* **BH** 37 theodbald.

Wǣr-beald *sm* **Ct** 24/12 węrbald. 25/14 wær§. 40/14 wer§.

Wern-beald *sm* **LV** 285 uernbald.

Wīg-beald *sm* **LV** 103, 15, 6, 83, 91; 206; 313, 97; 402, 8 uigbald.

Wiht-beald *sm* **LV** 276 uictbald. 479 uicht§. **Ct** 26/2 uuihtbaldes hlawe.

Wil-beald *sm* **LV** 418 uilbald.

Wine-beald *sm* **LV** 146 uinibald.

Wun-beald *sm* **Ct** 38/20 ~.

Wyn-beald *sm* **LV** 330, 57; 476 uynbald. **Ct** 49/12 wynbald.

Eaðu-gils LV.

heaðo *s* war.

Haðubald LV; haðo§ Ct. **Haduberct**, haðu§, hað§, heaðu§ LV; heaðoberht Gn; haðo§, heaðo§ Ct. **Haðuburg** LV. **Heaðufrith**, heað§, heaðuferð LV. **Haðugȳth** LV. **Hadulāc** BH; heaðo§ Gn. **Hadumund** LV. **Haðumēr** LV. **Heaðurēd**, headu§, haðu§, hadu§, heoðu§ LV; heaðo§ Gn; haðo§, heaðo§ Ct. **Heaðuric**, haðu§ LV. **Heaðuuald** LV. **Haðuuini** LV. **Haðuulf**, haduulf, heaðuulf, headuulf LV.

Eafa *sm* **BH** 205 ~ — eaba I. **LV** 171 eofa. **SG** 3 eaba.

Eafing *sm* son of E. **SG** 3 eabing. **Ct** 15/9; 16/8 ~.

Eafe *sf* **BH** 276 eabae.

Eafu *sf* **LV** 25, 38 ~.

þeafol *sm* **Ct** 5/7 theabul.

gonge-weafre *sf* spider. **VP** 38/12 ~an (aranea). 89/9 ~ (§).

geseah *prt* saw. **VP** 32/13; 36/25; 76/19; 96/4; 113/3; 118/96, 158; 141/5; **Hy** 7/70 gesaeh (vidit; §i *etc*). 54/10; **Hy** 7/36 gesæh.

for-seah *prt* despised. **VP** 21/25 ~saeh (despexit).

fore-seah *prt* saw before. **VP** 15/8 ~saeh (providebam).

sleahe *sf* slay, weaver's reed. **Cp** 1576 slahae (pectica).

gefeah *prt* rejoiced. **VP** 18/6; **Hy** 4/1; 10/1 gefaeh (exultavit).

Eahha *sm* **LV** 53, 94, 6 echha. **Ct** 5/7 aehcha.

Eahhe *sf* **BH** 137 acha *d*.

eax *sf* axle. **Ep** 13 aex (axis); **Ef**, **Cp** §. **Ef** 1149 § (§).

aexfaru Cp.

leax *sm* salmon. **Ep** 555 ~(isic); **Ef** lex; **Cp** laex. **Cp** 767 § (essox).

seax *sn* knife. **Cp** 625 saex(culter).

blōd-saex *sn* lancet. **Cp** 896 ~(flebotoma); **Ld** §.

scer-saex *sn* razor. **VP** 51/4 ~(novacula).

þeoh-saex *sn* short sword. **Cp** 1832 ~(semispatium).

Seaxan *pl* Saxons. **BH** 21 *saxonibus*. **SG** 12, 7 *orientalium* seaxonum, § seoxo(num).

Ēast-seaxan *pl* East Saxons. **Ct** 1/1, 6 ~sexanorum, *rex* ~sax'.

Middel-seaxan *pl* Middle Saxons. **Ct** 11/2 middilsaexum. 59/1 ~saxanorum.

Sūþ-seaxan *pl* South Saxons. **Ct** 7/3 suthsaxoniae.

West-seaxan *pl* West Saxons.

SG 11 ~seaxna lond. **Ct** 2/1 uestsęxanorum.

Seaxa *sm* **SG** 23 ~.

Seaxing *sm* son of S. **SG** 23 ~.

Sexbald BH. **Sexburg**, saex§ BH. **Seaxnēting** SG. **Seaxrēd**; §ing SG. **Sæxuulf**, saex§, sęx§, sex§, sax§ BH; saex§, *sœx*§ Gn.

weaxan *sv* grow. **Cp** 1955 waexit (surgit).

weax *sn* wax. **VP** 21/15; 57/9 wæx (cera). 67/3 węx. 96/5 wex. **Ct** 37/27 ðaet ~.

waexcondel Cp.

feax *sn* hair (of head).

Fexstān LV.

feaxnis *sn* head of hair. **Cp** 364 faexnis (capillatur).

Meahse-lōg Ct.

eahta *num* eight.

eahtategðan Mt.

hund-eahtatig *num* eighty. **VP** 89/10 ~aehtatiges (LXXX).

eahtian *wv* consider. **Ep** 836 aectath (perpendit); **Ef** aechtath; **Cp** aehtað.

eahtere *sm* censor. **Ef** 1167 †echtheri (censor, rimator, p'tiator).

leahtrog *sm* lettuce. **Ep** 247 leactrocas (corimbus); **Ef** §; **Cp** leactrogas.

geþeaht *sn* deliberation, council, advice. **VP** 12/2; 13/6; 20/12; 21/17; 32/11 geðaeht (consilium), 19/5 †gedaeh. 105/43 geðaehte (§io). 25/4; 110/1 gedaehte (§io). 32/10; 55/6 geðaeht (§ia). 82/4 geþæht. 32/10; 106/11 geðæht. 88/8 §e. 65/5 §um. 70/10 geðęht. 105/13 geðeht. **Hy** 7/57 §e. **Ct** 40/2 mid his geðeahte.

geþeahtian *wv* consider. **VP** 30/14 geðaehtende werun (consiliati sunt).

meahte *prt* could. **Mt** 37, 42 ~. **VP** 39/13 maehte (potui). 20/12; 128/2 §un (§uerunt).

Eatta *sm* **Gn** 107 ~.

Eatting *sm* son of E. **Gn** 107 ~.

geatwe *spl* trappings. **Rd** 10 geatum.

Eadu *sf* **LV** 40; 445.

sceadu *s*(*f*) shade, shadow. **Ep** 902 sceadu [u *over* o] (scena); **Ef** sceadu; **Cp** scadu. **Cp** 1954 sceadu *for* swaðu.

scaedugeardas Ep; sceadu§ Ef, Cp.

ofer-sceadwian *wv* overshadow. **VP** 90/4 ~ad (obumbrabit). 139/8 ~a (§a!).

scedeht *aj* shady. **VH** 6/6 ~um (umbroso).

beadu *sf* war.

Badufrith, beadu§, beodu§ LV. **Beadugils** LV. **Badugȳth** LV. **Beadheard**, bad§ LV; bada§, bead§ Ct. ?**Badhelm** [*or* ā?] LV. **Bað-hūn** LV. **Badumund** LV. **Badonōð**, bada§, bade§ Ct. **Badenoðingland** Ct. **Beadurēd**, badu§ LV. **Badusuið** LV. **Baduðegn**, beadu§ BH, LV. **Baduuald** LV. **Baduuini**, baduini BH, LV; beoduuini LV; beadwine Gn. **Baduulf**, beaduulf LV.

Headda *sm* **LV** 159 hadda. **Gn** 36 ~an *a.* 37, 50 ~. **Ct** 10/2 ~ *d.* 59/7 ~.

Ceadda *sm* **BH** 3 ~ *g.* 127, 95 ~. 195 ~ *d.* 207 ~an *a.* 246 ~ — cedda. **Gn** 34 ~.

Eappa *sm* **BH** 276, 281 ~. 281 ~an *a.*

ðri-nes *sf* trinity. **DA** 5 ða ~se. **VH** 12/5 seo~ (trinitas).

ðri-fedor Ep; ðrifeoðor Cp; tri§ Ef. **thriuuuintri** Ep; triumtri Ef; ðriuuintra Cp.

ni-hold [*under* ea].

twi-bille VP. **twiecge** VP. **tuiheolore** Cp. **twitælgad** VP.

diacon *sm* deacon. **Ct** 37/37.

hire *d* her. **VP** 3/3; 23/1; 67/11; 68/37 *etc* ~(illi; eā; §; §). **Ct** 38/2; 41/10, 0, 5 *etc*; 45/16, 20 ~.

hire *g* her. **VP** 3/3; 36/3; 57/5 *etc* ~(ejus; §; suas). **Ct** 37/37, 8; 38/2; 41/12, 6, 58, 68; 45/17 ~.

cirice *sf* church. **LP** 6 ~an *a.* **DA** 7 ~ean *pl.* **VP** 21/23 ~an (ecclesiae *g*). 21/26; 34/18 §micelre (§iā) *etc.* 67/27 § (§iis). 25/12 cirecum (§iis). **Ct** 37/8; 39/10 to ðære ~an. 45/31 ~um. 37/27 to † ciricican.

Cristes-cirice *sf* Christchurch. **CA** 8, 10, 7 ~circan *d.* **Ct** 37/2,

32; 39/2, 12; 40/3, 18; 41/59, 67; 42/5; 45/30, 4, 6 ~an *d.* 41/43, 71 kristes§. 41/44 kristes ~an *g.* 40/6 ~circcan *d.*

pirige *sf* peartree. Cp 1589 pirge (pirus).

bireð *prs* bears. VP 40/4 ~(ferat).

biren *sf* she-bear. Ct 30/12 ~e feld.

irre *aj* angry. VP 59/3; 73/1; 105/40; Hy 2/1 eorre (iratus). 17/8 § [*first* e *from* i]. Hy 5/23 eorre (§ae *pl*).

irre *sn* anger. VP 2/13; 29/6 *etc* eorre (ira). 68/25; 77/38 §ðin (iram); all§ (§) *etc.* 2/5; 6/2 §; §ðinum (irā) *etc.* 37/4; 77/50 *etc* §es. 87/17 §u (irae *pl*). 17/16; Hy 6/16 earres. 9/25 †eare.

irsian *wv* to be angry. VP 2/12; 4/5; 7/12; 78/5 eorsie, §iað, §að, §as (irascatur *etc*) *etc.* 17/48 eorsendum (iracundis). 123/3 †ersade.

irsung *sf* being angry. VH 5/12 eorsunge (iracundiae *g*).

seofon-stirri *s* pliades. Ep 762 sifunsterri (pliadas); Ef †fun~; Cp sibun§.

ā-firran *wv* remove Mt 48 afierr! VH 7/78 ~u (tollam). 103/29 ~es (auferes). 75/13 ~eð (aufert). 72/27 ~að (elongant). 39/15 ~en (auferant). 118/22 afir (aufer!). 50/13; 118/43; 140/8 ne § ðu (ne §as). 77/52 afirde (abstulit). 79/9 §es (transtulisti). 128/3 §un (prolongaverunt). 45/10 ~ende (auferans). 9/26 bioð ~ed (auferuntur). 119/5 §is (prolongatus est). 57/9 bioð afirde (auferentur).

onweg-āfirran *wv* remove away. VH 1/11 ~afirde (abstuli).

wirþeþ *prs* becomes, is. BDS I uuiurthit.

wirþe *aj* worthy. Ct 41/7, 36, 42 weorðe.

geor-wirþan *wv* disgrace. Ep 990 georuuierdid (traductus); Ef §; Cp georuuyrde.

first *sm* period of time.

fristmearc Ep; †frit§ Ef; first§ Cp.

first *sf* ceiling. Ep 595 fierst (laquear); Ef †firt; Cp ~hrof. Cp 1190~e (laquearia). 2028~(tigillum).

firsthrōf Cp.

smirwan *wv* smear, anoint. VP 140/5 smireð (inpinguet). 44/8; 88/21; Hy 1/6 §ede (unxit; §i; §it).

gesmirwan *wv* smear. Cp 676 gesmirwid (delibutus).

besmirwan *wv* besmear. Ep 534 bismiridae (interlitam); Ef †§a; Cp §e.

smirennis *sf* anointing. VH 1/6 ~enisse (unctionis).

smirwung *sf* ointment. VP 44/9; 132/2 smiring (cassia; unguentum).

geswirfeþ *prs* polishes. Cp 740 gesuirbet (elimat).

cirnel *sm* kernel. Cp 982 ~ (glandula). 1396 cirnlas (nucli).

Iurmin-burg LV. **Irminrēd** Ct. **Irminrīc** BH, iurmenric, §ing Gn.

or-firme *aj* squalid. Ep 933 orfiermae (†squalores); Ef orfermae.

orfirmnis *sf* squalor. Cp 1902 orfeormnisse (squalores).

cirm *s(m)* clamour. Cp 925 suoeg, ~(fragor). 1866 ~(sinnum).

birce *sf* birch. Ep 792 ~iae (populus); Ef §; Cp ~.

birhtu *sf* brightness. VP 89/17; Hy 6/8; 11/1 ~(splendor). Hy 6/10 ~(claritatem). Hy 6/24, 41~(splendore, claritudine). 109/3 ~um (splendoribus).

gebirhtan *wv* make bright, manifest. VP 41/9 ~e (declaravit).

firgen *s* mountain.

?**fergenberig** Rn. **firgingaett** Ep; § Ef; firgen§ Cp; firgingata Ld.

hirtan *wv* cherish. VH 12/15 hirt (fove!).

hirde *sm* shepherd. VH 3/5 heorda (pastorum).

Hirde *sm* LV 103; 319 hiordi.

cæg-hirde *sm* key-keeper. Cp 490 caeghiorde (clavicularius).

hors-hirde *sm* horse-keeper. Cp 1527 ~hi[o]rdas (pabulatores).

hriþ-hirde *sm* herdsman. **Cp** 313 hriðhiorde (bobulcus).

ðrili *aj* triple. **Cp** 29 ~(trilex). **Ld** 158 drili (triplex).

stileþ *prs* steals. **Cp** 589 ~ith (conpilat).

Uuil-tūn, úuil§ Ct.

Filið-lēag Ct.

milsc-apuldr Ep; milc§ Ef; mirc§ Cp.

til *prp* to. **Rn** 2/13 ~ anum. **CH** 6 ~ hrofe.

til *aj* good.

Tilbāeth LV. **Tilberht** LV, Gn, Ct. **Tilfrið** LV. **Tilhāeth** LV. **Tilhere** Gn, Ct. **Tilmon** BH, LV. **Tilrēd** LV, Ct. **Tilgeseltha** Ct. **Tilðegn** LV. **Tiluald** LV. **Tiluini** LV.

Til-geseltha Ct.

Tila-burg BH.

tilian *wv* aim at, tend, till. **Ep** 78 tilgendum (adnitentibus); Cp §; Ef §un. Cp 1567 tioludun (perstant).

tilung *sf* tending. **VP** 27/4; 98/8 teolunge (studiorum; §ia). 105/29 §um (§iis).

Tile *sm* **LV** 297 ~i. **Ct** 42/26 ~.

Tilese *sm* **LV** 95; 103, 8, 70; 211 tilisi.

Tilne *sm* **LV** 457 ~.

twili *aj* double. **Ef** 1151 tuili (biplex, duplex). Ld 157 †tili (bilex).

Dilra *sm* **Ct** 10/4 (dil)ran *g*.

dile *sm* dill (herb). **Ep** 21 dil (anetum); Ef §; Cp ~i.

ill *s* sole of foot **Cp** 400 weorras *vel* ~(callos). **Lr** 60 ~a (plantarum).

geille-rocad VP.

þille *sn* boarding. **Cp** 1988 ðille (tabulata). 1990 §(tabulamen).

gagul-swillan *wv* gargle. **Cp** 946 ~suille (gargarizet).

scilling *sm* shilling. **Ct** 47/15 ~a. 48/6 scill' *gpl*.

Scilling *sm* **Ct** 3/13 sci(lli)nges.

mene-scilling *sm* coin worn as an ornament. **Ep** 570 ~as (lunules); Ef meni§; Cp ~as.

Lilla *sm* **BH** 80 ~.

stille *aj* still, quiet. **VP** 75/10; Hy 12/13 ~(quietos).

un-stilnis *sf* agitation. **Cp** 106 ~(agitatio).

un-stilli[t] **LD** 252 ~(insolescit).

gestillan *wv* quiet. **Mt** 20 (ge)-stillde. **VP** 75/9; Hy 3/4 gestilde (quievit). 84/4 §es (mitigasti).

wille *vb* will. **Rd** 11 uil 3 *sg*. **CA** 8 ~að. **VP** 5/5 wellende (volens). 34/27, 7; 67/31 ~að (§unt). 21/9; 33/13 wile (vult). **Ct** 42/4 ic ~. 40/3 willa ic. 45/44 ic willio ⁊ ~. 40/20, 4; 41/4, 6; 45/19, 25, 7, 50; 48/3 (he)~. 45/32 §ęn. 41/10, 40; 45/39 (he) wile.

willa *sm* will. **VP** 142/10 ~an ðinne (voluntatem) *etc*. 20/3 § (§ate) *etc*. 5/13 godes§ (§atis) *etc*. 15/3 § (§ates). Hy 11/4 ~um (votis). **Ct** 41/1, 4, 9; 42/1, 18; 45/13 ~.

Uilbald LV. **Uilberct** LV. **Uilbrord**, uuil§ BH. **Uilburg** LV; wil§ Ct. **Uilcumae** LV. **Uilfarę̄s-dūn**, *id est*, *mons* uilfari — §færaes BH. **Uilfrid** BH; §frith LV; uuilfrið, uil§ Gn; uuilfridus, willfredi, §ferð Ct. **Uilgils** LV, Gn; §ing Gn. **Uilgȳth** LV. **Uilhāeth** LV. **Uilhelm** LV; wil§ Gn. **Wilhelming** Gn. **Willhere** Ct. **Uilmund** LV. **Uuilnōð** Ct. **Uilrēd** LV, Gn; uuill§, will§ Ct. **Uilrīc** LV. **Uilsig** LV. **Uilsuīð** LV. **Uilthegn** LV. **Uilðrȳth** LV. **Uiluulf** LV.

ān-willice *av* resolutely, pertinaciously. **Ep** 753 anuuillicae (pertinaciter); Ef §; Cp §e.

wilsum *aj* desirable. **VP** 18/11; 118/108 ~(desiderabilia; voluntaria). 67/10 ~ne (§iam). 105/24 ~e (desiderabilem).

wilsumlice *av* willingly. **VP** 53/8 ~(voluntarie).

willian *wv* desire. **VP** 33/13; 111/1 §að (cupit; §iet). **Ct** 45/44 ic willio ⁊ wille.

gewillian *wv* desire. **VP** 36/23; 41/2, 2 ~að (cupiet; desiderat, §). 44/12; 83/3; 118/20, 40, 174 ~ade (concupivit *etc*). 118/131 § (desiderabam). 105/14 ~adun (concupierunt). 61/11; 118/20 ~(concupiscere; desiderare).

gewillung *sf* desire. **VP** 105/14 ~e (concupiscentias).

Uillech *sm* **LV** 473 ~.

Cillincg *s* **Ct** 53/5 *portum quae dicitur* ~.

gillestre *sf* pus, matter, phlegm. **Ep** 833 ~istrae (pituita).

Tilli *sm* **LV** 169 ~.

bill *sn* bill. **Cp** 305 billeru (bibulta).

Bilfrith LV. Bilgils LV. Bilhāeth LV. Billheard Ct. Bilhelm LV. Bilstān. Bilsuið LV. Bilðegn LV. Biluald LV. Biluualch LV.

Cyni-bill *sm* **BH** 194 ~um. 195 ~ — ~bil — §.

twi-bill *sn* axe. **VP** 73/6 ~e (bipinnae *pl*).

wudu-bill *sn* hatchet. **Ep** 430 uudubil (falces); **Ef** uuidu§; **Cp** wudu§. 449 uuidu§ (falcastrum); **Ef** §; **Cp** wudu§. **Ld** 38 †uuitubil (runtina).

Billan-ōra Ct.

Billing *sm* **LV** 78, 9 ~.

silfren *aj* silver. **Rn** 7 siuilfur(n?).

be-silfran *wv* silver. **VP** 67/14 †besifrede (deargentatae).

ilca *prn* same. **DA** 19 to ðon ~e. **VP** 43/5 se ~cyning (ipse rex). 101/28 se ~earð (idem ipse es). 34/8; 73/6 *etc* in ðæt ~e (in id ipso). 61/10 in ðæt ~e (in id §um) *etc.* 73/2 in ðon ~an (in id ipso). **Hy** 7/10 ðes illce (hic ipse). **Ct** 37/16; 42/15; 45/36 ~an.

milceþ *prs* milks. **Ep** 628 ~iþ (morgit); **Ef** ~id; **Cp** ~it.

æt-fileð *prs* adheres. **VP** 93/20; 136/6 ~(adheret; §eat).

for-swilgeð devours. **VP** 20/10; 57/10 ~(devorabit; absorbet).

ā-dilgian *wv* destroy. **VP** 17/43 ~iu (delebo). 50/3, 11 ~a (dele!). 9/6 ~ades (delisti). 108/13, 4 sie ~ad. 68/29 sien ~ade.

dilgnis *sf* destruction. **Cp** 163 dilignissum (anastasis).

swilteð *prs* dies. **Pv** 2 suuyltit. **VP** 40/6; 48/18 ~(morietur).

Uilta-burg BH.

on-filt *s* anvil. **Cp** 1072 ~i (incuda). **Ld** 53 †osifelti (incus).

milte *sf* spleen. **Ep** 594 †multi (lien); **Ef** ~i; **Cp** ~; **Ld** ~ę. 970 ~i; **Ef** §; **Cp** ~(splenis). **Lr** 69 ~(splenem).

Ciltinne *s* **Ct** 11/3 in ~.

Uilta-burg BH.

hild *sf* war.

Hildiberct LV. Hildiburg LV. Hildgāringdenn Ct. Hildifriþ LV. Hildigils LV. Hilddigȳþ Rn; hildigyð, §gið **LV. Hildilid BH. Hildiþrȳþ Rn, LV. Hildiuald LV. Hilduini LV.**

Hild *sf* **BH** 199 ~ *abbattissa.* 211 hil[d]. 233 ~ae *g*— ~e I. 307 ~ae *g.*

Æþel-hild *sf* **BH** 156 aedil— aeðil~ I. **LV** 21 eðil~.

Beald-hild *sf* **BH** 362 baldhild — balthild — § [t *on er*].

Bōt-hild *sf* **LV** 30 ~.

Ēastor-hild *sf* **LV** 20 aestor~.

Friþ-hild *sf* **LV** 30 frið~.

Tīd-hild *sf* **LV** 47 ~.

Wulf-hild *sf* **LV** 37, 45 uulf~.

gescildan *wv* protect. **VP** 90/14 ~u (protegam). 30/21 ~es (§es) **Hy** 7/88 ~eð (defendit). 19/2, 3 ~e (protegat, tueatur). 16/8 †gesild (protege!) 26/5 ~e (protexit). 63/2 ~es (§isti). 26/4 siem ~ed (protegar). 60/5 sion § (§). **Hy** 7/88 bið§ (defenditur). 34/4 sien ~e (†confundantur).

gescildend *sm* protector. **VP** 17/3, 19; 26/1 *etc* ~(protector, §; defensor). 8/3 ~[i *over* e] (§em). **Hy** 7/75 ~(protectores).

gescildnis *sf* protection. **VP** 120/5 ~(protectio). 17/36; 35/8 *etc* ~nisse (§ionem, §ione).

scilden *sf* protection. **Ep** 1038 †clindinnae (tutellam); **Ef** scildinnae; **Cp** scildenne.

for-spildan *wv* destroy. **VP** 5/7; 20/11; 72/27; 142/12 ~es (perdis; §; §es; §§). 33/17 ~e (§at). 25/9; 27/3; 43/23 ne ~spild ðu (§as; §; †repellas). 118/95 ~en (perderent). 36/32 ~(§ere).

spilth *s* destruction. **Ep** 755 ~(pessum); **Ef**, **Cp** ~.

wilde *aj* wild. **Ep** 99 uuildae (agrestes); Ef §; Cp wildę (§is). Cp 450, 960, 3 ~goos (cente, gente, §). 1142 ~(indomitus). **Mt** 17 ~o *pl.* 18 ~an. **VP** 103/11 ~assan (onagri).

wilddēor, wildeor VP.

milde *aj* mild, gentle. **VP** 77/38; 78/9; 98/8, 102/3 ~(propitius). 85/5 ~(mitis). 24/9 ðа ~an (§es).

mildheort VP. mildheortnis, milheortnis VP. **Milrēd** VP, Gn, Ct.

gemildgian *wv* mitigate. **VP** 88/10 ~as (mitigas). 93/13 ~ie (§es).

milts *sf* pity. **LP** 1 ~e *g.* **VP** 129/4 milds (propitiatio). 102/5 §e (miseratione). 118/77, 156; 144/9 ~e (§es). 24/6; 50/3 §a (§um).

mildsian *wv* pity. **VP** 58/6 ~as (miserearis). 36/21, 6 *etc* ~að (§etur). 101/15 ~iað (§ebuntur). 108/12 ~ie (§eatur). 4/2; 6/3 *etc* ~a (§ere!). 76/10 ~ian (§eri). 29/11; 102/13 ~iende is, § bið (§tus est). 101/14 to §iende (miserendi ejus).

gemildsian *wv* pity. **VP** 24/11; 101/14 ~as (propitiaberis; misereberis). 66/2 ~ie (misereatur). 64/4 gemilsas (propitiaberis). 66/2 § ie (misereatur).

mildsiend *sm* pitier. **VP** 85/15; 110/4; 111/4 mildsend (miserator). 102/8; 144/8 ~ (§).

cild *sn* child. **VP** 18/8 ~e (†parvulis). 114/6 ~(§os). 118/130 ~um (§is). 8/3; 63/8 ~a (§orum). **Ct** 42/6, 12 ~ *pl*, ~a.

cildclāðas Cp. **cilda-trog** Cp; †ciltrog Ld.

stēp-cild *sn* orphan. **VP** 67/6 ~a (orfanorum).

Cilde-bergas Ct.

monn-cwild *s(m)* destruction. **Mt** 50 ~.

cwildeflōd VP.

gildeð *prs* requites. **VP** 93/23; Hy 7/89 ~(reddet; §it).

ā-gildes *prs* requitest. **VP** 61/13 ~(reddes).

Gilding *s* Ct 32/2 *agellam quod nos nominamus* ~.

Itha-mār BH.

R·chchriðe *s* LV 133 ~.

mid-hriþer *s* diaphragm. **Cp** 1041 ~hridir (ilia).

liþ *sn* limb.

lioðuwāc Cp; unlidouuac Ep; unliuduuac Ep; unlioþuwac Cp; unlioþuwacnis Cp.

liþere *sf* sling. **Cp** 939 liðre (funda).

stæf-liþere *sf* staff-sling. **Ep** 136 staeblidrae (ballista); Ef steb§; Cp staefliðre.

liþeren *aj* leather. **Ep** 31 lidrinae (scorteas); Ef lidrinn·; Cp liþrine.

geswiþerian *wv* settle down, calm. **Ep** 207 †gesuidradrae [*first* e *from* i] (constipuisse); Ef gisuderadae [*sec.* d *from* t]; Cp gesuedrade. **Ef** 368 gesuedradum (exoleverunt); Cp gesueðradun.

smiðlic *aj* wrought. **Cp** 847 ~e (fabrile).

wið *prp* against, towards. **DA** 14 ~. 20 ~ungetionu ⁊ ðiofum. **Bd**[2] 38 ~(contra). **VP** 3/2 ~me (adversum). 12/5 ~him (adversus). 14/3 ~ðæm (§). 22/5 ~him (§) *etc.* 108/15 ~dryhtne (contra). **Ct** 20/12 ~. 23/14, 5 uuið. 28/20, 1; 41/26; 44/7; 48/6.

wið-ðan-ðe. **wiðufan.**

wið-. standan, §end. sprecende. cwedenis. uuitsetnis. curun. lædan, §nis. cēosan. sōc.

wiðer-. uuidirhlinian, wiðerbroca, §ian.

Uuithig-ford Ct.

fiðere *sn* wing. **Mt** 8 fiðra *gpl.* **VP** 17/11; 54/7; 103/3 fiðru (pinnas). 138/9 §min (§). 67/14 § (§ae). Hy 7/21 § (alas). 90/4 §um. 16/8; 35/8; 56/2; 60/5; 62/8 §a (alarum).

gefiðred *aj* winged. **VP** 77/27; 148/10 ~e (pinnata *pl*; pennatae *pl*).

friþ *sm* peace. **Ct** 42/7 to friðe.

Friðubald LV. **Friðuberct** LV; frioðoberht Gn; freoðu§ Ct. **Frioðogeard**, freoðo§ Ct. **Friðugeorn** LV. **Frioðugils**, friðu§ LV. **Friðhelm**, frith§ LV. **Friðhild** LV. **Friðumund**, friodo§ LV: freoðo§ Ct. **Freoðorne** Ct. **Freoðorēd** Ct. **Friðuric** LV; freðo§ Ct. **Friduuald** LK; friðuuald, frioðuuald LV;

frioðowald Gn. **Friðuuini**, friðuini, frioðuuini, frioduuini LV. **Frioðuulf**, friðuulf, friuðuulf LV; frioðulf Gn. **Frioðulfing** Gn.

Æþel-friþ *sm* BH 8, 36, 8 aedilfrid—aeðil§ I. 38 aedilfridi—aeð§ I. 50 aedilfrid—aeðilfrið I. 53 ædilfrid — aeðilfrið I — aedilfrid. LK 4 aedilfrid. LV 401 eðilfrith. Gn 29 aeðilferð. 79 eðilfrið. Ct 5/6 aedilfridi. 17/6 æðelfrið.

Æþel-friþing *sm* son of Æþelfriþ. Gn 79 eðilfriðing.

Beadu-friþ *sm* LV 188; 269; 346, 76; 403, 5, 24 badufrith. 97 beadu§. 92 beo§.

Bēd-friþ *sm* LV 203 beetfrið.

Beorht-friþ *sm* BH 380 berctfrid. LV 162, 8; 231, 5, 87; 305, 39, 45, 55, 95; 432 berctfrith. 321, 4; 458 §ferð.

Beorn-friþ *sm* LV 85, 182, 91; 254, 8; 347; 407 ~th. 68 ~ð. Ct 40/12 ~ð. 25/13 ~ferð. 36/9 (biorn)-fer(ð). 31/6 biarnfreð.

Bil-friþ *sm* LV 54; 202, 52, 61, 6; 345 ~th.

Bōt-friþ *sm* LV 436 ~th.

Burg-friþ *sm* LV 119, 20 ~ð. 267; 353 ~th.

Cēol-friþ *sm* BH 331 ~d. 291 ~do *d.* LV 58 ~ð. 94; 187; 343 ~th. 302 ..lfrith.

Cœ̄n-friþ *sm* Ct 33/9 coenferð.

Cūþ-friþ *sm* LV 69; 176; 350, 63 cuthfrith. 112 §ð. Gn 39 cuðfrið. Ct 11/4 cuutfert.

Cyne-friþ *sm* BH 295 cynifrid. LV 119 cynifrið. 135, 59, 60, 74; 223, 54, 8, 73, 84, 8; 336, 77; 414 §th. 321; 435, 47, 73, 7, 80 §ferð. Ct 47/3; 48/10 ~ferð. 22/11; 23/12 §i.

Dæg-friþ *sm* LV 107 daegfrið. 264 §th.

Dene-friþ *sm* Gn 24 ~ð. Ct 15/5; 16/5 ~ferði.

Dōm-friþ *sm* LV 256 ~th.

Dycg-friþ *sm* LV 101, 24 ~th.

Ēad-friþ *sm* BH 92 ~d — eodfrid II. 115 ~d. LV 59, 83; 107, 32, 79, 87, 9, 94; 206, 56, 68, 78; 398; 425 eatfrith. 220; 440 eatferð. Gn 65 §. Ct 50/5 ~ferð. 55/9; 56/6 eat§.

Eald-friþ *sm* BH 333 aldfridi *lg.* LK 5 aldfrid. LV 3; 83 altfrith. Gn 107 aldfrið.

Ealh-friþ *sm* Rn 1/3 aft alcfriþu. BH 161 alchfrido — alh§ I, II. 180 alchfrido — alh§ I. 196 alc[h]§. 209 alchfridi *lg.* 209 alchfrid. 362 §i. LV 2 alchfrith. LN *ab* alchfriðo.

Ēan-friþ *sm* BH 130 ~d. 277 ~di *lg.* LV 91, 9; 126, 33; 236, 62, 94; 311, 63, 77, 85; 429 ~th. 435 ~ferð. Gn 29; 107 §. Ct 17/5 ~ð. 5/6 enfridi *lg.*

Ēan-friþing *sm* son of Ēanfriþ. Gn 107 ~ferðing.

Ecg-friþ *sm* Rn 1/7 ec*g*friþu [*case*?]. BH 219 ~do *ld* — ecfrido I. 233 ~dum — ec§ I. 234 ~di *lg* — ec§ I. 270 ~di *lg* — ęg§ — ec[g]§. LK 5 ~d. 8 ~di *lg.* LV 2; 221 ~th. Gn 55 ~do *ld.* 79; 100 ~ð. Ct 13/5; 15/3; 16/3; 30/14; 44/4; 50/5 ~ferð.

Gǣr-friþ *sm* LV 478 gerferð.

Gār-friþ *sm* LV 119 ~ð. 222 ~th.

Gūþ-friþ *sm* BH 332 gudfrid — gut[h]§ — gyð§. LV 101 guthfrith.

Hēah-friþ *sm* Ct 33/21; 51/11; 59/7 ~ferð. 49/11 haeh§.

Heaþu-friþ *sm* LV 139 heaðufrith. 240 heaðfrith. 376 haðuferth. 437 heaðu§.

Here-friþ *sm* LV 52 ~d. 59; 160, 76; 202; 397; 414 ~th. 456 ~ferð. Gn 22 *herefrið.* Ct 31/8, 10; 38/20 ~freð.

..efreðingdenn Ct. herefreðinglond (hę§) Ct.

Hilde-friþ *sm* LV 197; 215 hildifrith.

Hlēo-friþ *sm* LV 409 ~th.

Hrōþ-friþ *sm* LV 81 hroðfrith.

Hūn-friþ *sm* LV 138; 369 ~th. 154 ~ð. 469 ~ferd. Gn 21 ~ð. Ct 28/18; 30/18 ~freð. 35/13; 58/19 ~ferð. 33/15 ~frið.

Hyge-friþ *sm* LV 156; 235, 55, 7; 434 hygfrith. 312; 442, 64 hygferth.

Hygereðing-tun Ct.

In-friþ *sm* **LV** 252 ~th.

Land-friþ *sm* **LV** 101; 255 londfrith. 130 §ð.

Lēo-frith *sm* **LV**. 227 ~.

Lēod-friþ *sm* **LV** 172 liutfrith. 414, 20 liod§.

Mǣg-friþ *sm* **LV** 268 meifrith.

Mægen-friþ *sm* **LV** 13 ~th.

Nōþ-friþing *sm* son of Nōþfriþ. **Ct** 25/3 *in loca qui dicitur* noðfreðing.

Ōs-friþ *sm* **BH** 92; 115 ~d. 96, 119 ~di *lg.* **LV** 12 ~th. **Ct** 4/4 ~di *lg.*

Rǣd-friþ *sm* **BH** 237 raedfridum — § — § — §.

Sǣ-friþ *sm* **Ct** 30/17; 31/7; 38/17 sefreð. 45/59 sæ§.

Sele-friþ *sm* **SG** 23 ~ferð.

Sele-friþing *sm* son of Selefriþ. **SG** 22 ~ferðing.

Sige-friþ *sm* **LV** 234 sigfrith. 452 sigferð. **SG** 23 sigeferð. **Ct** 30/17; 31/8; 38/18, 8 ~freð. 31/9 ~fred. 40/14 sifreð. 45/57 sigfreð.

Sige-friþing *sm* son of Sigefriþ. **SG** 22 ~ferðing.

Tāt-friþ *sm* **BH** 308 ~d — ~ð I. **LV** 216; 338, 46; 432 ~th.

Tīd-friþ *sm* **Rn** 6 ~firþ. **LV** 123; 350, 79 titfrith. 330 ~ferð. 463 ~ferd. **Gn** 30, 63 ~ferð. **Ct** 19/5; 33/16 ~ð. 46/5 ~ðus. 49/8 ~ði *lg.* 12/4; 34/6 ~ferð.

Til-friþ *sm* **LV** 4; 53; 86; 221, 54, 90; 362, 90; 433 ~th. 122, 2 ~ð. 440 ~ferð.

Torht-friþ *sm* **LV** 252 torchtfrith. 387 torct§.

Tūn-friþ *sm* **LV** 206, 16 ~th.

þing-friþ *sm* **LV** 106 ðingfrith. **Gn** 100 ðincfrið. **Ct** 33/9 ðingcferð.

þing-friþing *sm* son of þingfriþ. **Gn** 100 ðincfri[ði]ing.

Wǣr-friþ *sm* **Ct** 32/3 †wer[f]eðes. 33/11 węrferð.

Weald-friþ *sm* **LV** 211 ualdfrith.

Wern-friþ *sm* **LV** 9 uernfrith. 365 ueren§.

Wīg-friþ *sm* **LV** 81; 230; 300, 65, 90 uigfrith. 102; 202, 5 uic§. 459 uigferð. **Ct** 33/4 wigferð.

Wiht-friþ *sm* **LV** 205, 72; 348 uictfrith.

Wil-friþ *sm* **BH** 127 uilfrid. 160 §o *ld.* 209 §um. **LV** 66; 111, 65, 98; 242, 51, 98, 9; 336, 50, 73 uilfrith. 375 §frið. 70; 465 §ferð. **Gn** 36 ~fridum. 37 uuilfridus. 46 uuilfrið. 54 uil§. 55 uilfrido *ld.* 57 .ilfrið. 60 uil§. **Ct** 1/6 uuilfridus. 9/5 §. 17/4 willfredi. 58/16 willferð.

Wine-friþ *sm* **LV** 361 uinifrith.

Wulf-friþ *sm* **Ct** 32/6 uulffreð.

Wyn-friþ *sm* **BH** 208 uynfridum. 228 §o *ld* — uin§ — uyn§. 246 uynfridum — uym§. 250 uynfrid —uuin§. 255 uynfrid—uym§. **LV** 261, 95; 350 uynfrith. **Gn** 34 ~ð.

niþer *av* down.

niþerra *aj cp* lower. **VP** 62/10; 85/13; 87/7 nioðerran (inferiora, §i; §i). 138/15 §um (§ibus).

niðerlic *aj* low. **Bd**[2] 18 niðirlices (ex infima). **VH** 12/6 ða ~an (ima).

niðerian *wv* condemn. **VP** 93/21 ~iað (condemnabunt).

geniðerian *wv* condemn. **VP** 36/33 geniderað (damnabit). 108/7 ~ad (condemnatus).

cwiþa *sm* womb. **Ep** 661 quiða (matrix); **Cp** §.

cwiþeþ *prs* says. **VP** 11/6; 65/4; 109/1 *etc* cwið (dicit; §at; dixit). 57/12 †cweð (dicet).

bið *vb* is. **Cp** 1555 ~slaegen (percellitur). **Mt** 39 ~. **VP** 9/17; 13/3; 38/6 *etc* ~(est). 33/10 wonu~ (deest). 9/19; 32/16, 17 *etc* ~(erit). 22/1 wonu~ (deerit). 77/38; 102/3 ~(fit). 9/23 ~inæled (incenditur), 24, 5 ~hered, ~bledsad (laudatur, benedicitur) *etc.* 60/3 §generwed (anxiaretur). 14/5 ne bið he onstyred (non commovebitur); 20/2; 32/21 ~geblissad (laetabitur) *etc.* 14/4 ~gelaeded (deductus est). 48/17 *etc* geworden~ (factus fuerit). 61/6 underðioded bid (subdita erit). 34/28 ~smegende (meditabitur). 102/13 mildsiende ~ (misertus est). 32/16 †bi gehęled (salvabitur). Ct 41/39, 40, 60 ~.

bist *vb* art. LP 10 bistu. VP 9/35; 17/26; 30/4 *etc* ~(eris). 17/27, 7 upahefen ðu ~, ðu ~ forcerred (electus eris, subverteris). 36/3 ~foeded (pasceris). 64/9 ~gelustfullad (delectaveris). 138/8 ðu ~et (ades). Hy 9/12 ~geced (vocaveris). 17/26 ðu bis (eris).

cyne-wiþþe *sf* diadem. Ep 877 cyniuuithan (ridimiculae). Ef §; Cp cynewiððan.

siþþan *av, cj* since. VP 75/8 nu seoðan (ex tunc). Ct 38/4; 39/7 siððan. 41/6, 23 sioððan.

is *vb* is. Cp 1398 ne huru is (numquid). 1532 aðroten is (perpessum est). Rn 7 ~. DA 2 ~. Mt 13 ~. VP 3/9; 5/10, 1 *etc* ~(est). 37/4; 141/5 ne is (non§; nec§). 4/7; 6/4 *etc* getacnad is; gedroefed is (signatum§; turbata§). 9/32 *etc* ofergeotul is (oblitus§). 11/3; 29/11 *etc* spreocende§; mildsiende§ (locutus§; misertus§). Ct 29/17; 37/45; 38/1; 39/11; 41/4, 8, 59, 66; 42/1, 4, 18, 20; 45/4, 5; 47/12 ~. 41/1 ís.

nis *vb* is not. VP 3/3; 5/10; 6/6 *etc* ~. 14/3 ~(non egit). Ct 38/11 ~.

his his. Rn 2/17 h(is). CH 2 ~. BDS 3, 4 ~. Rd 2 ~. LP 1, 12 ~. CA 9, 15 ~. Mt 24 *etc* ~. SG 2, 7 *etc* ~. VP 2/5, 5, 6; 17/51 *etc* ~(suā, suo, ejus; ipsius). 13/1 in ~heortan (in corde). Hy 1/10 ~agnum (ipsius). Ct 28/19; 34/8 *etc*; 38/3 *etc*; 39/7 *etc*; 40/22; 41/5 *etc*; 44/6 *etc*; 45/2 *etc*; 48/4 *etc* ~.

ā-ris- *prt* arose. VP 26/12; 53/5; 85/14 areosun (insurrexerunt). 19/9 aresun (resurreximus).

hrisian *wv* shake. Ep 434 risaendi (fibrans); Ef †ripendi; Cp risende. VP 21/8; 108/25 ~edon (moverunt).

hrisel *s* shuttle. Ep 851 ~il (radium); Ef, Cp hrisl. Cp 713 hrisle (ebredio). Rd 7 ~il.

lisit *prs* gathers. Cp 1200 ~(legit, collegit).

ðis *prn* this. Rn 1/2; 7/1 ~. DA 13, 4, 5 ~. VP 7/4; 23/6; 26/3 *etc* ~(istud; haec; hoc). Ct 23/14, 6; 24/8; 27/7; 28/18, 25; 37/16; 38/1; 39/1, 11, 3; 40/9, 9 *etc*; 41/47 *etc*; 45/41; 47/12 ~. 30/20; 34/17; 37/45; 38/15 þis. 41/65; 42/23, 4, 4, 5 ðiss.

ðisum *d. sg and pl.* VP 7/8; 9/16; 15/9 *etc* ðissum (hanc; isto; hoc). 17/18; 27/3; 33/19 § (his). 30/24 †ðeossu. Ct 45/1, 51 ðissum, þissum *sg.* 40/21 ðisem *sg.* 41/66 ðissem *sg.*

ðises *g.* VP 71/4 ðisses (hujus). Ct 34/19 þisses. 39/13 ðisses.

ðisne *a. m.* VP 74/8, 8; 79/15 *etc* ðeosne (hunc, §; istam). Ct 44/6 ~.

ðisse *d. and g. f.* CA 14 ðeosse *d.* VP 11/8; 30/5; 94/10 ~(hac; isto; huic). 73/18 ~(hujus). Ct 48/17 ~ *d.* 45/54 ðeosse *g.*

ðissa *g pl* Ct 42/18 ~. 24/8 ðeassa.

Uuis-lēag Ct.

cisir-bēam Ep; cy§ Ef; ciser§ Cp.

cisel *s* gravel. Ep 461 cisil (glarea); Ef cisal.

cisilstān Cp.

pise *sf* pea. Cp 1208 piose (lenticula). 1586 §an (pisum). 1867 ~an hosa (siliqua).

ā-bisgian *wv* occupy. VP 94/2 ~ien (praeoccupemus).

Bisi *sm* BH 248, 51 ~. Gn 27 ~.

geWisse *pl* BH 70 geuissorum. 138 *gens occidentalium saxonum qui antiquitus* geuissæ *vocabantur* — geuisse — §.

gewisslice *av* certainly. VP 50/18; 54/13, 3; 57/1, 12, 2 gewislice (utique).

miss-

misbyrd Ep; Ef, Cp §. **misthāgch** Cp. **misfoedan** VP.

missenlicnis *sf* variety. VP 44/10, 5 misenlicnisse (varietate).

Cissa *sm* LV 176 ~.

Cisseðe-beorg Ct.

bliss *sf* joy. VP 29/6; 96/11 blis (laetitia). 4/7; 15/11; 44/8 *etc* ~e (§iam; §iā, §iae *g*). 136/6 ~e mine (†§iae *g*).

blissian *wv* rejoice, gladden. VP

13/7 ~að (laetetur). 34/26; 47/12; 5/12 *etc* ~iað, ~ie, ~ien (gratulantur; laetetur; §entur). 18/9; 112/9; 125/3 ~iende (laetificantes; laetantem; §antes). 67/18; 86/7 ~iendra (§antium). 105/5 to ~iende (ad laetandum). 106/30 ~ende werun (§ati sunt). 149/2 †blisse (§etur). 30/8 blisie (laetabor). 31/11 §iað.

geblissian *wv* gladden. **VP** 20/7 ~as (laetificabis). 42/4 *etc* ~að (§at). 85/4 ~a (§a!). 88/43 ~ades (§asti). 9/3; 20/2 *etc* biom ~ad; bið§ (laetabor, §abitur). 59/8 biom ~að. 19/6; 34/15; 89/14 *etc* bioð ~ade; werun§; §sind (§abimur; §ati sunt; delectati sumus). 93/19 geblisadon (laetificaverunt).

bismer *s* contumely, insult, contempt. **VP** 88/35 do to ~e (faciam irrita).

bismerian *wv* insult, deride. **Rn** 2/8 bismærædu *prt pl.* **VH** 7/44 ~iu (irritabo). 58/9 ~as (deridebis). 2/4; 9/25; 36/13 ~að (inridebit; irritavit; inridebit). 73/10 ~ad (inritat). 24/3 ~iað (inrideant). 34/19, 24; 37/17 ~ien (insultent). 34/16 ~adon (diriserunt). 105/7, 16, 29, 32 ~adun (inritaverunt). 79/7; 106/11 ~edun (deriserunt; inritaverunt). 103/26 to ~enne (ad inludendum). 9/34 bismirað (irritavit). 104/23 bismarade (†intravit).

bismerung *sf* derision, contempt. **VP** 34/16; 43/14; 78/4 ~e (derisu).

bismernis *sf* contumely. **VP** 37/8 ~sum (inlusionibus).

risc *sf* rush. **Cp** 1165 ~(juncus).

riscthȳfil Ep; Cp §; †ryc§ Ef.

ēo-risc *sf* reed, flag. **Ep** 795 ~(paperum); Ef, Cp §. 960 §; Ef §; Cp §, leber (scirpea).

Wen-risc *s* the river Windrush. **Ct** 14/3 *fluvii qui nuncupatur* uuen~. 4 *fluvius* uuęn~.

fisc *sm* fish. **Cp** 1596 ~(piscis). **VP** 8/9; 104/29 ~as (§es). **Ct** 37/20 ~es.

fiscflōdu Rn.

gron-uisc *sm* a fish. **Cp** 66 netl *vel* ~(acus).

gegiscan *wv* block up, close. **Ep** 693 gigiscdae (oppilavit); Ef †gescdae; Cp gegiscte (§, clausit); Ld †gigisdae.

disc *sm* dish. **Ep** 786 ~(patena); Ef, Cp §. Cp 852 ~(ferculum).

biscop *sm* bishop. **Mt** 11 ~epes. 13 ~ep. **VP** 98/6 ~um (sacerdotibus). 131/16; **Hy** 8/17 ~as (§otes). **Ct** 34/20; 47/15 ~. 58/23 ~es. 28/9 ~epes land (*may be proper name in these four cases*).

biscopes-wīc Ct. biscopuuyrt Ep; Ef, Cp §.

Biscop *sm* **BH** 291 ~o. 362 ~. **LV** 78 ~us. 102, 7 ~.

Biscoping *sm* son of B. **LV** 107 ~.

ærce-biscop *sm* archbishop. **Ct** 40/2 ~es. 41/47 ~. 38/15 ercebisc'. 40/11 §. 34/9 arce ~e. 23/14 §biscep. 34/13 archi~. 45/55 ar' bisc'.

biscophād *sm* episcopate. **VP** 108/8 ~(episcopatum).

ǣ-rist *sf* resurrection. **VP** 138/2 ereste (resurrectionem).

þistel *sm* thistle. **Ef** 271 § (carduus); Cp ~.

þisteltuige Cp; †distyltige Ld.

þū-þistel *sm* sow-thistle. **Ep** 601 ~il (lactuca); Ef †popistil; Cp þuðistel.

wist *sf* banquet, delicacy. **VP** 138/11 ~um (deliciis).

nēa-wist *sf* nearness, vicinity. **VP** 21/12; 94/10 on neoweste (proxima; §us). **Hy** 6/24 in §ðinre (†comminatione).

wode-wistle *sf* hemlock. **Ep** 248 uuodaeuistlae (cicuta); Ef uuodeuuislae; Cp ~.

nistan *wv* build nest. **VP** 103/17 †~aðað (nidificabunt).

mistel *s* mistletoe. **Ep** 1083 ~il (viscus); Cp ~.

cisten-bēam Cp; †cistim~ Ef.

gistran *av* yesterday. **VP** 89/4 deg geostran (dies hesterna).

næs-gristle *sf* nose-gristle. **Ep** 174 naesgristlae (cartilaga); Ef §; Cp §e. **Lr** 36 ~an (internasso). 46 ~an (cartilagini).

candel-twist *s* pair of snuffers. Ef 382 †~thuist (emunctoria); Cp ~tuist.

wlisp *aj* lisping. Cp 271 uulisp (balbus).

stom-wlisp *aj* stuttering. Cp 277 ~(balbutus).

Ibe *sm* Ct 9/6 ~.

lifer *sf* liver. Ep 1057 libr (vicatum); Ef, Cp §. Ef 1128 len libre da (reniculus).

librlaeppan Ep; Ef, Cp §.

Lifna *sm* LV 207 ~.

Hlif-gesella Ct.

sife *s*(*n*) sieve. Cp 597 sibi (crebrum).

sifeþa *sm* siftings. Ep 428 siuida (furfures); Ef §; Cp sifiðan. Cp 216 sibaed (arbatae).

scrif- *prt* decreed. Ep 724 scribun (promulgarunt); Ef, Cp §. Cp 658 scriben (decerni).

for-scrifen *prt ptc* decreed. Ep 52 faerscribaen (addictus); Ef §scrifen; Cp ~.

Wifeles-berg Ct.

wifel *sm* weevil, beetle. Ef 310 uuibil (cantarus); Cp wibil. Cp 1498 wibl (panpila).

hnifol *s* forehead. Lr 28 h[n]eofulan (fronti).

clif *sn* cliff. VP 113/8 ~(rupem). 135/17 ~es (§is).

clifhlēp Cp.

clifeht *aj* cleaving. Ep 166 clibecti (clibosum); Ef, Cp §.

gif *cj* if. DA 10, 2 ~. Mt 50 ~. VP 7/4, 4, 5; 12/5 *etc* ~(si). Ct 23/15; 34/11, 2, 9; 37/19, 9; 38/3, 9; 41/4, 7, 14 *etc*; 45/11, 3, 5 *etc*; 48/18 ~. 38/8 gib.

for-gifeð *prs* grants. Ct 41/69 ~.

of-gifeð *prs* gives up, deserts. Cp 631 obgibeht (destituit).

gifeðe *aj* granted. Ct 41/8, 40 ~.

ā-drif- *prt* drove away. VP 87/6 ~ene sind (expulsi sunt).

onweg-ādrif- drove away. VP 41/10; 42/2; 43/3 *etc* ~e (reppulisti; §; expulisti). 35/13; 48/15 ~ene sind (expulsi sunt).

rift *s* veil, cloak, covering. Ep 801 ~(palla); Ef †ritf; Cp ~. Cp 1187 ~(laena). VP 103/6 ~(pallium)

bān-rift *s* leggings. Ep 1031 baan~ (tibialis); Ef §ryft; Cp †§rist.

cnēo-rift *s* napkin. Cp 21 ~ribt (mappa).

wāg-rift *s* curtain. Cp 624 ~ryft (curtina). VH 13/13 ~(velum . . templi).

rifter *sm* reaping-hook. Ep 430 sigdi riftr (falces; Ef §; Cp siðe riftras.

siftan *wv* sift. Ep 213 ~it (crebrat); Ef ~id; Cp ~ið.

swift *aj* swift. Cp 128 ~(alacer).

nift *sf* niece. Ep 734 ~(privigna, filia sororis); Ef, Cp, Ld §.

Sueord-hlincas *pl.* Ct 49/3; 52/4 ~. 15 ~um.

geswinc *sn* toil, affliction. VP 21/12 ~(tribulatio). 17/19 ~es (§ionis) *etc.* 80/8 *etc* ~e (§ione). 117/5 geswi[n]ce.

gescincio *spl* Cp 816 ~(exugia).

stincan *sv* smell. Cp 895 ~endi (flagrans). VP 134/17 ~ad (odorabunt).

sprincel *s* basket. Cp 875 sprinclum (fiscillis).

Uinc-ðrȳð LV.

læpe-wince *sf* lapwing. Ef 264 laepaeuincæ (cucuzata); Cp lepeuuince; Ld †laepiumcę.

finc *sm* finch. Ep 423 ~(fringella); Ef, Cp §; Ld †umc.

reagu-finc *sm* finch. Cp 283 ~(bariulus).

Wincel-cumb Ct.

drincan *sv* drink. VP 49/13 dri[n]co (potabo). 74/9 ~að (bibent). Hy 7/28 ~eð (§it). Hy 11/11 ~en (§amus).

Ing-uald BH; incwald Gn.

Ingi-brand Gn. §ing Gn.

Ingu-burg LV.

hring *sm* ring. Ep 410 hringiae (fibula); Ef ~ae; Cp ~e.

hringfaag Ep; Cp §; Ef †hrnig§, †hrinfag.

ēag-hring *sm* eye-ring. Lr 37 eg~um (rotis).

gyrdels-hring *sm* buckle. Ep

582 ~islrhingae (legula); Ef ~ils-hringe; Cp §. Cp 1226 § (lingula).

ymb-hringend *sm* surrounder. Ep 929 ~endum (stipatoribus); Cp §; Ef ~dringendum.

þing *sn* thing. Ep 709 oeghuuelci ðinga (omni moda); Ef §hadga; Cp oeghwelce ðinga. 845 aengi þinga; Ef §dinga; Cp aenge þinga. Ct 41/25 ðing. 37/15 ðas§ *pl.* 42/8; 45/10 §um.

Đingfrith LV; ðincfrið, §ing Gn; ðingcferð Ct. **þincggewrit** Ct.

• **geðinge** *sn* agreement. Cp 189 gethingio (aparitio). VP 48/8 ~(placationem). Ct 38/1 ~. 39/1; 41/71 ~a *pl.* 23/14 ~eo. 58/24 geðincgo.

ðingian *wv* intercede. LP 13 ðec fore ~iað.

geðingian *wv* intercede, agree. Cp 1522 ~adon (paciscitur).

þingung *sf* intercession. Ep 532 ~ae (interventu); Ef †ingungae; Cp ~e. LP 5 ðorh hiora ðingunge.

þingere *sm* pleader, advocate. Cp 89 ~(advocatus); Ld dingere (§ *etc*).

?**ymb-þringend** *sm* thronger round, *see under* ymbhringend.

eofor-þring *s* boar-throng, the constellation Orion. Cp 1464 ebur-ðring (orion); Ld †eburdnung. Ld 47 ebirdhring (§a).

Đingu *sf* LV 23 ~.

singan *sv* sing. LP 6, 9 sing! DA 14 sinc! VP 7/18 *etc* ~u (psallam). 29/13 ~e (cantet). 65/4 *etc* ~eð (psallat). 80/4 *etc* ~að (canite). 95/1; Hy 2/8 ~ad (cantate). 70/8 *etc* ~(§are). Hy 12/6 ~ende (canentes). 67/26 ~endum (psallentibus).

gesingan *sv* sing. Ct 37/35, 8 ~e.

singendlic *aj* singable. VP 118/54 ~ (cantabiles).

swinge *sf* stroke. VP 88/33 ~um (verberibus).

swinglung *sf* giddiness. Cp 2110 suinglunge (vertiginem).

ā-springan *sv* fail. Ef 334 ~endi (defectura); Cp §. VP 70/9 ~eð (defecerit). 17/38; 33/11 *etc.* ~að (deficiant; §ient). 67/3 *etc* ~en (§iant). 36/20 ~ende (§ientes).

āspringung *sf* failing. VP 141/4 ~e (deficiendo).

finger *sf* finger. VP 8/4 fingra (digitorum). 143/1; Hy 1/3 §as.

fingirdoccuna Ef; fingrdoccana Cp.

for-clingan *sv* shrink, wither. Cp 1744 ~endu (rigentia).

intinga *sm* cause. Cp 2115 uuordes ~(verbi gratia). VP 3/8; 72/13 ~an (causā). 9/5 § minne *etc* (§am). 73/22 § ðinne.

bringan *sv* bring.

gebrengan *wv* Ct 45/12 ~e.

forð-bringan *wv* bring forth. VH 11/1 ~ende (praeferens).

tō-bringan *wv* bring to. VP 28/1, 1, 2, 2; 95/7, 7, 8 ~að (afferte). Hy 6/35 ~eð (adferet).

in *prp* in. Ep 530, 50 ~; Ef, Cp ~. Cp 309, 1081, 1705, 1136, 1148 ~. Bl 19 ~. Rn 3/2 ~romæcæstri. BH 182; 210, 59; 334, 61, 7 ~. Bd[2] 39 in siðas (exitus). CA 7 ~. 10 in. DA 18 ~. Mt 13, 4, 7 *etc* ~. VP 2/4, 5, 5, 13 *etc* ~(in). Ct 3/3, 3, 4 *etc*; 44/7; 45/31, 2, 41 *etc*; 48/2, 2, 5 ~. *In* Ct 11/1, 3; 47/1, 1; 55/6 ~; 55/6 †iu *it is doubtful whether the* in *is English or Latin.*

in-, bærnis. tinga. uuerpan [*under* eo]. heldan. drencan. wendan. bryrdan. ǣlan. maethle. lihtan, §nis [*under* ē]. lēgan.

In-frith LV. **Ingeld** LV; ingild LV, SG, Ct; §ing SG. **Inuald** LV. **In-wines-burg** Ct.

Ini *sm* BH 283, 328 ~. LV 99 ~.

hine *prn acc* him. Rn 2/1, 16 hinæ. Mt 17, 22 *etc* ~. VP 2/13; 8/5, 6, 6, 7 *etc.* ~. Ct 45/18, 50 ~.

hiniongae BDS.

gerinen *aj* (*ptc*) diligent. Cp 24 ~(navum).

line-tuige Cp; †linaethuigae Ef; ~tuigle Cp.

on-hlinian *wv* lean on. Cp 1137 onhlingu [u *over* o] (innitor).

wiþer-hlinian *wv* lean against.

Ep 537 uuidirhliniendae (innitentes); Ef ✝~linienti; Cp wiðerhlingende.

sin-.

sinfullae Ep; § Ef; §e Cp; ✝fullae Ld. sinuurbul Ep; ✝ §uulfur Ef; siunhuurful Cp. sionuualt Cp.

spinel *s(f)* spindle. **Ep** 967 ~il (stilium *vel* fusa); Ef §; Cp ~. Cp 933 ~ (fusum). 1377 ~il (nitorium).

Uin-uaed BH.

Uuina *sm.* Ct 24/6 ~.

dæg-wine *s* daily expenses. **Cp** 806 daeguuini (expensa).

wine *sm* friend.

Uinibald LV. Uiniberct LV. Uinifrith LV. Uinilāc LV.

Wine *sm* **BH** 144 uini — uuini I — uuine. 146 uini — § I — uine [e *from* i]. 219 uini — uu§ I. 219 uine *d* — uu§ I. **LV** 461, 73 uini. **Gn** 17 *uuine*. **Ct** 45/59 ~.

Ælf-wine *sm* **BH** 297 aelfuini— aelb § — aelfuine — aelbuini. 377 ælfuini — aelfwine I. **LK** 8 ælfuini. **LV** 2; 144 aelfuini. 213 ael[f]§.

Æsc-wine *sm* **SG** 14 ~.

Æsc-wining *sm* son of Æscwine. **SG** 14 ~.

Æþ-wine *sm* **LV** 52; 175 aethuini. 162; 279 aeð§.

Æþel-wine *sm* **BH** 157 aediluini *g* — aeð§ I. 164 ediluinum — aeðiluuinum I. 214 ediluini—aeðiluini I. **LV** 121, 54; 219, 45, 53, 8, 72, 9; 304, 44, 80, 9; 449, 79 eðiluini. 313 aeðil§. **Gn** 43 aeðeluine.

Beadu-wine *sm* **BH** 252 baduuini — baduini I. **LV** 183; 215, 73, 7, 86, 90; 307, 87; 420, 9, 62 baduuini. 272; 380 baduini. 111 beoduuini. **Gn** 28 beadwine.

Bēag-wine *sm* **LV** 216; 300, 69, 70 beguini.

Beald-wine *sm* **LV** 64; 173; 237; 309; 451 balduini. **Ct** 3/8 baldwines healh.

Bēd-wine *sm* **LV** 263 beeduini. 363 bed§.

Beorht-wine *sm* **LV** 71, 84 berchtuini. 123, 4, 80, 5, 6; 222, 33, 7, 46, 57, 9, 75, 82, 4, 94; 300, 52, 68, 73, 83; 402, 5, 30 berct§. 328 berht§.

Beorn-wine *sm* **BH** 285 bernuini. **LV** 11, 74, 83; 141, 9, 76, 80, 4, 7, 94; 234, 43, 70, 3; 360, 4, 8, 77, 86; 411, 9, 25, 66, 9 ~uini. 281 b·oru·ini. **Ct** 35/11 ~.

Bēt-wine *sm* **LV** 322, 34, 93 betuini.

Bōt-wine *sm* **LV** 65; 177; 360 ~uini. **Ct** 14/6 ~ uuine.

Bregu-wine *sm* **Gn** 3 breguinus.

Burg-wine *sm* **Ct** 32/2 ~es.

Cent-wine, *sm* **Gn** 104 ~.

Cent-wining *sm* son of Centwine. **Gn** 104 ~.

Cēol-wine *sm* **LV** 128, 79; 290; 300, 1 ~uini.

Clȳd-wine *sm* **LV** 219 ~uini.

Cūþ-wine *sm* **LV** 82; 238, 65, 80, 4, 93 cuthuini. 456 cuð§. **Gn** 29 cuðuine. 85 cud . . e. **SG** 5 cuð~.

Cūþ-wining *sm* son of Cūþwine. cuðuining **Gn** 85. **SG** 5 cuð~.

Dǣd-wine *sm* **LV** 354 deduini.

Dæg-wine *sm* **LV** 208 daeguini.

Dōm-wine *sm* **LV** 388 domuini.

Ēad-wine *sm* **LV** 115, 8, 32, 41, 91, 3; 242, 83, 4, 96; 308, 52, 69, 70, 5; 415, 22, 63 ~uini.

Eald-wine *sm* **BH** 157 alduini *g* —§I. 371 §o *d*. **LV** 4; 86; 148, 73, 96; 264, 8, 97; 306, 50, 8, 92; 441 alduini. **Gn** 38 §e.

Ealh-wine *sm* **LV** 75; 373 alchuini.

Ealu-wine *sm* **LV** 12, 82; 140 aluuini.

Ēan-wine *sm* **LV** 127, 37, 52; 218, 38, 49, 88, 91; 300, 0, 49, 60, 8, 84; 413, 5, 6, 60 ~uini. **Gn** 89 §e.

Ēan-wining *sm* son of Ēanwine. **Gn** 89 ~uining.

Eard-wine *sm* **LV** 213 arduini.

Ecg-wine *sm* **LV** 178; 367 ~uini. **Gn** 46 ~uuine.

Ed-wine *sm* **BH** 41 aeduini *g*— —eduni—eduini—§. 41 aeduini *n*— ediuini—eduuine—eduini. 42 aeduini *n* — ediuini — eduuine — eduini. 42 aeduini — eduini — eduuine—eduini. 43 aeduini *g*—eduini—eduuini. 44

aeduine *d*—eduine—eduuine—eduine. 62 aeduini *n*—eduuine I—eduine [*sec.* e *from* i]. 74 aeduino *d*—eduuine I—eduine. 77 aeduino—eduuino—eduino. 82 ęduino. 82 aed§. 93 aeduini *g*—eduine I—eduini. 119 æduini *g*. LK 4 aeduini. LV 2; 89; 443, 60 eduini. Gn 73 §e.

Eorp-wine *sm* LV 61 ~uini.

Ēostor-wine *sm* LV 78 aesturuini. 153 aeostor§. 191 eostur§.

Folc-wine *sm* LV 110; 337 ~uini. Ct 8/5 ~uuinis *g*.

• **Folcuuining-lond**, folcw§ Ct.

Frēo-wine *sm* LV 125, 88; 476 friouini.

Friþ-wine *sm* LV 68 frioduuini. 457, 9 frioðuuini. 113; 303 friðuuini. 355 friðuini.

Gǣr-wine *sm* LV 291 geruini.

Gef-wine *sm* LV 84; 405 ~uini.

God-wine *sm* BH 347 ~uine *d*—~uino I.

Gūþ-wine *sm* LV 303 (guð)-uini.

Heard-wine *sm* LV 111, 92; 224; 378 ~uini.

Heaþu-wine *sm* LV 138, 41; 272, 92; 302, 27, 61; 421, 55 haðu-uini. 441 haduuini.

Helm-wine *sm* LV 11, 86; 107; 235, 70; 327, 61, 77; 427, 32 ~uini.

Help-wine *sm* LV 243; 347, 54; 402, 14 ~uini.

Here-wine *sm* Gn 41 *hereuuine.*

Hild-wine *sm* LV 230, 97 ~uini.

Hlēo-wine *sm* LV 443 ~uini.

Hlēof-wine *sm* LV 323 ~uini.

Hrǣþ-wine *sm* LV 230 hroeð-uini.

Hrōþ-wine *sm* LV 165; 477 hroðuini.

Hūn-wine *sm* LV 67 ~uini.

Hyge-wine *sm* LV 116, 89, 92, 3; 210, 26, 69; 304, 49, 96; 452 hyguini. 478, 81 hygine.

In-wine *sm* Ct 14/3 ~s burg.

Lēod-wine *sm* LV 470 lioduini.

Lēof-wine *sm* LV 87; 113; 240, 71; 358; 415 ~uini.

Mǣg-wine *sm* LV 186; 202, 93 meguine. Ct 5/3 §uuines (§uines).

Ō-wine *sm* BH 244 ouini *twice*—ouuini I.

Ōs-wine *sm* Rn 10 onswini. BH 123 osuini *g*—osuuini I. 162; 202 osuini *n*.

Peoht-wine *sm* Gn 68 pehtuine.

Pleg-wine *sm* LV 189, 91; 261, 76; 351 ~uini.

Sǣ-wine *sm* LV 118, 45; 359, 68; 473 saeuini.

Seol-wine *sm* LV 305 seoluini.

Sige-wine *sm* LV 63, 78; 339, 48, 88 siguini.

Tand-wine *sm* LV 14 tonduini. 199 tand§.

Tāt-wine *sm* BH 370 ~uini. Gn 3 §us. LV 62, 70; 133, 6, 79, 80; 230, 42, 81; 358, 79 ~uini. Ct 6/2 ~uuinus.

Tīd-wine *sm* LV 117, 43, 3; 202, 92; 377, 8, 80, 4; 429, 51, 3 ~uini.

Til-wine *sm* LV 53; 104, 7, 14, 82; 239; 321; 414 ~uini.

Torht-wine *sm* LV 66; 153 torchtuini. 270 torct§.

Trum-wine *sm* BH 274 ~uini. 313 triumuini—trum§—trum§. 319 ~uine *d*.

fin *s* heap. Ef 1169 ~(cella lignaria). 1186 ~(lignarium, ligneum).

fina *sm* woodpecker. Ep 648 ~(marsopicus); Ef pina; Cp ~; Ld uinu. 808 ~ *vel* higrae (picus); Ef, Cp §. Cp 1938 ~(sturfus).

finugl *s* fennel. Ep 451 ~ (finiculus); Ef ~; Cp finulae.

cinu *sf* chink. Ld 117 ~um (rimis).

cineht *aj* chinky, cracked. Cp 1739 cionecti (rimosa).

ginian *wv* jawn, gape, make a noise. Ep 149 ~ath; Ef § (battat); Cp geonath; Ld ginat. Cp 947 gionat (garrit). Cp 1467 geongendi (oscitantes).

ginung *sf* roaring. Cp 268 genung (barritus).

ginnis *sf* gap, interval. Cp 1126 ~se(intercapidine).

grin *sn* snare. **VP** 9/16 †~ ðissum (laqueo).

inn *av* in. **Ct** 41/20 in. 41/26; 42/13~.

inn-. inngang, in§. ingangende. ineardian. infeallan. ingefeallan. insendan. ingehygd. ingā. ingǣst. ingecēgan. ingefēoll. ingēotan. innēode, in§.

innerra *aj cp* inner. **VP** 102/1; 108/18 ða ~an (interiora).

innan *av* within. **VP** 44/14 from ~ (ab intus).

binnan *prp* within. **VP** 38/4 ~(intra). **Ct** 41/32.

innoð *sm* inside, womb. **Rd** 2 ~aðae *d.* **VP** 21/11; 57/4; 70/6; 109/3; 138/13 ~e (utero). 50/12 ~um (visceribus). **Hy** 9/14 ~as (§a).

innelfe *spl* entrails. **Ep** 504 innifli (interamen); **Cp** §; **Ef** inifli.

rinnelle *sf* rivulet. **VP** 64/11 ~an (rivos).

linnan *sv* cease.

blinnan *sv* cease. **VP** 36/8 blin [*or* blinn] (desine!).

scinn *s* magic. **Cp** 1611 scin (portentum). 1831 ~um (scenis).

scinhīow VP. scinlāecean Ep; § Ef, Cp.

scinnere *sm* magician. **Ep** 952 ~as; **Ef** scineras; **Cp** ~as (scienices); **Ld** †scinnenas. **Cp** 746 ~as (emaones).

heago-spinn *sn* cheek. **Cp** 962 heagaspen (genas). **Lr** 34 ~um (§is).

winnan *sv* labour. **VP** 126/1 ~að (laborant).

gewinn *sn* labour. **VP** 9/28 *etc* gewin (labor). 9/35 *etc* § (§orem). 77/51 *etc* ~es (§is). 77/46; 104/44 *etc* gewin (§es). **Hy** 6/14 ~um.

Finn *sm* **Gn** 110 ~.

Finning *sm* son of Finn. **Gn** 110 ~.

cinne *s* chin. **Lr** 32 ~ (mento).

on-ginnan *sv* begin. **Cp** 1463 ~endi (or). **VP** 146/7 ~að (incipite).

tin *s* projection. **Ep** 1024 ~(tignum); **Ef**, **Cp** ~.

tinnan *wv* stretch. **Bl** 18 tinde bogan (tetendit).

getwinn *sm* twin. **Cp** 12 getuin (gemellus).

binn *sf* bin. **VP** 80/7; **Hy** 6/38 ~e (cofino; praesepio).

swinsung *sf* melody. **Ep** 643 suinsung (melodium); **Cp** §; **Ef** † ruinsung. **Cp** 195 suinsung (armonia).

sinu *sf* sinew. **Cp** 1375 sionu (nervus).

Inta *sm* **LV** 337~.

Winta *sm* **Gn** 109 u~.

Winting *sm* son of Winta. **Gn** 109 u~.

Wintan-cæster, uintancæstir, uinta§ **BH**; wintanæ *civitatis* **Ct**.

winter *sm* winter. **SG** 1 wint *gpl* 10, 0 wintra *gpl*. **Ct** 41/63 §es dæg.

winterburna Ct.

þri-wintre *aj* three year old. **Ep** 780 thriuuuintri steor (prifeta); **Ef** †triuumtri steur; **Cp** † ðriuuintra steor.

flint *sm* flint. **Ep** 805 ~ (petra focaria); **Ef**, **Cp** ~.

minte *sf* mint. **Cp** 23 ~ (menta).

Cinta-stiogole Ct.

tintregian *wv* torture. **Mt** 45 tintergedon.

sind *vb* are. **VP** 11/2; 13/1; 17/37 *etc* gewonade ~; gewordne ~; ne ~ geuntrumad (sunt). 37/17 *etc* spreocende sind (locuti sunt). 43/18, 21 *etc* ofergeotele we ne ~, §ulæ we ~ (obliti sumus). 18/4; 24/6 *etc* ~ (sunt *absolute*). 35/11 rehte ~on heortan (recto § corde). 45/7; 143/15 sin (sunt). **Ct** 23/14 sint.

sindon *vb* are. **DA** 7 ~. **VP** 3/2; 11/3 *etc* gemonigfaldade ~un; spreocende § (sunt). 9/21; 11/5 *etc* § (sunt *absolute*). 9/16 gefestnade sindon (sunt). **Ct** 45/54, 5 ~. 27/7; 39/1 ~an. 28/18, 25; 37/7 siondan. 45/12 seondan. 37/44 siondon.

hind-berię Ep; Ef, Cp §; † §brere Ef. hindcaelf Cp.

Rind-burna Ct.

lind *sf* lime-tree, linden. **Ep** 1004 ~ (tilia); **Ef**, **Cp**, **Ld** §. 1017 ~ *vel* baest (tilio); **Ef** §.

Lindis-farnensis, ~faronensis **BH**. lindisfarorum BH, Gn.

Lindesse *s* Lindsey. **BH** 5 *in provincia* lindissi — ~isi. 43 *in provincia* ~issi — ~isi — ~issi — §.

sinder *s* cinder. **Cp** 1808 ~(scoria).

ǣ-swind *aj* slothful. **Cp** 1092 esuind, asolcen (iners).

ā-swindan *wv* become weak, wear away. **VP** 38/12; 118/139 ~ (tabescere). 111/10 ~eð (§et). Hy 7/47 ~ende (§entes).

sprindel *s* tenterhook. **Ep** 1025 ~il (tenticum); Ef §; Cp ~el.

wind *sm* wind. **VP** 17/11; 103/3 ~a (ventorum). 17/43; 34/5; 82/14 ~es. 134/7 ~as.

windfona Cp.

ēastnorþ-wind *sm* north-east wind. **Ep** 162 ~(boreus). Ef eustnorduind; Cp ~norð~. Cp 460 eostnorð~ (chorus).

sūð-wind *sm* south wind. **Cp** 252 ~uuind (auster).

sūðan-wind *sm* south wind. **VP** 77/26 ~(austrum).

westnorð-wind *sm* north-west wind. **Ef** 311 †uuestnorduuid (circius); Cp ~.

westsūþ-wind *sm* south-west wind. **Ef** 118 ~ (affricus); Ef uestsuduuind; Cp ~suð~. 452 uuestsuduuind (faonius); Cp ~ suð~.

westansūðan-wind *sm* south-west wind. **VP** 77/26 ~(africum).

windwian *wv* fan. **VP** 43/6 ~ iað (ventilavimus). 76/7 ~ ade (§abam).

windan *sv* wind.

windeloccas Cp.

wind *s*. **Cp** 1841 uuind (sclabrum). **Bd**[2] 72 ~um (slabris).

ðearm-gewind *sn* peritoneum (?) **Lr** 61 ~ (jugulam).

gearn-winde *sf* yarn-winder. **Cp** 1735 ~uuinde (reponile). **Ef** 1111 †giindi (conductium).

wudu-winde *sf* woodbine. **Ef** 348 uuidouuindae (edera); Cp uudu ~. Ep 1059 †wiuwindae (volvola *etc*); Ef uuidubindae; Cp uuduuuinde. 1082 uuiduuuindae (viburna); Ef §bindae; Cp uuduuuinde.

windel *s*(*m*) basket. **Ep** 173 ~il (cartellus); Cp §; Ef † pindil.

Bede-winde *s*. **Ct** 3/2 ~. 4 in ~an. 12 ~an *a*.

on-findan *sv* find. **Cp** 661 ~o (depraehendo).

for-grindan *sv* grind down. **Cp** 563 ~et (commolitio).

tind *sm* projection, beak. **Ep** 873 ~um (rostris); Ef, Cp §. Cp 1753 ~as (§i).

tindiht *aj* jagged, beaked. **Ep** 868 ~icti (rostratum); Ef §; Cp ~ecte.

gebindan *sv* bind. **VP** 149/8 to ~enne (ad alligandos).

gebind *sn*. **Ld** 83 †ebind (tentigo, tenacitas ventris).

wudu-binde woodbine. *under* ~winde *and* ~bindle. **Cp** 18 uuidu~.

wudu-bindle *sf* woodbine. **Ep** 559 uuidubindlae (involuco); Ef † uuydublindæ; Cp uudubinde; Ld § bindlae.

blind *aj* blind **VP** 145/8 ~e (caecos).

stær-blind *aj* **Cp** 1802 stae[r] ~ (scotomaticus).

him *d. sg* him. **Rn** 2/17 ~. **BDS** 2 ~. **DA** 13 ~. **Mt** 19, 21 *etc* ~. **VP** 2/6, 11; 4/4 *etc* ~. **Ct** 28/23; 34/15; 38/13, 4; 40/21; 41/11, 3 *etc*; 45/24, 5 *etc*; 48/2, 3 *etc* ~.

him *d. pl* them. **VP** 2/5; 5/12; 17/8; 21/19 *etc* ~. **Ct** 37/33; 38/5; 41/19, 37; 42/8, 11 *etc* ~. 45/11 heom.

rima *sm* rim. **Cp** 601 ~o (crepido).

bord-rima *sm* rim. **Ld** 112 ~remum (rimis *etc*).

tōð-rima *sm* gum. **Lr** 39 ~reomum (gingis).

lim *sn* limb. **Mt** 19 ~o. **VH** 12/2 liomu (artūs).

limwœrig Rn.

Limin *sf* Limen. **Ct** 35/4, 5, 6; 37/15; 52/12 ~um.

Liminēa Ct.

Liming *s* Lyminge. **Ct** 19/8; 27/4; 41/20 ~e *d*. 19/9 ~ingge *d*.

Limingēa Ct.

simle *av* always. **Ct** 37/30; 40/8; 41/67 ~.

niman *sv* take. **Rd** 14 ni(mæn) *sbj pl*. **VP** 138/9 niomu (sumpsero). 136/9; 138/10 ~eð (tenebit) Hy 4/16 § (§eat). 80/3; 93/15; 139/12 niomað (sumite; tenent; capient).

102/18 neomendum (retinentibus). Ct 41/15 to niomanne.

geniman *sv* take. VP 49/16 ~es (adsumes). 81/2 geniomað (sumitis). Hy 13/5 genioman (adsumere).

dǣl-niman *sv* participate. LP 11 bistu daelniomende.

dǣl-nimend *sm* participator. VP 118/63 daelniomend (particeps).

dǣl-niomenis *sf* participation. VP 121/3 ~(participatio).

Nim-stān LV.

Imma *sm* BH 300 ~. LV 202 ~.

Immin *sm* BH 205 ~.

himming *s* boot. Cp 1557 ~(pero).

hlimman *sv* resound. Rd 6 ~ith.

þurh-swimman *sv* swim through. Cp 2058 ðorhsuimmað (tranant).

gimm *s*(*m*) gem. VP 118/127 gim (topazion *a*).

grimm *aj* fierce. Bd² 37 grimre (diri *g*).

dimmnis *sf* dimness. VP 17/10; 96/2 dimnis (caligo). Hy 12/9 §nes (§).

trims *sm* a coin. Ep 31 ~as (asses); Ef †trynsas; Cp trymsas. Ld 80 trymisas (solidos).

limpan *sv* belong. Ct 28/15; 30/7 ~að. 28/25 ~ð. 37/16, 21 ~eð.

for-gelimpan *sv* mishappen. Ct 34/20 ~e.

be-limpan *sv* belong. Ct 29/15 †~oð. 45/10 ~að.

gelimplic *aj* suitable. Cp 548 ~e daele (conpetentes portiunculas). VP 31/6 †geliplice; 144/15 ~e (opportuno).

gelimplicnis *sf* opportunity. VP 9/10 ~sum (opportunitatibus).

timpana *sm* drum. VP 80/3 ~an (tympanum *a*). 150/4 §(§o). 149/3 timp' (§o). 67/26 plægiendra ~an (tympanistriarum).

cimbal *s* cymbal. VP 150/5, 5 cymbalan, ci§ (cymbalis).

cimbing *s* joint. Ef 291 ~; Cp ~ (commisura).

timber *sn* timber, building. VP 101/8 timbre (aedificio). 128/6 §a (§iorum).

timbran *wv* build. VP 88/5 ~iu (aedificabo). 27/5 ~es. 101/17 ~eð. 126/1, 1 ~ie (§averit), ~iað. 77/69 ~ade. 128/3 §un (fabricaverunt). 146/2 ~iende (aedificans). 117/22 ~ende (§antes). 88/3; 121/3 ~ed. 68/36 bioð ~ede.

getimbran *wv* build. VP 31/8 ~u (instruam). 50/20 sien ~ed (aedificentur).

for-timbran *wv* VP 62/12 ~ed (obstructam).

ic *prn* I. Cp 526, 1568~. Rn 2/4, 5 *etc* ~. Rd 3 *etc* ~. Lr 74~. CA 3, 14~. DA 2~. Mt 37, 47~. VP 2/6, 6, 7, 7, 8 *etc* ~. Ct 23/16; 30/20; 37/1 *etc*; 39/6; 40/1 *etc*; 42/1 *etc*; 45/1 *etc*; 48/8~.

Icel *sm* Gn 93 ··il·

Icling *sm* son of I. Gn 93 ~.

Ricula *sf* BH 54 *sorore* ~.

-lic. gafol~. ælmes~. næht~. middæg~. fæder~. gehæpplic, §nis. ealdor~. smiþ~. niþer~. missen~nis. singend~. gelimp~. micel~. regn~. reht~. ungereorded~. heofon~ hergend~. reced~. unāsecgend~. lufiend~. onscuniend~. hund~. wundur~. cyn~. gemynde~. gecynde~. symbel~. hyht~. nytt~. morgen~. ār~. swācend~. ungehǣlend~. ungehǣled~. ēce~. gǣr~. unrehtwīs~. gelōmlicnis. Cwoemlicu.

-lice. wlanclicae. framlicae. swīþfram~. fracadlicae. ælmes~. dæghwām~. lætlicor. hræd~. earfeþ~. scearp~. manigfeald~. seofonfeald~. ānwil~. gewis~. noht~. micel~. wrixend~. witod~. sibsum~. wer~. reht~. georn~, §liocar. sweotol~. herwend~. fremsum~. egesful~. wuldur~. geþungen~. gesundful~· wundur~. synder~. genyht~. genyhtsum~. horsclicae. snotor~. fǣcen~. fǣr~. dēgul~. frēo~. getrēow~. swīþ~. wearnwīs~. īdel~. cūþ~. sōþ~. sōþfæst~. tōhlicae. ēaþmōd~. roeþe~.

beswic- *prt* deceived. VP 76/3 neam biswicen (deceptus). 106/40 bisweocun (seduxerunt).

ǣ-swic *s* VP 48/14; 49/20; 68/

23; 105/36; 118/165; 139/6 eswic (scandalum). 140/9 §um.

bisuic-falle Cp.

swician *wv* wander. Ep 932 suicudae (spatiaretur); Ef §; Cp suicade.

smicer *aj* delicate. Cp 738 smicre (elegans, loquax).

stician *wv* pierce. Bd² 23 bioð stiocode (jugulamur).

sticung *sf* stabbing. Bd 3 ~(jugulum).

stricel *s* wheel. Ep 994 stricilum (trocleis, rotis modicis); Ef, Cp §.

spic *s* bacon. Ct 39/5 speces. 40/6; 41/30, 61 ~es.

spriceð *prs* speaks. VP 2/5; 14/3 *etc* ~(loquitur). 36/30 ~ed.

on-wicun *prt* gave way, retreated. Cp 437 †onwicum (cessere).

wice *s*(*m*) wich-elm. Cp 368 uuice (cariscus).

wrices *prs* avengest. VP 50/6 ~(†vincas).

Niclas *sm* CA 1 ~.

micel *aj* great. Cp 691 suiðe ~(difinis. VP 18/12 edlean ~(retributio multa) 46/3 cyning ~(magnus). 30/20 ~mengu (§a) *etc*. 102/12 swe ~(quantum *av*.) 35/7 ~u niolnis. 85/13 ~u mildheortnis. 118/165 ~u sib. 28/3 weter ~(multas). 103/25 lytelu ⁊ micel (magna *pl*). 71/18; 135/4 wundur ~u(§a). 96/1 eolond ~u (multae) *etc*. 24/7; 34/26 *etc* miclan. 135/17; Hy 1/7 *etc* §e. 67/12 megene §e (multā). 73/14 §es. 76/20; 98/3 *etc* §um. 21/26; 34/18 *etc* ~re. 31/6; 92/4 ~ra. 20/6 ~ne. Ct 28/20 miclum. 37/5; ~re.

micellic *aj* great. VP 91/6; 103/24 hu ~e sind were ðin (quam magnificata sunt opera tua!)

micellice *av* greatly, grandly. VH 2/9 ~(magnifice).

micelnis *sf* greatness. VP 8/2; 67/35 ~(magnificentia) *etc*. 70/8 §se ðine (§iam) *etc*. 28/4 §se (§iam = §iā) *etc*. 78/11 efter §se (magnitudinem). 150/2 §se (§inis) *etc*. 70/19; 105/21 §se (magnalia *a*.)

miclian *wv* magnify. VP 68/31 ~iu (magnificabo). 49/15 ~as (§abis). Hy 10/1 ~að (§at). 11/5; 21/24; 33/4; 71/17 ~iað. 125/2, 3 ~ade (§avit). 34/27 sie ~ad (§etur).

gemiclian *wv* magnify. VP 4/4; 14/4 ~að (magnificavit, §at), 30/22 ~ade (mirificavit) 137/2 ~ades (magnificasti). 9/39 ~a (†§are). 17/51 ~iende (§ans). 39/17; 56/11; 69/5; 103/1; 107/5 ~ad. 19/6, 8 bioð ~ade.

cwic *aj* alive. VP 123/3 ~e (vivos). Ct 45/9 mid ~e ęrfe.

cuicbēam Ep, Cp. Cuichelm, BH, Gn; c[u]uic§, quic§ BH. Cui[c]uald LV.

gecwician *wv* create. VP 50/12 ~a (crea!). 32/9 ~ad werun. 101/19 bið §. 103/30 bioð §e.

cwice *sm* couch-grass. Ep 464 †quiquae [*first* q *over* c] (gramen); Cp quice; Ef quicae. 1088 quicae [q *over* c] (virecta); Ef †cuiq*ue*; Cp quicae.

ticia *s* tick (insect). Ef 1130 ticia (ricinus).

pic *sn* pitch. Ep 820 ~(pix); Ef, Cp ~.

gebriceð *prs* breaks. VP 28/5; 45/10; 57/7 ~(confringet). 2/9; 55/8 ~es.

ofer-blic- *s* surface. BD² 44 ~bliocan (superficiem).

liccian *wv* lick. VP 71/9 liciað (lingent).

Liccidfeld, licid§ liccid§, liccit§, licit§, lyccid§, lyccit§ BH; liccid§, licced§ Ct.

ðicce *aj* thick. Lr 3 ~(denso). VP 28/9 ða ~an (condensa). Hy 6/6 ~um (§o).

sciccing *s* cloak. Ep 245 scicing (cappa); Ef scinccing; Cp scicging.

clader-sticca *sm* rattle-stick. Ep 116 ~(anate); Cp §; Ef ~stecca [d *from* t].

Hwiccas *spl*. BH 49 huicciorum. Gn 45 §. Ct 13/1 §. 15/1; 16/1 huuicciorum. 51/2 hu[u]icciorum.

flicce *sn* flitch. Ep 774 ~i (perna); Ef, Cp, Ld §. 804 ~ii (§). Ct 37/18 tua ~a.

bliccettan *wv* glitter. VP 143/6 ~e (corusca !).

. **bliccetung** *sf* glittering. VP 76/19; 143/6 ~e (coruscationes).

gesihþ *prs* sees. VP 9/35; 36/34; 90/8 gesist (vides; §ebis). 10/8; 48/11, 1, 20; 57/11 *etc* gesiȣ (§it *etc*). 63/6 gesiþ. 111/8 gesieȣ (videat).

for-sihst *prs* despisest. VP 9/22 forsist (despicis).

gesihȣ *sf* sight. VP 5/9; 9/20 *etc* ~e ȣinre (conspectu). 88/20 gesihde (aspectu). 79/10; 140/2 §. 142/2 gesi[h]ȣe.

gefihȣ *prs* rejoices. VP 20/2 ~(exultabit). 15/9 gefiht (§avit). 12/6; 13/7; 34/9 *etc* gefiȣ.

Siox-slihtre Ct.

wrixendlice *av* turn about, one by one. VP 32/15 ~(singillatim).

wrixlan *wv* reciprocate. Cp 1728 wrixlindum (reciprocis). 1736 uurixlende (reciprocatu).

mixen *s* dunghill. Ld 40 mixin (ruder). 105 mixinnum (§ibus).

be-twix *prp* between. Ct 44/7 ~.

geriht *sn* direction. Ct 20/16 on geryhte, straight on.

†nihtebred Cp.

Siox-slihter *s*. Ct 29/9, 9 ~slihtre *d*.

stihtian *wv* dispose. VP 111/5 ~aȣ (disponet).

gestihtian *wv* dispose. VP 72/15; 83/6; 88/4; 104/9 ~ade (disposui *etc*). 72/18; 83/7 ~ades. 82/6 ~adun.

wiht *sf* creature.

Uictbald, uicht§ LV; uuiht§ Ct. **Uictberct** BH; uichtbercht LV. **Uuihtbrord** Ct; **Uichtburg** LV. **Uictfrith** LV. **Wiohtgār** Ct. **[U]uictgils**, uict§ BH; uihtgilsing Gn. **Uictgȳth** LV. **Uichthāeth**, uict§ LV. **Uicthelm** LV. **Uihthere** Ct. **Uiohthūn** Gn; uuiht§, wioht§, uuiohtun, Ct. **Uichtlāc** LV. **Uictrēd** uuicht§ BH; uicht§ LV; uiht§ Gn; uuiht§, uiht§, wiht§, uueoht§, wioht§, wiaht§, wichred Ct; uihtreding Gn.

ō-wiht *sf* anything. Ct 48/19 on ~e.

nō-wiht *sf* nothing, VP 33/10 ~wonu biȣ (nihil). 38/6 §. 75/6 § *a*. 58/9; 105/24 fore ~(pro nihilo). 88/23 § *adverbial*. 14/4; 57/8 *etc* to ~e (ad nihilum). 55/8; 63/9 fore ~e (pro nihilo). 59/14 to niwihte. 35/5; 42/1 noht (non).

nohtlice *av* badly. VP 36/8, 9 ~(nequiter).

Uict-uari BH.

ful-wiht [*under* u].

frihtrung *sf* divination. Ep 10 frictrung (ariolatus); Ef †frictung; Cp ~.

pliht *sm* danger. VP 114/3 ~as (pericula).

igel *s*(*m*) hedghog. Cp 765 iil (ericius). 1023 § (histrix). VP 103/18 igles [*from* iles] (irinacis).

higre *sf* heron. Ep 156 ~ae (berna); Ef ~ę; Cp ~ae. 808 ~ae *vel* fina (picus); Ef §; Cp ~e; Ld ~ę. Cp 476 ~ae (cicuanus). 2064 ~ae (traigis).

rignan *wv* rain. VP 10/7 rineȣ (pluet). 77/24, 7 §, rinde (§it).

ȣignen *sf* servant. Cp 1531~ (pedissequa).

sige *sm* victory.

Sigibēd Ct. **sigbēacn** Ep; Ef §; sigebecn Cp; sigbecn Rn. **Sigbald** LV; sigebald, §ing SG. **Sigberct** BH, LV; sigberht, sige§ SG; sig..berht Ct; sigeberhting, sigberhting SG. **Sigburg** LV. **sigefęston** Bd². **Sigfrith** §ferȣ LV; sigeferȣ SG; sigefreȣ, §fred, sefreȣ, si§ Ct. sigeferȣing SG. **Sigefugl** SG. **Sigegār**, §ing Gn. **Siggēot**, §ing Gn. **Sighāeth** LV. **Sighāeh** Gn. **Sighard** BH, LV; si(gehard) SG; sigiheardi Ct. sigeharding SG; sigheardingmēduue Ct. **Sighelm** LV. **Sigheri** BH; §e SG. sighering SG. **Siglāc** LV. **Sigmund** LV; sige§ SG, Ct; sigemunding SG. **Sigenōȣ**, sig§ Ct. **Sigrēd** LV, Ct; sige§ SG, Ct. **Sigrīc** LV; sige§ SG. sigerīcing SG. **Sigscēat** LV. **sigisītha** Pv. **Sigȣrȳȣ** LV. **Si-**

guaru LV. Siguald LV. Siguini LV. Siguulf LV, Ct.

Ælf-sig *sm* LV 9; 90; 417, 22, 61, 76 aelf~.

Ealh-sig *sm* LV 116; 212 aluch~. 428 alch~.

Ēan-sig *sm* LV 391 ~.

Beorht-sig *sm* LV 361 berct~. 467 bercht~. Ct 45/28 berhtsige *d.*

Hūn-sig *sm* LV 65; 179; 217 ~.

Tīd-sig *sm* LV 330 ~.

Torht-sig *sm* LV 170 torct~.

Wil-sig *sm* LV 424 u~.

Wulf-sig *sm* LV 55, 64, 7, 92; 126, 30, 56, 90, 4; 249; 306, 72, 4, 85, 93, 6, 7, 8; 477 uulfsig. 246 uul[f]sig. 96 uulsig.

Wyn-sige *sm* Ct 44/4 ~.

sigel *s* seal. Ep 134 ~il (bulla); Ef §; Cp sigl. 408 ~il (fibula); Ef §; Cp sigl. 882 ~il (sibba); Ef §; Cp sigl.

Sigel-hearwan VP.

geswigra *sm* cousin. Ep 214 gesuirgion (consubrinus); Ef gisuirgian; Cp gesuigran.

āstig- *prt* ascended. VP 75/7; 121/4 asteogun (ascenderunt).

ofdūne-stig- *prt* descended. VH 3/21 ~steogun (discendunt).

ūp-stige *sm* ascent. VP 83/6; 103/3 ~(ascensus; §um).

Cinta-stigol *s(f)* Ct 29/5, 5 ~stiogole *d.*

Pēadan-stigel *s(f)* Ct 3/3 *ad* ~e.

stigu *sf* stye. Ep 45 ~(auriola); Ef, Cp §.

Wigora-cæster Worcester. Ct 33/8 wegoranensis.

be-wrig- *prt* covered. Bd[2] 71 wæs ~en (tegebatur). VP 31/1 biwrigen sind (tecta sunt).

ofer-wrig- covered. VP 84/3 ~e (operuisti). 70/13; 108/19, 29 ~en *ptc.* 72/6 §e.

on-wrig- uncovered. VP 17/16 ~en werun (revelata sunt).

wrigels *s* covering. VP 101/27 ~(opertorium). 60/5; 62/8 ~e (velamento).

ā-figen *ptc* fried. Ep 414 afigaen (frixum); Cp §; Ef ~en.

frignan *sv* ask. Cp 514 ~o (consulo). VP 10/5, 6 ~að, ~eð (interrogant, §at). 138/23; Hy 7/12 frign (§a!).

nigen *num* nine. Ct 48/2, 6 ~.

gigent *s(m)* giant. VP 18/6; 32/16 ~(gigas).

tigole *sf* tile. Cp 1992 tigule (tegula). VP 21/16 § (testa).

þæc-tigole *sf* roof-tile. Cp 1043 þaectigilum (imbricibus).

twig *sn* twig. Cp 1942 tuig (surculus). VP 57/10; 79/12 ~u (ramnos; palmites).

line-tuige *sf* linnet. Ef 309 linaethuigae; Cp ~(carduelis). Cp 913 linetuigle (fronulus).

þistel-tuige *sf* a bird. Cp 381 ~(cardella); Ld distyltige.

dern-licgan *sv* fornicate. VP 72/27 ~liggað (fornicantur). 105/39 ~ende werum (§ati sunt).

Sicga *sm* Gn 13 sicgga. Ct 17/6 sigcga.

ēar-wicga *sm* earwig. Ep 44 ~uuigga (auriculum); Ef †aeruuica; Cp ~; Ld ęruigga (§a).

Wicga *sm* LV 466 u~. Ct 12/6 wigga. 19/7 uuicggan *g.* 47/7; 48/14 ~. 49/11 uuigga.

strigdeð *prs* sprinkles. VP 147/16 ~(spargit).

on-strigdes *prs* sprinklest. VP 50/9 ~(asparges).

to-strigdeð *prs* scatters. VP 11/4; 93/23; Hy 7/14 ~(disperdat; §et; dispersit). 77/38 †tostrigeded (disperdet).

iteð *prs* eats. VP 68/10; Hy 7/83 ~(comedit; manducabit). 127/2 ites (§abis).

hit *prn* it. VP 34/15 hit nyston (ignoraverunt) *etc.* 104/24 ~(eum) *etc.* 39 ~ lihte (luceret) *etc.* Ct 29/7, 10, 1; 30/22, 3; 34/14; 37/19, 9, 28; 38/3, 5 *etc*; 39/8, 14 *etc*; 40/22; 41/5, 9 *etc*; 42/17; 45, 26, 39; 48/3 ~. 45/37 hít.

ðritig *num* thirty. Ct 41/60, 2 ~. 56/8 ~es.

tō-slit- *prt* tore asunder. VP 29/12;

73/15; 115/16 ~e (conscidisti; disrupisti; §). 140/7 wes ~en (erupta est). Hy 6/20 bið § (scinditur). Hy 13/14 § is (scissum est).

un-tōsliten *aj* (*ptc*) untorn. Cp 1048 ~(inextricabilis); Ld †anatreten (§es).

smit- *prt* smeared, defiled. Ep 437 †~or (funestavere); Ef, Cp ~on.

be-smit- defiled. VP 88/40 bismite (profanasti). 54/21; 78/1 bismeotun (contaminaverunt; coinquinaverunt). 73/7 bisme[o]ton (polluerunt). 9/26 bioð ~en (§uuntur). 105/39 bismiten wes (contaminata est).

un-besmiten *aj* (*ptc*) undefiled. VP 17/31 ~(inpolluta).

wrōht-spitel *aj* (*sm* ?) slandering. Cp 1943 ~(susurio).

wit *prn* we two. CA 5, 7 ~. Ct 37/6 ~.

wit- *vb* know. DA 10 ge.. ~en. VP 138/23 wite ðu (scito !). 38/5; 118/125 ~e (sciam). 9/21; 108/27 ~en (sciant). 4/4 weotað (scitote !) 58/14 §un (scient). 35/11; 86/4 §endum (scientibus). Ct 41/65 hie.. ~en.

neoton *pl* know not. VP 34/8 ~(ignorant).

wita *sm* sage, councillor. Ct 23/15 uuiotan *pl.* 45/2 weotum. 48/9 wotona.

Wita *sm* Ct 17/4 uu~.

ūð-wita *sm* sage, philosopher. Cp 1577 uðuuta (philosophus). VP 104/22 uðwiotan (seniores). 118/100 uðweotan (§).

gewita *sm* witness. VP 26/12 geweotan (testes). Hy 13/23 §a (§is). Ct 45/2, 54 §an, §on *pl.*

gewitnis *sf* witness. DA 11 on ~esse. Ct 24/9; 48/9, 17, 8 ~isse *d.* 39/14 ~esse *d.*

be-witian *wv* attend to. Ct 41/13 bewiotige.

witodlice *av* truly, for. VP 18/12; 22/4; 118/24 weotudlice (nam). Hy 13/13 § [t *from* d].

gewit- *prt* departed. VP 9/22 ~e ðu (recessisti). 104/41 geweotun (abierunt).

Uit-berct LV. Uitgils LV. Uitmęr LV.

wituma *sm* dowry. Ef 324 uu~ (dos); Cp ~ *vel* uuetma.

gewriten *prt ptc* written. Ct 45/41 ~.

ā-writen written. VP 39/8 ~is (scriptum est). 68/29; 101/19 bioð ~ (scribantur). 138/16 earun ~ (§entur). 149/9 ~ne (conscriptum). Ct 37/44 auuritene siondon. 45/54 sindon ~e. 45/43 awreotene *pl.*

gewrit *sn* writing, deed. Cp 413 ~(cautionem). VP 86/6 gewreotum (scripturis). Ct 23/16 ðis geuurit. 34/17 þis ~. 40/21; 41/66; 45/1 ~e *d.* 45/43, 9 gewriotu, §o. 42/18 §a *gpl.*

þing-gewrit *sn* deed. Ct 40/25 þincg~.

Writola-burna Ct.

wlite *sm* beauty. VP 20/6 micelne ~(decorem). 25/8; 92/1; 103/1 ~(§). 29/8 ~minum (§i). 49/2 ~es (§is).

on-wlite *sm* face. Lr 17 ~(patham).

ond-wlita *sm* face. VP 16/2; 139/14 ~an ðinum (vultu). 4/7; 68/30 § ðines; 41/6 § mines (§ūs). 10/8 ~wleota (§us). 20/13 ~wleotan (§um). 26/8, 8; 44/13 § ðinne. 15/11; 20/7 § ðinum *etc.* 41/12; 42/5; § mines *etc.* 33/6 § (§ūs *pl*). 33/17 § (§us). 20/10; 66/2; 79/17; Hy 13/4 ~wliotan. 37/4; 45/6 ~wleatan.

wlitig *aj* beautiful. VP 44/3 ~(speciosus). Hy 12/2 ~e (decoro).

flit- *prt* disputed. VP 63/6 fleotun (disputaverunt).

un-beflīten *aj* (*ptc*). Ct 45/14, 41 ~.

geflit *sn* dispute. Cp 417 ~(capistrinum). Bd² 61 ~(conflectum). VP 72/7 ~e (disputatione).

hnitu *s* louse-egg, nit. Ep 590 ~(lendina); Ef, Cp, Ld §.

citre *sf* cythara. VP 56/9 citere (cythara). 107/2 ~ (§). 32/2 in †~a (§ā). 42/4; 70/22; 80/3 *etc* ~an (§).

for-giteð *prs* forgets. VP 136/5 ~(obliviscatur).

on-giteð *prs* understands. **VP** 32/15; 40/2; 93/7; 106/43 ~(intelligit). 91/7 ~(§et). 18/13 †ongeteð (§it).

glitenian *wv* glitter. **Cp** 894 glitinat (flavescit, albescit); **Ld** glitinot (flavescit, color olei).

be-biten *ptc* bitten. **Ep** 616 bibitnae (mordicos); **Ef** §; **Cp** §e.

biter *aj* bitter. **Cp** 1073 bitrum • (rancidis). **VP** 63/4 bitre (amaram). 77/8 bitur (peramarum). **Hy** 3/17 sie bittreste (amarissima).

biternis *sf* bitterness. **VP** 9/28; 13/3; **Hy** 3/14 bitternisse (amaritudine). **Hy** 3/17 §nis (§o).

sittan *sv* sit. **VP** 9/5; 79/2; 98/1 sites (sedis). 9/29; 28/10; 46/9 §eð. 109/1 §e (§e!). 25/5 ~o (§ebo). 131/12; **Hy** 9/17 ~að. **Hy** 4/15 ~e (§eat). 100/6 ~en. 49/20; 106/10 ~ende (§ens, §entes).

gesittan *sv* sit down, possess. **VP** 24/13; **Hy** 7/10 gesiteð (possidebit; possedit). 78/11 gesite (posside!). 36/9, 11, 22, 9 ~að (§ebunt). 43/4 ~ad (§§). 68/37 ~að (†§ebit). 126/2 ~að (sederitis). 82/13 ~en we (possideamus).

feruuit-geornnis **Ep**; feruit§ **Ef**; feorwit§ **Cp**.

Witta *sm* **BH** 25 u~—uita. **LV** 305 u~. **Gn** 115 u~.

Witting *sm* son of Witta. **Gn** 115 u~.

fitt *sf* song. **Ef** 1144 fi[i]t (ampusatio, una lectio).

mitta *sm* measure. **Ct** 37/21 ~um. 37/22; 40/10 ~an fulne huniges.

and-mitta *sm* balance. **Ef** 380 hand~ (exagium); **Cp** ~.

hider *av* hither. **Cp** 1158 ~(istuc). 2148 ~ond †~(ultro citroque); **Ld** hidir †an didir. **VP** 72/10 ~(huc).

hidirrinȩ **Ld**.

tot-rid- *s* swing. **Ep** 689 ~an (oscillae); **Ef**, **Cp** §.

Hildi-lid *sf* **BH** 266 ~— hildilit [t *over* o].

Liding-denn **Ct**.

ðider *av* thither. **Ld** 10 hidir †an didir (ultro citro); **Cp** hider ond †hider. **VP** 49/5, 23; 121/4 ~(illic; quo, illuc). **Ct** 41/44 ~.

ymb-þridung *sf* deliberation. **Ef** 331 †~dritung (deliberatio); **Cp** ~ðriodung.

ā-sliden *ptc* slipped. **VH** 7/68 ~bið (lapsus fuerit).

slide *sm* slip. **VP** 55/13; 114/8 from slide (lapsu).

gesniden *ptc* cut. **Ef** 315 ~an (dolatum); **Cp** ~en.

scrid *sn* carriage, litter. **Cp** 270 ~(basterna). **Mt** 17 to ~e. 20 ðæt~. **VP** 67/18; **Hy** 5/5 ~(currus).

stride *sm* stride, step. **Cp** 1510 tuegen ~i (passus).

Widefing-denn **Ct**.

Uiduc *sm* **LV** 229 ~.

widwe *sf* widow. **VP** 108/9 ~(vidua). 93/6; 131/15; 145/9 ~an (§am). 77/64 § (§ae *pl*). 67/6 ~ena.

Widum- *s* **Ct** 47/11 bi weoduman.

hwider *av* whither. **VP** 138/7, 7 ~(quo).

huidirrynȩ **Ld**.

mid *prp w. d. instr. and a., av* with. **Ep** 796 mið naeðlae (acu); **Cp** §; **Ef** mid. **Rn** 2/9, 14, 5 miþ. 12 mith. **CA** 4, 5 ~. **Mt** 8, 22 *etc* ~. **Bd**[2] 1, 70 mið. **VP** 5/2, 13 ~ scelde, ~ earum (scuto, auribus) *etc*. **Hy** 11/15; 12/1 ~ ðy halgan gaste; ~ wlitige lehte (cum; decoro lumine) *etc*. 17/26; 48/18 ~ ðone halgan; ~ hine (cum) *etc*. 97/1 ~ ða swiðran his (dexterā ejus). 107/7 ~ ða swiðran ðinre. 104/12 mid ðy [d *from* ð]. **Ct** 28/5, 6; 30/6; 37/1, 5 *etc*; 38/7 *etc*; 40/1, 2 *etc*; 41/5; 42/2, 10 *etc*; 45/9, 9, 9 *etc*; 47/10, 1, 3 ~. 24/8 miþ. 48/3 mið.

mid-ðȳ-ðe.

clidren *s* clatter. **Ep** 928 brectme *vel* cliderme (strepitu); **Ef** clidrinnae.

ed-cwide *sm* relation, narrative. **Cp** 1729 eðcuide (relatio).

hwīt-cwidu *sm* (?) mastich. **Ep** 655 huuitquidu (mastice); **Cp** huitcudu.

glida *sm* kite. **Cp** 1313 glioda (milvus).

ā-gniden *s* rubbing. **Ef** 345 agnidinne (detriturigine); **Cp** agnidine.

gnidil *s* rubber, pestle. **Cp** 1597 ~(pistillus).

Tidi *sm* **LV** 200 ~.

trides *prs* treadest. **VP** 90/13 ~(conculcabis).

for-trideð *prs* tramples. **VP** 7/6 ~(conculcet).

te-tridit *prs* tramples. **Ef** 344 tedridtid (defecit); Cp ~(desicit).

Tuidi *s* river Tweed. **BH** 316 ~ *fluminis.*

ā-bid- *prt* waited. **VP** 118/95 abiodun (expectaverunt). Hy 7/2 sie ~en (§etur).

Iddes-hale Ct.

Hidda *sm* **LV** 274 ~.

Hiddi *sm* **LV** 159 ~.

Hiddila *sm* **BH** 285 ~ *a.*

Lidding *s* Lidding stream. **Ct** 11/2 ~e *d.* 3 *torrentis* ~.

ðridda *ord. num.* third. **Ct** 51/7 ~. 29/17 ~an.

Westan-widde *sf.* **Ct** 53/2 *regione quae dicitur* ~.

Nidd *s* river Nith. **BH** 365 *juxta fluvium* ~.

midd *aj* middle. **VP** 67/14 ~e (medios). 118/62 on ~e naeht (§iā nocte). Hy 2/11; 3/1 in midum ðin, in §daega (§io tui; §io). 73/11 of midum sceate [le *er. after* d] (§io sinu). 36/6; 54/18 on midne deg (meridie). Hy 11/13 midne deg (velut §ies). Hy 5/37 ðorh midne sę [ne *on er.*] (medium mare). Hy 5/13 in midre sae (§io).

middeglic VP. **midferh** Cp. **midhridir** Cp.

middel *sn* middle. **VP** 103/10 betwih ~ (medium). 135/14 ðorh ~ his (§). 21/15, 23 *etc* in midle (§io *w. g.*). 134/9 in § ðinum (§§). 101/25 § (dimidio). 56/5; 135/11 of § (medio). 103/12 of †mid.

Middilangli, §engli BH. **Middilsaexum** Ct.

gemidlian *wv* halve. **VP** 54/24 ~iað (dimidiabunt).

middun-geard CH; middan§ LP, DA, VH.

glidder *aj* slippery. **VP** 34/6 †glidd (lubricum). Hy 11/6 ~. Hy 12/12 glidderre (§o).

Tiddes-ford Ct.

biddan *sv* pray, ask. **CA** 15 ~að. **Mt** 47 ic ~o. **VP** 2/8; 89/13 bide (postula!; deprecare!). 29/9 ~u (§abor). 44/13; 121/6 ~að (§abuntur; rogate!). Hy 12/14 ~en we (§amus). 118/58; 141/2 ~ende eam (deprecatus sum). Hy 12/15 § (precantes). **Ct** 37/6 ~að. 37/40; 42/14 ic ~o. 30/22; 37/34; 40/18; 41/28 (ic) ~e.

gebiddan *sv* pray. **Rn** 1/5 gebid heo. 4/4 gebidæd! (gebidaed). 9/1 gibidæþ! 11/3 gibiddad! **LP** 1, 9 gebide! **VP** 31/6 gebideð (orabit). 5/8 ~a (orabo). 27/2; 137/2 ~u (oro; adorabo). 21/28 ~að (orabunt). 5/4 †gebidu (orabo).

bridd *sm* young bird. **Cp** 1687 brid (pullus). **VH** 3/10 § (§). **VP** 83/4; 146/9; Hy 7/21 ~as; ~um; ~as.

rip- *s* **VP** 125/6; 128/7 reopan (manipulos).

reopan *sv* reap. **VP** 125/5 reopað (metent).

wīn-reopan *sv.* **VP** 79/13 ~reopad (vendemiant).

swipe *sf* whip. **Ep** 641 suipan (mastigia); Ef †suibæ; Cp suiopan (§ium). 1051 auundre suipan (verbere torto); Ef §; Cp suiopan. Cp 891 §um (flagris).

scip *sn* ship. **Ep** 862 neb *vel* scipes celae (rostrum); Ef, Cp §. Cp 319 sundgerd in ~e (bolides). 1825 ~(scaphum). **VP** 47/8; 103/26 sceopu (naves). 106/23 §um.

hlæst-scip *sn* merchant vessel. **Cp** 1032 hlaest~ (honeraria).

ðēof-scip *sn* pirate ship. **Ep** thebscib (mimoparo); Ef §scip; Cp ~.

-scipe. wræcscype. þēodscipe. gehūs§. gefēr§ [*under* oe].

scripeþ *prs* scrapes. **Ep** 906 ~ith (scarpinat); Ef §; Cp ~ið; Ld †scribid.

clipian *wv* call. **VP** 4/4; 21/3; 27/1 *etc* cleopiu (clamavero *etc*). 64/14; 113/7 (2) §iað. 29/3; 85/3; 87/10, 4 §ade. 118/146; 119/1; 129/1 *etc* §ude. 3/5; 17/7; 26/7;

33/7 §ede. 17/42; 106/6, 13, 9, 28 §edun. 21/6; 33/18 §edon. 68/4 §iende (§ans). 16/6 cleapede. 21/25; 31/3 §ade.

cleopung *sf* calling. **VP** 5/2 ~e (clamorem). 17/7; 101/2; 143/14 ~(clamor).

gegripen *ptc* grasped. **VH** 9/16 ~ is (conpraehensus est).

Ripp *s* **Ct** 7/3 *silvam qui appellatur* ~.

Ripple-styde Ct.

ribb *sn* rib. **Cp** 585 rib (costa).

ribbe *sf* ribwort. **Ep** 184 ~ae (canis lingua); Ef §; Cp ~. **Ef** 280 ~ae (cynoglossa); Cp ~.

libban *wv* live. **VP** 118/17, 144; **Hy** 7/79 lifgu (vivam, §; §o). 37/20; 113/18 §að. 88/49; 117/17; 118/177 §e (§et; §am, §§). **Hy** 7/76 §an (§ere). 38/6; 142/2; **Hy** 3/21, 1 §ende (§ens). 54/16; 57/10 §ende (§entes). 41/3; 83/3 ðone §§; ðæm §endan (vivum). 26/13; 51/7; 55/13; 68/29; 114/9; 141/6; **Hy** 3/3 §endra. 38/12 §en (vivens). **Hy** 3/15 bið lifd (§itur). 21/27, 31; 48/10; 71/15 leofað (§it *etc*). 68/33; 118/175 liofað (§et). 17/47 leafað (§it). **Ct** 38/8 gib (he) .. lifige. 40/18 godes libgendes.

ofer-libban *wv* survive. **Ct** 38/4 ~lifde.

sibb *sf* peace. **VP** 37/4; 84/11; 121/7 *etc* sib (pax). 27/3; 33/15 *etc* ~e (pacem). 4/9; 28/11 *etc* § (§e). 13/3 *etc* § (§is). 40/10 §minre (§§).

mǣg-sibb *sf* family peace. **Ep** 109 megsibbi (affectui vel dilectione); Ef §; Cp §e.

un-sibb *sf* dissension. **Ep** 900 ~(seditio); Ef, Cp unsib. **Cp** 1871 ~ (simultas).

gesibb *aj* kindred. **Ct** 45/46 ~ra ęrfeweard.

sibsum *aj* peaceful. **VP** 36/37 ðæm ~an (pacifico). 119/7 ~(§us).

sibsumlice *av* peacefully. **VP** 34/20 ~(pacifice).

unsibbian *wv* disagree. **Ef** 323 ~adae (desidebat); Cp ~ade.

ðe *prn, av* which, when *etc*. **Rd** 10, 4. ða ði, ðeh ði. **LP** 3, 12 ~. **CA** 10 ~. **DA** 4, 6, 10, 6 ~. **Mt** 13, 47 ~. **SG** 11 ~. **VP** 2/10, 3 ða ~ (qui *pl*) *etc*. 7/3, 16 se ~, ðone ~ (qui, quam) *etc*. 79/2; 115/12; 118/1 de. **Ct** 20/13, 6; 28/25; 37/6, 7 *etc*; 38/2, 14; 39/11, 5; 40/3, 7, 19; 41/31, 6 *etc*; 42/2, 8, 20; 45/10, 54; 48/3, 17 ðe. 41/3, 7; 45/3, 12 *etc* þe.

ðætte. for-ðon-ðe. wið-ðan-ðe. ðā ðe (who). **ðā ðe** (when). **ðēah ðe. ðā-hwīle-ðe. for-ðȳ-ðe.**

seh-ðe.

se *prn, art* he, the. **Rd** 1 ~. **Ef** 320 ~; Cp ~. **Mt** 8, 15 *etc* ~. **SG** 2 ~. **Bd**[2] 4 ~. **VP** 7/6 ~ feond (inimicus) *etc*. 9/6 ~ arleasa (impius) *etc*. 2/4 ~ (qui) *etc*. 7/3 ~ ðe (qui) *etc*. **Ct** 20/17; 28/20, 2; 34/8; 37/33; 40/20, 0, 2; 41/31, 68, 8; 42/15, 5; 45/25; 47/13; 55/4 ~.

ne *av* not, nor. **Cp** 1398 ne huru is (numquid). **Rn** 2/4 (ni). 7 (n)i. **Rd** 3, 5, 5, 6, 8, 9, 13 ni. 7 ~. **DA** 9, 9, 12 ~. **Mt** 49, 9, 9 ~. **VP** 3/7 ~ ondredu ic (non timebo) *etc*. 5/5 ~ wellende (non volens) *etc*. 5/6; 6/2 *etc* ~ (neque). 9/32 ðæt he ~ gese (ne videat) *etc*. 90/12 ne otspurne (ne offendas). 37/2 n (neque). **Ct** 41/8, 37, 41; 45/26 ~.

nabban. næs. næbbe. nis. neoton. neom. nyllan. nyste. nolde. nǣfre. nǣnig.

ge *cj* ge .. ge both .. and. **Mt** 37 ~. **Ct** 37/13, 4, 4, 42, 2, 3; 42/21, 1 ~.

ge. martyrian. galan. laþian. staþolian, staþolfæstan. þafian, §ung. dafen, §ian. giþanc. strangian. gimang. crang. gangan. wanian. spannan, span. plantian. standan. band. giswom. hagian. hladan. tæl. hwæþer. gihwæs. liffæstan. fæstnian. hæftan, §ednis. scæft. giþræc. bræc. gædrian, §ung. bæd. sæt. wæterian. scæpen. gihæpplic, geheplicnis. gearwian, §ung. earnian, §ung. snearc. mearcian. feallan. gisalbot. healdan. sealde, §nis. manigfealdian. tealde. seah. þeaht, §ian. smirwan. birhtan. stillan. willian, §ung. scildan, §end, §nis. mildgian. miltsian. geswiðerian [*first* e *from* i *in Ep*]. fiþred. niþerian. Gewisse. wislice. blissian. gigiscian. swinc. scincio. singan. bringan. rinen. þinge, §ian. winn. twinn. niman. timbran. limp, §an,

§lic, §licnes. giswigra. sihþ *sbst.* fihþ. riht. miclian. cwician. briceð. sniden. witon. wita, §nes. sittan. welgian. gihwelc. writ, §en. teld. efenlician. segen. segnian. bregdenlice. sprec. brecan. setennis. fetod. met, §gian. medemian. leornian. feormian. sweorc. weorc. beorg. reordan, §nis. feohtan. sweotolian. hęrgian. nęrian. dęrian. cęrran. nęrwan. gigęrwan. gęrela. iehwęrfan. węrpan. sęllan. fęllan. tęllan. męltan. hęld. hnistun [*under*-ęsc]. ręstan. hęfigian. hęfeldian. stęfnan. swęncan, §ednis. scręncan. indręncan. lęngan. gimęngan, gimengedlice. gęnga. glęngan. ęndian, §ung. scęndan, §þu. węndan. węmman, ungewemmed. gifręmman. gigręmman. ręccan, recenis. fęccan. męcca. ręgnian. Gesęcg. sęttan. curon. fultumian. lustfullian, §ung. wuldrian. sufl. þungen, §lice. swungen. wuna. unnan. runnen. cunnan. sund, §fullice, §fullian. wundian. wundrian. ginumen. untrumian. brugdon. hroren. giþworen. gifyrþro. hyrstan. gidyrstig. wyrht. gybyrdid Ep, ge§ Ef. endebyrdan. inbryrdan. fyllan. fylgan. ēbylgan. þyld, §ig. scyldru. cnyssan. clystru. cyspan. tynge. myne. þynnian. wynsumian. mynd, §elic. cyndelic. trymman. nyclan. hyhtan. nyhtsum, §nis, §ian. gityhted. bycgan. hygd. dyde. cor, §en. boren. worht. worden. giþofta. onettan. illerocad. broc, §en. boht. togen. brogden. scota. strod. ārian. hālgian, §ung. stāl. singālian. clāsnian, §ung. þrāwan. māna. tācnian, §ung. gimāh. hāt, §an. wāt. rād. mād. brādian. grāp. lǣran. þwǣrian. hǣlan. dǣlan. lǣstan. þrǣstan. scǣnan. mǣne, §nis. hwǣm. rǣcan. nēalǣcan. hnǣgan. fǣttian. rǣdan. lǣdan. mǣdan. brǣdan. hwǣr. mǣre. bǣru. sǣlan, ungesǣlignis. fǣgon. brǣc. brǣcon. gelǣgeo. sǣton. wǣtan. giwǣde. brǣdan. hēran, §nis. lēfan (allow). lēfan (believe). gihēnan. ungisēne. tōgeēcan. hēhan. hēht. bēgan. þēde. fēa. frēas. cēas. rēafian. lēafa, §full, §sum. edlēanian, §end, §ung. bēacnend. flēah. þrēan. bēagian. nēat. gibēaten, unge§. strēad. sēo. fēo. frēo, frīgend. tēo (pull). tēo (adorn). tīung. ginēorð. fēoll. cēosan. trēowe, §lice. strēon, §an. ungetēon. giēode Ep, gaeadun Ef. þēodan. bēodan. sīþ. rīs. rehtwīsian, §ung. gisīwan. nīowian, ed§. liffæstan. wiif. hrīnan. līman. līc, §e, §nes, §ian. līhan. līhtan. swīgian. stīgan. wītan. wītnian. hwītian. cīd. grīpan. trūgung. hȳdan. nōm. bōcian. þōht *ptc, sbst.* sōht. gislōg Ef [=ti§]. mōt. unrōtsian. gistōd. eaþmōdian. gimōd. scōp. scoe. doe. foera, §ræden, §scipe. foerne. coelan. giroeþro. doeþ, doest. giroefa. droefan, §ednis. woenan. gifoegnis. moetan, §ung. loed. bloedsian, §ung. scroepnis. stoepan.

be *prp* by, about. **VP** 77/19; 86/3; 90/11 *etc* bi(de). 7/5 § gewyrhtum (merito). 34/7 *etc* §ungewyrhtum (gratis). **Ct** 20/17; 26/4; 28/14, 4; 29/4, 5, 12; 30/6; 56/8 ~. 47/11 bi.

be-. bihafaþ. bifangen. bigang, land§, §en. be, bifæstan. be, bigæt. bispearrian. biþearft. biswicfealle. be, bihealdan. befealdan. bismirwan. besilfran. bismer *etc.* biswicun. betwix. biwrigen. bismiten, unbe§. bewitian, unbefliten. bibiten. bīspell. begetan. becweden. benioþan. biheonan. bescęrian. bewęrian. be, bisęncan. binęmned. biþęccan. hēr-beufan. binumen. bicuman. bilucon. benuge. bibudon. bibyrgan. be, bigyrdan. bimyldan. becyme. bihygdignis. biworhte. be, biforan. bibohte. bigoten. be, bibod. beboden. begā· biswāc. biwrāh. biswāpan. biwǣgan. be, bigǣton. bifēng. bistēman. bidēpan. behēafdian, §ung. be, bilēac. bibēad. bilēoran. bihēold. biēode. be, bibēodan. bisīwan. biswīcan, §end. be, bitwīh. betwīhn. betwīnum. besmītan. bilūcan. bihȳran. befō. bicwōm.

blann. blinnan. būtan.

spere *sn* spear. **Cp** 528 speoru (contos).

nægl-spere *sn* nail-spear. **Cp** 2156 naeglsperu (unguana).

wer *sm* man. **Mt** 40 ~es. 45 ðone ~. **VP** 31/2; 33/9 *etc* ~(vir). 5/7 *etc* ~(§um). 17/26, 49 *etc* ~e. 146/10; **Hy** 6/14 ~es. 54/24; 75/6; 138/19 weoras. 25/9; 58/3 §um.

wergeld, wær§ Ct. **wermōd.** **wer**ð**ēode**, Cp.

Port-weorona *gpl* Ct 24/9 ~.

Uuiægen-weoras *pl* Ct 24/3 *villa regia añ* ~.

werlice *av* manlily. **VP** 26/14; 30/25 ~(viriliter).

werod *sn* host, army. **Cp** 109 weorod (agmen). **VP** 135/15 weorud (exercitum). Hy 5/5 weoreda (†§).

Uerlama-cæstir BH.

fer-uuitgeornnis Ef; § Ef; feor§ Cp.

teran *sv* tear. **Lr** 2 to teorenne (lacerandum).

Per-hamstede Ct.

Ber-uulf LV.

beran *sv* bear. **Ep** 790 berecorn ~ęndae (ptysones); Ef berendæ; Cp beorende. Cp 751 § (enixa). **Bl** 3 ~ende (fecundae). **VP** 90/12; Hy 13/17 beorað (portabunt; ferimus). 125/6; 143/13 §ende (portantes; fetosae).

forð**-beran** *sv* bear forth. **VP** 39/16 ~en (ferant).

un-beorende *aj* (*prs ptc*) barren. **VP** 112/9 ~(sterilem). Hy 4/10 ~u (§is).

un-beorendnis *sf* barrenness. **VP** 34/12 †~ednisse (sterilitatem).

fers *sn* vers. **LP** 7 ðas ~ *a*.

elothr *s*(*f*) lupin. **Ef** 386 ~; Cp elotr (electrum).

elone *sf* elecampane. **Ep** 697 ~ae (oridanum); Ef §; Cp eolone. Cp 1057 § (inola).

helor *s* scales, balance. **Ep** 607 ~(lanx); Ef §; Cp heolor. 988 ~(trutina *vel* statera); Ef §; Cp heolor.

twi-helor *s* balance. **Cp** 304 tuiheolore (bilance).

leloð**re** *sf* silverweed (?). **Ep** 607 lelodrae (lapatium); Ef, Cp ~. 861 lelothrae (radinape); Cp §; Ef lelothre.

stela *sm* stalk. **Ep** 215 ~(caulem); Ef §; Cp steola. Cp 432 § (cauliculus).

wel *av* well. **VP** 32/3; 35/4; 39/10 *etc* ~(bene). 34/21, 1, 25, 5; 39/16 ~ðe (euge). 39/16 ~ðæ (§). **Ct** 39/7 ~.

weldēd VP. **weldyde** VP. †**belhlēo**ð**riendum** VP. **welgelīcad** VP.

wela *sm* wealth. **VP** 40/4 weolan (opem). 61/11; 111/3 § (divitiae). 36/16 *etc* § (§ias). 36/3; 118/14 §um. 48/7; 51/9 *etc* §ena.

welig *aj* wealthy. **VP** 48/3, 17 weolig (dives). 9/29 §um (§itibus). 21/30; 33/11; 44/13; Hy 10/9; weolie (§ites).

welgian *wv* be prosperous.

welga *interj* (*imper*) hail! **Cp** 1015 ~(eja). **VP** 69/4, 4 weolga (euge!).

gewelgian *wv* enrich. **VP** 64/10 geweolgian (locupletare). Hy 4/14 geweolegað (ditat).

welor *sf* lip. **Lr** 30 weolure (labiae). **VP** 11/4; 15/4; 33/14; 39/10; 62/6; 65/14; 70/23 § (§ia). 30/19; 50/17; 62/4 weolere (§§). 11/5; 118/171 weolre (§§). 13/3; 16/1; 21/8 *etc* weolerum. Hy 3/15 § (†talibus). 16/4; 139/10 weolura (labiorum). 20/3; 58/13; weolera (§). Hy 6/32 †beolera (§). 11/3 welure (labia).

fela *aj* many. **VP** 39/6 feolu (multa *pl*). 65/16; 73/3 hu § (quanta *pl*). 77/3 hu fiolu (§). **Ct** 37/31 feola.

felofor Ep; †**felusor** Ef; **feolufer** Ct. **felofearth** Ep; **felufrech** Ef; **feoluferð** Cp. **Feologeld** Ct. **felosprāeci** Ep; §Ld; felu§ Ef, Cp.

gelostr *s* matter, pus. **Cp** 1970 ~(supuratio).

belone *sf* henbane. **Ep** 975 ~ae (sinfoniaca); Ef §; Cf ~.

Bel-daeg, §ing Gn.

snell *aj* quick, bold. **Ep** 77 snel (alacris); Cp §. Cp 823 § (expeditus, velox, fortis).

Snella *sm* **LV** 165, 209 ~.

spell *sn* story, news, narrative. **Ep** 869 ~i (relatu); Ef, Cp §.

spelbodan Cp.

bī-spell *sn* example, parable. **VP** 68/12 bispel (parabolam). 77/2 ~um (§is).

god-spellian *wv* preach the gospel. **VP** 67/12 ~iendum (evangelizantibus).

godspellere *sm* evangelist. **DA** 5 ~as.

spellung *sf* story-telling. **VP** 118/85 ~e (fabulationes).

fell *sn* skin, hide. **Cp** 1573 fel (pellis). **VP** 103/2 § (§em).

þrust-fell *sn* leprosy. **Ep** 139 blec thrustfel (bitiligo); **Ef** §; **Cp** blaec§.

stāne-gell- *s* pelican. **VP** 101/7 ~an (pellicano).

cellendre *sf* coriander. **Cp** 569 ~(coleandrum).

Tella *sm*. **LV** 98; 100; 334 ~.

self *prn* self. **VH** 3/14 ic †seofa (ipse). **Ps** 18/10; 35/2; 65/7 him seolfum (semet ipsā; §ipso; §ipsis). 41/7 me § (me ipso). 104/22 hine seolfne (semetipsum). **Ct** 34/15 seolfa. 41/25 siolf. 37 sylfum. 42/5 siolfne.

seolfboran Cp.

scelfan *sv* shake. **Rd** 7 scelfaeð.

elm *s(m)* elm-tree. **Ep** 1079 ~(ulmus); **Ef**, **Cp** §.

Elmhām(ens)is Ct.

Elmet *s* Elmet. **BH** 101 *in silva* ~.

helm *sm* helmet. **Cp** 418 ~es (cassidis. 422 ~(cassium).

Helmbǣd LV. **Helmgils** LV.
Helmstān Ct. **Helmðrȳþ** LV.
Helmuald LV. **Helmuini** LV.

Æþel-helm *sm* **LV** 387 eðil~. **Ct** 23/8 æðelhelmi. 33/18 aeþel~. 24/6 aeðelm.

Bād-helm *sm* **LV** 190; 204, 94; 358, 64 ~.

Beald-helm *sm* **LV** 50; 163; 404 bald~. 118 balð~.

Bed-helm *sm* **LV** 128 ~.

Beorht-helm *sm* **LV** 171, 6; 208, 10, 63, 98; 341, 92 berct~. 116 bercht~.

Beorn-helm *sm* **Ct** 33/16; 45/57; 47/5 ~. 56/7 biorn~. 31/6, 7; 38/16, 7, 9; 43/9 biarn~.

Bil-helm *sm* **LV** 107; 345 ~.

Bōt-helm *sm* **BH** 135 ~. **LV** 111 ~.

Burg-helm *sm* **BH** 276 ~. **LV** 88, 90; 428 ~.

Cēol-helm *sm* **LV** 217 ~. **Ct** 33/17 ~.

Cūþ-helm *sm* **LV** 157; 273 cuð~. 169; 255; 333; 47, 65; 468 cuthelm.

Cwic-helm *sm* **BH** 78 cuichelmo — qu§ 1 — cu§. 230 cu~ — qu~ 1. 269 cuichelmum — c[u]uic§ — quic§. **Gn** 10 cu~.

Cyne-helm *sm* **LV** 108, 25, 97; 260; 348; 415; cynhelm. **Ct** 12/7 cyn[h]elm. 49/9; 50/5 cynhelm. 51/10 ~.

Dæg-helm *sm* **LV** 98; 152, 2, 61; 417 daeg~. **Ct** 33/8 ~.

Drycg-helm *sm* **LV** 96 ~.

Dryht-helm *sm* **BH** 357 dryct-helme *voc.*

Ēad-helm *sm* **LV** 52; 465 ~.

Eald-helm *sm* **BH** 331; aldhelmum. **LV** 59; 103; 301, 19, 44; 418 ald~. **Gn** 24 §.

Ealh-helm *sm* **Ct** 47/6 alhhelm.

Eard-helm *sm* **LV** 448 ~.

Ed-helm *sm* **Gn** 86 ~.

Ed-helming *sm* son of Edhelm. **Gn** 86 edelming.

Forþ-helm *sm* **LV** 163; 335 forthhelm.

Frēo-helm *sm* **LV** 62; 286 frehelm.

Friþ-helm *sm* **LV** 123; 217 frið~. 220 frithhelm.

Gūþ-helm *sm* **LV** 207; 302, 70 guð~.

Gȳþ-helm *sm* **LV** 121 gyð~.

Lēof-helm *sm* **LV** 339 leob~.

Mǣþ-helm *sm* **LV** 96 maeð~.

Nōþ-helm *sm* **BH** 2 nothelmus, §i, §us, §o, §o. **Gn** 3 noðhelmus.

Ōs-helm *sm* **LV** 254 ~.

Peoht-helm *sm* **BH** 358 pecthelmo — peht§ 1. **LV** 194; 214; 356 pect~. 292 pecht~. **Gn** 68 peht~.

Pleg-helm *sm* **LV** 292; 346 ~. **Ct** 5/2 ~es tun.

Sige-helm *sm* **LV** 452 sighelm.

Swīþ-helm *sm* **BH** 189 suid~.

223 §um — suidelmum — suithelmum LV 198; 226, 33, 94; 344 suið~.

Tāt-helm *sm* LV 184; 280 ~.

Tīd-helm *sm* LV 172, 8, 85; 325, 79, 98; 401, 31 ~.

Torht-helm *sm* LV 120 torcht ~. 164, 70; 220; 342 torct~. Ct 17/4; 31/8; 58/16 ~. 53/7 ~i.

Weald-helm *sm* Ct 30/19; 31/10; 38/19; 45/59 ~.

Wīg-helm *sm* LV 271; 395 uig ~. Ct 28/8, 18; 30/15, 6; 31/6; 40/15; 55/10; 56/7; 58/18 ~. 28/9 ~es. 31/2 ~e. 38/17 †whelm.

Wiht-helm *sm* LV 206, 86; 400 uict~.

Wil-helm *sm* LV 80; 284; 429, 56 uil~. Gn 119 ~.

Wil-helming *sm* son of Wilhelm. Gn 119 ~.

Wulf-helm *sm* CA 2 ~.

Wyn-helm *sm* LV 160 u~. Ct 38/20 ~.

helma *sm* rudder. Cp 4 ~(clavis).

swelc *prn* such. Ct 39/9, 13 suelc. 14 suilc. 37/41 §e. 41/28, 31 swælc. 40 §um.

swelce *av* so, as. Ep 98 aend suilcae (atqueve); Ef §e; Cp suelce. Cp 238 †on suilce (§). CA 14 ~. VP 39/7 ec ~(etiam). Ct 37/42 suilce. 45/2 swylce.

hwelc *prn* which. Mt 47 (h)welc. VP 4/6; 6/6; 18/13 *etc* ~(quis). 29/10 ~ nyttnis (quae utilitas). 77/42 ~e dege (quā). 85/9 swe ~e (quascumque). 55/10; 101/3; 137/3 swe ~um dege (quacumque). Ct 38/10 ~. 45/18, 20, 49, 52 hwylc.

gehwelc *prn* each. Ep 842 gihuuelci uuaega (quocumque modo); Ef gihuelci uuegi; Cp ~i wega. VP 11/3 anra ~(unusquisque). 48/3 ~e (quique).

ǣg-hwelc *prn* each. Ep 709 oeghuuelci ðinga (omnimoda); Ef oeghuelci hadga; Cp oeghwelce ðinga. CA 11 eghwelce. VP 63/10 og~ (omnis). 64/3; 142/2 oeg~ (§). Ct 37/35, 6, 8 ęghwilc, aeg§, ęg§. 39/9; 45/22 eghwylce. 45/35 eghwylc. 40/9 eihwelc. 45/40 ęghwelce.

for-swelgan *sv* swallow, devour. VP 13/4 ~ad (devorant). 52/5 ~að (§). 34/25; 123/3 ~að (absorbuimus; deglutissent). 68/16 ~e (absorbeat). 106/27 ~ende wes (deglutita est). 140/6 ~ende werun (absorpti sunt).

swelgend *s(f)* gulf, abyss. Cp 2160 suelgendi (voragine). Ct 29/8, 8 ~e *d.*

welg *sm* willow. Bl 20 ~um (salicibus).

helt *s(mn)* hilt. Cp 359 ~(capulus). 414 ~(§um).

sweltan *sv* die. VP 48/11 ~ende (morientes). 81/7 ~að. 117/17 ~u.

smelt *sm* smelt (a fish). Ep 949 ~as (sardas); Ef, Cp §.

seld *sn* seat. VP 10/5; 44/7 *etc* ~ (sedis). 9/8 *etc* ~ (§em). 46/9 ~ halig (§em). 88/5 ~ ðin (§em). Hy 10/8 ~e (§e). 88/15; 96/2 ~es.

Seldrēd LV.

sundur-seld *sn* separate seat. VH 4/16 ~(solium).

ðrym-seld *sn* (glory-seat), throne. VP 9/5; 88/30 ~(thronum).

weard-seld *sn* guard-house. Cp 814 ~(excubias).

sceld *sm* shield. VP 34/2; 75/4 ~(scutum). 5/13; 90/5 ~e. 45/10 ~as.

Sceldes-ford Ct. **sceldreda** Ep; §hreða Ef.

pleg-sceld *sm* play-shield. Lr 11 ðine plægsceldæ (pelta).

meldian *wv* inform. Ef 342 † ~adum (deperuntur); Cp ~adun (defferuntur).

feld *sm* field. Cp 1796 ~(scamma). 1797 feltha (saltuum). VP 77/12 ~a (campo). 43 ðæm §. 8/8; 64/12 ~es. 95/12; 103/8; Hy 6/37 ~as. 131/6 ~um. Ct 47/11, 4 aet ~a.

felduuop Ep; Ef, Cp §.

Birene-feld *sm* she-bear's field. Ct 30/12 ~.

Gleppan-feld *sm* Ct 29/18 an ~a.

Hadfeld-geat Ct.

Hǣþ-feld *sm* Heathfield. BH 114 *campo qui vocatur* haethfelth—§feld I—§felth. 231 *in campo* hæthfelda—†haetfeldo I. 290 haethfelth—

§feld I. 378 *in campo* hæthfelda—haetfelda I.

Heofon-feld *sm.* **BH** 133 hefenfelth, *quod dici potest caelestis campus*—§feld [feld *from* fled]—§feld —§ felth.

Leanga-feld *sm* **Ct** 45/7, 15 on ~a. 28 an §.

Lencan-feld *sm* **Ct** 45/29 on lęncanfelda.

Licced-feld *sm* Litchfield. **BH** 243 lyccidfelth — licidfelt—liccid~ — licidfelth. 371 lyccitfeldensi—†licitfeldelsi — liccitfeldensi. **Ct** 33/3 ~ensis. 46/3, 3 liccidfeldensi, licced§.

Maser-feld *sm* **BH** 154 ~th—~th I—~th [*on er*].

Widmundes-feld *sm* **Ct** 1/4 uuidmundesfelt.

celd- *s* **Ct** 28/10 hwite ~an hec.

Cweld-gils, §ing Gn.

geldan *sv* pay, requisite. **VP** 7/5 ðaem ~endum (retribuentibus). 49/14 geld (redde!) 65/13 ~e (§am). 115/18; Hy 7/67 ~u. Hy 7/82 †gildu.

ā-geldan *sv* pay, sacrifice. **VP** 26/6 ~u(immolabo). 49/14; 93/2 ageld (§a!; redde!).

for-geldan *sv* pay for. **Ct** 34/14 (he) ~e.

dēofol-geld *sn* idol. **VH** 7/42 deofulgeldum (idolis).

Feli-geld *sm* **LV** 50 ~.

Felu-geld *sm* **Ct** 33/2; 34/17; 35/11; 49/11; 56/6; 57/6; 58/19 feolo ~.

In-geld *sm* **LV** 143 ~. 103, 44, 76, 81, 8; 207, 17, 65; 301, 41, 2, 58, 75; 411, 58 ingild. **SG** 4§. **Ct** 13/2 ~i *lg.*

Ingilding *sm* son of I. **SG** 4 ~.

wer-geld *sn* compensation. **Ct** 41/33 min wær ~ *a.* 45/13 min twa ~.

borg-gelda *sm* lender, creditor; debtor. **VP** 108/11 ~(fenerator). Hy 13/21 ~um (debitoribus).

teldian *wv* cover. **Cp** 591 ~at (conectit).

geteld *sn* tent. **Cp** 1997 ~(tentorium). **VH** 3/5 ~(tabernaculum *n*). Ps 17/12 *etc* ~ (§ *a*). 26/5, 5 *etc* ~e, ~es. 48/12 *etc* ~(§a). 64/5 *etc* ~um. 59/8 *etc* ~a. 25/8 †getedes (†~is).

elpend *sm* elephant. **Ef** 351 ~es ban (ebor); Cp ~baan.

elpendbaan Cp. elpanbaennum VP.

gehelpan *sv* help. **Bd**[2] 51 to ~enne (ad succurendum).

Help-rīc LV. **Helpuini** LV.

gelpan *sv* boast. **Cp** 1940 ~ende (subplaudens).

leðer *sn* leather.

lediruuyrcta Ep; § Ef; leðeruyrhta Cp; lediruyrcta Ld.

heals-leðer *sn* reins. **Ld** 5 halsledir (habenis).

gewald-leðer *sn* reins. **Cp** 1009 ~leðrum (habenis).

sueðrian *wv* calm. **Cp** 842 ~að (facessit).

weðer *sm* wether. **Cp** 1157 uueðer (istic). **Ct** 39/5; 40/6; 41/61, 2 weðras.

feðr-homan Cp.

ðri-feðor *aj* triangular. **Ep** 1039 ~fedor; Ef trifoedur; Cp ~feoðor (triquadrum).

cweþan *sv* say. **VP** 17/50; 41/10; 44/2 *etc* cweoðu (dicam *etc*). 3/3; 4/5, 6; 28/9; 34/27; 65/2 *etc* §að (§unt). 34/10; 67/5 cweodað. 65/3 cweoðad. 10/2; 138/20 cweaðað. 12/5; 117, 2, 3; 123/1; 128/1 cweðe (§at); Hy 3/13 § (§am). 34/25, 5; 69/5; 78/10 *etc* §en. 34/3 cweð! 70/11; 104/11; 118/82 cweoðende (§entes; §ens; §entes).

hearm-cweþend *sm* calumniator. **VP** 71/4 ~cweoðendra (†calumniatorem).

werg-cweoþan *sv* curse. **VP** 36/22 †wercweoðende (maledicentes). 61/5 ~cweodon [*last* o *over* e] (§ebant). 108/28 ~cweoðað (~ent).

ðes *prn m* this. **VP** 23/5, 8 *etc* ~(hic *sbst*, iste). 117/24 *etc* ~deg (haec). 54/13 ~se ðe (is qui). 103/26 ~ðone (iste quem). **Ct** 47/9 ~.

wesan *sv* be. **Cp** 819 ~draegtre (exerceri). **VP** 39/18; 118/151 wes (es).

æt-wesan *sv* be at hand. **Cp** 1054 aetweosendne (inminente).

tō-wesnis *sf* separation, discord. **Bd**[2] 41 ~nisse (defortii).

wesend *s(m)* bison. **Ep** 160 uusend (bubalis); **Ef** uesand; **Cp** weosend.

wesole *sf* weazel. **Ep** 650 uuesulae (mustella); **Ef** §; **Cp** uueosule.

cesol *s* gizzard. **Ep** 1054 ~(ventriculus, stomachus avis); **Ef** §; **Cp** ceonsol.

cesol *s* cottage. **Ep** 457 ~(gurgustium); **Ef** §; **Cp** ceosol; **Ld** chelor.

besma *sm* broom. **Cp** 1794 ~(scopa).

sess *s* seat. **Ep** 1021 ses (transtrum); **Ef** §; **Cp** saes.

cressa *sm* cress. **Ep** 917 ~ae (sinapio); **Ef**, **Cp** ~a. **Ef** 922 ~ae (sinapio). 1121 ~a (nascurcium). 1133 § (sinapiones *etc*). **Cp** 329 § (brittia).

lēac-cressa *sm* nasturtium. **Ef** 676 leccressae (nasturcium).

tūn-cressa *sm* garden-cress, nasturtium. **Ep** 676 tuun~ (nasturcium); **Cp** §.

gesca *sm* sob. **Ep** 958 iesca (singultus); **Ef** §; **Cp** ~. **Cp** 1857 ~slaet (singultat). 1996 ~(tentigo).

sester *sm* a measure. **Ct** 41/63, 3, 4 ~fulne huniges.

west *av* west.

Uuestburg Ct. **westdǣl** VP. **westmearc** Ct. **Westseaxna** SG; uestsęxanorum Ct. **westeweard** Ct. **westnorðwind** Cp; uu§ Ef. **westsuþwind** Ep, Cp; uu§ Ep; u§ Ef. **westansuðanwind** VP.

westan *av* from the west.

Uuestanae Ct. **Westanwidde** Ct.

norðan-westan *av* from the north-west. **Cp** 47 ~(a circio).

sūðan-westan *av* from the south-west. **Cp** 43 ~(ab affrico). 101 suþan~ (a fafonio).

Westarham Ct. **Uestorualcna** Gn. ·storualcning Gn.

nest *sn* nest. **VP** 83/4; **Hy** 7/20 ~(nidum).

nest *s* provisions. **Ef** 389 ~(epimenia); **Cp** §.

cest *sf* chest. **Ep** 231 ~(capsis); **Ef**, **Cp** §. **Ef** 1146 ~(sarcofagum *etc*). 1168 ~(cista *etc*). **Cp** 590 ~e (cornu). **Bd**[2] 65 ~e (capsulam).

efen *aj* even, level. **Cp** 92 efnum (aequatis).

efenherian, §herenis VP. **efenameten**, efenmeten VP. **ebnwege** Cp; **Efnuald** LV.

geefenlician *wv* level. **Cp** 1694 †geeblicadun (quadrare). **VP** 88/7 bið ~ad (aequabitur).

efennis *sf* equity. **VP** 9/5, 9; 16/2 *etc* ~se (aequitatem, §e, §em).

efne *av* evenly, indeed. **VP** 34/20 ~(quidem).

swefl *s* sulphur. **Cp** 1956 sue[f]l sueart (sulforia).

swefelrēc VP.

stefn *sf* voice. **Cp** 2164 stebn (vox). **Mt** 25 stef(n). **VP** 28/3, 4, 4, 5 *etc* ~(vox). 5/4; 6/9 *etc* ~e (vocem). 3/5 ~e minre (§e) *etc*. 18/4 ~e (§es). 92/4 ~um. 117/15 sefn.

wefan *sv* weave. **VH** 3/6 weofendan (texente).

ō-wef woof. **Cp** 482 ~(cladica).

wefl *sf* warp. **Ef** 300 uuefl (caldica); **Cp** ~ *vel* owef. **Cp** 1499 uuefl (panuculum). 2016 § (titica). **Rd** 5 ueflæ *pl*.

Fefres-hām Ct.

gefan *sv* give. **Ep** 525 gibaen uuaes (inpendebatur); **Ef**, **Cp** geben.

ā-gefan *sv* give. **VP** 21/26; 55/12 ageofu (reddam). 75/12 §að. 27/4; 50/14; 78/12 agef! 60/9 ~e (§am). **Hy** 12/3 ~e (§at). 64/2 bið ~en. **Ct** 37/26; 38/10; 40/9; 41/26, 9, 34, 68; 42/13 (he) ~e *sbj prs*. 39/13 agebe. 37/27 ágæfe. 41/19 ágefe. 41/16, 8 ~en *sbj prs pl*. 45/36 ageofen §. 39/3 agiaban. 41/67 sie ~en.

for-gefan *sv* grant, forgive. **VH** 13/23 forgef (ignosce!). 22 § [e *from* i]. **Ct** 30/20 (ic) ~geofu. 41/35 mon ~e *sbj prs*. 42/5 ~geofan.

of-gefan *sv* desert. **Cp** 699 ~en (distitutum).

forgefennis *sf* forgiveness. **VH** 13/10 ~gefenisse (indulgentiam).

gefu *sf* gift, grace. **LP** 11 ðorh ..

~e. **VP** 44/3 geofu (gratia). 83/12; Hy 11/8 ~e (§iam). Hy 12/2 ~e (§iā). Hy 11/5 męhtigre ~e (§iae *g*). 14/5; 67/30 *etc* ~e (munera). 67/19; 71/10 ~e (dona). 25/10 geofum. 44/13 gefum. **Ct** 38/15; 40/1, 11; 41/47 mid godes ~e. 37/1, 11 gæfe, mid gaefe. 45/49 þas geofe *a. pl.*

Gebmund BH, Gn; gemmund BH. **Gębredi** Ct. **Gefuini** LV.

Hroeð-gefu *sf* **LV** 42 ~gifu. 43 ~geofu.

Ōs-gifu *sf* **LV** 48 osgeofu.

Gefrin *s* Yeverin. **BH** 97 *villam regiam quae vocatur* ad~ — gebrin 1 — ~[vel b *written over*].

Repta-cæstir BH.

wefta *sm* weft. **Ef** 328 uueftan (depoline); Cp ~(deponile).

Gen-lād BH, Ct. **Geonuald** LV.

ðec *a* thee. **LP** 4, 12 ~. **Mt** 26, 47 ~. **VP** 2/7; 16/7; 19/10 *etc* ~(te). 44/9; 80/8, 8 *etc* dec. 72/23, 3 mid§. 69/5; Hy 12/6 ðæc.

spec-faag Cp.

sprecan *sv* speak. **DA** 12 ~. **Mt** 38 spræcan. **VP** 77/2; 80/9; Hy 7/1 spreocu (loquar). 49/7 sprecu. 5/7; 27/3; 30/19 *etc* §að. 34/20 §að (§uebantur). 16/4; 84/9 ~e (§uatur). 33/14 ~en (§uantur). 51/5; 74/6; Hy 4/6 spreocan. 11/3, 3; 16/10; 37/13 *etc* §ende is, sindun, wes, werun (locuti sunt *etc*). 62/12 §endra (loquentium).

yfel-spreocende *prs ptc* evil-speaking. **VP** 11/4 (maliloquam).

wið-spreocende *ptc* contradicting. **VP** 43/17 ~spreocen (obloquentis).

gesprec *sn* speech. **VP** 104/19; 118/50 *etc* (eloquium *n*). 118/38 ~ðin (§ *a*) *etc.* 118/41, 58 *etc* ~e. 5/3 ~es (orationis). 11/7, 7 ~(eloquia). 118/158, 62 ~ðin (§). 17/31; 18/15; 118/11, 103, 72 gespreocu (§). 18/4 § (loquellae). 118/148 ~u. 118/123 in +gesp (eloquium).

fore-spreoca *sm* advocate. **Ct** 41/45 ~.

wrecan *sv* avenge. **VP** 78/10 wrec (vindica!). 117/12 wreocu (§abor). 98/8 §ende (§ans). 117/10, 1 §ende eam (ultus sum). Hy 7/36 §ende wes (zelatus est).

ofer-wrecan *sv* overwhelm. **Cp** 1417 oberu[u]recan (obruere).

ǣrend-wreca *sm* messenger. **Bd**[2] 10 erendwrica (+legatis). **VP** 67/32 erendwrecan (legati *pl*).

frec *aj* greedy. **Cp** 1240 ~eo (lucor).

frecmāse Cp.

frecnis *sf* greediness. **Ep** 475 ~(glus); Ef, Cp §.

mec *a* me. **Rn** 5/3, 4 meh. 16/1, 1 ~. **Rd** 1, 3 *etc* ~. **Mt** 28 ~. **VP** 3/2, 5, 6 *etc* ~(me). 30/5 ~(mihi). 72/24; Hy 10/3 mic.

gecel *s* icicle. **Ep** 954 ~ilae (stiria); Cp §; Ef ~ile.

brecan *sv* break. **Cp** 1650 ~(proteri). **Ct** 45/52 (he) breoce.

gebrecan *sv* break. **VP** 17/43; 74/11 gebreocu (comminuam; confringam). 28/5 §endes (§entis).

tō-brecan *sv* break to pieces. **Mt** 19 (to)~.

egle *sf* dormouse. **Ep** 470 eglae (glis); Ef egilae; Cp, Ld ~.

Hegaer *sm* **LV** 167 ~.

regn *sm* rain. **VP** 71/6; Hy 7/2 ~(pluvia). 67/10; 134/7; 146/8 ~(§iam). 104/32 ~as (§ias).

regenuuyrm Ep; regn§ Ef, Cp.

smolt-regn *sm* mild rain. **Bl** 16 ~(torrens in austro).

regnlic *aj* rain. **VP** 77/44 ða ~an weter (pluviales).

reogol-warde, §weord Ct.

Lega-caestir BH.

leger-stōwe Ct.

þegen *sm* servant, officer. **Ep** 101 thegn; Ef degn; Cp þegn (adsaeculam, minister turpitudinis). **Mt** 36 ðegn. **VP** 102/21; 103/4 ðegnas (ministri; §os). **Ct** 28/20 ðegne [= ministro *line* 1]. 34/10; 48/2 §. 58/24 þegna.

ærn-þegen *sm* house-officer. **Ef** 1137 rendegn (aeditus, templi vel edis minister).

Ēad-þegen *sm* **LV** 88; 185; 233, 50, 79, 89; 302, 29, 46, 76, 97; 440 eatðegn. 130 eatdegn.

Ealu-þegen *sm* **LV** 146 aluðegn.

Eald-þegen *sm* **LV** 312 altðegn.

Beadu-þegen *sm* **BH** 323 badudegn — §deng — beaduðegn — baduðegn. **LV** 259 badudegn. 312 beaduðegn.

Bil-þegen *sm* **LV** 394 ~ðegn.

Cūþ-þegen *sm* **LV** 270; 310, 79, 99; 434, 7 cuthðegn.

Cyne-þegen *sm* **LV** 63 cynidegn. 121, 93; 230, 45; 343, 80, 93; 400 cyniðegn.

• **hors-þegen** *sm* groom. **Ep** 658 ~thegn; **Cp** ~ðegn (mulio).

Lēof-þegen *sm* **LV** 156 ~ðegn.

Til-þegen *sm* **LV** 102 ~thegn. 316; 442, 62 ~ðegn.

Wig-þegen *sm* **Gn** 22 ~ðegn. **Ct** 33/14; 57/7 §. 58/14 ~ðægn.

Wil-þegen *sm* **LV** 55 uilthegn. 123, 7, 30, 46, 8; 237; 305, 19, 75, 86; 404 §ðegn.

þegnian *wv* serve. **VP** 100/6 ðegnade (ministrabat).

þegnung *sf* serving. **Cp** 1081 ðegnunge (procinctu).

ā-ðegen *ptc* received, distended. **Cp** 700 ~(distentus).

segl *sm*.

segelbōsm Cp. segilgaerd Ep; § Ef; segl§ Cp.

ofer-segl *s* **Cp** 209 ober~ (artemon vel malus navis).

gesegen *ptc* seen. **LP** 13 ~ hæbbe. **Bd²** 62 gesegenne (conspicui). **VP** 83/8; 101/17 bið ~ (videbitur). 67/25 ~e sind (visi sunt).

for-segenis *sf* contempt. **VP** 122/4 ~(despectio).

segn *sm* banner. **Ep** 92 ~as (aquilae); Ef, Cp §. 567 seng (labarum); Ef, Cp ~. Cp 278 ~(ban). 1870 ~(signum). 2093 seign (vexilla); Ld segin.

gesegnian *wv* sign, mark. **VH** 13/17 ~ade (signati).

sweger *sf* mother-in-law. **Cp** 1877 su~ (socrus).

suegl-horn Cp.

snegl *sm* snail. **Ep** 217 lytlae ~as (cocleae); Ef, Cp §. 611 snel (limax); Ef, Cp §. 651 ~(maruca); Cp §; Ld snægl.

wegan *sv* carry. **Lr** 74 ic sio ~en (vehar).

forð-wegan *sv* carry forth. **VH** 11/13 †~eð (provehit).

weg *sm* way, road. **Ep** 91 an uueg aferidae (avehit); Ef uoeg; Cp weg. 842 gihuuelci uuaega (quocumque modo); Ef uuegi; Cp wega. 1050 iringaes uueg; Ef inges uueg; Cp iringes uueg (via secta); Ld §uuec. **Mt** 18 ~as. **Bd²** 58 ðorh wigas (tribia). **VP** 17/31; 48/14 *etc* ~(via). 5/9; 17/33 *etc* ~ minne. 5/11 on ~ adrif (expelle!); 17/23 on ~ adraf (reppuli); 18/6 to earnenne on ~(ad currendam viam); 88/42 ða leorendan on ~(transeuntes §am); 118/32 on ~ . . ic orn (§am cucurri). 2/12 ~e; 26/11 ~e ðinum *etc.* **Hy** 11/3 ~e (labere). 118/5 †~es mine (viae *pl*). 9/26; 15/11; 24, 4, 9, 10 *etc* ~as. 16/4; 17/22; 36/18 weagas. 13/3; 90/11; 118/3; 144/17 ~um; 61/10 ~um (stateris). 127/1 weogum. 36/5 wig ðinne. **Ct** 20/6, 12, 21 ðone ~. 31/3 ~. 43/3 cyniges hei ~.

uuegbrādae, uuaeg§ Ep; ueg§, uueg§ Ef; weg§, uueg§ Cp. **Wegbrand**, §ing Gn. **Uegdaeg**, §ing Gn. **weggedāl** Cp.

Bere-ueg *sm* **Ct** 5/2.

hēi-weg *sm* hay-road. **Ct** 43/3 ~.

gemǣr-weg *sm* boundary-road. **Ct** 3/10 ~es.

weall-weg *sm* wall-road. **Ct** 20/19 weal~.

on-weg-. āfirran. ādrifen. āwendan. āloceu. ādrāf. āsceaf. ādrīfan. gewītan.

-hwegu.

hwanon-hwegu *av* from anywhere. **Ep** 1095 huuananhuuoega (undecunque); Ef huuonan§; Cp huonanhuegu.

hwæs-hwegu *prn* of anything. **Mt** 35 ~.

twegen *num* two. **Cp** 1510 tuegen. **Rn** 3/1 twœgen. **VH** 7/59 ~. **Ct** 37/22 tuęgen. 41/18 twægen.

twega *gen* **VH** 6/2 twoega.

plega *sm* play. **Cp** 1477 plaega (palestra).

Plegberct LV; §berht Ct. Plegheard LV. Plegmund LV. Pleghelm Ct. Plegheri LV. Plegrēd Ct. plægsceldæ Lr. Pleguini LV. Pleguulf LV.

stæf-plega *sm* letter-game. Ep 577 staebplegan (ludi litterari); Ef scæbplega; Cp staefplagan.

plegian *wv* play. VP 46/2 plagiað (plaudite). 67/26 plægiendra timpanan (tympanistriarum). 97/8 plægiað (plaudent).

begen *prn* both.

bega *gen* Ct 34/12; 37/12 boega.

Bregu-suīd BH. **Breguini** Gn.

Bregunt-ford Ct.

blegen *s(f)* blain. Ep 1094 blegnae (vesica); Ef blegnæ.

stregdan *sv* scatter, sprinkle. VH 6/20 ~ende (aspargens).

tō-stregdan *sv* scatter. VP 53/7; 58/12 tostregd (disperde!; disperge!). 88/34 ~o (§am). 100/8 ~e (disperdam). Hy 7/52 ~e (dispergam). 82/5 tostrigden (§amus).

gebregdenlice *av* cunningly. VP 82/4 ~(astute).

for-bregdan *sv* snatch. VP 54/10 forbregd (praecipita!).

etan *sv* eat. VP 49/13 eotu (manducabo). 126/2 §að (§atis). 77/24; 101/5 §an. 58/16 to §enne. Hy 6/30 §ende. 105/20 §endes. 21/27 eatað. 26/2 eten (edant).

gesetennis *sf* position. VP 138/2 ~enisse (sessionem).

set *sn* seat, cattle-pen, stall. Ep 896 ~o (stabula); Ef, Cp §. Cp 339 seotu (bucitum).

setgong VP.

sǣ-geset *sn* sea-shore. Ep 728 saegesetu (promaritima); Ef saegaesętu; Cp saegeseotu.

ang-seta *sm* pustule. Ep 770 ~(pustula); Ef †~reta; Cp oncg~.

Bōbing-seata *sm* Ct 19/3 ~.

Hafing-seota *sm* Ct 19/2, 9 ~, ~an *g.*

Rūmining-seta *sm* Ct 5/4 ~.

setl *s(n)* seat. Ct 31/11 ~.

hēah-setl *s(n)* high seat, pulpit. Cp 1667 haehsedlum (pro rostris). VP 106/32 hehseotle (cathedrā).

weard-setl *s(n)* guard-house. Ct 29/11, 1 ~e *d.*

fetian *wv* summon, fetch. Ep 103 fetod (arcessitus vel evocatus); Ef fet[t]ad; Cp feotod.

gefetian *wv* Ep 105 ~odnae (accetum); Ef ~atnae; Cp gefeotodne.

fetor *s* fetter. Ep 778 ~(pedo vel paturum); Ef §; Cp feotur; Ld †fetor.

īsern-fetor *s* iron fetter. Ep 121 isęrn~ (balus); Ef isaern~; Cp ~feotor.

metan *sv* measure. VP 59/8; 107/8 meotu (metibor).

metrāp Cp.

efen-āmeten *ptc* compared. VP 48/13 ~(comparatus).

efen-meten *ptc* compared. VP 48/21 ~(comparatus).

gemet *sn* measure. VP 35/8; 77/57; Hy 7/14 to ðæm ~e (quemadmodum). 79/6 ~e (mensurā).

un-gemetlic *aj* immoderate. Bd[2] 1 mið ~re gitsunge (intemperans cupido).

ungemetnis *sf* extravagance. Bd[2] 3 ~se (dementiam).

gemetgian *wv* moderate. VP 101/10 ~ade (temperabam). Hy 12/11 ~ie (§et).

metod *sm* Creator. CH 2 metudæs.

cete *sf* cot. Cp 1002 ~an (gurgustione).

get *av* get.

nū-get *av* yet, still. VP 36/10; 76/8; 77/30 *etc* ~(adhuc).

be-getan *sv* obtain. VP 48/15 bigetað (obtinebunt). 68/36 bigeotað (adquirunt). Ct 37/20, 3; 41/8; 45/19, 37 begeotan. 47/9, 13 bigeten *prt ptc.*

for-getan *sv* forget. VP 44/11; 73/19 forget (obliviscere!; ne §aris).

on-getan *sv* understand. VP 100/2 ongeotu (intellegam). 2/10; 49/22; 93/8; Hy 7/11 §að (§ite). 72/17 ~e (§am). 5/2 onget! 35/4 ongeotan. 13/2; 52/3 ongeotende. Hy 7/58 ongeatan.

ond-get *sn* understanding. VP

15/7; 31/8, 9 *etc* ~(intellectum; §, §us). 77/72 ~e (sensu). 135/5 ~e (intellectu).

un-ondgetfull *aj* irrational. VH 7/62 ~e (insensati *pl*).

ofer-getol *aj* forgetful. VP 9/13 ~geotol (oblitus). 9/32; 41/10; 118/30, 61; 136/5 *etc* §ul. 43/18 §ele. 21 §ulæ [æ *from* u]. 77/11; 105/13, 21; 118/139 §ule. 101/5 offergeotul.

ofergetolnis *sf* forgetfulness. VP 9/19 ~geotulnis (oblivio). 87/13 §nisse (§ionis). 124/5 §nisse (obligationem).

ofergetolian *wv* forget. VP 118/16, 93 ~geoteliu (obliviscar). 12/1 §ulas. 43/24 §elas. 76/10 §elað. 9/18; 49/22; 77/7 §eliað. 58/12 §elien. 9/33 §ela! 102/2 §elian.

teter *sm* tetter, ringworm. Ep 128 ~(basis); Ef, Cp ~(balsis). 502 tetr (impetigo); Ef †teg; Cp ~. 766 tetr (petigo); Ef, Ld §; Cp ~. 791 spryng *vel* tetr (papula † pustula); Ef §.

Getling- *spl* Gilling. BH 165 *loco qui dicitur* in ~um. 202 *monasterio quod dicitur* in ~um.

Petrus *sm* Peter. Ct 41/33; 45/13 sancte Petre *d*.

mettoc *sm* mattock. Ep 565 ~as; Ef ~as; Cp meottucas (ligones). 586 ~as (§); Ef metocas. 878 ~as (rastros, ligones); Ef metticas; Cp ~as. 1003 maettoc (tridens); Ef ~; Cp awel, meottoc.

Bettu *sf* LV 45 ~.

ed-. scæft. eðcuide. welle. roc. mǣlu. lēan, §ian *etc*. geednīowian. wīt, §an.

smedoma *sm* fine flour. Cp 1606 smeodoma (polenta). Ld 74 smetuma (simila).

weder *sn* weather, air. Cp 2009 uu~ (temperiem). Bl 19 wedr (auram). VP 106/29 ~(§).

med-trymnis VP.

medomlice *av* suitably, fitly. Cp 696 meodomlice (dignitosa).

gemedomian *wv* condescend. VH 13/12 gemeodemad wer■ (dignatus es). 13/18, 20 §. 13/6 †gemeode ðu were.

ceder-bēam VP.

cweden *ptc* said. VP 41/4, 11 bið ~(dicitur). 86/3; 121/1 ~ sind.

be-cweden bequeathed. Ct 38/3 wes becueden.

fore-cweden *aj* afore-said. Ct 37/11, 6, 25 ~cuaedenan, §e, ~cuędenan. 40/16 ~an.

wiðcwedennis *sf* contradiction. VP 17/44; 30/21; 54/10; 79/7; 80/8; 105/32 ~enisse (†contradictionibus; §one; §onem; §onem; §onis; §onis).

cwedol *aj* soothsaying. Cp 689, 90 quedol (dicam, §as).

werg-cwedolnis *sf* malediction. VP 108/18 ~cweodulnisse (maledictionem).

hearm-cwedolian *wv* speak ill of. VP 118/122 hæarmcweodelien (calumnientur).

werg-cwedolian *wv* curse. VP 54/13; Hy 1/9 ~cweodelade (maledixisset; §it).

word-gecweodu *spl* agreement. Ct 45/12 ~.

be-tredan *sv* tread. VP 138/11 betreodað (conculcabunt).

for-tredan *sv* trample on. VP 56/4 ~treodendes (†conculcantes).

Deduc *sm* LV 106 ~.

gebed *sn* prayer. VP 4/2; 6/10 *etc* ~ min (orationem). 34/13 *etc* ~(§io). 60/2 ~e (§ioni). 103/23 to ~e (†operationem). 141/1 *etc* ~es. 101/18; 105/44; 144/19 gebeodu. 68/14 gebeded (orationem).

Bede-winde Ct.

Beoduca LV 102 ~.

bred *s*(*n*) board. Ep 1023 ~ (tabetum); Ef, Cp §.

bredīsern Ep; Ef, Cp §.

rihte-bred *s*(*n*) rule. Cp 1391 †n~ (noma).

gedd *s* song. Ef 374 ~i (elogio); Cp §.

screpan *sv* scrape. Cp 1828 scriopu (scalpio).

ā-screpan *sv* scrape off. Ef 354 †ascrefan (egerere); Cp ~. 375 ~aen (egesta); Cp ~en.

screpe *sf* scraper. Cp 1906 screope (strigillum). 1935 aeren screop (strigillus).

Iorotla-ford Ct.

heora *gpl* of them. **LP** 4; **Mt** 8 hiora. 23 ··ora. **CA** 12 ~. **SG** 9 hira. **VP** 5/10, 0, 1, 1 heara (eorum, §, §, suis) *etc.* 15/4; 54/16 § (illorum; ipsorum) *etc.* 48/15; 103/17 ~. 32/15 hiera. 124/3 hara. 143/8 †hea (eorum). Hy 1/9 he[a]ra. **Ct** 23/15; 30/21; 34/9, 10 *etc*; 37/8, 10 *etc*; 41/38; 42/9, 12 hiora. 42/10, 3, 9 ~. 38/5, 7 hira.

Heru-uald LV.

heorot *sm* stag. **VP** 17/34 ~utes (cervi). 103/18 ~etes (†§is). 28/9 ~etas. 41/2 ~ut.

heorotberge Cp. Herutēu BH. Herutford, heorut§, herud§, hered§. [*second* e *over* u] BH. Heoratlēag Ct.

speoru-līra Lr.

sweora *sm* neck. **Lr** 21, 45 swiran (cladam, ceutro).

weoruld *sf* world. **DA** 8 on ~olde **VP** 17/51; 40/14; 51/11 *etc* in ~(saeculum). 89/8 ~ ur (§ nostrum *a*). 105/1; 117/2; 135/1, 2 *etc* in ~e (§). 76/9; 89/2 *etc* from ~e (§o). 72/12 in ~e (§o). Hy 11/16; 13/32 in ðere ecan ~e (in sempiterna §a). 60/7; 77/2 *etc* ~e (§i). 9/6, 6, 37, 7 *etc* in ~ ~e (in §um §i). 47/15; 71/17; 72/26 *etc* in ~e (§a). 43/9 in weorulðe (§a). 54/20; 73/12; Hy 13/2 ær ~e (§a). 60/7 ~(§a). 60/5 in ~(§a). 144/13 ~a (§orum). 24/6; 101/29 werulde. 47/15 weorund. 101/29 weoruld [ld *from* n]. 135/4 weorulde [ld *from* n]. **Ct** 37/39 fore uueorolde. 40/20 wiaralde *g.*

weorldār Ct.

weoruldcund *aj* worldly. **Ct** 37/39 weorlodcundum.

Cerotaes-ei, ceortes ei BH; §eg Ct.

teorian *wv* tire. **Cp** 668 tiorade (desisse).

heorr *sm* hinge. **Cp** 423 heor (cardo). **VH** 4/17 ~as (§inis = §ines).

steorra *sm* star. **VP** 8/4; 148/3; Hy 8/5 ~an (stellas *etc*). 135/9 ~an (§as). 146/4 ~ena (§arum).

margen-steorra *sm* morning star. **VP** 109/3 ær ~an (luciferum).

swān-steorra *sm* evening star. **Cp** 2111 su~ (vesper).

feorr *av* far. **VP** 9/22; 21/2, 20 *etc* feor (longe). 37/12 § (a §).

feorran *av* from afar. **Rn** 2/12 fearran. **VP** 137/6; 138/3 ~(a longe).

ā-feorrian *wv* remove far. **VP** 54/8 ~ade (elongavi). 87/19 ~ades (§asti). 102/12 ~að (§avit). 70/12 ne afearra ðu (§is).

ceorl *sm* man, husband. **Cp** 2174 ~(uxorius).

Ceorl *sm* **BH** 93 cearli *lg.* **Ct** 20/24 ~i *lg.*

Ald-ceorl *sm* **LV** 98 † ~ceord. 206; 333, 51 ~. 379; 404 alt§.

eorðe *sf* earth. **Rd** 11 ofaer eorðu. **LP** 6 iorðan *d.* **Mt** 48 ~an *d.* **VP** 17/8; 32/5, 8 *etc* ~(terra). 9/39 *etc* ~an (§am). 44/17 *etc* alle § (§am). 7/6; 8/2, 10 *etc* § (§ā). 2/8; 17/16 *etc* § (§ae *g*). 46/8 alre § (§ae *g*). 23/1 *etc* ~ena. 48/12 ~um. 2/10; 46/10; 93/2 *etc* eordan. 23/1 earðe. 9/9; 11/7; 26/13; 45/9; 73/8 §an.

eorðcende VP. eorscripel Cp. eorðmata Cp. eordrestae Ep; § Ef, Cp.

heorþ *s* hearth. **Ep** 5 herth (arula); Ef herd. **Cp** 906 cyline, ~e (fornacula). **Ld** 126 herth (§um). **Bd**[1] hearth (arula).

heorðsuāepe Cp; herdusuepe Ld.

weorðan *sv* become, be. **BDS** uueorth[a]e *sbj.* **Ct** 45/47 ~eð.

geweorðan *sv* happen, become, agree (impers). **Ct** 34/21 ~e *sbj.*

for-weorðan *sv* perish. **VP** 9/6 ~ed (periet). 9/19; 36/28 *etc* ~eð (§ibit). 9/37; 36/20, 2 *etc* ~að. 9/4 ~weordað. 108/15 ~e (dispereat). 2/12; 67/3; 82/18 ~en. 91/8 § (intereant).

weorð *sn* worth, value, price. **VP** 43/13 ~e (pretio). 48/9; Hy 13/13 ~e (§ium). **Ct** 34/14 þæt wiorð. 45/20 mid halfe ~e.

weorðmynd uueorð§ Cp.

weorðian *wv* honour. **VP** 137/2 ~iu ⁊ gebiddu (adorabo). 80/10 ~as (§abis). 65/4 *etc* ~að. 44/12 *etc*

~iað. 113/6(2) § (†odorabunt). 94/6 ~ien. 21/30 ~adon. 105/19; 131/7 ~adun. 28/2 wearðiað.

geweorðian *wv* honour. Ct 37/9, 13 geuueorðiae.

weorðung *sf* honour. CA 9 to ~a.

georstu *interj* VP 114/4; 115/16; 117/25 ~ (o!).

smeoru *sn* ointment, fat, tallow. Ep 769 unamaelti †sperþi (pice sevo); Ef †cinamelti †spreui; Cp unamaelte smeoruue (§ saevo). 944 smeruui •(sevo); Ef §. Cp 1766 unslit smero (saevo). 1846 ~(sevo). 2154 ~(unguentum). Lr 35 smerum (buccis). VP 16/10; Hy 7/73 ~(adipem). 62/6; 72/7; 80/17; 147/14; Hy 7/27 smeorwe (§e).

speruuyrt Ep; smeruuuyrt Ef; smeoruwyrt Cp.

teoru *sn* tar. Ef 282 teru (cummi); Cp ~. Ep 858 teru (resina); Ef §; Cp ~. Cp 985 ~(gluten).

blæc-teoru *sn* black tar, naphtha. Ep 677 blaecteru (napta); Ef §; Cp §teoru.

trēo-teoru *sn* tree-tar, resin. Cp 279 treuteru (bapis).

hweorfan *see under* ę.

hweorf *s* whirl of a spindle. Cp 2108 huerb (vertil).

(hweorf)bānum Lr.

ceorfan *sv* cut. VP 128/4 ~eð (concidet).

ā-ceorfan *sv* cut off. VP 118/39 acerf (amputa!)

for-ceorfan *sv* cut down. VP 88/24 ~u (concidam).

eornan *sv* run. Mt 18 iornan. VP 18/6 to earnenne on weg (ad currendam viam). 57/8 ~ende (decurrens). 147/15 ~eð (currit).

ūp-eornan *sv* rise. VP 71/7 ~eð (orietur). 91/8 ~að (orientur).

eornest *s* earnest. Ep 945 eornęsti (serio); Ef ~esti; Cp ~isti.

leornian *wv* learn. VP 118/71, ~ade (discerem), ~ie (§am).

geleornian *wv* learn. VP 105/35 ~adun (didicerunt). 118/7 ~ade. (didici). Ct 34/16 ~ie.

liornǣre *sm* learner. Mt 35 ~a *gpl.*

georn *aj* willing.

Cundi-georn *sm* LV 346 ~.

Friðu-georn *sm* LV 225 ~.

Here-georn *sm* LV 267; 345 ~.

Wyrt-georn *sm* BH 20, 68 uurtigerno.

geornlice *av* willingly, carefully. Ep 708 ~(obnixe); Ef †~et; Cp ~. Cp 802 ~ (examusim, absolute, certe, vel exquisite). Ct 41/12 ~liocar *cp.*

georne *av* zealously, eagerly. LP 1 ~.

geornnis *sf* willingness, zeal. Ep 527 †geeornnissae (industria); Ef gyrnissæ; Cp geornis.

ferwit-geornnis *sf* curiosity. Ep 208 feruuit~ (curiositas); Ef feruitgernis; Cp feorwitgeornis.

beornan *sv* burn. VP 2/13; 49/3; 88/47 ~eð (exarserit; ardebit; exardescit). 7/14 †~edum (ardentibus).

beorn *sm* (bear), chief.

Beorn *sm* Rn 11/2 ~ae. LV 15, 85; 162; 290, 6; 380 ~.

Beornfrið LV, Ct; (biorn)ferð Ct; biarnfreð Ct. **Beorngȳth** LV. **Beornhǣð** LV, Ct. **Beornhēah**, †beon§, biarn§ Ct. **Beornheard**, bearnhard LV; †beorheard, bernhard, biornheard Ct. **Beornhelm**, biorn§, biarn§ Ct. **Beornmōd** LV, Ct; beormod Ct. †**Beornhōð** LV; beornnoð, beorn[n]oð, beornoð, bearnoð, b(ia)rnoð Ct. **Beornrēd** LV, Gn, Ct. **Beornðrȳð**, bearn§ Ct. **Beornweald** Ct. **Bernuini** BH; beornuini LV; §wine Ct. **Beornuulf** LV, Ct; biarnulf, bearnulf Ct.

Wigbeorn *sm* LV 466 u~.

Beornic *sm* Gn 82 ~

Bernicing *sm* son of B. Gn 82 ~.

feorm *sf* provision, feast, sustenance. Ct 41/69 ðas ~e.

feormfultum Ct.

feormian *wv* support, cherish. Ep 402 ~at (fovit); Cp §; Ef †caeormad.

gefeormian *wv* supply with provisions Ct 42/9 ~ien.

geormant-lāb Ep.

Earconberct, ercon§, eorcon§ BH; erconberht Gn; §ing Gn. **Ercongota**, eorcon§, earcon§ BH. **Ercunuald**, hercun§, ercon§, earcon§, eorcun§ BH; ercin§ LV; erconwald Gn; ercnuualdus Ct.

gesweorc *s(n)* clouding. VP 147/16 geswerc (nebulam).

weorc *sn* work. Ep 699 uuerci (opere); Ef uerci; Cp werci. Cd 3 uerc *pl*(?). VP 108/20; Hy 6/36 werc (opus). 85/8 §e ðinum *etc.* 8/4, 7 *etc* werc (opera). 9/17 *etc* §um. 76/12 *etc* ~a. 104/1; 110/3, 7 †wer (opera).

wundor-werc *sn* wonderful work. VP 138/14 wundur~ ðin (mira opera tua).

gewerc *sn* work. VP 91/5 ~e ðinum (facturā).

āl-geweorc *sn* fire-making. Ep 556 algiuueorc (ignarium); Ef algiuerc; Cp aalgewerc.

deorc *aj* dark. Cp 1994 duerc (teter).

beorc *s(f)* birch. Ep 132 berc (beta, arbor); Ef, Cp §. Cp 298 § (bitulus).

Beorcol *sm* Ct 9/7 bercol. 17/7 bercul. 33/21 ~.

þweorh *aj* perverse. VP 77/8; 100/4 ðuerh (pravum). 17/27; 77/57 ðweoran (perverso). Hy 7/8, 39 ðweoru (prava).

thuerhfyri Ep; Ef §; Cp þ§.

mid-ferh *s* youth. Cp 1164 ~(juventus).

ferht *aj* honest. Ep 748 ~(probus); Ef †fert; Cp ~.

beorht *aj* bright. VP 15/6; 71/14 berht (praeclara; §um).

Berctflēd LV. **Berctfrid** BH; §frith LV. **Berctgilsum**—berechgislum—bercht§ BH; berctgisl LV; bert§ Gn. **Berctgȳth** LV. **Bercthǣð** LV; berhthæð Ct. **Berctbelm**, bercht§ LV. **Berctheri** LV. **Bercthūn** BH, LV; bercht§ LV; †berhthum Gn. **Berctmund** LV; berht§ Ct. **Beorhtnōð** Ct. **Berctrēd** BH, LV; bercht§ LV, Ct; berht§ LV; beorhtredi Ct. **Berctsig**, bercht§ LV; berhtsige Ct. **Berctsuīð** LV. **Berctðrȳth**, berht§ LV. **Berctuaru** LV. **Berctuald** BH, LV, Ct; bercht§ LV; berhtuuald BH1, Ct; bericht§ Ct; berch[t]uald LV; bercuald Ct. **Berctuini**, bercht§, berht§ LV. **Berctuulf**, bercht§, berht§ LV; berchtwulf, berht§, beorhtuulf, biarhtwulf Ct; berh[t]uulf LV.

Beorht *sm* BH 313 bercto—berhto 1. LV 104, 13, 47; 297; 302, 49, 62, 80, 4; 408 bercht. 305, 84 berct. 274 berecht. 357 bercth.

Beorhte *sf* BH 30 bercta [*Frankish name*]—berchta 1—bercta. 65 berctæ *regina n*—berhtae 1—berctae. LV 23 berchtae.

Ægil-beorht *sm* BH 121 agilbercto [*Frankish name*]—aegilbericto—agilberhto. 143 agilberctus—§berictus—§berchtus. 146 agilberctus—egilberictus—agilberchtus. 218 agilberectum. Gn 17 agilberht.

Æl-beorht *sm* LV 65; 330; 451, 64 albercht. 124, 37, 9, 78; 215, 49, 9, 50, 0, 64, 8, 74, 7, 83; 320, 49, 71, 81, 92, 7; 400, 10, 34, 52 4, alberct. 86; 154 ael§. Ct 48/13 alberht.

Æþel-beorht *sm* BH 8 ædilbercto—edilbericto—aeðilberchto. 27 aedilberct—§berich—§aeðilbercht—aedilberct. 28 aedilberctum—§berictum—aeðilberchtum—§berctum. 32 aedilbercto—aedibericto—aeðilberchto—aedilbercto. 33 adilbercto [*in Latin document*]—aedilbericto—aeðilberhto—adiliberto. 34 aedilberct—§berict—aeðilbercht—aedilberct. 39 §o—aeðilberhto 1.—aedilbercto. 47, 54 §i—aeðilberchti—aedilbercti—55 §i. 55, 8 aedilberct—aeðilberht 1—aedilberct. 65 §—aeðilbercht 1. 75 aedilbercti—aeðilberchti 1. LV 3, 7, 7; 109, 9, 10, 78, 85; 220, 35, 43, 52, 91, 6; 308, 20, 40, 99 eðilberct. 259 edil§. 326; 470 eðilbercht. 474 §berht. Gn 62, 8 aeðil§. 80; 113 eðil§. 112 aeðel§. SG 7 æðelbe(rht). Ct 6/1, 2 aethilberhtus. 3 §i. 3 §o. 7/1 §berht. 4 §berhtus. 17/2 æðelberhti 3 §b[e]rhti. 29/1, 18 aeðælberht, aeðel§. 27/5 eþelbearht. 28/1, 3, 15, 9; 30/1, 4, 13 eðel§.

Æþel-beorhting *sm* son of Æþelbeorht. Gn 80, 113 eðilberhting.

Cēol-beorht *sm* LV 61, 99 ~bercht. 198; 205, 12, 71, 96 ~berct. Gn 8 *ceolberhtus*. Ct 22/12; 23/13 ~berhti. 47/4; 50/6; 58/15 ~berht. 57/8 ciol§. 3/13 ~brehtes. 31/10 cialbearht. 38/19 §barht.

Cœ̄n-beorht *sm* LV 236, 44 coenberct.

Cūþ-beorht *sm* Rn 9/2 cuþbœrec. BH 6 cudbercto—§bericto [ic *underdotted*] — §berchto. 234 §berct — §brect — §bercht. 313 §bercto — §berchto I. 321 cuthbercto. 324 cudbercti. 327 §i—cuðberhti I. LV 74, 98 cuthbercht. 131, 54; 248, 63, 71; 307 §berct. 219 cut[h]§. 245; 305 cut§. 418 cuð§. Gn 3 cuðberhtus. 49; 103 §berht. 65 cud§. Ct 7/4, 5 cuthberhto, §us. 17/2, 3 cutberhtus, §i. 17/4; 33/4, 13; 34/18 cuð§. 17/4 cuðberhtus.

Cūþ-beorhting *sm* son of Cūþbeorht. Gn 103 cuðberhting.

Cyne-beorht *sm* BH 5 cynibercti—§bericti [u *over the* y]— —§berhti. 272 §berctum. 286 §berct —cyneberht I. LV 60, 80; 463 cynibercht. 112, 4, 28, 60; 219, 32, 75; 304, 49, 55, 67, 74, 81, 7; 419 §berct. Gn 22, 43 cyneberht. Ct 9/2, 9 cyniberhtte, §ę. 12/4; 17/7; 18/4; 19/4; 32/10; 42/27; 47/6; 48/13; 51/11; 55/10; 56/7; 58/17; 59/6; ~berht. 15/5; 16/4; 52/16 §i.

Dæg-beorht *sm* BH 120 daegberecto [*Frankish name*]—daegberhto I. LV 235; 311, 62, 8, 82 daegberct. Ct 26/6 degberht. 44/2 deibearht.

Dene-beorht *sm* LV 108 ~berct. Gn 47 ~berht. Ct 12/3; 33/8; 34/5; 35/14; 51/2, 9; 54/5 §. 46/5 §us. 49/8 §i.

Dycg-beorht *sm* LV 360 ~berct.

Ēad-beorht *sm* BH 20▮ ~berct — ~brect. 322 ~bercto. LV 5, 8; 85; 125, 7, 35, 72, 7, 8, 81, 4, 91; 209, 21, 31, 4, 7, 7, 46, 51, 63, 6, 74, 89, 91, 95, 5, 5, 7; 307, 38, 45, 62, 2, 4, 71, 3, 3, 85; 400, 19, 24, 4, 8, 54 ~berct. 82, 90; 326, 7, 30 ~bercht. Gn 7; 13, 39, 65, 86 ~berht. Ct 8/4 §uo *ld.* 11/4; 32/9; 33/5, 12, 5, 7, 21; 51/10; 55/9; 56/5; 57/9; 58/17 ~berht. 22/8; 23/8 §i. 14/5 ~ber[h]tus.

Eald-beorht *sm* LV 53 aldbercht. 324 §berct. Gn 29, 50 aldberht. Ct 7/6 §i. 14/6 §us. 47/7; 57/2, 3, 3 aldberht. 5 §o. 34/4 ealdberht.

Aldberhting-tūn Ct.

Ealu-beorht *sm* LV 90 alubercht. 110, 72; 218, 59, 69; 376; 474 §berct. Gn 13 ~berht.

Ēan-beorht *sm* LV 69, 88; 121; 471 ~bercht. 113, 40, 70, 87, 9; 243, 98; 314, 5, 7, 50, 2, 9, 9, 67, 76; 420, 6, 52, 4, 9 ~berct. 476 ~berht. Gn 63 §. Ct 10/1, 3; 14/7; 51/10 §. 6/4 aeanberhti.

Ecg-beorht *sm* BH 126 ~berct —egberc — ~bercht. 136 ~bercto — —eg§ — ~berchto. 215 ~berct—eg§ —ecbercht. 216 ~bercte! — egberct — ecberhte. 216 ~berect — ~berct — ecberht. 220 ~berct — ~berict — ecberht. LK 10 ~berct. LV 5; 137, 80; 204; 307, 14; 423 ~berct. 15 ~bercht. Gn 60, 6; 112 ~berht. SG 3 §. Ct 21/5; 22/3; 23/3; 35/8; 58/17 §. 21/2, 3; 22/1, 2; 23/1, 2; 35/9; 36/5 §o. 21/4; 22/3; 23/3 §um. 22/8; 23/9 §i. 23/14 §es. 29/20 egcberht. 57/10 aecg§. 44/4 ecgbearht.

Ecg-beorhting *sm* son of Ecgbeorht. Gn 112 ~berhting. SG 3 §.

Eges-beorht *sm* Ct 5/7 egisberhti (§berichti).

Eorcon-beorht *sm* BH 122 earconberct—erconberht I. 148 earconbercto — §brecto — §berhto. 151 earconbercti—eorconberhti I—erconbercti. 236 erconberct—§bercht I. 294 earconberct—erconberht I. Gn 113 §.

Eorcon-beorhting *sm* son of Eorconbeorht. Gn 113 erconberhting.

Folc-beorht *sm* Ct 33/15 ~berht.

frēa-beorht *aj* very bright. VP 22/5 ~berht (praeclarum).

Friþu-beorht *sm* LV 183; 343

friðuberct. Gn 62 frioðoberht. Ct 33/15 freoðu§.

Gār-beorht *sm* LV 186 ~berct.

Ge-beorht *sm* Ct 14/6 geberh(tu).

Geng-beorht *sm* Ct 11/4 ~berht.

Gum-beorht *sm* Ct 4/4 ~bercti.

Gūþ-beorht *sm* LV 287 gut[h]berct.

Hǣþ-beorht *sm* LV 171 haeðberct.

Hālig-beorht *sm* LV 199 halegberct.

Hēa-beorht *sm* Gn 47 *heaberht*. Ct 21/6; 22/5; 23/5; 36/8; 41/54; 47/4; 48/15; 49/10; 50/4; 55/9; 57/7 ~berht. 19/6; 22/11; 23/13 §i. 8/1 ~berhcto. 33/20 heahberht. 58/14 haeberht (hea§). 24/11 ~bearht.

Heard-beorht *sm* LV 91 ~berct. Ct 9/6; 12/6; 15/8; 16/7; 49/10; 50/5; 51/10 ~berht. 19/7; 53/7 §i. 17/7 he[a]rdberht.

Heaþu-beorht *sm* LV 58 haduberct. 171, 5, 95; 236, 72, 83, 91; 313, 51, 6, 59, 74; 409, 18, 31 haðu§. 97; 436, 49 heaðu§. 206 hað§. Gn 7 heaðoberht. Ct 12/4; 19/4 haðo§. 12/5 heaðo§.

Here-beorht *sm* BH 235 heriberchto — hereberchto. 320 ~berct. 321 heri§. LV 51 ~bercht. 161, 8; 214, 32; 438 ~berct, 314 h(ere)§. Ct 33/7 ~berht. 24/4 ~bearht.

Hilde-beorht *sm* LV 103, 12; 253, 7, 96; 383 hildiberct.

Hlēo-beorht *sm* LV 201; 355; 452 ~berct.

Hrœþ-beorht *sm* Rn 4/2 roetberhtæ *d* (hroethberhtæ). LV 283 hroeðberct.

Hūn-beorht *sm* LV 129, 79, 87, 98; 248; 317; 415, 44, 57 ~berct. 465 ~bercht. Gn 30, 41 *hunberht*. Ct 48/12 ~bercht. 47/6; 58/15 humberht. 22/11; 23/12 §i.

Hwæt-beorht *sm* BH 381 huaetbercti. LV 61; 222, 95; 303; 406, 62 §berct. 92 §berht.

Hyge-beorht *sm* LV 63, 85; 472 hygbercht. 120, 4, 9, 33, 66, 81, 8, 92; 203, 24, 6, 8, 9, 34, 53, 5, 8, 67, 7, 76, 93, 9; 355, 7, 66, 74, 5, 85, 7, 9; 410, 8, 21, 37, 55 §berct. 329; 477 §berht. Gn 40. §berht. Ct 18/4; 19/3 ~berht. 15/4; 16/3 §i 33/3 hygberht.

Hyse-beorht *sm* Ct 33/9 ~berht.

Iæn-beorht *sm* Gn 4 iaenberhtus. Ct 18/3 §. 46/1 §i. 35/8 iaemberhti.

Land-beorht *sm* LV 104, 6 londberct.

Lēod-beorht *sm* LV 108, 12, 85; 357 liodberct. 437 §bercht.

Nōþ-beorht *sm* Gn 28 noðberht.

Ōs-beorht *sm* LV 13; 130 osberct. 92 osbercht. 326 osberht. Ct 26/7 §. 18/1 §o. 30/19 osbearht. 38/3 osbearte.

Ōsberhting-lond Ct.

Pleg-beorht *sm* LV 113 ~brect. 208; 366, 9, 94 ~berct. Ct 33/7 ~berht.

Rǣd-beorht *sm* LV 242 redberct.

Rīc-beorht *sm* BH 105 ~bercto — ~berchto I.

Sǣbeorht *sm* BH 39 sabercto—sabericto — saberhto — sabercto. 54 saberct—saberht I—saberct. 69 §i —saeberhti I — sæbercti. 375 sabercto — saeberchto. LV 89 saebercht. 283; 318 §berct. SG 14, 9 saberht. Ct 31/8; 43/9 sebearht.

Sǣ-beorhting *sm* son of Sǣbeorht. SG 14 saberhting. 19 sab(erhti)ng.

Sele-beorht *sm* LV 409 seliberct.

Seleberhtingc-lond, seleberhting § Ct.

Sige-beorht *sm* BH 106 sigberct—§bercht I—sigberct. 124 §i—sigberchti I. 124 sigbercto—§berchto. 169 sigberct—§berch—§berht. 171 §berctum — §berectum — §berchtum. 172 §berct—§berech. 184 §berct—§berecth—§berht. 185 §berctum—§berectum—§berchtum. 189 §bercto. LV 10, 2; 125; 238, 92; 379; 421 sigberct. 75 §bercht. SG 13 §berht. 22 sige§. Ct 26/8 sig.. erht. 24/6 ~bearht.

Sige-beorhting *sm* son of Sigebeorht. SG 13, 21 sigberhting, sige§.

Stīþ-beorht *sm* Ct 11/3 stidberht 1 §ae *d*.

Strēon-beorht *sm* LV 109 ~berct.

Swīþ-beorht *sm* BH 325, 9 suidberct—suitbercht I. 352 suidberctum—§berchtum I. 353 suidberct—suitberht I. LV 7; 207, 8, 25; 353, 83 suiðberct. Ct 40/14 swiðberht. 42/26 suið§.

Tand-beorht *sm* BH 292 tondberct. LV 260 §. 157 ton§.

Tāt-beorht *sm* LV 59 ~bercht. 100, 10, 77; 266, 86, 7, 9; 359; 420 ~berct.

Tīd-beorht *sm* LV 137, 53; 239, 52, 76, 88; 306, 19, 67, 71, 90, 0, 6; 411, 5, 59 ~berct. 382; 463 ~bercht. 479 ~berht.

Til-beorht *sm* LV 80; 468 ~bercht. 106, 14, 32, 40; 223, 65, 70; 319, 9, 67; 441, 4, 50 ~berct. 329 ~berht. Gn 62 §. Ct 33/17 §. 10/5 §i.

Trum-beorht *sm* BH 246 ~berct — ~brect.

Tūn-beorht *sm* BH 273 ~berctum. LV 239, 53, 85 ~berct.

Wendel-beorht *sm* LV 97 uendilbercht.

Wǣr-beorht *sm* LV 117; 295 uerberct.

Weren-beorht *sm* LV 64, 88 uernbercht. 122 §berct. Gn 40 uuærenberht. Ct 32/5; 46/4 uueren§. 33/4; 47/8; 48/15 weren§. 34/5 ueren§ (uu§). 49/7 uuerenbe[o]rhti. 43/8 ~bearht.

Wīc-beorht *sm* LV 62 uicbercht.

Wīg-beorht *sm* LV 56; 148 uigbercht. 123, 89; 235, 47; 364 §berct. Gn 24 uuigberht. Ct 12/4; 15/8; 16/7 §. 46/4 §us. 49/9 uigberhti. 33/11; 34/6 ~berht. 19/6 §i.

Wiht-beorht *sm* BH 328 uictberct—§bercht I. 349 uictberct—§berht I. LV 51 uichtbercht.

Wil-beorht *sm* LV 61, 84 uilbercht. 105, 20, 1, 56, 84; 218, 49, 52; 303, 47, 54; 432, 58 §berct.

Wine-beorht *sm* LV 177, 90; 277; 357, 85; 441 uiniberct.

Wit-beorht *sm* LV 188 u(it)berct.

Wyn-beorht *sm* LV 284; 360, 5 uynberct. Ct 15/8; 16/8 uuynberht.

Berhtening-lēag Ct.

beorhtnis *sf* brightness. VP 15/6 berhtnisse (praeclaris).

dweorg *s(m)* dwarf. Ep 686 duerg (nanus); Ef, Cp §. Ef 1176 duerh (humiliamanus).

duuergaedostae Ep; duergae§ Ef; duergedostle Cp.

beorg *sm* hill, mountain. Ef 1175 bergas (colles). Ct 20/13 ðæm ~e. 18 anne ~.

Cilde-bergas *pl* Ct 25/4 ~.

Cisseðe-beorg *sm* Ct 48/4 ~.

fergen-beorg *sm* Ferry-hill (?) Rn 3/5 ~berig.

Wād-beorg *sm* Ct 3/11, 1 ~e, wadb(eorge).

Wifeles-beorg *sm* Ct 30/20 ~berge.

Fearn-biorginga-mearc Ct.

beorg *sf* protection.

Æðel-beorg *sf* BH 74 aedilbergae—aeðilburgae [*last* e *er.*] I—aedilberge. 84 §am—aeðilburgam I aedilbergam. 84 ædilbergæ *d*—aeðilburgae I — aedilbergae. 85 §æ — aeðilburgae I—aedilbergae. 94 §ia *d* —aeðilburga [u *over* e] I—aedilberga. 117 §e *d*—aeðilburga I. 123 aedilbergæ *d*. 151 aedilberg—edilberc—aeðilburg [u *over* e]. 153 aedilberg —aeðilberg I—aedilburg [u *over* e].

brīost-biorg *s(f)* breastwork. Cp 1672 ~(propugnaculum).

līc-beorg *s(f)* coffin, sarcophagus. Cp 1771 ~(sarcofago).

gebeorg *sn* protection, refuge. Cp 1715 geberg (refugium). VP 9/10; 17/3 *etc* §. 90/9 § ðin (§a). 30/3 §es.

bān-gebeorg *sn* greaves. Cp 1426 baangeberg (ocreis).

woede-berge *sf* hellebore. Ef 388 †poedibergæ (elleborus); Cp ~. Cp 1017 woidi ~(helleborus).

heorte *sf* heart. **VP** 5/10; 12/6 *etc* ~(cor). 16/3; 25/2 *etc* ~an mine (§ *a*). 4/7 ~an minre (corde). 9/2 alre ~an (§) *etc.* 4/3; 7/11 *etc* on ~an (§) *etc.* 18/15; 24/17 ~an minre (§is) *etc.* 7/10; 18/9 *etc* ~an (§a). 4/5; 34/25 *etc* ~um (§ibus). 27/3 hortum.

heorthoman Lv.

mild-heort *aj.* merciful of heart. **VP** 77/38; 85/15, 5 *etc* ~(misericors).

reht-heort *aj* righteous of heart. **VP** 36/14 ða ~an (rectos corde). 96/11; 111/4 ~um (§is corde).

hāt-heortnis *sf* hot temper, fury. **VP** 73/1; **Hy** 2/2 ~(furor). 78/5 ~(zelus). **Hy** 6/25 †~iss (furore). 68/10 †~isse (zelus). 37/2 ~isse ðinre (furore) *etc.* 36/8 ~isse (§em).

mild-heortnis *sf* mercifulness. **VP** 24/6, 10 *etc* ~(misericordia). 6/5; 35/11 ~isse ðine (§am) *etc.* 20/8; 30/8 ~isse ðinre (§ā) *etc.* 5/8; **Hy** 9/14 ~isse (§ae *g*). 35/8; 39/12 ~isse (§as). **Hy** 1/6 ~heartnisse. 12/6 ~hertnisse. 16/7 ~heornisse (§as). 24/7 ~heor[t]nisse. 22/6 milheortniss. 106/31 ~heortis.

wœdend-heortnis *sf* madness **VP** 39/5 woedenheortnisse (insanias).

steort *s*(*m*) tail. **Cp** 404 ~(cauda).

heorda *sm* hards (of flax). **Cp** 1908 ~an (stuppa).

gereordan *wv* feed, satisfy. **VP** 131/15 ~u (saturabo). 80/17; 102/5 ~eð (satiavit; §iat). 104/40; 106/9, 9 ~e, gereo[r]de, ~e (saturavit; satiavit, §). 147/14 ~ende (~ians). 16/15 biom ~ed (§iabor). 103/13 bið ~ed (§abitur). 16/14 ~e sind (saturati sunt).

ungereordedlic *aj* insatiable. **VP** 100/5 ~re (insatiabili).

gereordnis *sf* refection, repletion. **VP** 22/2 † gereodnisse (refectionis). **Hy** 5/22 ~isse (§e). 105/15 §(saturitatem).

el-reord *aj* of strange speech, barbarous. **VP** 113/1 ~um (barbaro).

sweord *sn* sword. **Cp** 1927 sueorde (macera). **Mt** 24 sueorde *d.* **VP** 58/8; **Hy** 7/51, 83 ~(gladius). 44/4 ~ðin (§ium) *etc.* **Hy** 7/80 ~min (§). 34/3 ~(frameam). 9/7; 16/13; 21/21 ~e (frameā, †§eam, §eā). 43/4 *etc* ~e (gladio). 62/11 *etc* ~es (§ii). **Ct** 41/34 minum ~e.

Sueordhlincas Ct. **Sueordlēage** Ct.

meord *sf* reward. **VP** 126/3 ~e (mercis).

Eorpuald, earp§, erp§ **BH**; eorup§ **LV**. **Eorpuini** **LV**.

ā-weorpan *sv* throw away, out. **VP** 139/11 ~es (dejicies). 76/8 ~eð (proiciet). 50/13; 70/9 ne aweorp ðu (ne proicias). 54/23 § (jacta!). 16/11 ~ende (§ientes).

in-weorpan *sv* begin the web. **Ld** 34 inuuerpan †uuep (telam orditus).

tō-weorpan *sv* throw down, destroy. **VP** 51/7 ~eð (destruet). 8/3 ~el (§uas). 27/5; 58/12 toweorp (§ue!).

wande-weorpe *sf* mole. **Ep** 1045 uuandaeuui[o]rpae (talpa); **Ef** uuondæuuerpe; **Cp** wondeuueorpe.

weoloc *sm* whelk. **Ef** 267 uuylocas (cocleas); **Cp** uuiolocas. **Ef** 1109 uilucas (clauculas). **Cp** 594 wioloc (coccum).

uuylocbaso Ld. **uuilocrēad** Ep; †u[u]slucreud **Ef**; wiolocread **Cp**. **uuilucscel** Ep; uuyluc§ **Ef**; wiloc§, wioluc§ **Cp**.

Eolla *sm* **BH** 330 eallan *a* — § — ~an. 360 ~. **Gn** 13 ~.

Ceolla *sm* **LV** 413 ~.

Ciollan-dene Ct.

heolster *sm* hiding-place, retreat. **Ep** 867 helustras (recessus); **Ef** §; **Cp** heolstras. 901 helostr (secessum); **Ef**§; **Cp** heolstr. **VP** 17/12 ~ur (latibulum).

geolu *aj* yellow. **Ep** 242 gelu (crocus); **Ef**, **Cp** gelo. 432 gelu (flabum); **Ef** §; **Cp** ~. 458 gelu (gilvus); **Ef** §; **Cp** ~. 1064 ~(venetum); **Ef** geholu; **Cp** ~. **Rd** 10 goelu *neut.*

ǣger-geolu *s* yolk of egg. **Ep** 429 aegergelu (fitilium).

seolfor *sn* silver. **VP** 11/7; 65/10; 113/4; 134/15 ~ur (argentum). 67/31; 104/37 seolfre (§o). 118/72 §es.

ceolbor-lomb Cp.

meolc *s*(*f*) milk. **Bl** 11 from milcum adoen (ablactatus). **VP** 118/70; Hy 7/26 milc (lac).

milcdēondra VP.

eolh *s*(*m*) elk. **Ep** 233 elch (cerus); Ef §; Cp elh. 1001 elch (tragelafus vel platocerus); Ef, Cp §. Ld 139 elha (damma).

ilugsegg Ep; §seg Ef; †wiolucscel Cp.

seolh *sm* seal.

Seles-dūn Ct. **Selæs-ēu**, selaes§, seles§ BH; selesegi Ct. **Seoluini** LV.

sceolh-ēgi Ep; sceolegi Ef; scelege Cp.

feolhan *sv* enter, be joined to. **VP** 68/15 ðæt ic in ne fele (inhaeream).

æt-feolan *sv* adhere. **VP** 72/28 ætfealan (adhaerere).

ceoldre *sf* curds. **Cp** 1338 ~(muluctra); Ld celdre.

feoður-tēme VP.

neoðan *av* below.

nioðanweard, neoþouard Cp.

be-nioðan *prp* beneath. Ct 20/15 ~.

sweostor *sf* sister. **Ct** 41/39 minra swæstar suna.

eofor *s*(*m*) boar. **Cp** 179 eobor (aper). **VP** 79/14 ~ur (§).

Eoforhuaet LV. **eborsprēot** Ep; § Ef; eobor§ Cp. **eburðring** Cp; †eburdnung, ebirdhring Ld. **eborthrotae** Ep, Ef; §e Cp; aebordrotae Ef; eoburthrote Cp; eoforþrote Cp. **Eoforuulf** LV.

eofot *s* accusation, crime. **Cp** 1705 flitere in eobotum (rabulus); Ep, Ef ebhatis.

heofon *sm* heaven. **Rn** 2/6, 18. hea-funæs, h(*eafun*) ·· *g*. **CH** 6 heben. **Mt** 20, 2, 5 hiofonum. 37 in ~. 44 ~um. **VP** 49/4 ~en (caelum *a*). 10/5; 13/2 *etc* §e. 8/9; 21/32 *etc* §es. Hy 12/1 §es (poli). 8/2, 4; 17/10 *etc* §as. 2/4 §um. 67/34; 148/4 §a. 135/5 heofen [o *fr. other l.*]. 77/26 hiofene. 32/13 hiefene. **Ct** 45/50 ~es. 48/20 (heofnum).

Hefenfelth BH. **hebenhūs** Cp. **hefaenrīcaes** CH.

heofonlic *aj* heavenly, of heaven. **Mt** 26 hiofonlican. **VP** 77/24 heofenlic hlaf (manna). 67/15 §an (caelestis). **Ct** 40/22 hiabenlice.

leofaþ *under* libban.

seofon *num* seven. **Mt** 40 ~. 42 se·-fan. **VP** 118/164 seofen siðum (septies).

seofenfaldlice VP. **sifunsterri** Ep; †fun§ Ef; sibun§ Cp.

hund-seofentig *num* seventy. **VP** 89/10 ~um (lxx).

weofod *sn* altar. **VP** 25/6; 50/21 wibed (altare *a*). 83/4 § ðin (altaria). 42/4 to §e. 117/27 §es.

beofor *s*(*m*) beaver. **Ep** 399 bebr (fiber); Ef, Cp §. Ef 272 bebir (castorius); Cp beber; Ld bebor.

heonan *av* hence, from now. **VP** 92/2 nu hionan (ex tunc).

be-heonan *prp*, *av* on this side of. **Cp** 471 bi~ (cis). Ld 255 bihina (citra).

be-geonan *prp* beyond. **Ep** 1041 biginan (trans); Ef bigenan; Cp bigeonan.

Ēastr-geona *s* Eastry (in Kent). **Ct** 18/2 *in regione* ~.

Sūþer-geona *s* Surrey. **BH** 257 *in regione* suder~ — suðri[o]ena [na *hf er.*] I.

Beonna *sm* **LV** 178, 82; 239, 40, 50, 98; 371; 468 ~. **Ct** 12/5; 19/5; 33/6; 34/7; 46/6; 57/8; 58/14 ~. 15/7; 16/6 ~an *g*.

Beonnu *sf* **LV** 46 [*written over other letters*].

Beonne *sf* Ct 58/22 ~.

geond *prp* over, through. **DA** 6 gind. **Ct** 45/31 §.

geondgangend. **geondfæreþ**. **geondgā**. **geondsmēan**.

eom *vb* am. **VP** 2/6; 6/3; 21/7, 11 *etc* eam (sum). 118/109, 41, 53 ne eam (non §). 118/83 ne œam.

neom *vb* am not, aint. **VP** 76/3; 118/30, 60, 176 neam (non sum).

seoh *see* sēon.

feoh *sn* money. **CA** 5 mid uncre feo·

VP 14/5 feh (pecuniam). Ct 38/10 ðet ~. 39/13 ðis fiah.

pleoh *sn.*

Pleouald LV. **Pleoualch** LV.

Weohha *sm.* Gn 119 wehha.

Wehing *sm* son of W. Gn 119 ~.

Tihhan-hyl Ct.

Biohha-hǣma Ct.

seox *num* six. Ct 41/62, 2 sex.

reoht *aj* right. VP 24/8; 32/4 *etc* reht (rectus). Hy 11/9, 12; Hy 12/9 se §a geleafa (fides). 31/11 *etc* §e (recti *pl*); 35/11 §e sind on heortan (§o sunt corde). 7/11; 10/3 ða §an (§os); 13/6 ðere §an (justā); 25/12 ðæm §an (rectā); 57/2 ða §an (justa *pl*) *etc.* 124/4; 142/10 §um (rectis; §ā). 111/2 ðeara §ra (§orum). 72/1; 93/15 §re (§o). 50/12; 106/7 §ne (§um).

rehtmeodrencynn Ct. **rehtfęderen** Ct. **rehtheort** VP. **rehtwīs** *etc,* rechtwisnis, unrehwisnis VP.

un-reht *aj* wrong, unjust. VP 40/9 ~(iniquum). 118/118 ~(injusta). 26/12; 34/11 ~e (iniqui *pl*). 118/36 ~e gitsunge (avaritiam). 9/24; 36/38 *etc* ða ~an (iniqua *pl*; injusti *pl*). 139/12 ðone ~an (injustum). 42/1 ~um (iniquo). Hy 6/27 ~ra (§orum). 118/128 ~ne (§am).

unrehthǣmderum VP.

rehtlic *aj* right, fair. Ct 38/5 ~ast.

rehtlice *av* rightly. VP 18/9 ~(recte). Ct 34/15 ~.

un-rehtlic *aj* wrong, unrighteous. VP 118/126, 150 ~e (iniqui *pl*).

unrehtlice *av* wrongly, unjustly. VP 34/19; 37/20 *etc* ~(inique). 105/6; 118/78 ~(injuste).

reoht *sn* right. Ct 30/6 mid riahte. 38/14 mid ~e. 45/50 mid rehte.

un-reht *sn* wrong, wickedness. VP 40/7; 63/3; 91/10 *etc* ~(iniquitatem).

Uecta *sm* BH 25 ~ — uita.

feht *s* Ct 28/7 xx lamba ⁊ xx fehta.

feohtan *sv* fight. Rn 3/3 fegtaþ. VP 55/2 fehtende (bellans).

ofer-feohtan *sv* conquer. VP 34/1 ~feht (expugna!). 55/4 §að (debellant).

on-feohtan *sv* attack. VP 34/1 ða onfehtendan (inpugnantes).

gefeoht *sn* fight, battle. VP 26/3; 75/4 *etc* gefeht (proelium; bellum). 17/35, 40 to §e (proelium; bellum). 77/9; 139/8 §es. 45/10; 67/31 *etc* gefeht (bella).

þurh-gefeoht *sn* thorough fight. Ep 738 þorgifect (perduellium); Ef †dorhgifecilae; Cp þorhgefeht.

fleohta *sm* hurdle. Cp 600 flecta *vel* hyrþil (cratem).

wāg-flecta *sm* Cp 999 ~(graticium).

cneoht *sm* boy. VP 68/18; 85/16; 104/42 cnehte (puero; §; §um); 112/1 §as. Hy 9/3 §es. Hy 9/11; 10/9 cneht.

cēap-cneht *sm* Ef 349 ~cnext (empticius); Cp ~.

Peoht *sm* Pict.

Pectgils LV. **Pecthāeth** LV. **Pecthelm** BH, LV; peht§ BH, Gn; pecht§ LV. **Pecthūn** LV. **Pectuald,** pecht§ LV. **Pehtuine,** Gn. **Pechtuulf** LV.

sweotol *aj* manifest. Cp 770 seotol (evidens).

sweotullice *av* manifestly. VP 49/3 ~(manifeste).

gesweotulian *wv* manifest. VP 16/15 bið ~ad (manifestabitur), 50/8 ~ades (§asti). 24/14 sie gesweocelad (§etur). 147/20 †gesweocaðe (§avit).

Heott *sm* Ct 20/7 ~es dic.

Peott *sm* Ct 55/10; 56/7 piot. 58/16 piott (piot).

Beotting *sm* Ct 42/1 ~.

Eoppa *sm* Gn 80 ~. SG 4 ~.

Eopping *sm* son of E. Gn 80 ~. SG 3 ~.

here *s(m)* army. CA 4 haeðnum herge.

herebāecon Ep; here§ Ef, Cp. **Herebald** LV. **Herbeding-denn** Ct. **Heriberct** BH—hereberchto I; §berct LV; §berht Ct. **Heriburg** BH. **Herefordensis** Ct. **Herefrith** LV; §frið Gn; §freð Ct; · · efreðingdenn Ct; herefreðinglond (hę§)

Ct. Heregeorn. Heregils LV. Heregȳð LV; §geðe Ct. herehȳðe VP. Heremōd LV, Ct. herepað Ct. Herrēd LV. hererēaf VP, Bd². Heriric, here~ BH; § LV. haersearum Ef; here§ Cp. Heresuīt, §suith BH. heretoga VP. Hereðrȳð Ct. Hereuuald Gn; §wald Ct. Herewīc Ct. Hereuuine Gn.

Ælf-here *sm* Ct 29/22 ~.

Æþel-here *sm* BH 197 aedilheri. LV 266 edil§. Ct 28/17; 32/8 eðel~.

• **Beald-here** *sm* LV 52 balt~. 65 bald~. 204 balð~. Gn 6 ·aldhere.

Beorht-here *sm* LV 269 berctheri.

Cēol-here *sm* LV 104, 324 ~. 223 ~i.

Cnōf-here *sm* BH 172 *urbs* cnobheri—c[o]nobhere.

Cnobheres-burg, c[o]nobheres §, cnobheraes § BH.

Cœn-here *sm* LV 95, 8 coen~. 197 coenheri. Ct 35/14 §here.

Cūþ-here *sm* LV 74 cuthere.

Dōm-here *sm* LV 221 ~i.

Ēad-here *sm* Ct 33/4 ~.

Eald-here *sm* LV 166, 83; 263, 6, 85; aldheri. Ct 30/19 ~. 27/2 ~ *d*. 7 ~es.

Ealh-here *sm* LV 372 alcheri. Ct 24/4; 58/22 alhhere. 26/5, 6; 41/10, 8; 42/24 alchhere. 25/11 alahhere. 32/8; 39/11 ~.

Ēan-here *sm* BH 277 ænheri *g* —aean§—ean§—aen§.

Folc-here *sm* LV 227 ~i.

Forþ-here *sm* BH 80 fordheri—forð§ I—ford§. 359 fortheri—forðhere I. 372 fortheri—§e I. LV 122; 269 forð~. Gn 24 §.

Gisl-here *sm* Gn 13 ~.

Hlōþ-here *sm* BH 234 hlotheri *g*—§e I. 251 §e *d*. 300 §i *a*. Ct 4/1, 4 hlotharius, hlothari *lg*.

Ōs-here *sm* LV 78 ~. Ct 24/5 ~.

Ōs-hering *sm* son of Ōshere. Ct 38/1 ~es.

Pleg-here *sm* LV 164 ~i.

Regen-here *sm* BH 89 rægenheri —raegn§ I, II.

Sige-here *sm* BH 223, 4 sigheri —§e I. 256 §i. SG 13 §e.

Sige-hering *sm* son of Sigehere. SG 13 sighering.

Tandhere *sm* BH 164 tondheri —§e. LV 426 §i.

Tāt-here *sm* LV 173 ~i.

Tīd-here *sm* LV 95, 6; 200 ~.

Til-here *sm* Gn 46 ~. Ct 10/4 ~. 14/5 ~herus.

Torht-here *sm* Gn 49 ~.

Trum-here *sm* BH 183 ~i *d*—triumhere. 201 ~i— ~i I [i *over* e]. 203 ~ę *d*— § — ~ae — ~ę. 207 ~i *a*. 226 ~i *g*. Gn 33 ~.

Weald-here *sm* BH 267 ualdheri—uualdhere I. Ct 2/1, 3 ualdharius, ualdh·· 31/9 ~.

Wealh-here *sm* Ct 21/7; 40/13; 41/53, 6 ~. 22/5 uu~. 24/11 †uueahhere. 23/5 uualhhere. 25/13 walahhere.

Wīghere *sm* LV 200 uigheri.

Wiht-here *sm* Ct 49/12 uiht~.

Wil-here *sm* Ct 29/18 willheres trio.

Wulf-here *sm* Rn 1/12 ~. BH 147 uulfheri — §e I. 183 §i *g* — uulferi. 206 uulfhere *d*. 224 §ę *d*—§e—§e. 225 §i—§e I. 240 §i—§i I. 242 §i—uulferi. LV 11; 280; 383 uulfheri.

Wurm-here *sm* LV 196 uurmeri.

Wyn-here *sm* Ct 26/7 ~.

gehergian *wv* harry, invade. Bl' 24 ~edum (invasis).

for-hergend *sm* ravager. Ep 467 ferhergęnd (grassator); Ef fer~; Cp forhergen[d].

hergiung *sf* ravaging. Cp 821 ~(expeditio).

herian *wv* praise. CH 1 hergan *inf* [a *over dotted* e]. Mt 23 ~edon. VP 21/23 hergo (laudabo). 34/18; 55/5, 11, 1 *etc* §u (§abo). 21/24, 7; 62, 4, 6 *etc* §að (§ate, §abunt *etc*). 83/5 §ad. 106/32; 148/5, 12 *etc* §en (§ent). 17/4 §ende (§ans). 145/2; 147/12, 2; Hy 2/10 ~e (§a!). 101/19; 118/175; 150/6; Hy 3/20 ~.ð. 9/24; 33/3 bið ~ed. 105/5 sie §. 62/12 bioð ~eð. 43/9 bioð †here. 63/11 bioð ~ede. 150/2 hærgað.

efen-herian *wv* praise equally. VP 116/1 ~hergad (conlaudate).

hergendlic *aj* praiseworthy. VP 47/2; 95/4 ~edlic (laudabilis). 144/3; Hy 8/23 ~.

herenis *sf* praise. Cp 824 ~(favor). VP 55/12 ~isse (laudationis). 103/34; 110/10; 117/14; 146/1; 149/1; Hy 2/4 ~(§io).

efen-herenis *sf* VP 32/1 ~(conlaudatio).

here *s.* Cp 911 ~(fornaculum); Ld herth.

dur-here *s.* Ep 925 du:rhere (sualdam); Ef, Cp ~. 1053 duerheri [*first* e *hf er.* ?] (valba); Ef, Cp durheri.

swerian *sv* swear. VP 14/4 §eð (jurat). 62/12 swergað (§ant). Hy 7/78 §u (§abo). Hy 9/7 ðone §endan að (jusjurandum).

and-swerian *wv* answer. VP 101/24 ondsweorede (respondit). 118/42 §iu. Hy 3/12 §a! 13 §að (§ebit).

secgge-scere *sf* grasshopper. Cp 464 ~*vel* haman (cicad).

scerero *pl* shears. Ep 401 sceroro (forfices); Ef §; Cp ~.

īsern-scerero *pl* iron shears. Cp 903 ~uru (forfex).

be-scerian *wv* deprive. Ep 73 bisceredae (addicavit); Ef §idae. VP 20/3 §edes (fraudasti). 77/30 sind §ede. 83/13; Hy 7/50 ~ed; ~eð (§abit). Hy 7/52 biscergu (privabo).

werian *wv* defend. Cp 39 ~eth (abiget).

be-werian *wv* prevent. VP 33/14 ~e (cohibe!). 39/10 biwergu (prohibebo). 82/2 ne biwere (compescaris). 118/101 §ede (prohibui).

wer *sm* wier. Ct 43/4 halfne ~.

for-wered *aj* (*ptc*) worn out. Ef 1135 ~uerit (abusus).

Uern-bald LV. **Uernbercht** LV; uuærenberht Gn; uueren§, ueren§ Ct. **Uernfrith**, ueren§ LV. **Uerngȳth** LV **Uerenhāeth** LV. **Uernðrȳth** LV.

hwer *s*(*m*) kettle. Ep 563 huuer (lebes); Ef §; Cp huer. VP 59/10; 107/10 ~(olla).

ā-ferian *wv* carry away. Ep 91 an uueg aferidae [f *over* u] (avehit); Ef aueridae; Cp ~ide.

fere-scaet Cp.

generian *wv* save, preserve. VP 90/15 genergu (eripiam). 30/3; 39/14; 49/15, 22 §e *etc.* 81/4 §að. 34/10 §ende (§iens). 6/5; 7/2; 16/13 *etc* ~e! 21/21 § (erue!). 68/15 †gere! 17/49 ~es (eripies). 17/44 †genes (§). 21/9; 33/8; 36/40 ~eð. 88/49 § (eruet). 17/18; 33/5; 56/5 *etc* ~ede (eripuit). 114/8 †~ed (§). 53/9; 55/13 *etc* ~edes. Hy 3/17 § (eruisti). 17/30 biom ~ed. 123/7 §is.

mere *s*(*m*) lake. Ep 962 ~i (stagnum); Ef §; Cp ~. VP 106/35; 113/8 (1) in ~(§).

Meredenn Ct. **meremenin** Cp. **meresuīn** Cp.

Ēanburge-mere *s*(*m*) Ct 48/5 ~.

? **Hūs-merae** *s*(*m*) Ct 9/3 ~.

mere *sf* night-mare. Ep 558 mera (incuba, vel satyrus); Ef merae; Cp maere; Ld maerae. Ld 33 †menae (pilosi, incubi, monstri).

ā-merian *wv* test, purify. VP 11/7 amearad (examinatum). 17/31 § (§ata). 65/10 bið §. 16/3; 65/10 §edes.

gederian *wv* injure. VH 13/19 gedergan (ledere).

bere-corn Ep [*second* e *over* i]; ~Ef, Cp. **Bereueg** Ct.

berge *sf* berry. Cp 509 ~an (corimbos).

heorot-berge *sf* buckthorn-berry, blackberry (?). Cp 1333 ~(mora).

hind-berge *sf* a kind of berry. Ep 69 ~berię (acinum); Ef ~en; Cp ~beriae. Ef 352 ~brere (erimio); Cp ~.

wīn-berge *sf* grape. VH 7/28, 63, 4 ~an (uvae *g*, §a, §a).

ā-merran *wv* hinder. VP 77/31 amerde (impedivit).

cerran *wv* turn. VP 72/10 ~eð (revertetur).

gecerran *wv* turn. VP 17/38; 67/23; 88/24 ~u (convertar; §am;

§am). 65/6; 104/25; 113/8 ~eð (§it). 6/5; 79/15; 79/4, 8 *etc* gecer! (§ere; §ere; §e; §e). 18/8 ~ende (§ens). 22/3; 77/44 *etc* gecerde (§it). 29/12; 40/4 §es (§isti; versasti). 7/17 sic ~ed; 31/4 ~ed eam; 77/34 bioð ~ed *etc.* 7/12 sien gecerde; 9/18 bioð § *etc.* 21/28 sien gecered. **Ct** 40/24 ~.

ācerran *wv* turn away. **VH** 7/38 -u (avertam). Ps 12/1; 87/15 ~es (§is). 73/11 acers (§is). 33/15 acer (diverte!); 53/7 § (averte!); 26/9; 68/18 ne § ðu (§as) *etc.* 77/38; 80/7 acerde (§eret; divertit). 84/2, 4; 88/40, 4 §es (avertisti). 77/57 on weg §on (§erunt).

eft-cerran *wv* turn back, return. **VP** 103/29 ~að (revertentur). 145/4 ~eð (§etur). 77/39 ~ende (rediens).

forcerran *wv* turn aside. **VP** 43/24 ~est (avertis). 9/32; 13/7; 21/25 ~eð (§it). 52/7 ~ed (§it). 16/13 forcer (subverte!). 84/7 ~ende (convertens). 103/29 ~endum (avertente). 105/23 forcerde (averteret). 29/8; 43/11 §es (§isti). 6/11; 34/4; 39/15; 69/4 sien ~ed (§antur). 17/27 bist §(subverteris). 34/13 sie § (convertetur). 45/3 bioð § (transferentur). 58/15 sien § (convertentur). 58/7 sien ~ede (§). Hy 7/8, 39 cneoris ~edu (perversa). 69/4 sien forcerde (avertantur).

oncerran *wv* alter, change. **Ct** 34/17 oncærrende. 48/19 incerre.

forcerring *sf* turning aside. **VP** 9/4; 125/1 in ~e (convertendo).

erþling *sm* (husbandman), wren. **Cp** 302 erd~ (bitorius).

ærðelond Ct.

ers-endu Lt.

Mersa-hām Ct.

mersc *sm* marsh. **Ef** 289 merisc (cemetum); Cp mer[s]c (calmetum). 302 †merix (§). **Bl** 14 s·ltne ~(salsilaginem). **Ct** 28/24 ðem ~um. 30/11 of ~e. 54/2 cyninges~.

herste *sf* fryingpan. **Ld** 97 herst (craticulis ferreis factis). **VP** 101/4 in ~an (frixorium = §io).

herstan *wv* fry. **VP** 101/4 ~e sind (confrixae sunt).

derste *sf* dregs. **VP** 39/3 ~an (fecis). 74/9 dearstan [*from* derstan; *under* drosne] (fex).

herwan *wv* despise. **VP** 21/8 herwdun (aspernabantur).

herwendlice *av* with contempt. **Ep** 186 heruuendlicae (contemptum); Ef haeruendlicae; Cp †heuuendlice.

serwan *wv* plot. **Cp** 581 seruuende (convenientes).

generwan *wv* distress. **VP** 60/3 bið ~ed (anxiaretur). 142/4 § is (§iatus est). Hy 12/4 generwde (anxios).

gerwan *wv* prepare, dress. **VP** 131/16, 8 ~u (induam). Hy 12/1 ~ende (vestiens). 34/26 sien gerede (induantur).

gegerwan *wv* prepare, dress. **Ep** 196 †gegeruuednae (conparantem); Ef †gegeruednae; Cp gegaerwendne. 730 gigeruuid (praetextatus); Ef †gigarauuit; Cp gegeruuid. **VP** 92/1, 1; 108/18 gegereð (induit). 34/13 §ede (§uebam). 103/1 §edes. 131/9 earun gegered. 64/14 §e sind. 108/29 sien §e.

on-gerwan *wv* undress. **Rn** 2/1 (on)geredæ hinæ. **VH** 12/12 ongered (exuta).

gegerela *sm* dress. **VP** 44/10 ~an bigyldum (vestitu).

erfe *sn* inheritance. **VP** 46/5; 93/14 *etc* ~(hereditatem). 105/5 ~ðinum. 73/2; Hy 5/30 ~es. **Ct** 34/9 érfe. 40/19 ðis erbe. 41/2; 42/3, 14, 21 ærfe. 44/7 ęrbe. 48/2, 5, 7 ~. 40/3; 41/31 ærfe *d.* 45/9, 18 ęrfe *d.* 45/3, 48 ęrfes.

ærfegedāl Ct. **erfehond** Ct. **erfeland**, ærfelond Ct. **ærbenuma**, ærfe§ Ct. **ærfeweard**, ę§, e§ Ct. erfeweardnis, erfwordnis VP.

erfa *sm* heir. **Ct** 39/8 erbum.

hwerfan *wv* turn, wander. **Cp** 764 huerbende (errabiles). **VP** 108/14 ~eð (redeat).

gehwerfan *wv* change, exchange. **VP** 117/13 ~ed eam (versatus sum). **Ct** 28/23 iehwerfed.

cerfille *sf* chervil. **Cp** 456 ~(cerefolium).

for-wernan *wv* prevent. **Ct** 40/22 ferwernę.

dern-licgan VP.

ermðu *sf* misery. **VP** 68/21 ~(miseriam). 31/4 ~(in erumna). 87/19 § (miseriā). 11/6 fore § (§iam). 37/7; 139/11 ~um (§iis). 39/3 ~a (§iae *g*).

erce-biscop, ærce§, arce§, archi§ Ct.

serce *sf* shirt. **Ep** 18 ~ae (armilausia); Ef §; Cp ~.

Merce *pl* Mercians. **Rn** 1/11 myrcna *gpl*. **BH** 3, 93 ~iorum. 23 ~i. **Gn** 32 ~iorum. 97 mer ... *gpl*. 99, 102 mercna *gpl*. **Ct** 9/1 marcersium. 10/1 *etc* ~iorum.

Merce-cumb Ct. **Mercwælle** Ct.

merce *s* parsley. **Ep** 24 merici (apio); Ef †meru; Cp merice.

Bercingas *pl* Berkshire. **BH** 259 *loco* .. *in* berecingum — §un — bercingum — berecingum.

merhe *sf* mare.

Meran-worð Ct.

wergan *wv* curse. **Ef** 318 uuergendi (devotaturus); Cp ~endi. **VP** 73/3 ~ende wes (malignatus est). 91/12 § (§antes). 93/16 §um. 104/15 ~an (§ari).

wergcweoðan, wer§; wergcweodulnis; wergcweodelade VP.

ā-werged *aj* (*ptc*) cursed. **VP** 5/6 ~(malignus). 9/36 ðes awergdan. 14/4 se §a. 21/17; 63/3 ~ra (§antium). 25/5 § (§orum). 36/1 awergde (§antes). 100/4; 118/115 § (§os; §i). 118/21 § (maledicti). 143/10 §um (maligno).

āwergednis *sf* malediction. **VP** 9/28; 13/3; 108/18 ~nisse (maledictione).

fergen-berig [*under* eo] Rn.

bergan *wv* taste. **VP** 33/9 ~að (gustate).

Cert *s* Chart. **Ct** 25/3, 3; 28/9; 38/2, 9 ~ *d*. 55/5 *silva* .. *qui dicitur* ~. 6 Cymesinges ~.

Herding *sm* **LV** 333 ~.

werdan *wv* injure. **Cp** 1434 ~it (officit).

ā-werdan *wv* injure. **Ep** 1091 auuaerdid (vitiatum); Ef auuerdid; Cp †awended.

ferd *sf* expedition, army. **Ef** 373 fertd (expeditio); Cp faerd. **Cp** 810 ~un (§ibus).

ferdwīc VP.

Cerdic *sm* **BH** 309 *rege Brettonum* ~e.

Ceardicing *sm* son of C. **SG** 6 ~.

gerd *sf* twig, rod. **Ep** 614 toch ~(lentum vimen); Ef thoh §; Cp toh gęrd. Cp 2134 ~(virgultum). **VP** 22/4; 44/7 ~(virga). 73/2; 109/2; 124/3 ~(§am). 88/33 ~e (§ā). 2/9 in ~e iserre. 44/7 ger (§a).

hefel-gerd *sf* **Cp** 1219 hebel~(liciatorium).

segl-gerd *sf* sailyard. **Ep** 111 segilgaerd (antempna); Ef §; Cp ~gęrd.

sund-gerd *sf* sounding-rod. **Cp** 319 ~ in scipe (bolides).

scerpan *wv* sharpen. **VP** 139/4 ~tun (acuerunt).

ā-scerpan *wv* sharpen. **VP** 63/4 ~tun (exacuerunt). **Hy** 7/80 ~u.

gewerpan *wv* recover (from illness). **Cp** 572 geuaerpte (convaluit).

Sal-werpe *sf*. **Ct** 13/4 *fluvium qui dicitur* salu(uerpe). 6 saluuerpæ.

el-. reord. lende. ðēodig.

Seli-berct LV. **Seliburg** LV; sele§ Ct. **Seleferð**, §ing SG. **Selerēd**, SG, Ct; §ing SG. **selegescot** VP. **Seleðrȳð** Ct.

selen *s*(*f*) grant. **Ct** 44/8 sęlen.

Feli-geld LV.

cele *s*(*m*) keel. **Ep** 862 neb *vel* scipes celae (rostrum); Ef cæle; Cp caeli.

cele *s*(*m*) cold. **VP** 147/17 ~es (frigoris). **Hy** 8/8 ~(§us).

celiwearte Cp.

celeð *prs* cools. **Ep** 561 caelith (infridat); Ef cælid; Cp kaelið.

ē-celma *sm* chillblain. **Cp** 1500 ecilma (palagra).

ecilmeht *aj* with chillblains. **Cp** 1523 ~i (palagdrigus).

celic *s*(*m*) cup. **VP** 74/9; 115/13 calic (calix; §icem). 10/7 §es. 15/5 celces.

Celc-hȳð, caelic§ Ct.

Ella *sm* **LV** 140; 472 ae~.

Elle *sm* **BH** 46 aelli — aelle 1 [a *er.*]—

aelle. 60 §i — §e I — §i. **LV** 380 §i. **Gn** 73 §e.

Aelling *sm* son of Æ. **Gn** 73 ~.

elles-hwæt, ælles§ Ct.

ellen *s*(*n*) zeal. **VP** 118/139 ~(zelus).

elnian *wv* be zealous. **VP** 36/1 ~(aemulari). 36/1, 7 ~ende sie. 77/58 werun ~iende. 36/8 ~a! 72/3 ~ade (zelavi).

ellen *s* elder. **Ep** 893 ellaen (sambucus); **Ef** ellae; **Ep** ellaern. **Ef** 1131 elle (§a, lignum).

hell *sf* hell. **VH** 3/19 hel (infernus). 9/18 *etc* in ~e (§um). 6/6 *etc* § (§o). 85/13 § ðere nioðerran (§o). 17/6 *etc* § (§i). **Ct** 40/23 ~e wite.

heldīobul Cp. **helwearan** VH.

sellan *wv* give. **VP** 2/8; 31/8 ~u (dabo). 115/12; 131/4 ~u (retribuam; dedero). 104/11 ~e (dabo). 15/10; 17/48 seles (§is; das) *etc.* 20/7 §est (dabis). 13/7; 15/7; 40/3; 118/130; 120/3; 126/2 §eð (§it; tribuit; tradat; dat; det; dederit) *etc.* 12/6 selð (tribuit). 65/2; 80/3; **Hy** 7/5 ~að (date). 67/35 ~ad (§). 103/12 ~að (dabunt). 9/35; 103/27 selle (tradas; des). 19/5; 110/7; **Hy** 11/7 § (tribuat; det; donet). 27/4; 59/13 *etc* sele (da!). 118/17 § (retribue!). 27/3 ne sele (tradas). 26/11; 73/19 *etc* ne § ðu (§ideris; §as). 77/20 ~(dare). **Hy** 9/8; **Hy** 13/27 ~ende (daturum; §us). **Hy** 9/13 to § (ad dandam). 103/28 ~endum (dante). **Ct** 30/20; 45/8, 11, 23, 4, 8, 32, 8 ic ~o. 41/44; 42/20 ic ~e. 37/2 ~að. 37/15, 9; 41/13, 20; 45/26 ~e *sbj.* 41/11 sęlle *sbj.* 48/1 ic sile. 3 to siollanne.

gesellan *wv* give. **CA** 8 ~. **Ct** 37/24; 38/8; 45/22, 9, 34, 9 ~e *sbj.* 40/3 ~.

ā-sellan *wv* give away. **CA** 16 áselle *sbj.*

ymb-sellan *wv* surround. **VP** 7/8; 31/10; 54/11; 90/5 ~seleð (circumdabit). 31/7; 48/6 ~seled salde; ~eþ [þ *from other l.*] (§dedit). 47/13 ~að. 31/7 ~endum. 117/11 ~ende (§dantes). 3/7 ymsellendes.

Hlif-gesella *s* Ct 25/10 ~.

scell *sf* shell. **Ef** 376 scel (echinus, piscis); Cp §. Cp 560 ~um (concis).

musclan-scel *sf* mussel-shell. **Cp** 593 ~(conca).

weoloc-scel *sf* whelk-shell. **Ep** 182 uuiluc~(conquilium); **Ef** uuyluc~; Cp wiloc~. Cp 1487 wioluc~ (†papiliuus).

scelle *s* destruction. **Cp** 564 ~(concisium).

ā-stellan *wv* institute. **CH** 4 astelidæ.

on-stellan *wv* institute. **Ct** 42/17 ~en *sbj.*

welle *sm* spring, well. **VP** 35/10; **Hy** 11/2 waelle (fons). 17/16; 103/10 §an (fontes). 41/2 §um. 73/15; **Hy** 8/13 wællan (§) 113/8 (1) ~an (§es). **Hy** 2/5 †~u (§ibus). **Ct** 55/4 se hole ~.

Bōte-welle *sm* Botwell. **Ct** 59/2 ~wælle.

ed-welle *sm* whirlpool. **Ep** 1019 eduella (toreuma); **Ef** §i; Cp eduuaelle. 1068 edwalla (vertigo); **Ef** edualla; Cp eduuelle; **Ld** eduallę. Cp 137 edúaelle (alveum). 908 ~(fortex). 1798 eduuelle (scylla).

Merc-wælle *sm.* **Ct** 59/2 ~. 7 ~an boec.

Wassing-welle *sm.* **Ct** 28/2 †wasng~. 2, 7 *etc* ~an *d.*

Wilburge-welle *sm.* **Ct** 43/2 to ~an.

fell *sm* fall. **VH** 11/7 fael (casus).

gefellan *wv* fell. **VP** 105/26 gefaelde (prosterneret).

ā-fellan *wv* fell. **Cp** 1645 afael (praecipita).

ā-mællad *ptc* made empty. **VP** 74/9 ~(exinanita).

getellan *wv* account. **VP** 31/2 geteleð (imputabit). 143/3 §est (reputas).

Paelli *sm* **LV** 340 ~.

Til-geseltha *s.* **Ct** 25/9 ~.

elfetu *sf* swan. **Ep** 718 aelbitu (olor, cignus); **Ef** †ębitu; Cp aelbitu. Cp 30 § (tantalus).

haelf-trēo VP.

helfan *wv* halve. **Cp** 303 †herbid (bipertitum).

twelf *num* twelve. **Mt** 33 tuelf. **Ct** 41/67 ~. 37/9, 13. 5 tuælf.

eln *sf* ell. **Ld** 42 elin (cubitum).

selma *sm* bed. **Ep** 955 ~(sponda); Ef §; Cp benc §.

ǣ-welm *s*(*m*) source. **Ct** 20/5 æwielme *d*.

cwelman *wv* afflict, mortify. **VP** 36/14 cwaelmen (trucident). **Hy** 4/12 cwælmeð (mortificat).

Kælca-caestir, helca§ [he *on er*], faelcaestir BH.

welhisc *aj* foreign, Welsh. **Ct** 37/21 uuelesces.

Welhisc *sm*. **Ct** 4/6 uelhisci *lg*.

gunde-swelge *sf* groundsel. **Ep** 976 gundaesuelgiae (senecen); Ef §suelgae; Cp gundesuilge.

sadul-felg *sf* pommel of a saddle. **Ep** 818 ~ae(pella); Ef ~ae; Cp ~e.

faelging *sf*. **Cp** 1385, 1427 ~(navalia; occa).

telg *s*(*m*) dye. **Cp** 934 taelg (fucus, faex).

aet-taelg *s*. **Cp** 1732 ~(rediva).

twi-tælgad *ptc* twice-dyed. **VP** 108/29 ~e (deploide).

blǣst-belg *sm* (blowing-bag) bellows. **Ep** 454 blestbaelg (follis); Ef §; Cp blaes§. Cp 28 bloest§ (sublatorium).

ā-sceltan *wv*. **Cp** 697 ascaeltte (disolverat).

gemeltan *wv* melt *trans*. **VP** 21/15 gemaeltende (liquefiens). 57/9 gemælted (liquefacta). 74/4 gemaelted (§). 147/18 §eð (liquefaciet).

unā-melt *aj* (*ptc*) unmelted. **Ep** 769 ~maelti sperþi [=smerwi] (pice seuo); Ef †cinamelti; Cp. ~maelte.

elde *pl* men. **CH** 5 aelda barnum.

eldan *wv* delay. **Cp** 2065 ae[l]den (tricent). **VP** 77/21 aelde (distulit). 88/39 §es (§isti).

for-eldan *wv* delay, miss. **Pv** 1 domę foręldit.

aelding *sf* delay. **Cp** 677 ~(dilatio).

eldo *sf* old age. **SG** 10 ~ *g*. **Bd**[2] 31 nænig ældu (retna aetis). **VP** 70/9 aeldu (senectutis). 18 in § (senectā). 91/15 §. 11 § (§us).

eldra *comp*. elder. **Ep** 546 aeldrum (primores); Cp §; Ef ældrum. Cp 241 aeldra faeder (avus). 1855 aeldra (senior). **VP** 106/32 §ena (§um). **Hy** 7/13 ældran (§es tui).

ōhelde *aj* sloping, hanging. **Ep** 838 ohaelði; Ef oheldi; Cp ohældi (pendulus).

heldan *wv* incline. **Rn** 2/7 hælda *inf*.

āheldan *wv* incline. **VP** 26/9 ne ahaeld ðu (declines).

†inheldan *wv* incline. **VP** 143/5 inhæld (inclina!).

onheldan *wv* incline. **VP** 48/5 onhaeldu (inclinabo). 43/19 onhældes (declinasti). 9/31 onhęldeð (inclinabit). 74/9 ~haeldeð (§). 108/23 †onhaeð (declinat). 77/1; 118/21, 115; 138/19 ~haeldað (inclinate!; declinant; §ate!; §). 140/4 §e (§es). 16/6; 118/36 ~hæld (inclina!). 30/3; 44/11; 36/27 ~haeld (inclina!; §; declina!) *etc*. 87/3 ~hęld (inclina!). 17/10; 114/2; 118/51; ~haelde (inclinavit; §; declinavi) *etc*. 13/3; 20/12 §on (declinaverunt). 52/4; 101/12 §un (§). 54/4 ~hældon (§). 16/11 ~hældan (§are). 100/4; 124/5 ~haeldende (§antes). 103/5 bið §ed (inclinabitur). 45/7 §e sind (§ata sunt). 61/4 §um (§ato).

onheldednis *sf* inclination. **VP** 72/4 ~(declinatio).

geheld *sn* holding, custody. **VP** 89/4 gehaeld (custodia). 38/2; 78/1; 140/3 § (§iam). 76/13; 105/39 §um (observationibus). 129/6 §e (custodiā). 18/12 in gehælde (custodiendo).

hwelp *sm* whelp. **VP** 16/12 ~(catulus). 56/5 ~a. 103/21 ~as.

sweðel *sm* swathing. **Ep** 506 suedilas (instites); Ef §; Cp sueðelas. Cp 831 weðel (fascias). 833 suaeðila (fasciarum). **Ld** 72 suithelon (institis).

sceððan *wv* injure. **Mt** 49 ~e. **VP** 26/2 ~ende (nocentes). 34/1 ða ~endan (§). 86/34 ~u (§ebo). 104/14 ~an. 88/23 sceðeð.

un-sceððende *aj* (*ptc*) innocent. **VP** 17/26; 23/4 ~(innocens). 24/21 ~(§entes). 72/13 ða ~an. 17/

26 unscedendum. 25/6 unsceðende. 105/38 in~. 93/21 insceðende.

unsceðfull *aj* innocent. **VP** 14/5 ðone ~an (innocentem).

unsceðfulnis *sf* innocence. **VP** 40/13 ~nisse (innocentiam). 25/1, 11 § minre (§iā). 7/9; 17/21, 5; 83/13; 100/2 § *d*.

Ese *sm*. **BH** 4 ~i *g*. **LV** 214 ~i. **Ct** 28/16 ~.

Esne *sm*. **Gn** 50 ~. **Ct** 12/5; 14/7; 15/8; 16/7; 19/6; 20/5; 34/18 ~. 14/7 esn(e). 34/10 ~*d*.

Esning *sm* son of E. **Ct** 47/12 ~e.

gehnescan *wv* soften. **VP** 54/22 gehnistun (mollierunt).

rest *sf* rest, bed. **VP** 131/14 ðeos ~(requies). **Hy** 12/3 sie ~(quies). 131/5 ~e (requiem). 94/11 ~e mine (§). 114/7; 131/8 ~e ðine (§).

eorð-rest *sf* resting on the earth. **Ep** 219 eordrestae (cauneuniae); **Ef** §raestae; **Cp** §reste.

restan *wv* rest. **Ep** 443 ~aendum (feriatis, quietis, vel securis); **Ef** ~endum.

gerestan *wv* rest. **Cp** 854 ~ed (feriatus). **VP** 4/9; 54/7; **Hy** 6/34 ~u (requiescam). 14/1; 15/9 ~eð.

gest *sm* stranger.

gesthūs VP.

gesting *sf* exile. **Cp** 795 gestin[c]cum (exilia).

hefeð *under* hebban.

hefig *aj* heavy. **VP** 37/5 ~(grave). 34/18 ~um (§i). 34/13; 54/4 hefie (molesti). 4/3 hwefie (graves).

gehefegian *wv* weigh down. **VP** 31/4 ~ad is (gravata est). 37/5 ~ade sind.

hefeld *s* weaver's beam. **Ep** 602 hebild (liciatorium); **Ef** §. **Cp** 1232 hebeld (licium).

hebelgerd Cp. **hebeldðrēd** Cp.

gehefeldian *wv* begin the web. **VH** 3/7 ~ad (ordirer).

Lefilla *sm* **LV** 197 ~.

Lefincg *sm*. **LV** 235 ~.

cefes *sf* concubine. **Ep** 745 cebisae (pelices); **Ef** caebis; **Cp** cebise.

refsan *wv* intercept, reprove. **Ep** 523 r[a]ebsid uuaes (interceptum est); **Ef** repsit; **Cp** raefsit. 526 raefsed (interpellari); **Ef** refset; **Cp** raefsit. **Cp** 1082 rę̄fsde (intercepit).

ā-refsan *wv* intercept. **Ep** 511 araepsid (intercaeptum); **Ef** arepsit.

refsung *sf* interception. **Cp** 1068 raepsung (interceptio).

stefnan *wv* alternate. **Ep** 75 staefnęndra (alternantium); **Ef**, **Cp** §endra.

gestefnan *wv* alternate. **Ep** 864 gistaebnęndrae (reciprocato); **Ef** †gistaebnen; **Cp** gestaefnendre.

eft *av* again, afterwards. **Mt** 14 ~. **VP** 70/20 ~(iterum).

eftcerran. **eftryne**. **eftārās**.

Lęncan-feld Ct.

ðencan *wv* think. **VP** 37/19 ~o (cogitabo). **Hy** 3/14 ~u (re§). 9/23; 34/4; 39/15 ~að.

be-sencan *wv* sink *trans*. **VP** 68/3 bisencte (demersit). 16 bisence (demergat). **Hy** 5/7 ~te. 17 bisenctun.

swencan *wv* afflict. **Cp** 640 suenceth (defatiget). **VP** 17/39 ~u (adfligam). 41/10; 42/2 ~eð (§et; §it). 3/2; 12/5 *etc* ~að (tribulant). 16/9 ~tou (adflixerunt). 55/2; 105/42 § (†tribulavit; §averunt). 106/6 ~tun (†§arentur). 34/5; 105/11 ~ende (adfligens; tribulantes) *etc*. 59/14 *etc* ða ~endan (§antes). 77/42 ~endes (§antis). 43/8 ~endum (adfligentibus). 43/3 †swentes (adflixisti). 73/13 †senctes (contribulasti).

geswencan *wv* afflict. **VP** 68/21 ~ende (tribulantes). 30/10; 68/18 biom, bio ~ed (§or). 37/7 § eam (afflictus sum). 50/19 § (contribulatus). 105/32 § is (vexatus est). 63/2; 101/3; 119/1 § (tribulor; §or; §arer). 33/19 §re (§ato). 43/22 bioð ~te (afficimur). 105/44; 106/13, 9, 28 werun §(tribularentur). 106/39 § sind (vexati sunt). **Hy** 7/71 §(fatigatos). 93/5 †geswecton (vexaverunt).

geswencednis *sf* affliction. **VP** 118/143 ~(tribulatio). 43/24 *etc*

~nisse (§onem). 65/14 § minre (§one) *etc.* Hy 6/34 § minre (§onis) *etc.* 24/17 *etc* § (§ones). 33/5 *etc* ~nissum (§onibus). 33/20 † geswenced (§ones).

gescrencan *wv* trip up. VP 16/14 gescrenc (supplanta!). 17/40 ~tes. 36/31 bioð ~te. 139/5 ~an.

gescrencednis *sf* tripping up. VP 40/10 ~nisse (supplantationem).

tō-stencan *wv* scatter. VP 67/31 tostenc (dissipa!). 142/12; 143/6 ~es (disperdes; dissipabis). 32/10; 52/6 ~eð (§at). 43/3; 144/20 § (disperdet). 17/15 ~te (dissipavit). 17/41; 88/11 ~tes. 118/126 ~tun. 140/7 ~te sind.

tō-stencnis *sf* dispersion. VP 146/2 ~nisse (dispersiones).

wlencu *sf* pride. Cp 846 uu~(fastu).

drenc *s(m)* drink. DA 15 ofer ~e.

wyrt-drenc *s(m)* medicine. Cp 166 ~(antedo).

drencan *wv* give to drink. VP 35/9 ~es (potabis). 59/5 † drentes. 103/11 ~að.

in-drencan *wv* inebriate. VP 22/5; 64/11 ~ende (inebrians). 64/10 ~tes. Hy 7/82 ~u.

geindrencan *wv* inebriate. VP 35/9 bioð ~te (inebriabuntur).

benc *s(f)* bench. Cp 1895 ~, selma (sponda).

lencten *s(n)* spring. VP 73/17 lenten (ver).

†**lectinādl** Ep; lenctin§ Ef; §ald Cp.

engel *sm* angel. Mt 19 ~. 26 englas. VP 34/5 ~(angelus). Hy 1/5 ~(§um). 77/49; 96/7 *etc* englas. 8/6; 90/11 §um. 137/1 §a. Hy 7/15 †enga (§orum). 34/6 ængel.

Engle *spl* Angles, English. BH 21 anglis.

Ēast-engle *spl* East-angles. BH 290 estranglorum—ea§ I. Gn 117 eostengla *gpl.*

Middel-engle *spl* Middle-angles. BH 178 middilangli, *id est mediterranei angli*—§engli—§ęngli—§engli. 376 §angli—§engli—§aengli.

Sūþ-engle *spl* South-angles Ct 9/1, 8 sutangli *dicuntur*; suutanglorum.

Hengest *sm.* BH 24 ~ist—haengist I. 68 ~ist—haengest I. Gn 114 ~.

Hengesting *sm* son of H. Gn 114 ~.

leng *av* longer (of time). CA 7 lencg. VP 37/9; 118/8, 43, 51, 107 a hu ~e suiður (usquequaque). Ct 34/10; 38/8 ~.

lengu *sf* length (of time). VP 20/5; 22/6; 90/16 ~(longitudinem). 92/5 in ~(§ine).

gelengan *wv* lengthen. VP 97/6 gelengdum (ductilibus). 108/18 bið ~ed (prolongabitur).

þengel *sm* prince.

ðengles-hām Ct.

Sænget-hryg Ct.

ā-swengan *wv* swing, strike out. VP 135/15 ~de (excussit).

steng *sm* pole. Ep 209 stegn (clava); Ef stęng; Cp ~. Cp 2097 †seng (vectis).

strenge *aj* strong. VH 5/17 ðæm ~estan (validissimā).

strengu *sf* strength. VP 37/11; 42/2; 59/9; 107/9; 117/14; Hy 2/4 ~(fortitudo). 27/8 ~o (§). 67/36; 92/1 ~ (§inem). 58/10 ~o mine (§§). 38/12; 67/7; Hy 4/19; Hy 7/24 ~(§ine). Hy 4/9; Hy 6/10 ~(robore; fortitudini). 60/4 ~(§inis). 32/16 †streng (§inis).

strenge *sm* string. VP 32/2; 143/9 ~a (cordarum). 150/4 ~um (chordis).

tēn-strenge *aj* ten-stringed. VP 91/4 hearpan ~re (decacordo).

ðun-wenge *sn* temple (of head). Lr 31 ðunnwengan (timpori). VP 131/5 ~um (temporibus).

feng *sm* capture. Ep 727 faengae (captu); Ef §; Cp ~e.

ond-fengnis *sf* taking up. VP 82/9 ~nisse (susceptione).

ond-fenga *sm* taker-up. VP 41/10; 45/8, 12 *etc* ~ min (susceptor). 3/4 † ~e.

menga *sm* merchant. Ep 659 mengio; Cp 1285 §(mango).

mengan *wv* mix. Cp 565 ~et (confundit).

gemengan *wv* mix. Ep 543 gimaengdae (infici); Ef gimengdæ; Cp ~de. Cp 547 gemęngan (confici). 1055 ~ed (infestus). VP 74/9 § (mixto). 105/35 ~de werun (commixti).

gemengedlice *av* mixedly. Ep 750 gimengidlicę (permixtum); Ef gimaengidlicæ; Cp gemengetlic.

gemengung *sf* confusion. Ep 203 gimaengiungiae; Ef gemengiungae (confusione); Cp gemengiunge.

genge *s* (going, gang,) privy. Cp 1172 ~(latrina, atque ductus, cloacas).

Gengberht Ct.

fræt-genga *s*(*m*) apostasy. Cp 183 fraetgengian (apotasia).

næht-genge *sf* night-walker. Cp 1025 naect~ (hyna).

gegenga *sm* fellow-traveller. Ld 85 † gegenta (pedisequis, conviator).

ō-gengel *s* bolt, bar. Cp 1423 ~(obex).

geglengan *wv* adorn. VP 143/12 ~de (compositae *pl*).

Eni *sm.* BH 171 ~ *g.* Gn 118 ~.

Ening *sm* son of E. Gn 118 ~.

ened *s*(*f*) duck. Ep 17 aenid (aneta); Ef §it; Cp enid.

dop-ened *s* diver. Ep 419 ~aenid (fulix); Ef §; Cp dopp§.

þeneþ *under* þennan.

āwened *under* wennan.

mene-scillingas Ep, Cp; meni§ Ef.

menigo *sf* multitude. Cp 685 meniu (dilectum, exercitum). VP 30/20; 76/18 mengu (multitudo). 43/13 §o (§). 5/8; 32/16; 63/3 *etc* §u (§ine). 5/11; 9/25 *etc* efter § (§inem). 17/17; 36/11; 105/7 §u (§inis).

menen *sn* (virgin), handmaid, slave. Cp 2106 ~(vernacula). VP 85/16; 115/16; 122/2; Hy 10/3 ~es (ancillae).

mere-menin *sn* mermaid. Cp 1864 ~(sirina).

Glene *s* river Glen. BH 98 *fluvio* ~i.

Tenid *s* Thanet. Ct 4/1 in ~ *d.*

denu *sf* valley. VP 107/8 ~e (convallem). 83/7 ~e (§e). 64/14 ~e (§es). 103/10 deanum.

Ciollan-denu *sf* Ct 41/11 an ~e.

Cymenes-denu *sf* Ct 3/2 *vallem vocatam* ~.

haran-denu *sf* hare's valley. Ct 3/4 in vallu . . in ~e.

Līowsan-denu *sf* Ct 29/7, 8 ~e *d.*

stān-denu *sf* stone-valley. Ct 3/6 in ~e.

Turca-denu *sf* Ct 14/4 *vallis qui dicitur* ~.

Dene *sm* LV 292 ~.

Deneberct LV; §berht Gn, Ct. Denefrið Gn; §ferð Ct. Denewald Ct.

Denes *sm.* BH 131 denises burna, *id est, rivus* §i—§aes—dęnises, §i.

pening *sm* penny. Ct 45/22 ~a. 34 pęninga. 41/68 pendinga. 41/35 † pending *gpl* [*end of line*]. 41/33 pend' *a.* 41/22, 6, 7 § *gpl.* 39/12 pen' *gpl.*

henn *sf* hen.

hennfuglas, hen§ Ct.

edisc-henn *sf* quail. Ep 714 ~haen (ortigomera); Ef † ~henim; Cp ~hen. VP 104/40 edeschen (coturnix).

wudu-henn *sf* wood-hen. Cp 583 †wodhae (coturno).

ðennan *wv* stretch. VP 7/13 ðeneð (tetendit). 35/11 §e (praetende!) 10/3; 36/14 §edon (tetenderunt). 142/6 §ede (expandi). Hy 6/18 ~ende (tendens).

ā-ðennan *wv* stretch out. VP 54/21; 104/39 aðeneð (extendit; expandit). Hy 6/18 §es (extendes). 84/6 §e! (§as). 87/10; Hy 7/21 §ede (expandi; §it). 79/12; 137/7; Hy 5/20 §edes (extendisti). 63/4 §edun (intenderunt). 139/6 §edon (extenderunt). 43/21 ~að (expandimus). 59/10; 107/10 ~u (extendam). 103/2 ~ende (§ens). 124/3 ~en (§ant).

āðenenes *sf* extension. VH 7/48 ~(extensio).

ā-wennan *wv* wean. Cp 1957 awenide (suspenderat). VP 130/2 awened (ablactatus).

ofer-wennan *wv* be proud. Ep

538 oberuuaenidae (insolesceret); Ef §uenedæ; Cp §uuenide.

for-wened *aj* (*ptc*) insolent. Ep 548 feruuaenid (insolens); Ef † feruendid; Cp foruuened.

fenn *sn* fenn.

fenðacum Bd[2].

menn *under* mann.

mennesc *aj* human. VH 13/5 ~es (humani).

cennan *wv* bring forth. Rd 2 caend(æ). VP 7/15, 5 ~eð (parturit, peperit). 47/7; Hy 7/24, 45 ~ende (parturientes; nascentias, §). 2/7; 109/3; Hy 7/35 cende (genui; §; §uit). 50/7; Hy 4/11 § (peperit).

ā-cennan *wv* bring forth. VP 21/32 bið ~ed (nascitur). 44/17 acende sind (nati sunt). 77/6 bioð §(nascentur). Hy 8/11 ~ende (nascentia). Ct 45/47 acenned weorðeð.

ā-cenned *aj* brought forth. Hy 13/8 ~ne (editum).

ān-cenned *aj* only-born. Hy 11/15 ðæm ancendan (unigenito). Hy 13/31 §um (§).

eorð-cenned *aj* earthborn. VP 48/3 ~cende (terriginae).

frum-cenned *aj* firstborn. VP 88/28 ~ne (primogenitum).

ācennis *sf* birth. VP 106/37 ~se (nativitatis).

grennung *sf* grinning. Ep 852 graennung (rictus); Ef †graemung; Cp ~.

denn *sn* den, swine-pasture. Ct 29/16, 6 ~es. 29/15, 7 ~ *pl.* 28/12 stanehtan ~.

denbēra Ct.

Aeting-den *sn* Ct 25/8 ~.

Bleccing-den *sn* Ct 30/11 ~.

Herefreðing-denn *sn* Ct 30/10 · · efreðing~.

Herbeding-denn *sn* Ct 30/10 ~.

Hildgāring-denn *sn* Ct 25/9 ~.

Lāmburnan-den *sn* Ct 28/11 ~.

Liding-den *sn* Ct 25/8 ~.

Mere-denn *sn* Ct 25/8 ~.

Orrices-den *sn* Ct 28/11 ~.

Pafing-denn *sn* Ct 30/10 ~.

Sciofing-den *sn* Ct 55/7 sc[i]ofing~.

Telig-den *sn* Ct 28/11 ~.

Wīdefing-denn *sn* Ct 30/11 ~.

Pennel-tūn, pegnel§ BH.

stent. Cp 292 stęnt (becta).

Der-wente *s* Derwent. BH 79 *amnem* deruuentionem—dor§ I—derue§. 320 deruuentionis *fluvii*—dor§ I.

Sol-wente *s* Solent. BH 288 *pelago quod vocatur* soluente—§ II [u *dotted out*].

Cent *s*(*f*) Kent. Ct 41/32 binnan ~. 45/32 in cęnt.

Kentuald LV. Centwine, §ing Gn.

Centa *sm* LV 160 kaenta.

Centing *sm* son of C. Ct 1/5 cęntinces triow.

Quenta-uīc BH.

twentig *num* twenty. Ct 47/10 tuentigum.

tuentegða *aj* twentieth. Mt 39 ~an.

Pente *sf* river Pant. BH 188 ~æ *amnis g*—paentae—paente [*first* e *er.*]

ende *sm* end. VP 144/3 ~(finis). 9/7, 19 *etc* ~(§em). 38/5 ~minne (§em) 18/5; 45/10 *etc* ~as. 7/7 ~um. Ct 40/20 oð wiaralde ~.

geendebyrdan, endebyrdnis VP. endistaeb Cp; † stęb Ef.

ers-endu *npl* buttocks. Lr 53 ~.

geendian *wv* end. VH 3/7, 10 ~as (finies).

geendung *sf* ending. VH 6/40 ~e (consummatione).

ān-hende *aj* one-handed. Ep 626 ~i (mancus); Cp §; Ef anhaendi.

īdel-hende *aj* empty-handed. VP 7/5 ~(inanis). Hy 10/9 ~(§es).

Rendel *sm*. BH 191 rendlæs ham, *id est, mansio* ~ili—raendili I.

Rendlæs-hām, raendles § BH.

el-lende *aj* foreign. Cp 99 ~ (afiniculum, a finibus procul).

lenden *s* loins. Ep 216 lendnum (clunis); Ef laendum. 860 lęndino (rien); Ef lendino; Cp laendino. Ef 1128 len libre da (reniculus). Lr

24 lendana (talias). VP 44/4 ym lendan (femur).

lendebrēde Cp.

sendan *wv* send. VP 147/17, 8 ~eð (mittit). 19/3 ~e (§at). 17/15, 7 ~e (misit) *etc.* Hy 5/11, 6; Hy 6/27, 30 ~es (§isti). 21/19 ~on (§erunt). 77/9; 125/6 ~ende (mittentes).

in-sendan *wv* send in. VP 33/8 ~e (immittit). 39/4; 77/45, 9 ~e (inmisit). Hy 7/49 ~u (inmittam).

on-sendan *wv* send out. VP 42/3; 103/30; 143/6, 7 onsend (emitte!). 103/10 ~eð (§et).

ūt-sendan *wv* send out. VP 109/2 ~eð (emittet). 147/15 § (§it).

gescendan *wv* bring to shame, confound. VP 13/6; 43/10 ~es (confudisti). 24/20; 30/2 biom ~ed *etc.* 85/17; 128/5 sien ~ed. 21/6 werun ~e. 24/3, 4 sien ~e. 118/31 ~(confundere). 70/1 sie ges[c]ended. 118/78 sien gesende.

gescendðo *sf* confusion. VP 108/29 ~e (confusione).

gewendan *wv* turn. Cp 2056 geuuendit (transfert).

ā-wendan *wv* turn away, remove. VP 38/11; 118/29 awend (amove!).

onweg-āwendan *wv* remove away. VP 65/20 onweg ne awende (non amovit). 108/10 sien ~e (§eantur).

in-wendan *wv* change. VP 108/24 ~ed is (inmutata est).

on-wendan *wv* move, change. VP 101/27 ~es (mutabis). 35/12 ~eð (moveat). Hy 7/59 ~að (transmovebunt). 105/20 ~un (mutaverunt). 16/5 sien ~e (moveantur). 36/21 bið †~e (mutuatur). 101/27 bioð ~e (mutabuntur).

onwendednis *sf* commotion, change. VP 54/20; 76/11 ~(commutatio; in§). 43/13 ~nissum (commutationibus). 88/52 ~nisse (§em). 43/15 onwendnisse (commotionem).

lēof-wende *aj* amiable. Ef 1136 lebuendi (adfectuosus, amabilis).

Uendil-bercht LV.

Penda *sm* BH 115, 6 ~. 113, 26, 168 ~ *d.* 141; 206 ~an *g.* 204 § *g*—penda I. LK 7 ~. Gn 92 ~.

Pendgīth LV. Penduald LV. Penduulf LV.

Pending *sm* son of P. Gn 92 †peding.

bend *sf* bond. VP 106/14; 115/16; Hy 6/27 ~e (vincula). 106/10; 149/8; Hy 13/11 ~um.

ā-blendan *wv* blind. Cp 1941 ~eð (suffundit).

emer *s* a bird. Ep 909 ~(scorelus); Ef §; Cp omer; Ld emaer.

emel *s* beetle. Ef 257 æmil; Cp emil (curculio). Ep 484 aemil (gurgulio); Ef §; Cp emil. VP 104/34 ~(brucus).

Hemele *sm* Gn 39 ~.

fremðe *aj* strange, foreign. VP 68/9 ~(exter). Hy 7/23 ~(alienus). 108/11 ~(§i *pl*). 17/46, 6 bearn ~(§). 82/8 ~es cynnes (alienigenae *pl*). Hy 1/8 ~es cynnes men (§ *d*). 86/4 ~es (§). 18/14; 48/11; Hy 7/32 ~um. 43/21 ðæm ~an. 53/5 ða ~an. 80/10 ~ne. 136/4 ~re. 143/7 ~ra. 11 fremdra.

ā-fremðan *wv* alienate. VP 57/4 ~ae sind (alienati sunt).

āfremðung *sf* alienation. VH 6/28 ~e (alienatione).

fremu *sf* benefit. Ep 135 ~(beneficium); Ef §; Cp fre[o]mo.

freamsum *aj* beneficial. VP 68/17; 134/3 ~(benigna; §us).

freamsumlice *av* beneficially. VP 50/20 ~(benigne).

freamsumnis *sf* beneficialness. VP 51/5; 84/13 ~se (benignitatem). 64/12 § (§is).

Hemma *sm* LV 94; 100 ~. Ct 44/2 ~.

Hemmi *sm* LV 335 ~.

un-wemme *aj* undefiled. VP 17/24; 18/14 ~(immaculatus). 118/80 ~(§um *nom.*) 17/33 ~(§am). Hy 7/8 bearn ~(§i *pl*). 63/5 ðone ~an. 100/2, 6 ðæm §. 36/18 unwemra. 118/1 unwęmme (§i).

gewemman *wv* corrupt, injure. Ep 540 giuuaemmid (infractus); Ef geuemmid; Cp ungeuuemmid. VP 13/1 gewemde sindun (corrupti sunt). 52/2 § sind.

ungewemmed *see* gewemman.

fremman *wv* forward, perform. **Cp** 1649 ~endum (praestante). 1656 fremid (provehit).

gefremman *wv* forward, perform. **Ep** 725 gifraemith (provehit); Ef gifremit; Cp gefremið. 759 gifraemid (profetae); Ef gifremid; Cp gefremid. **VP** 16/5 gefreme (perfice). 7/14; 17/34 §ede (effecit; perfecit). 8/3; 30/20; 39/7 §edes (§isti). 30/19 sien §ed (efficiantur). 10/4; 67/10 †gefredes (perfecisti).

ful-fremed *aj* perfect. **VP** 88/38 ~(perfecta). 138/22 ~re (§o).

un-fulfremednis *sf* imperfection. **VP** 138/16 ~se mine (imperfectum *a*).

gremman *wv* irritate. **Ep** 580 graemid (lacessit); Ef gremid; Cp §ið. Cp 1195 ~(lacessere).

gegremman *wv* irritate. **Ep** 515 gigrę̄mid (irritatus in rixam); Ef gigremit; Cp gegremid. 593 gigraemid (lacessitus); Ef gigremid; Cp gegremid. **VP** 65/7 gegremedon (provocant). 67/7 ~að (§).

nemnan *wv* name. **Mt** 13 is ~ed. 50 ~eð.

be-nemnan *wv* name, settle. **Ct** 41/58, 66 hafað binemned. § is.

Hremping-wiic Ct.

laempi-halt Ep; †lemphi§ Ef; lemp § Cp; §hald Ld.

cempa *sm* fighter. **Ep** 481 caempan (gladiatores); Ef, Cp ~an. Ef 1148 ~(auctoracius i.g. monachus qui est ab exercitu electus). **Lr** 4 ~an (agonithetas). 6 ~an (anthletas)

tempel *sn* temple. **VP** 64/5 ~(templum *n*). 44/16 *etc* ~(§ *a*.). 78/1 ~ halig ðin (§ *a*). 5/8 *etc* temple. 67/30 § ðinum, ðæt (quod). 47/10 *etc* temples. 26/4 † tempe (templo).

Embe *sm* **LV** 440 ~.

Wemba-lēa Ct.

eced *s*(*nm*) vinegar. **VP** 68/22 ~e (aceto).

heced *s*(*m*) pike (fish). **Ep** 587 haecid (lucius); Ef, Cp §. 660 § (mugil); Ef hecid; Cp haeced.

recedlic *aj* palatial. **Cp** 1479 raecedlic (palatina).

lecþa *sm* leak. **Ep** 890 lectha (sentina, ubi multae aquae colliguntur in navem); Ef, Cp §.

blece *s* blight. **Cp** 2117 ~i (vitiginem); Ld §. Ld 24 § (pruriginem).

blecþa *sm* blight. **Ep** 1069 blectha (vitilago); Ef, Cp §.

Ecca *sm* **LV** 152 ~.

Ecci *sm* **LV** 200 ~.

Haecca-hām Ct.

Hecci *sm* **LV** 173; 201 ~.

reccan *wv* narrate, rule. **Cp** 139 ~eo (alligeo). **VP** 27/9 rece (rege!). 2/9; 79/2 §es. 22/1; 47/15; **Hy** 11/8 §eð.

gereccan *wv* direct. **VP** 5/9; 7/10; 24/5 *etc* gerece (dirige!). 24/9; 145/8; 100/7 §eð (§it; §; direxit). 95/10; 118/9 §eð (correxit; corrigit). 66/5 §es (diriges). **Hy** 9/17 to ~enne (ad §endos). 39/3 gerec:::hte (direxit). 77/8 gerehte (§). 118/128 § (dirigebar). 101/29; 139/12 bið gereht. 58/5 wes §. 36/23 bioð §. 118/5 sien §. 140/2 sie geræht.

ā-reccan *wv* recount; erect. **Ep** 204 arectae (concesserim; Ef §; Cp §e. Cp 818 arehtun (expresserunt). **VP** 144/14 areceð (erigit). **Hy** 9/2 arehte (erexit).

ūp-āreccan *wv* erect. **VP** 19/9 ~arehte sindun (erecti sumus).

ūp-reccan *wv* erect. **VP** 145/7 upreceð (eregit).

gerecenis *sf* direction, correction. **VP** 96/2 ~(correctio). 118/7; 138/3 ~se (directione; §em).

reccere *sm* director, ruler. **VH** 12/1 rec[c]ere (rector).

recceleās *aj* reckless. **Cp** 1646 ~(praefaricator).

ō-leccan *wv* soothe. **Cp** 1519 olectendra (palpantum).

leccan *wv* water. **VP** 103/13 ~ende (rigans).

ðeccan *wv* cover. **VH** 7/20 ðeceð (tegit).

bi-ðeccan *wv* cover. **VP** 103/3 biðeces (tegis). 54/6 biðehton (contexerunt).

ǥsleccan *wv* seize. **VP** 7/3 geslæcce [cce *in diff. ink*] (rapiat).

geoc-stecca *sm* part of a plough. ~(obicula). **Cp** 1424 ~.

specc *a s(m)* speck. **Cp** 1388 ~an (notae).

ā-weccan *wv* awake *trans.* **VP** 40/11 awece (resuscita!). 79/3 §(excita!). 87/11 §að (resuscitabunt). 112/7 ~ende (suscitans). **Hy** 4/14 awecende! (suscitans). **Hy** 12/13 ~e (§et). 77/5 awehte (suscitavit). 77/17; **Hy** 7/32, 41 §un (concitaverunt). 77/40, 58 §on (§). **Hy** 13/15 §es (resuscitasti). 77/26 awaehte (excitavit); **Hy** 6/27 §es (§asti). 77/65 awaeht is (§atus est).

wrecca *sm* exile, stranger. **Cp** 812 wraeccan (extorres). **Rn** 15 uræcko. **VP** 93/6 wrecan (advenam). 145/9 wręccan (§).

gefeccan *wv* fetch, seize. **Mt** 24 ~a(n).

hnecca *sm* neck. **Ep** 715 hreacca (occiput); **Ef** hręca; **Cp** hrecca. 720 snecca (occipitium). **Ef** 1165 ~(cervix, posteriora colli).

gemecca *sm* wife. **Ct** 37/1 ~. 41/5 minum ~an.

cweccan *wv* shake *trans.* **Lr** 12 cueccen (librent). **VP** 7/13 cweceð (vibrabit).

Deccan-haam Ct.

dreccan *wv* afflict. **Bd**[2] 27 ~ende (adficiens).

Bleccing-den Ct.

hlehhan *sv* laugh. **VP** 51/8 hlæhað (ridebunt).

ðwehð *prs* washes. **VP** 57/11 ðweð (lavabit).

ðwehs *prs* washest. **VP** 50/9 ðwes (lavabis).

slehð *prs* strikes, kills. **Cp** 1857 gesca slaet (singultat). **Bl** 15 sliet (concidet). **VP** 77/34 sleð (occiderit).

slehs *prs* strikest, killest. **VP** 138/19 sles (occideris).

ege *sm* fear. **VP** 13/3, 5; 18/10 *etc* ~(timor). 33/12 ~(§em). 2/11 *etc* ~(§e). 5/8; 118/38, 120 ~ ðinum.

egesa *sm* fear. **Rd** 13 egsan *g.*

Egisberht Ct. **egisigrīma** Ep, Ef; egis§, eges§ Ct.

egesful *aj* fearful. **VP** 46/3; 65/5; 75/8 *etc* ~(terribilis). 65/3 ~fulle. 75/12, 3; 105/22 §an. 98/3 §um. 144/6 ~ra (§iorum).

egesfullice *av* fearfully. **VP** 138/14 ~(terribiliter).

egðe *sf* harrow. **Ef** 395 egdae (erpica); **Cp** ~; **Ld** eg[i]ldae. **Cp** 1702 egiðe (raster).

egðere *sm* harrower. **Ef** 396 egderi (erpicarius); **Cp** ~.

Ægili *sm* **Rn** 3/9 ~.

Agilberct, aegil§, egil§ BH. **Egilmund** LV.

hege *sm* hedge. **Cp** 606 ~as (crates). **Ct** 26/5 be norðan ~.

Hegford Ct.

Regn-hæg LV [*under* hēah]. **Rægenheri**, raegn§ BH.

geregnian *wv* adorn. **Ep** 618 ~odae [*from* -ren-] (mendacio composito); **Ef** †geradnodae; **Cp** ~a[de].

slege *sm* stroke. **Cp** 582 slaege (conlisio).

Degsa *sm* **BH** 37 ~stan, *id est* ~lapis.

Degsa-stān, daegsa§ BH.

ecg *sf* edge. **Cp** 50 ~(acies *etc*).

Ecgbāeth LV. **Ecgbald** Gn; egc§ Ct. **Ecgberct**, eg§, ec§ BH; ecg§ LK; LV; §berht Gn, SG, Ct; egc§ Ct; aecg§ Ct; ecgberhting Gn, SG. **Ecgburg** LV; ę§ (æ§) Ct. **Ecgfriþu** Rn; ecgfrid, ec§, ęg§, ec[g]§ BH; ecg§ LK; §frith LV; §frið Gn; §ferð Ct. **Ecghēanglond** Ct. **Ecgheard** LV, Ct. **Ecghūn** Ct. **Ecglāf** Gn, Ct. **Ecgmund** LV. **Ecgrēd** LV. **Ecgrīc** BH. **Ecgsuīth** LV. **Ecguaru** LV. **Ecguald** LV, Gn; §ing Gn. **Ecguini** LV; §uuine Gn. **Ecguīo** LV. **Ecguulf** LV, Gn, Ct.

twi-ecge *aj* two-edged. **VP** 149/6 sweord ~(gladii ancipites).

Ecga *sm* **LV** 90; 432 ~.

Ecgi *sm* **LV** 175 ~.

ecgan *wv* harrow. **Cp** 1430 egide (occabat).

ā-lecgan *wv* lay down. **Rn** 2/16 alegdun.

Gesecg *sm* **SG** 16 ~.

Gesecging *sm* son of G. **SG** 16 ~.

Ant-secg *sm* **SG** 16 ants(ecg).

Ant-secging *sm* son of A. **SG** 16.

secg *s(mn)* sedge. **Ep** 463 segg (gladiolum); Ef ~; Cp saecg. Ef 251 †sech (carix); Cp ~; Ld †seic.

seggescere Cp.

eolh-secg *s(mn)* **Ep** 781 ilugsegg (papiluus); Ef §seg; Cp † wiolucscel.

secgwæll Ct.

secgan *wv* say. **VP** 9/2; 74/2 ~o (narrabo). 21/23 ~u (§). 9/12; 47/13; 93/4; 95/2 ~að (adnuntiate!; narrate!; pronuntiabunt; nuntiate!) *etc.* 78/13 ~ad (narrabimus). 9/15; 70/18; 72/28 ~e adnuntiem). 91/16 ~en (§ient). 77/4 ~ende (narrantes). 54/18; 117/17 seggo (§abo). 72/15 §u (§). Hy 2/9 §að (adnuntiate!) 91/3 to §enne (ad §andam). 65/16 seg[c]o. 106/22 †segen (adnuntient). 18/2; 21/32; 70/15; 87/12 segeð (adnuntiat; †§abitur; pronuntiabit; narrabit) *etc.* 29/10 §ed (adnuntiabit). 101/24 sege (enuntia!).

ā-secgan *wv* tell. **Cp** 720 asaecgan (edissere). **VP** 18/2 ~að (enarrant), 25/7 ic ~u (§em). 47/14 ~en (§etis).

un-āsæcgendlic *aj* indescribable. **Mt** 41 ~um [úná-].

forð-secgan *wv* utter. **VP** 70/17; 141/3 ~u (pronuntiabo; §io). 88/2 ~o (§iabo). 144/4 ~að (§iabunt). 31/5 ~segcgo (§iabo). 37/19 §a (§io). 147/19 ~seggende (§ians). 118/172 ~segeð (§iabit).

onsecgan *wv* offer, sacrifice. **VP** 4/6 ~að (sacrificate!). 53/8 †onsecg (§abo). 106/22 ~en (§ent). 115/17 ~u (§abo).

wecg *s(m)* wedge. **Cp** 626 waecg (cuneus).

Plecga *sm.* **LV** 310 ~.

Plec-gils LV.

hete *sm* hatred. **VP** 35/5; 51/5 ~(malitiam). 51/3; 77/72; 106/34 ~(§iā). 93/23 ~as. 139/3 heatas.

seten *sf* planting. **Cp** 1604 setin (plataria). **VP** 79/12 ~e (propagines).

hand-seten *sf* ratification. **Ct** 44/8 ~.

oem-seten *sf* shoot, slip. **Cp** 151 ~setinne wiingeardes (amtes).

hueti-stān Ef; huet[e]§ Cp. †ueostun Ld.

netele *sf* nettle. **Cp** 2168 netlan (verticeta).

Netelhæmstyde Ct.

mete *sm* food. **VP** 77/30; Hy 7/48 ~(esca). Hy 11/10 ~(cibus). 13/4 *etc* ~(escam). 68/22 ~minne (§). 106/18 alne ~(§). 64/10 ~(cibum). Hy 6/37 ~(escā). 77/18; 78/2; Hy 6/37 mettas (§as). 43/12 §a (§arum).

meteren Ct [*under* ærn].

swōet-mettas *pl* dainties. **VP** 54/15 swoet nome mettas (dulces capiebas cibos).

cetel *s(m)* kettle. **Ep** 168 ~il (cacabum); Ef, Cp §. Ef 350 § (enuum); Cp §. Cp 405 § (caldaria).

betera *aj* better. **VP** 62/4 betra (melior). 83/11 §e (§). 36/16 bettre (§ius).

Aetti *sm* **LV** 170 ~.

settan *wv* set, place. **Cp** 1478 ~(pastinare). **Rn** 1/2 ~on *prt.* 4/1 sœttœ (settae) *prt.* **VP** 11/6; 49/21 ~o (ponam; statuam). 12/2; 88/26, 8, 30; 131/11 ~u (ponam). 47/14 ~að. 109/1 ~e (§am). 77/7 ~en (§ant). 72/28 ~[a *over* e]. 32/7 ~ende (§ens). 20/10, 3 setes. 84/14; 103/3 §eð. 82/12, 4; 118/33; 140/3 sete! 17/33; 24/12; 38/2 ~e (posuit; statuit; posui) *etc.* 20/4; 49/18, 20 ~es *etc.* 72/9; 73/4; 78/1, 2 *etc* ~un (posuerunt). 118/110 ~en (†posuerunt). 45/9 sete (posuit). **Ct** 37/42 ic ~e *prs.*

gesettan *wv* set. **Ep** 191 gisettae; Ef gisette; Cp gesette (condidit). 542 þa gisettan; Ef §; Cp ge§ (inditas). 707 †ð giset[t]an (ordinatissimam); Ef †girettan; Cp gesettan. **VP** 17/44; 44/17 gesetes (constitues). Hy 6/41 §eð (statuit). 83/4 †gesetteð (reponat). 9/21; 26/11; 108/6; Hy 6/40 gesete (constitue!). 34/17 § (restitue!). 118/38 § (statue!). 17/34; 24/8 *etc* ~e (statuit). 104/21 ~e (constituit). 117/27 gese[t]te (§ui). 4/10; 8/7; 88/48 ~es (§uisti). 15/5 ~es (restituisti). 30/9 ~es (statuisti). 16/11 106/36 ~on (statue-.

runt; constituerunt). 139/3; 140/9 ~un (§uebant; statuerunt). 2/6 geseted ic eam (constitutus sum). 48/15 gesette sind (positae sunt). Ct 40/17 ic ~e *prs.*

ā-settan *wv* set. **Mt** 18 ásetton *inf.* **VP** 79/13 asetes ðu (deposuisti).

fore-settan *wv* place before. **VP** 53/5; 85/14~un (proposuerunt). 100/3 ~e (proponebam). 136/6 ~u (proposuero).

ofdūne-settan *wv* set down. **VH** 10/7 ~e (deposuit).

ofer-settan *wv* set over. **VP** 77/21 ~e (superposuit).

ofer-gesettan *wv* set over. **VP** 37/5 ~on (superposuerunt).

on-settan *wv* place on. **VP** 20/6 onsetes (imponis). 50/21 ~að (§ent). 65/12 ~es (imposuisti).

ongegn-settan *wv* set against. **Cp** 1415 ongensette (objecte).

tō-settan *wv* place to. **VP** 9/39 ~e (adponat). 61/11 ~(§ere). 68/28 tosete (§e!). 76/8 §eð (§et). 77/17 ~on (adposuerunt). 119/3 bið toseted (adponatur).

gesetnis *sf* settlement, will. **Ct** 37/42, 5 ðas gesettnesse; gesetnes *n.*

fore-setnis *sf* proposition. **VP** 48/5 foresetenisse mine (propositionem). 77/2 § (§ones).

wiþ-setnis *sf* opposition. **Cp** 1416 uuitsetnis (objectus).

nett *sn* net. **VP** 140/10 ~e (retiaculo).

nette *sf* **Ep** 702 ~ae (oligia); **Ef** † nectae; **Cp** ~ae. **Lr** 64 ~an (cum obligia).

Cretta *sm* **LV** 224 ~. **Gn** 109 ~.

Cretting *sm* son of C. **Gn** 109 ~.

Betti *sm* **BH** 182 ~. **LV** 161, 4; 266; 336 ~. 456 ~e.

Aed-uini, æd§, ęd§, ed§ **BH**; aed§ **LK**; ed§ **LV**; edwine **Gn**.

edisc *s* enclosure. **Ep** 147 ~(broel); **Ef** ~; **Cp** ~, deortuun. **Ct** 3/4 *agellum qui dicitur* tatan ~. 55/6 greotan edesces lond.

edischen **Cp**; **Ep**, **Ef** §; edesc§ **VP**. ediscueard **Ep**; **Ef**, **Cp** §.

heden *s* dress. **Cp** 409 ~(casla).

stede *sm* place.

Hanchem-stede *sm* Hempstead. **Ct** 1/5 ~.

Medesham-stede *sm* Peterborough. **BH** 254 ~i— ~ I.

Perham-stede *sm* **Ct** 8/2 ~.

Sonder-stede *sm* Sanderstead. **Ct** 45/5 an sonden~.

Stānhām-stede *sm* **Ct** 37/2, 17 æt ~.

Aeddi *sm.* **BH** 239 ~. 341 addi—aeddi II.

Hædde *sm.* **BH** 140 haedde—hedde I. 230 ~i—heddi—haeddi. 359 haeddi. **Gn** 18 haedde. **Ct** 1/7 haedde.

unā-sedd *aj* (*ptc*) unsatiated. **Ep** 541 ~ae (inopimum); **Ef** †unasettæ; **Cp** ~saedde.

Sledd *sm* **SG** 14 sle(dd).

Sledding *sm* son of S. **SG** 14, 19, 23 ~.

Cedd *sm* **BH** 3 ~i *g.* 125 ~— ~a I. 181 ~—ced I [*end of line*]. 125 ~o *d.* 190 ~e *d.* **Gn** 6 ~.

Cedda *sm* **Gn** 54 ~. 56 *pro* ~an.

Ceddan-lēage **Ct**.

Geddingas *pl.* **Ct** 58/8 æt ~incggum (~incgum).

ā-gleddian *wv* moisten. **Ld** 9 agleddęgo (labefacare).

treddan *wv* tread on, trample. **Ep** 749 treddun (proterunt); **Ef** treodun; **Cp** tredun.

bedd *sn* bed. **Ep** 243 ~(culcites); **Ef** ~; **Cp** bed. 971 bed (spatula); **Ef**, **Cp** §. **Ld** 65 berian †beed (lecti aurei). **VP** 6/7 bed min (lectum). 40/4; 131/3 §.

bedclēofum **VP**.

Beddan-haam **Ct**.

stepe *sm* step. **VP** 44/9 ~um (gradibus). 47/14 ~as.

sceppend *sm* creator. **CH** 6 scepen. **VH** 12/1; 13/1 ~(creator).

Feppingas *pl.* **BH** 182 *in regione quae vocatur* in ~um.

Gleppan-feld **Ct**.

Ebbe *sm* **LV** 131, 54; 250 ~i. 453, 63 ~.

Ebbella *sm* **Ct** 9/6 ~.

hebban *sv* raise. **VP** 98/9 ~að up (exaltate!). 36/34 hefeð up (§abit). 7/7; 20/14; 56/6, 12; 93/2; 107/6 hefe up (†exaltare!).

ā-hebban *sv* raise. **VP** 73/3 ahefe (eleva!).

ūp-āhebban *sv* raise up. **Bd**[2] 15 ~(tollere). **VP** 17/49 ~hefes (exaltabis).

on-hebban *sv* raise. **VP** 23/7, 9 ~að (tollite!).

ūp-hebban *sv* **VP** 27/2 ~u (extollo). 29/2; 117/28; 144/1 ~u (exaltabo). 62/5 ~u (levabo). 58/17 ~o (exaltabo). **Hy** 5/4 †uphebu (§). 33/4; 95/8; 98/5; 133/2 ~að (exaltemus; tollite!; exaltate!; extollite!). 106/32; **Hy** 8/22 ~en (exaltent; superexaltemus). 74/5 ~(exaltare). 3/4; 101/11 ~ende (§ans; elevans). 74/8; 144/14; 148/14; 149/4 ~hefeð (exaltat; adlevat; exaltabit; §). 27/9 ~hefe (extolle!).

Sebbe *sm* **BH** 224, 5, 30, 56 ~i. **SG** 19 ~. **Ct** 1/6 ~i. 1, 7 ~i *g*.

Sebbing *sm* son of S. **SG** 18 ~.

swebban *wv* put to sleep. **Cp** 1881 suebbo (sopio).

on-swebban *wv* put to sleep. **Ep** 942 ansuebidum (sopitis); **Ef** † ensuebitum; **Cp** onsuebdum. **Cp** 1851 onsuebbað (sepeliant).

webb *sn* web. **Ep** 1026 uueb (telum); **Ef** §; **Cp** web; **Ld** † uuep. 1030 uu[e]b (textrina); **Ef** uuęb; **Cp** ~. **Rd** 10 goelu godueb *a*.

webgerodes Cp. waebtaeg Cp.

god-webb *sn* precious cloth, purple. **Ep** 441 ~uuebb (fasces); **Ef** †guoduueb; **Cp** god§ (fasces, libri). **Cp** 2038 ~uuebbe (toga).

nebb *sn* beak, face. **Ep** 862 neb (rostrum); **Ef. Cp** §. **Cp** 1595 neb (piceca). **Lr** 29 ~e (rostro).

Cnebba *sm* **Gn** 93 ~.

Cnebbing *sm* son of C. **Gn** 93 ~.

Bebba *sf* **BH** 137 ~. 168 ~ae *g*.

spurul *aj* **Ef** 1162 ~(calcatiosus).

gecur- *prt* chose. **VP** 64/5 ~e (elegisti).

wið-curun *prt* rejected. **VP** 117/22 wid~ (reprobaverunt).

turl *s* ladle. **Cp** 2051 cruce, ~, scofl (trulla).

duru *sf* door. **VP** 73/6; 77/23 ~a (januas). 140/3 ~(ostium *a*).

du: rhere, duerheri [*first* e *hf er.*] **Ep**; durheri **Ef, Cp.**

Burra *sm* **LV** 225 ~.

ðurst *s(m)* thirst. **VP** 61/5; 106/33 ~(sitim). 68/22 ~e minum. 103/11; **Hy** 7/18 ðurs.

sin-hwurful *aj* round. **Ep** 1047 sinuurbul [b *over* f] (teres); **Ef** †sinuulfur; **Cp** siunhuurful.

curfun *prt* cut. **VP** 73/6 ~(exciderunt).

for-curfe *prt* cut off. **VH** 6/28 ~(praecidisti).

urn- *prt* ran. **VP** 49/18 somud ðu ~e (simul currebas).

ot-spurne *prt* kicked against. **VP** 90/12 ~ [t *over* f] (offendas).

burnun *prt* burned. **VP** 117/12 ~(exarserunt).

burne *sf* brook, torrent, spring. **Cp** 1185 ~(latex). **VP** 123/5 ~an (torrentem). 125/4 § (†§ens). 35/9 *etc* § (§ente). 17/5 *etc* § (§entes).

Burne *sf* Bourne. **Ct** 35/8, 9, 10 æt ~an. 37/29 §. 39/2 §.

Brade-burn- *s* Brabourne. **Ct** 30/5 to ~an.

Casing-burn- *s* **Ct** 52/12 *in loco ubi* kasingburnan *appellatur*. 14 æt ~an.

Denises-burna *sm* **BH** 130 ~, *id est, rivus* denisi — denisaes brunna — dęnises burnna.

Forsca-burna *sm* **Ct** 3/12 *fontem qui dicitur* ~.

Gylde-burne *sf* **Ct** 25/6 ~.

Lāmburnan-den Ct.

Rind-burna *sm* **Ct** 10/2 ~.

Scīra-burn- *s* Sherborne. **Gn** 19 ~bur' *ecclesiae*. 23 *scira' ecclesiā*. **Ct** 33/12 ~ensis.

winter-burna *sm* winter-torrent. **Ct** 27/4 ~.

Writola-burna *sm* **Ct** 1/5 ~.

wurma *sm* purple-fish. **Cp** 1353 ~an (murice).

corn-uurma *sm* corn-worm. Cp 2114 ~(vemiculus).

Uurmeri LV [*under* hęre].

wurmille *sf* wild marjoram. Ep 691 uurmillae (origanum); Ef ~æ; Cp ~.

Turca-denu Ct.

þurh *prp, av* through. Ep 741 þorh (per); Ef dorh; Cp ðorh. 757 þorch (§); Ef dorh; Cp ðorh. 760 þorch [c *hf er.*] (per); Ef dorh; Cp ðorh. Cp 1549 § (per). Rd 4 ðerh. 6 ðerih. LP 4, 11 ðorh. Bd² 58, 9 ðorh (per). VP 6/7; 7/12; 12/2 *etc* ðorh (per). Hy 13/7 †ðoh.

ðorhfaran. ðorhswimman. þorgifect, dorh§, ðorh§. **ðorhwunian. ðorhgute. ðorhbrogden. ðurhtēon. ðorhlēoran.**

furh *s*(*f*) furrow. Ep 884 ~um (scrobibus); Ef §.

furh-wudu Cp.

burg *sf* fort, city. Mt 13 (ðære) ~e *g*. Ct 20/14, 5 ða ~. 35/3; 36/10; 37/33 on byrg. 56/8 be norðan §.

Burgfrith LV. **Burgheard** LV. **Burghelm** BH, LV. **burglēod** Ep, Cp. **Burgnōð** Ct. **Burgrēd** Ct. **burgrūnae** Ep, Ef, Cp. **Burgsuīth** LV. **Burgðrȳð** LV. **burgwara** Ct. **Burgwines** Ct.

Æþel-burg *sf* BH 257 aedilburgæ *d* [u *over* e] — §e — aeðilburgae. 263 aedilburga — §bur[u]g — aeðilburga. 265 aedilburge *d* — edil§ — aeðilburga [*last* a *over* ę]. 266 aedilburgi *d* — aeðilburgae I. LV 30 eðil~. Ct 1/2 *tibi* hedilburge. 5/5 aethilburgae *g* (aedil§).

Bancorna-burg *sf* Bangor. BH 49 bancor[n]a~ — boncorna~ [a *over first* o] I — ~.

Cantwara-burg *sf* Canterbury. Ct 37/2; 58/24 ~byrg *d*.

Cnōfheres-burg *sf* BH 172 cnob~, *id est urbs* cnobheri — c[o]nobheresburrug — cnobheraes~ II.

Cūþ-burg *sf* LV 19/33 cuth~.

Cwœn-burg *sf* BH 93 quoenburga *d*. 338 quoenburg — quoin§ II. LV 23 cuoen~. Ct 51/11 cu[u]oen~.

Cyne-burg *sf* BH 181 cyniburgam — cymburgam. LV 22, 6, 31 cyni~

Cynn-burg *sf* Rn 1/9 *k*ynnburu*g*.

Dæg-burg *sf* LV 41 daeg~.

Ēad-burg *sf* LV 34, 42, 3 ~.

Eald-burg *sf* LV 31 ald~.

Ealh-burg *sf* LV 30 aluch~. Ct 39/6 ~. 1, 10 ~e *g*. 3 ~e *a*.

Ealu-burg *sf* LV 19, 29, 9 alu~. 44, 5 al~. Ct 58/23 alo~.

Ēan-burg *sf* LV 31, 9 ~. Ct 48/5 ~e mere.

Ecg-burg *sf* LV 27, 47 ~. Ct 58/23 ę~ (æ~).

Eormen-burg *sf* LV 18 iurmin~.

Gēan-burg *sf* Ct 34/8, 18 gæn~.

Hēa-burg *sf* LV 31 ~.

Hēan-burg *sf* Hanbury (in Worces.). Ct 47/1, 14 ~byrg, ~byrig *d*. 12 ~e *g*.

Heaþu-burg *sf* LV 21 haðu~.

Here-burg *sf* BH 338 heri~.

Hilde-burg *sf* LV 28 hildi~.

Hlēo-burg *sf* LV 43 ~.

Hrœþ-burg *sf* LV 30 hroeð~.

Hūn-burg *sf* Ct 20/22 ~e fleot.

Hyge-burg *sf* LV 42 hyg~.

Ingu-burg *sf* LV 19 ~.

Inwines-burg *sf* Ct 14/3 *usque* ~.

līc-burg *sf* cemetery. Cp 472 ~(cimiterium *etc*).

Œþel-burg *sf* LV 18 oeðil~.

Ōs-burg *sf* LV 22, 8 ~.

Rǣd-burg *sf* LV 25, 31, 41 red~.

Scīr-burg *sf* LV 24 ~.

Seax-burg *sf* BH 151 sexburg — §burc. 294 §burg — saexburg I.

Sele-burg *sf* LV 45 seli~. Ct 51/12 ~.

Sige-burg *sf* LV 45 sig~.

Sulmannes-burg *sf* Ct 14/2 sulmonnes§.

Tand-burg *sf* LV 37 tond~.

Tīd-burg *sf* LV 27, 35 ~.

Tila-burg *sf* BH 187 ~ — ~burug — ~ — ti[l]la~ [*first* l *later* ?].

Wǣr-burg *sf* LV 22, 31 uer~. CA 4 wér~. 12 for werburge. 14 wer~. 18 werbur(g). Ct 45/4 wer~. 8 §e *d*. 14, 33 §e *g*. 57 ~.

Wērburging-wīc Ct.

West-burg *sf* Westbury. Ct 15/2; 16/2 uu~.

Wiht-burg *sf* LV 44 uicht~.

Wil-burg *sf* LV 40, 1; 445 uil~. Ct 43/2 to ~e wellan.

Wilta-burg *sf* BH 354 u~, *id est, oppidum uiltorum.*

Wyn-burg *sf* LV 41 u~.

turtur *s* turtle-dove. VP 83/4 ~(turtur).

for-wurd- *prt* perished. VP 72/19; 82/11 ~un (perierunt; dis§). 118/92; Hy 3/18 ~e (perissem; perirem).

ā-wurp- *prt* threw out, down. VP 36/14 ~en (dejiciant). 73/6 ~un (dejecerunt). 72/18; 79/9; 49/17; Hy 3/18 ~e (§isti; ejecisti; pro§; §§). 105/27 ~e (dejeceret).

tō-wurp- *prt* destroyed. Cp 635 towuorpon (destituunt). VP 9/7; 59/3; 88/41 ~e (destruxisti). 10/4 ~un (§erunt).

wurpul *s* Cp 1936 ~(stenax).

Lull *sm* Ct 33/17 ~.

Lulla *sm* Ct 24/7; 27/6; 28/17; 30/18, 8, 8; 33/4, 14; 44/5 ~.

Lullede *sm* Ct 27/5 ~.

Lulling *sm* Ct 15/9; 16/8; 20/23; 24/10; 32/6; 43/8 ~. 59/3 ~es treo. 33/19 ~ingc. 32/7 luling.

Lulluc *sm* Ct 20/23; 25/12 ~.

wull(e) *sf* wool. Cp 1189 uul (lana). Rd 3 uullan *g.* VP 147/16 ~e (§am).

†uuilmod Ef; †wulf§ Cp.

wulluc *s* Ep 557 uulluc (involucus); Ef, Cp §; Ld uuluc.

full *aj* full. VP 9/28; 13/3 *etc* ful (plenum). 32/5; 74/9 *etc* § (§a; §us). 143/13 § (§a *pl*). 72/10 ~e (§i *pl*). Ct 42/3 ~um. 37/22; 40/10; 41/63, 3, 4 fulne. 40/23 fulre.

folclaemid Cp. fulfremed, unfulfremednis VP. fulgere Ct [*under* gearw]. fulnēh VP. fultēam, Ef [*under* ult]; fultum Cp.

-full. unondgetfull-. unsceðfull-. egesful, §lice. gelustfullian, §ung. gesundfullice, gesundfullian. synfull-. hyhtful. mānful. gelēaffull-. oestful.

hand-full *s(n)* handful. Ep 645 ~ful beouuas (manticum); Ef § beouaes; Cp, Ld hond§.

sin-fulle *sf* houseleek. Ef 387 ~ae (eptafolium); Cp ~. Ep 819 ~ae (palurus); Ef ~æ; Cp ~; Ld †fullae (paliurus *etc*). Cp 724 ~(eftafolium).

fullian *wv* confirm. Ct 37/12 ic ~iae.

Tulla *sm* LV 96 ~.

fulwiht *s(m)* baptism. CA 13, 7 ~. VH 13/10 ~(baptismum). Ct 45/37 ~. 42 ~e [*accent on* w] *nom.*

wulf *sm* wolf. Cp 1259 ~(lupus). Ep 183 uulfes camb (camellea); Ef §; Cp wulfes §.

Wulffreð [=~friþ] Ct. Uulfgār LV. Uulfgȳth LV. Uulfhāeth LV. Wulfhāt Ct. Wulfhēah Ct. Uulfheard LV, Gn, Ct; wulf§ Ct. Uulfhēd LV. Wulfhelm CA. Wulfhere Rn; uulfheri BH, LV. Uulfhild LV. uulfholu Cp. Uulflāf LV, Ct; wullaf Ct. wulfmod Ct (=wull§). Uulfrēd LV, Ct; wulfredus Gn; wulfred Ct. Uulfsig, uulsig LV. wulfwælles Ct. Uulfwīg Gn.

Āc-wulf *sm* LV 454 acuulf.

Ælf-wulf *sm* LV 70 aelfuulf.

Æsc-wulf *sm* LV 406, 23 aescuulf. Gn 28 §.

Æþel-wulf *sm* LV 12; 131; 237; 315; 403, 8, 48, 61, 67, 70 eðiluulf. 317; 412 eþil§. Gn 14 aeðiluulf. 29 æðel§. SG 1 æ(ðelwulf). 2 æðe(lwulf). Ct 20/1, 22; 22/3 æthel-uulf. 20/2 §e. 22/1, 2 §o. 22/7 §um. 21/5; 25/1, 10 aetheluulf. 21/2, 3 §o. 22/7; 23/3, 7 æðeluulf. 22/8; 23/8, 11; 24/9 §i. 23/1, 2 §o. 23/7 §um. 23/14 §es. 47/6 aeþeluulf. 25/11; 26/1, 6; 51/3, 9 aeðeluulf. 24/1 §us. 36/5 §o. 42/2 §e. 45/58 æðel~. 48/15 ae§. 44/3 ę§. 22/10 eðeluulfi. 27/1, 3, 4; 30/20; 31/5; 42/26; 43/7, 7 eðel~. 29/20 æðæluulf. 32/4 æðelulf. 7 eðelulf. 5, 6, 6 eðeluf. 24/3 aeðeu[u]lf. 4 aeðuulf.

Beadu-wulf *sm* LV 136, 8, 92; 322, 91; 418, 23, 8, 39 baduulf. Gn 69 beaduulf.

Beald-wulf *sm* LV 403 balduulf.

Bēo-wulf *sm* LV 342 biu[u]ulf.

Beorht-wulf *sm* **LV** 88, 91; 444, 69 berchtuulf. 147, 8, 9; 326, 8 berht§. 174; 244, 57; 308, 11, 21, 3, 62, 83; 404, 4, 7, 16, 26, 35, 43, 53, 5, 6 berct§. 149 berh[t]uulf. **Ct** 45/56 ~uulf. 31/5 biarht~. 47/9 berhtuulf. 48/8 §wulf. 1 bercht~.

Beorn-wulf *sm* **LV** 138, 43, 4, 5; 240, 6, 7; 323, 84; 400, 13, 6, 28, 33, 66 ~uulf. **Ct** 56/6; 58/9, 13~. 58/6 ~i. 7 ~o. 57/7 ~uulf. 57/1 §o. 58/3 §o (~wulfo). 30/15 biarnulf. 31/9 bearnulf.

Ber-wulf *sm* **LV** 200 ~uulf.

Bōt-wulf *sm* **LV** 66; 143, 4; 310, 8, 92; 457, 68 ~uulf.

Cēol-wulf *sm* **BH** 1 ~uulfo. 374 ~uulf—ceolulf. **LK** 6 ~uulf. **LV** 11; 121, 90; 340 §. **Gn** 44, 85 §. **Ct** 21/7, 7; 22/6; 55/1, 8; 56/1, 3, 4 ~. 23/6; 24/7, 11; 54/5 ~uulf. 53/7 §i. 41/56 ciol ~. 14/5 ~ulfus. 15/4; 16/4 §i. 44/2, 6, 6 ciolulf. 1 cialulf.

Cœ̄n-wulf *sm* **LV** 481 coenuulf. **Gn** 103 §. **Ct** 12/5; 19/3; 34/3; 35/4; 50/1, 4; 51/8, 8, 8; 52/13, 6; 53/5, 6; 54/1, 5 §. 12/2; 34/1; 35/15; 52/1; 53/6 §i. 12/2; 46/2; 49/1, 5; 53/1 §us. 51/3; 52/1, 7, 15; 54/4 §o. 56/2; 58/5, 5, 7 §wulf. 58/4, 7, 7, 9, 12, 3 §i. 51/1 coenu[u]lfi. 2 §[u]ulf.

Cūþ-wulf *sm* **LV** 8; 106, 37; 225, 32, 4, 8, 41, 64, 7; 306, 61, 83; 419, 25 cuthuulf. 182; 318, 95; 412, 36, 42, 7, 62, 71 cuð§. 316; 471 cud§. **SG** 5 cuð(uulf). **Ct** 22/12 cuðuulfi. 58/15 cuð~. 57/8 cuðulf. 23/13 §i.

Cūþ-wulfing *sm* son of Cūþwulf. **SG** 5 cuðuulfing.

Cyne-wulf *sm* **LV** 9; 63; 126, 39, 42, 93; 312, 4, 5, 8, 28, 30, 67, 72, 82, 99, 9; 413, 27, 40, 55 cyniuulf. **Gn** 66 cynwulf. **Ct** 33/17 cynulf. 3/1 ~.

Drēam-wulf *sm* **LV** 114 ~uulf.

Ēad-wulf *sm* **LV** 4; 72, 88; 139, 41, 5, 8, 9, 53, 84; 233, 4[illegible], 6; 308, 16, 7, 23, 5, 5, 6, 7, 9, 73, 5, 9, 91, 1, 3; 401, 5, 6, 7, 8, 11, 7, 24, 6, 30, 1, 3, 9, 9, 9, 40, 3, 3, 5, 8, 50, 7, 9, 61, 5, 82 ~uulf. 324 eod§. **Gn** 44 ~uulf. **Ct** 19/4; 29/20; 33/8; 34/6; 47/3, 4; 52/16; 57/11 §. 46/5 §us. 49/9; 53/7 §i. 50/1 §o. 26/7; 33/7; 48/14; 56/7; 57/8, 9; 58/14, 7, 8, 21; 59/6 ~. 12/3; 30/18 ~ulf.

Eald-wulf *sm* **BH** 103 alduulf. 289 §o. 302 §i — §ulfi 1. 371 §uulfo — §ulfo 1. **LV** 9; 14, 4, 92; 112, 25, 32, 3, 5, 5, 7, 50, 6, 7; 233, 6, 39, 87, 8; 303, 6, 10, 3, 26, 56, 81, 93, 4, 5, 9, 9; 402, 6, 6, 16, 21, 3, 30, 42, 60, 5, 73 alduulf. 387 aldulf. **Gn** 10, 41, 3; 118 alduulf. **Ct** 17/5, 6 ald~, 34/5; 53/6 §uulf. 46/4 §us. 49/8 §i. 12/3 aldulf. 33/3 aldulsus.

Eald-wulfing *sm* son of Ealdwulf. **Gn** 118 alduulfing.

Ēan-wulf *sm* **LV** 64, 71, 87; 127, 9, 59, 76; 241, 7, 98; 303, 5, 10, 5, 6, 8, 20, 8, 77, 91; 406, 7, 8, 9, 10, 6, 7, 31, 5, 6, 41, 61, 72, 3, 9 ~uulf. 89 ~ulf. 446, 9, 9 eonuulf. **Gn** 100 ~uulf. **Ct** 25/12; 29/20; 32/4; 47/8 §. 23/8, 8 §i. 22/8 ~i. 32/6; 43/7 ~ulf.

Ēan-wulfing *sm* son of Ēanwulf. **Gn** 100 ~uulfing.

Eard-wulf *sm* **LV** 9; 72; 141, 94; 248; 308, 9, 11, 70, 93, 5; 411, 2, 2, 38, 41, 68, 80 ~uulf. **Gn** 11 §. **Ct** 45/57, 8 §. 8/4, 4 §i, §us. 36/9 (eard)~. 31/7; 38/17 ~ulf. 8/1, 4 §us.

Earn-wulf *sm* **LV** 466 ~uulf.

Ecg-wulf *sm* **LV** 76; 128; 242, 4; 391; 406, 9 ~uulf. **Gn** 6 §. **Ct** 51/10 §. 20/23 §i.

Eofor-wulf *sm* **LV** 403 ~uruulf.

Friþu-wulf *sm* **LV** 134; 209 frioðuulf. 238 friðuulf. 464 friuðuulf. **Gn** 110 frioðulf.

Friþu-wulfing *sm* son of Friþuwulf. **Gn** 110 frioðulfing.

Gār-wulf *sm* **LV** 55 ~uulf. **Ct** 30/5 ~ulfi. 30/14, 9; 44/4 ~ulf.

God-wulf *sm* **Gn** 110 ~ulf.

God-wulfing *sm* son of Godwulf. **Gn** 110 ~uulfing.

Heard-wulf *sm* **LV** 316, 8, 25 ~uulf.

Heaþu-wulf *sm* **LV** 115, 81, 8; 244, 93; 309, 22, 84, 8, 96; 401, 27, 31, 56, 75 h[illegible]ðuulf. 182; 393 haduulf. 140, 2; 435 heaðuulf. 396 h..ðuulf. 146 headuulf.

Hrōþ-wulf *sm* LV 456, 9 hroð-uulf.

Hūn-wulf *sm* LV 120; 413 ~uulf.

Hyge-wulf *sm* LV 437, 80 hyg-uulf.

Hyse-wulf *sm* LV 134 hysiuulf.

Īsern-wulf *sm* LV 356 ~uulf.

Mǣg-wulf *sm* LV 422 meguulf.

Mōd-wulf *sm* Ct 24/5 modulf.

Nōþ-wulf *sm* Ct 21/7; 22/6; 25/14; 36/8; 41/55 noð~. 23/6; 24/5, 11 §uulf.

Ord-wulf *sm* Ct 29/21 ~uulf.

Ōs-wulf *sm* LV 7, 89; 178; 393, 9; 445 osuulf. Ct 19/8; 34/4; 35/12; 37/1; 57/4 §. 37/13, 32, 6 §es. 19/1 ~o. 58/19 ~. 12/6; 30/17; 43/9 osulf. 37/45 (os)ulf(es).

Peoht-wulf *sm* LV 443 pechtuulf.

Pend-wulf *sm* LV 111 ~uulf.

Pleg-wulf *sm* LV 8 ~uulf.

Rǣd-wulf *sm* LV 70, 91; 449, 61, 1, 76, 9 reduulf. Ct 17/6 red~.

Rīc-wulf *sm* LV 7 ~uulf.

Sæx-wulf *sm* BH 228 ~uulf — saex§ — saxulf — sexuulf. 253 sexuulfum — saex§ — saexulfum — sex§. 269 sexuulfum — saex§ — saexulfum. 272 sexuulfum — sęxulfum 1. Gn 34 saex~. 35 ~uulfum. 42 *post sæx* · · · ·.

Scēn-wulf *sm* LV 94 ~uulf.

Sige-wulf *sm* LV 14, 69; 132, 5; 320, 1, 3, 61, 88; 412, 6, 21, 2, 38, 54, 74, 80 siguulf. Ct 45/33 ~e. 34 sigulf. 60 siguulf.

Stīþ-wulf *sm* LV 189 stiðuulf.

Strēon-wulf *sm* LV 301 ~uulf.

Swīþ-wulf *sm* LV 86; 187; 390 suiðuulf. 296 suith§.

Tāt-wulf *sm* LV 91; 224, 31; 301, 19, 81, 8; 417, 48, 53, 74 ~uulf.

Tīd-wulf *sm* LV 118; 382; 425, 8, 52, 74, 6 ~uulf. Ct 47/6; 49/10 §. 59/5 ~.

Tiouulfinga-cæstir BH.

Tīr-wulf *sm* Ct 24/7 ~uulf.

Torht-wulf *sm* LV 127; 459 torctuulf. 425 torcht§.

þrȳþ-wulf *sm* BH 100 thryduulfi—thryth§ 1—§.

Wil-wulf *sm* LV 147 uiluulf.

culfre *sf* pidgeon, dove. VP 54/7; 67/14 ~an (columbae *g*). Hy 3/11 ~ (§a).

dulfun *prt* dug. VP 21/17; 56/7 ~(foderunt).

bulc- *s* Ct 3/7, 8 ~an pytte, § pyttes.

sulh *s*(*f*) plough. Cp 656 sules reost (dentalia).

swulung *sn* a measure of land. Ct 49/3; 52/5, 8 sulung. 28/21 fif §. 28/22; 39/12 §um. 34/19 ðrie sulong. 41/11 an half ~ *a*. 37/3 xx ~uncga.

for-swulgun *prt* swallowed. VP 123/4 ~(absorbuissent).

fultum *sm* help. Ef 360 fulteam (emolomentum); Cp ~. VP 9/10, 35; 17/3, 3 *etc* ~(adjutor). 19/3; 48/15 *etc* ~(auxilium). 21/20 ~ ðinne (§). 7/11; 37/23 *etc* ~ minne (adjutorium). 80/2 ~e urum (§i). 90/1 ~e (§io). 87/5 ~ie? (§io). 61/8 ~es (auxilii). 69/2 †fultu.

feorm-fultum *sm* sustenance. Ct 45/23 to ~e [*accent on first* m].

fultumian *wv* help. Ep 74 ~emendi (adstipulatus); Ef §. 95 §um (adsessore); Ef, Cp §. VP 88/22 ~eð (auxiliabitur). 85/17 ~ades (§iasti). 93/17 ~ade (§iasset). Ct 41/10 ~e *sbj*.

gefultumian *wv* help. VP 21/12 ~e (adjuvet). Hy 12/5 ~e (§es). 43/26; 69/6; 108/26; 118/86 ~e (§a!). 36/40; 45/6; 53/6 ~eð. 93/18 ~að (§abat). 118/175 § (§abunt). 106/12, 41 ~ade (§aret, §abit). Hy 7/74 ~en (§ent). 69/2 to ~iende. 88/44 ard gefultemiende (es auxiliatus). 27/7 ~ad (adjutus). Ct 40/4, 7 gefultemedan.

fultemend *s* support. Cp 928 ~(frutina).

scult-heta [*under* hǣta] Cp.

sculdor *s* shoulder. Ep 963 ~ur (scapula); Cp §; Ef sculdra.

wuldor *sn* glory. CA 9 wuldre *d*. VP 3/4; 16/15; 20/6 *etc* ~ur (gloria).

149/9 § ðis (§). 7/6; 62/3 *etc* § min, § ðin (§iam). 8/6; 48/15 *etc* wuldre. 23/7, 8, 9, 10 *etc* §es. 23/10 wuld[ra]es. 105/7 ~ur ðin (†mirabilia).

uuldurfadur CH.

wuldorfæst *aj* glorious. **VH** 5/18 wuldurfest (gloriosus). Ps 86/3 §e (§a).

wuldurlice *av* gloriously. **VH** 5/1 ~(gloriose).

wuldrian *wv* glorify. **VP** 90/15; Hy 6/39 ~iu glorificabor; gloriebor). 51/3 ~as (§iaris). 88/8 ~að (glorificatur). 5/12; 31/11; 96/7 ~iað. 105/47 ~ien. Hy 4/6 ~ende (gloriantes).

gewuldrian *wv* glorify. **VH** 5/8 ~ad is (glorificata est). Ps 48/7; 93/3 bioð ~ade (gloriabuntur). 73/4 § sind (§iati sunt). 138/14 † gewundra ðu earð (magnificatus es).

guldun *prt* paid, sacrificed. **VP** 105/37 ~(immolaverunt).

feor-stuþ *s* support. **Ef** 1110 ferstud (continuus). Bd[1] 2 feurstud (destina).

þus *av* thus. **Ep** 1037 ~suiþae (tantisper); Ef dus; Cp ðus. Cp 26 ac §(sicini). **Mt** 46 ~. **Ct** 37/13; 38/7 ~.

muscel *s* mussel. **Ef** 1117 musscel (genesco).

musclan-scel Cp.

cuscote *sf* wood-pigeon. **Ep** 829 cuscutan (palumbes); Ef ~ae; Cp ~.

tusc *s*(*m*) tusk, grinder. **Ef** 487 ~[n *dotted out after* u] (genuinum, intimum, vel dens); Cp ~ (genuino, naturale).

rust *s* rust. **Ef** 397 †rost (erugo); Cp ~.

lust *sm* desire. **VP** 9/38; 20/3 *etc* ~(desiderium). 102/5 ~ðinne (§). 77/30 ~e. 139/9 ~e minum. 9/38 ~as. 13/1 *etc* ~um (voluntatibus). 9/24 *etc* ~um (desideriis).

gelustfullian *wv* delight, take pleasure. **VP** 36/4 ~a (delectare !). 50/18 ~as (§aberis). 29/2; 91/5 ~ades (§asti). 44/9 ~adun. 15/9; 72/21 ~ad is (§atum est). 64/9 bist § (§averis). 76/4 ~ eam. 103/34 biom § (§abor). 34/9 bið ~að. 36/11 bioð ~ade. 67/4 sien §. 89/15 § sind. 118/14 gelusdfullad ic eam.

gelustfullung *sf* delectation. **VP** 15/11 ~e (delectationes).

thrust-fell Ep; Ef, Cp §.

uferra *aj comp.* above; after (of time). **VP** 103/3 ða ~an (superiora) 13 ðæm ~um. **Ct** 34/16 ~an dogor.

ufan *av* over, above. **Mt** 27 ~. **VP** 77/23 ~(desuper).

ufancumende VH.

hēr-beufan *av* here-above, before. **Ct** 45/43 ~.

wið-ufan *prp* above. **Ct** 20/11 ~.

lufu *sf* love. **Ct** 30/22; 42/14 for godes ~e.

Lufu *sf* **Ct** 40/1, 25, 15, 6 ~a, ~e *g*, lubo, §a.

lufe *sf* love. **CA** 6 for godes ~an. **VP** 108/5 ~an minre (dilectione). Hy 12/8 ~(amor). **Ct** 37/43 for higna ~on.

lufian *wv* love. **VP** 17/1 ~iu (diligam). 10/6, 8 *etc* ~að (§it, dilexit). 36/28 §(amat). 4/3; 5/12 *etc* ~iað. 25/8; 108/18; 118/97, 127, 40, 63 ~ade. 77/68; 118/47, 8, 113, 9, 59, 66, 7 ~ude. 114/1 ~ede. 50/8; 51/6 ~ades. 44/8; 51/5 ~edes. 77/36 ~edun. 108/4 ~eden. 118/165; 121/6 ~iendum. 144/20 † lifiende (diligentes). 46/5 † luade.

lufiendlic *aj* amiable. **VP** 83/2 ~e (amabilia).

sufl *s* **Ct** 37/31 ~a *gpl.*

gesufl *aj* **Ct** 37/24; 39/9 ~ra hlafa.

Wuffa *sm* **BH** 103 uuffa. **Gn** 119 ~.

Wuffing *sm* son of W. **BH** 104 uuffingas *etc.* **Gn** 119 ~.

Eald-uuft *sm* **Ct** 9/7 ~.

unc *prn* us two. **Rn** 2/8 uq*k*et *a.*

uncer *prn* our two. **CA** 5, 6 uncre. **Ct** 45/4, 12 ~. 37/5, 5 uncerra. 37/8 unce. 45/8 §um.

drunc- *prt* drank. **VP** 68/13; Hy 7/73 ~un (bibebant; §ebatis). 77/44 ~en (§erent).

druncen *aj* (*ptc*) intoxicated. VP 106/27 ~(ebrius).

druncennis *sf* intoxication. VH 11/11 †drincennisse (ebrietatem).

hungor *sm* hunger. Mt 49 (h)ungor. VP 58/7, 15; 104/16 hungur (famem). 32/19; Hy 7/47 hungre. 36/19 §es.

geðungen *aj* (*ptc*) virtuous. VH 12/8 ~(sobrius).

geðungenlice *av* virtuously. VH 11/11 ~(sobrie).

þung *sm* nightshade. Ep 23 thungas (aconita); Ef §; Cp ~as. Cp 736 ~(eleborus).

þrung- *prt* pressed, squeezed. Cp 2039 ~un (torquent).

ūtā-þrungen *ptc* pressed out. Ep 176 utathru[n]gaen (celatum); Ef utathrungen.

sungun *prt* sang. VP 68/13; 105/12 ~(psallebant; cantaverunt).

swung- *prt* beat. Cp 804 suungen (exalaparetur). Mt 9 wæs sungen. VP 72/5 †bið swungne (flagellabuntur).

geswungen *ptc* beaten. VP 72/14 wes ~(fui flagellatus).

ā-sprung- *prt* failed. VP 9/7; 63/7; 68/4 *etc* ~un (defecerunt) 89/7, 9 § (§imus). Hy 7/71 ~ne (defectos).

āsprungnis *sf* failing. VP 118/53 ~nisse (defectio).

healf-clungen *aj* (*ptc*) half-withered. Ep 931 halbclungni (semigelato); Ef §; Cp half§.

geong *aj* young. Bl 8 þa gingan eletriow (novella olivarum). VP 77/63; 148/12; Hy 7/51 gunge (juvenes). 67/26 iungra [u *over* o] (§um).

geongra *cp* younger. VP 36/25 gungra (juvenior). 118/141 iungra (adolescentior). Hy 1/1 iugra (§). 148/12 gingrum (junioribus). 118/9 ging (juvenior).

geongest *superl* youngest. VP 67/28 se gungesta (adulescentior).

tunge *sf* tongue. Cp 807 ~(lingua). Lr 18 ~an (liganam). VP 15/9; 21/16 *etc* ~(lingua). 11/4 *etc* ~an (§am). 11/5 §ure (§). 9/28 *etc* § (§ā). 38/2, 5 *etc* § minre (§§). 54/10 *etc* § (§as). 5/11; 13/3 ~um.

tungeðrum Lr.

hrǣc-tunge *sf* uvula. Lr 41 hrętungan (uvae).

þung *s* purse. Ef 297 ~(cassidele); Cp §.

un-. Unwana. æþele. stilnis. stillit. tōsliten. besmiten. befliten. sibb, §ian. berende. reht. gemetlic, §nis. ondgetful. gereordedlic. scęþþende. scęþful. węmmed, ge§. fulfręmednis. āsęcgendlic. āsędd. ofercumen. trum; geuntrumian. tǣlwyrþe. gewyrht. scyldig. cystig. trymnis. bryce. þyhtig. nytt, §nis. liþuwāc. gehǣlendlic; gehǣledlic. mǣle. fǣcne. gesǣlignis. ǣmete. hēre. gesēne. nēah. gebēaten. getīonu. hlīsa. wīs; rehtwīs *etc*. wīsdōm. cūþ. ondcȳþignis. sōfte. rōtsian. gefoerne. oferfoere. smoeþe.

Una *sm*. LV 214 ~.

hunig *s*(*n*) honey. VP 18/11; 118/103; Hy 7/25 ~(mel). 80/17 hunge (melle). Ct 37/22; 40/10; 41/63 ~es.

hunaegaepl Ep; †cæneg§ Ef; hunig§ Cp. **hunaegsūgae** Ep; huneg§ Ef; ~suge Cp.

þunor *s*(*m*) thunder, the god Thunder. Cp 1152 ~er (Jovem).

ðunurrād VP.

sunu *s*(*m*) son. Cp 1495 faedran ~(patruelis). DA 2 ~a *g*. Mt 28 ~. SG 2/7 ~. VP 2/7; 8/5 *etc* ~(filius). 79/16, 8 *etc* ~(§ium). 49/20 wið ~a (§). 71/2 ~a (§io). Ct 38/3; 41/40 ~a *d*. 45/23 ~ *d*.

brōðor-sunu *sm* nephew. Cp 916 ~(fratuelis).

stēop-sunu *sm* stepson. Cp 886 ~(filiaster).

on-scunian *wv* shun, abominate. Cp 177 anscungendi (aporians). VP 5/7 ~að (abhominabitur). 34/4, 26; 39/15; 68/7; 69/3; 82/18 ~ien (revereantur). 128/5 § (†revertantur). 5/11; 77/41; 105/33 ~edon (exacervaverunt). 55/6 § (execrebantur). 77/56; 104/28; 105/43;

Hy 7/31 ~edun (exacervaverunt). 73/18 ~ade (§avit). Hy 7/37 ~ad wes (§atus est). 70/24 ~iende bioð (reveriti fuerint). 118/163 § eam (abominatus sum). 105/40 †onsuniende wes (§). 106/18 †onscuiende wes (§ata est). 77/40 onscunedun [*first* u *over* y]. 106/11 onscynedun.

onscuniendlic *aj* hateful. VP 13/1; 52/2 ~e (abominabiles).

onscunung *sf* execration. VP 58/13; 87/9; 94/9 ~e (execratione; abominationem; exacervatione). Hy 7/32 ~ingum (abominationibus).

gewuna *sm* habit. VH 12/3 ~an (usui).

wunian *wv* dwell, remain. Cp 1140 ~at (inmoratur). CA 7 ~aden. Mt 21, 33 ~edon, ~ode. VP 24/13; 29/6 ~að (demorabitur). 32/11: 54/20 *etc* § (manet). 88/37 § (§ebit). 90/1 § (commorabitur). 54/8 ~ade (mansi).

ā-wunian *wv* remain. VP 105/11 ~ede (remansit).

ðorh-wunian *wv* continue. VP 101/13, 27 ~as (permanes). 9/8; 18/10; 60/8; 71/5, 17; 118/90 §að. 118/89 ~ad (§et). 5/6; 118/91 ~iað (§ebunt; perseverant).

Wun-beald Ct.

gemun- *vb* remember. VP 136/6 ~u (meminero). 104/5; Hy 2/8 ~að (mementote). Hy 9/7 ~an (memorare). 87/6 ~des (meministi).

Cuna *sm*. LV 341 ~.

cunelle *sf* thyme (?). Ep 246 ~illae (cerefolium); Ef §; Cp ~elle.

Cunen *sm*. LV 159; 203; 301 ~.

Cuneningas *spl*. BH 355 *regione in* ~um—cuniningum.

Buna *sm* LV 81; 277 ~. Ct 17/8 ~.

bune *sf* cup. Cp 436 ~an (carcesia).

unnan *vb* grant. Ct 41/4 ~. 42/15 ~en *pl.*

geunnan *vb* Ct 41/25; 45/25 ~.

gerunnen *aj* (*ptc*) coagulated. Cp 592 ~(concretum). VP 67/16 ~(coagulatus). 118/70 ~is (§um est).

ðunn-wengan Lr; ðunwengum VP.

sunne *sf* sun. VP 88/38; *103/19, 22 *etc* ~(sol). 57/9 *etc* ~an (§em). 18/6 *etc* § (§e). 49/1 *etc* § (§is).

sunnan-dege Ct. sunfolgend Cp.

spunnun *prt* span. Cp 1733 ~(reverant).

Nunne *sf* LV 19 ~ae.

cunnan *vb* know. VP 9/11; 118/79 ~un (noverunt). Hy 12/11 ~e (§erit). Ct 41/7 ~e.

on-cunnen *ptc* known. Cp 1389 ~(notatus).

cunnian *wv* try. VP 94/9 ~adun (probaverunt).

gecunnian *wv* try. VP 67/31 ~ade werun (probati sunt). 138/1 ~ades (§asti). 23 ~a (§a !).

ā-cunnian *wv* try, excuse. VP 16/3; 65/10 ~adest (probasti). 80/8 ~ade (§avi). 25/2 ~a (§a !). 140/4 to ~enne (excusandas).

on-cunnis *sf* excuse. VP 140/4 ~se (excusationes).

grunnettan *wv* grunt. Cp 998 ~(grunnire).

Tunna *sm* BH 300 ~. LV 115; 207 ~.

Tunnacaestir BH.

tunne *sf* tun. Cp 615 ~(cuba).

dunn *aj* dun. Ld 29 ~ę (lapides onichinos).

Dunn *sm* Gn 11 ~.

hunta *sm* hunter. Mt 24 ~an *a*.

huntian *wv* hunt. VP 90/3 ~iendra (venantium). 123/7 ~endra (§).

huntað *s*(*m*) hunting. DA 17 to huntade.

munt *sm* mountain. VP 47/3, 12 se ~(mons) *etc.* 23/3 *etc* ~(montem). 71/16 libanan ~(Libanum). 3/5 *etc* ~e. 28/5; 103/16 ðes ~es (Libani). 45/3, 4 *etc* ~as. 49/10 *etc* ~um. 17/8 *etc* ~a. 2/6; 10/2 †mont. 103/32 untas.

Undal- *spl* Oundle. BH 361, 6. *provincia quae vocatur* in ~um. *in provincia* §.

under *prp* under. Cp 1960 ~(sub). VP 8/8; 9/28; 13/3 *etc* ~ fotum, tungan, weolerum (sub). 17/39 ~ foet (subtus). Hy 6/33 ~ me (§).

underfēng. underðēodan.

hund *sm* dog. VP 21/21 ~es (canis). 104/31 ~es pie (cynomia). 21/17; 58/7, 15 ~as. 67/24 ~a.

roð-hund *sm* mastiff. **Cp** 1330 ~(molosus).

hundlic *aj* dog's. **VP** 77/45 ~e (caninam).

hund *sn* hundred. **Ct** 37/30; 41/26, 7, 35, 60 ~*pl.* 47/15 sex ~. 48/6 nigen ~.

hund-aehtatig VP. hundseofentig VP.

lund-laga Ep, Ef, Cp; ~leogan Lr.

sund-gerd Cp.

gesund *aj* sound, prosperous. **VP** 67/20 ~ne (prosperum).

gesundfullice *av* prosperously. **VP** 44/5 ~(prospere).

gesundfullian *wv* prosper. **VP** 36/7 bið ~ad (prosperatur). 117/25 ~a (§are!).

sundur-seld VH.

on-sundron *av* separately. **Ct** 41/21, 7 ansundran.

āswund- *prt* perished, decayed. **Ep** 1044 asuund[nan]*etc* (tabida et putrefacta); Ef asuunden. Ef 341 †asundnum; Cp asundun (§uerunt). **VH** 5/26 aswundun (tabuerunt).

wunden *ptc* wound. **Rd** 5 uundnae *pl.*

ā-wund- *prt* wound. **Ep** 507 auundun (intexunt); Ef §; Cp wundun. 985 auunden (torta); Ef, Cp §. 1051 †auundre (tortā); Ef auundenre; Cp awundere. Cp 1603 auunden (plectra).

wund *sf* wound. **VP** 68/27; **Hy** 13/26 ~a (vulnerum). 29 ~e (§era).

wundsweðe VP.

gewundian *wv* wound. **Rn** 2/15 *g*iwundad. **VP** 87/6 ~ade (vulnerati). 88/11 ðone ~edan. **Hy** 7/84 ~edra.

wundor *sn* wonder, miracle. **CH** 3 uundra. **Rd** 1 §um. **Mt** 34 ~er. **VP** *only in pl.* 9/2, 12; 25/7 *etc* ~ur (mirabilia). 77/32; 118/27 §um. 76/12; 77/11 *etc* §a.

wundurwerc VP.

wundurlic *aj* wonderful. **VP** 8/2, 10 *etc* ~(ammirabile). 64/6; 67/36 *etc* ~(mirabile; §is). 92/4; 135/18 ~e (§es). 130/1 ~um.

wundurlice *av* wonderfully. **VP** 44/5; 75/5 ~(mirabiliter).

wundrian *wv* wonder. **VP** 47/6 ~iende sindun (admirati sunt).

gewundrian *wv* make wonderful. **VP** 15/3 ~ade (mirificavit). 16/7 ~a (§a!).

funden *ptc* found. **Ct** 38/7 ~e.

mund *sf* protection.

mundbora Ep, Ef, Cp, Ct. mundbyrd Ep, Ef, Cp, Ct. mundlēu Cp; Ep §; mun§ Ef.

Æþel-mund *sm* **LV** 83; 131, 54; 288, 9; 322; 436, 8, 81 eðil~. 437 aeðil~. **Ct** 3/14 æðelmundes. 12/5; 16/7; 40/14 æðel~. 13/1, 4 §o. 15/2; 16/2 aeðelmundo. 19/6 §i. 44/2, 5 ęðel~. 38/16 eðel~. 15/8 ædel~.

Beadu-mund *sm* **LV** 100, 5, 93; 236, 90, 3; 321, 66, 6, 74, 6, 86; 462, 4, 74 badu~.

Bēag-mund *sm* **Ct** 23/4; 28/16; 30/18; 36/6; 40/12; 41/48 ~. 21/5; 22/4; 24/9; 42/24; 58/20 bæg~.

Beorht-mund *sm* **LV** 142, 86; 232; 451 berct~. **Ct** 33/12 berht~.

Cēol-mund *sm* **LV** 118/~. **Gn** 50 ~. **Ct** 12/6; 15/9; 16/8; 18/5; 32/5, 7; 43/8; 45/60 ~. 15/5; 16/5 i~. 33/21 (c)eol~. 19/7 ciolmundi. 27/6 cial~.

Cūþ-mund *sm* **LV** 186; 422 cuth~. 315, 7, 20 cuð~.

Cyne-mund *sm* **BH** 166 cyni~—cyne~ II. **LV** 5; 101, 9, 84; 233, 42; 349, 53, 6, 74, 98; 423, 34 cyni~.

Dæg-mund *sm* **LV** 152 daeg~. **Ct** 36/8 (daeg)~. 58/21 ~. 30/15; 40/13; 43/9 dei~.

Ēad-mund *sm* **LV** 72 ~. **Gn** 66 eað~. **Ct** 45/60 ~.

Eald-mund *sm* **LV** 321 ald~.

Ealh-mund *sm* **LV** 6; 62, 87; 122, 55, 82; 225 alch~. **Gn** 22 §. 62 alh~. **SG** 3 ealh(mund). **Ct** 15/6, 8; 16/6, 7; 19/5; 33/5; 34/7; 47/8 alh~. 46/4, 6 §us. 49/8 §i. 33/13 ~.

Ealh-munding *sm* son of Ealhmund. **SG** 3 ealhc~.

Ēan-mund *sm* **LV** 81; 153; 232, 3, 76, 94; 403 ~. 223 eon~. **Ct** 47/5; 56/6; 57/9, 9; 58/16, 6 ~. 44/1, 2, 6 ~e.

Ēast-mund *sm* **Ct** 28/15; 29/21; 30/14; 31/4; 44/3 ~.

Ecg-mund *sm* **LV** 127 ~.

Egel-mund *sm* **LV** 109, 63; 272 egil~.

Friþu-mund *sm* **LV** 79 friodu~. 223, 31, 80; 346 friðu~. **Ct** 33/9; 41/34 freoðo~. 41/38 §e.

• **Gār-mund** *sm* **LV** 214 ~.

Gef-mund *sm* **BH** 231 ~—geb~—gemmund—geb~. 270 gebmundum. 347 §o. **Gn** 10 geb~.

God-mund *sm* **Ct** 14/8 ~es.

Godmunddinga-hām, godmundinga§ **BH**.

Gūþ-mund *sm* **LV** 135 guð~. 277 guth~. **Ct** 35/12 guð~.

Hēa-mund *sm* **Ct** 30/13; 44/3 heah~. 35/11 ~.

Heaþo-mund *sm* **LV** 55 hadu~.

Hō-mund *sm* **LV** 201, 10 ~.

Hrōþ-mund *sm* **Gn** 120 hroð~.

Hrōþ-munding *sm* son of Hrōþmund. **Gn** 120 hroð~.

Hyge-mund *sm* **LV** 397 hygmund.

Nōþ-mund *sm* **Ct** 24/4; 28/18 noð~.

Ōs-mund *sm* **LV** 83; 278 ~. **Gn** 7 ~. **Ct** 21/6; 22/5; 23/5; 24/10; 30/16, 7; 31/6; 32/9; 33/17; 35/15; 36/7; 38/16; 40/13; 41/53; 42/26; 44/6; 58/20 ~. 20/23; 22/9; 23/9; 49/8 ~i. 46/5 ~us.

Pleg-mund *sm* **LV** 312 ~.

Sige-mund *sm* **LV** 166; 250 sigmund. **SG** 18 ~. **Ct** 28/18; 31/8; 38/19; 42/26 ~.

Sige-munding *sm* son of Sigemund. **SG** 18 ~.

Torht-mund *sm* **LV** 12 torct~. 89; 106; 467, 75 torcht~. 147 ~.

Wǣr-mund *sm* **LV** 50; 370; 478 uer~. **Gn** 11 uær~. 30 *uuermun[d]*. 46 uęr~. 94 uer~. **Ct** 15/6; 16/5 uuermundi. 17/7; 33/19; 38/20; 57/8 wer~.

Wǣr-munding *sm* son of Wǣrmund. **Gn** 94 uær~.

Wid-mund *sm* **Ct** 1/4 uuidmundes felt.

Wig-mund *sm* **LV** 149; 243; 446, 50, 70 uig~. **Ct** 15/7; 16/6 uuigmundi. 19/5; 23/5; 24/10; 33/6 uu~. 46/6 §us. 21/6; 22/5; 34/7; 36/7; 41/51; 42/25; 58/21; 59/6 ~. 23/12 ~i. 25/13; 43/8 wimund.

Wil-mund *sm* **LV** 143, 77; 234, 45, 70; 308, 10, 29, 94; 442, 48, 50, 63 uil~.

Mundlinga-hām Ct.

mundl.. Ep; munleuu Ef; mundleu Cp.

-cund. weoruld~. god~.

Cunda *sm* **Ct** 47/4 ~.

Cundwalh, §waling Gn.

gundae-suelgiae Ep; §suelgae Ef; §esuilge Cp.

grund *sm* ground, bottom. **VP** 64/8 ~(fundum). 68/16; **Hy** 5/8 ~(pro§). **Hy** 12/8 ~(†§§a). 68/15; 106/24 ~e (§§o). 68/3 ~ès. 129/1 ~um. 67/23 †grud.

grundsuopa Ef; grun[d]sopa Cp.

pund *sn* pound. **Ct** 37/18; 41/68, 9 ~ *pl.*

pundur *s* weight. **Cp** 1553 ~ (perpendiculum). **Ld** 36 pundar (§ *etc*).

pund *s* **Ct** 1666 ~(praesorium).

gebunden *ptc* bound. **Mt** 17 gebundenne. **VP** 19/9 gebundne sindun (obligati sunt). 67/7; 68/34 §(vinctos). 106/10 §(ligatos). **Hy** 13/11 §(ligati). 101/21 ~ra (vinculatorum).

ā-bunden *ptc* **Cp** 773 abundęn (expeditus).

þumle *spl* entrails. **Cp** 2140 tharme, thumle (viscera).

tunge-ðrum *s* tongue-ligament. **Lr** 43 ~(sublinguae).

sum *aj, prn* some. **Ep** 731 ~e daeli (partim); **Cp** §; **Ef** ~ae. **Mt** 35 ~um. **VP** 89/13 ~e hwile (aliquantulum).

-sum. wil~, §lice. sib~. frem~, §lice,

§nis. wyn~, §ian, §nis. genyht~, §ian, §nis. hērsumian. geleāf~.

Want-sumu *s* BH 28 u~—uuantsamu I—u[u]~ [e *over last* u *but one*].

sumur *sm* summer. VP 73/17 ~(aestatem). Hy 8/7 ~(aestus).

fruma *sm* beginning. Rn 1/6 ~an (?). LP 3 ~an *d.* 109/3; 118/160~(principium). 110/10~(initium). 73/2; 76/12 *etc* ~an (initio). Hy 13/2 § (primordio). 77/51; 104/36 § (primitias).

frumbearn VP. frumcenned VP.

numen *ptc* taken. VH 13/10 earun numene (tenebamur).

genumen *ptc* taken. Ep 100 ginumni; Ef ·enumini (adempto).

be-numen *ptc* taken away, deprived. Ep 102 binumni; Ef § (adempta). Cp 76 †gebinumini (§o). 104 binumini (ablata); Cp §e; Ef †binoman.

for-numen *ptc* destroyed. VP 7/10 sie ~(consumetur).

erfe-numa *sm* heir. Ct 40/9 ærbenumena. 42/17 mine ærfenuman.

cuman *sv* come. VP 39/8 ~u (venio). 33/12; 45/9; 65/16 *etc* ~að (§ite!). 67/32; 85/9; 125/6 ~að (§ient). 125/6 ~ende (§ientes).

becuman *sv* come. VP 57/8 bicumad (devenient).

ufan-cumende *aj* (*ptc*) rising. VH 9/15 ~(oriens).

ūp-cuman *sv* come up. VP 84/12; 96/11: 111/4 ~en wes (orta est; §; exortum est). 103/22 ~en is (ortus est).

un-ofercumen *aj* (*ptc*) un-overcome. Ep 536 unofaercumenrae; Ef unofercumenræ; Cp unobercumenre (indigestae).

cuma *sm* stranger. VP 68/9 ~(hospis).

Ēad-cume *sf* LV 45 eat~.

Tīd-cume *sf* LV 46~.

Wil-cume *sf* LV 20, 4 uilcumae.

guma *sm* man.

Gumbercti Ct. Gumuald LV.

brȳd-guma *sm* bridegroom. Cp 1669 ~(procus). VP 18/6 ~(sponsus).

dryht-guma *sm* Cp 1476, 1514 ~(paranimphus, paranymphus). Ld 124 dryct~ (§nimphi).

Gumeninga-hergae Ct.

trum *aj* firm, substantial. Lr 8 were ~e (firmum). VH 6/10 ~e (§am). Hy 7/25 ~um (§ā).

Trumberct BH. Trumheri BH; §here Gn. Trumuald LV. Trumuini, trium§ BH.

un-trum *aj* infirm. VP 6/3; 104/37 ~(infirmus). Hy 4/9 ~e (§i).

untrymnes *sf* infirmity. Mt 49 ælce untrymnesse *a.*

wyrtruma *sm* root. VP 51/7 ~an (radicem).

geuntrumian *wv* weaken. VP 25/1 biom ~ad (infirmabor). 30/11; 67/10 § is. Hy 4/12 § wes. 9/4 bioð §. 17/37; 108/24 § sind. 57/8 sien §. 87/10; 106/12 §e sind. 26/2 ~ede sind.

ā-crummen *ptc* crammed. Cp 843 ~(farsa).

Tumma *sm* LV 228 ~.

crump *aj* crooked. Cp 1411 ~(obunca).

Humbre *sf* Humber. BH 23 ~i *fluminis* — § [u *from* y]. 373 hymbrę *fluminis* — § — humbrę. Ct 22/10 *fluminis* ~ę. 23/11 § ~e.

cumb *sm* valley. Ct 20/10, o oð smalan ~. smalan ~es. 58/12 æt ~e.

Merce-cumb *sm* Ct 20/4, 4 on ~, ~es.

Mogan-cumb *sm* Ct 25/4 ~.

Wincel-cumb *sm* Ct 58/12 æt ~e.

dumb *aj* dumb. VP 37/14 ~(mutus). 30/19 ~e (§a *pl*).

ā-dumbian *wv* become dumb. VP 38/3, 10 ~ade (obmutui).

bi-luc- *prt* closed. VP 16/10 ~un (concluserunt). 30/9 ~e (§isti).

sucun *prt* sucked. VH 7/24 ~un (suxerunt).

Mucca *sm* LV 172 ~.

Tucca *sm* Ct 24/7 ~.

Plucca *sm* LV 199 ~.

bucc *s* beaver (of helmet). Ep 120 ~(buccula); Ef †bua; Cp buuc.

bucca *sm* he-goat. **VP** 49/9 ~an (hircos). 49/13; Hy 7/27 ~ena. 65/15 ~um.

suhterga *sm* nephew. **Cp** 915 ~(fratuelis).

ofer-fuhtun *prt* conquered. **VP** 108/3; 128/1, 2 ~(expugnaverunt). 119/7 ~(impugnabant).

sugu *sf* sow. **Ep** 912 ~(scrofa); Ef †ruga; Cp, Ld ~.

suge-sweard Cp.

fugol *sm* bird. **Ep** 1067 stalu to fuglum (*first* u *from* l); Ef fluglum; Ld fuglam (umbrellas). 1085 fuglaes bean (vicium); Ef flugles; Cp, Ld fugles. Ld 183 †fuglues benae (vicias). **VP** 8/9; 103/12; 148/10; Hy 8/14 fuglas (volucres). 78/2 §um (volatilibus). Hy 7/48 §a (avium).

fuguldaeg Ct. **fugultrēo** Cp.

Fugul *sm* **LV** 319 ~.

gōs-fugol *sm* goose. **Ct** 41/62 ~fuglas.

henn-fugol *sm* hen. **Ct** 37/18; 41/62 ~fuglas. 40/10 hen§. 39/5 henfugla.

Sǣ-fugul *sm* **Gn** 75 sae~.

Sǣ-fugling *sm* son of S. **Gn** 74 sae~.

Sige-fugl *sm* **SG** 15 ~.

Sigefugling *sm* son of S. **SG** 15 (~).

flug- *prt* fled. **VP** 30/12 ~un (fugiebant). 59/6 ~en (§iant). 113/5 ~e (§isti).

benug- *vb* enjoy. **Ct** 41/22 ~e *sbj pres.*

ā-tuge *prt* draw out. **VP** 21/10; 29/4 ~(abstraxisti). **Ct** 38/5 hia. ~.

dugunde *aj* (*ptc*) availing. **Ct** 37/18.

sucga *sm* titlark. **Ep** 422 sugga (ficetula); Cp §; Ef ~; Ld †suca.

frugn- *prt* asked. **VP** 34/11 ~on (interrogabant). 136/3 ~un (§averunt).

tō-strugde *prt* scattered. **VP** 43/12 ~(dispersisti). 105/23, 3, 7 ~(disperderet).

gebrugdun *prt* drew out. **VP** 36/14 ~(evaginaverunt).

Utel *sm* **Ct** 12/3 utol. 15/7; 16/6; 19/4 ~.

þrut *s* eruption, leprosy.

thrustfel Ep, Ef, Cp.

hnutu *sf* nut. **Ep** 15 †hrutu (abilina); Ef ~.

hnutbēam Ep, Ef, Cp.

haesel-hnutu *sf* hazelnut. **Cp** 33 ~(abelena).

ā-gut- *prt* poured out. **VP** 78/3 ~on (effuderunt). 105/38 ~un (§).

ðorh-gute *prt* poured through. **VP** 88/46 ~(perfudisti).

butre *sf* butter. **Ct** 37/20; 41/63 ~an *g.*

buturfliogae Ep; §o Ef; buterflege Cp.

Utta *sm* **BH** 166 ~. 167 ~ *d.* 182 ~an *g.* **LV** 78; 162; 215, 9, 30, 91 ~.

Lutting *sm* **LV** 171 ~.

Tutta *sm* **LV** 159, 60 ~.

Putta *sm* **BH** 227 ~ — put[t]a I. 230 ~ *d* — puta. 239 ~. **Gn** 10, 49 ~.

Puttan·ealh Ct.

lud-gaet Ep; Ef, Cp §.

wudu *sm* wood. **Bd**² 30 ~um (saltibus). **VP** 73/5; 79/14 ~a (silvā). 131/6 ~a (§ae *g*). 82/15 ~a (§as). 49/10; 67/31 *etc* ~a (§arum). **Ct** 20/16 ~a *d.* 28/6 ðem wiada. 39/6 weada *g.*

uuidubil Ep, Ef; uudu§ Ep; wudu§ Cp; †uuitu§ Ld. **uuidubindae** Ef; §binde, uudu§ Cp. **uuidubindlae** Ep; †uuydublindæ Ef; uudubindlae Ld. **uuduhona** Cp. **wodhae** Cp [*under* henn]. **uuydumer** Ef; Cp wudu§. **uudusnīte** Cp. **Wudotûn** Ct. **uuiduuuindae**, †wiuwindae Ep; uuidouuindae Ef; uuduuuinde, §winde Cp.

Dēra-wudu *sm* **BH** 335 in ~uuda, *id est, in silva* derorum — §u I.

furh-wudu *sm* pine. **Cp** 1590 ~(pinus).

bi-bude *prt* commanded. **VP** 7/7; 118/4 ~(mandasti).

on-bud *prt* commanded. **VP** 40/9 ~un (mandaverunt). 118/138 ~e (§asti). 43/5 ~e (§as).

Uddan-hom Ct.

Rudda *sm* **LV** 412 ~.

Cudda *sm* **LV** 78; 163 ~.

Tudda *sm* LV 336 ~. Ct 35/12; 58/20 ~.

Dudd *sm* Gn 21 ~. Ct 33/21; 35/14 ~.

Dudda *sm* Ct 14/1 dud[d]ono *d.* 24/2, 2 †iððan *d.* ~an *d.* 24/7; 28/16; 30/17, 9; 32/9; 43/8; 44/4 ~.

on-uppan *prp* upon, on. Ct 35/6 ~.

hupp-bān Lr.

Ubba *sm* Ct 15/9; 16/8 ~.

Bubba *sm* Gn 108 ~.

Bubbing *sm* son of B. Gn 108 ~.

hryre *sm* fall. VP 105/29; 143/14 ~(ruina). 90/6 ~(§ā). 109/6 ~as.

styria *sm* sturgeon. Ep 809 ~(porcopiscis); Ef §; Cp styrga; Ld styra. Cp 607 ~(cragacus).

styrian *wv* stir. Cp 1328 ~ið (movebor). Bd² 2 ~ede (exagitabat).

on-styrian *wv* stir. VP 28/8 ~eð (commovebit). 59/4 ~edes (commovisti). 9/27 *etc* biom ~ed (movebor). 14/5 *etc* § bið (commovebitur). 17/8 *etc* §e sind (commota sunt). 65/9 onstyrgan (commoveri).

on-styrenis *sf* movement. VP 88/10; 120/3 ~isse (motum; commotione).

styring *sf* moving. VP 105/30 sie ~(quassatio).

ā-spyrian *wv* track, investigate. VP 138/3 ~edes (investigasti).

ā-spyrgend *sm* tracker. VH 13/25 ~(investigator).

cyre *sm* choice. Cp 664 cyri (delectum, electio).

wal-cyrge *sf* war-goddess. Cp 771 ~(eurynis). 2017 uu~ (tisifone). 1018 walcrigge (herinis).

byres *s* borer. Ep 891 ~is (scalprum); Ef §; Cp byrs. 907 ~is (scalpellum); Ef §; Ld biriis. Cp 11 buiris (foratorium).

wyrrest *aj sprl* worst. VP 33/22 se ~a (pessima).

myrre *sf* myrrh. VP 44/9 ~(mirrha).

dēor-wyrðe *aj* precious. VP 18/11 ~ne (praetiosum). 20/4 ~um. 115/15 ~(§a *sg*).

un-tēl-wyrðe *aj* irreproachable. VP 18/8 ~[y *from* i] (inrepraehensibilis).

wyrð *s* honour, dignity. Ef 252 uuryd (culmus); Cp ~. Cp 1139 uyrðo (infula).

or-wyrð *s* ignominy. VP 82/17 mid ~e (ignominiā).

fyrðran *wv* promote. Cp 1673 ~u (proveho).

gefyrðro *sm* promoter. Ef 327 gifyrdro (ditor); Cp ~.

byrðen *sf* burden. VP 37/5 ~(onus). 80/7 ~ennum.

ðyrs *sm* giant. Cp 1457 ~(orcus).

wyrsa *cp* worse.

wyrsian *wv* get worse. VP 37/6 ~adon (deterioraverunt).

Hyrst *s* Hurst. Ct 55/6 †iu ~.

Sand-hyrst *s* Sandhurst. Ct 28/12 silva ~.

Snād-hyrst *s.* Ct 55/7 ~.

hyrst *sf* ornament. Cp 848 hryste (farelas).

gehyrstan *wv* adorn. Cp 849 ~i (falerata).

ðyrstan *wv* thirst. VP 41/3; 62/2 ~eð (sitivit). 106/5 ~ende (§ientes).

gedyrstig *aj* daring. Ep 81 gi~ (ausus); Ef †gedurstip; Cp ~. CA 16 ~.

byrst *sf* bristle. Ep 905 ~(seta); Ef, Cp §. Ef 1132 brysti (setes). 1182 §æ (§ *etc*).

Gyrwe *pl* BH 176, 254 gyruiorum. 292 guruiorum — gy§ — §§ — §§. 367 *loco qui vocatur* in gyruum.

tyrf *pl* pieces of turf. Cp 452 tyrb (cespites).

scyrft *s* Cp 1799 ~(scansio).

ymb-hwyrft *sm* circuit. VP 23/1 *etc* ~(orbis). 9/9 *etc* ~(§em). 11/9 *etc* ~e (circuitu). 78/4 ~e urum (§). 17/16 *etc* ~es (orbis). 43/14 ymhwyrfte. 48/2; 97/9 ymbhwyrf. 32/8 ~hwyrst. 49/12 ~hwerft.

ān-hyrne *aj, sb* unicorn. VP 21/22 ~era (unicornuorum). 28/6; 77/69 ~ra.

hyrnen *aj* of horn. VP 97/6 †hyrnes (corneae).

hyrnetu *sf* hornet. Ef 275 hirnitu (crabro); Cp hurnitu.

þyrne *sf* thorn-bush. Ep 317 thyrnae (dumus); Cp ~.

byrne *sf* corslet.

Byrnhom, §ing Gn; §ham Ct. Brynuald LV; byrnwald Ct.

wyrm *sm* worm. Rd 9 uyrmas. VP 21/7 ~(vermis).

uuyrmbaso Ld.

fāg-wyrm *sm* basilisk. VP 90/13 ~(basiliscum).

hand-wyrm *sm* Ep 126 †~[u]yrp (briensis); Ef honduyrp; Cp §uyrm. Cp 1193 hond~ (ladascapiae, §).

regen-wyrm *sm* earthworm. Ep 612 ~uuyrm (lumbricus); Ef regn§; Cp §wyrm.

trēo-wyrm *sm* caterpillar. VP 77/46 ~e (erugini).

wyrcan *wv* work. VP 5/7 *etc* wircað (operantur). 6/9 *etc* § (§amini). 14/2 §eð. 16/4 wirc! (opera *sbst*). 43/2; 67/29 wircende earð. 73/12 §is. 91/8 § werun. 27/3; 58/3; 93/16 *etc* §um. 63/3 §ra. Hy 1/3 wyrctun (aptaverunt).

wircnis *sf* operation. VP 106/23 ~isse (operationes).

þyrhel *aj* perforated. Ct 20/9 ðyrelan stane.

næs-ðyrel *sn* nostril. Lr 20 ~(michinas). VP 113/6 (2); 134/17 nes~ (nares).

þweorh-fyrhi *s* cross-furrow. Ep 881 thuerhfyri (salebrae); Ef §; Cp þuerh§.

gewyrht *s*(*n*) merit, desert. LP 2; DA 11 ~um. VP 7/5 bi § (merito).

un-gewyrht *s*(*n*) want of merit, deserts. VP 34/7, 19; 68/5 *etc* bi ~um (gratis).

Tyrhtel *sm* Gn 49 ~.

wyrhta *sm* worker, maker.

hrōf-wyrhta *sm* roof-maker. Ep 996 ~uuyrcta (tignarius); Ef ~huyrihta; Cp ~uuyrhta.

leðer-wyrhta *sm* leather-maker. Ep 155 lediruuyrcta (byrseus); Ef §uyrhta; Cp leðer§; Ld lediruyrcta.

meter-wyrhta *sm* metrician. Cp 1312 †meder~(metricius).

fyrhtu *sf* fear. VH 12/13 ~(pavor). Ps 30/23 ~ minre (pavore). 67/28 ~(§). 45/4 ~(†fortitudine). 88/41 ~(formidine). 54/5 fyr[h]tu (§o). 118/25 †fyhtu (pavimento).

ā-fyrht *ptc* frightened. Cp 237 hlysnende, ~e (attoniti).

wyrgan *wv* strangle. Cp 1926 ~eð (stangulat).

myrgnis *sf* mirth, melody. Cp 1352 ~(musica).

byrg *under* burg.

byrga *sm* security, bail. Ep 776 ~ea (presetuas); Ef §; Cp ~. 921 ~[e]a (sequester); Ef ~ea; Cp ~.

bi-byrgan *wv* bury. VP 78/3 ~de (sepeliret).

byrgere *sm* burier. Ep 760 ~as (vispellones); Cp §; Ef †buyrgenas.

byrgen *sf* tomb. Cp 1350 ~(murilium). VP 5/11; 13/3 ~(sepulchrum). 87/12 ~enne (§a). 48/12 § (§a). 67/7; 87/6 §um (monumentis).

wyrt *sf* herb, plant. VP 89/6 ~(herba). 103/14; 146/8 ~e (§am). 36/2 ~a (§arum).

wyrtdrenc Cp. wyrtruman VP. wyrtwalan VP.

bēo-wyrt *sf* sweet flag. Ep 20 biouuyrt (apiastrum); Ef biuyrt; Cp bio~. 657 biouuyrt (marrubium); Cp bio~.

biscop-wyrt *sf* bishop's weed. Ep 496 ~uuyrt (hibiscum); Ef, Cp §.

lǣce-wyrt *sf* ribwort. Ep 849 leciuuyrt (quinquenervia); Ef §uyrt; Cp §wyrt.

gelod-wyrt *sf* silverweed. Ef 379 gilodusrt; Cp ~(eptafyllon). Cp 725 ~(eftafylon).

gescād-wyrt *sf* rocket (?). Ep 1032 giscaduuyrt (talumbus); Ef gescan§; Cp ~.

smeoru-wyrt *sf* Ep 1078 speruuuyrt; Ef sm§ (veneria); Cp ~.

walh-wyrt *sf* dwarf elder. Ef 393 uualhuyrt (ebulum); Cp ~; Ld ualuyrt. Ep 518 uualhuuyrt (intula); Ef §uyrt; Cp §wyrt.

Uurti-gern BH.

hyrdel *sm* hurdle. Cp 600 hyrþil (cratem).

āð-swyrd *sf* oath-swearing. VP 104/9 ~e (juramenti).

wyrde *sbj prt* has become. DA 12 ~.

wyrd *sf* fate, Fate. Ep 764 uuyrdae (parcae); Ef §; Cp ~e. 980 †uuyd (sortem, condicionem); Ef uyrd; Cp~. Cp 897 ~(fortuna). 904 ~(fors); Ld uyrd. Ld 96 § (fatum).

for-wyrd *sf* destruction. VP 9/16 ~ ða (interitum quem). 34/7; 48/11; 108/13; 139/12 ~(§). 102/4; 106/20 ~e (§u). 54/24 ~e (§ūs *g*).

fore-wyrd *sf* predestination. Cp 162 ~e (antefata).

Twi-fyrde *s* Twyford. BH 318 ad tuifyrdi, *quod significat ad duplicem vadum.*

be-gyrdan *wv* gird. VP 44/4 begyrd (accingere!). 17/33; 92/1 bigyrde (praecinxit). 17/40; 29/12 §es. 64/7 §ed (accinctus). 108/19 sie §ed. 64/13 bioð §e. Hy 4/9 §e sind.

gyrdels *s* girdle. Ep 573 ~ils *vel* broec (lumbare); Ef, Cp §broec. Cp 321 ~(brahiale). VP 108/19 ~(zona).

gyrdislrhingae Ep; gyrdilshringe Ef, Cp.

byrde *aj* of high rank. Ef 1153 ~istrae (blaciarius, primicularius).

mis-byrd *sf* abortion. Ep 80 ~(abortus); Ef, Cp §.

mund-byrd *sf* protection. Ep 935 ~(suffragium); Ef §. Cp 1475 ~(patrocinium). Ct 42/7 to ~e.

gebyrded *ptc* fringed. Ep 228 †gybyrdid (clabatum); Ef ~id; Cp ~ed.

geende-byrdan *wv* order, arrange. VP 49/5 ~un (ordinaverunt).

endebyrdnis *sf* order. VP 118/91 ~(†ordinatione). 109/4 efter ~isse (ordinem). Hy 6/23 § (§e).

in-bryrdan *wv* touch, inspire. VP 29/13 biom inbr(yrd) (compungar). 108/17 ~edne (§unctum).

geinbryrdan *wv* VP 4/5 bioð ~e (conpungimini). 34/16 ~e sind (§uncti sunt).

onbryrdnis *sf* compunction. VP 59/5 ~isse (conpunctionis).

scyl- *vb* shall. CH 1 (we) ~un.

Mylen-tūn Ct.

cylen *sf* kiln. Cp 906 ~ine, heorðe (fornacula).

Ylla *sm* LV 338 ~.

hyll *sm* hill. VP 64/13; 71/3; 113/4, 6; 148/9; Hy 6/13; Hy 8/11 ~as (colles). 77/58 ~um. Ct 48/4 feower treowe hyl.

Broc-hyl *sm* Ct 9/8 ~.

sond-hyllas *pl* sandhills. Cp 125 ~(alga).

Tihhan-hyl *sm* Ct 48/5 ~.

syll *sf* sill, basis. Cp 275 syl (basis).

wið-styllan *wv* retreat. Cp 662 ~stylde (descivit, pedem retraxit).

nyllan = ne willan. VP 36/1; 102/2; 118/31 nyl (noli!). 4/5; 31/9; 61/11, 1, 1; 145/2; Hy 4/5 ~að (§ite!). Ct 41/14, 24, 5 (he) ~e.

fyllan *wv* fill.

gefyllan *wv* fill. VP 80/11; 90/16 ~u (adimplebo). Hy 5/15; Hy 7/47 § (replebo; consummabo). 15/11; 144/16 ~es (adimplebis; imples). 19/7 ~eð (impleat). 109/6; 126/5; 128/7 § (§ebit). 43/15 ~að (†in plebibus). 82/17 gefyl (imple!). Hy 10/8 gefylde (implevit). 21/27 bið ~ed (†saturabuntur); 25/10 *etc* §is (repleta est); 37/8 § is (conpleta est); Hy 7/29 § wes (satiatus est). 64/12 bioð †gefyld (replebuntur). 36/19 bioð §e (saturabuntur); 64/5 bioð §e (replebimur); 73/20 §e sind (§eti sunt) *etc.*

fyllnis *sf* fullness. VP 23/1; 49/12; 95/11 fylnis (plenitudo). 88/12 §nisse (§inem). 97/7 †fynis (§o).

gefyllnis *sf* fullness, consummation. VP 58/14 ~nisse (consummationis). 118/96 § (§e).

fylled-flood Cp.

Geard-cyll *s* Ct 35/5 æt ~e.

wylf *sf* she-wolf. Cp 1260 ~(lupa). Rn 3/2 wylif.

fylgan *wv* follow. VP 33/15 fyl[g] (sequere!).

gefylgan *wv* attain. Mt 51 (he) ~e.

æfter-fylgan *wv* follow after, pursue. VP 22/6; Hy 7/59 efterfylgeð (subsequitur; persequitur). 37/

21 †esterfylgende eam (subsecutus sum).

æfterfylgend *sm* successor. Ct 37/29 minum ~um.

tylg *av comp.* Ep 743 ~(propensior); Ef, Cp §.

geæ-bylgan *wv* make angry. VP 102/9 bið geebylged (indignabitur).

æbylgðu *sf* anger. VP 68/25 [y *over* u] (indignatio). 29/6 § (§ione). 77/49; 84/4 §e (§ionis; §). 77/49 ebylðu [ð *from* y] (§). 101/11 § ðinre (§).

egylt Cp 808 ~(excesus).

gyltan *wv* be guilty. VP 24/8 ~endum (delinquentibus).

ā-gyltan *wv* be guilty. VP 33/22 ~að (delinquent). 38/2 ~e (§am). 74/5 ~endum. 118/67 ~e (deliqui).

geðyld *sf* patience. VP 9/19; 70/5 ~(patientia). 61/6 gedyld.

geðyldig *aj* patient. VP 85/15; 102/8; 144/8 ~(patiens). 91/15 geðyldge. 145/7 §um.

scyld *sf* crime, guilt. DA 10 ~ *a*. VP 9/36; 50/5 ~(delictum *n*). Hy 12/11 ~(culpa). 31/5 ~(delictum *a*). Hy 11/6 ~(§am). 18/14; 39/7 ~e (delicto). 37/19; 50/4 ~e minre (peccato). 18/13; 58/13; 68/6 ~e (delicta). 24/7 †~(§). 50/7; 67/22; 126/2 ~um. 21/2 ~a (§orum).

scyldig *aj* guilty. Cp 1422 ~(obnoxius). VH 12/5 scyldge (reos).

un-scyldig *aj* innocent. VP 9/29 ðone unscyldgan (innocentem).

gescyldru *pl* shoulders. VP 90/4 ~um [d *from* t] (scapulis). Hy 7/22 ~(§as).

bi-myldan *wv* bury. Cp 1034 ~(humare).

gylden *aj* golden. VP 44/14 gyldnum (aureis).

bi-gyld *ptc* gilded. VP 44/10 ~um (deaurato).

Gylde-burne Ct.

ān-gylde *s* single fine. Ct 54/3 *singulare praetium ad penam, id est* ~.

byþne *s* keel. Cp 389 bythne (carina).

ysope *sf* hysop. VP 50/9 ~an (ysopo).

Hyse *sm* LV 239 hyssi. Ct 43/9 ~.

Hyseberht Ct. **Hysimonn** LV. **Hysenōð** Ct. **Hysiuulf** LV.

Ad-hysi *sm* LV 278 ~.

Hwīt-hyse *sm* Ct 47/8 ~.

Tāt-hysi *sm* LV 95 ~.

rysel *s* fat. Ep 2 ~il (axungia); Ef risil; Cp ~. Cp 219 risel (arvina).

hlysnan *wv* listen. Cp 82 ~ende (adtonitus). 221 §i (arectas). 237 §e, afyrhte (attoniti).

dysig *aj* foolish. VP 91/7; Hy 7/9 ~(stultus; fatua). 48/11 se ðysga (stultus). 93/8 dysge (§i).

Hyssa *sm* LV 101 ~.

cnyssan *wv* strike, knock. Rd 8 ~a *inf*.

gecnyssan *wv* VP 136/9 gecnyseð (adlidet). 88/45; 101/11 §edes (conlisisti; elisisti). 144/14; 145/7 §ede (elisos).

on-cnyssan *wv* strike against. VP 61/4 oncnysede.(impulsae).

frysca *sm* kite. Cp 340 ~(butio).

nyste = ne wiste. VP 34/11 nysse (ignorabam). 15 ~on (§averunt). 72/22 ~(nescivi). 81/5 ~un (nescierunt). Hy 7/34 ~un (§iebant).

cystig *aj* munificent. Ep 621 cistigian (munifica); Cp ~an. Cp 671 ~(devota).

un-cystig *sf* stingy. Ep 413 ~ *vel* heamol (frugus); Ef, Cp ~.

clyster *s(n)* cluster. Cp 318 clystri (botrum).

geclystre *sn* cluster. VH 7/25 (botyrum .. et lac).

hyspan *wv* revile. VP 2/4 ~eð (subsannabit). 40/8 ~ton (susurrabant).

cyspan *wv* fetter. VP 78/11 ~edra (compeditorum).

gecyspan *vb* VP 145/7 ~te (compeditos).

yferra *comp.* after. Ct 41/23 ~an dogre.

yfel *aj* bad. VP 63/6; 140/4 ~(malum). 11/3; 48/6 yflan. 26/5 ðæm †yfla. 36/19; 70/20 *etc* §e. 40/2; 93/13 *etc* §um.

yfeldēd VP.

yfel *sn* evil. BDS 4 yflaes. VP 14/3; 50/6 *etc* ~(malum). 9/27; 33/14, 5 *etc* yfle. 7/5; 20/12; 22/4 *etc* ~(mala *pl*). 34/26; 87/4; 106/26 yflum (§is). 106/39 §a (§orum).

yfelspreocende VP.

yfle *av* badly. VP 77/19 ~(male).

lyfesn *sf* charm. Cp 1413 lyb, lybsn (obligamentum). 1930 lybesne (strenas).

scyfel *sm* instigator, god of war. Ep 627 scybla: [y *over* i] (mafortae); Ef scybla; Cp scyfla.

Yffi *sm* BH 96 ~. 119 ~ *a*. Gn 73 ~.

Yffing *sm* son of Y. Gn 73 ~.

lyft *sf* air. Cp 1961 lybt (sudum, siccum). VP 17/12 ~e (aeris).

Hynca *sm* LV 208 ~.

ðyncan *wv* seem. Ct 37/42; 38/14 (hit) ~e.

drync *sm* draught. Cp 1008 ~(haustum). VH 11/10 ~(potus). Ps 22/5 ~ ðinne (poculum). 79/6 ~(potum). 101/10 ~minnė(§).

dryncan *wv* give to drink. VP 68/22 dryncton (potaverunt).

Brynca *sm* LV 196; 217 ~.

hyngran *wv* hunger. VP 49/12 ~iu (esuriero). 33/11 hyn[g]radun. 106/5, 36; Hy 10/8 ~ende (§ientes). 106/9 § (§ientem). 145/7 ~endum.

ē-spryng *s* well. VP 67/27 ~um (fontibus).

spryng *s* ulcer. Ep 175 spyrng [n *on er.*] (carbunculus); Ef, Cp ~. 791 ~(papula, pustula); Ef, Cp ~.

getynge *aj* talkative. VP 139/12 ~(linguosus).

Hyni *sm* LV 99 ~.

ryne *sm* course. VP 58/6 :yrn (occursum). Hy 11/13 ~(cursus).

eft-ryne *sm* running back. VP 18/7 ~yrn (occursus).

hider-ryne *aj* directed hither. Ld 131 hidirrinę.

hwider-rynė *aj* directed whither. Ld 130 huidirrynę (cujatis).

lynes *sm* axle. Ep 8 ~isas (axedones); Cp §. Cp 258 ~is (axredo).

gemyne *sbj prs* remember. Mt 28 ~ðu! VP 24/6 ~(reminiscere!). 73/2; 102/14; 105/4; 118/49; 131/1; 136/7 ~(memento!). 78/8 ~(memineris!). 88/48 ~(memorare!). 24/7 ~es (memineris). 21/28 ~en (reminiscentur). Ct 37/41; 42/11 (ge) ~en.

mynet *sn* coin. Ep 670 ~it (nomisma); Cp §; Ef munit.

mynetere *sm* money-changer. Cp 1392 miyniteri (numularius *etc*).

Cyni *sm* LV 239; 340 ~.

Cynibalþ Rn; §bald LV; cyne§ Ct. **Cyniberct** BH, LV; cyneberht BH, Gn, Ct; cyniberhtte Ct. **Cynibill** BH. **Cynibrē** Ct. **Cyniburg** BH, LV; cymburg BH. **Cynifrid** BH; §frith LV. **Cynigār** LV. **Cynigisl** BH, LV. **Cynegӯð** LV. **Cyniheard** LV; cyn§ LV, Gn; cyne§ Ct. **Cynhelm** LV, Ct. **Cynelāf**, cyn§ Ct. **Cynimund** BH, LV; cyne§ BH. **Cynirēd** LV; *cynered* Gn; cyrred Ct. **Cynrēou**, §reowing Gn. *Kyneswīþa* Rn. **Cyniðegn** LV. **cyneðrym** VP. **Cyniðrӯð** LV; cyne§, †cyne Ct. **Cynewald**, §ing Gn. **Cynuīse** BH. **cyniuuithan** Ep; Ef §; Cp cynewiððan. **Cyniuulf** LV; cynwulf Gn, Ct; cyne§ Ct.

cynedōm *sm* kingdom, rule. Ep 859 cyni~ (respuplica); Ef §; Cp ~doom. Cp 845 ~as (fasces). VH 4/22 ~(imperium).

cyning *sm* king. Rn 1/4 *kyniq*, 6 *kyninges*, 11 *kyng*. 2/5 *kyniqc*. VP 2/6; 20/2, 8 *etc* ~(rex). 19/10 *etc* ~(regem). 44/2, 15 *etc* ~e. 17/51 *etc* ~es. 2/10; 47/5 *etc* ~as. 88/28 *etc* ~um. 44/10 ~a. 44/14 † ~(regum). 5/3 cynin (rex). Ct 28/19, 20, 2; 45/25, 50; 48/1 ~. 42/2; 47/9 ~e. 28/5, 6, 8; 34/10; 43/4, 6; 44/7; 50/2; 54/2 ~es. 433 cyniges. 53/3 cynincges.

Cyninges-tún, k§ Ct.

Cynech *sm* LV 340 ~.

Cynicin *sm* LV 227 ~.

clyne *sm* lump of metal, mass. Cp 1291 ~(massa).

Byni *sm* LV 159 ~.

Bryni *sm* LV 221, 69; 340 ~.

ynnilaec Cp, Ef; hynni§ Ep; ynne§ Cp.

ðynnian *wv* thin. Bd[2] 80 ~ade (obtenuerað).

geðynnian *wv* thin. **VH** 3/11 ~ade sind (adtenuati).

Ðynne *sm* **Ct** 50/6 ~.

synn *sf* sin. **Bd²** 37 grimre ~e (sceleris). **VP** 58/5; 108/14 syn (peccatum). 31/2; 108/7 ~e (§ *a*). 24/11 ~e minre (§o). 24/18; 31/1; 84/3 *etc* ~e (§a). 50/11 *etc* ~um. 37/4 ~a (§orum).

synfull *aj* sinful. **VP** 36/20; 72/12 *etc* ~e (peccatores). 139/5; 140/5 *etc* ~es. 9/17, 24, 5 *etc* se ~a (peccator). 49/16 ðæm ~an *etc.* 9/36 ðes § *etc.* 9/18; 10/3 *etc* ða §. 36/40; 27/3 *etc* ~um; ðæm §. 3/8; 7/10 *etc* synfulra; ðeara §.

syngian *wv* sin. **VP** 118/11 ~ie (peccem). 40/5 ~ade (§avi). 77/32 ~adon. 105/6; Hy 7/7 ~adun. 81/2 ~iendra. 4/5; 77/17 ~. 50/6 synngade.

wynn *sf* joy.

Uynbald LV, Ct. **Uynberct** LV; uuynberht Ct. **Uynburg** LV. **Uynfrid**, †uin§, uym§ BH; uynfrith LV; §frið Gn. **Uynhelm** LV, wyn§ Ct. **Wynhere** Ct. **Wynnheardinglond** Ct. **Wynsige** Ct.

Eala-wynn *sf* Ct 39/4 ~e *a*. 11 ~e *d*.

wynsum *aj* pleasant. **VP** 33/9; 85/5 *etc* ~(suavis). 111/5; 131/1 *etc* ~(jucundus; §um). 80/3; 118/39 ~e.

wynsumnis *sf* pleasantness, rejoicing. **VP** 31/7 ~(exultatio). 88/16 ~isse (jubilationem) *etc.* 32/3 § (§ione) *etc.* 26/6 § (§ionis). 41/5 *etc* § (exultationis). 144/7 § (suavitatis). 149/6 § (exultationes).

wynsumian *wv* rejoice. **VP** 2/11; 80/2 *etc* ~iað (exultate!). 46/2; 80/2 *etc* § (jubilate!). 94/1, 2 ~ie we (§emus!). 131/16 § (exultabunt). 97/6 †wynsumuað.

gewynsumian *wv* make to rejoice. **VH** 11/7 ~ie (secundet).

Uynna *sm* **LV** 167 ~.

cynn *sn* race, family. **Ef** 1108 ~a (cunabula). **Mt** 21 cynn(a). **SG** 11 ~. **VP** 77/67, 8; 84/6 ~(tribum, §; progeniem). 48/20; 77/8, 8; 121/4, 4 cyn (§; genus, §; tribus, §). 44/18 *etc* ~e (progenie). Hy 13/5 ~es (generis). 82/8; Hy 1/8 fremðes § (alienigenae *pl*). 71/17; 77/55; 104/37 cyn (tribūs). **Ct** 41/6, 41 ~. 38/4, 12 ~es.

Kynnburug Rn. **Cynnrīc**, §ing SG.

Angel-cynn *sn* English race. **Ct** 45/42 ~es ealonde.

mon-cynn *sn* mankind. **CH** 7 ~æs.

reht-meodren-cynn *sn* direct mother's line. **Ct** 45/42 ~.

cynn *aj* fitting, proper. **Ct** 38/13 cyn.

cynlic *aj* fitting, proper. **Ct** 37/42 ~.

Bynna *sm* **Ct** 15/7; 16/7; 58/18 ~. 6/3; 10/4 ~an *g*.

Bynni *sm* **LV** 115, 62 ~. **Ct** 14/7 ~ *lg*.

mynster *sn* monastery. **Ct** 41/17 ... ster.

mynster-hāmas Ct. **mynsterlīfes** Ct.

Sūð-mynster *sn* Ct 57/4 ~. 57/5, 6; 58/4, 5 æt ~mynstre.

styntan *wv* stupify. **Cp** 1019 ~id (hebetat).

ā-styntan *wv* stupify. **Ep** 488 ~id (hebitatus); Ef, Cp §.

synderlice *av* specially, singly. **VP** 4/10; 140/10 ~(singulariter).

syndrig *aj* single. **VP** 6/7 ~ie (singulas). 7/12; 41/11; 144/2 § (§os). 61/13 ~um. 79/14 ~ing (singularis).

stryndere *sm* squanderer. **Cp** 1670 ~(prodigus).

uuyndecreft Cp; †uyrdicraeftum Rd.

hāl-wynde *aj* salutary. **VP** 78/9; 84/5 ~(salutaris). 67/20 se † ~(§). 26/9; 61/3, 7 se ~a. 61/8; 94/1; Hy 7/31 ~an. Hy 10/2 ~um. 27/8 ~wendra (§ium). 23/5 ~wendan.

weorð-mynd *s(fn)* honour, distinction. **Cp** 83 to ~um (fasces). 1053 uu~ (infula).

gemynd *sf* memory. **Mt** 48 mine ~ *a*. **Bd²** 87 neowre ~e (memoriā). **VP** 9/7; 108/15 ~(memoria). 101/13; 134/13 ~(memoriale). 33/17; 108/14; 110/4; 144/7; Hy 7/53 ~(memoriam). 96/12; 111/7 ~e

(§iae *d*; §iā). 102/18 †~(§iā). 29/5 gemydde (~iae *d*).

gemyndelic *aj* memorial. Bl 7 ~(memoriale).

gemyndan *wv* commemorate. VP 9/13 gemynd is (memoratus est).

gemyndig *aj* mindful. VP 6/6; 8/5 *etc* ~(memor). Hy 10/10 ~(recordatus). 41/5 ~ eam (§ sum). 108/16 nis ~(non est§). 77/39 ~ is (memoratus est). 44/18; 105/7 gemyndge (memores). 77/42 sind § (sunt recordati). 136/1 werun § (§aremur).

gemyndgian *wv* remember, mention. VP 70/16 biom ~ad (memorabor). 82/5 bið ~að (§abitur). 77/35 ~ade werun (§ati sunt).

Cundi-georn LV.

gecyndilic *aj* natural. Ep 480 ~an (genuino); Ef §.

tynder *sf* tinder. Ep 562 tyndirm (isca); Ef, Cp tyndrin; Ld tyndri. 685 ~ir (napta, genus fomenti); Ef †ryndir; Cp ~. Cp 1367 tyndre (neptam). Ld 19 tund[e]ri (cautere). 100 tindre (cautere, ferrum melius).

ymen *sm* hymn. VP 64/2 ~(hymnus). 39/4; 64/14 ~(§um). 99/4 ~um. 136/3; Hy 13/23 hymen. Hy 12/6 humen.

Hymora *sm* Ct 6/2 (hymoran) *d*.

fore-nyme *sm* taking before. Cp 1671 ~(praesumptio).

nymðe *cj* unless. VP 123/1 ~(nisi). 126/1, 1; Hy 7/60 nemðe. Hy 7/53 nybðe. 7/13; 93/17; 118/92; 123/2 nemne. Ct 34/17 nymne.

ūp-cyme *sm* rising. VP 49/1; 106/3; 112/3 ~(solis ortu). Hy 12/5 ~(exortum = -ū).

cym- *prs* come. Mt 25 cy̆m! VP 100/2 ~es (venies). 36/13; 49/3; 64/3; 108/18; 120/1; Hy 6/6 ~eð. 41/3 ~e (§iam). 34/8; 35/12; 54/16; 118/41 ~e (§iat). 118/77 ~en (§iant). 68/3; 79/3 cym (§i!). 65/5 ~að (§ite!).

be-cym- *prs* come. VP 101/2 ~e (perveniat).

for-cymeð *prs* comes before. VP 67/32 ~(praeveniet).

fore-cym- *prs* come before. VP 16/13 ~(praeveni!). 58/11; 87/14 ~eð (§iet).

forð-cymeð *prs* comes forth. Ct 45/47 ~.

tō-cymeð *prs* comes to. VH 6/3 ~(advenerit).

ūp-cymeð *prs* comes up. VP 64/11 ~(exorietur).

Cymesing *sm*. Ct 55/4 cymesinc. 6 ~es cert.

Cymenes-denu Ct.

cymin *s(mn)* cummin. Cp 475 ~(cinnamomum, resina).

Cymedes-halh Ct.

grymetian *wv* roar, grunt. VP 36/12 ~ad (frement). 111/10 ~að (fremet). 37/9 ~ede (rugiebam). 34/16 ~adon (striderunt). 21/14 ~iende (rugiens). 103/21 § (§ientes).

untrymnis *sf* weakness. VP 40/4 †untrynisse (infirmitate).

med-trymnis *sf* weakness. VP 15/4 ~isse (infirmitates).

þrymm *sm* force, glory.

ðrymseld VP.

cyne-ðrym *sm* royal power. VH 6/19 ~(sceptra).

mægen-ðrymm *sm* majesty. VH 6/7 megenðrym (majestas). 71/19 §drymme. 101/17 §ðrymme. 28/3; 144/5 ~drymmes. 71/19; Hy 5/10 ~ðrymmes. Hy 5/19 §ðrymmum.

trymman *wv* strengthen, confirm. Cp 577 trymide (commendabat). VP 36/24 trymeð (firmat). 63/6 §edun. 70/21 ~ende eart (exortatus es). Ct 48/8 ic ~e.

getrymman *wv* strengthen, fortify, confirm. VP 19/5 ~e (confirmet). 31/8 ~u (firmabo). 36/17; 92/1; 103/15 §eð (confirmat; firmavit; confirmet). 67/29; 118/28 getryme (§a!). Hy 7/87 §en (§ent). 74/4; 102/11; 104/24 §ede (§avi *etc*). 37/3; 40/13; 73/13; 79/16, 8 §edes. 110/8 getrymed (confirmata). 70/6 § eam. 87/8 *etc* § is. 88/14 sie § (firmetur). 89/2 were §. 138/16 bioð §. 59/11; 107/11 §e (munitam). 70/3 §e (§itum). 32/6 §e sind. 104/4 bioð §e. 50/14 getrime. Ct 45/44 sion getrymed.

trymenis *sf* strengthening. VP

17/3; 18/2; 24/14 *etc* ~(firmamentum). 104/16 alle ~isse (§*a*). 150/1; Hy 8/23 § (firmamento). 88/41 § (munitiones).

Pymma *sm* LV 84 ~.

ymbe *av, prp* around, about. Cp 1605 ymb ðæt (plus minus). VP 44/4 ym (circa). 77/28 ymb (§). Ct 37/8, 12, 5, 30; 40/2, 8; 41/1, 3, 67 ymb. 38/2 ~.

ymb- gangan. standnis. ymbegefrætwad. eardian. sealde. hringend. þridung. sellan, ymsellend. hwyrft. hycgan. clyppan. gā. swāpan. lǣdan. swǣpe. ēode.

Hymbre *spl* Northumbrians. BH 289 ~onensium—humbronensium.

Norðan-hymbre *pl* Northumbrians. BH 2, 23 nordanhymbrorum. 62 nardahymbrorum — norðan§ 1— nordan§. 64 §§ — norðan§ 1. 129 nordan§—nordon§ 1. 355 nordan§. LK 1 §§. Gn 51 *nordanhymbrorum.* 72 *nordanhymbra gpl.* 78 norðanhy(mb)r· *gpl.* 84 norðan'. 88 norðanhym'.

hymblice *sf* hemlock. Ep 185 ~ae (cicuta); Ef huymblicae; Cp hymlice.

symbel *s(n)* feast. VP 117/27 deg ~(diem solemnem).

symbeldeg VP.

symbelnis *sf* solemnity. VP 80/4 ~isse (solemnitatis).

symblian *wv* feast. VP 41/5 ~iendes (epulantis). 67/4 *~iað (§entur).

symbellic *aj.* festive. VP 73/8 ~e (festos).

genyclan *wv* crook. Ep 701 genicldae (obuncans); Ef gensccilde; Cp genyclede.

'**gycenis** *sf* itching. Ep 788 gycinis (prorigo); Ef §; Cp ~; Ld gyccae (§, urigo cutis).

un-bryce *aj* useless. Ep 522 ~i; Ef unbrycci; Cp ~(incommodum).

Ycca *sm* LV 214 ~.

for-ðryccan *wv* press, squeeze. VP 73/8 ~en (comprimamus).

ferðrycednis *sf* pressure. VP 31/7 ~se [c *cr. before* c] (pressurā).

stycce *sn* piece. VP 147/17 ~hlafes (frusta).

styccimēlum Ep; Cp §; Ef †sc§.

molegn-stycci *sn* Cp 953 ~, moling (galmulum).

crycc *s* crutch. Ep 571 ~(lituus, baculum curvum *etc*); Ef §; Cp cryc. VP 22/4 § (baculus).

fyxe *sf* she fox. Ct 20/8 ~an dic.

hyht *sm* hope. VP 13/6; 21/10 *etc* ~(spes). 72/28 ~minne (spem). 77/7; 118/49 ~(spem). 4/10; 15/9; 77/53 ~e (spe). 59/10; 93/22; 107/10 ~es (spei). Ct 37/4 fore ~e.

hyhtfull *aj* hopeful. Ct 1118 ~ful *vel* ðiendi (indolis).

hyhtlic *aj* hopeful, pleasant. Rd 12 ~.

hyhtan *wv* hope. VP 118/43 ~e (speravi).

gehyhtan *wv* hope. VP 12/6 *etc* ~u (sperabo). 68/4 § (§o). 43/7 *etc* ~o. 90/4 ~es (§abis). 20/8; 33/9 *etc* ~eð. 4/6; 5/12 ~að *etc.* 144/15 †gehyht (§ant). 7/2; 90/14 ~e (§avi; §avit) *etc.* 21/5, 5, 6 *etc* ~on (§averunt). 36/3, 5; 41/6 *etc* gehyht (§a!). 61/11; 117/9, 9 ~(§are). 25/1 ~ende (§ans). 31/10; 32/18 § (§antes). 16/7 ða §an (§antes). 30/20 ~§um. 17/31 ~endra. 85/2 ~endne. 51/9; 118/114 †gehyte (§avit; §avi). 9/11 †gehtað (§ent). 111/7 §an (§are). 118/74 §e (§avi).

un-þyhtig *aj* weak. Ep 1093 †unþyotgi egan (vitiato); Ef undyctgi; Cp unðyhtge.

flyht *s(m)* flight. Mt 8 ~e *d.*

flycti-clāð Cp.

genyhtfull *aj* abundant. Ep 723 genyctfullum (profusis); Ef §; Cp ~um.

genyhtlice *av* abundantly. Cp 38 genycthlice (abunde).

genyhtsum *aj* abundant. Bd[2] 42 genihtsumra (profusior). VP 24/11; 129/7; 67/16 ~(copiosum; §a; uberem) 67/17 ~e (§es). 91/11, 5 ~re (uberi). 109/6 § (copiosā). 122/4 ~um (abundantibus). 85/5 †gentsum (copiosus). ▪

genyhtsumlice *av* abundantly. **VP** 30/24 ~(abundanter).

genyhtsumnis *sf* abundance. **VP** 71/7; 121/6, 7 ~(abundantia). 29/7 minre ~isse (§iā) *etc.* 64/12; 103/28 § (ubertate).

genyhtsumian *wv* suffice, abound. **VP** 49/19 ~að (abundavit). 64/14 ~iað. 72/12 ~egende (§antes). 127/3; 143/13 ~iende (§ans; §antes). **Hy** 7/17 ~iendne (sufficientem).

dryht-dōmas VP. **dryhtguma** Cp; dryct§ Ld. **Dryctheim** BH. **Dryhtnōð** Cp. **Dryhtwald** Ct.

dryhten *sm* Lord. **CH** 4, 8 dryctin. **LP** 11 dryhtnes. **DA** 3 ~. **Mt** 46 dryhtne. **VP** 4/4; 6/2; 33/4 *etc* ~(dominus, §e; §um). 2/11; 7/18 *etc* dryhtne. 3/9; 11/7 *etc* §es. 2/4, 7 *etc* dryht' (§us). 3/7 *etc* § (§e). 9/25 *etc* § (§um). 4/6 *etc* § (§o). 2/6 *etc* § (§i *g*). 46/9; 47/12 *etc* dryh' = dryhten. 56/8 § = dryhtne. 87/10 ~[d *from* ð]. 19/7; 58/5 ðryhten. 120/5 ðryht*en*. 113/14 ryht' (§us). 118/168 drht' (§e). 14/1 dry[h]ten. 14/4 dryten. 24/8 dryt'. 83/2; 87/2 dryht (§e).

tyhtan *wv* incite, allure. **Ep** 85 tyctendi (adridente); Ef §; Cp §e. 509 tyctaend (inlex *etc*); Cp §endi; Ef tychtend. 936 tyc[h]tit (sollicitat); Cp ~eð. Cp 1122 tyhten[d] (incentor). 1153 tyhton (inridabant). 1887 ~o (sollicito). 1889 ~an (§are).

getyhtan *wv* incite, teach. **Ep** 533 gitychtid (inlectus); Ef getyctid; Cp ~id. Cp 820 ðare ~an (exercitatae).

for-tyhtan *wv* allure. **Cp** 483 faertyhted (clinici).

tyhtend *under* tyhtan.

tyhten *sf* incitement, alluring. **Ep** 513 tyctinnum (inlecebris); Ef §; Cp tychtingum. 516 §ae (incitamenta); Ef §; Cp tyhtinne. 579 †thyctin *vel* scocha; Ef tyctin; Cp tyhten (lenocinium).

tyhting *under* tyhten.

hyge *sm* mind.

Hygbald BH, LV, Gn. **Hygberct** LV; §berht Gn, Ct; hyge§ Ct. **Hygburg** LV. **Hygfrith** LV. **Hyglāc** LV. **Hygmund** LV. **Hygrēd** LV; hygereðingtūn Ct. **hygidoncum** (?) Rd. **Hygðrȳð** LV. **Hyguald** LV. **Hyguini** LV. **Hyguuulf** LV.

ryge *s*(*m*) rye. **Ep** 918 ~i (sicalia); Ef †ryg; Cp ~.

smygel *sm* retreat. **Ep** 199 smigilas (cuniculos); Ef smy§; Cp smyglas.

Strygel *sm.* **Ct** 33/11 ~.

hnygelan *spl* clippings. **Cp** 1678 hnyglan (putamina).

Trygel *sm.* **Gn** 120 tryg.l.

Trygling *sm* son of T. **Gn** 120 ~.

byge *sm* bend. **Cp** 1874 ~(sinus).

for-hycgan *wv* despise. **VP** 43/6 ~að (spernimus).

ymb-hycgan *wv* think about. **BDS** 3 to ~hycggannae.

hrycg *sm* back, ridge. **LV** 50 ~ (spinam).

Cadaca-hrycg *sm* **Ct** 25/8 ~ hrygc.

holhrycg-get Ct.

Sænget-hryg *sm* **Ct** 29/17 ~.

mycg *sm* midge. **Ef** 277 mi[c]hc (culix *etc*); Cp mygg. Ep 916 mygg (scnifes); Cp §; Ef ~.

Dycga *sm* **Ct** 33/11 ~.

Dycgberct LV. **Dycgfrith** LV. **Dycguio** LV.

Dryçg-helm LV.

gebycgan *wv* buy. **Ct** 34/20; 45/19 (he) ~e.

brycg *sf* bridge. **Cp** 1623 ~(pons). **Bd**[2] 8 ~(†pontes).

ofer-hygd *sf* pride. **VP** 72/6; 73/23 ~(superbia). 30/24; 100/7 ~(§iam). 16/10; 30/19; 58/13; 73/3 ~e (§iā). 35/12 ~e (§iae *g*).

gehygd *sf* understanding. **VH** 11/4 ~um (sensibus). **Hy** 12/12 ~e gliderre (§u).

in-gehygd *sf* consciousness, thought. **VH** 13/11, 24 ~e (conscientiā), ~e ure (§ = *g*.)

ofer-hygdig *aj* proud. **VP** 17/28; 118/69 ~ra (superborum). 88/11 ðone ~hygdgan. 93/2; 100/5

§um. 118/51 ꝺa †~hygdg [*last* g *on er.*] (§i). 118/21, 78 ꝺa ~hygdan (§os, §i).

bi-hygdignis *sf* sollicitude. **VP** 28/8 ~isse (†solitudinem).

oferhygdgian *wv* be proud. **VP** 9/23 ~aꝺ (superbit).

ā-rytran *wv* strip. **Ef** 372 aritrid (expilatam); Cp aþryid, ~id.

lytel *aj* little, small. **Ep** 217 lytlae sneglas (cocleae); Ef §; Cp §e. **VP** 36/10; Hy 1/1 ~(pusillum; §us). 36/16 ~(modicum). 103/25 ~u (pusilla). 41/7 ꝺæm lytlan (modico). 113/13 §e (pusillos). 136/9 ꝺa §an (parvulos). **Ct** 20/15 ꝺa lytlan burg.

lytelmōd VP.

lytling *sm* little one. **VP** 16/14 ~um (parvulis).

lytis-nā Ep; Ef §; Cp lytesna.

hlyte *s*(*m*) portion. **Cp** 1608 ~(portio).

snytru *sf* wisdom. **VP** 48/4 ~(sapientiam). 89/12; 103/24 ~(§iā). 146/5 ~e (§iae *g*). 106/27 snyttru (§ia). 36/30 § (§iam). 110/10 § (§iae *g*). 18/8 · · · ro (§iam). 50/8 syntru ꝺinre (§iae *g*) [*cp note to* 146/5].

scyti-halt Ep; †sestihalth Ef; scytehald Cp.

scytel *s* dart, arrow. **Ep** 632 ~il (momentum); Ef §; Cp ~. Ef 1177, 9 sciutil (jaculum; sagitta).

gyte *sm* flood. **Cp** 1127 ~(inundatio).

Tytel *sm* **BH** 103 tytili *g*.

brytnian *wv* distribute. **Ct** 37/26 he ~iȩ.

hlytta *sm* diviner. **Cp** 1886 hlytan [y *over* u] (sortilegos).

scyttels *sn* bolt. **VP** 106/16 ~ irenu (vectes). 147/13 ~(seras).

nytt *aj* useful. **Ct** 37/28; 41/11, 43 ~. 30/22 nyt.

un-nytt *aj* useless. **VP** 13/3 ~e (inutiles).

nytt *s*(*f*) use. **Ep** 93 to ~um (expensas); Cp §; Ef †nytum.

nytlic *aj* useful. **Cp** 38/14 †~as *sprl.*

nyttnis *sf* utility. **VP** 29/10 ~(utilitas).

un-nyttnis *sf* uselessness. **Ep** 678 ~(nugacitas); Ef, Cp §.

Nytta *sm* **LV** 209 ~.

grytt *sf* grits. **Ep** 823 ~(pollis); Ef gryt [*or* grytt?]; Cp ~.

grytte *sf* spider. **VP** 89/9 ~[*over* gongeweafre] (aranea).

Tyt · · ·, t · ttwianing Gn.

Tyttla *sm* **Gn** 119 ~.

Tyttling *sm* son of T. **Gn** 118 ~.

for-dyttan *wv* obstruct, close. **Cp** 1414 ~e (obstruit). **VP** 57/5 forduttænde (obturantes). 106/42 fordyt[t]ed (oppilavit).

pytt *sm* pit. **Ct** 20/4 on grenan ~.

Bulcan-pytt *sm* **Ct** 3/7, 8 to ~e, ~es.

styde *s* place.

Acustyde *s*. **Ct** 29/14, 4 ~ȩ, ~e *d.*

Bipple-styde *s*. **Ct** 29/13, 3 ~æ, ~ȩ *d.*

Netelhæm-styde *s*. **Ct** 45/34 an ~e.

Sondem-styde *s* **Ct** 45/15 on ~.

Uydiga *sm*. **LV** 167 ~[*or* uychga?].

Tydi *sm*. **LV** 117 ~.

or-tydre *aj* barren. **Cp** 723 †ontudri (effetum).

dyde *prt* did. **CA** 6 deodan. **Mt** 36 dede. **VP** 7/4, 16 *etc* ~(feci, §it). 17/22 ~(gessi). 35/3, 4 *etc* ~(egit; ageret). 9/5; 15/11 *etc* ~est (fecisti). 39/6; 49/21 *etc* ~es. 5/11; 9/16 *etc* ~un. 104/25 ~en. 38/12 †des (fecisti). 77/12 †dydede (§it). **Ct** 28/22 ~.

gedyde *prt* **VP** 75/10 ~(faceret).

wel-dyde *prt* benefited. **VP** 56/3; 114/7 ~(benefecit).

byden *s*(*f*) bucket. **Ef** 260 ~in (cupa); Cp ~. Cp 6 ~(doleus). 341 ~(bunia).

Budin-haam Ct.

Bydic-tūn Ct.

ā-ryddan *wv* strip. **Cp** 817 arydid (expilatam).

Syddensis *civitatis*. **Ct** 33/7 ~.

Cydda *sm* **Ct** 12/6 ~. 19/7 ~an *g*.

Cuddi *sm* **LV** 161 ~.

Dyddel *sm* **Ct** 42/26 ~.

hype *s(m)* hip. **Cp** 1041 midhridir, nioðanweard ~(ilia).

Hryp- *spl* Ripon. **BH** 210 in ~um. 332 §—rypum II.

eorð-crypel *sm* paralytic. **Cp** 187 eorscripel (applare).

yppe *sf* upper room. **Ep** 553 uppae (in aestivo coenaculo *etc*); Ef ~; Cp ~.

yppan *wv* manifest. **VH** 5/22 ~ed earð (exortus es).

forð-yppan *wv* manifest. **VP** 16/2 ~eð (§). 72/7 § (§iit). **Hy** 11/14 ~ypeð (prodeat).

clyppan *wv* embrace. **VP** 47/13 ~að (complectimini). 84/11 ~ende werun (§plexae sunt).

ymb-clyppan *wv* embrace. **VP** 118/61 ~ende werun (circumplexi sunt).

Pybba *sm* **Gn** 92 pypba.

Pybbing *sm* son of P. **Gn** 92 pypbing. 98; 101, 5 ~.

lybb *s* medicine, potion, charm. **Ep** 711 ~(obligamentum); Ef libb; Cp lyb, lybsn.

lypbcorn Ef; lyb§ Cp. **lyblāecan** Cp.

cēse-lyb *s* rennet. **Cp** 562 ~(coagolum).

holen-stybb *s(m)* holly-stump. **Ct** 3/10 ~stypbum.

or- þanc. fiermae, feormnis. georwirþan. wyrþ. †ontudri [*under* y]. oroþ. sorg. dāl. mǣte.

Or-rīces-denn Ct.

oroð *s(n)* breath. **Lr** 40 ~e (anile).

gehroren *ptc* fallen. **Bd²** 85 gerorenra (derutarum).

for-loren *aj* (*ptc*) lost. **VP** 30/13 ~(perditum). **Hy** 7/56 ~um (§o).

forlorenis *sf* perdition. **VP** 87/12; **Hy** 7/68. ~isse (perditione; §is).

forlor *s(n)* loss. **Cp** 144 ~(amisionem).

geþworen *ptc* beaten. **Ep** 605 githuornae fleti (lectidiclatum); Ef §e: Cp geþuorne.

snoro *sf* daughter-in-law. **Cp** 1393 ~(nurus).

smorian *wv* strangle. **Cp** 1926 ~að (stangulat).

Scor-ham Ct.

spora *sm* spur. **Ep** 226 ~; Ef, Cp § (calcar). Ef 1164 sporonus, ~(calcar).

hel-spure *sf* heel-spur. **VP** 48/6 ~an minre (calcanei). 55/7 § mine (§eum *a*).

hūn-spora *sm*. **Cp** 706 ~an (dolones).

sporettan *wv* kick. **VH** 7/29 ~eð (recalcitravit).

Wor *sm*. **Gn** 38 uuor. **Ct** 9/5 uuor.

felo-for *s* fieldfare. **Ep** 807 ~(porphyrio); Ef felusor; Cp feolufer. Cp 1445 § (onocratallus).

for *prp* for. **CA** 6, 6, 12, 2, 2 ~. **DA** 3, 4 ~. 5, 6, 7, 8 fer. **Mt** 9, 15 ~. **Ct** 23/15; 30/23; 37/24, 43; 38/11, 4; 39/3, 3, 10, 0; 40/6; 42/14; 45/22, 30, 6 ~. 30/22; 45/30 fer.

for-ðon, fore-ðon, §ðe, §ðæt. **for-hwon.** **for-ðȳ-ðe.**

fore *prp* before, for. **Rn** 2/3 ~. 9/1 ~æ. **BDS** 1 ~. **LP** 1, 6, 9, 13 ~. **VP** 5/9; 8/3 *etc* ~ feondum (propter). 7/8; 31/6 *etc* ~ ðissum (§ hanc; pro hac). 34/12 *etc* ~ godum (pro). 58/9; 105/24 ~ nowiht (§). 63/9 ~ §e. 6/8 ~ eorre (prae). 17/13 ~ sciman (§). 134/5 ~ allum (§). 6/5 ~ mildheortnisse ðine (propter). 24/7 ~ godnisse ðine (§). 47/12 ~ domas (§). **Ct** 34/14; 37/3, 4, 4, 28, 32 *etc*; 39/3; 41/20, 7 ~.

fore-. foraeweall. seah. spreca. cweden. settan, §nis. wyrd. nyme. forecymeþ, for§. gā, gǣþ, gǣst. sprǣcon. sǣgon. fēng. bēacn. cōm. foe·

foran *av* in front, before. **Ct** 37/30, 3 ~ to.

on **foranheafdum** VP.

beforan *prp* before. **VP** 5/6; 13/3; 25/3 *etc* bi~ egum (ante). 17/24 †biom him (coram); 21/26 § ondredendum (§). **Ct** 34/9; 37/43 ~.

for-. bærnan. gæf. faerslægen. træd. heardian. dealf. swealg. seah. spildan. gifeþ. clingan. timbran. gelimpan. sihst. trideþ. giteþ. geldan. gefan. segenis. bregdan. getan. tredan. weorþan. ceorfan. ferhergend. wered. cerran, §ing. wernan. eldan. ferwened. curfe. wurdon. swulgon. numen. lor. loren, §nis. wyrd. hycgan. þryccan. ferðrycednis. faertyhted. dyttan. corfen. hogian, §adnis. þrǣstan, §ednis. clǣman. gæfon. lætan, §nis. trædon. ferrēd, faer§. sēo. lēort. trūgadnis. nōm. cōm. sōc.

fnora *sm* sneezing. **Ep** 888 ~ (sternutatio); Ef †huora; Cp ~; Ld †nor.

walh-more *sf* turnip. **Ep** 794 uualhmorae (pastinaca); Ef §; Cp ~.

Mǫreb *s.* **Ct** 9/4 *silvam, cui nomen est* moerheb . 7 *in silva* ~.

Maeth-cor *sm.* **LV** 109 ~.

gecoren *aj, subst* (*ptc*) chosen, elect. **VP** 104/6 ~es (electi). 107/7 ða ~e ðine (§). 77/31; **Hy** 5/6 ~e (§os). 105/5 ~ra ðinra. 105/23 se ~a (§us). 88/20 ðone ~an. 59/6; 104/43 ða §. 88/4; 140/4 ~um.

gecor *sn* decision. **Ct** 23/15, 6 ~, eouuere ~e.

gor *s* dung. **Cp** 882 goor (fimum).

dora *sm* humble bee. **Ep** 119 ~ (atticus); Ef, Cp §.

geboren *ptc* carried, born. **Ef** 359 ~onae (exposito); Cp ~one.

sīð-boren *ptc* late-born. **VP** 77/70 ~um (postfaetantes = §e).

cēac-bora *sm* jug-bearer. **Cp** 176 caec~ (antulus).

mund-bora *sm* protector. **Ep** 934 ~(suffragator); Ef, Cp §. **Cp** 41/45 ~.

rǣd-bora *sm* councillor. **Ep** 551 redboran (jurisperiti); Ef, Cp §.

strǣl-bora *sm* arrow-bearer. **Ep** 114 strel~ (arcister); Ef, Cp §.

borettan *wv* brandish. **Ep** 1092 borę[t]it; Ef boretit (vibrat, dirigit); Cp ~ið.

bor *s* borer. **Cp** 7 boor (dasile). 1803 ~e (scalpro). 1806 ~(scalpellum). Ld 259 boor (scalpeum).

borian *wv* bore. **Ld** 14 †borgenti (terebrantes).

torr *sm* tower. **VP** 47/13; 121/7 ~um (turribus). 60/4 tor (§is). **Ct** 20/4 ðone ~.

worþ *s* landed property.

Hodo-worð *s* **Ct** 27/4 ~a.

Meran-worð *s* **Ct** 25/10 ~

worðig *s* court. **VP** 17/43 ~na (platearum). 54/12; 143/14 ~num (§eis).

Tome-worðig *s* Tamworth. **Ct** 50/4 ~.

forð *av* forth. **Ep** 529 a fordh (in dies); Ef a †forthe; Cp a †forht. **SG** 23 ðonan ~. **Ct** 20/20 ~ on. 39/8; 41/6 siððan ~.

Forthhelm LV. **Fordheri**, forð§, fort§ LV; forðhere LV, Gn. **Forðrēd** LV, Ct. **Forthuald** LV. **forðweard** Ct. **Forthuīo** LV.

forð-. framung. sægde. weard. bringan. beran. wegan. secgan. cymeþ. yppan. gā. lǣstan. lǣdan, gelǣdan. scēaf. lūtan. cȳþan. lōcian.

norþ *av* north.

norðdāel, noð§ VP. **norðeweard** Ct. **eastnorþwind** Ep; nord Ef; norð Cp. **†uuestnorduuid** Ef; westnorðwind Cp.

norðan *av* from the north. **Ct** 26/4; 28/14; 56/8 be norðan. 29/2 an ~.

Nordanhymbrorum BH, LK, Gn; norðan§, nordon§, nardahymbrorum BH; nordanhymbra, norðan§ Gn. **norðanwestan** Cp.

ēastan-norþan *av* from the north-east. **Cp** 44 ~(ab borea).

corðor **Ep** 1074 cortr (verberatorium); Ef cordr; Cp corthr.

hors *sn* horse. **Mt** 17, 8 ~ *pl.* 20 horssum. **VP** 31/9; 32/17 ~(equus). **Hy** 5/1 ~(equum). 146/10 ~es. 75/7; **Hy** 6/18, 30 ~(equos). 19/8 ~um.

horshiordas Cp. **horsa-lęge** Ct [*under* ēa]. **horsthegn** Ep; Cp §.

Horsa *sm* **BH** 24, 4 ~.

Horsel-get Ct [*under* gæt].

worsm *s*(*n*) matter, pus. **Ep** 777 uuorsm (pus); Ef †uuorsin; Cp †uuorm.

fors *s* waterfall. **Bl** 5 forsceta (cataracte).

horsclice *av* briskly. **Ep** 668 ~ae (naviter); Ef §; Cp ~.

forsc *sm* frog. **Cp** 1258 for[s]c (luscinius). **VP** 77/45 ~(ranam). 104/30 ~as.

. forsca-burna Ct.

gorst *sm* gorse, furze. **Cp** 97 gors(aegesta). 2162 ~(voluma).

dorste *prt* durst. **Rn** 2/4 (dars)te. 7 darstæ.

horweg *aj* muddy. **Ef** 340 horuaeg stiig (devia callis); Cp ~.

for-corfen *prt* cut off. **VH** 3/5 ~(praecisa).

Freoð-orne *sm* **Ct** 17/7 ~.

horn *sm* horn. **VP** 17/3; 74/5 *etc* ~(cornu). 80/4 ~e (tubā). 97/6; 150/3 ~es (§ae). 68/32; 74/11, 1 *etc* ~as. 117/27 horn (cornua). 21/22; 97/6 ~um. **Ct** 41/14 ænne ~.

hornblāuuere Cp. hornnaap Cp.

ān-horn *s* unicorn. **VP** 91/11 ~es (unicornis).

swegl-horn *sm* **Cp.** 1777 suegl~ (sambucus).

ðorn *sm* thorn. **Cp** 1834 ~as (sentes). **VP** 31/4 ~(spina). 57/10 ~as. 117/12 ~um.

Ðorndūn Ct.

hagu-ðorn *sm* hawthorn. **Ep** 19 haeguthorn (alba spina); Ef hagudorn; Cp hea[go]~. 956 haeguthorn (spina alba); hegu§ Ef; haegu~ Cp.

Hēagȳðe-ðorn *sm* **Ct** 34/3 æt ~e (hęgyðe§). 19 æt hægyðe §.

slāh-ðorn *sm* sloe-thorn. **Ep** 672 slachthorn (nigra spina); Ef §dorn; Cp slagh~. 957 slaghthorn (spina nigra); Ef †salach§; Cp ~.

ðēfe-ðorn *sm* buckthorn. **Ep** 880 thebanthorn (ramnus); Ef §thron; Cp ðeofe:ðorn.

swornian *wv* coagulate. **Ep** 198 suornodun (coaluissent); Cp §adun; Ef suarnadun.

corn *sn* corn. **Ct** 45/40 ~es.

cornuurma Cp.

bere-corn *sn* barley-corn. **Ep** 790 ~ [*second* e *over* i] berędae (ptysones); Ef, Cp ~.

lybb-corn *sn* medicinal seed. **Ef** 279 lypb~(cartamo); Cp lybcor[n]. Cp 459 lyb~ (chartamo).

grorn *aj* sad, agitated **Rn** 3/6 ~.

gnornian *wv* murmur. **VP** 58/16 ~iað (murmurabunt). 105/25 ~adun (§averunt).

Dorn-uuarara-ceaster Ct.

storm *sm* storm. **Ep** 682 ~(nimbus); Ef, Cp §. **VP** 49/3; 68/3, 16 ~(tempestas). 54/9; 82/16 ~e. 80/8 ~es.

orc *s(m)* pitcher **Ep** 698 ~(orcus); Ef, Cp §.

orc *sm* demon. **Cp** 1080 ~eas (immunes).

storc *s(m)* stork. **Ef** 259 ~(ciconia); Cp §; Ld storhc.

Dorcic *s* Dorchester. **BH** 140 ~.

Dorciccaestræ, dorcicæstrę, BH.

horh *s(n)* phlegm, mucus, filth. **Ep** 412 ~(flegmata); Ef, Cp §. **Ef** 1120 horch (muccus).

geworht *ptc* worked, wrought. **Cp** 567 gewarht (conderetur).

be-worht *ptc* bewrought. **Rd** 3 biuorthæ.

forhtian *wv* be afraid. **VP** 26/1 ~iu (trepidabo). 118/161; Hy 13/8 ~að (formidavit; pavescit). 103/7; Hy 4/20 ~iað (formidabunt). Hy 6/15 § (expavescent). Hy 6/2, 31 ~ade (expavi, §it). 52/6 ~adun (trepidaverunt). 13/5 †~aðum (§).

torht *aj* bright.

Torchtfrith, torct§ LV. **Torctgils**, torcht§ LV. **Torctgȳd**, to[r]chtgyð, troctgyd, †tora§, torchgyð BH. **Torcthāeth** LV. **Torcthelm**, torcht§ LV; torht§ Ct. **Torhthere** Gn. **Torchtmund**, torct§ LV. **Torctrēd**, torcht§ LV. **Torctsig** LV. **Torchtuini**, torct§ LV. **Torctuulf**, torcht§ LV.

torhtnis *sf* brightness. **Ep** 574 torchtnis (luculentum); Ef, Cp ~.

torhtian *wv* show. **Ep** 544 taecnaendi, torctendi (index); Cp §; Ef torchtendi.

organan *spl* organ. **VP** 136/2 ~an (organa). 149/4 ~§ (§o). Hy 1/3 § (§um *a*).

lorg *s* pole, distaff. **Ef** 1172 ~, couel (colum). 1173 ~ (§us).

sorg *sf* sorrow. **Cp** 67 ~ (anxietas *etc*). **Rn** 2/14 sorgu(m).

or-sorg *aj* secure. Ep 1034 †on~(tuta); Ef, Cp ~. Cp 573 ~(consors).

sorgian *wv* sorrow. Cp 169 ~endi(anxius); Ef §; Ef soȩr[g]ȩndi.

morgen *sm* morning. VP 5/4, 5; 54/18 *etc* on marne(mane). Hy 3/7, 9 of § (de§). 8 oð margen (ad§).

margensteorra VP. margentīd VP.

ǣr-margen *sm* early morning. VP 56/9; 107/3; 118/148; Hy 11/12 on ~(diluculo).

•**morgenlic** *aj* in the morning. Ep 729 ~; Ef morgendlic; Cp ~(matutinos).

borg *s(m)* bail, security. Ep 1090 ~(vadimonium); Ef, Cp §. Cp 856 ~ (foenus). Ef 1115 brog (fideius).

borggelda VP.

scort *aj* short. VP 104/12 ~um (brevi).

scortnis *sf* shortness (of time). VP 2/13 in ~isse (in brevi).

Port-weorona Ct.

portic *sn* porch. VP 72/17; 73/7; 82/13 halig ~(sanctuarium *a*).

Ord-uulf Ct.

hord *s(n)* treasure.

hordern Bl, VP; †hondern VH.

gold-hord *s(n)* treasure. VP 32/7; 134/7; Hy 7/66 ~um (thesauris).

gold-hordian *wv* hoard. VP 38/7 ~að (thesaurizat).

word *sn* word. Cp 2115 uuordes intinga (verbi gratia). VP 32/4 ~ (sermo); 44/2 ~ god (verbum *a.*) *etc.* 32/6 ~e; 118/114 ~e ðinum (§o) *etc.* 118/25 efter word dinum (§um). 104/8, 42 *etc* ~es. 5/2 ~(verba); 18/4 ~(sermones) *etc.* 16/4; 50/6 *etc* ~um. 102/20; 118/130 *etc* ~a. Ct 37/12 ðas uuord. 45/49, 56 þas ~.

wordgecweodu Ct.

geworden *ptc* become. VP 9/10; 17/19 ~ is (factus est) *etc.* 110/8 bibodu . . ~(facta). 13/1, 3 gewordne sind, § werun (facti sunt) *etc.* 32/9 werun ~[o *from* u] (facta sunt).

ford *sm* ford.

Onnan-ford *sm* Ct 10/2 æt ~a.

Bregunt-ford *sm* Brentford. Ct 2/2 ~.

Heg-ford *sm* Ct 28/14 be norðan ~e.

Here-ford *sm* Hereford. Ct 33/10 ~ensis.

Heorot-ford *sm* Hertford. BH 227 *ad locum* herutforda—heorut§ I. 248 herut~—§frod—heorut~—herud~ [u *dotted, and* e *wr. over*]. 377 ad herutforda — herud§ — §§.

•**Hrēod-ford** *sm* Redbridge. BH 286 hreut~, *id est, vadum harundinis* —hreud~ — hreout~ — hreut~ [u *dotted, and* od *wr. over*].

Iorotla-ford *sm* Ct 14/5 æt ~a.

Sceldes-ford *sm* Ct 36/3 æt ~a. 5 ~. 10 §æs.

Scūfeling-ford *sm* Ct 43/3 to ~e.

Slohtran-ford *sm* Ct 14/4 ~.

Stān-ford *sm* Stamford. BH 363 ~.

Tiddes-ford *sm* Ct 20/7 ~.

Wealdenes-ford *sm* Ct 20/21 ~.

Wiþig-ford *sm* Widford. Ct 14/3 uuithig~.

bord *sn* board, shield.

bordremum Ld. bordðeaca Cp; †borohaca Ep; brodthaca Ef.

borda *sm* fringe. Cp 479 ~(clavia). 1209 ~(lesta).

brord *s* point. Ep 782 ~(puntus); Ef broord; Cp †brond.

Wiht-brord *sm* Ct 8/5 †uuihtbrordis *g.*

Wil-brord *sm* BH 160 uilbrordum. 328, 30 uil~—uu~—uilbrod. 352 uil~.—§ I. 364 uilbrord — uilbrod — uilbrord.

Brorda *sm* LV 9 ~. Ct 15/7; 16/6 ~. 14/6, 7; 19/6 ~an *g.*

þòrp *s* farm. Ef 307 tuun *vel* ðrop (conpetum); Cp þrop.

ā-worpen *ptc* thrown out. VP 21/11; 30/23 ~ eam (jactatus sum; projectus §). 83/11 ~ bion (abjectus esse). 87/6 aworpne (projecti *pl*). 108/10 sien § (ejiciantur).

tō-worpen *ptc* scattered. Cp 636 toworpne (destitutae).

hol *aj* hollow. **Ct** 20/21 ðone ~an weg. 55/4 se †hole welle.

hol *sn* hole, cave. **Ep** 1072 hool (vorago); Ef, Cp §. Cp 416 ~um (caverniculis). 434 ~u (cavernas). 1900 ~(spiramentum) **Bd**² 12 ~um (cavernis).

holhrygcgete **Ct** [*under* geat].

wulf-hol *sn* wolf-hole. **Cp** 1261 uulfholu (lupinare).

holo-pannae Ep; Cp §.

holen *s*(*m*) holly. **Ep** 34 ~egn (acrifolus); Ef, Cp §; Ld †holera. **Ct** 20/13 ðæm beorge ðe mon hateð æt ðæm holne.

holenstypbum Ct.

cnīo-holen *s*(*m*) butcher's broom. **Ep** 879 ~aen (ruscus); Ef †cniolen; Cp ~; Ld cne~, †creholegn.

þol *s* rowlock. **Cp** 1820 thol (scalmus).

sol *sn* mud, wallowing-place. **Ct** 13/6 readan ~o.

Sol-uente BH.

Sola *sm*. **LV** 288 ~.

gescola *sm* fellow-debtor. **Cp** 578 ~an (condebitores).

molegn *s* **Ep** 477 ~(galmum); Ef moleng; Cp moling.

molegnstycci Cp.

liim-molegn *s* Ep 486 ~(galmilla); Ef lim~.

col *sn* burning coal. **VP** 17/9, 13; 139/11 ~u (carbones). 119/4 ~um.

colþrēd Ep; Ef, Cp §.

Colan-homm Ct.

hǣð-cole *sf* a plant. **Cp** 570 haetcolae (colomata).

dwolian *wv* err. **VP** 94/10 ~iað (errant). 118/110, 76 duolede, §ude (§avi). 57/4 ~edon. 106/4 ~edun.

Bola *sm*. **Ct** 57/11; 58/19 ~.

(ā)swollen *ptc* swollen. **Ep** 1018 suollaen (tuber, tumor); Ef †assuollan; Cp asuollen.

hnoll *s* top, crown of head. **Lr** 13 ~(gygram). **VP** 7/17 ~e (vertice).

Moll *sm* **LV** 407 ~.

cnoll *s*(*m*) top. **Cp** 1162 cnol (jugum). **VP** 67/22 § (verticem).

bolla, -e *smf* bowl. **Ep** 234 ~(cyatus); Ef ~ae. 965 ~(scifus); Ef ~ae; Cp ~. Cp 65 ~e (aceti cotilla, vas).

bēod-bolle *sf* table-bowl. **Cp** 627 ~ę (cuppa).

ðrot-bolla *sm* gullet. **Ep** 456 throt ~(gurgulio); Ef, Cp ~; Ld droh~. **Lr** 42 ~an (gurgilioni).

bolster *s* bolster. **Ef** 296 †bol (cervical).

olfenda *sm* camel. **Ef** 319 afyrid †obbenda (dromidus); Cp olbenda.

dolfen *ptc* dug. **VP** 93/13 bið ~(fodeatur).

dwolma *sm* chaos. **Ep** 181 du~ (chaos); Cp § (chaus, prima confusio omnium rerum); Ef dualma.

ā-solcen *aj* (*ptc*) torpid. **Ep** 531 ~aen (iners); Ef ~æn; Cp ~.

wolcen *sn* cloud. **VP** 103/3; 104/39 ~(nubem). 77/14 wolcne (§e). 98/7 §es. 17/13; 35/6; 76/18; 96/2; 134/7; **Hy** 8/10 ~(§es *pl*) 56/11; 107/5 ~u (§). 17/12; 67/35; 77/23; 88/7; 146/8 wolcnum.

folc *sn* nation, people. **VP** 49/7 *etc* ~(populus). 3/9 *etc* ~ðin (§um). 13/4 *etc* ~ min (plebem). 21/32 *etc* ~e. 49/7 israhela ~e (Israel). 3/7 *etc* ~es. 7/9 *etc* ~(populos). 17/50 *etc* ~um. 7/8 *etc* ~a.

Folcberht Ct. **Folcheri** LV. **folcland** Ct. **folcgeroebum** Ep; Ef, Cp §. **Folcuald** LV. **Folcuini** LV; §uuinis Ct; §wininglond Ct.

Folcan-stān Ct.

Rīc-folcyn *sf*. **LV** 21 ~.

oden-colc *s* **Ct** 20/11 on ~.

bolca *sm* gangway in ship. **Cp** 907 ~an (foras).

sun-folgend *s* marigold (?). **Cp** 1880 ~(solisequia).

dolg-suaþhe Bl.

holt *s*(*nm*) wood.

holtbana Ep; Ef, Cp, Ld §.

aler-holt *s*(*nm*) alder-wood. **Ep** 46 †alter ~(almeta); Ef, Cp, Ld ~.

smolt-regn Bl.

bolt *s*(*m*) bolt. **Ef** 1178 ~io (jactus).

hold *aj* faithful. **VH** 13/9 ~e (devotā).

hold *s*(*n*) carcass. **Ep** 415 ~(ferinum); Ef, Cp §.

scolde *prt* should. **Mt** 18 scealden.

wolde *prt* would. **Rn** 2/2 walde. **Mt**

16 (ne) §. **VP** 17/20; 39/9 *etc* § (voluit; §ui). 50/18 § (§uisses). 40/12 §es.

nolde *prt* would not. **CA** 7 nolðan. **VP** 35/4; 108/18 nalde (noluit). 39/7 §es. 77/10 §un.

folde *sf* earth. **CH** 9 ~[u]*a*. **Bd**² 16 of ~an (umo).

Folðrēd Ct.

molde *sf* mould. **Cp** 1760 ~(sablo).

gold *sn* gold. **Cp** 1401 smaete ~(obrizum); Ld ~. **CA** 5 ~e. **VP** 18/11b; 113/4 *etc* ~(aurum). 71/15 *etc* ~e. 67/14 *etc* ~es. **Ct** 41/32 ~es. 47/15 ~e.

goldhord, §ian VP.

Wīc-bold *s* Wichbold. **Ct** 54/5 uuit ~. 59/4 ~.

oð *prp* until. **VP** 9/32 *etc* oð ende (usque in). 13/1 *etc* oð enne (usque ad). 48/20, o oð in cyn, oð in ecnisse (§ in) *etc*. 103/23 oð to efenne (§ ad). 45/10 oð oð endas (§ ad). 70/17 oð nu (§ nunc). 106/26; **Hy** 3/9 ut (§ ad). **Ct** 20/7 *etc*; 40/20 ~.

oð-ðaet Ct; oð-ðæt, ot-ðet VP; oð-ðæt-ðe Ct.

oð-swīgan.

roð-hund Cp.

loða *sm* cloak. **Ep** 572 lotha [th *from* d] (lacerna); Ef §; Cp ~. 600 lotha (lodix); Ef §; Cp ~. 898 loda (sagulum); Ef §; Cp ~. Cp 1776 ~(sandalium). **Ld** 31 †loth (poderis, vestis *etc*).

On-both *sm*. **LV** 291 ~.

oððe *cj* or. **BDS** 4 aeththa. **CA** 17 ~. **DA** 11, 1, 2 ~. **Mt** 51, 1 ~. **VP** 8/5; 13/2; 14/1 *etc* ~(aut). 131/5 †oðð. **Ct** 34/20; 40/22; 41/24, 62 ~. 37/22; 41/17, 25, 37 oðða.

Osa *sm*. **Gn** 13 ~.

hos *s* pod. **Cp** 1867 pisan hosa (siliqua).

dros *s* dirt, ear-wax. **Ep** 39 ~(auriculum); Ef, Ld §; Cp dorsos.

drosne *s* dregs. **VP** 74/9 ~(fex).

gebrosnung *sf* decay. **VP** 15/10; 29/10 ~e (corruptionem).

geroscian *wv* **Cp** 1501 ~ade (pascsos).

ðrostle *sf* throstle. **Ep** 1011 throstlae (turdella); Ef §; Cp ~; Ld drostlae. Cp 2062 ~(trita).

frost *sm* frost. **Ep** 485 ~(gelu); Ef †frots; Cp forst. **VP** 77/47 §e (pruinā). **Hy** 8/9 §as (†§a).

nostle *sf* fillet. **Ld** 109 mihes ~um (odonis vitam, odon lineum est in pede).

costian *wv* try, tempt. **VP** 25/2 ~a (tempta!). 77/41; 94/9 ~adun. 34/16; 77/18, 56; 105/14 ~adon.

costung *sf* temptation. **VP** 17/30 from ðe ~e (temptatione). 94/9 ~e (§em).

grost *s* gristle. **Ld** 56 uuldpaexhsue *vel* ~(cartillago).

dweorge-doste *sf* pennyroyal (a plant). **Ep** 831 duuergaedostae (pulium); Ef duergaedostae; Cp duergedostle.

hosp *s*(*m*) contumely. **Cp** 1549 ~(hironiam).

hospettan *wv* ridicule. **Cp** 1963 ~etęt (subsannat).

cosp *s*(*m*) fetter. **Ep** 765 ~(puncto *etc*); Ef, Cp §.

fōt-cosp *s*(*m*) foot-fetter. **VP** 104/18; 149/8 ~um (compedibus).

ðrowian *wv* pay, suffer. **Ef** 365 throuadae (expendisse); Cp ~ode (expedisset). **Cp** 1568 ðrouuio (persolvio). **VH** 3/12 ~iu (patior). **Ps** 58/7, 15 ~ien, ~iað. 102/6 ~iendum. **Hy** 11/3 ~(perpeti).

geðrowian *wv* suffer. **Mt** 14 ~ade.

ðrowung *sf* suffering. **CA** 9 ~a *gsg*.

of *prp* of. **Ef** 369 ob (ex); Cp of, of. **Rn** 2/10 o(f). **Rd** 2, 14 ob. **Mt** 19, 44 of. **Bd**² 16 of. 46 of (de). **VP** 2/12; 8/3 *etc* of (de; ex). **Ct** 3/11; 30/11; 37/15, 6, 23; 40/3; 41/59; 45/34, 9 of. 39/2; 40/17 ob.

of-. slægen, §nis. gifeþ. gefan. obþwǣnan. slēa. slōg.

ofer *prp, av* over, on. **Ld** 134 ~ tua †nest (perende). **Rd** 11 ofaer. **DA** 15, 5, 6 ~. **VP** 2/6; 3/9 *etc* ~ sion; ~ folc (super). 120/5 ~ hond ðere swiðran (§). **Hy** 4/20 ~ him (§). 71/16 ~ bið upahefen (superextollitur). 13/7 ~ sion (†ex). 113/2(2) ofur. **Ct** 34/12; 41/58, 8; 42/12; 45/21, 33, 47; 48/4 ~. 42/7 ober.

ofer-. gangan. oberlagu. sceadwian. wrigen. blica. libban. obersegl. oberwrecan. getol. feohtan. oberwennan. settan, ge§. unofaercumen, unober§. fuhton. hygd, §ig. hoga. gā. wrāh. stǣlan. gǣst. sǣton. ēaca. lēoran, §nis. oberswīþan. wrīban. brū. cōm. oberfoeran. unoferfoere.

ofen *sm* oven, furnace. **VP** 20/10 ~(clibanum *a*).

ofet *s*(*n*) fruit. **Ep** 421 †obtt (fraga); Ef †obea; Cp obet.

hofer *s*(*m*) hump. **Ep** 459 hofr (gibbus); Cp §; Ef †hosr. Ep 1046 ofr (tuber); Ef o[f]r; Cp ~.

Hrof *sm.* **BH** 57 ~. 71 *civitatem* ~i.

hrofæs-cæstir, hrofaes §, hrofes § BH; §cestre Ct.

lof *sn* praise. **Cp** 2176 loob (ymnus). **CA** 11 ~. 8 ~e. **VP** 8/3 *etc* ~ (laudem). 21/4 *etc* ~(laus). 50/17 *etc* ~ ðin (laudem). 65/2 *etc* ~e. 25/7 *etc* ~es. 9/15; 72/28 *etc* ~u.

ā-scofen *ptc* pushed. **Bl** 2 ascoben (impulsus).

scofel *s* shovel. **Ep** 1022 scofl (trulla); Cp §; Ef †scolf. Cp 1483 scoble (palas).

glœ̄d-scofl *s* fire-shovel. **Ep** 1065 gloed~ (vatilla); Ef §; Cp §.

īsern-scobl *s* iron shovel. **Cp** 2081 ~(vatilla).

stofa *sm* bath-room. **Cp** 281 ~(balneum).

Clofes-hōh, clofacs §, clofęs §, BH; clofes §, clobes § Ct.

clofe *sf* buckle. **Ep** 653 clofae (mordacius); Ef ~æ; Cp clouae; Ld clox.

dofian *wv* be torpid. **Ef** 322 dobendi (decrepita); Cp dobgendi; Ld dobend.

offrian *wv* offer, sacrifice. **VP** 65/15, 5 ofriu (offeram). 67/30 §edun. 71/10 §adun. 75/12 §iað.

Offa *sm* **BH** 331 ~. **LV** 217, 28; 340 ~. **Gn** 94 off·. 100, 23 ~. **SG** 13, 5 ~. **Ct** 10/3; 11/1, 4; 14/1, 5; 15/1, 3; 16/1, 3; 18/1, 3; 35/9; 46/1 ~. 10/1; 14/4 ~an *g*. 12/1; 13/3 ~ani *g*. 35/9 ~ *rege*.

Offing *sm* son of O. **Gn** 94, 100 ~. **SG** 15 ~.

oflate *sf* (?) offering. **VP** 50/21 ~an (oblationes).

stofn *s*(*m*) stem. **Ld** 90 stofun (codex).

oft *av* often. **Pv** 1 ~. **Bd**[2] 45 ~(nonnulli). **VP** 77/40 swe ~ swe (quotiens). 105/43; 128/1, 2 ~(saepe).

Oftfōr BH, Gn.

geþofta *sm* companion. **Ep** 189 gidopta [ò *over* a] (contubernalis); Ef †gidogta; Cp ~. Cp 3 ~(coliferte).

on *prp* on. **Ep** 51 an; Ef, Cp on. 91 an uueg; Ef an; Cp on. Ef 370 an; Cp on, on. Cp 86 on. **Rn** 2/2, 11 on. 3/5, 7 on. **Bl** 6, 14, 20 on. **Rd** 6 an (?). **CA** 15 on. 15 ón. **DA** 2 *etc* on. **Mt** 9 *etc* on. **Bd**[2] 66 on. 89 (?) on. **VP** 5/4, 5 on marne (mane) *etc.* 23/4 on hondum (manibus) *etc.* 33/19, 9 on heortan; on gaste (corde, spiritu) *etc.* 6/11 *etc* on bec (retrorsum). 18/6 to earnenne on weg (ad currendam viam) *etc.* 54/18, 8, 8 on efenne, on marne, on midne deg (vespere, mane, meridie). 48/13 on are (in). 55/10 on . . dege (in) *etc.* 61/4 on men (in). **Ct** 20/3, 4, 4 *etc*; 25/3, 3; 26/5; 34/15, 6; 35/3, 4. 4 *etc*; 36/10; 37/6, 9, 9, 33; 39/15, 5; 41/65, 6; 42/3, 8, 12 *etc*; 43/4; 45/5, 6, 6 *etc*; 47/14, 5; 48/17, 8, 9; 52/12; 53/5, 5; 58/24 on. 20/2 †om homme. 20/14; 28/4, 6, 9, 10; 29/2, 7, 15, 7; 39/6, 7, 13, 4; 40/18, 21; 41/11, 43, 5; 43/5, 6; 45/1, 5, 17, 24, 7, 8, 33 an. 41/35 ðeran.

on-. gang. sand. anslægen. gægn. sæt. filte. hlinian. wlite. weg. feohtan. sendan. settan. sundron. uppan. cnyssan. swāpan. rǣsan. ǣht. hēaw. hrēosan. anscēot. answēop. līcnis. stīgend. oeþung.

on-. gann. sacan. anhæfd, a§. sægde, §nis. gæt. ginnan. wicon. wrigen. strigdes. giteþ. getan. cęrran. gęrwan. stęllan. hęldan. węndan. sęcgan. hębban. swębban. scunian *etc.* cunnen, cunnis. budon. styrian, §enis. bryrdnis. cnāwan. wrāh. ǣlan. sǣlan. drǣdan. lēsan. fēng. andlēac, on§. rēad. bēad. drēord. cnēow. bēodan. līhan. tȳnan. fō. foe. hrērnis. doen, doest. foehþ, foest. anoegun.

On-both LV.

onettan *wv* hasten. **Ep** 712 onettae

(occupavit); Ef †onete; Cp onette. Cp 107 ~ad (agitate).

geonettan *wv* hasten. **Ef** 717 †geomette (occupavit).

ðon *instr of* se. **VP** 30/14 in ~ ðonne (in eo dum) *etc.* 73/2 in ~ ilcan (in id ipso). 118/7 in ~ ðæt (in eo quod). 118/9, 49 in ~(in quo). 44/15 efter ~(post eam). **DA** 19 to ðon ilce. **Ct** 45/18 to ðan.

æfter-ðon *av, cj* afterwards, after. **Mt** 32 (æfter) ðon. **VP** 15/4 e~ (postea). 126/2 § (postquam).

ǣr-ðon *cj* before, until. **VP** 17/38 ~(donec). 38/14; 57/10; 89/2 *etc* ~(priusquam).

ēac-ðon *av* besides. **Ep** 846 aec þan (quinetiam); Ef § don; Cp § ðon. **VP** 8/8; 15/7, 9 *etc* ec ~(insuper).

for-ðon *av, cj* therefore, because. **VP** 3/6, 8; 4/10 *etc* ~(quoniam). 30/23; 72/6, 10 *etc* ~(ideo). 44/12; 71/12 *etc* ~(quia). 51/7 ~(propterea). **Hy** 7/4 ~(quando). 9/34 ~(propter quid). 108/16 ~(pro eo quod). 40/13 for †ðon unsceðfulnisse (propter). 106/33; 109/7; 117/28 *etc* fordon. 118/74, 128 †forðo. **Hy** 7/44 forþon.

for-ðon-ðe *cj* because. **CA** 6 ~.

for-ðon-ðæt *cj* in order that. **VP** 108/4 ~(pro eo ut). 115/10 ~(propter quod).

fore-ðon *av* therefore. **VP** 17/50 ~(propterea).

tō-ðon *av* to that degree, so. **CA** 16 ~. **Ct** 41/41 to ðan.

wið-ðan-ðe *cj* in consideration of. **Ct** 41/12, 22 ~.

ðone *acc. masc.* the, that. **LP** 10 ~. **Mt** 11 *etc* ~. **Bd**[2] 28 ~. **VP** 2/6; 4/4; 5/7 *etc* ~. 7/13, 6 ~(illum, eum) *etc.* 80/11 ~(illud). 24/12 ~(quam) *etc.* 79/16 ~ ~(eam quam). 77/41 ðon halgan. 105/9 sae § readan. **Ct** 20/4, 5; 26/12, 9, 20, 0, 1 ~. 45/30 þ~.

hwon *instr of* hwā.

for-hwon *av* wherefore, why. **Mt** 36 ~. **VP** 41/6, 10 *etc* ~(quare). 21/2; 41/6 ~hon (§).

tō-hwon *av* for what, wherefore. **VP** 4/3; 9/22; 48/6 *etc* ~(utquid). 113/5 (1) ~(quod). 113/5, 6 (1) ~ (quare).

ðonne *av* then, when. **LP** 4, 5 *etc* ~. **CA** 5 ~. **Mt** 22, 2, 48, 51 ~. **VP** 2/5; 18/14 *etc* ~(tunc). 2/13; 36/24 *etc* ~(cum). 4/4; 7/3 *etc* ~ (dum). 77/34, 4 ~ . . ~(cum . . tunc). 100/2 ~(quando). 118/171 ðon[n]e (cum). **Ct** 20/4, 4 *etc*; 25/4; 34/11, 2, 21; 37/11, 4, 9, 23; 38/7; 39/15; 41/8, 14 *etc*; 42/12, 8; 45/17, 45 ~. 23/16 (ðonne). 25/5; 34/13; 41/8, 25 *etc*; 45/4, 19 *etc* þ~. 29/3, 4, 5 *etc*; 45/47 ðanne. 45/21 þanne.

ðonne *av* than. **BDS** 2 than. **VP** 51/5; 117/8, 9 ðon (quam). 83/11 ðone (§). **Ct** 38/8, 9 ~. 12 ðanne.

hwonne *av* when. **VP** 2/12 ðylęs ~(ne quando). 58/12 ðylæs ~ (§). 49/22; 78/10 *etc* ne ~(§). 34/17; 40/6; 41/3 *etc* ~(quando?). **Ct** 37/33 ~.

ā-hwonne *av* ever. **VP** 37/17 ne [a]h[w]onne (quando).

ed-roc *s* rumination. **Ep** 876 ~(rumex); Ef §; Cp edric.

geille-rocad *aj* (*ptc*) hot-cockled. **VP** 77/65 ~(crapulatus).

rocettan *wv* belch. **VP** 18/3; 44/2 roccetteð (eructuat, §uavit); 144/7 §að. 118/171 rocetað.

loca *sm* flock of wool. **Ep** 448 ~(floccus); Ef, Cp §.

onweg-ā-locen *ptc* pulled away. **Bd**[2] 66 ~(evulsam).

ūtā-locen *ptc* pulled out. **VP** 128/6 sie ~ (evellatur).

locer *s* plane. **Ep** 853 ~aer *vel* sceaba (runcina); Ef §; Cp ~.

loc *s* enclosure. **Ep** 1028 gata ~(titule); Cp §; Ef gatan ~.

clūstor-loc *s* enclosure, passage. **Ep** 220 ~ae (caustella); Ef ~erlocae (clustella); Cp ~.

cealf-loc- *s.* **Ct** 41/59 et ~an.

ā-hlocian *wv* pull out. **Ef.** 364 ach[l]ocadum (effossis); Cp ~adum.

cocer *s(m)* quiver. **Rd** 14 cocrum. **VP** 10/3 ~e (faretrā).

geoc *sn* (yoke), a measure of land. Ct 42/20 XVI gioc.

geoc-led *s* a measure of land. Ct 35/6 an iocled. 49/4 ~. 52/6 (*de*)*mediam partem unius mansiunculae, id est*, an ioclet. 13 §.

gebrocen *ptc* broken. VP 31/4 bið ~(confringitur). 41/11 bioð §.

tō-brocen *ptc* broken up. VH 6/12 ~e sind (confracti sunt).

gebroc *sn* breaking. VP 105/23 ~e (confractione).

brocian *wv* afflict, molest. Ct 23/15 ~ie.

wiðer-broca *sm* adversary. VP 3/8 ~an (adversantes). Hy 4/20; Hy 5/11 §(adversarii; §ios). Hy 7/55 ~um.

wiðerbrocian *wv* oppose. VP 34/19 ~iað (adversantur). 73/10 ~að (†adversarius).

hocc *s* mallow. Cp 1288 ~ *etc* (malva).

locc *sm* lock (of hair). Ep 28 ~as (antiae); Ef, Cp §. Cp 1364 §(nazarei). Lr 15 ~um (iaris). VP 39/13; 67/22; 68/5 ~as (capillos *etc*).

winde-locc *sm* curly lock. Cp 473 ~a[s] (circinni).

socc *s*(*m*) sock. Ep 951 sooc (soccus); Ef §; Cp ~.

stocc *s* stock, trunk. Ct 29/4, 4 ðam won ~e.

Stocmēd Ct.

finger-docc- *s* finger-muscle. Ef 346 fingirdo[c]cuna (digitalium musculorum); Cp fingrdoccana.

brocc *s* badger. Ep 1008 ~; Ef †broa (taculus); Cp ~.

Brocces-hām Ct. **Brochyl** Ct.

oxa *sm* ox. VP 8/8; 65/15; 143/14 ~an (boves). Hy 7/25 oxna (boum). Ct 41/13, 21 ~an *pl.* 28/6, 6 oxnum.

fox *sm* fox. VP 62/11 ~a (vulpium).

box *s* box-tree. Cp 332 ~(bux).

crohha *sm* pot. Ep 171 crocha (citropodes *etc*); Ef chroca; Cp chrua, croha.

crohha *sm* saffron. Cp 1254 ~(luteum).

Slohtran-ford Ct.

dohtor *sf* daughter. VP 44/11; 136/8 ~ur (filia). 44/10, 3, 4; 47/12; 96/8 § *pl.* 143/12 ðohtur *pl.* 105/38; Hy 7/37 dohtra (§iarum). Ct 38/12 ~ar.

gebohte *prt* bought. Cp 741 geboht (empta). Ct 24/8; 42/2 ~ *prt*.

bi-bohte *prt* sold. VP 43/13 ~es (vendidisti). 104/17 biboht wes (venundatus est).

ofer-hoga *aj* despising, proud. VP 118/122; 139/6; Hy 10/7 ~an (superbi *pl, etc*). 122/4 ~um. *all without subst.*

hogian *wv* think. VP 93/8 ~iað (sapite). Hy 7/57 ~edon (§uerunt). 130/2 ~ade (sentiebam).

for-hogian *wv* despise. Cp 1154 ~hogd (irritum, inanem). VP 50/19; 101/18 ~að (spernit; sprevit). 21/25; 52/6; 68/34; 77/59, 62 ~hogde (sprevit). 88/39; 118/118 §es. 118/141 ~hogd (contemptus).

forhogadnis *sf* contempt. VP 106/40; 122/3 ~(contemptio; §ione). 30/19; 43/14; 118/22 ~nisse (contemptu; §; §um). 78/4 ~hogdnisse.

Baeg-log *sm.* LV 172; 208 ~. 290 baeglug.

Mogan-cumb Ct.

Iognes-homme Ct.

getogen *ptc* drawn. Cp 1918 ~um (strictis). 1927 getogone (strictā).

here-toga *sm* general. VP 67/28 ~an (duces).

trog *s*(*m*) trough. Ef 1140 ~(albeus, genus vasis). Cp 425 ~(canthera). 492 cilda ~(conabulum); Ld †ciltrog (cune, cunabula).

boga *sm* bow, vault. Ep 442 ~an (fornicem); Ef, Cp §. 453 ~(fornix, super columnis); Ef ~; Cp ~o. Cp 168 ~(antena). 410 ~(canda). 1607 ~(postena). Bl 18 ~an (arcem). VP 36/15; Hy 4/8 ~(arcus). 7/13 *etc* ~an (§um). Hy 6/19 § ðinne. 43/7 *etc* § (§u). 59/6 § (§ūs *g*).

geoc-boga *sm* yoke-bow. Cp 15 ~ (jungula).

sadul-boga *sm* saddle-bow. Ef 283 ~o (carpella); Cp ~.

Ocg *sm* Gn 86, 114 ~.

Ocging *sm* son of O. Gn 86 ocgting. 114 ~.

tō-strogden *ptc* scattered. VP 21/15 ~ sind (dispersa sunt). 58/16 bioð tostrogdne (dispergentur). 67/2 sien § (dissipentur). 91/10 bioð tostrodne (dispergentur).

gebrogden *ptc* drawn. VH 1/10 gebrogdnum (evaginato).

***ðorh-brogden** *ptc* drawn through. Cp 2046 ~(trajectus).

brogdettan *wv* shake, brandish. Ep 735 brocda[e]ttendi (palpitans); Ef brogdaethendi; Cp brogdetende. Cp 411 § *vel* deppetende (campus). 2132 brogde[t]teð (vibrat); Ep borȩttit.

otor *s*(*m*) otter. Ep 585 otr (lustrus); Ef †oct*er*; Cp otr. 914 ~(sullus); Ef otr; Cp ottor.

huōn-hlotum *av* minutely. Cp 1515 ~(parumper).

ā-ðroten *ptc* wearied. Cp 1532 ~ is (perpessum est).

þrote *sf* throat.

throtbolla Ep; ðrot§ Ef, Cp, Lr; †droh§ Ld.

æsc-ðrote *sf* a plant. Ep 450 aescthrotae (ferula); Ef aescdrotae; Cp ae~.

eofor-ðrote *sf* carline thistle. Ef 303 aebordrotae (colicum); Cp eoburthrote. Ep 927 eborthrotae (scasa); Ef §; Cp ebor~. Cp 27 ~þrote (scisca).

snotor *aj* wise. VP 106/43; Hy 7/9 snottur (sapiens). 48/11 snotre. 57/6 ðæm snottran.

þanc-snotor *aj* wise of thought. BDS 2 thonc-snotturra *cp*.

snotterlice *av* wisely. VP 46/8 ~(sapienter).

sele-gescot *s*(*n*) tabernacle. VP 14/1 ~e ðinum (tabernaculo).

scotian *wv* shoot. VP 10/3; 63/5 ~eden (sagittent). 63/6 ~edun. 75/9 ~ad is (jaculatum est).

scotung *sf* shooting. VP 54/22; Hy 6/23 ~e (jacula).

gescota *sm* fellow-shooter, archer. Cp 551 ~(commanipularius *etc*).

flota *sm* fleet. Cp 485 ~(clasis). Ef 1170 ~(classis, navis collectae).

ā-goten *ptc* poured out. VP 78/10 ~ is (effusus est) 79/17 ~(†effossa). 21/15; 72/2 ~e sind. 106/40 agetenis.

be-goten *ptc* poured over with. Rn 2/10 bi(*g*)ot(en).

tō-goten *ptc* poured away. VP 44/3 ~ is (diffusa).

Ercon-gote *sf* BH 122 ~a *d*. 149 earcongotæ *n* — §ȩ — eorcangota [e *er after last* a]. 152 earcongotam — eorc§ 1.

grot *sn* groats, coarse meal. Ld 149 ~(pollis).

cot *s*(*n*) cot. Ct 30/8 ~a *pl*.

cotuc *s*(*m*) mallow. Ep 656 ~(malva); Cp cottuc.

tot-ridan Ep; Ef, Cp §.

Tota *sm* Gn 13 ~.

Totta *sm* LV 345 ~. Gn 39 ~.

Botta *sm* Ct 5/6 ~.

Hodo-worða Ct.

Oden-colc Ct.

Ald-hod *sm*. Ct 4/5 ~i *g*.

gelod-wyrt Cp; gilodusrt§ Ef.

Sodom-wearena VH.

Wealh-stod *sm*. BH 373 ualch~ — uualstod 1. LV 114, 95; 214, 7, ualch~. Gn 49 †walhston.

gestrod *sn* rapine. VP 61/11 in ~u (rapinis).

god *smn* God, god. Rn 2/1 *g*od. LP 6 ~es. CA 6 *etc* ~es. 8 ~e. 13 ~. DA 7 ~es. Mt 9 ~e. 19 ~es. 23 ~. VP 3/7 *etc* ~ (deus), 13/2, 5 *etc* ~ (deum). 65/8 ~ urne. 17/7 *etc* ~e. 13/3 *etc* ~es. 46/3, 10 *etc* ~as. 85/8 *etc* ~um. 49/1 *etc* ~a. 65/19 †go (deus). Ct 40/3; 41/3 *etc*; 45/52 ~. 30/23; 37/3; 40/24; 42/5 ~e. 30/22; 37/1, 6 *etc*; 38/15; 39/6, 14; 40/1 *etc*; 41/32 *etc*; 42/12, 4; 45/13, 31; 48/19 ~es.

Godmundinga-hām BH. **Godmund** Ct. **godspellian** VP; §ere DA. **goduuebb** Ep; § Cp; guod§ Ef. **goduurēci** Cp; §wrecnis Bd².

Goduine BH. Godulf Gn; goduulfing Gn.

godcund *aj* divine. CA 9 ~an. Ct 37/9, 13, 40; 42/10 ~um. 37/34; 42/16 ~an. 37/41 ~e.

Goda *sm* Ct 26/7; 35/15 ~.

be-boden *ptc* commanded. Ct 40/21 ~ hebbe.

bebod *sn* command. VP 2/6; 18/9 *etc* bi~ (praeceptum). 118/96 § ðin (mandatum *a*). 93/20; 118/48 ~e. 98/7 bi~ (praecepta). 102/18; 118/143 §(mandata). 77/7; 88/32; 110/8; 118/4, 6 *etc* bibodu. 111/1 *etc* §um. 118/32, 5 §a. 7/7 bebode. 118/78 §um. 118/110 †bodum.

spell-boda *sm* orator. Cp 1461 spelbodan (oratores).

bodian *wv* preach. VP 2/6 ~iende (praedicans).

bodan *s*(*m*) bottom. Cp 10 ~(fundus).

bodig *s*(*n*) body. Ep 947 bodęi (spina); Ef §; Cp ~eg.

codd *sm* cod.

†goodaeppel Cp.

Dodda *sm* Ct 36/5 ~. 6 ~an *g*.

Podda *sm* Gn 49 ~.

open *aj* open. VP 5/11; 13/3 ~(patens).

lopust *s* lobster. Cp 1238 ~(locusta).

grund-sopa *sm* ground soap (a plant). Ef 312 ~suopa (cartilago); Cp grun[d]~.

dop-aenid Ep, Ef; dopp§ Cp.

dropa *sm* drop. VP 44/9 ~(gutta).

dropfaag Ep; Cp §; Ef †drofaxg.

dropettan *wv* drip. VP 71/6 ~etende (stillantia).

popig *s* poppy. Ef 253 ~eg (cucumis); Cp ~æg. Ep 824 ~aeg (papaver); Ef papoeg; Cp ~æg. Cp 1516 ~ei (§).

gers-hoppe *sf* grasshopper. VP 104/34 geres~ (locusta). 108/23 ~(§). 77/46 ~an (§ae).

stoppa *sm* cup. Ep 122 stappa [a *alt. to* o ?] (bothonicula); Ef, Cp ~.

hramsa-crop *sm* head of wild garlick. Ep 60 ~(acitelum); Ef § [o *over first* a]; Cp hromsan ~.

Cloppa-hām Ct.

Bobba *sm* Ct 10/4 ~an *g*.

cœren *s* sweet wine. Ef 313 coerim (dulcis sapa); Cp caerin. Ef 314 coerin; Cp § (defrutum). Cp 1368 carere (nectar, mel, vinum).

lœrge *pl* poles. Ep 1 loerge (amites); Ef §ae; Cp la[e]rgae.

sœrgan *wv* sorrow, be anxious. Ep 79 soęr[g]ęndi (anxius); Ef, Cp sorgendi.

œle *sm* oil. VP 54/22; 108/18; 140/5; Hy 7/25 ele (oleum). 22/5 *etc* §(oleo). 88/21 halgum §. 4/8 §es.

eletrīow Bl; VP §.

œm-setinne Cp.

cœcel *s*. Cp 1964 cecil (suffocacium).

œxen *pl* oxen. VP 49/10; Hy 6/38 oe~ (boves).

þrœhtig *aj* vigorous Cp 1556 ðro[e]htig (pervicax).

dœhter *dat*, *gen* daughter. VP 9/15; 72/28 doehter (filiae *g*). Ct 39/11 § *d*.

recetung *sf* eructuation. VP 143/13 ful ~e (plena eructuantia).

Oiddi *sm*. BH 276 ~.

dœppettan *wv* dip. Cp 411 brogdetende *vel* deppetende (campus).

ā *av* ever. Ep 529 a fordh (in dies); Ef, Cp §. VP 15/8; 17/23; 18/15 *etc* aa (semper). 37/9 *etc* a hu lenge swiður (usquequaque). 118/44, 4 aee in aee (semper in aeternum). Ct 48/9 a.

ou(ua)n(a). owiht. ahwonne.

ā-. galan. grafan. sprang. sten [*under* a]. assuant Ef. scacen. slacian. bær. ræfnan, unaræfnendlic. ahæfd, an§. cearf. heardian. wearp. geald. swealt. firran. dilgian. gildeþ. bisgian. drifen. springan. swindan. figen. writen. sliden. gniden *sbst*. biden. geldan. gefen. þegen. screpan. feorrian. ceorfan. weorpan. fęrian. męrian. cęrran. węrgan, §ednis. węrdan. scęrpan. sęllan. stęllan. fęllan. męllad. scęltan. unamęlt. hęldan. ręsan. swęngan. węnnan. węndan. blęndan. fręmþan, §ung. ręccan. węccan. lęcgan. sęcgan, unasecgendlic. sęttan. hębban. wurpon. ūtaþrungen. sprungon. sprungnis. wunian. cunnian. wundon. swundon. crummen. dumbian. tugon.

guton. spyrian, §iend. fyrht. gyltan. styntan. rytran. ryddan. worpen. assuollan Ef. solcen. scofen. onweg-alocen. ut§. blocian. þroten. goten. gā. rās. rāsian. swāf. onweg-adrāf. stāg. scādan. bād. rǣran. gǣlan. þrǣstan. þwǣnan. wǣgan. rǣdan. lǣdan. brǣdan. bǣre. wǣgon. wǣfon. rǣdan. slǣpan. lēsan, §nis. tēhþ. stēpan. þwēa. gēat. tēo. ūtalēoran. fēoll. wēoll. þēostrian. gēotan. brēotan, §nis. þēodan. hīþan. wrīþan. sīwan. rīsan. onwegadrīfan. dwīnan. rīman. stīgan. īdlian. bīdan. fūlian. scūfan. lūcan. drūgian. fȳred. tȳnan. þrȳan, þȳtan. hȳdan. hōf. grōf. þōht. woestan. froefran. doen. soedan. foedan.

nā *av* not. **VP** 9/39; 53/5; 76/8 *etc* no (non). 85/14 †non (non).

nowiht, noht, †niwiht. nalǣs.

lytes-nā *av* nearly. **Ep** 200 lytisna (concedam); Ef §; Cp ~.

ēaw·lā *interj.* **VP** 117/25 ~(o). 118/5 ~(utinam).

ðā *prn f sg* her *etc* **Ep** 707 †ð gisettan (ordinatissimam); Ef †a; Cp. þa. **DA** 4 ða. **Mt** 26 ða. **Bd**[2] 13 ða. **VP** 9/16, 6 ða (quem) *etc.* 21/21 ða angan (unicam) *etc.* 23/2; 30/20 *etc* ða (illam; eam). 97/1 mid ða swiðran his (dexterā) 107/7 mid ða swiðran ðinre (§). **Ct** 20/14, 5; 42/15; 45/42 ða. 45/32, 6, 7 þa.

ðā *prn pl* **Ep** 439 tha; Ef da; Cp ða. 542 þa; Ef, Cp ða. 576 tha; Ef §; Cp ða. **Bl** 8 þa. **DA** 5 *etc* ða. **Mt** 19 ða. **Bd**[2] 25 ða. **VP** 5/6 *etc* ða unrehtwisan (injusti). 9/24 *etc* ða unrehtan (iniqua). 18/12; 49/21 *etc* ða (ea; illa). 6/9; 9/23 *etc* ða (qui; quas). 5/7; 13/4 *etc* ða ða (qui). 43/11 *etc* § (eos qui). 4/9 in ða ilcan (in id ipsum). **Hy** 9/6 da. 30/24 þa. **Ct** 38/11; 41/42; 42/16 ða. 37/7 ða menn ða. 45/3, 14, 9, 20 þa.

ðā-ðe *rel.* (they) who. **Rd** 10 ða ði. **LP** 3 ~. **Mt** 44 ~. **VP** 2/10, 3 *etc* ~(qui). 5/7 § [e *from some other l.*] **Ct** 38/4 ~.

ðā *av, cj* then, when. **Rn** 2/2 þa. **CH** 7 tha. **Mt** 8 *etc* ða. **SG** 1 *etc* ða. **VP** 39/8; 47/6 *etc* ða (tunc). 118/32 ða (cum). **Ct** 28/23 ~.

nū-ðā *av* now, already. **VH** 12/4 ~(jam).

ðā-ðe *cj* when. **VP** 48/21; 106/6 ~(cum).

Sā-berct, sæ§ **BH**; saberht, §ing **SG**. **Saweard,** §ing **SG**.

sā *s* ladle. **Cp** 17 saa (libitorium).

Snā-hard LV.

ēu-wā *interj* woe! **Cp** 31 ~(va).

hwā *prn* who. **Ct** 23/15 h(ua).

gā *sv* go. **VP** 7/8 gaa eft (regredere!). 80/13; **Hy** 6/23 gað (ibunt). 121/1 § (ibimus).

ā-gā *sv* go out, pass (of time). **SG** 10 wæs agan.

be-gā *sv* exercise, take care of. **Ct** 41/13 (he) ~.

fore-gā *sv* go before. **VP** 88/15 ~gað (praeibunt).

forð-gā *sv* go forth. **VP** 44/5 ~gaa (procede!). 21/30; 71/9; 88/35 ~gað (§unt *etc*). 18/6 ~gande (§ens).

geond-gā *sv* traverse. **VP** 100/2 ~gan [or ~gau ?] (perambulabam). 8/9 ~gað (§ant).

in-gā *sv* enter. **VP** 5/8; 70/16; 131/3 ~(introibo *etc*). 41/5 ~(ingrediar). 42/2 ~(incedo). 25/4 in ne ga (non introibo). 41/10 ingaa (incedo). 42/4; 65/13 § (introibo). 142/2 ne ga ðu inn (non intres!). 62/10; 94/11 ingað (introibunt). 95/8 § (§oite). 99/2, 4 § (intrate). 117/20 § (§abunt).

ofer-gā *sv* cross. **VP** 17/30 ~gaa (transgrediar).

ymb-gā *sv* go round. **VP** 25/6; 26/6 ~gaa (circuibo). 58/7 ~gad (§uibunt). 58/15 utan ~gað (§§).

twā *fem* two. **Ld** 134 tua. **Lr** 27 ~(binas). **Ct** 37/36, 6, 7, 7 ~.

twā *neut.* two. **VP** 61/12 tu (duo). **Ct** 29/17; 37/38, 8; 41/19, 33; 42/18; 45/10, 3 ~. 37/18 tua.

bā *fem.* both. **Ep** 51 ba; Ef, Cp §.

bā *neut.* both. **Rn** 2/8 ba.

ār *sf* honour, mercy, prosperity. **VP** 98/4 ~(honor). 28/2; 67/35; 95/7 ~e (§em). 61/5 ~e mine (§em). 8/6 *etc* ~e (§e). 44/10 ~e ðinre (§e). Ct 30/21 to ~e. 45/53 ~e *g.*

Aruald BH.

weorld-ār *sf* worldly prosperity. Ct 45/53 ~e *g.*

ārlēas *aj* wicked, impious. VP 9/6, 23, 34 se ~a (impius). 10/6 ðone ~an. 11/9 ða ~an (§ii) *etc.* 16/9 ~ra *etc.*

ārlēaslice *av* wickedly. VP 17/22 ~(impie).

ārlēasnis *sf* wickedness. VP 5/11 ~nissa (impietatum). 31/5 ~nisse (§em). 64/4 ~nissum. 72/6 †arleas (§e).

ārlic *aj* honourable. Ct 42/11 ~.

ārian *wv* honour. VP 85/9 ~iað (honorificabunt). 85/12; Hy 5/3 ~iu (§abo; honorabo).

geārian *wv* VP 49/23 ~að (honorificabit). Hy 5/1 ~ad is (§atus est). 36/20 §e (honorati). 138/17 §e sind (honorificati sunt).

ār *s(n)* brass. Cp 255 groeni a[a]r (aurocalcum).

hār *aj* hoary, grey. Ct 20/13 an ~an stan.

ðāra *gpl.* LP 11 ðeara. Bd² 53, 86 ~. VP 7/10; 57/11; 111/2 ðeara. 13/3; 18/4; 25/10 *etc* § (quorum). Ct 36/10; 37/43; 41/6, 41, 60 §. 58/24 þeara. 37/7; 40/2 ~. 45/35 þara. 45/54 ðæra.

sāre *av* sorely, very. Rn 2/14 s(are).

sār *sn* sore, pain, grief. DA 14 ~e. VP 7/15, 7 *etc* ~(dolorem, dolor). 30/11 *etc* ~e. 40/4 *etc* ~es. 17/6 *etc* ~(§es). 93/19; 106/39 ~a.

sārgian *wv* be in pain, grieve. VP 68/30 ~iende (dolens). Hy 6/20 ~iað (§ebunt).

wār *s* seaweed. Ep 47 uaar [u *over* p] (alga); Ef uar; Cp waar; Ld †uac. Ef 1139 uar (§ marina).

Itha-mār *sm.* BH 162 ~, *de gente cantuariorum.* 177, 7 ~; ~ *d.*

māre *aj* greater, more. VP 113/13 ~um (majoribus).

gār *sm* spear.

Garberct LV. Garfrið LV. garlęc Ep; Ef §; Cp gaar§. Garmund LV. Garuald LV. Garuulf LV; garulf Ct.

Cēol-gār *sm* LV 95 ~.

Cūð-gār *sm* LV 84; 157, 81; 382 cuth~. 108, 34 ~.

Cyni-gār *sm* LV 427 ~.

Ēad-gār *sm* BH 271 ~um. LV 169, 88; 253, 60, 75, 81, 97, 9; 309, 22, 3, 48, 54, 89; 420, 79 ~. Gn 7, 43 ~. Ct 19/7 ~i. 38/18; 48/15 ~.

Hildgāring-denn Ct.

nafo-gār *sm* auger. Ep 1010 nabfogar (terrebellus); Ef †naboger; Cp §gaar; Ld nębu§. Cp 1754 nabogar (rotnum).

Sige-gār *sm* Gn 76 ~.

Sigegāring *sm* son of S. Gn 76 ~.

Wiht-gār *sm* Ct 27/6; 29/21 wioht~.

Wōp-gār *sm* Rn 1/3 ~*gar.*

Wulf-gār *sm* LV 365 uulf~.

bār *sm* boar. Ep 151 baar (berrus); Ef, Cp, Ld §. Ef 1163 § (caper, porcus dimisus).

āl-giuueorc Ep; Ef §; Cp aal§.

hāl *aj* VP 17/4, 28 ~(salvus; §um) *etc.* 7/3, 11 ~e (§um; §os) *etc.* 3/7; 6/5 *etc* ~ne (§um).

hālwynde VP.

hālig *aj* holy. I *with subst.* II *without subst,* holy one, saint. CH 6 ~eg. LP 2 ~ra II. CA 7, 16 halgan. 15 ~ra II. DA 3, 6, 7, 8 halgan. 4 ~an. 7 ~ra. Mt 11, 45 halgan. VP 17/26; 18/10 *etc* ~(sanctus) *etc.* 72/17; 73/7 ~ portic (sanctuarium). 42/1 ~re. 51/11; 78/2 ~ra (sanctorum) II. 50/13; 144/21 ~ne. 11/2 se halga II. 2/6; 3/5 *etc* §an. 4/4 ðone §an II. 15/3; 29/5 §e (§i *pl*) II *etc.* Hy 11/4 §es. 19/3 §um *etc.* 67/36; 73/3 §um (§is) II *etc.* 67/25; 76/14 in § (§o = 'sanctuary'). 47/2 †hagan. Ct 37/3 halgon. 39/7, 14 ~ra II. 45/55 halgan. 48/9, 18, 20 ðaere ~ran *g.* II.

Halegberct LV.

hālignis *sf* holiness. VP 95/6 ~(sanctitas). 29/5; 96/12 ~sse (§atis). 88/40; 144/5 § (§atem). Hy 5/32 § ðine (sanctimonium). Hy 9/10 § (§ate).

hālgian *wv* consecrate. **DA** 12 ~a!

gehālgian *wv* consecrate. **DA** 8 ~ode sien. VP 45/5 ~að (sanctificavit). 104/15 ða ~edan (christos). 105/28 ~ade werun (consecrati sunt).

gehālgung *sf* consecration. **VH** 113/2; 131/18 †~un (sanctificatio). 77/54, 69 ~e (§nis, §nem). 95/6 ~e (§ne). 131/8 ~e ðinre (§nis).

salt-hālgung *sf* consecration of salt. **DA** 18 ~uncge *d.*

wæter-hālgung *sf* **DA** 17 waeterhalguncge *d.* 19 waeterhalgunc.

hāl-stān Ef; haalstaan Cp.

sāl *s(m)* bond. **Cp** 1727 ~e (repagula).

gestāl *s* objection. **Cp** 1421 ~um (objectionibus).

sin-gāl *aj* continuous. **Cp** 1440 ~e (olim).

gesingālian *wv* continue. **VP** 88/51 ~ede (continui). 140/6 werun ~ede (§uati).

or-dāl *sn* ordeal. **DA** 10 ðæm ~e.

tō-dāl *sn* distribution. **VP** 77/54 ~es (distributionis).

ærfe-gedāl *sn* dividing inheritance. **Ct** 41/71 ~.

weg-gedāl *sn* road-dividing. **Cp** 672 ~(discidium).

āð *sm* oath. **VH** 9/7 ðone swergendan að (jusjurandum).

aðswyrd VP.

āðexe *sf* lizard. **Cp** 1182 ~(lacerta); Ld adexa. Ef 1119 adexe (§).

lāð *aj* hateful. **Ep** 514 lath (ingratus); Ef laad; Cp ~. 552 laath (invisus); Ef, Cp lath; Ld †luad.

ātur-lāðe *sf* a plant. **Cp** 293 ~(bettonica); Ld 70 †atersatha (nemias).

Waðol-gēot, ·að·· geoting Gn.

māðm *sm* treasure. **Ld** 12 madmas (exenia).

clāð *sm* cloth, clothes (*in pl*).

cild-clāðas *pl* swaddling-clothes. **Cp** 623 ~(cunae).

flycti-clāð *sm* patch. **Cp** 491′~ (commissura).

hās *aj* hoarse. **VP** 68/4 ~e (raucae *pl*).

ā-rās *prt* arose. **VP** 75/10 ~(exurgeret). 118/62 ~(surgebam). 138/18 ~(resurrexi).

eft-ārās *prt* rose again. **VP** 3/6 ~(resurrexi).

ā-rāsian *wv* convict, blame. **Cp** 1067 ~ad (interceptum).

ðās *sg fem acc* this. **VP** 26/4 ~(hanc). Ct 34/16; 37/42; 38/7; 41/43, 58, 69; 45/56; 48/8, 18 ~.

ðās *pl* these. **LP** 6 ~. **CA** 4, 7, 16 ~. **VP** 19/8, 8 ~(hii) *etc.* 43/18, 22 ~(haec, ista) *etc.* **Ct** 24/8; 37/11 *etc*; 40/16 *etc*; 45/49, 53 ~. 45/9, 43 *etc* þas.

snās *s* spit. **Ld** 144 snaas (veru).

wrās- *s* lump, knot. **Cp** 1387 wrasan, ost (nodus).

māse *sf* titmouse (?). **Ep** 806 ~ae (parrula); Ef §; Cp ~; Ld ~ae.

frec-māse *sf* titmouse (?). **Cp** 1192 ~(laudariulus).

cāsere *sm* emperor. **Mt** 15, 6, 24, 8, 40 ~. 44 ðone ~.

Cāsaer *sm.* LV 6 ~.

geclāsnian *sf* purify. **VP** 18/13; 50/4 ~a (munda!). 40/3; Hy 7/90 ~að (§et; §abit). 11/7 ~ad (purgatum). 18/14; 50/9 biom § (emundabor).

geclāsnung *sf* purification. **VP** 88/45 ~e (emundatione).

gāsric *s(m)* ocean. **Rn** 3/6 ~.

lāst *sm* track. **Cp** 769 on ~e (e vestigio). 1465 ~(orbitae).

braadlast-ęcus Cp; braedlaestuaesc Ef.

wāst *vb* knowest. **VP** 68/6, 20 ~(scis).

wrāst *aj* delicate. **Ef** 332 wrastum (delicatis et quaerulosis); Cp ~um end seobgendum. Cp 630 ~(delicatus).

hwāstrung *sf* murmur. **Ld** 7 uastru[n]g (murmur).

gāst *sm* spirit, angel, ghost, soul. **BDS** 4 ~ae. **DA** 3 ~es. **Mt** 47 minum ~e. **VP** 10/7 *etc* ~(spiritus). 30/6 ~ minne (§um) *etc.* 32/6 *etc* ~e. 17/16 *etc* ~es. 103/4; Hy 8/6, 18 ~as. 50/19; 77/8, 39; 142/4; 148/8 gas (§us). Ct 34/14 ~as. 41/43 minum ~e.

āwescniss *sf* disgrace. **VP** 34/26 ~e (reverentiā).

hrāw *s(n)* carcass. **Bd**[2] 22 hra (funerum).

lāwerce *sf* lark. **Ep** 1012 lauuercae

(tilaris); Ef lauuercæ; Cp lauricae; Ld laurice. Cp 142 lauricae (allauda). 1173 laurice (laudae).

hlāw *s(m)* mound.

Ōslāfes-hlāu *s(m)* Ct 58/11 ~.

Uuihtbaldes-hlāw *s(m)* Ct 26/3 et ~e.

geðrāwan *sv* twist. Cp 1730 geðraune (retorto).

sāwan *sv* sow. VP 125/5 ~að (seminant).

sāwol *sf* soul. Rn 1/5 sinna sowhula. 4/4; 11/3 der saule *d.* CA 6 saule *g.* 12 §um). VP 6/4 sawl (anima). 21/31; 24/13; 30/10 *etc* ~ul (§). 6/5 *etc* sawle (§am). 7/3, 6 § mine (§am) *etc.* 10/2 *etc* § (§ae *d*). 9/24 *etc* § (§ae *g*). 18/8; 26/12 *etc* § (§as). 77/18, 50 §um. 3/3 †salwle (§ae *d*). 55/7 †sawulf (§a). Hy 8/18 †sawe (§ae *pl*). Ct 37/32, 6, 6, 7, 8; 41/27; 45/22, 30, 6 sawle *a.* 30/21, 2 § *d.* 45/53 § *g.* 37/27, 8, 35 §um. 39/10; 40/7 saule *a.* 42/17 § *g.* 37/24, 40 §a *pl.* 37/5, 43 §a *gpl.* 39/15 sawale *d.*

saulðearfe Ct.

snāw *sm* snow. VP 148/8; Hy 7/4 ~(nix). Hy 8/9 ~(nives). 50/9; 147/16 ~(nivem). 67/15 ~e (§e).

crāwe *sf* crow. Ep 241 crauuae (cornacula); Ef §; Cp crauue. Ef 308 †crauua (cornix); Cp ~. Ef 1171 †crę (curnicula *etc*). Cp 401 crauue (carula). 950 cra[u]ue (garula).

on-cnāwan *sv* know. VP 50/5 ~u (agnosco). Hy 6/3 ~es (cognosceris). 9/17; 73/9; 91/7; 102/16 ~eð. 137/6 ~eð (agnoscit). 13/4; 52/5 ~að. 77/6 ~e (cognoscat). 66/3; 82/19 ~en. 138/23 oncnaw (§e!). 47/4 bið ~en (dinoscitur). 76/20 bioð §. 87/13 bioð oncnawne.

pāwa *sm* peacock. Ep 826 pauua (pavo); Ef, Cp §.

horn-blāwere *sm* horn-blower. Cp 454 ~blauuere (cereacus).

hǣwe-blāw *aj* blue. Ef 1152 hauiblauum (blata, pigmentum).

lāf *sf* I leavings, relic. II widow. Bd² 25 ~e (reliquia). 46 ~um (§is). VP 16/14 to ~e werun (superfuerunt). 72/25 to ~e †stodeð (restat). 20/13 ~um (reliquiis). 36/37, 8; 75/11 ~e (§ae *pl*). Hy 3/2 ~e (residuum *a*). Ct 38/1 ~e *g* II.

Angen-lāf *sm* Ct 1/3 ~labes haam.

Cyne-lāf *sm* Ct 28/17 ~. 29/21 cynlaf.

Dēor-lāf *sm* Ct 48/11 ~.

Ecg-laf *sm* Gn 29 ~. Ct 17/5 ~.

Frēa-lāf *sm* Gn 110 ~.

Frēa-lāfing *sm* son of Frēalāf. Gn 77, 83; 109, 16, 21 ~. 96 fr·· lafing.

Ōs-lāf *sm* LV 3 ~. Ct 58/11 ~es hlau.

un-lāf *s(f)* posthumous child. Cp 1622 unlab (posthumus).

Wīg-lāf *sm* LV 395 u~. Ct 47/1, 3; 59/1, 4, 5 uu~. 47/8, 9 ~, ~e.

Wulf-lāf *sm* LV 125 uulf~. Ct 24/6; 29/22 uulf~. 20/23; 22/9; 23/10 §i. 28/8; 33/15 ~. 26/8; 27/6; 28/15 wullaf. 28/1, 13, 9, 21 §e.

geormant-lāb *s* mallow. Ep 656 cotuc *vel* ~(malva).

hlāf *sm* bread, loaf. VP 77/24 heofenlic ~(manna). 36/25 *etc* ~(panem). 101/5 ~ minne. 13/4 *etc* ~es. 79/6 *etc* ~e. 40/10 *etc* ~as. Hy 4/9 ~um. Ct 37/17, 24, 31; 39/10; 40/5; 41/30, 60 ~a *gpl.* 39/4 hlaba *gpl.*

elmes-hlāf *sm* almsbread. Ct 40/5 ~es.

hwīte-hlāf *sm* wheat loaf. Ct 40/5; 41/61 ~a *gpl.*

hlāford *sm* I lord. II husband. Rn 2/6 ~ard. VP 104/21 §(dominum). 122/2; 135/3, 26 §a (§orum). Ct 38/2 hlabard II. 41/24, 42, 4 ~. 42/6 ~e. 37/7 ~as. 25 ~a. 41/4 ~um.

hlāforddōm *sm* lordship, jurisdiction. Ct 41/45; 42/8 ~e.

hlāfdie *sf* mistress. VP 122/2 ~ian (dominae *g*).

ā-swāf *prt* strayed. Cp 803 asuab (exorbitans).

scab-foot Ep; scaabfot Ef; scaffoot Cp.

clāfre *sf* clover. Ef 250 †trede clabre

(calta); Cp reade ~. 254 †huitti clabre (calesta); Cp huite ~.

onweg-ā-drāf *prt* drove away. **VP** 17/23 onweg ne adraf (non reppuli).

ān *aj, prn* I one. II alone. **Rn** 2/13 ~um II. **Pr** ana II. **VP** 26/4; 33/21 *etc* ~(unam; unum). 50/6 ~um (soli). 70/16; 148/13 ~es (§ius). 71/18; 76/15 *etc* ~a (solus). 13/1, 3 *etc* enne (unum). 61/12; 88/36 æne siða (semel). **Ct** 35/6; 40/5, 5; 41/11, 30 *etc*; 43/2; 49/4; 52/5, 6 *etc* ~. 31/11; 37/17; 45/28; 49/3 ·án. 20/17 anne. 41/14 ænne. 37/13 anes.

ancendan VP. anēge Cp. anfald Cp. angylde Ct. anhendi Ep; Cp, Ef §. anhorn VP. anhyrne VP. anmōd Ep; Cp §; Ef on§. anstigan Ep; Ef §. anuuald Ep; Ef §; Cp anuualda. anuuillicae Ep; Ef, Cp §.

nān *aj, prn* none, no. **Ct** 41/41 ~.

ānnis *sf* unity. **VP** 47/5; 70/10; 132/1 in ~isse (in unum). 40/8 in anisse (§). 48/3; 82/6; 101/23 in annesse (§).

ānga *aj* only. **VP** 24/16 ~(unicus *sbst*). 101/8 se ~(unicus). 21/21; 34/17 ða ~an mine (§am).

swān *sm* herdsman. **Ep** 961 suan (sabulcus); Ef †suam; Cp †snan. 431 suan (flabanus); **Ef, Cp §.**

suansteorra Cp.

scān *prt* shone. **Cp** 220 scaan (ardebat).

stān *sm* stone, rock. **Ld** 69 ungebatne ~e (lapide). **VP** 18/11 deorwyrðne ~(lapidem); 39/3 ~(petram); 103/18 ~(§a) *etc.* 20/4 deorwyrðem ~e (lapide); 26/6 ~e (petrā) *etc.* 101/15 ~as (lapides). 103/12 ~a (petrarum). **Ct** 13/6 *hii sunt termini*: huitan ~. 20/5 on denewaldes ~. 10 from ðyrelan ~e. 11 to græwan ~e. 12 huitan ~es. 13 an haran ~. 19 ðone ~. 19 ðæm ~e.

standene Ct. Stanford BH. stanegellan VP. Stanhamstede Ct. stanwal VP.

Ælf-stān *sm* **Ct** 30/15; 31/9; 38/18 e~. 47/7; 59/6 ae~. 48/12 †aef~.

Æþel-stān *sm* **Ct** 24/4; 25/11; 26/6 aeð~. 32/7 eð~.

Bēag-stān *sm* **Ct** 45/58 ~.

Bil-stān *sm* **LV** 275 ~.

Cēol-stān *sm* **Ct** 35/11; 49/12 ~.

cisel-stān *sm* **Cp** 975 cisil~ (glarea).

Cū-stāning *sm* **Ct** 29/10 ~a [u *over* y] mearcę. 10 ~a mearc [u *over* y]. 12 cusstaninga mearc [u *over* y].

Degsa-stān *sm.* **BH** 37 ~, *id est* degsa *lapis*—stán. 375 *ad* ~æ—daegsastanę I.

Ealh-stān *sm* **LV** 254 aluch~. **Gn** 25 *alhstan.* **Ct** 20/22, 4; 22/7; 23/7; 47/4; 58/15, 9 alh~. 22/9, 10; 23/9, 12 §i. 30/17; 38/18 ~.

Fæx-stān *sm* **LV** 257 fex~.

Folcan-stān *sm* **Ct** 41/20, 9 to ~e, æt ~e. 57/3 *monasterio quae nominatur* æt ~ę.

hāl-stān *sm* crystal. **Ef** 288 ~(crustulla); Cp haalstaan.

Hēah-stān *sm* **Ct** 33/18 ~.

Helm-stān *sm* **Ct** 22/11; 23/12 ~i.

Hūn-stān *sm* **Ct** 48/14 ~.

hwete-stān *sm* **Ef** 294 hueti~; Cp huet[e]~; Ld ueostun (cos).

Nim-stān *sm* **LV** 254 ~.

rede-stān *sm* **Cp** 1872 ~(sinopede).

tæfl-stān *sm* gambling-stone, die. **Ep** 172 tebel~ (calculus vel lapillus *etc*); Ef †tebiltan; Cp tebl~.

Wīg-stān *sm* **Ct** 30/14 ~.

stāneht *aj* stony. **Ct** 28/12 ~an denn.

flān *sf* arrow. **Ep** 937 ~um (spiculis); Ef, Cp §. Cp 353 flaan (catapulta).

mānfull *aj* wicked. **Ep** 512 maanful (infandum); Ef †meinfol; Cp mánful.

gemāna *sm* community. **Ct** 37/6 ðem ~on.

clāne *av* entirely. **Ct** 41/41 ~.

gānian *wv* yawn. **Ep** 690 ganaendae (oscitantes); Ef ~endæ; (Cp geongendi).

grānian *wv* groan, roar. Bl 9 ~ode (rugiebam).

bān *sn* bone, (leg) Rn 3/4 ~ *pl.* VP 6/3; 21/15, 8 *etc* ~ min (ossa). 37/4; 108/18 ~um.

baangeberg Cp. baanrift Ep; Ef, Cp §.

elpend-bān *sn* ivory. Ef 351 elpendes ban (ebor); Cp ~baan.

hupp-bān *sn* hipbone. Lr 52 ~(catacrinas).

hweorf-bān *sn* vertebra. Lr 56 ~um[?] (genuclis).

swir-bān *sn* neck-bone. VP 128/4; Hy 6/28 ~(cervices).

ām *s* weaver's reed. Ep 177 haam (cautere, ferrum); Ef fam; Cp aam. Rd 8 §.

hām *sm* home, homestead. Ct 37/24 aet ~.

hámscīre Cp.

Angenlāfes-hām *sm* Ct 1/4 ~labeshaam.

Beddan-hām *sm* Ct 1/2 ~haam.

Bōsan-hām *sm* Bosham. BH 277 ~hamm — bo[o]san haam — ~ I, II.

Brocces-hām *sm* Ct 29/16 ~ ðes dennes nama.

Budin-hām *sm* Ct 1/3 ~haam.

Cloppa-hām *sm* Clapham. Ct 45/6, 21 on ~.

Deccan-hām *sm* Dagenham. Ct 1/3 ~haam.

Elm-hām *sm* Ct 33/14 *~is* (= *~ensis*) *ecclesiae.*

Fefres-hām *sm* Faversham. Ct 28/5, 24 et~. 52/7; 54/2 febres~. 51/5 ~hám.

Godmundinga-hām *sm* Goodmanham. BH 91 godmunddinga~ — ~ I, II.

Hæcca-hām *sm* Ct 47/11 aet haecca~.

Hēah-hām *sm* Ct 8/3 ~haam.

Lēana-hām *sm* Lenham. Ct 28/4 to ~.

Mēdeshamstedi BH.

Mersa-hām *sm* Mersham. Ct 30/3 ~. 28/2, 3, 20, 2, 3; 30/4 et ~. 30/6 to ~. 12 *ad* ~.

Mundling-hām *sm* Ct 40/17, 9 et ~.

mynster-hām *sm* monastery. Ct 45/31 ~as.

Netelhamstyde, netelam§ Ct.

Perhamstede Ct.

Rendles-hām *sm* BH 190 *vico regio qui dicitur* rendlæs ~, *id est, mansio* rendili — raendles~ I.

Rīcinga-hām *sm* Ct 1/3 ~haam.

Rœginga-hām *sm* Ct 51/5 roegingahám.

Scor-hām *sm* Shoreham. Ct 55/5 ~ *silva.*

Stānhamstede Ct.

þengles-hām *sm* Ct 39/12 et ð~.

Ūla-hām *sm* Ct 27/2 ~. 27/3, 7 et ~. 3 ęt ~.

Westar-hām *sm* Ct 45/6 on ~.

Wīginga-hām *sm* Ct 36/5 uuigincgga~.

Wīc-hāma *s.* Ct 11/4 *in loco ubi dicitur ~.*

hāma *sm* cricket. Ef 256 ~an (cicade); Cp §. Cp 987 ~(grillus).

Hāma *sm* LV 210; 349 ~.

lām *s* loam, clay. Ep 48 laam (argella); Cp §; Ef ~ [l *over* sr]; Ld la[a]m. Cp 1227 laam (limus). VP 17/43 ~(lutum). 39/3; 68/15 ~e (§o). 68/3 ~(limum). 2/9 fęt ~es (vas figuli).

Lamburnan-den Ct.

fām *s(n)* foam. Ep 426 faam (famfaluca); Ef, Cp §.

āc *sf* oak. Ep 235 aac (color); Cp §. 863 § (robor); Ef, Cp §. BH 48 augustinæs ac, *id est, robur augustini.*

Aclāeh Ct. Acuulf LV.

ācweorna *sm* squirrel. Ep 911 aquearna (scira); Cp §; Ef aquorna; Ld acurna.

lāc *sn* gift. Cp 737 laac (elogia). 798 §(exenium).

Cūþ-lāc *sm* LV 431 cuth~.

Ēa-lāc *sm* LV 118 ~.

Ēad-lāc *sm* LV 348; 482 ~.

Ēan-lāc *sm* LV 112; 430 ~.

Heard-lāc *sm* LV 384 ~.

Heaþo-lāc *sm* BH 372 hadu~. Gn 28 heaðo~.

Hrœþ-lāc *sm* **LV** 110, 32, 97 hroeð~.

Hwæt-lāc *sm* **Ct** 17/5 huet~.

Hyge-lāc *sm* **LV** 122, 67; 229, ·67 hyglac.

Ōs-lāc *sm* **Ct** 28/16 ~.

Sige-lāc *sm* **LV** 290 siglac.

Wiht-lāc *sm* **LV** 197 uicht~.

Wine-lāc *sm* **LV** 221 uini~.

bi-swāc *prt* deceived. **VP** 14/4 †bswac (decepit). Hy 13/4 ~(§erat).

swācend-lic *aj* convenient. **Ep** 729 suacendlic (percommodos *etc*); Ef §; Cp suacenlic.

lioðu-wāc *aj* flexible. **Cp** 1010 ~(habile).

un-liðuwāc *aj* inflexible, rigid. **Ep** 521 unlidouuac (intractabilis); Ef unliuduuac; Cp unlioþu~.

unlioþuwācnis *sf* inflexibility. **Cp** 1052 ~(infestatio).

fācn *aj* deceitful. **Cp** 883 ~um (fictis).

fācn *sn* deceit. **Ep** 83 ~i (astu); Ef, Cp §. **VP** 31/2; 35/4; 54/12; 138/4 facen (dolus). 33/14; 49/19; 51/4 § (§um). 9/28; 23/4; Hy 12/13 ~e (§o). 72/18 fore ~e (†§os). Hy 11/9 ~es (fraudis). 37/13 facen (dolos). 14/3 facæn (§um).

facnlice *under* fǣcnlice.

tācor *sm* brother-in-law. **Ep** 598 ~(levir); Ef §; Cp ~ur.

tācn *sn* sign, wonder. **Cp** 694 ~e (dicimenta). **VP** 85/17 tacen (signum). 45/9 § (prodigia). 73/4, 4, 9; 77/43; 134/9 § (signa). 64/9 ~um (§is), 104/27 ~a (§orum).

rōde-tācn *sn* sign of the cross. **Ct** 38/15; 40/11; 41/48, 50; 42/23; 45/55; 48/9 ~e *d*.

getācnian *wv* sign, show. **VP** 18/3 ~að (indicat). 118/27 ~a (insinua). Hy 7/66 ~ad (signata). 4/7 § is (§um est).

getācnung *sf* signification. **VP** 59/6 ~e (significationem).

rā *s* roe. **Cp** 403 raha (capria). **Ef** 1161 raa (capriolus).

lāh *prt* lent. **Ct** 41/3 ~.

mis-thāgch *prt* misthrove. **Cp** 667 ~ (degeneraverat).

slāh *sf* sloe. **Cp** 289 slag (bellicum). slachthorn Ep; § Ef; salach§ Ef; slagh§ Ep, Cp; slah§ Cp.

Uāch *sm.* **LV** 161/2 ~.

bi-wrāh *prt* covered. **VP** 28/9 ~(revelavit).

ofer-wrāh *prt* covered over. **VP** 31/5; 68/11 ~(operui). 43/16; 68/8 *etc* ~(§uit). Hy 5/7 ~(cooperuit).

on-wrāh *prt* uncovered. **VP** 97/2 ~(revelavit).

flāh *aj* hostile. **Ep** 510 flach (infestus); Ef, Cp §.

gemāh *aj* importunate. **Ep** 519 gimach (improbus); Ef ge§; Cp ~. **Bd**[2] 38 ðæm gemaum (inprobis).

gemālicnis *sf* importunity. **VP** 9/22 ~issum (†opportunitatibus).

tāhe *sf* toe. **Cp** 141 tahae (allox).

āgan *vb* possess. **Rn** 16 (he) ah. **Ct** 45/14 (heo) age.

āgen *aj* own. **VH** 1/10 his agnum sweorde (ipsius). **Ct** 41/16 ~.

āgnettan *wv* appropriate. **Ep** 1096 agnaettae (usurpavit); Ef ~etæ; Cp ~ette.

hrāgra *sm* heron. **Ep** 42 ~ (ardea et dieperdulum); Ef, Cp, Ld §.

þrāg *sf* space of time. **Cp** 1064 ~e (interim).

ā-stāg *prt* ascended, discended. **VP** 17/9, 11; 46/6; 67/5, 34; 77/21, 31 ~(ascendit). 73/23 ~(†§at). 71/6; 132/2, 2 ~(discendit).

ofdūne-stāg *prt* discended. **VP** 17/10 ~(discendit).

wāg-ryft Cp; §rift **VP.** wagflecta Cp.

fāg *aj* variegated. **Ep** 61 faag (arrius); Ef, Cp §. Cp 841 § (farius).

fagwyrm VP.

drop-fāg *aj* drop-spotted. **Ep** 924 ~faag (stornus); Cp §; Ef †drofaxg.

hring-fāg *aj* ring-(circle-)variegated. **Ep** 798 ~faag (polimita); Cp §; Ef hrnig§. 984 ~faag (tonica polimita, a rotunditate circulorum); Cp §; Ef †hrinfag.

spec-faag *aj* speckled. **Cp** 22 ~(maculosus).

hnāg *prt* bowed. **Rn** 2/14 h(n)a*g*.

āte *sf* oats. **Ep** 599 atae (lolium); Ef atte; Cp ~. Cp 248 atę (avena). 291 § (bena).

ātor *sn* poison. **Ep** 141 atr (bile); Cp §; Ef art. **VP** 13/3; 139/4 atur (venenum). Hy 11/9 § (§a).

aturlāðe Cp; atersatha Ld.

hāt *aj* hot.

hatheortnis VP.

hātian *wv* get hot. **Ep** 206 haetendae (calentes); Ef †hattendae; Cp ~ende. **VP** 38/4 ~ade (concaluit).

hātan *sv* call, name. **Rd** 12 ~. **Ct** 20/13 ~eð. 41/1 ic ~e. 42/1 ic ~o. 45/1 ic ~u.

gehātan *sv* promise. **VP** 75/12 ~að (vovete).

gehāt *sn* promise. **VP** 64/2; 131/2 ~(votum). 55/9 ~e ðinum (promissione). 21/26; 49/14; 55/12 *etc* ~(vota). Hy 12/5 ~um.

slāt *prt* tore. **Cp** 433 sclat (carpebat).

tō-slāt *prt* tore. **VP** 77/13, 5 ~(interrupit). 104/41; 106/14 ~(disrupit).

smāt *prt* smeared. **Cp** 1121 ~(impingit).

wāt *vb* know. **Rd** 3 uuat ic. **VP** 36/18; 43/22 *etc* (novit). 72/11 ~ (scivit). 102/14 ~(scit). 88/16 wæt(§).

gewāt *prt* departed. **Cp** 576 geuuatu (concessit). **VP** 43/19 ~(recessit).

wlātung *sf* nausea. **Ep** 667 uu~ (nausatio, vomitus); Ef uulating; Cp uulatunc.

clāte *sf* burdock. **Ep** 144 ~ae (blitum); Ef, Cp ~. Ld 45 ~(lappa). Cp 2066 ~(tubera).

gāt *sf* goat. **Ep** 1028 ~a loc (titule); Cp §; Ef ~an loc.

Gata-tūn Ct.

firgen-gāt *sf* mountain goat. **Ld** 49 firgingata (hibicum).

tāt *aj*.

Tatberct LV. **Tatfrid** BH; §frith LV. **Tathāeth** LV. **Tathelm** LV. **Tatheri** LV. **Tathysi** LV. **Tatmonn** LV. **Tatnōð** Ct. **Tatsuīð** LV. **Tatuini** BH, LV; §us Gn; ~uuinus Ct. **Tatuulf** LV.

Tāte *sf* BH 75 ~ae *nom.* — ~ę 1. LV 28 ~ae.

Tātan-edisc Ct.

ād *s(m)* funeral pile. **Ld** 95 aad (rogus).

Ād-hysi LV.

ādl *sf* disease. **Lr** 73 ald (langor). Bd[2] 50 fulre ~e (peste). **VP** 102/3 aðle (languores).

lencten-ādl *sf* spring-fever. **Ep** 999 †lectin~ (tertiana); Ef lenctin~; Cp §ald.

-hād. wǣpned~.

Hāda *sm.* **LV** 258 ~.

gerād *sn* arrangement, condition. **CA** 11 to ðæm ~e ðæt.

brand-rād *s* **Ep** 4 ~(andeda); Ef brond~; Cp bran[d]rod; Ld †brondra.

hwēol-rād *sf* rut. **Ep** 710 huueol~ (orbita); Ef hueolraat; Cp §rád.

strēam-rād *sf* bed of stream. **Ep** 88 ~(alveus); Ef streum ~; Cp ~raad.

ðunur-rād *sf* thunder. **VP** 76/19 ~e ðinre (tonitrui). 103/7 § *g.*

Gen-lād *sf* Inlade. **BH** 345 *fluminis* ~ae. Ct 50/2 ~.

lād-tow VP.

Snād-hyrst C.

Theodoice-snād Ct 25/5 *silvam quem ~ nominamus.*

ā-scādan *sv* separate. **Bl** 1 þem ~ endum (inseparunt).

tō-scādan *sv* separate, distinguish. **VP** 42/1 toscad (discerne!). 49/4 ~e (§eret). 67/15; 81/1 ~eð (§it). 67/10 ~ende (segregans).

giscaduuyrt Ep; ge§ Cp; gescan§ Ef.

Wād-beorg Cp.

gemād *aj* mad. **Cp** 2105 gemaad (vecors).

Cāda *sm* **LV** 267 ~.

gād *sf* goad. **Cp** 1937 gaad (stiga).

grād *s* step. **VP** 47/4 ~um (gradibus).

pād *s* cloak. **Ep** 779 paad (praetersorim); Ef, Cp §. Cp 1676 § (praetersorium).

bād *prt* waited, expected. **VP** 54/9 ~(expectabam). 55/7; 68/21 ~(§avit).

ā-bād *prt* awaited. VP 39/2 ~(expectavi).

bād *s(f)* expectation. VP 38/8 ~(expectatio).

Badhelm LV [or = beadu§ ?].

Bāda *sm.* LV 85; 472 ~.

brād *aj* broad. Ct 3/6, 6 ~an leage.

braedlaestuaesc Ef; braadlaastęcus Cp; bradacus Ld. Bradeburne Ct. bradaelēac Ep; bradelec Ef; §laec Cp.

weg-brāde *sf* plantain. Ep 65 uuegbradae (arniglosa); Ef uegbradae; Cp ~. 793 uuaegbradae (plantago vel septenerbia); Ef uuegbradæ; Cp uueg~.

gebrādian broaden. VP 47/3 ~ende (dilatans).

braad-ponne Cp.

Brāda *sm* LV 471 ~.

rāp *sm* rope. VP 104/11; Hy 7/16 ~(funiculum). 77/54 ~e (§o). 15/6; 118/61; 139/6 ~as (funes).

met-rāp *sm* measuring-rope, sounding-line. Cp 319 ~, sundgerd in scipe (bolides).

bi-swāpen *ptc* clothed. VP 103/2 ~(amictus).

on-suāpen *ptc* clothed. Cp 1143 ~(instincta).

ymb-swāpen *ptc* clothed. VP 44/10, 5 ~(circumamicta).

gegrāp *prt* seized. VH 5/25 ~(adpraehendit).

grāpian *wv* feel, grope. Bd[2] 82 ~ade (adtrectat). VP 113/7 (2); 134/17 ~iað (palpabunt).

Sāba *sm* BH 70 ~ — sæba II [æ *from* a?].

sǣ *smf* sea. Mt 51 on sǽ. Bd[2] 56 ðæs ~s (pelagi). VP 68/35; 77/53 *etc* sae (mare *n*). 103/25 ðis § (hoc §). Hy 5/16 sæ [*from* m]. 97/7 sę. 65/6; 73/13 *etc* § *a*. 105/9 § ðon readan. 135/13 ðone readan §. Hy 5/37 ðorh midne sę [ne *on er.*] 88/13 sæ. 64/6 in sae (§i); 71/8, 8 from § oð § (§i..§e) *etc*. 105/7; Hy 5/6 in ðere readan §. 105/22; 135/15 in ðæm readan §. Hy 5/14 in midre §. 8/9, 9; 68/3 saes (§is). 32/7; 45/3; 64/8 sæs *etc* (§is). Hy 5/36 sae (§is). 23/2 sęas (§ia). Hy 8/12 sae (§ia). 92/4 †hæs (§is). Ct 20/9, 22 oð sǽ; to sǽ.

Saebald, §§ing Gn. Saberct, sae§ BH; sae§ LV; saberht, §§ing SG; sebearht Ct. Sefreð, sæ§ Ct. Saefugul, §fugling Gn. Saegȳþ LV. Saerēd LV. saegesetu Ep, Ef, Cp. †haesualwe Cp. Saeðrȳð BH, LV, Ct. Saeuald LV. Saeuini LV.

wīd-sǣ *smf* open sea. VH 5/7 ~sae (pelago).

wǣ *interj* woe! VP 119/5 ~(heu).

Wǣ *s* Ct 26/6 *villa qui dicitur* on uueę.

mǣ *av* more. VP 9/39; Hy 3/4 mae (ultra). 50/4; 61/3; 82/5; 87/6; 102/16 § (amplius). 51/5; 83/11 § (magis). 38/14 męe (amplius). 73/9 mę: (§). Ct 38/4 ma.

Mae-suith LV [= mægen§ ?].

in-gae *prs* enter. VP 72/17 ~(intrem).

ǣr *av, prp* before. BDS 3 aer. Mt 45 ~. VP 54/20 ~ weorulde (ante). 71/5 *etc* ~ monan (§). 77/34 ~ lehte (§). Hy 13/6 ~(§ *av*). Hy 4/9 ~ (prius). 73/12 aer. Ct 38/9 er ðonne. 42/17 ~ *av.*

ærmargen [*under* morgen] VP.

ær-ðon VP.

ǣrest *aj* first. Ct 45/5 et ęrestan.

ǣrest *av* first. CH 5 aerist. Rd 2 § [or aerest?]. SG 11 ~. Ct 20/3; 41/3 ~. 42/4 ærist. 48/10 aerist.

ǣra *sm* scraper. Cp 1935 aera (strigillus) [*see* ǣren].

ǣren *aj* brazen. Cp 1935 aeren screop (strigillus). VP 17/35 ærenne (†aereum). 106/16 ða ęrnan (aereas).

rǣran *wv* raise. CA 11 ~að.

ā-rǣran *wv* raise. VP 112/7 araerende (erigens).

ūp-rǣran *wv* raise up. VH 4/15 ~ende (eregens).

lǣran *wv* teach. VP 33/12; 131/12 ~u (docebo). 93/12; 118/171 ~es. 17/35 ~ed (docet). 93/10; 143/1 ~eð. 24/4, 5 lær (educe! doce!). 118/12, 26, 64, 6, 8, 108, 24, 35 § (doce!). 17/36 lærde (§uit). 104/22; Hy 7/22 § (doceret; §ebat). 70/17 §es. 118/99 ~ende (§entes). 50/15 lęru. 24/9 lerąð.

gelǣran *wv.* VP 2/10 bioð ~de (erudimini). 93/12 ~es (§ieris). 104/22 ~de (erudiret).

gelǣred *aj* learned. VP 89/12 gelærde (eruditos).

ðǣre *dat fem.* Cp 820 ðare getyhtan (exercitatae). Rn 4/4; 11/3 der saule. BDS 1 there. CA 7 ~. DA 3 ~. Mt 14, 28, 43 ~. VP 13/6; 15/8, 11 *etc* ðere. 18/12; 26/7; 74/4; 103/20 *etc* § (illā; quā; eā; ipsā). 59/7; 86/4 *etc* dere. 26/11; 109/1 ðe. Ct 20/8, 8, 19; 37/30; 42/7; 45/55 ~. 37/8; 48/9, 18 ðaere. 37/3, 31, 4, 41; 42/5 ðere. 39/10 ðare [ðære?] 45/11 þare.

ðǣre *gen fem.* DA 8 ðaere. Mt 12, 33 ~. VP 32/12; 121/3 ðere (cujus). Ct 48/20 ðaere.

mann-ðwǣre *aj* gentle, humane. VP 146/6 mon~ (mansuetos). 149/4 §ðuęre (§os). 24/9 ða §ðuęran. 36/11 ða §ðuaeran. 33/3 ða §ðueran.

monðwǣrnis *sf* gentleness. VP 89/10 ~ðuęrnis (mansuetudo). 44/5 ~ðwernisse (§inem). 131/1 alre ~ðuernisse (§inis).

geðwǣrian *wv* agree. VP 36/21 geðwaerað (commodat). 36/26 geþwærað (§). 111/5 geðwærað (§).

swǣr *aj* sluggish. Cp 633 suuęr (desis).

æt-gǣre *sn* javelin. Ep 440 aetgaeru (framea); Cp æt§; Ef aetgaru. Cp 167 aetgaere (ansatae). 839 †ægtęro (falarica).

glǣr *s* amber. Cp 1958 glaeres (sucini).

in-ǣlan *wv* set fire to. VP 96/3 inaeleð (inflammabit). 9/23 bið inælled [*second* l *dotted out*] (incenditur). 79/17 inaeled (incensa).

on-ǣlan *wv* set fire to. VP 77/21 onaeled is (accensus est). 78/5 bið § (accenditur). 77/38 onælde (†§et). 17/9 onęlde sind (succensi sunt).

hǣl *s* omen. Cp 1444 hael (omen).

hǣlsian *wv* take omens. Cp 251 haelsadon (auspicantur).

hǣlsend *sm* augurer. Cp 805 haelsent (extipices).

hǣlsere *sm* augurer. Cp 253 haelsere (augur).

hǣlu *sf* health, salvation. VP 3/3, 9; 19/7 *etc* haelu (salus). 37/4, 8; Hy 6/18 § (sanitas). 34/3; 59/13 hælu (salus). 107/13 hęlu (§). 13/7 *etc* haelu (salutare *a.*). 20/2; 41/6, 12 § ðine (§) *etc.* 66/3 § ðin (§). 84/8; 97/2 hælu' (§). 11/6 hęlu (§). 9/16; 12/6 haelu ðinre (§i); 21/2 § minre (salute) *etc.* 131/16 mid hælu (salutare *abl*). 17/3, 36 haelu minre, § ðinre (salutis) *etc.* Hy 13/13 ure § (§is). 50/16; 88/27; Hy 9/2, 13 hælu (§is). 17/47 hęlu (§is). 32/17; 37/23; 87/1 halu. Ct 37/5 fore..hela.

hǣlan *wv* heal, save. VP 6/3; 40/5 hael (sana!). 58/3 hæl (salva). 102/3; 146/3 haeleð (sanat). Hy 13/29 §e (cures).

gehǣlan *wv* heal, save. VH 7/77 gehaelu (sanabo). 33/19; 43/7 §eð (salvabit). 43/4 ~eð (§). 59/4 gehael (sana!). 97/1; 106/20 §de (salvavit; sanavit). 29/3, 4 §des (§asti, salvasti). 32/16 bi(ð) gehęled (§atur).

hǣlend *sm* Saviour. DA 3 haelende *d.* Mt 46 ~e crist! VP 24/5 haelend (salvator). Hy 2/3 hęlend (§). Hy 2/6 haelendes (§oris). Hy 6/39 §e (Ihesu).

ungehaelendlic *aj* incurable. VH 7/48 ~ (insanabilis).

ungehaeledlic *aj* incurable. VH 7/65 ~ (insanabilis).

þwǣle *sf* (?) towel. Ep 1060 thuelan; Ef, Cp § (vittas). Cp 1991 ðuaelum (taenis).

on-sǣlan *wv* unbind. Cp 634 onsaelid (desolutus).

ofer-stǣlan *wv* confute, convict. Ep 192 obaer[s]taelendi (convincens); Ef oberstęlendi; Cp §staelende. 194 obaerstaelid (convicta); Ef oberstaelid; Cp §ed. Cp 588 oberstaelid (confutat).

un-mǣle *aj* Cp 2143 ~o (virgo).

ā-gǣlan *wv* hinder. Cp 40/23 agele.

dǣl *sm* part. Ep 731 sume daeli (partim); Cp §; Ef dæli. Cp 548 gelimplice daele (conpetentes portiunculas). VP 10/7; 15/5; 72/26; Hy 7/16 dael (pars). 118/57; 141/6 § (portio). 49/18 ðæl (portionem). 62/11 daelas (partes).

daelniomende LP, VP; dælniomenis VP.

ēast-dǣl *sm* East. VP 102/12 ~dael (oriens). 67/34 §e. 74/7 ~dęle.

norð-dǣl *sm* North. VP 88/13 ~(aquilonem). 47/3 †noðdaeles. 106/3 ~dęle.

sūð-dǣl *sm* South. VP 125/4 ~daele (austro).

west-dǣl *sm* West. VP 74/7 ~e (occidente). 102/12 ~daele (occasu).

dǣlan *wv* divide, distribute. VH 5/14 daellu (partibo).

gedǣlan *wv* Ct 34/14 (he) gedæle. 45/31 gedęle. 37/31; 41/31 gedele.

tō-dǣlan *wv* divide. Cp 675 todaeldum (dilotis). VP 107/8 todaelu (dividam). Hy 7/13 §eð. 16/14 todael (dispertire!). 47/14 §að (distribuite). 65/14 §an. 77/54; 135/13 todaelde (divisit). 105/33 § (distinxit). 21/19 §un. Hy 5/12 todaeled is. 59/8 todęlu. 65/14 todęldun (distinxerunt). 105/34 § (disperdiderunt).

tō-dǣlnis *sf* division. VP 135/13 ~isse (divisiones).

ǣlc *prn* each. VP 38/6, 12; 77/51; 115/11; 127/4; 144/16, 21; 150/6; Hy 13/8 ylc (omnis *etc*). 44/18; 147/20 §re. 102/22 §ere. 104/36 §es. 104/36 oelc. Ct 39/2, 12 elce. 40/4 ęlce. 41/29, 32, 2 ælce, §um, §§.

hǣþ *s*(*n*) heath. Ef 269 haeth (calomacus); Cp haet; Ld het. Ep 1007 haeth; Ef haedth; Cp haet.

Haeðberct LV. haetcolae Cp. **Haethfeld**, hæth§, haet§ BH.

Bēd-hǣþ *sm* LV 114 ~haeth.

Beorht-hǣþ *sm* LV 155; 313, 4 bercthaeð. 285; 311, 63 §th. Ct 33/6 berhthæð.

Beorn-hǣþ *sm* LV 3 ~haeth. 274 ~haeð. Ct 48/16 ~haeð.

Bil-hǣþ *sm* LV 169; 205, 79; 334, 53, 72 ~haeth. 227 bilaeth.

Cēol-hǣþ *sm* LV 100 ~haeth.

Dǣd-hǣþ *sm* LV 184 dedhaeth.

Ēad-hǣþ *sm* BH 219 ~haedum—~hedum—~haedum I, II. 271 ~haed—~haet I. 272 ~haedum—~hedum—~[h]aedum. 273 ~haed—~hed. 274 ~haedum—~hędum. 377 ~haeth—~haet I. LV 173; 448 ~haeð. 261, 1, 81; 420, 2 ~haeth. Gn 43 ~haeð.

Eald-hǣþ *sm* LV 54; 119 aldhaeth.

Peoht-hǣþ *sm* LV 334, 5 pecthaeth.

Sige-hǣþ *sm* LV 204 sighaeth.

Tāt-hǣþ *sm* LV 123 ~haed. 175; 378 §th.

Taþ-hǣþ *sm* LV 164 taðhaeð.

Tīd-hǣþ *sm* LV 136; 247 ~haeth. 443 ~haeð.

Til-hǣþ *sm* LV 183; 336 ~haeth.

Torht-hǣþ *sm* LV 344 torcthaeth.

Weren-hǣþ *sm* LV 334 uerenhaeth.

Wīg-hǣþ *sm* LV 117 uighaeð. 256 §haeth.

Wiht-hǣþ *sm* LV 60 uichthaeth. 226, 56 uict§.

Wil-hǣþ *sm* LV 264; 419 uilhaeth. 473 uilhaeð.

Wulf-hǣþ *sm* LV 10, 86; 139; 304, 48, 68, 9; 475 uulfhaeth.

Hǣþe *sm* LV 196 haethi. 341 haeði.

hǣþen *aj* heathen. CA 4 haeðnum. Mt 44 hæðnan.

hǣþen-nis *sf* heathendom. CA 7 in ðære haeðenesse.

Maeth-cor LV. **Maeðhelm** LV.

in-mǣðle *sf* recklessness. Ep 549 inmaethlae (incuria); inmedlæ Ef; inmaeðle Cp.

gǣð *prs* goes. VH 6/10 ~(ibit). Ct 20/9 ~.

gǣst *prs* VP 43/10 ~(egredieris).

fore-gǣð *prs* goes before. VP 96/3 ~gęð (praeibit).

in-gǣð *prs* goes in. VP 78/11 ~(intret). 14/2 ingęð (ingreditur). 87/3 § (intret). 23/7, 9 ingaeð (introibit). 36/15 § (intret). 48/20 § (introibit).

ūt-gǣð *prs* goes out. VP 103/23; 145/4 utgaeð (exiet). 108/7 § (exeat). Hy 6/11 § (exibit).

fore-gǣst *prs* goest before. VH 9/12 ~(praeibis).

in-gǣst *prs* enterest. VP 31/8 ~(ingredieris).

ofer-gǣst *prs* traversest. VP 67/8 ~(transgredieris).

ūt-gæst *prs* goest out. VP 59/12 ut ne gæst (egredieris). 67/8 ~. 107/12 ut ne gęst.

Ecg-baeth *sm* LV 169 ~.

Til-baeth *sm* LV 174 ~.

lǣððu *sf* hatred, dislike. VP 24/19 laeððu (odio). 108/5 § (§ium *a*). 108/3 ~(§ii). 35/3 laeðu (§ium).

Ǣsica *sm*. BH 261 ~. Ct 5/7 aesica (aessica).

on-rǣs *sm* rushing on, assault. VP 45/5 onraes (impetus). Hy 6/17 ~(§).

rǣsan *wv* rush. Cp 1120 raesde (inruit).

on-rǣsan *wv* rush on. VP 58/4 ~dun (inruerunt). 61/4 onraesað.

lǣs *av* less.

nā-les *av* not. VP 6/2; 21/20; 37/2 *etc* ~(ne). 43/4 ~(nec). 9/19; 16/1; 21/3 *etc* ~(non). 113/1 (2) nalas (§).

ðȳ-lǣs *cj* lest. VP 33/14; 58/12 [y *from* u]; Hy 7/54 ~(ne). Hy 12/12 ~(nec). 2/12 ðylęs. 7/3 ðyles.

lǣssa *aj* less. VP 8/6 hwoene laessan (paulo minus *a*.) 93/17 ~an (§). 118/87 lęssan (§).

flǣsc *sn* flesh. Cp 2135 gebreded flaesc (viscera tosta). VP 72/26; 77/39 ~(caro). 101/6 ~e. Hy 13/7 ~es. 26/2; 77/27; 104/40; 118/120 ~(carnes). 37/8 flaesce. 15/9; 27/7; 62/2 flęsc (caro). 135/25 §e. 49/13; Hy 7/83 flęsc (carnes). 83/3; 108/24; 144/21 flesc. 37/4 §e.

lǣstan *wv* perform. Ct 40/21; 45/32 lestan. 42/16 leste *sbj prs*.

gelǣstan *wv* accompany, carry out, perform. Cp 574 to gelestunne (comitavere). Ct 41/70 ~e *sbj prs*. 41/66 gelęsten. 45/50 §an.

forð-lǣstan *wv* perform, supply. Ct 40/20 ~leste *sbj prs*.

geðrǣstan *wv* (twist), afflict. VP 146/3 geðręste (contritos).

ā-ðrǣstan *wv* twist out. Ef 358 ath[r]aestae (extorti); Cp aðręsti.

for-ðrǣstan *wv* afflict. VP 9/36 ~ðræst (contere). 3/8 §es (§uisti). Hy 5/4 §ende (§ens). 104/16 ~ðręste (contrivit). 47/8 §ende (conterens). 36/17 sien §eð. 123/7 §ed is. 33/21 bið ~dręsted. Hy 3/9 fordręste (contrivit). Hy 5/10 §es (conteruisti). 57/7 ~þręsteð. 104/33 ~ðreste (contrivit). 36/15 bið forðrested. 50/19 ~ðrested. 106/16 ~dreste (contrivit). Hy 13/16 §ende (conterens). 45/10 ~þreste [þ *from* w] (conteret).

forðrǣstednis *sf* contrition. VP 13/3 ~ðręstednis (contritio). 146/3 ~ðręstnisse. 59/4 ~ðrastnisse.

wrǣstan *wv* twist. Ep 499 úura[e]stendi (indruticans); Ef uraesgendi; Cp wraestendi [i *over* e].

mǣst *aj* most. VP 18/14 ðere ~an (maximo). Ct 37/26 maest. 38/12; 42/22 mest.

ǣw *sf* law. VP 18/8 ęew (lex). 36/31 ae (§). 118/72, 7, 85, 92, 174 aee (§). 118/142 ææ (§). 24/8; 26/11; 77/5; 104/45; 118/33, 4, 44, 53, 5, 7, 61, 70, 97, 104, 9, 13, 26, 53, 63 aee (legem). 24/12; 70/4; 118/136 ęe (§). 39/9 ae ðine (§). 77/1; 88/31 ae mine (§). 83/8; 118/102 ae (§). 77/10; 118/1 aee (§e). 118/29 § ðinre (§e). 129/4 fore § ðinre (§em). 118/18, 150 ęe ðinre (§e). 93/12 ae ðinre (§e). 9/21 aee (§is).

hǣwe *aj* blue. Ep 221 haeuui (cerula); Ef haui; Cp heawi. 473 hęuui *vel* grei (glaucum); Ef hauui *vel* grei; Cp heauui grei. Ld 62 haue (aeri).

hauiblāuum Ef.

-hǣwen *aj* Ld 64 syitor heuuin (iacynthini).

mǣw *s*(*m*) mew, sea-gull. Ep 610 †men (laris); Ef meu; Cp meau. Cp 135 § (alcido). 955 me[a]u (gabea).

ǣfre *av* ever. VP 7/3 ðyles ~(ne quando). 12/4 ne ~(ne unquam). 12/5; 90/12; 139/9; Hy 13/19 ne ~(ne quando).

nǣfre *av* never. Mt 42 ~.

ǣnig any. Ep 845 aengi þinga (quoquomodo); Ef §; Cp aenge. LP 12 ~. Mt 50 ~re. VP 87/12 ~(aliquis *subst*). 33/11 ængum (omni). Ct 41/7 ~. 48/18 aenig. 38/11 enig.

nǣnig none. Cp 1397 naenge (nullo). BDS 1 naenig. CA 16 ~. Bd[2] 31 ~. VP 138/16; Hy 13/24 ~(nemo). Ct 34/16, 6 ~; nænge. 38/4 neniggra.

ǣnli *aj* simple. Ld 156 aenli (simplex).

lǣn *s* loan. Ct 45/46 on lęne.

of-ðwǣnan *wv* moisten. Cp 1297 obðaenit (madidum).

gescǣnan *wv* shatter. VP 28/6 ~eð (comminuet). 67/22 § (conquassavit). 109/6 ~æð (§abit).

stǣnen *aj* stone. Ct 25/4 æt †stęnan steaple.

ā-stǣnan *wv* adorn. Cp 1931 ~aenid (stellatus).

wrǣne *aj* lascivious. Ep 835 uuraeni (petulans, spurcus); Ef ureni; Cp wraene. Cp 81 § (ad libidines).

gemǣne *aj* common. Ct 31/3; 45/4 gemene. 8 §um. 37/23 gemęnum.

gemǣnnis *sf* community. VH 13/8 ~isse (contubernium *a*).

clǣne *aj* clean, pure, chaste. CA 5 claene *instr*. 5 ~ *instr*. VH 12/7, 11 clęne, ~(castus). Hy 11/8 clęne (§os). 11/7 gesprec ~(§a *pl*). 50/12 heortan ~ (§um *a*). 23/4 clænre (mundo). Ct 37/17 clenra.

clǣnnis *sf* purity, chastity. VH 11/12 clęnnes (pudor). Ct 41/9, 14 clennisse. 45/11 mid ðare clęnnisse.

clǣsnian *under* ā.

Iaenberht Gn, Ct; iaem§ Ct. **Gænburg** Ct.

tǣnel *s* basket. Ep 403 taenil (fiscilla); Cp §; Ef tenil.

stic-tēnel *s* basket. Cp 872 ~.

elpan-bǣnen *aj* ivory. VP 44/9 ~baennum (eburneis).

wrǣnna *sm* wren. Cp 301 werna (birbicariolus).

Bīohha-hǣm *s* Ct 29/14 ~hema mearcę.

Liofs-hem *s* Ct 29/3 bromleaginga mearc ⁊ ~a.

Mōdinga-hem *s* Ct 29/5 ~a mearce.

Wic-hæm *s* Ct 29/12, 3 ~amearcę, wichema §.

Hanchemstede Ct. **Netelhæmstyde** Ct.

Haem-gils BH, LV.

hǣmed *sn* copulation, marriage. Cp 1036 hęmedo (hymeneos). Ct 41/15 oðer hemed *a*.

unreht-hǣmdere *sm* adulterer. VP 49/18 ~um (adulteris).

ðǣm *dat sg*. CA 9, 11 ~. DA 9 ~. VP 3/5; 5/8; 9/39, 9 *etc* ~. 35/8 *etc* to ~ gemete (quemadmodum). 19/10; 31/2 ~(quā, cui) *etc*. Hy 2/6 ~(illā). 26/1 dæm (quo). 138/9 ðęm [*from* ðęre]. Ct 20/12, 3, 7, 9; 34/13; 40/19; 41/59; 42/6 ~. 37/16; 48/3, 6 ðaem. 37/26; 45/26, 35, 7, 47 ðęm. 45/51 þęm. 28/5, 24, 5, 5; 30/7; 37/6; 38/9; 39/1, 2; 40/3; 41/13, 6, 9, 37; 45/18, 34, 40 ðem. 45/17 þem. 29/4, 4, 15 ðam.

ðǣm *dat pl*. Bl 1 þem. Mt 20 ~. Bl[2] 12, 29 *etc* ~. VP 9/29; 16/8; 17/18 *etc* ~. 31/9 ~(quibus). 89/15 dæm (§). 7/5 ðaem. Ct 41/59; 42/8 ~. 37/27; 47/10 ðaem. 41/66; 45/16 ðęm. 28/22, 3, 4; 39/2, 13, 39, 40; 40/6, 17; 41/29, 64 ðem. 45/11 þem. 3/9 ðam.

hwǣm *dat sg* whom. VP 38/7 ~(cui).

deghwæmlice VP.

gehwǣm *dat sg* to each. Pr 2 †gahuem.

fǣmne *sf* virgin. DA 9 ðaere faemnan *g*. VP 44/15 fęmnan (virgines). 77/63 faemnan (§). 148/12 †fęmman(§). Hy 7/51; Hy 13/8 ~an (§ine).

clǣman *wv* plaster. Cp 1433 claemende (offirmans).

for-clǣman *wv* Cp 1419 folclaemid (obturat). 1446 forclaemde (opilavit).

bǣm *dat* both. Ct 34/10 ~. 38/5 boem.

gerǣcan *wv* reach, attain. Ct 42/17 gerece.

-lǣca

scin-lǣca *sm* wizard. Ep 681 ~laecean; Ef ~lecan; Cp ~laecan (nebulonis).

lybb-lǣca *sm* wizard. Cp 408 lyblaecan (caragios).

genēa-lǣcan *wv* approach. VP 63/7 to geneolaeced (accedit). 90/7 to ne §eð (adpropiabit). 90/10 §eð (§). 31/6 §að (adproximabunt). 54/19; 90/10 to ne geniolaecað (adpropiant; accedent). 106/18 to §laehtun (adpropiaverunt). 140/4 genehlaecu (combinabor). 31/9 to ne ~að (adproximant). 33/6 to §(accedite!).

tō-nēalǣcan *wv* approach. VP 26/2 toneolicað (adpropiant). 87/4 §laeceð (§abit). 118/150 §laehton (§averunt). 148/14 §laecendum (§anti). 118/169 toniolaeceð (§et). Hy 6/3 §að (§averint). 54/22 tonialaehte (§avit). 37/12 †tolehlaecað (†§averunt).

fǣcne *aj* deceitful. Ep 938 faecni (subscivum); Ef §; Cp †fraecni. Cp 2112 faecnum (veterno). VP 11/3, 4; 30/19 weolure faecne (dolosa). 54/24 ða §an. 16/1 §um. 5/7 ðone ~an. 51/6; 108/3; 119/2, 3 faecenre. 42/1 facnum. 108/2 ðes §an.

un-fǣcne *aj* undeceitful. Ep 679 unfaecni (non subscivum); Cp §; Ef unfecni.

fǣcenlice *av* deceitfully. Cp 926 faecenlice (fraudulenter). VP 5/11; 35/3 faccen~ (dolose). 13/3; 34/20 faecen~ (§).

tǣcnan *wv* point out. Ep 544 taecnaendi (index); Ef §endi; Cp tacnendi.

fǣhan *wv* paint. Ep 785 faehit (pingit); Cp §; Ef †faethit. 797 faedun (pangebant); Cp §; Ef †fædum.

ǣht *sf* property, possession. VP 134/4 aeht (possessionem). 104/21 alre §e(§ionis). 77/48 §e(§iones). Ct 34/11 to alre ~e. 12 ~e *d.*

on-ǣht *sf* possession. VP 2/8 ~e ðine (possessionem).

ǣg *sn* egg. Ct 37/20 aegera *gpl.*

aegergelu Ep. **aeggimang** Ep; Ef, Cp §. **aegmang** Cp.

ǣg-. oeghwelc, og§, aeg§, ęg§, eg§, ei§. oeghwǣr, og§.

stǣgel *aj* steep. Ep 747 staegilrae (praerupta); Cp §e; Ef stegelræ.

wǣgan *wv* deceive. Cp 860 uuegið (fefellit).

ā-wǣgan *wv* elude, frustrate. Ef 356 auęgdæ (eluderet); Cp auuægde. Ct 39/14 awege.

bi-wǣgan *wv* frustrate. VP 131/11 biwaegde (frustrabitur). Hy 13/24 ~ (fallere).

hwǣg *s* whey. Ep 979 huaeg (seru); Ef §; Cp ~ (serum). 982 huaeg (serum, liquor casei); Ef huuaeg.

gehnǣgan *wv* prostrate. Cp 1929 ~ith (sternit).

hnǣgung *sf* neighing. Cp 1024 hnaeggiung (hinnitus).

caeg-hiorde Cp.

Āeting-den Ct.

ǣtren *aj* poisonous. Ep 576 tha.. aetrinan (toxica); Cp §; Ef etrina[ni].

scult-heta *sm* bailiff. Cp 799 ~(exactor).

hǣtu *sf* heat. VH 8/8 haetu (caumas *n*). Hy 11/9 §(calore). 18/7 §o (§). Hy 7/18 §u (§oris).

hǣtan *wv* heat. Ep 206 haetendae (calentes); Ef hattendae; Cp hatende.

smǣte *aj* beaten. Cp 1401 smaete gold (obrizum); Ld ymaeti §.

hwǣte *sm* wheat. VP 64/14 ~(frumento). 80/17; 147/14 ~es. 4/8 hwętes. Hy 7/27 hwaetes (tritici).

HuętedūnCt. hwętewestemVP.

hwǣten *aj* wheaten. Ct 37/17 huaetenra.

nǣtan *wv* annoy. Ep 752 naetendnae (proterentem); Ef §; Cp §ne.

firgen-gǣt *pl* mountain-goats. Ep 560 firgingaett (ibices); Ef §; Cp ~gaet.

Tǣtica *sm.* LV 171 taetica.

fǣtt *aj* fat. VP 67/16 fęt (pinguis). Hy 7/29 faet. 21/13; 143/14 faette (§es).

fǣtnis *sf* fatness. VP 62/6 faetnisse (pinguedine). 140/7 §nes (crassitudo).

fǣttian *wv* fatten. VP 64/13 faettiað (pinguescent). 22/5 §ades (impinguisti). Hy 7/30 §ade (incrassavit).

gefǣttian *wv.* VP 19/4 gefaettie (pinguefiat).

gerǣdan *wv* arrange. Cp 669 geraedit (digesto).

ā-rǣdan *wv* arrange, settle. Ef 366 aręddun (expedierant); Cp araeddun. Ct 34/8 aræddan.

rǣden *sf* condition, terms. Ep 123 redisnae (bacidones); Ef rędisnae; Cp raedinne. 212 raedinnae (condiciones); Cp §enne (§ione); Ef redinnae. 1035 raedinnae (taxatione); Cp §e; Ef redinnae. Ct 41/43 an ðas redenne.

gefœr-rǣden *sf* fellowship. VP 44/8 gefoerraedennum (consortibus).

lǣdan *wv* lead. Mt 26 ~að. 43 ~ed. VP 67/19 laedde (duxit). 136/3 laeddun (§erunt).

gelǣdan *wv* lead. Mt 20 ~æddon. VP 54/24; 79/2 ~aedes (deduces; §is). 7/6; 44/5; 59/11 §eð *etc.* 59/11; 138/10 §ed (§it; §et). 5/9; 85/11; 118/35; 138/23 ~aed! 141/8 § ut (educ!). 77/72 ~aedde (deduxit). Hy 5/35 §(†induxit). 22/3; 77/13 ~aed[d]e (deduxit; per§). 77/52 ~aede (perduxit). 76/21 ~aeddes (deduxisti). 65/11 ~ęddes (induxisti). 72/24 ~aedes (deduxisti). 21/16 ~aeddon (deduxerunt). 42/3 ~aedon (§). 14/4 ~aeded bið. 30/18 sien gelędde.

ā-lǣdan *wv* lead away. VH 4/13 eft alaedeð (reducit). Ps 22/2 aledde (educavit). 70/20 alaedes (reduxisti). 135/16 alaedde (transduxit).

forð-lǣdan *wv* lead forth, bring forth. VP 68/32 ~lędende (producentem). 134/7 ~laedeð (§it). 146/8 ~eð (§it).

forð-gelǣdan *wv* lead forth, produce. VP 57/10 ~aeden (producant). 103/14 §es (§es). 131/17 §u (§am).

in-gelǣdan *wv* lead in, bring in. VH 5/30 ~aedes (induces). 77/26, 54 ~aedde (induxit). 65/12; 87/8 §es (§isti).

tō-gelǣdan *wv* lead to, bring. VP 124/5 ~aedeð (adducet). 71/10 §að (§ent). Hy 7/23 ~aedde (adduxit). 42/3 ~aeddon (adduxerunt). 44/15, 6 sien ~aeded (adducentur).

ūt-lǣdan *wv* lead out. VP 134/7 ~aedende (educens).

ūt-ālǣdan *wv* lead out. VP 30/5; 142/11 ~ędes; ~aedes (educes). 36/6; 67/7 ~ędeð. 103/14 ~æde (§at). 17/20; 39/3; 77/53 *etc* ~aedde (eduxit). 135/11 ~ædde. 77/14, 6; 104/43; 106/30 ~ędde. 77/16; 80/11 ~edde.

wið-lǣdan *wv* lead away, take away. VP 108/23 †~laedde eam (ablatus sum). 136/3 ~laeddun (abduxerunt). Hy 3/4 ~laeded is (ablata est).

ymb-lǣdan *wv* lead round. VH 7/19 ~laedde (circumduxit).

wiðlǣdnis *sf* leading away, abduction. VH 7/71 ~laednisse (abductione).

hlǣder *sf* ladder. Ld 16 hlędrę (trogleis).

snǣdan *wv* cut. Ld 249 snędit (putat).

snaedil *vel* thearm Ef; §þearm Cp; snedildaerm Ld; snędelðearm Lr.

gemǣded *aj* (*ptc*) foolish. Cp 1134 gemędid (ineptus). 2083 gemaeded (vanus).

bǣdan *wv* impel. Ep 539 baedendrae (inpulsore); Ef bedændræ; Cp baeden[d]rae. Cp 822 baedde (exactum).

Bǣda *sm* BH 1 baeda—beda I. 380 baeda—§—be:da. LV 98; 105, 67; 216, 78 beda. Gn 108 §.

Bēding *sm* son of B. Gn 108 ~.

Bǣde *sm* LV 432 baede.

Helm-bǣd *sm* LV 10 ~baed.

brǣdu *sf* breadth. VP 17/20; 117/5 braedu (latitudinem). 118/45 brędе (§e).

gebrǣdan *wv* dilate. VP 4/2; 118/32 gebręddes (dilatasti; §aris). 17/37 gebraeddes. 34/21 gebręddon. 24/17 §e sind. Hy 4/2 gebraeded is. Hy 7/30 gebreded wes.

ā-brǣdan *wv* dilate. VP 80/11 abraed (dilata!).

ymb-swǣpe *sf* digression. Cp 147 ~suaepe (ambages).

heorð-swǣpe *sf* hearth-sweeper, daughter-in-law. Cp 1660 ~suaepe (pronuba); Ld 73 herdusuepe.

swǣpels , *s* robe. VP 103/6 ~(amictus).

ǣ-. ecambe. erest [*under* i]. esuind. eswic. geebylgan, ebylgðu. egylt. espryng. ęmōd.

suǣ *av* so. Ep 843 suae suithae (quacumque); Cp §; Ef suue. 844 suae suithae (quantisper); Cp §; Ef suue. 865 suae haldae (reclines); Cp §; Ef †suuaeldae. Ld 133 suæ-ald (totus). CH 3 sue. Mt 35, 6, 47 suæ. VP 13/4; 34/14, 4 *etc* swe (sicut). 34/14, 4 *etc* §(ita). 103/35 § ðæt (§ ut). 103/33 § longe (quamdiu). 147/20 § (taliter). 47/9, 9; 102/13 § .. § (sicut .. ita). 77/40 § oft § (quotiens). 145/2 § longe § (quamdiu). 41/2 swę. Ct 37/26; 41/6, 15, 22, 3, 3, 3; 42/9, 11, 4, 21, 2 swæ. 34/10, 0, 4, 5, 5, 7, 20; 37/10 suæ. 37/31 swae. 25/4; 37/22, 5 suae. 42/10, 7 swę. 37/22 suę. 38/5; 40/9; 45/20, 7 swe. 28/14, 20; 30/6; 38/10, 0, 0, 3, 3; 39/14; 40/8 sue. 45/18, 8, 20, 7, 7, 7, 48, 9, 51, 2, 3 swa. 39/9 se. ?41/28, 31, 40 se.

swe-hwet VP. **swe hwelc** VP. **swēswē swe** VP. **suae-ðēh** Rd.

swǣ-swǣ *av* as. VP 2/9; 17/34 *etc* swe swe (tamquam). 5/13; 7/3 *etc* §(ut). 9/30; 10/2 *etc* §(sicut). 57/8; 72/20 *etc* §(velut). 72/7; 73/5 §(quasi). 102/15 sweswe .. swe (sicut .. ita). 118/85 swe .. sweswe (ita ut). 124/1 swe se munt sion (sicut mons Sion). 57/9; Hy 7/2 swe †sw (sicut).

frǣ-. fraehraed. fræcūð.

gǣ *av* yes. BH 337 gae, *id est etiam* — gea [ea *on* er] I.

ǣrende *sn* errand.

erend-wrica Bd²; §wrecan VP.

geǣrendian *wv* fulfill a commission. Cp 1986 gierende (taxaverat).

hǣr *sn* hair. Cp 1594 her (pilus). Rd 4 §um.

hēre *sf* hair-cloth. VP 34/13; 68/12 heran (cilicio; §ium *a*).

ðǣr *av* there. Rn 2/12, 8 þer. 3/7 þær. Mt 21, 4, 33 ~. VP 22/2; 35/13 ðer (ibi). 49/23 *etc* §(illic). 52/6, 6 § .. § (§ .. ubi). 13/5; 131/7 § (ubi). 138/10 § (illuc). 13/5 der (illic). Ct 20/5, 7, 8, 22 ~. 41/22 þær. 37/6, 7, 23 ðaer. 42/6 ðęr. 29/15; 30/6, 8; 41/41 ðer. 28/15 ðerto. 45/25, 9 þerto. 41/34, 5 ðeræt, §an.

wǣre *prt* were. VP 49/21 ic węre (ero) *etc.* 98/8 §(fuisti). Hy 13/1 §(eras). Hy 13/18 § gemeodemad (dignaveris). 54/13 spreocende §(locutus fuisset) *etc.* 136/1 we werun gemyndge (recordaremur). 54/4, 19 §(erant). 86/6 §(fuerant). 13/3 *etc* gewordne §(facti sunt). 89/2 weren (fierent). Ct 34/11; 38/6 (he) were. 48/17 werun. 37/7 wæron.

wǣr *sf* agreement, treaty. Lr 8 were trume (pactum). VP 118/158 § (§).

Węrbald, wær§, wer§ Ct. **Uerberct** LV. **Uerburg** LV; wér§, wer§ CA; wer§ Ct. **†Wǣr-feðes**, węrferð Ct. **wærgeld**, wer§ Ct. **Uergils** LV. **Uuaerheard**, uuær§, uuerhard Ct. **Uermund** LV, Gn; uær§, uęr§ Gn; uuer§, wer§ Ct; uærmunding Gn. **Wernōð**, uuer§, uuęr§ Ct.

hwǣr *av* where. VP 41/4, 11; 78/10 *etc* hwer (ubi).

gehwǣr *av* everywhere. Bd² 84 gewaer (parumper).

œg-hwǣr *av* everywhere. Ep 1061 oghuuaer (vulgo, passim); Ef oeghuuer; Cp §huer.

fǣr *s(m)* danger. Cp 419 fer (casus).

fērlice *av* suddenly. DA 12 ~.

fēring *sf.* Cp 1085 ~e (insimulatione).

fēringa *av* suddenly. Cp 1051 ~(improvisu). Mt 35 ~. VP 63/6; 72/19 ~(subito).

wudu-mǣr *sf* wood-nymph, echo. Ef 347 uuydumer (echo); Cp ~mer.

mǣre *aj* famous. Ep 737 mere uueard (percrebuit); Ef, Cp §. VP 80/4 §um (insigni).

Æðel-mǣr *sm.* Ct 4/5 aedilmaeri *g.*

Ēad-mǣr *sm* LV 136, 9, 57 ~er. 157 ~aer.

Ēo-mǣr *sm* Rn 4/1 ~(eomaer) BH 78 eumer. Gn 93 ea~.

Ēamǣring *sm* son of Ēomǣr. Gn 93 ~.

Haðu-mǣr *sm* LV 183; 331 ~mer.

Ōs-mǣr *sm* LV 200 ~maer.

Swīð-mǣr *sm* LV 99 suiðmer.

Wit-mǣr *sm* LV 219 uitmęr.

gemǣre *sn* boundary. VP 59/8 ~(convallem). 103/9 ~(terminum). 2/8; 71/8; 73/17 ~u (§os). 21/28 § (fines). 64/14 § ך dene (convalles). 60/3; 104/31 ~um (finibus). 58/14; 104/33 ~a (§ium).

gemærweges Ct.

gǣr *sn* year. Ep 494 thy̆s geri (horno); Ef §; Cp þys gere. Cp 1030 þys § (§). Rn 1/6 *gear*. Mt 33, 40 gear *pl.* 42 §um. SG 2 healf § *a.* 7, 8, 9 § *pl.* VP 64/12 geres (anni). 30/11; 60/7; 76/6 ger *pl.* 89/4, 10 *etc* §a. Ct 39/2, 12; 40/4; 41/29; 45/22, 40 gere.

Gerferð LV. Geruald LV. Geruini LV.

gērlic *aj* yearly. Ep 94 ~ae (annua); Ef †gern-licae; Cp ~e.

ā-bǣre *prt* bore. VP 54/13 abere (supportassem).

bǣr *s(f)* litter. Ep 137 beer (basterna); Ef, Cp §.

den-bēre *sn* swine-pasture. Ct 28/11 *pascua porcorum quot nostra lingua ~a nominamus.* 25/7; 30/9 §.

gebēru *pl* gestures. Ep 492 ~(habitudines); Ef, Cp §. Cp 775 ~o (exegestus). 957 §(gestus).

-bǣre. wæstembere; wæstembiornis.

ǣl *s(m)* eel. Cp 174 el (anguila). 1331 eil (morenula).

Ēlge *s* Ely. BH 293, 4 ~. 295 ~ *regio a copia anguillarum nomen accepit.*

lǣl- *s* weal. Cp 2136 lelan (vibice).

sǣlan *wv* happen. Ct 41/38, 9 sęle, ~eð.

gesǣlan *wv.* Ct 41/41 gesele.

un-gesēlignis *sf* unhappiness. VP 13/3 ~(infelicitas).

strǣl *s* curtain. Ep 9 strel (aulea, curtina); Cp stregl [g *over* a]. Cp 1907 strel (stragua).

strǣl *smf* arrow. Rn 2/15 strelum. BD[2] 34 §as (tela). VP 90/6 §e flegendum (sagittā). 7/14; 10/3; 56/5; 63/8 *etc* §as. 17/15; 37/3; 44/6 §e *pl.*

strelbora Ep; Ef, Cp §.

æt-fǣlun *sm* adhered. VP 101/6 ~felun (adheserunt).

ed-mǣle *sn* festival. Cp 1790 edmelu (sacra, orgia).

fōt-mǣlum *av* step by step. Ef 834 ~melum (pedetemptim *etc*).

stycce-mǣlum *av* piece by piece. Ep 751 ~imelum (particulatim); Cp §; Ef †sc§. Cp 1528 ~imelum (passim).

þrēat-mǣlum *av* troop by troop. Ep 617 threatmelum (manipulatim); Ef † theat§; Cp þreat§.

wearn-mǣlum *av* troop by troop. Cp 994 ~melum (gregatim).

tǣlan *wv* blame. VP 37/21; 108/4 teldon, §un (detrahebant), 49/20 §es. 70/13; 100/5 telende, §ne (§entes, §§em). Hy 7/49 §ra (trahentium). 108/29 telað. Hy 6/25 §es.

untelwyrðe VP.

tēlnis *sf* blaming. VP 30/14 ~isse (vituperationem).

bǣl *s* bonfire. Ef 1157 beel (bustum, ustrina). Ld 95 § (rogus).

ǣðre *spl* kidney. Cp 1731 heðir (renes). VP 7/10; 15/7; 25/2; 72/21; 138/13 eðre (renes). Hy 7/27 §a (§ium).

ǣðm *s(m)* breath. Ep 89 ethm (adlitus); Cp aethm. Cp 2083 §e (vapore).

nǣðl *s(f)* needle. Ep 796 mið naeðlae (acu); Ef nedlæ; Cp nethle. Cp 66 netl (acus).

wǣðl *s(f)* (poverty). Cp 1554 weðl (penuria).

wēðla *sm* pauper. VP 39/18 *etc* ~(egenus). 73/21 *etc* ~(inops). 34/10 *etc* ~an (inopem, egenum). 108/17 §(mendicum). 71/13 §(inopi). 13/6 § (§is). 11/6; 139/13 ~ena (inopum).

wēðelnis *sf* poverty, beggary. VP 43/24 wedelnisse (inopiam). 87/

10; 106/41 ~isse (§iā). 106/10 §(mendicitate).

wēðlian *wv* be in want, beg. VP 33/11 ~adon (eguerunt). 36/25 ~iende (egens). 108/10 ~ien (mendicent).

rǣsian *wv* consider, conjecture. Cp 1448 resigan (opinare). VP 118/39 resenðe ic eam (suspicatus sum).

rǣsung *sf* reasoning, conjecture. Ep 190 resung (conjectura); Ef, Cp §. Cp 1737 §e (retiunculas).

lǣs *sf* pasture. VP 22/2; 94/7; 99/3 leswe (pascuae *g*).

blōd-lǣs *s(f)* blood-letting, bleeding. Ct 41/67 to higna ~lese.

þrǣs *s* fringe. Ep 583 thres (lembum); Ef ðres. 705 t[h]res (oresta); Ef thres; Cp ðres. Cp 1228 §, liste (limbus). 1264 §i (lymbo).

swǣsend *snpl* dainties. Cp 108 suoesendo (agapem). Ct 37/14, 25 suesendum, suęsenda *pl*. 42/16 ~um.

cǣse *sm* cheese. Cp 912 cese (formaticus). Ct 37/19, 20 caeses, ~a. 39/4 cesa. 40/6; 41/30, 61 §es.

ceselyb Cp.

blǣs *s* torch. Cp 1993 blesum (tedis).

blǣst *s* blast.

blestbaelg Ep; § Ef; blaesbaelg, bloest§ Cp.

ǣfen *sm* evening. VH 3/7, 9 efen (vesperam). Ps 29/6; 54/18; 58/7, 15 *etc* efenne.

ēfenlic *aj* evening. VP 140/2 ~e (vespertinam).

Swǣf-

Suebdaeg, §ing Gn. **Suæbhard**, suęb§ BH. **Suefred** BH; sueb§ Ct.

for-gǣf- *prt* gave. VH 13/10, 21 ~gefe (donasti; §aris).

ā-wǣfon *prt pl* wove. Rd 9 auefun.

wǣfung *sf* spectacle. Cp 1818 uuebung (scena).

un-ǣmette *sf* want of leisure, occupation. Ep 680 unemotan (negotia); Ef †unemo; Cp une[me]tta.

aemetgian *wv* be at leisure. VP 45/11 ~iað (vacate).

lǣce *sm* leech, doctor. Ep 746 leceas (phisillos); Ef, Cp §. Ld 254 lecas (sanguessuges). VH 13/26 lece (medicus). Ps 87/11 §as (§i).

leciuuyrt Ep; Ef, Cp §.

hēa-lēce *sm* physician. Cp 218 ~as (archiatros).

lēce-dōm *sm* medicine. CA 13 ecum ~e. Ct 30/21 †leedome.

strǣc *aj* strenuous. VP 11/6 strece (strenuos).

sprǣcon *prt* spoke. VP 118/23 sprecun (loquebantur).

sprǣc *sf* speech, statement, document. Cp 1852 spręc (sermo). Ct 34/16 ðas †prece.

fore-sprēc *sf* preamble. Ct 45/43 ðeos ~.

felo-sprǣce *aj* loquacious. Ep 1009 ~spraeci; Ef felusp'ici (trufulus); Cp §spreci; Ld ~spric.

god-wrǣce *aj* wicked, impious. Cp 1829 ~uureci (scevum).

godwrēcniss *sf* impiety. Bd² 36 ~um (uaemonibus).

gebrǣc- *prt* broke. VP 73/14 gebrece (confregisti).

gebrǣc *s* phlegm. Ep 775 gibrec (pituita); Ef gibreec; Cp gebrec. 856 gibrec (reuma); Ef, Cp ge§. Cp 2152 gibrec (umecta); Ld gebyraet. Ld 180 gibreci (sicunia).

mēos-gelǣge *sn* moss-tract. Ct 10/2 ~gelegeo.

gesǣg- *prt* saw. VP 34/22; 49/18 gesege (vidisti; §ebas). 39/13; 62/3 §(viderem). 21/8; 30/12 *etc* §un (§ebant). 47/9 *etc* §un (§imus). 34/21 §an (§erunt). 96/6 †gesgun (§§). 40/7 gesegen (§erent).

fore-sēge *prt* foresawest. VP 138/4 ~(praevidisti).

wǣge *sf* weight, a certain measure of weight. Ct 37/20 uuęge. 40/6 II węga. 39/4, 5 wege. 41/30, 61 III §a, an †weg.

efen-wǣge *s* counterpoise. Cp 98 ebnwege (aequipensum).

gefǣg- *prt* rejoiced. VP 96/8; 97/8; 113/4 gefegun (exultaverunt).

mǣg *sm* kinsman. Ep 164 meeg (contribulus); Cp meig. Ct 39/6;

44/6; 45/28, 33, 8 mege. 41/16 §as. 45/2 §um. 40/7 §a. 41/18 męgas.

megoualm Cp. Meifrith LV. meihand, meg§ Ct. megsibbi Ep; Ef, Cp §. Meiuald LV. Meguine LV, Ct. Meguulf LV.

fæderen-mǣg *sm* paternal relative. Ct 45/18 fędrenmega.

mǣgð *sf* family, nation, country Mt 14 ðære ~e *d*.

grǣg *aj* grey. Ep 473 hęuui *vel* grei (glaucum); Ef hauui *vel* §; Cp heauui§. Cp 850 greig (feruginius). 967 grei (gillus).

gregōs Ef.

īsern-grei *aj* iron-grey. Cp 865 ~(ferrugine).

Pǣga *sm*. LV 337 pega. Ct 33/9 ~.

brǣg *sm* eyelid. VP 10/5 bregas (palpebrae). 131/4 §um.

ǣton *prt* ate. VP 77/29; 105/28 eton (manducaverunt). Hy 7/73 §(edebatis). 78/7 etun (comederunt).

lǣtan *sv* let. VH 12/10 ne let ðu (sinas).

for-lētan *sv* leave, forsake, forgive. VP 9/11; 15/10 ~es, ~esde (derelinques). 33/23 ~eð (†delinquit). 36/28 *etc* §(derelinquit). 38/14; 48/11; 88/31 ~að (†remitte!; relinquent; dereliquerint). 24/18 forlet (demitte!). 26/9 *etc* §(derelinquas). 36/8 §(§e!). 118/53 ~endum. 36/25 ~enne (dereclictum). 31/1 ~letne sind (remissae sunt). 9/35 †forlen is (derelictus est).

forlētnis *sf* remission. VH 9/14 ~isse (remissione).

frīo-lēta *sm* freedman. Cp 1218 ~an (libertabus); Ld †friulactum. 1224, 2104 ~(libertus; vernaculus).

sǣton *prt* sat. VP 68/13; 118/23; 121/5; 136/1 setun (sedebant *etc*).

gesēt- *prt* possessed. VP 138/13 ~e (possedisti). 104/44 ~un (§erunt).

ofer-sēton *prt* occupied. VP 21/13 ~(obsederunt). 58/▮ ~un (occupaverunt).

-sǣtan *spl*.

Creg-sētna haga. Ct 29/7, 8 ~.

Magon-sētum. Ct 35/4 on ~.

sētian *wv* lie in wait for. VP 9/30, 0 ~að (insidiatur).

sētung *sf* ensnaring. Ep 72 ~ae (aucapatione); Ef §; Cp §e.

strǣt *sf* high-road, street. Ct 20/15 to ~e. 43/3 stret. 6 §e *d*.

Stretlēg Ct.

wǣt *aj* wet. Ep 604 huet (licidus); Ef huaet; Cp huæt. Rd 1 ueta.

wētan *wv* wet. VP 6/7 ~u (rigabo).

gewētan *wv*. Cp 1298 geuueted (madefacta).

or-mǣte *aj* immense. Ep 640 ormetum (molibus); Ef, Cp §.

be-gǣt- *prt* got. CA 4 begetan. Ct 38/11, 4 begetan. VH 5/29 bigete (adquaesisti). Ps 72/12 §(obtinuerunt).

on-gēt- *prt* understood. VP 138/3 ~(intellexisti). 27/5; 63/10; 81/5; 105/7 ~un (§erunt).

blǣtan *sv* bleat. Cp 282 bletid (balatus).

hæfre-blēte *sf* a plant. Ep 124 †hraebrebletae (bicoca); Ef hebre§; Cp haebre~.

rǣd *sm* advice, what is advisable. Ct 37/26; 42/22 red.

Redbald LV. Redberct LV. redboran Ep, Ef, Cp. Redburg LV. Raedfridum BH. Redgȳth LV. Reduald BH — ręduuald 1. Reduulf LV; §wulf Ct.

Ælf-red *sm* LV 15 ae~. CA 3, 12, 4 |§. 18 aelfre(d). SG 9 ~. Ct 24/7; 45/44, 56 ~. 29/19; 47/7; 59/6 ae~. 45/41 §es. 45/1, 8 ę~. 45/1 §e. 45/22, 36 §es. 27/5; 32/1 e~.

Æþel-red *sm* Rn 16 æð~. BH 156 aedilredo—aeð§ 1. 233 aedilredum—aeðel§ 1. 298 aedilred—ędilredh — aedilred. LV 3; 12 eðil~. Gn 92 aeðil~. SG 8 æðered. Ct 29/19, 21 aeðæl~, æðel~. 26/7 ęð~. 27/7; 31/1, 3, 3, 5; 32/8; 42/27 eð~. 30/2 §o. 45/39 §es. 29/19 aeðerred. 24/5, 7 aeðered, æðered. 45/55 §. 44/3, 4 ęðered. 7 §es. 28/15; 30/13, 3; 32/1, 9 eðered. 31/5 §i.

Beadu-red *sm* LV 134 · · · du§. 439 badu~.

Beald-red *sm* LV 243; 403, 23, 75, 81 bald~. Ct 48/15 §. 21/4; 22/2; 23/2 §o.

Beorht-red *sm* BH 380 berct~. LV 3, 4; 131; 246, 6, 79; 402, 29, 30, 48, 54 §. 69, 91; 467, 77, 81 bercht~. 325; 471 berht~. Ct 22/12; 23/13 ~i. 48/11 bercht~.

Beorn-red *sm* LV 4, 5; 134, 8, 57; 327, 89; 402, 4, 7, 33, 42, 53, 75 ~. Gn 123 ~um. Ct 31/7 ~.

Burg-red *sm* Ct 48/12 ~.

Cēol-red *sm* LV 130; 386, 94, 6 ~. Gn 40 *ceolred.* Ct 22/9; 23/10 ~rædi. 48/11 ceored.

Cǣn-red *sm* BH 331 coin~— coen~ I. 369 §. 370 §o. LK 5 coin~. LV 4, 5; 476 coen~. SG 4 §. Ct 2/2 §i.

Cœ̄n-reding *sm* son of Cœ̄nred. SG 4 co(enred)ing.

Cūþ-red *sm* LV 55; 155, 6, 92; 249; 388, 92; 409, 24, 32 cuth~. 146; 320, 5; 405, 29, 47 cuð~. Ct 12/6; 17/8; 29/22; 33/10; 34/3; 51/12; 57/10; 58/18 §. 34/1; 49/7 §us. 52/16 §i. 49/1 cuðrędus.

Cyne-red *sm* LV 155 cyni~. Gn 14 *cyneredus.* Ct 47/5; 57/8; 58/15 cynred. 22/11 cyrredi.

Ēad-red *sm* LV 8; 14, 5; 144, 4, 9, 56; 249, 55; 309, 16, 7, 20, 2, 2, 7; 412, 4, 39, 46, 7, 55, 5, 62, 3, 8, 78, 80, 1 ~. Ct 27/5; 33/5, 7; 48/15 ~. 45/38, 41 ~e, ~es.

Eald-red *sm* LV 62; 144, 8; 323, 83; 409, 17, 35, 6, 46, 57, 60, 4, 7, 71 ald~. Gn 40 *aldred.* Ct 4/5 aeldredi. 10/3; 31/9; 47/7; 48/12, 3, 4, 6; 56/7; 57/11; 58/18, 9; 59/7 ald~. 30/14; 39/3 ~. 39/10 ~es. 10/1 aldréd.

Ealh-red *sm* LV 89 alh~.

Ēan-red *sm* Rn 16 ~. LV 6; 12, 5, 6; 135, 6, 42, 8; 247, 50; 306, 65, 98; 410, 8, 30, 0, 4, 5, 46, 50, 3, 63, 72 ~. Ct 33/6, 7.

Eard-red *sm* Gn 28 ~.

Ecg-red *sm* LV 71, 2; 248; 413, 45, 65, 71 ~.

Fold-red *sm* Ct 12/5 folð~.

Forþ-red *sm* LV 307, 9; 411, 75 forð~. Ct 19/5; 31/4; 33/5 §. 48/1 §e. 46/6 f[o]rðréd.

Friþu-red *sm* Ct 33/19 freoðo~.

Gearu-red *sm* LV 282 georo~.

Gǣf-red *sm* Ct 4/4 gębredi.

Hēa-red *sm* Ct 33/20 ~.

Heard-red *sm* LV 60, 84; 128; 260, 81; 351, 85; 446, 58, 66, 72 ~. Gn 29, 63 ~. Ct 18/4 ~raed.

Heaþo-red *sm* LV 15; 129; 324, 92; 429, 41 heaðu~. 68; 469 headu~. 54 hadu~. 180; 310 haðu~. 451 heoðu~. 134 · · · dured. Gn 47 heaðo~. 69 *heaðored.* Ct 15/4; 16/4 haðoredi. 19/4 §red. 33/8 heaðo~.

Here-red *sm* LV 440, 7, 73 herred.

Hūn-red *sm* LV 458, 70 ~. Ct 23/4 ~ræd. 21/6; 22/4; 24/10; 25/13; 36/7; 43/7; 58/20 ~.

Hwæt-red *sm* Rn 1/2 ~. LV 92; 195; 242; 408, 33 huaet~.

Hyge-red *sm* LV 325; 437 hygred.

Irmen-red *sm* Ct 4/5 ~inredi.

Mild-red *sm* LV 3; 82; 279 milred. Gn 46 §. Ct 10/3; 27/6 §. 20/24 milræd.

Œþel-red *sm* Ct 1/1 ho·ilredus. 6 oedelraedus. 8 odilredus.

Ōs-red *sm* BH 359 ~. LK 5 ~. LV 4 ~.

Pleg-red *sm* Ct 43/1, 6 ~, ~e.

Rīc-red *sm* LV 82 ~.

Sǣ-red *sm* LV 71 sae~.

Sæx-red *sm* SG 19 seax~.

Sæx-reding *sm* son of Sæxred. SG 19 seax~.

Seld-red *sm* LV 402 ~.

Sele-red *sm* SG 21 ~. Ct 33/10 ~ręd. 36/10 · · elered.

Sele-reding *sm* son of Selered. SG 21 ~.

Sige-red *sm* LV 7; 13, 3, 4, 4, 67; 265; 407, 47, 68 sigred. SG 21 ~. Ct 47/5; 48/13; 51/9 sigred. 47/15 §e. 55/9; 56/5, 5; 57/10; 58/17; 59/6 ~.

Swǣf-red *sm* **BH** 268 suefredo. **Ct** 1/8 suebredi.

Swīþ-red *sm* **LV** 145; 213; 427 suið~. **Gn** 4 *suiðredus*. **SG** 18 swið~.

Til-red *sm* **LV** 471 ~. **Ct** 35/14 ~.

Torht-red *sm* **LV** 182 torct~. 439 torcht~.

Tūn-red *sm* **Ct** 55/10 ~.

þrȳþ-red *sm* **BH** 326 thruid~—thryded—thrydred. **LV** 60 thryth~.

Uht-red *sm* **LV** 145; 410 ucht~. 336 uch[t]~. **Ct** 10/1, 3 uhct~. 13/1 ~us. 24/7; 57/10 ~.

Wiht-red *sm* **BH** 315 uict~—uuicht~ I. 346 ui[c]tredo—uict§ I. **LV** 67 uicht~. **Gn** 112 u~. **Ct** 5/1, 5 uuihtredus, uuihtredi (uihtredus, §i). 17/2 ~i. 48/11 wichred. 47/5 uueoht~. 58/16 wioht~. 58/21 wiht~ (wioht~). 30/15 wiaht~.

Wiht-reding *sm* son of Wihtred. **Gn** 112 u~.

Wil-red *sm* **LV** 88 uil~. **Gn** 30 *uuilred*. **Ct** 22/12; 23/13 uuillredi, uuilredi. 58/15 will~.

Wulf-red *sm* **LV** 15; 447, 66 uulf~. **Gn** 4 §us. **Ct** 24/4; 34/5, 13, 7; 43/9; 47/8; 48/14; 55/8, 9; 56/4; 58/18 ~. 34/9 ~e. 35/15 ~i. 56/2 ~o. 24/4; 30/14; 33/3; 35/1, 10; 36/1, 6; 37/11; 51/2, 9; 52/2, 7, 7, 15, 6; 54/3, 5, 6; 57/5, 7; 58/6; 59/5 uulf~. 49/7; 57/2; 58/4, 13 §us. 51/1, 4; 52/1 §i. 51/8; 52/2, 15; 53/1; 54/1; 55/1, 4; 57/1; 58/3; 59/2 §o. 34/4 §us (wulfredus). 20/24 uulfræd.

rǣdan *sv* read. **DA** 15 rede *inf*. 16 reda *inf*.

be-rǣdan *sv* betray. **Ep** 800 birednae (prodimur); **Cp** §; **Ef** biraednae.

ā-rǣdan read. **CA** 11 árede. **Ct** 37/37 arede.

dæg-rǣd *s*(*n*) dawn. **VH** 11/13, 4 degred (aurora). 13 §(crepusculum).

ðrǣd *s*(*m*) thread. **Cp** 876 ðred (filum). **Ld** 103 dredum (lineolis). **Rd** 6 ðret.

col-ðrēd *s*(*m*)(coal-thread), plumb-line. **Ep** 763 ~þred (perpendiculum); **Ef** ~draed; **Cp** ~.

hebeld-ðrēd *s*(*m*) weaver's thread. **Cp** 1233 ~(licia).

sǣd *sn* seed. **VP** 20/11; 21/24, 5, 31 *etc* sed (semen). 88/5 § ðin *a*. 17/51; **Hy** 10/11 ~e. 125/6 sed (§ina).

spǣd *s* spittle. **Cp** 1575 sped (petuita).

wǣd *s*(*f*) dress. **Cp** 164 waede (antemne).

gewǣde *sn* dress. **Rd** 12 giuæde.

-flǣd

Ælf-flǣd *sf* **BH** 198 aelffledam—aelbfledam—aelffledam—aelbfledam. 314 aelbfled—ęlffled I. **LV** 18, 36 aelfled. **Ct** 13/5 ~.

Alh-flæd *sf* **BH** 179 alchfledam—alh§ I.

Berct-flēd *sf* **LV** 38 ~.

Ēan-flǣd *sf* **BH** 81 ęanfled—ean§ I, II. 118 ~fledam—~fledan I. 201 aeanfled—enflet—eanfled. 202 aeanfled—ean§ *other three*. 209 ~fled. 314 §e *d*—ęnflædæ. **LV** 18 eanfled.

nǣdre *sf* serpent. **Bd²** 13 ða earman nedran (anguiculum). **VP** 90/13 nedran (aspidem). 57/5 §(serpentis). 139/4; 148/10 §(§es). 57/5 §(aspides). 13/3; 139/4; **Hy** 7/65 §ena.

mǣd *sf* meadow. **Cp** 25/5 hearde méd. 26/4 *prata* . . longan med. 43/6 §. 42/21 medwe *g*. 28/14; 30/6 §a *pl*. 43/5, 5 §um.

Medeshamstedi BH.

Aling-mēd *sf* **Ct** 26/4 ~.

Sighearding-mēd *sf* **Ct** 52/11 ~uue *a*.

Stoc-mēd *sf* **Ct** 28/14 ~.

cwǣd- *prt* said. **VP** 11/5; 63/6; 70/10 *etc* cwedun (dixerunt). 34/21; 40/6 *etc* §on. 88/3, 20; 89/3 §e (§isti).

†**werg-cweodon** *prt* cursed. **VP** 61/5 ~ (*second* o *over* e) (maledicebant).

grǣd *s*(*m*) grass. **VH** 7/4 ofer gred (gramen).

grǣdig *aj* greedy. **Ep** 500 gredig (inhians); **Ef**, **Cp** §. **Cp** 146 gredge (ambrones).

trǣdon *prt* trod. **Cp** 1640 tredun (proterunt); **Ep** treddun; **Ef** treodun.

for-trǣdon *prt* trod down. VP 55/3 ~tredon (conculcaverunt).

dǣd *sf* deed. Cp 728 deid (effectum). VP 63/10; Hy 11/6 dede (facta; actūs). 142/5 §um (factis).

Dedhāeth LV. daedlata Pr. Deduini LV.

wel-dēd *sf* benefit. VP 77/11 ~a (benefactorum).

yfel-dēd *sf* illdeed. VP 34/17 ~um (malefactis).

Dēda *sm*. BH 109 ~.

on-drǣdan *sv* fear. VP 3/7 *etc* ondredu (timebo). 26/1; 55/11 §o. 26/3 *etc* §eð. 90/5 §es ðu. 21/24 *etc* §að. 21/25 *etc* §e (§eat). 66/8 §en (metuant). 48/17 ne ondred ðu. 88/8 to §enne (metuendus). 14/4 *etc* §ende (timentes). 32/18 ða §endan. 21/26 *etc* §endum. 33/8 *etc* §endra.

bǣd- *prt* prayed, asked. VP 39/7 bede (postulasti). 77/18 §en (peterent). 104/40 §un (petierunt).

Caed-baed *sm*. Gn 108 ~.

Caedbaeding *sm* Gn 108 ~.

Rath-bēd *sm* BH 349 *regi* ~o [Frisian name].

Sigi-bēd *sm*. Ct 9/6 ~.

lende-brǣde *sf* loins Cp 1262 ~brede (lumbulos).

gebrǣdan *wv* roast Cp 2135 gebreded flaesc (viscera tosta).

bredipannae Ep; Cp §; Ef breiti§.

blǣd *s*(*m*) blast. Ep 445 blaeed (flamina); Ef bled; Cp blęd.

Blaedsuith LV.

blǣdre *sf* bladder. Ep 1077 bledrae (vesica); Ef §; Cp bledre.

slǣp *s*(*m*) sleep. VP 75/6; 126/2; 131/4 slep (somnum). 72/20 §e. Hy 12/2, 11 §es (soporis, somni).

slēpan *sv* sleep. VP 120/4 ~eð (obdormiet). 67/14 ~að (dormiatis). Hy 12/12 §(somnient). 3/6 ~ ongon (somnum coepi). Hy 12/10, 0 ~(dormire). 77/65; 87/6 ~ende (§iens; §ientes). Hy 13/5 §ra.

ā-slēpan *sv* sleep. VP 12/4 ~e (obdormiam).

scǣp *sn* sheep. VP 79/2; 118/176 scep (ovem; ovis). 8/8; 43/12, 22 *etc* §(oves). Hy 1/5 §um. 64/14 *etc* §a. Ct 37/18 scęp *pl*. 41/14 §a.

wǣpen *sn* weapon. VP 34/2; 45/10; 56/5 wepen (arma). Hy 6/24 wepna (§orum).

wēpned-hād *sm* male sex. Ct 45/47 ~es.

nǣp *s*(*m*) turnip. Ep 1363 naep (napi); Cp § (§is); Ef nep.

hē *prn* he. Rn 2/2; 3/7 ~. CH 3, 5 ~. LP 4 ~. Mt 9 *etc* ~. VP 9/25, 9 *etc* ~. 9/9; 18/6 *etc* ~ (ipse). 32/9 hie (§). Ct 34/13, 5; 37/26; 38/3; 39/7; 40/19, 23; 41/12; 45/19; 48/5, 19 ~.

ðē *prn dat* thee. LP 1 ~. DA 10 ~. VP 2/8; 5/5 *etc* ~ (tibi). 15/1; 26/7 *etc* de. 6/6 ðæ (§).

ðē *acc*. DA 2, 10 ~. VP 4/2; 5/11; 7/8 *etc* ~(te).

wē *prn* we. Bd² 23 ~. VP 11/5; 19/6, 6 *etc* ~. Ct 41/46; 48/17, 20 ~.

mē *prn dat* me. Rd 5, 6, 7, 13 ~. VP 2/7, 8 *etc* ~. 3/8 *etc* ~(mihi). 38/11; 39/12 †frome (a me). Ct 30/22; 40/3, 7; 41/3, 4 *etc*; 42/22; 45/45, 6, 6 ~.

mē *acc*. VP 3/7, 7; 4/2 *etc* ~(me). Ct 37/41; 42/4 ~.

gē *prn* ye. DA 4, 9, 10 ~. VP 2/12; 4/3; 7/13 *etc* ~. Ct 30/22; 37/39, 41 ~.

Cyni-brē *s*. Ct 9/4 *silvam quam nominant* ~.

hēr *av* here. Rn 3/3 ~. DA 8 ~. Mt 37 ~. VP 131/14 ~(hic). Ct 37/43 haer-beforan. 45/43, 54 ~beufan; ~.

gehēran *wv* hear. Cp 1011 ~es thu (heus). LP 4 ~eð. Mt 37 ~. VP 25/7; 90/15 ~u (audiam; ex§). 5/4; 21/3; 37/16 ~es *etc* (exaudies). 4/4; 19/7 *etc* ~eð (§iet). 57/6; 93/9 ~ed (†§ient; audiet). 33/12; 48/2 ~að (§ite!) *etc*. 19/2; 84/9; Hy 7/1 ~e (exaudiat *etc*). 33/3; 140/6 ~en. 4/2; 12/4; 44/11 *etc* geher! 3/5; 6/9; 29/11 *etc* ~de. 4/2; 16/6 *etc* ~des. 43/2; 47/9; 77/3 *etc* ~dun. 102/20 to ~enne (ad audiendam). 37/15 geherrende (§ens). 18/4 bioð ~de. 105/2 ~de (§tas).

hērnis *sf* obedience. **Ct** 48/3 mid eaðmodre ~se.

gehērnis *sf* hearing, obedience. **VP** 17/45 ~se (obauditu). 50/10 § minre (auditui *d*). 111/7 § (§u). Hy 6/1 § ðine (§um).

hērsumian *wv* obey. **VP** 17/45 ~ade (obaudivit). 65/8 ~iað (§ite!).

hērcnian *wv* listen. **Mt** 36 ~ade.

un-hēre *aj* fierce. **Ep** 983 hunhieri (trux); Ef unhyri; Cp †unhiorde.

Dēre *pl* **BH** 45 deiri *vocarentur iidem provinciales*. 193 derorum — § — §. 335 §—deirorum 11.

Derauuda BH.

brēr *s* briar. **Ep** 68 breer (anguens); Ef, Cp §. Cp 1355 braer (murus). 2057 §e (tribuli).

hēla *s*(*m*) heel. **Lr** 57 ~an (talos). 59 ~um (calcibus).

helspuran VP.

stēle *s* steel. **Ep** 49 steeli (accearium); Ef, Cp ~i; Ld stel. Cp 1431 staeli (ocearium).

mēle *s*(*m*) basin. **Ep** 56 meeli (alvium); Cp §; Ef †§u. Cp 250 ~i (avum).

ēðung *sf* laying waste, destroying. **Cp** 1399 ~(obolitio).

sceld-hrēða *sm* phalanx, testudo. **Ep** 997 ~reda *etc* (testudo); Ef ~.

ā-lēsan *wv* release. **Cp** 774 alieset (eximet). **VP** 33/23; 48/8, 8 *etc* ~eð (redimet). 7/3 ~e (§at). 24/22; 25/11 *etc* ales (§e!). 30/6; 70/23; Hy 13/6 ~des. Hy 13/19 ~de (redemptos). 106/2 § werun.

on-lēsan *wv* loosen. **VP** 36/21; 145/7 ~eð (solvit). 101/21; Hy 12/4 ~e (§at). Hy 12/6 ~að. 68/5; 104/20 ~de (exsolvebam; solvit).

tō-lēsan *wv* loosen, destroy. **VP** 119/4 ~es (†desolatoriis). 88/45 ~des. (dissolvisti). Hy 7/71 ~de (dissolutos. Hy 12/2 §(solutos). 34/16; 72/21 § sind (dissoluti sunt; resoluti §).

ā-lēsend *sm* liberator. **VP** 18/15 ~(redemptor). 69/6; 77/35 ~(liberator).

ā-lēsnis *sf* redemption. **VP** 129/7 ~(redemptio). 110/9; Hy 9/2 ~isse (§ionem). 48/9 § (§ionis).

tō-lēsnis *sf* destruction. **VP** 72/19 ~isse (desolationis).

cēsnis *sf* niceness (in eating). **Ep** 406 ciisnis (fastidium); Ef †ciinis; Cp †cymnis (§, odium).

Gēsus *sm* Jesus. **Rn** 1/1, 13 *gessus*.

geðēwan *wv* subdue. **Cp** 1965 geðedum (subjugatis).

gelēfan *wv* allow. **Ep** 1089 gilebdae (concesserim); Ef gilepdae; Cp gilefde.

gelēfan *wv* believe. **Mt** 9 gele(fde). **VP** 26/13 ~u (credo). 67/19; Hy 13/9 ~að. 115/10; 118/66 ~de (§idi). 77/22; 105/12, 24 ~dun. 77/32 ~don.

thēban-thorn Ep; § Ef; ðeofe§ Cp.

slēbe-scōh Cp.

hēng *prt* hung. **VP** 136/2 ~un (suspendimus).

fēng *prt* seized, took. **SG** 1 *etc* ~.

bi-fēng *prt* clasped, seized. **VP** 47/7 ~ (adpraehendit). 39/13 ~on (comprachenderunt). Hy 5/24 ~un (§). 105/46 §(ceperant).

fore-fēngun *prt* anticipated. **VP** 76/5 ~(anticipaverunt).

on-fēng *prt* took, received. **VP** 3/6; 17/36 *etc* ~(suscepit). 14/3, 5; 17/17 *etc* ~(accepit). 29/1 *etc* ~e (suscepisti). 16/12; 39/12 ~un (§erunt). 47/10 § (§imus).

under-fēng *prt* undertook. **DA** 4/4 ðu ~e, (ge) ~an.

gehēnan *wv* humiliate. **Ef** 371 †giheldae (exauctoravit); Cp geheende. **VP** 17/28 ~es (humiliabis). 74/8 ~eð. 104/18 ~dun. 37/9 ~ed (§iatus).

gerēn *snf* snare. **Bd**[2] 69 girenum (laquiis). **VP** 34/8; 123/7 giren (laqueus). 10/7 § (§eos). 68/23 in §e (§eum). 24/15; 34/8; 90/3; 123/7; 139/6 §e (§eo). 140/9 §e ða (§eo quem). 34/7 §e (§ei *g*). 56/7; 63/6; 139/6; 141/4 §e (§eos). 65/11 in gerene (§eum). 9/31; 30/5 § (§eo). 17/6 § (§ei *pl*). 118/110 § (§eos).

on-sēn *sf* face. **VP** 9/32 *etc* onsiene (faciem). 12/1; 26/9 *etc* § ðine (§). 9/4; 49/21 § ðinre (§ie) *etc*. 81/2; 82/17 § (§ies *pl*). 41/3 biforan onsien (§iem).

un-gesēne *aj* unseen. Ef 333 †ungiseem uard (disparuit); Cp ~ weā.

Scēn-uulf LV.

strēn *sf* bed. VP 6/7; 62/7 ~e mine (stratum). 40/4 alle § (§). 131/3 § minre (stratūs).

tēn *num* ten. VP 32/2; 67/18; 90/7; 143/9 (decem) Hy 7/59 ~(dena). Ct 37/30; 41/26, 62; 47/11, 2, 4, 4, 6 ~.

tenstrenge VP.

ðrēo-tēne *num* thirteen. Ct 41/35 ~.

fīf-tēne *num* fifteen. Ct 41/69 ~.

Treent *s* river Trent. BH 109 *fluvio* ~ — ~ I, II. 205 *fluvio* treanta — §e. 297 *juxta fluvium* treanta.

bi-stēman *wv* besteam. Rn 2/9 ~i(d).

gēm-nis *sf* care. VP 39/18 ~isse (curam).

feoður-tēme *aj* four-teamed. VH 5/34 ~um (quadrigis).

Drēmca *sm.* LV 95 dremka. 104, 99 ~.

bēme *sf* trumpet. Cp 571 ~(concha). 2015 beeme (thessera). VP 46/6 ~an (tubae *g*).

ēce *aj* eternal. CH 4, 8 eci. CA 13 ecum. Mt 33 ecan. VH 13/1 ~(eterne!). 76/6 ~(§os). 77/66 ~(sempiternum). 104/10 cyðnisse ~(eternum). Hy 11/16; 13/32 ðere ~an (sempiternā). Hy 11/5 ~es. 75/5; 138/24 ~um. 111/7 æcre. Ct 42/14; 48/2, 5, 7 ~. 42/3, 21 æce. 37/4 aecan. 44/7 in ęc ęrbe.

ēcelic *aj* eternal. VP 23/7, 9; Hy 6/13 ~e (aeternales).

ēcnis *sf* eternity. VP 5/12; 9/6 *etc* in ~isse (eternum). 9/8 in ecnesse (§).

geēcan *wv* increase. VP 40/9 ~eð (adiciet). 70/14 ~u (§iam). 104/24 ~te (auxit).

tō-geēcan *wv* add to. VP 60/7 ~es (adicies). 113/14 ~e (§iat).

ot-ēcan *wv* increase. VP 68/27 ~tun (addiderunt).

rēc *sm* smoke. VP 17/9; 36/20; 67/3; 101/4 ~(fumus).

swefel-rēc *sm* vapour of sulphur. VP 10/7 ~(sulphur)

smēc *sm* smoke, vapour. VH 12/11 ~(vaporem).

smīcan *wv* fumigate. VP 103/32; 143/5 ~að (fumigabunt *intr*).

mēce *sm* sword. Cp 1341 ~(mucro). VP 56/5 ~(machera).

gehēhan *wv* exalt. VH 4/14, 22 geheð (sublimat, §abit).

ūp-hēhan *wv* exalt. VP 9/15 uphest (exaltas).

ā-tēhð *prs* draws out. VP 9/30 atið (abstrahit).

hēhst *sup* highest. VP 9/3; 12/6; 65/4; 91/2 ~a (altissime). 17/14 se ~a (§us). 90/9 hest (§um). 45/5, 7; 82/19; 86/5; 91/9; 96/9 se §a. 7/18; 20/8; 90/1; Hy 9/11 ðes §an. 49/14; 56/3 ðæm §an.

nēhst *sup* nearest. VP 72/17; 138/5 ða nestan (novissima). Hy 7/39 ot §(in novissimo). Ct 45/17 sio neste hond.

nēsta *smf* neighbour. VP 27/3; 34/14; 87/19 ðone ~an (proximum). 11/3; 14/3 *etc* ðæm §. 37/12, 2 ða §, ða § mine (§i). 44/15 ða § his (§ae *pl*). 121/8 fore ~um.

hēht *prt* commanded. Mt 16, 29, 42 ~. Ct 39/15 het.

gehēht *prt* promised. VP 131/2 ~(vovit).

lēhtan *wv* shine. VP 104/39 lihte (luceret). Hy 12/10 §eð (§eat).

in-lihtan *wv* shine, illuminate. VP 12/4; 17/29; 30/17; 118/135 inliht (inlumina!) 17/29; 75/5 ~es. 118/130; 145/8 ~eð. 66/2 ~e (§et). 117/27 ~e (inluxit). 76/19 ~on (§erunt). 96/4 ~un (§erunt). Hy 9/16 ~. 18/9; Hy 11/2 ~ende. 138/12 bið ~ed. 33/6 bioð ~e.

inlihtnis *sf* illumination. VP 26/1; 43/4; 138/11 ~(inluminatio). 77/14; 89/8 inlihtnisse (§ione).

ēg *sf* island.

Beardan-ēg *sf* Bardney. BH 156 ~eu—~ig II [ig *over* eu].

Cerotes-ēg *sf* Chertsey. BH 258 ~aes ei, *id est ceroti insula* — ceortes ei I. Ct 45/22, 30 to ceortesege.

Heorot-ēg *sf* Hartlepool. BH 199 heruteu, *id est insula cervi* — §eig II. 303 §eu—§ei II.

Læstinga-ēg *sf* Lastingham. **BH** 3 ~eu—†luestinga eu—lęstinga eu. 194 laestinga eu—§enga eu—§inga ig [ig *over* eu] II. 218 laestinga eu—§ eg [g *over* u] II. 241 in læstinga e—leśtinga he—laesting e. 245 §eu. 363 in læstinga æi—†luestingua æi—laestinga ei.

Peartan-ēg *sf* Partenay. **BH** 109 *de monasterio* ~eu—§ei [i *from* u] II. 158 ~eu—~ea.

Seles-ēg *sf* Selsey. **BH** 279 selæs eu, *quod dicitur latine insula vituli marini*—selaes§—seles§—selaes ei. 360 selæs eu. **Ct** 33/20 ~i *ecclesiae.*

ān-ēge *aj* one-eyed. **Cp** 1239 ~(luscus).

sceolh-ēge *aj* squinting. **Ep** 981 ~i (scevus, strabus, torbus); **Ef** sceol§; **Cp** scel~.

hēg *sn* hay. **VP** 36/2; 102/15; 103/14 *etc* ~(faenum). 104/35 all ~ (§ *a*).

heiweg Ct.

Hēga *sm*. **Ct** 28/3 [h]ega.

lēg *sm* fire. **VP** 82/15; 105/18 ~(flamma). 28/7 ~(§am).

in-lēgan *wv* inflame. **VP** 104/19 †inlegagede (inflammavit).

lēgitu *sf* lightning. **VP** 17/15; 96/4; 134/7; **Hy** 8/10 ~e (fulgura). **Hy** 7/80 ~ (fulgur). **Hy** 6/24 ~e (§oris).

strēgan *wv* strew. **Ep** 899 stridae (struere); **Ef** streidæ; **Cp** streide (struerer).

cēgan *wv* call. **VH** 11/4 ~en (vocemus). 146/4 ceð (§at). 49/1 cede (§avit).

gecēgan *wv* call to, invoke. **VP** 17/4; 114/2, 4; 115/13; **Hy** 7/5 ~u (invocabo). 137/3 § (§avero). 101/3 ~o. 19/10; 48/12; 74/2; 79/19; 98/6; 104/1; **Hy** 2/7 ~að. 85/5; 144/18; 146/9 ~endum. 55/10 geceigo. 49/15 gece! 101/25 § (revoces). 41/8 geceð (invocat). 88/27; 90/15 § (§abit). 4/2 gecede (§arem). 17/7; 24/20; 30/18 § (§avi). 104/16 §(vocavit). 80/8 §es. 13/5; 52/6 §un. 78/6; 98/6 §on. **Hy** 9/12 bist geced.

in-gecēgan *wv* call in. **VP** 117/5 ingecede (invocavi).

tō-gecēgan *wv* call to. **VP** 49/4 togeceð (advocavit).

dēgol *aj* secret. **VP** 43/22; **Hy** 13/24 ða deglan (occulta; secreta).

dēgullice *av* secretly. **VP** 100/5 ~ (occulte).

dēgulnis *sf* secret. **VP** 9/30; 138/15; **Hy** 6/30 in ~isse (in occulto). 30/21 in §(in abdito). 9/29 ~issum (occultis). 16/12 §(abditis). 142/3 §(obscuris). 10/3; 63/5 degelnisse (occulto; §is). 80/8 §(abscondito). 18/13 §um (§is).

gedēglian *wv* hide. **VP** 9/16; 30/5; 34/8 ~adon (occultaverunt). 77/4 sind ~ad. 138/15 nis §.

gebēgan *wv* bend. **Cp** 71 gebegdum (aduncis). **Lr** 70 §(turtuosis). **VP** 72/20 ~es (rediges). 77/59; **Hy** 11/6, 7 ~eð (§it; §§, retundat). 56/7 ~don (incurvaverunt). 37/9 ~ed (incurvatus). 68/24 §(incurva). 72/22 § eam (redactus sum).

bēgir *spl* berries. **Ep** 143 ~(bucina); **Ef** §; **Cp** beger (baccinia).

hlēt *s* lot. **VP** 21/19; 124/3 ~(sortem). 77/54 ~e (§e).

scēte *s* sheet. **Cp** 1776 ~(sandalium).

flēte *s* cream. **Ep** 605 githuornae ~i (lectidiclatum); **Ef** §; **Cp** ~. 1075 ~i (verberatrum); **Ef** †~u; **Cp** ~. **Cp** 605 ~(crama).

Seax-nēt *sm*.

Seaxnēting *sm* son of S. **SG** 15 ~.

nēten *sn* beast. **DA** 20 ~a *gpl.* **VP** 8/8; 148/10; **Hy** 8/15 ~u (pecora). 67/11; 103/25 §(animalia). **Hy** 6/2 netna (§ium).

Frīu-bēt *sm*. **LV** 333 ~.

Beet-frith LV. **Betmon** LV. **Betgils** LV. **Betscop** LV. **Betuald** LV. **Betuini** LV.

Monn-ēd *sm*. **Ct** 23/8 ~i *lg.*

Ēda *sm*. **LV** 239; 427, 78 ~.

Aedgils BH; eed§ LV. **Edgȳth** LV. **Edhelm**, edelming Gn. **Edrīc** BH; eed§ LV; edric, §ing Gn; ędric Ct.

Uulf-hēd *sm*. **LV** 458 ~.

for-rēd *prt* betrayed. **Ep** 739 ferred (proscribit); **Cp** faerred (§scripsit).

geðēde *sn* language. **VP** 30/21 geðieda (linguarum).

scēd *prt* divided. **Ct** 29/7, 10, 1 ~.

nēd *sf* compulsion. **Cp** 420 ~(casis). **VP** 37/13; **Hy** 3/12 ~(vim).

neidfaerae BDS. **nedðearfnis** VP.

hæft-nēd *sf* captivity. **VP** 13/7; 52/7; 67/19; 77/61; 84/2; 125/1 heft~ (captivitatem). 125/4 §ure (§). 123/6 in §(captione). **Hy** 7/84 §e (captivitate).

nēdan *wv* compel. **Bd**[2] 21 neddan (cogunt). **VP** 117/13 ~ed (impulsus). 58/13 sien nedde (compellantur). **Hy** 7/41 §un (§pulerunt).

Pēde *sm*. **Ct** 9/7 ~.

Preed *sm*. **LV** 200, 26 ~.

Bēd-hāeth LV. **Bedhelm** LV. **Beeduini** LV.

Bēdca *sm*. **SG** 15 ~.

Bēdcing *sm* son of B. **SG** 15 ~.

clif-hlēp *s(m)* cliff-leap. **Cp** 1558 ~(pessum).

ā-stēpan *wv* bereave. **VP** 108/9 asteapte (orfani).

nēp-flōd Cp.

cēpe *s* onion. **Ef** 286 cipae (caepa); Cp ynnilaec, cipe. **Cp** 1791 cipe (scolonia).

bi-dēpan *wv* dip. **VP** 67/24 sie ~ed (intinguatur).

ēa *sf* river. **Ct** 30/6 beeastan ee. 44/7 eum.

ealond VP, Ct; eo§ VP. eorisc Ep; Ef, Cp §.

Grafon-ēa *sf* Graveney. **Ct** 52/9; 53/3 ~eah. 51/6 aet ~aea. 52/14 æt ~æa. 53/5 on ~ęa.

Homel-ēa *sf* river Hamble. **BH** 288 *fluminis* ~ — ~ae [vel a *over* ae] II.

Liming-ēa *sf* Lyminge. **Ct** 5/1 *in loco qui dicitur* ~ae.

Limin-ēa *sf* river Limen. **Ct** 5/4 *fluminis quae appellatur* ~aea. 7/2 ~aea. 19/2 ~ea. 7/4 *in loco qui dicitur* ~iaee. 6/1 *juxta* ~aee. 7/3 in ~iaeae.

Westan-ēa *sf*. **Ct** 4/2 uuestanae.

Ēa-lāc LV. **Ēaðrȳð** LV.

ðwēa *sv* wash. **VP** 6/7; 25/6 ðwea (lavabo).

ā-ðwēa *sv* wash. **VP** 50/4 aðuaeh (lava!).

slēa *sv* strike, kill. **VP** 58/12 ne slęh ðu (occideres). **Hy** 7/77 slea (percutiam).

of-slēa *sv* kill. **Mt** 25 ofslean *inf*. **VP** 9/29 ofsle (interficiat). 61/4 ofsleað (§itis). **Hy** 5/15; 7/76 ofslea (§iam; occidam).

gefēa *sm* joy. **Mt** 33 ðone gefean. **VP** 118/111 ~(exultatio). 29/12 in gefean (gaudium). 50/10 gefian (§*a*). 20/7; 125/2, 5; **Hy** 2/5 § (§io).

fēa *aj pl* few. **VP** 106/39; 108/8 ~(pauci). 16/14 feam. 104/12 ða feastan.

fēanis *sf* fewness. **VP** 101/24 ~isse (paucitatem).

frēa-berht VP.

frēa *sm* lord, the Lord. **CH** 9 ~.

Frēa-lāf, §ing Gn.

Wūsc-frēa *sm* **BH** 96 uusc~ — uúsc~ I — uusc~ II. 118 §frean *a*. **Gn** 73 §frea.

Uuscfrēa-ing *sm* son of W. **Gn** 73 ~.

flēa *sv* flay. **Cp** 659 flean (deglobere).

ēar *sn* ear (of corn). **Cp** 1892 ~(spicas).

ēare *sn* ear. **VP** 9/38; 91/12 ~(auris). 16/6 *etc* ~ ðin (§em). 17/45 ~an (§is *g*). 17/7; 33/16 *etc* § (§es). 5/2 *etc* §um.

earuuigga Ep; Cp §; Ef aeruuica; Ld ęruigga.

ēarendel *s(m)* dawn. **Ep** 554 ~il (iuuar); Ef oerendil; Cp ~.

tēar *sm* tear. **VP** 38/13; 41/4; 55/9 ~as (lacrimas). 6/7 *etc* ~um. 79/6; 83/7 ~a (§arum).

ðwēal *s(n)* washing. **Ef** 326 thuachl; Cp ðhuehl (delumentum). **Cp** 1991 ðuaelum (taenis).

ēað-mōd *etc*, ead§, geaðmodades, geeðmodedan VP; eaðmod, §nis Ct.

hrēatha-mūs Ep, Ef; hreadae§ Ep; hreada§ Ef; hraeðe§ Cp.

sēað *sm* pit. **VP** 68/16; 93/13 ~(puteus; fovea). 7/16 *etc* ~(lacum). 7/16 *etc* ~(foveam). 56/7 ðone ~ (§). 54/24 ~(puteum). 39/3 ~e (lacu).

dēað *sm* death. **Mt** 9 ~ *a*. **VP** 33/22

etc ~(mors). 12/4 ~e. 7/14 *etc* ~es. 6/6 ðeaðe. 114/3 deðes.

deothdaege BDS.

lēas *aj* false, deceitful. **VP** 32/17; 115/11 ~ (falsus; mendax). 39/5; 61/10 ~e (falsas; mendaces). 57/4 ða ~an (falsa).

-**lēas**. fæder~. recci~. ār~ *etc*. treuleusnis Ep [*first* u *er*]; treulesnis Ef. frēond~.

lēasung *sf* deceit, falsehood. **Ep** 426 ~(famfaluca); Cp §; Ef laesung. Ld 171 §ae (famfelucas). **VP** 4/3; 5/7 ~e (mendacium *a*). 58/13 ~e (§io).

wēas *wv* by chance. **Bd**[2] 54 ~(casu).

gefrēas *prt* froze. **Cp** 1402 gefreos (obriguit).

gecēas *prt* chose. **VP** 24/12; 32/12; 46/5 ~(elegit). 131/13, 3, 4 ~ (§, preelegit, preelegi).

ēast *av* east.

eastdǣel VP. **Estranglorum**, ea§ BH; eostengla Gn. **easthalf** Ct. **Eastsexanorum** Ct. **eastsūth** Cp. **easteweard** Ct. **east-norþ-wind** Ep; § Cp; eust§ Ef; eost§ Cp.

ēastan *av* from the east. **Ct** 30/6 be ~ ee.

eastannorþan Cp. **eastansūdan** Cp.

Ēast-mund Cp.

Aestor-hild LV. **Eosturuini**, aeostor§, aestur§ LV.

Ēastorege *sf* Eastry. **Ct** 34/8 to éastorege. 35/2 *in regione* easterege. 10 on easterege. 3 *in regione* eosterege. 7, 10 on eostorege. 4, 7 on eosterge. 36/4 *ad* eastrege.

Eastrgeona Ct.

ot-ēawan *wv* show. **VP** 16/15 ~u (apparebo). 49/23; Hy 7/38 §(ostendam). 4/6 ~eð (§it). 41/3 ~e (†parebo). 58/12; 79/4, 8, 20; 84/8 oteaw (ostende!). 79/1 § (appare!). 62/3; 77/11 ~de (apparui; ostendit). 59/5; 70/20 ~de (§isti). 17/16 ~don (apparuerunt). 90/16 oteowu (ostendam). 91/8 §dun (apparuerunt). Hy 6/4 odeawes (ostenderis).

ēaw-lā VP; **euwa** Cp.

heard-hēaw *s* chisel. **Ef** 262 ~heui (ciscillus); Cp ~heau; Ld haerdhaeu.

on-hēaw *sm* trunk. **Cp** 507 ~as (codices).

sēaw *s*(*n*) sap. **Bd**[2] 83 sea (sucum).

scēawian *wv* behold. **VP** 118/15, 8 ~iu (considerabo). 9/35 ~as. 36/32 ~að. 27/5 ~iað. 141/5; Hy 6/1 ~ade. 21/18 ~edun. 93/9 scewað.

scrēawa *sm* shrew. **Ep** 649 screuua (musiranus); Cp screauua; Ld scraeua.

Cēawlin *sm* **BH** 60, 1 caelin *rex occidentalium saxonum, qui lingua eorum* ceaulin *vocatur*. 194 caelin. 195 § — cęlin 1. **LV** 222 celin. **SG** 6 ceaul[i]n.

†**Ceaulniing** *sm* son of C. **SG** 5.

glēaw *aj* prudent. **Cp** 1768 gleu (sagax). **VP** 118/98 ~ne (prudentem).

glēawnis *sf* prudence. **Cp** 203 gleaunisse (argutiae). **VP** 48/4; 104/22 ~isse (prudentiam).

dēaw *s*(*m*) dew. **Cp** 1752 ~e (roscido). **VP** 132/3; Hy 7/3; Hy 8/5 ~(ros).

hēafod *sn* head. **Rn** 2/17 (h)*eaf*(du)m. **VP** 3/4; 17/44; 21/8 *etc* heafud (caput). 22/5 § min (§ *a*). 7/17; 20/4 *etc* heafde. 43/15; 68/5 *etc* heafdes. 65/12; 73/13; 108/25; 109/6; Hy 6/28 heafud (capita). 67/22; Hy 6/27 §u (§). 82/3 heofud (§ut). 39/13 †heasdes. **Ct** 20/6, 11, 4, 8 ~.

heafudponnan Lr.

foran-hēafod *sn* forehead. **VH** 13/17 on ~heafdum (frontibus).

be-hēafdian *wv* behead. **Mt** 43 ~.

behēafdung *sf* beheading. **Mt** 43 to ðære ~a.

here-rēaf *sn* spoil. **Bd**[2] 76 ~(spolia). **VP** 67/13; 118/162; Hy 5/14 ~(§).

wæl-rēaf *sn* spoil. **Ep** 642 uuaelreab (manubium); Ef uuel§; Cp waelreaf.

rēafian *wv* rob, plunder. **VP** 108/11 ~ien (diripiant). 68/5 ~ade (rapui). 21/14 ~iende (§iens). 34/10 ~iendum (§ientibus).

gerēafian *wv* **VP** 49/22 ~ie (rapiat). 9/30 ~ (§ere). 43/11 ~adon (diripiebant). 88/42 ~edon (§uerunt).

89/10 bioð ~ade (corripiemur). 9/30 geræafie (rapiat). 103/21 †geraflen (§iant).

lēaf *sn* leaf. **VP** 36/2 ~(holera).

gearwan-lēaf *sn* mallow. **Cp** 1288 hocc, cottuc, *vel* ~(malva); **Ef** geormantlab.

gelēafa *sm* faith. **VP** 77/37; Hy 7/40; Hy 11/10; Hy 12/11 ~(fides). Hy 11/9, 12; Hy 12/9 se rehta ~ (§). 32/4 ~an (§e). Hy 13/17 †gelean (§ei).

gelēaffull *aj* pious. **LP** 10 ~ę.

gelēafsum *aj* credible. **VP** 92/5 gelæfsume (credibilia).

onweg-ā-scēaf *prt* pushed away. **VP** 77/60, 7 ~(reppulit).

forð-scēaf *prt* pushed forth. **Bl**[2] 14 ~(propulit).

scēaf *sm* sheaf. **Ep** 30 sceabas (areoli); Cp §; Ef scebas. 468 sceabas (garbas); Ef, Cp §.

dēaf *aj* deaf. **VP** 37/14 ~(surdus). 57/5 ~e (§ae).

ēan-

Ean-bald LV, Gn. **Eanberht** LV, Gn, Ct; aean§ Ct. **Eanburg**, LV, Ct. ęanfled, aean§, ean§, ęn§ en§ BH; ean§ LV. **Eanfrid** BH; §frith LV; §ferð, §ferðing Gn; §frið Ct. **Eangeard** Ct. **Eangȳth** LV. **Eanheri**, aean§, aen§, æn§ BH. **Eanlāc** LV. **Eanmund** LV, Ct; eon§ LV. **Eanrēd** Rn, LV, Ct. **Eanðrȳth** LV. **Eanuald**, eon§ LV. **Eanuini** LV; §uine, §uining Gn. **Eanuulf** LV, Gn, Ct; eon§ Gn; eanuulfing Gn.

hēan *aj* humble, abject. **VP** 9/39 ~an (humili). 81/3 ~ne (§em). 112/6 ða ~an (§ia).

Hēan-byrig Ct.

Lēana-hām Ct.

lēan *sn* reward. **Cp** 743 ~(emolumentum). **Ct** 42/16 ða ~.

ed-lēan *sn* retribution. **VP** 18/12 ~(retributio). 27/4 *etc* ~(§ionem). 118/112 ~e. 102/2 ~(§ones). **Ct** 37/4 fore aedleane.

lēanian *wv* reward. **Ct** 30/23 ~ie.

geedlēanian *wv* requite. **VP** 40/11; Hy 7/81 ~iu (retribuam). 130/2 ~as. 17/25; 30/24 *etc* ~að. 17/21 ~ad (§uit). 141/8 ~ie. 27/4 ~a! 17/21 ~ade. 136/8; Hy 7/9 ~ades. 84/3 §(remisisti). 31/5 ~edes. 34/12 ~edun. 37/21 ~edon.

geedlēanend *sm* rewarder. **VH** 13/28 ~(remunerator).

geedlēanung *sf* requiting. **VP** 54/21 ~e (retribuendo).

Mēan-uarorum BH.

bēan *sf* bean. **Ef** 284 ~(cicer); Cp §. Cp 844 ~(favo).

fugles-bēan *sf* vetch. **Ep** 1085 ~aes ~(vicium); Ef flugles~; Cp ~; Ld ~e (viciam, pisas agrestes). **Ld** 183 fuglues benae (vicias).

Bēan *s* [=Blēan?]. **Ct** 25/6 *in loca qui vocatur* ~.

Beanseta Cp.

Blēan *s* Blean forest. **Ct** 28/5 to ~ ðem wiada. 53/6 on ~.

ēam *sm* uncle. **Rn** 4/3 eomæ (§ae) *d.*

hēamol *aj* miserly. **Ep** 413 uncystig *vel* ~(frugus); Ef †healful; Cp ~ul.

strēam *sm* stream. **Ep** 855 ~(rema); Ef, Cp ~; Ld streum. 1033 †streum (torrentibus); Ef †streaumum; Cp ~um.

streamrād Ep; § Cp; streum§ Ef.

flēam *sm* flight. **VP** 88/24 ~(fugam). 141/5 ~(§a).

Drēam-uulf LV.

bēam *sm* tree. **Ct** 29/6, 6 earnes ~e *d.*

ceder-bēam *sm* cedar. **VP** 91/13 ~(cedrus). 28/5, 5; 36/35; 79/11; 103/16; 148/9 ~as.

ciser-bēam *sm* cherry-tree. **Ep** 237 cisir~ (cerasius); Ef cysir~; Cp ~.

cisten-bēam *sm* chestnut. **Ef** 249 †cistim~ (castania); Cp ~.

cwic-bēam *sm* aspen. **Ep** 238 cuic~ (cariscus); Cp §.

hnut-bēam *sm* nut-tree. **Ep** 671 ~(nux); Ef, Cp §.

mōr-bēam *sm* mulberry-tree. **VP** 77/47 marbeamas (moros).

wanan-bēam *sm.* **Ep** 418 uu~ (fusorius); Ef uuonan~; Cp ~.

ēac *av* also. **Ep** 846 aec þan (quinetiam); Ef § don. Cp § ðon. **Rn** 1/4 ~. **CA** 14 ec swelce. **VP** 39/7 ec swelce (etiam). **Ct** 45/51, 3; 52/

11 ~. 37/9 æc. 37/14, 27, 8, 34, 40; 48/17 aec. 45/2 ec swylce.

ofer-ēaca *sm* residue. Ct 45/31 ðone ~ęcan.

geēacnian-*wv* conceive. VP 7/15 geecnað (concepit). 50/7 §ad eam.

be-lēac *prt* closed. VP 77/50, 62 belec; bilec (conclusit).

on-lēac *prt* opened. Ep 872 and~ (reserat); Ef §; Cp onlaec.

lēac *s*(*n*) leek. Ep 64 laec (ambila); Ef, Cp §.

leccressae Ef.

brāde-lēac *s*(*n*) leak. Ep 895 ~aeleac (serpillum); Ef ~lec; Cp ~laec.

gār-lēac *s*(*n*) garlic. Ep 16 ~lęc (alium); Ef ~lec; Cp gaarleec.

ynne-lēac *s*(*n*) onion. Ep 62 hynnilaec (ascolonium); Ef ynnilec; Cp ~laec. Cp 448 ynnilaec, cipe (cepa).

caec-bora Cp.

cēace *sf* cheek. VP 31/9 cecan (maxillas).

gēac *s*(*m*) cuckoo. Ef 265 gęc (cuculus); Cp gaec. Cp 965 ~(geumatrix).

geacaes-sūrae Ep; gecaes Ef; gęces Cp; iaces Ef; ieces Cp; acac Ef.

bēacn *sn* beacon, sign. Rn 4/3 be*k*un (becun). 11/2 becun. VP 77/43; 104/5 becen (prodigia). 104/27 becna (§iorum).

bæcenfȳr Bd[2].

fore-bēcen *sn* prodigy. VP 70/7; 134/9; Hy 5/19 ~(prodigium).

here-bēacn *sn* banner. Ep 919 ~baecon (simbulum); Ef ~becon; Cp ~benc. Cp 1971 ~bæcun (symbulum).

sige-bēacn *sn* trophy. Ep 992 sig~ (tropea, signa); Ef †beanc; Cp ~becn. Rn 1/2 þis si*g*becn.

bēcnian *wv* beckon. VP 34/19 ~adon (annuebant).

gebēcnend *sm* beckoner. VP 72/14 ~(index).

hēah *aj* high. VP 46/3 heh (summus). 98/2; 112/4; 137/6 §(excelsus). Hy 2/8 § (§um). 77/35; Hy 7/14 se hea (§us). 77/17, 56 ðone hean (§um). 18/7 ðæm §(summo). 76/11; 81/6 ðes §(excelsi). 17/34; 41/8; 73/5; Hy 6/41 ða § (§a *pl*). 137/6 ða §(alta). Hy 4/6 ða §(sublimia). Hy 12/12 ða §(alta). 103/18 muntas heae (excelsi). Hy 7/55 honda ure hea (§a *sg*). 135/12 heam (§o). 63/7 to heortan heran (altum). 88/28 heane (excelsum). Mt 21 (on) hea dune.

Heaberht Gn, Ct; heah§, hae§ Ct. **Heaburg** LV. **hehcraeft** Rd. **Heahferð** Ct. **Heagȳðe-ðorne**, hę§, hæ§ Ct. **Heahhaam** Ct. **healēcas** Cp. **Heahmund**, heamund Ct. **Hearēd** Ct. **haehsedlum** Cp, hehseotle VP. **Heahstān** Ct.

Æþel-hēah *sm* LV 68 edilhech. 165 eðil§. Ct 33/2 ae~. 35/14; 51/11 aeð~. 52/17 acd~. 33/6 æþelhæh.

Beorn-hēah *sm* Ct 31/8; 40/14 ~. 45/58 †beon~. 30/16; 38/16 biarn~.

Regen-hēah *sm* LV 372 regnhaeg.

Sige-hēah *sm* Gn 6 sighaeh.

Wulf-hēah *sm* Ct 45/58 ~.

Ecgheannglond, ecgheang§ Ct.

hēa-nis *sf* height. Cp 1960 under haehnisse (sub cono). VP 7/8; 67/19; 68/3 in heanisse (altum; §; altitudinem). 102/11 efter § (§). 17/17 §(summo). 55/4; Hy 6/22 §(altitudine). 70/19 §(altissimis). 72/8, 11; 101/20 §(excelso). 92/4 §(§is). 143/7; Hy 9/15 §(alto). 94/4 §(altitudines). 71/16; 112/5; 148/1 §um (summis; altis; excelsis). Hy 3/12 in ~(§o). 11/9 efter hehnisse (altitudinem). 18/7 oð §(summum).

lēah *sm* meadow. Ct 3/6, 6 to brad(an) leage; *illo septo* bradan leage. 29/3, 4 langan § *d*.

Āc-lēah *sm* Ockley. Ct 49/6 ~laeh.

Berhtening-lēag *sm* Ct 25/6 ~.

Brōm-lēag *sm* Bromley. Ct 29/2 ~. 27/4 †~teag.

Bromleaginga-mearc Ct.

Ceddan-lēag *sm* Ct 29/2, 15 ~e *d*.

Crōg-lēah *sm* Crowle. Ct 47/16 ~lea *d*.

Fearn-lēah *sm* Farleigh. Ct 45/38 on ~lege.

Filið-lēag *sm* Ct 3/3 in ~e.

Godmundes-lēah *sm* Ct 14/8 ~.

Heorat-lēag *sm* Hartley. Ct 25/9 ~.

Horsa-lēag *sm* Horsley. Ct 45/7 ~lęge. 27 ~lege.

Hūs-lēah *sm* Ct 30/10 † ~neah.

Hr · · lēag (= hrīþra-?) *sm* Ct 25/3 ~.

Pægna-laech *sm* BH 213 ~ — paegnalech—pęgnalech.

Strēt-lēg *sm* Streatley. Ct 5/3 ~.

Sueord-lēag *sf* Ct 20/18 ~e wælle.

Wemba-lēah *sm* Wembley. Ct 58/8, 10 æt ~lea.

Wis-lēag *sm* Ct 10/2 uu~.

ðēah *cj* though.

ðēah ðe *cj* though. Rd 14 ðeh ði. VP 22/4; 137/7 ðæh ðe (etsi; si). 38/7 ðaeh ðe (quanquam). 61/11 daehðe (si).

swā-ðēah *av* however. Rd 11 suae ðeh.

flēah *prt* fled. VP 113/3 fleh (fugit).

geflēh VP 142/9 ~(confugi).

flēah *s(f)* flea. Ep 813 ~(pulix); Ef †floc; Cp flęh.

nēah *aj, av, prp* near. VP 5/6 neh ðe (juxta). 33/19; 118/151; 139/6 §. 140/7 § helle (secus). 84/10 § *w.d.* (prope). 144/18; Hy 7/68 §.

nehgehūsum VP. **nehlǣcan**, †leh§, nio§, neo§, nia§ VP. **neowest** VP.

ful-nēh *av* nearly. VP 72/2, 2 ~(pene).

un-nēg *aj, av* away from. Rn 3/1.

nēor *av* nearer. Bl[2] 33 nior (propior). Ct 38/11 ~.

tō-getēah *prt* drew to. VP 118/131 ~eh (adtraxi).

ēage *sn* eye. Ep 1093 †unþyotgi egan (oculo); Cp §; Ef ægan. Lr 16 egan (conas). DA 14 egna *gpl.* VP 6/8 *etc* ege (oculus). 93/9 § (§um). 100/5 egan (§o). 16/8; Hy 7/20 § (§i *g*). 12/4; 16/2 § min (§os: §i *pl*) *etc.* 5/6 *etc* §um. 17/25; 30/23; 37/11 §ena.

eghringum Lr.

ēagor *s* flood, tide. Ef 316 aegur (dodrans); Cp egur.

lēag *s(f)* lye. Ep 591 ~(lexiva); Ef læg; Cp laeg.

ðrēagan *wv* rebuke, chastise. Cp 180 biað þreade (aporiamur). Mt 41 ðreade. VP 49/8 dregu (arguam). 68/16 ðrege (urgeat). 117/18 §ende (castigans). 49/21 ðreu (arguam). 37/2 ðrea! (arguas). 6/2, 2 dreast, ðreast (arguas, corripias). 93/10, 0 ðreað (§it, arguet). 140/5, 5 §(corripiet, increpabit). 104/14; 105/9; 117/18 ðreade (corripuit; increpavit; castigavit). 9/6; 38/12 ðreades (increpasti; corripuisti). 67/31 §(†increpa). 118/21 dreades (§asti). 15/7 ðreadun (§averunt).

geðrēagan *wv* VP 37/2 geðrea (corripias). Hy 3/16 geðreas (§ies).

ðrēang *sf* rebuking. VP 37/15 ~e (increpationem). 17/16 § (§one). 103/7 § ðinre (§§). 149/7 § (§ones). 38/12 §um. 75/7; 79/17 dreange.

ðrēa *sf* rebuke, castigation. Ep 53 thrauu (argutie); Cp thrauuo; Ef trafu. VP 90/10 ~(flagellum). 31/10 monge drea (§a). 34/15 ~(§). 37/18 to ðream.

smēagan *wv* penetrate, examine, consider. VP 62/7; 118/16, 34, 47, 117; 142/5; Hy 3/11 smegu (meditabor). 118/69, 115 § (scrutabor). 118/2 §að (§antur). 108/11; 118/148 §e (§etur; meditarer). 7/10; 63/7 §ende (scrutans; §antes). 34/28; 70/24 bið smegende (meditabitur). 35/5 § is. 76/7, 13; 118/70; 142/5 § eam. 37/13; 89/9 werun §. 63/7 § werun. 36/30 bið smead. 118/129 scmegende wes. Ct 40/1 wes ~ende.

geond-smēad *ptc* investigated. Cp 750 ~(enucleata).

smēang *sf* meditation. VP 18/15; 118/24, 77 *etc* ~(meditatio). 48/4 smea[n]g (§). 38/4 ~e minre (§ione) 63/7 smeaunge (scrutinio).

flēag *prt* flew. VP 17/11, 1 fleg (volavit).

tēag *s* tye. Ep 964 teac (sceda); Ef ~; Cp taeg. Cp 19, 1300 § (mantega). 2010 tegum, fodrum (tehis).

waeb-taeg *s* Cp 1231 ~(linea).

bēag *sm* ring, crown. Cp 1339 baeg (munila). VP 20/4; 64/12 beg (coronam).

Baeglog, §lug LV. Beagmund, bæg§ Ct. Beagnōþ Rn. Beag-stān Ct. Bægswīð Ct. Beguini LV.

earm-bēag *sm* bracelet. Ld 54 ermboeg (armilla).

rand-bēag *sm* boss. Ep 153 ~(buculus); Ef, Cp rondbaeg; †nord§ Ld. Ef 1156 randbæg (bucula, umbo).

• **gebēagian** *wv* crown. VP 5/13; 8/6 gebegades (coronasti). 102/5 §að (§at).

Ēata *sm* BH 212, 2, 2, 71, 3; 317 ~. 274; 334 ~ *d*. 348 ~ *d*—æata. LV 205 eota. 256; 329, 56, 6, 61 ~. Gn 55 eota. 65, 87 ~. 56 ~an *d*.

Ēating *sm* son of Eata. Gn 86 ~.

ðrēat *sm* troop. Ef 369 threatae (falange); Cp ðreote. Rd 6 ðrea[t] *or* ðrea[t]un. VP 67/14 ~as (cleros). 149/3; 150/4 ~e (choro).

threatmēlum Ep; theat§ Ef; þreat§ Cp.

ðrēatian *wv* threaten. Cp 1275 þreatende (maceratus). 2169 threatade (urguet). Mt 15 ~ade.

scēat *s(m)* lap. VP 78/12 ~(†sinūs). 128/7 ~(§um). 34/13 †seate (§u). 73/11 ~e ðinum. 88/51 ~e minum.

Sig-scēat *sm*. LV 8; 155 ~.

nēat *sn* animal. VP 72/23; 134/8; 144/16 ~(jumentum; pecus; animal). 35/7; 49/10; 77/50; 106/38 ~(jumenta). 48/13, 21; 103/14; 146/9 ~um. 77/48 net (§a).

genēat *sm* companion. Cp 1117 genaeot (inquilinis).

earn-gēat *s* vulture. Ep 40 ~(arpa); Ef aerngeup; Cp ~geot; Ld arngeus. Cp 233 ~(asapa).

ā-gēat *prt* poured out. VP 41/5 ~(effudi).

grēat *aj* big. Ct 55/5 greotan edesces.

gebēaten *ptc* beaten. Ep 140 gibeataen!(battuitum); Ef gebeatten; Cp ~.

un-gebēaten *ptc* unbeaten. Ld 69 ~batne stane (lapide impolito, non exciso).

ēad *sn* prosperity.

Eadbald BH, LV, Gn, Ct; aeod§ BH; eod§ BH, LV; eadbalding Gn. Eadberct BH, LV; §berht Gn, Ct. Eadburg LV. Eatcume LV. Eodfrid BH; eadfrid BH; eatfrith LV; §ferð LV, Gn, Ct; ead§ Ct. Eadgār BH, LV, Gn, Ct. Eadgȳd BH. Eadhāeth BH, LV; §haeð Gn. Eadhelm LV. Eadhere Ct. Eadhūn LV, Ct. Eadlāc LV. Eadmēr LV. Eadmund LV, Gn, Ct. Eadrēd LV, Ct. Eatðegn LV. Eatðrȳð LV. Eaduald LV, Ct; eod§ LV. Eaduini LV. Eaduulf LV, Gn, Ct; eod§ LV.

Ēada *sm* LV 116, 35, 77, 91; 210, 73; 372, 92; 411, 6, 9, 23 ~.

ēadig *aj* prosperous, blessed. VP 31/2; 33/9; 39/5 ~ (beatus). 40/3 ~ne. 32/12 ~u *sg*. 2/13; 31/1; 83/5; 105/3; 118/1, 2; 127/1 eadge *pl*.

ēadignis *sf* happiness. Mt 34 ðære eadinesse *g*.

rēad *aj* red. Ef 250 rede clabre (calta); Cp ~e. Ep 404 ~(flavum, fulfum); Ef ~; Cp reod. Cp 1758 ~(ruber). VP 105/7, 9, 22; 135/13, 5; Hy 5/7 ~an (rubro *etc*). Ct 13/6 ~an solo.

uuretbaso Ld.

wioloc-rēad *aj* purple. Ep 169 uuilocre[a]d (coccum bis tinctum); Ef †u[u]slucreud; Cp ~.

rēadan *spl* tonsils. Lr 65 ~(toleam).

on-rēod *prt* reddened. Cp 1129 ~(inluit).

lēad *s(n)* lead. VH 5/17 ~(plumbum).

gestrēad *prt* plundered, destroyed. B[2] 26 ~(conroderet).

dēad *aj* dead. VP 30/13 ~(mortuus). 87/6; 113/17 ~e *pl*. 87/11 ~um. 105/28 ~ra. 142/3 deode *pl*.

deadraegelum Cp.

dēadlic *aj* deadly, mortal. Ep 439 tha deatlicostan (funestissima); Ef deudlicustan; Cp dead§. VP 78/2 ða ~an (mortalia).

Pēada *sm*. BH 124 ~ *d*—peda. 179 ~ *d* — ~ II [*first* a *over* o]. 204 ~ *d*— ~an I — peada [*first* a *over* o; peoda *in margin*]. 205 ~ — ~ II. Ct 3/3 ~an stigele.

bi-bēad *prt* commanded. **VP** 132/3 ~(mandavit). **Ct** 39/11 be~.

on-bēad *prt* commanded. **VP** 41/9; 77/5, 23; 90/11; 104/8; 110/9; 148/5 ~(mandavit).

bēo-brēad *sn* honeycomb. **VP** 18/11 bio~ (favum). 118/103 bia~ (§).

hēap *s(m)* heap. **Cp** 1912 ~(strues).

stēapol *s* steeple. **Ct** 25/5 æt stęnan steaple.

cēap *sm* purchase.

ceapcnext Ef; §cneht Cp. ceapstōu Cp.

lond-cēap *s(m)* purchase of land. **Ct** 48/6 to ~e.

gēap *aj* open. **Cp** 1493 ~um (pandis).

drēapian *wv* drip. **VP** 67/9 ~edun (distillaverunt).

drēapung *sf* dropping. **VP** 71/6 ~(stillicidia). 64/11 ~ingum.

Ēo-mǣr Rn; eumer BH; eamær, §ing Gn.

hēo *prn* she. **VP** 85/11 hie. **Ct** 34/11, 2; 41/69; 45/11, 2, 27, 7, 9 hio. 45/13, 5, 6 ~. 38/5, 9; 41/9, 25 hia.

Hēuuald, heauald BH; heouald LV.

Rīuualch LV.

lēo *sf* lion. **VP** 21/14 ~(leo). 90/13 leon (leonem). 16/12; 21/22 § (§is). 34/17 leom (§ibus). 56/5; 57/7; 103/21 leona (§um). 7/3; 9/30; 16/12; Hy 3/8 lea (leo).

Lēo-frith LV.

Hlēo-berct LV. **Hleoburg** LV. **Hleofrith** LV. **Hleouald** LV. **Hleouini** LV.

þrēo three.

ðrēotēne Ct.

sēo *fem.* **VP** 17/36; 38/8 *etc* sie *article.* 20/9 *etc* § *prn.* 31/7; 57/6 *etc* § (quae). 25/10 seo swiðre. **Ct** 29/12; 37/33; 45/17 sio. 39/11; 40/22 sia.

gesēo *sv* see. **VP** 105/5 to geseonne (ad videndum). 5/5; 117/7; Hy 3/2 gesio (§ebo). 39/4; 106/42 gesioð (§ebunt). Hy 13/25 gesionde (§ens). 16/2; 33/9; 35/10; 45/9, 11; 51/8; 65/5; 113/5 (2); 113/74; Hy 7/75, 5 gesiað (§eant; §ete *etc*). 26/13; 33/13 gesian (§ere). Hy 6/20 geseað (§ebunt). 15/10 gesean (§ere). 8/4 gesie (§ebo). 72/3 gesiende (§ens). 26/4 gese (§eam). 9/32; 13/2; 52/3 § (§eat). 88/49 § (§ebit). 68/24, 33; 85/17; 118/37 gesen (§eant). 127/5, 6 gesee (§eas). 9/14; 24/18; 36/37 *etc* geseh (§e!).

sehðe *interj* behold! **VP** 7/15; 36/36; 38/6 *etc* ~(ecce). 10/3; 122/2 sehde. 131/6 seððe. 118/40 sehð.

for-sēo *sv* despise. **VP** 26/9; 54/2; 137/8 ~seh! (despicias).

sēo *sf* pupil (of the eye). **VP** 16/8 sean (pupillam). Hy 7/20 sian (§).

fēo *wv* hate. **VP** 10/6 fiað (odit). 34/19; 96/10 § (§erunt, §ite). 44/8 feodes (§isti). 25/5; 54/13; 100/3; 138/21, 2 fiode (odivi *etc*). 30/7 §es. 17/18 §on. 67/2; 68/5; 73/23; 82/3; 85/17; 105/41; 119/7; 128/5; 138/21; Hy 7/82, 9; Hy 9/6 §un. 104/25 §en (§irent). 35/5 fiede (§ivit). 24/19; 37/20; 43/8, 11; 73/4 §on. 5/7 fedest (§isti). 20/9; 33/22 figað (§erunt). 88/24 figende (§ientes). 17/41 ða §an. 68/15 §um. 105/10 §ra.

fēond *sm* enemy. **Mt** 49 fiond. **VP** 7/6; 12/3; 40/12; 142/3 se ~(inimicus). 12/5; 42/2; 54/13; 73/3, 10, 8 ~ (§). 8/3 ~(§um). 41/10; Hy 13/4 fiond (§; hostis). 88/23 se § (inimicus). 30/9; 43/17; 54/4 *etc* ~es (§i *g*). Hy 12/13; Hy 13/15 fiondes (hostis *g*). 40/3 ~(†inimici *g*). 6/8, 11; 9/7 *etc* ~ (§os; §i *pl*; §i *pl*). 16/9; 26/2, 6 *etc* fiond (§; §; §os). 5/9; 7/5; 8/3 *etc* ~um. 43/11; 68/19; Hy 7/89 fiondum. 7/7; 16/14; 17/41 *etc* ~a. 88/43 feonða. 44/6; 135/24; Hy 7/54; Hy 9/9 fionda. 9/14; 26/11 fiendum. 9/4 fienda min (†inimicum). 9/26 § (§orum). Hy 5/14 feond (§us).

fīong *sf* enmity. **VP** 118/104, 28, 63 ~e (odio). 138/22 fulfremedre ~e (§). 118/113 fienge (§).

gefēo *sv* rejoice. **Bd**[2] 67 gefegan (exultant). **VP** 9/16; 74/10; Hy 6/39 gefio (exultabo; gaudebo; §). 5/12; 32/1 gefioð (exultabunt; gaudete). 12/5; 31/11; 34/27; 50/10; 67/5 70/23; 88/17; 89/14; 95/12, 2; 67/4, 144/7; 149/5 gefiað (exultabunt *etc*). 88/13 gefeað (§). 9/3; 30/8; 62/8; 91/5 gefie (§abo). 95/11 gefee (exultet). 39/17; 47/12; 66/5; 67/4; 69/5; 149/2 gefen (§ent). 94/1; 117/24 § (§emus). Hy 2/10 gefeh (§a!).

frēo *aj* free. **VP** 87/6 frea (liber).

Friubet LV. Frehelm LV. friolēta Cp; friulactum Ld. **Friumon LV. Friouini LV.**

frēolice *av* freely. **VP** 93/1 ~(libere).

frīodōm *sm* freedom. **Ct** 47/9 ðes ~. 47/10, 3 ~. 42/3 ~e.

frīols *s*(*m*) freedom. **Ct** 44/7 ~.

gefrēo *wv* free. **Lr** 11 ~ia [a *alt. to* o] (libera!). **VP** 90/14 ~igu (§abo). 143/10 ~eas (§as). 33/20; 40/2; 48/16 *etc* ~eað (§abit). 36/40 ~eoð (§abit). 90/3 ~iað (§abit). 81/4 ~igað (§ate!). 7/2; 21/22; 30/2 *etc* ~ea (§a!). 56/4; 71/12; 80/8 *etc* ~eode (§avit; §avit; §avi). 21/5; 76/16 ~eodes (§asti). 33/7; 105/21 ~iode (§avit). 106/6; Hy 9/5 ~eade (§avit). 43/8; 73/2; Hy 5/22 ~eades (§asti). 33/18 ~ede (§avit). 106/28 †gefre (§avit). 123/7 ~eode sind (§ati sumus). 59/6 sien ~iad (§entur). 107/7 sien ~ead (§entur). Hy 9/10 ~eade (§ati *pl*).

gefrigend *sm* liberator. **VP** 17/3, 48; 39/18 ~(liberator). 143/2 gefrigen (§).

flio *s* albugo. **Ep** 12 ~(albugo); Ef, Cp ~.

flēo *sv* flee. **VP** 138/7 fleom (fugiam). 103/7 fleoð (§ient). 54/8 fleonde (§iens). 67/2 flen (§iant).

Gīu-haep LV.

milc-dēond *sm* suckling. **VP** 8/3 ~ra (lactantium).

Tīouulfinga-cæstir BH. **Tiuuald,** tiouald LV.

getēon *sv* draw. **VP** 31/9 geteh (constringe!).

ā-tēon *sv* deal with. **Ct** 38/10, 3 (he) atee; ateon *inf.* 42/22 to ationne.

ðurh-tīon *sv* accomplish. **Ct** 42/10 ~.

tēon *wv* prepare, adorn. **CH** 8 tiadæ.

getēon *wv* arrange, decree. **Ct** 45/45 geteod habbe.

getīung *sf* preparation. **Ep** 97 gitiungi (apparatione); Ef get[o]ing [o *doubtful*]; Cp ~e.

twēon *wv* doubt. **Cp** 175 tuigendi (anceps).

bēo *vb* be. **Cp** 180 biað þreade (aporiamur). **Rd** 5 biað *pl.* **CA** 14 beon *inf.* **Bd**[2] 23 we bioð stiocode (jugulamur). **VP** 15/4; 17/4, 24 *etc* biom (ero). 9/3, 27 *etc* § geblissad (laetabor); § onstyred (movebor). 30/10 § geswenced (tribulor). 15/8 ne § ic onstyred (ne commovear). 118/15; 142/7 beom. 68/18 bio geswenced (tribulor). 24/7; 36/7 bio (esto!). 31/9 bion (fieri). 83/11 aworpen § (abjectus esse). 118/59 § gecerred (converti). 12/5 ic beam. 30/3 bia (esto!). 18/15; 44/18; 62/11 bioð (erunt). 4/5 § geinbryrde (conpungimini) *etc.* 9/4 § geuntrumad (infirmabuntur) *etc.* 9/18 § gecerde (convertantur) *etc.* 9/26, 6 § besmiten, § afirred (polluuntur, auferuntur) *etc.* 18/14 § waldende (fuerint dominati) *etc.* 2/10 bi[o]ð. 21/27; 72/5 bið (saturabuntur *etc*). 36/9, 20; 43/22; 79/8 biað. **Ct** 37/6 bion *inf.* 41/46 bian *inf.*

bēo *s*(*f*) bee. **VP** 117/12 bian (apes).

biobrēad, bia§ VP. **Biuuulf LV. biouuyrt** Ep; biuyrt Ef; biowyrt Cp.

ēored *s*(*n*) troop of cavalry. **VH** 5/34; 6/18 ~ud; ~(equitatus).

se oritmon Ef; se eorod§ Cp.

Īuring *sm* **LV** 199 ~.

lēoran *wv* pass, depart. **VP** 61/7 ~u (emigrabo). 56/2; 89/6; Hy 5/28 ~eð (transeat). 79/13 ~ad (§eunt). Hy 11/12 ~e (§eat). 36/36; 72/9 ~de (§ivi; §iit). 17/13 ~don. 41/8; 65/12; 72/7 ~dun. 88/42 ða ~endan (§euntes). 140/10 ic †leareore (§eam).

ūt-ā-lēoran *wv* depart. **VP** 51/7 ~eð (emigrabit).

bī-lēoran *wv* pass by. **VP** 143/4 ~að (praetereunt). 89/4; 148/6 ~de (§iit; †§ibit). 128/8 ~dun (§ibant).

ofer-lēoran *wv* pass over. **VP**

118/119 ~liorende (praevaricantes). 136 ~don (transierunt).

ðorh-lēoran *wv* pass through. VP 65/6; 89/6; 102/16 ~eð (pertransivit; §eat; §iit). 103/10, 20 ~að. 104/18; 123/5, 5 ~de (§ivit *etc*). 76/18; 87/17; 104/13 ~dun.

lēornis *sf* departure. VH 6/35 ~isse (transmigrationis).

ofer-lēornis *sf* passing over. VP 100/3 ~isse (praevaricationes).

hlēor *sn* check. Ep 438 ~(frons); Ef, Cp §. 482 ~(genas); Ef, Cp §. Cp 86 on hlior rouuit (adplaudat). LP 5 ðin ~ *a*.

swēor *sm* father-in-law. Ep 1062 suehoras (vitelli); Ef, Cp sueoras. Ef 1099 sueor (vetellus); Cp §. Cp 552 § (consobrinus). 1878 †sur (socer).

stēor *sm* bullock. Ep 596 ~(ludaris); Ef, Cp §. 780 thriuuuintri ~(prifeta); Ef steur; Cp ~.

stēor *sf* steering.

steorrōðor Cp.

stīora *sm* steerer. Lr 5 ~an (proretas).

stēoran *wv* steer. VH 5/21; Hy 11/8 ~des; ~eð (gubernasti, §et).

Uīuri *s* river Wear. BH 291 *fluminis* ~. 303 §.

Uiuraemūda, uu§ BH; †u[i]uræmoda LK.

frēorig *aj* cold, chill. Rd 1 ~.

genēorð *aj*. Ef 276 ginehord (contentus); Cp ~.

cnēoris *sf* generation, family, race. Ep 903 †~issa (sanguinis); Ef ~issae; Cp cniorisse. VP 21/32; 144/4, 4; Hy 3/4; Hy 6/36 ~(generatio). 77/6 ~ oderu (§). Hy 7/39 ~ðweoru (§). 72/15; Hy 7/8 ~(natio). 73/8 ~(cognatio). 9/27, 7 *etc* ~isse (generatione, §em). 77/4 § oðerre (§e). Hy 7/12 § (nationis). 64/11; Hy 10/4 § (generationes). 78/10 *etc* §um. Hy 7/12 §a (nationum). 104/8 cneorrissa (generationes). 88/2 cnerisse. 95/10 cneorisum.

dēor *sn* wild beast. Mt 23 de(or) *pl*.

Deorlāf Ct. Deornōð, dior§ Ct. deortuun Cp. Diarweald Ct.

Dīar *sm* Ct 43/9 ~.

wildēor *sn* wild beast. Mt 21 (wil)deor *pl*. VP 79/14 ~(ferus). 49/10 ~(§ae). 73/19; 78/2 ~um. Hy 7/49 ~a. 103/11, 20; 148/10; Hy 8/15 wilddeor (bestiae).

Dīora *sm* Gn 11 ~. Ct 25/11 di[o]ra. 30/19 diara.

Dīori *sm* LV 361, 9; 408 ~.

Dēoring-lond Ct.

Dīorente *s*. Ct 55/5 ~.

dēor-wyrðe VP.

fīorða *aj* fourth. LP 5 ~an.

for-lēort *prt* left, abandoned, allowed. VP 37/11 ~(deseruit). 39/13; 70/11; Hy 7/30 ~(dereliquit). 118/87 ~(§ui). 80/13 ~(dimisi). 104/20; Hy 10/9 ~(§it). 104/14 ~(permisit). 21/2; Hy 7/35 ~e (dereliquisti). 16/14 ~un (reliquerunt). 26/10 ~on (de§).

on-drēord *prt* feared. VP 63/10; 118/120; Hy 6/1 ~(timuit *etc*). 54/20; 63/6; 76/17; 77/53 ~un.

hwēol *sn* wheel. VP 76/19 ~e (rotā). 82/14 hwiol (§am).

huueolrād Ep; hueol§ Ef, Cp.

nēolnis *sf* abyss. VP 35/7; Hy 6/21 niolnis (abyssus). 41/8, 8 § §se (§us §um). 76/17; 77/15; 106/26; 148/7 §se. 103/6 ~. 32/7; 70/20 ~se. 134/6 ~sum.

gīululing *s*. Ct 1699 ~(quintus).

cēol *s(m)* ship. Ep 230 ~(celox); Ef, Cp §.

Ceolbald LV. Ceolberct LV; §berht Gn, Ct; ciol§, cial§ Ct. Ceolfrid BH; §frið LV. Ceolgār LV. Ceolhāeth LV. Ceolheard CA. Ceolhelm LV, Ct. Ceolhere LV. Ceolmund LV, Gn, Ct; ciol§, cial§ Ct. Ceolnōð Gn, Ct; ciol§, cial§ Ct. Ceolrēd LV, Gn; §ræd, ceored Ct. Ceolstān Ct. Ceolðrȳth LV. Ceoluald LV; ceolwald, §ing SG. Ceolward Ct. Ceoluini LV. Ceoluīo LV. Ceoluulf BH, LK, LV, Gn, Ct; ciolulf, cial§ Ct.

ā-wēoll *prt* flowed out. Ef 355 uueol (exundavit); Cp a§. Cp 1133 auueoll (incanduit).

fēoll *prt* fell. Mt 27 ~. VP 117/13 ~e (caderem).

gefēoll *prt*. VP 54/5; 57/9;

104/38 gefeol (cecidit). 15/6; 19/9; 26/2 *etc* ~un (§erunt). 56/7 § (inciderunt).

ā-fēoll *prt* fell. Bl 2 ~(versatus sum).

in-gefēoll *prt* fell in. VP 7/16 ~(incidit).

hēold *prt* held. SG 1, 2, 7, 8, 9 ~. VP 16/4; 17/22; 118/55, 67 ~(custodivi). 118/167 ~(§ivit). 118/168 ~(servavi). Hy 6/31; Hy 7/19 ~(§ivit). Hy 4/18 ~(servabit). 77/10 ~on (custodierunt). 70/10; 77/56; 98/7; 118/136, 58 ~un (custodiebant *etc*). 77/57 §(observaverunt). 90/11 hiolden.

bi-hēold *prt* beheld. Rn 2/13 bi(h*ea*)l(d). 18 (bi)h*ea*(l)du(n).

hlēoð *s.* Cp 1843 hliuða (scuporum).

hlēoðrian *wv* sound, resound. Ep 508 hlaeodrindi (increpitans); Ef †hleodendri; Cp hleoþrendi. VP 17/14; 28/3 ~að (intonuit). Hy 4/21 ~að (tonabit). 57/3 ~iað (concinnant). Hy 12/7 § (†concinat). 49/19 ~ade (concinnavit). 45/4; 82/3 ~adun (sonaverunt).

wel-hlēoðriende *ptc* well-sounding. VP 150/5 †belhleoðriendum (bene sonantibus).

newe-sēoða *sm* pit of stomach. Ep 505 neuu*n*seada (ilium); Ef naensida. Ef 1180 naensood (ilium neisn').

Giuþeas *pl* Jews. Rn 3/3 †~u.

eahta-tēoða *num* eighteenth. Mt 11 ~tegðan.

rā **ge-rēose** *sf* spine-muscle. Ef 1181 iesca, hregresi (inguen).

hrēosan *sv* fall. VP 144/14 ~að (ruunt).

on-hrēosan *sv* assail. Ep 520 anhriosith (ingruerit); Ef onhrisit; Cp onhrioseð.

ðēos *fem nom* this. VP 76/11; 108/27; 118/50, 6; 131/14 ~(haec). Ct 45/43.

flēos *sn* fleece. Rd 3 fliusum. VP 71/6 ~(vellus *a*).

nēosian *wv* visit. VP 88/33 ~iu (visitabo). 8/5 ~as. 105/4 niosa! 58/6 to §enne. 64/10 §ades. Hy 9/1, 15 neasede, §ade (§avit). 16/3 §ades.

mēos-gelegeo Ct.

gecēosan *sv* chose. VP 118/122 geceos (elege!).

wið-ceōsan *sv* reject. VP 32/10, 0 ~eð (reprobat).

brēosa *sm* gadfly. Ep 27 briosa (asilo); Ef, Cp §. 1016 §; Ef § (tabanus); Cp §; Ld briusa.

rēost *s* part of a plough. Cp 656 sules ~(dentalia).

ðēostre *aj* dark. Bd² 12 ðiostrum (obscuris). VP 17/12 ~weter (tenebrosa). ?34/6 ~(tenebrae).

ðēostru *spl* darkness. Cp 152 þiustra (ambulas). VP 138/12, 2 ~(tenebrae). Hy 8/8 deostru (§). 17/12; 103/20; 104/28; Hy 12/9 ~(§as). 17/29 ~min (§). 81/5 in ~(§is). 138/11 on ~(†§ae). 54/6 ~o (§ae). 87/7 ~um [*or* ðeastrum?]. 90/6 *etc* ~um.

ā-ðēostrian *wv* darken. VP 104/28 ~ade (obscuravit). 138/12 bioð §. 68/24 sien aðiostrade. 73/20 aðeastrade sind.

mæsse-prēost *sm* mass-priest. Ct 34/10 ~prioste. 37/35 messepriost. 41/32 §preoste.

bēost *s* beestings. Ep 703 ~(obestrum); Ef †beoth; Cp ~. Ef 261~; Cp ~(colostrum); Ld beust. Ef 1183 ~(†lantantia).

brēost *sn* breast. Lr 22 ~(crassum). VP 21/10 ~um (uberibus). 35/9 § (ubertate). Hy 13/25 ~a(pectorum).

briostbiorg Cp.

ēow *sf* ewe. Ct 41/20, 1 eawa *gpl*.

ēowod *sf* flock of sheep. VP 77/52 eowde (gregem). 73/1 § ðinre (§is). 78/13 §es. 49/9; 77/70 §um.

ēow *prn dat.* you. DA 10 ~. VP 65/16 ~(vobis). Ct 30/23 ~. 37/42 iow.

ēow *acc.* DA 2, 10 ~. VP 33/12; 128/8 ~(vos). Ct 23/16 ~. 30/22 iow.

ēowic *acc.* you. VP 113/14, 4; 128/8; Hy 7/74 ~(vos).

ēower *poss.* your. VP 30/25 ~ heorte (vestrum). 68/33 ~ sawul. 77/1 eare ~. 80/4 eowerre. 23/9 ~es. 23/7; 104/11 eowres. 33/6; 47/14; 57/3, 10; 61/9; 94/8, 9;

113/14; 133/2 §e. 4/5, 5; 138/20; Hy 4/7 §um. Ct 23/15, 6 eouuer, eouuere.

Ēowa *sm* Gn 98, 101 ~.

Ēowing *sm* son of E. Gn 98,101 ~.

ēowister *sm* sheepfold. Cp 1274 eouuistras (mandras).

Rīuuala *sm* LV 211 ~.

Cyn-rēou *sm* Gn 104 ~.

Cynrēowing *sm* son of C. Gn 103 ~.

hrēowsian *wv* repent. VP 105/45; 109/4 ~ade (paenituit; §ebit).

mund-lēu *s* basin. Ep 1055 mundl·· (vescada); Ef munleuu; Cp ~. Cp 561 ~(conca).

lēower *s* Lr 10 ~(pernas).

Līowsan-denu Ct.

ðēow *sm* servant, slave. Mt 26 ~. VP 18/12 ~(servus). 77/70; 104/17 ~(§um). 118/122 ~ ðinne (§um). 108/28 ðeo (§us). 88/4; 118/65 ~e. 34/27; 79/5; 85/4; 88/40; 104/6; 129/2 ~es. 89/16; 101/15 ~as. 96/10 ~a. 30/17; 85/2; 88/21; 104/26; 115/16, 6; 118/23, 125, 135, 40; 142/12; 143/10 ðiow. 18/14; 26/9; 118/17, 38, 49, 76, 124; 135/22; 142/2 §e. 118/84 §es. 89/13; 104/25; 133/1; 134/1, 9; Hy 8/17 §as. 134/14; Hy 7/70 §um. 33/23; 68/37; 78/2, 10; 88/51; 101/29; 122/2 §a. 131/10 ðieowe. Ct 37/38 ðiow. 41/33 §e. 37/6 §as.

lād-ðēow *sm* leader. VP 9/21 aee ~tow (legislatorem). 30/4; 54/14; 103/17 § (dux). Hy 5/25 §as (duces).

ðīwen *sf* servant. Ct 40/16 ~.

ðēowdōm *sm* servitude. VP 103/14 ~e (servituti). 146/8 ~es ((†§).

ðēowian *wv* serve. VP 2/11; 71/11 ~iað (servite). 21/31 ðiowað (§iet). 99/2; 118/91 §iað. 101/23 §ien. 105/36 §edun. 80/7 ðeowdun. 17/45 ðeawde. Hy 9/10 ðiwgen (§iamus).

ðīowincel *sn* little servant. VH 4/10 ~u (famelici).

sēowun *prt* sowed. VP 106/37 ~(seminaverunt).

snēowan *vb* snow. Ep 669 †hsniuuith (ninguit); Ef sniuidh; Cp s[ni]uwið.

snīð-strēo *s* Ep 973 snid~ (sisca); Ef §streu; Cp ~. Cp 13 snithstreo (gacila).

uuēowera-get Ct.

fēower *num* four. Mt 17 fiow(er). Ct 41/34, 61; 48/4 ~.

fēowertig *num* forty. VP 94/10 ~um (quadraginta).

flēowun *prt* flowed. VP 77/20; 104/41; 147/18 ~(fluxerunt; §; fluent).

tō-flēowun *prt* flowed away. VP 96/5 ~(fluxerunt) Hy 6/12, 3 ~(de§).

on-cnēow *prt* knew. VP 19/7; 40/12; 49/11; 70/15; 139/13; 118/75, 152; 134/5 ~(cognovi). 90/14; 103/19 ~(§it). 55/10; 100/4 ~(agnovi; agnoscebam). 39/10; 138/2, 5; 141/4 ~e(cognovisti). 72/16 ~e (cognoscerem). 141/5 ~e (agnosceret). 13/3; 73/5; 77/3 ~un. 78/6 ~un(noverunt). 17/45 oncnew. 138/1 §e (cognovisti). 94/11 §un.

cnēow *sn* knee. VP 108/24 ~ min (genua).

cnioholaen Ep; Cp §; cniolen Ef; cneholen, †cre§ Ld. cneoribt Cp.

grēow *prt* grew. Cp 2138 greouue (viresceret).

trēow *sn* tree. VP 104/33 trew (lignum). 79/11; 95/12; 103/16 § (arbusta; ligna; §). 148/9 treo (§). 95/10 § (§o). 73/5 trea (§orum). Ct 1/5 triow. 29/18 trio. 59/3 treo. 48/4 feower ~e hyl.

treuteru Cp. **treowyrm** VP.

ele-trēow *sn* olive. Bl 8 þa gingan ~tri[o]w (novella olivarum). VP 51/10 ~(oliva). 127/3 ~(trea (§arum). Hy 6/37 ~tres (§ae).

fīc-trēo *sn* figtree. VP 104/33 ~trew (ficulneas). Hy 6/35 ~(ficus).

fūle-trēo *sn* black alder. Ep 36 fulaetrea (alneum); Cp §treo; Ef falatreu.

fugul-trēo *sn* perch. Cp 150 ~ *vel* reftras (amites).

haelf-trēo *sn* VP 31/9 ~(camo).

plūm-trēu *sn* plumtree. Cp 1598 ~(plunas).

tel-trēo *sn* Cp 488 ~(clus).

wīn-trēow *sn* grape-vine. **VP** 127/3 ~(vites). Hy 7/62 ~treo (§).

getrēowe *aj* faithful. **VP** 88/38; 144/13; Hy 7/6 ~(fidelis). 110/8 ~bibodu (§ia). 18/8 cyðnis.. ~u. 100/6 ða ~an (§es). 88/29; Hy 11/8; Hy 12/10 ~um.

trēulēasnis *sf* perfidy. **Ep** 726 ~le: snis [u *er.*] (perfidia); Ef treulesnis; Cp ~.

getrēowlice *av* faithfully. **VP** 11/6 getrew~ (fiducialiter). Hy 2/3 ~(§).

getrēowan *wv* trust. **Ep** 436 gitreeudae (foederatas); Ef getreudæ; Cp getreuuade. Cp 857 getriowad (foederatus). **VP** 10/2; 24/2 ~u (confido). 56/2 ~eð. 2/13; 48/7; 113/8 (2); 124/1; 134/18 ~að. Hy 7/72 ~dun. 117/8, 8; 145/2 ~.

bēow *s* corn. **Ep** 645 handful †beouuas (manticum); Ef beouaes; Cp ~es; Ld baeues.

blēow *prt* blew. **VP** 147/18 ~(flavit).

blēow *prt* flowered. **VP** 27/7 ~(refloruit).

Ēof *sm* **Ct** 30/16 iab. 41/52 iof.

Īubi *sm* **LV** 175 ~.

hīofian *wv* lament. **VP** 34/14 ~ende (lugens).

lēof *aj* dear. **VP** 28/6 se ~a (dilectus). 67/13 ðes ~an. Hy 7/29 se liofa. **Ct** 41/15, 7, 24, 5 liofre *cp*. 42/14, 22 liofast. 45/48 ~ust.

Leofrith LV. **Leobhelm** LV. **Liofshēma** Ct. **Leofðegn** LV. **Leofuini** LV.

lēofwende *aj* amiable. **Ef** 1136 lebuendi (amabilis *etc*).

Lēofa *sm* **Ct** 32/1 liaban *d*.

Hlēof-uini LV.

ðēof *sm* thief. **DA** 20 ðiofum. **VP** 49/18 ~(furem).

ðeofscip Cp; Ef theb§; Ep theb·scib.

sēofian *wv* sigh, complain. **Cp** 645 wrastum end seobgendum (delicatis et querulis).

Sc[i]ofing-den Ct.

bed-clēofa *sm* bedroom. **VP** 9/30; 35/5 ~an (cubili) 4/5; 103/22; 104/30; 149/5 ~um.

dēofol *sn* devil. **VP** 108/6 ~(diabolus). Hy 7/33 deoflum (daemoniis). Hy 13/4 dioful (diabolus). 90/6 diofle (daemonio). 105/37 §um (§iis). 95/5 ðioful (§ia).

deofulgeld VP.

hel-dīobul *sn* hell-devil. **Cp** 1457 ~(orcus).

Pēuf *sm* **LV** 199 ~.

Pēufa *sm* **LV** 216 ~.

Strēonaes-halch, streunaes §, streanæs §, strenæs §, strenes § BH.

Strēon-berct LV. **Streonuulf** LV.

gestrīon *s*(*n*) gain, property. **Cp** 510 ~(commercium). 1470 ~(patrimonium).

gestrīonan *wv* get, beget. **Ct** 41/36, 7 ~en.

Tyt-wīan *sm* **Gn** 121 tyt····.

Tyttwīaning *sm* son of T. **Gn** 120 t·ttwianing.

Kīona *sm* **LV** 480 ~.

tēona *sm* injury. **Cp** 1125 tionan (infestationes). **VP** 102/6 tionan (injuriam). 145/7 ~an (§).

ungetīon *sn* injury. **DA** 20 ~u.

frēond *sm* friend. **VP** 87/19 ~(amicum). 138/17 ~(§i *pl*). 37/12 freod (§i *pl*). **Ct** 40/4, 7 friond *pl*, §a. 38/8 friandum.

frēondlēas *sm* friendless. **VP** 9/39 ðæm ~an (pupillo).

Rēumwalus *sm* Remus. **Rn** 3/1 ~.

lēoma *sm* ray of light, brilliance. **Ep** 478 ~(globus); Ef leuma; Cp. ~. 554 ~(iuuar); Ef, Cp §. Hy 11/3 lioma (jubar).

gēomrung *sf* lamentation, groaning. **VP** 78/11 geamring (gemitus). 6/7; 11/6; 37/9 §e *d*. 101/6 §e minre (§us). 17/5 §e (§ *pl*). 30/11 §um. 37/10 gemrung. 101/21 §e.

gēoc *sf* consolation, help. **LP** 1 gece *g*.

ðēoh *s*(*n*) thigh. **Ef** 295 th~ (coxa); Cp thegh. **Lr** 25 ðeeoh [o *from* c] (bathma).

þeohsaex Cp.

lēoht *sn* light. **VP** 4/7; 86/

6 *etc* leht (lumen). 42/3 § ðin (lucem). 35/10 *etc* §e. Hy 11/2, 2 §es (luminis; lucis).

lehtfaet Cp, VP.

lēht *aj* light. VP 18/9 ~(lucidum).

lēogan *sv* lie. VP 88/36 legu (mentiar). 65/3; Hy 6/36 §að. 26/12 legende wes. 77/36; 80/16 § werun. 17/46 ligende werun.

flēogan *sv* fly. VP 49/11; 77/27 ða flegendan (volatilia). 90/6 flegendum (volante). 54/7 fligu (volabo).

flēge *sf* fly. Cp 1354 ~ (musca). VP 77/45 ~an (muscam). 104/31 hundes pie (cynomia).

buter-flēge *sf* butterfly. Ep 817 buturfliogae; Ef §fli[o]go; Cp ~(papilio).

gēoguð *sf* youth. VP 42/4 iuguðe mine (juventutem). 128/2 § minre (§ute). 70/5, 17; 128/1 guguðe minre (§ute). 143/12 § (§ute). 24/7 †guiuðu (§utis). 87/16 guðe (§ute). 102/5 guðuð (§us).

Iutas *pl* Jutes. BH 21 ~is. 21 ~arum —io§. 22 ~arum.

ðēote *sf* torrent. Cp 884 þeotum (fistulis). VP 41/8 ~ena [a *over* e] (cataractarum).

Sceut-uald LV.

an-scēotan *sv*. Ef 377 anseot (extentera); Cp ansceat (exintera).

ūt-sciotan *sv* shoot out, project. Ct 20/17 ~eð.

sprēot *s*(*m*) pole, spear. Ep 211 ~um (contis); Cp §; Ef spreutum.

eofor-sprēot *s*(*m*) boar-spear. Ep 1052 ebor~ (venabula); Ef §; Cp eobor~.

flēot *sm* aestuary, fleet. Ep 107 ~as (aestuaria); Cp §; Ef fleutas. Ef 1126 fliute (ratis).

Am-flēot *sm* Ambleteuse. BH 35 *sinu maris qui* vocatur ~eat.

Ealh-flēot *sm* Ct 52/11 ~. 54/2 alh~

Hūnburge-flēot *sm* Ct 20/22 ~.

Mearc-flēot *sm* Ct 53/4 *fretum qui nominatur* ~.

clēot *s* cloth. Cp 1585 clut, ~(pittacium, os peri).

ā-gēotan *sv* pour out. VP 141/3 ~u (effundam). 61/9 ~að. 34/3; 68/25; 78/6 ageot (§e!). 13/3 to ~enne.

in-gēotan *sv* pour in. VH 11/4 ingeot (infunde).

Gēoting *sm* son of Gēot. Gn 110 ~.

Angen-gēot *sm* Gn 81 ~. 94 · · g · · geot.

Angen-gēoting *sm* son of A. Gn 81, 94 ~.

Sig-gēot *sm* Gn 75 ~.

Sig-gēoting *sm* son of S. Gn 75 ~.

Waðol-gēot *sm* Gn 95 ~.

Waðol-gēoting *sm* son of W. Gn 15 · að · · geoting.

grēot *s*(*n*) sand, gravel. Rn 3/7 greut.

bēot *prt* beat. Bd[2] 52 biotan (caedebant).

ā-brēotan *wv* destroy, root out. VP 145/9 ~eð (exterminabit). 77/45 abreotte (§avit). 36/9 biað §. 79/14 †abreoette (§avit).

ābrēotnis *sf* extermination. Bd[2] 86 ðara ~issa (exterminia).

ēode *prt* went. Mt 33 ~. VP 80/14; 130/1 ~(ambulasset; §avi). 118/3; Hy 5/37 ~un(§averunt). 54/15 ~on(§avimus). 125/6 § (ibant). 106/7 ~en (irent).

geēode *prt* went to; gained, conquered. Ep 76 gihiodum (adgrediuntur); Ef gaeadun; Cp geeodun. Cp 453 ~(cessit). SG 11 ~on.

bi-ēode *prt* practiced. VP 76/7, 13 ~(exercitabam; exercebor). 68/13 ~un (§ebantur).

in-ēode *prt* entered. VP 17/7; Hy 5/34; Hy 6/32 ~(introivit). 37/7 ~(ingrediebar). 108/18 ~(intravit). 68/2; 131/7 ~un (introierunt; introivimus). 40/7 inneodan (ingrediebantur).

ūt-ēode *prt* went out. VP 18/5; 80/6; Hy 1/8 ~(exivit; exiret; exivi). 87/9 ut ne ~(egrediebar). 40/7 ~on (†egrediebatur).

ymb-ēodun *prt* surrounded. VP 87/18 ~ (circuierunt).

rēod-naesc Cp.

hrēod *s*(*n*) reed. Ef 290 ~(carectum); Cp §; Ld reod. Cp 9 ~(ferula). 1007

~(harundo, canna). **VP** 44/2 ~(calamus).

Hreodford, hreot§, hreout§ BH. h) eodpōl Ct.

burg-lēod *sm* mayor. **Ep** 620 ~(municeps); Cp ~liod. **Bd**² 17 § (§).

lēode *pl* people. **Ct** 23/15 ~a *gpl.*

lond-lēod *sm* inhabitant **VP** 38/13; 118/19; 119/6 ~(incola). 119/5 ~(incolatus). 104/12 ~e(§ae *pl.*)

Liodberct LV. **Liodfrith,** liut§ LV. **Liudhardo** BH. **Lioduald** Gn; li·dualding Gn. **Lioduini** LV.

Līoda *sm* **LV** 358 ~.

þēod *sf* people, nation. **VP** 32/12 eadigu ðiod (gens). Hy 7/56 § (†agens). 104/13 in ðeode (gentem). Hy 7/43, 3 in ðiode (§). 42/1 ðeode haligre (§e). 104/13 § (§). 82/5 ðiode (§). 105/5 ðeode ðinre (§is). 2/8; 9/6, 12, 6, 8, 20, 1, 37, *etc* § (§es). 58/6 deode (§es). 71/11 ðeoðe (§es). 46/2, 4; 64/8; 65/7, 8; 66/5, 5 *etc* ðiode (§es). 21/28; 95/7; 105/41; 113/4(2) ðeoda (§ium). 88/51; 95/5; 97/2; 110/7 ðioda (§ium). 104/44 dioda (§ium). 17/48; 81/8 ðeodum (§ibus). 43/12 †ðeodu (§ibus). 43/15; 45/11; 66/3 ðiodum. 21/29 ðeada (§ium). 45/7 §e(§es). 134/15 ðiada(§ium). 17/44; 32/10; Hy 7/15 ðieda (§ium).

Theodbald BH. **Theodric** LK, LV. **theodoicesnād** Ct.

wer-þēod *sf.* **Cp** 1381 ~ðeode (nixu).

ðēod-scipe *sm* discipline. **VP** 17/36 ~ (disciplina). 49/17; 118/66 § (§am). Hy 7/57 ðiod~(§a).

el-þēodig *aj* foreign. **VP** 38/13 ~ðeoðig (peregrinus).

geþēodan *wv* join. **Cp** 91 geþiudde (adplicuit). **VP** 67/26 tosomne geðeode (conjuncti).

ā-þēodan *wv* separate. **CA** 17 áðeode *sbj.*

tō-geþēodan *wv* join to. **Bd**² 40 ~ðioded (adjuncta).

under-þēodan *wv* subject. **VP** 143/2 ~ðeodende (subiciens). 17/48 §es (subdidisti). 8/8 ~deodes (subjecisti). 36/7 ~ðioded bio (subditus esto!) § bið (§a erit). 59/10 sindun ~ðeoded (subditi sunt). 61/2 ~deoded (§a erit). 46/4 ~ðeodde (subecit). Hy 7/60 ~ðiodde (subdidit). 107/10 § sind (subditi sunt).

þēodning *s* **Ct** 14/2 *torrentis qui vocatur* theodningc.

uuēod-hōc Cp; uuead§ Ep, Ef.

cēod *sm* pouch. **Cp** 1282 ~as (marsuppia).

Crīoda *sm.* **Gn** 92 ~. **SG** 6 criodo.

Crīoding *sm* son of C. **Gn** 92 ~ **SG** 6 ~.

Pīuda *sm.* **LV** 119 ~.

gebēodan *sv* announce, command. **Ct** 37/33 ~e. 48/21 gebeod · n *inf.*

bi-bīodan *sv* command. **VP** 30/6 ~u (commendo): **Ct** 37/12, 5, 28; 41/28; 42/12 ic bebeode. 48/17 bibeodað. 39/8 he §. 39/6; 40/18 ic bebiade. 41/64 bibeadeð.

on-bēodan *sv* enjoin. **VP** 67/29 ~biod (manda!).

bēod *s(m)* table. **VP** 68/23 biod (mensa). 22/5; 77/19, 20 ~(§am). 127/3 ~es. **Ct** 30/21; 42/13 ~e.

beodbolle Cp.

hēope *sf* wild rose. **Cp** 1858 ~an (sicomoros).

on-swēop *prt* swept on, blew on. **Ep** 32 ansueop (atflarat); Cp onsueop; Ef †asueus. Cp 100 †ansuaep (afflarat).

step-cilda VP. **steupfaedaer** Ep; †staupfotar Ef; steopfaeder Cp; steuffeder Ld. **steopmōder** Cp. **steopsunu** Cp.

wēopun *prt* wept. **VP** 77/64; 125/6; 136/1 ~(ploraverunt; flebant; flevimus).

crīopung *sf* creeping. **Ep** 696 ~ae (obreptione); Ef cr[i]upungae; Cp cr[i]opunge.

dēop *aj* deep. **VP** 91/6 ~e (profundae).

hīe *prn fem acc* her. **Mt** 28 hio. **VP** 7/3 ~. 7/6; 23/2; 39/15;

47/4, 13 *etc* ~ (eam). 118/34 ~(illam). Ct. 41/20 ~. 41/14 hia. 45/11 hio.

hīe *prn pl* they. **Rn** 2/16 hiæ. 18 hi(æ). 3/2 hiæ. **CA** 8, 11 heo *fem.* **Mt** 20 hio *neut.* **VP** 9/21, 3 *etc* ~. 19/9; 21/18 *etc* ~(ipsi). 2/4, 4, 5 *etc* ~(eos). 5/11; 17/38 *etc* ~(illos). 72/27; 84/11 ~(se). 17/39 hio (illos). Ct 28/23; 34/21; 37/34; 41/18, 37, 65, 5; 42/8, 9 hie. 37/29 hiae. 45/32, 44, 52 hio. 36 híо.

ðrīe *num* three. **Mt** 39 ðr[i]o. **VH** 5/6 ðreo foeðan (ternos). Ct 34/19 ~ sulong. 41/60 ðreo hund.

ðreotēne Ct.

sīe *sbj* be. **BDS** 2 ~. **Lr** 74 ic sio wegen (vehar). **CA** 16 seo. **DA** 8 sien. **VP** 7/10, 7 ~(consumetur, convertetur) *etc.* 6/6 ~(sit) *etc.* 32/22 *etc* ~(fiat). 26/4 ic siem. 60/5 ic sion. 38/14: 70/1 ic sie. 8/5; 36/1, 7 *etc* ðu ~. 95/9 si : onstyred [e *er*] (commoveatur). 6/11, 1 sien gedroefde, § forcerred (conturbentur; avertantur) *etc.* 34/5, 6 *etc* § (fiant). 7/13 ge sien. Ct 34/13, 7; 37/19, 9, 27, 33; 38/10, 1; 40/8; 41/7, 7 *etc*; 42/8, 14, 22 ~. 37/39; 42/18 sien. 42/11 siȩ. 39/8, 15; 40/21, 3 se. 41/44 [se]. 45/13, 4 seo. 45/18, 21, 6, 37, 40, 2, 8 sio. 45/44 sion *pl.*

slī *s* a fish. **Ep** 1015 ~(tincti); Ef, Cp §. Ld 221 slii (tinct, lupus brevis).

scīa *sm* leg. **Ef** 299 ~ (crus); Cp §.

Wii *s.* **Ct** 28/4 to ~.

Frī-gȳð BH.

cīan *spl* gills. **Ep** 158 ~ (branciae); Ef, Cp §; Ld chyun.

Īringes-weg *sm* milky way. **Ep** 1050 ~aes ueeg (via secta); Ef inges §; Cp ~ uueg; Ld ~uuec.

hīred *sm* family. **VP** 106/41 heoredas (familias).

speoru-līra *sm* calf of leg. **Lr** 55 ~an (suras).

swīra *sm* neck. **Lr** 21,45 ~an (cladam, centro).

swirbān VP.

scīr *sf* office, authority. **Ef** 721 †scur (procuratio); Cp sciir. Cp 692 ~(dispensatio). **VP** 70/15 ~e (negotiationes). 90/6 ~e †geondgongendum (negotio).

Scirabur' *ecclesiae* Gn; sciraburnensis Ct.

hām-scīr *sf* home-office. **Cp** 719 hámscire (edilitatem).

scīran *wv* decree. **Ep** 86 scirde (actionabatur); Ef, Cp §. Cp 688 ~o (disceptavero).

scīr *aj* clear. **Ep** 941 sciir (sublustris); Ef §; Cp ~. **VP** 74/9 ~es wines (vini meri).

Scīr-burg LV.

wīr *s* myrtle. **Ep** 637 †uuyr (martus); Ef §; Cp uuir (myrtus).

fīras *spl* men. **CH** 9 ~um.

Tīr-wald Ct. **Tiruulf** Ct.

hwīl *sf* while, time. **Bd²** 48 wilum (nunc). **VP** 89/13 sume ~e (aliquantulum). 93/8 ~um (aliquando).

ðā-hwīle-ðe *cj* while. **CA** 13/7 ~. Ct 39/8; 41/9 ~. 45/32, 7 þa ~ þe. 41/6; 45/42 ða ~þe.

fīl *s(f)* file. **Cp** 1234 fiil (lima); Ld §. Ld 39 § (§ *etc*).

mīl *s(f)* mile. **Cp** 1314 miil (milium).

Pīl-heard Ct.

ā-hīðan *vb* **VP** 79/14 ~ende wes (depastus est).

hrīðer *s(n)* ox, bull. **Ct** 37/17; 39/5; 40/5 ~. 41/30, 61 hriðr.

hrīðhiorde Cp. **hr · · leag** Ct.

līðercian *wv* soothe. **Ep** 722 lithircadae (promulserit); Ef §æ; Cp ~ade.

sīð *sm* journey, time. **LP** 5 fiorðan ~e. **Bd²** 39~as (exitus). **VP** 61/12; 88/36 æne ~a (semel). 118/164 seofen ~um (septies).

sīðfæt Mt, Bd², VP.

sigi-sīth *sm* victorious expedition **Pr** 2 ~a.

Uid-sīth *sm* **LV** 179 ~.

gesīð *sm* companion, retainer. **Cp** 1407 ~as (optimates).

sīð *av* late.

sīðboren VP. **sīð ðan.**

sīðe *sf* scythe. **Ep** 430 sigdi riftr (falc..s); Ef §; Cp ~ riftras.

sliðen *aj* cruel. Cp 1130 sliden (infastum).

swīþ *aj* strong.

Suiðbald LV. **Suidberct**, suitbercht BH; suiðberct LV; ~berht, suið§ Ct. **suiðfromlice** Cp. **Suiðgils** LV. **Suidhelm**, suit§, suidelm BH; suiðhelm LV. **Suiðmēr** LV. **Suiðrēd** LV, Gn; sw§ SG. **Suiðuald** LV. **Suiðualch** LV. **Suiðuulf** LV.

Æþel-swīþ *sf* LV 46 eðilsuið.

Beadu-swīþ *sf* LV 40, 4 badusuið.

Bēag-swīþ *s(f)* Ct 58/22 bægswið.

Beorht-swīþ *sf* LV 26 berctsuið.

Bil-swīþ *sf* LV 20 ~suið.

Blæd-swīþ *sf* LV 21 blaedsuith.

Bregu-swīþ *sf* BH 308 ~suid—§t I.

Burg-swīþ *sf* LV 34 ~suith.

Cyne-swīþ *sf* Rn 1/10 *kyne*swiþa.

Eald-swīþ *sf* LV 33 altsuith.

Ealh-swīþ *sf* LV 27 alchsuið.

Ecg-swīþ *sf* LV 24 ~suith. 39 §ð.

Here-swīþ *sf* BH 302 ~suid—§t I.

Mæ-swīþ [=mægen§ ?] *sm* LV 80 maesuith.

Tāt-swīþ *sf* LV 22 ~suið.

Wil-swīþ *sf* LV 24 uilsuith. 37 §ð.

Ȳþ-swīþ *sf* LV 26 ythsuið.

Swīþa *sm* LV 101 suitha.

swīþe *av* excessively, very. Ep 843 suae suithae; Ef suidae; Cp suiðe (quacumque). 844 suae suithae (quantisper); Ef †sidae; Cp suiðe. 1037 þus suiþae; Ef suidae; Cp suiðe (tantisper). Cp 691 suiðe micel (difinis). VP 6/4, 11 swiðe (valde). 18/11; 85/15 *etc* § (multum *w.aj*). 119/6 § londleod (§incola). 36/23; 45/2 *etc* §(nimis). 30/12; 46/10 §(nimium). 30/20; 62/2 *etc* (quam). 22/5 swide(§).

swīþor *av cp* more. VP 37/9; 118/8, 43, 51, 107 a hu lenge swiður (usquequaque).

swīþre *aj cp, sbst* right (hand). VP 17/36; 20/9 *etc* sie swiðre ðin (dextera). 25/10 seo § heara (§); 136/5 sie § min (§) *etc*. Hy 5/9 † sie § honda ðine (§ manus tua). 137/7 § ðin (§). 72/24 hond ða swiðran mine (§am). 73/11; Hy 5/20 ða § ðine (§am). 88/26, 43 ða § his; ða § (§am). Hy 7/79 ða § mine (§am). 97/1 mid ða § his (§ā). 107/7 mid ða swiðran ðinre (§ā). 89/12 †swiðre ðin (§am). 15/11 ðere swiðran ðinre (§ā). 44/10 to § ðire (a §is). 90/7; 108/31; 109/5 to ðere § ðinre (a §is). 108/6 to ðere § his. 109/1 to ðe § minre. 141/5 to ðere §. 59/7 ðinre dere § (§ā). 120/5 ofer hond ðere § ðinre (manum §ae tuae). 15/8 to ðere swiðra. 16/8 ðere swiðra [a *over* e] ðinre (§ae *d*). 19/7 §an his (§ae *g*). 76/11 §an ðes Hean (§ae *g*). 79/18 ðere †swið ðinre (§ae *g*). 138/10 †swið (§a).

swīþlice *av* excessively, extremely. VP 20/2; 103/1; 118/48, 140, 67; Hy 6/13 swiðlice (vehementer).

ofer-swīþan *wv* overcome. Cp 2137 obersuiðo (vinco). Mt 42 ~suiðan. VH 4/8 ~swiðed is (superatus est). 6/41 ~swiðe(vincam).

swiðian *wv*. Cp 885 suiðigað (figite).

snīð-strēo, smith§ Cp; snid§ Ep, Ef.

stīð *aj* stiff, strong.

Stidberht Ct. **Stiðuulf** LV.

ā-wrīðan *sv* bind. VP 146/3 ~eð (alligat).

nīð *sm* malice, hate. VP 7/10; 54/16 ~(nequitia). 49/19 ~e. 72/8 ~as. 27/4 ~um.

mīðan *sv* conceal. Cp 681 ~ið (dissimulat).

mīðl *s* bit. Cp 1770 ~um (salibaribus).

crīþ *vb* Cp 1807 criid (scaturit).

æt-clīðan *sv* adhere. Bd[2] 64 ~ende (aderentem).

cwīðan *wv* lament. VP 77/63 sind ~de(lamentatae).

blīðe *aj* cheerful, glad. Ef 77 *blidi* (aldcris). VH 11/10, 1 ~(laeti; §us).

Bliththrȳdae BH. Bliðuald LV.

īs *sn* ice. VP 148/8 ~ (glacies).

īsern *sn* iron. Ep 25 isęrn (alchior); Ef isaern; Cp ~. VP 104/18 iren (ferrum). 106/10 ~e.

isęrnfetor Ep; isaern§ Ef; isern§ Cp. iserngrēi Cp. isernsceruru Cp. isernscobl Cp. Isernuulf LV.

bred-īsern *sn* chisel. Ep 883 ~(scalbellum); Ef §isaern; Cp ~.

mearc-īsern *sn* branding-iron. Ep 227 †mearisern; Ef †merisaen; Cp ~iseren.

īsern *aj* iron. VP 2/9 iserre (§eā). 106/16 irenu (ferreos). 149/8 irnum.

ā-rīsan *sv* arise. VP 11/6; 56/9; 107/3 ~u (exsurgam). 26/3 ~eð (insurgat). 93/16 §(exsurget). 3/2; 123/2 ~að (insurgunt; §erent). 77/6 §(exurgent). 126/2 § (surgete). 40/9; 67/2 ~e (resurgat; ex§). Hy 7/74 ~en (exsurgant). 3/7; 7/7, 7 *etc* aris (§e!). 126/2; Hy 13/9 ~(surgere; re§). 17/40; 43/6; 91/12 ~ende (insurgentes). 101/14 § (exsurgens). 34/11; 72/20 § (§entes). 17/49; 58/2 §um (insurgentibus). 108/28 †ariað (§unt).

gerīs *s*(*n*) fury. Cp 1707 ~(rabies).

hlīsa *sm* fame. Bd² 28 ðone lisan (famam).

un-hlīsa *sm* infamy. Ct 48/20 unhlis··.

wīs *aj* wise.

reht-wīs *aj* righteous. VP 7/12; 10/8 ~(justus) *etc.* 10/4 se ~a (justus) *etc.* 5/13 ðone ~an (§um) *etc.* 31/11 ~e (§i) *etc.* 7/10 ~ne *etc.* 33/20 ~ra *etc.* Hy 8/18 †~re (§orum). 117/20 ~wisse (§i).

un-rehtwīs *aj* unrighteous. VP 35/2 se ~a (injustus). 5/6; 36/28 ða ~an (§i). 24/4 ða § (iniqui). 118/113 ða § (§os). 17/49 ðæm § (§o). 50/15 ða urehtwisan (§os). 74/5 ðæm ~um (§is). 119/2; 139/5 § (§is). 24/19 ~re (§o). 64/4 ~ra (§orum).

un-wīs *aj* unwise. Cp 983 ~(glebo). VP 73/18; 91/7 ~(insipiens). 13/1; 48/11; 52/1 se ~a. 38/9; 73/22 ðæm ~an. 75/6; 93/8 ~e (§entes). Hy 7/43 ~e (§entem). 48/13, 21 ~um.

wīsdōm *sm* wisdom. VP 18/3; 93/10; 118/66; Hy 9/13 ~(scientiam). 72/11; 138/6 ~(§a). Hy 4/7 ~a (§arum). Ct 34/15 on his ~e.

un-wīsdōm *sm* unwisdom. VP 21/3 to ~e (insipientiam). 37/6 ~es (§ae). 68/6 minne ~(§am).

unreht-wīslic *aj* unrighteous. VP 68/5 ~e [*dotted* e *after* s] (injusti).

and-wīsnis *sf* experience. Cp 778 ~ (experimentum).

reht-wīsnis *sf* righteousness. VP 35/7; 118/75 ~(justitia; aequitas) *etc.* 5/9 ~sse ðine (†justitia) *etc.* 9/9 § (§ā) *etc.* 4/2 § minre (§ae *g*) *etc.* 118/54 § (justificationes) *etc.* 118/48 §um (§ibus) *etc.* 10/8 ~nesse (aequitatem). 44/5 rechtwisnisse. 21/32 ~ssnisse [*second* s *dotted*]. 35/11; 70/21 rehwisnisse. 34/27; 37/21; 39/11; Hy 5/21 ~winisse. 118/26 †~wis (justificationes).

unreht-wīsnis *sf* unrighteousness. VP 7/4, 17 *etc* ~(iniquitas). 118/133 all ~ss (injustitia). 7/15 ~sse (§am). 50/3 § mine (iniquitatem) *etc.* 17/24 § (§ate) *etc.* 17/5 § (§atis) *etc.* 31/1 § (§ates) *etc.* 38/9 §um (§atibus). 73/20 §a (§atum). 35/13 unrehwisnisse. 58/5 †nurehtwisnis. 37/19 †~ss (iniquitatem). 35/4 ~wisse (§as). 93/20 ~nise.

gereht-wīsian *wv* justify. VP 81/3 ~iað (justificate). 72/13 ~ade (§avi). 50/6 sie ~ad. 142/2 bið §. 18/10 §e (§ata).

gerehtwīsung *sf* justification. VP 88/32 ~e (justificationes).

wīse *sf* manner, arrangement, thing. VP 63/4 ~an bitre (rem). 100/3 §. Hy 13/1 ~ena (rerum). Ct 38/7; 41/58; 45/56 ðas ~an *a.* 42/15 §. 45/54 ðeosse wīsan *g.*

wearn-wīslīce *av* obstinately. Ef 338 uernuislicæ (difficile); Cp ~.

Cyn-uīs *sf.* BH 196 *reginam* ~e — ~ę.

gīsl *sm* hostage. Cp 1400 ~as (obsides). Rn 3/3 ~.

Gislheard Rn, gils§ Ct. Gislhere Gn.

Aðđi-gils *sm* **LV** 279 ~.

Badi-gils *sm* **LV** 328 ~.

Beadu-gils *sm* **LV** 446 ~.

Beorht-gils *sm* **BH** 176 berctgilsum — berechgislum — bercht§ — berct§. **LV** 124, 97; 247, 77; 343, 63, 4 §gils. **Gn** 27 bert§.

Bet-gils *sm* **LV** 245 ~.

Bil-gils *sm* **LV** 196 ~.

Cūþ-gils *sm* **LV** 113; 377; 401, 12 cuth~. 479 cuð~.

Cweld-gils *sm* **Gn** 109 cu~.

Cweld-gilsing *sm* son of Cweldgils. **Gn** 108 cu~.

Cyne-gils *sm* **BH** 139 cynigilso—§gislo—§—§. **LV** 87; 127, 40, 6; 391; 421, 51 cyni~.

Ēd-gils *sm* **BH** 312 aed~. **LV** 219 eed~.

Eald-gils *sm* **BH** 364 aldgilso—§gislo—§. **LV** 241, 76; 314, 6; 420, 77 ald~.

Eaþu-gils *sm* **LV** 424 eaðu~.

Friþu-gils *sm* **LV** 212 frioðu~. 342 friðu~.

Hǣm-gils *sm* **BH** 356 haem~. **LV** 51; 202; 338 §.

Helm-gils *sm* **LV** 10; 244 ~.

Here-gils *sm* **LV** 390 ~.

Hildi-gils *sm* **LV** 145, 75; 224 ~.

Hūn-gils *sm* **LV** 180; 438, 77 ~.

Hwæt-gils *sm* **LV** 125, 65 huaet~.

Peoht-gils *sm* **LV** 271; 380 pect~.

Plec-gils *sm* **LV** 102; 275; 355 ~.

Rīm-gils *sm* **LV** 227 ~.

Swīþ-gils *sm* **LV** 105; 212, 59, 61; 378 suið~.

Torht-gils *sm* **LV** 278 torct~. 337 torcht~.

Tūn-gils *sm* **LV** 116; 211 ~.

Wǣr-gils *sm* **LV** 293 uer~.

Wiht-gils *sm* **BH** 25 uictgilsi—§§—§gisli—§. **Gn** 115 uiht~.

Wiht-gilsing *sm* son of Wihtgils. **Gn** 115 u~.

Wil-gils *sm* **LV** 138, 72, 89, 288; 445, 55 u~. **Gn** 74 §.

Wil-gilsing *sm* son of Wilgils. **Gn** 73 u~.

Wit-gils *sm* **LV** 108; 283 u~.

gīsl-hād *sm* being a hostage. **Cp** 1418 ~(obsedatus).

līste *sf* fringe. **Ep** 583 ~an (lembum); Ef, Cp §. **Cp** 1228 ~(lembus).

Crīst *sm* Christ. **Rn** 1/1 *k*risttus. 2/11 krist. **DA** 3 ~. **Mt** 46 ~. 9 *etc* ~e. **VP** 19/7 *etc* ~ (Christus). **Hy** 6/26 ~as. **Ct** 40/11; 41/48; 42/23; 45/55; 48/8, 17 ~es. 41/50 kristes.

crīsten *aj* Christian. **Ct** 39/8 ~.

crīstnes *sf* christianity. **DA** 4 for ðære cristnesse.

īw *s* yew. **Ep** 1005 iuu (taxus); Ef, Cp §.

hīw *sn* hue, colour. **Cp** 188 hio (color). **VP** 44/5 heow ðin (speciem). 46/5 hiow (§). 44/12 hiow ðin (§). **Hy** 13/5 § (formam). 44/3; 67/14 §e (§ā; specie). 49/2, 11 §es (§ies).

scin-hīow *sn* illusion. **VH** 6/22 ~es (fantasiae).

hīowian *wv* form, fashion. **VP** 93/9, 20 ~ede, ~as (finxit, fingis).

gehīowian *wv*. **VH** 11/6 ~að (informet). 103/26; 138/5 §ades. (formasti). **Hy** 13/3, 7 †~adas, ~ades (plasmasti, §averas). 118/73 ~adun (§averunt). 32/15 gehiewade [w *from some other letter*] (finxit).

gehēowung *sf* forming. **VP** 102/14 ~e (figmentum).

hīwa *sm* member of a family, inmate, monk. **Ct** 39/3 ~um. 41/24, 42 higan *pl.* 37/34, 41; 42/9, 10, 4, 5, 9 higon *pl.* 30/21; 37/26; 39/13; 40/6; 41/21, 7, 9, 59, 66; 42/6, 13, 20 §um. 37/14, 23, 43; 41/67 higna *gpl.* 40/17 hiium. 31/3, 3 hina *gpl.* 40/3 hiona *gpl.*

hīgid *sfn* hide of land. **Ct** 48/2, 5 nigen ~a, tu §. 45/24 (ane)s hides. 28 †án §e *a.* 45/24 II hida. 45/5, 6 *etc*; 47/10, 1 *etc* §a *gpl.*

ðrīwa *av* thrice. **LP** 5 ðriga.

sīwan *wv* sew. **Cp** 1773 siouu (sarcio).

gesīwan *wv.* Ep 886 gisiuuid (sarcinatum); Ef ge§; Cp gesiouuid. Cp 68 gesiuwide (adsutae). 508 gesiowed (consutum). Cp 1374 gesiuwid (netum). 1774 gesiowid (sarcinatum).

ā-sīwan *wv.* Ep 796 mið naeðlae [a]siuuid (pictus acu); Ef asiuuid; Cp asiowid.

be-sīwan *wv.* Ep 699 bisiuuidi uuerci (opere plumario); Ef †bisiuuisidi; Cp bisiudi.

-wīu

Cēol-uīo *sm* LV 266 ~.

Dycg-uīo *sm* LV 257 ~.

Ecg-uīo *sm* LV 216 ~.

Forth-uīo *sm* LV 79 ~.

Ōs-uīo *sm* BH 64 osuiu—osuuiu I —osuiu. 126, ·55 osuiu. 159 §—osuuiu I. 218 ~ —osuiu—osuuiu. 184 osuiu *d*—osuuiu I. 123 osuiu *d* —†osino—osuio. 166 osuio *d*—osuuiu I. 212 osuiu *d*—osuio—§. 221 osuio [*last* o *over* u] *d*—osuiu I. 222 osuio *d*—osuiu—§. 236 osuio *d* —osuiu—§. 180 osuiu *g*. 185 § *g* —§ I. LK 5 osuiu. LV 2 osuio. Gn 79 §.

Ōsuīing *sm* son of O. Rn 1/4 oswiuq. Gn 79 osuing.

Wīwara-wīc Ct.

nīwe *aj* new. Bd² 87 neowre (recente). VP 127/3 neowe plant (novella). 32/3; 95/1 neowne (novum). 68/32; 80/10 niowe (novellum; recens). 143/12 § plant (novella). 39/4; 97/1; 143/9 niowne (novum).

nīowinga *av* newly. VH 7/34 ~(novi recentes).

genīowian *wv* renew. VP 50/12 ~a (innova!).

geednīowian *wv* renew. VP 38/3 geedneowad is (renovatus est). 102/5 bið ~ad. 103/30 ~as.

clīwe *s* clew, ball of thread. Ep 472 cleouuae (glomer); Ef cleuuae; Cp clouue.

gīw *s* vulture. Cp 986 gig (gripem).

glīw *s*(*n*) mirth, joke, music. Ep 398 gliu (facitiae); Ef §; Cp glio (facetia). 550 in gliuuae (in mimo *etc*); Ef gluuiae; Cp gliowe. Cp 354 glio (cabillatio). 948 gliu (gannatura).

Tīw *sm* Ep 663 tiig (mars); Ef, Cp §.

brīw *s*(*m*) porridge. Ep 767 briig (pulenta); Ef, Cp §.

ifig *s* ivy. Ef 392 ifeg (edera); Cp ifegn; Ld ibaei (hederam).

līf *sn* life. VP 29/6 *etc* ~(vita). 7/6 ~ min (§am) *etc*. 16/14 *etc* ~e. 15/11 *etc* ~es. Ct 45/51, 1 ~e. 34/10, 3; 37/4; 38/10; 41/38 ~es.

liffæst Ct. **geliffestan** VP.

mynster-līf *sn* monastic life. Ct 41/25 ~es.

hlīfian *wv* tower, overhang. Cp 1317 hlibendri (minaci).

wīf *sn* woman, wife. Cp 173 ald uuif (anus). VP 108/9; 127/3 ~(uxor). Ct 34/8; 45/4 ~. 41/9, 14 wiif. 22 wíif. 42/6 wiib. 42/4, 12 ~es.

geuiif *s* fate. Ld 94 ~(furtunam, fatum).

fīf *num* five. Ct 28/21, 2; 29/15; 41/27 ~ hund.

fiftēne Ct.

fīftig *num* fifty. Ct 37/38; 41/60 ~.

fīfalde *sf* butterfly. Ep 768 ~(papilio); Ef uiualdra; Cp fiffalde. Ef 1134 fifeldae (spalagius, musca venenosa). Ld 135 ~ae (animalus).

clīfe *sf* burdock. Ep 613 cliþae (lappa); Ef clifae; Cp clibe. Cp 978 ~(glitilia).

ā-drīfan *sv* drive away. VP 118/10 ne adrif ðu (ne repellas).

onweg-ādrīfan *sv* drive away. VH 7/43 ~u (repellam). 87/15 ~es. 93/14 weg ne adrifeð. 94/3 on weg ne §. 5/11 onweg adrif (expelle). 61/5; Hy 13/18 ~(repellere).

gehrīnan *sv* touch. VP 103/32 ~eð (tangit). 104/15 ~. 143/5 gehrin!

līn *s* linen, cloth, napkin, towel. Ep 634 liin (manitergium); Ef † lim; Cp ~.

līnen *aj* linen. Ep 1081 †linnin ryhae (villa); Ef, Cp linin.

ðīn *prn* of thee, thine. Lr 11 ~e. LP 5 ~. VP 6/6; 41/7; 62/7 *etc* ~(tui). 3/9, 9 *etc* ~(tuum, tua). 2/8, 8 *etc* ~e. 4/7 *etc* ~es. 5/12 *etc* ðinne. 26/8 ðin[n]e. 5/8, 9; 6/2 *etc* ðinre. 16/14 of honda ðinra. 30/2; 44/10; 90/7; 118/106 ðire. 7/7 *etc* ðinra (tuorum). 108/28 *etc* din. 114/7 *etc* §e. 5/13 *etc* §es. 83/5 *etc* §um. 120/8 dinne. 118/68; 142/11 *etc* dinre. 137/8 dinra. 64/5 ðinnum.

swīn *sn* pig. **Ep** 972 suin ւ suadu (suesta); Ef, Cp §. Cp 1966 suin (suis). **Ct** 40/5; 41/62 suin. 41/21; 45/10, 25, 9, 9 ~a *gpl.*

suínhaga Ct.

mere-suīn *sn* porpoise. **Cp** 315 ~(bacarius).

swīnen *aj* pig's. **Cp** 1968 suinin (suellium). **VP** 16/14 ða swinnan (porcina).

scīnan *sv* shine. **VH** 11/3 ~ende (micans).

wīn *sn* wine. **VP** 68/13 *etc* ~(vinum). 59/5 *etc* ~e. 4/8 *etc* ~es. **Ct** 37/22 uuines.

uuinaern Ep; § Ef; win§ Cp. **winbergan** VH. **winfaet** Cp. **wiingeardes** Cp; **wingeard** VP. **winreopað** VP. **wintrēow** VP.

mīn *prn* my. **Bl** 21 ~. **Lr** 9 ~es. **CA** 4 mín. **Mt** 25, 8 §. 26, 48 ~e. 47 mi[n]um. 50 minne. **VP** 18/14; 24/7, 16 *etc* ~(mei). 2/7 *etc* min (meus). 5/2, 3, 9 *etc* ~e, ~es, ~um. 5/9 *etc* ~ne. 3/3, 5 *etc* ~re. 7/9 *etc* ~ra. 41/6 minis (mei). 102/1 mi = min. 39/10 minne *pl* [*first* n *dotted out*]. Hy 10/2 minnum. **Ct** 37/1; 41/1 *etc*; 42/1 *etc*; 45/4 *etc* ~. 37/32; 40/2; 41/16 *etc*; 42/17 *etc*; 45/30; 48/8; ~e. 42/4; 45/3 *etc* ~es. 37/29; 41/3; 45/2 *etc*; 48/1 ~um. 39/6; 40/17 ~em. 42/7, 21; 45/21 ~ne. 30/21, 2; 42/9, 16, 6 ~re. 41/39 ~ra swæstar. 40/7, 9; 41/45; 42/3, 4; 45/18; 56/8 ~ra.

cīnan *sv* crack. **Ep** 495 ~aendi (hiulca); Ef, Cp ~endi.

tō-cīnan *sv* crack. **Ef** 343 tecinid; Cp ~it (dehiscat).

Tīn *s* Tyne. **BH** 336 ~o *amne.* 367 *amnem* ~am—a~—§.

twīn *sn* twine, cloth. **Ep** 138 †tuum (byssum); Ef tuigin; Cp tuin.

ā-dwīnan *sv* waste away. **Ep** 1044 †aduinendanan *etc* (tabida *etc*).

rīm *s*(*n*) number. **VP** 38/5; 39/6 ~(numerum). 39/13; 103/25; 104/34; 146/5 ~(§us). 104/12 ~e scortum. Hy 7/15 efter ~e.

rīman *wv* count. **VP** 138/18 ~u(dinumerabo). 146/4 ~eð (numerat).

ā-rīman *wv* count. **VP** 21/18 ~don (dinumeraverunt). 89/12 ~ (§are).

Rim-gils LV.

hrīm *s*(*m*) hoarfrost. **Cp** 1653 ~(pruina).

līm *s* lime, cement, glue. **Ep** 133 ~(bitumen); Ef ~; Cp liim. Cp 449 § (cementum, lapidem).

liimcaluuer Cp. **liimmolegn** Ep; lim§ Ef.

gelīman *wv* cement, glue. **Cp** 539 ~ed (conglutinata).

scīma *sm* brightness. **VP** 17/13 ~an (fulgore). Hy 11/3 § (nitore).

strīman *vb* **Ep** 695 ~aendi (obnixus); Ef, Cp ~endi. Cp 1132 § (innixus).

caluuer-clīm *s.* **Cp** 427 ~(calvarium).

grīma *sm* mask. **Ep** 646 ~(mascus); Ef, Cp §. 904 ~(scina); Ef §. 953 ~(scina, nitatio); Ef §. Cp 1279 ~(masca).

eges-grīma *sm* terror-mask. **Ep** 569 egisi~ (larvula); Ef §; Cp egis~. Cp 1351 ~(musca).

glīman *sv* **Ld** 125 ~ith (sevit).

rīce *aj* mighty, of high rank. **Rn** 2/5 riicnæ.

Ricbercto BH. **Ricfolcyn** LV. **Ricrēd** LV. **Ricðrȳth** LV. **Ricuulf** LV.

Ælf-rīc *sm* **BH** 129 aelfrici *lg.*

Æþel-rīc *sm* **LK** 3 aedil~. **LV** 117; 280, 7; 300, 57 eðil~. **Gn** 79; 118 §. **Ct** 9/5 aethil~. 24/6; 25/12 aeð~. 32/5, 7 æð~. 26/8 ęð~. 32/8 eð~. 27/5; 43/7 eðeric.

Æþel-rīcing *sm* son of Æþelrīc. **Gn** 79; 118 eðil~.

Al-rīc *sm* **BH** 370 ~um. **LV** 248; 386 ~.

Cūð-rīc *sm* **LV** 266, 80; 339 cuth~. **Ct** 28/8 ~es dun. 35/13 ~.

Cynn-rīc *sm* **SG** 6 ~.

Cynn-rīcing *sm* son of Cynnrīc. SG 6 cynnr(icing).

Ecg-rīc *sm* BH 171 ~e *d.*

Ēd-rīc *sm* BH 315 ~. LV 198 eed~. Gn 90 ~. Ct 4/3 ędrico.

Ēd-rīcing *sm* son of Ēdrīc. Gn 90 ~.

El-rīc *sm* Ct 30/19 ~.

Friþu-rīc *sm* LV 251 friðu~. Ct 25/11 freðo~.

Hale-rīc *sm* LV 174 ~.

Heaþu-rīc *sm* LV 120 heaðu~. 223 haðu~.

Help-rīc *sm* LV 11; 146, 64; 237, 93; 356 ~.

Here-rīc *sm* BH 302 ~rici *lg*—heri§—§. 309 ~—heri~. LV 169 ~.

Irmen-rīc *sm* BH 66 irminrici *lg.* Gn 114 iurmen~.

Irmen-rīcing *sm* son of Irmenrīc. Gn 114 iurmen~.

Mægen-rīc *sm* LV 117; 213 mae~.

Or-rīc *sm* Ct 28/11 ~es den.

Ōs-rīc *sm* BH 129; 307 ~. 162 ~i *lg.* LK 6 ~. LV 4 ~. Ct 20/23; 23/9 ~i. 22/9 ósrici.

Sige-rīc *sm* LV 401 sigric. SG 21~.

Sige-rīcing *sm* son of Sigerīc. SG 21~.

Þēod-rīc *sm* LV 79; 116; 212; 354 th~. LK 3 §.

Wil-rīc *sm* LV 318 u~.

Rīcinga-haam Ct.

rīce *sn* kingdom, rule. Rn 1/6 ~es. SG 1/8, 9 ~ *d.* VP 21/29; 102/19; 144/13, 3 ~ (regnum). 104/13 ~ (§o). 44/7; 144/11, 2 ~es (§i). 45/7 ~ (§a). 67/33; 78/6; 101/23; 134/11 ~u (§a).

heofon-rīce *sn* kingdom of heaven. CH 1 hefaenricaes.

rīcsian *wv* reign, rule. VP 9/37; 46/9; 95/10: 96/1; 98/1; 113/2; 145/10 ~að (regnabit). 92/1 ~ad (§). Hy 5/33 ~as (§as). 44/5 ~a (§a!).

līc *sn* body. Rn 2/17 (l)icæs. Ct 41/21, 3, 6 minum ~e.

licbeorg Cp. **licburg** Cp. **lichoma**, Lr., VP.

gelīc *aj* like. VP 27/1; 34/10 *etc* ~ (similis). 113/8 (2); 134/18 ~e (es). Hy 13/4 ~ne. ? Ct 42/18 [*under* gelīce].

gelīce *av* similarly, alike. Cp 1517 ~(pariter). VP 67/7 ~ (similiter). Ct 42/18 ~[*or neut. pl.* ?]

gelīcnis *sf* likeness. VP 143/12 ~(similitudo). 43/15; 48/5; 57/5; 105/20 ~isse (§inem).

on-līcnis *sf* likeness, image. Bd[2] 60 ~(instar). VP 38/7 ~isse (imagine). Hy 13/3 § (§is). 72/20 onlicnesse.

līcian *wv* please. VP 114/9 ~iu (placebo). 68/32 ~að (§ebit). 55/13 ~ie(§eam). 52/6 ~iendra.

gelīcian *wv* please. LP 3 ~edon. VP 39/14 ~að (complaceat). 34/14 ~ie (†§ebam). 18/15 ~ien. 25/3; 43/4 ~ade.

wel-gelīcian *wv* please well. VP 67/17; 146/10, 1; 149/4 ~ad is (beneplacitum est). 76/8 § sie. 101/15 § hefdun. Hy 1/7 wes §. 68/14; 118/108 §e (§i, §a). 88/18; 105/4; 140/5 §um.

Tūn-līc *sm.* LV 338 tu[u]nlic.

sīcettan *wv* sigh. Cp 1757 s'cetit *etc* (singultat).

bi-swīcan *sv* deceive. VP 61/10 ~en (decipiant).

bisuīcend *sm* deceiver. Ep 545 ~ (inpostorem); Ef bisuiccend; Cp bisuuicend.

snīcan *sv* creep. Bd[2] 5~ (repere). VP 103/25 ~ende (reptilia).

scrīc *s* shrike (bird). Ep 1013 ~(turdus); Ef screc; Cp ~; Ld †scruc.

wīc *sn* dwelling. Ct 36/10; 56/8 ~ a *gpl.*

Uicbercht Lv. **Wicbold**, uuit§ Ct. **Wichāma** Ct. **Wichæma-mearc** Ct. **uuicgeroebum** Cp.

Biscopes-uuīc Ct 7/2 ~.

Quenta-uīc BH 238 *portum cui nomen est* ~.

ferd-wīc *sn* camp. VP 26/3 ~(castra). 77/28 ~a. 105/16 ~um.

Here-wīc. Ct 30/8 ~.

Hremping-wīc Ct 19/2 ~wiic, *et alio nomine* hafingseota.

Werburging-wīc Ct 56/4 ~.

Wiwara-wīc Ct 28/4, 6 an ~. *in alia* ~.

wīcing *sm* pirate.
uuicingsceadan Ep; Ef §; Cp wicinsceaðan.
fīc-trēo VP.
dīc *sm* ditch. Ct 20/8 ~ *a.* 8 díc *n.* 5, 20 ðone díc.
pīc *s* point. Cp 49 piic(acisculum).
pīcung *sf* pricking. Cp 1933 ~ (stigmata).
Bīca *sm.* Ct 3/1 ~an *d.*
gelīhan *sv* lend. Ct 45/46 gelið.
þīhan *sv* flourish. Cp 1118 hyhtful *vel* ðiendi (indolis).
geþīhan *sv* receive, accept (?). Ct 41/40 geðian.
sīhan *sv* strain. Ef 384 siid (excolat); Cp §.
Al-wīh *sm.* LV 165 aluych. 73 aluich. Gn 43 alouuioh. 98 ~.
Alwing *sm* son of A. Gn 98 ~.
ofer-wrīhan *sv* cover. VP 139/10 ~wrið (operiet), 146/8 †~w[i]rð (§it). 103/9 ~wrean (§ire).
on-wrīhan *sv* uncover. VP 36/5; 118/18 onwrih (revela!).
tīhan *sv* accuse. DA 10 tihð.
be-twīh *prp* between. VP 6/8 ~ alle (inter). 9/12; 25/6; 36/1; 56/10 *etc* ~ (§). 15/3; 54/19 bi~ (§). Ct 11/2 bituih.
betwihgongend VP.
betwīhn *prp* between. Ep 546 bitui[c]n aeldrum (inter primores); Ef bituichn; Cp bitun. Cp 1310 bituihn (mentagra).
betwīhnum *prp* between. VP 33/4 betwinum (invicem).
þīhsl *s* shaft. Ep 1043 dislum (temonibus); Ef dixlum; Cp þixlum. Ef 1147 dixl (arquamentum).
waegne-þīxl *s* carriage-shaft. Cp 205 ~ (archtoes).
Piichil *sm.* LV 173 ~.
Lict-uald LV.
gelīhtan *wv* alleviate. VH 12/3 ~e (allevet).
swīgian *wv* be silent. VP 49/3 ~að (silebit). 31/3; 49/21 ~ade (tacui). 38/3 § (silui). 106/29, 30 ~edon, ~adon. 27/1; 34/22; 38/13; 82/1; 108/2 ~a!
geswīgian *wv.* VH 4/19 ~iað (conticescent).
oð-swīgan *wv* cease speaking. Mt 35 oðsuigde.
stīgan *sv* ascend, descend. VP 67/19 ~ende (ascendens). 118/118 § (discendentes).
gestīgan *sv* Rn 2/2 *gistiga.*
ā-stīgan *sv* ascend, discend. VP 29/10 ~o (descendo). 131/3; 138/8 ~u (ascendero). Hy 6/17 ~es (§es). 7/17; 48/18; 132/3 ~eð (descendit). 23/3 § (ascendit). 21/30; 106/23; 113/17 ~að (discendunt). 103/8; 106/26 §(ascendunt). Hy 6/34 ~e(§am). 54/16; Hy 7/2 ~en (descendant). 143/5 astig (§e!). Hy 13/20 ~(§ere). 105/7; Hy 6/17 ~ende (ascendentes; §ens). 27/1; 142/7 ~endum (descendentibus).
ofdūne-stīgan *sv* descend. VP 103/8; 106/26 ~að (discendunt). 138/8 dunestigu (§ero). 29/4; 87/5 §endum.
ūp-stīgan *sv* ascend. VH 5/6, 35 ~ende, §um (ascensores; §ibus).
on-stīgend *sm* mounter. Hy 5/2 ~ (ascensorem).
stīg *sf* path. Ef 340 horuaeg stiig (devia callis); Cp ~. VP 22/3 ~e (semitam). 138/3 § mine (§). 26/11; 118/35 § (§ā). 8/9; 24/4 *etc* § (§as). 16/5 *etc* ~um. 77/50 styge.
ān-stīg *sf* narrow path. Ep 1042 faestin *vel* ~an (termofilas); Ef ~a.
wīg *s* war.
Uigbald LV. **Uigberct** LV; uuigberht Gn, Ct; uig§, wig§ Ct. **Uigbeorn** LV. **Uigfrith** LV; wigferð Ct. **Uigfūs** LV. **Uighāeð** LV. **Uighard,** uuigheard BH; uig§ LV; wig§ Ct. **Uighelm** LV; wig§, †whelm Ct. **Uigheri** LV. **Uiglāf** LV; uu§, w§ Ct. **Uigmund** LV; uu§, wimund Ct. **Wigstān** Ct. **Wigðegn** Gn, Ct.
Uuigincgga-hām Ct.
Alu-uīg *sm.* Ct 17/5 ~.
or-wīge *aj* unwarlike. Cp 1145 ~(inbellem).
Uulf-wīg *sm* Gn 60 ~.
slītan *sv* tear. Ld 99 ~endę (laciniosa).
snīte *sf* snipe. Cp 64 snite (acegia).

wudu-snīte *sf* wood-snipe. Cp 428 uudu~ (cardiolus).

be-smītan *sv* defile. VP 88/32, 5 ~að, ~u (profanaverint, §abo).

gewītan *sv* depart. Ef 335 geuuitendi (decidens); Cp ~endi. Lr 7 ~e (pereat a me). VP 6/9 ~að (discedite). 79/19 § (§imus). 38/14 ~e (abeam). Hy 4/6 ~en (recedant). 21/12; 37/22 gewit! (discesseris). 34/22 § (discedas). Ct 38/9; 41/41 (he) ~e.

onweg-gewīt *s* departure. VP 115/11 ~e (excessu).

ed-wīt *sn* reproach, disgrace. VP 14/3; 21/7 *etc* ~ (opprobrium *a*; § *n*). 68/20 ~ min (improperium *a*). 122/4 ~e(†§). 68/10 ~(§ia). 73/22 ~a (improperiorum). 118/22 ędwit.

edwītan *vb* reproach. VP 43/17 eðwetendes (exprobrantis). 73/10 edwetede (improperavit). 68/10 ~endra. 118/42 ~endum. 73/18 edwitte (improperavit). 34/7; 101/9 §un. 41/11; 88/52 edwiton. 78/12; 88/52 edwitun.

wīte *sn* punishment, torture. Mt 41 ~um. VP 72/4 ~(plagā). 38/11; 63/8 ~u(§as; §ae). Ct 40/23 ~.

wītnian *wv* punish. Cp 1349 uuitnath (multabitur). VP 36/28 bioð wicnade (punientur).

gewītnian *wv* VP 78/11 gewicnedra (punitorum).

wītedōm *sm* prophecy. Bd[2] 57 witedo[o]m (baticinatio).

wītega *sm* prophet. Cp 698 uuitgan (divinos). VP 73/9; Hy 9/11 witga (propheta). 104/15 §um. Hy 9/4 §ena. 126/4 §ena (excussorum).

wrītan *sv* write. VP 44/2 ~endes (scribentis). Ct 38/16; 40/12, 2, 3; 41/47 *etc*; 45/56 ic ~e. 42/23, 4, 4, 5 ic ~o. 41/1; 42/1; 45/1 ~.

wrītere *sm* writer. VP 44/2 †writ (scribae *g*).

hwīt *aj* white. Ef 254 huitti clabre; Cp huite clafre (calcesta). Ct 13/6 huitan stan. 20/12 § stanes. 25/9 ~an ::::... 28/10 ~e celdan hec.

huuitquidu Ep; huitcudu Cp. huitfōt Ep; Ef Cp §. **hwitehlāfa** Ct. **Hwithyse** Ct.

Huīta *sm* LV 419, 40, 80, ~. Gn 39 ~.

Hwīting *sm* Ct 24/12 ~. 36/10 (wi)ting.

Huītae *sf* LV 28 ~.

gehwītan *wv* whiten. VP 50/9 ic biom ~ad(dealvabor). 67/15 beoð gehwitte (§abuntur).

hwītel *s(m)* cloke. Ef 1127 huitil (racana).

flītan *sv* dispute. Ef 330 ~ad (disceptant); Cp ~at.

flītere *sm* disputer. Ep 854 ~ (rabula); Ef, Cp §.

bītul *s(m)* beetle (insect). Ep 145 ~um (blattis); Ef, Cp §.

īdel *aj* useless, vain. Cp 421 idle (casso). VP 5/10; 59/13 ~(vanum, §a). 107/13 ~u hęlu. 11/3; 40/7 ða idlan. 93/11; 106/9 idle (§ae; inanem).

idelhende VP.

īdellice *av* vainly. VP 30/7 ~(supervacue). 34/7; 38/7; 88/48 ~(vane).

īdelnis *sf* vanity. VP 38/6, 12 ~(vanitas). 4/3; 30/7 *etc* ~isse (§atem). 51/9 *etc* § (§ate). 25/4 § (§atis). 126/1, 2 in § (in vanum). 23/4 in § (in §o). 61/10 ~nesse.

ā-īdlian *wv* make vain. VP 136/7, 7 ~iað (exinanite).

Īda *sm* LK 1 ~. Gn 80 ~.

Īding *sm* son of I. Gn 80, 6, 90 ~.

Īdi *sm* LV 218 iidi.

Īdle *sf* a river. BH 88 ~æ — ~ae I.

sīde *sf* side. Cp 1256 ~(lumbus). Lr 23 ~an (madianum). VP 47/3 on ~an(latera). 90/7 § ðire (§e). 127/3 ~um.

hrīder *s(n)* sieve. Cp 14 ~(glebulum).

scīd *s* shingle. Ep 943 ~um(scindulis); Ef, Cp §.

strīdan *sv* stride. Ep 1086 ~it (varicat); Ef, Cp §; Ld stritęd.

wīd *aj* wide.

widsāe VP. Uidsīth LV. **Widmundes-felt** Ct.

wīde *av* widely. Rd 11 uidæ.

gīdsung *sf* greed. Ep 82 gitsung

(appetitus); Ef §; Cp ~. **Bd² 1** ungemetlicre ~e (†cupido). **VP** 118/36 unrehte §(avaritiam).

gecīd *sn* strife. **Bd² 35** ~(litigia).

tīd *sf* time. **Mt** 12, 40 ~ *n*. **VP** 80/16; 101/14 *etc* ~(tempus *n.*) 74/3 ~(§ *a.*). Hy 7/54 longe ~(tempore). 36/39 on ~(§). Hy 13/27 on cuðe ~ (§). 20/10; 70/9 *etc* in ~ (§). 9/26; 33/2 *etc* in alle ~ (§). Hy 7/58 in towordre ~e (§). 30/16 ~e (§a). 88/46 ~a (§um). **Ct** 37/33 sio ~. 37/12 ~ *a*. 37/8 unce ~e. 37/13 ~e *d*. 37/30 to ðære ~e. 37/41 aet ðere ~e. 42/9, 16 minre ~e *d*. 37/25 ~um.

Tidbald LV. **Tidberct** LV. **Tidburg** LV. **Tidcume** LV. **Tidfirþ** Rn; §ferð LV, Gn, Ct. **Tidhāeð** LV. **Tidhelm** LV. **Tidhere** LV. **Tidhild** LV. **Tidhūn** LV. **Tidsig** LV. **Tiduald** LV; §weald Ct. **Tiduini** LV. **Tiduulf** LV, Ct.

margen-tīd *sf* morning time. **VP** 48/15; 72/14 in ~(in matutino). 62/7; 100/8 in ~(in §is). Hy 13/22 on ~ (§o tempore). 29/6 to ~e (ad §um). 64/9 ~e (§i). 129/6 gehaelde ~e (custodiā matutinā).

Tīda *sm*. **Ct** 30/16 ~.

bīdan *sv* wait. **Cp** 1296 ~(manere). **VP** 51/11 ~u(expectabo). 24/3; 68/7; 103/11, 27; 141/8; Hy 3/20 ~að. 39/2 ~ende (§ans).

ā-bīdan *sv* await. **VP** 32/20 ~eð (sustinet). 36/9 ~að (expectant). 26/14, 4 abid (§a!, sustine!).

brīdels *s* bridle. **Ep** 127 ~(bagula); Ef brigdils; Cp ~. Cp 1248 ~um (lupatis). **VP** 31/9 ~e(freno).

rīpan *sv* reap. **VP** 128/7 ~eð(metit).

rīpung *sf* ripening. **VP** 118/147 ~e(maturitate).

gegrīpan *sv* seize. **VP** 17/38 ~o(compraehendam). 7/6 ~eð (§at). 34/8 § (adpraehendat). 2/12 ~að (adprehendite). 70/11 § (comprae·hendite). 68/25 ~e(§at). 34/2 gegrip (adpraehende!).

Uu-heard [= uuīg§ ?]. LV.

hū *av* how. **Ld** 132 hu ald (quotus). **Mt** 37 hú. **VP** 8/2, 10 *etc* ~(quam). 10/2; 72/11, 9 *etc* ~(quomodo). 4/3 *etc* ~ longe (usque quo). 12/1 *etc* ~ longe (quousque). 65/16 *etc* ~ feolu (quanta). 70/20 ~ monge (§as). 118/84 ~ monge (quot). 37/9 *etc* a hu lenge swiður (usque quaque). **Ct** 41/1; 42/1 ~.

ðū *prn* thou. **Cp** 1011 geheres thu (heus). **DA** 4 ~. **Mt** 28, 48 ~. **VP** 2/7, 9 *etc* ðu earð, ðu reces(es tu, reges). Hy 13/2 ðu (qui). 9/22 gewite ðu *etc*. 21/12 ne gewit ðu *etc*. 41/6, 12 *etc* earðu. 15/10 ne forletesde. 39/18 wes ðe. 34/22 ne gewit †ð.

þū-þistil Ep; †popistil Ef; ðuðistel Cp.

nū *av* now. **CH** 1 ~. **CA** 8 ~. **VP** 2/10; 11/6 *etc* ~(nunc). 70/17 oð ~(usque §). 112/2; 120/8 *etc* of ðissum ~(ex hoc nunc). 75/8 ~ seoðan (ex tunc). 92/2 ~ hionan (ex tunc). 117/3 ne (nunc).

nu-get VP. **nu-ðā** VH.

cū *sf* cow. **Cp** 2085 cuu (vacca). **Ct** 53/3 cua *gpl*.

cucaelf Ef, Cp. **Custaningamearc**, cusstaninga § [u *over* y] Ct.

bū *neut* both. **Mt** 37 bú.

brū *s* eyelid. **Lr** 38 bruum (tautonibus).

ofer-brū *s* eyebrow. **Lr** 33 ~bruum (supercilis).

ūr *s*(*m*) bison. **Ep** 1097 ~um (uris); Ef, Cp §.

ūre *prn* our. **DA** 3 ~. **VP** 8/2, 10 dryhten ur (noster) *etc*. 11/5 ur is dryhten. 32/20, 1 sawul ur, heorte ur *etc*. 34/21 *etc* egan ur. 65/12 heafud ur *pl*. 11/5 *etc* ~ *fem a*. 21/5 *etc* ~ *masc.pl*. 11/5 *etc* ~*fem.pl*. 19/6, 8 *etc* ~es. 39/4 *etc* ~um. 34/14; 65/8 *etc* urne. 34/25; 84/10 ure = urre *d*. Hy 13/13, 24 ure = urre *g*. 89/10, 7; 135/24; Hy 13/25 ura *gpl*. **Ct** 48/18 ure gewitnisse *a*.

hūru *av* perhaps. **Cp** 1398 ne ~ is (numquid).

sūre *sf* sorrel. **Ep** 974 ~ae (salsa); Ef §; Cp ~. Cp 1785 ~(saliunca).

gēaces-sūre *sf* sorrel. **Ep** 63 ~aes surae (accitulium); Ef gecaes †sarae; Cp gęces~. Ef 263 iaces †sura (calciculium); Cp ieces surac. Ef 1101 †acacsore (acidus).

scūr *s(m)* shower. VH 7/3; 8/5 ~(imber).

Stūr *sf* Stour. Ct 9/3 *juxta fluvium vocabulo* ~. 26/4 *fluminis qui dicitur* stúr. 24/3; 43/4 ~. 24/2 *fluminae* st[u]ræ. 28/14 be ~e. 30/5 *ab oriente* ~e. 30/4 *ab occidente* ~. 4/4 *in* sturia. 51/8 ~e *fluminis*.

brȳd-būr *s(m)* bride-chamber. VP 18/6 ~e (thalamo).

gebūr *sm* husbandman. Ep 163 gibuur (colonus); Cp gebuur.

ūle *sf* owl. Cp 378 ulae (cavanni). 1382 ~(noctua, ulula). 2150 ulae (ulula).

Ula-hām Ct.

scald-hūlas *spl* seaweed (?) Cp 1491 ~(paupilius).

Hūlan *sm* LV 334 ~.

fūl *aj* foul. Cp 1031 ~e (olido). DA 16 ~. Bd[2] 50 ~re (feda).

fūlae-trēa Ep; §treo Cp; falatreu Ef.

fūlian *wv* rot. VP 37/6 ~adun (computruerunt).

ā-fūlian *wv* rot. Ep 1044 ~odan *etc* (putrefacta *etc*); Ef ~at.

mūl *s(m)* mule. VP 31/9 ~ (mulus).

Muul *sm* LV 336 ~.

Cūlingas *pl* Cooling. Ct 50/2 *in loco quae appellatur* ~. 6 ~a boc.

ūð-wita Cp, VP.

sūð *av* south, southward. Ct 34/20; 41/17 ~.

suðdǣl VP. **Sutangli**, suutanglorum Ct. **Suðmynster** Ct. **suþrador** Bl. **Suthsaxoniae.** **suðeweard** Ct. **suðuuind** Cp. **westsuþ-wind**, uuestsuduuind Ep; -sud- Ef; -suð- Cp.

east-sūth *av* south-eastwards. Cp 41 ~ (ad euronothum).

sūðan *av* from the south, south. Ct 29/11 ~.

suðanwestan, suþan§ Cp. **suðanwind** VP. **westan-suðanwind** VP.

ēastan-sūdan *av* from the south-east. Cp 40 ~ (ab euro).

Sūþrege *s* Surrey. Ct 21/2; 22/1 *in regione* suðregię. 23/1 § suðregiæ. 45/31 in ~um.

Sudergeona, suðri[o]ena BH.

mūð *sm* mouth. VP 9/28 *etc* ~(os *n*). 38/10 *etc* ~ minne (os *a*). 5/10 *etc* ~e. 32/6 ~es. 48/14 muþe (þ *on other l.*). 49/16; 65/14; 72/9 mud. 57/7 §e. 18/15; 61/5; 137/4 §es.

Uiurae-mūþ *sm* Wearmouth. BH 381 ad ~muda—§—uu§. LK 9 aet u[i]uræmoda.

gūð *sf* war.

Gut[h]berct LV. **guðfona** VH. **Gudfrid**, gut[h]§, gyð§ BH; guthfrith LV. **Gudhard** Ct. **Guðhelm** LV. **Guthmund** LV; guð§ LV, Ct. **(Guð)uini** LV.

Gūða *sm* LV 369 ~. Ct 1/7 guda.

cūð *aj* known. VP 38/5; 75/2 ~(notum; §us). 54/14 ~a min (§us meus). 15/11 *etc* ~e. 31/5 ~e (cognitam). 87/9 ~e mine (notos). 30/12 ~um minum (§is). Hy 2/7 cyðe.

†**Cudbald** BH; cuth§ LV. **Cudberct**, cuth§, cuðberht BH; cuthberct, cut[h]§, cut§, cuð§ LV; cuðberht, cud§ Gn; cuthberht, cut§, cuð§ Ct; cuðberhting Gn. **Cuthburg** LV. **Cuðfrið** LV, Gn; cuutfert Ct. **Cuthgār** LV. **Cuthgils** LV. **Cuðheard**, cutheard LV. **Cuðhelm**, cuthelm LV. **Cuthere** LV. **Cuthlāc** LV. **Cuthmund**, cuð§ LV. **Cuthrēd** LV; cuð§ LV, Ct. **Cuthrīc** LV; cuð§ Ct. **Cuthðegn** LV. **Cudusald** BH; cuth, cuð§ LV. **Cuthuini**, cuð§ LV; cuðuine, cud · · · e Gn; cuðwine, §ing SG. **Cuthuulf**, cud§ LV; cuðuulf LV, Ct; §ing SG.

un-cūð *aj* unknown. VP 50/8 ða ~an (incerta).

frǣ-cūð *aj* contemptible. Cp 695 frae~ (despectus).

cūðlice *av* certainly, indeed. Bd[2] 49 ~(sane). VP 87/6 ~(quidem).

cūðian *wv* be known. VP 78/10 ie~ (innotescat). 143/3 ~ades (§uisti). Hy 6/2 ~as (§ueris).

ūs *prn dat., acc.* us. VP 4/6; 11/5 *etc* us (nobis). 4/7 ofer us (nos). 43/6 in us (§). 19/10; 43/26 *etc* us (§). Ct 42/10, 1 us *a., d.*

ūsic *acc.* us. VP 5/13; 11/8, 8 *etc* ~(nos). 79/7 †sic.

hūs *sn* house. Cp 705 ~es (domatis) DA 18 ~um. Mt 49 húsum. VP

103/17 *etc* ~(domus). 5/8 ~ ðin (§um) *etc.* 26/4 *etc* ~e. 25/8 ~es. 48/12 ~(domos). 73/20 ~a. 64/5 hyses.

Husneah (= huslēah) Ct. Husmerae Ct.

eardung-hūs *sn* tabernacle. VP 32/14; Hy 5/31 ~e (tabernaculo, habitaculo).

gest-hūs *sn* inn. VP 54/16 ~um (hospitiis).

heben-hūs *sn* ceiling. Cp 1180 ~(lacunar).

gehūsscipe *sm* home. VP 44/11 ~(domum). 134/19, 9, 20 ~(§us). 97/3 gehuscipe.

nēh-gehūs *sm* neighbour. VP 30/12; 43/14; 78/4, 12; 79/7; 88/42 ~um (vicinis).

hūsincel *sn* little house. VP 101/7 ~e (domicilio).

Hūsa *sm* LK 4 hussa. Ct 47/4 ~.

hūsl *sn* eucharist. DA 9 þys ~e.

lūs *s(f)* louse. Ep 812 luus (peducla); Ef, Cp §.

ðūsend *sn* thousand. VP 89/4; 90/7; 104/8; Hy 7/59 ~(mille). 3/7; 83/11; 90/7; 118/72 ~(milia). Hy 7/59 ~u(§). 67/18 ~um. 67/18 †ðused. Ct 38/9 x ~a. 41/19, 33 twa ~a. 34 feower ~a *pl.* 45/10 twa þusendu.

fūs *aj* eager. Rn 2/12 ~æ *pl.*

Uig-fūs *sm* LV 10; 370 ~.

mūs *sf* mouse. Ep 664 ~(mus, muris); Ef §; Cp muus. 977 ~(sorix); Ef §; Cp mús.

muusfalle Cp. mushabuc Cp.

hreaða-mūs *sf* bat. Ep 978 hreatha~ (stilio, vespertilio); Ef §; Cp hraeðemu[u]s. 1098 hreadae~ (vespertilio); Ef hreadam's; Cp hraeðemuus.

Cūsa *sm* Ct 9/7; 10/4 ~.

Ūusc-frēa, uúsc§ BH; uusc§ Gn; uuscfreaing Gn.

clūstor-locae Ep; §loc Cp; clusterlocae Ef.

dūst *sn* dust. VP 29/10; 102/14 ~(pulvis). 7/6; 17/43; 21/16; 77/27; 103/29 ~(pulverem). Hy 4/14 ~e (§e). 43/25 dusðe. 34/5 dus (pulvis).

scūwa *sm* shade. VP 43/20; 79/11; 101/12; 108/23; 143/4 scua (umbra). 16/8; 87/7; 106/10, 4 §an (§ā). 22/4 §an (§ae *g*).

ūf *s* owl. Ep 142 uuf (bubu); Ef, Cp §. 161 § (bufo); Ef §.

þūf *s(m)* banner. BH 111 *genus vexilli quod romani tufam, angli vero appellant* thuuf—§ 1—thuf.

ā-scūfan *sv* push. Cp 1644 ~ið (praecipitat). Lr 47 ~e (retrudas).

Scūfeling-ford Ct.

Cūfa *sm.* Ct 33/14 ~.

hūn *sm* cub.

Hunbald LV. Hunberct LV, §berht Gn, Ct, hum§ Ct. Hunburg Ct. Hunfrið LV, Gn, Ct. Hungils LV. Hungȳth LV. Hunrēd LV, Ct. Hunsig LV. hunsporan Cp. Hunstān Ct. Hunualdi BH, §uald LV, §wald Ct. Hunuini LV. Hunuulf LV.

Ælf-hūn *sm* Gn 30 ae~. Ct 15/6; 16/5 ~i.

Æþel-hūn *sm* BH 95 aedil~ — aeðil~ 1—aedil§. 214 edil~—aedel~ 1. 216 edil~ — aeðil~ [i *alt. to* e] 1. Ct 7/5 aeðelhuni. 34/9 æðelhune. 34/18; 41/50 æð~. 35/11; 36/7; 57/6; 59/7 aeð~.

And-hūn *sm* BH 283 ~o.

Beadu-hūn *sm* LV 328 baðhun.

Beald-hūn *sm* LV 289 balð~.

Beorht-hūn *sm* BH 282 berct-huno. 334 §hun. LV 74 bercht~. 136, 205; 358, 89 berct~. Gn 40 †berhthum.

Ēad-hūn *sm* LV 278 ~. Ct 22/7 ~hún. 23/7 ~.

Eald-hūn *sm* LV 168; 286, 97 ald~. Ct 35/8 §. 8 §o.

Ealh-hūn *sm* CA 1 ~. Ct 24/5; 32/9 ~. 35/14 ealhun. 48/10 alch-hun.

Ecg-hūn *sm* Ct 48/16 ~.

Peoht-hūn *sm* LV 222; 359 pect~.

Rǣþ-hūn *sm* Gn 40 *rethhun.* Ct 23/12; 53/7 reðhuni. 55/8; 57/7; 58/14 §hun. 22/11 ræðhuni. 47/3 raeþ~.

Suiðhūnincglond, suiðhuning§, suithhuning§, Ct.

Tīd-hūn *sm* Ct 33/18 ~.

Wealh-hūn *sm* Ct 85 uuealh-hunes.

Wiht-hūn *sm* Gn 13 uioht~. Ct 12/4; 33/20 uu~. 46/5 §us. 49/9 §i. 19/5; 34/7 wioht~. 15/6; 16/6 uuiohtuni.

Hūna *sm* LV 160 ~.

hūne *sf* horehound. Ep 657 ~ae *vel* biouuyrt (marrubium); Cp ~.

burg-rūn *sf* sorceress. Ep 761 ~ae (parcas); Ef ~æ; Cp ~e.

tūn *sm* enclosure, farm. Ef 281 tuun (cors); Cp §. Ef 307 § *vel* ðrop (conpetum); Cp §. Ct 3/2 ·· erra-tuun. 43/2, 3 an healf ~, healfne ~. 44/6 ðisne tuun.

Tunberct BH, LV. tuuncressa Ep, Cp. Tunfrith LV. Tungils LV. Tu[u]nlic LV. Tunrēd Ct. tuntih Ct. Tunuald LV.

æppel-tūn *sm* orchard. VP 78/1 eappul~ (pomorum).

Bōsing-tūn *sm* Bossingham. Ct 32/4 *ad* ~e.

Bydic-tūn *sm* Ct 55/8 ~.

cæfer-tūn *sm* court-yard. Ep 1058 cebęrtuun; Ef †caebertuum; Cp caebrtuun (vestibulum). VP 83/3 ceafurtune (in atria). 73/4; 99/4 §es (§o, §a). 95/8 §as (§a). 91/14; 115/19; 121/2; 134/2 §um (§is). 133/1 ceafortunum (§is). 83/11 ceaful§.

Cyninges-tūn *sm* Kingston. Ct 21/1; 22/1 ~tún. 23/1 k§.

dēor-tūn *sm* park. Cp 324 edisc, ~tuun (broel).

Ealdbeorhting-tūn *sm* Ct 56/3 aldbęrhting~.

Gāta-tūn *sm* Gatton. Ct 45/24 an ~e.

Hygereðing-tūn *sm* Ct 59/3 ~.

Mylen-tūn *sm* Milton. Ct 55/2 ~.

Pennel-tūn *sm* Kinneel. BH 16 ~ — pegnel~ — ~tuun.

Pleghelmes-tūn *sm* Ct 5/2 ~.

Wil-tūn *sm* Wilton. Ct 22/7 úuiltún. 23/7 uuiltún.

Wudu-tūn *sm* Wooton. Ct 48/2 in wudotune.

dūn *sf* down, hill. Mt 21 (on) hea dúne.

Duunuualla Ct. Dunuualhi Ct. Dunwalinglond Ct.

Cūðrices-dūn *sf.* Ct 28/8 ~.

Huete-dūn *sf* Wotton. Ct 45/24 on ~e.

Onnan-dūn *sf.* Ct 10/3 ~duun.

Seles-dūn *sf.* Ct 45/5, 15 on ~e.

Đorn-dūn *sf.* Ct 50/3 ~.

Ueta-dūn *sf.* BH 338 ~.

Wilfæres-dūn *sf.* BH 162 uilfarę̄s dun, *id est mons uilfari*—§aes duun—§es dún—uilfæraes dun.

of-dūne *av* down. VH 7/45 ~(deorsum). Ct 20/6, 7, 8, 20, 1 ~.

ofdūne-. stigun. settan. stāg. dune, ofdune-stīgan.

Dūn *sm.* Ct 6/2; 28/16 ~.

Dunwalinglond Ct. Duunuuallan Ct.

Dūnincg *sm* son of D. Ct 43/10 ~.

Dunincg-land Ct.

brūn *aj* brown. Ep 159 bruun (burrum); Cp §; Ef †bruum. 433 bruun (furvum); Ef, Cp §. Ef 1145 § locar (aquiluus fulvus).

bru[u]nbesu Ep; Ef, Cp bruun§. Brunheard Ct.

brūn *sn* cloth. Ep 837 stefad bru*n* (perstromata, ornamenta); Ef staefad †brum; Cp steba.

rūm *aj* roomy, wide. VP 30/9 ~ne (spatioso). 103/25; 118/96 ~(§um); latum).

Rūmining-seta Ct.

ðūma *sm* thumb. Ep 821 thuma (pollux); Ef §o; Cp ~.

plūme *sf* plum. Ep 822 ~ae (prunus); Ef §; Cp ~ę. Cp 1600 ~ae (plumum).

plumtrēu Cp.

ā-lūcan *sv* pull out. VP 24/15 ~eð (evellet).

ūt-ālūcan *sv* pull out. VP 51/7 ~eð (evellet).

bi-lūcan *sv* close. VP 34/3 biluc (conclude!). Hy 12/9 §eð (clauserit).

Mūca *sm* Ct 33/12; 55/9; 56/5 ~.

Mūcel *sm* Ct 28/16; 29/20; 30/13; 31/4; 48/12, 3, 4; 54/5; 56/6; 58/18. 47/12, 6 ~e. 47/5, 7 mucoel. 57/10 mucael.

crūce *sf* pot. **Ep** 989 ~ae (trulla); Ef §; Cp ~. 1056 · · · · ae; Ef crucae (urciolum); Cp 2165 waeter~.

fȳr-crūce *sf* crucible. **Cp** 621~ (cucuma).

waeter-crūce *sf* water-pot. **Cp** 2165 ~(urciolum).

brūcan *sv* enjoy, use. **Cp** 254 ~ende (ausurae). **CA** 10 to ~en(ne). **Ct** 39/13; 41/5; 45/21, 6 ~e. 42/8 ~en. 41/12; 42/13, 5, 21 to ~anne. 45/48 to ~enne.

Pūch *sm* **BH** 340 ~.

Ūchtrēd, uc[h]t§ **LV**; uhct§, uht§ Ct.

ðrūh *sf* pipe. **Ep** 1000 thruu[c]h (tubo); Ef thruch; Cp ~.

wæter-ðrūh *sf* water-pipe. **Ep** 232 uua[e]terthruch (caractis); Ef †uaeterthrouch; Cp uuęterþruh. Cp 372 waeterðrum (canalibus).

mūha *sm* heap. **Cp** 46 ~(acervus).

sūgan *sv* suck. **Ep** 455 suggit (fellitat); Ef, Cp §.

hunig-sūge *sf* honeysuckle. **Ep** 615 hunaegsugae (ligustrum); Ef huneg§; Cp ~.

Cūga *sm* **LV** 203 ~.

getrūgung *sf* confidence. **VP** 88/19 ~(adsumptio).

fortrūgadnes *sf* confidence. **VP** 51/6 ~isse (praecipitationis).

ā-drūgian *wv* dry up. **VP** 89/6; 101/5 ~að (arescat; aruit). 36/2; 128/6 ~iað (arescent; exaruit). 21/16; 101/12 ~ade(§; arui). 105/9 ~ad wes (siccatum est).

drūgung *sf* drying. **VP** 77/17; 105/14; 106/4 ~e(siccitatem; §e; §e).

būgan *sv* bow. **Rn** 2/4 (b)ug(a) *inf.*

ūt *av* out. **VP** 40/7 uteodon ut (†egrediebatur foras). **Ct** 20/16 ut on. 29/13 ut to.

ūt-. gang. Utbigeht (Ct). cwealm. sendan. āþrungen. ālocen. gǣþ, gǣst. lǣdan, ā§. alēoran. scēotan. ēode. ālūcan. ātȳnan.

ūtan *av* outside. **VP** 58/15 ~ ymbgað (circuibunt). **Hy** 7/50 ~(a foris).

būtan *av, prp, cj* outside, without, except, unless. **Cp** 1967 ~ toðum (suaeder). **VP** 9/27 ~ yfle (sine malo). 3/8; 14/2; 17/32, 2 *etc* ~ (§). **Hy** 4/4 ~ ðe (extra). **Hy** 7/76 ~ me (praeter). **Ct** 28/24, 4, 4 ~ *w.d.* 40/23 bute *cj.*

ūte *av* outside. **VP** 30/12 ~(foris).

Ūtel *sm* **Gn** 50 ~.

hrūtan *sv* snore, resound. **Cp** 1923 ~ende (stertens). **Rd** 7 ~endum.

forð-lūtan *sv* lean forward. **VP** 94/6 ~eu (procidamus).

lūtian *wv* hide. **VH** 13/26 ~iendra (latentium).

hlūtor *aj* clear. **Ep** 578 hlutrae (liquentes); Ef §; Cp §e.

clūt *s(m)* cloth. **Ep** 789 ~(pittacium); Ef, Cp §.

grūt *s(f)* groats, coarse meal. **Cp** 1619 †gruiit (pollinis). **Ct** 41/30 ~a *g.*

Ūda *sm* **LV** 345 ~.

Hūda *sm* **Ct** 24/6; 25/12 ~. 22/9; 23/9 ~an *g.*

Lūdeca *sm.* **Ct** 57/10 ludęca.

Cūda *sm* **LV** 220 ~.

Crūd *s.* **Ct** 32/3 ~es *silba.*

Tūda *sm* **BH** 126; 212 ~. 127 ~ *d.* **Gn** 53 ~. **Ct** 33/19 ~.

Dūda *sm* **Ct** 58/22 ~.

Dūde-mon Ct.

Dūduc *sm.* **Ct** 24/6; 25/12; 26/7; 27/6; 32/8 ~.

ūp *av* up. **VP** 49/4 ~(sursum). 113/3 (2) upp (§). **Ct** 20/7, 10, 6; 48/20 ~.

ūp-. stige. ' eornan. āreccan. hebban. āhebban. cuman. cyme *sb.* cymeþ. rǣran. hēhan. stīgan. āhōf.

ðȳ *prn instr* the, that; *av* therefore, *w. comp* the. **Pr** 2 thi *av.* **VP** 17/27, 7 mid ðy upahefenan, mid ðy ðweoran (cum). **Hy** 11/15; **Hy** 13/30 §. 108/19 mid ðy (quā). **Ct** 41/12, 69 ðy *w. comp.* 47/11, 3 mid ðy londe.

ðy-lǣs.

for-ðȳ-ðe *cj* because. Ct 41/69 ~.

mid-ðȳ *cj* while, when. VP 4/2; 48/13 *etc* ~ (cum). 21/25; 30/23; 31/3 *etc* ~(dum). 105/44 mið ðy (cum). 100/5; 105/44; 108/7; Hy 12/8 mitte (cum).

cȳ *pl* cows. VP 67/31 cye (vaccas). Ct 41/13, 20, 1 ~.

cȳe *sf* chough (bird). Ep 240 chyae (cornicula); Ef ciae.

bi-hȳran *wv* hire. VH 4/10 ~dun (locaverunt).

fȳr *sn* fire. Mt 44 fy'r. VP 17/9 *etc* ~(ignis). 104/32, 9 ~forbernende, ~.. hit (§em). 11/7 *etc* ~e. 10/7 ~es.

fyrcrūce Cp. fyrpannae Ep; Ef, Cp §.

bēcen-fȳr *sn* beacon-fire. Bd[2] 7~ (farans).

fȳren *aj* fiery. VP 118/140 ~(ignitum).

ā-fȳred *ptc* castrated. Ef 319 afyrid †obbenda (dromidus); Cp ~ olbenda.

þȳre *spl* dwellings. Cp 1292 ~(mapalia). 1294 ~(magalia); Ld byrae.

sȳl *sf* column. VP 74/4 ~e (columnas). 98/7 ~e(§ā).

cȳlle *s(m)*. Cp 231 kylle (ascopa). VP 32/7; 77/13 ~ (utrem). 118/83 ~ (uter).

ȳð *sf* wave. VP 41/8; 106/25, 9 ~e (fluctūs. *pl*). 64/8; 88/10 ~a (§uum). Hy 5/13 yde (§ūs *pl*).

Yth-suīð LV.

ȳðgian *wv* fluctuate, flow. VP 77/20 ~adon (inundaverunt).

ȳðgung *sf* fluctuation. VP 54/23 ~e(fluctuationem).

Ȳthan-caestir BH.

þrȳþ *sf* strength.

Thryduulfi—thryth§ BH. Thruidrēd—thryd§ BH; thryth§ LV.

Ælf-þrȳþ *sf* LV 38 aelfðryth. 42 §dryð. Ct 2/2 (aelfdrydę) *g*. 50/4 ęlfðryð. 51/9 aelfþryð. 53/6 §þryþ.

Æþel-þrȳþ *sf* BH 95 aedilthryd —aeðilðryð 1—aedilthryd. 232 edil§—aediltryd—aeðilðryt 1. 245 aedilthryde *d* — aedyldrydę — aeðilðryda [i *alt. to* e]. LV 32, 2, 4 eðilðryth. 41 edildryð.

Beorht-þrȳþ *sf* LV 33 berctðryth. 46 berhtðryð.

Beorn-þrȳþ *sf* Ct 19/8 ~ðryðe *g*. 37/1 ~ðryð. 32/6 §e *g*. 45 bearnðryðe *g*.

Blīþ-þrȳþ *sf* BH 353 bliththrydae *d*—§yðe 1.

Burg-þrȳþ *sf* LV 23, 4 ~ðryð.

Cēol-þrȳþ *sf* LV 25 ~ðryth.

Cwēn-þrȳþ *sf* LV 25, 33 cuoenðryth. 29 §dryth. Ct 57/4 quoenðryðae *lg*. 5, 5 §am. 6 §e [*among nominatives*]. 58/6 cwoenðryðam (§þryðam). 9 §ðıyð (coenþryð). 13 cwoenðryð (§þryð). 23 cwænðryðe *g*.

Cyne-þrȳþ *sf* LV 24, 5, 36 cyniðryth. 28; 444 §ðryð. 40 §ðryd. 41, 4 §dryð. Ct 13/4; 38/8; 59/5 ~ðryð. 47/3 ~ðryþ. 35/5 ~ðryðae *ld*. 38/1 ~ðryðe *g*. 4 § *a*. 38/7 †cyne.

Ēa-þrȳþ *sf* LV 20, 39 eaðryð. 37 eaðryth.

Ēad-þrȳþ *sf* LV 39, 42 eatðryð. 47 eatdryd.

Eald-þrȳþ *sf* LV 26 aldðryth. 32, 4 alt§. 34 al[t]§.

Ealh-þrȳþ *sf* CA 12 for alhðryðe. 18 §ðryð. Ct 45/8 §dryðe *d*. 14 §ðryðe *d*.

Ēan-þrȳþ *sf* LV 36, 8 ~ðryth. 42, 6, 7 ~dryth.

Helm-þrȳþ *sf* LV 32~ ðryth.

Hildi-þrȳþ *sf* Rn 8 ~. LV 26 ~ðryth. 47 ~dryð.

Hyge-þrȳþ *sf* LV 42 hygðryð.

Ōs-þrȳþ *sf* BH 155 osthrydae *g*—ostrydę—osðryðę. 298 osthryd—§id—§yð. 380 §yd. LV 37 osðryth. 44 osðryð. 3 9 ostðry

Rīc-þrȳþ *sf* LV 26, 9 ~ðryth.

Sǣ-þrȳþ *sf* BH 149 saethryd—§ith—§ðryth—saedryd. LV 36 saeðryth. 44 §ð. Ct 48/10 §ð.

Sele-þrȳþ *sf* Ct 57/2, 2 ~ðryð.

Sige-þrȳþ *sf* LV 31 sigðryth. 48 ~ð.

Wern-þrȳþ *sf* LV 28, 32 uernðryth.

Wil-þrȳþ *sf* **LV** 24/37 uilðryth. 45 §dryð.

Winc-þrȳþ *sf* **LV** 20 uincðryð.

here-hȳð *sf* booty, prey. **VP** 16/12 to ~e(praedam).

hȳð *sf* landing-place, harbour. **Ef** 329 †hydde (deconfugione, statione); Cp ~ae. **VP** 106/30 in ~e (portum).

Caelic-hȳth *sf* **Ct** 12/2 ~. 18/3 celchyð.

cȳðan *wv* make known. **Cp** 1150 to ~enne (intimandum). **VP** 49/7; 80/9 ~u(testificabor). 54/18 §(adnuntiabo). **Ct** 41/1 ~e. 42/1 ~o. 45/1 ~.

forð-cȳðan *wv* announce. **VP** 118/26 fordcyðde (enuntiavi).

cȳðnis *sf* testimony. **VP** 18/8; 80/6; 121/4 ~(testimonium). 102/18 ~ (†testamentum *a*). 118/129, 44 ~ (†§ia). 49/16 ~isse mine (testamentum *a.*). 24/10 § (§). 43/18 *etc* § *d.* 104/8 *etc* § *g.* 24/10 *etc* § (testimonia). 118/31 *etc* ~issum. 118/14 ~issa. 24/14 cyðnes (testamentum).

cȳðere *sm* witness. **VP** 34/11 ~as(testes). 88/38 ~ (†§).

un-ond-cȳðignis *sf* ignorance. **VP** 24/7 ~isse (ignorantiae *g*).

ðȳs *prn instr.* this. **Ep** 494 thys geri (horno); **Ef** §; **Cp** þys. **Cp** 1030 §. **DA** 9 þys [y *over* u].

-gȳþ

Gyðhelm LV.

Ælf-gȳþ *sf* **LV** 33, 6, aelfgyth. **Ct** 58/22, 2 §gyð.

Æþel-gȳþ *sf* **LV** 20, 1, eðilgyth.

Beadu-gȳþ *sf* **LV** 20, 38 badugyth.

Beorht-gȳþ *sf* **LV** 27 berctgyth. 43 berhtgið.

Beorn-gȳþ *sf* **LV** 30, 5, 5, 6 ~gyth. 43 ~gið.

Cyne-gȳþ *sf* **LV** 48 cynigyð.

Ēad-gȳþ *sf* **BH** 261 ~gyd *three times*— ~ð 1 *once*. **LV** 22 ~gyð.

Eald-gȳþ *sf* **LV** 35 aldgyth.

Ēan-gȳþ *sf* **LV** 21 ~th.

Eard-gȳþ *sf* **LV** 35 ~th. 40; 445 ~ð. 47 ~gið.

Ēd-gȳþ *sf* **LV** 27 ~th.

Frī-gȳþ *sf* **BH** 310 ~gyd — ~gid — ~gyð.

Hēa-gȳþ *sf* **Ct** 34/3, 19 æt ~gyðe ðorne (hęgyðe), hægyðe §.

Heaþu-gȳþ *sf* **LV** 33 haðugyth. 40 §gið.

Here-gȳþ *sf* **LV** 23 ~ð. 30 ~th. **Ct** 28/9 ~geðe land. 41/58, 64 ~gyð.

Hilde-gȳþ *sf* **Rn** 8 hilddi[*g*]yþ. **LV** 40 hildigið. 445 §yð.

Hūn-gȳþ *sf* **LV** 22 ~th.

Ōs-gȳþ *sf* **LV** 21, 2 ~th. 43 ~ið. 47 ~id.

Pend-gȳþ *sf* **LV** 19 ~gith.

Rǣd-gȳþ *sf* **LV** 25 redgyth.

Sǣ-gȳþ *sf* **LV** 34 saegyth.

Torht-gȳþ *sf*. **BH** 263 torctgyd—troctgyd—torchgyð. 264 torctgyd—†toragyd—to[r]chtgyð.

Weald-gȳþ *sf* **LV** 19 ualdgith.

Wern-gȳþ *sf* **LV** 27 uerngyth.

Wiht-gȳþ *sf* **LV** 28 uictgyth.

Wil-gȳþ *sf* **LV** 25, 7, uilgyth. 39 §ið.

Wulf-gȳþ *sf* **LV** 32 uulfgyth.

Hȳsica *sm*. **LV** 9 hysca. 385 ~.

ȳst *s* storm. **VP** 106/25, 9 ~es, ~ (procellae, §am). 10/7; 148/8 ~a (§arum).

fȳst *sf* fist. **Lr** 49 ~e(pugnas).

hȳf *sf* hive. **Cp** 133 ~i (alvearia).

risc-ðȳfel *sm* bed of rushes. **Ep** 517 ~thyfil (jungetum); **Ef** †ryc§; Cp ~.

scald-ðȳfel *sm* sea-weed. **Ep** 58 ~thyflas (alga); **Ef** ~thyblas (§e); Cp ~hyflas *vel* sondhyllas.

·Cȳna *sm*. **LV** 130 ~.

Cȳnia *sm*. **LV** 213 ~.

ā-tȳnan *wv* exclude. **Cp** 792 ~ið(explodit, excludit).

ūt-atȳnan *wv* exclude. **VP** 67/31 sien ~ed (excludantur).

on-tȳnan *wv* open. **VP** 48/5; 77/2 ~u (aperiam). 144/16 ~es. 37/14 ~eð. 117/19 ~að. **Hy** 6/29 ~að (adaperient). 50/17 ontyn!

7/16; 38/10; 77/23; 118/131 ~de. 21/14 ~don. 103/28 ~endum. 105/17 ~ed wes. 108/2 § is.

Tȳcan-ōra Ct.

rȳhe *sf* blanket. Ep 1020 ryae (tapeta); Ef hryhae; Cp rye. 1080 ryhae (villosa); Ef §; Cp rye. 1081 linnin ryhae (villa); Ef §; Cp ryee. Ld 120 rihum (tapetibus).

ā-þrȳan *wv.* Cp 789 ~id, arytrid (expilatam).

scȳhan impel. Ep 654 scyhend (maulistis); Ld §; Cp scyend.

drȳge *aj* dry. VP 65/6 in ~(aridam). Hy 5/36 ðorh ~(siccum). 94/5 ða ~an (arida). 104/41 in ~um (sicco).

ā-drȳgan *wv* dry. VP 73/15 ~des(exsiccasti).

ȳtmest *aj superl* uttermost. VP 134/7 ðere ~an eorðan (extremo). 138/9 ðęm utmestan sæs (postremo).

ā-ðȳtan *wv.* Cp 739 ~ið(eliminat).

strȳta *sm* ostrich. Cp 1932 ~(strutio).

cȳta *sm* kite. Cp 333 ~(butio).

gehȳdan *wv* hide. Cp 42 gehyddum (abditis).

ā-hȳdan *wv* hide. VP 18/7 ~e(abscondat). 26/5 ~eð. 30/21 ~es (§es). 55/7 ~að. 118/19 ahyd! 39/11; 54/13 ahydde (§i; §erem). 34/7 §on. 139/6 §un. 63/6 §en. 37/10 nis ~ed. 68/6 sind ahydde. 118/11 ahyd[d]e (§i). 30/20 ahydes (§isti). 141/4 †ahydun (§erunt).

gehȳdnis *sf* convenience, opportunity. Cp 1449 ~(oportunitatem).

hlȳdan *wv* sound. VH 12/7 ~eð (concrepet).

Cȳda *sm.* LV 251 ~.

Clȳd-uini LV.

Bȳda *sm.* LV 167 ~.

brȳd *sf* bride.

brydbūr VP. **brydguma** Cp, VP.

Hrȳþ *sm.* Gn 120 ~.

Hrȳþing *sm* son of H. Gn 120 ~.

ō-. wæstm. wef. helde. gengel. leccan.

Ō-uini BH.

Hō-mund LV.

fō *sv* seize, take. Ct 41/19 fon *sbj. pl.*

on-fō *sv* receive. Mt 47 ~fóh! VP 115/13 ~fou (accipiam). 49/9 ~foo (§). 74/3 ~fo (accepero). 48/2; Hy 7/58 ~foð (percipite; §ient). 67/17 § (suscipitis). 5/2; 16/1; 38/13; 53/4; 83/9; 85/6; 142/1 ~foh (percipe!). 118/116 § (suscipe!). Hy 13/12 ~ (§ere). 146/6 ~fonde (§iens).

be-fō *sv* seize. VH 5/14 ~foo (compraehendam).

tō *prp, av* to. Ep 93 to nyttum (ad); Ef to; Cp tó. 1067 to fuglum; Ef, Cp, Ld to. Cp 83 to (ad), 574 to gelestunne (comitavere). 815 to aseodenne (expendere). 1150 to cyðenne (intimandum). BDS 3 to ymbhycggannae. Lr 2 to teorenne. LP 6 to. CA 8 *etc* to. 13 tó. DA 9 *etc* to. 9 tó. Mt 17 *etc* to. 21 tó. SG 2 *etc* to. Bd² 40, 51 to. VP 2/5 *etc* to him (ad). 10/2 to minre sawle (animae meae). 28/1 to dryhtne (domino). 140/6 to stane (petrae). 15/8 to ðere †swiðra (a) *etc.* 2/7 *etc* to dege (hodie). 16/14 *etc* to lafe werun. (superfuerunt) 35/8 *etc* to ðæm gemete (quemadmodum). 58/6 to niosenne (ad visitandas) *etc.* 101/14 to mildsiende (miserandi) *etc.* 105/5 to blissiende (ad laetandum) *etc* 31/6 to ne geneolaecað (non ad proximabunt) *etc.* Ct 3/5 *etc*; 20/8 *etc*; 27/4; 28/4 *etc*; 29/2 *etc*; 30/5 *etc*; 34/8 *etc*; 37/2 *etc*; 39/2 *etc*; 40/6 *etc*; 41/5 *etc*; 42/5 *etc*; 43/2, 3; 45/10 *etc*; 48/2 *etc*; 59/3 to. 28/15 ðerto.

tō-. samne. heald. settan. cymeþ. ðon. hwon. strogden. scādan. dǣlan, §eðnis. nēalǣcan. gelǣdan. geēcan. gecēgan. getēah. brōht.

inn-tō *prp* into. CA 8 ~. Ct 30/21 into.

tō-. standan. scacan. strægd. strigdeþ. tetridit. sliten. wesnis. stregdan. brecan. weorpan. stencan. wurpon. strugde. worpen. brocen. goten. dāl. slāt. flēowon. tecīnan. flōwan. tislōg.

dō *vb* do. LP 5 do! VP 11/6; Hy 2/3; dom (agam). 30/25; 36/9; doð (agite; §unt). 102/20, 1; 105/3 *etc* § (facitis, §; §iunt). 75/11 ðoð (agent). 30/24 dooð (faciunt). 67/5 dood (§ite). 88/35 do (faciam). 59/14 don (§iemus). 6/5; 19/10 *etc* do (fac!). 21/20 do (§ias). 11/2; 27/9 *etc* doo (fac!). 26/14 § (age!). 17/20 § (†fecit). 3/7; 30/17; 33/15 doa (fac!). Hy 3/14 § (†fecerim). 9/17; 17/51 *etc* donde (faciens). 24/4 *etc* § (ientes). 33/17 ða §an. 70/4 §es (agentis). 36/7 *etc* §um. 25/4 ðondum. 74/5 don (agere). 108/16; 125/2, 3 § (facere). 142/10 doan (§). 67/21 to donne (faciendi). Hy 11/7 to § (gerendi). 118/112, 26 to § (ad faciendas, faciendi). Ct 39/15 don *inf.*

wel-dō *vb* benefit. VP 124/4 ~doa (bene fac!).

gedō *vb* do. VH 7/76 gedom (faciam). Ct 37/34 hie gedon. 42/6 gedoan *inf.*

ōr *s* beginning. CH 4 or *a.*

Billan-ōra *sm* Ct 29/17 ~ is ðes (dennes) nama.

Tȳcan-ōra *sm* Ct 25/4 ~.

swōr *prt* swore. VP 23/4; 109/4; 131/2, 11; Hy 9/8 ~ (juravit). 88/4; 94/11; 118/106 ~ (§avi). 88/50 ~e (§asti). 101/9 ~un (§abant).

for-suōr *prt* forswore. Cp 660 ~ (defotabat).

uuōr-hana Ep; §hona Ef; worhona Cp.

Oft-fōr *sm.* BH 306 ~. Gn 46 ~.

Hrōð-fōr *sm.* LV 212 ~.

fōr *s* pig. Ep 810 foor (porcaster); Cp §; Ef ~; Ld foor (porcastrum).

†mar-bēam VP.

hōlunga *av.* in vain. Ep 683 ~ (nequaquam); Ef, Cp §.

swōl *s* heat. Ef 274 suol (camos); Cp §. Cp 415 §e (caumati).

stōl *sm* stool, seat. Cp 2059 stool (tripes).

wōl *s(f)* pestilence. Lr 1 wól (mortalitas).

hrēod-pōl *s(m)* reed-pool. Ct 20/16 on ~pól.

bōl *s* eel. Cp 1337 bool (murenula).

ōðer *prn* other. VP 108/8 ~(alter). Hy 4/4; Hy 7/76 ~(alius). 77/6 oderu *f sg.* 47/14; 104/13 oðrum (alterā; §um). 77/4; 101/19 oðerre (§ā) Ct 41/15, 25; 42/18, 9 ~. 34/16 oðre. 29/16 §es. 45/19 oðoro *pl* 28/20; 34/20 §um.

ōþel *s* country, native land. Rn 3/1 oþlæ *d.*

rōðor *s(n)* rudder. Ep 986 rothor (tonsa); Ef †rohr; Cp roðr.

stēor-rōðor *s(n)* rudder. Cp 1520 ~ (palmula).

Hrōð-fōr LV. **Hroðfrith** LV. **Hroðmund**, §ing Gn. **Hrothuaru** LV. **Hroðuald** LV. **Hroðuini** LV. **Hroðuulf** LV.

hlōþ.

Hlotheri BH; hlotharius, hlothari *lg* Ct.

hlōðere *sm* Bd[2] 4 se [h]loðere (rethor).

þōþor *s(m)* ball. Ep 787 thothor (pila); Ef thorr; Cp thothr. Ef 1124 thothur (§).

sōð *aj* true. VH 11/2 ~ (verus). VP 18/10; Hy 7/5 ~e (vera).

sōð *av* truly, indeed. VP 49/8 ~ (autem). 50/7, 8; 55/4; 58/16 ~ (vero).

sōðfæst *aj* truthful, honest. LP 13 ~festę *pl.* VP 85/15 ~fest (verax).

sōðfęstlice *av* honestly. Ct 45/44 ~.

sōðfestnis *sf* truth. VP 5/10; 24/10 *etc* ~ (veritas). 14/3 *etc* ~se (§atem). 24/5 § ðinre (§ate) *etc.* 30/6 § (§atis). 11/2 § (§ates). 88/3 soðfes[t]nis.

sōðlice *av* truly, indeed. VP 2/6; 3/4 *etc* ~ (autem). 9/27, 32 *etc* ~ (enim). 54/14; 88/39 ~ (vero). 57/2 ~ (vere). 73/9; Hy 13/6 ~ (jam). 72/13; Hy 13/28 ~ (ergo). 31/6 hweðre ~ (verum tamen). 48/16 § sodlice. 54/20; Hy 7/62 †soðl (enim).

wōþ *s* eloquence. Ep 564 uuoþ (lepor, subtilitas); Ef p'uod; Cp wooð. Ep 444 †þoot (facundia, eloquentia); Ef †puoo[d].

Wōþ-gār Rn.

fōþor *s(n)* food; covering, case; load. Ef 378 fothr; Cp foth[r] (emblema); Ld fodor. Cp 138 fothur (alitudo). Ct 39/6 IIII foðra.

nōþ.

Noðberht Gn. **Noðfreðing** Ct [*under* friþ]. **Noðheard,** not§ Ct. **Nothelmus** BH; noð§ Gn. **Noðmund** Ct. **Noðwulf** Ct.

Æþel-nōþ *sm* Gn 8 aeðilnoð. Ct 8/13 æðelnoðes. 34/2 §noðo. 8, 18 §noð. 7/6 aethelnothi. 8/6 §es. 43/10 e[ðel]noð.

Beadu-nōþ *sm* Ct 21/7 badonoð. 26/2 §e. 22/5; 36/7; 41/54; 42/1, 27 badanoð. 23/5; 24/11; 42/25 bade§.

Badenoðing-land Ct.

Bēag-nōþ *sm* Rn 12 beagnoþ [*or* beog§]. Ct 33/19 ~noð.

Beorht-nōþ *sm* Ct 31/4 ~noð. 34/5 berht§.

Beorn-nōþ *sm* LV 450 †~hoð. Ct 12/6; 21/6; 22/5; 49/10; 51/10; 56/5; 57/9; 58/16 ~noð. 19/7 §i. 50/4 beorn[n]oð. 23/5; 45/59; 48/14 beornoð. 31/10 bearnoð. 38/18 (b(ia)rnnoð.

Burg-nōþ *sm* Ct 28/17 ~noð.

Cēol-nōþ *sm* Gn 4 *ceolnoðus.* Ct 21/5 ~noth. 21/2, 2, 4; 22/1, 2, 3 §o. 22/10; 23/4, 11; 24/3; 25/12; 32/7; 34/5; 38/15; 40/11; 42/23; 47/3 ~noð. 23/1, 2, 3 §o. 40/2 §es. 29/18; 30/15; 41/47; 44/3 ciolnoð, 36/6 §noth. 31/5 cialnoð. 27/5 §us. 22/4 †ceolnotht.

Dēor-nōþ *sm* Ct 35/12 ~noð. 58/20 § (dior§).

Dryht-nōþ *sm* Ct 32/8; 35/13 ~noð.

Hyse-nōþ *sm* Ct 21/6; 23/4; 24/10; 25/13; 42/25 ~noð. 36/8 (h)yse§. 22/4 ~noth.

Sige-nōþ *sm* Ct 28/16; 30/15 ~noð. 29/20 sig§.

Tāt-nōþ *sm* Ct 26/6 ~noð.

Wǣr-nōþ *sm* Ct 33/2; 35/11; 57/6 wernoð. 57/9 uuer§. 49/11 uuęr§.

Wil-nōþ *sm* Ct 35/13 nuilnoð.

tōð *sm* tooth. Cp 1967 butan ~um (suaeder). VH 11/6 ~(dentem). Ps 56/5 ~as. 34/16; 36/12; 123/6 ~um. 111/10 todum.

toðreomum Lr.

brōður *sm* brother. SG 8, 9 broðor, broðar. VP 48/8 ~(frater). 34/14 ~urne (fratrem). 132/1; Hy 1/1, 7 ~ (§es). 21/23; 121/8 broðrum. Ct 41/10 ~ar *n.* 38/3, 12 § *g.* 41/36 § *npl.*

broðorsunu Cp.

gebrōðru *pl* brothers. Rn 3/1 twoegen gibroþæra.

ōs *sm* god.

Osbald LV. **Osberht** LV, Ct; §inglond Ct.. **Osburg** LV. **Osfrid** BH, Ct; §frith LV. **Osgeofu** LV. **Osgȳth** LV. **Oshelm** LV. **Oshere** LV, Ct. **Oshering** Ct. **Oslāc** Ct. **Oslāf** LV, Ct. **Osmäer** LV. **Osmōd** Gn, Ct; §ing Gn. **Osmund** LV, Gn, Ct. **Osrēd** BH, LK, LV. **Osrīc** BH, LK, LV, Ct. **Osðrȳð** BH, LV. **Osuald** BH, LK, LV; §weald Ct. **Onswini** Rn; osuini BH. **Osuīu** BH, LK; §uio LV, Gn; oswiuq Rn. **Osuulf** LV, Ct.

ōsle *sf* ouzel. Ep 665 ~ae (merula); Ef §; Cp ~ę.

Hacanōs *s* Hackness. BH 310 *monasterio quod appellatur* ~ [*later* (?) *accent on* o].

gōs *sf* goose. Ep 117 goos (anser) Ef, Cp. Ef 1103 ~ (§). Cp 450, 960, 3 wilde goos (cente, gente, §).

gosfuglas Ct.

grǣg-gōs *sf* grey goose. Ef 1104 gregos (anser silvatica).

Bōsa *sm.* BH 271, 3; 306 ~. LV 86; 342 ~. Gn 56 ~. 58 ~ *d.*

Bosanhamm, bo[o]sanhaam BH.

Bōsel *under* oe.

segl-bōsm *s*(*m*) swell of sail. Cp 412 ~(carbasus).

ōst *s* protuberance, knot. Ep 688 ~ (nodus); Ef, Cp ~.

fōstur-bearn Ep; foetribarn Ef; fostorbearn Cp. **fostor-faeder** Cp.

blōstme *sf* blossom. VP 102/15 ~e (flos).

rōwan *sv.* Cp 86 on hlior rouuit (adplaudat).

stōw *sf* place. CA 14 ðeosse ~e *d.* VP 36/36; 75/3 ~(locus). 25/8; 36/10 *etc* ~e (§um). 70/3 ~e getrymede (§um). 22/2 *etc* § (§o). 62/3 in wetrigre ~e (in inaquoso). Ct 42/5, 7 ðere §, ðære § *d.*

cēap-stōu *sf* market. Cp 510 ~ (commercium).

cualm-stōu *sf* place of execution. Cp 2 ~ (calvariae locus).

leger-stōw *sf* resting-place. Ct 41/26 wið ~e.

stōwian *wv.* Cp 1713 stouuigan (retentare).

flōwan *sv* flow. VP 67/3 ~eð (fluit).

tō-flōwan *sv* flow away. VP 61/11 ~en (affluant).

blōwan *sv* blow, flower. VP 89/6; 91/13; 102/15; 131/18 ~eð (floreat *etc*). 71/16; 91/14 ~að.

ōfer *s*(*m*) bank. Cp 1271 obr (margo).

Ōfa *sm* LV 15, 89; 251; 404, 34, 58 ~. Ct 9/6; 30/18; 36/9; 38/19 oba. 17/6 ~.

ōfost *s* haste. Ep 757 þorch obst (per anticipationem); Ef obust; Cp obst.

hōf *prt* raised. Mt 22 hóf. 23 ~on. VP 85/4 ~ (levavi).

ā-hōf *prt* raised. Rn 2/5 (ahof). 3/5 ~. VP 77/70 ~ (sustulit). 118/48 ~(levavi).

ūp-hōf *prt* raised. VP 120/1; 122/1 ~ (levavi). 60/3 ~e (exaltasti). 113/6 ~un (†exultastis). 92/3, 3 § (elevaverunt).

ūp-āhōf *prt* raised. VP 24/1; 142/8 ~ (levavi). 26/6, 6 *etc* ~(exaltavit). 105/26 ~(elevavit). 88/43 ~e (exaltasti). 82/3 ahofun up (extulerunt).

hrōf *sn* roof. Ep 609 ~(lacuna); Ef §. Cp 2013 ~(tholus). CH 6 til ~e.

hrofuuyrcta Ep; Ef, Cp §.

first-hrōf *sn* ceiling. Cp 1176 ~(laquear).

frōfur *sf* consolation. VP 118/24 ~(consolatio). 93/19 frofre (§iones).

cōfa *sm* chamber Cp 1583 ~(pistrimum).

cōfincel *s*(*n*) little chamber. Cp 1587 ~(pistrilla).

Cnōb-heri; c[o]nob§, cnobheresburg, conob§ BH. **Cnob-ualch** LV.

ā-grōf *prt* engraved. Rn 1§ ~.

glōf *s*(*f*) glove. Ep 631 gloob (manica); Ef glob; Cp ~.

Bōfa *sm* LV 167; 226 ~. Gn 89 ~, Ct 24/5 boba. 55/9; 56/6; 57/11 ~.

Bōfing *sm* son of B. Gn 89 ~.

Bobingseata Ct.

sōfte *av* gently. Cp 1848 ~(sensim).

un-sōfte *av* uncomfortably. DA 12 ~.

sōna *av* soon. VP 36/20 ~(mox). 39/16 ~(confestim). 69/4 ~(statim).

spōn *s* Cp 972 ~(gingria).

hwōn *av* somewhat. VP 76/4 ~(paulisper).

huonhlotum Cp.

mōna *sm* moon. VP 71/7; 88/38 *etc* ~(luna). 8/4; 73/1 *etc.* ~an (§am).

mōnað *sm* month. CA 12 ~e. Mt 11, 39 monðes. SG 1 VII ~. VP 80/4 monðes (mensis). Ct 37/9, 12, 5, 30; 40/8; 41/67 tuælf *etc* ~.

Brōn *sm* LV 96 brón.

ōma *sm* rust, mildew. Cp 1039 ~an (igni sacrum). Ld 88 ~ (igni sacer).

brond-oom *s* mildew. Cp 1757 ~(rubigo).

ōmig *aj* rusty. Cp 866 omei (ferruginem, obscuritatem ferri).

Rōm *s*(*f*) Rome. Mt 14 in rom(e).

Romæcæstri Rn.

Rōmwalus *sm* Romulus Rn 3/1.

lōma *sm* tool, utensil. Ld 21 ~um (colomellas).

gelōma *s* utensil. Cp 2172 ~(utensile).

gelōmlicnis *sf* frequency. VP 117/27 ~sum (confrequentationibus).

nōm *prt* took. Ep 113 naamun (auserunt); Ef noumun; Cp ~un. VP 54/15; 72/24 ~e(capiebas; tenuisti).

genōme *prt* tookest. VP 64/5; 72/24 ~e (adsumpsisti).

for-nōmun *prt* destroyed. VP 118/87 (†consummaverunt).

cwōm *prt* came. Rn 2/12 kwomu. Mt 19, 21 ~. 25 cwóm. 44 cuom. VP 82/9; 95/13, 3 *etc* ~(venit). 104/19 ~e (§iret). 43/18; 54/6; 77/34; 78/1; Hy 7/34 ~un.

bi-cwōmun *prt* came. VP 34/15 tosomne ~(convenerunt). 84/11

§ bicomun (obviaverunt). Hy 5/7 ~(devenerunt).

for-cuōm *prt* obtained. Cp 1409 ~, bigaet (obtenuit).

fore-cwōm *prt* came before. VP 118/147 ~com [*last* o *from* u?] (praeveni). 17/6 ~on (praevenerunt). 20/4 ~e (§isti). 67/26 ~un. 17/19; 118/148 ~comun.

ofer-cuōm *prt* obtained. Cp 1420 ~(obtenuit).

gōma *sm* palate. VP 68/4 ~an (fauces). 21/16; 118/103; 136/6; 149/6 ~um.

dōm *sm* judgment, glory. Rn 3/3 ~. Pr 1 ~ę. VP 96/2 *etc* ~(judicium *n*). 9/5; 16/2 ~ minne (§ *a*) *etc*. 9/8 *etc* ~e. 9/26; 17/23 *etc* ~as.

Domfrith LV. **Domheri** LV. **Domuini** LV.

-dōm. martyrdóm. camp~. cynedoom. hlāford~. lǣce~. frīo~. þēow~. wīs~.

dryht-dōm *sm* judgment. VP 9/17 ~as (judicia).

brōm *s* broom. Ep 465 broom (genista); Cp ~.

Bromlēag, §inga-mearc Ct.

ōcusta *sm* arm-pit. Ep 38 ~(ascella); Ef, Cp §.

wēod-hōc *s*(*m*) weed-hook. Ep 887 uuead~ (sarculum, ferrum); Ef §; Cp ueod~.

Hooc *sm* Ct 1/7.

hrōc *s* rook. Ep 469 hrooc (grallus); Ef, Cp §; Ld ~.

gelōcian *wv* look. VP 118/6; Hy 3/3 ~iu (respicio; aspiciam). 34/17 ~as ðu (respicies). 32/14 *etc* ~að (respexit). 36/13 § (prospicit). 94/4 § (conspicit). 101/20 § (prospexit). 103/32 *etc* § (respicit). 9/30; 10/5; 65/7 ~iað (§iunt). 12/4; 21/2 *etc* ~a (§e!). 21/20; 83/10; 118/132 § (aspice). 32/13; 39/2; 65/18; Hy 6/12 ~ade (prospexit; respexit; conspexi; aspexit) *etc*. 30/8 ~ades (respexisti). 21/18 ~adon (conspexerunt). Hy 3/12 ~ende (aspicientes).

forð-lōcian *wv* look forth. VP 13/2 ~að (prospexit). 52/3; 84/12 ~ade (§).

for-sōc *prt* refused. Ef 339 ~(detractavit); Cp forsooc.

wið-sōc *prt* renounced. Mt 16 ~e. 51 wiðsóce. VP 76/3 ~(negavi).

flōc *s* flat fish. Ep 802 flooc (platisa); Cp §; Ef ~; Ld 163 †folc.

cōc *sm* cook. Ef 287 †coacas (culinia); Cp ~as.

bōc *sf* beech. Ef 1113 ~(fau, arbor).

bōc *sf* book. Ct 50/6 ~.

boclond Ct.

lond-bōc *sf* land-book, deed Ct 56/8 ~.

gebōcian *wv* book, settle by deed. Ct 28/21 ~ade.

brōc *sm* brook. Ct 20/7, 7, 9, 10 on ~. 21 on bróc. 9 to ~e.

brōc *s* breeches. Ld 256 brooc (suricus).

Clofes-hōh *sm*. BH 250 ~ho[c]h—clofaes hooh—clofęs §—clofaes§. Ct 15/3; 16/3 clobeshoas. 46/2 clofes §. 17/1 ~hos. 46/3; 57/1; 58/2, 6 æt ~houm.

scæft-lōh *s* spear-strap. Ep 106 sceptloum (amentis); Ef, Cp §. 489 scaeptloan (hastilia telorum); Cp §. Cp 145 sceptog (amentum).

þōhe *sf* clay. Ep 3 thohae (argillus); Ef th[o]ę; Cp thoae.

þrōh *s* hatred. Ep 874 throh (rancor, invidia, odium); Ef throch; Cp troh.

scōh *sm* shoe. Cp 395 ~(caliga).

schonegl Cp.

slēfe-scōh *sm* slipper. Cp 1879 socc, slebe ~(soccus).

steppe-scōh *sm* Cp 1969 ~(subtalaris).

scōere *sm* shoemaker. Cp 1962 ~(sutrinator); Ld scoehere.

wōh *aj* crooked. Ct 29/4, 4 ðam wón stocce.

wlōh *s* fringe, ornament. Ep 1066 uulohum (villis); Ef §; Cp uuloum. Cp 2142 u[u]loh (villus).

crōh *sm* shoot, twig. Ep 773 cros (pampinus); Ef, Cp crous.

tōh *aj* tough. Ep 581 toch (lenta, tarda); Ef †thoch; Cp ~. 614 toch gerd (lentum vimen); Ef thoh; Cp ~.

tōhlice *av* toughly. **Ep** 1063 tholicae (uscidae); Ef †tochtlicae; Cp ~. Cp 1033 tolice (huscide).

Ōhta *sm.* **BH** 66 octa.

ðōhte *prt* thought. **Bd²** 78 ~on (moliuntur). **VP** 51/4; 76/6; 118/59 ~ (cogitavit; §i; §§). 20/12; 34/20; 61/5; 72/8; 82/4, 4, 6; 139/3, 5, 9 ~un. 40/8 ~on.

geðōht *ptc* thought. **Cp** 670 ~(decreta).

ā-þōht *ptc* thought. **Cp** 566 ~(commentum).

geðōht *sm* thought. **VP** 75/11; 118/118 ~(cogitatio). 54/23 gedoht ðinne (cogitatum). 32/10, 1 *etc* ~as (cogitationes). 5/11 *etc* ~um. 75/11 geþohta.

sōhte *prt* sought. **Ep** 756 sochtae (petisse); Ef †scochtae; Cp ~. **VP** 26/8 *etc* ~e (quisivi). 33/5 § (inquisivi). 76/3 *etc* § (exquisivi). 37/13, 3 ~on (querebant; inquirebant). 53/5; 62/10; 85/14 ~un (quaesierunt). 118/155 § (exquisierunt). 9/36 bið ~(requiretur).

gesōht *ptc* sought. **Bd²** 74 ~e (repetitam).

ā-sōht *ptc* sought out. **VP** 110/2 ~(exquisita *pl*).

wrōht *sf* accusation. **Ep** 524 uuroctae (insimulatione); Ef uurochtae.

wrohtspitel Cp.

brōhte *prt* brought. **Cp** 629 ~e(detulerat). **VP** 77/29 ~e (obtulit).

tō-brōht *ptc* brought. **VP** 44/15 sien ~(adferentur).

Meahse-lōg *s.* **Ct** 43/6 ~.

ðwōg *prt* washed. **VP** 72/13 ~(lavi).

slōg *prt* struck, killed. **VP** 77/20, 51, 66 *etc* ~(percussit). 3/8; 68/27 ~e (§isti).

of-slōg *prt* killed. **VP** 77/31, 47; 104/29 *etc* ~(occidit). 100/8 ~(interficiebam). 93/6, 6 ~un (interficerunt, occiderunt).

tō-slōg *prt* destroyed. **Ep** 195 ti~(concidit); Ef gi~; Cp ~.

crōg *s* pot. **Ep** 584 croog (lagoena); Ef, Ld §; Cp ~. Ld 79 ~(lagonam, vas lapideum, ollo).

Crōg-lea Ct.

dōgor *s(n)* day. **Ct** 34/16 uferrau ~. 41/23 yferran dogre.

bōg *s(m)* shoulder. **Ep** 67 boog (armos); Ef, Cp §.

brōga *sm* terror. **Rd** 13 ~um. **VP** 87/17 ~an (terrores).

un-rōt *aj* sad. **VP** 41/6, 10, 2; 42/2, 5 ~(tristis).

geunrōtsian *wv* sadden. **VP** 34/14; 37/7; 54/3 ~ad(contristatus). 68/21 were ~ad.

sōt *s* soot. **Cp** 944 sooth (fulgine).

wrōtan *sv* root, turn up. **Cp** 1959 ~u(subigo).

wrōt *s* snout. **Ep** 152 uurot (bruncus); Ef urot; Cp ~.

fōt *sm* foot. **Cp** 1566 ~(pes). **Mt** 23 ~as. **VP** 9/16; 25/12 *etc* ~(pes). 90/12 ~ðin (pedem). 120/3 ~ðinne (§). 8/8; 17/10 *etc* ~um. 98/5; 109/1 ~a.

fotcospum VP. **fotmēlum** Ef.

hræfnes-fōt *sm* ranunculus. **Ep** 848 hraebnęs foot (quinquefolium); Ef hræfnæs §; Cf hraefnes §. 1084 hraefnaes fot (quinquefolium).

hwīt-fōt *aj* white-footed. **Ep** 55 huit§ (albipedius); Ef §; Cp §foot.

scāf-fōt *aj* splay-footed. **Ep** 832 scabfoot (pansa); Ef scaabfot; Cp scaffo[o]t.

mōt *vb* may. **CA** 14, 7 ~e. **Ct** 37/6; 41/46 ~en.

gemōt *sn* meeting. **Cp** 584 gemoot (contio, convocatio populi). **VP** 67/31 ~(concilium).

bōt *sf* reform, repentance. **Ct** 40/23 to fulre ~e.

Botfrith LV. **Bothelm** BH, LV. **Bothild** LV. **Botuald**, LV. **Bote-wælle** Ct. **Botuini** LV; §uuine Ct. **Botuulf** LV.

Bōta *sm.* **LV** 155 ~.

hōd *s* hood. **Ep** 239 hood (capitium); Ef, Cp §.

rōd *sf* cross. **Rn** 2/11 on ~i. **VH** 13/16 ðorh ~e (crucem).

rodetācn Ct.

wearg-rōd *sf* gallows. **Ep** 409 uue[a]rg~ (furca); Ef uaergrod. Cp 930 waergrood (furcimen).

hlōdun *prt* drew water. Cp 247 nomun, ~(auserunt).

þōden *s* whirlwind. Cp 136 ~(alcanus).

snōd *s* hood. Ef 301 ~(cappa); Cp ~.

stōd *prt* stood. VP 25/12; 81/1; 105/30 ~(stetit). 37/12, 2 ~on. 131/7; Hy 6/11 ~un.

gestōd *prt* stood. Rn 2/17 gistoddun. VH 6/26 ~e(existi).

æt-stōd *prt* stood by. VP 35/5; 44/10; 108/31 ~(adstitit).

wōd *aj* mad. Ef 383 uuoda; Cp ~a(epilenticus). Cp 1044 ~an(inergumenos).

Wōden *sm* Cp 1309 ~(mercurium). BH 25 uoden—uuoðen II [uu *over* w, *which is on er.*] Gn 76, 83; 116, 21 uoden. 109 uuoden. 95 ~.

Wōdning *sm* son of W. Gn 76; 115, 21 uodning. 83, 95; 109 ~.

fōdor *s*(*n*) case, sheath. Cp 2010 fodrum, tegum (tehis).

fōdrere *sm* forager. Bd[2] 20 †fodraðas (annonus).

frōd *aj* wise, old. Ep 758 f[r]odrae (provectae); Ef ~rae; Cp ~re.

Frōd *sm.* LV 97 frood. Ct 5/6 ~i *lg.*

flōd *sm* flood. Cp 1; 342 flood (adsida; bubla). VP 64/10 ~(flumen). 79/12 ~(§ *a*). 71/8 ~e. 45/5 ~es. 23/2; 65/6; 77/16 *etc* ~as(flumina). 73/15 § (fluvios). 88/26; Hy 6/16, 6 ~um.

cwilde-flōd *sm* destructive flood; deluge. VP 28/10 ~(diluvium). 31/6 ~e(§io).

fisc-flōdu *sm* fish-flood, sea. Rn 3/4 ~.

fylleþ-flōd *sm* high tide. Cp 20 fylledflood (malina).

nēp-flōd *sm* ebb, low tide. Cp 16 ~flod (ledo).

flōde *sf* channel, gutter. Ep 597 flodae (lacunar); Ef §; Cp ~; Ld ~a (antoni lacuna). Ct 20/8, 8, 19 ðære ~an *d.*

mōd *sn* mind, spirit. VP 123/3 ~(animus). Hy 11/13; Hy 12/8; ~(mens). Hy 11/8; Hy 12/10 ~(mentem). 76/6; Hy 7/11; Hy 13/9 (§e). 105/40; Hy 10/7 on ~e(animo; mente). 115/11; 118/53 ~es(§is; animi). Hy 12/3 ~(mentes).

modgidanc CH. **Modulf** Ct.

Æþel-mōd *sm* LV 6 aeðil~. Gn 24 aeðel~. Ct 3/13 æðel~us. 17/6 æðel~. 18/4 aethil~. 25/2 aethel~e. 11 aeðel~. 26/7 §. 27/5; 28/15; 32/8; 38/2; 43/6, 7 eðel~. 38/1 §es. 38/11; 43/1 §e.

Beorn-mōd *sm.* Gn 11 ~. Ct 33/2; 34/6; 51/9; 56/4; 58/14 ~. 35/10 ~us. 47/4 beormod. 49/8 ~i.

Here-mōd *sm* LV 190 ~. Ct 29/19; 30/14; 31/4; 35/12 ~.

Hwæt-mōd *sm* LV 255 huaet~.

Ōs-mōd *sm* Gn 101 ~. Ct 36/9 ~.

Ōs-mōdin *sm* son of Osmod. Gn 101 ~.

wer-mōd *s* wormwood. Ep 66 uuer~ (absintium); Ef uermodae; Cp ~.

ǣ-mōd *aj* out of mind, distracted. Cp 149 e~(amens).

ān-mōd *aj* unanimous, resolute. Ep 202 ~ (contumax); Ef on~; Cp ~mood. VP 54/14 ~(unanimis). 67/7 ~modde (§es).

ēað-mōd *aj* humble. VP 17/28 ~(humilem). 33/19; Hy 8/19; Hy 10/8 ~e (§es). 137/6 ~an(§ia). 73/21 ead~(§is). Ct 40/16 ~. 48/3 ~re.

lang-mōd *aj* constant. VP 7/12 long~(longanimis).

lytel-mōd *aj* pusillanimous. VP 54/9 ~um(pusillanimo).

ēað-mōdlice *av* humbly. VP 130/2 ~(humiliter).

ēað-mōdnis *sf* humility. VP 9/14 *etc* ~se (humilitatem). 118/153 § mine (§em). 118/50 § minre (§e). 135/23 § (§e). 118/92 ~nise. Ct 37/5 mid micelre ~se.

geēað-mōdian *wv* humiliate. VP 9/31; 54/20; 146/6 ~að(humiliabit; §; §iat) *etc.* 34/13; 80/15 ~ade(§abam; §assem). 43/20 *etc* ~ades. 93/5; 104/18 ~edun. 34/14 wes ~ad; 38/3 ~ad eam; 43/25 ~ad is *etc.* 105/42, 3 ~ade werun. 106/17 ~ade sind. 89/15 118/75 geaðmodadės. 142/3 §ade. 118/107 geeaðmoddad eam. 50/10 ða geeð-modedan.

gemōd *aj* agreed. **Ep** 201 gimodae (conjurati); Ef gimode; Cp gemode.

mōdig *aj* proud. **Rn** 2/3 modig.

Mōding *sm* Ct 29/4, 5 ~a hema mearce.

mōdor *sf* mother. **Mt** 12 ~ *g*. 27 ~ *n*. **VP** 26/10; 50/7; 86/5 ~ur (mater). 112/9; 130/2 §(matrem). 108/14 §(matris). 21/10, 1; 70/6; 138/13 § minre (§). **Ct** 38/12 ~ar *n*.

stēop-mōder *sf* stepmother. **Cp** 1390 ~(noverca).

mōderge *sm* cousin. **Cp** 587 ~(consobrinus, filius patruelis).

gōd *aj* good. **VP** 5/13 *etc* ~es (bonae). 33/13 *etc* ~e. **Ct** 37/21 ~es.

†goodaeppel Cp. **godspellian** VH; §ere DA.

gōd *sn* good; goods, property. **BDS** 4 ~aes. **LP** 12 ðeara ~a. **VP** 13/1, 3 *etc* ~(bonum *a*). 33/11; 85/17 ~e(§o). 4/6; 12/6 *etc* (§a *pl.*) 24/13; 37/21 *etc* ~um (§is). 15/2 ~a minra (§orum). **Ct** 37/41 mid godcunde ~e. 40/7 to ~e. 37/34; 40/16, 20; 45/49 ðas ~. 37/9, 14, 23, 40, 0; 42/10 ~um *pl.*

gōdnis *sf* goodness. **VP** 24/7; 36/3; 118/65, 6 ~se(bonitatem). 105/5 § (§ate). 118/68 § dinre (§ate).

blōd *sn* blood. **Rn** 2/9 ~æ. **VH** 7/87 ~(sanguis). 9/13 *etc* ~(sanguinem). 29/10 *etc* ~e mine. 15/4 *etc* ~um. 5/7 *etc* ~a.

blodlēs Ct. **blodsaex** Cp, Ld.

rōpnis *sf* liberality. **Cp** 1229 roopnis (liberalitas).

scōp *prt* created. **CH** 5 ~.

gescōp *prt* **VH** 7/11 ~(creavit). Ps 73/2; 88/13 ~e(creasti).

Bēt-scōp *sm.* **LV** 107 ~.

wōp *sm* weeping. **VP** 29/6 ~(fletus). 12 ~ minne (§um). 101/10 ~e. 6/9 ~es. Hy 12/4 ~as(luctūs).

cōp *s* coat. **Ef** 390 ~; Cp cóp (ependiten). Cp 760 ~ (erenditen).

grōp *s* pit. **Ld** 150 groop (scropis).

gescoė *pl* shoes. **VP** 59/10 ~(calciamentum). 107/10 gesc[o]e.

foe *sbj prs* take. **Ct** 34/11, 1, 3; 41/5, 31, 4, 42, 68; 45/35. 41/16, 65 foen. 41/19 fōn. 45/16, 7 feo.

on-foe *sbj prs* receive. **VP** 30/14; 138/20 onfoen (acciperent, §iant). 71/3 §(suscipiant).

fore-foe *sbj prs* anticipate. **VP** 78/8 ~(anticipet).

doe *sbj prs* do. **Mt** 48 ~. **VP** 39/9 ~(faciam). 36/8; 79/3 ~ (§ias). 13/1, 3; 21/9; 52/2, 4; 55/5, 11 ~(faciat).

gedoe *sbj prs.* **VP** 30/3; 70/3; Hy 6/26 ~(facias). 7/3 ~(§iat). **Ct** 37/28; 41/2, 11 ~. 41/43 gedoen. 30/22 ge gedeo.

Oeric BH.

hroeran *wv* stir.

on-hrērnis *sf* agitation. **Bl** 12 onhrernisse (commotionem).

woerig *aj* weary. **VH** 12/3 ~u (fessās).

lim-wœ̄rig *aj* lim-weary. **Rn** 2/16 ~næ.

ofer-foeran *wv* travel over. **Cp** 747 oberfoerde (emenso).

foernis *sf* travelling. **Ep** 530 in ~sae (transmigratione); Ef fornissæ; Cp ~se.

gefoera *sm* I companion. II wife. **CA** 4 min gefera II. **Ct** 45/3 gefeorum.

gefoerraedennum VP.

un-oferfoere *aj* impassable. **Cp** 1144 ~(intransmeabili).

geferscipe *sm* brotherhood. **CA** 10 ðæm ~.

un-gefoerne *aj* impassable. **VP** 62/3 in ðæm ~an(in invio). 106/40 in ~um.

soel *av* better. **Ct** 41/69 ~.

soelest *av* best. **Ct** 37/27; 38/11; 42/9 ~. 45/4 seolest.

coelan *wv* cool. **VH** 12/11 ~ende (refrigerans).

gecoelan *wv* **VP** 38/14 sie ~ed (refrigerer).

coelnis *sf* coolness. **VP** 65/12 in ~se (in refrigerium).

oeðel *sm* country, native land. VP 21/28; 95/7 oeðlas (patriae).

Oeðilburg LV. Ho·ilrēdus, odilredus Ct. Oidiluald, oiðil§, oedil§, oid§ BH; oedil§ LV; oeðil-wald, oeðeluuald Gn.

on-oeðung *sf* breathing on. VP 17/16 ~e(inspiratione).

roeðe *aj* fierce. Cp 851 ~ (ferox). Bd[2] 29 reðun (investis). VH 11/7 ~(asperos).

? Rethhun Gn; raeþ§, ræð§, reð§ Ct.

roeðelice *av* fiercely. Cp 2116 ~(violenter).

roeðra *sm* rower. Ep 875 roedra (remex); Ef §; Cp ~.

geroeðro *pl.* Ep 14 giroedro (aplustra); Ef geroedra; Cp ~.

Roetberht (hroeth§) Rn; hroeðberct LV. Hroeðburg LV. Hroeð-geofu LV. Hroeðlāc LV. Hroeð-uald LV. Hroeðuini LV.

smoeðe *aj* smooth. Cp 1610 ~um (politis). VH 12/7 ~u(canora).

un-smoeðe *aj* rough. Cp 232 unsmoþi (aspera). 1830 ~i(scabro).

foeða *sm* troop. Cp 787 ~an(phalange). 840 ~ (falanx). VH 5/6 ~an(statores).

moeðe *aj* tired.

mēðnis *sf* fatigue. Bd[2] 55 ~se (lassitudine).

toeð *pl* teeth. Lr 19 ~(sennas). VP 3/8; Hy 7/49 ~(dentes). 57/7 †toð (§).

wong-toeð *pl* grinders. VP 57/7 ~(molas).

doeð *prs* does. VP 9/24 ~(gerit). 14/5; 19/7; 36/5 *etc* ~(facit *etc*). 68/36; Hy 3/23 doð (§iet). Ct 37/10, 25, 8 ~.

gedoeð *prs* LP 12 ~. VP 7/11 ~(facit). 36/40; 40/3; 71/4, 13; 144/19 ~(faciet).

doest *prs* dost. VP 35/7 does 17/28; 87/11; 118/84 ~ (facies). 16/7; 76/15 ~(§is).

gedoest *prs* dost. VP 55/8 ~ (facies).

on-doest *prs* undoest. Cp 1888 † ondest (solvas).

broeðer *d* brother. VP 49/20 ~ ðinum (fratrem).

Oesa *sm.* Gn 80 ~.

Oese *sm.* Gn 114 ~.

Oesing *sm* son of O. Gn 80 ~. 114 o(esing).

Oese-walum Ct.

goes *pl* geese. Ct 37/18; 39/5; 40/10 ~.

Ploesa *sm* Ct 52/16 ~.

Boesel *sm* BH 307 bosel. 308 §um. 316, 7 boisil—bosil I. 319 boisil—boisel I. 348 boisili—§ I. 348 boisil —§ I. LV 51 ~. 196 bosil. 207 boesil. Gn 46 bosel.

Oisc *sm* BH 66 ~. 68 ~ *d.*

Oiscing *sm* son of O. BH 67 ~.

oest-ful *aj* gracious. Cp 2161 ~(voluter, cupido votium).

woeste *aj* desert. VP 68/26 ~u (deserta). 74/7 ~um (§is). 108/7 wostu (§a).

woesten *sn* desert. Mt 19 in westenne. VP 67/8 ~ (†deserto). 28/8; 106/33, 5 ~(desertum *a*). 106/4 in ~(solitudine). 54/8; 101/7 ~ne(§). 62/3; 77/19, 40, 52; 94/9; 105/9, 14, 26 § (deserto). Hy 7/18 § (heremo). 64/13 ~nes (deserti). 77/15 wostenne (heremo). 135/16 weosten (desertum *a*).

ā-woestan *wv* lay waste. VP 78/7 ~un(desolaverunt).

foetri-barn Ef (= foestribearn).

oefstan *wv* hasten. VP 69/2 oefesta (festina!) Hy 5/24 ~un(§averunt).

oefestung *sf* hastening. Cp 474 oefsung (circinatio). VP 77/33 ~e(festinantiā).

geroefa *sm* officer. Ep 197 giroefan (censores); Ef, Cp ~an. 223 giroefa (commentariensis); Ef, Cp ~. Cp 1674 ~an(proceres). Ct 34/8 se gerefa. 41/1, 49 ~. 71 ~an *g.*

folc-geroefa *sm* officer of the people. Cp 48 ~geroebum actionaris).

wīc-geroefa *sm* bailiff. Cp 2011 uuicgeroebum (teloniaris).

froefran *wv* console. VP 22/4 ~ende werun (consolata sunt). 68/21 § (§antem). 85/17 § were. 118/50

§ wes. 134/14; Hy 7/70 bið ~ed. 118/76, 82 frofrie (§etur), §es. 76/3 §an. 118/52 §ende eam. 125/1 §ende (§ati *pl*). Hy 2/2 §ende earð.

ā-froefran *wv* console. **Cp** 1210 afroebirdun (lenirent).

Coifi *sm* BH 90, 0 ~. **LV** 340 ceefi.

gedroefan *wv* disturb, trouble. **Rn** 2/14 *gi*(d)rœ(fe)d. **VP** 41/12; 42/5 ~es (conturbas) *etc*. 2/5; 20/10 ~eð. 17/15 ~de (§avit). 41/6 ~des (†§as). 17/5 ~don. 87/17 ~dun. Hy 6/31 ~ende (turbantes). 6/3 ~ed sindun; 4, 8 ~ed is (§ata est, §atus est) *etc*. 6/11 sien ~de; 17/8 ~de sind; 45/4, 4 ~de werun *etc*. 36/24 bið †~ede. 89/7 †gedroefd sind. 103/29 beoð ~eð. 75/6 gedrefde sind. 108/22 gedr[o]efed is. 59/4 gedrofdes. 45/3 bið †gedroed.

gedroefednis *sf* troubling, disturbance. **VP** 43/16 ~(confusio). 30/21 § (conturbatione). 70/13; 88/46 § (confusione). 68/20 gedroefnisse (§ionem).

woenan *wv* hope, think. **Cp** 87 uuoende (adcommodaturus).

gewoenan *wv*. **VP** 49/21 ~des (existimasti). 72/16 ~de (§abam).

woeninga *av* perhaps. **VP** 118/92; 123/3, 4, 5; 138/11 ~(forsitan).

hwoene *av* somewhat. **VP** 8/6; 93/17 ~laessan (paulominus). 118/87 hwene lęssan (§).

coene *aj* bold.

Coenberct LV. **Coenferð** Ct. **Coenhard** Ct. **Coenhere** LV, Ct. **Coinrēd** BH, LK; coen§ BH, LV, SG, Ct; coenreding SG. **Coenuald** Ct. **Coinualch**, coenualh BH; §ualch LV; §walh Gn, Ct; coenwaling Gn. **Coenuulf** BH, Gn, Ct.

Coena *sm* **LV** 244 (coen)a. 295 ~. 389 koena.

cwoen *sf* queen. **VP** 44/10 ~(regina).

Quoenburg, quoin§, cuoen§ BH; cu[u]oen§ Ct. **Cwoenðrȳth** LV; §ðryð, quoen§, coen§, cwæn§ Ct.

groene *aj* green. **Cp** 255 ~i aar(aurocalcum). Ct 20/4 on grenan pytt.

græs-groene *aj* grass-green. **Ef** 298 gręsgro[e]ni (carpassini); **Cp** graesgroeni.

gedoen *ptc* done. **VH** 12/4 ~u(per acto).

ā-doen *ptc* taken from. **Bl** 11 from milcum ~(ablactatus).

fram-ādoen *ptc* removed. **Ep** 870 ~re(remota); Cp fromadoenre; Ef †framadϸændrae.

on-doen *ptc* **Cp** 1056 ~(ingesta).

boen *sf* prayer, request. **LP** 2 ~um. **VP** 118/170 ~(postulatio). 6/10; 16/1 *etc* ~e mine (deprecationem). 21/25 § (precem). 87/3 to § minre (§). 27/2, 6 *etc* § (deprecationis). 19/7; 36/4; 105/15 § (petitiones). 33/16; Hy 12/5 § (preces). 101/18 bene (§).

Soemel *sm*. **Gn** 74 ~.

Soemling *sm* son of S. **Gn** 74 ~.

cwoeman *wv* please. **Bl** 13 quemde (conplacebam).

Cuoemlicu *sf* **LV** 29 ~.

doeman *wv* judge. **Cp** 440 doema (censeo). **BDS** 5 ~id uueorthae. **VP** 74/3 ~u [u *from* a] (judicabo). 9/5 *etc* ~es. 50/6 ðoemes. 66/5 ~est. 9/9, 9 *etc* ~eð. 97/9 ~æð (§abit). Hy 4/21 ~ed (§abit). 2/10 *etc* ~að. 57/2 ~að bearnum (§ate filii). 5/11; 7/9, 9 *etc* doem !. 9/39; 71/2 § (†§are). 95/13; 97/9 ~an. 57/12 †doende (§ans). 9/20 sien ~ed. 108/7 bið ~ed. 36/33 bið †omed (§abitur). 95/10 domeð (§abit).

doema *sm* judge. **VP** 7/12; 49/6; 74/8; Hy 13/23 ~ (judex). 67/6; 140/6; 148/11 ~an(§ices).

theodoice-snād Ct.

soecan *wv* seek. **VP** 26/4, 8; 118/145; 118/33 ~u (requiram, §; §; exquiram). 36/10 ~es (quaeris). 9/25 ~eð (inquiret). 9/34; 43/22; ~eð (requirit). 30/24; 60/8 ~eð (§et). 36/32 ~eð (querit). 4/3; 34/4; 68/33 ~að (itis; §unt; §ite) *etc*. 21/27; 68/7 ~að (requirunt). 77/7; 118/2 ~að (exquirant; §unt). 77/34 ~að (†inquirebant). 82/17 ~ad (querant). 141/5 ~e (requirat). 103/21; 140/45

~en (querant; exquirant). 33/15; 118/176 soec (inquire; require). 9/13; 13/2; 52/3 ~ende (querens; requirens; §). 9/11 ða §endan (quaerentes). 24/10 ~endum (requirentibus). 23/6; 73/23; 104/3 ~endra (§entium; querentium; §). 23/6 socendra (§). 33/11 socende (inquirentes). Ct 40/1 wes ~ende.

froecne *aj* dangerous.

frēcennis *sf* danger. **Mt** 50 in ænigre ~se.

coecel *s(m)* cake. **Ep** 993 coecil (tortum); Ef, Cp §.

boec *sf, d, g, pl* book(s). **CA** 4 béc *pl.* 7, 16 beoc *pl.* **VP** 68/29 ~(libro). 138/16 ~ ðinre (§). 39/8 ~(§i *g*). **Ct** 19/9; 24/8; 28/19; 36/10; 59/8 ~ *pl.* 27/7 bec *pl.* 28/25 (boc) *pl.* 42/19 ~um.

boece *sf* beech. **Ep** 22 ~ae (aesculus); Ef boeccae; Cp ~. 417 ~ae; Ef boecce (fagus); Cp ~. Ef 391 beccae (esculus); Cp ~.

broec *sf* breeches. **Ep** 573 gyrdils *vel* broec; Ef gyrdils broec; Cp §.

on-foehð *prs* receives. **VP** 47/4 onfoeht (suscipiet). 23/5; 108/8 onfoeð (accipiet; §iat). 48/16 § (acceperit). 145/9; Hy 10/9 § (suscipiet; §it). 48/18 onfoð (accipiet).

onfoest *prs* receivest. **VP** 50/21 ~(acceptabis).

oehtan *wv* persecute. **VP** 17/38 ~u(persequar). 82/16 ~es(§ueris). 7/6 ~eð. 34/3; 68/5; 70/11 ~að. 100/5 ~e(§uebar). 34/6; Hy 5/14 ~ende (§uens). 118/150, 7 § (§uentes). 108/17 § wes. 68/27; 118/86, 161 § werun. 43/17 §es. 7/2; 30/16; 108/31; 118/84, 121; 141/7 §um. 142/3 ohtende wes.

oehtend *sm* persecutor. **VP** 26/12 ~ra(persequentium)

on-oegnan *wv* fear. **Rd** 13 anoegun.

Roeginga-hām Ct.

swoeg *s(m)* sound. **Ep** 446 suoeg (fragor); Ef, Cp §. Cp 1027 sueg (hora). **VP** 18/5; 41/5 ~(sonus). 64/8 swo[e]g (§um). 9/7 ~e(sonitu). 76/18 ~es(§ūs). 150/3 swoge(sono).

wroegan *wv* accuse. **Ef** 342 meldadum *vel* †roactum; Cp ~dun(defferuntur). Cp 663 ~de (defert).

foegan *wv* join.

gefoegnis *sf* joining. **Ep** 889 gifoegnissae (sarta tecta); Ef gefegnessi; Cp ~se.

foeging *sf* joining. **Cp** 1163 ~(junctura).

swoete *aj* sweet. **VP** 24/8; 118/103 ~(dulcis; §ia). 18/11 ~ran (§iora).

swoetmettas VP.

swoetnis *sf* sweetness. **Cp** 148 suoetnis (ambrosea). **VP** 30/20; 67/11 ~se(dulcedinis; §ine). 20/4 swetnisse (§inis).

foet *sm d, pl* foot, feet. **VP** 65/6 ~(pede). 13/3; 17/34, 9; 21/17 *etc* ~(§es). 113/7 (2) fo[e]t (§§).

moetan *wv* meet, find. **Cp** 1432 ~te (offendit).

gemoetan *wv* find. **VP** 20/9; 118/162 ~eð (inveniit; §it). 83/4 ~ed (§it). 131/5 ~e (§iam). 35/3; 68/21; 88/21; 114/3 gemoette (§iret; §i *etc*). 75/6; 106/4; 114/3; 131/6 §un. 9/36; 20/9 bið ~ed. 16/3 nis ~ed (est inventa). 72/10 bioð ~ed (invenientur). 45/2 gemoetun (§erunt). 36/10 gemotes (§ies). 36/36 wes gemoted (inventus est). 118/143 gemo[e]ttun (invenerunt).

gemoeting *sf* meeting. **VP** 61/9 ~(conventus). 101/23 in ~e (in conveniendo). Hy 2/7 ~e (adinventiones).

groetan *wv* greet. **Ep** 210 ~u(convenio vel adjuro); Cp §; Ef †gloetc. Cp 1305 ~o(mereo).

geloed *s.* **Ep** 229 †gloed(catasta). Ef geleod; Cp ~.

ā-soedan *wv* satiate. **Cp** 1789 ~ (satiare).

stoeda *sm* steed. **Ef** 1143 ~(amisarius et homo for).

spoed *sf* prosperity, riches. **Ep** 815 ~(proventus); Ef, Cp §. 940 ~(successus); Cp, Ef §. Cp 1648 ~(praesidium). **VP** 38/6, 8 ~e mine, sie ~ (†substantia; §). 68/3; 88/48 ~ (§). 108/11 spodo (§iam). 138/15 sped §ia).

woedan *wv* be mad. **Ep** 575 †uuoendendi (lymphatico); Ef †uuodenti; Cp ~endi. Cp 273 uuoedende (bachantes). 1221 ~endi (limphaticus).

†**poedibergæ** Ef; woedeberge, woidi§ Cp. **woedenheortnis VP.**

foedan *wv* feed. **Rn** 3/2 fœddæ. **VP** 30/4; 79/6 ~es(enutries; cibabis). 32/19; 80/17 ~eð (alat; cibabit). 77/72; Hy 1/2 ~de (pavit; pascebam). Hy 7/24, 36 fo[e]dde (cibavit), ~endne (alentem). 77/71 ~(pascere). 36/3 bist ~ed (§ceris).

ā-foedan *wv* feed, nourish. **Cp** 580 ~de (confoti). **VP** 54/23 ~eð (enutriet).

mis-foedan *wv* nourish ill. **VP** 48/15 ~eð (depascit).

foedils *s* feeding. **Cp** 134 ~(altilia).

moeder *sf, g* mother. **VP** 49/20; 68/9 ~ ðinre, minre (matris).

rehtmeodrcynn Ct.

gloed *s*(*f*) redhot coal. **Ef** 304 ~(carbo); Cp §. Cp 1657 ~e (prunas).

gloedscofl Ep; Ef, Cp §.

broedan *wv* breed, cherish. **Cp** 899 feormat, broedeth (fovet).

bloedsian *wv* bless. **VP** 15/7; 25/12 *etc* bledsiu (benedicam). 5/13 *etc* §as (§es). 48/19 §as (benefeceris). 28/11; 144/21 §að. 48/14; 65/8 *etc* §iað. 62/5; 66/2 *etc* §ie (benedicam; §at). Hy 8/10 §ie (†§ite). Hy 8/20 §ien we (§amus). 27/9; 102/1 *etc* §a! 44/3 *etc* §ade. 84/2 §ades. 61/5 §adon. 64/12; 131/15 §iende (§ens). 36/22 §iende (§entes). 9/24; 111/2; 127/4 bið §ad.

gebloedsian *wv* bless. **VP** 17/47; 27/6; 30/22 *etc* gebledsad (benedictus). 48/19; 111/2 bið §. 71/17 sie §. 118/12; Hy 8/22 § earð. 113/15(2) §e (benedicti). 71/17 bioð §e. ?**Ct** 37/39 sien geblitsade [*under* blīþsian].

bloedsung *sf* blessing. **VP** 3/9; 128/8 bledsung (benedictio). 20/4, 7 in §e (§ne, §nem); 23/5 §e (§nem) *etc.* **Ct** 40/22 sia hiabenlice §.

gescroepnis *sf* convenience. **Cp** 568 ~ (conpedium).

gestoepan *wv* begin. **Cp** 1149 ~id (initiatum).

woepan *sv* weep, bewail. **VP** 94/6 ~en(ploremus). Hy 13/22 ~ende (deflentes).

groepe *sf* pit. **Ep** 948 ~um (scrobibus); Ef, Cp §. Cp 1172 genge, ~(latrina, atque ductus cloacas). **Ld** 150 groop (scropis).

ARRANGEMENT OF GLOSSARY.

Vowels: **a, æ, ea, i, e, eo, ę, u, y, o, œ; ā, ǣ, ǣ**(=Mercian *ē*), **ē, ēa, ēo, ī, ū, ȳ, ō, œ̄.**

Consonants: **h** (initial); **r, l; þ, s, w, f; nc, ng, n, m; c, h** (non-initial), **g, t, d, p, b.**

cg is considered as *gg*, *x* as *hs*.

The words are arranged primarily according to the vowel of their rootsyllables, then by the following cons., and lastly by the first of the preceding vowels and conss.

Compounds are treated in full under their second elements in the alphabetical order of the initial letter of the first elements, all the forms of the first elements being also enumerated under their own vowels, but without references. Thus *ealdor-mann* is to be sought under *a*, the various spellings of the first element being also enumerated under *ea*.

The different inflections of words are separated whenever their vowels differ (*wœs* under *æ* etc.).

The words are generally put under their oldest vowel (generally the Mercian); but *all* etc are put under *ea*.

CONTRACTIONS.

Bd (Northumbrian Bede-glosses p. 123). **Bd²** (Bede-glosses 179). **BDS** (Bede's Death-song 149). **BH** (Names in Bede's History). **Bl** (Blickling Glosses 122). **CA** (Codex Aureus 174). **CH** (Cædmon's Hymn 148). **Cp** (Corpus). **Ct** (Charters.) **DA** (Durham Admonition 175). **Ef** (Erfurt). **Ep** (Epinal). **Gn** (Genealogies 167). **Hy** (Vespasian Hymns). **Ld** (Leiden). **LK** (List of Kings 148). **LN** (Lorica Names 174). **LP** (Lorica Prayer 174). **Lr** (Lorica Glosses 171). **Mt** (Martyrology 177). **Pv** (Proverb 151). **Rd** (Leiden Riddle 149). **SG** (Saxon Genealogies 179). **VH** (Vespasian Hymns). **VP** (Vespasian Psalter).

(~) denotes repetition of the whole or part of the head-word, (§) similarly of the preceding word.

a etc = accusative. *la* = Latin accusative. The other contractions require no explanation.

INDEX TO GLOSSARY.

Words with prefixes are referred to under the root syllable, compounds under the second element, thus *ahebban* must be sought under *h*, *Eadwulf* under *w*. Derivatives in *-dom*, *-fæst*, *-full*, *-had*, *-leas* go under the first element, thus *soþfæst* must be sought under *s*. *ȝ*, *k*, *qu*, *u*(*u*) cons. must be sought under *æ*, *c*, *cw*, *w* respectively, *th* and *ð* under *þ*.

CORRECTIONS AND ADDITIONS.

P. 13, l. 2. *from bottom, read* slightly from (*instead of* slightly but).
P. 16, l. 24. urbanus *is not in Ep.—only in Ef.*
P. 35, gl. 16. *add* lancola : cellae *after* nepflod.
P. 35, gl. 31. *add* vertellum: uerua.
P. 37, gl. 55. 1431 (1428).
P. 38, gl. 50. *add* anconos : uncenos both.
P. 41, gl. 166. antedoque (antedo).
P. 42, gl. 117. *add* alapiosa: calua.
P. 42, gl. 121. *add* bothon : a : embrin.
P. 43, gl. 216. sibæd (sibaed).
P. 44, gl. 124. 294 (194).
P. 45, gl. 292. stęrt (stęnt).
P. 45, gl. 299. seolfbonan (seolfboran).
P. 45, gl. 308. bothoma : embrin.
P. 46, gl. 162. 312 (212).
P. 47, gl. 344. 155 (135).
P. 47, gl. 360. catabatus: romei.
P. 47, gl. 372. -ðru[u]m (-ðrum).
P. 47, gl. 393. græs- (graes-).
P. 49, gl. 397. *add* caraðrion : laurice — e *over* i.
P. 49, gl. 424. *add* catagrinas : bleremina mees.
P. 51, gl. 495. *the ms. has* sanguiñ.
P. 55, gl. 599. aves *added u. l. after* territat.
P. 55, gl. 599. *add* cripta : ascussum. crepundia : maenoe.
P. 55, gl. 617. *after* mygg *add* longas tibias habet.
P. 57, gl. 708. *add* dracontia: gimro dicitur.
P. 59, gl. 723. ortudri (ontudri).
P. 59, gl. 723. *add* effoth : bąt.
P. 59, gl. 726. *after* eff. *add* velociter.
P. 59, gl. 727. *after* eff. *add* expeditus.
P. 61, gl. 813. *add* expediam : arecio.
P. 63, gl. 851. *after* roeðe *add* ferae similis.
P. 63, gl. 852. *after* disc *add* vasculum.
P. 65, gl. 911. *transfer* [126] *to* 906.
P. 65, gl. 931. *add* fundi : grundus.
P. 67, gl. 989. *after* quice *add* gramina.
P. 69, gl. 1054. -endre (-endne).
P. 75. *note.* ni.
P. 75, gl. 1234. *add* [39].
P. 79, gl. 1347. *add* mulgit : milcit.
P. 79, gl. 1368. *after* mel *add* vel.
P. 81, gl. 1391. rihte- (nihte-).
P. 83, gl. 1479. *add* panice : ruseam.
P. 83, gl. 1482. *add* parabsides : gauutan.
P. 84, gl. 733. propropera (prae-).
P. 84, gl. 759. provectae — v *over* f (profetae).
P. 86, gl. 764. *add* parabsides : gabutan.
P. 87, gl. 1578. *add* phitecus : apa.
P. 89, gl. 1651. *add* prosapia : ob cniorisse.
P. 92, gl. 859. *add* 1719.
P. 93, gl. 1706. rationato (-atio).
P. 93, gl. 1758. *add* rubisca : saeltna. rubisca : raedda, rabisca.
P. 95, gl. 1793. *add* scrobibus : furum.
P. 96, gl. 930. maesttun (maestun).
P. 96, gl. 946. strenuae (strenue).
P. 101, gl. 1967. *add* sunt : sint.
P. 106, gl. 1892. *add* vel *after* vimbrat.
P. 106, gl. 1099. —vetellus.
P. 106, gl. 1100. —yripeon.
P. 107, gl. 2131. awerded (awended).
P. 107, gl. 2171. usia : suernit.
P. 111, gl. 3. fatescit (pa-).
P. 111, gl. 6. *add* soeue : su.
P. 111, gl. 8. *add* lurida : pox.
P. 111, gl. 9. agleddę go : : : : : : : .
P. 111, gl. 10. hiðir (hidir).
P. 111, gl. 11. *after* arguta *add* vel argumenta.

P. 111, gl. 22. poccas (poaas).
P. 112, gl. 31. *erase this gloss.*
P. 112, gl. 38. uitu- (uuitu-).
P. 112, gl. 39. ffil (fiil).
P. 112, gl. 40. gaborind (gaba-).
P. 112, gl. 41. *erase; see AHG.* 591 *note* 1.
P. 112, gl. 42. *add* lappa: clitę.
P. 112, gl. 46. [h]reod (reod).
P. 113, gl. 76. *add before* sarra, imitatio vel grina.
P. 125, gl. 21. prologue (epilogue).
P. 133, gl. 24. uictgilsi ([u]u-).
28. uant- (uu-).
P. 136, gl. 84. ædilbergæ (ædib.)
P. 137, gl. 116. osuald (osualdus).
P. 139, gl. 169. *add—after* ejus.
P. 141, gl. 235. *add* 1 *after* hereberchto.
P. 143, gl. 284. *read* 1 *for* C[1].
P. 145. *the line-numbering has been omitted from here to end.*
P. 147, gl. 362. *for* [4] *read* [1].
P. 147, gl. 366. *for* [1] *read* [2].
P. 147, gl. 376. *add* 1 *after* saeberchto.
P. 147, *note* 2 *add* 1 *after* in.
P. 151, gl. 14. ni(mæn.
P. 179, gl. 11. lond (bond).
P. 186, gl. 9. *os* 'mouth.'
P. 204, ps. 14. womb[2] (womb[1]).
P. 237, ps. 35. *transf.* Libani *to the Latin.*
P. 237, ps. 38. soðlice (-líce).
P. 251, ps. 5. hiow (hiop).
P. 288, ps. 5. gewinnum(-un).
P. 333, ps. 14. scit (sit).
P. 354, l. 7. *from b.* 1 (1) *etc.*
P. 406, l. 27. cwaecung (ew-).
P. 412. *erase note.*
P. 428. *note* 7 *add* St.

Lightning Source UK Ltd.
Milton Keynes UK
UKHW012147081218
333475UK00008B/1017/P

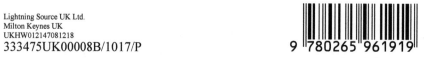